Medical Legal Aspects of Medical Records

Second Edition

Volume II: Clinical Specialty Records

Patricia Iyer, MSN, RN, LNCC
Barbara J. Levin, BSN, RN, ONC, LNCC

Contributors

John A. Amaro, DC, Dipl.Ac.(IAMA), Dipl. Ac.(NCCAOM)

Kathleen C. Ashton, APRN, BC, PhD

Barbara Mladenetz Weber Berry, MSN, RN

Gloria Blackmon, AAS, BSN, RN-BC, LNHA

Bruce Bonnell, MD, MPH

Douglas R. Briggs, DC, Dipl.Ac.(IAMA), DAAPM

Steven Charles Castle, MD

Stacy S. Cohen, DC

Kimberly Combs, LMT

Barry C. Cooper, DDS

Yvonne D'Arcy, MS, RN, CRNP, CNS

Susan G. Engleman, MSN, RN, APRN, BC, PNP, CLCP

Marjorie Eskay-Auerbach, MD, JD

Mary Fakes, RN, MSN

Hilary J. Flanders, MPH, RN-BC, RRT

Kelly A. Jaszarowski, MSN, RN, CNS, ANP, CWOCN

Elliott M. Korn, MD

Jo Anne Kuc, BSN, RN, LNCC

Michael T. Lennon, PharmD, MBA, RPh, JD

Jeffrey M. Levine, MD

Susan Masoorli, RN

Joanne McDermott, MA, RN

Wanda K. Mohr, RN, FAAN, PhD

Scott A. Mullins, AAS, EMT-P

Jane O'Rourke, MSN, RN, CNAA

Ann M. Peterson, EdD, MSN, RN, CS, LNCC

Sally Russell, MSN, RN

Gwen Simons, PT, JD, OCS, FAAOMPT

Ginny Tucci Starke, MSN, RN

Keith M. Starke, MD, FACP

Dana Stearns, MD

Jill Thomas, RNC, CWOCN, LNHA

Angela Tobias, RN, BSN, MSHSA, LNCC, CHCC

Howard Yeon, MD, JD

L&J **Lawyers & Judges Publishing Company, Inc.**
Tucson, Arizona

 **Lawyers & Judges Publishing Company, Inc.**

P.O. Box 30040 • Tucson, AZ 85751-0040
(800) 209-7109 • FAX (800) 330-8795
e-mail: sales@lawyersandjudges.com
www.lawyersandjudges.com

Library of Congress Cataloging-in-Publication Data

Medical legal aspects of medical records / [edited by] Patricia Iyer, Barbara J. Levin. -- 2nd ed.
    p. cm.
  Includes bibliographical references and index.
  ISBN-13: 978-1-933264-79-0 (v. 1 : softcover : alk. paper)
  ISBN-10: 1-933264-79-9 (v. 1 : softcover : alk. paper)
  ISBN-13: 978-1-933264-80-6 (v. 2 : softcover : alk. paper)
  ISBN-10: 1-933264-80-2 (v. 2 : softcover : alk. paper)
  1. Medical records--Law and legislation--United States. I. Iyer, Patricia W. II. Levin, Barbara J.
  [DNLM: 1. Medical Records--legislation & jurisprudence--United States. WX 33 AA1 M36 2010]
  KF3827.R4I98 2010
  344.7304'1--dc22
                                    2010002580

ISBN 13: 978-1-933264-80-6
ISBN 10: 1-933264-80-2
Printed in the United States of America
10 9 8 7 6 5 4 3 2 1

To my family, who has supported my writing for 30 years and is proud of my accomplishments. Love, Pat

Our deepest thanks to Mary Ann Shea and Aaron Levin who have dedicated so much of their time reviewing this book. We appreciate your insight and passion for this publication.

With love, this dedication is for Margie (sister), Barry (cousin) and their families. A package of seeds is planted and out of this a beautiful garden grows and spreads knowledge, generosity and kindness to everyone around them. Your uncanny ability to see only the good in people is reflected in the passion of your lives. Thank you for sharing these family gifts with those around you! Thank you Pat for being such an inspiration to me! With love, Barbara

Contents

Preface

The seeds of this book were sown in 2003 when we recognized the need for a comprehensive book that would shed light on the complex world of medical records. Although the book originally was intended to focus just on medical records, each author took advantage of the opportunity to provide a wider glimpse into the subject matter. Thus, the reader will come away from this book gaining broader knowledge about healthcare delivery, which will assist in analyzing medical records and details. The text is intended to benefit attorneys, paralegals, legal nurse consultants, risk managers, and anyone else with a keen appreciation of the nuances of medical records.

This second edition of the text has grown to reflect changes in the medical-legal arena. This includes new chapters on e-discovery, hospital-acquired conditions, attorneys' use of medical records in medical malpractice claims, physical therapy records, and respiratory care records as well as updating of other chapters. The growth of the book has necessitated dividing it into two volumes. Volume One gives an overview of the foundations of medical records. Volume Two focuses on the medical records generated within clinical specialties.

Within our work lies a crucial analysis of the data. While our roles may differ, reviewing medical records to locate the clues is essential as this makes a difference on the direction of the case. Consider Gandhi's expression: "To the world, YOU (the attorney, legal nurse consultant or healthcare provider) are one, BUT to that one (client or patient), YOU are their world." We are confident this comprehensive reference will assist you with your work.

The editors appreciate the assistance of Arlene Klepatsky, RN, JD in contributing cases for the first edition.

We are indebted to our authors, who shared their expertise with us and patiently worked through the process of turning ideas into an outline and thus into a finished manuscript. Their persistence and knowledge produced informative chapters. We appreciate our attorney clients, who helped us all as independent legal nurse consultants to grow in our own careers. We offer thanks to the American Association of Legal Nurse Consultants for providing us with an opportunity to meet each other and serve the organization as presidents of its Board of Directors. Lastly, we are indebted to our families, who watched the gestation of this book and its continuation into a second edition, and cheered us on.

Patricia Iyer
Barbara Levin

Chapter 1

Complementary and Alternative Medicine— Chiropractic, Acupuncture, and Massage

Douglas R. Briggs, DC, Dipl.Ac.(IAMA), DAAPM, John A. Amaro, DC, Dipl.Ac.(IAMA), Dipl. Ac.(NCCAOM), Kimberly Combs, LMT, and Stacy S. Cohen, DC

1.1 Chiropractic
A. Introduction

Chiropractic treatment is a branch of the healing arts which is concerned with human health and disease processes. It is deeply rooted in the Chinese health tradition, which focuses on the creation and maintenance of health. Chiropractic may be defined as a non-surgical and drug-free method of healing that is based on the premise that dysfunction of spinal alignment can be the causal root of a variety of ailments. The concept of the relation between spinal alignment and the function of the nervous system to maintain health is fundamental to chiropractic.[1] Doctors of chiropractic are physicians who consider humans as a physical, mental, social beings and give special attention to structural, spinal, musculoskeletal, neurological, vascular, nutritional, emotional, and environmental relationships.

TIP: Chiropractic is a drug-free, non-surgical science, and as such does not include pharmaceuticals or incisive surgery.[2]

B. History

The concept of manipulation of the spine to alleviate discomfort and heal disease has existed for thousands of years. Writings from China and Greece written in 2700 B.C. and 1500 B.C. mention spinal manipulation and the maneuvering of the lower extremities to ease low back pain. Hippocrates, the Greek physician who lived from 460 to 357 B.C., also published texts detailing the importance of spinal manipulation. In one of his writings he declared, "Get knowledge of the spine, for this is the requisite for many diseases."[3] The ancient Egyptians and Native American tribes also used various techniques to restore spinal function. The earliest records of manipulation are cave paintings depicting the delivery of spinal manipulations dating back to 17,500 B.C.[4] (See Figure 1.1.)

In the United States, the practice of spinal manipulation began gaining momentum in the late nineteenth century. In 1895, Daniel David Palmer founded the chiropractic profession in Davenport, Iowa. Palmer was well-read in medical journals of his time and had great knowledge of the developments that were occurring throughout the world regarding anatomy and physiology. Palmer was a practitioner of magnetic healing, a practice similar to the modern Asian art of QiGong. Palmer was treating a deaf janitor who worked in his building. He noted a torsion in the upper dorsal spine and upon "racking the vertebrae back into position" the man's hearing was restored. Palmer postulated that the majority of human diseases were the result of displaced articulations in the spine and axial skeleton. He maintained that the role of the chiropractor was to adjust any and all articular displacements in the human body. One of Palmer's early patients gave the profession its name by combining the Greek words *chiro* (hand) and *praktikos* (done by).[5] In 1897, Daniel David Palmer began the Palmer School of Chiropractic, which has continued to be one of the most prominent chiropractic colleges in the nation.[6]

In 1906, Palmer's son, B.J. Palmer, took over the school and is credited with the development of the chiropractic profession. By 1910, the Palmer School had courses in x–ray studies and was the first to use this new technology to detect spinal misalignments. In 1935, B.J. Palmer established a research clinic at the school and is credited with developing a prototype of the electroencephalogram, or EEG. Although he agreed with his father's philosophy regarding the relationship of skeletal misalignments and disease, he refined chiropractic theory to concentrate only on the spinal vertebrae.[7]

Figure 1.1 *Detail of spinal manipulation. Taken from an etching on a tortoise shell shield in a Shaolin temple in China, known to be at least 3000 years old. Rubbings provided courtesy of Dr. John Amaro and the International Academy of Medical Acupuncture.*

Throughout the twentieth century, doctors of chiropractic gained legal recognition in all fifty states. A continuing recognition and respect for the chiropractic profession in the United States has led to growing support for chiropractic care all over the world. The research that has emerged internationally has yielded incredibly influential results, which have changed perceptions of chiropractic care. The report *Chiropractic in New Zealand* published in 1979 strongly supported the efficacy of chiropractic care and elicited medical cooperation in conjunction with chiropractic care. The 1993 *Manga Study* published in Canada investigated the cost effectiveness of chiropractic care. The results of this study concluded that chiropractic care would save hundreds of millions of dollars annually with regard to work disability payments and direct healthcare costs.[8]

Doctors of chiropractic have become pioneers in the field of non-invasive care promoting science-based approaches to a variety of ailments. A continuing dedication to chiropractic research could lead to even more discoveries in preventing and combating maladies in future years.[9]

C. Philosophy

Chiropractic is based on the belief that structure affects function. The spinal cord is the pathway for all sensory nerve impulses that reach the brain and all motor nerve impulses that relay brain impulses to the appropriate muscles and viscera. Spinal misalignments (called *subluxations*) interfere with the normal transmission of these nerve impulses and blood supply. Chiropractic believes that when a nerve is irritated by a spinal subluxation, the resulting nerve impulse will be abnormal and disease will result because of the body's inability to adapt and react properly. Correcting these spinal misalignments by manipulative therapy removes the interference with the nerve transmission and blood flow, and allows the body's normal healing mechanisms to restore health.[10] A doctor of chiropractic is one who is involved in the treatment and prevention of disease, as well as the promotion of public health, and a provision of wellness approach. As a profession, the primary belief is in natural and conservative methods of health care. Doctors of chiropractic have a deep respect for the human body's ability to heal itself without the use of surgery or medication. These doctors devote careful attention to the biomechanics, structure, and function of the spine, its effects on the musculoskeletal and neurological systems, and the role played by the proper function of these systems in the preservation and restoration of health.[11] It should also be noted that the practice of chiropractic is based in science. It does not have any ties to

a religious belief or practice. The chiropractic profession is a healing discipline.

Chiropractic is not anti-medical. Rather, the profession developed as an alternative to allopathic medicine. Both professions share the same core philosophy of helping patients, although they use different means to help the patient achieve optimal health. The chiropractic profession focuses on the spine to alleviate neural and articular irritation through manual therapies, where the allopathic profession uses more interventional means such as pharmaceuticals and surgical procedures. It is now recognized that cooperation between the two disciplines will often produce a higher quality of care and a better patient response.

A natural extension of the art of manipulation of the spine is the effect it will have on physically and neurologically related tissues. Chiropractors are often able to treat non-spinal conditions with manual therapies. It is important to recognize that many health conditions may be effectively treated with chiropractic care (Figure 1.2). Even in cases where medical co-management is indicated or necessary, chiropractic may be effective in promoting the healing response.

D. Education

TIP: Educational requirements for doctors of chiropractic are among the most stringent of any of the healthcare professions.

According to the Council on Chiropractic Education, doctors of chiropractic are trained as primary care providers. Doctors of chiropractic—who are licensed to practice in all 50 states, the District of Columbia, and in many nations around the world—undergo a rigorous education in the healing sciences, similar to that of medical doctors. The practice and procedures which may be employed by doctors of chiropractic are based on the academic and clinical training received in and through accredited chiropractic colleges, and include, but are not limited to, the use of current diagnostic and therapeutic procedures. Such procedures specifically include the adjustment and manipulation of the articulations and adjacent tissues of the human body, particularly of the spinal column. Included is the treatment of intersegmental aberrations for alleviation of related functional disorders.

TIP: In some areas, such as anatomy, physiology, rehabilitation, nutrition and public health, DC students receive more intensive education than their MD counterparts.

How Chiropractic May Treat Visceral Conditions

Otitis media in children. Often in infants the eustacian tube lies in a more horizontal plane and is more prone to serous blockage—leading to infection. Gentle manipulation of the upper cervical spine may help to drain this fluid and prevent the congestion leading to and associated with infection.

Environmental allergies. Many of the nerves to the membranes and vessels of the sinuses come from the upper cervical nerve roots. Irritation of the nerves at this level may produce an over-reaction of the allergic response. Alleviation of this neural interference may help to reduce sinus congestion. Also, manipulation of the sinuses and upper cervical tissues will help with circulation and promote drainage of the sinus cavities.

Asthma. Several factors must be considered when dealing with conditions such as asthma. Asthma is an over-reaction of the lung tissues to an irritant. Again, this may be exacerbated by irritation of the nerve roots to the lungs at the respective spinal level. Also, functional locking of the thoracic spine will limit the full motion of the thoracic cage, thereby limiting the normal vital capacity. Manipulation can alleviate the nerve root irritation, restore the spinal function, and facilitate the natural healing responses in the body.

Figure 1.2 *How a chiropractic may treat visceral conditions.*

Table 1.1
How Well Educated is Your Chiropractor?

Chiropractic Hours+	Subjects	Medical Hours*
366.4	Anatomy/Embryology	184.6
120.0	Biochemistry	108.4
197.0	Microbiology/Public Health/Biostatistics	155.3
105.9	Cell Biology/Histology	130.7
312.8	Physical Diagnosis/Clinical Medicine	200.5
141.4	Neuroscience	114.0
561.2	Physiology/Pathology	542.3
66.7	Nutrition	21.5
29.4	Pharmacology	99.0
1900.8	Total Hours	1556.3

+ An average of required pre-clinical instruction hours during the first two years at 14 chiropractic schools.
* Average number of required pre-clinical instruction hours during the first two years of the medical school curriculum as listed in the 2000 Curriculum Directory, published by the American Medical Association (AMA).
• Reference for data in chart: *How Well Educated is Your Chiropractor?* (2002) Parker Professional Products. Dallas, TX.

The Council on Chiropractic Education requires that students have 90 prerequisite hours of undergraduate courses with science as the focus. The typical applicant at a chiropractic college has already acquired nearly four years of pre-medical undergraduate college education, including courses in biology, inorganic and organic chemistry, physics, psychology, and related lab work. Doctors of chiropractic must then complete 10 semesters or 5 academic years at an accredited chiropractic college. The complete curriculum includes a minimum of 4,200 hours of classroom, laboratory and clinical experience (Table 1.1). Approximately 555 hours are devoted to learning about adjustive techniques and spinal analysis in colleges of chiropractic. Because of the hands-on nature of chiropractic, and the intricate adjusting techniques, a significant portion of time is spent in clinical training. In medical schools, training to become proficient in manipulation is generally not required of, or offered to, students. An individual studying to become a doctor of chiropractic receives an education in both the basic and clinical sciences and in related health subjects. Like other primary healthcare doctors, chiropractic students spend a significant portion of their curriculum studying clinical subjects related to evaluating and caring for patients. The intention of the basic chiropractic curriculum is to provide an in-depth understanding of the structure and function of the human body in health and disease. The educational program includes training in the basic medical sciences, including anatomy with human dissection, physiology, and biochemistry. Thorough training is obtained in differential diagnosis, radiology and therapeutic modalities. Typically, as part of their professional training, chiropractice students must complete a minimum of a one-year clinical-based program dealing with actual patient care. Those intending to become doctors of chiropractic must also pass four levels of national board examination and all exams required by the state in which the individual wishes to practice. The doctor must also meet all individual state licensing requirements in order to become a doctor of chiropractic. Depending on the state involved, the agency that regulates chiropractic practice might be the State Board of Chiropractic or the Division of Professional Regulation.

As doctors, chiropractors may use a variety of modalities to care for patients and treat different conditions. What distinguishes chiropractic is the use of manipulation techniques to restore spinal function and alleviate nervous, soft tissue, and joint dysfunction. A doctor of chiropractic is able to both diagnose and treat patients, separating them from non-physician status providers, such as massage therapists, physical therapists, or acupuncturists.

This extensive education prepares doctors of chiropractic to diagnose healthcare problems, treat the problems when they are within their scope of practice, and refer patients to other healthcare practitioners when appropriate.

E. Goals of Care

There is a common misperception that when pain has disappeared, healing is completed and treatment should be stopped. However, the goal of care should go beyond the mere resolution of symptoms and continue on to include the restoration of structural and functional stability. An understanding of the phases of healing will enhance the patient's response to care and minimize residual sequelae.[12]

The purpose of the manipulative procedures and therapies utilized by chiropractic physicians is the restoration of normal and stable functional joint mechanics. It is sometimes misunderstood that the goal of chiropractic treatment or manipulation in general is the production of an audible sound or "joint cavitation." Patients may often say they go to a chiropractor so he can "crack their back." According to the current understanding, this sound is produced from small nitrogen gas bubbles in the joint space. These bubbles form in response to functional irritation in the joint. As the joint is gently mobilized, the gas bubbles shift position and are dissipated back into the surrounding tissues. However, if there are no bubbles in the joint, no audible sound will be produced. The purpose of the manipulation is the restoration of joint function, not the production of a specific sound.

TIP: Although manipulation often produces an audible sound, it should never be assumed that this sound is desirable or necessary.

Patients may often state that they are able to twist themselves into a position to produce a similar type of sound, which they equate with manipulation. It must be understood that it is physically impossible for an individual to create adequate leverage to restore functional motion to a hypomobile articulation in their own body.

F. Nomenclature

Every profession has its own terminology. A common example of this is the use of the term *subluxation*. From its root, the word is medically defined as a partial or incomplete dislocation of an articulation. Chiropractors have adopted this term to address any alteration in the normal functional mechanics of an articulation. Chiropractic uses standard medical terminology—primarily those of orthopedics, radiology, neurology, and physical therapy. Unfamiliar terms generally relate to specific chiropractic adjustments or maneuvers. The terms are specific to the chiropractic profession as defined by the American Chiropractic Association.[13] The glossary at the end of this text contains some of the terms.

As the educational requirements for chiropractors and medical doctors are very similar, chiropractors should be able to clearly document a patient's condition using standardized terminology (HNP = Herniated Nucleus Pulposus, IVF = Intervertebral Foramen, SLR = Straight Leg Raise test, and so on). Unless there is a very specialized technique being used, orthopedic maneuvers and evaluation protocols are the same amongst MDs and DCs and should be easily referenced and understood.

Historically, the disciplines of chiropractic and osteopathy were identical. Over time, the profession of osteopathy has shifted toward a more contemporary medical focus. Manipulation procedure and technique is now typically an elective topic in an osteopathic education. As a general rule, most osteopaths do not focus the majority of their practice on manipulative therapies, but standard medical protocols, while chiropractic has continued to focus on manipulation as the primary method of treatment.

G. Phases of Musculoskeletal Healing
1. Acute
Personal injury attorneys may handle claims in which the plaintiff sought the care of a chiropractor after trauma, such as may result from a motor vehicle accident. Typically, a rear end collision will result in acute pain. The acute stage

is the initial stage of response to injury. This phase of healing is often confined to the first 72 hours following a trauma; however, the active process of inflammation may continue beyond this time. Soft tissue injuries, especially of the spine and larger muscle groups, may not manifest the classic symptoms of injury (i.e., pain, inflammation, or hematoma) for several hours or days following the causal incident.[14]

Early intervention is essential. During the time immediately following injury, the body will respond with active inflammation. It is critical to minimize the inflammatory response as the extent of inflammation bears a direct relationship to the resulting fibrosis of repair. The application of cold therapies to the site of injury produces a localized decrease in blood flow and tissue metabolism, and minimizes the inflammatory response by arteriolar vasoconstriction. Failure to control the initial inflammatory reaction will lead to further tissue damage, often worse than that of the original injury. A common misconception is that immediate activity is beneficial; however, it is clear from the literature that no tissue healing can begin until the active inflammatory response is resolved. There is a common notion that after 72 hours, ice is no longer effective or warranted; however, cryotherapy is effective as long as there is active inflammation in the tissues. More active/aggressive therapies during this phase of healing will exacerbate the soft tissue inflammatory reaction and reinforce the potential of chronic irritation. During this phase, supportive bracing (i.e., soft collar, circumferential wrist support) will also help to limit excessive movement and limit the stresses on the weakened regional tissues.[15]

The patient should be cautioned regarding excess activity to avoid additional injury. Conservative treatment is warranted even in the absence of obvious inflammation.

TIP: Often patients will self-manage with heat as it provides some pain relief. However, this may also accelerate the reactive inflammatory response and produce greater latent irritation. The immediate prescription of rest and ice will greatly reduce both healing time and cost.[16]

As the immediate inflammation is controlled, gentle passive mobilization should be incorporated to promote regional circulation and facilitate the removal of metabolites from the tissues. Light chiropractic mobilization techniques, such as myofascial release, distraction, and neuromuscular re-education (NMR) may be performed on a daily basis during this time. In-office modalities, such as electric muscle stimulation, may be used to massage or "pump" the region of injury. The patient may continue to use ice or transcutaneous electrical neurostimulation (TENS) as home therapy. Supportive bracing should be continued, as the tissues are often still weak and easily re-injured. The patient may also be instructed in appropriate stretching exercises to minimize the formation of adhesions in the tissues.[17]

Depending on the severity of injury, this acute phase of the healing cycle may last anywhere from 72 hours to 6 weeks. Care during this time must focus on the control and resolution of tissue inflammation. Aggressive or active therapies during this phase may further damage the tissues and initiate subsequent inflammation. It is also important to establish patient compliance at this time, as the resolution of acute inflammation is often the greatest alleviation of pain. However, the resolution of pain is not the end-goal of care. The end of the acute inflammation is the time the body begins the physiologic process of tissue repair and remodeling.[18]

2. Reparative

More aggressive treatments must be incorporated to facilitate the regeneration of the damaged tissues once inflammation has been controlled. This phase is characterized by the synthesis and deposition of collagen (scar formation). Mobilization during this phase is important for two reasons:

- The fibers of the collagen scar are deposited randomly into the tissues, and must be trained in order to produce a "functional scar."
- The restoration of functional joint mechanics minimizes further tissue irritation from biomechanical/ structural imbalance.[19]

The reparative phase may last up to 6 weeks, even with appropriate care. Chiropractic manual therapy and therapeutic modalities (low-volt galvanic muscle stimulation, ultrasound, acupuncture, and so on) may continue at a schedule of three times a week to facilitate the ongoing healing process. The patient should continue home stretching and use of supportive bracing, as indicated.[20]

3. Rehabilitative

As inflammation resolves and the stability of the soft tissues is restored, the focus of care should shift toward rehabilitation. Ideally, the patient is free from resting pain by this time. The patient should be introduced to a progressive regimen of therapeutic exercise to restore postural and functional stability. Active resistance exercise, such as using free weights, will improve the orientation and strength of the collagen scar and help return the patient to her pre-injury functional capacity. During this phase, passive modalities are often palliative and not of significant benefit. Mobilization should be continued on a decreasing frequency schedule (tapering from two times weekly to once weekly) to ensure proper joint mechanics and maintain function. Active rehabilitation exercises should be the focus of care at this point, ideally at a schedule of 3 times weekly from 4 to 12 weeks depending on the extent of tissue weakness and instability. During this time the patient should continue home stretching exercises, with a focus of establishing an ongoing, self-directed program of therapeutic exercise to minimize future injury due to biomechanical instability.[21]

Patients often show improvements in function following a rehabilitation program for low back pain (LBP). The functional improvement score is influenced by age, symptom duration, and inclusion of mobilization/manipulation and strengthening and flexibility exercises.[22] The amount of time until a patient's condition stabilizes depends on the severity of the injury, the type of tissue injured (muscles heal and stabilize faster than ligaments and tendons), the patient's physical fitness and level of activity, the patient's motivation to exercise and stretch, the reduction of risk factors such as smoking, postural and ergonomic stressors, genetic factors, and the patient's emotional state.

TIP: It is not unusual for soft tissue injuries of the neck and spine to require 14-18 months for complete resolution; however, the course of treatment may range anywhere from 6 months to 2 years or more. Again, regular appropriate evaluation protocols must be followed to document the patient's condition, response to care, and progress with treatment.[23]

---

4. Supportive

Patients who reach a level of biomechanical stability, he should return to their full complement of daily activities. If a rational course of care has been followed, they should be well into the lifestyle of following a daily protocol of moderate stretching and strengthening activities. As a patient attains this level in the treatment regimen, it is reasonable for the chiropractor to monitor the condition for a period of several weeks to ensure that no residual irritations or latent sensitivities are manifest before formally closing care.[24]

From a case management perspective, there must be a point where active treatment in relation to an injury is concluded (the patient has reached Maximal Medical Improvement or MMI). The American Medical Association defines MMI as that point in time when a patient's "condition or state is well-stabilized and unlikely to change substantially over the next year, with or without treatment. There may

be a change in the patient's condition, but further recovery or deterioration is not anticipated."[25] The AMA defines disability as an "alteration of an individual's capacity to meet personal, social, or occupational demands or statutory or regulatory requirements because of an impairment. Disability is a regional outcome, contingent on the environmental condition in which activities are performed."[26] Based on these very wide criteria it is not always easy to determine a specific time that a functional disability is permanent or MMI has been achieved. However, with an appropriate perspective, consistent documentation, and focused objective testing, a reasonable determination can be made.[27]

5. Maintenance

Typically, once patients are able to pursue their daily activities for 10-14 days without treatment, care is not considered consistent enough to create additional functional improvement. At this time patients may be offered the opportunity to pursue "wellness care" to monitor their condition and offset any of the functional stresses of daily living. Many chiropractors advocate periodic visits to maintain health and function. The physical and postural stresses of daily activities continue to have an impact on the body regardless of one's level of activity. However, these treatments should not be billed into an injury claim unless there is a defined residual demonstrating the need for periodic care to be able to continue a minimum level of daily functional or work-related activities.[28]

H. Evaluation Protocols

In addition to standard evaluation procedures, chiropractic physicians are trained to examine the functional component of a condition. Along with the normal battery of standardized orthopedic evaluation protocols, there are specialized biomechanical evaluations utilized by chiropractors. The information derived from the patient interview and clinical history establishes a baseline for the functional evaluation and will guide the experienced physician to a differential diagnosis. Orthopedic maneuvers and diagnostic studies may then be pursued to rule out or define the cause of the patient's complaints.

1. Objective assessment

The basic elements of examining a patient include: vital signs, observation and inspection, palpation, neurological evaluation, range of motion studies, clinical laboratory, orthopedic tests, and diagnostic imaging. A thorough patient interview should provide the basis for a differential diagnosis. Then orthopedic and neurological testing, coupled with appropriate diagnostic studies, must be pursued to confirm or rule out possible diagnoses. A treatment plan cannot be derived without a working diagnosis.

a. Neurologic

Chiropractic physicians are trained to perform routine neurological examinations. The neurological evaluation involves locating the lesion; testing deep tendon, superficial, and pathologic reflexes; testing cranial nerve and brainstem function; measuring of body parts; grading muscular strength; and testing gross sensory perception.

b. Orthopaedic

Orthopedic tests are based on the kinetic activity of the patient. These maneuvers are performed to duplicate the patient's complaint or symptom. Orthopedic maneuvers may be positive or negative, and may increase or decrease the patient's symptom complex. Correlation of the patient's complaints with orthopedic findings becomes another objective finding. It is reasonable that a physician perform multiple maneuvers so that the patient is not aware of which specific faculty or sensory modality is being examined. This allows the examiner to further differentiate an organic complaint from one that may have a psychological or hysteric basis. It should also be noted that simply a positive or negative notation is not adequate; there must be documentation of the significance of the findings linked to the patient's complaint, diagnosis, and treatment plan.

c. Biomechanical

There are a number of formalized techniques and postural reflexes utilized in the chiropractic profession to diagnose the torsions in the spine and their effect on the extremities.

2. Leg length

Comparison of a patient's leg length is a common assessment notation. It is important to remember that measurement of a true anatomical leg length deficiency is only possible with full-length radiographic study. In the majority of patients, actual leg length discrepancy is negligible. As the acetabulum is not centralized on the pelvis, torsion in the pelvis or unilateral iliolumbar myospasm may cause an apparent leg length discrepancy. It is important to understand the difference between a true anatomical and functional short leg. If a heel lift is given to a patient without an actual deficiency, the patient will most likely experience an increase in her symptom complex.

3. Pottenger's Saucering

A relative flattening of the dorsal column produces a number of different issues. When palpating the regional spinous processes, one may feel a relative indentation at a specific level. This finding is referred to as Dishman's Syndrome, Pottenger's Saucering, or simply as an anterior thoracic segment. This finding may indicate postural tension. Anterior wedging of the mid-dorsal spine is often found in patients with respiratory problems. Not only does locking of the segments irritate the nerve roots supplying the lung tissues, but it also limits the ability of the thoracic cage to expand, causing a decreased vital capacity.

4. Cervical syndrome

It has long been known that the spinal tissues compensate for dysfunction at one level by becoming hypermobile at an articulation above or below the level of problem. Cervical syndrome is an example of this. Leg length is compared and noted when the patient is lying prone. The patient is then asked to rotate his head left and right. Cervical rotation to one side or the other will change the resting tone in the paraspinal tissues and affect the difference in leg length. This demonstrates how torsion in the cervical spine may cause a functional imbalance in the pelvis. When this is observed, it is referred to as a cervical syndrome.

5. Diagnostic imaging and studies

The primary reason for utilizing diagnostic procedures is to obtain the most accurate and proper diagnosis of the patient's condition, so that care may be specific for the problem. Studies should not be performed as a matter of protocol, but to confirm or define a clinical differential based on the examination. Imaging is useful, but has limitations, and findings must be correlated with the patient's history and objective evaluation. A second reason would be the need for proper documentation of the patient's condition and progressive response to treatment. Chiropractic physicians may draw from a battery of diagnostic procedures based on the patient's clinical history and the initial assessment finding.

a. Plain film radiography

TIP: Spinal radiographs are nearly always produced to rule out fracture, dislocation, anomaly, or bone pathology.

Chiropractic radiographs are used in biomechanical analysis to establish an initial understanding of the patient. Spinal views are performed in the upright/weight-bearing position to evaluate the spinal structures under gravitational load. There are numerous protocols to measure and define articular dysfunction. Understanding of the normal functional relation and positioning of the articulations will give a chiropractor the ability to infer what is happening with the associated tissues, even though they are not visualized on the study. Degenerative changes are commonly viewed, even on asymptomatic patients. Such findings should not automatically infer a diagnosis, but lend to an overall understanding of the patient's clinical picture.

b. Video Fluoroscopy

Video Fluoroscopy (VF) is used when a functional study of the joint is warranted. VF should be used when there is biomechanical abnormality not adequately demonstrated by plain film stress studies or other examination methods. It may be used when there is clinical indication of significant instability or in cases of fixation or ligament laxity.

c. Computerized Tomography

Computed Tomography (CT) is used for more detailed appreciation of skeletal pathologic processes, which can help evaluate suspected intervertebral disc protrusions or herniations, facet disease, or central canal and lateral recess stenosis. A CT scan is indicated if spinal disease is suspected and is not well identified on plain films, and the patient is not responding to care. A CT scan is especially useful for the appreciation of bone and calcifications and surpasses MRI in this regard.

d. Magnetic Resonance Imaging

The computerized, thin-section images produced by MRI are most effective at evaluating neurologic structures, and are often the preferred method for defining disc degeneration and herniation. MRI is considered superior for evaluation of suspected spinal cord tumors, intracranial disease, and various types of central nervous system disease. High field MRI currently provides the most detailed images and should be considered the gold standard for evaluating soft tissue conditions.

Although MRI is useful in the identification of small differences within and along similar soft tissues, it will not always reveal regional inflammation.

TIP: When a region of the body is inflamed, the fluid content is uniformly increased in those tissues, and the MRI will often be read as normal or negative, as there is no one specific finding.

A patient may have legitimate complaints and positive orthopedic examination findings, but in the absence of disc herniation, may very well present with a negative MRI. Therefore, MRI results must be correlated with history, interview, and examination findings. A finding of disc herniation

or endplate inflammation will help to identify which level of the spine needs specific attention. Evidence of an annular tear would be a contraindication for traction therapies, as there is an increase of stretch receptors in the annular fibers.

e. Positional MRI

Conventional MRI studies require that patients be positioned in a horizontal plane for the study to be performed. With the advent of Position MRI (pMRI) patients may be scanned in their position of pain or symptoms—flexion, extension, lateral bending or rotation. Such positioning allows for more accurate assessment and diagnosis.

f. Diagnostic ultrasound

Diagnostic ultrasound (DxUS) has primarily been used for the evaluation of the gastrointestinal and genitourinary tracts, and in the assessment of obstetric and gynecologic conditions. This modality is particularly useful in the evaluation of the musculoskeletal system. Although it does not provide the same quality of image as CT or MRI, there are many advantages to this type of study:

- It is non-invasive.
- It may be performed in an office.
- There is an absence of ionizing radiation.
- It is relatively low cost.
- It is a fast procedure.
- As it is nondestructive to tissues, frequent examinations of the same region may be performed without tissue damage.
- It does not require contrast material.
- It does not depend on the function of an organ to visualize the anatomy.

TIP: Another valuable difference is that DxUS is able to differentiate between recent/acute injury and previous trauma and chronic irritation.

---

g. Nerve conduction velocity

Pain is difficult to evaluate and define as areas of body sensation overlap and complaints may come from a primary locus or be referred from a different location. Nerve conduction is an excellent test for the evaluation of peripheral sensory nerves. The clinical utility of Evoked Potentials (EPs) and Nerve Conduction Velocities (NCVs) is based on their ability to:

- demonstrate abnormal nerve function,
- reveal the presence of clinically unsuspected malfunction in a sensory system when demyelinating

disease is suspected because of symptoms and/or signs in another area of the central nervous system,

- define the anatomic distribution of a disease process, and
- monitor objective changes in a patient's status.

NCV testing is a relatively simple procedure, which is often performed in the office at minimal expense. Also, the human body cannot decipher between small differences in stimulating electrical currents, making this test essentially "malinger-proof." NCV should not be confused with an electromyelogram (EMG), which is used to evaluate the motor aspect of a nerve.

h. Range of motion

Range of motion testing is still the established standard that many insurance companies and other third parties rely upon to measure impairment. Any range of motion that is less than normal may indicate or be a result of injury, degenerative changes, and disease process. Regional spinal motion is a compound motion as the motion above and below the measurement points compounds the difficulty of measuring spinal segments mobility. Normal values may vary dramatically depending on the reference source used. Observation or measurement by goniometer cannot accurately assess motion of the spine. Dual inclinometry is the most accurate way to measure spinal motion, as it will measure the difference in motion between the two measurement points. The American Medical Association states that for a study to be valid, motion values must be calculated from a series of at least three repetitions of a movement which must fall within a deviation of 5 degrees or 10 percent, whichever is larger.[29] The American Medical Association has provided standardized guidelines for functional assessment of a patient. Abnormal spinal motion should be regularly monitored as part of the patient's evaluation criteria. Computerized dual inclinometry testing will accurately quantify this data to demonstrate the patient's progressive response to treatment.

i. Manual muscle testing

Manual muscle testing is the most frequently used procedure to initially assess muscle strength and function in patients with neurologic disorders. One can develop a general impression of the relative strength and integrity of the muscle-joint complex being tested, based on the reaction to the amount of pressure applied. Unfortunately, this testing is often performed in an extremely subjective manner and the finding will vary greatly depending on the examiner, patient condition, and other testing variables. Standardized testing using manual load cell equipment is recommended as it provides more accurate assessment, reproducible results, and intra-examiner variability. The American Medical Association has provided standardized guidelines for functional assessment of a patient. An imbalance in muscular strength should be regularly monitored as part of the patient's evaluation criteria. The use of manual load cell equipment will accurately quantify this data to demonstrate the patient's progressive response to treatment.

6. Outcomes assessment

The measurement of pain and its effects on daily activities is largely dependent on the efforts of the examiner and the information given by the person experiencing pain. Unfortunately, there is no serum level of pain that can be monitored. Pain data may be questioned due to patient anxiety, inability to describe pain, and need for secondary gain. Further, non-pain sensations such as tingling, numbness, and paresthesia may be confused with pain. Cultural and gender differences in pain perception and treatment must be recognized before initiating pain management therapy. It is recommended that pain assessment tools be used to initially assess the patient's discomfort.[30] Standardized outcomes assessment evaluation questionnaires, such as the SF36, Zung, or Oswestry, may be used to assess a patient and monitor progress. These forms are comprised of condition-specific questions to help define a degree of disability in different categories. The questions are often phrased in a way that makes it difficult for the patient to manipulate the data. After completion, the information obtained may be used to indicate the accuracy of a patient's claims of pain or limitation, or his perceived level of pain and limitation.

Follow-up studies may help to validate the patients' response to treatment. Questionnaires such as the Oswestry Low Back Disability Index and Neck Disability Index are often used to assess a patient's level of disability and gradual response to care as a measurement tool to define when a patient may return to work. Short health surveys, such as the SF-36, have been developed over the last 20 years to measure different aspects of a patient's condition. Responses are calculated and compared to recognized normative data. If the normative data for a patient is at a higher number than the patient's score, and the patient's condition has not reached a plateau, additional care may be indicated. This information may be useful to examiners, patients, and insurance company case managers if additional care is needed ("medically necessary") to return the patient to a "mean" level of function—especially if the condition is not supported by other documentation.

The stresses of the healing process, and the limitations of lifestyle during this time, may have a significant impact on the patient. The psychological condition of a patient has an enormous impact on the healing process and must be considered when evaluating a patient or recommending a treatment plan. The Beck Depression Inventory (BDI) is perhaps the most frequently used depression screen and outcomes measure used in clinical pain practices. The Zung Depression Index is a similar measurement tool. The presence of depression is common when patients have had lingering pain or irritation. Comorbid psychiatric disturbances are not the only psychological factors that can influence the course of pain treatment. Pain, particularly persistent pain, is not often directly tied to specific pathophysiology, but rather is linked to integrated perceptions arising from neurochemical input, cognition, and emotion. The mind greatly influences the intensity of pain. Evaluation and monitoring of the psychosocial component of a patient's condition can give a better understanding of her perception of her injury and limitations, and provide greater insight into the needs of the patient through the healing process.[31] Chapter 18, *Pain Assessment and Management,* addresses this issue in greater depth.

7. Case study: herniated disc

Failure to perform and document an appropriate evaluation, as well as failure to act on worsening symptoms may expose the chiropractor to liability, as this case study shows.

The chiropractor began treating the patient for pain in the mid and upper back during the mid-1980s. He continued to treat the patient for this same concern sporadically for more than a decade. On May 7, 1998, the patient returned to the chiropractor with low back pain he experienced after lifting his lawnmower into the bed of his pickup truck a few days earlier. He rated his pain a "5" on a 1-10 scale.

The chiropractor recorded positive findings on the Valsalva Test and the Straight Leg Raising Test, and the remainder of the examination form was left blank. The chiropractor did not perform any new x-ray studies. The differential diagnosis was a sprain/strain in the lumbar region along with spinal subluxations. The patient was treated with electric muscle stimulation and a side-posture rotational manipulation to the lumbar spine. The patient was instructed to return on Monday, May 11.

The patient arrived for his May 11 appointment using a crutch—his pain had increased significantly since his last appointment and he was now experiencing numbness, tingling and weakness into his legs. The chiropractor repeated the Straight Leg Raising Test, which was again positive, but he did not test the patient's reflexes or perform additional testing. The chiropractor explained that the numbness was due to pressure on the sciatic nerve. However, he never clarified whether it was a disc, muscle, or bone applying the pressure. Again, the same treatment was applied, and the patient was in such discomfort that he did not go to work that day. He was instructed to return for treatment in three days.

At his May 14 appointment, the patient said his problems were exacerbated when he bent over and twisted to get a window cleaner out of the cupboard the day before. The resulting pain was so severe that he collapsed. Since then, the pain had begun radiating into both legs and feet. The chiropractor continued to treat with EMS and side-posture rotational manipulation.

The following morning, the patient called the chiropractor's office to report that he was numb from the waist down and could not walk. The chiropractor ordered an MRI and scheduled a surgical consult for May 18. On May 16, when the patient's condition continued to decline, his brother took him to the emergency room where he was diagnosed with a subacute L4-5 herniated disc and L5-S1 lumbar stenosis with acute severe cauda equina syndrome. The patient underwent emergency L4-5 and L5-S1 decompressive lumbar laminotomies and radical L4-5 microdiscectomy.

The patient sued the chiropractor for malpractice. His attorney claimed that while the chiropractor may not have caused the cauda equina syndrome, the doctor failed to promptly diagnose and refer the patient. The attorney also presented credible expert testimony that timely surgical intervention and decompression of a cauda equina disc must occur within hours—not days—to avoid significant damage.

The patient claimed economic damages for past and future medical bills, lost past and future wages, and life care needs of more that $2 million. The patient sought non-economic damages for excruciating pain and debilitating cramps and spasms from his hips down to his toes lasting 15 to 20 minutes; erectile dysfunction and deadened sexual sensations; difficulty with his bowels and constipation; and poor foot control that resulted in frequent stumbling.

The chiropractor's defense team reviewed the case with two chiropractors and two neurosurgeons. These experts concluded that there was a 30 to 35 percent chance the case would be lost for more that the chiropractor's $1 million policy limit. As a result, the chiropractor chose to settle for $765,000.[32]

Despite being familiar with the patient's history, the chiropractor failed to recognize a new condition. When a patient presents with a new complaint, doctors should set aside all previous opinions, findings, and assessments and use a new approach to ensure a fresh, complete, and comprehensive evaluation. The recent injury and new complaints should have been a red flag.

New symptoms or complaints should trigger a new evaluation and no change in complaints should be another red flag. The standard of care requires consideration of a change in management approach when a patient's condition worsens.

The chiropractor did not perform a thorough evaluation or order any new diagnostic studies despite the new history of injury. Information derived from the objective assessment is part of the data needed to arrive at a correct diagnosis. In litigation, plaintiffs may claim that "if only" more comprehensive or symptom-related tests would have been performed, a proper evaluation could have been made and the patient appropriately treated.[33]

I. Scope of Practice

TIP: Doctors of chiropractic are most commonly known to treat individuals with neuromusculoskeletal complaints, such as headaches, joint pain, neck pain, low back pain and sciatica.

Chiropractors may also treat patients with osteoarthritis, spinal disc conditions, carpal tunnel syndrome, tendonitis, sprains, and strains. However, the scope of conditions that doctors of chiropractic manage or provide care for is not limited to neuromusculoskeletal disorders. Chiropractors have the training to treat a variety of non-neuromusculoskeletal conditions such as allergies, asthma, digestive disorders, otitis media (non-suppurative) and other disorders as new research is developed. State laws, as well as the nation's antitrust laws, may allow doctors of chiropractic to utilize ancillary healthcare procedures commonly referred to as being in the common domain. Particulars of chiropractic scope of practice are determined by case law and statute. If there is a question, consult the local codes to determine the appropriate scope of practice.

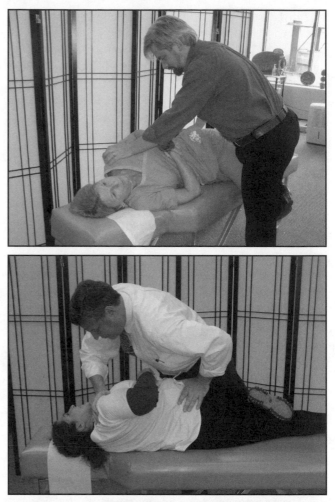

Figures 1.3 (top) and 1.4 (bottom) *Different views of a typical low back manipulation. The upper hand stabilizes the shoulder back, while the lower hand brings a specific thrust into the articulation (in Figure 1.4 the hand is positioned on the ilia to bring a lateral traction across the sacroiliac joint). However, this maneuver also be used for the sacrum, lumbar segments, and occasionally the lower dorsal segments. The chiropractor's lower leg is positioned across the patient's thigh to help provide gentle traction into the regional tissues; although typical, it may not be performed on all low back maneuvers.*

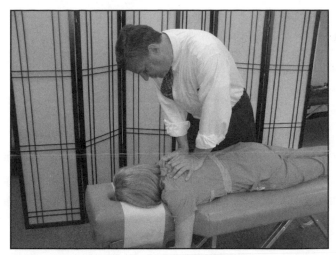

Figure 1.5 *An example of typical hand setup for a mid-dorsal adjustment. It should be noted that the line of correction force is not straight down, but on an angle toward the head, along the plane of the facet articulations.*

Figure 1.7 *Another type of cervical manipulation. In this type of manipulation, the right hand cradles the neck, and the fingers traction the fixated segment. The left hand helps to stabilize the position of the head during the maneuver.*

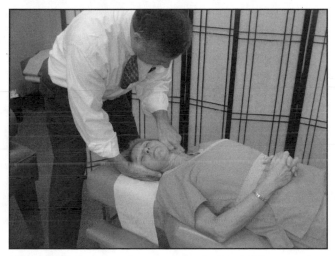

Figure 1.6 *Position for a manipulation of the cervical spine. The right hand cradles the head, the left hand delivers a controlled thrust along the joint plane to restore motion to a fixated segment.*

1. Manipulation techniques

As a healing art, chiropractic practices may seem diverse when comparing different practitioners as there is a wide variety of theories, procedures, and techniques practiced. With the growth of the profession, there has been a development of various specialized protocols to evaluate, define, and treat joint dysfunction. Practitioners of these specialized protocols often have a very specific series of examinations they will use to evaluate a patient's spine, and a core set of manipulation techniques to then treat the identified joint dysfunctions.

Depending on the manipulation protocol being practiced, a variety of manipulation techniques, treatments, and procedures may be used to restore joint function and promote healing. There are over 150 different types of formalized chiropractic techniques currently defined. The technique a doctor may use depends on several factors, including educational background, personal and professional experience, and preference. In general, unless there is a specific question regarding a procedure, it is not necessary to identify the technique utilized. See Figures 1.3–1.8.

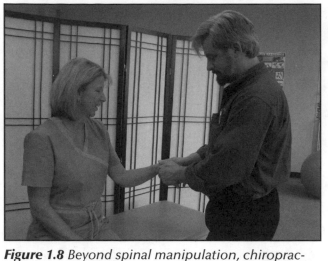

Figure 1.8 *Beyond spinal manipulation, chiropractors use specialized manipulation techniques to correct joint dysfunction in all parts of the body. This illustration demonstrates a common treatment for carpal tunnel syndrome.*

Figure 1.9 *The Activator instrument.*

a. Diversified

Diversified is the most common chiropractic technique used. It is a formalized protocol of manipulating each spinal level. Although this protocol is specific to chiropractic, there are osteopathic and physical therapy manipulation maneuvers that look very similar; however those maneuvers are more general and are limited in their ability to restore spinal function.

b. Gonstead

This technique is named after the developer of the system, Dr. Clarence Gonstead. This technique is known for its protocol of radiographic evaluation and specific mea-surement of spinal misalignment. Formalized manipulation techniques developed by Dr. Gonstead are employed to restore spinal function when articular lesions are discovered.

c. Lumbar distraction/Cox

This technique focuses on conditions of the lumbar spine with particular emphasis on the intervertebral disc. It requires the use of a special manipulation table to gently distract the lumbar articulations, reduce adhesions, and promote the circulation of fluids in the disc material.

d. Nimmo

Developed by Dr. Raymond Nimmo, this technique focuses on the neurologic reflex arc as a root of myospasm. The intensified reflex arc causes hypermyotonia which will in time produce vertebral misalignment and other skeletal deviations, as well as create trigger points which generate a barrage of noxious impulses which interfere with the function of the nervous system.[34] There is a specific protocol of manual therapies including trigger point therapy, stretching, and myofascial release to alleviate the congestion and restore musculoskeletal function.

e. Activator

This is a high-speed, low-force chiropractic technique utilizing a special impact hammer to deliver a dynamic thrust of controlled force into a specific segment at a specific line of drive at a high speed. See Figure 1.9.

f. Thompson

This technique also requires a specialized adjusting table. Once subluxations are identified, the use of a drop mechanism in the table is used to create an impulse into the articulation and restore mobility.

Chiropractic techniques continue to be researched and developed, helping the profession stay on the cutting edge of conservative health care. Due to the impact of scientific research, the chiropractic profession has seen advances once deemed impossible.

- The Agency for Health Care Policy and Research (AHCPR), now Agency for Healthcare Quality (AHRQ), guideline for *Acute Low Back Problems in Adults* recommended spinal manipulation for low-back pain; federal grants for chiropractic research are a reality;
- the Department of Defense formed a committee to introduce chiropractic services to the U.S. military;

- political victories are being won on the federal, state, and local levels;
- some managed care organizations are beginning to recognize chiropractors as gatekeepers; and,
- there is an ever-growing public awareness of the benefits of chiropractic care.[35]

2. Modalities

Chiropractic physicians may often use therapeutic modalities as part of their scope of care to facilitate healing in a patient. Chiropractic physicians are trained to use these therapy modalities and must pass a national board examination as part of their licensure requirements.

Chiropractors differ on the use of modalities. The two main schools of thought are referred to as "straights" and "mixers." The straights represent the conservative side of chiropractic and rely on spinal manipulation of the vertebrae as their primary therapeutic tool. The mixers are more progressive and incorporate a wide range of alternative healing methods beyond spinal manipulation.[36]

Each modality has its clinical indications, contraindications, and precautions that must be observed if the modality is to be applied safely and effectively. This requires knowledge of the biophysics involved, the physiologic responses and their modification by the technique used and the pros and cons in achieving a specific therapeutic purpose.[37]

a. Electric muscle stimulation

Electric muscle stimulation is use of an electrical current to affect the myoneural junction—where the nerve goes into the muscle. Use of this modality will help to override the neural reflex associated with muscular spasm, increase local circulation, and alleviate pain.

b. Thermal modalities
i. Ice

Ice is arguably the best immediate anti-inflammatory and analgesic remedy available. The pain response in the body is often a result of localized inflammation. Cryotherapy is effective in controlling and reducing localized inflammation, and also in numbing the pain associated with the inflammatory process. As long as there is identifiable inflammation in the tissues, cryotherapy is indicated to reduce the inflammatory reaction.

ii. Warming therapies

Warming therapies, such as moist heat, are ideally suited for promoting circulation in an area of congestion or adhesion prior to mobilization. The increase in local microcirculation helps to soften muscular rigidity, and to flush the lactic acid and metabolites associated with myofascial adhesion.

TIP: Warming therapies typically produce a comforting effect; however application of heat over an area of acute or chronic inflammation will tend to perpetuate the symptom complex.

---

c. Ultrasound

High frequency sound waves are often used to break up localized congestion in tissues—reducing adhesions and helping to flush metabolites. Soundwaves are usually used in conjunction with manipulative or active stretching exercises to facilitate function in a joint complex.

d. Acupuncture

Acupuncture is within the scope of chiropractic practice in many states, but is discussed in greater detail as a separate modality in Section 1.2.

e. Rehabilitation

The ultimate goal of chiropractic care is the restoration of spinal postural and functional stability. Whenever there has been a trauma to the spinal tissues, there will be some degree of residual weakness as the inflammatory reaction subsides. At that time it is appropriate to pursue a formalized protocol of functional rehabilitation or therapeutic exercise to reduce adhesions, facilitate formation of a functional scar, and restore stability to the spinal tissues. The goal of active rehabilitation is to improve the effectiveness of the chiropractic adjustments. As chiropractic care moves from alleviation of pain to functional restoration, patients are able to be more actively involved in their care. Such involvement gives patients an understanding of their role in the healing process, and a portion of the responsibility for recovery.

J. Pain Management

Pain is an unpleasant sensory and emotional experience associated with actual or potential tissue damage.[38] Modern research has revealed that diseases and injuries are resolved by a complex set of responses. These responses are coordinated by several signaling systems within the body's normal physiology. According to the current understanding, the primary signaling system affected by acupuncture is the nervous system which not only transmits signals along the nerves that comprise it, but also emits a variety of biochemicals that influence other cells of the body. The nervous system, with over 30 peptides involved in transmitting signals, is connected to the hormonal system via the adrenal gland,

and it makes connections to every cell and system in the body.[39]

In all pain-related cases, the patient should remain the center of care with a myriad of therapies and healthcare professionals impacting the treatment approach and management.[40]

K. Case Management

Given their educational background and training, chiropractors should appropriately diagnose and treat disorders of the neuromusculoskeletal system. However, the scope of conditions that doctors of chiropractic manage is not limited to neuromusculoskeletal disorders. Spinal irritations may exacerbate or mimic visceral complaints, and organ dysfunction may refer pain to the spine. It is the obligation of the physician to carefully assess the patient's localized, regional, and referred complaints. Although a chiropractic physician's primary focus is the spine, he is expected to recognize visceral disease conditions, and to make appropriate referral when indicated.

TIP: If a treatment plan has not made a documentable change in a patient's condition within a six-week period, alternate modalities must be considered including co-management with other professionals.

When a doctor begins a care plan, it is implied that (1) the abnormal or disease state has been identified by the doctor so that the criteria for proper application of treatment can be applied, and (2) the doctor has an understanding of the mechanisms of action and their predictable effects on the pathologic processes involved.[41]

Regular re-assessment of a patient's progress should be used to inform decision making in ongoing conservative management of patients with musculoskeletal symptoms. A methodological approach that considers change in parameters such as patient impairments is likely to be a useful guide for decision making during ongoing patient management, but only when the change being reassessed can be directly linked to functional goals. Changes in active range of movement or centralization of pain appear to be better indicators of treatment effectiveness than changes in either pain intensity or assessment of joint position.[42]

L. Standards of Care

It should be standard practice within any chiropractor's office that any patient, including those already under care presenting with a new problem, should be re-examined. Upon completion of the examination, any procedure used must be determined by the nature and scope of the disorder presented (i.e., the diagnosis). After diagnosis, the doctor must judge for herself whether the case should be treated, co-managed, or referred.[43]

1. Patient records

It is not only necessary, but also the acceptable standard of care for any healthcare practitioner to fully document the patient's condition, the treatments rendered, and the patient's progress. Patient records are viewed as files of evidence, which third-party liability carriers use to evaluate adequacy of treatment. Obviously the patient records of different healthcare providers will vary according to the type of treatment rendered. However, every provider in every discipline is accountable for the care provided to a patient. Records must consistently define the patient's condition, clearly objectify the findings during the course of treatment, and document the patient's progress.[44]

Chiropractic terms and abbreviations vary from practitioner to practitioner and often depend on the physician's background and training. Chiropractic records should be summarized in the same manner as other medical records. Procedures performed in the office should be described in detail. It is reasonable to expect that records be clear, concise, and legible. The dilemma from the non-chiropractor reviewer perspective is that the chiropractic records are often difficult to interpret. If the chiropractor has used idiosyncratic abbreviations and terms, it is reasonable that the reviewer ask that the chiropractor translate the records. The attorney who needs to understand the records should plan on meeting with the chiropractor, expecting to pay for his time, and go through the crucial records. Another alternative is to ask the chiropractor to prepare a narrative report that explains the records, treatment, and prognosis. See Figures 1.10 and 1.11.

2. Risk management

As with any other healthcare discipline, the chiropractic profession is held to a standard of professional, ethical, and legal conduct. The starting point for evaluating the extent of a doctor's liability to a patient is identifying any duty the doctor owes that patient. The chiropractic care is judged by the performance standard of the average chiropractor. The law expects the chiropractor to perform at the reasonable level of an average qualified chiropractor, or if the chiropractor claims a specialty, at the reasonable level of the average chiropractor in that specialty. Care that falls below this level sets the stage for a charge of malpractice if the patient is injured as a result.[45]

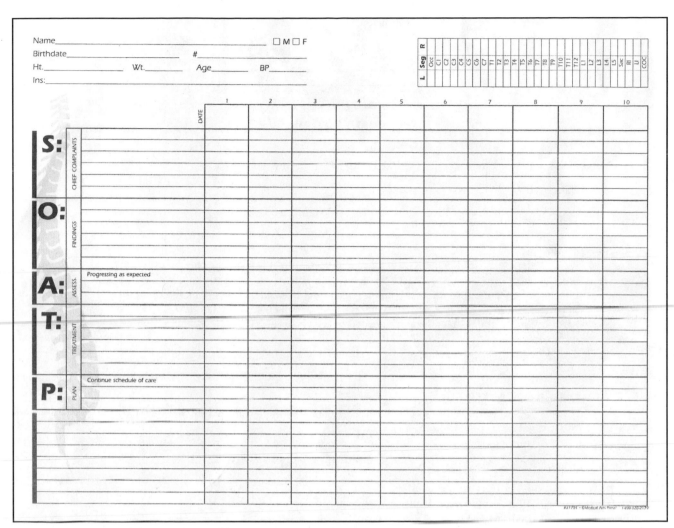

Figure 1.10 Often chiropractors will use a "travel card" system as a way to daily note on a patients' progress. There are many varieties of this card. The above example allows the patient to grade the severity and frequency of pain, and the doctor's findings. Other versions may include spinal regions manipulated or therapies performed. Such systems are good for daily tracking of a patient's progress, but should not be a substitute for regular evaluation and documentation.

Patient: John Smith
Patient ID# 12345

Date of Service: 2/3/04

Subjective:
        Mr. Smith returns today. He notes an improvement in his neck pain and shoulder tension. He also comments that the pains into his left arm and hand are improved since last week. He continues to have limiting tension in his back, and is still unable to raise his arms over his head without increasing his pain complaints.
Mr. Smith also states that he has not needed to take his Rx. pain medication the last 2 days.
Today he grades his neck pain at a 5, his shoulder at a 6, and his L arm soreness at a 7. (scale of 1-10, 1 = minimal pain, 10 = severe pain)

Objective:
        Trigger points noted in the mid-trapezius bilaterally, levator scapulae, and left rhomboid.
        Anterior segment at T4, fixation on motion at C5-6.

Diagnosis:
        847.1   Cervicodorsal strain
        739.1   C5 articular dysfunction
        729.1   Myositis
        723.4   Cervical neuritis on L – C5
        739.2   T4 articular dysfunction (compensatory)

Plan:
        Patient is responding to treatment.
Continue Chiropractic manipulation at schedule of three times weekly until re-evaluation in 2 weeks. Also continue electric muscle stimulation to the cervicodorsal spine to reduced congestion and pain. Mr. Smith is to continue cryotherapy to the affected area 15 minutes per hour as needed to minimize swelling. Anticipate beginning active therapies following re-eval, pending patient progress.

Douglas R. Briggs, DC, Dipl.Ac.(IAMA)

NEWARK
1536 Kirkwood Highway
Newark, DE 19711-5716
302.454.1200
fax: 302.454.1238

WILMINGTON
St. Francis Hospital
Suite 533, MSB
7th & Clayton Streets
Wilmington, DE 19805
302.575.8330
fax: 302.575.8382

HOCKESSIN • PIKE CREEK
202 Lantana Drive
Lantana Square
Shopping Center
Hockessin, DE 19707-8807
302.239.1600
fax: 302.239.1919

GLASGOW • BEAR
650 Plaza Drive
Four Seasons
Shopping Center
Newark, DE 19702-6369
302.453.4043
fax: 302.453.4484

REHOBOTH • LEWES
26 Midway Shopping Center
Rehoboth Beach, DE 19971-9735
302.645.6681
fax: 302.645.6621

Figure 1.11 Computerized SOAP note.

While the criteria for professional performance are generally established by usual and customary practices, this does not imply that there is not more than one acceptable method to reach a therapeutic goal. Different surgeons use different techniques to accomplish the same goal. Likewise, the chiropractor may select from several acceptable procedures and techniques available. The ones that are selected should be determined by the doctor's knowledge, training, experience, skill and clinical judgment. However, providing healthcare services which measure up to the applicable standard of care is only one of the doctor's duties. Chiropractors are trained in patient examination and treatment and are expected to act in the best interest of the patient.

Some of the major issues in healthcare litigation today include managed care organizations (MCOs) or health maintenance organizations (HMOs) and their cost management procedures, which impact patient care. Unfortunately, this often limits patient care options. This may create potential problems for the doctor in failing to properly diagnose or refer a patient for continued care or diagnostic testing. It is the responsibility of the chiropractor to appropriately examine a patient and pursue appropriate diagnostic evaluation. Records should show a clear plan of care and explain the logic of the studies performed. If studies are warranted but not obtainable, it is reasonable that the doctor refer the patient to the primary provider or another professional for the necessary examination. It is unreasonable for a chiropractor to offer medical advice or instruction outside of her appropriate scope. Again, particulars of chiropractic scope of practice are determined by case law and statute. If there is a question, consult the local codes to determine the appropriate scope of practice.

Depending on the state involved, the agency that regulates chiropractic practice might be the State Board of Chiropractic or the Division of Professional Regulation.

On occasion, malpractice insurance rates have been used to demonstrate the relative safety of chiropractic care. Comparison of malpractice premiums can be used. But it is an apples to oranges comparison because chiropractors have low liability in that they do not prescribe medications or perform invasive surgery; therefore, the rates would be expected to be less. Chiropractors nationwide on average pay about $1500 for malpractice insurance. Medical doctors may pay ten to one hundred times more than that. But the difference in premiums is not really a valid measure of safety but rather of less invasive types of procedures with less potential for malpractice incidents.[46]

3. Case study: discontinuation of medication

In the following case, the chiropractor clearly practiced beyond the scope of her training.

In *United States vs. Chiropractor* (Ref # CR-02-253) on March 9, 2004, the chiropractor was sentenced in a federal mail fraud case. She received an 18-24 month prison sentence; a fine of $9,000 and restitution of $631; relinquishment of her chiropractic license; and the order never to practice chiropractic again. Ten days later, she was sentenced in county court for violating Pennsylvania chiropractic regulations and ordered to pay a fine of $500 and serve three to six months in prison (which would run concurrent to the federal sentence).

The chiropractor was prosecuted for billing Medicaid for spinal manipulation for neck and shoulder problems. In fact, she was treating the plaintiff, a 30-year-old woman, for her chronic epilepsy. The plaintiff's fiancée, a Jehovah's Witness, wanted her to discontinue her medication. The chiropractor told the plaintiff that her treatment would eliminate the seizures and that she had to discontinue taking the anticonvulsive medications, which had successfully managed her condition for 20 years.

On the last visit to the chiropractor's office before her death, the plaintiff was wheelchair-bound, wearing adult diapers, choking on her own vomit, and had bitten through her tongue. On the night of her death, the chiropractor was taped telling the plaintiff's caretakers that the seizures (which were now occurring every 10-15 minutes) were part of her body detoxifying for the years of taking anticonvulsive medication. The chiropractor also said that under no circumstances should the plaintiff be taken to a hospital because they would give her anticonvulsive medication that would kill her. The chiropractor also told them that the patient would go into a deep sleep and awake drug-free. She never awoke.[47]

There are many issues in this case, some of which cannot be discussed as they have not yet been released in the public records. The case was settled before going to trial when tapes of the doctor's comments to the caregivers were found to contradict her deposition testimony.

First, the doctor was practicing beyond the appropriate scope of her license, and then fraudulently billing for her care. In Pennsylvania, chiropractors are not licensed to prescribe medication. Therefore they are also not able to direct a patient to discontinue or change dosing of prescribed medications. Although there have been times when chiropractic care has been helpful in treating epilepsy, it is inappropriate to immediately discontinue anticonvulsive medications—especially if they have controlled the patient's condition for an extended time. Appropriate chiropractic care must be co-managed with the prescribing medical physician so that medication dosages may be monitored and gradually decreased accordingly.

Also, at the time of her last visit, the patient was clearly not responding to treatment in an appropriate manner. Even if the chiropractor had believed that the medications were dangerously toxic, she should have referred the patient to another physician for evaluation and other treatment options. To mandate that the patient pursue no other course of treatment suggests a professional bias and an over-confidence on the part of the chiropractor.

4. Contraindications

It is commonly recognized that any therapeutic procedure or agent that has a potential for effectiveness has a potential for harm. Prior to any therapy being administered, the doctor is expected to be knowledgeable in the indications for, contraindications to, and the physiologic effects of all therapies utilized. Moreover, prior to utilization, the patient should be informed about what to expect from the therapy.[48]

Common contraindications to manipulation include:

- fracture or acute instability,
- active cancer metastasis, and
- vascular compromise.

However, the human body is a dynamic biological organism, and examination will determine when treatment parameters may require modification as the active processes of healing and rehabilitation progresses.[49]

The reported frequency of adverse reactions following spinal manipulation (adjustment) is rare; however, research constantly strives to reduce the risks even further. Generally, contraindications may be classified as vascular, traumatic, infectious, arthritic, psychological or metabolic. In addition, underlying congenital and acquired deformities and weaknesses should always be evaluated, since many do not become symptomatic until after trauma. Specific disorders within these classifications may not automatically contraindicate chiropractic adjustment because of their existence; but their presence and degree should be recognized and carefully considered prior to modifying treatment if necessary. All precautions taught in an accredited college of chiropractic and those dictated by sound clinical judgment should be observed.[50]

5. Vertebro-basilar stroke

The most common question regarding chiropractic care is the issue of manipulation-induced strokes. Vertebrobasilar strokes are not the most common cause of litigation against chiropractic physicians (less than 5%), yet they are among the most serious, well known, and feared, since they can result in permanent neurologic deficit, quadriplegia or death.[51] It must be recognized that VBS following a manipulation does occur; however, the incidence is very low. VBS usually occurs following a specific type of high velocity/low amplitude type of manipulation in a rotated position that compromises the vertebral artery. This risk is minimal in the general population. Common everyday activities, such as stargazing, rapidly turning the head while driving, and having a shampoo at a salon may cause aneurysm leading to a stroke. There are standardized maneuvers to screen for potential compromise of the vertebral artery, and they should be performed on every patient at initial examination as a routine screening tool. However, there is no sure way to define if a particular individual is at higher risk. It is difficult to anticipate and lessen a risk that is virtually nil.[52]

A Canadian study, reported in the October 2, 2001, issue of the *Canadian Medical Association Journal* (CMAJ), put the risk of stroke following neck adjustment at 1 in every 5.85 million adjustments. The study, which was based on patient medical files and malpractice data from the Canadian Chiropractic Protective Association, evaluated all claims of stroke following chiropractic care for a ten-year period between 1988 and 1997.[53]

TIP: It is reasonable to screen patients for warning signs of VBS; however, there are no definitive diagnostic maneuvers. It is therefore vital to know how to recognize the signs of a CVA or VBS, and to be able to treat the patient accordingly. Prompt treatment can result in total remission, or regression of neurologic deficits.[54]

Treatment should stop immediately if signs of vertebral artery injury present after manipulation. No further attempt at manipulation should be pursued. If the patient's symptoms quickly resolve, it may indicate a transient VBS resulting from slight arterial damage or spasm; or proprioceptive dizziness. Further examination and/or referral for additional diagnostic assessment is necessary if signs and symptoms do resolve. Alternate forms of treatment should be considered for this patient on future visits. If the symptoms progress and do not abate, this could be a medical emergency and requires immediate transportation to the hospital for medical intervention.[55]

6. Case study: stroke

This case describes serious injuries that occurred after chiropractic manipulation.

In January 2001, the plaintiff presented to a chiropractor for the first time. She had a sore neck, headache and back pain, which had emerged after shoveling snow with her husband. The chiropractor treated the discomfort through cervical spine manipulation. The patient was then directed to lie in a "therapy bed," but it was occupied. So she went to the reception desk to get an appointment card for the following Monday. At that moment she became suddenly ill and destabilized. She had a sudden onset of acute vertigo with nausea and vision disturbance that seemed to cut off half of whatever she focused on. She thought perhaps she was getting the flu, and she left the office. That evening at home she continued to feel ill with nausea, dizziness, loss of balance, and a visual field cut. The symptoms waned over the weekend and were mostly gone by Monday when the patient returned to work. When the workday was over, her husband took her to the chiropractor for her scheduled appointment. She was under the impression that she was to spend time in the previously occupied therapy bed. She did not realize that she had been scheduled for another adjustment. The patient told the chiropractor about her sudden feeling of malaise just as she was preparing to leave the office during the previous appointment date, as well as her symptoms over the weekend. She reported her symptoms of dizziness and nausea and vision problems. The chiropractor assured her that her symptoms were a normal reaction to the treatment. The medical record notes read "aura after treatment" to describe the patient's complaints and symptoms. The chiropractor then took the patient back for another manipulation. The patient's husband waited in the reception room.

After the manipulation treatment, the patient got up to walk from the treatment room to one of their therapy beds where she was supposed to lay for five or ten minutes. Her husband was present during her walk from the treatment room to the therapy bed, and noticed that she was walking sideways and that she was very pale. He also observed her staggering while exiting the therapy bed area. She quickly went straight past him to go outside to vomit. She complained of her neck hurting. She came back into the clinic and went into the

bathroom for over thirty minutes. The chiropractor checked on her repeatedly while she was in the bathroom. Throughout, the patient was holding her neck and complaining of severe pain and vomiting. The chiropractor suggested that she place an ice pack on her neck, and then told her husband to bring the vehicle around to the back of the building to load her in and take her home. The patient was observed to be hardly able to walk. The patient's husband had to physically lift his wife into their vehicle and then took her home and placed her in bed. She was reportedly barely responding, and even a sip of water caused her to "choke." He then telephoned a nearby emergency room and was told to bring his wife into the emergency room immediately. Within minutes of their arrival at the hospital, a CT scan of her head was done. In consult with a neurologist at another facility, an immediate transfer was arranged.

The working diagnosis was vertebral artery ischemia versus complete dissection following recent chiropractic adjustment. A left vertebral artery dissection was diagnosed. The dissection had caused a stroke principally in the cerebellum. The patient was twenty-eight years-old at the time of her injury, working full time with four school-age children. She has not been able to return to work. She claims permanent disability as a result of the left vertebral artery dissection. The plaintiff's chiropractic expert opined that the plaintiff should not have received any adjustment of her cervical spine on the second occasion, after she experienced adverse symptom reactions immediately following her first manipulation appointment. To have dismissed these complaints as a normal reaction to the treatment and merely label them as "an aura" was outside the acceptable standards of chiropractic care. The plaintiff's neurology expert opined that she would not have gone on to suffer a completed stroke if the second chiropractic manipulation had not been done. He was also prepared to testify that the stroke was the cause of her current disability. The case settled at mediation, prior to suit being filed, for $720,000, according to the published account.[56]

M. Summary

It is important to understand the paradigm of the chiropractor in the scope of case management. The goal of care should go beyond the mere resolution of symptoms and continue to include the restoration of structural and functional stability. An understanding of the phases of healing will enhance the patient's response to care and minimize residual sequelae. The standard of care is to move the patient through the phases of healing and return her to functional status. Clearly, appropriate regular evaluation and thorough documentation is critical to define the patient's condition, progress, and the rationale for continued or modified treatment. Achievement of maximum medical improvement must be the criteria that all healthcare practitioners follow. Chiropractic care has the advantage of more physician involvement, less invasive care, and better patient outcomes, often at a lower cost.[57] The clinician should use complementary and alternative medicine (CAM) therapies as adjuvants when evidence exists for their beneficial effect.[58]

1.2 Acupuncture

Acupuncture and chiropractic have a long historic affiliation, as they are both parts of the scope of what is now termed "traditional" Chinese medicine. Acupuncture may be very powerful as a stand-alone technique, yet traditionally it is more effective when combined with other healing practices. Acupuncture is an ancient art which has grown and developed with time, and many of the terminologies used have been carried forward. Often, this older, more poetic vocabulary is difficult to translate into the current medical terminology. Yet modern research continues to reveal the effectiveness of this treatment modality.

Acupuncture was originally taught through the chiropractic colleges in this country, until the profession expanded and developed its own educational standards and national certification examination. Acupuncture is becoming a more respected and recognized modality within the chiropractic profession, and as a stand-alone treatment. It is necessary to understand the background and application of the art.

A. History

Acupuncture has gained recent popularity in this country as an isolated treatment for any number of conditions, yet historically it is only a part of the system of traditional health care that has evolved in China over the last 6,000 years. It should be understood that this philosophy of health care extends beyond China, and includes Japan, Korea, Tibet, and many other nationalities and cultures. Acupuncture is a general term that refers to no specific style of treatment, and may encompass hundreds of geographical variations and different styles vaguely based on similar ideas. Chiropractic and acupuncture have a long affiliation. D.D. Palmer was well-versed in Chinese medical theory, and much of his early chiropractic protocols were based on oriental medical principles.

There are three general levels of acupuncture in use today:

- **Treatment of tender (ashi) points**. A style made popular by the "barefoot doctors" of China. Essentially stimulation of areas of localized tenderness, it is very similar to trigger point therapy and may be confused with massage techniques.
- **Treatment of conditions by "recipes."** This is a very common technique practiced throughout the acupuncture profession.
- **Meridian balancing** is considered the highest level of acupuncture therapy. The patient is evaluated for systemic imbalances, irrespective of condition, and treated to restore balance to the entire body.

B. Philosophy

Oriental medicine understands illness as a disruption or imbalance in an individual's *qi* ("chee"), the Chinese term for life force or vital energy. This approach also involves the application of different modalities for different facets of a patient's condition. *Tui Na*, which has evolved into the modern practice of chiropractic, was used to address myofascial adhesions and articular dysfunctions. Acupuncture is the branch of classical Chinese medicine concerned with restoring balance to the meridian system. This concept of an energetic system is foreign to Western medical science, but continues to be researched throughout Asia, primarily Japan. Described simply, there is a network of "bioenergy" called qi, which flows in a regular pattern around and through the body. At times these pathways run parallel to circulatory and nervous systems, yet they are independent from them. If there is an imbalance in the natural flow of qi, there will be a spillover effect into the associated body region or system. The goal of Oriental medicine is to restore homeostasis to the body as a whole. Acupuncture is used to clear the blockage and facilitate healing when it is determined that there is an energetic imbalance.

C. Diagnostics

Historically, diagnosis of the internal condition of a patient was performed by a careful evaluation of the patient's physical presentation. Diagnosis in the traditional model is theoretical and from a Western perspective very vague—focusing more on the interrelations of the organ systems than a specific diagnosis. As modern diagnostics are able to define the physiologic state of the patient much more quickly and accurately, practitioners should use every diagnostic tool available to appropriately evaluate a patient's condition. If there is any question of significant disease or pathology, the practitioner is obligated to refer for appropriate medical evaluation and co-management.

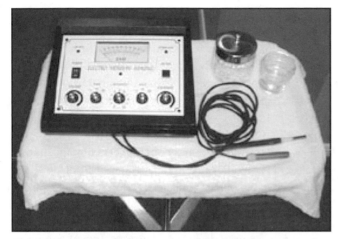

Figure 1.12 Micro-current used for electro-acupuncture and meridian balancing.

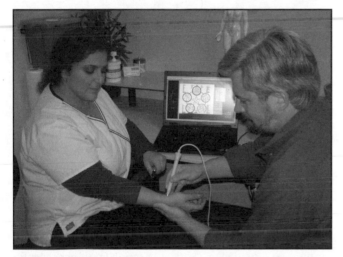

Figure 1.13 Contemporary acupuncture evaluation using computerized meridian imaging.

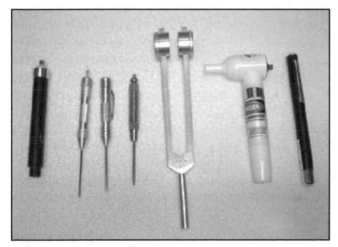

Figure 1.14 Contemporary acupuncture tools. From left to right: piezo-electric stimulator; 3 different tei-shin (non-piercing needle); 128 cps tuning fork; 2 632nM HeNe lasers.

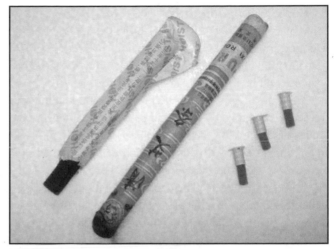

Figure 1.15 The use of moxibustion in classical acupuncture was to warm the tissues. Shown are stick moxa and Korean "stick-on" moxa.

A simple form of evaluation is the palpation of *ah-shi (ouch) points*, commonly referred to as trigger points in Western medicine. These points are often both diagnostic (indicative of a condition) and therapeutic (promoting a benefit) when handled properly.[59] See Figures 1.12 and 1.13.

TIP: The most modern of acupuncture diagnostic procedures is the Japanese art of *Ryodoraku* (also known as Electronic Meridian Imaging or EMI).

This technique involves the use of a probe to test the electrical resistance to current at specific points on the wrists and ankles. The theory is that this evaluation will provide a representation of the relative imbalances of the primary energetic system as a whole. While this type of evaluation will provide direction to treat meridian imbalances, it does not indicate all the points that might be treated for a specific condition.

D. Modalities

Contrary to common perception, acupuncture is not the use of only needles. Needles are one modality the acupuncturist may use to treat imbalances in the meridian system. Historically, finger pressure (called acupressure in the U.S.) and blunt probe pressure were the original tools of acupuncturists. Modern modalities also include the use of laser ("cold" HeNe laser at a frequency of 632nM), microcurrent, and electric muscle stimulation. Vacuum cupping is used to pull circulation into an area of congestion. Vibration stimulation (128 cycles per second) is effective to reduce myofascial adhesion. Moxibustion (burning of the herb mugwort to heat an area) and diathermy are used to promote regional circulation.[60] With the advent of new and equally effective methods of stimulation, the use of needles is becoming secondary.[61] See Figures 1.14–1.15.

E. Pain Management

Microcurrent, cold laser, and electric stimulation via the acupuncture needle are all valid methods of reducing pain and inflammation, integrating the function of the body's systems, and facilitating a healing response.

Fibromyalgia is one of the most difficult conditions to treat medically today. The progressive muscular tension and adhesion, along with the associated pain, is difficult if not impossible to treat with conventional methods. Patients often develop secondary visceral and psychosocial complaints due to the chronic pain. The danger of treating chronic pain with medication is that the patient ultimately requires higher doses to maintain the same level of relief. Such conditions may be effectively treated with a combination of both acupuncture and chiropractic. The application of acupuncture modalities for pain relief, coupled with manipulation of the joint complexes and controlled rehabilitation of the regional tissues, can greatly improve patients' functional abilities and their quality of life. In all pain-related cases, the patient should remain the center of care with a myriad of therapies and healthcare professionals impacting the treatment approach and management.[62] See Figure 1.16.

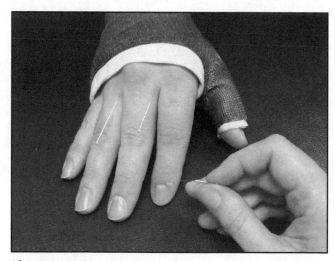

Figure 1.16 *Acupuncture may be used to reduce pain and promote healing for a variety of injuries.*

F. Case Management

Within the case management system, it is reasonable to expect that acupuncture will primarily be used for pain management. This does not preclude acupuncture as a legitimate modality for treating visceral or other organic conditions; however, extensive discussion in those directions is beyond the scope of this text.[63]

Pain, either by traumatic injury or some pathologic process, is often the driving reason for a patient to seek care, and enter the case management system. Pain level is entirely subjective, and may often be modified by the patient depending on her perception, constitution, psychological state, and need for secondary gain. Although there is no serum pain level to monitor, there are a number of orthopedic maneuvers designed to screen for malingering that can be employed effectively.[64] This remains a controversial area. The diagnosis of the cause(s) of pain depends on the skillful interpretation of its often-subtle features.[65]

As acupuncture becomes more mainstream, it is imperative for the individual practitioner to appropriately evaluate the patient's complaint, validate the differential diagnosis, and recommend appropriate treatment. Almost 90% of all diseases either begin with pain or have pain as a prominent symptom at some time during their course.[66] When a patient has pain, either acute or chronic, care must often focus on the alleviation of symptoms before other treatments can be incorporated to facilitate healing. Acupuncture, coupled with some forms of electrical stimulation, can be effective in the management and treatment of acute and chronic pain, in part at least through the biologic activation of neurohormonal and neurotransmitter systems.[67]

G. Standards of Care

1. Patient records

As discussed above, it is the standard of care for any healthcare practitioner to fully document the patient's condition, the treatments rendered, and the patient's progress. Obviously the patient records of different healthcare providers will vary according to the type of treatment rendered. However, every provider in every discipline is accountable for the care provided to a patient. Records must consistently define the patient's condition, clearly objectify the findings during the course of treatment, and document the patient's progress.[68]

Acupuncture terms and abbreviations vary from practitioner to practitioner and often depend on the physician's background and training. The records should be summarized in the same manner as other medical records. Procedures performed in the office should be described in detail. It is reasonable to expect that records be clear, concise, and legible. The dilemma from the non-acupuncture reviewer perspective is that the records are often difficult to interpret. If the practitioner has used idiosyncratic abbreviations and terms, it is reasonable that the reviewer ask that the acupuncturist translate and explain the records. The attorney who needs to understand the records should plan on meeting with the provider, expecting to pay for his time, and go through the crucial records. Another alternative is to ask the provider to prepare a narrative report that explains the records, treatment, and prognosis.

2. Risk management

Obviously, the greatest concern with acupuncture is the insertion of a needle into the tissues. As part of licensure, acupuncturists are required to pursue specific training in clean needle technique. Chiropractic and allopathic physicians are trained in phlebotomy, and have already met this requirement. Training in acupuncture also guides the practitioner in appropriate needle placement and insertion.

3. Contraindications

There are times when certain acupuncture treatments are not recommended. Standard precautions are indicated whenever utilizing needle therapies. Blood-borne diseases and clotting disorders are obvious health concerns that must be ruled out during consultation. Contemporary practitioners must pass a national clean needle technique examination as part of the licensure requirements. Other contraindications include deep needling over the thoracic cage, electro-stimulation across the cortex and cardiac regions, and heat modalities over areas of infection or inflammation. Additionally, there are more subtle precautions associated with the patient's condition, such as avoiding needle stimulation of certain points during pregnancy. As these points are different for the individual, it is the responsibility of the practitioner to act in the best interest of the patient.[69]

H. Summary

Acupuncture is a principle, not a technique. Some states have considered the use of acupuncture needles a medical procedure and therefore outside of the chiropractic domain. Even in those states forbidding the use of needle acupuncture, chiropractors are able to use non needle meridian therapy techniques under the physiotherapy laws, as it was obvious that needles were not necessary to positively affect an acupuncture response. It is important to understand that there is no difference between "meridian therapy" and "acupuncture" philosophically, theoretically, clinically, or practically. There is only a difference in semantics.[70]

1.3 Massage
A. History

The use of touch is a natural and instinctive means of relieving pain and discomfort. When a person bruises or injures themselves, it is common to touch or rub that part of the body for relief. Most ancient cultures practiced some form of healing touch. This was usually performed by someone in the tribe with specialized training (i.e., shaman or priest). Massage evolved simultaneously in Japan, China, Egypt, Greece and Rome. In 1814, Per Henrik Ling is credited with developing what we currently recognize as Swedish Massage. At the time it was referred to as "Medical Gymnastics." Medical Gymnastics incorporated a series of active and passive movements with massage. These active and passive movements, when added to the manual therapies, helped release the joints of their restriction and adhesion. Ling divided his movements into three forms: active, duplicatable and passive. In an active movement the patient performs the activity. Now we name this Therapeutic Exercise, duplicated movements performed by the patient and the therapist. For example, the therapist might move a limb while the patient resists. We now refer to this as Resistive Exercise or PNF. When the therapist moves the limb without resistance from the patient, this is called passive movement. We now identify this as Range of Motion and Stretching.[71]

B. Philosophy

Massage is a natural, instinctive method for relieving pain and restoring healthy body functions. Pain can be soothed away while bringing relief from nervous tension and fatigue. The effects of massage differ according to the individual needs and goals of the patient. It is not uncommon for the effects of massage to change from one patient to another. This is partly due to the mental and emotional reactions patients may experience with massage.

Massage believes in the structural unity of the body. Nothing exists in isolation. Dysfunction in one area of the body can create dysfunction in another area. For example, muscular tension or trigger points in the hip can create an altered gait pattern that can create pain in the neck or shoulder.

C. Effects of Massage
1. Physiological effects of massage

Physically, massage increases metabolism, hastens healing, relaxes and refreshes the muscles, and improves the detoxifying functions of the lymphatic system. Massage helps to prevent and relieve muscle cramps and spasms and improves circulation of blood and lymph, thereby improving the delivery of oxygen and nutrients to the cells as it enhances the removal of metabolic wastes. Massage therapy is effective as pain management in conditions such as arthritis, neuritis, neuralgia, whiplash, muscular lesions, sciatica, headaches, muscle spasm, and many other neurological and muscular conditions.[72]

2. Effects of massage on the muscular system

Massage encourages the nutrition and development of the muscular system by stimulating its circulation, nerve supply, and cell activity. Regular and systematic massage causes the muscles to become firmer and more elastic. Massage is also an effective means of relaxing tense muscles and releasing muscle spasms.[73] Massage is useful in managing more generalized soft tissue injuries as well. Fibrotic tissue responds well to the specific approaches of connective tissue massage (particularly deep transverse friction). Studies indicate that massage may reduce the formation of adhesions and the scarring that often results from soft tissue injury.

3. Effects of massage on the nervous system

The effects of massage on the nervous system depend on the direct and reflex reaction of the nerves stimulated. The nervous system can be stimulated or soothed depending on the type of massage movement applied. Stimulation of the peripheral nerve receptors could have reflex reactions affecting the vaso-motor nerves, internal organs, pain perception, or the underlying joints and muscles of the areas being massaged.[74] Massage stimulates various sensory receptors. Various feedback loops are activated that intervene and adjust various homeostatic processes. The sensory stimulation from massage disrupts an existing pattern in the central nervous system (CNS) control centers, resulting in a shift of motor impulses, most often in the peripheral nervous system, that re-establishes homeostasis. Usually both the somatic and autonomic divisions of the peripheral nervous system are influenced as balance is restored.

Massage is able to directly work on specific nervous system-related complaints. The effects of massage on myofascial trigger points are a result of stimulation of proprioceptive nerve endings, changes in sarcomere length, release of enkephalin, and stretching of musculotendinous structures that initiate reflex muscle relaxation through the Golgi tendon organ and spindle receptors. Massage is also valuable in treating nerve impingement such as entrapment or compression. Impingement often occurs at major nerve plexuses because of the structural arrangement of the body. The specific nerve root, trunk, or division affected determines the condition, such as thoracic outlet syndrome, sciatica or carpal tunnel syndrome. Therapeutic massage techniques work in many ways to reduce pressure on nerves. Mechanically stretching the muscles will soften the connective tissue and interrupt the pain-spasm-pain cycle caused by protective muscle spasm that occurs in response to pain.

4. Effects of massage on the circulatory system

Massage affects the quality and quantity of blood with the increased flow of blood to the massaged area. This improves cellular nutrition and elimination of cellular waste. The work of the heart is reduced. Massage also helps improve the blood making process which results in an increase in the number of red and white blood cells.

5. Psychological effects of massage

Massage promotes relaxation while muscle tension and pain are reduced. Massage also helps patients become more aware of where they are holding tension and where they have tight muscles or painful areas. By getting in touch with these areas, the patient can begin to focus on relaxing them both during the massage and on a daily basis.[75]

Massage is the application of touch to aid the healing process. Therapeutic massage is more concisely defined as the scientific art and system of assessment, and systematic, manual application of a technique to the superficial soft tissue of the skin, muscles, tendons, ligaments and fascia, as well as to the structures that lie within the superficial tissue. This is accomplished by use of the hand, foot, knee, arm, elbow, and forearm. The manual technique involves systematic application of touch, stroking, friction, vibration, percussion, kneading, stretching, compression or passive and active joint movements within the normal physiologic range of motion. Also included are adjunctive external applications of water, heat, and cold for the purposes of establishing and maintaining good physical condition and health by normalizing and improving muscle tone, promoting relaxation, stimulating circulation and producing therapeutic interactions among all body systems. These intended effects are accomplished through the physiologic energetic and mind/body connections in a safe, non-sexual environment that respects the patient's self-determined outcome for the session.[76]

The simple act of touch alone can be a soothing experience. The skillful act of touch can help reduce pain, promote circulation, alleviate congestion, and facilitate the healing response. For some patients the experience can be purely mechanical—the release of myofascial adhesions. For others, the experience can be much more emotional. The effects of massage can be classified as either mechanical or reflexive. Mechanical effects are direct physical effects of the massage techniques on the tissues they contact. Reflex effects of massage are indirect responses to touch that affect body functions and tissues through the nervous or energy systems of the body.

D. Education

The practice of massage therapy involves a core curriculum. Coursework focuses heavily on anatomy, but also includes physiology, physical examination, orthopedic testing, medical terminology, record keeping, body mechanics, hygiene, and different techniques and therapies. Licensure is dictated by state laws. Not every state requires licensing and in certain states licensing is determined by the individual city or township. The generally accepted standard for licensing is passing of the national exam, established by the National

Certification Board for Therapeutic Massage and Bodywork (NCBTMB). Currently this exam is the accepted standard in 33 states. However, there is work in progress to develop an alternate exam that will also be accepted by various states along with or in place of the NCBTMB's exam.

To be considered eligible to take the NCETMB or NCETM a candidate must have completed a minimum of 500 hours of instruction from a school that has a NCB Assigned School Code.

The program of study must include:

- 300 hours (60%) delivered in-class (face-to-face) or in a distance education format (CD, DVD, online, videotape, telecourse, hybrid course, etc.), or in some combination of both. (Please note that not all states accept distance education when reviewing for licensure.)
- 200 hours (40%) of hands-on instruction delivered *in-class* (face-to-face) only.

The program of instruction must include:

- 200 hours of massage and bodywork assessment, theory, and application instruction.
- A minimum of: 125 hours of instruction on the body systems (anatomy, physiology and kinesiology).
- 40 hours of pathology.
- 10 hours of business and ethics instruction (a minimum of 6 hours in ethics).
- 125 hours of instruction in an area or related field that theoretically completes the massage program of study.[77]

Some states are adopting a two-tiered licensure process for applicants. The first tier generally has less educational and testing requirements and may be titled as "certification" by the state. An applicant who is licensed under the lower tier is generally limited in her scope of practice. For example, Delaware has two tiers. The first is a "Certified Massage Technician." Applicant are required to have completed 300 hours of education and to be CPR (cardiopulmonary resuscitation) certified. Applicants are also restricted from performing therapeutic massage. They are also not able to bill insurance for their services. The next tier is "Licensed Massage Technician." A therapist who is licensed by the state of Delaware has completed a minimum of 500 hours of education, is CPR certified and has passed the national exam (NCETMB or NCETM). This therapist is able to perform therapeutic massage and is able to bill insurance for services.[78] See Figures 1.17 and 1.18.

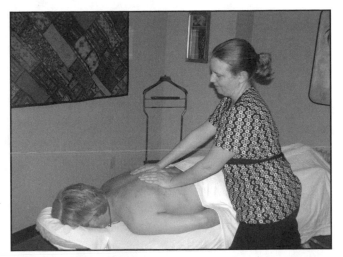

Figure 1.17 *Massage.*

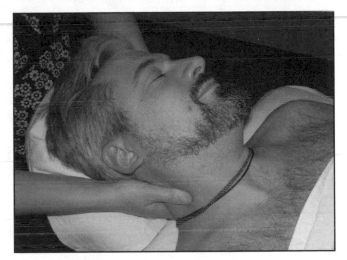

Figure 1.18 *Massage.*

E. Techniques

There are a myriad of specialties that fall under the umbrella of massage. There is, however, a core of basic techniques that each specialty uses. The techniques are the same; the difference is the manner in which they are applied.

1. **Effleurage**—light gliding strokes. This is typically the preferred methods to warm the tissues for more focused bodywork. Gentle strokes parallel to the muscle fibers have a soothing effect, and will stimulate superficial circulation and lymphatic flow. Stronger pressure will activate connective tissue and proprioceptors. By altering the pressure, drag, speed, direction, and rhythm, the therapist can introduce tension, bending and compression forces.

2. **Petrissage**—requires that the tissues be lifted, rolled, and squeezed. This technique works ver-

tically to the muscle fibers and has the effect of stretching both the tendons and Golgi tendon receptors, stimulating a reflex relaxation in the muscle.

3. **Compression**—also called ischemic compression or direct pressure. Compression involves controlled focused pressure down into the belly of the muscle to spread the spindle cells and cause a reflex contraction in the tissue.

4. **Tapotement**—quick, gentle forces in succession down across the area to create a rhythmic compression of the tissues.

5. **Friction**—small deep movements in an area to create a shear force. This is to stimulate "therapeutic inflammation" or a localized increase in circulation.

6. **Vibration**—the application of compression followed by back and forth motions while maintaining pressure to stimulate the tissues.

7. **Shaking**—is used to relax a muscle group or limb by literally lifting and shaking the tissues. This is to warm and relax the tissue prior to more direct therapy.

8. **Rocking**—a rhythmic technique used to calm and relax.

F. Different Modalities of Massage Therapy

1. **Swedish**—Based on Western concepts of anatomy and physiology and employs the traditional techniques (effleurage, petrissage, etc.). This system also employs joint movements, stretching and range of motion exercises.

2. **Asian approaches**—(Amma, acupressure, shiatsu, jin shin do, do-in, hoshino, tuina, watsu, Tibetan point holding, and Thai Massage.) Derived from original Chinese concepts, these manipulations and stretches focus on specific areas of the body to elicit responses in the nervous and circulatory systems. Pressure or joint movement is applied to stimulate specific points. The goal is to achieve therapeutic changes in the person through the regulation of chi (life force energy).

3. **Structural and postural integration approaches**—(Bindegewebs massage, Rolfing, Hellerwork, Looyen, Pfrimmer, Soma, and Bowen therapy.) These techniques focus more specifically on the connective tissue structure to influence posture and biomechanics. The approaches are systematic and effective because they are grounded in the fundamentals of physiology and biomechanics. Practitioners of these styles have received an extensive education.

4. **Neuromuscular approaches**—(Neuromuscular techniques, muscle energy techniques, strain/counterstrain, orthobionomy, Trager, myotherapy, proprioceptive neuromuscular facilitation, reflexology, and trigger points.)

5. **Craniosacral and myofascial approaches**—(Craniosacral therapy, myofascial release, soft tissue mobilization, deep tissue massage, and connective tissue massage.) These systems focus more specifically on the various aspects of both mechanical and reflexive connective tissue functions. Both light and deep pressure are used. Cross-fiber friction is frequently utilized as well.

6. **Manual lymphatic drainage**—(Vodder lymph drainage.) This system uses the anatomy and physiology of lymphatic movement with both mechanical and reflexive techniques to stimulate the flow of lymphatic fluid.

7. **Applied kinesiology**—(Touch for health, applied physiology, educational kinesiology, and three in one concepts.) This system is frequently used within the chiropractic discipline. A specific muscle testing procedure is used for evaluation. Asian meridians and acupressure are some of the corrective measures. Others rely on osteopathic reflex mechanisms.

8. **Integrated approaches**—(Sports massage, infant massage, equine massage, on-site or seated massage, prenatal massage, and geriatric massage.) These styles of massage focus on a specific type of population.

G. Case Management

Massage is able to function in both a wellness and therapeutic capacity. Each focus is more accurately defined by its generally accepted scope of practice. There is no formal scope of practice for massage therapy. Each state and professional organization has adopted its own, but there are some generally accepted principles.

TIP: Medical massage vs. wellness massage—Practitioners of medical massage work within the context of the healthcare system. Their approach to treatment is more scientific or problem-solving oriented versus the intuitive, nurturing approach of wellness massage. The focus of medical massage is on producing functional outcomes, whereas wellness massage focuses more on patient comfort. In a medical massage setting, care is terminated when the therapeutic goals are reached. In a wellness setting, care is terminated at the patient's discretion.[79]

---

1. Wellness massage scope of practice

This is a non-specific approach to massage that focuses on assessment procedures to detect contraindications to massage and the need for referral to other healthcare professionals, and on the development of a health-enhancing physical state for the patient. The plan for the massage session is developed by combining information, desired massage outcomes, and directions from the patient with the skills of the massage practitioner to provide an individualized massage session aimed at normalizing the body systems. The goals of this session are reduced stress, decreased muscle tension, relief of pain related to soft tissue dysfunction, and increased circulation.

2. Medical/rehabilitative massage scope of practice

Massage therapists develop, maintain, rehabilitate or augment physical function; relieve or prevent physical dysfunction and pain; and enhance the well-being of the patient. Methods include assessment of the soft tissue and joints, as well as treatment by soft tissue manipulation, hydrotherapy, remedial exercise programs and patient self-care programs.

The massage therapist will perform an assessment of the patient and from that information a treatment plan is developed. It is not uncommon for a portion of the assessment to take place during the treatment. The therapist may use certain techniques to assess the tissue and then use the same or similar techniques, altered slightly in intensity to correct the situation. The therapist may utilize several areas of assessment, the first of which is done when interviewing. Information is gathered regarding the patient's health history, history of the complaint and any related complaints. The therapist may also perform a posture assessment. This helps identify areas where the body's symmetry is off. Right and left sides will never be identical but they should be similar. This helps the therapist to understand where the postural stresses on the joints are. A therapist may also perform a gait assessment. The patient is observed walking toward and away from the therapist. The therapist notes any deviation in the gait phases from heel strike to toe off. The position of the feet in relation to the pelvis can highlight areas of postural stresses. Range of motion is often used to assess a joint. A therapist can visually assess whether a joint's range of motion falls into the normal range, or if it is reduced or excessive. The therapist is also able to assess the joint by how the joint feels at the end of the motion. This is called end feel. How the joint feels at the end of motion can indicate muscle spasm, edema, loose cartilage or meniscal tissue.

Palpation is probably the most commonly used assessment tool for the massage therapist. For example changes in skin temperature over a specific area indicate the presence of edema or a trigger point. Also, adhesions in the skin, muscle tissue or fascia indicate binding scar tissue. Massage therapists are also able to perform muscle testing to determine areas of tension or adhesion. The three most common muscle tests are strength testing, neurologic muscle testing, and applied kinesiology. The purpose of strength testing is to discover whether the muscle is responding with sufficient strength to perform the required body functions. The purpose of neurologic muscle testing is to discover whether the neurologic interaction of the muscles is working smoothly. Applied kinesiology relies on muscle strength or weakness as an indicator of body functions. This is similar to a biofeedback mechanism.

H. Standards of Care
1. Patient records

As with any healthcare discipline, it is reasonable to expect that the care provided be clearly documented. The patient's case history should be reviewed, as well as relevant assessment and orthopedic findings. The massage therapist should record the findings on a specific visit, the areas treated, the particular therapies used, and the patient's response to care.[80] The generally accepted method of charting for massage therapists is the SOAP format (Subjective, Objective, Assessment, Plan).

The massage therapist should perform a thorough assessment that includes a patient history, observation, and examination. This will help disclose problems and the physiological basis for the patient's complaints. The therapist will generally notice how the patients hold their bodies and how they move. The massage therapist may also utilize various manual tests to help more precisely determine the tissues or conditions involved. The therapist will then generally develop a treatment plan formulated using information from the intake and medical history forms, the interview, and preliminary assessment. In this treatment plan, the therapist will formulate session goals and may choose massage techniques.[81]

2. Risk management

As with any other healthcare discipline, the massage profession is held to a standard of professional, ethical, and legal conduct. Care is judged by the performance standard of the average massage therapist. The law expects the practitioner to perform at the reasonable level of an average qualified massage therapist, or if a specialty is claimed, then at the reasonable level of the average practitioner in that specialty. Care that falls below this level sets the stage for a charge of malpractice if the patient is injured as a result.

While the criteria for professional performance are generally established by usual and customary practices, there is more than one acceptable method to reach a therapeutic goal. Different surgeons use different techniques to accomplish the same goal. Likewise, the massage therapist may select from several acceptable procedures and techniques available. The ones that are selected should be determined by the practitioner's knowledge, training, experience, skill and clinical judgment. However, providing healthcare services which measure up to the applicable standard of care is only one of the practitioner's duties. Massage therapists are trained in patient examination and treatment and are expected to act in the best interest of the patient.

3. Contraindications

Contraindications to massage are considered either general or regional. Regional contraindications are those that relate to a specific area of the body. General contraindications are those that require a physician's evaluation before any massage is indicated. Massage is indicated for musculoskeletal discomfort, circulation enhancement, relaxation, stress reduction, and pain control. It is also indicated in situations in which analgesics, anti-inflammatory drugs, muscle relaxants, and blood pressure, antianxiety and antidepressant medications may be prescribed. Therapeutic massage can support the use of these medications, manage some of the side effects and in mild cases may be able to replace them.

There are situations where massage is contraindicated until the patient has received permission from a doctor to continue. These conditions include diabetes, recent diagnosis of heart disease, or cancer. Massage is not necessarily contraindicated for those with cancer. Current research indicates that massage can support the immune system's battle with cancer cells.[82] Certain conditions preclude massage absolutely. Massage is contraindicated when the patient has a fever. A fever signifies that the body is trying to isolate and eliminate invading pathogens. Massage would tend to work against the defense mechanisms of the body. It is generally recommended that if the patient's body temperature is over 99.4°F, then massage should not be performed. Massage may be performed once the fever is reduced for 24 hours. Massage is contraindicated if the patient has an acute cold or influenza. Giving massage to a person with an acute viral infection will intensify the illness. Massage is indicated once the acute period is over. Massage is contraindicated in the presence of a possible blood clot, uncontrolled high blood pressure, unstable heart conditions, and locally over the site of varicose veins.

1.4 Integrative Medicine

It becomes clear from a review of the history of the different healing practices that much of what has been called "alternative" or "complementary" has traditionally had an integrative focus.

According to the National Center for Complementary and Alternative Medicine (NCCAM) at the National Institutes of Health, integrative medicine "combines mainstream medical therapies and CAM therapies for which there is some high-quality scientific evidence of safety and effectiveness."[83]

In other words, integrative medicine "cherry picks" the very best, scientifically validated therapies from both conventional and CAM systems. Integrative medicine is a healing-oriented medicine that takes into account the whole person (body, mind, and spirit), including all aspects of lifestyle. It emphasizes the therapeutic relationship and makes use of all appropriate therapies, both conventional and alternative.

The principles of integrative medicine include:

- A partnership between patient and practitioner in the healing process
- Appropriate use of conventional and alternative methods to facilitate the body's innate healing response
- Consideration of all factors that influence health, wellness and disease, including mind, spirit and community as well as body
- A philosophy that neither rejects conventional medicine nor accepts alternative therapies uncritically
- Recognition that good medicine should be based in good science, be inquiry driven, and be open to new paradigms

- Use of natural, effective, less-invasive interventions whenever possible
- Use of the broader concepts of promotion of health and the prevention of illness as well as the treatment of disease
- Training of practitioners to be models of health and healing, committed to the process of self-exploration and self-development[84]

TIP: Preventive care versus early detection—Often these two terms get used interchangeably, but they are entirely different. Preventive care focuses on attaining and supporting overall health and well-being—through care, good nutrition, exercise, and rest. Early detection is just that, *detection*. Mammograms are used for detection of breast cancer—and the earlier found the better, but they do not serve to *prevent* breast cancer. Understanding the differences in these terms may offset confusion when evaluating a care plan.

Until recently, pain management has been a very isolated practice, often relying on the use of medication to mask symptoms. The current trend is the integration of different practitioners to address the various physical and mental aspects of the pain patient.[85] The idea of integrative medicine is not new—the Greek physician Hippocrates advocated massage and gymnastic exercise.[86]

It is well documented throughout the literature that ongoing pain leads to a cascade of physical and psychosocial limitations. The pain patient, especially when dealing with chronic pain, faces the physical challenges of pain and the progressive neuromuscular and emotional issues of the pain complex. Medication for pain may be reasonable but will not necessary address an underlying joint dysfunction with myofascial adhesion. Manipulation is effective in promoting joint function, but without appropriate rehabilitation exercise to restore stability the effects of manipulation may show little lasting benefit.[87]

It is incumbent on the pain practitioner to recognize the specific needs of the individual patient and to pursue the best combination of treatment options for that patient. Even in cases of chronic pain, one should be able to document some progressive response to care, or at least the tangible maintenance of a functional baseline. With a course of care, every patient should show a progressive—though possibly very gradual—evolution toward improvement, and it is reasonable to expect that the care plan for this patient would evolve as well. Ideally, the long term goal of any pain management care plan is to reduce patients' needs for pain medication and increase their functional capacity.

Additional Reading

Bagnell, K.G. *Pre-Natal Chiropractic Care* USA, Instant-publisher.com. 2005

Boswell, M.V., Cole, B.E. *Weiner's Pain Management A Practical Guide for Clinicians*. Boca Raton, FL: Taylor & Francis Group; 2006

http://www.chiroweb.com/forum/important.html

www.fcer.org (The Foundation for Chiropractic Education and Research)

www.chiroaccess.com (Manual Alternative and National Therapy Index System—MANTIS)

www.chiro.org (The Chiropractic Resource Organization)

www.acatoday.com (American Chiropractic Association)

Savoie, S. "Common Documentation Mistakes And How You Can Avoid Them" http://www.ncmic.com/microsites/Examiner/Documentation.aspx, retrieved 11/28/09

Endnotes

1. Appleby, K. and Tarver, J. *Medical Records Review* (3rd ed.) Gaithersburg, MD: Aspen Law and Business; 1999.

2. Retrieved 8/15/04 from www.amerchiro.com.

3. See note 2.

4. See note 1.

5. *Id.*

6. See note 2.

7. See note 1.

8. See note 2.

9. *Id.*

10. See note 1.

11. See note 2.

12. Briggs, D.R., Curley, D.M., Cohen, S.S., Mahoney, J.J. "Understanding Chiropractic Case Management." *Journal of Legal Nurse Consulting*. Vol 14, No. 2; April 2003: 9-13.

13. Received 8/18/04 from the American Chiropractic Association.

14. See note 12.

15. *Id.*

16. *Id.*

17. *Id.*

18. *Id.*

19. *Id.*

20. *Id.*

21. *Id.*

22. Badke MB, Boissonnault WG. "Changes in Disability Following Physical Therapy Intervention For Patients With Low Back Pain: Dependence On Symptom Duration." *Arch Phys Med Rehabil.* 2006 Jun; 87(6):749-56.

23. See note 12.

24. *Id.*

25. Cocchiarella, L., and Andersson, G. B. J. *Guides to the Evaluation of Permanent Impairment* (5th ed.). United States: American Medical Association; 2001.

26. *Id.*

27. *Id.*

28. See note 12.

29. See note 25.

30. *Managing Pain in the Primary Care Office.* (CD-ROM) Family Practice - Pain Education Project. Sponsored by The Ohio State University Medical Center, Center for Continuing Medical Education. September, 2004.

31. Yeomans, S.G. *The Clinical Application of Outcomes Assessment.* Stamford, CT: Appleton & Lange; 2000.

32. Bickner, B.J. Doctor fails to act in timely manner, Case Study: 102431. *NCMIC Examiner*; Fall 2004: 2-3.

33. *Id.*

34. Laws, S., Franklin, D.J. *The Receptor-Tonus Technique* (Available from: Holistic Health Enhancement, 1210 n. 24th St., Quincy, IL 62301).

35. Retrieved on 8/31/04 from http://www.fcer.org/html/research.htm.

36. See note 1.

37. Sportelli, L. "Cervical Adjustment Leads To Standard Of Care Allegations," Case Study: 4892002731. *NCMIC Examiner*; Summer 2000: 2-3.

38. See note 30.

39. Briggs, D.R., Curley, D.M., Amaro, J.A. "Acupuncture in the Contemporary Healthcare System." *Journal of Legal Nurse Consulting*; Winter 2005.

40. See note 30.

41. See note 37.

42. Tuttle, N. "Is it Reasonable to use An Individual Patient's Progress After Treatment as a Guide to Ongoing Clinical Reasoning?" *Journal of Manipulative and Physiological Therapeutics.* June 2009.

43. *Id.*

44. See note 39.

45. See note 37.

46. Received from Dr. Sportelli, NCMIC on 8/31/04.

47. Perle, S. "J'Accuse (I Accuse)" *Dynamic Chiropractic*; May 20, 2004:10.

48. See note 37.

49. See note 12.

50. See note 37.

51. Terrett, A.G.J. "Current concepts in vertebrobasilar complications following spinal manipulation." Des Moines, IA: *NCMIC Group, Inc*; 2001.

52. *Id.*

53. Retrieved 8/31/04 from http://www.fcer.org/html/News/CCPA-stroke.htm.

54. See note 51.

55. *Id.*

56. Laska, L. "Failure to Timely Diagnose and Treat Artery Dissection Following Manipulation." *Medical Malpractice Verdicts, Settlements and Experts*, April 2003: 5-6.

57. See note 12.

58. See note 30.

59. Yennie, R.D. *Modern and Classical Acupuncture*. Kansas City, MO: Acupuncture Society of America and Texas Chiropractic College. Post-Graduate Advanced Acupuncture Fellowship Series conducted in Raleigh, NC; 2004.

60. See note 39.

61. Amaro, J.A. *Acupuncture*. Carefree, AZ: International Academy of Medical Acupuncture and Seneca Falls, NY: New York Chiropractic College. Post-Graduate Fellowship Series conducted in Greensboro, NC; January-August 1996.

62. See note 30.

63. See note 39.

64. See note 12.

65. Jaskoviak, P.A. *Applied Physiotherapy*. Second Edition. Arlington, VA: American Chiropractic Association. 1993.

66. See note 39.

67. *Id.*

68. *Id.*

69. *Id.*

70. Amaro, J.A. "Acupuncture Vs. Meridian Therapy: Is There A Difference?" *Dynamic Chiropractic*; July 29, 2004:18.

71. Fritz, S. *Mosby's Fundamentals Of Therapeutic Massage* (3rd ed). St. Louis, Missouri: Mosby; 2004.

72. Beck, M. *Milady's Theory and Practice of Therapeutic Massage* (3rd edition) Albany, NY; Milady Publishing 1999.

73. *Id.*

74. *Id.*

75. *Id.*

76. See note 71.

77. www.ncbtmb.org.

78. http://dpr.delaware.gov/boards/massagebodyworks/index.shtml.

79. http://www.larryswanson.com/medical-massage-vs-wellness-massage.htm.

80. See note 72.

81. *Id.*

82. See note 71.

83. http://www.drweil.com/drw/u/id/ART02054.

84. Retrieved 8/17/09 from http://www.drweil.com/drw/u/id/ART02054.

85. Weiner, R. *Innovations In Pain Management—A Practical Guide For Clinicians*. Vol. 1. Orlando, FL: Paul M. Deutsch Press, Inc; 1993.

86. See note 71.

87. Slosberg, M. "Update on Manipulation and Exercise." *Dynamic Chiropractic*; July 15, 2009: 32.

Chapter 2

Dental Records

Barry C. Cooper, DDS

2.1 Introduction

This chapter provides members of the legal profession with an overall understanding of dentistry. It aids readers in becoming competent to review dental cases and understand what type of expert dental advice is needed for a specific case. The text describes terminology of dental and oral anatomy as well as dental disorders and their diagnostic and therapeutic procedures. The discussion in this chapter is not complete; it should not be interpreted as a statement of standard of care but rather as a guide in evaluating dental cases using the available dental records. The various dental specialty and non-specialty areas of practice concentration are described in terms of which type of dentist is most appropriate to treat various dental conditions. The contents of adequate dental records are discussed, as they are necessary for the evaluation of dental disorders and injuries and their treatment. The qualifications of dental expert witnesses and types of demonstrative material for court testimony are described.

2.2 Background of Dentistry—Terminology
A. Hard Tissues

The skull is composed of many bones. The bones most relevant to dental issues are the maxilla, mandible, zygomatic arch, and temporal. The rear or base of the skull, called the occiput, connects (articulates) with the cervical spine (neck), which consists of seven vertebrae. (See Figure 2.1.)

Bony Structures	Muscles
1. Articular Eminence	A. Temporalis
2. Glenoid Fossa	B. Masseter
3. External Auditory Meatus	C. Internal Pterygoid
4. Condylar Head	D. External Pterygoid
5. Meniscus-Disk	
6. Maxilla	
7. Mandible	

Figure 2.1 The head.

1. Maxilla

The maxilla, or upper jaw, holds sixteen teeth in the adult. The portion of the maxilla that holds the teeth is called the alveolar bone. There are fewer teeth in a child, depending on the child's age.

TIP: The adult teeth are customarily numbered beginning with the upper right third molar (wisdom tooth). This is tooth #1. The numbers continue around the dental arch to the left third molar #16. In this numbering system the mandibular (lower) teeth are numbered #17-32 beginning at the lower left third molar and continuing through the right third molar #32.

The complete adult dentition includes thirty-two teeth. There is also an older tooth numbering system, which assigns numbers 1 through 8 to each of the four quadrants (quarters) of the upper and lower dental arches. In this system, there are four sets of numbers 1-8. The numbers are designated within a bracket that shows the location of that quarter (quadrant) of the mouth: upper right, upper left, lower right, and lower left. Number 1 is assigned to each of the four central incisor teeth in the midline of the mouth. Numbers proceed in each quadrant from front at the midline (central incisors) to the last tooth in the back (third molars) from #1 through #8. Tooth #8 is the third molar (wisdom tooth). As an illustration, the upper right third tooth from the

center is the cuspid. It would be designated as tooth #6 in the commonly used 1-32 numbering system, described first. In the older quadrant numbering system it would be designated as 3/. Note the bracket symbol shows that this is the third tooth in the upper right quadrant as you look face to face at the person.

TIP: It is important to recognize which numbering system each dentist is using when dental records are being reviewed. When a single patient has been or is contemporaneously treated by multiple dentists, the two numbering systems may appear in different dental office records. (See Figure 2.2 and Figure 2.3.)

---

2. Mandible

The *mandible* is the lower jaw and, like the maxilla, holds sixteen teeth in the adult with full dentition. The third molars customarily erupt in the patient in his early twenties. However in children, the full complement of deciduous (primary) teeth is ten in the upper jaw and ten in the lower jaw. By approximately age twelve all of the primary teeth are lost and replaced by permanent teeth. In addition, the permanent molars erupt into the mouth behind, not in place of the primary teeth. These are commonly called six- and twelve-year molars, meaning the first and second molars. The third molars (wisdom teeth) erupt behind (posterior to) the second molars.

Maxillary-Upper Adult Teeth

8	7	6	5	4	3	2	1	1	2	3	4	5	6	7	8
1	2	3	4	5	6	7	8	9	10	11	12	13	14	15	16
Mol	Mol	Mol	Bic	Bic	Csp	Lat	Cen	Cen	Lat	Csp	Bic	Bic	Mol	Mol	Mol
32	31	30	29	28	27	26	25	24	23	22	21	20	19	18	17
8	7	6	5	4	3	2	1	1	2	3	4	5	6	7	8

Mandibular-Lower Adult Teeth

Mol-Molar, Bic-Bicuspid, Csp-Cuspid, Lat-Lateral, Cen-Central

Figure 2.2 Teeth numbering systems.

Upper Teeth

A	B	C	D	E	F	G	H	I	J
Mol	Mol	Csp	Lat	Cen	Cen	Lat	Csp	Mol	Mol
T	S	R	Q	P	O	N	M	L	K

Lower Teeth

Note: In the mouth of a child with some permanent (adult) and some deciduous (primary) teeth, the permanent teeth are numbered and the deciduous teeth are designated by letter. This is called a mixed dentition.

Figure 2.3 Children's teeth primary-deciduous.

The mandible is a horseshoe-shaped bone with the two rear ends bent upward extending towards the base of the skull in front of the ears. The lower portion of the mandible that holds the teeth is called the *body of the mandible*. The actual part of the body that holds teeth is called the *alveolar bone*. The midpoint of the mandible is the *symphysis*. It may become the site of a traumatic injury that can result in a fracture. The part of the mandible that extends upward behind the third molars is called the *ramus*. Each ramus ends in two projections. The forward one is the coronoid process to which the temporalis muscle tendon attaches behind the *zygoma* or *zygomatic arch* (cheek bone). The rear uppermost projection of the mandible is the condyle. There is one condyle on each side of the jaw.

The surfaces of the teeth are identified as follows:

- mesial—faces the midline of face,
- distal—faces the rear of the mouth,
- lingual—faces the tongue,
- labial—faces the lips,
- buccal—faces the cheeks,
- incisal—edges of the four center teeth top and bottom, and
- occlusal—chewing surface of the back teeth.

The condyle is shaped like a fist and is oriented on a horizontal, but angular, position with the inner end tilted slightly backwards and the outer end forwards. The left and right condyles each fit into depressions or sockets (*glenoid fossa*) in the undersurface of the temporal bone. Between the two bones of the skull and mandible is a cartilage disk, also called a meniscus. The disk is held in place by ligaments on both the inner and outer sides and also in the rear. A small muscle holds (stabilizes) the disk in place in the front. Capsular ligaments hold the entire joint together. The inner surfaces of the joint socket and condyle are lined with synovial protective tissue and *articular cartilage*.

TIP: Together, the condyle, fossa, disk, and attachment structures comprise the *temporomandibular joint*.

These various bony and soft tissues are discussed later when they may become participants in disorders of the temporomandibular joints.

The *zygoma* (cheek bone) or zygomatic arch mentioned above is not part of the dental structures but may be the site of a traumatic facial injury and can have an effect if it is displaced and impinges on the opening movements of the mandible.

The *dentition* (teeth) is divided into anterior (front) and posterior (back) teeth. The anterior teeth in the maxilla and mandible consist of symmetrically placed pairs of teeth described from the midline as central incisors, lateral incisors, and cuspids (canines). The posterior teeth in each quadrant beginning behind the cuspids are first and second bicuspids (premolars) and three molars.

Upper molars usually have three roots. The area beneath the crown between the roots is called the *trifurcation*. Lower molars usually have two roots. The area beneath the crown between the roots is called the *bifurcation*. The part of every tooth that is visible in the mouth is called the *anatomic crown* or coronal portion.

TIP: Note that the term crown is also used for a dental restoration that completely covers that portion of the tooth.

The natural crown is covered with a crystalline coating called *enamel*. Under the enamel is a less hard substance called *dentin*. In the center of the crown is a hollow chamber called the *pulp chamber* (root canal). It is continuous with the canal that runs down the concealed portion of the tooth below the gum, called the *root*. In a healthy state the entire root canal is filled with blood vessels and nerves. This is called the pulp of the tooth. The vitality of the *pulp* can be compromised by decay or trauma, sometimes requiring the removal of its contents and filling. This is called *endodontic treatment* (root canal therapy).

The root portion of the tooth is not visible in the mouth that is in a state of good periodontal health. It lacks the enamel coating and instead has a softer coating called *cementum*. The tooth is attached to its bony socket in the alveolar bone by periodontal connective tissue (called the periodontal ligament). In *periodontal disease*, the attachment of the tooth and its bony support are reduced and a portion of the tooth's root may become exposed. The teeth may become mobile (movable). Tooth mobility is classified as Class I (mild), Class II (moderate), and Class III (severe).

The term *dental occlusion* refers to the way in which the upper and lower teeth fit together (interdigitate). In the normal occlusal relationship, the outermost portion of the upper teeth overhangs the outermost part of the lower teeth by one or two millimeters. In the anterior teeth this is called the *vertical overbite*. The horizontal relationship between the upper and lower front teeth is called the *overjet*. When the upper and lower front teeth do not overlap, the condition is called an open bite. When any of the lower teeth (front or back) are outside the upper teeth in occlusion the condition is referred to as a *cross bite*. An *anterior open bite* indicates the lack of anterior tooth contact in any occluding position of posterior teeth. An *edge-to-edge bite* is when the upper and lower teeth touch with no overlap. Abnormal (aberrant) occlusal relationships are called *malocclusion*. A traditional orthodontic classification of occlusal relationships is called the *Angle Classification*.

- Class I represents a normal occlusion with a normal anterior posterior relationship of the jaws.
- Class II relationship is when the mandibular dental arch is posterior to the maxillary dental arch.
- Class III relationship is when the mandibular arch is anterior to the maxillary dental arch and is often indicative of an anterior crossbite.

The Angle Classification actually refers to the relationship of upper to lower first molars.

B. Soft Tissues

1. Extraoral—facial

The lips are the significant dental *extraoral/facial structures* on the face. The portion of the upper and lower lips that is visible is called the *vermilion*. It is normally bilaterally symmetrical. Discussion of the remainder of the face is not within the scope of this chapter.

2. Intraoral—within the mouth

Intraoral structures include the following: tongue, cheeks, the inner surfaces of the lips, the *gingiva* (gums), soft and hard palate, and the floor of the mouth. The rearmost part of the oral cavity is the *oropharynx*, which is the entry to the throat. Suspended from the soft palate is a projection called the *uvula*. It is sometimes the site of surgical intervention when it obstructs breathing, as are the tonsils and adenoids, which are at the rear of the oropharynx.

The gingiva covers the alveolar bone of the maxilla and mandible. In a state of good health, the gingiva is normally smoothly contoured, pink, and firm. It covers the attachment of the root of each tooth to its bony socket. The gingiva and the periodontal attachment fibers constitute the *periodontal* (around the tooth) tissues. In the mandible below the gingiva and in the maxilla above the gingiva is the tissue called the *alveolar mucosa*, which extends to the point where the lips and cheeks attach to the lower mandible and maxilla. Inside the cheeks near the first upper molars there is an opening of a saliva duct. There are also saliva ducts beneath the tongue in the front floor of the mouth.

The mandible is held in place and moved to function in speech, breathing, swallowing, and eating by groups of muscles divided into two groups that exist on both sides of the jaw: those that open the mouth and those that close it. The opening muscles are called *depressors* and include the *lateral (external) pterygoids and digastrics*. The muscles that move the jaw to close the mouth and chew food are called *elevators* and include the *temporalis, masseters* and *medial (internal) pterygoids*. These receive their nervous supply from the mandibular division of the *trigeminal nerve*, which is the fifth (V) cranial nerve. There is also a branch of the facial nerve that provides stimulation (innervation) to the posterior digastric muscles.

The remaining facial muscles are called the muscles of expression. They receive their nervous innervation from the *facial nerve*, which is the seventh (VII) cranial nerve. Description of the rest of the nervous system related to the head and neck is not within the scope of this chapter. There are interrelationships between the sensory and motor nerves and the central nervous system as well as the autonomic nervous system. This permits complex activities and can cause complex responses to injuries and dysfunction.

C. Injuries to Soft and Hard Tissues

TIP: Soft tissue injuries in the oral cavity and lips include lacerations, abrasions, incisions (cutting), and infections. Soft tissue injuries can result from foreign objects in the mouth and inadvertent biting of the cheeks, lips or tongue. In addition, soft tissues can be the sites of various diseases.

Hard tissue injuries include fractures of the maxilla and mandible and teeth, as well as infection or neoplastic diseases within the bone. Trauma to the maxilla may involve the alveolar bone that houses the teeth. Trauma to the mandible (jaw) can occur from an impact to either the front or sides of the jaw. Trauma to the chin area can cause a fracture in the center (symphysis) or in the body of the mandible. Trauma can also cause a fracture beneath the upper rear terminal end of the mandible, called the condyle. The thin area below the condyle is called the neck of the condyle, which can also be the site of a fracture.

The zygoma (cheek bone) can also be fractured due to a trauma. If this bone does not heal in its proper place and protrudes inwardly, it may interfere with the forward movement of the mandibular ramus as the mouth opens. It also can impinge on muscles that attach to the inner surface of the zygoma and may restrict mandibular movement on opening. Lower facial fractures may necessitate surgery to restore stability with the use of plates and wires. Swelling and pain are often extensive before and after surgery.

Teeth can be decayed, which is called *dental caries*. Teeth can be fractured or broken by traumatic forces applied to the face, by hard foreign objects in the mouth, or by sudden, unexpected, and unprotected violent contact between upper and lower teeth. Teeth can also fracture due to extensive decay that undermines the integrity of the tooth with or without trauma.

Teeth can become worn due to noxious habits such as *bruxism* (grinding the teeth together). The term *abrasion* describes an artificial wearing away of tooth structure other than by chewing food (mastication). An example is excessive tooth brushing wearing away the tooth structure at the gum line. This can also be caused by clenching and bruxing the teeth. The process is called *abfraction* in which microfractures of enamel occur due to excessive forces theoretically bending the rigid tooth. *Avulsion* describes a traumatic process in which teeth are forcibly knocked out of the alveolar bone.

D. Restorative and Therapeutic Dental Terminology

Crowns are complete coverings that are fabricated to restore lost tooth structure, to provide anchorage for a prosthesis (bridge) that replaces adjacent missing teeth, or for cosmetic reasons. Teeth that serve as anchors for a *fixed bridge* (cemented) are called *abutments*. Crowns on these teeth are abutment crowns. The missing teeth that are replaced by the fixed bridge are called *pontics*. A fixed bridge (fixed partial denture) can be attached to natural teeth and can also be attached to dental implants. *Dental implants* are devices that approximate the form of teeth roots and are inserted into the alveolar bone. Crowns and bridges can be attached to (retained by) these dental implant fixtures. Crowns are fabricated of high noble (containing precious metals) or non-high noble metals covered with porcelain (ceramics). Crowns can also be made of nonmetallic materials. Temporary bridges are made of plastic (acrylic) materials and serve as temporary restorations during the fabrication of durable bridges or during the months during which dental implants are undergoing *osseous integration* (attachment) to the alveolar bone. Temporary removable bridges (partial dentures) are also made for children who lose teeth and their replacement must await maturity.

Defects in teeth that involve less extensive loss of tooth structure are repaired by a variety of dental restorations, including gold, amalgam, porcelain, and composite tooth-colored materials. An *onlay* is a restoration that covers the chewing surface of a tooth and can also include one or more of the sides of the tooth. An *inlay* fits inside part of the coronal part of the tooth and can also include one or more of the sides of the tooth. Following root canal therapy, some teeth require the placement of a post into the root canal and a core build up necessary to retain a crown.

Teeth that are either decayed or fractured horizontally beneath the gum line may require a surgical procedure to expose more of the remaining tooth before the tooth can be restored. This periodontal surgical procedure is called *crown lengthening*. Vertically fractured teeth that run down the root cannot be restored, and the remaining root must usually be extracted. The treating dentist decides on the restorability of a tooth.

There are three ways in which teeth can be replaced when more that one tooth is missing in the dental arch. Tooth retained and implant retained fixed bridges have been described above. *Removable partial dentures* are prostheses that attach with arms (clasps) to natural teeth and replace multiple teeth on either or both sides of the mouth in a single dental arch (maxilla or mandible). When all teeth in a dental arch are missing they can be replaced with a *complete denture* or fixed bridge that is retained by dental implants.

Periodontal treatments include *curettage*, which is the removal of calculus (tartar) and other debris or tissues above and below the gums. *Gingivectomy* is a surgical procedure to remove part of the gingival tissue. This includes crown lengthening described above. Periodontal surgical treatment can also include plastic procedures to reshape the bony supporting structures around the teeth. *Bone augmentation* utilizes synthetic materials or bone grafts to stimulate or add bone to the alveolar ridges to aid in retention of dental implants or dental prostheses. Soft tissue grafts are used to augment or improve gingival form and appearance.

Oral surgery procedures involve extraction of teeth, and repair of fractured bones. Bony surgery to change the position and relationships between the maxilla and mandible is called *orthognathic surgery*. Surgery to the temporomandibular joints includes a variety of procedures, including the following: lysis (cutting fibrous adhesions), and lavage (irrigation) arthroscopy, and open joint surgery. Open joint procedures include repositioning or replacement of the disk, condylar reshaping (*arthroplasty*), and either partial or total replacement of bony joint components. Bony fractures are either corrected (reduced) by an open procedure in which the skin or intraoral soft tissues are opened to gain access to the bony structures or by a closed procedure that does not involve entry into the soft tissues.

Endodontic treatments involve root canal therapy, which is the removal of all tissue and debris in the pulp canal and filling of the canal with an inert material. In certain situations, endodontic treatment also includes the surgical removal of the tip of the root and removal of pathological material called an *apicoectomy*, sometimes accompanied by bone augmentation procedures to maintain bony anatomic form. In situations where the tooth pulp is only partially injured, a surgical procedure called a *pulpotomy* is performed. This involves the removal of the portion of the pulp within the crown of the tooth.

Orthodontics is the portion of dental treatment that repositions the teeth in the dental arches to achieve a proper esthetic and functional alignment of teeth within each dental arch and interdigitation of teeth between the maxillary and mandibular arches.

Non-surgical treatments for temporomandibular disorders (TMD) include the use of physical medicine modalities to dental structures. These include, but are not limited to, the following:

- electrical stimulation (transcutaneous electrical neurostimulation or TENS),
- ultrasound,
- massage,
- exercise,
- heat and cold application,
- injection of trigger points in muscles, and
- nerve block injections.

Sometimes internal derangements within the temporomandibular joint (TMJ) either of disk displacement or condylar dislocation (hyperextension) can be reduced (corrected) by manual manipulation of the mandible.

TIP: A variety of oral appliances are used. The appliances are often referred to as splints, *orthoses, orthotic appliances*, biteguards, or *nightguards* and are made of either soft or hard plastic or more durable materials. Depending on the design and usage, they may be for fulltime or part-time use.

A dental provider should describe the specific design, material type, therapeutic purpose, and usage instructions for the specific appliance made to treat a specific patient.

Sometimes long-term treatment is necessary, which could include reshaping or restoration of the teeth or orthodontic movement of teeth, all of which would be designed to improve the dental occlusion, the interdigitation of teeth, or bite. Some dentists have been trained to use computerized measurement devices in the management of TMD. They are American Dental Association (ADA) and Food and Drug Administration (FDA) approved for this purpose. They use mandibular tracking (computerized mandibular scan/CMS), surface electromyography (EMG), and electrosonography (electrovibratology).

2.3 Extent of Dental Records

The extent of dental records varies for each dental patient and the type of provider. The list that follows includes all possible records. A determination of the completeness of the available records must be made for each case when reviewing dental records.

- Treating dentist chart records. Initial patient input information related to medical history should be obtained through a patient-completed questionnaire. Initial examination findings are reported in words and/or schematic tooth diagrams that include the following: a listing of present and absent teeth, periodontal pocket measurements if significant, and measurements of tooth mobility if present. Daily chart notes should include the date and a description in word or symbols of new findings, services rendered, treatment recommendations, referrals to specialists, and comments by patients.
- Treating dentist narrative reports if written.
- Treating dentist laboratory and pharmaceutical prescriptions.
- Referral slips or chart notations related to referrals to dental and medical specialists.
- Specialist dentists/physician reports or records.
- Radiographs or radiographic reports by treating dentist and other doctors.
- Diagnostic casts (models) of the teeth before and during treatment.
- Diagnostic testing data and/or reports.
- Photographs of intraoral and adjacent structures pre-treatment or post-trauma.

2.4 Disorders of Dental/Oral and Adjacent Structures

A. Disorders of Hard Tissues

Hard tissue disorders include dental caries (decay) with possible extension into the dental pulp and periapical (root end) pathology. Traumatic tooth injuries include breakage of tooth structure and breakage of dental restorations within or covering teeth. This can include fracture of dental crowns and in an allied condition, breakage of dental replacement prostheses (complete and removable partial dentures) and dental implants. Depending on the extent of tooth fracture, the tooth may or may not be restorable. A vertically fractured tooth extending down the root cannot be restored and must be extracted. Horizontally fractured teeth above the gum line can be restored but may require root canal therapy before a dental restoration (post-core and crown) can be fabricated.

Traumatic injuries to bone can involve the maxilla with the tooth-bearing alveolar bone and the mandible including its alveolar bone, symphysis, body, ramus, and condyles. Fracture of the zygoma, if displaced inward, can affect mandibular and muscular function. Fractures sometimes require the placement of plates screwed to the bony parts or arch bars attached to the upper and/or lower teeth. The upper and lower arch bars are sometimes wired together to immobilize the jaw during healing. Pathology in bone can arise from tooth structures, periodontal disease, developmental aberrations, and other diseases of bone.

B. Disorders of Soft Tissues

Soft tissue disorders include periodontal disease ranging from gingival inflammation to advanced destruction of gingival and periodontal supporting tissues with extension to the alveolar bone. Traumatic injuries can arise outside of the mouth, penetrating into the interior intraoral tissues. Intraoral traumatic injuries can also arise directly within the mouth from foreign objects or during dental or medical procedures. These can include laceration, abrasion of soft tissues, or damage to the nerves within the oral cavity. Neoplastic and other diseases can also affect the intraoral soft tissues.

C. Temporomandibular Disorder

This is a collective term that describes a group of disorders that can involve the hard and soft tissue structures within the temporomandibular joints. *Arthrosis* or *arthropathy* denotes pathology (disease) within a joint. TMDs that involve the temporomandibular joints include

- condylar fracture,
- osteoarthritis (degenerative joint disease),
- rheumatoid arthritis (a systemic joint inflammatory disease), and
- internal derangement in which there is disk displacement with or without recapture on opening.

When the disk has suddenly been dislocated forward or laterally preventing translation (forward movement) of the condyle, the condition is called an *acute closed lock*. If it is not treated or fails to respond to conservative treatment or does not resolve, it can become a *chronic closed lock*. In the latter condition, the disk shape may not be compatible with its being simply reseated on top of the condyle by external manipulation of the jaw.

Fibrosis within the joint may also have occurred. Intracapsular (within the joint) TMDs can also include the following:

- disk perforation,
- *synovitis* (inflammation of the joint lining tissues),
- *retrodiscitis* (inflammation of the tissues that attach behind the disk),
- *hemarthrosis* (bleeding in the joint),
- *fibrosis* (adhesions),
- *ankylosis* (a condition of bony immobility in the joint), and
- systemic diseases and developmental aberrations.

Temporomandibular disorders can also involve inflammatory conditions of the structures that support and encapsulate the TMJ joint (*capsulitis*). Temporomandibular disorders most often involve dysfunction of the muscles that posture and move the mandible. These are called masticatory or craniomandibular muscles. Disorders of muscles include:

- *myalgia* (pain),
- *hyperalgesia* (hypersensitivity causing increased pain perception),
- *myospasm* (hyperactivity),
- *contracture* (total spasm), and
- *myositis* (inflammation).

Temporomandibular disorders often involve a complex of muscle and TMJ joint elements. Temporomandibular disorders affect one or both sides of the face and cause a wide variety of symptoms and clinical presentations unique to each patient. Symptoms can include:

- pain in dental and other facial, head, and neck areas,
- alteration or limitation of jaw movement, and
- clicking or crackling (*crepitation*) sounds in the jaw joints on jaw movement and destruction of tooth structure or tooth bony support.

TMD can be caused or precipitated by direct facial/dental or mandibular trauma. It can also be caused or precipitated by indirect trauma to the head and neck. This can occur during motor vehicle, trip and fall, or other accidents, or direct facial or head injuries sustained during an assault. TMD can also result from dental or medical procedures that involve or traverse the oral cavity. Some patients have a preexisting TMD or a quiescent disorder that is exacerbated during a traumatic incident or during dental or medical procedures.

TIP: TMD can exist in a subclinical state unknown to a person until activated as a result of a traumatic event. These are important considerations in establishing possible causal relationships between traumatic events and a temporomandibular disorder.

2.5 Dental Procedures/Treatments

Procedures and treatments have been described in the terminology section above. In this section a partial list of procedures with appropriate providers is defined. In all areas of treatment the treating dentist must be able to establish his training and expertise in areas of ADA-approved specialties, board specialty certification, or eligibility to establish qualifications. In some of these areas, the general dentist may have the requisite skills to treat.

The following disciplines are recognized by the American Dental Association (ADA) as *Dental Specialties.*

- Orthodontics,
- Periodontics and Implantology,
- Prosthodontics,
- Pedodontics,
- Endodontics,
- Oral and Maxillofacial Surgery,
- Dental Public Health,
- Oral (Dental) Radiology, and
- Oral Pathology.

There are other areas of practice concentration in dentistry that are not recognized by the ADA as specialties including

- esthetic dentistry,
- implants,
- cosmetic dentistry,
- temporomandibular disorders (TMD), and
- orofacial and craniofacial pain.

2.6 Complications of Treatment
A. Appropriate Treatment

All treatments that are considered medically (dentally) necessary based on sound diagnostic procedures and patient desires are appropriate. Properly performed dental treatments may result in untoward results that may not be due to deviation from the standard of care. Commonly occurring posttreatment complications should be explained to patients prior to treatment. The treating dentist must obtain an *informed consent* in a form customarily used in that practice. The occurrence of untoward results must be evaluated on a case-by-case basis assisted by the services of a dental expert in the field.

TIP: Examples of untoward results include alteration in normal sensation, undiagnosed infection of the bone (osteomyelitis), fractured teeth or alveolar bone during tooth extraction, and implant or dental restoration failure.

B. Failure to Provide Sufficient or Appropriate Treatment

The *scope of dental practice* is established by each state regulatory board. The *standard of care* is established by the governmental bodies responsible for professional conduct and by the dental profession itself operating through professional organization peer review committees. The American Dental Association (ADA) has written a series of *parameters* for various areas of dental practice that are not standards of care. The ADA and each state's dental associations have separately established Codes of Ethics with which to guide dentists in conducting ethical dental practice. The treating dentist must personally provide all necessary dental treatment or refer to an appropriate dental or medical provider when necessary. Failure to do either may constitute a deviation from the standard of care. This determination must be made on a case-by-case basis depending of the nature of necessary treatment and the availability and nature of referral resources. A treating dentist is not responsible for diagnosing or treating clearly medical conditions for which dentists are not customarily trained. When multiple dental treatment options would be considered appropriate, the dentist should present (and document) treatment options explained to the patient.

TIP: Failure to complete treatment undertaken is a deviation from the standard of care unless the discontinuation of treatment was initiated by the patient or an appropriate referral to another practitioner was made.

The following case, where delay in treatment and subsequent complications were alleged, serves as a reminder that bad outcomes can result from malpractice.

In August 2005, a fifty-eight year-old woman developed intermittent, unexplained lower right jaw pain, not localized to a tooth. Three lower teeth became mobile in February 2006. The defendant general dentist referred the plaintiff to the defendant peridontist with a tentative diagnosis of acute periodontal abscess. The peridontist agreed and recommended extraction of the loose teeth. The peridontist also diagnosed a leukoplakia type white lesion in the anterior floor of the mouth which he misdiagnosed as an aspirin burn. The leukoplakia allegedly cleared up and in May 2006, the defendant peridontist charted a new leukoplakia ten to fifteen millimeters away. Clindamycin was prescribed but the lesion persisted. The plaintiff was referred back to the defendant dentist to refer to an oral surgeon for evaluation of the lesion and possible biopsy. That week the plaintiff began treatment with the defendant oral surgeon, whose differential diagnosis was traumatic injury from a temporary bridge or tongue fussing versus dysplasia or neoplasm. Biopsy was not recommended. In November 2006, when the plaintiff had a large invasive leukoplakia lesion, a biopsy was finally performed. Stage IV squamous cell cancer was diagnosed. The plaintiff was still receiving treatment at the time of trial. The general dentist settled for a confidential amount. The peridontist was given a no cause verdict. A jury returned a verdict against the oral surgeon for $15 million.[1]

C. Providing Treatment When Medical Necessity is Not Established

There are general dental criteria for the medical necessity of each dental service rendered. However, it is the responsibility of the treating dentist to establish the medical necessity of each diagnostic and treatment service rendered to a specific patient based on available data for that patient. Providing a service for which the provider has not established the medical necessity may not be appropriate.

D. Providing Inadequate Treatment

Providing incomplete or inadequate dental treatment is a deviation from the standard of care. Inadequate treatment can include failure to perform appropriate diagnostic and treatment procedures or failure to refer to appropriate providers for conditions commonly acknowledged to be included in the scope of dental practice. If radiographs are obtained they should be of diagnostic quality. Incomplete caries removal, incomplete debridement or filling of patent (open) root canals, improperly fitting or designing dental restorations (e.g., crowns and dentures) are considered to constitute inadequate dental treatment. Failure to diagnose properly could result in a worsening of dental conditions requiring more extensive treatments at a later date or perpetuation of patient discomfort. Inadequate dental treatment may require replacement of restorations with possible changes in design and extent or complexity.

2.7 Documentation Practices
A. Patient History Questionnaire

Each dental office uses a different written questionnaire. It should include a medical history to provide essential information that could affect dental treatments. Examples include: cardiac status, the need for antibiotic premedication, compromised blood clotting, and other relevant information. In the absence of a formal questionnaire, the dental office records should include this information.

B. Dental Examination Charting

Dental examination findings should be reported in the form of a schematic diagram or in written form. It should include teeth that are missing or damaged, restorations necessary, restorations present (optional), and periodontal status. The latter should include measurements of significant periodontal pockets around all teeth and tooth mobility if either is present. If there are no periodontal findings, a note of that should be included to document that the examination was conducted.

TIP: Positive findings of an intraoral soft tissue examination should be reported or no findings should also be noted.

If the patient is being examined for a *temporomandibular disorder* (TMD), the examination notes should include mandibular range of motion in protrusion, lateral excursions, and in maximum opening (measured between the edges of the upper and lower incisor teeth).

The temporomandibular joint examination includes palpation of the joints on the outside of the face and within the outer ear by finger application and joint sounds analysis (*auscultation*) with a stethoscope if sounds are present. The type of sound that emanates from a temporomandibular joint suggests the type of pathology or dysfunction present. Popping or clicking suggests disk dislocation with recapture on jaw movement. *Crepitus* that sounds like the crackling of stiff parchment suggests bony rubbing. This is an indication of a more advanced, severe degenerative joint disease of long standing. This difference is significant in analyzing the time of onset of a TMD and etiological (causative) elements.

Reports of pain or discomfort on palpation of muscles within the mouth and around the head, face, and neck are also essential symptoms to record during a comprehensive clinical dental examination. Negative findings should also be recorded. Sometimes models or casts of the teeth are valuable in analyzing the status of a patient and designing treatment plans. If taken, it is the responsibility of the treating dentist to establish their medical necessity specifically for that patient.

C. Dental Treatment Records (Chart Notes)

Chart notes should include the following:

- **Services rendered.** All services rendered at each visit should be dated and detailed in a readable form. This should include anesthetic administered, teeth treated, and materials used in restorations. Any untoward results during or following treatment should be documented.
- **Dentist recommendations.** This should include treatment recommendations and options, patient instructions when given, and referrals to dental or medical specialists. Compliance or lack of compliance with dental recommendations should be recorded.
- **Patient comments.** Patient comments during dental visits or subsequently regarding treatment recommended or received and referral options should be noted.
- **Telephone conversations.** Calls to or from patients should be recorded and described for other than routine office appointment calls.
- **Appointment compliance.** Cancelled or missed (broken) appointments should ideally be documented in some form in the dental office records. Some dentists note this on the daily chart records, others on ledger cards, appointment book, or in the computer scheduling program. Although not essential, this information is valuable in establishing patient compliance patterns.

D. Reports from Consulting and Treating Specialists

Oral reports from specialists should be noted in the dental chart. Written reports should be included in the dental record. Additional material sent by the specialist such as radiographs, radiology reports, and pathology reports should be included as well.

E. Dental Laboratory and Pharmaceutical Prescriptions

Copies of dental laboratory prescriptions should be kept with the dental records or maintained in a separate place for a reasonable time. Prescriptions for medications should be noted in detail within the dental chart or maintained as a photocopy of the prescription.

F. Referral Notes to Specialists

A doctor's referral to medical or dental specialists may be documented in the dental chart notes or in a separate written prescription form. Telephone call referrals should also be noted in the chart. Some specialists provide printed referral forms for this purpose. A copy of that form should be included in the dental records.

G. Radiographs (X-Rays)

The medical necessity of specific dental radiographs must be established by the dental provider and is specific to each patient. Failure to obtain necessary radiographs or obtaining excessive radiographs that are not medically necessary is inappropriate. Radiographs appropriate to making the correct diagnosis and planning treatment should be obtained and maintained as documentation of the pre-treatment dental status. Some dental procedures appropriately use radiographs to document successfully completed treatment. Examples include

- completion of endodontic (root canal) treatment,
- fit check of crowns and fixed bridges,
- implant placement, and
- bony *osseous integration* of implants.

Dental radiographs obtained by the treating dentist or sent by the specialist should be kept as long as the dental records are kept.

Intraoral periapical dental radiographs include images of several complete teeth from root to crown and the surrounding bone. *Bite wing radiographs* include only the crown portions of both upper and lower teeth. *Occlusal* radiographs include one full dental arch, either maxillary or mandibular.

Extraoral radiographs of dental structures include panoramic (also known as orthopantogram) and lateral transcranial views of the left or right temporomandibular joints. There are a series of views on one film with various positions of the mandibular condyles at opened and closed mouth. Tomographs can also be taken of the temporomandibular joints. Full lateral skull images include the following:

- cephalometric images (for orthodontic and for orthognathic surgical diagnosis and treatment planning),
- submental vertex (the jaw from below),
- anterior/posterior views of the front or back of the skull, and
- sinuses and cervical spine area films.

Appropriate Treatment and Providers

Dental caries (tooth decay) removal: general practitioner, prosthodontist, endodontist.

Tooth restoration or replacement: general dentist, prosthodontist.

Pulp pathology (root canal therapy) and periapical pathology (apicoectomy at root end): endodontist or general practitioner.

Periapical surgery: endodontist or oral surgeon.

Tooth extraction: oral and maxillofacial surgeon, general practitioner or periodontist.

Periodontal disease: periodontist or general practitioner.

Temporomandibular joint surgery: oral and maxillofacial surgeon.

Fractures of maxilla or mandible: oral and maxillofacial or head and neck surgeon.

Malocclusion orthodontic treatment: orthodontist or general practitioner with appropriate training.

Orthognathic surgery to correct maxilla/mandible skeletal malrelationships: oral and maxillofacial surgeon.

Temporomandibular disorders (conservative, non-surgical): general practitioner or any dental specialist with appropriate training.

Dental implant placement: periodontist, oral and maxillofacial surgeon, or general dentist with appropriate training.

Dental hygiene: includes obtaining necessary tooth cleaning (prophylaxis curettage), dental radiographs, dental examination, oral soft tissue screening, periodontal examination with pocket and tooth mobility determination and documentation, by general dentist or dental hygienist.

Figure 2.4

More elaborate imaging of portions of the skull includes arthrograms of the TMJ, CT (Computerized Tomography), and magnetic resonance images (MRI). Special CT scanning techniques can be obtained in order to plan for dental implant placements. The medical necessity of each type of radiograph must be established by the dental provider for each patient examined. MRI imaging is performed in medical radiology facilities with radiologists providing reports. CT scanning is performed in specialized facilities as well. The plain films described above are performed in either equipped dental offices or medical radiology facilities.

There are a group of computerized measurement devices available that some dentists and their staffs use in diagnosis and treatment planning. These include

- electrical pulp vitality testing,
- electronic apex locators (in endodontic treatment),
- electromyography of facial, masticatory (chewing) muscles (EMG),
- computerized mandibular tracking (CMS),
- electrosonography (electrovibratology) of TMJ joint sounds, and
- Doppler auscultation of TMJ sounds.

TIP: With all diagnostic procedures, it is the responsibility of the treating doctor to establish the medical necessity of each procedure employed for each patient.

2.8 Use of a Dental Expert Witness
A. Treating Dentist or Dentists

Treating dentists provide valuable information as to the status of a patient prior to a subject incident and also following an incident before treatment, the need for treatment, and the treatment performed. When multiple dentists perform contemporaneous treatment, they can provide corroboration of the status of a patient, the medical necessity of treatments rendered, and the quality of treatment rendered by other dentists. The attorney must determine the qualifications of treating dentists to serve as experts in the subject case and their ability to testify.

B. Dental Expert or Experts Appropriate to the Subject Case

The type of expert or experts required to evaluate a case depends on the conditions that required treatment and whether multiple types of dentists provided treatment. An appropriate general practitioner or specialist would have to be considered for each area of dental practice involved.

The attorney or legal nurse consultant must determine which areas of dental practice are involved in a specific case by the treatments rendered and the conditions that were treated in order to select the appropriate dental or medical experts. Determining the credentials of the defendant is essential in selecting a similarly trained individual.

In the following Oregon case, the qualifications of the testifying expert were questioned.

A patient brought a medical malpractice action against a dentist. The patient alleged that the dentist was negligent in the administration of nitrous oxide, causing hypoxia and cognitive defects. The trial court refused to allow the testimony of the patient's expert as to medical causation of the injuries, stating that the expert was a neuropsychologist, not a medical doctor. The case was appealed.

The appellate court opined that Oregon law does not require an expert witness testifying about medical issues to be a licensed medical doctor. If the expert has specialized training and experience that can help the jury better understand the case, there is no reason to exclude the testimony. The field of specialization of the expert witness affects the weight to be given to the testimony, not its admissibility. The trial court's decision was reversed.[2]

C. Qualifications of Non-Treating Experts

Qualifications of dentists who are board certified or board eligible in ADA recognized specialties are established by that level of recognition. In practice areas not designated as ADA-recognized specialties, the dentist's expertise must be confirmed on an individual basis. This includes consideration of continuing dental education through ADA-certified teaching entities, authorship of scientific articles published in refereed journals, and research in which the dentist is a principal investigator. Another qualifying credential is a faculty appointment in a dental or medical school in which the dentist teaches the subject of the purported expertise.

D. Medical Experts if Appropriate to the Subject Case

When a plaintiff has medical and dental issues, it may be necessary to use both medical and dental experts. This may be the case even when the subject case involves only the dental treatment because medical conditions may affect the patient and the dental treatments rendered. Examples of conditions include diabetes, which affects changes in the periodontal tissues, and fibromyalgia, which affects changes in pain perception.

E. Demonstrative Evidence for Trial

Illustrative materials can be used to describe injuries and treatments provided. They can be in the form of schematic illustrations or three-dimensional models of the teeth, skull, facial muscles, and temporomandibular joints. They can be illustrations of dental restorations if that is the subject of the case. In a case where the adequacy or inadequacy of dental restorative treatment rendered is the issue, illustrative material could include actual dental models before and after treatment, if they are available. Dental radiographs and photographs also pre-treatment and post-treatment are valuable and can be viewed, preferably with optical or digitalized magnification. As an example, in the case of dental restorations such as fixed bridges or crowns, the accuracy or inaccuracy of the fit of the restorations can be demonstrated in part on dental radiographs. All of the above described illustrative materials give the treating dentist as well as the dental experts for the plaintiff and defense an opportunity to explain the relevant dental issues to the judge and jurors.

2.9 Summary

Although this chapter is not intended to provide a complete description of all phases of dental disease, injuries, and treatment, it does present a comprehensive overview of dental issues. It should provide legal personnel with enough information to review and understand the nature of dental records related to a subject case and guide in the selection of appropriate dental experts.

Endnotes

1. Laska. L. "15 Million Verdict Returned Against Oral Surgeon in Michigan For Failure to Biopsy Lesions In Mouth." *Medical Malpractice Verdicts, Settlements and Experts*, October 2009. Pg 5-6.

2. *Cunningham v. Montgomery*, 143 Or App 171, rev den, 324 Or 487. 1996.

Chapter 3

Home Care Records

Barbara Mladenetz Weber Berry, MSN, RN

3.1 What Is Home Care?

Home care is a term with broad applications. It implies some type of "care service" in the home setting and could refer to professional as well as nonprofessional services. Professionals may include registered and licensed practical nurses, physical, speech, respiratory, and occupational therapists, social workers, nutritionists, and spiritual counselors. Paraprofessionals are primarily home health aides and therapy assistants; the latter are authorized in some states to work in home care under the supervision of the professional therapists.

There is also a distinction within the industry that separates *certified* and *non-certified* agencies. An organization that is certified means one that has the ability to obtain reimbursement from Medicare, the federally sponsored healthcare program for citizens aged sixty-five years and older. These agencies may bill their regional Medicare insurance intermediary directly for services they provide to clients. This privilege does not come easily. Medicare-certified agencies are heavily regulated and, in addition to meeting the government's "Conditions of Participation" for the Medicare program, they must meet requirements for licensure as home health agencies in their state. Many also voluntarily meet national accreditation standards with either The Joint Commission (TJC) or Community Health Accreditation Programs (CHAP). Medicare services are intermittent or brief in duration and generally available to the client who demonstrates a potential for rehabilitation. The presence of a chronic condition generally does not support eligibility for Medicare services. The exception to this rule is hospice care. Clients may elect to participate in the Medicare hospice benefit if they have a prognosis of less than six months of life expectancy and are no longer seeking treatment.

Non-certified agencies are much less regulated, and each state determines the type of license that they need in order to operate. In some states, a license through the state's department of consumer affairs is the requirement to provide healthcare staffing. These agencies may provide nurses or aides to perform brief, intermittent visits to the home or private duty arrangements where a client may secure round-the-clock assistance. They may charge the insurance company or the client privately but are unable to bill Medicare.

TIP: There are also home health staffing registries that may operate with a business license and merely link a clinician with a client for a finder's fee. However, these entities do not assume responsibility for the actions of the clinician.

Almost half of the home care agencies are voluntary nonprofit: 42 percent are proprietary and 9 percent are government based.[1]

Within this industry, there is a range of services that are included under the umbrella of home care. Table 3.1 depicts five main categories in this area of specialization: chronic, outreach/preventative, acute, specialty, and high technological care. Within each domain, the potential exists for litigation to arise. An example is provided in each category to demonstrate this point.

- A client receiving *chronic* care may sue because a live-in aide was negligent in fulfilling her duties and, as a result, caused the client to sustain a fall.

Table 3.1
Continuum of Home Healthcare Services

Chronic	Outreach/ Preventative	Acute	Specialty	High Technological
♦ Live-In Aides	♦ Early Maternity Discharge	♦ Skilled Nursing	♦ Palliative and Hospice Care	♦ Infusion Therapy -Antibiotics -Chemotherapy -Hydration -Pain Management -Enteral Feeding -Heparin
♦ Personal Care	♦ Flu Campaign	♦ Rehabilitation -Physical Therapy -Occupational Therapy - Speech Therapy -Restorative Nursing	-Traditional - Pediatric - Inpatient/Respite - Bereavement	
♦ Companions	♦ Employee Health Screening		♦ Pediatrics and Neonatal	♦ Ventilator Care
♦ Homemakers		♦ Medical Social Work		
♦ Meals On Wheels	♦ Communicable Diseases, Maternal Child Health Issues		♦ High Risk Antepartum	♦ Telemonitoring (Pacemaker)
♦ Adult Day Care		♦ Home Health Aides	♦ Medicaid Waiver	♦ Apnea Monitoring
♦ Long Term Maintenance/Respite	♦ Community Health Screening	♦ Nutrition	♦ Joint Clinical Protocols -Congestive Heart Failure	♦ Photo Therapy
♦ Case Management	♦ Nutrition	♦ Laboratory Tests		♦ Cardiac Monitoring ♦ EKGs
♦ Personal Emergency Response System	♦ Liaison/Intake	♦ Medical Supplies and Equipment	♦ Private Duty Nursing	♦ X-Rays
	♦ Community Education	♦ Central Intake and Case Management	♦ Mental Health	♦ Respiratory Therapy
	♦ Bereavement Support Groups		♦ Continence Program	
			♦ Wound Care	

With permission of JoAnne Ruden and Barbara Weber Berry.

- A client may allege professional malpractice occurred because of an injury received during the administration of a flu vaccine at a community *outreach* program.
- An *acute* care client may pursue litigation because a home physical therapist neglected to follow the therapy protocol prescribed by the orthopaedic physician, and as a result, the client sustained further injury to the extremity.
- A *specialty* care client may resort to legal action if the visiting nurse did not meet the standards of care for a wound procedure or failed to report a significant change to a physician and it deteriorated as a result of this negligence.
- Finally, a client requiring *high technological* home health services may seek legal recourse for an infection at the site of infusion therapy that was acquired as a result of the nurse's poor technique.

The environment is the factor that differentiates this specialty from others in health care. Providing services in a client's home is much different than an institutional setting. It is unlikely that there will be any other healthcare staff present to act as witnesses. On occasion, joint visits are made, but that is the exception. For that reason, the importance of documentation is paramount. The chart is the document that is the core piece of evidence that demonstrates the actions of the clinicians.

This chapter emphasizes the importance of documentation in home care and how the legal professional may analyze the areas that commonly demonstrate documentation deficiencies.

At present, home care is a non-dominant sector of the healthcare arena. However, industry trends show that more consumers are choosing home care, provided that is an option to them. For example, today an individual requiring intravenous therapy for Lyme's disease could easily be treated at home instead of being hospitalized.

Demographers predict that there will be more grandparents than grandchildren as the baby boomers age, and this bodes positively for the growth of the home care industry. In 1996, an estimated 2.5 million individuals received care from 13,500 home health and hospice care agencies in the United States.[2] Litigation is minimal in this industry at the present time; however, with increased growth, it is anticipated that lawsuits will rise concomitantly.

3.2 Documentation in Home Care

The medical record in home care is as diverse as the many types of agencies performing home health services. A certified agency must conform to many federal and state standards, and if accreditation is chosen, those standards as well. The record is generally "sectioned" into the following components: physicians' orders, admission, nursing, aide, therapies, billing, and consents.

TIP: Every certified home health agency in the country must complete a standardized assessment tool, OASIS (Outcome and Assessment Statistical Information Set), on all Medicare and Medicaid clients.

OASIS consists of ninety mandated questions. These responses are transmitted to the state health department and then forwarded to Medicare for benchmarking purposes. In addition to including the client's diagnoses and surgeries, this document is an evaluation of the client's living arrangement, supportive assistance required, activities of daily living, all body systems and wounds, and medications.

The data derived from OASIS drive the care plan that is the guide for the clinician. Many agencies follow clinical intervention tools that match the client's diagnosis and specify care measures for each visit. These "care paths" are very paper-intense processes. Some agencies are automating their records.

All of the information collected by the clinician must coordinate with the physician's orders. Each discipline within the agency that services the client must also have supporting orders for its interventions. Orders must be renewed by the physician every sixty days with a progress note from the agency.

Non-certified agencies do not require the same extent of documentation required of Medicare providers. However, Medicaid providers must subscribe to the requirements of their state's Medicaid program. The agencies also must obtain physician orders and demonstrate documentation for all services provided by the disciplines.

The least regulated home care agency is one operating with a license to provide healthcare staffing. If the agency is not billing one of the governmental programs, it may have simplistic documentation requirements. In fact, if the client is paying privately, and the service is homemaking/personal assistance, physician's orders for care are not customary. However, an order is generally necessary for paraprofessional services if an insurance company is being billed.

3.3 Risks in Home Care

There are numerous circumstances that create risks in the home care environment and these may potentially contribute to allegations of malpractice.

A. Inadequate Communication Between Nurses

Areas of risk that may give rise to litigation are described below. These include

- inadequate communication between nurses resulting in loss of coordination of care,
- inadequate planning of care between disciplines,
- imprecise communication between the physician and the nurse,
- improper provision of specialized services,
- inadequate coordination of care between providers of care, and
- potential for staff dishonesty.

First, agencies offering home health services typically provide care twenty-four hours per day, seven days a week.

TIP: Unless a client secures a "live-in" arrangement, there will always be the transition of care from one nurse to another. Complete documentation to transfer vital information is essential as a safeguard to risk management concerns.

Most home health agencies use their weekday staff to case manage the clients. Evenings, nights, and weekends are considered *after-hours*. These shifts are managed by a staff that usually does not work the traditional shift of daytime hours, Monday through Friday. Because of this situation, the potential exists for information to "fall through the cracks," and this is often the basis for a litigious situation.

As a legal professional reviewing a home health chart, note the days of the week and time of the visits. Assess the continuity of care by noting the different nurses involved in a case. The greater the number of staff involved, the higher the probability that there is a lack of coordination among them. Home care agencies should have an established protocol to assure that the staff who are responsible after hours and weekends are documenting their assessments, even telephonic, to communicate necessary information to the day staff.

Weekends and evening/night after-hours are sometimes high-risk shifts, and this is magnified because some of the nurses who work at these times are *per diem* employees. They work occasionally and are often not present enough to command a thorough knowledge of the agency's practices. While the status of "per diem" itself does not indicate less than optimum functioning of a nurse, some professionals consider them the weaker links in the system.

B. Inadequate Planning and Implementing Care Between Disciplines

In addition to multiple nurses servicing a client, there is a second element that contributes to risks in home care. The disciplines offered in most home care agencies include nursing, physical, speech, and occupational therapies, social work, nutrition, and home health aide services. Some clients require more than one discipline to provide all the necessary care. For example, a client who has sustained a stroke would have most or even all of the aforementioned disciplines provide home visiting.

It is imperative in this situation that there is internal coordination of these disciplines, and typically, it is the nurse who acts as the *case manager*. The goals of the nurse must be known by the therapist and vice versa. The home health aide must be instructed by the professional disciplines in the unique aspects of care of the client. Home care agencies should have policies on "coordination of services." A timely transfer of information between disciplines is essential. An example of how poor interdisciplinary communication may lead to litigation is described.

A client's family was instructed to use a transfer board to move the client from the bed to a chair. The physical therapist taught the client and family how to do this safely. However, the therapist did not share (either verbally or in writing) this information with the nurse and the home health aide. The aide, unaware of the transfer board teaching, independently struggled with the client while performing a transfer, and the client was hurt in the process.

In this scenario, the physical therapist should have communicated to the nurse and aide the goal to have the client and family successfully use a transfer board. In addition, the therapist should have made a joint visit with the home health aide to demonstrate the correct procedure and observe that the aide was capable of doing this independently.

C. Imprecise Communication Between the Physician and the Nurse

A third potential risk area in the home healthcare environment is the method in which information is transmitted. Previously addressed was the need for communication to be documented and shared among disciplines. A serious concern is the exactness and specificity of the communication, including the physician's orders for care. In a home health agency, it is typical to have an intake nurse, or a department in a large organization, responsible for receiving client referrals for service. These referrals may come from doctors, staff within hospitals and possibly even the families or clients themselves who are seeking assistance.

TIP: Transmission of accurate information from intake to the clinician in the home providing care is a critical area for potential liability.

There is usually an *intake form*, typically labeled a referral and treatment plan, that elicits demographic data, recent medical information that includes dates of hospitalization, diagnosis, surgery, and specific physician orders for all home health disciplines, including the frequency of their visits. This is often faxed to a home health agency to initiate services prior to the receipt of the original copy. The exactness of the order prescribed by the physician cannot be underestimated.

TIP: Any breach in communication can be the foundation for medically unauthorized care.

A case example involving the lack of adherence to the prescribed treatment plan that subsequently led to legal action against the home health agency is described. This hypothetical example also includes the issue of multiple nurses who did not compare their clinical findings with the previous nurse's documentation.

A patient was discharged from the hospital with two skin ulcers, close to each other, on his buttocks. The larger ulcer had a debridement, and the secondary ulcer, partially concealed by skin folds, was slowly healing with wound care. The initial orders specified to "check debrided ulcer for signs and symptoms of infection and secondary ulcer— wound care per protocol." Care was prescribed for one to three visits per week for nine weeks.

Although the admitting nurse on the weekend was very thorough and addressed *both* ulcers in her notes, the plan for visits to continue was ignored, and the client's care was stopped without any explanation or call to the physician. Five days later, the intake nurse received a faxed order from the physician ordering daily wound care and documented the physician's concern of an infection. Orders for the cleansing of the ulcer were specified by the physician in detail, but the intake nurse did not clarify to which ulcer these orders pertained. The nurse erroneously wrote the orders to apply to the debrided ulcer site and did not address the infected secondary ulcer.

Unfortunately, multiple nursing staff assigned to the case did not question the intake nurse's order from the physician. They only treated the debrided ulcer site and ignored the secondary infected ulcer. In fact, the notes of the previous clinician were not properly evaluated by the nurse each day, as evidenced by the apparent discrepancies in comparative ulcer measurements that went unquestioned.

The client's condition continued to deteriorate, and finally the physician ordered two nursing visits per day. At last, the correct ulcer was treated, and healing occurred within six months. However, the client sought legal action against the home health agency.

This example stresses the fragility of communication within a home health agency and depicts how a seemingly minor misunderstanding can escalate to a case of malpractice.

D. Improper Provision of Specialized Services

The movement toward specialized services is a fourth area of potential risk within home health agencies. The emphasis on maintaining patients out of the hospital has brought more advanced technological services to the home setting. Providing intravenous nutrition or medications (infusion therapy) and monitoring for pre-term (early) labor are common examples of this trend. The home health agency that can tout an ability to deliver the specialized services is in demand by insurance companies trying to avoid costly hospitalizations. However, an agency that desires to promote itself as specializing in certain areas must demonstrate that its staff has the required training and continuing education to perform these skills. Staff must also receive a baseline of competency testing to ascertain these clinical skills, and this should be repeated annually. The Community Health Accreditation Program (CHAP) cites this in its most recent standards of home health practice.[3] Specialized services usually involve specialized equipment. Inadequately trained nurses may be ineffective in problem solving when intervention is required.

Offering specialty services requires that the agency maintain a staff that is capable of delivering this level of service whenever the need arises. After-hours and weekend shifts present challenges in most home health agencies to ensure staff coverage. Providing a specialized infusion therapy nurse at that time can be difficult. Clearly, an agency cannot accept responsibility for a client and admit the case if it has specialty staff limited to only certain hours.

The plaintiff's decedent suffered from Duchenne Muscular Dystrophy and was nearly paralyzed. He required continuous mechanical ventilation. Advantage Nursing Services was under contract to provide the patient with twenty four hour home care. The decedent's ventilation tube became disconnected while the LPN on duty was asleep in another room. When the LPN awoke she heard the alarm, but by the time she reached the patient, he was unconscious and had no pulse. The plaintiff claimed the LPN had not been trained to effectively administer CPR to an intubated patient and that the LPN had been negligent in falling asleep. The plaintiff also claimed that Advantage's hiring practices were insufficient in that there was no investigation of applicants' self-reported qualifications and experience. The defendant argued that there was an orientation and preceptorship in place. The defendant also argued that the death was due to the decedent's medical condition and was not related to the LPN sleeping on the job or inadequate administration of CPR. A $579,000 settlement was reached.[4]

E. Inadequate Coordination of Care Between Providers of Care

The fifth and most complex risk for home health agencies is their relationship to other entities serving the client. The home healthcare agency frequently does not "stand alone" as the sole provider of services. It often coordinates with other organizations on behalf of meeting a client's needs. The home health agency that provides the intermittent services of the nurse, home health aide, therapist, nutritionist, or social worker can interface with many other organizations. One example of a joint effort may be the collaboration between an infusion company that independently provides drugs and a specialized staff of intravenous nurses and the home health agency, both engaged in home visits to the client. The infusion company may be contracted by the insurance company for the specialty service of infusion therapy, but the home care agency is performing other skilled services that the client requires.

TIP: In these situations, it is critical to have a clear delineation of the roles of each organization. It is also important that the client understand what constitutes an emergency and who should be contacted in that event.

Although the home health nurse functions as the case manager for a client and coordinates all the care (therapies, social work, nutrition, and aides) provided internally through the home care agency, communication and cooperation with other external providers is often a critical component to achieve attainment of client goals. Social service organizations often provide complementary assistance to home health care. However, both work autonomously, yet collaborate together for the client's welfare.

Probably the most common example of external agency coordination occurs with a Medicare-certified home health agency that supplies the client's skilled care and minimal aide services and a homemaker company that is providing a supplement to the Medicare services. This supplement can be paid for privately or perhaps subsidized by welfare.

As a legal professional encountering a myriad of names and titles on a client's record, it is important to identify the representatives of the agency that are named in the suit. Next, identify where the other staff are employed and determine the relationship between the two agencies. Also, investigate the background of the agencies and be aware of how they are regulated, specifically their licensing, certification, and accreditation standards.

A lack of coordination among agencies serving the client can have serious consequences as depicted in the following case example.

A client was receiving skilled nursing services for wound care due to an amputation. Although the nurse was from a certified home health agency, the client also received an aide from a homemaker/home aide staffing firm. The latter provided the client two aide visits per day, and the goal was to maintain this chronic welfare client in his own home. The nurse visited until the wound healed but maintained the patient on a long-term program after the acute phase and continued only bimonthly nursing visits.

The client's primary caregiver was the aide from the staffing firm, which was responsible for that component of the care, including direct supervision of the aide. Communications regarding any nursing concerns were to be directed to the home healthcare nurse at the certified agency. The sentinel event was a fall that the client sustained and an "agreement" he made with the aide not to disclose this due to his fear of being sent to a nursing home.

The previously closed wound reopened, and the aide did not report this. The aide staffing firm was lax in its direct supervision of the aide, and the deteriorating wound condition went unrecognized for two weeks. The nurse from the certified agency made her routine bimonthly visits and immediately assessed the seriousness of the client's condition, and notified the physician. The patient required more surgery,

and the family sued the home aide staffing firm for severe negligence. (Unpublished settlement.)

In this situation, the home aide staffing firm was liable because its employee did not react in a responsible manner and notify the agency or the nurse from the certified agency. The lack of coordination with the certified agency in regards to the wound contributed to the poor medical outcome for this client.

Some welfare programs offer consumer choice options that allow the client to receive monies to hire aide services or obtain an aide through a staffing firm. Many clients are choosing to hire their own aides.

TIP: Hiring a private aide has a greater potential for liability due to the lack of checks and balances on the independently hired aide, and it is anticipated that legal actions will increase with the growth of these programs.

F. Potential for Staff Dishonesty

An acknowledged fact of life within the home care industry is the risk associated with unscrupulous staff who takes advantage of the independent environment of home care. Deceitful behaviors can range from the lack of reporting deterioration of a client's condition to fraudulent notes or timesheets.

It is unusual for one employee of the agency to be the sole provider of care to a client. Typically, there are checks and balances on clinicians through this routine relief of staff for each other's absences. It is expected that each practitioner has also reviewed the previous clinician's notes and compared findings to the former report. Any significant discrepancy or negative progression in a client's condition is an event that warrants consultation with a supervisor. Management oversight should mitigate the possibility of any clinician concealing an adverse event. Agencies are required to have corporate compliance plans as part of their training requirements for employees. Staff should be educated regarding the serious consequences of dishonest behavior as well as the Draconian measures the government initiates against agencies that have committed fraud. Nonetheless, there are actual case studies that highlight an agency's vulnerability by the actions of dishonest staff.

The first example involves a patient who was a chronic smoker and set herself on fire when the home health aide was out of the room. The aide and the registered nurse failed to report the burns to the agency. In a phone call to the patient's physician, the home care nurse minimized the extent of the burns. The medical record contained an inadequate description of the seriousness of the burns. The second- and third-degree burns were discovered a week later when the patient fell, hitting her head, and was evaluated by the rescue squad. She died two weeks later in a burn unit. This case settled in an unpublished settlement.

Another unpublished actual case that settled involved a home care aide who was assigned to care for a debilitated woman in her home. The aide decided to take another job as an aide in a hospital. Without the knowledge of her employer, she asked a friend to care for the home care patient while the aide was completing orientation at the hospital. The patient's pressure sore worsened during this time. When the deception was exposed, time sheets in the patient's medical record showed that the aide was documenting as if she were caring for the patient during the same hours she was in the hospital on orientation. The two-fold issues in this situation involved falsification of time sheets and impersonation of an agency employee.

In summary, it is impossible to remove all the risks cited above from the realities of home health care. However, a responsible agency will ensure that the issues of communication via professional documentation, collaboration among disciplines, supervision of staff, and coordination of services, both internally and externally, will be addressed to minimize legal consequences.

3.4 At-Risk and Non-Compliant Client

The organization must define its admission criteria in order for a home health agency to serve clients who are appropriate for home care. Generally, agencies cite the need for

- the client to be mentally and physically able to learn to care for herself or have a responsible caregiver who will accept that role,
- adequate physical resources in the home for safe and effective client care,
- an environment that is safe for the client and agency's staff, and
- a client who does not require more than intermittent services (brief visits by the different clinicians a few times per week).

TIP: In this era of shortened hospital stays, it is not unusual for an agency to be referred an inappropriate case.

Clients have many rights, including the right to be in their own home. However, the agency has the right to determine if a client is appropriate for its services and does not have to accept all clients. It is important that the organization articulate its admission criteria and also include within this definition that a client will be accepted for services *after* the first visit, which is an evaluation to determine a client's appropriateness for the services offered by the home health agency. If the client does not meet the admission criteria, he and the family, as well as the physician and the referral source, are notified. Inappropriate referrals rarely occur if there is good discharge planning between the facility the client is leaving and the home health agency. If an inappropriate referral is made, it is in the agency's best interest to refuse the client. Accepting an inappropriate case subjects the agency to many risks, and it is much more difficult to discontinue services than to refuse it in the first place.

An even greater challenge is the client currently on service, who earlier met the admission criteria, but now has deteriorated and become physically or mentally incapable of meeting her care needs. If the client has no one to assume this responsibility, the agency must confront this situation. If possible, it is the best strategy to make the decision to deny further services at the time the patient is rehospitalized. Generally, that allows the hospital social work staff to make alternate long-term-care arrangements for the client. It is the agency's responsibility to notify the family and hospital as soon as the client is admitted, that she is no longer a candidate for home health services and the reason for this decision. It is recommended that this be clearly documented in the clinical record and the physician also advised.

If the client remains at home without an intervening hospitalization, and it is evident that the client's needs are greater than the capabilities of the home healthcare agency, the agency must commence action to terminate services. This must be a well-documented process in order to avoid abandonment charges. Initially, the agency's clinician with the best relationship with the client and family should address this topic and offer whatever assistance the family will accept with making alternate long-term plans. Generally, the social service staff of the organization is best qualified in assisting with this.

The communication addressing this topic should include the family or caregivers, provided the client consents to their involvement. Often it is necessary to visit in the evening or weekends to facilitate this dialogue. The medical record should reflect the efforts of the staff to present the concern for the client's safety in relation to the client's existing physical or mental condition. The documentation on the home care record should clearly specify the agency's attempt to connect the client and/or caregiver with alternative living arrangements. If the client and family respond positively to a transfer to a long-term-care facility, it is desirable if the agency can maintain the client on service until he is admitted elsewhere.

Notification of Termination of Care within Thirty Days

Date

Dear Client:

Our Agency's professional practice policies specify that when a client is physically and/or mentally unable to care for himself/herself, there must be a responsible primary caregiver who is capable of assuring 24-hours a day responsibility for the client. This is essential for the client to be eligible for continued services.

Your medical condition requires that you have 24-hours per day supervised care and we have discussed this with your physician. This letter is to notify you that your needs exceed the scope of intermittent home health care offered by this Agency and we must terminate services to you within 30 days of this letter which is

_____.

Since we are interested in helping you obtain adequate care for your situation, we strongly recommend that you seek placement in a supervised facility, such as a nursing home. Our social work staff has presented information to you regarding long-term-care arrangements and we would facilitate a transfer to such a facility for you. We have advised your physician of our recommendation and the potential termination of Agency services.

We are concerned for your safety and hope that you will seek alternate living arrangements as soon as possible.

Sincerely,

Executive Director

C: Client's Physician
        Family Member (if applicable)

Figure 3.1

The client who is resistive to leaving the home creates problems for the home health agency. The agency must then send the client, family, and physician a letter outlining why the patient is no longer a candidate for home care and review the efforts that have been made to assist them with alternative plans. The letter concludes with a date that will officially terminate the client from services. A minimum notification of two weeks is essential, but thirty days is desirable. A sample of this letter is provided in Figure 3.1. A common example of this problem arises when a client requires more than intermittent care and truly needs a live-in caregiver in order to remain safely in the home.

There are times when the agency cannot grant a two-week notice prior to discharging a client. This is usually a scenario that exposes the agency to being at-risk due to a safety concern in the client's environment that places the organization's staff in jeopardy. In this situation, the client and family are advised of the risk and asked to remedy the situation immediately. The physician is also apprised of the matter. (Figure 3.2.) If the family and patient do not comply, a final visit is made that prepares the client for discharge, and arrangements to obtain follow-up care are documented.

Notification of Safety Problem

Date

Dear Client:

This letter is to notify you that our Agency is being prevented from providing effective home health services in your home. In order to provide these services, we must be assured of our clinicians' safety in the home and the client's cooperation in allowing our personnel to perform their duties in a safe environment. This has not been our experience in your case.

We would like to be of service to you and have discussed this matter with your physician. However, unless the following circumstances are remedied immediately, we will have to cease providing our services in your home:

(Identification of caregiver safety issues that must be corrected.)

I understand that the Agency requires that I (or my responsible caregiver) correct the safety issue described above, as a condition to receiving future services from it.

_____   _____
Client/Responsible Caregiver Signature   Agency Representative Signature

If you would like to discuss this matter further, please contact the Director of Patient Care Services.

Sincerely,

Executive Director

C: Client's Physician
       Family Member (if applicable)

Figure 3.2

An example of an at-risk situation occurred when a mentally unstable client kept a gun in his apartment. After notifying the client and his sister about this being a safety risk for staff, the physician and welfare program, his payer, were also advised. When he would not remove the gun, the agency discharged him with a recommendation for follow-up care at a clinic and documented all of these actions.

Another difficult situation is posed when the non-compliant client's actions place the client at risk. In this scenario, the agency may be liable if there is no documentation that supports the agency's concern and attempt to remedy the matter. An example of noncompliance may be a situation involving a client who is at risk of falling and refuses to obtain rails in the home and wear an emergency activation device. The home health agency clinician recognizes that without these assistive devices, this client is unsafe for home care. Therefore, the best strategy is to develop an agreement with the client that specifies adherence to certain conditions (obtaining rails on the stairs and in the bathroom and wearing a "help signal" device) as a prerequisite for services to continue. Both the agency representative and the client sign this contract, and it is advisable for the clinician and a manager to deliver this to the home and discuss the matter.

If the client refuses to cooperate with this proposed agreement, or denies that there is a problem, then a certified letter to the client, physician, and family is necessary. It should outline that the client, family, and physician have been previously advised about the safety risk that the client faces and that no action has been taken to remedy the situation. Since agency policies mandate a safe environment for the delivery of client care, the agency must terminate services when this condition is not met. (Figure 3.3.) The details surrounding the client's decision need to be documented in the medical record.

An unpublished case example of how a non-compliant client can cause an agency to be at risk and be sued is described.

A woman who lived in an apartment complex received the assistance of a home health aide. The client was a double above the knee amputee. Allegedly, she refused to use a seat belt while being pushed in a wheelchair. This refusal was not documented in her record. One day, the aide pushed her onto an elevator. When the doors opened in the lobby, the floor was not level. In the process of attempting to push the wheelchair out of the elevator, the client was tipped forward out of the wheelchair. The impact of her fall caused a fractured hip.

Since the patient was nonambulatory, no surgical correction was undertaken. The case settled for an unpublished amount. During the deposition of the aide, she revealed that she had two Social Security cards, one of which she bought on the street. This admission tarnished the aide's credibility.

This example stresses the need for the home health agency to protect itself by thorough documentation when unsafe client behaviors or conditions are evident. Letters to the client, family, and physician are further reinforcement of the agency's attempt to remedy an unsafe situation.

3.5 Home Care Cases

The following are examples of actual cases that were settled in the courts and recently publicized.

In the first example, the plaintiff's decedent, age seventy-three, suffered from end stage chronic obstructive lung disease. She was receiving hospice care in her home from the defendant home health agency in Missouri. In March 2002, the decedent fell in her kitchen while under the care of a certified nurse assistant. She was hospitalized with a broken arm and dislocated shoulder but died eight days later after the family decided not to place her on a ventilator and had returned her to her home. Prior to the incident, the physician's prediction of the patient's prognosis was for a six-month life expectancy, although in his deposition he testified that she had as long as three years of life expectancy. The plaintiff claimed that the nurse assistant failed to properly monitor and assist the decedent at the time of the fall and that the nurse assistant was not properly trained. The plaintiff also claimed that the increased pain, immobility, and treatment caused by the fracture contributed to the woman's death. The agency contended that all training was proper and that the nurse assistant was not at fault for the fall. The defense also contended that the decedent had only days to live and that she had a very poor quality of life before and after the fall. According to a published account, a $450,000 settlement was reached. The defendant agency was bankrupt at the time the case was filed, but liability insurance coverage was available.[5]

In this case, the home health record would have been subjected to scrutiny in regard to the documentation that described the patient's fall. The record should have also noted what measures the aide took to avert this accident. The training of the aide in relation to falls prevention would have been assessed, and the agency records may have been examined.

Termination of Services Letter

Date

Dear Client:

We have previously advised you and your physician of certain conditions in your home which have
prevented our Agency from providing safe and effective home health services to you. We can only service
clients if the home environment is safe for them. The client safety issues in your home have not been
remedied in spite of our request to do so.

Since Agency policies mandate a safe environment for the delivery of client care, the Agency must terminate
services when this condition is not met. Therefore, we are hereby notifying you that effective _____
_____ we will no longer provide services in your home.

Should you wish to obtain health services elsewhere, we would attempt to try to facilitate this. Please let us
know if you want to pursue other arrangements for care.

Very truly yours,

Executive Director

C: Client's Physician
        Family Member (if applicable)

Figure 3.3

In a second case, a healthy child born in an Illinois hospital had a different blood type than his mother. A sample of blood was obtained from him at birth to determine if this would be a problem. However, the defendant doctor who obtained the blood did not have it tested immediately, and within three days, the newborn suffered brain damage (bilirubin encephalopathy) as a result of blood incompatibility. He died at the age of sixteen days. The plaintiff alleged that several defendant doctors and a home healthcare agency were negligent for failing to perform the testing in a timely manner, despite the efforts of the mother to have it done. The defendants denied any negligence and claimed that the infant's death was due to Sudden Infant Death Syndrome, rather than to any acts of omissions on their part. The jury returned a $30,000,000 verdict to the plaintiff.[6]

In this second example, the home care agency's order for services authorized by the physician would have been closely examined to determine the established time frame that was prescribed by the doctor for the bilirubin test.

3.6 Recommendations for Reviewing the Home Care Record

The final segment of this chapter outlines the process to review the home care record and describes the information a legal professional requires in order to understand fully the accountability of the agency.

First, determine what type of home care agency is involved in the lawsuit. Is it certified or not? The answer to this question will alert the reviewer to the regulations that must be adhered to by the organization.

Second, ask who was billed for the service(s) the client received. Even in non-certified agencies, if contracts are held with the state for Medicaid (indigent) services, then the organization must meet the criteria of that particular program.

Third, ascertain if multiple agencies are involved with the case. Sometimes, the client does not understand the professional versus nonprofessional's role and misdirects the accusation.

Finally, ask questions about what internal policies and procedures the agency would follow in regard to the incident that led to legal action. For example, if the wound care ordered by the physician was specified as "per agency protocol," determine exactly what this written procedure includes.

The medical record created by a home health agency can be overwhelming. Most organizations have adopted many standard forms to help clinicians address all the critical issues. The industry admits it is the most paper-intense specialty in health care. All of this magnifies the task of reviewing a home care record.

To initiate a home care chart review, a basic approach is recommended:

- Ask if the record includes all previous admissions to the organization or only the episode in question.
- Divide the papers into categories, if the chart is not already sectioned.
- Isolate physician orders, beginning with the most current.
- Separate treatment notes by discipline: nursing, therapies (physical, occupational, speech), aides and allied health (social work and nutrition).
- Identify all admitting information, including the referral form and any documents received from the referring physician or institution.
- Check if the patient or family signed agency consent forms.
- Classify all billing and insurance information together.

Aside from the documents in the record, the legal reviewer may wish to see an occurrence report that described the incident. Typically, these are maintained by the quality assurance or risk management departments.

Also, it may be helpful to view agency records on continuing education of staff to determine if clinicians are kept current on procedures. This is true especially if the legal issue involved a task that is a basic skill set that would constitute a standard of practice. For example, if a client was injured while a home health aide was performing a transfer, ask when was the last inservice the agency offered to teach transfer techniques?

Finally, consider using the skills of nurse expert witnesses. These individuals can contribute their years of experience and education in quickly assessing the merit of a case.

3.7 Summary

In summary, this chapter began with a description of the many facets of home care and the accountability associated with the various agencies, depending on their regulatory status. The latter affects the documentation requirements of the agency, and this overview was provided. The author discussed the risks within the home care industry and offered examples of at-risk and non-compliant clients and proposed suggestions to reduce agency liability when confronted with these situations. Actual cases settled in the courts were reviewed, in context to their significant findings relative to the home care record. Finally, the last segment of the chapter outlined a straightforward approach to the home care record in the legal review process.

Endnotes

1. Wunderlick and Kohler. (Editors). *Improving the Quality of Long-Term Care*. p. 53. Washington, D.C.: National Academy Press. 2001.

2. *Id.*

3. Community Health Accreditation Program (CHAP). *Home Health Standard of Excellence*. p. 25. New York, NY. 2002.

4. Laska, L. "Death After Ventilation Tube Becomes Disconnected While Home Health Nurse is Asleep" *Medical Malpractice Verdicts, Settlements, and Experts*. November 2009, p. 21.

5. Laska, L. "Woman Falls While with Home Health Agency Nurse Assistant." *Medical Malpractice Verdicts, Settlements, and Experts*. September 2004, p. 20–21.

6. Laska, L. "Failure to Test Bilirubin of Newborn Leads to Brain Damage and Death." *Medical Malpractice Verdicts, Settlements, and Experts*. August 2004, p. 25.

Chapter 4

Independent Medical Examination

Marjorie Eskay-Auerbach, MD, JD

4.1 Introduction

Independent Medical Examinations or IMEs, also referred to as Defense Medical Examinations (DME) and Insurance Medical Evaluations, are currently a mainstay of the medical-legal system. In most cases, the examination consists of a patient interview and physical examination; psychiatric and psychological IMEs do not generally have a physical examination component. The procedural rules governing IMEs vary across jurisdiction; however, an IME is broadly defined as a health assessment conducted by a physician, not otherwise involved in the care or treatment of the individual, at the request of a third party.[1]

The examiner is often expected to answer questions of causation, appropriateness of treatment, need for additional care, and sometimes disability, posed by the requesting party. Other issues that may arise include the presence or absence of pre-existing medical conditions, apportionment of findings, and impairment ratings. These examinations may occur in the context of a work-related injury, disability, or personal injury litigation.

If the examination is performed well, and findings and conclusions are reported in a detailed and unbiased manner, the IME may provide sufficient information to allow for settlement of a particular issue. Alternatively, if the examination is poorly performed, so that the examinee reports that "the doctor spent five minutes with me" or the conclusions are clearly unfounded or obviously biased, the report will provide ample ammunition for opposing counsel to discredit the physician's opinions.

Independent medical examinations have been referred to as defense medical examinations by plaintiff's counsel, to highlight the assumption that the physician conducting the examination has a defense bias. Much of the information available on the Internet, using the search term "independent medical examination" relates to educating patients about what to expect or discussing the defense bias assumed to be present. It is the responsibility of the entity requesting the IME to recognize the reputation of the evaluating physician, and the risk that accompanies hiring a physician with a reputation for bias to conduct the examination. It is, of course, unrealistic to assume that there is no such thing as a work-related accident or that every motor vehicle crash is disabling, and requesting parties may consider the physician's "track record" when making a choice.

In the context of litigation, and most frequently in the workers' compensation arena, independent medical examinations may be conducted to determine medical "impairment ratings." These ratings are performed, by definition, only when the patient's condition has reached maximum medical improvement. The values for impairment ratings are most commonly computed using the AMA Guides to the

Evaluation of Permanent Impairment. The ratings are often used in calculations that vary from state-to-state and at a federal level to determine the financial compensation for a given condition.

IMEs involve critical analysis of all relevant medical and some non-medical information that may affect the ultimate outcome of the medical condition being evaluated. For the attorney or claims adjuster, a detailed report, including a comprehensive history (obtained from the examinee) and medical record review, will reflect the examining physician's efforts to obtain data related to the examinee's altered condition and the events leading up to it.

4.2 The Examiner's Role
A. Physician-Patient Relationship

An IME has already been described as a medical examination performed by a healthcare professional who is not involved in the treatment of the examinee, for the purposes of providing specific information about the examinee to a third party. Most often, an IME is requested for clarification of the medical component of a medical-legal issue, such as causation or appropriateness and relatedness of care. The examiner's role, as a neutral and disinterested party, is to determine the facts related to the incident in question, and associated medical conditions, and to arrive at a conclusion with respect to those issues. It is the examiner's responsibility to explain to the patient that the physician is conducting an evaluation and will not provide treatment or medical advice. Unlike a regular medical examination, in which a patient seeks the opinion of a medical care provider, the opinions of the IME physician are not explained to the examinee but are discussed in the final report.

Many physicians believe because the IME is conducted at the request of a third party, there is no physician-patient relationship, and therefore no potential liability for malpractice. However, several recent court decisions have challenged that interpretation. In 2004, the Michigan Supreme Court found that if the IME's alleged negligence caused injury to an individual while performing an examination, the physician could be sued for malpractice. In *Dyer v. Trachman*, 470 Mich 45 (2004), the Supreme Court held that an IME physician has a limited physician/patient relationship with the examinee giving rise to limited duties to exercise professional care. This would include the duty to perform the examination in a manner that does not cause physical harm to the examinee. In this particular case, the plaintiff had recently had surgery on his shoulder and advised the physician conducting the exam that his surgeon had placed restrictions on his range of motion. Apparently, the examining physician caused damage to the shoulder repair by performing passive range of motion, necessitating another procedure.

In the case *Christine Stanley v. Robert R. McCarver, Jr., M.D., Osborn Nelson & Carr Portable X-Ray, Inc.*, 204 Ariz. 339, 63 P.3d 1076 (App.2003), Ms. Stanley, a registered nurse, was required to undergo a chest x-ray for employment purposes. Dr. McCarver interpreted the chest x-ray and reported abnormalities that required serial x-rays for further evaluation. He provided that report to Osborn, Nelson & Carr, and they forwarded the information to the employer. Ten months later, Ms. Stanley was diagnosed with lung cancer. She alleged she would have been diagnosed earlier if she had been notified of Dr. McCarver's report. The trial court granted Dr. McCarver summary judgment because there was no physician-patient relationship with Stanley. However, the Arizona Court of Appeals reversed and found that when an employer has referred a person for an examination, a physician has a duty to exercise reasonable care in conducting the examination, and this duty includes communicating any matter of concern or abnormalities about the examination directly to the person examined. This issue had not been addressed previously in Arizona. The Arizona Supreme Court concluded that the absence of a formal doctor-patient relationship does not necessarily preclude the imposition of a duty of care and affirmed the portion of the Court of Appeals opinion imposing a duty but vacated the remainder of the opinion and remanded the case for further proceedings.

In more recent Arizona litigation, the Court of Appeals found that "a formal doctor patient relationship need not exist for a duty of reasonable care to arise." *Ritchie v. Krasner*, 1 CA-CV 08-0099. The court held that when a doctor, in the context of performing an IME at the request of the insurance carrier, reviewed patient records, conducted an exam and rendered a report which was relied upon by the carrier and the worker, he assumed a duty to conform to the legal standard of care for one with his skill, training and knowledge.

The court found this duty to exist even though the doctor showed the examinee a written limited liability agreement, stating specifically that no physician-patient relationship was created in the context of performing an IME. The court found that although the agreement made clear to the worker that there was no doctor/patient relationship, this did not obviate the doctor's duty of care. Subsequently, some experts have said the appeals court decision represents an expansion of an IME's legal duties and could have a chilling effect on their participation in certain evaluations.[2] The ramifications of this recent decision have not been fully appreciated.

The physician conducting the IME may also have a duty to inform the examinee of medical findings unrelated to the condition being evaluated. The courts differ on this issue, but the recent trend is that "the IME physician has a duty to take reasonable steps to ensure that the patient is advised of significant medical findings."[3] The *Stanley* case, described above, also discussed this issue. The AMA also endorses the duty to disclose in its ethical opinions. That opinion goes on to state that when appropriate, the physician should suggest that the patient seek care from a qualified physician.[4]

In a practical context, the IME physician may advise the examinees to seek care from their primary care physician. Furthermore, notation that this recommendation was made may be included in the IME report.

B. Expert Testimony

It is important that physicians preparing the report recognize that they may be called to testify as an expert witness. The attorney or adjuster may want to consider this when selecting a physician to perform an IME. The opinions and testimony of independent medical examiners and expert witnesses should be held to the same scientific and ethical standards expected in clinical practice. This requires that experts stay current in their field of expertise and revise their opinions accordingly, based on new information. Opinions and testimony should be honest and based on current scientific evidence. (See Section 4.9 for a discussion of evidence-based medicine.)

The need to remain current with respect to the medical literature relevant to a particular specialty may be more easily accomplished by the busy practitioner who stays up to date based on the demands of caring for patients. However, the IME physician has the same obligation with respect to providing scientifically valid opinions.[5] In many communities, physicians who have retired from operating and general patient care may provide IMEs. Regardless of their clinical experience over the years, they should remain current with respect to the medical literature related to a given topic. Attending annual meetings, reading medical journals, and participating in specialty organizations are all methods of staying informed about changes in a particular medical field.

4.3 Choice of an IME Physician

In choosing a physician for an IME or evaluation, it is important to recognize that for the purposes of this particular occasion, the physician is a medical expert rather than a medical care provider. The skill set of the physician in the context of an IME differs from that of a treating physician, in that no long-term relationship is anticipated. A great deal of information related to the event in question has to be obtained in a single interview. Furthermore, since the exam is most commonly performed in the context of litigation, there may be an adversarial feeling on the part of the patient who is being evaluated. Certain physician personalities are better suited to this type of interaction, which may be viewed as an academic effort rather than an opportunity to treat the patient.

The IME physician may be a medical doctor, doctor of osteopathy, or chiropractor who has an area of medical expertise such as occupational medicine, orthopedic surgery, neurology, psychiatry, or other specialties. State statutes vary with respect to who qualifies as an examiner. It is important that examiners limit their opinions to those within their true area of expertise. In choosing an IME physician, the attorney or adjuster should be familiar with the physician's experience in the area of medicine that is being considered. Most attorneys requesting IMEs will ask the examining physician for a curriculum vitae (CV), which outlines education and experience. It is best to avoid asking IME physicians to express opinions about issues outside their area of expertise.

TIP: The physician who performs an IME is selected because of training, experience, qualifications and ability to produce a well-written report and to articulate expert medical opinions in legal settings. When evaluating the physician's CV, look for current contributions to the medical or legal literature, teaching and speaking engagements, and/or activity in a specialty organization.

The quality of an IME will vary among examiners. This is a function of interest, experience, and time invested in the examination and report. There is special certification as an Independent Medical Examiner available from the American Board of Independent Medical Examiners (ABIME). This certification requires that the physician attend specific continuing medical education courses aimed at teaching the proper methods of performing an IME and use of The *AMA Guides to the Evaluation of Permanent Impairment*. ABIME provides courses designed to prepare the physician for its certification examination, which must be repeated every few years. The American Academy of Disability Evaluating Physicians (AADEP) also provides additional training in disability evaluations and has requirements for membership and fellowship. The physician who maintains an association with such an organization may be more informed as to current impairment and disability-related issues. Certification is neither required, nor a substitute for integrity, thoroughness, or experience in performing IMEs.

4.4 Differing Legal Perspectives on IMEs and Caveats

IMEs are requested far more frequently by defense attorneys and insurance carriers, presumably because the claimant or plaintiff's attorney views the treating physician as his medical expert. The nature of litigation is generally such that there needs to be an equally qualified expert on the opposing side. In general, plaintiffs' attorneys view IMEs as potentially harmful with respect to their cases. It is in the best interest of the defense attorney or insurer to have a qualified and reputable examiner perform the examination, in part because the qualifications and reputation for bias form the basis for much of the plaintiff's attorney's questions, as the attorney tries to impugn the expert's integrity during deposition, in a hearing, or in court.

A. Bias

Often the plaintiff's attorney will take the position that a physician who performs a large number of these exams over the course of a professional career has a bias towards the defense, in part because remuneration from such a practice may exceed that of clinical practice (particularly for the physician who does not perform procedures or surgery). In reality, it may be accurate to assume that payment for IMEs, which require hours of evaluation and report writing, far exceeds reimbursement for an initial patient evaluation in the context of providing patient care, particularly in the settings of health insurance, managed care, liens, and worker's compensation. The alternative view is that physicians who make IMEs a large part of their practice have actually taken the time to develop a level of expertise in conducting evaluations and to review thoroughly medical records and related information, so that an accurate assessment and a thoughtful report are generated. Lawyers who are active in litigation are generally aware of those physicians whose practices they consider unfair, and whose opinions they consider biased.

Although an applicant's or plaintiff's attorney will often imply that the IME physician's goal is to defeat the claim, a more realistic view of the situation may be that the legal system has created a dynamic requiring experts on each

"side." Increasingly, attorneys on both sides of the bar are using deposition and trial testimony databases as a resource for information regarding expert witnesses. There are listservs available for the legal practitioner community (e.g., trial lawyers associations) that provide information about a particular physician's performance in the context of the members' experience.

TIP: It is common for the plaintiff's attorney to question the IME physician, sometimes relentlessly, during deposition or trial, about what portion of his practice is devoted to performing IMEs, and how much income is derived from this type of practice. Perhaps more valuable information is related to what percentage of evaluations are performed at the request of defense attorneys or carriers, and what percentage is performed at the request of plaintiffs. Presumably, physicians who have provided fair opinions on a regular basis will be asked to evaluate injured persons for both sides.

Questioning of the physician during a deposition or during testimony may be structured to imply that the opinions provided in the report favor the party requesting and paying for the examination, most frequently, the defense. The assumption is often made that the physician is or will be unduly influenced by the party paying for the IME. A conflict of interest does exist in this setting; however, it may be managed by fair and accurate reporting of examination findings and opinions based on scientific evidence. Therefore, it is advantageous for the party requesting the examination to seek out an IME provider who has developed a reputation for fairness and whose opinions are grounded in peer-reviewed medical literature. The requesting party who has chosen a fair and unbiased examiner must, however, also be prepared for the situation in which the examiner's findings are not necessarily in his favor.

Diagnoses such as "soft tissue injury," "chronic whiplash," and "chronic sprain/strain" are non-specific, and may be difficult to defend. Bias should not be assumed in such cases; if there are no objective findings on physical examination or imaging studies, subjective complaints of pain can be found insufficient to support a claim.

B. Expertise of Treating Physician versus IME Examiner

The defense attorney or adjuster must be aware that the treating physician is ethically obligated to be an advocate for the examinee. In many cases, if the injury has not been life-threatening or has not required surgical intervention, the examinee will be under the care of her primary care physician.

The physician-patient relationship may have a long history, with expectations on the part of the patient. Although the primary care physician may be extremely knowledgeable with respect to a broad range of conditions, she may not be as comfortable providing medical opinions about more specific conditions, long-term complaints, or chronic pain issues in a medical-legal setting.

TIP: Although the plaintiff's attorney will often view the treating physician's relationship with the patient as a sufficient rationale for the treatment provided, it may be useful to consider whether that treating physician is adequately trained to address the condition that is being treated. In the context of litigation, a specialized physician may be used as an expert for either the plaintiff or defense, depending on the rules in a particular jurisdiction.

The IME physician may be put in the position of unintentionally discrediting the treating physician, particularly if he is a specialist and the treating physician is a primary care physician. The plaintiff's attorney may use this to his advantage. The most frequently asked question in this situation is, "Doctor, don't you think that the treating physician is in a better position to assess the patient's condition than you are? After all, you only spent at most an hour with Mr. X." From a purely clinical standpoint, if the IME examiner has an area of expertise, she may be more competent to address the examinee's condition at a given point in time (the time of the IME).

It is important to remember that the purpose of an IME is very different from the goal of providing treatment. The IME physician is conducting an assessment of the examinee and is obligated to remain objective. In contrast, the treating physician will often be more focused on managing the patient's reported symptoms and concerns about his condition. Causation is often incidental to the treating physician's assessment.

In some cases, perhaps in an effort to establish rapport with a patient, the treating physician may verbalize an opinion as to the relationship between an injury and the need for intervention (e.g., surgery). Unless the statement is documented in the medical records, the physician may not recall having made that connection at the time of deposition or trial. Unfortunately, this is a difficult issue to manage retrospectively, particularly in the absence of documentation.

C. Medical Necessity and Treatment Guidelines

In both the treatment and IME settings, the diagnosis drives treatment recommendations. However, in an IME, the appropriateness and efficacy of treatment that has already been provided is also considered. For the physician providing care, symptomatic relief and palliative measures are most important. Critical evaluation of the extent of treatment may rely on the use of treatment guidelines, discussed below.

Some attorneys choose to refer their clients to a physician who strongly advocates for extensive care in a setting where there is a financial relationship among providers of physical therapy modalities, chiropractic treatment or massage. Treatments are recommended based on intermittent medical evaluations performed by the physician, presumably to lend credibility to the treatment plan. Treatment plans are often designed in response to the patient's persistent pain complaints; however, these complaints are considered subjective, rather than objective, and are often difficult to substantiate based on physical examination findings. In the case of *soft tissue injuries,* in which the diagnosis is characterized as a sprain or strain, there may be little in the way of objective findings to support extended periods of treatment (greater than three months). Treatment guidelines (discussed below) may support criticism of extensive treatment by the physician performing the IME.

TIP: In cases where "soft tissue injuries" are the medical conditions at issue, there is frequently a paucity of objective findings on physical examination and imaging studies often fail to demonstrate any anatomic changes. The patient/examinee may have complaints of ongoing pain, stiffness or spasm in the neck or low back region; however, physical findings are generally limited to tenderness to palpation and restricted range of motion. These findings are considered subjective, since they are based on examinee response or participation. Diagnoses such as these are nonspecific and difficult to substantiate with objective information, since physical examination and imaging studies do not demonstrate the condition.

Another consideration in the assessment of treatment for any given condition is the implementation of treatment guidelines such as the ACOEM guidelines, ODG or state developed ones. Guidelines, although intended only to "guide" treatment, have been adopted in some states for use in the workers' compensation setting, and may impact the availability or duration of treatment for a condition. These guidelines are based on consensus in some cases and evidence-based medicine in others. The recommendations are not case specific, and guidelines may fail to address relevant conditions. However, they are designed to provide recommendations for appropriate treatment of some common medical diagnoses and conditions.

Clinical guidelines have become increasingly popular, because they often provide a summary of the current literature about a particular condition. They may be created by professional medical associations, specialty groups, commercial entities and state panels. Carriers may implement some form of these recommendations, in an effort to reduce the variations in the delivery of care. Guidelines also reduce the delivery of inappropriate care and may support the introduction of new clinical information into practice. The process of guideline development continues to evolve, and criteria defining quality are being developed.[6]

The National Guideline Clearinghouse™ (NGC), available online, is a resource for selected guidelines, and accessible to the public. Some of the information provided may be valuable for assessing the quality of the information provided. The NGC is located at www.guideline.gov. ACOEM guidelines and ODG guidelines are available commercially. Some private insurance companies, such as BCBS and Cigna, have select guidelines used for authorization of procedures and treatment available on the Internet.

D. Documentation Issues

Medical records documenting patient care are intended to contain adequate information to allow another practitioner to take over care. The information contained in the medical records produced by the treating physician (often referred to as office notes or progress notes) should be sufficient to justify the need for continued care. Effective documentation of care during treatment is frequently provided in the "SOAP note" format—subjective, objective, assessment, and plan. In addressing each of these components, the provider should take care to articulate the patient's *subjective* complaints, *objective* findings that are consistent with those complaints, an *assessment* or a synthesis of that information, and a *plan* of care. If the assessment reached by the treating physician is that the patient's condition remains unchanged over several weeks despite treatment, it is appropriate to acknowledge that and to change the treatment plan or make a referral to another provider.

The treating provider who fails to articulate objective findings on examination, and the relationship of treatment to those findings in the medical records, makes it easy for the independent medical examiner to be critical of the medical necessity of the treatment. (Figure 4.1.) Although this may be characterized as "bias," the trend in medicine is towards objective assessment of the need for treatment (medical necessity) and validation of the effectiveness of treatment in providing the desired outcome (see discussion of EBM below).

S: "My neck aches on the right side, into the shoulder."

O: Persistent tenderness to palpation in the right shoulder region.

A: CMT (chiropractic manipulative therapy), hot packs, and ultrasound.

P: Return as scheduled, three times per week.

Figure 4.1 Example note A.

S: "My neck aches on the right side, into the shoulder."

O: Range of motion is restricted in rotation to the left, there is palpable muscle spasm in the trapezius region on the right, no neurological findings noted in the right upper extremity.

A: Persistent neck pain, probable strain/sprain without radiculopathy (neurologic involvement of the arm).

P: CMT is recommended three times per week with modalities, and reassessment after one week; if no response is noted, consider referral to Dr. X for other treatment recommendations.

Figure 4.2 Example note B.

Notes such as those provided in the second part of the example (Figure 4.2) are much more difficult to criticize, because all the components of the SOAP evaluation have been addressed and the physician has provided an alternative treatment in case the initial treatment is not effective. The examiner who provides opinions in the IME report is obligated to support conclusions regarding the necessity of care with information obtained from the medical record, the examinee's history, and the current medical literature.

4.5 Scheduling an IME or Record Review

In the optimal scenario, physicians performing the IME will have structured their practices so that a certain amount of time is devoted specifically to IMEs. The exams are very time consuming and require careful review of medical records, which should be performed by the examining physician rather than a nurse or other office personnel.

Most states have statutory requirements with respect to notice for IMEs, and this will generally require scheduling appointments weeks in advance. Examining physicians will usually have a fee schedule that includes charges for the evaluation, review of additional records and cancellation policies for both examinations and testimony. Since it is often impractical to fill the time slot allotted for an IME on short notice, and the physician may have already reviewed the medical records, a cancellation fee, either full or part of the original fee, may be requested.

It is to the advantage of both the requesting party and the examining physician to have the medical records available at least five to seven days prior to the examination, so that the examining physician has sufficient time to review them. The depth and completeness of the report is improved when the requesting party provides all the necessary and appropriate medical records. Review of the records prior to the evaluation will allow the examiner to ask more probing questions.

A detailed record review may provide adequate information to determine causation, which is very frequently the primary issue in cases that have been referred for IMEs. If several years have passed since the accident in question, there may have been intervening events or the examinee may have poor recall of the events and treatment that occurred early on in the course of treatment; medical records contemporaneous with the injury and treatment are an invaluable source of information. It is often the case that a physical examination late in the course of events will provide very little additional information about causation.

4.6 Structure of the Independent Medical Examination and Report

Although there is no formal measure of a thorough IME, the most complete reports will provide clear responses to the questions posed by a requesting party, with substantiation of those opinions by examination findings and scientific medical opinions. Opinions provided in IME reports should be scientifically based and substantiated with information obtained through a review of medical records and radiographic studies, an interview with the examinee to obtain the examinee's current complaints, history of injury and treatment, and a physical examination. Each of these topics is discussed in greater detail below.

A cover letter or "purpose letter" that clearly poses the questions that have prompted the examination can facilitate an organized and coherent report. Some third-party companies that provide IME scheduling services will also supply a standard set of questions that require responses. The depth and completeness of the report is improved when the requesting party provides all the necessary and appropriate medical records and formulates a specific request for information. Some examples of questions that are typically part of a purpose letter are provided in Figure 4.3.

1. Is there objective medical evidence of an injury?
2. What is the patient's diagnosis and/or diagnoses?
3. Are the identified conditions causally related to the work-related injury? Discuss the etiology for each diagnosis.
4. Are there any underlying medical conditions or behavioral components present that might be hindering the recovery?
5. Is any of the present impairment or symptoms related to the natural aging process or an underlying disease process that in your opinion would have caused the symptoms anyway? If so, please explain.
6. Has the claimant reached a permanent and stationary status? If no, please outline your recommended treatment plan (including type, frequency, duration of treatment, and anticipated date of discharge.)
7. Can the claimant return to work without restrictions? If work is restricted, please indicate specific restrictions and duration. Are the work restrictions permanent?
8. Has the claimant's injury resulted in permanent impairment in accordance with AMA Guidelines? If so, please rate the impairment per the AMA Guidelines (edition should be stated).
9. If there is a pre-existing condition that has resulted in permanent impairment, please rate the pre-existing condition in accordance with AMA Guidelines (apportionment).
10. Is supportive care needed? If so, please provide specific recommendations and duration.
11. Do you have any additional thoughts after reviewing the records/performing the examination?

Figure 4.3 Typical IME questions.

A. General Organization

A physician who is experienced in performing independent medical examinations will have a standard format for the examination. In cases where a third party is involved in scheduling, specific organization of the report may be requested. However, the essential elements of an independent medical examination remain the same. As is the case in an initial evaluation or a specialty consultation, the text of the report will contain a description of the examinee's current complaints, a history of present illness, past medical history, current treatment, and physical examination. A summary of the medical records reviewed and conclusions or responses to questions posed by the requesting party are unique to an IME.

TIP: Although there are some technical differences in terms of presentation of the information obtained in an IME, the health information (outside of a detailed review of medical records) elicited from the examinee is similar to that obtained in a thorough initial evaluation or consultation of a patient in the treatment setting.

TIP: A cover letter with specific questions outlining the information that is expected from the examination allows the examiner to maintain autonomy with respect to providing information, including conclusions about diagnosis, causation and appropriateness of care. In the absence of a letter, the evaluating physician may find it necessary to call the requesting party. This may raise issues about "independence" of the conclusions.

B. Components of the Examination

1. Interview

It is recommended that the interview portion of the examination be performed with the examinee in street clothes. This portion of the examination may, in fact, take the longest time. Information relating to the current chief complaint or main complaint and treatment details, as well as past medical history, is obtained during the interview. In cases where a number of years have passed since the incident in question, the history is more important because the patient will have had treatment and may actually have improved.

It is important that the examining physician retain objectivity during the interview of the examinee. This does not preclude establishing rapport with the examinee, which facilitates the interaction and makes it much easier to obtain information. The examinee may be sufficiently comfortable to ask questions regarding treatment, and the IME physician should refrain from providing medical information in response, unless there is a specific health risk to the patient that requires medical attention. In cases where the claimant or plaintiff is angry or hostile during the course of the examination, it becomes more difficult for the physician to elicit relevant information regarding the current symptoms, injury and treatment. This may make accurate assessment of the examinee's condition more difficult. Figure 4.4 provides some tips that have been suggested by plaintiff's or applicant attorneys.

Information obtained during the course of the interview may be compared with information gleaned from the medical record review. The IME physician will generally call attention to any discrepancies between these sources of information. Credibility of the examinee may be at issue, and will be highlighted in the event that there are significant differences between the medical records and the information provided by the examinee.

For example, JS was involved in a motor vehicle accident and subsequently reported back pain. He was referred to physical therapy, and notes documenting that treatment reflected gradual improvement in his condition. Subjective complaints stated, "back pain is gone. I feel great," and he was discharged from therapy. Nine months later, JS presented to a neurosurgeon with recurrent back pain and right leg pain. The neurosurgeon's initial consultation indicated that JS reported no improvement with physical therapy. At the time of the IME, the examinee continued to complain of back pain and right leg pain, and reported that no treatments to date had been effective. The medical records reflected findings at the time treatment was provided. A discrepancy between that information and the examinee's narrative report of treatment at a later date may cause the IME doctor to question the accuracy of other historical information presented at the time of the interview. If the records were reviewed prior to the interview, the examining physician may ask additional questions to clarify the inconsistencies.

The examinee may request to tape the IME (if permitted in the venue), and in that case, most IME educators advise that the physician do the same. A legal nurse consultant may be requested to observe and document the IME. This individual may be asked to testify in court if the IME physician's report of the exam is markedly different from the one observed by the nurse. *Legal Nurse Consulting Principles and Practices* covers this subject in greater detail.[7]

The following tips will help assure that you are treated fairly by the IME doctor.

1. Your lawyer or someone from the law firm should accompany you and monitor the exam.

2. Approach the doctor and the exam with a courteous and pleasant attitude. Do not be hostile or un-friendly.

3. The doctor will ask you questions about the accident. Do not discuss specific details, rather speak in general terms. The doctor can call your lawyer to discuss details.

4. Wear a watch to the examination.

5. Record the time the doctor begins the examination and the time examination ends.

6. Tell the doctor if anything hurts, even if it is mild pain. If you do not tell the doctor, the record will reflect that you do not have pain, when, in fact, you may have pain.

7. Do not let the doctor push you farther than you feel comfortable. Again, if you endure discomfort in silence, the record will not be an accurate reflection of what you are experiencing.

8. Do not resist unnecessarily, either. If you do, the doctor will record evidence of resistance on the medical report.

9. Do not say something hurts if you do not feel pain. The doctor will know if you are being honest.

10. Watch for tricks. For example, if you complain of back pain, but bend over to pick up an object the doctor "accidentally" dropped, the doctor will note this in the report.

11. Write a summary immediately following the exam.

12. Call your lawyer immediately after the exam.

From www.branchlawfirm.com/accident-and-injury-help.html, accessed 9/7/09

Figure 4.4 Tipsheet: independent medical exam.

Observation of independent medical examinations, most often by the plaintiff's attorney, is sometimes agreed to by the physician, or court-ordered. This could be interpreted as a benefit for the evaluator, since the observation (and recording) process may preclude the examiner from being accused of some wrongdoing.[8] However, if it is assumed that medical and psychological evaluations are scientifically based, the extensive literature available on this topic must be considered. Research in the field of social psychology has reliably reported that observation by a third party changes the examinee's presentation in an unpredictable manner. The examinee's perception of the observer as an ally, a stranger, an expert and personality characteristics of the examinee are among some of the recognized factors.[9]

TIP: Some attorneys may advise their client to be prepared for an examination, and may take the time to review with the examinee the past medical history, previous injuries and treatments related to the current condition. There are now several websites and informational videos that address preparation for an IME and what the examinee can anticipate. See Figure 4.4.

2. Current chief complaint

At the time of the evaluation, the examinee is asked to state her primary complaint in her own words. This is often recorded in the report with quotation marks, reflecting that the physician has tried to accurately document the examinee's description of the condition at issue. Those examinees who have been involved in the process of litigation for an extended period of time may even state their chief complaint in the form of a diagnosis. Since this information may not be entirely accurate, it is appropriate to have the examinee clarify her symptoms, rather than to express a diagnosis that she has heard from other providers of care. For example, an examinee may state her chief complaint as, "I have a bulging disc at L4-5." That statement provides no useful description of the examinee's symptoms or ability to perform activities of daily living at the time of the evaluation.

The chief complaint is subjective by definition, because it reflects the examinee's own perceptions of her condition. The examinee will often provide information about perceived limitations as a result of this condition, and this provides additional valuable information to the examiner. This initial information may also set the tone for the examination.

In the case of an examinee who states that he has "pain all over," the examining physician may register this complaint as so nonspecific that it cannot reasonably be related to the precipitating incident. From a technical and professional standpoint, it is the job of the examiner to remain objective throughout the course of the exam. Global complaints of total body pain, or even an intake form that reveals a myriad of complaints, may make it difficult for the examining physician to objectively hear the examinee's rendition of his injury and current symptoms. The IME physician is required to develop the necessary skills to listen to the examinee's complaints without dismissing them. In an environment where the physician is no longer able to hide behind the notion that there is no physician-patient relationship created in the IME setting, this has become a more sensitive issue. (See Section 4.2.)

3. History of present illness/treatment history

This portion of the report is intended to record the examinee's report of the injury or events leading to development of the condition and the subsequent treatment. The *history of present illness*, often abbreviated "HPI" in the medical records, refers to the precipitating incident and medical treatment that has led to the need for the IME. It should contain a detailed account of the examinee's recollection of what occurred at the time of the incident, whether emergency care was needed or provided, and the immediate subsequent events. Additionally, the examinee's history of treatment and her response to such treatment, as recalled, should be reported in this section.

The detail with which information obtained during the interview is recorded is, in part, a function of the examining practitioner's reporting skills. Some IME educators recommend that the examiner dictate the history during the course of the evaluation, ensuring more accurate reporting. However, it is common for the IME physician to take handwritten notes during the examination and to dictate findings after the examination is completed.

The examiner, rather than a nurse or assistant, is most qualified to obtain the information contained in the history of present illness. The depth of the history is dependent on both the skill of the examiner in asking specific questions of the examinee, and the detail that is provided by the patient. As might be expected, there are physicians who ask leading questions, which in the setting of an IME may be intimidating to the examinee and result in the physician not being corrected, even if information is presented inaccurately. Unfortunately this misinformation then becomes a part of the IME report. There are examinees who are not able to articulate their complaints or history well for whatever rea-

son. Arrangements should be made by the requesting party to have an interpreter available for the examination if there is any question about the examinee's ability to communicate (e.g., language barrier, head injury, or deafness).

TIP: Direct quotations from the examinee included in the report may alert the plaintiff's attorney to the examining physician's attitude towards the examinee.

When tension exists in the exchange the examiner may choose to describe the tenor of the interview. The attitudes of the examinee and the examiner play a role in determining the quality of the interaction and, therefore, the amount of information that can be obtained. If the examinee was belligerent, or passive in response to many questions, this information can be stated in an objective and professional manner in the report. On occasion, it is very difficult to elicit information from the examinee because he has poor recall of the events. An examinee may have been advised by counsel to provide short answers or only to respond that the necessary information is contained in the medical records. This may not only compromise the quality of the examination, because insufficient historical information is provided by the examinee, but may also serve to place the examiner on guard with respect to the veracity of the examinee. Regardless, it is reasonable for the examining physician to state those difficulties in the report as long as it is done in a professional and non-judgmental manner.

Psychosocial risk factors, sometimes referred to as "psychological yellow flags" have been described in the medical literature and may help to identify a patient at risk of developing chronic pain and disability at an early stage in her condition.[10] The biopsychosocial model of back pain and disability emphasizes the interaction between the injured person and her social environment. The social environment includes family, friends, associates at work, employers, and health professionals as well as the compensation system (personal injury or workers' compensation). These interactions influence the person's behavior, level of distress, and attitudes and beliefs about her condition. A patient with several "yellow flags" may be at higher risk for abnormal illness behavior. These yellow flags should be reported by the examiner. For the treating physician, awareness of the behavioral issues is important because such a patient may be at increased risk for treatment failure with conventional treatments such as medication, manipulation, exercise, and surgery. A biopsychosocial approach, which facilitates integration of physical, medical, and psychological treatment efforts, can enhance response to treatment. In patients where these issues are a concern, the patient has continued complaints of pain and limited function regardless of appropriate intervention. Opinions or comments by the evaluating physician will often include a discussion of future treatment, with recommendations that treatment should be oriented toward reducing dependency on medication and other passive forms of treatment and encouraging the development of self-treatment skills.

Yellow flags alert the evaluating physician and the treating physician that there may be underlying issues presenting as non-anatomic conditions, including family interactions, financial stresses, job-related stresses, and other non-physical conditions that deserve further exploration. There tends to be more skepticism on the part of the examiner with respect to conditions of long duration, particularly when the examinee manifests a number of yellow flags and has no objective anatomic lesion, or has had multiple treatments, even surgeries, with no improvement in his condition.

Often, there has been a time lapse of several years between the event leading to the IME and the evaluation, which may result in some holes in the historical information. The medical records can be used to fill in the historical details that are absent, and some physicians will integrate information from the medical records into the history provided by the examinee to preserve or complete the chronology. Most physicians will include a record review as a separate part of the IME report, which is preferable; otherwise, it may be difficult to discern what information was provided by the examinee, and what information was gleaned from the medical records.

4. Current condition

The examinee's current condition and treatments, activity level, and functional level, including daily activities, are reported. The examinee's current functional level includes work activities, activities at home, abilities, limitations, and medications/treatment. It may be useful to ask the examinee how she spends a typical day. Answers to this type of question allow the examiner to understand the examinee's perception of her limitations and condition.

There are several self-assessment scales that have been validated in the medical literature. These include a number of multiple choice assessments, such as the Oswestry Disability Assessment, that reflect a person's self-perceived functional limitations with respect to such activities as pain, sitting, standing, walking, and getting dressed.[11] The *AMA Guides to the Evaluation of Permanent Impairment, Sixth Edition* has added recommendations for self-assessment tools. The Pain Disability Questionnaire is a newer functional status measure for musculoskeletal conditions in general.[12] Other tools include the QuickDASH, recommended

for upper extremity assessment, and the American Academy of Orthopedic Surgeons Lower Extremity Questionnaire. The patient can complete these brief questionnaires in the office, prior to being seen. Experienced examiners will compare their own evaluation of the patient's condition and its effect on functional abilities with the examinee's self-perception. This may provide insight into the possibility of symptom magnification.

5. Review of systems

This portion of the examination generally includes a brief review of symptoms associated with each of the major systems, including the heart, lungs, gastrointestinal system, genitourinary system, and musculoskeletal system. Many offices will have the examinee complete an intake form that includes a review of systems and past medical history. This information may alert the examiner to some other underlying medical conditions, or suggest a preoccupation with health-related issues.

6. Past medical history

The examinee's past medical history will detail any medical conditions that have required medical intervention in the past. Depending on the condition for which the examinee is being evaluated, the past medical history (PMH) may have more or less significance. Consider as an example, the patient with a history of fibromyalgia, diagnosed by a primary care physician, who subsequently requires treatment for chronic musculoskeletal complaints after a motor vehicle accident. This information is essential, and may provide a basis for apportionment in some settings.

The examinee's past medical history should include information as to whether the individual has had previous conditions or injuries causing the same or similar symptoms. The examining physician may perceive the examinee as less than forthcoming if information related to previous injury is not provided on questioning, but is apparent after review of the medical records. Treatment provided for a previous injury and whether or not there was complete resolution of the condition prior to this event are relevant to issues of apportionment. Other chronic medical conditions such as hypertension, diabetes, asthma, chronic obstructive pulmonary disease, or heart disease should be reported here, regardless of their relationship to the condition at hand.

There is little medical literature reflecting a systematic review of the accuracy of self-reported previous axial pain and co-morbid conditions. However, a recent study demonstrated that a large number of patients who were seen for persistent pain complaints related to a motor vehicle accident (MVA) and pursuing compensation claims and/or retaining an attorney, underreported a past history of axial neck or back pain or other serious co-morbidities, including a history of drug or alcohol use and psychological problems.[13] This finding demonstrates the importance of pre-incident medical records to all parties involved.

7. Social history

In the litigation environment, the examinee's social background and habits may provide additional information regarding support systems and other psychosocial factors that have influenced the examinee's response to injury and treatment. This section generally includes information about level of education, marital status, and any history or current use of tobacco, alcohol, or street drugs.

8. Vocational status

This portion of the report should include the examinee's current and past history of employment, with a description of types of work (heavy labor, clerical, or sedentary) and duration. The examinee's description of his relationship with the current employer may provide information about the work environment.

9. Physical examination

The physical examination will usually be tailored to the symptoms or complaints for which the examinee is being evaluated. For example, an examination of the musculoskeletal system focusing on range of motion, muscle strength, and neurologic findings is appropriate for the examinee with orthopedic complaints, and neck or back pain. Although musculoskeletal conditions are the most common reason for independent medical examinations, and will be discussed in greater detail, other systems often require evaluation in cases where exposure to possible toxins, stress, or other issues plays a role. It is possible that more than one expert will be necessary to evaluate the involved systems.

The expert examiner will determine, at the time of the evaluation or prior to evaluation and after reviewing the medical records, if additional diagnostic tests are necessary to establish the examinee's medical condition in an objective manner. The evaluating physician must be familiar with both the indications for such a study and the interpretations. For the examinee with a cardiac condition, the physical examination may be insufficient to provide information about cardiac function. Cardiac diagnostic testing, including graded treadmill testing and echocardiography, may be indicated to assess accurately cardiac function. In the case of pulmonary disease, pulmonary function tests provide more useful information than the physical examination with respect to

lung function. Symptoms of shortness of breath and claims of limited endurance are nonspecific. Pulmonary function testing (PFT) measures lung volume, expiratory flow rate, and gas exchange to evaluate current pulmonary function. The results of such evaluations may be important in determining the short- and long-term limitations of the examinee. Although previous testing may be available for review, the professional and technical staff are factors in the performance and interpretation of such testing, and the examining physician will request repeat studies if there is a question with respect to the quality or age of the previous studies.

In other medical conditions, such as peripheral vascular disease and peripheral neurologic disorders, the examinee's past medical history plays a greater role in the overall assessment. A history of hypertension (elevated blood pressure), chronic tobacco use, and/or diabetes mellitus may clarify the etiology of some symptoms or raise issues related to apportionment for underlying medical conditions that existed before the condition in question. For example, peripheral neuropathy affecting the hands and feet, and often described by the examinee as a burning sensation, can be related to underlying diabetes mellitus, which is not uncommon. Neurodiagnostic testing is required to confirm this diagnosis and/or to differentiate it from other conditions that cause similar symptoms.

C. Musculoskeletal IME

The majority of IMEs are performed for conditions related to the musculoskeletal system, specifically the neck and back. A complete examination of the neck and back has both a musculoskeletal component and a neurologic component. The emphasis on one or the other may be determined in part by the specialty of the physician performing the examination (chiropractor, neurologist, neurosurgeon, orthopedic surgeon, spine specialist, or physiatrist).

In general the examination will contain:

- a reference to the overall appearance of the examinee including weight, conditioning, and general health;
- a description of gait and balance, the use of any assistive devices, ability to walk on toes and heels;
- measurements of range of motion of the cervical and/or lumbar spine, including flexion (bending forward), extension (bending back), lateral side bends (bending from side to side), and rotation (Figure 4.5); and
- neurologic assessment of the upper and/or lower extremities.

**Range of Motion of the Lumbar Spine
(AMA Guides, Fifth Edition)**

Flexion (bending forward)   60+ degrees*
Extension (bending back)   25 degrees
Lateral Bending (side bending)   25 degrees

*hip flexion angle is assumed to be 45+ degrees for these measurements

**Range of Motion of the Cervical Spine
(AMA Guides, Fifth Edition)**

Flexion (chin to chest)   50 degrees
Extension (looking upward)   60 degrees
Lateral bending (ear to shoulder)   45 degrees
Rotation (looking side to side)   80 degrees

Figure 4.5 *Range of motion guides.*

Objective findings refer to the findings on physical examination that are quantifiable on some level. The *AMA Guides to the Evaluation of Permanent Impairment,* Fifth Edition, considers spinal range of motion to be an objective measure of function.[14] Range of motion has the advantage of being observable and quantitatively measurable; however, it can be argued that it lacks objectivity in that it is prone to voluntary restriction. It is incumbent upon the examiner to determine whether the examinee has put forth maximum effort, and it may be necessary to repeat range of motion several times to assess validity. These caveats have resulted in the elimination of range of motion measurements for determination of impairment in the cervical, thoracic and lumbar spine in the *AMA Guides to the Evaluation of Permanent Impairment,* Sixth Edition.[15]

TIP: There is some controversy as to whether range of motion of the cervical or lumbar spine is an objective finding because the examinee can control active range of motion.

Upper extremity neurologic function is supplied by nerve roots from the cervical spine (neck); and lower extremity neurologic function is supplied by nerve roots from the lumbar spine (low back). This portion of the exam includes evaluation of reflexes, muscle tone and bulk, muscle strength and sensation. Comparison of one side to the other may be important to ascertain abnormalities. In performing this portion of the exam, the examiner is looking for patterns

of altered function that correspond to a particular nerve root. This information supports the presence or absence of radiculopathy. Sensory examination is based upon the examinee's report and therefore must be considered subjective. If the examining physician chooses to limit his description of objective findings to the presence of neurologic findings, then in many cases of both neck and back injuries, the examinee will be found to have no objective findings at all. The predominant findings in soft tissue injuries or sprain/strain injuries are:

- complaints of pain in a non-radicular distribution (not corresponding to a particular nerve root),
- palpable muscle spasm, which is usually intermittent and nonspecific for a diagnosis, and
- trigger points which are nodular areas of tenderness which cause referred pain when palpated and are also nonspecific for a diagnosis.

Neurodiagnostic tests may be appropriate in orthopedic and neurologic conditions. These tests are most valuable when they are performed to differentiate between central and peripheral neurologic disorders. Neurologic disorders are often difficult to evaluate, because subjective complaints of pain and dysesthesia (burning pain) are not objectively measurable. The IME physician may be critical of the use of inappropriate testing; for example, neurodiagnostic studies are not indicated less than three weeks after injury, because any neurologic changes are not measurable until then. Likewise, clinical evaluation should provide sufficient information for the ordering physician to identify a specific diagnosis (C6 radiculopathy, carpal tunnel syndrome) for which the testing is being performed. Neurodiagnostic studies are indicated as confirmatory studies for suspected diagnoses.

A controversy that may arise has to do with the examinee's report of what transpired during the examination. The examinee may report that the examining physician only spent five minutes in the room or did not perform an examination. It is important that a thorough examination be performed and reported; however, the duration of the physical examination may be appropriately brief and will vary based on the condition being evaluated. There are examples of musculoskeletal physical examinations available for review at numerous websites; those from medical schools are likely to be reliable resources.

4.7 Review of Medical Records

Medical records should be thoroughly reviewed by the physician conducting the IME. In the case where the injury is several years old, medical records documenting contemporaneous care may provide information essential to understanding the medical history. Medical records are also useful for documenting resolution of symptoms, exacerbation of symptoms, and intervening incidents.

Findings in the medical records may be reported either chronologically or by provider. In general, they will most probably be organized in the format in which they were received by the examining physician. In cases where services that obtain records are used, the records will generally be organized by provider. Although the medical records can be reported selectively, it is important that the information be accurately reported. Dates of service, diagnostic studies, and providers' impressions are all relevant to the review. Physical therapy and chiropractic care are often provided for management of musculoskeletal conditions. Notes from the providers of these services may include valuable information about the patient's level of activity, compliance with treatment recommendations, and response to treatment.

TIP: Examination of the musculoskeletal system includes evaluation of soft tissue findings in addition to neurologic findings. However, because these soft tissue findings are not objectively quantifiable, they are much more difficult to defend.

4.8 Medical/Legal Controversies
A. Non-Organic Signs (Waddell's Signs)

The medical-legal environment, in particular the defense environment, will often exclude or discount complaints of pain or treatment provided for complaints of pain if there is an absence of "objective findings" on physical examination. Many of the complaints with which examinees present are pain related and have no objective measure. This does not mean that the examinee does not have pain; however, there are many issues attendant to the evaluation of pain, and because pain is a subjective experience, it cannot be adequately measured or quantified in a manner that allows for relative comparisons. Chapter 18, *Pain Assessment and Management*, covers this topic in depth.

In 1980, Waddell and colleagues developed a standardized assessment of behavioral responses to examination. The signs were associated with other clinical measures of illness, behavior, and distress and were not isolated to medical-legal settings.[16] Waddell's assessment and subsequent literature made it clear that multiple signs might suggest that the patient does not have a straight-forward clinical problem; however, this was not meant to be interpreted as evidence of malingering or even suspicious behavior. Instead, this literature acknowledges that significant physical impairment may produce high levels of distress.[17] The identification of

a behavioral component to the examinee's presentation does not preclude pathology that requires further investigation and/or treatment and may make discernment of true clinical findings more difficult.

Behavioral signs are indications that are consistently reliable and reproducible for identifying non-structural problems. These are often referred to as "Waddell's signs," based on the literature described above. The initial description of these signs included superficial tenderness, nonanatomic tenderness, axial loading, simulated rotation, distraction straight leg raising, regional weakness, regional sensory change, and overreaction to examination.[18]

Superficial tenderness means tenderness or discomfort caused by light touch or gentle palpation by the examiner. Physical back pain does not cause skin tenderness. *Non-anatomic tenderness* is illustrated by tenderness on palpation of multiple spinous processes at the midline, in the absence of direct trauma to that area or suspicion of a compression fracture, or extension of pain into unrelated areas. *Axial loading* is performed by pushing down on the examinee's head and is considered a positive Waddell's sign when the examinee complains of back pain. This action does not directly load the spine, and should not cause back pain. *Simulated rotation* is accomplished by rotating the shoulders and pelvis in unison in the standing patient. This does not stress any structures in the back and should not be painful. *Distracted straight leg raise* occurs whenever the hip is flexed and the leg is extended. The patient is not aware that straight leg raise is occurring, hence the term *distracted*. Patients with organic pain have the same or similar results on both the standard straight leg raise and the distracted straight leg raise test. (In both cases this maneuver should reproduce radicular leg pain, not low back pain.) The examinee who has severe pain on straight leg raise, with no other apparent physical findings or consistent complaints, will raise suspicions of a behavioral component to her presentation.

Regional muscle weakness may be described as weakness of an entire upper or lower extremity. For example, specific ankle motions such as dorsiflexion (toes pointing toward the body) and plantarflexion (toes pointed away from the body) are performed by muscles that are innervated by different nerve roots. Weakness of more than one muscle group suggests involvement of multiple nerve roots, which is not common, and requires further neurologic evaluation for a more generalized condition or tumor. Sudden uneven weakness or the sudden letting go of a muscle may be described as *cogwheeling*, *giving way*, or *breakaway* weakness. In patients with true physical weakness consistent with nerve or muscle pathology, the muscle is smoothly overpowered, or the muscle contraction cannot even be initiated, and this is reproducible. Patients with non-organic weakness cannot duplicate this response. *Regional sensory pain* such as widespread numbness on one side of the body or one-quarter of the body is also suspect. Numbness in a "stocking-glove distribution" may reflect a peripheral neuropathy. Stocking distribution (the area covered by a sock) or glove distribution (the area covered by a glove) rarely has a traumatic cause but may be consistent with a peripheral neuropathy. *Overreaction* includes disproportionate grimacing, tremor, collapse, inappropriate sighing, guarding, bracing, and rubbing the reportedly involved area. These can all be characterized as exaggerated behaviors and non-reproducible or nonspecific responses to a stimulus.[19] Appropriate interpretation of these findings is that the examinee is in distress, although there may be no objective findings to support an anatomic or physiologic reason for the examinee's ongoing complaints. The predictive value of behavioral signs in identifying a behavioral component to the examinee's presentation is greatly improved with three or more positive signs.[20] It is essential to remember that these non-organic signs are only part of a comprehensive clinical assessment. They must be interpreted critically within the context of the whole picture.[21]

A comprehensive evidenced-based review by Fishbain and others of over 50 studies showed Waddell's signs do not correlate with psychological distress. They do not discriminate organic from non-organic problems. They may represent organic phenomenon. They are associated with poor treatment outcome and greater pain levels. They are not associated with secondary gain.[22]

TIP: Behavioral symptoms such as those listed above are distinct from the usual physical symptoms associated with a condition and are more closely related to psychological distress. Assessment of the patient should be based on the whole clinical picture, and isolated behavioral symptoms may generally be ignored. See Figure 4.6.

Somatoform disorder is another term used in the context of evaluating the patient whose predominant complaint is pain. This describes physical symptoms, which suggest a physical disorder for which there are no organic findings or known physiologic mechanisms. The patient may become preoccupied with health-related issues and symptoms. The medical symptoms patients experience may arise from both medical and psychiatric illnesses. Anxiety disorders and mood disorders commonly produce physical symptoms. The creation of physical symptoms in a somatoform disorder is not intentional.[23] This presentation further complicates evaluation of the patient. Patients with chronic pain of uncertain etiology should not be presumed to have psychogenic pain.[24] In the context of an IME, examinees who present with obvious behavioral components to their examination increase the complexity of the evaluation. Patients with complaints of pain and without objective examination findings are often characterized as having "functional overlay," or a "supratentorial component" to their pain. An alternative interpretation would be that the patient is in some distress and has pain that is not amenable to surgery or not responsive to traditional treatments.

Signs	Physical Disease	Illness Behavior
Tenderness	Musculoskeletal distribution	Superficial, nonanatomic, widespread
Simulated rotation	+/- Nerve root pain (radicular)	Low back pain
OR Axial loading	Neck pain	Low back pain
Muscle weakness	Anatomically appropriate	Regional, jerky, giving way
AND/OR Sensory findings (pain, numbness)	Dermatomal (associated with particular nerve root)	Regional (stocking-glove distribution)
Distracted straight leg raise	Limited on formal exam, not improved on distraction	Marked improvement with distraction
Overreaction	Not present	Present

Figure 4.6 *Summary of Waddell's signs.*

TIP: The most obvious difficulty in assessing the examinee who presents with non-anatomic complaints is the lack of "objective findings" on physical examination. Conventionally, objective findings have been described as reproducible neurologic findings including loss of strength or decreased reflex, and limited range of motion. This presents an advantage for the defense, because complaints of pain cannot be objectively quantified.

Malingering, in contrast to non-organic findings, is generally described as the intentional production of false or exaggerated symptoms motivated by external incentives such as obtaining compensation, avoiding work, receiving medications, and so on. Malingering is not considered a mental illness, nor are there validated clinical methods of assessment to identify malingering in patients who present with pain complaints. The individual may falsify all his symptoms or exaggerate the effect that the symptoms have on activities of daily living. A marked discrepancy between the individual's claimed symptoms and the medical findings on examination can be anticipated.

B. Chronic Pain

Chronic pain is a major public health problem with medical and lost productivity costs estimated at $120 billion. Fifty million people in the U.S. are either partially or completely disabled by pain.[25] The International Association for the Study of Pain (IASP) has described pain as an unpleasant sensory and emotional experience with actual or potential tissue damage described in terms of such damage.[26] Current medical literature regarding chronic pain suggests that there may be sensitization of the central nervous system that leads to prolonged suffering and disability even after the source of pain has been addressed. The pattern of pain for which many chronic pain patients are at risk is independent of the anatomic locations where the chronic pain condition may be located, and therefore the assessment of chronic pain does not follow the traditional biomedical model.[27]

TIP: The physician needs to document in her report the basis for indicating that a pain-related condition is unratable. The necessary details for this explanation are well outlined in Chapter 18 of the *Guides, Fifth* and in Chapter 3 of the *Guides, Sixth*.

The details of evaluating pain for the purposes of an IME cannot be adequately elaborated on here. The IME report should indicate that the physician recognized chronic pain as an issue. More recently, it is common to obtain IMEs in the worker's compensation setting to evaluate use of expensive long-acting narcotic medications. Assessment of pain and the need for medications to manage it is a very controversial issue. Chronic noncancer pain requires management of medication regimens tailored to the individual. In general, the use of opioids in chronic noncancer pain is intended to improve the individual's function. Improved function should be documented in the medical records, if a recommendation for chronic opioid use has been made. In addition, accumulating evidence suggests that opioids may cause opioid-induced hyperalgesia; opioid therapy aiming at alleviating pain may cause patients to be more sensitive to pain and potentially aggravate their preexisting pain.[28]

The assessment of pain for the purposes of determining an impairment rating using the *AMA Guides to the Evaluation of Permanent Impairment, Fifth Edition* has been a contentious issue. However, use of the *Guides* has been mandated in many jurisdictions, and the lack of consensus or peer-reviewed literature addressing pain and impairment does not mitigate its importance. The *Guides, Fifth*[29] made an effort to facilitate the practical assessment of pain for the explicit purpose of assigning an impairment for pain. Chapter 18, *Pain,* characterizes pain as ratable or unratable. A ratable pain-related impairment, for the purposes of using the *Guides, Fifth*, however, requires an underlying objective condition that could reasonably be determined to result in pain. The presence of an unratable impairment does not imply that the pain is fabricated or unreal; however, a condition may be considered unratable if the symptoms are vague or suggest a controversial diagnosis, or symptoms and limitations cannot be related to any well-defined medical disorder. Unratable impairments have no associated quantitative measure of impairment, only a qualitative one. *Master the AMA Guides, Fifth Edition*, recommends that the decision that a pain-related impairment is unratable be interpreted as a result of the limitations of medical science and impairment evaluations, rather than the authenticity of the examinee's pain reports.[30]

The more recent sixth edition of the AMA Guides provides a significantly different methodology for evaluating and rating pain. The focus of the most recent edition of the *Guides* is consistency and reproducibility. As a result, the complicated issue of pain has been addressed by limiting the circumstances in which a pain-related impairment is appropriate.

In the *Guides, Sixth*, numerical ratings exclusively for pain can be determined only for a recognized medical condition (e.g., headache) that is not otherwise ratable using Chapters 4 through 17, which cover the major organ systems of the body.

Pain ratings for conditions covered by the other chapters are accounted for by a modifier used in the impairment calculation, in an effort to capture the burden of illness associated with those conditions.[31]

4.9 Impressions and Professional Opinions

TIP: The most valuable reports are those that answer the questions at hand. The experienced physician will answer only the questions posed by the requesting party. The attorney or adjuster requesting the IME can assure that she receives the necessary information by asking the appropriate questions in a cover letter accompanying the medical records or confirming the examination issues that require a medical opinion. In a case where the issues are unclear, the requesting party may ask for "comments" in addition to the other medical opinions; however, there is some risk associated with an open-ended question.

The experienced physician will answer only the questions posed by the requesting party. A cover letter with explicit questions to be answered will facilitate the writing of a report. If the requesting party does not formulate specific questions, the evaluating physician may have to call for clarification. This may raise issues of bias, in that any conversation about the results of the examination could be perceived as unduly influenced by such an interaction. It is best for the requesting party to formulate questions in advance and to include them in a cover letter with the medical records. An additional benefit is that the examining physician can direct the questioning to the salient issues.

The examiner is asked to state his opinions to a reasonable degree of medical probability and may need to be educated with respect to the legal definition of certainty. Most medical practitioners are not familiar or comfortable with causation from a legal perspective. As professionals trained in the sciences, medical practitioners require a higher level of certainty (95%) in order to make an association between an event and result. This is in contrast to the greater than 50% level accepted in the legal setting. The text *Master the AMA Guides, Fifth Edition*,[32] provides a detailed discussion of causation that may be a useful reference for physicians and attorneys who work with physicians.

It is important to recognize that the evaluation is intended to assess the patient's condition at that specific point in time. Although the patient's history of injury and response to various treatments are contributory to understanding the patient's condition, these are not determinative with respect to diagnosis or prognosis. Physical examination findings will reflect the patient's condition after treatment, whether she has responded well or not.

4.10 Evidence-Based Medicine

New information is available almost in real-time, and this is true in medicine as well as other sciences. The content of medical school classes and residency training programs completed by a physician quickly becomes outdated. Many physicians attend continuing medical education courses, and some specialties require recertification for board exams, which ensure some familiarity with current medical science. Physicians who are active in practice are required to stay current, and more recently are being expected to practice according to the tenets of evidence-based medicine.[33] These evidence-based medicine standards should apply to IME physicians and physician-experts as well.

The practice of EBM is described as "the conscientious, explicit and judicious use of current best evidence in making decisions about the care of individual patients."[34] The phrase "the best evidence available" is recognition that there may be limited literature on many clinical topics; however, where research is available, the level of accuracy is improved.

Of course, it is assumed that physicians will base their decisions—and in the case of IMEs, their opinions—on the best available medical evidence. This evidence has often represented extrapolations of scientific principles and logic, rather than established facts based on data derived from patients. There recently has been an increase in the number of high-quality clinical studies and a corresponding increase in the quantity and quality of clinically valid evidence concerning many conditions.[35] As the quantity of valid evidence increases so does the requirement for each of us to develop the skills necessary to assimilate, evaluate and make best use of that evidence for patients. Often we fail to identify or address our daily needs for clinically important knowledge, leading to a progressive decline in our clinical competency.

The practice of EBM requires evaluation of the medical literature with respect to the methodology of the clinical studies that are reported. The value of information in the medical literature is organized in a hierarchy, so that the most informative studies, usually randomized controlled trials, are at the top, and expert opinion is at the bottom of the pyramid. The studies may be referred to as Levels 1-5: Level 1 which includes randomized controlled trials and metanalyses (analysis of information from multiple studies) to Level 5 or expert opinion.

Evidence-based medicine is not only valuable in a clinical setting, but in the medical-legal setting there could be significant improvement if IME physicians and expert witnesses were required to support their positions, not only based on scientific facts, but on an evidence-based standard.[36] This would eliminate citing only medical literature that supports a particular position, particularly when that position is no longer an accurate reflection of the current science. Furthermore, a physician who is considered an expert in a particular field should be familiar with the medical literature. Online searches for updates on a particular topic and systematic reviews (authors have searched, reviewed and analyzed the literature) are easily accomplished.[37]

TIP: EBM is commonly misconstrued as requiring a valid study finding to be supported by Level 1 evidence. The use of EBM requires only that the "best available evidence" be used to substantiate validity.

4.11 Role of the AMA Guides

IMEs are regularly performed in the workers' compensation setting to determine whether a patient has reached maximum medical improvement (MMI) and, if so, to determine a permanent impairment rating. More recently, IMEs are being obtained in the personal injury setting for the purposes of determining permanent impairment ratings using the *AMA Guides to the Evaluation of Permanent Impairment,* now in its Sixth Edition (2007). The Fifth Edition is still used in many states.

The *Guides* was first published in 1971 in an effort to provide a standardized, objective approach to medical impairment ratings. It has undergone several revisions since that time, reflecting changes in scientific evidence and prevailing medical opinion.[38] The *Guides* remains primarily a consensus document with respect to actual impairment values, because there is very little scientific literature addressing the topic of impairment values. The use of permanent impairment percentages to calculate financial compensation is not a scientific or medical determination, but rather legislative or statutory and variations in use of the *Guides* is jurisdictional. The *Guides* is not intended as a reference for evaluation of disability.

The *Guides* does provide a form of guidance used by physicians to conduct an IME and to evaluate impairment. The text is organized around the various physiologic systems such as the respiratory system, the gastrointestinal system, the extremities, and the spine, so that each may be independently addressed. A whole person impairment (WPI) can be determined by adding or combining impairments according to the *Guides, Fifth.*

The primary goal of the *Guides* is to provide a standardized method for assessing permanent impairment. By using the methods described, multiple examiners should arrive at the same calculation for an impairment within a small variance. The text is used most frequently in the workers' compensation setting but may also be applied in the personal injury setting where permanent impairment requires quantification.

The first two chapters of the Fifth and Sixth Editions of the *Guides,* are devoted to the practical application of its methods. The approach to calculating impairment is significantly different in the *Guides, Sixth,* in response to changes in the World Health Organization model of disablement, the International Classification of Functioning, Disability and Health (ICF).[39] Impairment evaluations are defined and distinguished from an IME and according to the *Guides, Fifth,* impairment evaluations may be less comprehensive than IMEs.[40] Furthermore, impairment evaluations for the purposes of calculating a permanent impairment are not performed until the patient has reached maximum medical improvement. An IME may be performed to determine whether the patient has reached MMI or requires additional treatment.

4.12 Summary

Independent medical examinations continue to be a mainstay in the medical-legal system. A thorough examination, complete review of the medical records, and well-written report can provide useful and objective information regarding the examinee's condition. Attorneys and other requesting parties should critically evaluate the content of the IME report for objective information and support of conclusions grounded in the examination findings, the examinee's history of injury and treatment, and the current medical literature.

Endnotes

1. Baum K, "Independent Medical Examinations: An Expanding Source of Physician Liability." *Ann Intern Med.* p.142:974-978. 2005.

2. http://www.ama-assn.org/amednews/2009/08/10/prca0810.htm.

3. *See* Note 1.

4. Council on Ethical and Judicial Affairs, American Medical Association, *Code of Medical Ethics: Current Opinions, Opinion 10.03, Patient-Physician Relationship in the Context of Work-Related and Independent Medical Examinations.* 2004-2005 edition. Chicago: American Medical Assoc; 303-4. 2004.

5. Schofferman J, "Opinions and Testimony of Expert Witnesses and Independent Medical Examiners." *Pain Medicine* 8(4);p. 376-382. 2007.

6. Jencks SF, Huff ED, Cuerdon T. "Change in the quality of care delivered to Medicare beneficiaries, 1998-1999 to 2000-2001." JAMA; p. 289:305-312. 2003.

7. Iyer, P. (Editor). *Legal Nurse Consulting Principles and Practices*. Second Edition. Boca Raton, FL: CRC Press. 2003.

8. Barth R J. "Observation Compromises the Credibility of an Evaluation."*AMA Guides Newsletter*, July/August 2007, AMA Press, Chicago.

9. *Id.*

10. Waddell, G. and D.C. Turk. "Clinical Assessment of Low Back Pain" in Turk, D.C. and R. Melzack. (Editors). *Handbook of Pain Assessment*. Second Edition. Chapter 23. New York, NY: The Guilford Press. 2001.

11. Fairbank, J.C. and P.B. Pynsent. "The Oswestry Disability Index." *Spine*. 25, p. 2940–52. 2000.

12. Anagnostis, Christopher PhD; Gatchel, Robert J, PhD; Mayer, Tom G. MD. "The Pain Disability Questionnaire: A New Psychometrically Sound Measure for Chronic Musculoskeletal Disorders." *Spine*. 29, p 2290-2302. 2004.

13. Carragee EJ. "Validity of self-reported history in patients with acute back or neck pain after motor vehicle accidents." *The Spine Journal*. 8, p. 311-319. 2008.

14. Cocchiarella, L. and G.B.J. Andersson. (Editors). *Guides to the Evaluation of Permanent Impairment*. Fifth Edition. Chicago, IL: AMA Press. 2000.

15. Rondinelli R, (Editor) *Guides to the Evaluation of Permanent Impairment*. Sixth Edition. Chicago, IL: AMA Press. 2007.

16. Main, C.J. and G. Waddell. "Behavioral Responses to Examination: A Reappraisal of the Interpretation of Nonorganic Signs." *Spine*. 23, p. 2367–71. 1998.

17. *See note* 10.

18. *Id.*

19. *Id.*

20. *Id.*

21. Waddell, G. "Nonorganic Signs." *Spine*. 29, p. 1393. 2004.

22. Fishbain DA; Cutler RB; Rosomoff HL; Rosomoff RS, "Is there a relationship between nonorganic physical findings (Waddell signs) and secondary gain/malingering?" *Clin J Pain*. 2004; 20(6):399-408.

23. Aronoff, G.M. "Evaluating and Rating Impairment Caused by Pain" in Demeter, S.L. and G.B.J. Andersson. (Editors). *Disability Evaluation*. Second Edition. St. Louis, MO: Mosby. 2003.

24. *Id.*

25. Griffin, R M. "The Price Tag on Pain." WebMD. n.d. 7 January 2005. http://my.webmd.com/content/article/57/66051.htm?z=1832_103590_2010_hz_02.

26. *See note* 14.

27. Robinson, J.P. "Disability Evaluation in Painful Conditions" in Turk, D.C. and R. Melzack. (Editors). *Handbook of Pain Assessment*. Second Edition. New York, NY: The Guilford Press. 2001.

28. Angst, MS. Clark JD. "Opioid-induced hyperalgesia: a qualitative systematic review. *Anesthesiology*. 104. p. 570 -87. 2006.

29. *See note* 15.

30. Cocchiarella, L. and S. Lord. *Master the AMA Guides Fifth: A Medical and Legal Transition to the Guides to the Evaluation of Permanent Impairment*. Fifth Edition. Chicago, IL: AMA Press. 2001.

31. *See note* 15,

32. *See note* 29.

33. *See note* 5.

34. Sackett DL, Rosenberg WM, Gray JA, Haynes RB, Richardson WS. "Evidence-based medicine; what it is and what it isn't." *BMJ*. 312. P.71-2. 1996.

35. Rosenberg WM, Sackett DL. "On the need for evidence-based medicine." *Therapie*. 51. p. 212-7. 1996.

36. *See note* 5.

37. *Id.*

38. *See note* 14.

39. *See note* 15.

40. *See note* 14.

Additional Reading

Buchanan, L. *Getting the most out of the legal nurse consultant's observation ofan IME*. www.medleague.com.

Chapter 5

Office-Based Medical Records

Keith M. Starke, MD, FACP and Ginny Tucci Starke, MSN, RN

5.1 Introduction

The role of medical records in physician offices has experienced a dramatic evolution in the past fifty years. The original purpose of medical records was to simply jog the physician's memory regarding pertinent history, physical exam, diagnosis, or treatment specifics. In the 1950s and 1960s, index cards were frequently used to store brief bits of information. Considering the limited number of therapeutic interventions available at the time, index cards were sufficient to list the necessary information of a patient or even a whole family. No medical record data were submitted to insurance companies. Communication with other physicians was less frequent and typically accomplished orally.

Over the course of the last fifty years, the ability to communicate information has grown exponentially with the technology boom. Medical advancements and new therapies have multiplied as technology has increased. Numerous specialties exist to manage and utilize the many facets of medicine available to treat patients. In addition, the lone physician, previously called the GP or general practitioner, is being replaced now by large group practices. Within these large practices rests the potential for many physicians to be involved in an individual patient's care. The primary need for a medical record remains to assist the treating physician in delivering therapeutic options. However, the need to document the pertinent findings and treatments of a patient has changed from a memory jog to a communication necessity.

The increase in information and the requirement to organize and transmit medical information has molded the format of office medical records. Medical records are required to support billing, document complex treatment protocols, support decision making for test ordering, pharmacy, and other medical interventions, and to communicate information to other physicians and patients. Index cards have become inadequate for these needs. Handwritten notes are also inadequate if they are illegible, since they cannot support all of the above needs. The most commonly used methods of medical documentation are handwritten, transcribed, or dictated notes prepared with a voice activated computer dictation system. Electronic medical records (EMR), the newest method of medical record documentation, are just beginning to emerge in the physician's office and will be the documentation tool of the future.

While this chapter refers to the recorder of the note as a physician, it is important to remember that office records may be prepared by physician assistants or nurse practitioners. Their documentation follows the same patterns described in this chapter.

5.2 Paper-Based Systems

Paper-based systems can fulfill the requirements of recording and communicating patient information. However, these systems are often limited by obvious inadequacies.

- Handwritten notes are frequently illegible and may be limited to superficial pieces of information. It is also difficult to record the important information of a complex case in a relatively brief amount of time.
- Dictated records tend to be more complete because of the speed of dictation, but the degree of accuracy of dictation may depend upon the completion of the note by the physician in a timely manner.
- Transcription errors can occur in transcribed notes. When this happens, the physician will often find the error in review of the notes, but the system is not fail-safe. Attorneys should clarify any statements that appear confusing or out of place.
- Paper medical records are unavailable or inaccessible at the time of the visit approximately 30 percent of the time. The records may be in a physician's private office, at the nursing station, or in the billing, insurance, or satellite office.[1]

The standard requirement for paper-based medical records includes the patient's name and date on each page. All notes should be signed and dated, regardless of whether they are handwritten or transcribed. However, on handwritten notes, the physician's signature is often illegible or abbreviated as initials. There is no universal method of organizing the documents contained in physician office records. This can be a source of frustration. Ideally, the office medical records will be organized in such a manner that physician-patient encounter notes, problem, medication, allergy, and immunizations lists, as well as test results are found with ease. Nursing documentation is frequently located within the physician notes but can also be kept separately. Phone call records may be found in a separate part of the chart, within the physician notes, or in a completely separate log. In some circumstances, it may be important to ask the attorney to request a complete file containing every piece of documentation pertaining to the plaintiff.

TIP: Attorneys should clearly state a request for all billing records in letters of request for medical records. A simple, direct statement requesting the medical record in its entirety, billing records, and any separate logs kept involving patient care (if appropriate) should suffice.

It is important to realize that consulting physician notes, hospital records, physical therapy updates, and other documents sent to the physician from an outside source will not necessarily be included when the medical record is requested by an attorney. Although a portion of these records may incidentally be sent, separate requests to each provider should be made to assure that a complete copy of medical records is compiled. Billing records are usually organized in a completely different system by the front desk or billing department. By comparing billing statement dates to office note dates, the attorney can verify he has received the complete medical record.

5.3 Sections of Information Found in the Office Records Related to the Patient

Office medical records are typically not as voluminous as hospital records but have a number of sections to review. The method of organization for the following sections is variable from office to office. In addition, some physicians will keep laboratory, radiology, and correspondence next to the corresponding office visit note. The following list details components that may be found within office records.

- Contact, demographic, insurance, and consent forms. (Copies of a patient's advanced directive and power of attorney may be found here as well.)
- An initial history. (This is typically completed during the first visit to the physician office by the patient before meeting with the physician.) The history summarizes:
  ◊ current medications,
  ◊ allergies,
  ◊ past surgeries,
  ◊ previous hospitalizations,
  ◊ prior illnesses,
  ◊ vaccination record,
  ◊ social history: includes employment, marital status, lifestyle habits such as smoking, alcohol intake, seat belt usage, exercise, the presence advanced directives in place and power of attorney,
  ◊ family history: records the cause of death of parents and siblings or current illnesses of these family members, and
  ◊ check-off list of symptoms previously or currently experienced.

Once the initial history is obtained, the physician office will frequently make a separate and continually updated list of medications, allergies, and vaccinations, as well as a patient problem list of all chronic illnesses or conditions. These are sometimes consolidated into one summary sheet and kept highly visible on the left hand side of the patient file as it is opened. In some cases, the initial history is updated as it changes with the date recorded next to the new information. Office records should also include:

- Physician office notes of visits, including weight, blood pressure, pulse, complaints, examination findings, diagnoses, and treatment.
- Laboratory, radiology, EKG, and other medical procedure results, which may or may not be divided into separate sections. Test results should have some notation either on the test report itself or within the physician office notes that the results were reviewed by the physician, communicated to the patient, and that follow-up was given to the patient, if necessary, to evaluate the results or monitor the findings at a specific time interval. This can be accomplished through a phone call, letter, or follow-up office visit. Some physicians simply initial the test results. Routine and normal results may be communicated to the patient by the office staff following a specified office procedure.
- Correspondence and consultation notes with other physicians, outpatient services such as physical therapy, and letters sent to or received from the patient.
- Phone call records. These are frequently inserted before or after office visit notes to maintain an easily readable time sequence of events.
- Letters and e-mails from patients.
- Health maintenance or preventative care may be in an organized section or simply found throughout the chart. Items typically noted include vaccinations, routine screening tests or procedures such as mammogram or colonoscopy, education, and health habits such as smoking or exercise.
- Billing records may or may not be kept within the body of the medical record.
- On occasion, copies of prescriptions for medications or therapeutic treatments will be found.
- Return to work or excuse from work/school notes.
- Disability records.
- Copies of hospital records such as discharge summaries, histories and physicals, operative reports, and consultations from other physicians are not always included and may be incomplete if present.

5.4 Electronic Medical Records

At this time, electronic medical records (EMR) are not widely used in physician offices. Clearly, however, the widespread replacement of paper-based medical record systems with EMR is coming. These EMR software programs can vary in function from simple data storage to systems that allow for note-building constructed in real time. Real-time construction embeds a time stamp when the system was accessed and information entered. Thus, the delay between dictation and transcription of the office note is eliminated.

A. Formats

A basic EMR may function as a simple storage system. In this instance, the handwritten or transcribed office notes are scanned into the EMR database. The most significant advantage of this type of EMR system over a paper-based medical record is that charts and information are not lost. Also, assuming that the information is scanned into the system promptly and in the correct file, the notes are preserved in their original form and cannot be altered.

A more sophisticated system in which the notes are actually built from templates within the system offers several additional advantages over paper-based systems. Templates of various formats serve as a guide for physicians to construct problem, medication, and allergy lists, perform a thorough physical exam, and consider basic treatment options. In addition, alerts for drug interactions or allergies are available which decreases the potential for medical errors.

The various sections of an EMR are the same as a paper-based system. When an EMR is used in an office, the physician sees links on the computer screen to enter data into a particular section. Unfortunately, a hard copy of the EMR often prints in random order, making organization and review of the printed EMR a challenging process. Legal nurse consultants can be of great value in the identification of missing records and chart organization.

TIP: Be aware that EMR systems can have an override function that gives the physician freedom to modify the templates, enter further information, or entirely skip functions available in the EMR system.

B. EMR Advantages

The EMR offers several advantages over paper-based systems, such as

- ability to write more complete notes,
- no time delay between note construction and entering the information into the medical record,
- legible, easy-to-read information,

- usually contains a link to the billing system,
- no opportunity for lost files,
- the information can be kept current without confusion or repetition that is often found in paper-based medical records,
- prescription writing systems improve completeness of medication documentation,
- elimination of the need to transport medical records physically from one destination to another,
- elimination of volumes of medical records, decreasing the overall cumbersomeness of patient records, and
- increased accessibility of the records.

C. EMR Disadvantages

Despite the overwhelming advantages to entice physicians to convert their paper-based medical record systems to an EMR system, the EMR poses a unique consideration. There is a general concern that tampering can occur by a third party altering the medical record. Although the potential exists, the EMR and its supporting database are designed to discourage and prevent tampering with the records by a third party. Many EMR programs require two electronic signatures for every entry when completed. Any additional information or change to an entry is typically required to be documented as a separate addendum entry. Unless there is collusion between the physician and the administrator jointly to alter the record, or if the physician's password to use the electronic signature is compromised, tampering with the EMR is very difficult. If tampering is suspected, the electronic trail is traceable and would likely require investigation by an expert in EMR technology.

Implementation of widespread electronic medical records is limited by the barriers listed below:

- physician resistance to emerging and often unfamiliar technology,
- start up, maintenance, and upgrade costs, and
- patient records and information security.[2]

D. Interrogatories

Consider the following questions to include in interrogatories for use with EMR records.

- What EMR software program is used?
- Who has privileges to access the system?
- What time stamping functions does the EMR system have?
- How are signatures handled?
- Does the EMR software allow additional information to be added to a completed entry at a later time? Does the office have a policy for how these changes or additions are to be made and tracked?
- What security functions for privacy of information does the EMR system contain?
- Is a printed version of the EMR generated on a regular basis? How often? Where is this printed version stored?
- What facility is responsible for storing the EMR database information?

Improved patient care logically stems from clear communication that projects a high level of accuracy and consistency. EMRs now provide an important tool to assist in the achievement of this goal. Refer to Chapter 6, *Computerized Medical Records*, in Volume I, for more information.

5.5 Governing Organizations' Documentation Guidelines

TIP: Ask if the physician office is part of a larger organization and whether or not that organization has participated in the TJC or NCQA approval process.

The Joint Commission (TJC) and National Committee for Quality Assurance (NCQA) provide a framework of standards to help assure patients receive the best possible quality of care. It is important to establish whether a facility has been accredited by either of these organizations. In addition, when a case requires review of medical records from a Health Maintenance Organization (HMO), asking for policies on documentation requirements could be beneficial to determine if a particular standard of care is applicable.

Only organizations that are TJC approved are obligated to adhere to the guidelines the organization sets forth as the accepted standard of care. Primary care facilities most commonly JC approved are those owned by hospitals, such as ambulatory care centers. TJC provides guidelines to which the center is expected to adhere. TJC medical record guidelines are listed under the title of "information management." The guidelines are general in nature and periodically change.[3,4] Therefore, the reviewer should refer to the appropriate standards in place at the time the patient received care. The guidelines notably do not specify exactly how the information should be organized into the medical record or give a specific timeline for entry of information. Each file is considered unique and has to be considered in context of the entire situation.

NCQA gives accreditation to health plans that have met the requirements of a thorough evaluation.[5] The evaluation from NCQA considers these categories: staying healthy, getting better, living with illness, qualified providers, and access/service. Under these categories, items such as health screening policies, disease management, and treatment plans are scrutinized. If a health plan organization is approved, the organization is given a rating such as excellent, commendable, or accredited, depending on how well the organization has met the criteria of the NCQA. Physicians who are part of an organization that is NCQA approved have been evaluated as part of their credentialing process to be a "qualified provider," which includes a physician's attention to medical record documentation recommendations. Thus, if a physician is part of an organization that is NCQA approved, she has proven in the past to demonstrate an acceptable level of proficiency.

5.6 Physician Notes

Physician notes can be quite diverse based on physician preference and the type of problems typically encountered in a particular specialty. There is no one format that must be followed. Furthermore, busy physicians may record very little detail of their thought process or discussions with the patient. However, regardless of format, a thorough office note should record assessments that are subjective in nature, vital signs, objective findings of a physical exam, impressions or opinion of what the findings mean, and a treatment plan that summarizes all of the physician's recommendations to diagnose, monitor, or treat the patient's problems. Lastly, physicians use a multitude of abbreviations to make efficient use of their time. Some of these abbreviations may not readily be found in medical abbreviation resources. Legal nurse consultants can be quite beneficial in the area of interpreting the physician's office notes.

Patients make appointments with physicians for different reasons. Thus, the office note structure is typically consistent with the reason for seeking the physician in the first place. There are three main reasons patients see physicians: a chronic problem, an acute problem, or a physical exam during a time of wellness.

A. Chronic Problem Notes

Office visits for chronic medical problems are usually scheduled well in advance and are often non-emergent on the day the patient is seen in the physician office. The focus of the chronic problem office visit is a comprehensive evaluation of the entire disease process that is occurring. Sometimes there are multiple diseases or conditions that are monitored during this type of visit. Subjective questions about how the patient is feeling and the physical examinations performed look for positive and negative findings that indicate whether or not complications are occurring, or likely to occur, from

the disease. The physical exam may be specific to the disease but tends to cover all of the major organ systems of the body, for example, lungs, heart, liver, kidneys, and so on. Based on the findings, the physician's opinion should state whether the disease process is improving, stable, or advancing in severity. Laboratory work that is appropriate for the condition may be included to bolster this opinion. Treatment plans map out how to avoid complications, identify ways to continue to evaluate the severity of the disease, and limit any associated discomfort. Follow-up is generally suggested for a specific time frame in the future, barring any acute problems that arise. The follow-up frequency may be abbreviated as RTO (return to office) or RTC (return to clinic) followed by a time frame such as one month. This may be recorded as "RTO 1 mo."

B. Acute Problem Notes

Acute medical problems require more urgent care. Some offices refer to acute visits to the physician as "sick visits." These problems or illnesses arise quickly and are often accompanied by various symptoms that cause discomfort or alarm for the patient. It is common for patients to call the physician with an acute problem and be evaluated in the office within a day or two. Notes that evaluate acute medical problems are very limited in the length and scope of the examination. The history and physical exam focus on the body system that is having the problem at the time, for example, an ear, nose, and throat exam for a complaint of a sore throat. The physician gives a diagnosis of the condition and appropriate treatment or lists the symptom with the potential diagnoses that could be the causative factor and the plan for how to evaluate the problem. Follow-up evaluations for acute medical problems are typically recommended within a few days to a few weeks' time or may be documented as "call back or RTO if no improvement."

C. Physicals

The words *physical exam, check up,* or *preventative health exam* should be identified under the heading of *chief complaint* or at the top of the page. These examinations are similar to those performed the first time a patient comes to see a physician. The patient's complete history is recounted on the history form, allergies and medication routines are verified, health and safety habits are reviewed, and a thorough accounting of any symptoms experienced from each of the body systems is documented. A complete head-to-toe examination follows. The physical exam is a screening examination for any existing medical problems or for conditions that could occur in the future, based on risk factors found during the office visit. Thus, the physician's assessment states whether or not disease is present and which diseases should be further screened for by diagnostic testing. An example of wording for the assessment section of the office note could be *normal physical exam* or *has risk factors for coronary artery disease*. Treatment plans discuss the specific testing that should occur, if any, or potentially document a referral to a specialist. Vaccination updates may be noted in the treatment section as well as preventative health testing recommendations. An example of a treatment plan following a physical exam could be *will do stress test, consider risk factor modification, blood lipid testing, and return in 3 months*.

There are several sources for the suggested frequency of physical exams and specific preventative health testing. These include:

- American Cancer Society for appropriate timing of screening or preventative testing,[6]
- American College of Physicians,[7]
- American College of Obstetrics and Gynecology,[8]
- American Academy of Family Practice,[9] and
- U.S. Preventative Task Force Recommendations.[10]

TIP: There may be some variation in recommendations from different organizations for the same healthcare screening test.

5.7 Referrals or Consultations

Physicians refer patients to physicians who possess different specialty certifications, outpatient ambulatory care settings such as physical therapy, mental health facilities, and home health companies as needed. These referrals are also called consultations. Sometimes physicians simply seek validation from other physicians regarding their plan of treatment. The plan section of the physician office records note when referrals are made. The physician may document the following:

- Reason for the consultation. What question needs to be answered or service provided by the referral or consultation?
- Recommendations for specific treatments the consultant believes should be performed.
- A request for "assumption of care." Will the consultant take over the general care of the patient, as in the case of an internist referring a cancer patient to an oncologist?

Physicians will often write a letter to request a consultation in addition to the notation made in the plan of care. This letter would be part of the medical record.

5.8 How to Evaluate Office Medical Records

The task of reviewing office medical records involves a new dimension of investigative abilities. On initial review, the office-based medical record may seem simplistic compared to hospital or nursing home records. However, despite its frequent brevity, the office medical record provides insight not only about the problem at hand but the overall health of the patient and the factors that may have played a role in the development of the illness. The reviewer should ask the following questions when evaluating office medical records.

- Is there a clear and appropriate plan of care?
- What is the style of the notes?
- Are the office notes linked to the plan of care?

A. Clear and Appropriate Plan of Care

TIP: The plan of care is not one document. It is found by linking together the individual office note entries.

When reviewing office records, it is important to know as closely as possible the physician's thought process in coming to a conclusion. This is found in the plan of care. To identify the physician's plan of care it is imperative to review all of the office notes instead of one or two isolated entries. Consider the overall style and content of the notes, the findings that are repeatedly evaluated and tracked, the laboratory values that help identify and follow problems, lists of potential diagnoses, and consultations or referrals to other specialists.

B. Style of the Notes

Look for consistency of style. Are the notes of similar length and detail? Most physicians follow a set pattern of structuring an office note. Some styles are more narrative in nature. Many physicians choose an outline style of office note. In general, the information is organized into four broad categories. These categories are subjective information, objective information, assessment or diagnosis, and plans for treatments and monitoring of patient conditions. Hence, the common format of "SOAP," or subjective, objective, assessment, and plan, finds its roots in these categories.

1. Subjective information

TIP: The subjective findings or complaints of the patient should direct how detailed the various parts of the physical exam will be and which diagnostic testing will be performed.

**Example of a Chronic Problem Office Note using a SOAP Format
(Subjective, Objective, Assessment and Plan)**

S   Patient present for 3 month check on diabetes. Has been doing reasonably well. No new complaints, except for slight numbness in toes. Her FBS (fasting blood sugars)* have been averaging 135 and 4:00 P.M. are around 160. Continues to follow her diabetic diet and exercise. She saw the dietitian 4 months ago.

O   ROS (Review of Systems)
General: Weight stable. Energy levels unchanged
Resp (respiratory): No SOB or wheezing
CV (cardiovascular): No chest pains or heaviness in the chest. No tachycardia
GI (gastrointestinal): Appetite good. No nausea or vomiting. No change in bowel habits
MS (musculoskeletal): No joint chest or pains
Neuro (neurological): Slight numbness in the toes which is new. It is bilateral and worse at night

Medications: Metformin 500 mg bid, Glyburide 5 mg at hs (hour of sleep)

PE (Physical Exam)
Vitals: P74 BP 122/76 R12
Skin: No rashes or changes in skin integrity
Eye: Fundoscopic exam is normal without retinopathy
Neck: Carotids 2+ without bruit. No thyroid or lymph node enlargement
Lungs: Clear to A&P (auscultation and percussion)
Heart: RRR (regular rate and rhythm), normal S1 and S2. Grade II/VI SEM (systolic ejection murmur) at LLSB (left lower sternal border) which does not radiate
Abd (abdomen): Normal BS (bowel sounds). Soft and non-tender. No masses.
Ext (extremities): Pulses 2+. No ulcers. Slight callous. Normal vibratory sense and pinprick.

A   1. Diabetes Mellitus Type II, not adequately controlled
2. Early signs of peripheral neuropathy without objective evidence at this point

P   1. Check labwork, including Lipids, HgA1c (test for long-term blood sugar control) and BMP (Basal Metabolic Panel)
2. Since fasting BS are still elevated, will double up on Metformin
3. If cholesterol is elevated, will start a statin (medication to lower cholesterol)
4. Continue to monitor foot exam for neuropathy
5. Return in 3 months

* Verbalized home reports of blood sugar readings are under the subjective category whereas laboratory blood sugar reports would be listed under assessment category.
Note: Parentheses transcribe word(s) of the abbreviation used.

Figure 5.1 *Chronic problem notes.*

Example of an Acute Problem Office Note using a SOAP Note
(Subjective, Objective, Assessment and Plan)

S   Sore throat and fever for 24 hours. He is having difficulty swallowing. Temp up to 102.5 at home. No sinus drainage or cough. Appetite poor. Has taken Tylenol with minimal relief. Sister had bronchitis recently, but no other family member has been sick.
NKA (No known allergies)

O   P (pulse): 104 BP (blood pressure)-106/70 T (temperature)-102.4 degrees
R (respiration): 14
Gen (general): WDWN (well developed, well nourished) black male adolescent, obviously feeling poorly
Skin: Warm and sweaty
Ears: TMs (tympanic membranes) clear. No exudates
Nose: Mucous membranes pink. No purulence
Throat: Pharynx markedly erythematous with exudates on the pharynx. Both tonsils markedly enlarged red and swollen
Neck: Bilateral, tender and swollen anterior cervical lymph nodes
Lungs: Clear to A&P (auscultation and percussion)

A   Pharyngitis, probable strep

P   Strep culture. Start Amoxicillin 500mg tid (three times a day) #30 (dispense 30 pills)
Call for results of culture. Call if no improvement in 72 hours or if symptoms worsen

Note: Parentheses transcribe word(s) of the abbreviation used.

Figure 5.2 Acute problem notes.

A subjective information section, in addition to being labeled just *S*, can also be recorded as *CC* for chief complaint, *HPI* for history of present illness, or simply noted as *history* or *hx*. In this section, the patient is asked to state the problem he is experiencing in his own words. A patient may state vague complaints such as "I feel terrible." Then, when questioned further, he narrows the problem to "my chest hurts sometimes." Both statements are important indicators of what the patient is experiencing. It is clear the physician is hearing the perceived problem accurately when a patient's words are quoted in the office medical record. The patient history is often the best lead a physician has in accurately diagnosing medical conditions. When no subjective information is present in the office note, it should raise questions in the reviewer's mind about the physician's level of completeness and attention given to patient concerns. Be aware that sometimes the physician's staff will complete this section of the examination. Note whether or not the handwriting is different in the subjective complaints section. Ultimately, the subjective findings or complaints of the patient should direct how detailed the various parts of the physical exam will be and which diagnostic testing will be performed.

2. Objective information

The objective (O) information recorded should begin with a review of systems, abbreviated "ROS." A review of systems is a summary of patient complaints from all body systems in addition to the chief or primary complaint that brought the patient to the physician. This is followed by a physical examination. The results of the physical exam and vital sign findings are a critical component of objective information. The physical exam can be written as *O* for objective or *PE* for physical exam. The information recorded here should be expressed in clear and concrete terms. Unfortunately, more than a few physicians record the absence of abnormal findings with the abbreviation *WNL* for within normal limits, *OK*, or a zero with a slash through its center. Consider the example of the patient who is complaining of abdominal pain. Physical exams which result in documentation of "*abdomen WNL or OK*" do not indicate results of abdominal assessments such as softness of the abdomen, the presence of bowel sounds, or distention. This vague type of documentation opens the door for questions concerning the type and accuracy of exams that were performed as well as the thoroughness of an exam, making defense of an alleged incomplete physical exam more difficult. Furthermore, it is hard to understand the plan of care when the reviewer is uncertain from the physician's note what the findings truly were.

TIP: Objective physical exam findings should include information relevant to each complaint the patient has offered.

There should also be an obvious link between subjective complaints described and the depth of the physical exam. As previously discussed, notes for an acute problem visit are typically more focused on the immediate problem at hand, whereas chronic problem notes may be more general and evaluate more systems of the body. Objective physical exam findings include information relevant to each complaint the patient has given. If a patient complains of both abdominal pain and shortness of breath, detailed exams of both the abdomen and lungs should be documented. A clear pattern of linking patient complaints with appropriate physical exam is evidence of a physician who is less likely to miss an important diagnosis.

3. Assessment and diagnosis

The word *assessment* in physician notes is often called *impressions* or, sometimes, *differential diagnosis*. The reviewer may see the abbreviations *A* for assessment, *I* for impressions, or *D* for diagnosis. All of these terms reflect the physician's medical opinion of the problem at that moment in time, based on all of the physician's findings. The results of laboratory and diagnostic tests that have been performed may be included here as well.

TIP: A differential diagnosis is the physician's thinking process: a list of all possible diagnoses that the physician is considering and will be confirmed or eliminated by further evaluation.

Patients very often come to the physician with confusing symptoms that could be related to a number of medical conditions. An example of this would be the symptom of fatigue. If a patient presents with a confusing or complex problem that requires further investigation, the physician may list all of the potential diagnoses that could be occurring. This listing is referred to as a differential diagnosis. This is the physician's thought process, a list of the possibilities that are going through her mind to be confirmed or eliminated by further evaluation. It is a positive sign to see a listing of potential diagnoses in the office medical record, indicating the physician is considering the various causes of the problem.

4. Plan

Appropriate treatment options or diagnostic testing can begin once the physician's opinion of the problem is established. This is recorded in the plan section of the office note and is the medical recommendation of the physician for that visit. The abbreviations *P* for plan and *Tx* for treatment can be used. In general, the plan section of the office record is an outlined approach to resolving patient problems. Physician plans may contain:

- appropriate medical treatments,
- instructions on how to prevent further problems or a worsening of the condition,
- testing for suspected problems,
- patient education, and
- a specific time interval for when the next follow-up visit should occur.

Ideally, the goals of treatment are included in the plan. For example: "Goal for total cholesterol of 180 mg." If multiple problems are present, then the plan section will often prioritize which problems require the most urgency by numbering the steps to be taken in ascending order of importance. However, some EMR software programs automatically list problems and their treatments chronologically, based on the date of occurrence. When a medical problem is more complex than the physician is trained to treat or with which he is unfamiliar, referral to another physician should be made and documented in the physician's plan. Accordingly, the plan section of subsequent follow-up visits should state whether or not the described complaint has resolved, improved, stabilized, or worsened. Thorough follow-up notes comment on what therapies were effective and define changes made to ineffective therapies.

A dispute about the plan of care was at the heart of the following case.

The plaintiffs claimed that for a period of time before his death the decedent sought treatment from the Defendant #1 at his office with complaints of severe shortness of breath and a history of difficulty breathing when sleeping and with any movement. Plaintiffs claimed the defendant diagnosed and treated the condition as an upper respiratory bacterial infection when, in fact, he had congestive heart failure. The plaintiffs contended that on January 7, 1997, the plaintiff went to defendant's office with worsening symptoms, including an inability to lie down when sleeping, or orthopnea, and defendant scheduled an echocardiogram for January 13, 1997, to investigate possible congestive heart failure. On January 10, 1997, the plaintiff contacted defendant's office and told Defendant #2 that his condition had worsened. After consulting with Defendant #1, Defendant #2 advised decedent that an antibiotic was being prescribed. Plaintiffs contended that no other instructions were given to decedent. On January 12, 1997, he was taken to the hospital because his condition worsened, and he died at the hospital later that day. Plaintiffs claimed that defendants' negligent failure to diagnose and treat decedent's condition and failure to refer him to a specialist caused his death.

Defendants denied negligence and contended that the plaintiff was instructed to go to the emergency room on January 10, 1997, after his condition did not improve with the antibiotic treatment. Defendants asserted that standards of care were met regarding the plaintiff's diagnosis and treatments. A settlement of $712,5000 was reached during mediation.[11]

5. The physician's signature

TIP: Physician offices provide training for medical residents who may perform examinations; however, the supervising physician is ultimately responsible for the examination.

As previously discussed, at the end of every office visit, the signature of the physician who performed the examination must be present. This also applies if the note was dictated and typed. Medicare reimbursement guidelines require further medical record documentation by the attending physician when supervising residents. At a minimum, these guidelines call for identification of the service provided, the participation of the teaching physician in providing the service, and notation about whether the physician was physically present.[12]

C. Linking the Individual Office Notes into a Plan of Care

After evaluating the plan of care and the style and content of office notes, compare them to each other chronologically. The reviewer should see an ongoing plan of care emerging that reflects both treatment of the short-term problem and a plan for identifying how the problem will be monitored in the future. As an example, assume a patient complains of occasional and brief chest pain during the night. The office note documents a thorough physical exam. The physician collects blood, and an EKG is performed. The physician's diagnosis considers a heart valve problem, and the plan recommends

an echocardiogram test. The plan also states the patient is to return to the physician office in two weeks. The next visit should document the results of the echocardiogram test and comment on how the results confirm the suspected diagnosis or change the next step of the plan. For example, the second office visit note might state the echocardiogram revealed a minor heart valve leak. The plan section should outline any useful treatments such as medication or referral of the patient to a cardiologist, if appropriate. Subsequent office visit plan sections may comment on how well the patient is tolerating the medication and whether or not the original chest pain has resolved, as well as the findings of the cardiologist. By comparing each office note to the previous one, the reviewer can evaluate whether or not comprehensive follow-up was done.

It is helpful for attorneys to identify the plan of care in the office records. Defense counsel may want to use the plan of care to demonstrate a reasonable and prudent line of thinking by the physician. Plaintiff's attorneys may find important information regarding inappropriate treatments.

TIP: By remembering to consider each office visit in the context of the whole plan of care and not in isolation, the attorney avoids misinterpretation of the medical office record.

5.9 Is the Physician the Only Examiner?

TIP: In most states, nurse practitioners or physician assistants must work under the direction of a physician and adhere to a policy about conditions they can treat and how.

Many primary care and specialty practices today use nurse practitioners (NP) and physician assistants (PA) to assist the physician in treating patients. In general, the role of the nurse practitioner or physician assistant is to perform patient exams and treat common problems specific to a particular medical specialty. Any problem that is out of the ordinary or does not resolve with routine protocol requires that the supervising physician examine the patient. In most instances, the nurse practitioner or physician assistant works with a physician under a clear policy that guides what duties are to be performed and how the physician will oversee the care provided. The physician and the employing company are responsible for establishing this guideline. Counsel may request to see a particular office's policy for use of a nurse practitioner or physician's assistant. Another term for this agreement between a physician and a nurse practitioner or physician's assistant is *collaborative agreement* or *collaborative practice agreement*.

State regulations govern the extent of duties a nurse practitioner or physician assistant is allowed to perform. For example, the ability to prescribe medications varies from state to state. For nurse practitioners, the appropriate state regulations to review are those that discuss nursing practice. Specific regulations may include in their titles the term *advanced practice nurse* (APN) or *advanced practice registered nurse* (APRN). Medicare regulates reimbursement issues for nurse practitioners.[13] Physician's assistants are licensed under the state medical board. Thus, state regulations pertaining to physician assistants will likely be listed under regulations pertaining to physicians and surgeons. Medicare also regulates reimbursement issues for physician assistants.[14] The guidelines for nurse practitioners may be slightly different than those for physician assistants in any given state. When reviewing a case that involves the actions of a nurse practitioner or physician assistant, it is beneficial to be familiar with the individual state regulations.

The physician may initial the notes of a physician's assistant, acknowledging that he reviewed the assessment and care plan. Such was the case in the following suit.

In *Deceased Thirty-Eight-Year Old Man v. Anonymous Physician, Physician's Assistant, and Pulmonologist*, according to the defendant doctor's office records, the plaintiff's decedent had a history of obesity and smoking and a family history of hypertension and heart disease. On June 10, 1999, the decedent presented to the defendant's office complaining of shortness of breath on climbing one flight of stairs. He was evaluated by a physician's assistant, the Defendant #2, and diagnosed with possible bronchitis/pneumonia. He was treated with an antibiotic and instructed to stay out of work. A chest x-ray was obtained and the interpreting radiologist noted bilateral interstitial infiltrates and a heart size at the upper limits of normal. The radiologist recommended correlation with clinical findings and follow-up. On June 30, 1999, the physician's assistant saw the patient again, and he reported to her that he felt shortness of breath when walking merely fifty to one-hundred yards and also when climbing stairs. The patient was once again diagnosed with bronchitis/pneumonia and restarted on antibiotics. The defendant doctor initialed the charts for both the June 10 and June 30 visits, thus acknowledging and affirming the physician assistant's assessment and care plan. The defendant doctor documented a plan to obtain pulmonary function tests. A pulmonologist evaluated

the patient on August 5. The first defendant doctor initialed the record, thus acknowledging and affirming the specialist's assessment and documented plan of care.

On August 16, 1999, the decedent was found by his wife at home, in evident cardiac arrest. He was transported to a nearby hospital, where efforts to resuscitate him were unsuccessful. The plaintiff's family contended that the defendants were negligent when they failed to respond to the decedent's persistent symptoms of shortness of breath, his positive family history of cardiac problems, and his x-ray findings of an enlarged heart. The parties agreed to pretrial settlement for the sum of $1,500,000.[15]

5.10 Is There Office Nurse Documentation?

Documentation by the office nurse may be found in the medical record depending on how involved registered nurses are within a particular physician's office. The office nurse may record the chief complaint or document patient statements and actions observed. These statements can become sources of valuable information.

In one case, a patient fell during the discharge process from a hospital and alleged a two-week delay in diagnosis of a broken hip. The plaintiff alleged calling the physician's office twice before receiving an appointment with the physician. However, the physician's nurse testified and her chart notes reflected that the patient was told to come to the office directly, but that the patient declined. The plaintiff ultimately admitted to not following the physician's office's advice. A defense verdict was handed down.[16]

Counsel may need to ask for any handwritten sections of the medical record even if electronic medical records are used by the physician's office to be sure to obtain notes entered by a nurse or other staff member.

5.11 Does the Office Have a Protocol for Performing and Communicating Test Results?

TIP: An office that does not have in place a system to communicate test findings runs the risk that a patient may be uninformed of a catastrophic problem, and treatment could be delayed.

Most physicians' offices request many laboratory and diagnostic tests on patients. It is important to know whether or not the office uses a protocol to track and inform timely the patients of test results, and if so, what this protocol states. The norm of physicians' offices is to have a protocol to handle test results. Defense and plaintiff's attorneys will be interested in reviewing this protocol, to see if the protocol was followed. If not, where did the system break down and who was responsible? Tracking records of laboratory results may show how well the protocol has worked or not worked previously. This helps to establish a pattern of appropriate care delivered by a particular office. If there is no written policy, one may question staff to establish what their office standards were for reporting test results. This will be fruitful in identifying a consistent system.

In a New Jersey case, critical lab testing was not done. The plaintiff mother's obstetrician/gynecologist ordered a test for cystic fibrosis. The lab claimed it did not receive a request for the cystic fibrosis test. The obstetricians did not realize the test was not performed until the child was born with cystic fibrosis. The plaintiff claimed negligence in the failure to perform the proper testing. A $2 million settlement was reached.[17]

In another New Jersey case, the plaintiff underwent prostate-specific antigen tests in October 2004, August 2005 and March 2006. The results were all above 4. The plaintiff claimed the defendant failed to take action. The plaintiff later had a biopsy at the urging of his son, a urologist. The test revealed prostate cancer, which had spread. The plaintiff claimed his chance of survival had dropped from ninety percent to sixty percent due to a delay in diagnosis. The defendant claimed the test results were normal for a man his age and that he was told to return a few weeks after the first test, but did not do so. A $1.5 million settlement was reached.[18]

5.12 How Does the Office Handle Phone Call Documentation?

TIP: Request any separate phone logs that may be kept regarding the date in question.

With a greater number of patients needing health care than there are physicians available, physicians' offices maintain a hectic pace on many days. A brief phone call that is not documented creates a loss of a potentially important inter-

action between the physician and the patient. The reviewer should examine the medical record for phone call documentations and note whether or not the physician spoke directly to the patient or whether office staff handled the request or question. The reviewer should look to see if there is documentation by the physician in response to specific patient complaints. Sometimes the staff may have communicated with the physician and a response was given to the patient by the staff. Although not the ideal, this is acceptable in many cases, often resulting in the patient coming to the office to be examined by the physician. The office policy should define criteria for the types of situations the office staff can answer on their own. This is often limited to relating normal laboratory findings, authorizing prescription refill requests, and changing schedules. Nurse practitioners are able to return phone calls for physicians to obtain additional assessment information and respond if the problem is routine in nature. Documentation of consultation with the physician should be found in the file for unusual or persistent problems. A direct question to the physician and the patient about any other communication that took place could be of benefit.

A woman's small intestine was perforated just below the stomach during an upper endoscopy. This perforation was not detected. That afternoon the plaintiff developed nausea and vomiting, and called the defendant's office. The plaintiff was told nausea was common and given a prescription for a medication. The plaintiff worsened and she again called the office. She was sent to the hospital for x-rays. She was so weak she had to use a wheelchair and be held up for the x-rays. Shortly after, she had a cardiac arrest and suffered brain damage. She maintained the physician was negligent in injuring the intestine and in failing to properly respond to her phone calls. The plaintiff claimed she should have been seen in response to her phone calls. The physician maintained that perforation was a known complication of the procedure and blamed poor communication by the plaintiff for any delay in seeing her, maintaining she did not adequately describe the seriousness of her condition. The defendant also claimed that if she was vomiting and seriously ill, she should have gone to an emergency room on her own. The plaintiff countered this by arguing that she had called the defendant twice and had followed the advice each time. A $12 million gross verdict was returned, which was reduced to $6,120,000 for comparative fault.[19]

5.13 Is There Documentation of Referral When Necessary?

Appropriate referral to other physicians is a highly situation-specific issue, yet should be generally addressed in any discussion of office medical record evaluation. To screen the records for appropriate referral, first look at the date of the initial complaint and then at the follow-up appointments.

- Did the complaint resolve with the initial treatment or did it persist? Was the initial treatment provided appropriate?
- Is the physician qualified to treat the problem?
- Was the complaint related to an entirely different area of medicine than the treating physician's specialty, such as the complaint of chest pain voiced during a visit to a kidney specialist?
- Would a procedure that the treating physician is not certified to perform have helped the problem?

Emergent problems require prompt referral. An example of this would be when an internist suspects a diagnosis of appendicitis and immediately refers the patient to a surgeon. Attorneys should seek expert opinion to establish whether or not appropriate referral was indicated but should be aware that opinions on this issue could vary.

5.14 Are There Red Flags Present in the Medical Record?

There are several tip-offs that the standard of reasonable medical care has likely been breached or, worse, the medical record has been altered in some way. Legal counsel should pay close attention when:

1. The notes prior to an event in question are lacking the detail necessary to project a clear image of the patient's condition and, following the event, the notes are very detailed or paint a picture of physician attentiveness.
2. The copy of the office medical record has black lines near an entry or the entry is not aligned with the rest of the notes on a page, indicating an entry may have been rewritten and then pasted over the original note or that an additional entry was added to the medical record at a later time. The original record should be reviewed for evidence of tampering.
3. The notes are not signed. Sometimes this is simply an oversight or poor office procedure, but it requires analysis to assure the physician is the true examiner.

4. A diagnosis of "stress" is made without further evaluation of patient complaints, particularly if the complaints are persistent.
5. A pertinent complaint disappears from the office notes after noting it for several entries without clear evidence the problem was resolved.
6. There is documentation that phone calls were placed to the office by the patient, but a clear response was not given.
7. Office policies are requested, and counsel is informed there are no written policies or procedures to guide office management.
8. The time sequence of the office entries is incorrect or does not make sense with the sequence of events.
9. The writing style of the physician or nurse practitioner changes at any point. Look for consistent, legible documentation as a sign of professionalism.
10. There is a bill for an office visit, but there is no corresponding office note in the file.

When any of these red flag alerts is raised, the attorney for either plaintiff or defense should consider a more in-depth analysis of the record. Forensic document examiners, though costly, can provide invaluable information with regards to tampering. Legal nurse consultants can help further explain the nuances involved in the clinical office setting. Refer to Chapter 15, *Tampering with Medical Records*, and Chapter 16, *Forensic Examination of Medical Records*, both in Volume I, for more information.

5.15 Patient Behavior

The patient, of course, plays an important role in the medical system. Be sure to review office medical records for indicators of patient noncompliance or instances when the patient deviates from the suggested medical advice. These instances may include:

- multiple cancelled appointments (Note that individual offices may have specific abbreviations for missed appointments such as *NS* for no-show, *DNKA* for did not keep appointment, and *NSNC* for no-show, no-cancel. The office note may include whether or not the patient voiced a mitigating factor for the cancellation, such as weather, lack of transportation, or illness of self or others.),
- refusal to attempt lifestyle changes that promote health such as smoking cessation, weight loss, and decreased alcohol consumption,
- documentation the patient refused a suggested medication to treat a medical problem,

- stopping medications prior to the prescribed date, such as the case with antibiotics,
- stopping medication without informing the physician because "it didn't help," or
- not returning to the office for follow-up appointments for prolonged periods of time.

TIP: Health care is a joint venture between physician and patient. A physician cannot promote wellness and treat illness if the patient is not cooperative and compliant with the plan of care.

Consider patient behavior in light of other medical records as well. Are there records from emergency rooms after the patient stopped taking or changed the recommended dosage of prescribed medication, or stopped treatments such as physical therapy? For patients experiencing pain, is the patient in pain seeing multiple providers and acquiring narcotic medication from each provider, suggesting narcotic drug abuse? Plaintiff's counsel benefits and can better prepare a case by knowing the documented behavior and attitude demonstrated over time by their clients.

5.16 Summary

TIP: Contacting a legal nurse consultant to provide medical record analysis provides both defense and plaintiff's counsel with valuable healthcare system experience and medical knowledge in a time-saving manner.

In summary, despite the seemingly straight-forwardness of office medical records, a sharp eye and thorough review are essential to have accurately interpreted information about a case. Asking the key questions about the physician's plan of care, office policy and procedure, and the plaintiff's behavior while staying alert for red flags can unlock the information contained in the medical records. The combined effort of legal counsel and nurse consultants to scrutinize the above questions is helpful in obtaining the discovery needed for solid case preparation.

Endnotes

1. Sloin, C. "Computerized Medical Records in Physician Offices: Risk Management Considerations." *The Executive Page*. vol. 5, no. 4, July 1997, p. 1.

2. *Id.*

3. JCAHO guideline IM 7.2. JCAHO Ambulatory Care Standards Crosswalk: Clinical Program Module II. p. 5. 2001.

4. JCAHO guideline IM 7.6. JCAHO Ambulatory Care Standards Crosswalk: Clinical Program Module II. p. 5. 2001.

5. National Committee on Quality Assurance. www.ncqa.org.

6. American Cancer Society screening recommendations. www.cancer.org.

7. American College of Physicians clinical guidelines. http://www.acponline.org/sci-policy/guidelines/.

8. American College of Obstetrics and Gynecology. http://www.acog.org.

9. American Academy of Family Practice Clinical Policies. http://www.aafp.org/x132.xml?printxml.

10. U.S. Preventative Task Force Recommendations also called the Agency for Healthcare Research and Quality. http://www.ahrq.gov/clinic/uspstfix.htm.

11. Verdict Reporter, Inc. 2004. www.verdictreporter.com.

12. 42 C.F.R. 415.172(b).

13. 42 C.F.R. 410.75.

14. 42 C.F.R. 410.74.

15. Laska, L. "Failure to Treat Enlarged Heart Leads to Death from Myocardial Infarction." *Medical Malpractice, Verdicts, Settlements, and Experts.* November 2003, p. 8–9.

16. Laska, L. "Patient Fell during Discharge Process." *Medical Malpractice Verdicts, Settlements, and Experts.* June 2004, p. 25.

17. Laska, L. "Failure to See That Testing for Cystic Fibrosis is Done." *Medical Malpractice Verdicts, Settlements, and Experts.* July 2009, p. 33

18. Laska, L. "Perforation of Small Intestine During Upper Endoscopy." *Medical Malpractice Verdicts, Settlements, and Experts.* August 2009, p. 16-17.

19. Laska, L. "Failure to Act on High PSA Tests." *Medical Malpractice Verdicts, Settlements, and Experts.* May 2009, p. 24.

Chapter 6

Ophthalmology Records

Elliott M. Korn, MD

6.1 Introduction

This chapter explains various eye examinations in the adult patient, and is written to aid the attorney in understanding the detection, diagnosis, and appropriate responses to ocular situations. The goals of the ophthalmologist are to

- identify certain risk factors,
- identify the presence or absence of ocular signs and symptoms,
- diagnose eye aberrations, and
- initiate further diagnostic treatments and/or referrals.

A strong knowledge base and understanding of the many ocular conditions will aid in the medical-legal development of liability cases or defense of a liability claim.

6.2 Providers of Eye Care

A comprehensive eye examination is best performed by an eye medical doctor ophthalmologist (Eye M.D.), a doctor of medicine or osteopathy specifically trained to distinguish normal from abnormal states of the eye. An ophthalmologist has training in

- the pathological and disease processes of the eyes,
- systemic disorders associated with ocular symptoms, and
- skills in medical decision making and surgery.

The ophthalmologist's knowledge of medical and surgical management of eye conditions allows for the most complete patient care in diagnosis and treatment.

TIP: Many people confuse the backgrounds of ophthalmologists, optometrists, and opticians.

Ophthalmologists are doctors who have received eight or more years of training after undergraduate education, including four years of medical school, one year of internship, and at least four years of residency. An *optometrist* (O.D.) is a person skilled in testing for defects of vision in order to prescribe corrective glasses and who may treat minor conditions of the eye with eye drops and other medicines. Optometrists generally receive four or more years of training after college. *Opticians* are not doctors, but eye care professionals who adjust and repair glasses, instruct patients in contact-lens use, and grind and assemble spectacles. Opticians receive their training either "on the job" by apprenticeships or from technical schools.

6.3 Visual Acuity
A. Central Visual Acuity
Medical records contain descriptions of central visual acuity. The term 20/20[1] is used to describe normal distance vision measured at a distance of twenty feet. Visual acuity for distance is recorded in the Snellen Notation. The numerator is the test distance in feet or meters and the denominator is the distance at which the smallest letter seen by the patient would subtend five minutes of arc at which an eye with 20/20 vision would see that letter. A similar Snellen Notation, or Jaeger standard point type notation, may be used for near vision, that is, J is 20/25 near vision.

TIP: A person with 20/20 vision can see clearly at twenty feet what should normally be seen at twenty feet. A person with 20/100 vision must be as close as twenty feet to see what a person with normal vision (20/20) can see at one hundred feet.

The term 20/20 may not mean perfect vision. Some people may have 20/10 vision. The Snellen Notation (20/10) only indicates the sharpness or clarity of vision at a distance. Other important visual components include

- side vision,
- eye coordination,
- depth perception,
- focusing ability, and
- color vision.

TIP: The attorney should find the earliest medical record to determine the best corrected vision the client had before the change occurred.

B. Legal Blindness
Under federal guidelines, a patient is considered legally blind when the best corrected vision in the better eye is 20/200 or less at distance and a near central visual acuity of 14/140. Also, legal blindness is present if the visual field of the better eye is twenty degrees or less, no matter what the best corrected acuity is achieved. The visual field is defined as that area within which objects are distinctly seen by the eye in a fixed position.

6.4 Clinical Examinations
There are many ocular complaints that are nonspecific; hence, in such cases, a comprehensive history of the patient, an eye exam, and an adnexa (the eyelids, lacrimal glands, and so on) exam should be done. The ocular exam contains the history, examination, diagnosis, additional laboratory or radiological testing, and treatment modalities. These items listed above are basic areas in the exam and are not meant to exclude any additional tests as deemed necessary.

A. Basic Eye Examination
The basic eye examination includes a general medical history, previous eye diseases, symptoms, surgeries, outcomes, and an examination of the anatomical and physiological state of the eye.

1. History
A detailed history of the patient includes the following data:

- demographic data: name, birth date, race, and gender,
- other relevant healthcare providers,
- chief complaint and history of the present illness,

- current status of visual function including the patient's estimate of visual status, needs, current ocular symptoms, and present use of eyeglasses or contacts,
- any type of corneal refractive surgery (radiokeratotomy, photokeratectomy, or Lasik surgery),
- past history including prior eye diseases (example: congenital such as amblyopia, crossed eyes, injuries, surgeries, or other treatments and medications), and
- past history of allergies, allergic reactions to medicine, medication use (ocular or systemic), and current medical conditions or surgeries. The patient's most recent eye exam with the latest glasses refraction should be included.

2. Family history

Information needed to make a proper diagnosis regarding the family history includes the following:

- poor vision in other family members or pertinent familial ocular or systemic disease,
- medications: systemic or ophthalmic, and
- social history: married/single, occupation, alcohol use, smoker/non-smoker.

3. Eye examination

The first important question the ophthalmologist asks the patient is the major reason the patient is being seen. Other useful information to help direct the examination include

- the location of complaints,
- the duration of the symptoms,
- the presence and nature of any pain,
- any discharge,
- redness, and
- a change in visual acuity.

4. Visual acuity

Unless the eye has been splashed with chemicals requiring immediate irrigation, the first step in the eye examination is to record the visual acuity by identifying letters, numbers, or figures with glasses on and off. This should be done up close in the reading position and at the distance of twenty feet. It is necessary to examine each eye individually and then together. Visual acuity is recorded as VA and/or VAd, for visual acuity at distance, or VAn, meaning visual acuity at near. The record will give the patient's refractive errors (W) in terms of ametropia (no glasses needed), myopia or nearsightedness (i.e., -2.50), hyperopia or farsighted-

ness (i.e., +2.50), or with astigmatism (i.e., plano +2.50 × 180 or plano -2.50 × 180). Use of a pinhole (PH) may be recorded as well.

5. External exam

The external exam (adnexa) includes

- eyelid position,
- eyelash direction,
- lacrimal apparatus, and
- relevant facial features.

6. Extraocular muscles and motility

The exam includes documentation of

- pupil size,
- pupil shape, and
- pupil reaction to light and accommodation.

7. Slit lamp (Biomicroscopy)

The slit lamp exam (SLE) incorporates the use of a tabletop microscope to examine the conjunctive (conj), sclera, cornea, anterior chamber depth, iris, and lens.

8. Eye pressure

The intraocular pressure is measured either by the Goldman tonometer (Tapp) or by Tonopen (Tp).

9. Gonioscopy

Use of the gonioscope involves evaluation of the angle of the eye with a special lens placed onto the cornea. This test is done when there is concern about narrow angle glaucoma, vascularization, or synechiae (closing of the angle).

10. Retina/fundus

The retina or fundus of the eye is positioned posterior to the iris and lens. Evaluation of this part of the eye may require a dilated pupil for optimal examination of the peripheral retina. Refer to Figure 6.1 for the anatomy of the eye.

11. Visual field

The visual field is the area of space in which objects are seen by the eye in a fixed position. The retinal sensitivity is best in the macula (fine vision center) and decreases in direct proportion to the distance that the rod and cones (visual receptor cells) are from the macula. The same is true of the visual field examination as the farther out the object is, the less clear it becomes. Ophthalmologists examine the fields by perimetry (Goldman, Humphrey, and so on) to detect defects in the visual fields.

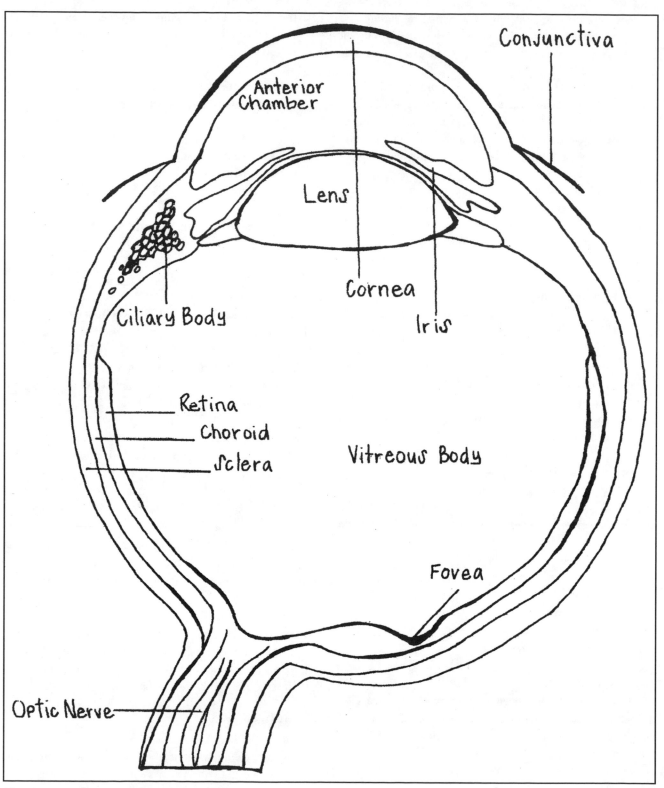

Figure 6.1 *Anatomy of the eye.*

a. Confrontation test. This test is performed with the examiner and patient facing each other about a half yard apart while the examiner wiggles a finger in each of the four quadrants of the visual field and the patient responds if she sees the finger. This method, however, only detects gross defects.

b. Screening machines. Screening devices for rapid field examination, such as the Harrington-Flock, Glubuck screen, and Friedman field analyzer, though not used as routinely, are still found.

c. Automated computer-assisted perimetry. More sophisticated instrumentation which presents multiple stimuli (flashes of illuminated dots) in automated patterns is recorded automatically by the patient pushing a small button when he sees the lighted dot. Charts are used to record the visual fields.[2] Refer to Figure 6.2. An exhaustive discussion of the gross and microscopic anatomy of the visual pathways is beyond the scope of this chapter. With present-day technology, it is possible to isolate a defect from the ganglion cell layer of the retina to the optic nerve, chiasm, and through the optical radiation of nerve fibers to the visual cortex center in the back of the brain.

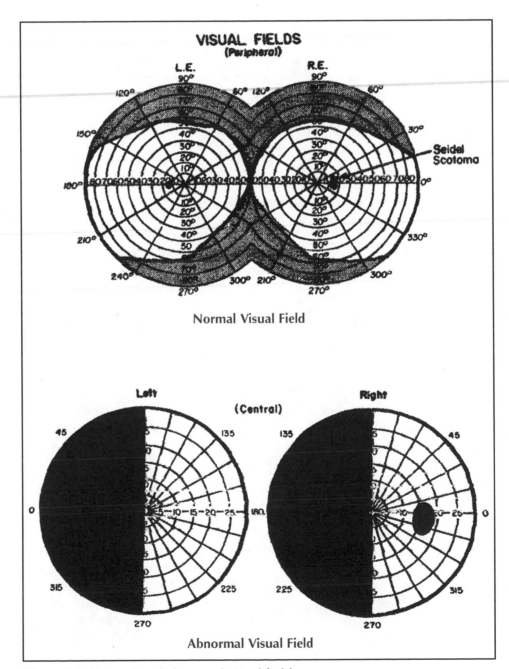

Figure 6.2 *Normal and abnormal visual fields.*

B. Additional Tests

Using the patient's history, symptoms, signs, and examination, additional tests may be indicated. These tests listed below are not part of a routine eye examination.

- *Gonioscopy*—Examination of the angle of the eye.
- *Color Vision Testing*—Multicolored numbers used to detect color blindness.
- *Amsler Grid*—Used to detect macular or fine vision abnormalities.
- *Visual Fields by Perimetry*—Area within which objects are distinctly seen by the eye in a fixed position.
- *Lacrimal Evaluation*—To determine obstruction of tear flow from the puncta through the nasolacrimal duct.
- *Fluorescein Angiography*—Intravenous infusion of dye to evaluate retinal fluid leakage in the back of the eye.
- *Stereophotography of Optic Disk*—Photographs of the optic nerve especially in the care and treatment of glaucoma patients.
- *Microbiology and Cytology*—Determination of the bacterial cause of an infection especially of the cornea and in endophthalmitis cases.
- *Radiologic Testing*—X-ray testing.
- *Electrophysiological Testing*—Testing to determine conductive defects in either the retinal nerve fibers or the optic nerve.

6.5 Eye Symbols and Abbreviations

Interpretation of the ophthalmic medical record can be difficult and time consuming. The medical record is broken down into five parts: the vision evaluation, the adnexa, the slit lamp biomicroscopy, the retinal exam, and ophthalmic tests. Abbreviations and terms are found within the ophthalmologic record. Refer to Figure 6.3.

6.6 Refractive Errors

The refractive error[3,4] occurs when parallel rays of light go into the non-accommodating (relaxed state of the lens) eye and are not focused on the retina. The following conditions are due to low or moderate refractive errors (refer to Figure 6.4):

- myopia[5] (nearsightedness), which is less than six diopters (amount of calibration),

- hyperopia (farsightedness), which is less than four diopters, and
- regular astigmatism (unequal refractions in different meridians of the eye), which is less than three diopters.

High refractive errors in each eye are greater than the above range of three to six diopters. Presbyopia (the lens is less pliable and unable to change shape) develops with aging and results in deficient accommodation for near work in a patient whose distance refractive error is fully corrected by glasses, contacts, or surgery. Refer to Figure 6.5 for definitions.

TIP: It is best to define any previous refraction errors such as a prescription for glasses in order to compare previous eye refractions before a determination of loss is assessed. This will help aid in determining whether a trauma (examples: corneal laceration, retinal detachment, ocular trauma) is the cause for the change in visual acuity.

Elective Lasik surgery planned to correct refractive errors can go awry. Dr. Dello Russo in New Jersey was sued after the plaintiff developed epithelial abrasions of both eyes during Lasik surgery. She had pain and difficulty with her vision immediately after the surgery. The plaintiff suffered scarring of both corneas and persistent eye fatigue and blurred vision. The plaintiff claimed the procedure should have been stopped when the epithelial abrasion occurred. An $821,000 settlement was reached. This was one of fourteen similar cases in this venue involving the same defendants.[6]

6.7 Ocular Structures
A. Cornea

The cornea sits in the sclera like a watch glass. Refer to Figure 6.6. The periphery of the cornea where the sclera meets the cornea is called the limbus. Perilimbal vessels stop here and do not invade the clear cornea unless a disease state occurs. The cornea contains 72 percent to 82 percent water. There are no blood vessels or lymph vessels in the cornea. However, there are strong sensory innervations which make the cornea very sensitive to touch and pain. In normal light, the cornea appears grayish but transparent. Infiltrates of the cornea appear grayish to yellow and scars appear gray-white. Corneal leukoma appears as a dense white scar. Leukoma adherence is caused by traumatic irido-corneal adhesions.

Symbol	Interpretation
C/D	Evaluation of the optic nerves cup to disc ratio, i.e., important in glaucoma evaluations.
A/V	Artery/Vein Comparison
Mac	Macula or Fine Vision Center
Ret	Retinal Layer of the Eye
PVD	Posterior Vitreous Detachment. The pulling away of the jelly-like vitreous from the retina.

Example: 2+ dot/blot Heme.
With PVD inferior

There is a moderate amount of dot hemorrhages in the retina with an inferior vitreous detachment from the retina, i.e., seen commonly in diabetics.

Examples: Retinal Detachment and Retinal Hemorrhage

Tests	
F/A	Flourescein Angiogram
ICG	Indocyanide Green
OCT	Optical Coherence Tonography
HRT	Heidelberg Retinal Tomography
G Dx	Assesses the thickness of the retinal nerve fiber layer around the optic nerve.

Procedures	
Cryo	Cryotherapy
ALT	Argon Laser Trabeculoplasty
SLT	Selective Laser Trabeculoplasty

Contact Lenses	
GP	Gas Permeable Hard Lens
DW	Daily Wear Soft Lens
EW	Extended Wear Soft Lens

Figure 6.3

Symbol	Interpretation
Pupils	
Size	How big the pupil is, i.e., 2 mm, 3 mm, etc.
Shape	The shape of the pupil, i.e., oblong, circular, etc.
Reaction to Light	How fast the pupil reacts to light.
APD	Afferent Pupillary Defect. Abnormal dilation of the pupil compared to the other when stimulated with a bright light.
Example: 2 mm R s APD	The pupil is 2 mm, round with no afferent pupillary defect.
Slit Lamp Biomicroscopy (SLE)	
Conj	Conjunctiva
Corn	Cornea
Epith	Corneal Epithelium or Top Layer
Stroma	Corneal Stroma or Central Portion
Endo	Corneal Endothelium or Bottom Layer
CCT	Central Corneal Thickness
Gut	Guttae
Arc	Arcus senilis
AC	The cornea in front of the iris.
Depth	Deep or Shallow
Cells	Inflammatory Cells or Red Blood Cells
Flare	Inflammatory Debris
Iris	Colored Part of the Eyeball
Lens	
Clarity	The color intensity of the lens: clear, yellow, brown.
Capsule: Ant/Post.	The clear membrane surrounding the lens.
Cortex	The material around the central nucleus of the lens.
Nucleus	The central portion of the lens.
IOP	Intraocular Pressure
TA	Eye pressure by tonometer tool, by applanation of the top surface of the cornea.
Tp	Eye pressure by a tonometer in the shape of a pen, which is held in the hand.
Example: TA 28/30	The intraocular pressure by tonometry is 28 in the right eye and 30 in the left eye; a sign of glaucoma.
Fundus	Examination of the posterior area of the eye, i.e., vitreous cavity, retina, choroid, optic nerve, and vessels.
Dil	Dilation
N 2.5% (Neo)	Neosynephrine 2.5%
M 1% (Myd)	Mydriacyl 1%
C 2% (Cyc)	Cyclocyl 2%

Figure 6.3 *(continued)*

Abbreviations

Symbol	Interpretation
CC	Chief Complaint
HPI	History of the Present Illness
VA sc	Visual Acuity without Correction
VA cc	Visual Acuity with Correction
OD	Right Eye
OS	Left Eye
OU	Both Eyes
W or CRX	Present Glasses or Current Glasses
MR	Manifest Refraction (Testing for New Glasses)
J or N	Near Vision (at 14 cm)
PH	Pinhole Exam
Examples: VA cc OD 20/20	The visual acuity at distance with glasses is 20/20 for the right eye.
VAN sc OS 20/20	The visual acuity at near without glasses is 20/20 for the left eye.
Adnexa/External	Accessory Parts to the Main
Lids	Eyelids
Lash	Eyelash
Lacrimal gl.	Lacrimal Gland
Lacrimal drainage	The tear outflow system from the puncta to the nasolacrimal duct.
Orbits	The bony structure around the eyeball.
Lymph Nodes	The glands around the eyeballs, in front of the ear and neck.
Motility/EOM	Movement of the Extra-ocular Muscles
Primary Gaze	Eye alignment looking straight ahead.
Orth	Orthotropic. Eyes are straight.
Ductions/Versions	Turning movement of the eyes.
E(T)	Esophoria
E T	Esotropia
X(T)	Exophoria
X T	Exotropia
Hypo	Hypotropia
Hyper	Hypertropia
Example: EOM 5ΔRET	The right eye turns inward 5 diopters of power.
VF	Visual Fields
Conf	Confrontational Visual Fields
Gold	Goldman Visual Fields
Humphrey	Humphrey Visual Fields
Example: VF Conf	The confrontational visual fields show right superior quadrant of both eyes are abnormal and additional tests are needed, i.e., Goldman or Humphrey.

Figure 6.3 (continued)

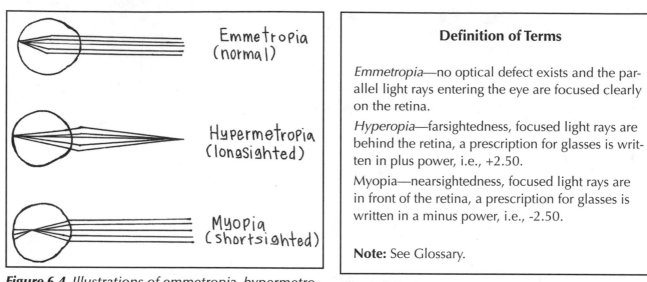

Figure 6.4 *Illustrations of emmetropia, hypermetropia, and myopia.*

Definition of Terms

Emmetropia—no optical defect exists and the parallel light rays entering the eye are focused clearly on the retina.

Hyperopia—farsightedness, focused light rays are behind the retina, a prescription for glasses is written in plus power, i.e., +2.50.

Myopia—nearsightedness, focused light rays are in front of the retina, a prescription for glasses is written in a minus power, i.e., -2.50.

Note: See Glossary.

Figure 6.5

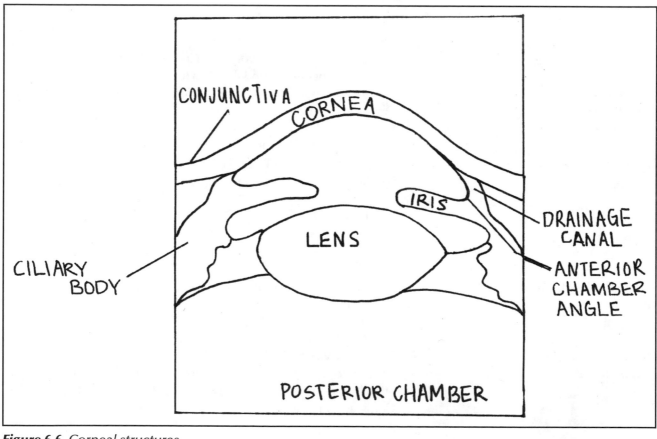

Figure 6.6 *Corneal structures.*

1. Corneal edema

Corneal stromal edema (central portion) can be due to any traumatic or degenerative damage. The cornea appears gray in the area of the edema. Epithelial (top layer) damage produces very little stromal edema. Corneal edema due to acute elevation in eye pressure (glaucoma) causes the cornea to become dull and lose its normal sheen. A microscopic examination (slit lamp) of the epithelium shows droplet-like swelling, which can become confluent or rupture. This causes pain or an ache. The patient has symptoms of colored halos around lights and progressive clouding of the vision. Excessive wearing of poor eye-fitting contact lenses may case similar epithelial edema.

TIP: The attorney needs to be aware that medical-legal issues resulting from failure to diagnose other problems, usually glaucoma, occur when symptoms were thought to be from contact lenses. As a result, the glaucoma was not diagnosed because the clinician did not do a complete eye examination.

In severe trauma such as corneal laceration or surgery, the epithelium may grow over the back layer of the cornea endothelium resulting in stromal edema. This can also result in a secondary glaucoma.

2. Arcus senilis

Arcus senilis is a common dystrophy of aging. Intracellular lipid deposits form a ring about 1.5 mm wide inside the limbus (edge of the cornea where it joins the sclera), but separated from the limbus by a clear space.

3. Corneal sensitivity

There exist various causes of increased or decreased corneal sensitivity. Corneal anesthesia is seen in herpes simplex, neuroparalytic keratitis (loss of trigeminal innervation), diabetes, herpes zoster, and psoriasis. A minor decrease in sensitivity is part of any stromal edema. Hypoesthesia can occur after cataract surgery, retinal detachment, and Lasik surgery. Increased corneal sensitivity is seen in traumatic injuries, infections, or degenerations of the cornea.

4. Corneal vascularization

Workplace or personal injury suits may evolve as a result of thermal and severe chemical burns to the cornea. Lye or strong acids can cause deep corneal vascularization due to inflammatory corneal edema. The vessels from the limbus grow into the corneal stroma. This gives the cornea a fleshy appearance. Vascular ingrowths in the pupillary region will cause decreased and distorted vision. Superficial vascularization has etiologies. The vessels are a continuation of the conjunctival vessels. They may be seen with acne rosacea, vitamin B deficiency, and mild ocular trauma.

5. Corneal abrasion

In corneal abrasions the epithelium (top layer of cells) has been scraped or disturbed, leaving a denuded area on the cornea. The defect stains yellow/green with fluorescent dye. Abrasions occur with ocular trauma, foreign bodies trapped under the lid, misdirected lashes, or lid margin lesions. Abrasions can cause severe pain, foreign body sensation, photophobia (painful response to light), lacrimation (tearing), and/or blepharospasm (sustained, involuntary closing of eyelids). If severe enough, ciliary injection (redness) and pupillary constriction may occur. There may be slight dullness of the corneal reflex in the area of the abrasion.

6. Recurrent corneal erosions

Recurrent erosions (abrasions) may occur days, weeks, or months after a corneal injury. It can be presumed that the adhesion between the epithelium and the underlying corneal tissue was inadequate. Tears evaporate during sleep, thus causing the epithelium to adhere to the lid. Upon waking, the epithelium is pulled off as the eyes are opened. The patient may complain of severe pain, photophobia, and/or blepharospasm. Recurrent erosions occur more frequently if the injury is caused by organic matter such as leaves, twigs, wood, and so on. Other common causes of these erosions can be attributed to fingernails, hair brushes, and mascara brushes.

Treatment of recurrent erosions consists of eye lubrication gels or ointments at night as well as tear replacement drops during the day as needed. In some cases, patching the eye may be necessary.

TIP: Incomplete healing of an abrasion may lead into a recurrent erosion or corneal ulceration with secondary visual loss. Failure to treat or follow up can be below the standard of care.

7. Superficial punctate keratitis (SPK)

SPK is seen as scattered, fine punctuate loss of corneal epithelium on the surface of the cornea when stained with fluorescein. Symptoms include pain, foreign body sensation, tearing photophobia, and blepharospasm. Signs may include ciliary injection, conjunctival redness, and mild lid edema. Topical anesthetics should not be prescribed for pain relief. SPK is commonly encountered due to overexposure to UV light (welding, sun lamps, exposure to the sun, or snow skiing). The patient develops symptoms six to eight hours after exposure. Healing occurs within forty-eight hours with or, in most cases, without treatment. SPK may be seen due to exposure to hydrogen sulfide in textile manufacturing, radiation to the cornea for ocular tumors, tear gas, household sprays, and tar fumes.

Treatment for SPK includes use of ocular lubricants such as drops or ointments and patching of the eye for a few days. If a chemical solution is the cause of the SPK, patching may not have to be administered in order for the patient to tear excessively in an effort to cleanse the eye faster. Residual vision impairment is rare regardless of the etiology.

8. Dry eyes/SPK

Dry eyes can cause SPK. There are many causes for dry eyes[7] with secondary conjunctivitis sicca. Chemical or radiation burns, removed sections or diseases of the lacrimal gland, infections, viruses, and medical effects must be ruled out. Refer to Section 6.8.D for more information.

9. Corneal ulcers

A corneal ulcer[8] can be defined as a local necrosis of corneal tissue due to an invasion by microorganisms. The causes of such corneal ulcers include

- trauma,
- contact lenses,
- chronic blepharitis,
- chronis keratitis,
- infectious diseases,
- lacrimal sac infections,
- fungus,
- abrasions, and
- corneal exposure due to eyelid injuries or defective closure of the lids (i.e., seventh cranial nerve palsies).

Chronic use of topical anesthetics (tetracaine, ophthaine) or excessive use of topical steroids can cause corneal erosions with delayed healing and secondary ulceration.

TIP: Topical anesthetics should never be prescribed to the patient for self-administration. Severe corneal ulcers have resulted in such therapy. This would be a case of medical malpractice.

Corneal exposure can be caused by

- exposure keratitis (lagophthalmos) or improper lid closure from trauma of the seventh cranial nerve,
- Graves disease,

- cicatrical (scarred) ectropion (outturning of the lid), or
- coma.

The exposed cornea develops infiltrates, ulcerations, vessel in-growth, and rarely perforation. Bell's phenomenon turns the globe up and out during sleep, which explains why it is usually the lower third of the cornea that is affected. A rare complication of secondary infections may cause panophthalmitis leading to secondary glaucoma, phthisis bulbi, or loss of the eye. Symptoms of a corneal ulcer may include

- mild to severe pain,
- photophobia,
- blepharospasm,
- tearing, and
- blurred vision.

Early on, the corneal lesion is seen as a dull, grayish, circumscribed superficial infiltration; however, its progression leads to necrosis, and it suppurates to form an ulcer. It stains yellow/green with fluorescein. Ciliary injection (redness) is common and in chronic, undiagnosed, or untreated cases, blood vessels may grow in from the limbus, which is called pannus. The ulcer may then spread to involve the width of the cornea, or it may possibly penetrate even deeper.

The deeper the ulcer, the more symptoms and complications will accompany it. Healing leaves a fibrous tissue scarring with opacification and decreased vision over the pupillary margin if the ulceration is central over the pupil.

Treatment of a corneal ulcer is aggressive with topical dilating drops (for pain relief from secondary iritis), antibiotic drops, ointments, and in some cases, subconjunctival antibiotic injections with oral or intravenous antibiotics.

10. Secondary corneal degenerations

Band keratopathy is an opacification with calcium deposition in the epithelium and superficial stroma which progresses from the periphery to the center of the cornea in the area between the eyelids. This may be caused by a perforation injury, burns, chronic iridocyclitis, inflammation, and chemical irritation such as Mercury vapors and calcium bichromate. Band keratopathy impairs vision by clouding the cornea.

11. Corneal pigmentation

Hemosiderosis cornea or blood staining of the cornea develops after blood has been in the anterior chamber of the eye for some time. It is more common with high intraocular pressure and a markedly damaged globe. Pain occurs with high pressure, but normally the eye is free of irritation; however, the vision decreases. To prevent prolonged blood staining, the massive hemorrhage should be surgically irrigated out if it has not resolved on its own in 1 to 2 weeks.

Pigmentation may also result from chemical and medication use. The causes of pigmentation can include phenol, especially carbolic acid damage, aniline, chloroquine, indomethacin, chlorpromazine, phenothiazines, and amiodaron.

12. Metal deposition in the cornea

Metallic foreign bodies such as copper (chalcosis), silver (argyrosis), siderosis (iron containing), and gold (chrysiasis), either internally, locally, or parenterally may stain the cornea. Rarely, after intramuscular injection (gold therapy for rheumatoid arthritis) there may be resultant staining of the cornea. Removal of the offending substance by stopping intake or scraping the foreign body off will resolve the situation without problems. In the rare case of a secondary corneal ulcer from a foreign body, additional treatment would be administered as necessary.

13. Bullous keratopathy

Bullous keratopathy is a condition caused by excessive fluid accumulation in the cornea from severe trauma with secondary inflammation inside the eye, corneal lacerations, post-intraocular surgery (i.e., cataract surgery), or aging, especially in patients with Fuch's Endothelial Dystrophy. The fluid-filled bubbles on the surface of the cornea may cause pain and decreased vision. Treatment of this corneal condition includes topical dehydrating agents, soft contact lenses, and, if severe enough, a corneal transplantation.

B. Lens

The lens (Figure 6.7) is a transparent organ found behind the pupil and iris and in the posterior chamber of the eye in front of the vitreous, or the transparent jelly of the globe. The lens bends (refracts) rays of light so they are focused on the retina. The lens is the organ that accommodates or makes adjustments for seeing near objects and objects at a distance. Presbyopia occurs with increasing age as the lenses lose their elasticity to focus light rays on the retina. A *cataract* is a clouding of the lens of the eye which in turn reduces the amount of incoming light, resulting in diminished

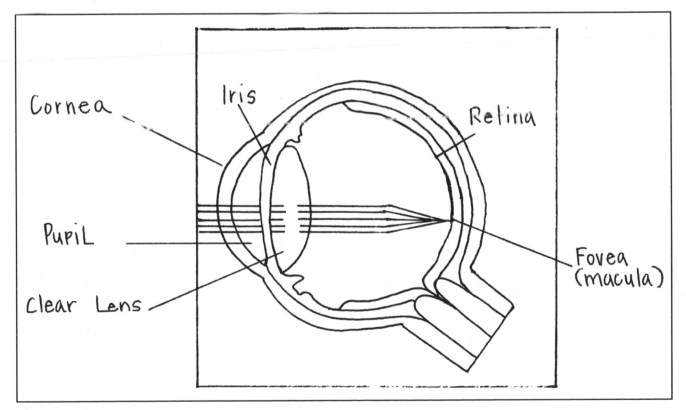

Figure 6.7 *Lens.*

vision. Cataracts begin for many people after birth, though some people are born with them fully developed. During youth, the lens is colorless and transparent. With increasing age, the lens becomes yellow/brown. Increasing brown coloration leads to brunescent cataracts with resultant very poor vision. Developmental cataracts occur congenitally or during early life from nutritional, toxic, inflammatory, or hereditary metabolic causes (galactosemia, rubella, etc.). Degenerative cataracts occur from aging, x-rays, heat from infrared rays (glassblower cataracts), trauma, systemic diseases (diabetes), uveitis, or from medications (steroids). In fact, 80 percent of people over seventy-five-years old have poor vision as a result of cataracts. We may all suffer from cataracts at some time in our lives.

Symptoms of cataracts can be described as looking through a waterfall or piece of wax paper. Patients sometimes complain of glare, hazy, foggy, or painless loss of vision. Under biomicroscopy (slit lamp), the lens fibers appear more yellow. Depending on the location of the fiber, cloudiness is indicative of either an anterior subcapsular, nuclear, or posterior subcapsular cataract. Infections that develop after surgery can threaten the eye. The standard of care requires the ophthalmologist to document findings, including normal ones.

Surgical intervention with placement of an intraocular lens is now the medical procedure of choice. Most cataract surgeries are performed by phacoemulsification, though some still use an extracapsular cataract technique.

In *Anita Clark-Nelson v. Dr. Richard Multack, D.O.*, the defendant ophthalmologist performed surgery to remove a cataract formation from the plaintiff's right eye at Olympia Fields Osteopathic Hospital. Two months later, the plaintiff, a forty-two-year-old woman, lost vision in her right eye, which is now nearly blind. Vision in her left eye is normal. The plaintiff contended that cataract surgery was contraindicated given her visual acuity and moderate interference with daily activities, and surgery should have been deferred at least ninety days due to a recent bout of chronic iritis. The plaintiff further alleged the defendant was negligent in failing to administer topical steroids three to seven days before surgery as a preventative measure to combat anticipated inflammation associated with cataract surgery. The plaintiff claimed the vision loss was caused by extraordinary postoperative inflammation which led to macular edema. The defense asserted the cataract surgery was warranted and a thirty-day period of quiescence was a sufficient,

conservative, and reasonable waiting period under the standard of care. The defense also argued that the diabetic plaintiff's loss of vision was due to either some type of ischemic event in the eye or extraordinary macular edema regardless of timing of surgery. The hospital settled for $55,000 prior to trial. The jury returned a defense verdict for the physician. Plaintiff's post-trial motions were pending, according to the *Cook County Jury Verdict Reporter.*[9]

Traumatic cataracts occur when contusion rosettes appear under the anterior, and rarely the posterior, lens capsule after severe blunt ocular trauma. In this circumstance, however, visual loss is minimal. Perforation rosettes are feathery opacities (opaque areas) composed of fluid-filled vacuoles (small cavities) that may disappear if the perforation site closes by itself. If lens protein has been released, a chronic inflammatory (phakogenic) reaction may occur. A severe iritis with pain, redness, and decreased vision with elevated eye pressure is seen. A secondary glaucoma also commonly occurs in this situation.

Treatment should consist of intense anti-inflammatory and anti-glaucoma measures, as well as possible surgical intervention if needed.

TIP: Intense follow-up is indicated if a suspected perforation of the lens has occurred. Failure to diagnose and appropriately treat deviates from the standard of care.

In *George Gill v. Azeb Telahun, M.D., et al.*, the plaintiff, a forty-seven-year-old married massage therapist, presented to the defendant ophthalmologist group for treatment of cataracts. Lab studies were performed three times during a four-month period, and the plaintiff underwent four separate surgeries on his eyes during that time. All three lab assay reports showed markedly elevated blood glucose levels. Eighteen months later, the plaintiff developed sores on his right foot for which he sought treatment with another physician, at which time he was diagnosed with diabetes. The sores failed to heal properly, resulting eventually in amputation of the plaintiff's right leg below the knee, and amputation of his left foot's great toe, followed by several lengthy hospitalizations. The plaintiff is very tall, at six feet and eight inches in height, and his rehabilitation was slow and complicated. The plaintiff alleged that with the type of cataracts he had, his age, and the three elevated blood sugar lab readings, the defendants should have had strong suspicion of a diagnosis of diabetes. The plaintiff also alleged negligence in failing to inform him of the likelihood of diabetes or to refer him to a physician for medical management. The plaintiff also claimed that the defendant's negligence resulted in a twenty-month delay in diagnosing the diabetes, which was the proximate cause of his damages. The defendants contended that they told the plaintiff repeatedly to see a physician and that the plaintiff refused. The plaintiff's counsel reported that hospital records for the cataract operations indicated the plaintiff's health was excellent at the time of his admissions, and that the office chart was devoid of a referral except for one undated and unsigned entry in the margins. According to *Metro Verdicts Monthly*, the jury in this case returned a plaintiff verdict for $5,100,000 including $800,000 for pain and suffering.[10]

C. Retina

The retina is the innermost layer composed of light sensitive neurons surrounding the posterior chamber where the vitreous body is located. The outer retinal layers are the sensory epithelium, including the rods and cones (visual cells), which are nourished by diffusion from the choroids (blood supply) of the eye. The inner retinal layers of neurons form the optic nerve. The retinal vessels supply only the inner retinal layers. These retinal vessels are end arteries such as cerebral vessels. Pre-retinal hemorrhages appear as round lakes of blood found between the retina and the vitreous. These are usually seen in younger patients. Causes of this type of hemorrhages can include

- subarachnoid hemorrhage,
- vascular disorders (diabetes, periphlebitis, arteriosclerosis, and vein thrombosis),
- blunt trauma,
- vitreous detachment, and rarely
- vicarious menstruation.

Complications are usually rare, and the blurred vision that accompanies this condition usually goes away.

Intra-retinal hemorrhages that are more superficial have a feathery striate (streaks) appearance which corresponds to the nerve fiber layer. Intra-retinal hemorrhages in the deeper layers are punctate or blot-like. Cotton-wool spots are fluffy, gray-white, poorly demarcated lesions found over and under the retinal blood vessels. They usually disappear in a few weeks. Cotton-wool spots are seen in

- severe hypertension,
- eclampsia,
- blood dyscrasias (pernicious anemia, leukemia),
- lead or mercury poisoning, and
- infections (sepsis, TB).

TIP: Pay attention to the ophthalmologist's notes or drawings as to the appearance and size of hemorrhages. This will aid in determining if the blood in the retina was iatrogenic or not, as in the case of globe penetration during a retrobulbar injection.

---

1. Retinal edema (Berlin's Edema)

Direct trauma to the eye causes retinal edema which appears as a diffuse gray discoloration of the retina. There is an immediate decrease in vision. Small petechial hemorrhages may occur. The edema usually resolves in twenty-four to forty-eight hours with no residual effects.

2. Retinal detachment

A retinal detachment[11] is a pulling away of the neurosensory retina from the underlying choroids (blood supply to the outer retinal layer). It can progress rapidly, becoming more extensive and bullous with undulating folds.[12] Subjective symptoms include:

- painless flickering (flimmering) vision,
- flashing lights, and
- a gray dark curtain occasionally appearing in the peripheral vision.

There is a comparable visual field loss in the case of retinal detachment.

Retinal tears or holes are of utmost importance in detachments.[13] Horseshoe tears comprise about 60 percent of tears. These occur in moderate (3-6 diopters) myopia patients (nearsightedness), aphakics patients (post-cataract removal), and trauma. Operculated (covered) and atrophic holes appear as round or oval holes in the peripheral retina. Operculated and atrophic holes occur in about 30 percent of retinal detachments. Refer to Figure 6.8.

Ora (the edge of the retina) tears found in the inferior temporal area can occur days or years after trauma. Macular holes and cysts affect the fine vision center of the eye. Though rare, they occur in highly myopic patients, degeneration, or after trauma.

Causes of primary retinal detachments include myopia, senile, aphakic, traumatic, or degeneration. Idiopathic detachments, tumors, exudative uveitis, intraocular hemorrhages, or foreign bodies can be diagnosed with additional tests.

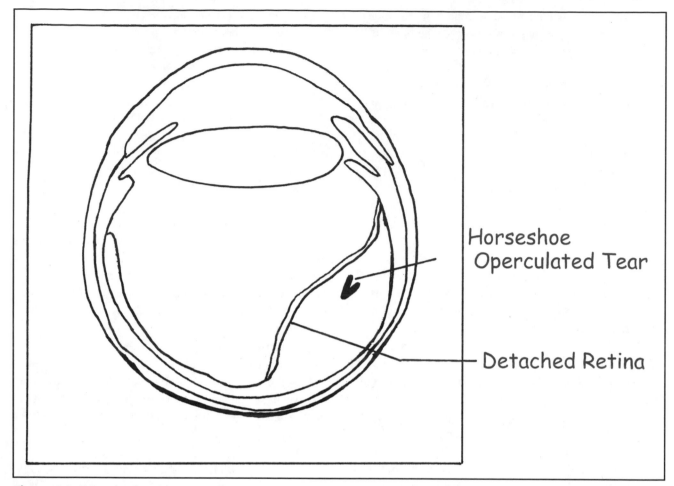

Figure 6.8 *Detached retina.*

Secondary detachments are seen with inflammation, renal disease, malignant hypertension, eclampsia, or other retinal conditions.

TIP: Common causes of claims are failure to diagnose the detachment, along with inadequate examinations because the pupil was not dilated and indirect ophthalmoscope was not used, or the contralateral eye was not carefully examined.

In *June Severson, Ednar Severson v. Dr. Raymond Alberts, Raymond Albers, M.D., S.C.,* the plaintiff, a sixty-year-old woman, was seen by the defendant Dr. Alberts for vitreous hemorrhage. She alleged that there was an diagnosed tear of the retina and that she was not properly instructed on when to come back. She returned to the defendant's office on December 14, and at that time was given an eye occluder but was not seen by the defendant. The patient later experienced loss of vision in her eye and returned to the office on January 7, 2000, at which time she had chronic macula off detachment of the retina. Two repair surgeries were performed but were unsuccessful. Another procedure was performed to remove silicone oil from the plaintiff's eye, and eventually the eye was enucleated (removed). The defense argued there was no tear on December 8, since the defendant was able to see the entire peripheral retina and the patient was properly instructed but did not return accordingly to medical instructions. This case resulted in a $94,000 jury verdict, according to the *Illinois Jury Verdict Reporter.*[14]

3. Traumatic retinal damage

Attorneys may handle claims involving traumatic retinal damage. Common mechanisms of injury include a direct blow to the eye from being punched, a fall, or from projectile objects. Retinal edema (Berlin's edema) evolves within twenty-four to thirty-six hours. It can be seen anywhere in the retina. Depending on the severity of the trauma, vision can return completely, or residual impairment may occur.

Retinal contusions from trauma with hemorrhages and secondary pigment changes, as well as macular holes, can cause marked visual field loss and permanent visual disabilities. A perforating injury with hemorrhages, secondary scarring, inflammation, or infection leads to secondary detachments, endophthalmitis, and phthisis (shrinkage of the globe).

TIP: Missing a small detachment despite an extensive examination with a dilated pupil is not substandard care, but failure to suspect or look for it often is.

---

4. Purtscher's traumatic retinopathy

Purtscher's traumatic retinopathy is seen in compression injuries to the chest, body, or blows to the head. Characteristic findings include flame-shaped and large blot hemorrhages and exudates usually near blood vessels. Considerable permanent damage can occur in this situation. A similar picture may develop with fractures of the long bones and fat emboli but usually resolves without late complications or visual loss.

Standard modalities in the prophylactic treatment[15] of retinal breaks and retinal degenerations include cryotherapy and laser photocoagulation. These treatments increase chorio-retinal adhesions. Depending on the type and severity of the detachment, surgical intervention with a buckling (placement of a silicone band around the eye) or other techniques may be required. Complications include redetachment, epimacular membrane proliferation, or infection.

In *Timothy Von Schmidt v. Jacqueline Watskin*, a forty-nine-year-old former truck driver was examined on March 3, 1998 by his regular ophthalmologist after complaining of flashing sensations in his visual field, limited vision, and a puzzling black spot in the left eye. The ophthalmologist diagnosed a retinal detachment and called in another specialist, the defendant Dr. Jacqueline Watskin, who scheduled surgery with the patient for March 4, but because no operating suite was available on that date, delayed it to March 5. By then, the size of one tear had increased, a second tear had developed, and blood was in his eye. The plaintiff alleged that a more complex operation should have been performed to hold the damaged retina in place via fluid or gas. When the patient continued to hemorrhage, Dr. Watskin performed a complex procedure, but the eye deteriorated and required removal one year later. The same condition existed with the right eye, but went undetected because Watskin failed to examine it for several months. Surgeries to repair it failed and left the patient legally blind. This action was resolved with payment of a $600,000 settlement, according to a published account.[16]

D. Uveal Tract

The uveal tract consists of the iris, ciliary body, and choroids. The iris is the circular pigmented membrane behind the cornea and is perforated by the pupil. The ciliary body connects the choroids and the iris. The choroids are the vascular layer of the eye.

1. Uveitis

Uveitis is an inflammation of the uveal tract. Anterior uveitis (iritis, iridocyclitis) and posterior uveitis (choroiditis, chorioretinitis) may be acute, recurrent, chronic, granulomatous, or non-granulomatous.

a. Anterior uveitis. The causes of anterior uveitis are numerous. Symptoms may include moderate to severe pain, sensitivity to light (photophobia), tearing (lacrimation), and blurred vision. Intense redness surrounding the cornea at the junction of the white sclera occurs. Inflammatory cells are found behind the cornea in the anterior chamber where the aqueous humor is located.

Anterior uveitis lasts a few days to weeks and may be recurrent. Neglected or chronic anterior uveitis may lead to secondary open angle glaucoma, corneal disease, or cataracts.

Treatments include intensive steroid drops and dilation of the pupil. In severe cases, systemic or subconjuctival corticosteroids may be required. Close ophthalmic care by an eye M.D. is needed to watch and monitor the severe cases in which eye pressure is increased due to steroid use.

TIP: It is common knowledge that prolonged steroid use may cause glaucoma and cataracts. In some cases the receptionist may be asked to approve telephone requests for refills. Refills may not be approved by telephone except in unusual circumstances concerning glaucoma therapy. As a defense against claims the physician must write "The above directions regarding refills may not be altered by telephone." A carbon copy is kept in the record.

Complications associated with systemic steroid use are justified if there are strong indications for systemic therapy. Cases have been reported when topical steroids would have controlled inflammation and the risks of systemic steroid use were not justified.

b. Posterior uveitis. Posterior uveitis involves the choroids and retina called chorioretinitis. Common symptoms include blurred vision, photophobia, and distortion of the size and shape of objects (metamorphopsia). Pain and tearing are less common and less severe. Complications include retinal detachments, secondary glaucoma, cataracts, and endophthalmitis.

Treatments with systemic steroids and pupillary dilation are similar to those of anterior uveitis previously discussed.

2. Trauma

Penetration and retention of an iron foreign body can lead to a brown-yellow discoloration of the iris (siderosis). Copper foreign bodies cause a gray-blue discoloration of the iris known as chalcosis iridis. Blunt trauma can lead to hemorrhages, mydriasis (pupillary dilation), iridoplegia, traumatic heterochromia, and lens subluxation.

E. Optic Nerve

The retina is an extension of the brain. The optic nerve is a condensation of all the retinal fibers which form a cerebral tract to the brain. The optic nerve begins in the eye and is made up of all the inner retinal neurons. The optic nerve is 1.5 to 1.7 mm in diameter, more oval than round, and has a delicate pink color.

1. Optic neuritis and papilledema

Optic neuritis is an inflammation of the visible portion of the optic nerve head when viewed with an indirect ophthalmoscope. Optic neuritis appears as an opaque, gray-red swelling with blurring of the margins of the nerve head. There are many causes. Some of the more pronounced ones are

- multiple sclerosis,
- viral illness,
- occlusive vascular disease,
- tumors,
- infections (syphilis), and
- chemicals (lead, ethanol).

Optic neuritis results in an immediate (one to two days) decrease in vision with diverse visual field loss. Treatment for optic neuritis is usually performed with intravenous or oral steroids and removal of the offending substance. Fortunately, spontaneous remission can occur.

Papilledema is a gray-red swelling with a glassy, transparent appearance and hyperemia (redness) of the optic disc head, usually associated with increased intracranial pressure. Papilledema usually involves both eyes (bilateral). Etiologies include

- brain tumors,
- head trauma,
- hemorrhages,
- meningitis,
- severe hypertension,
- renal disease, and
- pulmonary emphysema.

Vision is not initially affected, but the blind spot on the visual field testing is enlarged. Optic atrophy results if elevated intracranial pressure lasts a long time (weeks to months). Optic atrophy is associated with decreased vision and various visual field changes. Treatment involves identification and lowering of the intracranial pressure by surgical or medical means.

2. Trauma

A severe blow to the head, usually the face or occiput (back region of the head), can result in unilateral blindness (rarely bilateral) with pupillary abnormalities and can be revealed through a normal ophthalmic exam. This may be caused by an optic canal injury which occurs in 1 to 5 percent of severe head trauma cases. The reason is due to the shearing or tearing effect at the junction point where the nerve is fixed in the bony optic canal and free intracranial portion. The optic atrophy develops approximately ten to fourteen days later. In contrast, damage from bony fragments, hemorrhages, torn nutrient blood vessels, or optic nerve edema will not result in complete vision loss, and some recovery will be obtainable.

Trauma to the head with sudden vision loss, visual field defects, or slow progressive vision loss with optic atrophy and field defects may be secondary to opticochiasmatic arachnoiditis (inflammation of the delicate membrane interposed between the dura mater and pia mater).

F. Extraocular Muscles

The eye is unique in its ability to move independently. There are six muscles connected to the globe (sclera) that determine the mechanical features that both generate and limit the motility of the eye.[17] These six muscles (innervated by cranial nerves III, IV, and VI, respectively) are involved when the eye moves, but only one or two muscles actually regulate each principal direction of movement.

Deviations of the eye, whether temporary or permanent and from whatever etiology, are termed

- exotropic (eyes are divergent to one side away from nose),
- esotropic (eyes are convergent or crossed), or

- hypertropic (eyes have vertical deviation upwards or downwards).

Different tests are used to determine fixation and the objective angle of deviation. When an extraocular muscle is paretic (weak or paralyzed), the opposing muscle exerts a greater control of its own direction of action, thus resulting in a patient's complaint of double vision.

Examination by an ophthalmologist will determine the direction of the diplopia and any other ocular deviations. This examination should also identify the affected muscle involved and the cranial nerve (III, IV, or VI). Because a metabolic, neurologic, myopathic, or cardiovascular disorder may be the cause of the muscle palsy, additional tests may be indicated, unless the palsy is caused as a result of trauma.

Blow-out fractures result from a sudden rise in intra-orbital pressure (fist, tennis ball, fall onto face, and so on). This causes an orbital floor fracture through which orbital tissue herniates into the maxillary sinus and becomes entrapped. (Refer to Figure 6.9 for a drawing of this anatomy.) If the inferior rectus and inferior oblique muscles become entrapped, the result will be a restriction of upward gaze above the midline and a decrease in the downward gaze of the globe. Cutaneous sensitivity in the area of the inferior orbital nerve (cheek, upper gums, and teeth) may occur as well as enophthalmos (abnormal recession of the globe).

Diagnosis with x-ray or CAT scans will delineate the size of the fracture. Surgery using a mesh or metallic/plastic plate over the fracture site may be needed. In rare occurrences, if the nerve has been traumatized, muscle palsy will result. This can be treated with extraocular muscle surgery to help realign the eyes. A blow-out fracture can also result in injury to other portions of the eye, such as the retina, lens, or lacrimal system.

G. Conjunctiva

The conjunctiva is the delicate membrane lining the undersurface of the eyelids and covering the eye up to and around the cornea. Many people are familiar with the term "conjunctivitis" or "pink eye." There are several causes of red eye,[18,19] such as bacterial, viral, or fungal infections, herpes, and metastatic cancers. The transparent conjunctiva has no color whatsoever. With any insult to the conjunctiva, redness, drainage, and itching can evolve.

TIP: With any conjunctiva laceration or foreign body penetration, the important question to consider is whether or not the globe has been perforated. Treatment of any physical damage to the conjunctiva, whether chemical, thermal, or ultraviolet light, consists of anti-inflammatory medication or antibiotics.

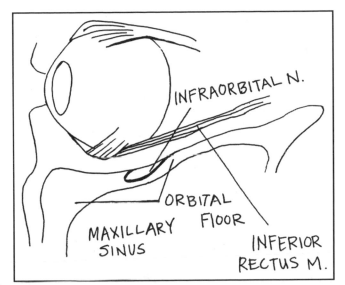

Figure 6.9 *Eye socket.*

H. Eyelids

The eyelids are composed of different tissues including

- skin,
- sweat and oil glands,
- blood and lymphatic vessels,
- nerves,
- fibrous connective tissue,
- smooth and striated muscles, and
- the conjunctival mucus membrane.

Most of the structures can be involved in any disease process, trauma, or neoplastic situations.[20] The eyelids protect and lubricate the cornea as well as help drain the tears into the lacrimal system.

1. Facial nerve paresis (weakness) (VII nerve)

Facial nerve paresis (VII facial nerve) can be caused by trauma, tumors, or inflammatory processes. The orbicularis muscle becomes paretic, causing lagophthalmos (inability to shut the eyelids completely) of the lower eyelid. This causes the lower third of the cornea to be exposed. This may also cause drying of the cornea with secondary corneal erosions, ulcers, and even perforations. Treatment consists of essential wetting and lubrication materials. Surgical intervention is necessary and involves tightening the eyelid or performing a tarsorraphy (closure of the eyelids).

2. Ptosis

Ptosis is the drooping of the upper eyelid and involves the levator palpebrae superioris muscle. Multiple causes include:

- congenital,
- birth trauma from forceps,
- neurological,
- myasthenia gravis,
- Horner's syndrome,
- inflammation, or
- a localized process of the lids such as pemphigus, chemical burns, chalazions (styes), or tumors.

Surgical intervention is necessary in most cases in order to reattach the levator muscle and to elevate the lid.

3. Ectropion

Ectropion, or eversion of the lid, occurs when the lower lid falls away from the eye. Tears pool along the lid margin because the punctum (opening on the edge of the lid margin to the lacrimal canaliculus) is no longer in contact with the lacrimal lake along the eyelid margin. Symptoms can include epiphora (tearing), chronic conjunctivitis, and irritation made worse by consistent rubbing of the eye by the patient.

Factors that give rise to the eyelid ectropion include

- aging,
- scarring after chemical or thermal burns,
- skin diseases such as ichthyosis (dry, rough, scaly skin),
- scleroderma,
- facial nerve palsies, or

- any significant traumatic or inflammatory shrinkage of the skin.

The conjuctiva becomes thickened, dry, and hyperemic. Surgical intervention with a possible skin graft is indicated.

4. Entropion

Entropion is an inversion or turning inward of the eyelid. When the lid turns inward, the lashes rub on the conjunctiva and the cornea. This causes chronic irritation, corneal abrasions, erosion, and possible ulcerations. Entropion is usually caused by aging due to laxity of the eyelid or from scarring of the conjunctiva as a result of chemical burns, ocular pemphigoid, trachoma, or symblepharon formation (adhesions of the eyelid to the eye). Treatment is surgical.

I. Lacrimal System

The lacrimal system[21] encompasses the lacrimal gland, which makes tears, the puncta (opening on the eyelid margin), the canaliculi (conduits through which tears pass from the puncta to the lacrimal sac), the lacrimal sac (chamber that holds tears before negative pressure, with each blink, pushes them into the nasolacrimal duct), and nasolacrimal duct (canal that extends down inside the lateral wall of the nose and opens into the nose). Refer to Figure 6.10. The passage of tears is not a passive process or due to gravity, but rather from eyelid closure and the surrounding muscles of the eyelids.

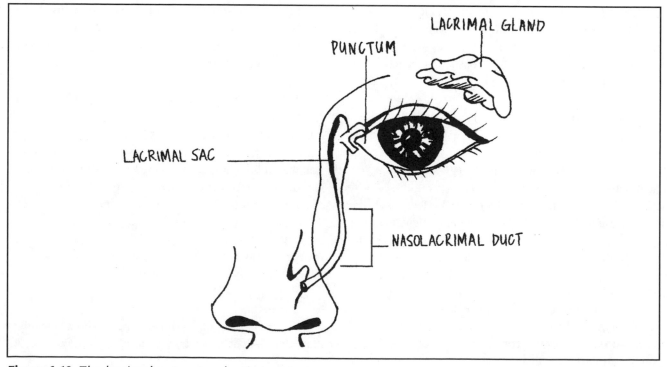

Figure 6.10 *The lacrimal or tear production system.*

Diseases of the lacrimal apparatus are caused by

- congenital anomalies,
- aging (weakened eyelid pump action),
- malposition or eversions (ectropion),
- inflammations,
- trauma,
- senile atrophy,
- tumors,
- infections,
- foreign bodies,
- concretions (hardened mass),
- cilial hairs,
- inflammations (pemphigoid, Stevens-Johnson syndrome),
- nasal and mid-facial fractures,
- post-rhinoplasty,
- sinus surgery, or
- orbital decompression which can cause tearing, chronic eye infections, irritations, and dacryocystitis.

Dacryocystitis is stenosis of the mucus duct that for any reason allows accumulation of mucoid, pus, and dilation of the lacrimal sac. Superinfection may occur, leading to an acute infection of the lacrimal sac with cellulitis. Periorbital cellulitis is an infectious inflammatory process in the loose tissues beneath the skin and around the eyelids. Cellulitis is dangerous because the infection may extend directly to the cavernous sinus to the brain. Symptoms include pain, redness, swelling in the area of the lacrimal sac, tearing, conjunctivitis, fever, and leukocytosis (elevation of white blood cell count).

Medical treatment consists of hot compresses, topical antibiotic drops, and oral, or in severe cases, intravenous antibiotics. Once the acute infection has subsided, surgical intervention is taken to open a passageway directly from the lacrimal sac into the nose (dacryocystorhinostomy).

6.8 Disease States
A. Glaucoma

Glaucoma[22] is distinguished by increased intraocular pressure resulting in damage to the retinal nerve fibers and optic nerve with impairment of the visual field from a slight loss to total blindness. Aqueous (water) secretions by the ciliary body epithelium occupy the anterior and posterior chambers of the eye. The amount of aqueous humor is carefully regulated to maintain the shape of the eye. The aqueous flows from the posterior chamber around and through the pupil, into the anterior chamber, the chamber angle (trabecular meshwork), Schlemm's canal, and via aqueous veins into episclera veins back into the blood stream. The normal pressure ranges from 10 to 20. Pressures above 23 are considered suspect for glaucoma. Intraocular pressures and blood pressures are not related. Figure 6.11 shows the loss of retinal nerve fibers by the amount of cupping or enlargement of the cavity within the optic disc.

TIP: The medical record will record the intraocular pressures as TA = (a number), for example, TA = 18.

---

1. Acute angle closure glaucoma

There are two principal forms of glaucoma. The acute form, called narrow angle glaucoma, causes an acute angle closure attack. There is almost unbearable eye pain, brow ache, and head pain, with or without nausea and vomiting.

The patient experiences rainbow colors followed by cloudy vision and finally marked loss of vision. There is rapid visual field constriction. Corneal edema, marked conjunctival redness, and swelling may occur. The pupil is dilated, and the anterior chamber is flat. The eye feels rock hard with eye pressures of 80-100 mm Hg.

Treatment of the acute form of glaucoma calls for topical and systemic agents with laser iridotomy (opening a hole in the iris), which will break the angle closure attack.

2. Chronic open angle glaucoma

The second primary form of glaucoma is called chronic open angle glaucoma. This is common, does not usually cause pain, and affects the vision very gradually with progressive loss of the peripheral visual field. When uncontrolled, this type of glaucoma leads to late loss of central vision and ultimate blindness. The disease is bilateral, but usually asymmetric in the degree of involvement. Excavation of the optic disc, nasal shift of vessels crossing the disk margin, and later optic atrophy occurs. Chronic steroid therapy[23] (drops or orally), or drugs used to treat epilepsy can cause increased resistance to aqueous outflow with pressure elevation, especially in cases where a predisposition for glaucoma exists. Remission is usually spontaneous once medication is stopped.

Treatment of chronic open angle glaucoma consists of an array of topical medications. If pressure cannot be controlled, laser trabeculoplasty or selective laser trabeculoplasty is performed. Surgical filtering procedures are a last resort due to persistent uncontrolled eye pressures.

TIP: A large portion of medical-legal claims are due to failure to diagnose the condition until severe optic nerve damage had occurred. Failure to measure the eye pressure for a long period of time and careless observation and recording of the optic nerve and visual fields are difficult to defend.

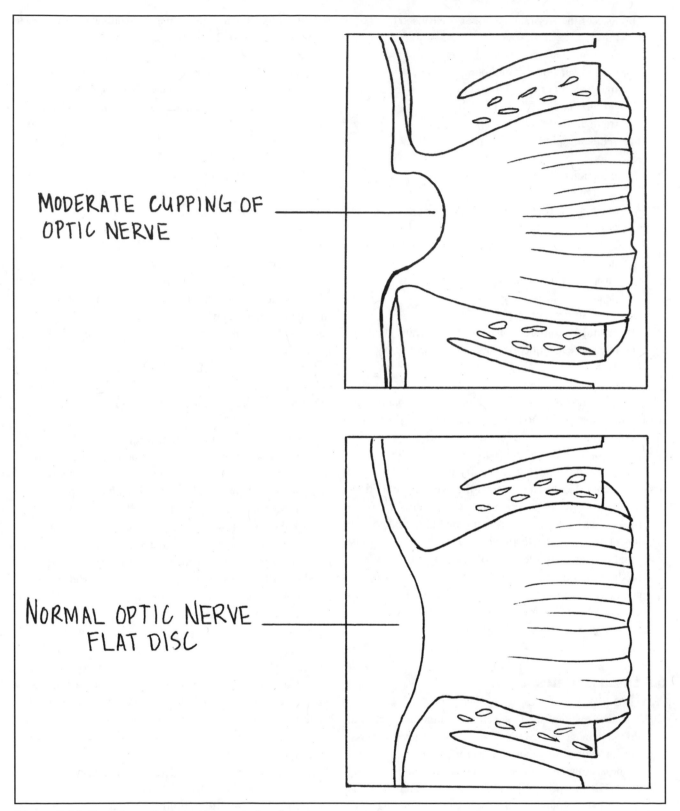

MODERATE CUPPING OF
OPTIC NERVE

NORMAL OPTIC NERVE
FLAT DISC

Figure 6.11 *Cupping of the optic nerve in glaucoma.*

3. Secondary glaucoma

Secondary glaucoma[24] is usually due to an intraocular disorder, commonly from anterior uveitis. This is caused by an interference with the flow of aqueous humor from the posterior chamber through the pupil and into the anterior chamber to the trabecular meshwork (drainage channels from the angle of the eye). Inflammation in the eye may prevent aqueous escape by causing complete posterior synechia (adherence of the iris to the capsule of the lens), or the inflammation may plug the trabecular meshwork with exudates. Other common causes are

- pigmentary glaucoma,
- pseudoexfoliation,
- glaucoma from blood or macrophages,
- blunt trauma, and
- tumor cell obstruction.

The most severe ocular inflammations lead to an elevation in intraocular pressure. Iridocyclitis[25] should raise the suspicion of secondary glaucoma as seen in herpes zoster, scleritis, trauma (increased anterior chamber protein and hemorrhage), and burns.

Central retinal vein thrombosis or diabetic retinopathy can cause rubeosis of the iris due to vascular dilation and new vessel formation at the papillary border and angle of the iris. These abnormal vessels can block the angle and cause elevated intraocular pressure.

A swollen lens[26] (intumescent cataract) can cause angle closure glaucoma. Injury to the lens by blunt trauma, perforation, or cutting into two pieces may release lens proteins which obstruct the trabecular meshwork in the angle of the eye. Anterior or posterior luxation of the lens can cause an acute pressure rise, but the posterior luxation causes glaucoma less often.

Prolonged loss of the anterior chamber after eye surgery, trauma, perforation, or corneal foreign bodies may lead to synechiae (adhesions) formation and secondary glaucoma. Anterior chamber hemorrhages, and rarely vitreous hemorrhages of longstanding durations may cause pressure elevations.

The sixty-nine-year-old plaintiff suffered from glaucoma and was in need of cataract surgery. The plaintiff claimed that the defendant ophthalmologist failed to monitor and control the glaucoma prior to the cataract surgery. The plaintiff lost vision in that eye. During discovery, it was determined that the defendant had altered his records to show that the injury was the plaintiff's fault for not using eye drops. The alteration was discovered when the records for the lawsuit were compared to the records that the plaintiff had taken to the hospital for emergency surgery to try to save the eyeball. The trial court granted the motion to amend the complaint to request punitive damages. However, the case settled for an undisclosed amount.[27]

TIP: The healthcare provider should never alter the records, especially once there is any litigation contemplated. Altered records may make the entire case indefensible.

B. Diabetic Retinopathy

The emergence of diabetic retinopathy,[28] a major cause of blindness, is associated with the duration and the severity of diabetes.[29] Retinopathy can be particularly severe in juvenile and chronic adult-onset diabetes.[30,31] Retinopathy can be expected after five to eight years of having diabetes. Sixty percent of diabetics after fifteen years have the disease of retinopathy. Hypertension has an additional deleterious effect.

Early on, isolated dot and blot or striate retinal hemorrhages (microaneurysms) appear in what is called stage I. In stage II, striate hemorrhages and white or yellow sharply delineated paracentral hard exudates are present. Circinate retinopathy (surrounding of the fine vision area known as the macula lutea) is a possible development. Fluorescein angiography (intravenous dye through the veins) helps show exudations across vessel walls in retinal photographs.

Stage III is characterized with more massive hemorrhages and exudates, with early neovascularization[32,33] (new vessel growth), and tissue organization known as retinitis proliferans.

The most severe form, stage IV, involves proliferative retinal neovascularization with large hemorrhages, often in the vitreous, with marked retinitis proliferans (tissue organization and scarring) and secondary traction detachment of the retina. Secondary detachment with retinitis proliferans is the most common cause of blindness in longstanding diabetics. Hemorrhagic secondary glaucoma nearly always associated with rubeosis of the iris is one of the more common complications of severe diabetic retinopathy.

TIP: The majority of claims involving diabetics center around poor vision after photocoagulation, failure to treat with panretinal photocoagulation, delay in therapy, and a poor visual result.

The plaintiff, a seventy-year-old woman, underwent laser treatment for diabetic retinopathy from 1992 to 1999. Within the scope of that treatment,

Dr. Joseph Younger performed several photocoagulation procedures on the plaintiff's eyes. She claimed that Dr. Younger failed to obtain her consent for the photocoagulation treatment and that he failed to provide adequate information about the treatment, its reasonable alternatives, and its associated risks. She also claimed that Dr. Younger did not inform her of the risks she could incur if the photocoagulation treatment was not performed. The plaintiff contended that Dr. Younger performed unnecessary photocoagulation to her right eye on March 19, 1998, that he performed excessive photocoagulation to her right eye on April 9, 1999, and that he performed excessive photocoagulation to her left eye on March 17, 1998, and again on April 16, 1999. Dr. Younger claimed that the plaintiff required laser therapy to decrease the progression of her diabetic retinopathy. He contended that the amount of photocoagulation performed was necessary to address the leakages in the vessels of her eyes. He also contended that her failure to keep appointments led to the progression of her diabetic retinopathy. He added that she failed to schedule and undergo cataract surgery. According to the *New York Jury Verdict Reporter*, the jury rendered a defense verdict on liability. Post-trial motions were pending.[34]

TIP: It is an established fact that many patients do not remember the preoperative warnings concerning complications, especially if they can be vision threatening.[35,36] It is best to have the patient write in the medical record what she understands after being properly informed. This evidence cannot be denied because it was written in the patient's own hand. A printed form given to the patient to read at home and sign is also effective.

Control of diabetes and high blood pressure is extremely important. Argon laser photocoagulation of proliferating neovascular tufts may reduce the degree of retinal edema along with the frequency and severity of the bleeding events. Surgical intervention with vitrectomy and removal of traction vitreous bands to prevent total retinal detachment may be indicated.

Diabetic retinopathy may be a factor in litigation. For example, a delay in diagnosis of diabetes may result in a worsening of retinopathy. A diabetic with pre-existing retinopathy may suffer trauma to the eyes, which may worsen vision. Questions may arise about the expected progressive loss of vision due to diabetes versus the sudden loss from the trauma. Medical malpractice suits may arise from improperly performed surgery to treat retinopathy.

C. Macular Degeneration

Age-related macular degeneration[37,38] (AMD) is the major cause of irreversible vision distortion and loss in Caucasians who are fifty years and older. Over thirteen million Americans have this condition.

The incidence and progression increases with advancing age.[39] Ninety percent of AMD cases are the "dry" form, consisting of drusen (hyaline material in choroid), pigment clumping, and atrophy in the macula. The remaining 10 percent of AMD cases are the "wet" form consisting of neovascularization with hemorrhages and accumulation of fluid under the fine vision center or macula. People over seventy-five have a 30 percent chance of developing AMD, whereas in people under fifty-five it is rare to develop AMD.

AMD affects men and women equally. It is more common in people with gray, blue, or green eyes because they have less pigment in the retina. Nearsighted (myopic) people and those people who work or spend a lot of time outside (ultraviolet exposure) have a greater chance of getting age-related macular degeneration.

Early symptoms include blurred vision with close work, seeing straight lines as wavy, and diminishing color vision.[40] There may be dimming, blurring, or an actual "hole" or black spots in the vision. Light sensitivity and poor night vision may precede the development of AMD.

Light and dark adaptation, such as the ability to find a seat in a dark movie theater, is delayed. Rarely is there total blindness. Instead, the loss of central vision and the inability to see straight ahead become noticeable. Looking at a clock or face becomes increasingly more difficult. Peripheral vision is relied upon more and more in patients who suffer from AMD. Refer to Figure 6.12.

Treatment includes laser photocoagulation, photodynamic therapy, pharmacologic (kenalog, retisent, posurdex), and vascular endothelial growth factors to prevent neovascularization. In addition, phase I gene therapy trials are underway.

Vitamins, minerals, and Omega-3 fatty acids are being used due to positive results from the Age-Related Disease Study (AREDS) revealing a decreased likelihood of having advanced age-related macular degeneration if incorporated into a daily health regimen.[41] Other treatment techniques being evaluated are submacular surgery, dye-enhanced photocoagulation, external beam radiation therapy, and macular translocation.

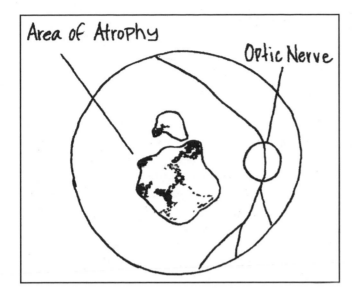

Figure 6.12 *Macular degeneration.*

D. Dry Eye Syndrome

Dry eyes are a common condition occurring more frequently in elderly patients[42] consisting of symptoms of ocular irritation, burning, stinging, foreign body sensation, blurred vision, photophobia, contact lens intolerance, redness, mucosal discharge, and increased blinking.[43,44] Treatment helps improve the symptoms, but the disease is not curable.

Dry eyes is not sight threatening in the majority of patients. If there is non-reversible deficiency of tear production or a chronic condition causing increased evaporation, chronic symptoms distinguished by a waxing or waning of symptoms occur over time.

Other associated conditions such as blepharitis or meibomianitis[45] (oil gland infection of the eyelid) are more likely to cause dry eyes. Also, Sjogren's syndrome, rosacea,[46] lacrimal gland diseases such as sarcoid, lymphoma, AIDS, and Stevens-Johnson syndrome produce tear deficiency due to inflammation, scarring, and goblet cell loss in the conjunctiva.

Increased corneal exposure as seen in eyelid malpositions such as ectropion from trauma, cranial nerve VII palsies, thyroid disease, thermal burns and scleroderma, usually cause corneal drying. If these factors are not treated, the result can be corneal decomposition and ulceration with possible loss of the eye.

In addition to the patient's history, the ophthalmologist should obtain additional information such as the usage of topical medication (artificial tears, antihistamines, glaucoma medications, vasoconstrictors, and corticosteroids). Details should be gathered concerning

- contact lens wear,
- eyelid surgery (ptosis repair, blepharoplasty, entropion/ectropion repair),
- chronic ocular surface inflammation (ocular cicatrical pemphigoid, Stevens-Johnson's, rosacea, atrophy),
- menopause,
- autoimmune diseases,
- Sjogren's syndrome,
- rheumatoid arthritis,
- systemic lupus erythematosus (scleroderma), and
- any systemic medications (psychotropic drops, anti-histamines, diuretics, hormones, hormonal antagonists, anti-depressants, anti-cholinergics, cardiac anti-arrhythmic drugs, isotretinoin).

Examination with the slit lamp biomicroscope reveals abnormal tear film debris, foam, or decreased height of the tear meniscus. The cornea will exhibit

- localized drying,
- punctuate epithelial erosions,
- filaments,
- mucus plaques,
- thinning,
- scarring, and
- possible pannus formation.

Tests include measuring tear break-up time, examining the corneal surface staining pattern with rose Bengal, fluorescein, or lissamine green, and performing the Schirmer (a paper tear strip) test.

After Lasik surgery, some patients experience a dry eye symptom. After time and tear replacement, the symptoms may disappear.

Treatment may be medical or surgical. Most cases are treated for tear deficiency by elimination of factors such as medications, environmental causes, or by correction of eyelid infections and inflammations. Artificial tears, ointment, and humidification of the environment are the mainstay of treatments. Newer drops such as cyclosporine drops (restasis) are now approved by the FDA.

Punctal plug occlusion[47] with cautery or silicone punctual plugs is common. Surgical correction of eyelid deformities (ectropion/entropion) is the most important to prevent corneal decompensation.

In severe ectropion from chronic VII nerve palsies, a lateral eyelid tarsorraphy (suturing of the upper and lower lid together) is needed.

E. Damage from Ultraviolet Light and Ionizing Radiation

Ultraviolet rays are absorbed into surface tissues of the cornea. With exposure, multiple diffuse epithelial (top layer cells) punctate erosions are formed. Usually there is a latent period of several hours between the exposure time and clinical symptoms. These cases are usually seen in welders, and those who suffer snow blindness and exposure time without adequate protective absorbent glasses. Common symptoms from corneal involvement include severe pain, foreign body sensation, blepharospasms, and excessive tearing.

Retinal photocoagulation from sun gazing with inadequate protection results in macula damage and edema. Such heat coagulation heals with a retinal pigmented scar.

Glassblowers and iron foundry workers exposed to short infrared wavelength light for more than ten years may develop a posterior subcapsular cataract. These same people can develop heat-related exfoliation of the outer cortex of the anterior lens known as glass-blowers cataract.

Ionizing radiation, due to excessive exposure to x-rays and radiation, leads to redness and loss of lashes. The cornea and conjunctiva become edematous and even necrotic. Cataract formation can occur in days or up to one to two years and is usually a posterior subcapsular cataract.

Attorneys may be involved in these cases if the employer failed to provide protective equipment to workers exposed to occupational sources of eye damage.

F. Thermal and Chemical Burns

Litigation may follow damage to eyes due to burns. First degree thermal or chemical burns result in hyperemia, cornea stippling or erosion, tearing, and blepharospasm of the eyelids. Second degree burns involve conjunctiva edema, corneal epithelium loss, and stromal edema with eyelid blepharospasm. Third degree burns are severe with necrosis and coagulation of tissues. The conjunctiva is white, anemic, and devoid of fine blood vessels. The cornea is white and opaque with total anesthesia.

Acid burns result in coagulative necrosis which prevents further penetration of the acid; therefore, the prognosis is better than in lye burns. Alkali burns cause liquefaction necrosis, allowing for deeper penetration of the chemicals. Ammonia burns are the most dangerous, often leading to corneal perforation after eight to ten days. Ocular lime burns are common. Lime causes severe burns with deposition of calcium salt in the cornea and the conjunctiva. The resulting white corneal and conjunctival appearance result in the term "boiled fish eye."

Tear gas and other chemical irritants fired at close range result in superficial chemical burns and embedded foreign body material. There is also a chance of secondary iridocyclitis and glaucoma depending on the severity of the exposure.

G. Ocular Trauma

1. Foreign bodies

Conjunctival foreign bodies, located in the upper cul-de-sac of the upper lid, may lead to corneal erosions which appear as multiple, parallel, fluorescein staining lines on the cornea. Lid eversion is necessary to remove the object.

Corneal foreign bodies, usually metal, glass, dust particles, or insects, can soon cause pain, redness, tearing, photophobia, and marked conjunctival redness. Removal of the object and antibiotic therapy will prevent a secondary corneal ulcer. A hidden perforation has to be considered with any corneal or scleral injury after a hammer blow, explosion, or use of a high-speed machine.

TIP: The usual reason for a claim in an ocular foreign body case is failure to diagnose. Commonly, a foreign body was missed because only one modality for diagnosis and localization was obtained, e.g., ultrasound, CAT scan, or x-rays. Though it is not reasonable to take x-rays in every instance of a suspected corneal foreign body, if the history is one of metal hitting metal, this should be thought of immediately.

---

2. Perforating injuries

Perforating injuries to the eye are readily diagnosed if there is

- a corneal laceration,
- a loss of the anterior chamber depth,
- an iris tissue incarcerated in the perforated or scleral tissue, especially at the limbus (junction of the sclera and cornea), and
- a hypotony (low intraocular pressure).

In a Virginia case, the fifty-seven year old patient was scheduled for a cataract removal on the right eye. Just prior to the surgery, a nurse anesthetist punctured her eyeball twice while inserting the needle for the superotemporal anesthetic injection. On the first postoperative day, the ophthalmologist and retinal specialists diagnosed a vitreous hemorrhage and then a double perforation. The plaintiff suffered a permanent macular scar while eliminating vision in the right eye, rendering her legally blind. The defendant claimed the double perforation was a risk of the procedure. A $450,000 verdict was returned.[48]

X-ray examination for foreign bodies is mandatory. Ultrasound examination is also helpful. If a metallic foreign body is present, an attempt at removal should be made using a magnet.

Perforating injuries carry a risk of

- endophthalmitis,
- sympathetic ophthalmia (described below),
- phthisis bulbi (shrunken globe),
- secondary glaucoma,
- retinal detachment,
- cataracts,
- siderosis, and
- chalcosis.

Brain involvement must be considered when the orbit has been penetrated by stab injuries (knives, sticks, and so on) or residual pieces of wood are retained in the orbit. Intraocular iron-containing foreign bodies lead to siderosis. Siderosis can occur of the iris, lens (with secondary cataract formation), and vitreous. Retinal siderosis ultimately leads to retinal atrophy and optic nerve atrophy.

TIP: A majority of claims involving siderosis are indefensible because the destruction was so advanced by the time the diagnosis was made that the result was blindness. A foreign body must be searched for in every case.

Intraocular chalcosis (copper retention) leads to corneal discoloration and a sunflower cataract (chalcosis lentis). Some changes in the retina vitreous may occur. Intraocular glass, depending on the location, may cause corneal decomposition, glaucoma, and retinal detachments. Intraocular vegetable matter (wood, leaves, and so on) can cause a marked inflammatory reaction and must be removed. Secondary complications include all of the above, especially endophthalmitis.

3. Sympathetic ophthalmia

Sympathetic ophthalmia may be seen potentially many years after a penetrating injury. Inflammation of the *uninjured*, sympathizing eye occurs no earlier than ten days, usually four to eight weeks, but potentially many years or decades after the trauma. This is considered an auto-immune process appearing as a chronic iridocyclitis after a perforating injury. Symptoms in the sympathizing eye include

- decreased accommodation (in young patients),
- decreased dark adaptation,
- iridocyclitis,
- photophobia,

- flare, and
- cells in the anterior chamber and secondary posterior synechia (scarring of the iris to the anterior lens capsule).

There is danger of secondary glaucoma, potentially leading to hypotony with phthisis bulbi, and retinal detachment. Treatment includes aggressive anti-inflammatory steroid medication either by drops, orally, or intravenously.

4. Blunt trauma

Blunt trauma to the eye can occur as a result of a blow, airbag deployment, paintball shot at the face, fall, and so on. Blunt trauma to the retina is known as commotion or the more severe form, contusion retinae. Ophthalmoscopy reveals gray (edema) discoloration of the retina area that is involved in the trauma. In some cases a cherry red spot means the macula has been involved. Vision loss is severe. In commotion retinae, the edema resolves with full restitution of vision, whereas contusion retinae can lead to scar formation with residual visual loss or distortion.

Blunt trauma to the eye can cause transitory corneal edema with corneal conjunctival limbal blood vessel dilation (ciliary injection). Photophobia, pain, and lacrimation are common. Sudden severe vision loss due to anterior chamber hemorrhages from a ruptured iris vessel may occur. The blood sinks and results in a horizontal fluid level (hyphemia). Secondary glaucoma is a risk as is corneal hemosiderosis due to corneal staining.

Moderate to severe blunt trauma to the iris may cause dilation to the pupil (traumatic mydriasis). The pupillary response to light and dark is incomplete. Iridodialysis is the disinsertion of the peripheral iris leading to distortion of the pupil in that area of trauma.

TIP: Many claims are based on delay in therapy. Blunt trauma resulting in a dense hemorrhage in the eye or an acute fracture of the bony orbit with severe swelling can delay diagnosis of a retinal detachment. In these situations, ultrasound may need to be done repetitively. There may be a long latent period between the trauma and the occurrence of the detachment.

---

5. Globe rupture

Globe rupture can occur with direct or indirect trauma by severe pressure against the bony orbit. The iris, lens, or other intraocular contents may be expelled from the eye. Posterior rupture is characterized by marked hypotony (decreased pressure), a deepened anterior chamber, and intraocular hemorrhage. Trauma to the lens can cause subluxation and cataracts.

Subluxation of the lens into the anterior chamber can lead to an acute glaucoma attack. Cataract formation can develop anteriorly, posteriorly, or in the sutures of the lens. Surgical removal of the lens may be indicated if vision is impaired.

Retinal detachments can occur in any case of trauma to the globe. In fact, trauma can prematurely precipitate a retinal detachment in patients so inclined. Even macular holes seen in patients with myopia or retinal degeneration can occur at times following ocular trauma.

Optic nerve damage with severe globe or periorbital trauma and vision loss can be due to fractures in the bony portion of the optic canal or hematoma in the optic nerve sheath. A contrecoup action, with the mass of the brain pulling and stretching the optic nerve, can also result in acute visual loss. Avulsions of the nerve head, though very rare, can also occur.

H. Endophthalmitis

Endophthalmitis[49] remains a devastating complication of either intraocular surgery (cataract, glaucoma, muscle surgery) or penetrating ocular trauma. This severe infection of the intraocular tissues is caused by bacteria or fungus. Early diagnosis and treatment are imperative to the outcome and residual visual function.

Since cataract extraction is the most common intraocular surgery, endophthalmitis occurs more frequently after this procedure.

Postoperative bacterial endophthalmitis develops anywhere from one to four days after surgery. The signs and symptoms include

- crescendo pain,
- lid edema,
- conjunctival swelling and redness,
- corneal haziness,
- anterior chamber inflammation (some with hypopyon or pus cells), and
- vitritis.

Less virulent bacteria may cause endophthalmitis, which is delayed for more than one or two weeks, especially if topical endophthalmitis may present itself in a similar fashion, with a latent period of several days to weeks.

TIP: The majority of claims are due to delay in treatment. In a postoperative patient who complains of pain, redness, and poor vision, it is difficult to defend the delay in examination and administration of antimicrobials.

Diagnostic techniques include tapping the anterior chamber fluid and vitreous to culture for bacteria and fungal organisms.

Intensive antibiotic treatment, including topical, subconjunctival injections, or intravenous and intravitreal injections of medication, is started as soon as possible to sterilize the eye. Anti-inflammatory (steroids) therapy to limit the damage, especially in the retina, is also administered. In some cases, surgical intervention (vitrectomy) is combined with antibiotics to more rapidly eliminate infectious material and aid in the diffusion of the antibiotics.

TIP: Claims based on insufficient prophylactic antibiotics or the wrong choice of antimicrobials are usually easily defended. It has not been proved that prophylactic antibiotic treatment will prevent eye infections. At least the doctor was thinking ahead to try to prevent an infection.

Besides poor visual outcomes, potential loss of the eye must be explained to the patient as a possible complication of this condition.

TIP: The claim is always defensible despite a bad result if proper antibiotic therapy was given in a timely manner and by acceptable routes of administration.

I. Functional Visual Loss

If a patient complains about decreased vision or a peripheral field defect in either a single eye or both eyes after a comprehensive eye exam reveals no abnormalities, then a diagnosis of functional visual loss is considered.[50,51] A neuro-ophthalmologic or neurological consultation is essential to ensure a real organic disease is not present. Patients may be malingering for secondary gain such as those involved in a lawsuit claiming severe visual loss after a minor accident or those for whom a clear motive is not evident.

Patients with functional visual loss should undergo definitive diagnostic testing as quickly as possible to avoid unnecessary non-invasive or invasive tests, due to their own false-negative and false-positive results.

Numerous clinical tests performed by an ophthalmologist can be performed to diagnose functional visual loss. These indirect and direct tests will aid in frank assessment of the visual function. Major causes of decreased vision with normal visual fields include cataracts, retinal macular problems, a refractive error, amblyopia from childhood, or a functional visual loss. Remember, functional visual loss is a diagnosis of exclusion.

6.9 Summary

When the reader began this chapter, it may have seemed possible to interpret simply and quickly ophthalmologic records. However, the content of this chapter has presented an overview of the complexities of eye conditions, terms, and abbreviations. Advances in medical eye science and technology show how many changes have occurred in the last thirty to forty years. Unlike with today's capabilities, traumatic eye injuries, medical inflammatory, or infectious conditions previously resulted in vision loss or even loss of the eye. Ophthalmologic innovations, better nutrition, surgery, and technological advances are paving the way for longevity and anti-aging aspects of visual health.

Endnotes

1. Klein, R. et al. "The Beaver Dam Eye Study: Visual Acuity." *Ophthalmology*. 98, p. 1310–1315. 1991.

2. Bajandas, F.S. *Neuro-Ophthalmology Board Review Manual*. SLACK Incorporated. 1980.

3. American Academy of Ophthalmology. "Basic and Clinical Science Course, Section 3: Optics and Refraction and Contact Lenses." p. 146–149. San Francisco, CA: American Academy of Ophthalmology. 1994.

4. American Academy of Ophthalmology: *Comprehensive Adult Eye Evaluation, Preferred Practice Pattern*. San Francisco, CA: American Academy of Ophthalmology. 1997.

5. Saunders, K.J. "Early Refractive Development in Humans." *Surv Ophthalmol*. 40, p. 207–216. 1995.

6. Laska, L. "Lasik Surgery causes Epithelial Abrasion, "*Medical Malpractice Verdicts, Settlements, and Experts*. February 2009, p. 35

7. American Academy of Ophthalmology. *Dry Eye Syndrome, Preferred Practice Pattern*. San Francisco: American Academy of Ophthalmology. 1998.

8. Schein O.D. and E.C. Poggio. "Ulcerative Keratitis in Contact Lens Wearers: Incidence and Risk Factors." *Cornea*. 9 Suppl 1, p. 55–58. 1990.

9. Laska, L. "One Eye Nearly Blind Following Cataract Surgery." *Medical Malpractice Verdicts, Settlements, and Experts*. March 2003, p. 39.

10. Laska, L. "Failure to Diagnose Diabetes from Tests Performed in Conjunction with Cataract Surgery." *Medical Malpractice Verdicts, Settlements, and Experts*. January 2004, p. 48.

11. Regillo, C.D. and W.E. Benson. *Retinal Detachment: Diagnosis and Management*. Third Edition. Philadelphia, PA: Lippincott-Raven. 1998.

12. Byer, N.E. "Natural History of Posterior Vitreous Detachment with Early Management as the Premier Line of Defense Against Retinal Detachment." *Ophthalmology*. 101, p. 1503–13. 1994.

13. Hilton, G.F., E.B. McLean, and D.A. Brinton. *Retinal Detachment: Principles and Practice*. Second Edition. Ophthalmology Monography. San Francisco, CA: American Academy of Opthalmology. 1995.

14. Laska, L. (Editor). "Eye Lost After Retinal Detachment Left Undiagnosed." *Medical Malpractice Verdicts, Settlements, and Experts*. May 2003, p. 43.

15. American Academy of Ophthalmology. "The Repair of Regmatogenous Retinal Detachments, Ophthalmic Procedure Assessment." *Ophthalmology*. 103, p. 1313–24. 1996.

16. Laska, L. "Former Truck Driver Loses Sight After Failure of Physician to Timely Perform Retinal Reattachment Surgery." *Medical Malpractice Verdicts, Settlements, and Experts*. January 2004, p. 48.

17. Von Noorden, G.K. *Binocular Vision and Ocular Motility: Theory and Management of Strabismus*. Fifth Edition. St. Louis, MO: Mosby-Year Book. 1996.

18. Foster, C.S. and M. Calonge. "Atopic Keratoconjunctivitis." *Ophthalmology*. 97, p. 992–1000. 1990.

19. Gutierrez, E.H. "Bacterial Infections of the Eye" in Locathcher-Khorazo, D. and B.C. Seegal. (Editors). *Microbiology of the Eye*. p. 63–64. St. Louis, MO: CV Mosby Co. 1972.

20. Jones, L.T. and J.L. Wobig, J.L. *Surgery of the Eyelids and Lacrimal System*, Birmingham: Aesculapius. 1976.

21. McCord, C.D. Jr. "The Lacrimal Drainage System" in Duane, T.D. (Editor). *Clinical Ophthalmology*. Philadelphia, PA: Harper and Row. vol. 4, ch. 13, p. 1–25. 1981.

22. Krupin, T. and M. Fertl. "Glaucomas Associated with Uveitis" in Ritch, R., M.B. Sheilds, and T. Krupin. (Editors). *The Glaucomas*. p. 1205–1223. St. Louis, MO: Mosby. 1989.

23. Fraundfelder, F.T., J.R. Samples, and F.W. Fraundfelder. "Possible Optic Nerve Side Effects Associated with Nonsteroidal Anti-Inflammatory Drugs." *J. Toxicol-Cut. and Ocular Toxicol*. 13, p. 311–316. 1994.

24. Rich, R. and M.B. Shields. *The Secondary Glaucomas*. St. Louis, MO: CV Mosby Co. 1982.

25. Panek, W.C. et al. "Glaucoma in Patients with Uveitis." *Br J Ophalmol*. 74, p. 223–227. 1990.

26. Rosenbaum, J.T. et al. "Chemotactic Activity of Lens Proteins and the Pathogenesis of Phacolytic Glaucoma." *Arch Ophthalmol*. 105, p. 1582–1584. 1987.

27. Laska, L. *"Anonymous Sixty-Nine-Year-Old Plaintiff v. Anonymous Ophthalmology." Medical Malpractice Verdicts, Settlements, and Experts*. June 2004, p. 42.

28. Center for Disease Control and Prevention. "Prevention of Blindness Associated with Diabetic Retinopathy." *Morbidity and Mortality Weekly Report*. March 19, 1993, p. 42–3.

29. The Diabetics Control and Complications Trial Group. "Early Worsening of Diabetic Retinopathy in the Diabetes Control and Complications Trial." *Arch Ophthalmol*. 116, p. 874–86. 1998.

30. Davis, M.D. et al. For the Early Treatment Diabetic Retinopathy Study research Group. "Risk Factors for High-Risk Proliferative Diabetic Retinopathy and Severe Visual Loss." ETDRS Report #18. *Invest Ophthalmol Vis Sci*. 39, p. 232–52. 1998.

31. Javitt, J.C. and C.P. Aiello. "Cost-Effectiveness of Detecting and Treating Diabetic Retinopathy." *Ann Intern Med*. 124, p. 164–9. 1996.

32. Ferris, F. "Early Photocoagulation in Patients with Other Type I or Type II Diabetes." *Trans Am Ophthalmol*. Soc. 94, p. 505–37. 1996.

33. Klein, R. "Hyperglycemia and Microvascular and Macrovascular Disease in Diabetes." *Diab. Care*. 18, p. 258–68. 1995.

34. Laska, L. (Editor). "Failure to Describe Potential Risks of Photocoagulation Treatment." *Medical Malpractice Verdicts, Settlements, and Experts*. July 2003, p. 44.

35. Priluck, I.A. et al. "What Patients Recall of Preoperative Discussion After Retinal Detachment Surgery." *Am J Ophth*. 87, p. 620. 1979.

36. Robinson, G. and A. Avd Merav. "Informed Consent: Recall by Patients Tested Postoperatively." *Bull Am Coll of Surgeons*. 62, p. 7. 1977.

37. American Academy of Ophthalmology. *Age-Related Macular Degeneration, Preferred Practice Pattern*. San Francisco, CA: American Academy of Ophthalmology. 1994.

38. Bressler, N.M., S.B. Bressler, and S.L. Fine. "Age-Related Macular Degeneration." *Surv Ophthalmol*. 32, p. 375–413. 1998.

39. Klein, R. et al. "The Five-Year Incidence and Progression of Age-Related Maculopathy." The Beaver Dam Eye Study. *Ophthalmology*. 104, p. 7–21. 1997.

40. Sunness, J.S. et al. "Visual Function Abnormalities and Prognosis in Eyes with Age-Related Geographic Atrophy of the Macula and Good Visual Acuity." *Ophthalmology*. 104, p. 1677–91. 1997.

41. Mares-Perlman, J.A. et al. "Association of Zinc and Antioxidant Nutrients with Age-Related Maculopathy." *Arch Ophthalmol*. 114, p. 991–7. 1996.

42. Schein, O.D. et al. "Prevalence of Dry Eye Among the Elderly." *Am J Ophthalmol*. 124, p. 723–8. 1997.

43. Baum, J. "Clinical Manifestations of Dry Eye States." *Trans Ophthalmol SOC UK*. 104, p. 415–23. 1985.

44. Schein, O.D. et al. "Relation Between Signs and Symptoms of Dry Eye in the Elderly: A Population-Based Perspective." *Ophthalmology*. 104, p. 1395–401. 1997.

45. Mathers, W.D. "Ocular Evaporation in Meibomian Gland Dysfunction and Dry Eye." *Ophthalmology*. 100, p. 347–51. 1993.

46. American Academy of Ophthalmology. *Blepharitis: Preferred Practice Pattern*. San Francisco, CA: American Academy of Ophthalmology. 1998.

47. American Academy of Ophthalmology. "Punctal Occlusion for the Dry Eye: Ophthalmic Procedure Assessment." *Ophthalmology*. 104, p. 1521–4. 1997.

48. Laska, L. "Double puncture of eyeball by Nurse Anesthetist Prior to Cataract Surgery." *Medical Malpractice Verdicts, Settlements, and Experts*, June 2009, p. 35.

49. Forster, R.K. "Endophthalmitis" in Duane, T.D. (Editor). *Clinical Ophthalmology*. vol. 4, ch. 24. Hagerstown: Harper and Row. 1982.

50. Keltner, J.L. et al. "The California Syndrome. Functional Visual Complaints with Potential Economic Impact." *Ophthalomolgy*. 92, p. 427–435. 1985.

51. Thompson, H.S. "Functional Visual Loss." *Am J Ophthalmol*. 100, p. 209–213. 1985.

Chapter 7

Emergency Medical Services Records

Mary Fakes, RN, MSN and Scott A. Mullins, AAS, EMT-P

7.1 Introduction

Emergency Medical Services (EMS) are the systems in place that respond to pre-hospital incidents of injury and illness. These systems include dispatchers, first responders, emergency medical technicians, paramedics, nurses, physicians, and the equipment and training to accomplish their missions.

7.2 History and Development of EMS Systems

The early organized care of the sick and injured began during the late 1700s when Napoleon Bonaparte appointed Baron Dominique-Jean Larrey to institute a medical patient care system for the French Army.[1] This decision was made after discovering that wounded soldiers left on the field for several days had an increase in complications as well as suffering. By 1797, Barron Larrey had developed a system that sent trained medical personnel to the wounded soldiers on the battlefield. This benefited Napoleon's conquest efforts. The special carriage designed by Baron Larrey that allowed the medical personnel to access the wounded became known as ambulance volante, or flying ambulance.[2] The concept of providing for removal of the sick, injured, and dead from battlefields existed in some form since the early Greek and Roman times; it was Baron Larrey who put some organization to the system.

TIP: Baron Larrey is considered the "father of emergency medical services" due to all of his precepts of emergency medical care that are still used today: 1) rapid access by trained personnel to the patient, 2) treatment in the field and stabilization of the patient, with 3) rapid transportation back to the medical facility, while 4) providing medical care en route.[3]

The utilization of EMS systems has not always been smooth in the United States. During the Civil War, both sides suffered in their abilities to manage the care of the wounded soldiers in the field. McSwain notes that during the Second

Battle of Bull Run in August of 1862, on the Yankee side alone, 3000 wounded lay in the field of Bull Run for three days and 600 lay there for a week.[4]

The Geneva Convention of 1864 recommended that hospitals, the sick and wounded, and personnel involved in medical care and ambulances were to be considered neutral. Furthermore, safe passage was to be provided for all involved in the medical care of the sick and wounded.

By 1865, the first ambulance service was started in the United States in Cincinnati at Cincinnati General Hospital.[5] Other services followed across the country. The original method of notification for the need of EMS services involved the hospital running a bess, which triggered a weight to fall, lighting the gas lamp which woke the physician and driver.[6] This system also caused the harness and saddle to drop from the ceiling onto the horse and the stable doors to open.

Modern Emergency Medical Services (EMS) has its roots in the 1960s following the publication of the National Academy of Science's "White Paper" titled "Accidental Death and Disability: The Neglected Disease of Modern Society" in 1966.[7,8,9] This paper brought to light the deficiencies in providing pre-hospital and emergency care in the country. The federal government began to organize EMS and trauma care. Prior to 1966, there were unregulated and disconnected methods for people to receive care before they arrived at the hospital. In many places, the local funeral home was the only resource that could transport a person lying down to the hospital.

Funeral homes were still the only methods of emergent transportation for the sick and injured in some areas of the country as late as 1975, even within thirty miles of a metropolitan area such as St. Louis, Missouri.[10] Care rendered at the time was limited to placing the sick or injured person on a stretcher and perhaps delivering oxygen as the care and transport were being managed by a funeral director, embalmer, or other unlicensed funeral home staff members.

Further expansion of the EMS movement occurred in 1966 when individual states gained authority to set the standards, implement programs, and regulate EMS through the 1966 Highway Safety Act.[11] Subsequent federal and state initiatives were responsible for the refinement and improvement of the care rendered to citizens during the next two decades after the "White Paper." That document suggested that the quality of pre-hospital care was an important determinant of surviving sudden injury. This recognition stimulated the development of federal funding through the Highway Safety Act of 1966. Subsequent to the enactment of the law, education was determined to be the most appropriate response. Funds were allocated to develop a National Standard Curriculum (NSC) for emergency medical technicians. It took five years for the contractor to deliver the first National Standard Curriculum in response to model legislation recommended by the National Highway Transportation Safety Administration (NHTSA). Many states adopted the NSC in the form of either law or rules. The curriculum and the scope of practice became intertwined. In 1973, Congress passed the Emergency Medical Services Systems Act (PL 93-142).[12] This law provided grants and other funding mechanisms to establish regional EMS systems including training and manpower. Additionally, the National Highway Transportation Safety Administration created a curriculum that evolved into the current forty-hour First Responder Program developed primarily for police officers. The first meeting of the National Registry of Emergency Medical Technicians (NREMT) took place in 1970 to provide uniform standards for credentialing of ambulance attendants.[13] In 1975, the American Medical Association first recognized the EMT-Paramedic as an allied health occupation.[14] NHTSA published the EMS Agenda for the Future as a guide for the continued advancement of Emergency Medical Services.[15]

7.3 Types of Services
A. First Responders

Resources to provide a local ambulance service are limited in many locations. Rural areas tend to have services that are responsible for large geographical areas so that they are fiscally capable of providing any level of service. Volunteer fire departments and ambulance squads are usually the first responders in these areas. There is a wide range of training for first responders. They may have had only an American Red Cross First Aid Class as their education. In 1970, NHTSA created the forty-hour First Responder Course which became the standard of education for first responders.[16] These providers may not document much about their activities at an accident scene because there is little within their curriculum that deals with documentation.

Rural locations are not the only places where first responders offer services. In urban and suburban locations, many fire departments and police departments respond to emergency calls but do not transport the patient. The educational level of the personnel can range from basic to advanced life support. These organizations benefit from the direction of physicians.

TIP: The documentation provided by the first responders often does not arrive with the patient to the hospital but follows later. Many states require first responders to submit documentation if they are under the direction of a physician and are licensed by the state.

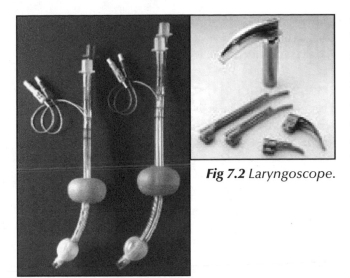

Fig 7.2 *Laryngoscope.*

Figure 7.1 *Combitube®.*

B. Basic Life Support Transport

The least educated level of transport ambulance service is the Basic Life Support or emergency medical technician (EMT) level. In many states, this level of service provider is referred to as an Emergency Medical Technician-Basic (EMT-B). All states license or regulate ambulance services that transport people based on the Department of Transportation guidelines. Basic life support ambulances are staffed with a crew of at least one basic EMT and possibly a first responder trained driver. State statutes vary on the minimum training level of the ambulance crew. EMT-Bs can provide oxygen therapy, automatic defibrillation, spinal immobilization, splinting, or insertion of a multilumen airway such as the Combitube® (Figure 7.1).[17] They cannot generally administer IV fluids or medications. In addition, an EMT-B generally cannot use a laryngoscope, which is an illuminating instrument inserted into the pharynx to permit visualization of the pharynx and larynx to place an endotracheal tube or breathing tube.[18] (Refer to Figure 7.2.) They are not educated to perform complex diagnostics such as electrocardiography (EKG). Because of the cost of education and advanced equipment, and limited funding, basic life support ambulance services are the only services available in many parts of the country. Since these services are licensed and regulated by the state, documentation standards for basic life support ambulance services vary state to state.

C. Advanced Life Support Transport

The highest level of education within the National Standard Curriculum (NSC) is advanced life support (ALS) or EMT-Paramedic.[19] Emergency services are provided under the direct supervision of a physician medical director and include invasive and pharmacological therapies for injuries

or illnesses. Some of these therapies include manual defibrillation, electrocardiography, endotracheal intubation, intravenous fluid therapy, and the administration of medications. Since these services involve advanced therapies, they also have requirements for comprehensive documentation. These services are almost always involved in a form of quality review by their physician medical director which includes a review of the documentation. The ambulance crew for advanced life support service is composed of at least one paramedic who has the education and skills to perform the advanced procedures listed above. The paramedic's documentation is more detailed than that of the EMT-B and includes a thorough systems assessment, similar to that seen in nursing assessments documented on the patient care report.

D. Ambulance Districts

Ambulance districts are political subdivisions that are created to provide a tax support for the provision of emergency medical services. Ambulance districts have broad legal powers to provide ambulance service. Typically an elected board of directors has statutory authority to levy taxes, impose fees for service, enter into contracts for services, enact ordinances, purchase equipment, hire staff, and provide for the administration and successful provision of the ambulance service. The ambulance district has much the same authority as a county level subdivision of government, although its sole function is the provision of ambulance services.

E. Fire Protection Districts

Fire protection districts are political subdivisions that are legally empowered to offer emergency medical services as well as fire protection services. These tax-supported entities have less power than ambulance districts for providing emergency medical services. While they also have an elected board of directors and the authority to do many of the same activities as an ambulance district, their primary function is to provide fire protection services. In some states fire protection districts can only provide first responder and emergency transports and no other services. Medical records generated during transportation of a patient would need to be obtained directly from the fire protection district.

F. Hospital-Based Programs

Many areas have hospital-based EMS services that transport both emergency and non-emergency patients. These services may have more requirements for documentation than public entity services because they have to meet both state and hospital regulations. There may be circumstances in which hospital-based systems are held accountable for more than the normal EMS regulations because the system is hospital-based. An example is that the hospital-based ambulance would follow stricter Consolidated Omnibus Budget Reconciliation Act of 1985 (COBRA) regulations since they are an actual service performed by the hospital.[20] The hospital-based service would be required to comply with any and all Medicare program regulations as they apply to the hospital's responsibility in treating individuals with emergency medical conditions under the provisions of the Emergency Medical Treatment and Labor Act (EMTALA).[21,22] The hospital-based service would be the entity responsible for keeping the medical records of patients transported by them.

G. Private Services

There are many localities that contract with private businesses to meet the needs of their area for ambulance services. Most of these companies bid on the emergency contracts in order to provide non-emergency services, which are certainly more profitable than the emergency services. For example, non-emergency services include transporting patients to their homes or nursing homes. The difference in for-profit versus not-for-profit may cause some documentation issues. Generally these documentation issues would have to do with their billing practices such as Medicare billing.

H. Air Medical Ambulance Transport

Most air ambulance services (Figure 7.3) are either private business ventures or are affiliated with a major hospital group or trauma center. These services can be either rotary winged (helicopter) or fixed wing (airplane). Helicopter services are used to provide time-critical transport either from facility to facility or from the primary scene to a specialty resource center such as a tertiary care facility or a specialized trauma hospital. Fixed wing services (Figure 7.4) move patients over long distances from facility to facility. These services have to comply with federal government regulations of the Federal Aviation Administration (FAA) and state regulations.[23] In addition, air medical ambulances may voluntarily be accredited by the Commission on Accreditation of Medical Transport Systems (CAMTS).[24] Due to the significant health issues of patients being transported, there is a greater need for in-depth documentation. In addition to emergency transports, there are a variety of specialized transport situations in which a higher level staffing such as critical care nurses, respiratory therapists, and even physicians is needed. This results in a higher level of treatment as well as increased documentation requirements. These entities maintain medical records for patients they transport. There may be additional requirements if the transport crosses state boundaries. Specialized equipment may be used on these flights such as newborn isolettes, intraaortic balloon pumps (IABP), and others based on the patient's condition and the necessity for the transport.

I. Other Types of Services

There are locations in the United States where the ambulance service is provided by a volunteer organization that charges fees for service and also bills insurance and Medicare. Since these are licensed by the individual state they have to adhere to the same documentation rules as tax-supported, hospital-based, or private ambulance services. There may not be any living facilities for the staff of some of these services. They may respond from their homes to the ambulance garage to pick up the vehicle and travel to the scene. There can be significant delays in the crew's response when this is the situation. Additionally the crews are "on the clock" from the time they are dispatched, so if there is an accident or incident in their personal vehicles before they get to the ambulance then they might be covered by workers' compensation or even the service's liability insurance. These situations certainly would require additional documentation.

Figure 7.3 *Air medical ambulance (helicopter).*

Figure 7.4 *Air medical ambulance (airplanes).*

J. Nonmedical Transport Services

The nonmedical transport services have become big business due to Medicare billing affecting the marketplace. These services transport passengers who have conditions that preclude them from using a normal car or van. This category includes wheelchair patients and others who must be transported lying down. There are few regulations since these passengers do not have a medical condition that requires care from the driver or attendant (if there is one). The only documentation that is necessary is a certification by the patient's physician that the patient does not need medical treatment or monitoring during the transport. One of the main issues with these types of services is that the transferring facility and the receiving facility must agree on the transfer and have a physician certify that no medical care is needed. Many laws do not identify the people being transferred by these services as "patients" but as "passengers."

TIP: The federal government's reimbursement program requires significant justification for the use of an ambulance for routine transfers, so these cost-effective services are becoming much more popular.

7.4 EMS Certifications

EMS professionals are often mandated by state law or medical direction to maintain certain credentials beyond their basic licensure. In some states, maintaining certain certifications is necessary in order to re-license. Some of the common certifications or credentials may include

- Basic Life Support Healthcare Provider (BLS),
- Advanced Cardiac Life Support (ACLS),
- Advanced Cardiac Life Support Experienced Provider (ACLS-EP),
- Pediatric Advanced Life Support (PALS), and
- Pre-Hospital Trauma Life Support (PHTLS).

The BLS Healthcare Provider Course teaches cardiopulmonary resuscitation (CPR) skills for helping victims of all ages (including providing ventilation with a barrier device, a bag-mask device, and oxygen); use of an automated external defibrillator (AED); and relief of foreign-body airway obstruction (FBAO).[25] It is intended for participants who provide health care to patients in a wide variety of settings, including pre-hospital and in-hospital settings. The participant of this program receives a course completion card upon successful completion of a written examination and practical skills.

First responders are often credentialed in a Heartsaver Automated External Defibrillator (AED) course.[26] Heart-

saver AED, a comprehensive course for the first responder, is designed to teach CPR, use of an automated external defibrillator (AED), and relief of foreign-body airway obstruction to all lay rescuers, particularly those who are expected to respond to emergencies in the workplace. It is specifically designed for lay rescuers who are required to obtain a course completion card documenting completion of a CPR AED course.

The ACLS Provider Course offers the knowledge and skills needed to evaluate and manage the first ten minutes of an adult ventricular fibrillation/ventricular tachycardia (VF/VT) arrest.[27] Providers are expected to learn to manage ten core ACLS cases:

- a respiratory emergency,
- four types of cardiac arrest,
- simple VF/VT,
- complex VF/VT,
- PEA (pulseless electrical activity),
- asystole (no heart rate),
- five types of prearrest emergencies,
- bradycardia (slow heart rate),
- stable tachycardia,
- unstable tachycardia (rapid heart rate),
- acute coronary syndromes, and
- stroke.

The course is eight to sixteen hours in length and is intended for healthcare professionals who staff emergency, intensive care, or critical care departments, such as physicians, nurses, emergency technicians, paramedics, respiratory therapists and other professionals who may respond to a cardiovascular emergency. The participant of this program receives a course completion card upon successful completion of a written examination and practical skills. The card has an expiration date of two years from the date of the course completion.

The American Heart Association (AHA) developed a program for healthcare professionals who previously completed the ACLS Provider course and were looking for increased information and challenges.[28] The ACLS-EP course provides greater complexity and variety to the ACLS cases. The course is a ten-hour class that allows for the participant to renew the ACLS provider status and covers four additional skills and discussion stations. The advanced material includes toxicology, environmental emergencies, electrolyte imbalances, and complicated myocardial infarction management. The course is specifically designed for the paramedic who practices in high run volume departments or works for critical care companies such as air medical transport agencies. Physicians and critical care and emergency department nurses can also benefit from the material. Like all other AHA programs, the participant of this program receives a course completion card upon successful completion of a written examination and practical skills. The card is valid for two years from the date of the course completion.

The intended audience for a PALS course is pediatricians, house staff, emergency physicians, family physicians, nurses, paramedics, respiratory therapists, as well as pre-hospital professionals who are responsible for the well-being of infants and children.[29] The goal of the PALS program is to provide the participant with the information needed to recognize pediatric patients at risk for cardiopulmonary arrest. The course teaches strategies to prevent the arrest. There is a didactic portion to the program as well as multiple skills stations for the participants to practice the cognitive and psychomotor skills needed to resuscitate and stabilize pediatric patients in respiratory failure, shock, or cardiopulmonary arrest.

The Pre-Hospital Trauma Life Support (PHTLS) course is a continuing education program created to provide EMS education in the handling of trauma patients.[30] The program is designed to enhance and increase knowledge and skill in delivering critical care in the pre-hospital environment.[31] The program includes identification of the mechanism of injury, recognition of life-threatening injuries, and content about the related pathophysiology as well as how to assess and manage trauma patients. The course was developed by the National Association of Emergency Medical Technicians (NAEMT) and the American College of Surgeons Committee on Trauma. The program also yields a certification card upon successful completion of a written and practical examination. Basic Trauma Life Support (BTLS) programs have varying degrees of credentialing from the basic for the EMT-B or First Responder to the Advanced for the paramedic or other advanced provider.[32] While similar in course content, the BTLS programs are credentialed through BTLS International and also offer course certification cards.

The Critical Care Emergency Medical Transport Program[SM] (CCEMTP) is designed to prepare nurses and paramedics to function effectively as members of a transport team.[33,34] The intensive program works to bridge the gap between hospital and pre-hospital care and transport for the team members. The program includes information on the special needs of the critically ill during transport and how to maintain the stability of hospital equipment and procedures during transport.[35] The program typically includes two weeks of classroom instruction and can include an optional thirty-two to forty-hour clinical component. The program offers a three year certification through the University of Maryland-Baltimore.

There are a number of other programs that specialize in educating pre-hospital and hospital professionals about specific patient populations such as burn victims, pediatric, obstetrical, and geriatric patients. A key to understanding the certification or credential is to look to the credentialing organization and determine the history of the organization and the requirements for instructor status. In addition, prerequisites for the program can give a clue to the level of difficulty of the program. The more pre-course requirements there are, the greater level of information is provided and tested during the course.

7.5 Types of Patient Transports

There are three basic types of patient transports

- from the scene of the accident or illness to the hospital,
- from the medical facility to medical facility, and
- from the medical facility to a patient's residence or long-term-care facility.

A. Emergency Transport

When a person has an injury or illness and cannot travel to a primary physician (if she has one), the patient calls for transport by an ambulance. A variety of providers offer this service. Public providers or private companies respond to these calls for assistance. Once a provider responds to a call, a legal duty to the caller is established. Dispatchers may also engage in directing treatment over the phone if they are trained and have the capability to do so. The documentation necessary for this type of transport should be comprehensive enough to accommodate the dispatch instructions if they are used and first responders' treatments if they are not involved in transport.

These reports should include the description of the location where the patient was picked up. An address or facility name is usually used. There should be sufficient patient identification information, including home address, phone number, Social Security number, or driver's license number if available, and the patient's date of birth. Some demographic information is generally used for statistical purposes. Response times should be noted, although some of the times in rural services may not be completed until the crew returns to the base so it may not be included in the patient care report that is left with the patient. The reason for the transport should be noted even if the actual provider impression is different. There are times that the patient verbalizes only one complaint. This should be thoroughly documented in addition to the actual physical assessment findings of the responding crew members. The assessment findings may differ from the complaints offered by the patient. For example, the patient may describe burning pain in the center of his chest as indigestion. The alert EMS crew would be assessing for signs of a heart attack and documenting color, pulse rate, intensity of pain, and so on. In this instance, clear documentation should state as to what was verbalized versus what were the actual physical findings by the EMS crew. Once the patient is being transported and treated, there should be significant detailed documentation on the patient assessment including

- vital signs, such as pulse, respiratory status, blood pressure,
- level of consciousness, and
- signs and symptoms of injury or illness.

The time the assessment was made should be recorded. Once the assessment is completed, there should be documentation of all therapies that are performed on the patient including status before and after each therapy. The more invasive the therapy, the more detailed the documentation must be.

TIP: If the paramedic places an endotracheal tube in the patient there must be a detailed assessment of the patient's respiratory and neurological status prior to and after the intubation. This should include verification of proper tube placement and the methods by which it was verified. The tube must be confirmed to be in place by several methods such as direct auscultation, end tidal CO_2 monitoring, esophageal detector devices or pulse oximetery.[36,37] There should be documentation of the respiratory status after the intubation and what steps were taken to maintain correct tube placement during transport.

Narrative documentation that supplements and supports all nonnarrative documentation of assessments and therapies (on flow sheets) performed during the transport should be completed. Any difficulties, incidents, or other factors that were encountered during the transport should be documented. The record needs to include a statement describing the condition of the patient when he arrived at the receiving facility and the name or signature of the person who received the patient report and took over the patient's care.

EMS professionals are expected to follow the appropriate standards of care. Careful stabilization of a potentially spinal-injured patient is essential, shown in the following case.

James T. Edwards v. Hillsborough County involved James T. Edwards, who was then twenty-nine years old, and who had suffered repetitive falls resulting in a head injury. 911 was called, and the 911 operator advised that Mr. Edwards should be moved, so he was placed into a chair. At that time, Mr. Edwards was able to move his arms and legs. Hillsborough County EMS responded, and the EMS run sheet documented the history that the patient fell down. EMS personnel grasped Mr. Edwards by the arms and legs and carried him with his body drooped in a "U" shaped position, then placed him on the stretcher for transfer to the emergency room. Upon arrival in the emergency room, Mr. Edwards was placed in a Philadelphia collar. The medical record documents that the patient was not previously immobilized, and no purposeful movement in the upper extremities or lower extremities was present, and priapism was noted. X-rays revealed subluxation of C6-C7 with spinal cord compromise. The plaintiff claimed the EMS paramedics failed to stabilize or immobilize Mr. Edwards' neck, head, or his spine prior to initiating movement and transport. The paramedics testified that head, neck, and back immobilization equipment was available to them, yet they did not follow the Hillsborough County protocol for patient transport, and they acknowledged failing to immobilize Mr. Edwards' neck and spine in any manner. The protocol also mandated that patients such as Mr. Edwards be transported to a trauma center. Mr. Edwards was instead transported by EMS to a local community hospital ill equipped to handle emergency care of his serious neurological injuries. The defendant initially disputed liability and advanced arguments that the plaintiff's condition was a proximate result of the falls that he sustained and not the result of negligence of the Hillsborough County paramedics. Ultimately this action was resolved in a $2,400,000 settlement, with the assistance of a claims bill passed by the Florida Legislature.[38]

In the case of *James T. Edwards v. Hillsborough County*, the plaintiff claimed that the EMS providers failed to stabilize and immobilize Mr. Edwards who had fallen and had documented abrasions and edema to the cranial area and had a Glasgow Coma Score of 9 (indicating a moderate head or brain injury). There are several areas that can be addressed. Mr. Edwards was involved in a fall, and he had motion of all four extremities upon the arrival of the EMS crew and documented head injuries. EMS has the duty to perform an examination sufficient enough to discover the presence of life-threatening conditions, even when the patient's initial presentation does not make him appear to be critically ill. In addition, the patient must be protected from further harm until a thorough medical evaluation can take place in a controlled environment such as an emergency department to rule out injuries such as spinal damage. High levels of suspicion should be maintained for neck injuries from falls. The adult skull weighs more than seventeen pounds and rests on a small segment of the cervical spine, similar to a bowling ball on a broom stick handle.[39] Sudden deceleration such as from a fall can generate sufficient force to fracture or dislocate the vertebrae.[40] Assumption of spinal cord injuries should be maintained until ruled out medically.

The duty to render appropriate care for potential spinal cord injuries was ignored. The treatment is the same regardless of where the potential spinal cord injuries are located. The skill of spinal immobilization from a seated position, such as the position in which Mr. Edwards was found, is a testable station during the National Registry of Emergency Medical Technicians licensure examination.[41] The emergency personnel should have performed assessment pre- and post-immobilization of sensory and motor function in all four extremities if the patient was responsive. Internal policies and procedures in this case were not followed when the patient was carried by the arms and legs, and no spinal precautions were initiated until the patient arrived without movement at the community hospital. In addition, had the EMS agency's protocols been followed, the patient would have initially been transported to a tertiary care facility where a higher level of care could have been rendered to minimize or eliminate potential long-term neurological deficits.

In this incident the EMS professionals failed to provide the level of care that was required by Mr. Edwards. Through this breach of duty Mr. Edwards was physically harmed. Prior to the treatment rendered by the EMS personnel, Mr. Edwards was able to move all extremities. After treatment his condition had significantly deteriorated.

B. Facility-to-Facility Transports

When a patient has a need that cannot be fulfilled at the facility, there must be a transport to a facility that can meet that need. This transport might be either emergent or non-emergent. The state-mandated documentation is still required. This pre-hospital care report (PCR) documentation varies from standardized trip sheets, that are computerized and sent into the state for review, to handwritten documentation. There may be additional records, including a physician statement that the transfer is medically necessary and an acknowledgment by the receiving facility's staff that they will accept the patient. The same documentation of assessments, signs, and symptoms of injury or illness, therapies, changes in the patient status, and a detailed narrative should be completed. Additionally, there may be records that are transferred from the sending facility to the receiving facility. In the following case, the plaintiff alleged that key documents indicating pain medication given to the patient were not sent with him.

In *Bryan McMullen v. Sherif T. Elamir, M.D.*, a Texas man who suffered a hip dislocation went to the hospital, where he was first given pain medication. He claimed that after he was transported to another hospital, the defendant doctor gave him inadequate pain medication, resulting in several hours of pain and suffering. The defendant argued that the patient's medication record did not arrive with him from the transferring hospital, and that once it did, the medications were adjusted appropriately. According to *East Texas Trial Reports*, the plaintiff reached a settlement with the ambulance company. The jury verdict was for the defendant doctor.[42]

There are facility-to-facility transfers in which the patient requires specialized care that is not within the scope of practice of the EMS crew. When this is the case, a healthcare provider such as a registered nurse, respiratory therapist, or even a physician may accompany the patient. In these situations, the documentation of the EMS crew might not be as detailed as that of the higher level provider because the crew is just operating the conveyance and not specifically performing primary care for the patient. Most often, the EMS patient care records refer the reader to the documentation of the healthcare provider who accompanied the patient and performed the assessments and treatments. A healthcare provider at the receiving facility may be asked to sign a form indicating transfer of responsibility. (Figure 7.5) In compliance with HIPAA (Health Insurance Portability and Accountability Act), the patient may be given a copy of the squad's privacy statement. (Figure 7.6)

Alarm Number _____   Date _____   **Eureka Fire Protection District**   Patient Name _____

No ECG Strip Attached

No ECG Strip Attached

I have received the transfer of care of the above named patient on this date from the Eureka Fire Protection District personnel and have received a report on the patient's condition, assessment, and therapies rendered to this patient by the Eureka Fire Protection District personnel.

Care Transferred To:

Signature _____

I have received a copy of the Private Health Information Policy of the Eureka Fire Protection District.

Patient Signature _____

Figure 7.5 Care transferral form—ECG strip.

Eureka Fire Protection District

Eureka, Missouri

Privacy Policy

[ ]   Copy of Private Health Information Policy left with Patient Care Report for patients that are unable to sign.

THIS NOTICE DESCRIBES HOW MEDICAL INFORMATION ABOUT YOU MAY BE USED AND DISCLOSED AND HOW YOU CAN GET ACCESS TO THIS INFORMATION. PLEASE REVIEW IT CAREFULLY.

Purpose of this Notice: Eureka Fire Protection District is required by law to maintain the privacy of certain confidential healthcare information, known as Protected Health Information or PHI, and to provide you with a notice of our legal duties and privacy practices with respect to your PHI. This Notice describes your legal rights, advises you of our privacy practices, and lets you know how Eureka Fire Protection District is permitted to use and disclose PHI about you.

Eureka Fire Protection District is also required to abide by the terms of the version of this Notice currently in effect. In most situations we may use this information as described in this Notice without your permission, but there are some situations where we may use it only after we obtain your written authorization, if we are required by law to do so.

Uses and Disclosures of PHI: Eureka Fire Protection District may use PHI for the purposes of treatment, payment, and healthcare operations, in most cases without your written permission. Examples of our use of your PHI:

For treatment. This includes such things as verbal and written information that we obtain about you and use pertaining to your medical condition and treatment provided to you by us and other medical personnel (including doctors and nurses who give orders to allow us to provide treatment to you). It also includes information we give to other healthcare personnel to whom we transfer your care and treatment, and includes transfer of PHI via radio or telephone to the hospital or dispatch center as well as providing the hospital with a copy of the written record we create in the course of providing you with treatment and transport.

For payment. This includes any activities we must undertake in order to get reimbursed for the services we provide to you, including such things as organizing your PHI and submitting bills to insurance companies (either directly or through a third party billing company), management of billed claims for services rendered, medical necessity determinations and reviews, utilization review, and collection of outstanding accounts.

For healthcare operations. This includes quality assurance activities, licensing, and training programs to ensure that our personnel meet our standards of care and follow established policies and procedures, obtaining legal and financial services, conducting business planning, processing grievances and complaints, creating reports that do not individually identify you for data collection purposes.

Reminders for Information on Other Services. We may also contact you to provide you with other information about alternative services we provide or other health-related benefits and services that may be of interest to you.

Use and Disclosure of PHI Without Your Authorization. Eureka Fire Protection District is permitted to use PHI without your written authorization, or opportunity to object in certain situations, including:

For Eureka Fire Protection District's use in treating you or in obtaining payment for services provided to you or in other healthcare operations;

For the treatment activities of another healthcare provider;

To another healthcare provider or entity for the payment activities of the provider or entity that receives the information (such as your hospital or insurance company);

To another healthcare provider (such as the hospital to which you are transported) for the healthcare operations activities of the entity that receives the information as long as the entity receiving the information has or has had a relationship with you and the PHI pertains to that relationship;

For healthcare fraud and abuse detection or for activities related to compliance with the law;

To a family member, other relative, or close personal friend or other individual involved in your care if we obtain your verbal agreement to do so or if we give you an opportunity to object to such a disclosure and you do not raise an objection. We may also disclose health information to your family, relatives, or friends if we infer from the circumstances that you would not object. For example, we may assume you agree to our disclosure of your personal health information to your spouse when your spouse has called the ambulance for you. In situations where you are not capable of objecting (because you are not present or due to your incapacity or medical emergency), we may, in our professional judgment, determine that a disclosure to your family member, relative, or friend is in your best interest. In that situation, we will disclose only health information relevant to that person's involvement in your care. For example, we may inform the person who accompanied you in the ambulance that you have certain symptoms and we may give that person an update on your vital signs and treatment that is being administered by our ambulance crew;

To a public health authority in certain situations (such as reporting a birth, death or disease as required by law, as part of a public health investigation, to report child or adult abuse or neglect or domestic violence, to report adverse events such as product defects, or to notify a person about exposure to a possible communicable disease as required by law;

For health oversight activities including audits or government investigations, inspections, disciplinary proceedings, and other administrative or judicial actions undertaken by the government (or their contractors) by law to oversee the healthcare system;

For judicial and administrative proceedings as required by a court or administrative order, or in some cases in response to a subpoena or other legal process;

For law enforcement activities in limited situations, such as when there is a warrant for the request, or when the information is needed to locate a suspect or stop a crime;

For military, national defense and security and other special government functions;

To avert a serious threat to the health and safety of a person or the public at large;

For workers' compensation purposes, and in compliance with workers' compensation laws;

To coroners, medical examiners, and funeral directors for identifying a deceased person, determining cause of death, or carrying on their duties as authorized by law;

Figure 7.6 Privacy policy—Eureka, MO.

If you are an organ donor, we may release health information to organizations that handle organ procurement or organ, eye or tissue transplantation or to an organ donation bank, as necessary to facilitate organ donation and transplantation;

For research projects, but this will be subject to strict oversight and approvals and health information will be released only when there is a minimal risk to your privacy and adequate safeguards are in place in accordance with the law;

We may use or disclose health information about you in a way that does not personally identify you or reveal who you are.

Any other use or disclosure of PHI, other than those listed above will only be made with your written authorization, (the authorization must specifically identify the information we seek to use or disclose, as well as when and how we seek to use or disclose it). You may revoke your authorization at any time, in writing, except to the extent that we have already used or disclosed medical information in reliance on that authorization.

Patient Rights: As a patient, you have a number of rights with respect to the protection of your PHI, including:

The right to access, copy or inspect your PHI. This means you may come to our offices and inspect and copy most of the medical information about you that we maintain. We will normally provide you with access to this information within 30 days of your request. We may also charge you a reasonable fee for you to copy any medical information that you have the right to access. In limited circumstances, we may deny you access to your medical information, and you may appeal certain types of denials.

We have available forms to request access to your PHI and we will provide a written response it we deny you access and let you know your appeal rights. If you wish to inspect and copy your medical information, you should contact the privacy officer listed at the end of this Notice.

The right to amend your PHI. You have the right to ask us to amend written medical information that we may have about you. We will generally amend your information within 60 days of your request and will notify you when we have amended the information. We are permitted by law to deny your request to amend your medical information only in certain circumstances, like when we believe the information you have asked us to amend is correct. If you wish to request that we amend the medical information that we have about you, you should contact the privacy officer listed at the end of this Notice.

The right to request an accounting of our use and disclosure of your PHI. You may request an accounting from us of certain disclosures of your medical information that we have made in the last six years prior to the date of your request. We are not required to give you an accounting of information we have used or disclosed for purposes of treatment, payment or healthcare operations, or when we share your health information with our business associates, like our billing company or a medical facility from/to which we have transported you.

We are also not required to give you an accounting of our uses of protected health information for which you have already given us written authorization. If you wish to request an accounting of the medical information about you that we have used or disclosed that is not exempted from the accounting requirement, you should contact the privacy officer listed at the end of this Notice.

The right to request that we restrict the uses and disclosures of your PHI. You have the right to request that we restrict how we use and disclose your medical information that we have about you for treatment, payment or healthcare operations, or to restrict the information that is provided to family, friends and other individuals involved in your health care. But if you request a restriction and the information you asked us to restrict is needed to provide you with emergency treatment, then we may use the PHI or disclose the PHI to a healthcare provider to provide you with emergency treatment. Eureka Fire Protection District is not required to agree to any restrictions you request, but any restrictions agreed to by Eureka Fire Protection District are binding on Eureka Fire Protection District.

Internet, Electronic Mail, and the Right to Obtain Copy of Paper Notice on Request. If we maintain a website, we will prominently post a copy of this Notice on our website and make the Notice available electronically through the website. If you allow us, we will forward you this Notice by electronic mail instead of on paper and you may always request a paper copy of the Notice.

Revisions to the Notice: Eureka Fire Protection District reserves the right to change the terms of this Notice at any time, and the changes will be effective immediately and will apply to all protected health information that we maintain. Any material changes to the Notice will be promptly posted in our facilities and posted to our website, if we maintain one. You can get a copy of the latest version of this Notice by contacting the Privacy Officer identified below.

Your Legal Rights and Complaints: You also have the right to complain to us, or to the Secretary of the United States Department of Health and Human Services if you believe your privacy rights have been violated. You will not be retaliated against in any way for filing a complaint with us or to the government. Should you have any questions, comments or complaints you may direct all inquiries to the privacy officer listed at the end of this Notice. Individuals will not be retaliated against for filing a complaint.

If you have any questions or if you wish to file a complaint or exercise any rights listed in this Notice, please contact:

Eureka Fire Protection District
Eureka, Missouri

Effective Date of the Notice: October 1, 2003
Eureka Fire Protection District
Notice of Privacy Practices

IMPORTANT: THIS NOTICE DESCRIBES HOW MEDICAL INFORMATION ABOUT YOU MAY BE USED AND DISCLOSED AND HOW YOU CAN GET ACCESS TO THIS INFORMATION. PLEASE REVIEW IT CAREFULLY.

As an essential part of our commitment to you, Eureka Fire Protection District maintains the privacy of certain confidential healthcare information about you, known as Protected Health Information or PHI. We are required by law to protect your healthcare information and to provide you with the attached Notice of Privacy Practices.

The Notice outlines our legal duties and privacy practices respect to your PHI. It not only describes our privacy practices and your legal rights, but lets you know, among other things, how Eureka Fire Protection District is permitted to use and disclose PHI about you, how you can access and copy that information, how you may request amendment of that information, and how you may request restrictions on our use and disclosure of your PHI.

Eureka Fire Protection District is also required to abide by the terms of the version of this Notice currently in effect. In most situations we may use this information as described in this Notice without your permission, but there are some situations where we may use it only after we obtain your written authorization, if we are required by law to do so.

We respect your privacy, and treat all healthcare information about our patients with care under strict policies of confidentiality that all of our staff are committed to following at all times.

PLEASE READ THE DETAILED NOTICE. IF YOU HAVE ANY QUESTIONS ABOUT IT, PLEASE CONTACT OUR PRIVACY OFFICER.

Figure 7.6 *Privacy policy—Eureka, MO. (continued)*

C. Facility to Home or Nursing Home

There may be a need to return a discharged patient home for further convalescence or to a rehabilitation or nursing facility. Commonly these patients cannot be transported without an ambulance. The state defines documentation for these transports. The patient condition that requires ambulance transfer should be documented on the report as well as initial assessment of the patient including basic vital signs. Details of the patient's condition on arrival at the receiving facility or the patient's home should be documented as well as reassessment of the patient as needed. There may be no one at the home to receive the patient. EMS crews should document if the patient is received at home by someone or if the patient is going to be left alone. (Figure 7.7)

A routine transportation from a dialysis center to a home can turn into a medical emergency, as the following case describes.

> A seventy-one year-old woman was being transported by the defendant ambulance company from a dialysis center to her home. As the ambulance employees were wheeling her on a stretcher through the parking lot, the wheels of the stretcher became stuck in a large rut in the pavement. The stretcher tipped over, causing the woman to fall and strike her head on the pavement. The woman was secured with every available strap on the stretcher, but suffered severe head injuries; she died three days later. The plaintiff claimed the EMTs failed to maintain a proper lookout and navigate the parking lot appropriately. Discovery revealed a report from a quality improvement manager from the ambulance company which determined that the incident was caused by both the inattention of the ambulance personnel and the unsatisfactorily maintained parking lot. A $750,000 settlement was reached.[43]

7.6 Transport and Crew Responsibilities
A. Patient Safety

EMS professionals are responsible for a wide range of activities during patient care and transport. The key to a successful transport is the assurance of the safety of the crew and the patient. It is not possible to help the patient if the EMS crew is injured before care can be rendered, so the first area of responsibility is to keep them safe.[44] Though typically emergency scenes are usually safe, they can also be unpredictable and care must be taken at all times to ensure everyone's safety.

The driver of an emergency vehicle is expected to use care when rushing to or from an accident scene. The same hazards that are present for the EMS provider are present for the patient and bystanders at an accident scene. The EMS professionals must be concerned with their safety as well as the safety of those in their care and in the immediate area of the response scene.

TIP: Incidents that affect patient safety must be documented on the patient care report. These can include motor vehicle crashes, patient handling accidents, medication or treatment errors, or even if the crew uses all safety equipment while transporting the patient.

It is a troubling fact that emergency crews attempting to help others are sometimes risking their own lives. There have been several instances in which EMS crews have been shot, wounded, or died while doing their job. In February 2004, a lieutenant with the Lexington Kentucky Fire Department was shot and killed after she responded to a call for help. In Kansas City, Missouri, a paramedic was shot when a sniper opened fire on emergency crews at the scene of a house explosion.[45] Any situation that imperils the EMS crew needs to be fully described and documented in the crew's report. A major cause of EMS crew injuries and deaths are vehicle accidents.

B. Life-Threatening Transport

The most crucial ambulance transport is reserved for those patients who would die without the initial stabilizing treatment and rapid transport to an appropriate facility. These transports range from 4 percent of the patients transported as reported by the Eureka Missouri Fire Protection District to as much as 60 percent of the total ambulance transports in the City of New York.[46,47] The patients who are transported when they have a life-threatening illness also need the most interventions by the crew.

> A Massachusetts case involved a three-year-old boy who choked on a piece of candy in a store. An ambulance arrived; the paramedics placed an endotracheal tube. It was not inserted into the lungs, caused hypoxia, cardiac arrest and permanent brain damage. The plaintiffs claimed the endotracheal tube was placed into the esophagus instead of the trachea. During the discovery process, the plaintiffs sought access to various records of the defendant regarding the incident, particularly the records prepared in connection with the cardiac monitor strips. The documents could never be found. The defendant contended the tube was properly inserted. The court ruled that the plaintiff would be entitled to a spoliation of evidence instruction. The parties then settled for $1.3 million.[48]

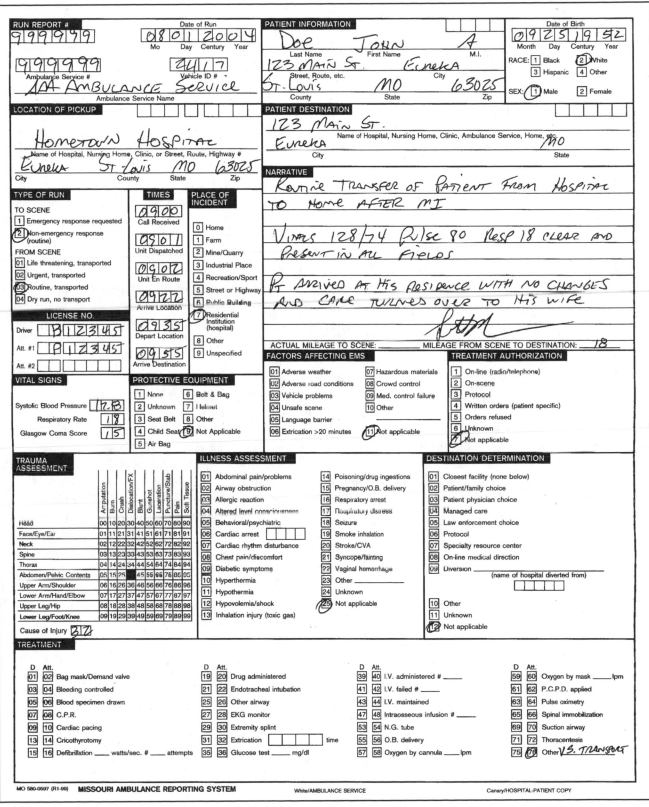

Figure 7.7 *Out of hospital license manager (computerized)—routine transfer home.*

There needs to be a greater detailed documentation since they require more treatments. These are the patients who would die if interventions were not provided by the EMS crews. Medication therapies to counteract allergic reactions, IV therapy for trauma patients, and advanced airway management procedures are all examples of treatment that is necessary for patients with life threats. See Figure 7.8 for a patient care report example.

C. Urgent Transports

The vast majority of emergency transports are urgent in nature but not life threatening. These make up from 96 percent of patients transported in the Eureka Fire Protection District to only 40 percent of the total ambulance transports in the City of New York.[49,50] While not as treatment intensive as life-threatening transports, many treatments are performed for these patients, requiring thorough documentation. There needs to be adequate documentation since treatments are performed. Examples of urgently transported patients might include a patient with a fractured ankle from a skiing accident to a person who suffers from dehydration while working outside on a very hot day. Figure 7.9 is an example of an urgent transport patient care report.

D. Routine Transports

When patients are transported from facility to facility for routine appointments or therapy, the documentation needed is significantly less than if treatments are being performed on the patient. Often patients need to go to another facility for a diagnostic test or outpatient procedure. Skilled nursing facilities may have to send residents to get x-rays, CT scans, MRIs or other diagnostic procedures and the resident can not travel by car or van. In this situation, the ambulance is just conveying the resident. The crews are simply monitoring the resident's status and not providing treatments or other therapies.

TIP: Routine transport documentation tends to be brief and concise because the crews are observing but not treating the patient.

E. Patient Restraints

Patient restraints are sometimes necessary for the safety of the patient and the crew. Patients prone to violence or who cannot follow commands may need to be restrained.

Pre-hospital providers do not routinely use medications to restrain patients. However, during routine transports pre-medication may be used when the physician determines that it is most appropriate. If this approach is used there must be documentation accompanying the patient that includes the medication used, the dose, and specific instructions on emergency procedures.

Physical restraints are common tools used by ambulance crews under strict medical direction. Most medical directors have established criteria for physical restraint use and the documentation that must be completed. Patients needing to be physically restrained are those who pose a safety threat to themselves or others due to intoxication, mental disorders, or other physiological criteria. Physically restraining a patient is not undertaken lightly. Often additional crew members are brought for support for the patient that has to be restrained. The rear of the ambulance is not without its share of potential weapons. (Figure 7.10) During transport an unrestrained patient with violent intent can create a perilous situation for the crew.

7.7 Medical Direction

Every pre-hospital provider must be supervised by a medical director. This physician assumes the ultimate responsibility of the medical direction, or the oversight of the patient care aspects, of the EMS system. What this means varies greatly from state to state and from medical director to medical director. Most medical direction involves standing orders or protocols that the crew can follow when the patient meets the criteria established in that protocol. The EMS professional is operating as a designated agent of the physician.[51] The EMS professional has the authority to give medications and provide emergency care as an actual extension of the medical director's license to practice medicine, even though the physician may not even be in verbal contact with the responding unit when care is rendered.

EMS systems have developed standing orders because physicians cannot be always accessible. These policies and procedures are approved by the medical director and authorize the EMS professional to perform particular tasks or skills based in certain situations.[52] An example of a standing order may be to administer oxygen to a patient who is in congestive heart failure without waiting to speak to a physician in the medical control emergency department. (Figure 7.11)

```
Service No  189049              OUT OF HOSPITAL CARE REPORT          Unit No.  2417
Inci#  04-9999999   Pt#  0001         License Manager                Alarm Date 08/01/2004
FDID#  09518
```

Incident No 04-9999999 Onset Date / / Onset Time	Location Type
Crash No Trauma ID 911 Used 2 E911	5 Street or Highway
Scene Address Station 1 Shift N	Response Code to Scene
I 44 EAST BOUND & ANTIRE RD /EUREKA, MO 63025	1 Emergency
	Highest Experience Level at Scene
	3 Paramedic/Firefighter
Township EU District 02 County STLCO Census 2215.00	Lights & Siren to Scene?
Mutual Aid None Occupancy	4 Emergent, with lights or siren

Patient # 000001 Name DOE, JOHN A	Times	Response Analysis
Address 123 MAIN ST	Dispatch Notified 09:00:00	Dispatch 00:00:00
	Unit Notified 09:00:00	En Route 00:02:00
Rm Phone		
City Eureka St MO Zip 63025	Unit Enroute 09:02:00	To Scene 00:03:00
Race White Gender M DOB (09/25/1951) Age 52 yrs 10 mos	Arrived Scene 09:05:00	To Pt/Vict 00:00:00
SSN 111-11-1111 Primary Physician		On Scene 00:10:00
Dispatched For MVC	Arrived Pt/Vict 09:05:00	Transport 00:20:00
Type of Service 1 Emergency Response Requested	Enroute to Dest 09:15:00	
Chief Complaint		Tot Resp Time 01:00:00
Provider Impression T22 MVC, driver	Arrived Dest 09:35:00	
Tx Authorization 1 On-line		Out of Srv 01:15:00
Injury Sustained? Yes	Cleared 10:00:00	ALS Response
Injury Intent 3 Unintentional	Back in Service 10:15:00	Total Miles
Mechanism of Injury NA Not Applicable		
Human Factors Affecting Care	ALS Arrival	Loaded Miles 18.00

Patient Prior Medical History	Factors Affecting EMS Care	Prior EMS Care Given	Safety Equipt Worn by Patient
13 None	11 Not Applicable		1 None

Injury/Illness Detail

Type	Area	Severity	Primary Symptom	Job Rel?

Basic Vitals

Time	LOC	Airway	Resp Rythm-Effort/Qlty	Pulse Rythm/Quality	Skin	Cap Refill	Bleeding	Pupils-L/R	Posture
09:06:00	V	Head Tilt -		Regul-Thready	Normal	2 secs	Hemorrhage	1 / 1	Supine
09:16:00	V	Head Tilt -		Regul-Thready	Normal	2 secs	Hemorrhage	1 / 1	Supine
09:26:00	V	Head Tilt -		Regul-Thready	Normal	2 secs	Hemorrhage	1 / 1	Supine

Secondary Vitals

Time	Pulse	Resp	Temp	BP	PaO2	Skin Appearance	Eye/Mtr/Vrbl	GCS	RTS	Cardiac
09:06:00	110	12	Unk	90/60	92mmHg	Moist/Diaphoretic	4 6 4	14	12	Sinus Rhythm
09:16:00	100	Unk	N/A	100/0*	98mmHg	Moist/Diaphoretic	4 6 4	14	99	Sinus Rhythm
09:26:00	94	Unk	N/A	110/0*	98mmHg	Moist/Diaphoretic	4 6 4	14	99	Sinus Rhythm

* Denotes Blood Pressure Reading by Palpation or Doppler

Procedures Performed

P - Procedure Failed

Time	Procedure	Notes	Staff Id	Attempts
09:06:00	P02 Bag mask/Demand valve		241060	1
09:06:00	P04 Bleeding controlled		241060	1
09:06:00	P76 Assessment, Vital Signs, Transp		241060	1
09:07:00	P68 Spinal immobilization		241060	1
09:07:00	P64 Pulse oximetry		241060	1
09:08:00	P40 IV administered	X 2 R AND L AC 500 CC BOLUS EACH 14 GA ANGIOCATH	241060	1
09:09:00	P70 Suction airway		241060	1
09:10:00	P22 Oral or Nasal tracheal Intubati	7.5 MM TUBE CLEAR LUNG SOUNDS R ABSENT LEFT 22 CM	241060	1
09:12:00	P72 Thoracentesis	NEEDLE DECOMPRESSION LEFT CHEST GOOD LUNG SOUNDS A	241060	1

```
08/04/2004       08:49                                              Page     1
```

Figure 7.8 *Motor vehicle accident report.*

```
Service No  189049                    OUT OF HOSPITAL CARE REPORT              Unit No.  2417
Inci#  04-9999999    Pt#  0001              License Manager                    Alarm Date 08/01/2004
FDID#  09518
```

Exposure Precautions Taken

Staff Member	Precaution Type
241052 Steve Mann	02 Gloves
241060 Scott Mullins	02 Gloves

Medications Administered

Time	Medication	Staff Id	Dosage

Disposition

Transported to D30 Not Listed	Dest Determined by 07 Specialty Resource Center
Mode of Transport 01 Ground	Diverted To
Agency Tiered With	Patient Disposition 01 Life threatening, transported
Lights/Siren from Scene? Emergent, with lights or siren	Pulse on Transfer NA Not Applicable

Insurance

Type	Policy #	Group #	Insured Name

Patient Narrative

RESPONDED FOR A MVC. ON SCENE EXTRICATED 52 Y/O MALE PATIENT UNRESTRAINED DRIVER OF A ROLLOVER HIGH SPEED MVC.
PATIENT RESPONDS TO VERBAL STIMULI PATIENT SNORING RESP 12 PER MINUTE. AIRWAY OPENED WITH JAW THRUST. PATIENT
EXTRICATED TO BACKBOARD WITH FULL SPINAL IMMOBILIZATION. ENROUTE ORAL AIRWAY INSERTED. MEDICAL CONTROL CONTACTED WITH
REPORT AND RECEIVED ORDERS FOR INTUBATION AND IV FLUID BOLUS. PAT IENT INTUBATED AS ABOVE. LUNG SOUNDS ABSENT LEFT
SIDE. NEEDLE DECOMPRESSION COMPLETED TO PATIENT LEFT CHEST. GOOD LUNG SOUNDS ALL FIELDS. VITALS ASSESSED AS ABOVE.
SECONDARY SURVEY PATIENT HAS MULTIPE LACERATIONS AND ABRASIONS TO HEAD CHEST AND LOWER EXTREMITIES. POSSIBLE BILATERAL
FEMUR FRACTURES. IV'S ESTABLISHED AS ABOVE VITALS REASSESSED. PATIENT VENTILATED 20 X PER MINUTE WITH 100% O2.
ARRIVED AT TRAUMA CENTER AND TURNED OVER CARE TO TRAUMA TEAM IN ROOM 4

Officer/Member Making

```
Signature_____          Signature_____
Officer Name   Mullins, Scott                      Member Name Mullins, Scott
                              08/04/2004                                      08/04/2004


Signature_____
Attending Physician
```

Figure 7.8 *Motor vehicle accident report. (continued)*

```
Service No  189049              OUT OF HOSPITAL CARE REPORT          Unit No.  2417
Inci#  04-9999999   Pt#  0001          License Manager              Alarm Date  08/01/2004
FDID#  09518
```

Incident No 04-9999999 Onset Date / / Onset Time	Location Type
Crash No Trauma ID 911 Used 2 E911	0 Home
Scene Address Station 1 Shift N	Response Code to Scene
123 MAIN ST /Eureka, MO 63025	1 Emergency
	Highest Experience Level at Scene
	3 Paramedic/Firefighter
Township EU District 02 County STLCO Census 2215.00	Lights & Siren to Scene?
Mutual Aid None Occupancy	4 Emergent, with lights or siren

Patient # 000001 Name DOE, JOHN A		Times	Response Analysis
Address 123 MAIN ST		Dispatch Notified 09:00:00	Dispatch 00:00:00
	Rm Phone	Unit Notified 09:00:00	En Route 00:02:00
City Eureka	St MO Zip 63025	Unit Enroute 09:02:00	To Scene 00:03:00
Race White Gender M DOB {09/25/1951} Age 52 yrs 10 mos		Arrived Scene 09:05:00	To Pt/Vict 00:00:00
SSN 111-11-1111 Primary Physician		Arrived Pt/Vict 09:05:00	On Scene 00:15:00
Dispatched For CHEST PAIN			Transport 00:20:00
Type of Service 1 Emergency Response Requested		Enroute to Dest 09:20:00	
Chief Complaint			Tot Resp Time 01:00:00
Provider Impression M08 Chest Pain/Discomfort		Arrived Dest 09:40:00	
Tm Authorisation 1 On-line			Out of Srv 01:15:00
Injury Sustained? No		Cleared 10:00:00	ALS Response
Injury Intent 3 Unintentional			
Mechanism of Injury NA Not Applicable		Back in Service 10:15:00	Total Miles
Human Factors Affecting Care		ALS Arrival	Loaded Miles 18.00

Patient Prior Medical History	Factors Affecting EMS Care	Prior EMS Care Given	Safety Equipt Worn by Patient
13 None	11 Not Applicable		9 Not Applicable

Injury/Illness Detail

Type	Area	Severity	Primary Symptom	Job Rel?

Basic Vitals

Time	LOC	Airway	Resp Rythm-Effort/Qlty	Pulse Rythm/Quality	Skin	Cap Refill	Bleeding	Pupils-L/R	Posture
09:08:00	A	Patent			Normal	N/A	None	1 / 1	Supine
09:12:00	A	Patent			Normal	N/A	None	1 / 1	Supine
09:20:00	A	Patent			Normal	N/A	None	1 / 1	Supine
09:30:00	A	Patent			Normal	N/A	None	1 / 1	Supine
09:35:00	A	Patent			Normal	N/A	None	1 / 1	Supine

Secondary Vitals

Time	Pulse	Resp	Temp	BP	PaO2	Skin Appearance	Eye/Mtr/Vrbl			GCS	RTS	Cardiac
09:08:00	80	18	N/A	146/84	98mmHg	Normal	4	6	5	15	12	Sinus Rhythm
09:12:00	76	16	N/A	146/84	99mmHg	Normal	4	6	5	15	12	Sinus Rhythm
09:20:00	76	16	N/A	140/80	99mmHg	Normal	4	6	5	15	12	Sinus Rhythm
09:30:00	78	16	N/A	142/82	99mmHg	Normal	4	6	5	15	12	Sinus Rhythm
09:35:00	78	16	N/A	142/80	99mmHg	Normal	4	6	5	15	12	Sinus Rhythm

```
08/04/2004        07:37                                              Page      1
```

Figure 7.9 *Urgent transport report.*

```
Service No  189049                OUT OF HOSPITAL CARE REPORT          Unit No.  2417
Inci#  04-9999999   Pt#  0001           License Manager               Alarm Date 08/01/2004
FDID#  09518
```

* Denotes Blood Pressure Reading by Palpation or Doppler

Procedures Performed

Time	Procedure	Notes		Staff Id	F - Procedure Failed Attempts
09:10:00	P64 Pulse oximetry			241060	1
09:10:00	P28 EKG monitor	SINUS RHYTHM		241060	1
09:10:00	P76 Assessment, Vital Signs, Transp			241060	1
09:11:00	P60 Oxygen by mask	15 LPM NRB		241060	1
09:14:00	P40 IV administered	NS 1000 ML, TKO RATE 18 GA 1 1/4" LEFT AC		241060	1

Exposure Precautions Taken

Staff Member	Precaution Type
241052 Steve Mann	02 Gloves
241060 Scott Mullins	02 Gloves

Medications Administered

Time	Medication	Staff Id	Dosage
09:14:00	19 Normal Saline	241060	
09:15:00	34 Baby Aspirin	241060	325 Milligram
09:18:00	18 Nitroglycerin	241060	0.04 Milligra
09:23:00	18 Nitroglycerin	241060	0.04 Milligra
09:23:00	18 Nitroglycerin	241060	0.04 Milligra
09:32:00	16 Morphine	241060	2 Milligrams

Disposition

```
Transported to  D30 Not Listed           Dest Determined by  02 Patient/Family Choice
Mode of Transport  01 Ground              Diverted To
Agency Tiered With                        Patient Disposition 02 Urgent, transported
Lights/Siren from Scene?  Emergent, with lights or siren    Pulse on Transfer   NA Not Applicable
```

Insurance

Type	Policy #	Group #	Insured Name

Patient Narrative

RESPONDED TO A RESIDENCE FOR A PATIENT WITH A CC OF CHEST PAIN. ON SCENE PATIENT IS A 52 Y/O MALE C/AX3 WITH COMPLAINT OF SUB STERNAL CHEST PAIN AN 8 ON A 1-10 SCALE. ASSESSED VITALS AS ABOVE. PLACED PATIENT ON O2 15 LPM PER NRB MASK. ATTACHED ECG MONITOR SHOWING SINUS RHYTHM. CONTACTED MEDICAL CONTROL ENROUTE WITH REPORT.   RECEIVED ORDERS FOR IV NS TKO, ASPIRIN 325 MG PO, NITRO .04 MG X 3 Q 5 MINUTES BASED ON PAIN. IF PATIENT NOT PAIN FREE AFTER NITRO MORPHINE SULFATE 2 MG EVERY 5 MINUTES UNTIL PATIENT PAIN FREE. IV ESTABLISHED AND ASPIRIN ADMINISTERED, NITRO ADMINISTERED. VITALS REASSESSED AS ABOVE. PAIN NOW A 6. SECOND NITRO GIVEN AFTER 5 MINUTES PAIN NOW A 4 THIRD NITRO GIVEN AFTER 5 MINUTES PAIN NOW A 2. VITALS REASSESSED AS ABOVE. MORPHINE 2 MG GIVEN IV PUSH AFTER FIVE MINUTES PATIENT NOW PAIN FREE. ARRIVED AT HOSPITAL AND TURNED OVER CARE OF PATIENT TO ER NURSE IN ROOM 4

Officer/Member Making

```
Signature_____          Signature_____
Officer Name  Mullins, Scott          08/04/2004           Member Name Mullins, Scott          08/04/2004


Signature_____
Attending Physician
```

```
08/04/2004        07:37                                                        Page    2
```

Figure 7.9 Urgent transport report. *(continued)*

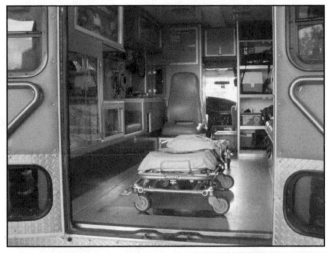

Figure 7.10 Ambulance.

POLICY AND PROCEDURE MANUAL FOR PRE-HOSPITAL EMS
Office of Paramedic Education

CATEGORY: Pre-Hospital Patient Care

TITLE: Adult Cardiac Emergencies—Congestive Heart Failure

Characterized by respiratory distress, basilar crackles (rales), jugular vein distension and possible peripheral edema.

1.   Establish and maintain an airway; administer oxygen at 12-15 liters per minute if tolerated well by the patient. Assist ventilations as necessary.

2.   Obtain vital signs and a brief history, noting the onset of dyspnea, any associated chest pain, and any prescribed medications the patient is taking. Place the patient on a cardiac, oxygen saturation, and CO2 monitor (if available).

3.   Sit the patient upright and let his legs dangle.

4.   Contact medical control with patient report and request orders. If, for whatever reason, contact with medical control cannot be established, pre-hospital emergency healthcare, professionals may continue as follows:
     a)   Establish an IV line of Normal Saline at a TKO rate.

5.   Medical Control may give further orders including:
     a)   Nitroglycerin tablet(s) sublingually if BP>100 mm Hg. systolic or Nitrolingual spray sublingually
     b)   Furosemide (Lasix) 40 mg. IV push
     c)   Morphine Sulfate 2-4 mg. IV push
     d)   Patients with CHF should never receive albuterol
     e)   Transport the patient to the hospital in an upright position. Monitor vital signs, respiratory status and cardiac rhythm en route.

Effective Date: October 1, 1993   Revision Date: August 12, 1999

Figure 7.11 Policy and procedure—cardiac emergencies.

A medical director may provide direct supervision via radio or telephone for more complex cases and rely less on standing orders. There are almost always certain procedures or situations where the medical director will require contact. These can include

- the administration of narcotic medications,
- refusal of care,
- do not resuscitate documents,
- major invasive skills, including
- endotracheal intubation,
- surgical cricothyrotomy (allows rapid entrance into the airway for temporary ventilation and oxygenation of patients for whom the airway control is not possible by other methods), and
- pericardiocentesis (insertion of a large hollow needle into the pericardial sac surrounding the heart to remove accumulated fluid), to name a few.[53, 54]

These situations tend to have a greater liability associated with them so the situation warrants medical direction and detailed documentation.

Medical directors also are involved with the educational aspect of the pre-hospital provider's work. Continuing education is a requirement for all EMS providers. The medical director must insure quality of care by conducting evaluation of selected calls and review of the EMTs' and paramedics' skills to assure that the patient is getting the best treatment possible. Much of the review and follow up is based on the documentation provided by the EMS professional.

7.8 Documentation

TIP: There are multiple methods of documentation in use in the pre-hospital arena. The most common are the traditional paper-based records. Recently, electronic formats are becoming more prevalent.

No matter what format is used, there are several items that should be documented in the patient care report. There should be as much patient identification information as possible. The patient's name, address, date of birth, Social Security number, telephone number, and insurance information should be recorded. The scene of the incident or where patient contact was first made should be noted, as well as the date. Specific times, including when the call was received by the dispatcher, when the units were dispatched, when the units responded, when they arrived at the scene, when they departed the scene for the hospital, and when they arrived at the hospital, should be documented. Additionally, the time the crew was available or returned to service should be noted. These times can establish the time frame that the patient was experiencing the injury or illness. Comparison can be made with the recorded progress of the patient in the emergency department. For instance, if a patient was exhibiting the signs and symptoms of a stroke and was being transported from a rural facility, she might not be a candidate for specific therapies due to the time of transport. Initial patient assessment findings should be noted as well as continuing assessments, especially after therapies. There should be a pre-therapy assessment and a post-therapy assessment. Routine assessments should be based on the patient's condition. Assessments would be documented closer together for the more serious patients and farther apart for the less serious patients. All therapies should be thoroughly documented. Changes in patient status should be noted as the transport takes place. Patient medical history, medications, and allergies should be documented as well. The identity of the person accepting the patient should also be recorded. A rule of thumb is that the care of the patient should never be turned over to a person of lesser experience or licensure than the EMS provider. Most patients are relinquished to a nurse or a physician in the emergency department.

Specific protocols and therapies may direct documentation. The issues of patient restraint and refusal of care are of particular importance for detailed documentation and are explained further in the chapter.

Abbreviations are frequently used for the sake of expediency when completing patient care reports. Often these abbreviations take the form of a kind of shorthand and are not decipherable except by the writer. Since this would prove to be impossible to interpret by anyone other than the writer, many medical direction physicians publish approved abbreviations within their protocols and standing orders. The appendix of this textbook includes abbreviations that are often noted in EMS records.

In addition to abbreviations, there are also many terms that are used to describe the kinematics or mechanism of the injury by the EMS provider. These descriptions are important in that they lead the healthcare providers to suspect occult or hidden injuries based on the mechanism of injury. For example, an adult jumps from a window and lands on his feet. He then complains of bilateral heel pain. A corresponding lumbar injury should be suspected until proven otherwise due to the mechanism of injury. An appropriate description of the events surrounding the injury should be thoroughly documented. Commonly used terms are described below.

A. T-Bone

A T-bone is a description of a side impact collision when one vehicle strikes a second vehicle directly on the side. (Figure 7.12) The EMS record may include a description of the number of inches or feet of intrusion. This term refers to how far the car was dented by the second vehicle. The medical record of the person sitting next to the side of the car that was hit may describe injuries on the side of the body next to the damaged portion of the car. Additionally, the individual may be thrown into other portions of the interior of the car, sustaining injuries on other parts of the body.

Figure 7.12 *T bone.*

B. Head On

This term is a description used to describe a motor vehicle crash where one vehicle strikes another vehicle front to front. (Figure 7.13) This occurs when the individual is pushed forward and backward by the impact. Intrusion of the engine into the passenger compartment may result in the crushing of extremities or the chest from impact with the steering wheel or dashboard. The medical record may describe bruising on the chest or knees.

Figure 7.13 *Head on.*

C. Rear End

This occurs when one vehicle strikes another from the rear (Figure 7.14). This type of impact may result in acceleration/deceleration injuries. Complaints of neck, low back, and head injuries are commonly documented.

Figure 7.14 *Rear end.*

D. CID

A cervical immobilization device is used to maintain stabilization of the cervical spine of patients in which the mechanism of injury leads one to suspect a cervical spine injury (Figure 7.15).

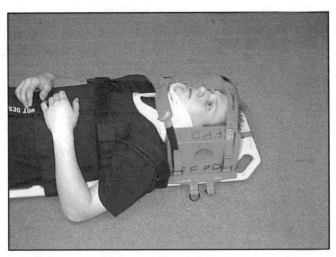

Figure 7.15 *CID.*

E. C-Collar

A cervical collar is a device that is also used to assist in the maintenance of stabilization of the cervical spine of patients where there is mechanism to suspect a cervical spine injury. Hard cervical collars are typically applied when trauma to the cervical spine is likely (Figure 7.16).

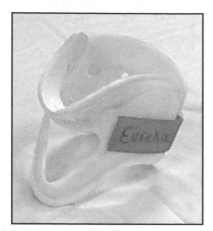

Figure 7.16 C-collar.

F. KED

A Kendrick Extrication Device is a tool used to help extricate victims of motor vehicle accidents. (Figure 7.17) The medical record may document the amount of time it took to extricate the patient from the vehicle. Documentation of extrication time is imperative in pre-hospital records based on the accepted theory that there is a "Golden Hour" for a serious trauma patient to begin definitive treatment. The documentation of the time of extrication becomes crucial for the patient care report.[55] Extended extrication times greatly reduce the pre-hospital provider's ability to deliver a trauma patient to a trauma center for definitive care within the "Golden Hour." Many studies have shown that there is a greatly increased mortality rate if the seriously injured trauma patient does not receive definitive care within the "Golden Hour."[56]

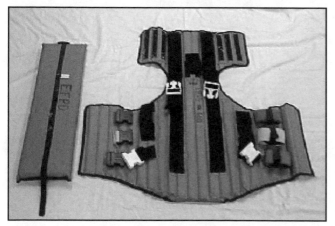

Figure 7.17 KED.

G. Traction Splint

Traction splints are designed to be used by patients who have upper leg fractures. They have a variety of names and manufacturers and are often referred to by the manufacturer's name like Hare® Traction Splint or Segar® splints. The concept behind the traction splint is to place traction on the leg to stabilize the fractures and minimize further injury and decrease bleeding. (Figure 7.18)

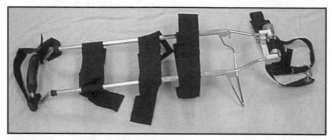

Figure 7.18 Traction splint.

H. PASG or MAST

Pneumatic Anti Shock Garment and Medical Anti Shock Trousers are devices designed to improve blood pressure for patients who have multiple system trauma. There are significant research controversies with these devices. (Figure 7.19)[57,58]

Figure 7.19 PASG or MAST.

I. Backboard

A backboard (bb)/rigid board is designed for use in spinal immobilization procedures. (Figure 7.20) The management for a suspected unstable spine such as injuries sustained from a fall or motor vehicle crash is to immobilize the patient in a supine position on a rigid longboard in a neutral inline position. This neutral inline immobilization position should include the head, neck, torso, and pelvis to prevent any further movement of the suspected unstable spine that could result in damage to the spinal cord.[59] Spinal immobilization follows the principles of fracture management of immobilization to the joint above and below the suspected injury. The anatomy of the spinal column and the interaction caused by forces that affect other parts of the body attached to it require that the principle of immobilization extend from the head to the legs.[60]

Figure 7.20 *Backboard.*

J. Level of Orientation

The EMS squad typically documents the status of the patient on their arrival and during transport. A&O×3 means that the patient was alert, and knew who he was, where he was, and the date. A&O×4 means that the patient was oriented ×3 and remembered events leading up to the arrival of the squad, such as how the accident occurred. Some squad members use the term CA&O×3 for conscious, alert, and oriented. A patient who has suffered a head injury and possible concussion might be asked to name the president as a method of evaluating confusion. Loss of consciousness may be documented as "+ LOC."

The Glasgow Coma Scale (GCS) is a frequently used method of evaluating the patient's level of responsiveness. Figure 7.21 depicts this scale. Internationally the GCS is recognized as the method used in the assessment of head injury severity and degree of coma.[61,62] The overall score ranges from 15 to 3 and is the sum of the best responses in three categories:

- eye opening,
- motor response, and
- verbal response.

The ability to score or use the tool appropriately has enabled providers to make meaningful comparisons between a series of assessments on the patient and accurately assess the level of injuries.[63]

Scene behavior is an area of documentation that will serve as a mental or neurological status baseline for later care and comparison. Many times a patient at the scene of an incident may display behaviors that change prior to arrival at the hospital. Pre-hospital providers should accurately describe behaviors observed on the scene and document these on the patient care report. Often treatments rendered by these providers may improve or alter the patient's behaviors once treatment has begun.

Glasgow Coma Score

The GCS is scored between 3 and 15, 3 being the worst, and 15 the best. It is composed of three parameters: Best Eye Response, Best Verbal Response, Best Motor Response, as given below:

Best Eye Response. (4)
1. No eye opening.
2. Eye opening to pain.
3. Eye opening to verbal command.
4. Eyes open spontaneously.

Best Verbal Response. (5)
1. No verbal response.
2. Incomprehensible sounds.
3. Inappropriate words.
4. Confused.
5. Oriented.

Best Motor Response. (6)
1. No motor response.
2. Extension to pain.
3. Flexion to pain.
4. Withdrawal from pain.
5. Localising pain.
6. Obeys Commands.

Note that the phrase "GCS of 11" is essentially meaningless, and it is important to break the figure down into its components, such as E3V3M5 – GCS 11.
A Coma Score of 13 or higher correlates with a mild brain injury, 9 to 12 is a moderate injury, and 8 or less a severe brain injury.

Teasdale G., Jennett B., LANCET (ii) 81-83, 1974.
www.trauma.org/scores/gcs.html

Figure 7.21

Documentation of the level of a patient's responsiveness can be crucial in establishing pain and suffering, as the following case illustrates.

In this action, the plaintiff contended that the defendant landlord of an apartment building negligently permitted a discarded couch to remain in the lobby for a three-day period, notwithstanding provisions in the code requiring that the lobby be used for ingress and egress only. The plaintiff contended that the extended presence of the couch in the lobby permitted an unidentified arsonist to start a fire which resulted in the death of the twenty-three-year-old decedent, who was sleeping in a third-story apartment when the fire started. The decedent had attempted to escape down the stairs and suffered extensive third degree burns and smoke inhalation, which the plaintiff contended caused severe pain for at least twenty minutes. They contended that the decedent suffered third degree burns over most of his body. The plaintiff would have presented one of his acquaintances to testify that the decedent was crying out for his mother as he was being brought to the ambulance. The defendant denied that this testimony was accurate. The defendants contended that because of the administration of extensive amounts of pain medication once the decedent was placed in the ambulance, it was clear that he could not experience pain. The plaintiff would have maintained that although the hospital records did not reflect overt signs of consciousness, the ambulance records revealed that the decedent was uncontrollable as he was being taken from the building. The plaintiff's forensic pathologist would have contended that in view of the severe nature of the burn injuries, it was highly likely that the decedent continued to experience some level of pain and suffering for the twenty to thirty minutes before he expired. The case settled prior to trial for $600,000 with the landlord paying $500,000 and the architect $100,000. The plaintiff, who would have argued that the pain medication would not prevent the decedent from experiencing some level of pain from the severe burn injuries, also would have argued that irrespective of this issue, records supported the plaintiff's claims that the decedent was in severe pain when taken from the building.[64]

In this case, the EMS records would have been used to document the level of awareness.

K. Multiple Systems Trauma

A patient who is described as having suffered multiple systems trauma experienced trauma that affects more than one organ system in the body. Generally, this is a more severely traumatized patient. Figure 7.22 describes procedures used by EMS to treat this patient.

L. Single System Trauma

This term is used to identify a patient who experiences trauma that affects only one organ system in the body. For example, a patient who has fractured an arm has suffered an orthopedic injury. A single system trauma patient usually has less severe injuries.

M. Seat Belt and Airbag

The squad members may document about whether the seat belt of the victim was broken during the impact. Seat belt abrasions may be seen on the patient's neck, chest, or abdomen. The squad may document that the airbag was deployed. Airbag injuries to the face may be noted.

N. Trauma Center

A trauma center is a hospital with resources kept readily available to treat the most severely traumatized patients. These resources include

- a team of emergency room personnel specially trained in the management of the trauma patient,
- trauma surgeons,
- available operating room staff and equipment, and
- physicians in specialties such as vascular, neurological, and orthopedic surgery.

Many states regulate the designation of a trauma center based on these resources. Emergency department records of trauma centers are often structured to permit documentation of when each of the trauma personnel were notified of the arrival of the trauma victim. It is common for the EMS squad to call the hospital prior to their arrival. This notification permits the emergency department to begin the process of alerting the trauma team to the patient's impending arrival.

O. Car versus Pedestrian

The EMS record may identify the mechanism of injury such as "car versus pedestrian," which refers to a car striking a pedestrian. Other common terms are car versus tree, bus versus pedestrian, car versus bike, and so on. This term is often carried over to the emergency department records.

POLICY AND PROCEDURE MANUAL FOR PRE-HOSPITAL EMS
Office of Paramedic Education

CATEGORY: Pre-Hospital Patient Care

TITLE: Trauma–Multiple System Trauma (MST)

---

1. Treatment of the MST patient in the field should be aimed at securing an airway, oxygenation, ventilation, treating life-threatening injuries, and transporting.

2. Rapidly assess and extricate the patient utilizing PHTLS/BTLS techniques
   Standing orders may be utilized to begin ALS care—see section 800.100.

3. Begin transport of the patient as soon as possible to the closest appropriate hospital as indicated by Medical Direction or section 300.300—Triage and Transport—Trauma Patients.

4. Use of air medical services may be considered when appropriate. See section 300.600 - Utilization of Air Medical Services.

5. Consider PASG for control of blood loss, management of pelvic fractures, or long transport times with the unstable MST patient. PASG is contraindicated in patients with pulmonary edema, traumatic diaphragmatic herniation, or known hemorrhage above the diaphragm. Inflate with order from Medical Direction if the patient is hypotensive (BP<90 mm Hg).

6. Unless the patient is entangled in wreckage and extrication is required, IV LINES SHOULD BE STARTED EN ROUTE TO THE HOSPITAL. LR or NS are the fluids of choice and should be started with 14 or 16 gauge catheters. One IV line is indicated in a patient who is normotensive. Two IV lines should be established in the hypotensive patient.

7. Complete stabilization of the patient in the field is not essential. Continue stabilization enroute to the hospital. Delays at the scene may cause harm!

8. Notify Medical Direction of the potential for a serious trauma patient as soon as possible to expedite activation of the appropriate resources.

Figure 7.22 Policy and procedure—multiple system trauma.

P. Star Pattern on the Windshield

A star pattern is a distinctive pattern of breakage created when an object strikes the windshield during a vehicle collision. It resembles a star burst pattern. EMS records containing this phrase identify that a victim's head struck the windshield. This impact creates the potential for a head or spinal injury.

Q. Passenger Numbering

Generally passengers are numbered from the driver across the front seat from left to right, then the rear seat left to right and so on. Not all reports are numbered in this fashion or numbered at all.

R. Car Pillars

The car pillars are the posts that join the roof to the body of the vehicle. They are labeled from front to back A, B, C and so on, and either driver side or passenger side.

7.9 Refusal of Care

EMS services do not transport every patient they encounter. Patients have the ability to refuse care if they are competent adults. Generally these patients are involved in a minor incident that does not potentially have serious consequences such as the minor motor vehicle crash (MVC) where there is not a serious mechanism of injury (the fender bender in a parking lot). (Figure 7.23) A minor laceration or minor illness for which the patient can see a private physician is an example of a situation that may warrant refusal of care. Most physicians providing medical direction require direct overview of the refusal with contact by phone or radio so that the physician can evaluate the assessment by the field personnel and determine if the patient should be advised to be treated or transported. There should be complete documentation to outline the reason for the call and the assessment findings. The reason for treatment refusal and the evidence that the patient understands the risks of refusing treatment should be recorded. The patient may be asked to sign a form indicating refusal of treatment. (Figure 7.24) Such a form was crucial in mounting a successful defense in the following New York case.

> In *Patricia Dunham, Adminx. of the Estate of Bobby A. Dunham, deceased, et al. v. City of New York, et al.*, the plaintiff called 911 in the early morning in March 1997. Her fifty-one-year-old husband had been suffering from severe headaches for two hours. Emergency medical services personnel arrived six minutes later and found the decedent's

blood pressure to be moderately elevated, but an otherwise normal examination was obtained. The decedent and the plaintiff signed a document indicating that he had refused transportation to a hospital. Twenty-one hours later the decedent experienced a seizure-like episode. He was taken to a hospital and diagnosed with a ruptured cerebral aneurysm. He died the next day. The plaintiff claimed that the emergency services personnel had discouraged the decedent from going to the hospital. The defendants denied this and contended that the decedent expressed a desire to stay home. According to a published account, a defense verdict was returned.[65]

7.10 Do Not Resuscitate

Many people are concerned with the possibility of their health deteriorating to the point of becoming a burden on their loved ones. People with terminal illnesses may elect to prepare documents that outline what the healthcare providers should do in the event of a serious life-threatening event. Many decide to have the providers forego heroic measures for resuscitation. Some elect that nothing be done. Generally there is a physician statement that the plan of care has been discussed with the patient and the patient's immediate family, and then the document is notarized. Figure 7.25 is an example of a protocol that directs how the EMS crews should respond to the do not resuscitate orders. Frequently, the EMS crews must follow the patient's wishes even at the direct disregard of the family members who are present and are requesting treatment for the patient. The need for complete documentation on the report is vital to rebut the possible litigation from family members. A copy of the do not resuscitate order is a helpful addition to the report.

7.11 Controlled Substances

Some of the most effective treatments accomplished in the pre-hospital setting utilize controlled substances. The Controlled Substances Act (CSA), Title II of the Comprehensive Drug Abuse Prevention and Control Act of 1970, is the legal foundation of the government's fight against the abuse of drugs and other substances.[66,67] There are five schedules of controlled substances: schedules I, II, III, IV, and V. (See Figure 7.26.) EMS providers are authorized to use medications in schedules II, III, IV, and V. Morphine and Demerol are Schedule II medications, and Valium and Versed are Schedule IV medications. State agencies also regulate the use of these medications.

```
Service No  189049               OUT OF HOSPITAL CARE REPORT          Unit No.  2417
Inci# 04-9999999    Pt# 0001           License Manager               Alarm Date 08/01/2004
FDID# 09518
```

Incident No 04-9999999 Onset Date / / Onset Time	Location Type
Crash No Trauma ID 911 Used 2 E911	5 Street or Highway
Scene Address Station 1 Shift N	Response Code to Scene
131 EUREKA TOWNE CENTER DR /EUREKA, MO 63025	1 Emergency
	Highest Experience Level at Scene
	3 Paramedic/Firefighter
Township EU District 02 County STLCO Census 2215.00	Lights & Siren to Scene?
Mutual Aid None Occupancy	4 Emergent, with lights or siren

Patient Info	Times	Response Analysis
Patient # 000001 Name DOE, JOHN A		
Address 123 MAIN ST	Dispatch Notified 09:00:00	Dispatch 00:00:00
	Unit Notified 09:00:00	En Route 00:02:00
City Eureka St MO Zip 63025 Rm Phone	Unit Enroute 09:02:00	To Scene 00:03:00
Race White Gender M DOB (09/25/1951) Age 52 yrs 10 mos	Arrived Scene 09:05:00	To Pt/Vict 00:00:00
SSN 111-11-1111 Primary Physician	Arrived Pt/Vict 09:05:00	On Scene
Dispatched For MVC	Enroute to Dest	Transport
Type of Service 1 Emergency Response Requested		Tot Resp Time 01:00:00
Chief Complaint	Arrived Dest	
Provider Impression T22 MVC, driver		Out of Srv 01:15:00
Tx Authorization 1 On-line	Cleared 10:00:00	ALS Response
Injury Sustained? Yes	Back in Service 10:15:00	Total Miles
Injury Intent 3 Unintentional		Loaded Miles 18.00
Mechanism of Injury NA Not Applicable	ALS Arrival	
Human Factors Affecting Care		

Patient Prior Medical History	Factors Affecting EMS Care	Prior EMS Care Given	Safety Equipt Worn by Patient
13 None	11 Not Applicable		6 Belt & Bag

Injury/Illness Detail

Type	Area	Severity	Primary Symptom	Job Rel?

Basic Vitals

Time	LOC	Airway	Resp Rythm-Effort/Qlty	Pulse Rythm/Quality	Skin	Cap Refill	Bleeding	Pupils-L/R	Posture
09:06:00	A	Patent			Normal	0 secs	None	1 / 1	Supine

Secondary Vitals

Time	Pulse	Resp	Temp	BP	PaO2	Skin Appearance	Eye/Mtr/Vrbl	GCS	RTS	Cardiac
09:06:00	76	16	0.00	132/74	0mmHg	Normal	4 6 5	15	12	Sinus Rhythm

* Denotes Blood Pressure Reading by Palpation or Doppler

Procedures Performed
F - Procedure Failed

Time	Procedure	Notes	Staff Id	Attempts
09:06:00	P76 Assessment, Vital Signs, Transp		241060	1

Exposure Precautions Taken / Medications Administered

Staff Member	Precaution Type	Time	Medication	Staff Id	Dosage
241052 Steve Mann	02 Gloves				
241060 Scott Mullins	02 Gloves				

Disposition

Transported to NA Not Transported	Dest Determined by 12 Not Applicable
Mode of Transport 01 Ground	Diverted To
Agency Tiered With	Patient Disposition 04 Dry Run No Transport
Lights/Siren from Scene? Emergent, with lights or siren	Pulse on Transfer NA Not Applicable

Insurance

Type	Policy #	Group #	Insured Name

Patient Narrative

RESPONDED FOR A MVC. ON SCENE MINOR MVC NO DAMAGE TO VEHICLE. PATIENT 52 Y/O M THAT REFUSES TREATMENT OR TRANSPORT.
NO APPARENT INJURIES. VITALS ASSESSED AND MEDICAL CONTROL CONTACTED FOR REFUSAL APPROVAL, APPROVED

```
08/04/2004       09:00                                                  Page    1
```

Figure 7.23 Refusal of treatment report.

```
Service No  189049                OUT OF HOSPITAL CARE REPORT            Unit No.  2417
Inci# 04-9999999   Pt# 0001            License Manager                Alarm Date 08/01/2004
FDID# 09518

                                  Officer/Member Making
_____


Signature_____        Signature_____
Officer Name   Mullins, Scott          08/04/2004   Member Name Mullins, Scott              08/04/2004


Signature_____
Attending Physician
```

```
08/04/2004        09:00                                                      Page    2
```

Figure 7.23 Refusal of treatment report. (continued)

Eureka Fire Protection District

Refusal of Treatment and / or Medical Care

ADDRESS _____

CITY _____ STATE _____ ZIP CODE _____ PHONE (___) _____

D.O.B. _____ B/P _____ PULSE _____ RESP _____

INJURY OR ILLNESS _____

MEDICAL CONTROL # _____ DR. _____ NAME OF EMT OR EMT-P _____ LIC. # _____

  I hereby voluntarily acknowledge and state that I have been advised by the above named Emergency Medical Technician, or Paramedic, regarding the state of my present physical condition in that I have been advised that my medical condition warrants transportation by ambulance service.

  I hereby voluntarily refuse said ambulance transportation as recommended by the aforementioned Emergency Medical Technician, or Paramedic and I do hereby for myself, my heirs, executors, administrators and assigns forever release and fully discharge said Emergency Medical Technician, Paramedic, or Physician Medical Control harmless in regard to my decision to refuse ambulance vehicle transportation. I also acknowledge that I have been provided with a copy of the Private Health Information Policy of the Eureka Fire Protection District.

_____
PATIENT

_____
WITNESS

_____
WITNESS

Figure 7.24 *Refusal of treatment/medical care.*

POLICY AND PROCEDURE MANUAL FOR PRE-HOSPITAL EMS
Office of Paramedic Education

CATEGORY: Pre-Hospital Patient Care

TITLE: Miscellaneous—Do Not Resuscitate Orders

This policy is written in accordance with MO 19 CSR 30-40, effective February 26, 1995 and it's subsequent interpretation by the Bureau of EMS and their legal council on November 11, 1995 entitled Procedures for Outside the Hospital Do Not Resuscitate (DNR) Request. Requests are orders by a patient's physician to refrain from initiating cardiopulmonary resuscitative measures in the event of cardiac or respiratory arrest. **DNR Requests are compatible with maximal therapeutic care and the patient may receive vigorous support (i.e., airway, IVs, drugs) up until the point of cardiac or respiratory arrest.**

Fire and EMS service administrators are encouraged to notify long-term-care facilities of the presence of this form so that it may be completed for those patients wishing not to be resuscitated. It shall be made clear to these facilities that this DNR Request form is the most easily recognized and honored in the pre-hospital setting.

Pre-hospital emergency care providers shall honor the DNR Request form when properly executed and presented. Procedures for acceptance of DNR request forms include:

1. If the validity of the DNR form is questioned, resuscitation should begin and medical control shall be contacted immediately to determine whether the DNR order is to be honored.

2. The DNR Request form shall be signed and dated by the patient or their legal representative and witnessed and signed by the patient's physician.

3. The revocation provision shall remain unsigned in order for the DNR Request Form to remain in effect.

4. The DNR Request forms shall be with the patient at the time of the pre-hospital care provider's arrival.

5. Medical control shall be contacted and informed of the presence of the DNR form.

6. If the DNR request is presented after basic life support/advanced life support procedures are implemented, the pre-hospital care provider shall consult with medical control prior to termination of resuscitation efforts.

7. The pre-hospital care provider shall assist appropriate agencies in documentation of the existence of the DNR request form on the provider's patient care report form.

8. The DNR request form shall remain with the patient.

9. The patient has a right at any time to rescind the DNR request form.

10. The primary obligation of the EMS crew shall be resuscitation, not verification of DNR documents.

Figure 7.25 Policy and procedure—do not resuscitate orders.

U.S. SCHEDULE OF CONTROLLED SUBSTANCES
Under the Jurisdiction of the Federal Controlled Substances Act

Schedule I
These substances have a high potential for abuse and do not have a currently accepted medical use. Examples include: LSD, heroin, mescaline, peyote. They are not obtainable by prescription but may be legally procured for research, study, or institutional use.

Schedule II
These substances have a high abuse potential and a high liability for significant or severe physical or psychological dependence. A non-renewal prescription is required to obtain these substances. Examples include: opium derivatives, other opioids, short acting-acting barbiturates, secobarbital, morphine, meperidine, cocaine, and amphetamines.

Schedule III
The potential for abuse is less than Schedule I or II drugs with a moderate to low physical dependence but a high psychological dependence. This includes certain stimulants and depressants that have not previously been included in the schedules and preparations containing limited amounts of certain opioids. Prescriptions are required for these scheduled drugs and are refillable up to five times within six months if indicated by the physician. Examples include: chlorphentermine, glutethimide, mazindol, paregoric, phendimetrazine.

Schedule IV
This classification has a lower potential for abuse than the previous schedule and prescriptions are required. Examples include certain types of tranquilizers or psychotropics, choral hydrate, valium, Phenobarbital, meprobamate.

Schedule V
This schedule includes drugs with less potential for abuse than previous schedule. Preparations contain limited quantities of the prescribed narcotics and are generally intended for use as an antitussive (cough) or antidiarrheal medication. The medication may be distributed without a prescription provided that certain criteria are met such as it is distributed by a pharmacist to some one over the age of 18 years and a record of the distribution is kept alone and other specific criteria are met.

Figure 7.26

TIP: The basis for documentation pertaining to controlled substances can be divided into two areas; storage and administration.

Storage documentation focuses on a two-person inventory system when the control of the medications changes hands at shift change. Security for storage almost always consists of a dual locking storage facility on the ambulance or at the squad's building. There is a physical inventory documented any time the storage cabinet is opened. An example of an inventory document is shown in Table 7.1. Another type of storage documentation consists of the base supply storage. Usually two people check the inventory when the medicines need to be replenished, issued to ambulances after administration, and on a periodic basis.

Administration documentation includes the information on the patient care record and on the medication storage documents. The following information is recorded:

- the alarm number,
- patient name,
- date,
- time of administration,
- prescribing physician's name and if possible signature, and
- medication name and dosage and any amount wasted.

Table 7.2 is an example of the form for medication administration.

7.12 Communications

Even with standing orders and protocols, there is a very real need for the pre-hospital providers to be able to communicate effectively and efficiently with their medical control (director) physician. Unusual patient presentations, certain procedures, refusal of care, and termination of resuscitation efforts in the field are all situations that require physician oversight. For years, radio communication was the prime method of the EMTs' and paramedics' contact with the hospital. With the advancement of technology, the cell phone is now the primary means of communication. Advanced diagnostics such as 12 lead electrocardiography are now routinely transmitted via cell phone to the receiving facility. Much of the communication between the pre-hospital providers and the hospital is recorded in the event that an incident later requires review. This is typically done by the hospital.

7.13 Termination of Resuscitation in the Field

There are certain situations in which a patient is not responding to heroic resuscitative efforts. Many EMS services medical directors will allow, after consultation with the physician, termination of the resuscitation effort without transporting the patient to the hospital. In certain cardiac rhythms such as asystole (a cardiac rhythm associated with no discernible electrical activity on the ECG and often referred to as "flat line") there is little to be gained from transporting the patient to the hospital only to be pronounced dead shortly after arrival.[68,69] The documentation required for these cases is directed by medical direction protocols (Figure 7.27) and will include all of the patient care interventions, the orders from the medical control physician, the situation surrounding the call for assistance, and an electrocardiogram of the patient's rhythm.

Cummins notes that asystole rarely is associated with a positive outcome. After a thorough assessment of the patient, efforts should be directed at assisting the family and friends that may be present to understand the situation and why prolonged efforts are unnecessary, futile, often unethical, and ultimately dehumanizing if not demeaning.[70]

7.14 Summary

The assessment, management, and transport of the critically ill and injured is a highly stressful activity for the professionals involved in this area of medicine. The scope of practice varies from state to state as well as from agency to agency. In one area EMTs may be able to perform certain basic procedures and levels of care while in another the same procedure is out of their specified scope of practice. Verification of specific laws or policies governing the level of licensure of the pre-hospital professional is necessary to understand their responsibilities and limitations while rendering aid to the sick and injured. Review of the EMT professionals' documentation will yield valuable information about the status of the patient at the scene and enroute to the hospital.

Table 7.1
Daily Controlled Substance Inventory

Eureka Fire Protection District   # 211A R7/04
DAILY CONTROLLED SUBSTANCE INVENTORY
UNIT NUMBER 2417   This form must be changed monthly.   MONTH_____ YR_____

DATE	TIME	DEMEROL	MORPHINE	VALIUM	VERSED	TAG #	ONCOMING SIGN	OFFGOING SIGN

SEE REVERSE SIDE FOR ADDITIONAL DOCUMENT REQUIREMENTS

Table 7.2
Medical Control Report

Eureka Fire Protection District   # 211D R7/04
CONTROLLED SUBSTANCE USAGE RECORD

TICKET#	DRUG/DOSE	WASTE	TOTAL	SIGNATURE	SIGNATURE	PATIENT NAME	PHYS NAME	DATE	TIME	COMMENTS

DRUG REPLACEMENT

DATE	TIME	DRUG	AMOUNT	BY WHOM

TAG REPLACEMENT

DATE	TIME	OLD TAG#	NEW TAG#	# KEYS PRESENT	SIGNATURE	SIGNATURE	REASON FOR USE

POLICY AND PROCEDURE MANUAL FOR PRE-HOSPITAL EMS
Office of Paramedic Education

CATEGORY:　Pre-Hospital Patient Care

TITLE:　　　　Miscellaneous—Termination of Resuscitation in the Field

---

Purpose

Studies have shown that patients in asystole or pulseless electrical activity (PEA) who do not respond to Advanced Cardiac Life Support procedures within fifteen to twenty minutes will not survive in the emergency department. Continued resuscitation efforts are traumatic to the patient, patient's families, costly, and hazardous to the EMS crew transporting the patient. This policy is intended as a guideline with the clear understanding that the medical control physician must have the latitude to make decisions based on the patient's best interest.

Procedure

1. Assess Airway, Breathing, Circulation (ABCs).
2. If breathing and pulse are absent, begin basic life support (BLS) and Advanced Cardiac Life Support (ACLS) procedures. Factors that may influence this step would be clear evidence that a patient would refuse ACLS efforts (i.e., a declaration of intent) or a clear indication of futility (i.e., a terminal illness or verifiable absence of breathing and cardiac output for longer than fifteen minutes).
3. ACLS protocols should be followed for approximately 20 minutes by ACLS providers or by online medical control.
4. If during the resuscitation effort
    a) there is no return of a palpable pulse greater than 60 for five minutes,
    b) the patient shows no continued neurological activity (i.e., motor response, eye opening or spontaneous respirations [not agonal]), and
    c) the patient remains in asystole or pulseless electrical activity, the paramedic should notify the online medical control physician. A decision will be jointly made as to terminating resuscitation efforts in the field.
5. Arrests in trauma, drownings, poisonings, hypothermia, hyperthermia, and children are excluded from this policy and will have resuscitation efforts continued and be transported. Patients in refractory ventricular fibrillation or refractory ventricular tachycardia will also be transported.
6. As a general rule, all patients age 18 and younger who present or progress to cardiopulmonary arrest will be resuscitated and transported.
7. If the resuscitation effort has been terminated, the paramedic will have the responsibility of informing the family that the patient has been declared dead by the medical control physician. If the family has questions about the decision, they will be referred to the medical control physician. ·
8. After the resuscitation effort has been terminated and the family informed, the paramedic will inform the law enforcement agency having jurisdiction (if they are not already present on the scene) that a death has occurred. The paramedic shall remain on the scene until law enforcement officers arrive on the scene. The paramedic will then determine the appropriateness of leaving the scene based on an assessment of the family's needs at that point.
9. If there is any doubt in the paramedic's mind about termination of the resuscitation efforts in the field, full resuscitation efforts should continue while the patient is transported to the appropriate emergency department.
10. When resuscitation efforts are terminated in the field, a copy of the Patient Care Report Form for that patient is to be forwarded to the Coordinator of the Office of Paramedic Education within 72 hours of the call. The report and radio/telephone report will be reviewed by the Coordinator of Paramedic Education and the EMS Medical Director. At a minimum, the narrative should include the details of the resuscitation efforts including any and all interventions performed (IV, drugs, intubation). Further, documentation of the reasons the resuscitation was terminated should also be documented (history of cancer, extensive down time, etc.).

Figure 7.27 Policy and procedure—termination of resuscitation in the field.

Endnotes

1. McSwain, Jr., N. "Short History of EMS." www.Firehouse.com. 2004.

2. *Id.*

3. *Id.*

4. *Id.*

5. *Id.*

6. *Id.*

7. *Id.*

8. LeMire, J. *History of Emergency Medical Services (EMS).* University of Florida, Office of Medical Informatics. 2000.

9. Santa Barbara Public Health Department. Emergency Medical Services History.

10. Lemme Funeral Home records. 1995.

11. *See* note 9.

12. National EMS Research Agenda. National Highway Transportation Safety. 2001.

13. National Registry of Emergency Medical Technicians History of the NREMT.

14. National EMS Research Agenda. National Highway Transportation Safety Administration. History of EMS Research. 2001.

15. *Id.*

16. *See* note 14.

17. Limmer, D. and M. O'Keefe. *Emergency Care.* Tenth Edition. Upper Saddle River: Pearson Prentice Hall. 2005.

18. *Id.*

19. "Emergency Medical Technician Paramedic: National Standard Curriculum (EMT-P)." National Highway Transportation Safety Administration. www.nhtsa.dot. gov.

20. Federal Register Part II. Department of Health and Human Services, Centers for Medicare and Medicaid Services. 2003. 42 C.F.R. Parts 413, 482, and 489. http://www.medlaw.com/.

21. *Id.*

22. Leaver, M. "EMTALA—At Last." *Healthcare Review.* 16, (10), p. 15. 2003.

23. FAA Regulations. http://www.faa.gov/avr/afs/faa/8400/8400_vol3/3_001_03.htm.

24. ARCH Air Medical Service, Inc. CAMTS. 2002. http://www.archairmedical.com/About_us. html.

25. American Heart Association. 2004. http://www.americanheart.org.

26. *Id.*

27. *Id.*

28. *Id.*

29. *Id.*

30. Basic Trauma Life Support International. 2004. http://www.btls.org/.

31. *Id.*

32. *See* note 30.

33. Centers for Emergency Medicine. 2003. http://www.centercm.net/education/CCEMTP.htm.

34. UMBC-Emergency Medicine. 2004. http://ehs.umbc.edu/.

35. Centers for Emergency Medicine. 2003. http://www.centerem.net/education/CCEMTP.htm.

36. Cummins, R. (Editor). *ACLS Provider Manual.* American Heart Association: Dallas. 2002.

37. Wang, H. et al. "Recommended Guidelines for Uniform Reporting of Data from Out-of-Hospital Airway Management: Position Statement of the National Association of EMS Physicians." *Pre-Hospital Emergency Care* Philadelphia. January-March 2004.

38. Laska, L. "Failure to Properly Stabilize and Support Head Injury Patient Results in Permanent Quadriplegia." *Medical Malpractice Verdicts, Settlements, and Experts*. October 2003, p. 16–17.

39. *See* note 17.

40. *Id.*

41. National Registry of Emergency Medical Technicians. The Nation's EMS Certification. Exam Coordinators Documents. http://nremt.org/downloads/spinalimmoblizationseated.pdf.

42. Laska, L. "Texas Man Claims He Was Given Inadequate Pain Medication for Hip Dislocation." *Medical Malpractice Verdicts, Settlements, and Experts*. April 2003, p. 26–27.

43. Laska, L. "Stretcher tips Over in Parking Lot While Woman is Being Returned From Trip to Dialysis Center." *Medical Malpractice Verdicts, Settlements, and Experts*. November 2009, p. 11.

44. *See* note 17.

45. "'Worst Nightmare': Domestic Dispute Call Turns to Tragedy." http://cms.firehouse.com/content/article/article, jsp?id+26153&sectionID=17.

46. Eureka Fire Protection District. 2003 Response Report. Eureka, MO.

47. City of New York Fire Department. 2003 Statistics. http://www.nyc.gov/html/fdny/pdf/stats/ems_cwsum_cy03.pdf.

48. Laska, L. "Failure to Properly Insert Endotracheal Tube in Child Blamed For Brain Damage." *Medical Malpractice Verdicts, Settlements, and Expert*, January 2009, p. 9

49. *See* note 47.

50. *See* note 48.

51. *See* note 17.

52. *Id.*

53. *See* note 36.

54. Desai, K. "Pericardiocentesis." *eMedicine*. April 2002.

55. McSwain, N. (Editor). *PHTLS Basic and Advanced Prehospital Trauma Life Support*. Fifth Edition. St. Louis: Mosby, Inc. 2003.

56. *Id.*

57. *Id.*

58. Mercy Memorial Hospital. MAST. http://www.mercymemorial.org/EMS/mast.htm.

59. *See* note 55.

60. *Id.*

61. *Id.*

62. Cardona, V. et al. *Trauma Nursing From Resuscitation Through Rehabilitation*. Second Edition. Philadelphia: W.B. Saunders Co. 1994.

63. *Id.*

64. Kessler, B. and C. Harvey. "$600,000 Recovery-Defendant Landlord Allows Discarded Couch to Remain In Lobby for Three Days." *Jury Verdict Review and Analysis*. March 2004, p. 10.

65. Laska, L. "Plaintiff Claims Emergency Medical Services Personnel Discouraged Transport to Hospital." *Medical Malpractice Verdicts, Settlements, and Experts*. December 2004, p. 15.

66. U.S. Drug Enforcement Administration. Controlled Substances Act. http://www.usdoj.gov/dea/agency/csa.htm.

67. Shannon, M., B.A. Wilson, and C. Stang. *Nurse's Drug Guide*. Upper Saddle River: Pearson Education, Inc. 2003.

68. Caggiano, R. "Asystole." *eMedicine*. November 2004.

69. *See* note 36.

70. *Id.*

Chapter 8

Emergency Department Records

Dana Stearns, MD

8.1 Introduction

Providers of emergency medicine intersect with the legal arena in two key ways. First, the emergency department is often a point of entry to the hospital. A significant percentage of hospital admissions arrive through a visit to the emergency department. Emergency department records contain initial impressions of the patient's condition upon arrival to the hospital. The often cryptic records contain essential information regarding the patient's past and present status and document the primary actions taken to treat the issues warranting acute intervention. Second, care delivered in the emergency department may come under scrutiny when an untoward outcome has occurred. These records often hold the keys for evaluation of whether or not the standards of care were followed.

This chapter describes principles of care delivery in the emergency department. These include a description of how emergency staff members evaluate patients and decide how and when treatments are indicated and a discussion regarding how triage assessment is performed and how patients are prioritized. The methods of documentation and record keeping are discussed. Patient case presentations are included throughout the chapter providing examples of how these issues are addressed.

A. Principles of Communication

Emergency medicine is like any other field of business: the patient is always right. Within reason, the patient is the boss. The patient is a team member—the most important one. Everything hinges upon her agreement with the staff's assessment and the plans or options.

Patient education is the cornerstone of good care. When a patient answers a question incorrectly or is unable to provide an answer, staff must ask themselves if they asked a question in a way that the patient does not understand and consider rephrasing it rather than concluding that the patient lacks the intelligence to provide the information. Using medical terms and jargon with patients is a common mistake by ED staff members that results in confusion and frustration.

Language barriers pose a unique problem, such as patients for whom English is not their first language. Translating information into terms that the patient understands provides improved understanding and hence more direct involvement in ongoing care. An interpreter can be very helpful in facilitating communication but still may not provide all the necessary information due to the language barrier and the potential for privacy or cultural invasion issues preventing the patient from entering into conversation.

ED patients expect certain actions and behaviors during their interactions with the ED team, many of which are listed below.

1. Trust

Anything that creates an opportunity to maintain or improve a trusting patient-staff relationship must be upheld. Simple actions and behaviors include

- sitting with patients,
- eye contact on the patients' level and not above them,
- acknowledging other family members present,
- asking for opinions, and
- continuously asking if the patient understands and what staff can do to improve the situation.

Simply sitting with a patient sends a message that the staff truly cares and is interested in his problem. A famous twentieth century physician, Sir William Osler, said, "Know when to say I don't know and your patient will respect you more." A close mentor and friend has taught for years to "leave your ego at the door…you can reclaim it on the way home."

TIP: A conservative and humble demeanor reduces the chance that mistakes will be made from overconfidence. It is often true that the more participants the better in medicine, provided that the patient is well informed and there is a point person assigned to explain everyone's ideas and opinions as well as the progression of the patient's evaluation.

2. Attention

Patients want the ED staff to listen to them. They request that their issues be interpreted and used when a list of possible explanations is offered to address their problems and options for treatment.

3. Courtesy and empathy

Patients expect the ED staff to be attentive to their needs and to recognize and respect the specific aspects of each unique situation. ED staff may have worked with patients with similar types of problems and concerns in the past but perhaps not exactly the same as the patient's. Every situation is unique. Patients and their families might confront situations differently than other patients have in the past. ED staff members should be cognizant of this and act accordingly by providing services that might be of assistance and specific to the patient's and the family's needs.

4. Empowerment

Patients are searching for explanations of their problems and treatment options. It is their right to have each fully explained. Most importantly, it is the patient's right to make the final treatment decision. ED staff members are advisors. The patient is in charge.

5. Respect

ED staff must respect the patient's decisions even if they are contrary to what was recommended. If a competent patient understands and accepts the risks of refusing certain treatment, the ED staff should be respectful of this and attempt to do what they can to assist the patient.

B. Access to Care

TIP: Every person has the right to be seen in an emergency department. Staff members are unable to turn patients away, even if the hospital does not provide the services that a patient might require.

If a person arrives in an ED requesting an evaluation, the staff must provide one. At times, however, the patient's needs may exceed the capabilities of the emergency department and its associated hospital. The ED staff must locate a facility whose staff is capable and willing to accept the patient in transfer once initial stabilization has been completed and the staff feels that the benefit of transfer outweighs the risks.

EMS personnel have the right to decide the priority of a patient's issues and then choose whether the closest facility should receive the patient, even if the facility does not provide specific services for the patient's needs or the institution is on divert to ambulance traffic due to patient volume and acuity overload. The following example describes this dilemma.

> EMS personnel inform the local community hospital that they have a multiparous female patient in active labor. They believe that the patient is crowning and that delivery of the newborn is imminent. The local facility has no OB/Gyn capability. Can the ED staff reject this patient and send EMS elsewhere? In this particular case, it will be the responsibility of the ED staff to prepare a section of the department and contact additional assistance as needed for delivery (on-call pediatrician, surgeon, and anesthesiologist). Crowning is a condition in which the baby's head has advanced beyond the cervix into the vaginal vault, stretching the introitus (opening). Such a condition in a mother who has delivered children in the past suggests a likelihood that her present labor is likely to be more rapid than her last. It is more likely that this baby will arrive before EMS has enough time to reach another facility with full obstetrical services. Such a patient is considered high priority and should be taken to the closest ED. After the situation has been evaluated and stabilized by the ED physician and appropriate consulting services available, the mother and child can be transferred on to a full obstetrical and pediatric facility.

With increased potential risk of complications and the need for continued invasive monitoring or treatment during transport, the ED physician can determine whether ED staff, including a nurse and/or physician, should accompany the patient. In certain situations, public and private critical care services have been created for such transport needs. Nevertheless, the continued care of the patient remains the responsibility of the ED physician until received in person by the accepting MD. See Chapter 7, *Emergency Medical Services Records*, for additional information on the role of EMS personnel.

C. Principles of Diagnosis
1. Medicine is common sense

If a patient states something is wrong, the ED staff must believe the patient. The challenge is to determine whether or not the problem is life threatening and demands intervention or how soon the issue must be definitively addressed. Appropriate care and follow-up instructions are necessary to ensure that the problem is resolving or that its cause is be-

ing diagnosed. Although ED staff members strive to provide definitive answers to their patients, this is sometimes impossible. This process includes identifying the possible causes that might make the patient significantly ill if not identified and treated.

2. Differential diagnosis

Hospital staff members are trained to consider problems that could make a patient extremely ill very quickly if not recognized, and to rule out these possibilities before considering illnesses less likely to cause such harm. Although there is often a single issue causing the ailment that brings a patient to seek help, its cause could include a wide range of options, each of which must be considered. This list of possible explanations is commonly called the differential diagnosis. Emergency department records often list these in the physician's history and examination, whether it is handwritten, computer generated, or dictated. Options might include the most common to the extremely rare disorder. The evaluation that ensues includes examination and testing in an effort to identify or eliminate choices on this list, narrowing the possible diagnoses.

Emergency medicine tends to maintain pessimism when it comes to the differential diagnosis. Worst case scenarios that fit the history and physical exam data top this list. Further evaluation and diagnostic testing follow to assist in ruling in or ruling out these choices of the differential diagnosis. ED staff members are sometimes unable to conclude a single definitive cause for a patient's problem. Identifying the cause is ultimately the goal of the evaluation. Eliminating the differential diagnoses that could create significant morbidity or mortality if left unidentified and untreated is a high priority. Life-threatening causes are treated first and then the patient is referred to the primary physician or a specialist for further care.

3. When in doubt, observe or admit

If a definitive diagnosis cannot be made, the patient is observed for a possible evolution of the ailment in a monitored environment where staff members can continuously reevaluate the patient's condition. Further diagnostic testing and treatments can be arranged during this observation period. The decision to admit the patient does not mean responsibility for the patient automatically passes to another service. The ED physician must determine the correct decision for further treatment, the appropriate service must be identified and contacted, and a staff physician on that service must have accepted and agreed to assume responsibility for the patient. The details of these interactions and the time of this transfer should be documented in the patient's chart.

Triage Levels

Level I   **Highest acuity/priority.** These patients are taken for evaluation as quickly as possible to the area in the ED that has the highest level of critical care services and the lowest patient/nurse ratio.

Level II   **High acuity.** The patient's condition requires emergent evaluation by ED staff but not at the expense of a Level I patient. Level II patients do not require the same level of care or services as Level I and might be placed in an area with a moderate patient/nurse ratio.

Level III   **Moderate/Urgent acuity.** The patient's condition should be evaluated as soon as possible but not at the expense of withholding care to Level I and II patients. These patients might be seen in the order that they arrived, but if the ED is at capacity and there is a wait, the triage nurse as well as the ED physician in charge may prioritize one Level III patient over another depending upon bed space availability, ancillary testing needs during the workup, and the availability of other services.

Level IV   **Urgent acuity.** The patient's condition should be evaluated as soon as possible after all higher level patients have been seen and assessed. Level IV patients are usually placed in an area with the highest patient/nurse ratio and are seen in the order that they were triaged (i.e., first come, first served).

Figure 8.1

8.2 The Triage Process

A patient is usually first greeted by a triage nurse who begins an evaluation by asking the patient to describe reasons for the visit. A history of the condition and brief evaluation including vital signs and focused physical examination are obtained. An assessment of the condition and a plan of action follow. This portion of the evaluation includes a decision about the urgency of the patient's condition. This is done by categorizing the condition and its potential severity. The triage nurse also compares that patient's condition to the other patients who are already present in the department at the time of the triage encounter. A simple form of triage designation would include

- Very Sick (critically ill requiring immediate attention),
- Sick (urgently ill, requiring attention quickly but not at the expense of the critically ill), and
- Moderately Sick (injury or illness that is not immediately risking life or limb and can be seen when time is available after the more urgently ill patients have been seen).

A more formalized method of communicating these categories is shown in Figure 8.1. (See also Section 8.3.B.)

The key to all triage is to remember that an assessment is fluid and evolving. What is noted as minimally urgent may evolve over time into something life threatening.

TIP: Triage staff must be aware continuously of the population in the waiting room and their problems and be ready to provide reassessment and re-triage as needed. Further, the staff should inform the patients that if they believe their situation is escalating they should feel free to approach the triage staff at any time for a re-evaluation.

A twenty-four-year-old man presented to the ED with severe chest pain. His vital signs were as follows: blood pressure 132/88, pulse 126 beats per minute, respirations 18 breaths per minute, temperature 99 degrees, and oxygen saturation 99 percent on room air. He appeared otherwise healthy and described no recent illnesses or previous history of similar chest discomfort. The ED was busy that evening, and the triage staff member thought the patient was stable and triaged him to the waiting room.

Two hours after the initial triage, the patient returned to the triage officer complaining of severe pain, requesting to be seen immediately. The staff member told the relatives that the department was busy and that he would be seen as quickly as possible after those patients with more serious illness were seen first. Shortly thereafter, the patient collapsed in the waiting room. Advanced cardiopulmonary resuscitation was required to revive the patient. The patient suffered a severe myocardial infarction. A toxicological analysis revealed large quantities of cocaine in his system. He later admitted to smoking large amounts of the drug at a party earlier that evening but thought it had nothing to do with his symptoms and did not offer the information. The patient recovered but suffered from significant heart failure.

If a patient presents to the ED with medical complaints, it should be assumed that there is a legitimate need for attention until proven otherwise. It is up to the ED staff to determine if the issue is emergent. It is their responsibility to offer a plan of action that is reasonable, is acceptable to the patient, and follows the appropriate standard of care.

8.3 Documentation of Triage and Treatment
A. Importance of Documentation

A purpose of documentation is to record the presentation, evaluation, assessment, and proceedings of a patient encounter. Such detail might otherwise be long forgotten afterward unless it is included in the patient's chart. Medical staff members are taught that thorough documentation in the ED chart is necessary. It is used to establish that treatment and disposition followed the standard of care. The interventions and outcomes are recorded for the purpose of providing quality medical care. The information is consistently available for the patient and staff actively involved in the case as well as off-service or consulting staff. The medical record provides a chronological proceeding of the entire event or encounter. Documentation is discussed with ED staff members as part of their education prior to bedside application and reinforced as a priority during medical education discussions.

Medical staff members are taught that documentation should include as much relevant information as possible. Such information should include the patient's history, the staff's objective findings, and laboratory and other evaluative data. The medical staff's overall assessment of the patient's condition should be entered, including a list of possible causes of the patient's condition. Potential treatment options, including the patient's chosen option, are important and helpful to all members involved. Medical professionals must document the patient's consent to treatment, including invasive procedures. Charting should include

- explanation of the risks and benefits of the procedure that were presented to the patient,
- medications or treatments given to the patient,
- timing and mode of administration of such treatments, and

- both subjective and objective outcomes of the interventions.

Documentation is a challenge for busy ED staff members who are constantly presented with acute, emergent situations requiring action, leaving little time to list the information that was collected prior to, during, and after the encounter. As a result, ED staff members search for ways to maximize data collection with time efficiency. The description below is one of several examples of data collection and documentation used not only by triage staff members but also nurses and physicians.

B. SOAP Note

SOAP notes are brief and focused documentation of the patient evaluation. They are used in a triage setting to inform the staff of what issues are to be expected as the patient is being formally and longitudinally evaluated. SOAP is an acronym denoting the four parts included in this type of documentation (subjective, objective, assessment, plan).

- **Subjective.** The patient's complaint; why a patient has decided to come to the ED at this time.
- **Objective.** Physical exam findings that corroborate the complaint (vital signs, fever, cursory physical exam findings including wheezing, coughing, vomiting, tissue swelling, bony deformity, or laceration).
- **Assessment.** The examiner's conclusions on what is happening to the patient. (See Chapter 5, *Office-Based Medical Records*, and Chapter 21, *Physician Documentation in Hospitals and Nursing Homes*, for additional information about SOAP charting.) ED triage staff members will likely include a sense or level of acuity of the patient's condition. This will be used to compare a given patient's condition with another's in an effort to determine who might require ED staff members' attention and resources more urgently.
- **Plan.** After triage, the plan is usually to admit a patient to the ED for a more detailed evaluation. Other options include being seen directly at triage, treated and released by an ED physician, or referral directly to a clinic or facility which might be more capable of evaluating and treating the patient's complaint. This latter option is not done without the ED physician having seen and approved the referral, the receiving staff having been informed of the patient situation and agreeing to accept him in transfer, and most importantly, the patient agreeing

with and approving the referral and transfer from the ED.

C. History (HX)

ED staff routinely use a series of standardized questions to guide them in the solicitation of information pertinent to the patient's case. These are often abbreviated as noted below and usually include the following information:

1. Chief complaint (CC)

What brings the patient to the ED at this time?

2. History of present illness (HPI)

What are the circumstances surrounding the evolution of the problem or issue that has made the situation emergent? For example, a person's breathing problems began several days before arrival but were manageable similarly to previous breathing problems. The person's breathing status suddenly became progressively worse despite her usual interventions to the point where the patient feared that things would worsen unless ED intervention was sought.

3. Past medical history (PMH)

This includes any medical illness or problem that patients have experienced over their lifetime. The problems might be ongoing or quiescent. The issues might require continued or occasional medication or other medical interventions including physical therapy and rehabilitation.

4. Past surgical history (PSH or SHX)

It is important to know what surgical procedures the patient has undergone in the past. What organs or tissues have been altered, removed, transplanted, or replaced? Operative procedures result in some form of scarring during the healing process. This may have led to complications and debilitation contributing to current symptoms. This is especially true for intra-abdominal surgical procedures because scarring in the peritoneal cavity may lead to bowel, biliary, or fallopian tube obstruction.

5. Medications

Current prescribed and over the counter (OTC) medications, dose, route, and frequency of administration are noted.

6. Allergies/adverse drug reactions

Medications and/or environmental exposures have caused rashes, throat tightness, difficulty breathing, or wheezing. Patients often describe medication allergies that manifest as gastrointestinal upset such as abdominal cramps, nausea, vomiting, or diarrhea. While such adverse reactions may indeed be true allergic responses, these are quite rare without respiratory and/or dermatological manifestations. Medical staff members often suggest that patients refrain from taking medications that produce such symptoms and categorize these under allergies when in fact the patient is not at risk for the morbidity and mortality of true chemical hypersensitivity. The patient, however, often confuses the concept and misperceives the effects. This is common and not the fault of the patient; rather it is the lack of adequate communication and education by the healthcare provider.

7. Social history (SH)

This subject includes, but is not limited to,

- occupation,
- domestic (married/single/dependents),
- smoking history,
- alcohol use, and
- illicit drug use.

8. Family history (FH)

Are there any family members, living or deceased, with significant medical problems such as heart disease, diabetes, elevated cholesterol, or stroke? This information is valuable to the ED physician because these conditions have a familial link, and this knowledge can assist in the diagnosis of the patient's current problem.

D. Review of Systems (ROS)

Many medical problems can manifest as issues with more than one organ system. The patient may be focused upon one or two main issues or manifestations. A series of questions regarding specific organ systems is asked by ED staff in an effort to glean additional information regarding the main complaints or to discover additional concomitant problems. These questions are usually asked sequentially from one system to the next and from head to toe. These responses are recorded in the medical records together with pertinent information as described above. Some ED records provide these questions under the history section of the chart.

TIP: Computer-based programs also exist to facilitate the process, allowing the physician to check the pertinent items that should be added to the record.

Answers to the questions related to the following systems should be documented in the patient's chart.

1. General

The healthcare provider inquires about constitutional symptoms. Is there fever, chills, malaise, weight loss, night sweats, loss of appetite, or fatigue?

2. Head, eyes, ears, nose, throat (HEENT)

This assessment includes documentation of

- abnormal swelling, bruises, cuts, or deformities of the scalp or skull. A normal assessment is recorded as "normocephalic";
- vision problems, conjunctival redness, swelling, or discharge;
- hearing difficulties, earache, discharge, blocked sensation, pain, redness, or swelling of the ear, nasal congestion, pain;
- discharge or bleeding, loss of smell sensation; and
- throat pain, swelling and difficulty swallowing or breathing.

3. Neck

Difficulty breathing, swallowing or speaking, tightness, abnormal mass, swelling or lump, and localized or generalized neck pain are noted.

4. Chest/respiratory

Is there any difficulty breathing, wheezing, cough or congestion, purulent or bloody sputum production, pleurisy (chest discomfort upon inspiration), or diffuse or focal chest wall tenderness upon palpation or chest wall/upper extremity motion? Does the patient experience dyspnea (difficulty breathing) with exertion or notes such symptoms with progressively less exertion than in the past? Does the patient have difficulty breathing at rest? Does the patient wake up from sleep with shortness of breath? Can the patient lie flat at night? If not, how many pillows does the patient use to sleep comfortably?

5. Chest/cardiovascular

Is there discomfort that is focal or radiating across the chest, neck, jaw, upper extremities, or abdomen? Does this discomfort occur with exertion and relieve with rest? Has this discomfort become progressively more frequent with progressively less exertion? Has the discomfort occurred with exertion in the past but has now recently occurred at rest as well? Does the discomfort awaken the patient at night?

6. Abdominal

Does the patient experience nausea, vomiting, and/or pain? Where is the pain located? Is it focal or diffuse? Does the pain radiate to the groin, genitals, or back? Is the discomfort associated with meals, defecation, or urination? Has the patient had similar abdominal pain in the past? Is the pain crampy, colicky, sharp, or piercing? Has the patient noted blood in vomit or stool? Has the patient noticed any abnormal swelling or masses along the abdominal wall or in the groin?

7. Genitourinary

Is there blood in the urine? Is the patient noting discolored, foul smelling, or burning urine? Is there pain in the lower pelvis or flank/back region? Is the pain constant and dull or crampy/colicky in nature? Has the patient experienced similar discomfort in the past? When was the patient's last menstrual period (LMP)? When was the LMP prior to the previous one? Is the patient experiencing abnormal vaginal discharge or bleeding? Has the patient been pregnant in the past?

8. Back/musculoskeletal

Are there deformities or swollen or discolored areas of the soft tissues or bones of the extremities or torso? Does the patient experience joint swelling, redness, or painful motion? Does the tenderness augment (increase) with active or passive movement? Was the complaint and finding spontaneous or the result of trauma? How long did it take for the condition to evolve?

9. Neurological

Has the patient had a change in mental status such as confusion, difficulty concentrating, disorientation, or delirium? Has the patient experienced any changes in the senses such as vision or hearing loss? Is there a change in motor strength or sensation of the muscles and skin of the face, torso, or limbs? Has the patient experienced seizure-like activity? Has the patient experienced incontinence of urine or stool? At what time exactly did such symptoms begin? If an exact time is unclear, when was the person last seen healthy and without such symptoms?

10. Hematological/immunological

Does the patient have a history of bruising or bleeding easily? Is she taking medications that "thin the blood" or make it more difficult for bleeding to stop? Does the patient have swelling, pain, or discoloration of a limb or a history of varicose veins, inflammation of superficial veins, (phlebitis), deep venous thrombosis (DVT), or pulmonary embolus? Does the patient have a history of autoimmune inflammation or is she taking steroids or other anti-inflammatory medications to reduce such conditions? Has the patient received chemotherapy or other immunosuppressant medications that might increase the risk of spontaneous infection?

11. Skin

Does the patient note any discoloration, raised or bumpy areas, or itchiness of the skin such as a rash or abrasion? Is this condition diffuse or localized? Are there any bumps, masses, or sores on the skin? Do these conditions itch or hurt? Is the skin generally dry, taut, and tender to touch or with limb motion? Is the skin thin or emaciated, easily bruised, torn or lacerated? Are wounds easily healed? Is there evidence of neglect? Are bruises consistent with the described mechanism of injury? Are there signs of physical abuse? Does the skin have poor turgor (indicating dehydration)?

12. Endocrine

Does the female patient suffer from irregular, heavy, or severely painful menses? Does the patient suffer frequent headaches or difficulty with vision? How is the patient's energy level? Is the patient hyperactive, nervous, jittery, suffering from sleeping difficulties, or losing weight? Does the patient lack energy or fatigue easily? Is he having difficulty rising from sleep? Is the patient intolerant of heat or cold climate conditions?

13. Psychiatric

Is the patient suffering from low, labile, or persistently elated mood? Is the sleeping pattern, appetite, ability to concentrate, ability to initiate sleep, or rise from bed in the morning altered in any way? Does the patient feel that people do not understand his concerns? Does the patient feel paranoid or claim knowledge of conspiracy? Does the patient exhibit delusional behavior that appears bizarre to friends and family but completely normal to the patient?

E. Physical Examination (PE)

Completion of the patient's history is then followed by a physical examination. The triage evaluation is often very superficial and focused. The examination is often incomplete and minimally obtrusive as the ED is not very private. The full exam is usually performed by the ED physician and nurse assigned to be the primary providers for the patient and is done in the privacy of the examination room. The examination usually follows the same order as is listed under the historical review of systems (ROS). This prevents an organ system or region of the body from being overlooked. Important findings, including normal data, are then recorded by the physician, nurse, or both and listed alongside the history to complete the initial evaluation.

8.4 Diagnosis (DX)
A. Leaving No Stone Unturned

The information gleaned is used to create the history of the condition that brought the patient to the ED. These data are combined with a list of objective findings that are discovered using the standardized physical examination. While some conditions might not require a full examination of the patient from head to toe, others certainly do, as many illnesses are capable of involving more than one organ system. It is therefore advised that a full physical examination be performed on all patients.

A patient's distraction may result in the physician missing extremely important information from an objective examination by relying solely upon the patient's subjective complaint. Distraction is a condition in which a patient might have multiple ailments occurring simultaneously, but when asked the patient complains only of the one causing the most discomfort.

TIP: The discomfort of a single condition may be significant enough to mask that of another problem with equal if not more life-threatening severity.

> Consider this patient:
> A person has suffered from a "belly ache" for the last twenty-four hours, keeping him from work and too uncomfortable to eat. While getting out of bed to use the toilet, he trips and breaks his ankle. Upon EMS arrival or ED presentation, on which pain will the patient likely fixate?

The human anatomy is blessed with a nervous system that is multifaceted. Nerves in the brain collate information and stimuli from the outside world and send messages to systems. The brain receives information from the outside world through the five senses and the peripheral sensory nervous system. Outside of the brain, these sensory afferent nerves usually travel alongside or piggyback upon motor or efferent nerves that leave the brain for peripheral organ or limb destinations. The nerves of the limbs or on the skin, known as the somatic sensory nerves, are incredibly point-specific. A person with an itch or a pinprick on the forearm will be capable of describing exactly where the noxious stimulus is located. Thus cuts, bruises, and fractures of the skin tissues or bones tend to be extremely intense and focal—very easy to interpret and their location easy to describe.

The involuntary nervous system helps the brain control multitudes of bodily functions that would be extremely complicated and distracting. Thus this system contains a series of sensory afferent nerves and motor efferent nerves that control these functions. Examples include peristalsis of digestion or transport of urine through the ureters. The internal organs that assist with digestion or urination lie deep within the body and send sensory impulses back to the brain. Unlike the skin surface or the extremities, these sensory nerves send very vague messages of sensation that the brain has difficulty interpreting. Thus if given the choice, the brain will fixate upon the more sharp and specific sensory impulses at the expense of the more diffuse and vague. This helps to explain why a patient may fixate upon the ankle pain and "forget" about his abdomen.

TIP: It is essential that the ED staff ask specific questions regarding events prior to ED presentation that might describe the "forgotten" symptoms.

The review of systems is also designed to assist the staff as well as the patient with recalling any recent or current complaints or concerns. Even more importantly, the physician should perform a thorough physical examination from head to toe that includes this patient's abdomen. Although not attentive to his subjective complaint of abdominal pain, the patient will likely note significant objective tenderness when the physician taps, shakes, or palpates his abdomen. It was the additional information from the physical examination that alerted the physician to this patient's abdominal condition. Evolving appendicitis was discovered, and appropriate treatment was arranged.

A man presented to an ED shortly after being involved in a motor vehicle crash when his pickup truck was struck on the driver's side by an eighteen-wheel tractor trailer in an intersection. There was significant damage to the vehicle, resulting in a prolonged extrication of the victim. While the patient was awake and alert with stable vital signs during the entire pre-hospital setting as well as in the ED, he complained of significant left jaw pain and left knee pain. The ED triage and staff nurse assigned to the patient documented significant jaw deformity and tenderness but noted no evidence of knee trauma or tenderness on examination. The ED physician noted no evidence of trauma during his evaluation of the patient either, though he made no notation of actually examining the limbs above or below the knee, which was recorded as "unremarkable." The ED physician did make note of the deformed jaw and arranged to have the patient admitted to the oral surgeon for definitive management of a jaw fracture. Then the patient made several

complaints of knee pain to the physician who explained that the pain was likely due to a contusion as there were no significant examination findings.

The patient continued to note severe left knee pain upon any weight bearing throughout his hospital stay, and this was duly noted by the nursing staff. One nurse carefully examined the patient and noted significant left hip pain on motion and weight bearing, but this went unheeded by the physician staff who called the condition a serious knee contusion that would resolve with rest and gradual increased activity. The patient was discharged three days after the accident with improved jaw pain but continued intense hip pain. He saw his chiropractor a few weeks later for persistent severe knee pain. This clinician noted similar findings to the nurse caring for the patient and ordered an x-ray of the patient's hip. The x-ray revealed a severe fracture of the acetabulum in his pelvis which was so significantly eroded that usual conservative treatment was no longer advisable. Ultimately the patient required a total hip replacement.

B. Inability to Communicate

Medical students are taught that 20 percent of their patients will be unable to provide a chief complaint or a history of illness that has brought them to the ED. The ED staff must continue to provide care until there is up-to-date documentation of an advance directive or a family member who can provide documentation that she has the power to make medical decisions for the patient. A patient may arrive from home or a nursing facility with verbal information regarding DNR, but no advance directive is documented and no one with power of attorney is present. The ED staff must proceed with all aggressive medical intervention within a reasonable standard of care in attempts to resuscitate the patient until such documentation can be obtained.

A semiconscious or unconscious patient who presents to the ED is commonly prioritized as a Level I patient until evaluated by the ED physician and re-prioritized. Obvious reasons for this are based upon common sense. If a patient is unconscious, he may be incapable of protecting the airway, leading to choking, aspiration, and suffocation. While the list of possible causes of acute change in mental status is long, there are several easily recognized and treatable causes (hypoxia, hypoglycemia, opiate overdose) whose identification should not be delayed. If these have been treated or ruled out from evaluation, it makes conditions such as acute stroke, myocardial infarction or infection more easily recognized and treated as quickly as possible. It can be considered a luxury in such cases to have a history of present illness, available medical records, or a person who witnessed the patient become symptomatic to provide some insight into an etiology. When this is not possible, there is an accepted progression of physical examination that the ED staff members follow in sequence for all patients who present with a change in mental status.

8.5 Patient Management

A. Airway

Evaluation of the airway encompasses the mouth, nose and throat, and trachea. Is there any evidence of narrowing or obstruction as observed by difficulty inhaling or exhaling? The patient may display sonorous inspirations from the tongue or soft palate if she is somnolent or unconscious. An anxious, agitated patient who cannot speak may point to the mouth or throat from a complete obstructed airway. A barking cough on exhalation may be heard from a two-year-old suffering from acute viral tracheitis, also known as croup. Loss of the airway implies a lack of oxygenation and ventilation. Without immediate intervention, this will always lead to death. Therefore, all airway issues are addressed as a top priority.

> A sixty-six year-old man went to the emergency department with a complaint of light-headedness and facial numbness. The decedent had a history of non-insulin dependent diabetes, hypertension, hypercholesterolemia and asthma. Initial lab reports supported a diagnosis of renal insufficiency and hyperkalemia. He was given medication to decrease potassium. Within minutes he became panicked and short of breath and stated that he was having an asthma attack. His Albuterol inhaler provided no relief. The attending emergency department physician was apprised of the situation. Four attempts over ten minutes to intubate the decedent were unsuccessful, and the decedent was eventually intubated by the anesthesiologist. His pulse returned, but he had suffered anoxic encephalopathy and died four days later. The defendant emergency department physician took the position that the decedent's obesity, combined with his significant asthma attack, made intubation difficult. A $400,000 settlement was reached.[1]

B. Breathing

Is the patient adequately providing oxygen to his system? How is the patient breathing? What is the respiratory rate? How is the patient's demeanor with breathing? Does the patient appear distressed? Is he having trouble breathing in or out? Is the patient wheezing? Can the patient speak? If so, can he speak full sentences or only whisper one or two words? Is the patient coughing or vomiting, suggesting a mechanical obstruction in the airway resulting from sputum or aspiration? What is the patient's current level of oxygenation?

TIP: An oxygen saturation monitoring device (called pulse oximetry) can be quickly and non-invasively applied providing real-time data and can be used for titration of oxygen supplementation.

C. Circulation

What are the patient's heart rate and blood pressure? The human system is designed to provide necessary circulation to the brain and the heart at all costs and at the expense of all other organs. This is the cornerstone of advanced cardiac and trauma life support in all patients. The brain tissues live for less than ten minutes without oxygen; the heart muscle will survive for less than twenty minutes. Thus the human system will adjust the body's circulation to maintain adequate blood flow to these organs for as long as possible while shunting blood flow away from less "vital" and more adaptable organ systems such as the muscles of the arms and legs, the abdominal organs, and the kidneys.

> A Massachusetts woman who was eight months pregnant went to the emergency department because she had shortness of breath. She had an elevated heart rate but a normal blood pressure. An EKG showed a wide complex tachycardia. The emergency department physician called the defendant, her treating obstetrician. The decedent had seen the obstetrician the day before for complaints of a cough. The emergency department physician advised the obstetrician the patient's heart rate was elevated and her blood pressure was normal. The defendant recommended Labetalol, which is designed to significantly reduce blood pressure quickly. The Labetalol was administered and the decedent's blood pressure began to drop to dangerously low levels. The fetal heart rate was lost on the fetal monitor. A cesarean section was performed. Shortly after delivery the decedent went into cardiopulmonary arrest and the woman died. The plaintiff claimed that the use of Labetalol was inappropriate. A $1.99 million verdict was returned.[2]

There are specific examination findings that, together with the history and/or mechanism of injury, can make ED staff highly suspicious of circulatory compromise. Such findings might include an increased heart rate, a falling blood pressure, and a sense of lightheadedness or feeling faint, especially when sitting up or standing from a supine position. A patient might appear gray, ashen, or pale, have very dry mucous membranes, or note a reduction in urine output and/or urinate small amounts of very concentrated urine. Options for the improvement of circulatory volume include oral (PO) and/or intravenous (IV) hydration. ED staff might ask permission and place an IV catheter attached to solutions such as normal saline (sodium chloride solution) that are used to add volume to the vascular system in an effort to improve circulation to the entire system.

D. Cervical Spine

Many patients are unable to provide ED staff with an adequate history of the events surrounding their need to present to the ED. The patient might have sustained a trauma such as collapsing onto a hard floor or falling down stairs. As a result, the patient's spine, especially the cervical spine bones of the neck, is at significant risk for injury. In addition, the spinal cord within the vertebral column is at risk for permanent injury if cervical or spinal bony injury is left unnoticed.

TIP: All patients who present with altered mental status, with an unclear history of events that lead them to the ED, or who are incapable of providing an adequate subjective and objective physical examination must have their spines, especially the cervical spine, immobilized and evaluated. Such patients might include the unconscious or intoxicated, those with distracting injuries such as concurrent head or facial injury, as well as those who are amnesic of the events leading to their ED presentation.

A Massachusetts woman was admitted to the emergency department after being involved in a collision in which her vehicle was struck in the rear. She complained of neck and bilateral shoulder pain. An examination revealed diffuse neck tenderness, among other things. She was given Percocet and removed from the backboard. The Percocet provided no relief from pain. X-rays were ordered and the emergency room found them normal except for degenerative joint disease. The patient's hard cervical collar was removed; she continued to complain of neck and back pain and was given stronger pain medication with some relief. She was then discharged with a diagnosis of acute cervical

muscle strain. Six days later, she was brought back by ambulance to the same emergency department on a backboard with a cervical collar in place. At this time, she could not feel her arms, was suffering visual and auditory hallucinations, and was unable to lift her arms. The triage nurse also documented limited hand grip bilaterally. The emergency room physician noted the cervical spine films performed at the time of the first visit had not been read by a radiologist. A radiologist then reviewed them and called them essentially normal. A CT scan of the neck was ordered and then cancelled. The physician maintained that the radiologist told him it was an inappropriate study. The radiologist testified he did say this, but also told the emergency room physician to repeat the plain film series of the spine. The emergency physician denied this was recommended. The plaintiff was admitted to the hospital with a diagnosis of altered mental status secondary to medication. Two days later, the plaintiff had no use of her arms and legs and was transferred to another hospital. The plaintiff was rendered quadriplegic despite surgery. The plaintiff claimed the first emergency department physician and the radiologist who subsequently reviewed the x-rays failed to recognize the abnormalities at C5-6 suggesting ligament damage. The plaintiff claimed the second emergency room physician was negligent in failing to perform any diagnostic imaging studies of the cervical spine. A $2.9 million settlement was reached.[3]

E. Disability

What is the mental status of the patient? Is the patient awake, alert, and oriented to person, place, and time of presentation, or somnolent or lethargic and minimally responsive to verbal commands or even painful stimulus? The possible causes of such conditions are extremely broad. However, there are several possible conditions that ED staff can quickly diagnose and treat at the bedside using a minimum of testing and intervention.

- **Hypoxia.** One cause of disability is hypoxia (lack of oxygenation). Supplemental oxygen is commonly used in the ED. It is delivered by nasal cannula, face mask, or via an endotracheal tube and ventilation device. Evaluating oxygen saturation with a non-invasive monitor device as well as the application of oxygen to patients can quickly improve or reverse many such conditions.

- **Hypoglycemia.** Another possible cause of disability is hypoglycemia or low blood sugar levels. While bedside glucometer devices and "stat" laboratory testing are helpful in determining serum levels, ED staff is instructed to act quickly in the administration of IV glucose solutions. When such testing is not timely or unavailable, the untoward effects of hypoglycemia are far more serious than the possible complications of transient hyperglycemia from the intervention.

- **Narcotic ingestion.** It is not uncommon to encounter a patient who has ingested, inhaled, or injected an amount of opiate or narcotic substances that has rendered him confused, somnolent, or apneic (not breathing). The antidote is naloxone, which can be quickly and easily administered in small increments to prevent the patient from anoxic injury from asphyxia or aspiration. The drug returns the patient to a functionally alert and oriented state.

A seventy-two-year-old woman arrived to the ED from a religious service after becoming acutely lethargic and confused. Witnesses stated that she was well prior to and throughout the service but suddenly slumped down in her pew, her skin became gray and sweaty, and her speech became slurred. The patient was controlling her airway and breathing without difficulty. EMS was called and noted her condition unchanged when they arrived five minutes later. The patient's vital signs appeared normal, and she had no other focal findings upon evaluation. The patient was taken directly to the ED where the triage nurse noted her condition to be Level I (highest priority). She was transported to the acute care area. ED staff quickly administered oxygen, inserted an IV catheter, drew several blood laboratory values, and placed her on a cardiac monitor. Fearing that the lab results would take too long, the ED staff gave the patient IV doses of dextrose sugar solution, thiamine, and naloxone opiate antidote and prepared for a stat head CT scan. The patient suddenly "awoke" from her semiconscious state having no complaints and asking her whereabouts. She admitted to being a diabetic on oral medications who took her usual dose that morning but did not eat much breakfast fearing that she would be late to church services. Her serum glucose lab value returned dangerously low. The remaining workup was completely normal, and she was discharged with instructions on avoiding accidental hypoglycemia.

F. Exposure

ED staff must request to examine the entire patient as the condition or situation arises. In the case of acute mental status changes or trauma, ED staff is instructed to remove all clothing to allow for a complete examination of the body, including the extremities and the back of the torso to search for clues that could lead to the diagnosis.

A patient arrived somnolent with heavy alcohol on his breath. EMTs found him collapsed at the foot of the steps outside a local pub. The presumption was that the patient had stumbled and fallen down the steps. However, upon examination after removing his clothing, there were no contusions, bruises, or abrasions on the dorsal extremities (forearms, hands, shins, shoulders) that one would expect if one fell down stairs and attempted to protect oneself from injury. Upon inspection of the patient's back, a large blue swollen area on the skin was noted over the patient's left flank. Evaluation of the patient's abdomen including a CT scan revealed a shattered left kidney that required emergent removal. When the patient regained consciousness, he stated that he had been assaulted and stuck in the flank with a baseball bat.

G. Fluid Status

Is there enough blood volume to perfuse the vital organs (the brain and heart)? Is there enough volume in the system to adequately perfuse the remaining organ systems? Medical staff members use a series of signs, symptoms, and laboratory values to determine this. They are reminded not to rely too heavily on one test or value but to take the entire patient presentation and objective data into consideration. For example, a patient's vital signs of heart rate and blood pressure in one or several body positions (lying down, sitting, standing) can be used to assess volume status. As the patient loses volume the heart has less blood volume to pump around the circuit. The brain and nervous system then instruct the heart to beat harder and faster to maintain flow forward and selectively shunt blood away from less vital organs to the more sensitive ones. The result is an increase in heart rate. Over time, however, the heart and vascular shunting can no longer compensate for such loss and the blood pressure begins to decrease overall. However ideal, there are many conditions where the "obvious" vital sign adjustment to volume loss does not occur. For example, an athletic female in her twenties or thirties, an adolescent male, or a young infant might have very strong heart tissue capable of beating harder and stronger for long periods without a compensating increase in heart rate to a degree expected in otherwise healthy individuals. As a result, staff can miss evolving or imminent severe volume depletion if vital signs are the only data used to determine hydration status.

Another classic example of missing the signs of volume depletion is in the elderly frail man with a heart condition who is taking medications designed to keep his pulse rate low so as to reduce stress on his heart. Should he suffer from a case of diarrhea or vomiting that dehydrates him, his heart will be unable to respond to the decreased volume. His heart rate might remain low and his blood pressure might begin to slip precipitously and without warning. Other signs and symptoms of reduced volume or flow include dry mucous membranes of the oral cavity and ocular conjunctiva, dry, frothy saliva, and decreased skin turgor and elasticity.

TIP: If there is such compromised volume that the system is no longer capable of compensating, there can be a reduction of flow to the vital organs, resulting in neurological symptoms including lightheadedness, dizziness, or feeling faint. This is commonly seen when a patient sits up or stands from a reclined or lying down position. The medical record may refer to this as postural or orthostatic hypotension.

A reduction of flow to the heart muscle can lead to palpitations from irregular heart rhythms or chest discomfort from myocardial ischemia. Volume depletion can also lead to a decrease in urine output with a production of small amounts of dark, concentrated urine if the kidneys are working properly. Clinicians can ask a patient about her urine output or actually collect this information by asking the patient to save urine or by placing a Foley catheter into the bladder to monitor urine output over time. Dehydration, blood loss, or poor cardiac muscle function (congestive heart failure, myocardial infarction) may result in low blood pressure. As the kidneys receive less blood flow, they perceive the system as dehydrated and will begin to conserve salt and water. This produces darker, more concentrated urine in very small amounts. ED staff members can use this information to assist with the diagnosis and monitor such symptoms or findings during treatment.

H. Gastrointestinal Status/Aspiration Risk

ED staff members are instructed to assume that a patient's stomach is full until proven otherwise. Physicians are concerned with gastric contents as such material can be regurgitated into the oral cavity and aspirated into the trachea and lungs causing a severe inflammation and respiratory compromise. It takes an average of two hours for ingested material to pass through the pylorus of the stomach and enter the small intestine. Thus more often than not during the day, a patient's stomach has material that can be aspirated. Further, it is common to encounter a patient who presents having accidentally ingested materials. For example, a three-year-old boy may ingest cleaning fluid that he finds under the sink or an eighty-year-old woman may misunderstand her doctor and ingest several more prescription medications than actually instructed. A person might have a depressed mood and describe having ingested a bottle of unknown pills.

In each case above, should the patient become nauseated or have a change in mental status as a result of the ingestion, she will be unable to protect the airway. ED staff must continuously monitor these patients for aspiration risk and consider mechanically protecting the patient's airway through intubation. Other considerations include removing the material from the stomach either by simply allowing the stomach to do so over time with close observation, by mechanical gastric lavage (pumping the stomach), or more commonly, by encouraging rapid transit. This is accomplished through the administration of substances designed to reduce material assimilation and produce a catharsis (using activated charcoal or a high osmotic salt solution). In addition, nearly 10 percent of all gas inhaled during respiration is ingested into the stomach to return at some later time from above or below. If large amounts of gas are ingested quickly as with active ventilation using a bag-valve mask (BVM) or a mechanical ventilator, this can lead to progressive stomach distention and promote regurgitation of gastric contents and lead to aspiration. A gastric tube (nasogastric tube, Salem sump) should be inserted into the stomach from the nose or mouth and left open to air or connected to small amounts of suction to allow decompression and gastric content removal, thereby reducing aspiration risk.

I. History of Present Illness (HPI)

Obtaining this information is extremely important but not at the expense of the concepts listed above. ED staff members are instructed to address all of these aspects above in sequence and with repetition and constant re-visitation. Meanwhile, they are attempting to glean as much information regarding the present condition as possible. Failure to address the ABCs (airway, breathing, circulation) above in exchange for history gathering could lead to acute progressive and irreversible compromise.

This evaluation takes a very brief period of time and can save a significant amount of guesswork on the part of the ED staff. Once these more easily recognizable causes of illness are ruled out and/or monitored for new changes and treated, other causes can be investigated.

J. Treatment (TX)

Once a patient has been taken from triage into a treatment area, the ED staff will begin a series of procedures to provide ongoing care to the patient. This would include placing the patient on oxygen if this has not already been done. In addition, an intravenous (IV) catheter is inserted into a vein and blood products are drawn. Some blood tests may be saved in a container in the patient's room for later use should the ED physician deem this necessary, while others are sent directly to the lab with a "stat" request. A plastic IV catheter is left in the patient either unattached to tubing or connected to some form of intravenous solution. Common solutions include saline (sodium chloride solution) or dextrose (a concentration of sugar in water solution). (See Chapter 11, *Intravenous Therapy Records*.)

Bedside blood testing might occur at this time, such as finger stick glucose testing or arterial blood gas analysis. The patient might also be placed on a continuous oxygen saturation and cardiovascular rhythm monitor. These devices are connected to the patient via small infrared monitors on the finger or toe as well as through a blood pressure cuff to the arm or thigh and electrocardiogram leads glued with self-adhesive to the chest and limbs. This will provide the ED staff with up-to-the-minute oxygenation and cardiovascular parameters.

8.6 The Trauma Patient

Very few patient presentations can be more shocking, gruesome, and disconcerting than a victim of trauma. The multi-trauma patient can be one of the more challenging cases in a busy ED. Since it is very likely that any one injury could have fatal consequences, the ED staff has to decide which injury to focus on while evaluating and treating such a patient. The ED staff should follow accepted standards of evaluation and treatment progression guidelines established by the American College of Surgeons Committee on Trauma. Some emergency department records are formatted to permit documentation of the categories of medical consultants (trauma surgeon, neurosurgeon, orthopedic surgeon) who were alerted to the impending arrival of a trauma victim. The form may include a space to record the name of the person who was notified and the time. Once the patient arrives, the primary survey begins.

The primary survey (airway, breathing, circulation) follows the same sequential and systematic approach as the evaluation of the patient with acute mental status changes previously described. Interventions for a given system being evaluated are performed at the time that they are needed and not deferred at the expense of completing the remainder of the survey.

TIP: Physicians remind students and staff, "You are stuck on A. Stabilize A before moving on to B, otherwise you will lose your patient."

The secondary survey includes a full head-to-toe physical examination, searching for evidence of trauma and/or hemodynamic compromise. This evaluation is not performed until all of the systems of the primary survey are evaluated and considered stable. These examination findings are then combined with the history to create the assessment and plan of action. The plan includes interventions to stabilize, maintain stabilization, and evaluate the patient for signs or symptoms of impending compromise.

Staff members must realize that the traumatic condition is in evolution. An organ system's condition at the time of initial evaluation might be radically changed in a very brief period of time. Hence these patients have their hemodynamic and neurological status continuously monitored by staff until it is deemed that they have been stabilized.

A close mentor and colleague teaches, "Death begins in Radiology" to his students and residents. This is not in any way meant to degrade or demean the radiology staff. Rather, it is meant to remind emergency medical and surgical staff members that it is not the radiologists' responsibility to monitor and treat the patient but to perform radiological examinations for the trauma staff.

TIP: The Radiology Department is not equipped to perform effective resuscitations similar to an ED, OR, or ICU. Therefore, the patient must be sufficiently stabilized in the ED before going for radiological evaluation. Medical records should define who accompanied the patient to the Radiology Department.

ED staff must accompany any trauma patient with a suspicious set of findings or mechanism of injury in order to intervene if there is an acute and/or evolving compromise. The management of a trauma patient is illustrated in Appendix 8.1.

8.7 Documentation of Patient Management
A. Treat the Patient, Then Document

ED staff is instructed to document all patient evaluation and care proceedings. While standard history/physical examination checklists exist for staff needs during the triage and initial evaluation process, many emergency departments provide continuation sheets. Continuation sheets usually contain areas and titles as guides for staff notes (vital signs, temperature, oxygen saturation, medications, oral/IV fluid input, and gastric and urine output). There is also space available for staff to list multiple assessments and interventions. Staff members are reminded to document the time at which evaluations, assessments, or interventions are carried out. Nursing staff members are especially adept at this practice. They are often excellent at documenting the timing and procurement of various tests and procedure interventions as well as medication administration. Other important data might include

- all subjective complaints,
- history of present illness,
- medications/allergies,
- past medical, surgical, family, and social history,
- continued and/or evolved subjective complaints or symptoms and the timing of such complaints that have ensued since the patient's arrival,
- all objective findings, including the patient's physical examination upon arrival, and
- any additional examinations that have occurred as well as the timing of the repeated examination.

Nursing staff usually note the time of the ED physician's evaluation and examination as well as the timing of any other patient encounter with a consultant physician, interventionalist, or technologist. For example, the ED staff might have requested that a staff cardiologist evaluate the patient. ED staff will document the consultant's name, time of consultation, and time of consultant's arrival. ED staff might request a radiological evaluation such as an x-ray or ultrasound.

TIP: Staff members are instructed to document the time that the patient underwent the test. If the patient had to leave the ED for a test or procedure, the departure and return times should be noted, as well as which staff members, if any, accompanied the patient.

The documentation about and management of an intoxicated patient is illustrated in Appendix 8.2.

Assessments of the patient evaluation should be documented. This should include not only nurses' impressions of the patient but the staff physicians' and consultants' as well. Such documentation is often used by other hospital staff for the purposes of continued evaluation and treatment. This is beneficial to all staff involved in the patient's care, allowing colleagues to get a sense for what possible conditions have been considered and at what times during the evaluation. In addition to direct verbal communication between staff members, written documentation should be reviewed regularly and updated throughout the patient's stay, creating

additional means of communication and reducing unnecessary testing and analyses. Written documentation provides a vehicle for thoughts and impressions when direct verbal communication between staff members is impossible for periods of time.

Everyone involved in a patient's care wishes to know the causes of the issues at hand. While a simple solution is indeed possible, there are usually multiple possible causes for a patient's condition. It is up to the entire team (patient, family members, nursing and physician staff members) to work together to find the answer. The possible causes are commonly referred to as the differential diagnosis (abbreviated as DD or DDx). The term suggests that while one problem might well exist, the patient's condition and its associated symptoms often have many other possible explanations, some of which might be occurring simultaneously. It is up to the entire team and their combined experience to come up with the list of possibilities. The true diagnosis cannot be found until it becomes listed as one of the differential diagnoses. The team can then begin to rule out members of this differential list by considering each diagnosis in conjunction with all of the data to decide which are more or less likely to be the cause. If one of the differential diagnoses remains a viable possibility but cannot be ruled in or out using the data obtained, decisions are made to consider additional testing in the ED or as an outpatient, or the patient is admitted for continued evaluation. Commonly, there is space provided on the ED chart for the physician to describe her impressions and differential diagnosis.

TIP: Computerized and verbal dictation systems allow the physician to document more extensively because the physician is not confined by a space on the paper record. ED staff members are encouraged to provide this information in the written record on continuation sheets or as an addendum, especially if the diagnostic options are narrowed by data gleaned during the patient's evaluation.

B. Plan

Assessments are made using all data including the subjective history, objective findings, and the results of any laboratory, radiological, or any other testing modalities. The staff's intention to proceed with a particular test or procedure following an evaluation is generally considered an effective plan of action to narrow the differential and treat the condition. This aspect of the evaluation is called the plan. The more complex the patient's condition or broad the differential diagnosis, the more often the team must alter the plan of action. Such intention usually begins with a decision to apply various treatment modalities, including interventions or procedures to resuscitate, improve, or maintain the patient's current condition while moving forward with additional testing that will narrow the differential diagnosis.

As the actual diagnosis is discovered, the plan usually evolves into a detailed and focused set of treatment options that are discussed and reviewed with the patient and mutually agreed upon by the team. The treatment options, benefits, and risks are documented with specific reference to the particular patient's situation. Each option is reviewed in detail with the patient and the timing and details of this discussion should also be recorded. If the treatment involves a particular invasive procedure or medical regimen that bears some risk to the patient, the patient should be fully informed of these, and a dated and timed consent form should be provided and signed by the patient or legal guardian and attached to the record. The current or final diagnosis at the time of patient disposition from the ED is commonly listed in the designated section on the written, computer-generated or dictated chart.

C. Disposition

Ultimate plans for future evaluation or treatment should be devised. In many cases, the patient's condition makes these decisions fairly easy. For example, if a patient's asthmatic condition has improved remarkably after arrival to the ED and the patient feels much better after interventions such as medications and oxygen therapy, the ED staff might determine that the condition has stabilized enough to allow discharge. Although the staff might conclude this, the patient should make the final decision. Ultimately the patient knows her condition better than the staff and will be able to give staff members a sense for how tenuous the condition might be. Such information offered by the patient should be documented as it will prove extremely helpful for the current situation as well as possible future visits for a similar occurrence. As in the example above, the asthmatic patient told staff that she typically improves clinically when given medications initially but if discharged too early she becomes symptomatic once again and must return. Given this information, the staff might proceed more cautiously, offering the patient additional medications and observation, thereby preventing a poor outcome.

When staff members consider a disposition to home, it is wise to ask about and document the living situation. For example, does the elderly patient with a broken ankle live in a third-story apartment with no elevator? Is he actually mobile with crutches or a walker or is his balance and upper body strength quite poor? While appearing as common sense issues to consider, such social conditions are easily

missed when discharging a patient. ED staff members might consider holding or admitting a patient for such reasons, allowing case managers and social service providers the opportunity to obtain services for the patient's management.

8.8 Summary

Treating ill patients in a busy emergency department is an ongoing challenge. Prioritizing one patient's condition over another's continues to be risky business and if done incorrectly may lead to a serious morbid or mortal outcome. Emergency medicine in North America continues to work alongside hospital administrations to provide improved facility resources and accommodation availability for what appears to be an increasingly ill patient population. Such efforts assist but do not eliminate the medical and nursing staff's risk and responsibility for the provision of timely and effective care within acceptable standards.

Staff must remain vigilant and attentive to the continuous evolution of illness and adhere to established methods to assist in the identification of serious or potentially serious illness before significant complications occur. These include obtaining an extensive history of the present illness together with other relevant past medical information. An extensive physical examination should accompany the subjective information. The procurement of diagnostic testing follows an assessment of the patient's condition.

The ED professional prioritizes life-threatening conditions that could account for the presenting problem. Only when these severe conditions have been successfully eliminated from the list can less threatening conditions, however commonplace, be considered. If any situations prevent life-threatening conditions from being eliminated despite full use of facilities at the emergency department's disposal, arrangements are made to admit and observe the patient's condition for evolution and further evaluation. This is done only after the treating physician is successful in obtaining and contacting a colleague whose team is willing and able to accept the patient.

If a patient's condition has stabilized and a threat no longer exists, that patient may be discharged or transferred to the care of a physician and team who will continue to care for and monitor the patient's condition. Whenever possible, all dispositions are reviewed and left to the discretion of the patient. It must be understood and is paramount in all care education that the patient is at all times empowered to make informed decisions regarding her care. The patient should be made an active member of the treatment team and privy to all diagnostic and treatment options available based upon the advice of the medical staff. Exceptions to this include a condition in which the patient suffers from an acute mental status change and hence is not capable of making informed decisions. In this situation, an advanced directive is evaluated, or next of kin, preferably with power of attorney, is asked to participate in the decision-making process.

Endnotes

1. Laska, L. "$400,000 Massachusetts Settlement For Man's Death After Multiple Attempts at Intubation Fail." *Medical Malpractice Verdicts, Settlements, and Experts*, March 2009, p. 13.

2. Laska, L. "Obstetrician orders Labetalol for Pregnant Woman With Elevated Heart Rate and Normal Blood Pressure." *Medical Malpractice Verdicts, Settlements, and Experts*, August 2009, p. 32.

3. Laska, L. "Failure to Note Abnormality in Cervical Spine on X-ray Following Auto Collision." *Medical Malpractice Verdicts, Settlements, and Experts*, August 2009, p. 13.

Appendix 8.1
The Most Common Cause of Low Blood Pressure or Shock in a Trauma Patient Is Due to Blood Loss until Proven Otherwise

Paramedics arrived after being called to the scene of a man lying by a park bench. He was unconscious with a feeble pulse and sonorous respirations. His empty wallet lay in the grass nearby. A small amount of blood was found on the grass by the patient's head where a large scalp laceration was noted. The medics immediately immobilized the patient while turning him onto his back, intubated the airway while securing his cervical spine, began assisted ventilations using an ambu bag, and administered 100 percent oxygen. They found that he had clear lungs bilaterally, CO_2 detection on the endotracheal capnometer device indicating tracheal intubation, and no evidence of abdominal distention suggestive of esophageal intubation.

The paramedics then noted a feeble pulse in the neck and groin but none at the wrists or feet. Appropriately concluding that the patient's blood pressure was low, the medics proceeded to place two large-bore IV catheters and began an infusion of saline solution. After sliding the patient onto a spinal immobilization board and placing him in the ambulance, the med-

ics proceeded to examine the patient further while driving to the local ED. They noted no other obvious bony deformities of the cervical spine, chest, abdomen, or extremities. A repeat set of vital signs consisted of a pulse rate of 100, blood pressure of 60/00, and spontaneous respiratory rate of only 3. There were no witnesses at the scene. The patient had only a driver's license but no other identifiers of medical history, medications, or allergies. They radioed the facility, a Level I trauma center, describing the incident that they encountered, presenting the patient, his examination findings, and their interventions prior to and during transport. The medics concluded that the patient had been assaulted, possibly mugged, and were concerned that he was suffering from a severe head injury.

After hearing the paramedics' transmission, the triage nurse and covering ED physician categorized the patient as a Level I, highest priority, notified the covering trauma team and neurosurgeon, prepared a critical care bed in the ED and notified the radiology staff to have a portable x-ray machine and the CT scanner open and prepared for this patient. The triage staff and nurses assigned to the patient began the ED evaluation documents, noting the time of transmission, who was notified in the hospital for the event, and who was present prior to the patient's arrival. The ED physician, nurse, and the trauma team were waiting in the room. A second nurse was assigned to scribe the findings of the team leader, and a third was assigned as a runner for medications, additional IV tubing, monitoring devices, and miscellaneous items. The ED physician assumed the role of examiner and positioned herself at the foot of the bed and assigned each trauma team member a specific role and position around the patient. The trauma surgeon assumed the role of team leader, standing at the foot of the bed where she could observe the proceedings and suggest interventions as needed.

Paramedics brought the patient directly into the critical care bed as instructed by the triage nurse. He remained unconscious with assisted ventilations using the ambu bag, and his color was ashen gray. The ED physician listened to the patient's breathing and checked the position of the endotracheal tube while the nurse placed the patient on the heart monitor and checked the blood pressure. Repeated vital signs were noted: heart rate 100, blood pressure 80/50, and a spontaneous respiratory rate of 12. Oxygen saturation was noted to be 100 percent. The patient did not respond to verbal or painful stimulus. The team leader agreed with the ED physician and ordered the patient to be ventilated at a rate of 20/minute in an effort to protect the patient's brain. Orders included continuation of normal saline solution as a rapid infusion to a total of 1.5 liters and 4 units of type O packed red blood cells to be administered immediately if the blood pressure did not normalize from the saline. As the trauma team cut away the patient's clothes, the ED physician surveyed the patient for evidence of trauma. She noted a large gaping scalp laceration on the side of the head with minimal bleeding. The remaining examination of the head and neck was normal. She found no evidence of trauma to the chest, abdomen, extremities, or back during the examination. Neurologically, while the patient was unresponsive to verbal or painful stimulus, his pupillary and extremity reflexes were all normal to both the ED physician and the neurosurgeon.

The patient's spine was kept immobile in a cervical collar and on a stiff slide board. A catheter was inserted into the patient's bladder for continuous urine production monitoring. A nasogastric tube was inserted and attached to low suction. No gastric contents were noted. Blood samples were obtained, including a blood type analysis, and sent to the lab. The history was reviewed with the paramedics. The team agreed that after stabilization of the patient's vital signs, immediate evaluation of the patient's brain and cervical spine was indicated. In addition, as no other history could be obtained and the patient was unconscious and unable to provide an objective examination, an abdominal CT scan was to be performed along with the head scan, if possible. The radiologist was informed and asked to stand by.

After saline infusion, the patient's vital signs were recorded: heart rate 92, blood pressure 80/50, and respirations 12. Oxygen saturation remained at 100 percent. The trauma surgeon suggested immediate infusion of two units of blood while a portable x-ray machine was used

to image the chest and pelvis. A bedside ultrasound machine was used by the ED physician and trauma surgeon to image the heart and abdomen in search of evidence of free fluid. None was noted. The nurse scribe continued to document all examination data and the timing of all fluid and blood administration as well as vital signs, oxygen saturation, and urine output. Although the neurosurgeon suggested that a CT scan be performed as quickly as possible, she agreed with the team that the patient required stabilization of his heart rate and blood pressure before being transported to the scanner.

After infusion of two units of blood, the patient's vital signs were noted: heart rate 80 and blood pressure 96/60. Oxygen saturation remained at 100 percent. A radial pulse was detected, and the team obtained an arterial blood sample for analysis. The blood bank forwarded two units of type-specific blood which were then administered to the patient. The large scalp laceration began to bleed profusely as the blood pressure improved, and a team member closed this wound using layers of suture with excellent hemostasis (control of bleeding). Vital signs were noted after the repair and during the continued blood transfusions: heart rate 78, and blood pressure 104/68. The patient began to move his fingers. The chest and pelvis x-rays were developed and read as normal. Blood tests returned, noting a low hematocrit of 30 (normal 38-45). The patient's skin appeared to return to a normal coloration, and urine was noted from the bladder catheter. A radio-opaque contrast material was instilled down the patient's nasogastric tube in preparation for the abdominal CT scan. The nurse scribe noted the vital sign values and the time.

With improvement of the patient's vital signs, the trauma team agreed that the patient was sufficiently stable to be transported with physician and nurse escort to the CT scanner. This was accomplished with continued stabilization of the patient's vital signs and gradual improvement of the patient's neurological status. The head CT noted a large scalp hematoma but no evidence of intracranial trauma. The cervical spine and abdominal CT were also normal.

Upon return to the ED, the team met to review the case. Repeated vital signs continued to show improvement; the neurosurgeon noted the patient was able to respond appropriately to verbal commands. He coughed through the endotracheal tube. Mild sedation was required. The ventilator was adjusted to allow the patient to breathe on his own without hyperventilation. The trauma surgeon suggested that the patient be admitted to her service in the ICU for continued one-to-one nursing monitoring as well as trauma and neurosurgical evaluation.

The patient did very well and was extubated the following morning. He was able to recount that he was seated at a park bench in a secluded park but recalled nothing further. Based upon the data obtained from the case, it was concluded that the patient suffered a blow to the head and sustained a large scalp laceration that nearly exsanguinated him. He suffered from a closed head trauma, a concussion, but no parenchymal (brain tissue) damage. After monitoring the patient's vital signs and neurological status for several days, the physician felt the patient was stable for discharge. The team sent him home with a series of written instructions provided by both the physician and nursing staff. These reviewed his case and evaluation findings in detail and several aspects of continued home monitoring. He was given a post-closed head injury definition and checklist of concerning symptoms, and he was told to return immediately to the ED for evaluation should any of such signs or symptoms of complications arise or if he had any questions or concerns. He was also provided with a wound care definition and checklist that included how to care for his scalp laceration, how to identify signs of wound infection, and when to return for suture removal. An appointment with the trauma service was arranged and documented for the patient. Neurosurgical follow-up was also arranged. After the patient reviewed the material and had additional questions answered by the staff, he signed his patient education instructions indicating his understanding and went home. The patient returned a few days later to the trauma clinic for suture removal from his scalp. Team members noted significant healing of the wound without evidence of complication. They documented that the patient had no other physical or psychological complaints and his physical exami-

nation was otherwise normal. The patient did not attend his neurosurgical appointment.

Appendix 8.2
Management and Documentation of the Intoxicated Patient

A twenty-four-year-old male was brought to the ED by police officers after being pulled over for dangerous driving, and they suspected that he was under the influence of alcohol. Officers observed the patient drive away from a local pub and became concerned when he passed through a stop sign. The police thought they smelled alcohol on his breath and noticed slurring of his speech and the inability to stand without assistance. The patient refused a roadside breathalyzer test. Police transported him directly to the emergency department.

After the triage nurse took the history from the police, he noted the patient aroused to verbal command, could protect his airway, and had stable vital signs. The nurse documented these findings and admitted the patient into the ED, triaging the patient as a level II (stable airway and vital signs but somnolent and at risk for airway compromise, possibly due to drug ingestion) and documenting his assessment. The nurse placed him on a cardiac monitor, applied oxygen via nasal cannula, and established IV fluids. The ED physician immediately met the patient. The patient admitted that he "drank a few beers" earlier that evening but denied any other drug ingestion. The patient denied any recent trauma, illness, or significant past medical history. He denied any medication use or illicit drug abuse but admitted to occasional alcohol consumption.

After completing a full physical examination, the ED physician ordered the continuation of monitored hemodynamics, oxygenation, and neurological status. She documented her findings. The physician's assessment included acute alcohol intoxication but could not rule out the possibility of simultaneous drug ingestion creating the symptoms. She requested a blood alcohol level (BAL), serum and urine toxicological analysis searching for other drugs of abuse including opiates, cocaine, benzodiazepines, barbiturates, phenothiazines, cyclic antidepressants, amphetamines, acetaminophen, and aspirin.

The patient remained hemodynamically stable and continued to arouse to verbal command with improved slurred speech and sensorium. The nurse recorded the times and extent of each improvement in the patient's condition. The toxicological analysis revealed a blood alcohol concentration (BAC) of 260 mg/dl. There were no other substances discovered.

Blood alcohol levels (BAL, BAC) are expressed in milligrams per deciliter (mg/dL) in most hospitals. An alcohol level of 100 mg/dL is the equivalent of 1 part alcohol in 1000 parts of solution (blood). Therefore, 100 mg/dL would be equal to a 0.1 percent concentration. In many states, 80 to 100 mg/dL represents the threshold concentration above which a person is legally intoxicated when driving (DWI, DUI).

Most alcoholic beverages contain approximately ten grams of ethanol. Alcohol concentrations vary from ten ounces (300 cc) of regular beer (5 percent ethanol content), four ounces of wine (12 percent ethanol content), or one ounce of vodka (40 percent ethanol content or 80 "proof"). The average person can metabolize approximately one drink (10 grams) or 300-500mg/dL per hour. Therefore for the patient described above, it would take approximately five hours from the time the blood alcohol level was drawn until he had a concentration that was below the legal limit.

Blood alcohol concentrations and associated clinical findings may be categorized as follows:

- intoxication 100-150 mg/dL,
- loss of muscle coordination, 150-200 mg/dL,
- decreased level of consciousness, 200-300 mg/dL, and
- obtundation (stupor), coma and death, 300-600 mg/dL.

Scientific studies suggest that many motor vehicle drivers become impaired at a level of 80 mg/dL. However, impairment may begin as low as 20 mg/dL and is common at 50 mg/dL.

The physician recorded her repeat examination findings and instructed the nurse to continue monitoring the patient for an additional five hours. The patient's mental status continued to improve over this period. The physician and nurse observed him ambulate steadily when he was completely alert and oriented. These findings were documented, and the patient was given instructions to avoid alcohol intoxication, to return to the ED with any concerns, and was discharged. The final diagnosis was recorded as "Acute Ethanol Intoxication."

Chapter 9

Critical Care Records

Kathleen C. Ashton, APRN, BC, PhD

9.1 Introduction to Critical Care Nursing

Attorneys, paralegals, legal nurse consultants, and others involved in medical-legal issues need to understand how to read critical care documentation. The evaluation of damages or deviations from the standard of care can hinge on being able to decipher critical care notes. The injuries sustained as a result of an accident may be sufficiently severe to necessitate admission to a critical care unit. Patients may be transferred to a critical care unit following a change in condition or a medical mishap elsewhere in the hospital. The evaluation of conscious pain and suffering is based in part on critical care documentation. For all of these reasons, being able to decipher critical care documentation can assist the legal professional in the handling of a claim.

In the 1960s, the first cardiac care units were set up in response to the recognition of the need for specialized care for individuals with similar complex conditions. For the first time critical care healthcare providers were able to focus their efforts on a group of patients with issues in common. The rates of patient survival soared dramatically.

This concept of grouping patients with similar concerns was soon expanded to include patients with primarily neurological issues, followed by those with surgical problems and later, those who had experienced a traumatic episode. For individuals with non-surgical, non-trauma issues, medical intensive care units were established. Large university teaching hospitals and urban medical centers could support several specialized units, while community hospitals developed a single unit for focused care that became known as an Intensive Care Unit. Here individuals with potentially fatal illnesses or conditions receive specialized care from healthcare professionals with advanced skills, experience, and in most cases, certification. The more current and generic term used to refer to the care rendered in such units is critical care.

9.2 Types of Units

TIP: The trend today is towards more specialized units according to the patient's diagnosis and age, if the institution can support them.

This facilitates the availability of a more experienced and appropriately prepared staff to handle the specific needs of this patient group. Typical units in use today are neonatal or neurological intensive care units (both of which use the acronym NICU), pediatric intensive care units (PICU), surgical intensive care units (SICU), cardiac intensive care units (CICU or CCU), cardiovascular intensive care units (CVICU), post-anesthesia care units (PACU), and maternal or medical intensive care units (both of which use the acronym MICU). As acronyms occasionally can stand for different units in varied settings, it is wise to investigate the way a particular institution classifies a particular unit. Nursing units that are a step below intensive care units in terms of the acuity level of patients are referred to as stepdown or intermediate care units.

9.3 Standards of Critical Care Nursing

The American Association of Critical Care Nurses (AACN) is a professional nursing organization that was established in 1969 as the Association of Cardiovascular Nurses. Its purpose was to assist in educating nurses working in the recently developed intensive care units of that time. Recognizing the need to encompass all of critical care nursing, the organization became the AACN in 1971 to represent all nurses who render care to critically ill individuals with complex diagnoses in the various units. As the largest specialty nursing organization in the world, it promulgates standards for critical care nursing practice through its numerous professional publications.[1] Standards for practice can also be obtained from the American Nurses Association's various practice statements.[2]

The Society for Critical Care Medicine provides practice guidelines for physicians and other providers in critical care. Many useful documents and information can be found on their website at www.sccm.org/Pages/default.aspx.

9.4 The Practice of Critical Care Medicine and Nursing

Critical care medicine encompasses an array of practitioners who ideally work together to bring the best possible care to the patient. Typical providers include respiratory therapists, occupational therapists, pharmacists, pastoral care providers, social workers, as well as nurses and physicians. Patients in critical care areas are frequently seen by several doctors in a twenty-four-hour period. In large teaching hospitals, interns and residents attend to patients under the auspices of the attending physician. In organizations without a teaching program, the attending physician will generally consult one or more specialty physicians when the patient has complex medical problems.[3]

Specially trained and certified physicians provide critical care in a variety of settings, including the critical care unit and the emergency department. Following a residency and fellowship in critical care medicine, physicians can become board certified in critical care medicine through successful completion of the certifying examination and appropriate experience.

Intensivists, or critical care physicians, are specialists in critical care who have taken supplemental training (and/or certification) after completing medicine, surgery, or an-

esthesiology residencies. In many ICUs, non-critical care physicians deliver the bulk of the care, often while also attending to their routine non-ICU daily duties. Frequently, the complex ICU patient is cared for by a whole array of physicians practicing individual specialties; in such cases a patient may have a surgeon, general internist, family physician, pulmonologist, cardiologist, nephrologist, infectious disease specialist, and hematologist all writing orders and managing individual aspects of care at different times of the day.[4]

Frequently, critical care units are using the services of intensivists in conjunction with other providers. Numerous organizations, including Leap Frog Group (http://www.leapfroggroup.org/home), regulatory agencies, and third-party payers, are encouraging hospitals to ensure appropriate intensivist support exists in their ICUs.

TIP: Critical care nursing is the diagnosis and treatment of human responses to actual or potential life-threatening illness.[5] The scope of critical care nursing practice is defined by the interaction of the critical care nurse, the critically ill patient, and an environment that provides adequate resources for the provision of care.

Patients enter the critical care environment to receive intensive care for a variety of health alterations. The continuum of patients presenting for care ranges from the patient in need of frequent monitoring, yet requiring little intervention, to the patient with multi-system failure requiring interventions to support the most basic of life functions. While the environment generally supports a nurse-to-patient ratio of one to two, depending on patient needs, one nurse may care for three patients and, occasionally, a patient may require the assistance of more than one nurse to survive. The support and treatment of these patients requires an environment in which information is readily available from a variety of sources and is organized in such a manner that decisions can be made quickly and accurately. Information is obtained through a balance of both human intervention and technological assistance. Indeed, the critical care environment is highly technical by nature.[6]

9.5 Documentation Issues

Documentation challenges in the critical care area relate to the intensity of care, the performance of highly repetitive, technical tasks at frequent intervals, and complex patient problems.[7] Timely, comprehensive, and meaningful documentation is a challenge for even the most competent and experienced critical care practitioner. The process of documentation is quite time consuming with estimates of more than one-half hour of paperwork generated for every hour of patient care delivered in a hospital unit.[8]

9.6 Types of Records and Systems

While many of the documentation systems currently used in critical care are based on the traditional paper medical record, the advantages of computerized, automated bedside records for this environment are well recognized. Many units are in the process of moving to computerized records. Computers that are interfaced with vital bedside monitoring equipment can provide continuous data printouts. Interfaces also assist in the active treatment of patients, requiring little physical intervention by the nurse. For example, researchers have developed a closed-loop system interfacing infusion pump to bedside monitor. The system automatically delivers the appropriate dose of prescribed drugs in response to the patient's blood pressure measurement. Both simple and complex calculations are completed in an instant. Laboratory values and other ancillary information can be readily available at the bedside, negating the need for the professional to "seek and find" pieces of pertinent information on which to base further treatment decisions. Despite these advantages, critical care information systems have not seen widespread acceptance. This is probably due to the cost of systems both in terms of hardware and the ongoing technical support required to maintain the system.[9]

In lieu of an automated charting system, the introduction of the microprocessor in the 1970s created an explosion of computer driven bedside equipment on into the 1980s and continuing to this day. This equipment has affected the critical care environment, and subsequently, the documentation of care provided. State-of-the-art computerized patient monitoring systems and other lifesaving devices such as external defibrillators have the capacity to capture, store, and record patient vital signs and significant events. Indeed, critical care professionals frequently rely on these (particularly the bedside monitoring systems) to capture vital signs as they become involved in the active assessment and treatment of highly unstable patients. In these cases, the nurse will document retrospectively based on the information stored by the device. Frequently, nurses use these printouts as "addendums" to flow sheet charting. As a result, a review of nursing documentation will include a curious mix of handwritten and computerized records.[10]

TIP: When reviewing documentation, the attorney would do well to compare the times noted on the handwritten documentation with the printed times in the monitoring printouts. There can be many explanations in addition to the obvious ones.

The author served as an expert witness on an interesting case in which the nurse purposely set her watch ten minutes fast to avoid being late for work each day. During a code, there was a discrepancy in response time after the alarm sounded. Through discovery it became evident that while the inaccurate watch setting enabled punctuality, it raised a question of delayed response to a life-threatening situation. A late entry in the nurses' notes contained the statement, "according to Jane Doe's watch," which clearly raised a red flag.

Research has shown that rather than take nurses away from the bedside, automated information systems can actually lead to increased time available for direct patient care. In a study assessing changes in nurses' activities after installation of an ICU information system, Wong and colleagues[11] found that installation of the system decreased the percentage of time ICU nurses spent on documentation by more than 30 percent. In this study, nurses used almost half of this time savings on a direct patient care task such as patient assessment.

Taking technology a step further, more than 150 hospital systems across the nation are using eICUs, or virtual ICUs to meet the standards of physician coverage set forth by regulatory groups. Using virtual ICU software, a board certified critical care intensivist monitors patient parameters from a distant setting where data from several units are being tracked. Using video, voice, and data software and hardware, the remote staff can monitor patient parameters, check ventilator settings, and review test results. The software gives a more comprehensive picture of the patient as it analyzes all of the data together to spot trends or detect subtle changes. The virtual ICU is the brainchild of two intensivists from Johns Hopkins Medical Center and is being used to leverage the scarcity of intensivists and support the nursing staff in critical care units.[12] Documentation issues in this setting are not fully recognized yet but could conceivably become troubling when coupled with system failure and down times.

9.7 Use of Computerized Records

Saving time is one important impetus for the initiation of computerized or electronic medical records (EMR). Another advantage is the improved legibility of entries in the electronic record and still another is the ability to link records to other departments for information sharing. Critical care units currently use any combination of bedside monitors connected directly to a computerized record, an electronic documentation system, an electronic medication administration recording system, or a barcoding system for medication administration. Some systems are comprehensive; others are phased in by increments over a period of time. Each program has inherent capabilities and limitations which must be understood by users and evaluators. Critical care professionals are oriented to the system through tutorials and workshops and are then provided with an access code and a resource for problems or questions that may arise in using the system. Only professionals who have completed the orientation tutorial receive an access code that can then be used to track use of the system by each person. Additionally, most units keep a supply of the formerly used paper flow sheets and other records on hand to use in times of computer down time or system failure.

TIP: Some EMR systems allow changes or corrections in documentation either electronically or by hand.

Most facilities have policies governing such changes as well as other aspects of documentation by use of the EMR. Printing of the EMR occurs on a scheduled basis and can also be accomplished at the end of each admission in some systems. Other important issues involving EMR systems include security concerns, such as tracking and monitoring activity on the system, capturing hidden passwords, recording all keystrokes, clipboard activity, menus and mouse clicks, data storage, backup and recovery, and accountability of healthcare providers. It is often helpful to obtain the hospital policies on documentation when evaluating documentation using computerized records.

In evaluating the record, the reviewer must first make certain a complete electronic record has been provided by the facility. Signs that may signal tampering when using EMRs are inconsistent format, print style, or font, inconsistencies among different sources, and inconsistencies in time stamps among different EMR components or between handwritten and electronic records. Refer to Chapter 6, *Computerized Medical Records*, in Volume I, for more information.

9.8 The Bedside Flow Sheet

The flow sheet is the cornerstone of bedside critical care nursing and respiratory therapy documentation. (Respiratory therapists are often involved in documentation regarding ventilators.) A well-constructed, comprehensive flow sheet communicates and reflects the standard of care of the major patient population served by the unit. The data are organized so that assessments and routine interventions are predetermined, cueing the nurse to ensure that documentation is complete and addresses all essential areas of nursing intervention. Depending on the patient population served, the cues will vary. For example, the flow sheet of the Cardiovascular Intensive Care Unit (CVICU) may have very

specific assessment parameters that cue the nurse to document the quality and amount of chest tube drainage hourly, whereas the records of the Coronary Care Unit (CCU) may not specify this parameter since patients with an acute MI do not routinely have chest tubes.[13] The actual process for designing a flow sheet is beyond the scope of this discussion; however, Figure 9.1 lists information sources for a critical care flow sheet.

TIP: Flow sheet design is as variable as the organizations that create them.[14]

Information Sources for a Critical Care Flow sheet

- Documentation standards of professional associations such as the American Nurses Association (ANA) or the American Association of Critical Care Nurses (AACN).
- Specific standards of care as defined by specialty organizations and current literature.
- Equipment considerations: calibration, alarms and alert settings, functional settings.
- Institution and unit policies and procedures.
- Pertinent patient safety issues: restraints, skin protocols, nutritional assessment.
- Clinical data: intake & output, vital signs, assessments, arterial blood gases, medication administration, hemodynamic parameters such as Swan-Ganz catheter readings or intracranial pressure monitoring.
- Laboratory and other ancillary departmental information.

Figure 9.1

Some organizations create forms that open out like a road map. For example, the flow sheet may be the size of four 8.5"×11" pieces of paper that folds out to be 32"×11" but may contain as many as eight sides. A landscape orientation presents information across the sheet with all significant parameters viewed in light of recorded interventions. Other organizations prefer to keep the pages in a portrait orientation, such as the format of this page. The pages may be folded in to create a compact document. Regardless of the form of presentation, information such as vital signs, medication administration, laboratory test results and other ongoing assessment and intervention data are generally placed conspicuously. Other, more routine or "scripted" information, such as nursing interventions or total body assessments, will be embedded more strategically. Generally, the time column is left blank, allowing the nurse to designate, based on patient status, the frequency of vital signs or other significant events. As a result, one form or a compilation of many forms may represent a twenty-four-hour period of documentation. This timed charting is done as events unfold as opposed to block charting which is generally used in the narrative note that describes an overall snapshot of the patient's condition for a period of time.[15] Appendices 9.1 and 9.2 are examples of critical care flow sheets.

Organizing the critical care documentation can be challenging. Dates are not always written on each sheet. A twenty-four-hour period may be contained on four to ten single sheets. The reviewer must be careful not to shuffle the pages out of the order in which they were supplied by the facility. It is advisable to look for cues that indicate how many pages are in each set of flow sheets. Some facilities mark the pages as 1 of 8, and so on. Other forms are designed to have the nurse assigned to care for the patient sign the bottom of each page. Understanding the format of the flow sheet will help identify missing pages.

A. Use of the Flow Sheet for Documentation

The purpose of the flow sheet is to provide an ongoing, continuous record of the patient's status over time. This may be in increments of a few minutes to each hour. It is essential to remember, however, that the flow sheet is but a piece of the total picture for documentation of the nursing process. It is used in conjunction with the progress notes and other essential pieces of documentation to describe the total delivery of nursing services to the client. It is essential that documentation include attention to all aspects of the nursing process: assessment, diagnosis, planning, intervention, and evaluation. The documentation of the patient's response, progress or deterioration, and the achievement of outcomes is an essential part of documentation.[16] Ideally, the nurse possesses an understanding of the purpose and use of the flow sheet as a means of documenting nursing care. Particular areas of ongoing nursing assessments that may be documented on a flow sheet are IV site rotation (IV sites are routinely changed every 72 hours), infection protocols such as ventilator associated pneumonia (VAP), restraint monitoring, turning and repositioning schedules, skin integrity assessments, titration of IV drips, fluid challenges, and drug holidays (e.g., suspension of sedation). Alternatively, separate flow sheets may be used for each of these parameters.

Assessment is an important area captured in the flow sheet. Baseline and ongoing assessments are pivotal in providing safe and competent nursing care. Two recent cases demonstrate the importance of documenting ongoing assessments.

The plaintiff's decedent, age seventy-one, was admitted to the defendant facility in April 2004 due to fevers and renal failure. At the time, the decedent had a tracheotomy and was ventilator dependent. The decedent had a medical history significant for coronary disease, COPD, and congestive heart failure. On the second day of his admission, the decedent's respiratory concerns were addressed. The nursing interventions included tracheotomy care by monitoring secretions, providing ventilator support and monitoring his vital signs and oxygen saturation levels. The plaintiff claimed that it was known to the staff that the decedent had a recurrent habit of flicking off the finger unit which measured his oxygen saturation level. The decedent was being weaned from the ventilator and was tolerating being weaned from the ventilator and had made attempts to speak. One evening the defendant took over the decedent's nursing care around 7:00 P.M. Around 8:30 P.M. a large mucous plug was suctioned. Around 9:00 P.M. the defendant recorded the decedent's vital signs. About fifty-five minutes later a code was called. About five to ten minutes before the decedent was found unresponsive a student nurse in the ICU heard an alarm sounding in the decedent's room. She approached the defendant and was told to go check the alarm. Upon entering the room the student nurse noted that the decedent was unresponsive and without a pulse. The pulse oximetry finger unit was detached from the decedent's finger and the pulse and blood pressure alarms were sounding. The defendant was attending another patient and did not respond to the alarm until another nurse summoned him. The defendant did not respond to assist the decedent until the student nurse and/or other nurse indicated that there was an emergency with his patient. When the code was called a large mucus plug was extracted from the decedent's tracheotomy. By this time the decedent had been deprived of oxygen for about five to ten minutes. The decedent was bag-ventilated and CPR and ACLS were given. After about twenty minutes the decedent was stabilized. He never again regained consciousness. A subsequent EEG was consistent with diffuse brain damage. The decedent was discharged to a skilled nursing facility about two weeks later. He died in early July 2004 from complications of his anoxic brain injury. The defendant claimed that there was no requirement that he monitor the decedent with any increased frequency despite the mucous plug previously encountered. The defendant was further prepared to testify that he was unable to respond to the alarm any sooner due to the other patient he was treating at the time. A $700,000 settlement was reached. [17]

In another case, the nurses failed to assess a patient who was developing neurological impairment.

The plaintiff was a sixty-eight-year-old woman who underwent surgery on a Friday to remove a kidney due to cancer. The defendant anesthesiologist placed an epidural catheter infusing with 0.125 percent Marcaine preoperatively for the purpose of postoperative pain control. On Sunday, two days following surgery, the patient began to experience signs and symptoms of neurological impairment involving her legs, including sensation of unusual heaviness in both legs, and altered vital signs. Thereafter, the hospital intensive care unit nursing staff failed to perform adequate assessments to determine the nature and full extent of any impaired neurological status or to alert the defendant anesthesiologist regarding the observed changes in neurological function. Although these changes had been reported on Saturday, at a time in which the catheter did not appear to be working properly, the anesthesiologist did not come to the hospital to examine her, or to examine the dysfunctional catheter, at any time during the weekend. On Monday morning, while making rounds, her surgeon noted she could not move her legs and asked the anesthesiologist to see the patient. However, the anesthesiologist failed to examine the patient on that date, but did issue an order to discontinue her epidural catheter. He gave no instructions to the nursing staff to assess the plaintiff's motor functions, and ordered that she be transferred from ICU to a regular medical ward—where she remained hospitalized and paralyzed from the waist down for another twenty-four hours without examination or evaluation of the cause of her paralysis.

During rounds on Tuesday, the surgeon again requested that the anesthesiologist perform an emergency evaluation of the plaintiff, since she remained paralyzed. Although noted by the anesthesiologist that the patient had been paralyzed for more than twenty-four hours, he again did not conduct a thorough evaluation or initiate treatment of her neurological deficits. The plaintiff was transferred later in the day to a tertiary care center for further neurological work-up. The plaintiff suffered arachnoiditis from her epidural catheter. Subsequent treatments proved unsuccessful, and she remained paralyzed from the T8 level down, with permanent bowel and bladder dysfunction. The plaintiff's experts contend that her anesthesiologist was negligent in failing to examine her when her catheter did not appear to be working properly and when her neurological status and vital signs adversely changed on Sunday. Furthermore, the anesthesiologist failed to instruct properly nurses caring for the plaintiff to assess for changes in neurological status and to report changes to him. Experts also criticized the nursing staff for failing to perform proper neurological evaluations and to appreciate that changes in the plaintiff's motor functions and vital signs. Had the plaintiff's epidural catheter been properly managed, changes in status been timely reported, and evaluation and treatment begun early on Monday morning, the plaintiff's experts believed the plaintiff would not have suffered complete paralysis of her legs or loss of bowel and bladder functions. This action was resolved in a $1,200,000 settlement, according to a published account.[18]

B. Casual or Rote Charting

Experienced critical care nurses are well versed in the use of flow sheet documentation, but the attorney may detect a few of the common pitfalls when reviewing these documents. These include casual or rote charting and relying too heavily on the flow sheet.

TIP: Casual or rote charting is defined as the practice of casually checking off certain parameters in the same manner as the previous nurse caring for the patient.[19]

An example of casual charting occurs when going through the head-to-toe assessment prompts, the night nurse checks the boxes as the evening nurse had done in the prior shift. The nurse will then use the nurses' notes or hourly entries to chart the actual specific assessment information. This may result in an obvious discrepancy if the patient's condition has changed or there are inconsistencies in the actual level of care provided.[20]

A second version of casual charting occurs when the nurse ignores the preprinted assessment altogether and documents in the nurses' notes: "Assessment as previously noted."[21] Such broad sweeping statements do not take into account subtle changes in patient status that may be quite significant. From a legal standpoint, such statements might represent a dereliction of the responsibility to provide ongoing assessment of the patient. Dating and timing entries for the actual time completed assist in properly documenting ongoing assessments of the patient.

The accuracy of charting comes into question when the patient's condition is inconsistent with the documentation. The following case hinged on the credibility of notes that stated that the patient refused continuous passive motion therapy.

The plaintiff, age forty-four, underwent heart surgery in January 2005, which involved a percutaneous repair of patent foramen ovale of the heart. Two hours later she developed hypotension from bleeding into the sack surrounding her heart. She progressed to tamponade, which caused a cardiac arrest. Emergency pericardialcentesis was performed. CPR was performed until a surgical team could be assembled. The plaintiff then underwent surgery to repair the leak. The plaintiff suffered hypoxic brain damage. She suffered total blindness for a while and severe vision problems for several months. The plaintiff claimed that she is mentally disorganized, has severe short term memory deficits and has a permanent tremor in her dominant hand. The plaintiff alleged negligence in the failure to respond to the leaking blood. The plaintiff also claimed that the nurse failed to accurately chart the developments as they occurred and that the monitoring equipment failed. The plaintiff maintained that if the tamponade had been timely diagnosed in the early stages, she would not have suffered a cardiac arrest and would not have suffered hypoxic brain damage. The defendant claimed that there was no negligence and that no equipment malfunctioned. According to a published account a defense verdict was returned.[22]

C. Reliance on the Flow Sheet

At times nurses improperly depend too heavily on the flow sheet to describe the entire course of care delivered, resulting in the flow sheet becoming the only evidence of care rendered.[23] In addition to observations, the nurse is required to evaluate and document the patient's response to nursing care provided. By documenting solely on the flow sheet, the nurse neglects to evaluate nursing care rendered, to make

recommendations for nursing care, or in general to give evidence of professional nursing care beyond that which can be checked off on a flow sheet. Although hospital policy differs, most institutions require a narrative or written note using some standard format at regular intervals or whenever there is a significant change in patient status. A written note in addition to the flow sheet documentation may also be used to focus attention on an ongoing patient care issue, thus providing information on progress made or resolution of the issue. In any case, the flow sheet may be insufficient to document delivery of total nursing care.

9.9 Physician Documentation

Documentation by physicians in critical care differs from documentation in other settings in terms of length and detail of the progress note. The note will typically begin with data regarding abnormal vital signs. The patient may be described as afebrile (without fever). The maximum temperature in the preceding twenty-four hours may be noted as "T Max." The current temperature may be documented as TC. The patient with an elevated heart rate might be described as "tachy" for tachycardia. A slow heart rate may be described as "brady" for bradycardia. The note may state the range of pulse rates, such as 100-120 beats per minute. Physicians tend to include test results, laboratory data, and other details not always seen in notes in less intensive settings. The array of physicians involved in the care of a critically ill individual necessitates a more detailed note to convey subtle and vital information concerning changes in condition and implications for patient prognosis. The plan of care can drastically change from moment to moment in an ICU, and precise and comprehensive documentation can preclude many pitfalls. Some units rely on preformatted notes to ease the amount of actual writing. Other units have instituted computerized documentation for physicians.

Typically, documentation will include an identification of the author by specialty or status, a review of the previous visit or time of documentation, a statement of sources for the note such as nursing staff or tests performed, a complete review of body systems, and an identification of the priority problems. Some physicians also document all of the medications the patient is currently receiving. The plan of care is included as well as any expectations or reactions to recent changes.

One area in electronic documentation that has been shown to be problematic is the practice of some nurses entering orders for physicians. If there is an issue with a particular order, both the physician and the nurse can be implicated if the nurse entered the physician's order into the record. This is an ongoing issue involving physicians who abdicate responsibility and rely on nurses to perform this function. Chapter 21, *Physician Documentation in Hospitals and Nursing Homes*, has additional information on this subject.

9.10 Comparison of Records by Type of Institution—"Magnet" Status

TIP: Healthcare institutions that have earned the "Magnet" designation from the American Nurses Credentialing Center are recognized as places where nursing practice is exceptional and the nursing staff attrition rates are low.

Nurses are attracted to Magnet Hospitals for the supportive environment and superb nursing opportunities that they offer. A list of hospitals and healthcare facilities that have earned magnet status is available on the American Nurses Association website: www.nursingworld.org. Currently 5 percent of hospitals nationwide have earned this designation. One attraction of these Magnet Hospitals is attention to documentation resulting in a system that is both user-friendly and beneficial in terms of capturing and recording pertinent patient data. Nurses using these systems are able to effectively and efficiently document the care rendered. In many instances, the documentation system in use has been developed with much input from the nurses using the system in their practice, as opposed to a system mandated by nursing administration.

9.11 Special Circumstances Encountered in Critical Care

As a specialized environment for the delivery of nursing care, critical care units present some unique challenges to effective documentation of care.[24] Some of these challenges and their implications are addressed below.

A. Unresponsiveness

The unresponsive patient presents a special challenge to documentation. This person is dependent upon caregivers for every need, yet in most cases, the patient cannot convey his needs to the nurse or physician. Family members or friends must provide a history and other information necessary for planning and providing care. This information as well as its source must be documented. Baseline data assessment provides the foundation upon which care is provided and changes in status are noted. An objective assessment of the neurological system forms the basis of ongoing assessments used to establish a prognosis and track deviations in either direction. One common tool used to evaluate level of consciousness (LOC) as well as ongoing neurological as-

sessment is the Glasgow Coma Scale (GCS). The scale is useful for making an objective determination of progress, despite its origin as a research instrument used to evaluate prognosis and recovery from head injuries. The total score on the GCS ranges between 3 and 15 and provides an objective measure of patient progress. See Figure 7.21 for this scale. Prognosis can be evaluated based on the trend toward improvement and consistency of assessment data. The lower the score, the worse the prognosis.

In addition to the GCS, some institutions use a modified Ramsey Scale (RS) to measure the patient's level of sedation. This measure tests the responsiveness of the patient and is especially useful in the patient who is receiving numerous medications. (See Figure 9.2.)

Another important assessment parameter in the unresponsive patient is the respiratory system, particularly airway assessment. The unresponsive patient is without benefit of secretion control and is at risk for obstruction of the airway. Documentation in this area should include lung assessment of normal and abnormal sounds, rate, depth, and quality of respirations, breath sounds associated with suctioning, times and results of suctioning, and laboratory values as ordered, such as arterial blood gases.

Skin integrity is compromised in the unresponsive patient, making this a crucial area for documentation. All skin areas must be assessed and findings documented, especially vulnerable areas such as over bony prominences, as well as the eyes and mouth that are prone to dryness and breakdown due to dehydration and loss of natural lubrication. Fluid and nutritional status is related to skin integrity as well as bowel and bladder function and output. These are areas that are crucial to document in the unresponsive patient. Prevention measures are especially important in this area and should be documented at regular intervals. Examples of prevention measures are various types of pressure minimizing mattresses, frequent turning and repositioning, and heel protectors or boots.

Modified Ramsey Scale	
1	Patient anxious, agitated, or restless
2	Patient cooperative, oriented, and tranquil
3	Patient responds to commands only
4	Patient responds to gentle shaking
5	Patient responds to noxious stimulus
6	Patient has no response to firm nailbed pressure or other noxious stimuli

Figure 9.2

Safety interventions and patient response to the interventions are important to document, including how intravenous and other lines are protected if the patient is restless. Aspiration precautions and other safety interventions should be noted as indicated. Teaching is directed to the patient's family, including times that they were encouraged to assist in caring for their loved one. Documentation should include instruction given and the family's response and actions, with an eye towards patient needs upon discharge, especially if family members will be the care providers.

B. Shock

TIP: Shock is a common sequelae of many disease states in a critical care unit. It can be categorized as cardiogenic, hypovolemic, or distributive.

Ongoing and concise documentation can assist in identification of the type of shock the patient is experiencing. Cardiogenic shock results from the impaired ability of the heart to pump blood, and hypovolemic shock results from a loss of circulating or intravascular volume. Distributive shock results from a maldistribution of circulating blood volume and can be further classified as septic, anaphylactic, and neurogenic. Septic shock is the result of microorganisms invading the body; anaphylactic shock is the result of a pronounced antibody-antigen response. Neurogenic shock results from a loss of sympathetic tone.[25]

A flow sheet is extremely useful for the types of ongoing documentation of vital signs, fluid balance, tissue perfusion, and laboratory test results that comprise care of the patient in shock. Care is aimed at preventing shock or preventing the rapid deterioration that can accompany the shock state. The record must reflect attention to prevention of complications or further deterioration.

The foremost parameters to document in shock are airway, breathing, and circulation (the ABCs). Attention to these parameters is a priority and takes precedence over all other interventions. In general, vital signs, including pulse, respiration, blood pressure, and pulse oximetry are typically recorded every fifteen minutes, or more often as indicated, until the patient becomes stable; then every two to four hours or upon changes in the patient's condition. Frequently, these parameters are being continuously, electronically monitored.

If mechanical ventilation is required, the time of intubation, the person performing it, and the size of the endotracheal tube plus the delivery of preoxygenation are all important aspects to be documented. The status of the tube and ventilator settings must be recorded at least every four hours. The five information points essential for the nurse or respiratory therapist to record are ventilator mode, tidal volume, respiratory rate (both set and actual), oxygen, and any added features such as positive end expiratory pressure (PEEP) or continuous positive airway pressure (CPAP). Airway maintenance including suctioning must be documented when performed. A chart entry concerning the nature of the secretions can give some insight into patient status. Blood-tinged secretions are often the unavoidable consequence of frequent suctioning, while thick yellow or green secretions may signal an infection.

Drug therapy and volume replacement are cornerstones of the treatment of shock. Intravenous medications must be accurately titrated and recorded in detail. Fluids and blood products must be carefully managed with complete documentation, including the patient's response to treatment. Intake and output are usually recorded hourly. Additional areas of importance for documentation are hemodynamic monitoring parameters such as arterial line or Swan-Ganz catheter measurements, results of arterial blood gas (ABG) analysis, and other interventions such as intra-aortic balloon pump therapy (IABP), including a description of the integrity of the insertion site and distal tissues.

C. Cardiopulmonary Arrest

Interruption or cessation of cardiac or respiratory function is not limited to the critical care area but is a possibility in any setting. Standardized flow sheets have been developed and are in use in most facilities to document details of an untoward event and the response of the healthcare team. One nurse usually acts as the recorder in a code situation and will ideally review all notations with the physician after the crisis has passed. Both individuals should sign the document, indicating agreement with its contents. Assessment and intervention are almost simultaneous processes in the midst of a fast-paced code situation. Documentation should include any observations prior to the code, the time of the initial call for help from the first responder, plus all assessments and interventions, including pertinent negatives.

Examples of interventions would be defibrillation or electrical shock, medications, intubation, or other resuscitative procedures. Essential data would include responses to interventions, absence of rhythm, pulse, or respirations. Examples of common terms used to denote heart rhythms include pulseless electrical activity (PEA), bradycardia or slow rhythm, normal sinus rhythm (NSR), and ventricular fibrillation or "V-fib" which requires defibrillation. Cardiac rhythm strips are routinely included as part of the documented resuscitative effort. The code sheet will reflect times cardiopulmonary resuscitation (CPR) was performed, delivery of medications or defibrillator shocks, blood tests and other actions during the code. If resuscitative efforts are unsuccessful and the code is terminated, documentation should include the physician's name, the time, and any specifics concerning the patient's condition, including the essential data. When the patient is successfully resuscitated, the type and time a viable rhythm returns and vital signs will also be recorded.

Standard Advanced Cardiac Life Support (ACLS) protocol should be followed in a code situation. All individuals working in critical care are required to be ACLS certified and current in their certification. Timing of a code may be difficult to determine. Ideally, when an arrest is recognized a code is called and resuscitative measures are begun within 3 to 5 minutes, the time it takes for brain death or anoxic encephalopathy to occur. Because no standard clock is routinely used to document the initiation of resuscitation, reliance on documentation for accurate timing is problematic at best.

D. Termination of Life Support

Termination of life support is a very delicate area and must be handled with the utmost respect and concern for the patient and family. Documentation should reflect the consideration given to the issues involved. The presence or absence of an advance directive in the patient's record must be noted, as well as whether it was read and brought to the attention of the appropriate party. All people notified of the decision to terminate life support should be listed along with the time contacted and their responses. Conversations with family members and offers of counseling or other support should be noted. Documentation should include any physical care of the patient just prior to or after termination, the time and name of the person who turned off the equipment, and those present. Additionally, any interventions provided for the patient or family should be recorded.

E. Organ Donation

The Uniform Anatomical Gift Act permits recovery of organs from a deceased individual who has given prior permission. It also permits the deceased patient's family to give consent for the donation of the patient's organs. Medicare and Medicaid reimbursement is contingent on hospitals reporting all cardiovascular and brain deaths to the local procurement organization. The United Network for Organ Sharing (UNOS) must be notified whenever a potential donor dies, and eligibility for donation is then determined through the local procurement organization. This referral assists in identifying potential donors to increase the number of desperately needed organs. The Network provides skilled interventions for the family and support for the nursing staff, taking on the responsibilities and documentation associated with the process. The patient record should include the date and time of the patient's death, the name of the person notified at the local procurement organization, and the organ's suitability for transplantation. Healthcare providers in the critical care area are frequently confronted with the issue of organ donation given the types of patients involved at this level of care.

In the following case, the issue was whether a mother gave approval for a cornea donation. Failure to obtain a written consent from the mother complicated the defense of the nurses.

In *Andrews et al. v. George Lanier Memorial Hospital*, the decedent, eleven-year-old Steven Shealy, sustained an asthmatic attack. He was taken to the emergency room at George Lanier Memorial Hospital. Despite aggressive intervention, the boy died two days later. At the time of death, his mother, Cynthia Shealy, was present at the hospital. A nurse, Jason Ivey, engaged in conversation with her regarding the possibility of her donation of her son's corneas for immediate transplantation. The mother initially was unsure and replied, "It doesn't matter." Ivey perceived this as a "yes" response. However, there was some dispute at the hospital about whether the mother needed to sign an official form, legally authorizing transfer of ownership of her son's tissue. Before it was determined that she did in fact need to sign, the mother had left the hospital and had returned to her home. In the interim, the boy's father, Steven Andrews, had arrived at the hospital. The father was certain that he did not want the organs to be donated, citing a deeply held religious conviction. Still, Nurse Ivey was undeterred and sought to gain the mother's approval. He telephoned her at home and repeated the question. Again, the mother replied, "It doesn't matter." Ivey again understood this as a "yes" response and, along with a second nurse, signed the consent form based on the perceived content of the telephone call with the decedent's mother. A second call was then placed to the Alabama Eye Bank, which sent an agent to the hospital, and the boy's corneas were gathered and then transplanted. Later that same day, the parents learned what had happened.

In the progress of litigation, an important fact dispute arose. When Ivey called the mother at home, after expressing lukewarm, "It doesn't matter" wording, the mother recalled that she then verbally withdrew her consent. Nurses Ivey and Strength remembered the content of the mother's disclosures very differently—maintaining that she had explicitly advanced her consent for organ harvesting/transplantation. The plaintiffs alleged that the hospital failed to comply with the established ethical and legal guidelines which require consent to be in writing. They also argued that Nurse Ivey later created a bogus consent form, for the benefit of the eye bank, when in fact consent had never been given. Both parents prevailed, with the mother awarded $85,000 and her husband awarded $15,000.[26]

F. Self-Removal of Tubes and Lines

The following are some of the types of tubes used in critical care units.

- Breathing
  - endotracheal (ETT)
  - tracheostomy
- Nutrition
  - naso- or orogastric (NG or OG)
  - percutaneous endoscopic gastroscopy (PEG)
- Dobhoff tube (DHT)
  - central intravenous catheters (CIC)
- Elimination
  - Foley catheters
  - nephrostomy tubes (kidney)
  - dialysis catheters
- Drainage of various body secretions
  - Jackson-Pratt (JP)
  - Hemovac
  - Penrose drains
  - jejunostomy (jejunum)
  - chest tubes

Patient self-removal of these tubes constitutes a life-threatening emergency that requires an immediate response. In addition, self-removal usually results in trauma such as tearing of urinary tract tissue with a Foley catheter or aspiration (inhalation of stomach contents) with a nasogastric tube removal. The reviewer should examine the charting to see if it includes important areas of documentation such as:

- all assessment findings and nursing interventions when the situation is first identified,
- how the situation became known, such as through an alarm sounding or by witnessing the act,

- the respiratory parameters,
- vital signs,
- the call for help, including time and person notified, and
- any immediate resuscitative efforts.

TIP: The reviewer should note that upon reintubation the medical record should include the name of the physician performing the procedure, the size of the tube, markings for placement, method of securing the tube, any tests to confirm tube location, and the patient's response, including restraints, if indicated.

9.12 Sources of Liability

This section discusses common issues which affect the healthcare provider in critical care. These include

- omission of critical thinking,
- inadequate evaluation of patient status,
- missing or incomplete documentation of changes in patient condition prior to an arrest and resuscitation, and
- missing documentation of physician notification of changes in a patient's condition.

A. Omission of Critical Thinking

Critical thinking forms the basis for quality documentation.[27] Critical thinking requires the use of judgment in several areas: initially evaluating the patient's status, making decisions about treatment options, and evaluating the effectiveness of interventions.

If critical care professionals are expected to form judgments, then failure to record those judgments could be seen as providing less than the standard of care.[28] The critical care physician heavily relies on the nursing documentation. The recording of critical judgments requires that the professional goes beyond the flow sheet data which documents only passive observations. Consider the following nursing progress note.

Extubated at 2300. Vital signs stable. Respirations at 20/min. On oxygen at 3 liters/min via nasal cannula. Mediastinal and leg dressings dry and intact. Monitor shows normal sinus rhythm (NSR) with occasional premature ventricular complexes (PVC). Pacer off. Chest tubes draining dark red. Foley draining amber urine. Nasogastric (NG) tube in right nares and to low suction. Report given to family and physician. Resting at intervals.[29]

With the exception of the description of the drainage, this note gives no more information than could readily be found on the flow record. The nurse cared for this patient for eight hours, recorded hourly data on the flow sheet and wrote this note. It fails to describe if the patient is improving, deteriorating, or what the nurse actually did to affect the patient's move toward the achievement of outcomes.[30]

According to Chase,[31] a meaningful note identifies what patient problem or major issue was the focus of nursing care. In the example above, the nursing care of this patient focused on interventions to maintain a patent airway. Incentive spirometry was done every hour, the patient was encouraged to cough and deep breathe frequently, and the nurse ensured that the aerosol treatments were provided. In addition, the nurse maintained the oxygen enriched air, did frequent respiratory assessments, and checked arterial blood gases periodically. While all of these interventions and assessments could be pieced together by reviewing the flow sheet, what could not be captured is the actual evaluation of the effectiveness of these interventions. The nurse should use the nursing progress note to document critical thinking in terms of describing the patient's response to interventions and judgments about the patient's progress.[32] For example:

> *Extubated and placed on nasal cannula @ 3 liters/min. Respirations are regular and easy @ 20/minute. Experienced mild anxiety immediately following extubation which subsided with targeted encouragement. Oxygen saturation (SaO2) 95-100 percent. Providing periods of rest between coughing and deep breathing and use of incentive spirometer. Alert and oriented with clear speech. Aerosol treatments by respiratory therapist. Patient taught to splint chest to cough. Is able to cough and expectorate clear sputum. Patient maintaining a patent airway with gas exchange as documented on data sheet.*[33]

This note demonstrates a relationship between the patient problem, interventions provided, and the patient's response. This note clearly states that this patient is breathing without difficulty and is tolerating the removal of the endotracheal (ET) tube. It also describes nursing's unique contribution to this patient's outcome of being able to breathe unassisted.[34]

Chase[35] provides an additional description of documentation that demonstrates critical thinking:

- focus on major patient problems that need care,
- reporting judgment about data,

- inclusion of patient responses to interventions, and
- documentation of patient outcomes.

B. Inadequate Evaluation of Patient Status

Croke[36] identified six major categories of issues which formed the basis of various lawsuits, one of which was failure to document. Included in this category is failure to note

- a patient's progress and response to treatment,
- a patient's injuries,
- pertinent nursing assessment information such as drug allergies,
- a physician's medical orders, and
- information from telephone conversations with physicians such as time, content, and actions taken.[37]

The practice of documenting judgments provides an ongoing evaluation of the patient's progress or deterioration and helps to explain the rationale for treatments or interventions initiated.[38]

C. Documentation of Changes in Patient Condition: Arrest and Resuscitation

As previously mentioned, documentation of arrest and resuscitation efforts presents special challenges. While some arrest situations are anticipated due to a recognition of the deteriorating patient condition, many are not.[39]

Organizations vary as to the amount of support they provide to the professionals who are attempting to resuscitate an arrested patient. In larger organizations, structured teams of nurses and physicians may respond, while in others, the nurse proceeds with support from the unit staff via standard written protocols. The challenge of documentation of these events lies in the fact that it is an extremely stressful situation, particularly if unanticipated, and it requires the nurse to attend to very specific details in very rapid succession.[40]

TIP: The timing that is recorded may be imprecise. Attorneys can be led astray if they believe, as they want to, that times are exact.

One important thing to look for in documentation is the timing of response as recorded in the notes and compared to monitored or electronic timing. Documentation must explain the delays. In the critical care area, unanticipated arrest situations are generally heralded by an alarm. Almost every piece of critical care equipment attached to the patient has an alarm capability. Experienced nurses are able to distinguish which alarms require immediate investigation, such as the ventilator or the heart monitor, and which alarms do not. Sophisticated, state-of-the-art electrocardiographic (EKG) monitoring systems provide different sounds for varying levels of alarm situations, assisting the nurse to identify, on the basis of sound alone, the presence of potentially lethal cardiac dysrhythmias.[41]

Many critical care flow sheets will designate an area in nursing interventions for the documentation of alarm status to cue the nurse, not only to document concerning this very important issue, but to check to make sure that all alarms are on and the parameters are set to the appropriate limits for that patient.[42] Parameters for a cardiac monitor, for example, may be set at a low of 50 beats a minute and a high of 120. The alarm will go off if the heart rate drops below 50 or rises above 120. Even with the alarms activated, there must be a nurse to respond to the signal. Chapter 10, *Patient Safety Initiatives and Medical Records,* in Volume I, addresses this issue within the context of a patient safety goal.

TIP: Most organizations provide a code sheet for the documentation of resuscitation efforts.

Like the flow sheet, the code sheet will cue the nurse to document important facts about the specific episode. Because the arrest situation is associated with a significant change in patient condition and may be linked to unexpected poor outcomes, it is imperative that events are documented clearly and accurately. In fact, documentation of these events is so important that organizations will frequently designate in the policy and procedure who is to assume the role of recorder. Figure 9.3 lists key items that should be documented on a code sheet.[43]

Documentation of the arrest and resuscitation efforts is made on the code sheet and cardiac rhythm strips. The flow sheet and the nurses' progress notes should reflect assessment data prior to and preceding the code. It is important that the code sheet, progress note, rhythm strips, and the flow sheet document a consistent recording of timed events to reflect accurately the care provided. Evaluation consists of comparing the documented data to the current Advanced Cardiac Life Support (ACLS) standard of care. Because this is such an important clinical issue, many organizations have a system whereby each and every arrest situation is evaluated in a formalized manner with feedback to the providers regarding their performance and adherence to current standards of care. Indeed, consequences of not providing the standard care in these instances can be devastating and costly.[44]

Key Items Found on a Code Sheet

- Time and type of arrest (pulselessness/breathlessness).
- Initiation of CPR.
- Rhythm initially and after medications/defibrillation/external pacemaker.
- Intubation /O^2 therapy/ABGs.
- Time and watts (joules) of defibrillation, response to defibrillation.
- Medications and IVs: type, route, dose and time, as well as name of person administering.
- Pupillary reactions.
- Members of the resuscitation team.
- Patient outcome including disposition (where sent if transferred).

Figure 9.3

D. Documentation of Change in Patient Condition: Physician Notification

With many physicians caring for one patient, the nurse is responsible for coordinating and organizing the implementation of prescribed treatments and ensuring that information is communicated to the appropriate physician. Most routine information is communicated via the flow sheet, through other written reports, or verbally during physician rounds. Ongoing information describing the patient's condition is relayed either in person as the physician makes additional rounds or via telephone. Each communication with the physician should be documented either in the progress note or comments section of the flow sheet.[45]

With a significant change in the patient's condition, a physician, preferably the physician who admitted the patient, should be contacted immediately after the nurse completes the assessment. In large teaching hospitals, the intern or resident may be contacted as the "on-call" physician. Whether a notification is made to the resident or the attending physician, the nurse must document the notification and also note the response of the physician to the call. Failure to report important changes to a physician or allowing the patient's condition to deteriorate over time without insisting that the physician see the patient is below the standard of care. When working with residents or interns, the nurse may need to insist that the resident notify the attending physician in cases where the nurse judges that the patient is not responding to treatment by the resident. Names of individuals involved should always be documented.[46]

TIP: If, after notification, the attending physician is not responsive at a level that matches the severity of the patient's condition, the nurse may need to reiterate the concerns to the physician. If, after repeated notification, the patient's condition continues to deteriorate, the nurse must consult with the next level in the chain of command as defined by organizational policy and procedure.[47]

The chain of command may involve a nursing supervisor (who provides "next-step" information) or perhaps the physician who is the director of the critical care unit. It is important that the nurse document each attempt to obtain physician intervention.[48]

The following cases involve issues related to the documentation of changes related to bleeding, and informing the physician of these changes.

The plaintiff's decedent underwent surgery on a Friday to reconnect his small intestine with his rectum, having had his colon removed some time earlier because of colitis. The surgery was successful. The decedent had been on Coumadin because of prior bypass surgery. When he came out of surgery he was placed back on the Coumadin and was also given Lovenox. On the first postoperative day his hematocrit dropped. On the second postoperative day it was noted that he had a bloody bowel movement, the hematocrit dropped further and the INR climbed above therapeutic levels. On the second postoperative day (a Sunday) the decedent received a morning dose of Lovenox. He was seen by a physician covering for the attending surgeon, as well as residents and nurses. After the early morning hours, he was not seen again until the next morning by anyone other than nurses. The lab work on postoperative day two was available at around noon on Sunday. At 9:30 p.m. a first-year resident gave an order by phone that the Coumadin for that night not be given. No one had any recollection of the reason for that order. There was another recorded note by a nurse indicating that there was some bleeding from the wound site. The wife claimed that there was a substantial amount of blood when she saw her husband that evening and when she brought it to the nurse's attention, was told that it was normal. The dressing was changed on two occasions. There was a dispute over whether the nurse did or did not administer the Coumadin that evening. The Pyxis records indicated that Coumadin was withdrawn

from the Pyxis dispenser along with other medications around 9:45 P.M. and not until the next morning at 4:30 was it, allegedly, replaced. Throughout the night, there was one recording of vital signs, which were low to normal. On the third postoperative day, at 5:30 A.M., the decedent was seen by a medical student who noted that the decedent told him that he'd been bleeding that night and he noticed that the abdomen was moderately swollen. About a half hour to an hour later the attending physician did see the decedent and discussed the findings with the medical students doing the rounds, but no further action was taken. A nurse entered the room around 7:30 A.M. and was told by the decedent that he was tired and had been awake all night, so she did not do an examination, but she noted that even under the covers the abdomen seemed to be swollen. At 7:58 A.M. the lab called the floor and told the floor that the INR was further increased, as was the PT and the PTT. Nothing was done. About fifty minutes later the man went into arrest and did not survive. The plaintiff claimed that from noon on Sunday the decedent should have had additional lab study performed to see if there was bleeding, that the residents did not properly notify other senior residents of the situation and that the nurses did not notify the residents of the bleeding. The plaintiff also claimed that the stop Coumadin order was not followed and that when the nurses received information of the increased INR on the third postoperative day a physician should have been immediately notified. A confidential settlement was reached during trial.[49]

The plaintiff, age seventy-one, underwent an elective abdominal aortic aneurysm repair surgery in August 2003. After the surgery the plaintiff had documented pulses in both feet and movement of all extremities, but when she was transferred to the ICU she was reported as having loss of sensation and movement in both legs. The plaintiff later lost pulses in both feet and the lost pulses were documented throughout the overnight shift of one of the ICU nurses. When the surgeon returned to the hospital the following morning, he determined that the aortic graft repair had occluded, requiring a second surgery to re-establish blood flow. The plaintiff was left with partial paralysis of her legs which ultimately resulted in amputation of both legs below the knee. The plaintiff claimed that the hospital was liable for its nurses' failure to recognize the signs and symptoms of the graft occlusion, failure to contact a doctor about the changes in the patient's condition and failure to obtain intervention. The defense argued that the nurses acted reasonably and appropriately, including keeping the surgeon fully updated on the patient's condition throughout the night. According to Cook County Jury Verdict Reporter a $4,741,000 verdict was returned.[50]

The nurse has a responsibility to assess correctly a patient situation, notify the appropriate individual to obtain a remedy, and then document the process. In situations where the response is not effective or nonexistent, documentation must reflect all attempts to obtain appropriate interventions and all measures taken to insure safe and effective patient care.

9.13 Summary and Recommendations

Clear, concise documentation of nursing care in the critical care setting reflects the level of nursing care provided. When appropriate documentation is lacking, the nursing care is called into question and the burden falls on the nurse to prove that care was rendered despite the absence of documentation.[51] The use of an EMR system has been shown to free up the nurse for patient care activities but has some drawbacks in implementation. In using either method of documentation, entries are ideally made as close as possible to events to decrease the chance of errors or charting based on memory.

Recommendations for reviewing documentation and determining accuracy and reliability include the following.

1. Consider the intent of the flow sheet and check for thoroughness in all areas to be filled out.
2. Compare the activities recorded to patient outcomes. Narrative notes should link patient problems to interventions to outcomes. Look for judgments about the patient's progress.
3. Check for consistency between the flow sheet and the progress notes.
4. Compare the code sheet with the organization's designated instructions for completion. Look for compliance with current ACLS standards of care as well as the standards of the American Association of Critical Care Nurses.
5. Check for documentation of every communication with medical providers including name of person contacted, time of contact, response and time of response, and action initiated as a result of the communication.[52]

Endnotes

1. AACN. http://www.aacn.org/AACN/mrkt.nsf/vwdoc/HistoryofAACN. Retrieved May 24, 2004.

2. American Nurses Association. *Principles for Documentation*. Washington, D.C.: Author. 2002.

3. Kretovics, A.M. "Intensive Care Documentation" in Iyer, P. and Camp, N. *Nursing Documentation: A Nursing Process Approach*. Fourth Edition. p. 14–25. Flemington, NJ: Med League Support Services, Inc. 2005.

4. Cohen, L. "Pain and Suffering in the Intensive Care Unit" in Iyer, P. (Editor). *Medical Legal Aspects of Pain and Suffering*. Tucson, AZ: Lawyers and Judges Publishing Co. 2003.

5. American Association of Critical-Care Nurses *Standards for Nursing Care of the Critically Ill*. Upper Saddle River, NJ: Prentice Hall. 1989.

6. *See* note 3 at 14–25.

7. *Id.*

8. American Hospital Association. *Patients or Paperwork? The Regulatory Burden Facing America's Hospitals*. Chicago, IL: Author. 2001.

9. *See* note 6.

10. *Id.*

11. Wong, D.H. et al. "Changes in Intensive Care Unit Nurse Task Activity After Installation of a Third-Generation Intensive Care Unit Information System." *Critical Care Medicine*. 31(10), p. 2488–2494. 2003.

12. Nowlin, A. "Get Ready for the Virtual ICU." *RN*. 67(8). August 2004. p. 52–55.

13. *See* note 3 at 14–2.

14. *Id.*

15. *Id.*

16. *Id.*

17. Laska, L. "Failure to Properly Monitor Man on Ventilator." *Medical Malpractice Verdicts, Settlements, and Experts*. August 2008. p. 19.

18. Laska, L. "Arachnoiditis Develops from Epidural Catheter for Pain Management." *Medical Malpractice Verdicts, Settlements, and Experts.* September 2003. p. 4.

19. *See* note 3 at 14–3.

20. *Id.*

21. *Id.* at 14–4

22. Laska, L. "Failure of Nurse to Chart Developments Relative to Bleeding Following Heart Surgery." *Medical Malpractice Verdicts, Settlements, and Experts.* September 2008. p. 21.

23. *See* note 3 at 14–4.

24. Urden, L.D., K.M. Stacy, and M.E. Lough. *Thelan's Critical Care Nursing: Diagnosis and Management.* Fourth Edition. St. Louis, MO: Mosby. 2002.

25. *Id.*

26. Laska, L. "Parents Deny Giving Consent for Cornea Harvesting from Deceased Son." *Medical Malpractice Verdicts, Settlements, and Experts.* October 2003. p. 23.

27. Chase, S. "Charting Critical Thinking: Nursing Judgments and Patient Outcomes." *Dimensions of Critical Care Nursing.* March–April 1997. p. 102.

28. *Id.*

29. *See* note 3 at 14–22.

30. *Id.*

31. *See* note 27.

32. *See* note 29.

33. *Id.*

34. *Id.*

35. *See* note 27.

36. Croke, E. Nurses, Negligence, and Malpractice. *American Journal of Nursing.* 103(9), p. 54–64. 2003.

37. *Id.*

38. *See* note 3 at 14–23.

39. *Id.*

40. *Id* at 14-24.

41. *Id.*

42. *Id.*

43. *Id.*

44. *Id* at 14-24, 14-25.

45. *Id* at 14-25, 14-26.

46. *Id* at 14-26.

47. *Id.*

48. *Id.*

49. Laska, L. "Failure to Notify Physicians of Swelling in Abdomen and Abnormal INR Levels Following Surgery to Reconnect Small Intestine With Rectum." *Medical Malpractice Verdicts, Settlements, and Experts.* August 2008. p. 18-19.

50. Laska, L. "Failure to Notify Physicians of Diminished Pulses in Feet After Abdominal Aortic Aneurysm Repair." *Medical Malpractice Verdicts, Settlements, and Experts.* October 2008. p. 18.

51. Gialanella, K. Documentation. *Advance for Nurses.* 6(14), p. 23–25. 2004.

52. *See* note 3 at 14–27.

Chapter 10

Diagnostic Testing

Bruce Bonnell, MD, MPH

10.1 Introduction

This chapter addresses the role of testing in the evaluation of the patient suspected of having disease. It is intended as a brief introduction to diagnostic tests. As there are a huge number of potential tests, only the most common forms of diagnostic tests are covered. Given the complexity of interpretation, no attempt is made to make this a text useful in interpreting results of the tests discussed. Sufficient detail is provided to allow a layperson to decipher some of what is routinely encountered in medical records.

A. Definitions and Examples

There are two general categories of tests defined by their intended purposes. Those used to screen a population for a disease (i.e., a mammogram used to screen an asymptomatic—without symptoms—patient for breast cancer) are known as *screening* tests. Those used to diagnose a suspected condition (i.e., a mammogram performed to look for a breast mass in a patient with a breast lump) are known as *diagnostic* tests. This chapter reviews the proper use of and pitfalls arising from selected diagnostic tests. The discussion of screening tests is left to others. Figure 10.1 lists tests routinely ordered in patients with specific medical conditions.

All testing should be dictated by *standards of care*. Courts define a standard of care in terms of the degree of skill and expertise normally possessed and exercised by a reasonable and prudent practitioner relative to colleagues with the same level of training in the same or similar circumstances.[1] With respect to diagnostic testing, standard of care is determined after study of the efficacy or "validity" of specific tests in certain contexts. A valid test produces a relevant and meaningful result. There exists a number of statistical indices helpful in determining which tests are valid and in which contexts. A detailed review of the statistics is beyond the scope of this text.

	CBC	Sma7/LFTs	ABG	Blood Culture	UA/Urine Culture	CXR	KUB	Bone Film	CT Head	CT Abd	MRI	NIVs	EKG	CK/Troponin	Echo
Fever	×			×	×	×									
Respiratory Failure			×			×							×		
Abdominal Pain	×	×			×		×								
Bone Pain/ Suspected Fracture								×							
Head Trauma								×	×						
Stroke									×		×				
Deep Vein Thrombosis												×			
Typical Chest Pain						×							×	×	
Congestive Heart Failure						×							×		×
Kidney Stone					×		×			×					

Figure 10.1 Commonly ordered tests under certain general clinical scenarios. (See text for abbreviations.)

Sensitivity. This is the likelihood of a test being positive if the patient has a disease. One hundred patients with a disease are tested and ninety-nine are positive. Therefore, the test is 99 percent sensitive. This does *not* mean that if a patient is tested and turns up positive that there is a 99 percent certainty of that patient having a given disease.

Specificity. This is the likelihood of a test being negative if the patient does *not* have a disease. One hundred patients without a disease are tested and ninety-nine are negative. Therefore the test has a specificity of 99 percent. This does not mean that if a patient is tested and turns up negative that there is a 99 percent certainty of that patient not having a disease.

- A *true positive test* is a positive test in the presence of disease.
- A *false positive test* is a positive test in the absence of disease.
- A *true negative test* is a negative test in a patient who does not have a disease.
- A *false negative test* is a negative test in a patient who has a disease.

Positive predictive value. This is the likelihood of a patient with a positive test actually having a given disease. This will vary with any number of characteristics of the group to which a patient belongs as well as with the quality of the test. For example, a twenty-year-old patient who is an intravenous drug abuser (IVDA) has a positive HIV test. (Intravenous drug abuse is a strong risk factor for HIV.) This would be considered much more likely to be indicative of disease than the same test in a ninety-year-old spinster living in a nursing home.

The positive predictive value depends upon the prevalence of disease within a group. *Prevalence* is the number of cases of a disease existing in a given population at a specific period or moment of time. Consider the case of a twenty-year-old IVDA with thrush (a symptom seen commonly in patients with AIDS). His HIV test comes back positive. If the prevalence of HIV in twenty-year-old IVDA patients with thrush is 50 percent, it can be demonstrated that it is 99 percent certain that this patient has HIV. The *positive predictive value* of an HIV test is 99 percent in twenty-year-old IVDAs with thrush.

Now consider the example of a ninety-year-old man with thrush in the nursing home. Thrush can also be associated with other diseases commonly seen in the elderly. His HIV test comes back positive as well. Let us say the prevalence of HIV in ninety-year-old nursing home patients with thrush is 1 percent. It can be demonstrated that it is only 50 percent certain that this patient has HIV. The *positive predictive value* is 50 percent in ninety-year-old nursing home patients with thrush.

Negative predictive value. This is the likelihood of a patient with a negative test *not* having a given disease. For example, a twenty-year-old patient twists her ankle and is complaining of pain. Her plain x-ray is negative. This patient is likely to be diagnosed with a sprained ankle rather than a fracture based just upon this film. The same film and symptom complex in a ninety-year-old nursing home patient may not rule out a fracture. The reason is that the ninety-year-old is much more likely to have osteoporosis than the twenty-year-old and therefore is more likely to sustain a fracture. *There is a higher prevalence of disease.* Additionally, plain x-rays are often much less sensitive in detecting fractures in the elderly than in younger patients.

Clinical scenario

Consider the case of a ninety-year-old male who falls and complains of right hip pain. He is unable to walk after his fall due to pain. An x-ray is done immediately following the fall and is read as negative. Should further work up be done? Assume that 30 percent of male patients in this age group with falls who cannot walk afterwards have suffered a fracture. (The prevalence of disease is 30 percent.) Let's assume that, due to age-related changes in bone, plain films are only 50% sensitive for detecting fractures in this setting. We are interested in the negative predictive value of an x-ray in this setting. That is, how confident should we be that a negative film excludes a fracture? After doing the calculation we get an 82 percent negative predictive value. This translates as an 18 percent chance of missing a fracture in this patient based just on the plain film. One should likely consider further work up to exclude a fracture in this patient.

Consider the case of a twenty-year-old who falls and cannot walk afterwards. Let's assume that in healthy young people plain films are 90 percent sensitive for detecting fractures. Further, let's assume that the prevalence of disease with this scenario is the same as in the older individual (in truth it is likely to be lower). The negative predictive value here is 98 percent. This translates to only a 2 percent chance of missing a fracture. Further work up might likely be deferred.

It is unlikely that any provider could quote actual statistics for any given scenario. That said, the relative prevalence of disease in a given group (high or low) and general knowledge of the sensitivity and specificity of specific tests (good or bad) should play a role in everyday decision making by the provider.

TIP: In general, when testing a member of a population where the disease prevalence is high and where the clinical scenario is reasonable, a provider should be circumspect about negative test results.

B. Responsibilities of Personnel

TIP: It is the responsibility of the ordering provider to make sure that test results are reviewed and acted upon in a prudent and timely manner. A provider who does not review the results of tests they have ordered should not use this as an excuse for a missed diagnosis. A provider who does not follow up on positive results should not use this as an excuse for not treating a disease.

A forty-seven-year-old New York clerical worker, presented to the defendant gynecologist for an annual examination and a Pap smear. She claimed she was not informed of the results of the Pap test. She returned three months later with complaints of increased bleeding and dizziness, but the defendant performed no other test at that time. Six months later, she returned for another Pap test, which was positive for stage IB cervical cancer with intense vascular invasion. After she was notified of the result, the patient sued the gynecologist. She claimed that the delay in diagnosis forced her to undergo a radical abdominal hysterectomy, including a bilateral salpingo-oophorectomy, as well as radiation and chemotherapy. The defendant claimed that she informed the plaintiff that the first Pap test result was slightly abnormal and that the plaintiff failed to follow up, noting that her records indicated that the plaintiff missed a scheduled appointment. According to the *New York Jury Verdict Reporter*, the parties settled for $1,750,000 prior to jury selection. *Maria Mejia v. Johanna Shulman M.D.*, Bronx County (NY) Supreme Court, Index No. 24792/98.[2]

Some frequently ordered tests, such as certain plain x-rays, MRIs, and CT scans, require extensive training to interpret properly. In this case it is the responsibility of the radiologist (or other specialist) to report positive findings of immediate concern *directly* to the ordering provider or the covering physician at the time of interpretation. It is not sufficient to dictate an interpretation and hope that the ordering provider takes note of it. Frequently, radiologists will include this as part of their official report, for example, "Interpretation discussed with Dr. Johnson at 2:30 P.M."

The American College of Radiology Practice Guidelines state: "In those situations in which the interpreting physician feels that immediate patient treatment is indicated (e.g., tension pneumothorax), the interpreting physician should communicate directly with the referring physician, other healthcare provider, or an appropriate representative. If that individual cannot be reached, the interpreting physician should directly communicate the need for emergent care to the patient or responsible guardian, if possible." "In those situations in which the interpreting physician feels that the findings do not warrant immediate treatment but constitute significant unexpected findings, the interpreting physician or his/her designee should communicate the findings to the referring physician, other healthcare provider, or an appropriate individual in a manner that reasonably ensures receipt of the findings."[3]

TIP: Laboratory personnel should report critical values and other abnormalities (such as positive blood culture results) either directly to providers or to nursing staff. A notation to this effect should be included in the report.

"Critical values" are defined by the institution and may go by other names, e.g., "panic values." A notation is generally made on the official report of who was notified. It is the responsibility of the laboratory staff to obtain, secure, and transport specimens in an appropriate manner and to notify the ordering provider or nursing staff when a specimen is inadequate (e.g., insufficient quantity of blood, specimen kept unrefrigerated for an extended period) or not obtainable.

After their July 2004 meeting on National Patient Safety, the Joint Commission on Accreditation of Healthcare Organizations published the following guideline which took effect January 1, 2005: "All values defined as critical by the laboratory are reported directly to a responsible licensed caregiver within time frames established by the laboratory (defined in cooperation with nursing and medical staff). When the patient's responsible licensed caregiver is not available within the time frames, there is a mechanism to report the critical information to an alternate responsible caregiver."[4] Refer to Chapter 10, *Patient Safety Initiatives and Medical Records*, in Volume I, for additional information on the TJC Patient Safety Goals.

It is the responsibility of nursing staff to report significant laboratory abnormalities to providers when they become aware of them. Notation of such notification should be made in the nursing notes, e.g., "Dr. Johnson notified of sodium level of 158 at 11:30 P.M."

C. Urgency of Testing

The term "stat" (from the Latin *Statim*) is an American medical term meaning "immediately." Stat orders are orders requiring immediate action. Results of tests ordered stat need to be received within a reasonably short period of time. In the acute care setting, one should refer to the hospital policy regarding time frames. Typically, results are available within minutes to hours of the test being requested (depending upon the test). Review of results by a medical professional should take place soon after they are available. Routine testing generally takes place at intervals established by the institution (frequently the next day). If a test is ordered with the expectation of results having an immediate impact upon patient treatment or if delay of diagnosis could potentially harm the patient, then tests should be ordered stat and results reviewed promptly.

D. Treating the Patient

Diagnostic tests should never be ordered blindly. The history and physical exam should always guide the clinician in his selection of appropriate testing. When interpreting results, the clinician should always consider findings of the history and physical exam. The context and rationale for ordering a test should dictate how it is interpreted and what actions are taken. Treating the test alone may lead to further complications, as the following scenario illustrates.

An elderly patient presents to a rehabilitation hospital after a hip fracture. The patient appears well other than having evidence of having undergone recent surgery. On routine blood work the patient is noted to have a white count of 13,000 with a normal differential. She is started on antibiotics for a presumed infection. She subsequently develops antibiotic-associated diarrhea resulting in multiple further complications and a prolonged hospital stay.

Specific categories of diagnostic testing are addressed in the next section of the text. Clinicians should be familiar with the nature and limitations of and indications for each of the following tests. Many of these tests require the expertise of sub-specialists to perform and interpret. There is little debate about the usefulness and proper performance of these tests and procedures in the contexts described.

10.2 Diagnostic Tests Involving Blood Work

A. Basic Definitions and Considerations

"Blood work" includes tests conducted upon cellular components of blood (hematology) and tests conducted on the non-cellular components of blood, i.e., "serum" (chemistries). When a phlebotomist draws blood, she typically collects it into color-coded tubes treated with chemicals appropriate for specific tests. For example, blood used for cell counts is treated with an anticoagulant and is collected in a red-topped tube.

Normal values for blood work are typically defined using results from a "normal" population. These are usually young individuals without significant pathology of any sort. They are often not representative of the typical patient seen in the hospital setting. Therefore, abnormal values on any number of tests are frequently encountered even in reasonably healthy patients. Normal values for commonly ordered tests vary from setting to setting. The reviewer should consult the range of normal values printed with the laboratory results.

Practitioners typically (and appropriately) respond more to a change in a baseline value in an appropriate clinical setting than to the actual value itself. A hematocrit of 25 in an asymptomatic patient with chronic anemia may not be that distressing. The same value in an otherwise healthy person complaining of fatigue should sound alarm bells.

Reproducibility is another factor to consider when observing a particular laboratory value. The majority of tests in a good laboratory may vary as much as 8 percent above and below the true value. For example, the hematocrit (percentage of blood volume occupied by cells) of a patient with a true hematocrit of 30.0 might reasonably come out as anywhere from 27.6 to 32.4. A practitioner might view a subtle change in a laboratory value as variability in testing rather than resulting from pathology.[5] Additionally, how a sample is obtained, for example, from a central line or from a vein, can impact results.

Critical values are results potentially requiring immediate action. Critical values are defined in a rather subjective manner by nonstandard measures determined by the reporting laboratory. Again, the appropriate action is determined by the baseline value, the patient's condition, and the clinical acumen of the practitioner.

B. Complete Blood Count with Differential (CBC with Diff)

For efficiency, practitioners have adopted a form of shorthand to note routine hematological results. (See Figure 10.2.)

The hematocrit (HCT) is the percentage of the volume of a blood sample occupied by cells. It is different in males and females. This is potentially of value in a patient who has a loss of blood. In shorthand, 42 would represent 42 percent of a blood sample represented by cells.

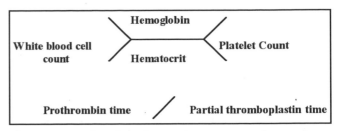

Figure 10.2 *Shorthand notation commonly used to depict routine hematologic test results.*

The hemoglobin is the respiratory protein of red blood cells. Hemoglobin transports the majority of oxygen in the blood. It is expressed in grams per deciliter. It is less frequently observed than the hematocrit, as it parallels it and adds little. In shorthand, 11 would represent 11 grams of hemoglobin per deciliter. Of potential interest, hemoglobin is measured in the laboratory while hematocrit is calculated. Therefore, hemoglobin is the more accurate of the two measures in evaluating for blood loss.

The leukocyte or white blood cell count (WBC) is expressed as the number of white blood cells per cubic millimeter. This is elevated in medical conditions such as infection, stress, or acute bleeding and depressed in patients with immunosuppression such as in people receiving chemotherapy. Generally, a number in excess of 10,000 per milliliter is considered abnormal. In shorthand, 10 would represent 10,000 white blood cells per ml.

The differential is a breakdown of the types of white blood cells represented in a sample. Common terms encountered are "left shift or bandemia" and "neutropenia." Left shift or bandemia are terms referring to an increase in immature white blood cells. These include blasts, promyelocytes, myelocytes, metamyelocytes, and band neutrophils. Infectious processes typically produce this phenomena.[6]

Neutropenia is an abnormally low number of neutrophils. This is common in immunosuppressed states such as cancer and AIDS. Neutropenic patients often will be placed on "reverse precautions" (in isolation), as they are more vulnerable to infection. Neutropenia is commonly defined as having fewer than 1000 neutrophils per cubic milliliter of blood (some institutions use a value of 500). A patient with a WBC of 3.0 with 10 percent neutrophils would have 300 neutrophils per milliliter and therefore would be neutropenic. The lower the number of neutrophils, the higher the risk of infection (e.g., a patient with 300 neutrophils per ML is at greater risk of infection than someone with 800 neutrophils per ML).

The platelet count (PLT) is expressed as the number of platelets per milliliter. Platelets are intimately involved in the mechanism allowing blood to clot. Abnormalities in the platelet count may indicate any number of disorders but are nonspecific. In shorthand, 150 would represent 150,000 platelets per milliliter.

C. Coagulation Tests

Coagulation tests include the partial thromboplastin time (PTT), prothrombin time (PT), and the international normalized ratio (INR). These tests are useful in monitoring patients undergoing anticoagulation therapy for a stroke or myocardial infarct (among other clinical scenarios) and for long-term prevention of stroke in patients with atrial fibrillation.

The INR is the most common coagulation test seen in routine outpatient clinical practice. The most common condition treated by anticoagulation is atrial fibrillation. Patients with atrial fibrillation in combination with certain other risk factors (such as age) have a markedly elevated risk for embolic stroke. By anticoagulating these patients with a drug called Warfarin (a.k.a. Coumadin) these patients' risk for stroke can be markedly reduced.

TIP: Unfortunately, Warfarin is one of the most common drugs associated with adverse reactions, most often bleeding. It is therefore essential to try to maintain the INR within a therapeutic range of between 2.0 and 3.0. There are clinical scenarios where a higher or lower goal is suggested.

Frequent monitoring (most commonly every month or even more frequently in some patients) is required to prevent complications. In general values much above 3.0 require a reduction in dosage and a repeat blood test in the next few days. Values below 2.0 require a dosage increase.

D. Serum Tests

The basal metabolic profile or SMA7 and the comprehensive metabolic profile are blood tests conducted on serum. For efficiency, practitioners have adopted a form of shorthand to note routine serum test results. (See Figure 10.3.)

The creatinine, or CRE, is a breakdown product of muscle and is useful in detecting and assessing renal failure. If the patient's weight, age and gender are known, a rough estimate of kidney function can be made using the creatinine. Formulas also exist which allow calculation of kidney function without knowledge of the patient's weight.

The blood urea nitrogen or BUN is sometimes useful in assessing kidney function in conjunction with the creatinine. It is, however, much less specific than the creatinine for renal failure. For example, the BUN is commonly elevated in patients with gastro-intestinal bleeding.

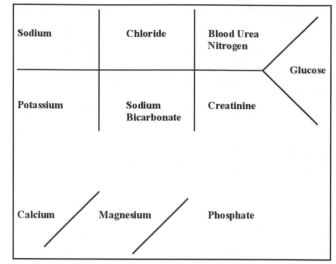

Figure 10.3 *Shorthand notation commonly used to depict routine SMA7 results plus calcium, magnesium, and phosphate.*

The ratio of BUN to CRE is sometimes useful in determining if a patient is in acute or chronic renal failure and the severity of the renal failure. Generally, an elevated BUN/CRE ratio indicates that the condition is acute rather than chronic. An increased BUN/CRE ratio is often seen in dehydrated patients. The sodium (Na) is also useful in determining a patient's fluid status. Elevated sodium almost invariably indicates dehydration. A low sodium is non-specific and may be present in any number of clinical scenarios.

The sodium bicarbonate (sometimes reported as $NaHCO^3$ or incorrectly as CO^2) level is useful in the "acidotic" or "alkylotic" patient. In conjunction with a patient's arterial blood gas (discussion to follow), the bicarbonate level helps to determine if the patient suffers from a metabolic or respiratory derangement and the acuity of the derangement. This is often essential to guide treatment. Figure 10.4 demonstrates how notation is used in a typical SOAP note format.

Liver function tests or LFTs test for a number of substances. The total, direct, and indirect bilirubin may reflect the synthesis, secretion, and storage of bile. An elevated total bilirubin may result from any number of insults to the liver but can also result from hemolysis (rupture of blood cells) or even fasting. Indirect or conjugated bilirubin is often a sign of obstruction or cholestasis. Isolated direct bilirubin elevation is often the result of processes taking place outside of the liver such as hemolysis. The alanine aminotransferase (ALT or SGPT) and aspartate aminotransferase (AST or SGOT) are enzymes in the liver, which serve a synthetic function and may be released due to liver cell injury or death (such as in acute hepatitis). An elevated alkaline phosphatase (Alk Phos) is nonspecific and may result from any number of processes. Bone disease or fracture commonly result in an increase in this enzyme.[7]

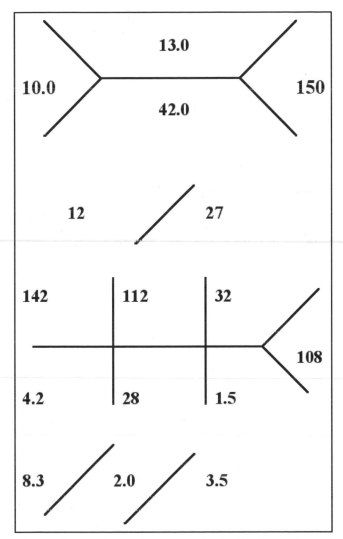

Figure 10.4 *Lab results in a typical SOAP note format*

E. Arterial Blood Gases (ABGs)

The arterial blood gas is a sample drawn into a heparinized tube from the patient's radial or occasionally the femoral or brachial artery. An extremely useful tool, it allows the evaluation of a patient's oxygenation and acid/base status. It is an essential tool in adjusting the treatment of the patient on mechanical ventilation. It is sometimes used in prognosticating how likely a patient undergoing CPR is to survive. The ABG will indicate the pH (acidity) of the patient's blood and the amount of oxygen and carbon dioxide and occasionally carbon monoxide dissolved in the blood. The interpretation of this test is rather complicated. (Please see the suggested reading list for a reference containing a detailed discussion

of the interpretation of this test.) Even experienced physicians frequently misread ABGs. This may lead to incorrect or even harmful treatment.[8] An extremely low level of oxygen in a sample (less that 40 mmHg) likely indicates that the sample was drawn from a vein rather than an artery (a common mistake) and may result in a patient being incorrectly diagnosed as hypoxic.

F. Newer Blood Tests

The d-dimer test is a very sensitive but non-specific method of determining if a blood clot exists. A low value is quite reassuring that a blood clot is not present whereas a high value is generally not helpful.

The Brain Naturitic Peptide test (BNP) is useful in cases when congestive heart failure is suspected. A low level is reassuring that the patient is not suffering from CHF. A very elevated level may confirm the diagnosis. An intermediate level is rarely helpful. Unfortunately, other clinical factors can impact BNP levels. For example, renal failure tends to raise them.

TIP: When in doubt, repeating a blood test is preferable to precipitous action. The prudent practitioner should be wary of unanticipated results.

10.3 Microbiology
A. The "Micro" Lab

Most hospitals with laboratory facilities have a microbiology laboratory dedicated to the study of pathogens, including bacteria and viruses, recovered from bodily fluid excretions, secretions, and tissues. This chapter discusses the study of bacteria. Bacteria are most commonly cultured (grown) from blood, sputum, or urine.

B. Blood Cultures

Blood is usually cultured when there is a suspicion of systemic infection. Situations in which blood cultures may be drawn include febrile illness not believed to be related to a viral syndrome (such as influenza) or when a bacterial infection is suspected despite the absence of fever (such as in the delirious elderly patient).

TIP: Blood cultures should be drawn in a febrile patient who is unstable and, whenever possible, should be collected prior to the start of antibiotics. A frequent mistake is to start antibiotics before drawing blood cultures. This may result in missed or delayed diagnosis.

There are two terms often (and frequently incorrectly) used interchangeably: "bacteremia" and "sepsis." The term bacteremia is defined as "the presence of viable bacteria in the blood." Sepsis is a broader term defined as "the presence of various pus-forming and other pathogenic organisms, or their toxins, in the blood or tissues." Bacteremia may be transient and benign; sepsis is always pathologic. "Septic shock," frequently referred to as "sepsis," is "a state of profound mental and physical depression associated with sepsis."

The appropriate method of blood culture collection may be found in any basic medical procedures text. Most suggest collecting 10 to 20 ml of blood per culture from an adult or 1 to 6 ml from an infant or child. Blood should either be collected from two separate sites or from the same site at least twenty minutes apart. Each set of blood cultures should consist of at least two bottles, one for aerobic and one for anaerobic cultures. Studies have shown that the sensitivity of two to three separately collected blood cultures within a twenty-four-hour period in establishing the cause of clinically significant bacteremias is nearly 100 percent and the sensitivity of a single blood culture within the same period is approximately 80 to 90 percent.[9,10]

Thus, if multiple blood cultures are drawn on a febrile patient within a 24-hour period and they turn up negative, it is reasonable to conclude that the patient is not bacteremic.

Once bacteria are cultured, they are usually identified using special stains. The gram-stain is the most frequently used. Gram staining allows the pathologist to classify bacteria as gram positive or gram negative. It can be determined if the bacteria grow best in an oxygen-rich environment (aerobic bacteria) or an oxygen-poor environment (anaerobic bacteria). Bacteria are then exposed to various antibiotics to determine to which they are sensitive.

TIP: Any growth in a blood culture is considered a positive (and clinically undesirable) result. Any positive result must be immediately reported verbally to either the patient's nurse or physician. A notation is usually made in the record of who was notified and when.

Several reports are generated for each positive culture. A preliminary result will usually state that there is growth and identify what the bacteria look like and from which bottle they grew. For example the report might say "gram-positive cocci in clusters from the aerobic bottle." Subsequent reports will determine the type of bacteria and ultimately the sensitivity of the bacteria to various antibiotics.

Particularly worrisome results include early (less than twenty-four hours after collection) growth or growth in multiple cultures. Such results may indicate a high degree of bacteremia.

Gram-negative bacteria are especially troublesome because they can rapidly lead to septic shock. Resistant organisms are becoming more common as broader spectrum antibiotics are gaining wider use. Infections with resistant bacteria require more potent and expensive antibiotics to treat and often require isolation of the patient from other patients and increased care by providers to avoid contamination ("precautions").

Blood cultures contaminated by skin flora are common and usually due to sub-optimal sterilization of the venipuncture site. The most common bacteria isolated from contaminated cultures are described as "coagulase-negative staphylococcus." These do not contain the enzyme coagulase found in staphylococcus aureus (a particularly virulent bacteria). So-called "coag-negative staph" are usually not pathogenic and are therefore usually ignored, though exceptions exist.[11,12] Coag-negative Staph gram stain as "gram positive cocci in clusters." If this is the preliminary read on a blood culture, the initial conclusion is likely to be that the blood culture was contaminated. Providers often will wait for further data before treating such a test result rather than exposing a patient to potentially harmful antibiotic treatment.

C. Urinalysis and Urine Culture

Urinalysis (UA) and culture are routinely done in settings where a urinary tract infection is suspected. A urinalysis and culture are part of the standard work-up for any fever in a patient without an obvious source of infection. Another common circumstance when this is done is in the elderly patient with a change in mental status.

Specimen collection is typically accomplished by having the patient urinate into a sterile container, a "clean-catch" specimen. Where the patient is too disabled or delirious to accomplish this task, the bladder is catheterized to obtain the specimen.

The presence of nitrites, bacteria, or leukocytes in a urinalysis may indicate an active urinary tract infection, while the presence of significant numbers of epithelial cells may represent contamination. In the appropriate context, a positive UA is evidence enough to begin empiric treatment with antibiotics.

A colony-forming unit (cfu) is a measure of growth used in evaluating a positive urine culture. The growth of skin flora, colony counts of less than 100,000, or growth of multiple organisms usually represents contamination.

TIP: Colony counts greater than 100,000 may indicate infection. One exception to the colony count rule is for specimens obtained by sterile catheterization; here any growth may be indicative of infection.[13,14,15]

The presence of an indwelling catheter complicates matters. Ninety-five percent of the time, the urinary tract in these patients is colonized by bacteria. In the appropriate context, positive cultures should not be ignored. These bacteria may lead to infection and are responsible for two-thirds of all febrile episodes in catheterized patients. In one study, acute pyelonephritis (kidney infection) was identified in one-third of dying patients with indwelling catheters. Many of these patients were afebrile (without fever).[16]

A verbal report of a positive UA or culture is less frequently given than for blood cultures. The assumption is that the provider will check these results in a timely manner. The rationale is that it is less likely that a positive urine result will be of critical importance, while a positive blood culture result often is.

D. Sputum Cultures

Sputum is a third commonly cultured bodily substance. Sputum collection is appropriate whenever a pulmonary infection is suspected. Appropriately collected sputum which is gram stained and cultured may reveal the bacteria causing pneumonia or bronchitis and direct the choice of antibiotics.

Collection methods vary, from the patient producing a specimen after coughing (the least invasive approach), to inducing sputum production by provocation with an inhalant, to invasively obtaining a specimen by bronchoscopy. Finding more than twenty-five epithelial cells in a stained specimen at 100-power magnification indicates contamination by oral flora and should lead to the specimen being discarded. If fewer than five epithelial cells are found in the specimen, it is reassuring that the sample is not contaminated by oral flora. The presence of many leukocytes may indicate an active infection.[17,18]

As with all cultures, several reports are usually generated for the sputum culture. The initial report will indicate the morphology of the bacteria or the presence of suspected oral flora. (Oral flora are a benign finding.) Subsequent reports will detail what pathogenic bacteria are growing and the antibiotics to which they are sensitive. As with urine culture results, sputum results are less frequently called directly to the provider.

10.4 Imaging Tests
A. General Considerations

Imaging tests involve the use of various forms of energy to generate images of the internal structures of the body. The use of x-rays (plain films and Computerized Axial Tomography or CAT scans), radio waves (Magnetic Resonance Imaging or MRI), and sound waves (ultrasound) are discussed.

TIP: Which test is chosen depends upon the sensitivity and specificity of these tests for detecting a suspected pathology, practical matters such as availability of equipment and personnel, and the ability of the patient to undergo a test.

As with all tests, the responsibility of the ordering provider is to choose the test to order and to make sure that results are obtained and acted upon in a timely manner. The interpreting radiologist is responsible for directly alerting the ordering provider or a surrogate of significant abnormal findings. The radiologist is responsible for reading and reporting any abnormalities the film contains. For example, an otherwise unremarkable plain film of the abdomen done for abdominal pain also demonstrates pneumonia in the left lower lobe. The report should indicate both that the abdomen is benign in appearance and that there is a left lower lobe pneumonia. The radiologist should suggest an appropriate follow-up study, e.g., "a chest x-ray should be considered to further evaluate this process."

Unlike most other tests, x-ray "results" may be quite subjective and often dependent upon the experience of the reader. Even two radiologists occasionally differ over the interpretation of a film.

Imaging tests usually undergo interpretation by multiple providers. For example, a chest x-ray may be read by medical house-staff or the ordering provider, the radiology resident, and a radiologist. The medical house-staff or radiology resident may give an informal reading or "wet-read." A preliminary report or "draft" is prepared in written form by the radiology resident. Once the radiologist has reviewed ("overread") the film and report, a final or signed interpretation is prepared. It is important to understand that the version referred to in the record as a "wet read" or "draft report" will not have been reviewed with the same scrutiny or by as trained an eye as the final read.

As with all tests, it is important for the physician to treat the patient rather than the film. In most circumstances, the clinical status of the patient trumps any radiological finding.

B. Plain Films
1. Definition

Plain films, or x-rays taken without the use of a contrast medium, are still the mainstay of radiology. They are simple to obtain and (with the exception of mammograms) require the least amount of training to interpret. They are generated by passing x-rays from an x-ray tube through the body. Some of the x-rays are absorbed by the structures in the body casting "shadows" on a film placed on the other side of the patient. Denser structures (such as bone) appear white on the x-ray film.

2. Chest films

Chest x-rays (CXRs) are the oldest and still the most common technique used to image the lungs and other structures in the thoracic cavity. Chest x-rays are of two varieties referring to how they are obtained.

The usually preferred technique is to x-ray the patient with the film placed in front of the patient and the x-ray tube in the back (the posterior to anterior or PA view). This is augmented by a lateral view with the right side of the patient closest to the film. The PA/lateral technique is preferred in most instances because it reveals more detail and is less subject to distortion.

An alternative method is the anterior to posterior or AP film. Here the situation is reversed with the x-ray tube in front and the film in the rear. No lateral is obtained. The AP film is usually obtained only if the patient is unable to be positioned to obtain a PA and lateral film (e.g., the patient is critically ill and unable to leave the intensive care unit or is intubated or on a back board) or if an AP film will suffice (e.g., checking for the correct placement of a central line or naso-gastric tube).

AP films are often obtained using portable equipment that can be brought to the patient's bedside. In such cases the film may be referred to in the record as a "portable film." All "portable chest films" are AP films.

TIP: As with all imaging studies, some will turn out poorly. So called "sub-optimal studies" may result from "under-penetration" of x-rays (i.e., due to obesity), "respiratory artifact" (i.e., blurring due to breathing), movement artifact, or any one of a number of other causes.

When clinically indicated, sub-optimal studies need to be repeated. The reading should contain a reference to the quality of the film if it is suboptimal, e.g., "Pneumonia cannot be excluded due to under penetration and poor inspiratory effort. Should clinical suspicion for pneumonia exist, this film should be repeated."

False negative x-rays are a common occurrence. For example, pneumonia in an elderly patient who presents in a dehydrated state may not be evident on the initial chest film. The x-ray should be repeated after hydration if clinical suspicion of disease is high.

Atelectasis is an absence of gas from a part or the whole of the lungs. Often a non-pathologic condition, atelectasis is sometimes impossible to differentiate from pneumonia on a plain film. In such instances the interpretation may read,

"Atelectasis vs. pneumonia, clinical correlation is advised." This means that the radiologist was unable to determine if the patient has pneumonia and should suggest to the provider to either act on her clinical suspicion or repeat the film.

Congestive heart failure (CHF) is frequently identified on CXR. CHF is suggested by a combination of any of the following:

- "cephalization" or engorgement of the vessels in the upper lobes on CXR,
- "Kerley B lines" representing thickened interlobular septa (engorged lymphatic vessels),
- "pulmonary interstitial edema" representing excess fluid in the lung tissue,
- alveolar edema representing fluid in the air sacs of the lungs (usually in the inner two-thirds of the lung producing a "bat-wing" appearance),
- pleural effusions representing fluid on the diaphragm, or
- cardiac enlargement.

One or more of these signs may be present depending upon the severity or chronicity of CHF.[19]

Other findings suspicious for pathology include masses, cavitation (holes) or lymphadenopathy (enlarged lymph nodes). Often, the suggestion is to obtain a more detailed study such as a CAT scan of the chest.

3. Abdominal films

Kidney-ureter-bladder (KUB) radiography involves a single plain image of the abdomen. It is usually the first film performed when intra-abdominal pathology is suspected. It is frequently sufficient to reveal pathology, but often other imaging techniques are required.

TIP: "Free air" (air in the peritoneal cavity) may be indicative of a perforated bowel, although it may be a normal finding in the setting of recent abdominal surgery. Ileus, a condition which may result from an absence of peristalsis or obstruction of the bowel due to paralysis or mechanical cause, is usually identifiable on KUB. Frequently, kidney stones will be identified on KUB, though the preferred study for suspected kidney stones is an abdominal CAT scan ("a stone protocol").

---

4. Skeletal films

In the majority of cases, x-rays of skeletal structures are sufficient to diagnose fractures. In certain circumstances (i.e., in elderly or osteopenic patients) plain films are sometimes insensitive and additional studies may be required.

Rarely does a single view suffice. A fracture may be visible only from a certain perspective. Additionally, the complexity of a fracture is often seen only when several views have been obtained.

TIP: Fractures may not be evident immediately following an injury. If clinical suspicion is high, follow-up plain films or a more sensitive study (such as an MRI, CAT scan, or bone scan) may be in order. Individuals may have benign abnormalities, such as additional vertebrae. These are only of academic interest.

Plain films of the cervical spine are an essential part of the work-up for traumatic neck injury. They are key in the evaluation of patients with neck pain following motor vehicle accidents or head injuries. Cervical films consist of four views: the dontoid, anterior-posterior, lateral, and right oblique. It is essential to visualize all seven cervical vertebrae. A "swimmer's view" may occasionally be obtained to supplement other cervical films.[20]

5. Mammography

Mammography is an imperfect radiological technique requiring a high degree of training and experience to interpret. It is (unfortunately) the only routine screening test for breast cancer. It is also the essential initial test following discovery of a suspicious lesion on manual breast exam. Abnormalities suggestive of breast cancer include distinct, irregular "crab-like" densities, clusters of five or more microcalcifications in an area less than 1 cm, or architectural distortion without a benign explanation.[21]

Mammography is far from an ideal diagnostic test. For example, 80 percent of microcalcifications are benign (i.e., the specificity is 20 percent).[22] Under optimal circumstances, screening mammography is 90 to 95 percent sensitive for detecting occult breast cancer. Supplemental studies, such as ultrasonography, are frequently employed. Ultrasonography is particularly useful in distinguishing solid from cystic (fluid-filled) masses.[23]

C. Computerized Axial Tomography (CAT or CT scans)

1. Introduction to the CAT scan

Computerized Axial Tomography (CAT or CT) employs x-rays obtained from multiple angles and integrated by complex computer manipulation to generate high quality cross-sectional images of bodily structures. CAT scans may utilize intravenous (IV) and/or ingested (oral) contrast (radio-opaque substances which highlight areas of interest) to distinguish vascular and gastrointestinal structures. Use of intravenous contrast is relatively contraindicated in patients with renal failure because it may worsen kidney function.

TIP: CAT scans are particularly useful in demonstrating disease within the chest or abdominal cavities. They are less useful in demonstrating disease in the brain. MRI studies have mostly supplanted the use of CAT scans of the brain, the exception being in acute head trauma where a non-contrast head CT may be the preferred study.

There are circumstances where CAT scans are performed even though an MRI might be more informative. CAT scans are often done if there is a need for the study to be rapidly completed. A CAT scan can be accomplished in minutes versus a much longer period to perform an MRI. A CAT scan may be the only option if a patient has a pacemaker or metal in the brain, eye, or back making an MRI impossible.

2. CAT scan of the brain

The head or brain CAT scan is useful in identifying gross abnormalities and is the preferred test to demonstrate the presence of abnormal collections of blood. Head CAT scans are superior to MRI in detecting fractures and foreign bodies. They are the preferred study in patients with head trauma or acute change in mental status. They are less useful in identifying subtle anomalies such as ischemic strokes (so-called lacunar infarcts) or demyelinization caused by multiple sclerosis or abnormalities in the brain stem for which MRI is the better study. A CAT scan of the brain with intravenous contrast is superior to a "non contrast" CAT scan for identifying brain tumors and vascular anomalies such as aneurysms, though in such cases an MRI is preferred.[24]

3. CAT scan of the chest

The chest CAT scan is often the preferred study to demonstrate intrathoracic pathology such as lung cancer or vascular abnormalities. It is the diagnostic procedure of choice for studying the mediastinum and pleura. It is usually indicated if plain x-ray films suggest an abnormality requiring further investigation such as a mass, cavitary lesion (a hole), lymphadenopathy or vascular abnormality such as an aortic aneurysm. Contrast dye should be used when indicated (i.e., to evaluate vascular or mediastinal structures).[25]

4. CAT scan of the abdomen

The abdominal CAT scan, usually performed with both oral and IV contrast, is useful in identifying intra-abdominal pathology. It is frequently the study of choice for the initial evaluation of the trauma patient; patients with suspected kidney stones, abdominal aortic aneurysms, intraperitoneal or retroperitoneal bleeding or abscesses; or the evaluation of the acute abdomen.[26] It may complement other studies such as ultrasound in the evaluation of diseases of the kidney, liver, and pancreas.

5. CAT scan of the skeleton

Skeletal CAT scanning is the preferred test in the evaluation of complex fractures particularly of the skull. In patients with osteoporosis with recent injury, CAT scanning may identify occult fractures not visible on plain films, though MRI is preferred in most instances.[27] For evaluation of bulging or frankly herniated discs, bone tumors or bone metastasis, and spinal osteomyelitis, MRI is the superior study.[28,29]

D. Magnetic Resonance Imaging (MRI)
1. Introduction to MRI

MRI involves no ionizing radiation. MRI is based instead on the interaction between radio waves and hydrogen nuclei (protons) in the body subjected to a strong magnetic field. All substances in the body contain hydrogen in the form of H_2O or water. In a powerful magnetic field, protons will all orient themselves in a certain direction. When subjected to a radio pulse, these protons absorb the energy briefly then pop back to their original state (a process called "relaxation"), releasing energy at the same frequency as the radio pulse. The time it takes these nuclei to "relax" (the "relaxation time") varies depending upon what the tissue is composed of (bone, blood, muscle) and the proton density (i.e., how much water there is in the tissue).[30]

TIP: MRIs require patients to be subjected to a strong magnetic field. If a patient has a pacemaker metallic heart valve or metal in the brain or eye, exposure to this magnetic field can have catastrophic consequences.

MRIs usually cannot be accomplished on intubated patients due to the metal in the ventilator. Additionally, MRIs take a long time to perform limiting their usefulness to patients who can lie still for a prolonged period. The typical MRI requires the patient to be bodily inserted into the machine (though "open MRIs" do exist which do not require such confining circumstances). Patients suffering from claustrophobia or agitation may not be able to tolerate an MRI. Additionally, a patient's weight may determine the need for an open MRI. There are weight limits with closed MRIs.

2. T1 versus T2

Two different strengths of radio energy are used in MRIs. Images resulting from these are referred to as T1 and T2. On T1 images, non-flowing fluid such as cerebral spinal fluid (CSF) appears dark, and fatty tissue appears bright. On T2 images, the reverse is true. Flowing fluids (blood) appear dark on both T1 and T2 imaging. With regard to the brain, T1 imaging is usually superior in demonstrating normal anatomy, while T2 imaging is best at demonstrating pathology (such as strokes and cerebral edema) and portraying arteries and veins.[31]

3. Preferred uses for MRI

With the exceptions described in prior sections, MRI is the preferred modality for imaging the brain, spinal cord, soft tissues (ligaments and tendons in orthopedic injuries), tumors of the kidneys and adrenal glands, and areas of bone with artifact on CAT scan. It is also more sensitive and specific than either a CAT scan or bone scan in detecting osteomyelitis (infection of bone), bone metastases, or occult fracture. Major drawbacks include the length of time it takes to obtain an MRI image and the fact that critically ill patients requiring life support equipment containing metal (e.g., ventilators) cannot be imaged. Patients with pacemakers or those with intracranial metallic clips (among others) cannot undergo an MRI.[32]

4. Gadolinium

Gadolinium-diethylenetriaminepentaacetic acid ("Gadolinium" or "Gad") is a paramagnetic agent serving as contrast in MRI. Among other uses, Gad helps enhance T1 imaging of the brains of subjects suffering an acute stroke.[33] It is also the preferred imaging technique for evaluating abscesses of the brain and spinal column.[34,35]

TIP: Gad cannot be used in patients with renal insufficiency due to a common and potentially fatal reaction.

E. Ultrasonography

Ultrasonography is a technique where high frequency sound waves are projected into a body organ, cavity, or vessel. The "echo," returning sound waves, is detected and translated into an image. A radiologist or other professional with specialized training interprets this image. Ultrasonography is often the preferred study of the heart (i.e., an echocardiogram in a patient with congestive heart failure or valvular disease), certain forms of kidney disease (i.e., acute or chronic renal failure), and in the pregnant patient for evaluation of the uterus, ovaries, and fetus. It is the study of choice to identify deep venous thromboses (blood clots) of the veins of the arms and legs (non-invasive venous studies or NIVS; lower extremity noninvasive studies or LENIS). Ultrasonography is often useful in gall bladder or liver disease and pancreatitis. It may play an integral part in biopsy procedures allowing imaging of tumors of interest in the thyroid, breast, or solid internal organs such as the liver and kidney. It is sometimes helpful in evaluating and aspirating pleural or peritoneal fluid. Ultrasonography often is the initial test to look for blockages of peripheral arteries (i.e., non-invasive arterial studies or non-invasive carotid studies) and to image the aorta for aneurysms.[36]

F. Bone Scan

A bone scan involves imaging of the skeleton after injection of a radioactive tracer, usually technetium diphosphate or gallium. Areas "lighting up" (showing up bright) on bone scan have a higher amount of metabolic activity and blood flow. Bone scanning may be useful in detecting bone metastases, occult fractures, and osteomyelitis and in certain pain disorders (such as reflex sympathetic dystrophy). However, specificity is low, and other tests (such as MRI or CT) are often preferred. Certain forms of cancer (myeloma) will not show up on bone scan.[37,38]

10.5 Testing in Cardiology
A. Introduction to Testing in Cardiology

Patients with suspected coronary artery disease (CAD) or other forms of heart disease are subjected to a broad variety of tests. The ones discussed in this section rarely are used under other circumstances. Some, such as the electrocardiogram and certain blood tests, are ordered and interpreted routinely by general internists, family practitioners, and other providers. Stress tests with imaging and echocardiograms may be ordered by these providers but usually require a cardiologist (or in some cases a radiologist) to interpret them. Cardiac catheterization is the province of the interventional cardiologist or radiologist and only occurs with the advice and under the guidance of such a specialist. Some of these tests, such as cardiac catheterization, may entail substantial

risk and should involve a detailed and well-documented discussion of potential risks and benefits.

B. The Electrocardiogram (ECG or EKG)

The oldest, most basic, and easiest test in cardiology to perform and interpret is the electrocardiogram. The electrocardiogram records the changing potentials (strength and direction) of the electrical field imparted by the heart. It is the only practical means of recording the electrical behavior of the heart.[39]

TIP: ECGs are the procedure of first choice in the evaluation of chest pain, syncope, or dizziness.

An initial ECG, followed by serial ECGs, should be performed on any patient with typical chest pain (pain characteristic of ischemic heart disease) until the patient has returned to a stable condition. An ECG is indicated in all patients with known cardiovascular disease or dysfunction during the initial evaluation and should be repeated as indicated to evaluate short- and long-term responses to therapy known to produce electrocardiographic changes. A baseline ECG is warranted in patients at increased risk for heart disease, such as those with diabetes or high blood pressure, with follow-up ECGs at one to five year intervals. ECGs may be used as a screening test to risk-stratify patients undergoing surgery (though evidence here is less strong).[40]

The standard ECG is composed of twelve "leads." Each lead offers a different perspective on the heart. There are three pairs of bipolar leads (the limb leads I, II, III) and nine unipolar leads, consisting of three limb leads (aVr, aVl and aVf) and six precordial leads (V1-V6). Together these twelve leads help portray a three-dimensional portrait of the heart's electrical activity.[41] (Figure 10.5)

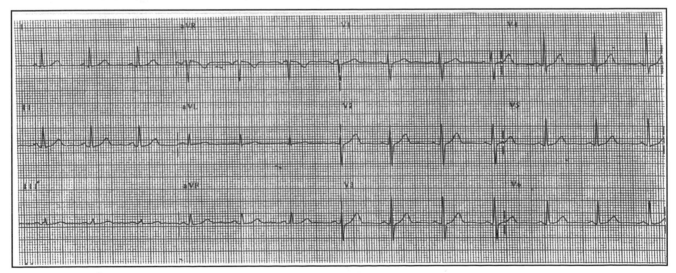

Figure 10.5 *A normal twelve-lead ECG.*

In emergency situations (such as in an ambulance) or for routine monitoring on a telemetry unit, only one lead is observed (most frequently lead II). This "rhythm strip" offers a limited perspective on the status of the heart and should not be relied upon to make a firm diagnosis. It is quite useful in monitoring for arrhythmias and is typically the only monitoring available when conducting a "code" following cardiac arrest.

TIP: When interpreting an ECG report, it is important to realize that there is no such thing as a "normal" ECG. Two perfectly healthy individuals will likely have different ECGs due to variations in their size, gender, and other factors.

There are situations when a normal ECG indicates pathology (e.g., when abnormalities visible on prior ECGs disappear and the ECG appears normal). There are "typical" findings on an ECG usually indicative of a normally functioning heart. The ECG represents a snapshot of the heart at a particular point in time. Whenever possible, a prior ECG should be obtained and compared to the current ECG. When reviewing an ECG interpretation, the phrase "no change from prior" should generally be taken as reassuring. "New" findings are often of concern. All primary providers of medical care should be competent in interpreting ECGs. With few exceptions, there is no need for a cardiologist to interpret an ECG.

It is sometimes impossible to interpret an ECG due to artifacts on the tracing. Missing a diagnosis due to baseline artifact, misplaced, or missing leads is no excuse. In the majority of instances, when an ECG is not interpretable it needs to be repeated.

ECGs, though necessary and useful tools in identifying pathology, are rarely sufficient to formulate a diagnosis. For example, the World Health Organization criteria for the diagnosis of a myocardial infarct (MI or heart attack) require two of three elements be met, only one of which is "evolutionary changes on serially obtained ECGs." The other two are a typical clinical presentation and a rise and fall in cardiac markers (defined below). Indeed, diagnostic ECGs are obtained in only half of emergency room patients presenting with MI.[42] In other words, the ECG is only 50 percent sensitive in diagnosing MI in this situation.

C. Blood Tests to Rule Out Myocardial Infarction

TIP: Cardiac markers are serially obtained blood tests attempting to detect certain enzymes and other proteins released from injured or dying cardiac muscle cells. The most commonly used cardiac markers are creatinine kinase and its isoenzymes and the troponins.

Creatinine kinase (CK) is an enzyme found in many tissues of the body. An elevation in the total CK is very sensitive for MI, rising four to eight hours after injury and returning to normal within two to three days. Unfortunately, elevations are common in patients with numerous pathological and non-pathological conditions. For example, elevations occur following vigorous exercise and after receiving intramuscular injections. Therefore, an elevated CK has low specificity. To improve the specificity of this marker, levels of certain isoenzymes, forms of CK found more commonly in the heart (CK-MB), are determined and compared with the level of CK in a simultaneously drawn sample. A ratio of CK-MB mass to CK activity greater than 0.025 or 2.5 percent generally indicates cardiac muscle injury. An elevated ratio may be seen in skeletal muscle injury and is unreliable if the CK is within normal range. Measurement of serial markers is essential as a typical rise and fall pattern over a course of twenty-four to forty-eight hours, and is diagnostic for MI.

Troponins are molecules found in skeletal and cardiac muscle. The cardiac forms of troponin differ from those found in skeletal muscle, making detection of troponin elevation highly sensitive and specific for MI. (Exceptions, such as in the patient with renal failure, exist.) The two most common forms of troponin which are measured are troponin I and troponin T. Troponin levels begin to rise about three hours following injury and stay elevated for more than a week.[43] Again, serial enzyme measurements are essential.

Typically, three sets of enzymes are drawn eight hours apart. Lack of the typical pattern of enzyme rise and fall is usually sufficient to "rule out" an MI.

D. Stress Testing

Stress testing in patients with known or suspected coronary artery disease (i.e., patients with chest pain or exertional shortness of breath) is often indicated.

A thirty-seven-year-old construction worker presented to the emergency room with intermittent chest pain and pain radiating to his neck and left shoulder. A two-pack-per-day smoker, he also reported shortness of breath during exertion in the preceding month. He was admitted to the hospital under the care of the defendant doctor. The defendant ordered a number of tests, which yielded a diagnosis of pulmonary disease. A year later, the patient suffered a fatal heart attack. An autopsy revealed diffuse coronary artery disease. The decedent's widow contended that the defendant should have performed further testing which would have revealed this coronary artery disease and allowed lifesaving measures to be performed. The defendant argued that the pain the decedent experienced upon admission to the hospital was consistent with costochondral pain rather than a cardiac condition and that no abnormalities suggestive of cardiac disease were found in the tests that were performed. According to *New York Jury Verdict Reporter*, the jury returned a $15,000,000 verdict for the plaintiffs. *Donna Ventura, Individually, and as Adminx. of the Estate of Paul Ventura v. Mitchell Lipton M.D.*, Kings County (NY) Supreme Court, Index No. 13250/99.[44]

Tests are divided into those where "stress" is induced by exercise (an exercise tolerance test or ETT) and those where chemicals are used to simulate a "stress" response. Sometimes imaging of the heart is involved.

In general, if the patient can exercise, an ETT is indicated as it has superior prognostic value. In this type of test the patient exercises on a treadmill or bike. The intensity of exercise is gradually increased (intensity is measured in metabolic equivalents or METs on a scale of 1 to 10). Serial vital sign measurements and ECGs are performed. Results are given as diagnostic, non-diagnostic (indeterminate), or normal based upon the level of exercise attained and changes in the ECG and vital signs. The ETT is reasonably sensitive and specific in appropriately chosen subjects. It should not be performed as a screening test for very low-risk asymptomatic patients due to a high false positive rate in this population.[45]

When a patient cannot exercise (due to age, deconditioning, arthritis, or other condition) chemical stress testing is indicated. Often chemical stress tests are combined with imaging. Three different types of chemical stress tests are commonly employed: dipyridamole (or persantine), adenosine, and dobutamine. After injection, dipyridamole and adenosine both cause dilation of coronary arteries. Simplistically put, diseased arteries do not respond in the same way as normal arteries. Blood flow will increase only to areas supplied by non-diseased vessels. A relative lack of blood flow (and therefore lack of tracer) to an area of heart muscle indicates disease in the coronary arteries supplying that portion of the heart.

Some patients (e.g., those with chronic lung disease) cannot tolerate dipyridamole or adenosine. In such cases, or due to provider preference, dobutamine may be used. Dobutamine increases myocardial contractility, heart rate, and blood pressure. Imaging may be accomplished using radiation or with echocardiography. In the latter instance, ischemia is inferred by visualizing abnormal motion of the heart with exercise. Typical changes on serial ECGs may also be demonstrated.[46] Echocardiography offers the advantage of visualizing the anatomy and function of the heart while under stress.

Myocardial perfusion imaging uses radioactive substances or tracers. The two most commonly administered substances are Thallium-201 (Thallium) and Technetium-99-sestamibi (Sestamibi). These are absorbed by heart muscle then rapidly decay (change into other substances). In the process they emit x-rays (in the case of Thallium) or gamma rays (in the case of sestamibi) which are detected by a camera forming an image of the heart. Heart muscle requires an intact blood supply in order for the tracer to reach it. Lack of absorption of tracer implies that a diseased vessel supplies that area of the heart.

In Thallium testing, a single injection is given at peak exercise (or after giving a chemical stressor). Images are obtained immediately after injection and several hours later. Imaging is commonly by Single Positron Emission Computed Tomography (SPECT), which allows horizontal and vertical images of the heart to be produced. A normal finding is homogeneous uptake of Thallium throughout the myocardium. A defect is a relative or absolute lack of uptake in an area of myocardium. Defects may be "fixed" (i.e., tracer is not absorbed with recovery from exercise) or "reversible" (i.e., tracer is absorbed with recovery). Fixed defects generally indicate "dead" myocardium, which is not salvageable. Reversible defects imply living or salvageable heart muscle. An additional finding with Thallium testing may be "lung uptake" which commonly indicates exercise-induced left ventricular dysfunction.

In Sestamibi testing, two injections are required. The first injection occurs at peak exercise, the second several hours later. Images are obtained using a gamma camera and reconstructed and interpreted as with Thallium images (see above). Images obtained using Sestamibi are generally of better quality. An additional advantage of Sestamibi imaging is that "ECG-gated images" can be obtained, effectively allowing assessment of regional wall motion and wall thickening during the cardiac cycle and a determination of left ventricular ejection fraction (a measure of the squeeze of the heart muscle).

The selection of an appropriate stress test is often not straightforward. Selection depends on how strong the provider's suspicion for heart disease is, how capable the patient is to perform exercise, baseline ECG abnormalities, and what equipment is available. For example, in a patient with a "left bundle branch block" (a type of ECG abnormality), interpretation of the ECG is impossible, and therefore imaging is always required. In patients with a highly typical presentation for angina, the false negative rate for stress testing is much higher than for those with low risk. Such patients may go directly for cardiac catheterization.[47]

E. Cardiac Catheterization

TIP: Cardiac catheterization and angiography (left heart catheterization) involve the injection of contrast directly into the coronary arteries accompanied by x-ray imaging. This allows direct visualization of the coronary arteries and carries the additional advantage that direct therapeutic intervention (such as angioplasty and stenting) may be accomplished. The main drawback is that potentially nephrotoxic contrast must be used.

Catheterization is accomplished by cannulating the femoral or brachial artery and threading a catheter into a position where contrast may be injected into the coronary arteries. Catheterization is indicated for patients in whom the presence or absence of coronary disease should be determined with reasonable probability in order to improve management or when patients at high risk for complications of ischemic heart disease should be identified. Associated risks include pseudo-aneurysm formation, bleeding, and acute renal failure due to contrast (among others). Informed consent is essential.[48]

F. Echocardiogram

After the ECG, the echocardiogram ("echo") is the most commonly ordered test in cardiology. Echocardiograms are ultrasounds of the heart. There are three commonly performed types of echocardiogram, the m-mode, two-dimensional, and Doppler echocardiogram. The m-mode echocardiogram generates an ice-pick ("one-dimensional") view of the heart. The two-dimensional echocardiogram generates a pie-shaped view of the heart. Doppler echocardiography demonstrates velocity and direction of blood flow in the heart and is used in conjunction with m-mode or two-dimensional echocardiography. Echocardiograms may be indicated in patients with newly diagnosed congestive heart failure, newly detected heart murmurs, and in patients with suspected valvular disease or cardiomyopathy. They are commonly ordered following an MI to determine if there is significant resulting dysfunction.[49] Suboptimal echocardiograms are common in patients whose body habitus interferes with imaging, i.e., obese persons.

A typical clinical scenario is as follows. A sixty-three-year-old male arrives in the emergency room with crushing sub-sternal chest pain and ECG changes consistent with an MI. He receives thrombolytics (clot dissolving drugs) in the emergency room, and his symptoms resolve. He is diagnosed with an MI through elevations in his troponins and CK-MB index. An echocardiogram is done, and significant cardiac dysfunction is noted. A stress test is considered, but due to the patient developing congestive heart failure, a cardiac catheterization is suggested. This reveals multiple diseased vessels. The catheterization is complicated by acute renal failure and the development of a pseudo-aneurysm. The patient subsequently undergoes a coronary artery bypass graft (CABG) operation. His recovery is uneventful.

10.6 Summary

Diagnostic testing plays a critical role in modern medicine. When used appropriately it can lead to prompt diagnosis and lifesaving treatment. When improperly used it may lead to additional suffering, iatrogenic complications, and added expense. A reasonable familiarity with the most common tests is essential for interpreting any medical record.

Endnotes

1. Hollowell, E.E. and B.H. Bloch. Coproviders and institutional practice in Sanbar, et al. (Editor). *Legal Medicine*. Fifth Edition. p. 508. St. Louis, MO: Mosby. 2001.

2. Laska, L. (Editor). "Failure to Notify New York Woman of Abnormal Pap Test Results Leads to Delay in Diagnosis and Treatment of Cervical Cancer—Hysterectomy, Radiation, Chemotherapy." *Medical Malpractice Verdicts, Settlements, and Experts*. August 2003, p. 20.

3. *American College of Radiology Practice Guideline for Communication: Diagnostic Radiology*. January 1, 2002.

4. "2005 Joint Commission National Patient Safety Goals: Practical Strategies and Helpful Solutions for Meeting These Goals." Joint Commission Sentinel Event Advisory Group. July 2004.

5. Ravel, R. *Clinical Laboratory Medicine*. Sixth Edition. p. 2–3. St. Louis, MO: Mosby.

6. *Id* 56-57.

7. Gomella, L.G. *Clinician's Pocket Reference*. Sixth Edition. p. 71–72. Norwalk, CT: Appleton and Lange. 1989.

8. Marino, P.L. *The ICU Book*. p. 415–426. Malvern, PA: Lea and Febiger. 1991.

9. Holmes, N.H. *Diagnostic Tests*. p. 457–458. Philadelphia, PA. 2003.

10. Woods, G.L. and J.A. Washington. "The Clinician and the Microbiology Laboratory" in Mandell, et al. (Editor). *Principles and Practice of Infectious Diseases*. Fourth Edition. p. 177. New York, NY: Churchill Livingstone. 1995.

11. *Id*.

12. Waldvogel, F.Z. "Staphylococcus Aureus" in Mandell, et al. (Editor). *Principles and Practice of Infectious Diseases*. Fourth Edition. p. 1759. New York, NY: Churchill Livingstone. 1995.

13. *See* note 10 at 176.

14. Sobel, J.D. and D. Kaye. "Urinary Tract Infections" in Mandell, et al. (Editor). *Principles and Practice of Infectious Diseases*. Fourth Edition. p. 662. New York, NY: Churchill Livingstone. 1995.

15. *See* note 7 at 112.

16. Warren, W.W. "Nosocomial Urinary Tract Infections" in Mandell, et al. (Editor). *Principles and Practice of Infectious Diseases*. Fourth Edition. p. 2609–10. New York, NY: Churchill Livingstone. 1995.

17. *See* note 10 at 173–174.

18. *See* note 7 at 111.

19. Steiner, R.M. and D.C. Levin. "Radiology of the Heart" in Braunwald, E. *Heart Disease*. Fifth Edition. p. 219–220. Philadelphia, PA: Saunders Co. 1997.

20. McKown, K.M. "Common Musculoskeletal Symptoms" in Rakel, R.E. *Saunders Manual of Medical Practice*. p. 737–8. Philadelphia, PA: W.B. Saunders Company. 1996.

21. Henderson, C. "Breast Cancer" in Wilson, J.D. et al. (Editors). *Harrison's Principles of Internal Medicine*. p. 1615–16. Twelfth Edition. New York, NY: McGraw Hill, Inc. 1991.

22. *Id*.

23. *See* note 9 at 621–622.

24. King, D. "MRI or CT in CNS Imaging" in Rakel, R.E. *Saunders Manual of Medical Practice*. p. 1061. Philadelphia, PA: W.B. Saunders Company. 1996.

25. Friedman, P.J. "Imaging in Pulmonary Disease" in Wilson, J.D. et al. (Editors). *Harrison's Principles of Internal Medicine*. Twelfth Edition. p. 1040–42. New York, NY: McGraw Hill, Inc. 1991.

26. Ben-Menachem, Y. and R.G. Fisher. "Radiology" in Feliciano, D.V. et al. *Trauma*. Third Edition. p. 208–10. Stamford, CT: Appleton and Lange. 1996.

27. *Id*.

28. *See* note 24.

29. Braunwald, E. et al. (Editors). *Harrison's Principles of Internal Medicine*. Fifteenth Edition. p. 827. New York, NY: McGraw Hill, Inc. 2001.

30. DeLaPaz, R.L. and J.P. Mohr. "Magnetic Resonance Scanning" in Barnett, H.J.M. et al. (Editors). *Stroke*. Third Edition. p. 227–29. New York, NY: Churchill Livingstone. 1998.

31. *Id*.

32. *See* note 7 at 164-165.

33. *See* note 30.

34. Wispelwey, B. and W.M. Scheld in Mandell, et al. (Editor). *Principles and Practice of Infectious Diseases*. Fourth Edition. p. 892–3. New York, NY: Churchill Livingstone. 1995.

35. *See* note 29.

36. Rakel, R.E. *Saunders Manual of Medical Practice*. p. 164, 276, 283–4, 379, 396, 483, 536–8. Philadelphia, PA: W.B. Saunders Company. 1996.

37. Mankin, H.J. "Back and Neck Pain" in Wilson, J.D. et al. (Editors). *Harrison's Principles of Internal Medicine*. Twelfth Edition. p. 121. New York, NY: McGraw Hill, Inc. 1991.

38. *See* note 9 at 671-672.

39. Fisch, C. "Electrocardiography" in Braunwald, E. *Heart Disease*. Fifth Edition. p. 108. Philadelphia, PA: Saunders Co. 1997.

40. Lee, T.H. "Practice Guidelines in Cardiovascular Medicine" in Braunwald, E. Heart Disease. Fifth Edition. p. 1940–41. Philadelphia, PA: Saunders Co. 1997.

41. Fisch, C. "Electrocardiography" in Braunwald, E. *Heart Disease*. Fifth Edition. p. 110–111. Philadelphia, PA: Saunders Co. 1997.

42. Antman, E.M. and E. Braunwald. "Acute Myocardial Infarction" in Braunwald, E. *Heart Disease*. Fifth Edition. p. 1202. Philadelphia, PA: Saunders Co. 1997.

43. *Id*. at 1202–1204.

44. Laska, L. (Editor). "New York Construction Worker Dies of Heart Attack—Widow Sues Doctor Who Examined Him One Year Earlier, Alleging Failure to Detect Coronary Artery Disease." *Medical Malpractice Verdicts, Settlements, and Experts*. October 2003, p. 28.

45. Chaitman, B.R. in Braunwald, E. *Heart Disease*. Fifth Edition. p. 160–1. Philadelphia, PA: Saunders Co. 1997.

46. Wackers, F.J., R. Soufer, and B.L. Zaret. "Nuclear Cardiology" in Braunwald, E. *Heart Disease*. Fifth Edition. p. 289–90. Philadelphia, PA: Saunders Co. 1997.

47. *See* note 46 at 273-295.

48. *See* note 40 at 1949.

49. Feigenbaum, H. "Echocardiography" in Braunwald, E. *Heart Disease*. Fifth Edition. p. 53–57. Philadelphia, PA" Saunders Co. 1997.

Chapter 11

Intravenous Therapy Records

Susan Masoorli, RN

11.1 Introduction

Peripherally inserted central catheters (PICC lines), central venous catheters (CVCs), implanted ports, tunneled catheters, triple lumen catheters, midlines and peripheral intravenous (IV) catheters are all types of devices used to access the vascular system (veins) for the infusion of medications and solutions. People who enter the healthcare system have a high probability of having one of these devices inserted for IV therapy. Even though the practice of accessing veins was developed in the 1600's, research and production of new improved and safer devices has escalated dramatically within the past 10 years. There are over 500 million peripheral catheters and 5 million central venous catheters inserted annually in the United States.[1] IV catheters are inserted in hospitals, long-term care and rehabilitation facilities, patient homes, physician offices, occupational health, work sites and schools. Clinicians must act as patient advocates and a firewall to prevent bad practices from occurring. The Institute for Healthcare Improvement (IHI) and The Joint Commission give permission to all healthcare workers to stop bedside poor practices such as breaking sterile technique during a central venous catheter insertion. In addition Medicare and various insurance agencies have elected not to reimburse hospitals for vascular access infections that occur during a hospital admission. Infections and many other vascular access and IV therapy complications are preventable. The dramatic increase in the number of infusion therapy malpractice cases is due directly to the lack of competently trained healthcare providers inserting and monitoring the various types of vascular access devices and IV therapies or could be attributed to inadvertent attention to detail by otherwise competent healthcare providers.

11.2 Peripheral Vascular Access Devices

Peripheral veins can be accessed for the infusion of fluids and medications or the withdrawal of blood. Peripheral veins are defined as the superficial veins of the upper extremities. Medical records should include a notation about the type of device that was used to start intravenous fluids. There are three types of peripheral intravenous devices: short stainless steel needles, midline catheters and catheter over-the-needle devices.[2]

A. Butterfly

A short stainless steel needle is commonly called a *butterfly* and has a beveled or slanted tip and integral plastic extension tubing. These devices are currently used on a very limited basis, due to the high risk of infusion-related complications.[3] The advantage for using this type of device is that they are easier to insert and a visible flash of blood will be detected in the plastic extension tubing, which signifies that the needle tip is seated within the blood vessel. However, the sharp beveled tip of the needle remains in the vein. If the vein moves, or the needle moves within the vein, the risk of vein puncture is substantial. Vein puncture will result in the leakage of blood into the tissue, causing a hematoma (bruise) to form or the leakage of medications and solutions into the tissue (infiltration). If the drugs have the potential to burn the tissue (extravasation), resulting tissue and muscle injury can occur. In the recent past, clinicians involved in short-term procedures requiring the injection of medications, such as in the radiology department for the injection of contrast agents, often selected this type device. Stainless steel needles are not the device of choice for any type of infusion, for any duration of time. These devices are primarily used for withdrawing blood for analysis.

TIP: These devices are particularly dangerous in the pediatric and geriatric populations, since their veins are very fragile and prone to needle puncture.[4]

B. Catheter

1. Catheter over-the-needle device

The most appropriate peripheral venous access device is the catheter over-the-needle device which is defined as a catheter that is less than or equal to three inches in length. There are many brands on the market, but all have the same design elements. There are more steps to access a vein using an IV catheter as opposed to a stainless steel needle. However, once the catheter is positioned properly within the vein, the risk of IV-related complications is significantly reduced. Catheter over-the-needle devices are two-piece devices: a catheter and a needle. The plastic catheter sits over the beveled needle. When the needle enters the vein, a flash of blood will be visible in the flash back chamber. The beveled needle is removed and the plastic catheter is fully advanced into the vein. Today, most catheters are designed to soften and mold to the contours of the vein after the needle is removed, thereby reducing the incidence of vein puncture and irritation. According to the Infusion Nurses Society (INS) Standards of Practice, short peripheral access devices should be rotated to a new vein site every seventy-two hours.[5] However, the Centers for Disease Control (CDC) Intravascular Guideline recommends peripheral IV devices should be rotated every 72-96 hours.[6] It is a federal law passed in 2001 that all IV catheters must have a needle safety device to prevent contaminated needlestick injury.

2. Catheter insertion documentation

There are specific documentation requirements for the insertion of vascular access devices.[7] The documentation for peripheral catheters should include

- date and time of insertion,
- type of device,
- length of IV catheter,
- gauge of IV catheter,
- anatomical name of the accessed vein,
- number of attempts,
- patient tolerance of the procedure, and
- signature of person inserting the device.

A correctly written example of documentation following a catheter insertion is shown below.

Sample Note
Date/Time
#22 gauge one inch Braun Introcan inserted into left mid cephalic vein on first attempt.
1000ml NSS infusing by gravity at 100ml/hr. Patient states "I did not feel the stick at all"
—H. Bradley, RN

TIP: The current INS Standards of Practice state that all peripheral intravenous devices should be rotated every seventy-two hours or upon suspected complication or therapy completion. The longer the same peripheral device remains in place, the higher the complication rate.

All intravenous site rotations should be documented on the infusion therapy flow sheet or the nurses' progress notes. The documentation should also include an assessment of the condition of the site from where the catheter was removed and the reason the intravenous device was removed. This information should be recorded in the nurse's progress notes.

3. Midline catheter

A midline catheter is defined as a peripheral catheter that is between three and eight inches in length.[8] Specially trained nurses can insert this device at the bedside. An introducer needle is inserted into a vein slightly above the antecubital fossa (inner aspect of the elbow) into the basilic or cephalic vein. The catheter is advanced through the introducer needle to below the shoulder in the axillary vein. The introducer needle is then removed, leaving the catheter in place. According to the INS Standards of Practice, midline catheters can remain in place for up to four weeks.[9] Review of the literature shows there is evidence of higher risk of venous thrombosis (blood clot) with this catheter type. Many hospitals restrict or prohibit the use of midline catheters because of the complication. Only medications approved for peripheral IV catheters can be infused through midline catheters.

4. Midline catheter documentation

The documentation for midline catheters should include

- date and time of insertion,
- type of device,
- anatomical name of the access vein,
- gauge of device,
- length of catheter,
- external length of catheter,
- number of attempts,
- patient tolerance of procedure, and
- signature of person inserting the device.

A correctly written example of documentation prepared after a midline catheter insertion is shown below.

Sample Note
Date/Time
A 20 gauge BD midline catheter inserted into right basilic vein, one inch above the antecubital fossa on the first attempt. 2cm of catheter is external. Patient states "My elbow is a little sore."
—B. Waters, RN

This is required documentation content by the Infusion Nurses Society. In most cases, the documentation of the insertion of an intravenous access device is found in the medical or nursing progress notes. However, the procedure may be documented on the intravenous flow sheet. In specialty areas, such as the emergency room and outpatient surgery, there are often specified areas on the nursing assessment forms to document the insertion of the intravenous device.

C. Insertion Site Selection
The INS Standards of Practice state that areas of joint flexion, such as the wrist area and the antecubital fossa (elbow area), should be avoided as insertion sites,[10] as this increases the risk of complications due to joint movement. The best location for the insertion of peripheral IV devices is in the forearm. The cephalic and basilic veins are straight and large in diameter. Refer to Figure 11.1. These should be the first choices. The metacarpal veins on the back of the hand

are the first choice only when the patient is scheduled for surgery. Anesthesia providers must have access to the IV site for the injection of additional medications as well as to assess the IV site during the intraoperative procedure. The Standards also state that the IV devices should not be inserted into the legs of adult patients as this increases the risk of thrombophlebitis which is the inflammation of the vein with a clot formation.[11] This can result from slower blood flow through the veins in the lower extremities due to an increased number of large semilunar valves. Arms of patients with impaired drainage due to axillary lymph node removal related to metastatic breast cancer or head and neck cancer should not be used for peripheral IV insertions. The impaired drainage of fluid from the arm can cause swelling to occur (lymphedema) making assessment of the IV site for complications more difficult. Arms of patients with functioning AV shunts or fistula for dialysis should also be avoided because the venous anatomy may be compromised.

The preservation of peripheral veins in patients with chronic kidney disease who may need hemodialysis in the future has taken on a new sense of urgency. Patients with chronic kidney disease, Stage 3 or greater, or a serum creatinine level greater than 2.0 mg/dl may need a fistula for hemodialysis. It is the position of the Association for Vascular Access (AVA)[12] and the American Society of Diagnostic & Interventional Nephrology (ASDIN) that the veins in the forearm should be preserved for future fistula placement. The primary sites for peripheral IV access in these patients are the metacarpal veins in the hands. This practice should continue only if the vein is appropriate and safe for catheter cannulation and IV infusion.

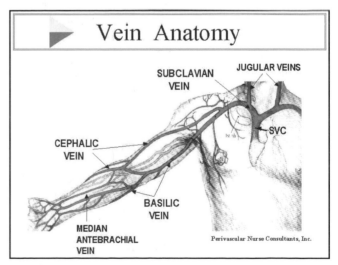

Figure 11.1 *Veins of arms. (Courtesy of Perivascular Nurse Consultants, Inc.)*

D. Gauge Selection

The clinician who inserts a peripheral IV catheter is responsible for assessing the diameter and condition of the vein. The vein should be straight, smooth, soft and pliable for approximately one inch in length. Hard and sclerosed (scarred) veins are often seen in the IV drug abuser population. The diameter of the catheter should be 50% of the diameter of the vein, which will allow for blood to flow around the IV catheter. This acts as a cushion to prevent the IV catheter from rubbing and irritating the vein lining (causing phlebitis).[13] The higher the number of the catheter gauge, the smaller the diameter of the catheter. A 24-gauge catheter is very small in diameter, and is appropriate for neonatal, pediatric and geriatric patients. A 22-gauge catheter is appropriate for most adult IV infusions. A 2-gauge catheter is most appropriate for adult blood transfusions and minor surgery. However, in adult patients with poor peripheral vein access, a 22-gauge catheter can be used for blood transfusions.[14] An 18-gauge catheter is appropriate for trauma patients and operations with a high risk for large amounts of blood loss. Large bore 16 and 14 gauge catheters are most appropriate for major trauma and major surgeries. The selection of the appropriate gauge peripheral IV catheter is the responsibility of the clinician inserting the device. The IV insertion documentation should always include the size and length of the catheter used.

TIP: The IV insertion documentation should always include the size and length of the catheter used.

11.3 Central Venous Access Devices

Central venous catheters (CVC) are defined as catheters whose tips rest in the vena cava.[15] The superior vena cava (SVC) is the largest vein in the body and sits in the center of the chest just above the heart.[16] The inferior vena cava (IVC) can be accessed by inserting a catheter into the femoral vein in the groin area. Both the SVC and IVC drain blood into the right atrium of the heart. Because the rate of blood flow in these veins is substantial, they are the safest locations for all CVC catheter tips.[17]

A. Non-Tunneled Central Venous Catheters

Non-tunneled central venous catheters were the first type of centrally placed catheters and to this day have the highest complication and fatality rate when not properly inserted and monitored. Currently physicians and specially trained nurses can insert these catheters at the bedside, in the operating room, or in interventional radiology. It is highly recommended that these catheters should be inserted using ultrasound for vein visualization. Using the old "land-mark system" is a deviation from the standard of care.[18] The catheters are inserted into the subclavian or internal jugular vein. The subclavian vein is located under the collar bone, whereas the jugular vein is located on the side of the neck. A large-bore needle is inserted into the vein, and a six to eight inch long catheter is advanced through the needle with the catheter tip resting in the superior vena cava. This catheter is associated with high infection rates (sepsis), pneumothorax (lung puncture and collapse), and the entry of air into the venous system (air embolism). This catheter has the highest mortality rate related to these complications. This type of catheter can be inserted relatively quickly into critically ill patients who need large vein access for rapid infusions and multiple life saving drugs, such as in cardiac arrests and major trauma.[19]

The attorney, paralegal, legal nurse consultant, or expert witness (reviewer) should be able to locate the insertion site by review of the medical record. The name of this catheter type is often abbreviated as CVP for central venous pressure catheter or TLC for triple lumen catheter or SC for subclavian catheter. It is the standard of care that all types of central venous catheters require a chest x-ray post insertion to determine catheter tip placement in the SVC.[20] Some facilities require signing of an informed consent for the performance of catheter insertion. Physicians rarely document any information related to the catheter insertion, other than "catheter inserted."

B. Tunneled Catheters

TIP: Tunneled catheter brand names include Hickman, Broviac, and Groshong.

Tunneled catheters are durable and are considered to be among the safest of central venous catheters. These catheters are generally inserted by physicians in the operating room under anesthesia.[21] As with non-tunneled catheters, the subclavian or jugular vein is accessed, and the catheter is advanced into the superior vena cava. However, from the catheter insertion site below the collar bone to the nipple point on the chest, a blunt tipped introducer is advanced under the skin creating a subcutaneous tunnel through which the catheter is advanced. The catheter will exit somewhere on the patient's chest. All tunneled catheters have an attached cotton cuff which sits within the tunnel. Scar tissue will grow around the cuff in about 10 days after catheter insertion.[22] The cotton cuff has two functions: to anchor the catheter in place and to prevent bacteria from migrating up the tunnel and into the venous system. This catheter was initially designed for transplant patients who were severely immunocompromised and at extreme risk for infection. This catheter is often used in patients requiring long-term daily infusions, such as Total Parenteral Nutrition (TPN), for the rest of their lives.[23]

Many clinicians are under the misconception that *Groshong* denotes a specific type of catheter. The term denotes a unique catheter tip design, which is available on all types of central venous catheters. Open tipped catheters are catheters with straight cut tips, where all IV solutions exit the catheter at the distal tip. Groshong tipped catheters have a black plug which covers the catheter tip. A three-way slit valve is on the distal side of the catheter, which allows the valve to open by pressure and permits the IV solutions/medications to enter the venous system. When negative pressure is applied by pulling back on a syringe plunger to withdraw blood, the valve opens inward and allows the removal of blood.[24] When the catheter is not being used, the valve remains in a closed position inhibiting the reflux of blood or air into the catheter and entering the bloodstream, which could be a potentially fatal situation. Groshong tipped central venous catheters are in limited use and are usually utilized based on the inserter's catheter preference.

C. Peripherally Inserted Central Catheters (PICC)

Peripherally inserted central catheters (PICC) are the newest central venous catheters. They were used initially in the neonatal population but now are exceedingly popular in the adult population and are primarily used for long-term IV antibiotics. However, PICC catheters have been used successfully for hydration, chemotherapy, and parenteral nutrition. These are the longest central venous catheters, approximately twenty-five inches in length. Specially trained nurses, physicians, and radiologists can insert these catheters at the bedside. A large vein is accessed just above the antecubital fossa usually the basilic or brachial veins.[25] The catheter is advanced up the arm into the subclavian vein which is located under the collar bone and down into the superior vena cava. The catheter tip rests just above the heart. These catheters have a low incidence of catheter related complications when inserted and monitored properly and are often used in home care where patients or caregivers are instructed to self administer their intravenous medications.[26] It is the standard of Care and the recommendation of AVA, Joint Commission and CDC that all central venous catheters including PICC lines, should be inserted using ultrasound to locate the vein, to assess the condition of the vein and to assess adjacent structures in order to minimize insertion related complications such as arterial puncture and nerve injury.[27] The documentation for PICC insertion should include

- date and time of insertion,
- catheter gauge, brand and lot number,
- anatomical name of the access vein,
- type of introducer used,
- if a guidewire was used,
- total measured length of catheter,
- external length of catheter,
- radiographic confirmation of anatomical location of catheter tip,
- patient response to procedure, and
- signature of person inserting the device.

Sample Note
Date/Time
4 Fr Bard Per-Q-Cath, lot #5064, with guidewire inserted into left basilic vein via 20 gauge microintroducer with ultrasound. Catheter measured 50cm total length with 1cm remaining external. Patient states "My arm feels fine." Patient sent to x-ray for confirmation of tip placement.
—S. Huang, RN

Date/Time
Catheter tip confirmed in superior vena cava. Verbal report obtained from Dr. Smith. Will use catheter for 8:00 P.M. dose.
—M. Alvarez, RN

D. Implanted Ports

TIP: Implanted ports are devices that are totally under the skin and are inserted by physicians in the operating room or by Interventional Radiology.

A subcutaneous skin pocket is made on the chest, and the port housing with a self-sealing silicone gel center is placed into the pocket and sutured to the chest wall.[28] The catheter is inserted into the subclavian or jugular vein and advanced with the final catheter tip placement in the superior vena cava. The port pocket is then sutured closed once the catheter tip is correctly placed. The advantage of this device is that because the port is totally under the skin, there is little or no care in between usage of the port. The clinician will feel the metal back of the port and obtain a 3-ml blood return when ports are properly accessed.[29] In order to use ports, a special non-coring Huber needle is pushed through the skin and into the port. These needles are available in various gauges and lengths. These devices are the catheters of choice for oncology patients who require long-term intermittent chemotherapy infusions. Ports can remain in place for many years and have a low complication rate when properly inserted and monitored. Insertion documentation is commonly located on the surgical operative report. Verification of catheter tip placement is on the chest x-ray or fluoroscopy report. Ports can be inserted into veins, arteries, the liver, spinal column, pleural space and abdominal cavities for the infusion of IV fluids or the withdrawal of bodily fluids such as ascites.

11.4 Site Monitoring Documentation

TIP: All peripheral and central catheters can be disconnected from a continuous IV fluid source. A resealable end cap is attached to the catheter hub. This may be documented as a saline lock (SL), intermittent lock (IL), and by the other terms as well. This device is part of routine nursing practice that limits unnecessary IV fluids and allows for greater patient mobility. The IV sites must be assessed frequently for early symptoms of IV catheter complications.

The frequency of assessing and monitoring the intravenous puncture site is dependent on many factors, including the age of the patient, the type of medications/solutions infused, the IV flow rate and the type of vascular access device. Pediatric and geriatric patients require more frequent vascular access device assessment because of the fragility of their veins.[30] Vesicant medications/solutions (drugs with the potential to burn the skin and tissue if they leak out of the vein and into the surrounding tissue) require more frequent monitoring to prevent serious injury.[31]

Examples of vesicant drugs are

- sodium bicarbonate,
- calcium chloride,
- calcium gluconate,
- concentrated potassium chloride solutions,
- adriamycin,
- dilantin, and
- phenergan.

Examples of non-vesicant drugs are

- ancef,
- cipro,
- heparin,
- sodium chloride, and
- penicillin.

Peripheral intravenous access devices inserted into small veins are more prone to puncture the vein as compared to catheters that are inserted into the larger veins of the forearm. Non-vesicant pediatric infusions should be assessed hourly at a minimum. The insertion site of vesicant pediatric infusion should be assessed every thirty minutes at a minimum. Adult non-vesicant solutions should be assessed every four hours and vesicant infusions every hour at a minimum. Institutional policies should stipulate the frequency of catheter site assessment and documentation requirements. Many hospital policies state that IV sites should be assessed every shift (a shift can be 8, 10 or 12 hours). Assessing the IV site every 8-12 hours is not sufficient to prevent serious IV-related complications from developing and it is a deviation from the standard of nursing care. The assessment of a vascular access device should include the condition of the skin at the catheter insertion site, the surrounding skin area, the flow rate, adverse reactions to medications and solutions, and any infusion-related complications.[32] The assessment should be documented in the nurses' progress note flow sheets, on the intravenous flow sheet on the medication administration record (MAR), or on the treatment administration record (TAR). Facility policy may specify other locations.

11.5 Legal Issues

The question in many IV therapy malpractice cases is "Was the right catheter inserted into the patient?" The physician orders the IV medication or solution on the physician order sheet. In most cases, the type of access device is not specified by the physician. The nurse reviews the IV orders and determines if a peripheral access device is appropriate based on the type of therapy, length of therapy, and the condition of the veins in the patient's arms. If the patient is not a candidate for a peripheral access device, the nurse notifies the physician and asks that a central vascular access device be inserted. It is the nurse's responsibility to infuse safely the medications/solutions through the appropriate intravenous device. There are many algorithms available on the Internet to assist in proper vascular access device selection for specific patients. (See www.accessabilitybybard.co.uk.)

A. Vascular Access Organizations

TIP: There are several sources of standards of care for infusion therapy.

The Infusion Nurses Society (INS) is a nationally recognized nursing organization that has established the scope of practice, competencies, and educational requirements for the administration of infusion therapy. The organization publishes Standards of Nursing Practice which are applicable to all nurses in all settings who administer any type of infusion therapy. Standards have been published in 1981, 1990, 1998, 2000 and 2006. Currently a committee has been created to review and update the Standards for publication around 2010. These Standards have been used at trial to establish if the standard of nursing care has been met.

The Oncology Nurses Society (ONS), a nationally recognized nursing organization, published *Vascular Access Device Guidelines* in 1996 and 2004. They also published *Chemotherapy and Biotherapy Guidelines and Recommendations for Practice* in 2000 and 2009. These guidelines provide information to healthcare professionals who specialize in the care of cancer patients and infusion related therapies such as blood transfusions and intravenous chemotherapy. The guidelines are very broad and non-binding and are meant to assist the clinician with proper infusion techniques.

The Association for Vascular Access (AVA), formerly known as NAVAN, is a nationally recognized multidisciplinary organization composed of physicians, nurses, pharmacists, and catheter manufacturers who specialize in vascular access. The organization has published position papers on specific issues such as catheter tip position and internal jugular PICC lines.

The Society of Interventional Radiologists (SIR) is a nationally recognized organization composed of physicians, nurse practitioners, and physician assistants who insert vascular access devices in the radiology department. The organization publishes guidelines for practice and has developed a comprehensive curriculum for training clinicians on the appropriate procedures for insertion of vascular access devices. In addition to the publications of the aforementioned organizations, a literature search can be performed to find evidence-based research and a review of published data to support vascular access device related issues.

The Centers for Disease Control & Prevention (CDC) published *Guidelines for Prevention of Intravascular Device Related Infections* in 1996 and 2002. Currently, a committee has been convened to update these Guidelines. With over 500,000 reported catheter related blood stream infections each year the government is very concerned about the cost to both patients and the healthcare system. This document addresses infection related issues for all indwelling catheters, including peripheral and central venous access devices. CDC's information is meant to be used in establishing institutional policies and procedures. The CDC discourages routine site rotation for *central venous catheters*. The organization states that central venous catheters should be removed when therapy is complete or when there is evidence of a catheter related complication.

The Food and Drug Administration (FDA) is required to review manufacturer's data for marketing a new catheter. In addition, the FDA must review the product information sheet and directions for use before the product can be marketed. MedWatch, which is a mandatory reporting service for catheter related adverse reactions, can be helpful when tracking a history of problems for a specific vascular access device, medication, or infusion equipment such as IV pumps.

Still, with all these organizations providing vascular access device information, standard of care issues can be difficult to identify. Many routine practices associated with the insertion, care, and maintenance of vascular access devices have not been validated by evidence-based research.

B. Standard of Care Issues
1. Clinical competency

Every state has a Board of Nursing whose main responsibility is to license qualified nurses. It is the responsibility of the hiring facility to provide competent qualified nurses to care for their patients. INS and Joint Commission also recommend validation of competency for nursing procedures as deemed necessary by the facility.[33] Nurses who are required to administer intravenous chemotherapy are expected to have documented training on chemotherapeutic agents, mode of action, infusion techniques and adverse reactions.

TIP: Hospital personnel files should include documentation of orientation programs, validated competencies, and in-service continuing education programs which were attended by the nurses. Providing incompetent nurses to deliver infusion therapy is a deviation of the standard of care.

---

2. Policies and procedures

All regulating bodies, including the state Boards of Nursing, The Joint Commission, and the Infusion Nurses Society, require that nurses have access to current institutional policies and procedures. Many hospitals and other healthcare facilities provide updated nursing policies and procedures in each nursing unit on computers for easy access. These policies should be reviewed annually and approved by an organizational committee. The manual should include the institution's procedures for insertion, care, and maintenance for all vascular access devices, infusion therapies, and infusion related equipment. The manual should provide information to the staff on when, where, and how to document pertinent patient events. There must be an order by a physician for a nurse to initiate infusion therapy. The order should include the therapy, rate of flow, dose, frequency and the signature of the physician. However, it is the responsibility of the nurse to use critical thinking skills to determine if the order is appropriate and if the vascular access device is appropriate for the ordered therapy.

3. Informed consent

All patients have the right to accept or refuse treatment without the threat of retribution. Informed consent should include a description of the vascular access device, a description of the insertion procedure and identification of probable complications, and vascular access device options if applicable. Signed consent forms are most commonly used for insertion of central venous pressure catheters, tunneled catheters, implanted ports, and PICC lines. Identification and description of the consent process in the progress notes is also acceptable.

4. Number of attempts

TIP: The INS Standards of Practice stipulates that only two attempts per practitioner should be made when inserting a vascular access device, but does not limit the number of attempting practitioners.[34]

In some cases patients who have been repeatedly punctured trying to access their veins have successfully sued for assault. The staff's inability to carry out treatment may have significant adverse clinical results.

In a recent South Dakota case, a two-year-old child was admitted to the hospital with severe dehydration. The same nurse attempted unsuccessfully to insert a peripheral IV catheter sixteen times. The child was unable to receive fluids, sustained a cardiac arrest and died. The result was an out of court settlement with the hospital for substantial damages (unpublished settlement).

5. The use of armboards

Armboards can be used to stabilize an area of joint flexion (wrist and elbow) to prevent the catheter from moving. Roller bandage should not be used to anchor or secure the extremity to the armboard as this will prevent assessment of the IV site.[35] The use of armboards and their removal should be documented in the nurse's progress notes. Hospitals should have written policies which describe the appropriate use of armboards. If armboards are used, nursing assessment and documentation should include the color and temperature of the skin. The nurse must check the nail beds for color and capillary refill which denotes how well the blood is circulating to the hand. Armboards should be applied in a manner that allows for unimpeded visualization of the IV site.[36]

6. Appropriate infusion solutions and medications

According to the INS Standards of Practice the following IV solutions/medications are not appropriate for infusion into peripheral veins through peripheral IV catheters and midline catheters:[37]

- Continuous vesicant infusions such as Dopamine and many chemotherapy drugs
- Total Parenteral Nutrition (TPN); reviewers (expert witnesses, risk managers, legal nurse consultants, and attorneys) should look on the TPN order sheet to determine the glucose (sugar) and amino acid (protein) concentration. The sugar concentration should not exceed 10% and the protein should not exceed 5%. This is an issue in many neonatal IV extravasation malpractice cases.
- Drug pH; the pH of the drug should not exceed 9 or go below 5. A commonly infused antibiotic, Vancomycin, has a pH of 2.4 and should be infused through a central venous catheter.
- Drugs with an osmolality greater than 600 mOsm/L.

It is the responsibility of the nurse to determine that the ordered drug is appropriate for the type and location of the IV device that the patient has in place. Infusing caustic drugs through small veins can result in permanent vein damage and is a deviation from the standard of care.

11.6 Vascular Access Device Complications

This section discusses the most common complications related to peripheral and central venous catheters which result in malpractice claims.

A. Peripheral Access Devices
1. Nerve injury

Nerve injuries related to peripheral IV device insertion and phlebotomy have been reported in the medical literature since the late 1990s. A neuroma (scar tissue on the nerve) can form on the surface of the nerve when the needle makes contact with the nerve. Permanent progressive nerve injury can be the result when the nerve fibers are cut with an IV needle.[38]

Needle injury to the radial nerve during peripheral vascular access device insertion is a common needle insertion injury which can result in Reflex Sympathetic Dystrophy (RSD) which has been renamed Complex Regional Pain Syndrome (CRPS).[39] This can be a permanent, progressive, painful disability. Needle injury to the median nerve in the antecubital fossa (inner elbow) during a blood drawing procedure can result in this injury. Important issues related to nerve injuries are the angle of the needle during the insertion procedure and how far the needle is initially inserted. The higher the angle, the higher the risk for nerve contact. The maximum angulation of the needle during insertion should be 0-15 degrees. Only the tip of the needle should be inserted initially to minimize nerve contact. The distal one-third of the cephalic vein, just above the thumb, should be avoided because the radial nerve is superficial in this area. The inner aspect of the wrist above the palm of the hand should also be avoided, as the median nerve is superficial in this area.[40] Injury to the distal median nerve can result in carpal tunnel syndrome. When the needle makes contact with the nerve, the patient will complain of an immediate "electric shock" sensation down the arm into the fingertips and/or numbness or tingling. Ulnar nerve injury has been reported with the improper insertion technique of a PICC line. This procedure should be performed using ultrasound to identify and locate the vein and the nerve, which will reduce the opportunity to contact the nerve.[41] The appropriate intervention is to remove the needle immediately. Documentation of the adverse event should be found in the progress notes, on an unusual occurrence form or a variance report.

The expertise of the phlebotomist was an issue in the following case.

The plaintiff, age 17, went to a Foundation Hospital in February 2006 for a routine venipuncture. The plaintiff claimed that the angle used by the phlebotomist to insert the needle was inappropriate, causing a deep needle stick to the right median nerve in the right cubital fossa. The plaintiff claimed that she suffered complex regional pain syndrome with extreme burning pain in the right arm and hand, swelling of the right arm and hand, right arm discoloration, stiffness to the joints in the right arm, uncontrollable muscle spasms in the right arm and an overall lack of strength. The plaintiff underwent some physical therapy for the arm, but was unable to continue it due to pain. The plaintiff claimed that she was told that she would require surgery with a dorsal column stimulator to send electric impulses into her right arm to alleviate the pain. The defendant maintained that any injury which the plaintiff sustained should have resolved within a year. According to published account an arbitrator awarded $959,700.[42]

The deviation from the standard of care was the angle of the needle during the blood drawing procedure. The higher the angle, the more opportunity to hit the median nerve. This was a deciding factor determined by the jury to have caused the injury.

2. Infiltration

Infiltration occurs when the vascular access device punctures the vein and non-vesicant solutions or medications enter the surrounding tissue.[43] The main symptoms of infiltration are swelling and coolness around the IV site. The IV site is cool because the IV fluids that are leaking under the skin are not body temperature. Nurses are required to assess the IV site by palpation and visualization through the intact transparent IV dressing.[44] At the first sign of an infiltration, the infusion should be stopped and the IV device removed. The most important issue related to infiltration malpractice cases is the amount of IV fluid in the tissue. *Small* infiltrations are not always preventable. *Large* infiltrations are preventable with frequent and proper IV site assessment. Nurses should measure and document the size of the swollen area.[45] The routine application of warm or cold compresses to the infiltrated site and/or elevation of the affected extremity without a physician order are a deviation from the standard of nursing care. Ongoing, frequent assessment of the IV site for skin changes is required. In the event of a large infiltration, the physician should be notified immediately if the patient complains of numbness and tingling within the swollen area. This is a symptom of a nerve compression injury which can result in compartment syndrome. If not treated appropriately a surgical fasciotomy (opening the skin to relieve pressure within the tissue) may be required to prevent permanent nerve injury.[46]

In the following case, the lack of site assessment and size of the infiltration were the two issues at trial:

The plaintiff, age 43, was diagnosed with nasal airway obstruction and surgery was recommended for the nose. Before the surgery, performed in June 1996, an IV line was placed on the top of the plaintiff's right hand near her wrist for administration of anesthesia and fluids. The plaintiff began to feel severe pain in the hand and arm where the IV had been placed and was fully awake and in pain for the entire surgery. The IV line placement was not checked during the surgery. At the end of the surgery the plaintiff was unable to move her right arm due to massive swelling. In the recovery room the patient's hand and arm were elevated and warm compresses were applied. The plaintiff suffered infiltration of the IV into the tissue of the arm, instead of the circulatory system. The arm was painful and swollen for several weeks after surgery. Two years after the procedure the plaintiff underwent two surgeries to recompress the radial and ulnar nerves. The plaintiff was left with large scars. The plaintiff also claimed that she continued to experience stiffness, loss of mobility and range of motion, burning throbbing, aching and general pain in the right arm and hand. The nurse anesthetist claimed that it was the anesthesiologist who started the IV. The anesthesiologist claimed that his only contact with the plaintiff was when he examined her in the recovery room. According to published accounts a $500,000 settlement was reached.[47]

3. Extravasation

Extravasation occurs when the vascular access device punctures the vein and vesicant solution enters the tissue. A vesicant is a medication/solution that is capable of burning the skin and surrounding tissue.[48] The most important identifiable symptoms of extravasation are swelling and coolness around the IV site. Patients may or may not complain of burning or stinging during the extravasation. Extravasation may result in blisters, blackening of the skin, and eventually skin loss and can cause significant tissue, muscle and nerve injuries requiring skin debridements, skin grafting, and in many cases amputation. Extravasation is significantly more damaging to the skin, muscle and nerves than infiltration. Nurses who infuse vesicants must be extra vigilant when assessing the IV site for the earliest possible symptoms of extravasation. There are many recommendations for antidotes to reverse adverse tissue effects; however, there is no research data that validate the use of these antidotes.[49]

TIP: There are no known antidotes for extravasations caused by electrolytes.

Non-chemotherapy vesicants are administered by nurses on a daily basis. These can include IV solutions that contain calcium, magnesium and concentrated potassium chloride. There are no antidotes for these extravasations. In addition, there are chemotherapy drugs that are very dangerous vesicants, including anthracyclines such as Adriamycin. New on the market is an FDA approved drug to reverse the tissue damage associated with anthracycline extravasations. Totect has been proven to reverse the tissue damage associated with anthracycline extravasations.[50] However, it must be infused as soon as possible and within six hours of the extravasation event. This is the only FDA approved drug which will reverse potential tissue damage related to anthracycline extravasations. For all other chemotherapy vesicant

extravasations, prevention is the best treatment, since there are no reliable treatments.[51]

In the following case, site assessment was the main issue at trial:

> The plaintiff, age 55, was hospitalized in April of 2003. The plaintiff claimed that the ICU nurse was negligent in failing to timely assess the IV site, initiate the appropriate intervention and call a physician about the development of an IV extravasation of calcium gluconate. This caused severe pain, swelling and dark nail beds. The plaintiff also claimed that the orthopedic hand specialist physicians were negligent in failing to diagnose and treat an unrecognized forearm compartment syndrome and in failing to timely diagnose and treat a recognized hand compartment syndrome within the six-hour window of opportunity to re-establish blood flow before the tissue in the arm and hand died. The plaintiff's right arm and hand lost circulation for eight and one-half hours, became necrotic, died and ultimately required a mid-forearm amputation. According to a published account a $450,000 verdict was returned.[52]

The compartment syndrome was a result of a large amount of IV fluid in the tissue. The calcium burned the tissue in the arm which resulted in the amputation. The jury found negligence in all counts.

TIP: The key clinical issue for infiltration and extravasation is the amount of solution in the tissue.

> In the following case, the plaintiff, a 34-year-old man working as a child care provider, was a cancer treatment patient at the defendant's hospital. While receiving IV treatment involving ABVD chemotherapy, there was an extravasation that went unappreciated during the full administration of the treatment, despite the plaintiff raising specific complaints regarding pain and discomfort. As a consequence, the claimant developed a five by five centimeter dark tender area over the dorsum area of the hand, hypersensitivity, limited motion of the right finger, a "swan neck" deformity of the small finger and some Reflex Sympathetic Dystrophy with chronic pain, all of which are deemed to be permanent. The defense alleged the IV was properly administered, and that the area of injury was not at the site of the IV. This case proceeded to trial, where the jury awarded the plaintiff $322,000.[53]

TIP: Removal of the access device, immediate physician notification, appropriate nursing interventions and surgical intervention should be documented along with the patient's complaints in the progress notes. Many of these patients require extensive follow-up care with orthopedists, vascular surgeons, and plastic surgeons to treat the damaged areas.[54]

B. Central Venous Catheter Complications
1. Catheter malposition

TIP: All central venous catheter tips must be verified by x-ray to be in the superior vena cava prior to use.

The standard of care for infusing through any type of central venous catheter is to verify the location of the catheter tip radiographically by chest x-ray prior to use. The positions of INS, ONS, SIR, AVA, and the FDA are that correct catheter tip location is in the superior vena cava (SVC). Optimal tip location is the distal one-third of the SVC or the atrial caval junction.[55] When catheter tips rest in other venous locations, such as the subclavian or the brachiocephalic vein, the incidence of thrombus (clot) formation and vein perforation increases exponentially. The only exception is for hemodialysis catheters, which can reside in the right atrium of the heart because of the required high pressures during the dialysis procedure. Nurses who infuse through central venous catheters must have x-ray confirmation of tip placement prior to use. If the catheter tip is not in the SVC, the catheter should not be used for any infusion of any type for any duration of time. The result of infusing through malpositioned catheters can be permanent injury and in many cases has resulted in patient fatalities.[53] The best tip location is in the SVC, which is straight for approximately three inches in the center of the chest allowing the catheter to rest inside the vein without making contact with the vein wall. Blood flows through the SVC at a rate of 2000 mls/minute which allows for maximum dilution of the medication/solution with blood, eliminating complications such as vein irritation and perforation. Hospitals should have specific policies stating that central venous catheters require radiographic confirmation of the catheter tip in the SVC immediately after catheter insertion. The catheter cannot be used for any infusion until x-ray confirmation is obtained.[56]

In the following case the initial x-ray report showed the catheter tip in the wrong place:

> The plaintiff, an 11-month-old girl, developed respiratory distress after cardiac catheterization. Upon admission to the recovery area, the child had an elevated heart rate and respiratory rate. Her lower extremity pulses were diminished, indicating poor perfusion. Four days later, the cardiologist placed a central venous catheter in the patient jugular vein. An x-ray report indicated that the tip of the catheter appeared to pass into the right atrium of the heart, and to lie a little beyond the margin of the heart. The plaintiffs contended that the cardiologist rendered substandard care when he failed to adjust the position of the catheter before it was used to infuse IV fluids. The next day the child suffered cardiorespiratory arrest and despite respiratory efforts, died. X-ray of the lungs showed that the IV fluid completely filled the right lung. Autopsy revealed that the jugular catheter was outside the vein, in the neck passing through parietal pleura into the right pleural cavity. The defendants claimed they provided proper care. The case settled for $2.4 million.[57]

If the doctors and nurses had verified correct catheter tip placement prior to infusing the catheter the child would not have died.

The next case resulted in a substantial settlement during trial. The events were marked by physician miscommunication.

> The decedent was admitted to the hospital by defendant Dr. Mac with a presumed diagnosis of Crohn's disease. Defendant ordered a central venous catheter for the purpose of infusing IV fluids and Total Parenteral Nutrition, which was performed by defendant Dr. Z, a general surgeon. Dr. Z positioned the catheter in the right atrium of the decedent's heart. Dr. Z allegedly discovered the catheter was incorrectly positioned in the decedent's heart after reviewing the chest x-ray films, but the plaintiffs claimed Dr. Z left the catheter in decedent's heart and ordered it could be utilized in that position. Plaintiffs also alleged Dr. Z was negligent in failing to withdraw the catheter from the right atrium into the superior vena cava and failing to inform decedent and Dr. Mac that the catheter was in a position that could result in the perforation of the heart and a cardiac tamponade. Dr. Z admitted he fell below the standard of care when he left the catheter in decedent's heart. Plaintiffs alleged Dr. Mac, a gastroenterologist, discovered the catheter was positioned in decedent's heart but did not reposition it or request that Dr. Z reposition it. Dr. Mac left town

for a medical conference without informing the on-call physician, defendant Dr. H, of the misplaced central venous catheter, which was infusing IV fluids and TPN. Dr. Mac denied liability and claimed that reliance on Dr. Z to place the catheter properly was appropriate and the standard of care did not require a gastroenterologist to know it was dangerous to leave the catheter in the patient's heart.

The decedent awoke in the night with complaints of chest pain, chest tightness, and a blood pressure of 68/44. Hospital nurses contacted Dr. H, who believed the decedent was having either a cardiac event or pulmonary embolism and ordered diagnostic tests. Decedent's condition continued to deteriorate over the next hour and ten minutes until a code was called. Plaintiffs claimed that the catheter perforated decedent's heart and deposited TPN in the pericardial sac, which caused an acute cardiac tamponade. The defense claimed that cardiac tamponade was not the cause of death. A defense expert admitted that the catheter perforated the decedent's heart and deposited TPN in her pericardial sac, which caused a fatal arrhythmia. S Health Systems settled prior to trial for a confidential amount. During trial, the matter settled for $1,200,000 (unpublished verdict).

2. Catheter malfunction

TIP: The only reliable method to determine if the central venous catheter is still in a vein and is functioning properly is to aspirate (withdraw) 3mls of blood prior to each infusion.

Lack of a substantial 3ml free flowing blood return is indicative of a catheter malfunction.[58] Lack of blood return could be the result of a catheter tip outside the vein, causing the intravenous fluid to enter the chest cavity, or of a catheter that has broken inside the patient. However, the most common reason for lack of blood is the presence of a fibrin sheath completely encapsulating the outer catheter surface as well as the catheter tip. Symptoms include the ability to infuse solution/medications without resistance, but little or no blood can be aspirated from the catheter. Evidence-based research has proved that all central venous catheters will become encapsulated in a fibrin sheath within ten days of the catheter insertion.[59] This appears to be the body's protective mechanism against the foreign body catheter. The fibrin sheath will continue to grow if not removed on a timely basis. If no blood return is obtained, a physician's order for the instillation of Cathflo (Alteplase) should be obtained. Cathflo is the only FDA approved drug for catheter clearance. This procedure is painless to the patient and has few associated risks. Infusing through a fibrin sheathed catheter increases significantly the risk of blockage of the vein with a blood clot, thrombus formation, and extravasation. Salvaging the catheter, as opposed to catheter removal, is the appropriate intervention.

Nurses do not always document that they have verified proper functioning of the central line prior to medication administration. They may testify that this is their normal routine. In the following case, the nurse was asked to explain the term "no blood return." The nurse assigned a benign meaning to the term. However, "no blood return" was interpreted to mean that the device was not functioning properly. Major clinical damages resulted from this incident.

> The plaintiff, age 69, had cancer in her right breast and went to an oncology clinic for chemotherapy. She underwent two treatment sessions through an intravenous needle positioned into an access port surgically implanted above her left healthy breast. During the third session, the chemotherapy drug Adriamycin leaked out of the port and into the left breast tissue. As a result, the healthy breast became necrotic and the plaintiff required a mastectomy and breast reconstruction. The plaintiff claimed that the needle was improperly positioned during the third treatment session, causing it to become dislodged. The plaintiff also claimed that the nurses had failed to properly monitor her, which allowed a full bag of Adriamycin to be administered into the healthy breast tissue. According to a published account a $500,000 verdict was awarded.[60]

> Mrs. P was diagnosed with non-Hodgkins lymphoma. She was to receive six cycles of Adriamycin, Oncovin, and Cytoxan in an outpatient facility. Prior to her first cycle she received an implanted port. On cycle one, two, and three the nurse noted a positive blood return, and the chemotherapy was infused without incident. The fourth cycle documentation noted that no blood return was obtained, but the port flushed easily and the chemotherapy was infused. The fifth cycle documentation revealed "mediport accessed with 20 gauge huber needle, no blood return—flushes freely. Pre meds given. Adriamycin 85 mgms in 50 cc's over 15 minutes—halfway through infusion patient complained of discomfort. Area appeared swollen, ice applied. Dr. notified."

Mrs. P returned to the clinic two days later with her chest and breast swollen, red, hard, and blistered. There was a large infected cavity. A large area of slough encompassed the entire breast and nipple. Follow up with a surgeon resulted in a mastectomy due to the extreme amount of tissue damage.

The nurse testified that "no blood return" means that there is a fibrin sheath on the end of the catheter—but this was normal and to be expected. It was not an indication that the port was malfunctioning. The jury awarded $1,000,000 to the plaintiff (unpublished settlement).

Confirmation of the central venous catheter tip location can be found on chest x-ray or fluoroscopy reports. Once tip placement has been confirmed, the location should be recorded on the Medication Administration Record (MAR). A physician's order "OK to use" does not provide the anatomical location of the catheter tip and is an invalid order. Central venous catheters used in hospitals, home care, long-term care, outpatient facilities, and so on must follow the same rules. Nurses should document in the progress notes the presence and amount of blood flow obtained prior to each infusion. Using central venous catheters without verifying a blood return is a gross deviation from the standard of care.[61]

3. Air embolism

Air embolism may cause anoxic encephalopathy; it is defined as the presence of air within the vascular system. The exact amount of air required to cause damage and/or death is controversial. However, most experts agree that a minimum of 15mls (1/2 ounce) of air bolus can result in transient or permanent neurologic deficits. Minor to major strokes, permanent vegetative states and fatalities have been reported to be caused by intravascular air embolism.[62]

How does air enter the vascular system? There must be a direct or indirect opening into the vascular system. This can occur when the IV catheter is removed at the completion of the therapy or the catheter is accidentally pulled out by the patient. The direct opening into the vascular/venous system must be above the level of the heart while the patient simultaneously changes her intrathoracic pressure (chest pressure). This is done by crying, laughing, sneezing, coughing, yelling, vomiting, deep breathing, etc. The change in chest pressure will allow air to enter the vascular/venous system through the catheter exit site. Seconds is all the time needed for air in the vascular system to enter the right ventricle, causing an "air lock."[63] The air will prevent

any blood from entering the pulmonary circulation and/or causing a displacement of blood to the brain. This will result in a drop in blood pressure, a rapid pulse rate and confusion followed by lack of consciousness and possibly death. Subclavian and in particular jugular vein access sites and catheters are high risk for air embolism because they are located above heart level. Physicians and nurses who insert these catheters should be cognizant of risk of air embolism during the insertion procedure. It is especially important to prevent air from entering the vascular system when the wire is removed from the introducer needle before the catheter is inserted. Many catheter manufacturers discuss this risk in the FDA approved product and insertion procedure information included on all product trays.[64]

Healthcare providers who care for patients with subclavian or jugular vein catheters also need to understand the risk of air embolism. Air can enter the vascular system when the IV tubing is changed, when catheter end caps are changed and when the catheter is discontinued or removed. Any time the catheter is opened to air, the nurse should instruct the patient on the Valsalva Maneuver. The patient takes a deep breath and holds it, while the IV tubing/cap is changed. This maneuver stabilizes the intrathoracic chest pressure and prevents air from entering the open catheter. The Joint Commission and INS recommend that only Leurloc connections (screw-on) be used to prevent accidental IV tubing/cap disconnection.[65]

When the central venous catheter is removed, application of a gel based ointment (neosporin, triple antibiotic, etc.) should be applied liberally to the venous opening, followed by a transparent dressing. The gel based ointment will prevent air from entering the venous system. The INS Standards state that the catheter exit site should be assessed every 24 hours until the site is epithelialized (scab formation). The scab will prevent air from entering the vascular system and then the dressing can be removed.[66]

What should the healthcare provider do if air embolism is suspected? Immediately stop further air from entering the vascular system by pinching the open IV catheter or covering the opening to the vascular system. Once this is accomplished, turn the patient on her left side, place her in the Trendelenburg Position (head down, feet up) and notify the physician. The positioning will allow the air to rise to the top of the right ventricle and permit the blood to flow into the pulmonary circulation. A surgeon can use CT scans to visualize the air and can employ intracardiac needles to remove the air.[67]

With the increase in the number of jugular vein catheter sites, the number of air embolism cases is increasing. Air embolism in peripheral IV catheters is rare because the vein opening is below heart level. Most peripheral IV embolism cases are due to pumped or injected air into the venous system. As of October 1, 2008, Medicare has classified IV catheter related air embolism as a "never" event. Medicare reported 45 air embolism cases in 2006. Medicare, as well as many other insurance companies, will not reimburse hospitals for the treatment of air embolism. Air embolism can be difficult to diagnose and almost impossible to treat with success. Education of the healthcare providers is essential for the safety of the patients.

From a legal perspective, hospitals should have Central Venous Catheter Removal Policy and Procedures, which detail the application of ointment to prevent air embolism. Only physicians and trained registered nurses can remove central venous catheters. There should be documentation in the nurses' personnel file that their competency has been validated and they are permitted to remove central venous catheters.

In the following case the defendant hospital admitted that the nurses did not follow hospital policy:

The plaintiff, age 51, was admitted to the hospital in September 2003 for revision of an implantable morphine pump used to control pain. Prior to the plaintiff's discharge, the defendant nurse removed the right subclavian central venous catheter. After removal of the central venous catheter, the plaintiff sustained a stroke. The plaintiff claimed the removal of the catheter, while the plaintiff was seated in an upright position, caused an air embolism which resulted in a right frontal lobe infarction. Prior to the trial, the defendants admitted negligence in the training of its nurse, violation of policy and procedures regarding removal of the IV catheter and negligence by the nurse in removal of the IV catheter. The defendants did not admit that removal of the IV catheter was the legal cause of the stroke and argued that the blood clot was due to a dilated cardiomyopathy. According to Florida Jury Verdict Reporter a $3,826,991 verdict was returned.[68]

4. IV catheter-related sepsis / infection

Each year many thousands of catheter related infections are reported. According to the CDC, catheter related bloodstream infections are the eighth leading cause of death in the United States. Staph Epidermidis, an organism commonly found on the skin, is most often the source of the infection.[69] Using sterile technique, cleansing the skin properly with Chlorhexidine prior to catheter insertion and us-

ing maximum barrier precautions (sterile draping the patient from head to foot) will significantly reduce the incidence of infection.[70] Catheter-related infections have been litigated with minimal success even when the patient dies. There are many extenuating circumstances which may have contributed to the infection; however, it is difficult to prove in a court of law that there was a deviation from the standard of care. Important evidence of infection such as sudden temperature elevations, positive catheter tip cultures and positive blood cultures should be documented in the patient's record.[71]

In the following case the peripheral IV catheter remained in place for five days, which is longer than the three day standard of care:

The plaintiff, a 48-year-old woman, suffering from chronic Hepatitis C, was released from the hospital with instructions to a home health care agency to provide her with a hep-lock IV therapy of saline solution for five days. The home health care nurses left the IV in longer than reasonable, failed to recognize symptoms of infection, and failed to timely return to effectively monitor the patient's IV site after conclusion of the treatment. The plaintiff's arm was so severely infected with a staphylococcus infection that the cephalic vein had to be removed from the wrist to several inches above the elbow. After two surgeries attempting to remove scar tissue from the radial, nerve, without reduction in severe pain, the patient opted for dissection of the nerve to alleviate the pain. This procedure resulted in residual numbness at the nerve distribution. Reflex Sympathetic Dystrophy developed in the arm and this was treated by placement of a spinal cord stimulator that the patient will require for the remainder of her life. The jury rendered a verdict in the amount of $2,383,181 for the injured plaintiff and $75,000 for the spouse.[72]

11.7 Conclusion

The number of infusion and vascular access device malpractice cases has increased dramatically over the past five years. Many vascular access injuries result in serious tissue damage and sometimes the demise of the patient. Standards of care and standards of practice issues can easily be identified in many malpractice cases. Hopefully, the number of malpractice cases will increase the awareness of healthcare professionals to the seriousness of the injuries that can result from negligent vascular access device insertion and care.

Endnotes

1. Centers for Disease Control and Prevention. "Guidelines for Prevention of Intravascular Catheter Related Infections." *MMWR*. August 9, 2002.

2. Plumer, A.L. *Principles and Practice of Intravenous Therapy, Seventh Edition*, Philadelphia PA., Lippincott, Williams and Wilkins 2007.

3. *Id.*

4. Schelper, R. "The Aging Venous *System*." *Journal of Vascular Access*. Fall 2003, p. 8-10.

5. *Infusion Nursing Standards of Practice*. INS, 10 Fawcett Street, Cambridge, MA 02138 November 2006.

6. *See* note 1

7. *See* note 5

8. *See* note 2

9. *See* note 5

10. *Id.*

11. *Id.*

12. "NAVAN Position Statement." *Journal of Vascular Access Devices, Summer* 1998 p. 9-11.

13. Terry. J. et al. *Intravenous Therapy Clinical Principles and Practice, Third Edition* Philadelphia, PA: W.B. Saunders Company 2009.

14. Acquillo, G. "Blood Transfusion Flow Rates." *Journal of the Association of Vascular Access* Winter 2007 Vol. 12, No. 4.

15. Vesely, T. et al. "The Diverse and Conflicting Standards and Practice in Infusion Therapy." *Journal of Vascular Access Devices*. Fall 2002.

16. Ray, C., *Central Venous Access,* Philadelphia, PA, Lippincott Williams & Wilkins 2001.

17. *Id.*

18. Wise, M. et al. "Catheter Tip Position: A Sign of Things to Come." *JVAD,* Summer 2001.

19. *IV Therapy Made Incredibly Easy,* Lippincott, Williams & Wilkins, Philadelphia, PA 2006.

20. Sorrell, D. *Access Device Guidelines: Recommendations for Nursing Practice & Education* Pittsburgh, PA, Oncology Nurses Society 2004.

21. *See* note 16

22. *See* note 1

23. Wilson, S. *Vascular Access: Principles and Practice, Fourth Edition.* Mosby - St. Louis, MO. 2002.

24. Phillips, L. *Manual of IV Therapeutics, Fourth Edition,* FA Davis, Philadelphia, PA 2005.

25. *Id.*

26. *See* note 2

27. *See* note 1

28. *See* note 23

29. *See* note 2

30. Masoorli, S. "Pediatric Infusion Therapy: Small Children at High Risk." *Journal of the Association for Vascular Access,* Fall 2003, p. 42-43.

31. *See* note 5

32. *Id.*

33. *See* note 24

34. *See* note 5

35. *Id.*

36. *Id.*

37. *Id.*

38. Schull, P. *IV Drug Handbook.* McGraw-Hill, New York, 2009.

39. Horowitz, S. "Venipuncture-Induced Causalgia: Anatomic Relations of Upper Extremity Superficial Veins and Nerves, and Clinical Consideration." *Transfusion,* September 2000, Vol. 40.

40. Masoorli, S. "Nerve Injuries Related to Vascular Access Insertion and Assessment." *Journal of Infusion Nursing,* November / December 2007: Vol. 30 No. 6.

41. *See* note 39

42. Laska, L. "Teenager Claims Venipuncture Caused Median Nerve Injury With CRPS." *Medical Malpractice Verdicts, Settlements and Experts*. March 2009 p. 26.

43. Fabian, B. "Intravenous Complications: Infiltration," *Journal of Infusion Nursing,* July/August 2000.

44. *See* note 5

45. Masoorli, S. "Legal Issues Related to Vascular Access Devices and Infusion Therapy." *Journal of Infusion Therapy,* May/June 2005: Vol. 28 No. 38.

46. *See* note 40

47. Laska. L. "IV Infiltration (Extravasation) Causes Arm Injuries and Need for Multiple Surgeries." *Medical Malpractice Verdicts, Settlements and Experts.* November 2004, p. 2.

48. *See* note 5

49. *Id.*

50. Oncology Nurses Society *Chemotherapy and Biotherapy Guidelines and Recommendations for Practice, Third Edition* 2009.

51. *Id.*

52. Laska, L. "Failure to Timely Inform Physician of IV Infiltration (Extravasation)." *Medical Malpractice Verdicts, Settlements and Experts*. July 2007, p. 20.

53. Laska, L. "Extravasation from IV Results in Pain, Deformity of Finger and RSD." *Medical Malpractice Verdicts, Settlements and Experts*. April 2006, p. 25.

54. *See* note 5

55. *See* note 15, 23

56. *See* note 5, 15, 24

57. Laska, L. "Death of 11-Month Old Girl Following Cardiac Catheterization Blamed on Misplaced Central Venous Line." *Medical Malpractice Verdicts, Settlements and Experts*. September 2002, p. 5 and 6.

58. *See* note 15, 45

59. *Id.*

60. Laska, L. "Adriamycin Leaked During Chemotherapy Treatment Causing Need for Mastectomy." *Medical Malpractice Verdicts, Settlements and Experts*. May 2009, p. 37.

61. *See* note 4

62. Froede, R. *Handbook of Forensic Pathology, Second Edition*, Northfield, IL, 2003.

63. Hadaway, L. "Air Embolus" *Nursing 2002,* October 2002.

64. *See* note 62

65. *See* note 5

66. *Id.*

67. *See* note 62

68. Laska, L. "Air Embolism from Inappropriate Removal of (CVC) IV Line Blamed for Stroke." *Medical Malpractice Verdicts, Settlements and Experts*. June 2007, p. 17.

69. *See* note 1

70. *Id.*

71. *Id.*

72. Laska, L. "Home Healthcare Service Causes Serious Infection in Arm." *Medical Malpractice Verdicts, Settlements and Experts*. September 2001, p. 24.

Chapter 12

Long-Term Care Records

Gloria Blackmon, AAS, BSN, RN-BC, LNHA, Patricia Iyer, MSN, RN, LNCC,
Angela Tobias, RN, BSN, MSHSA, LNCC, CHCC and Jill Thomas, RNC, CWOCN, LNHA

12.1 Introduction

The quality of care in assisted living facilities, long-term acute care hospitals, subacute, and nursing home beds affects a large portion of the population either directly (as residents) or indirectly (as relatives of a resident). This chapter provides information about the medical record in use in long-term care settings.

12.2 Assisted Living

The Assisted Living Federation of America (ALFA) defines an assisted living residence as a special combination of housing, personalized supportive services, and health care designed to meet the needs, both scheduled and unscheduled, of those who need help with activities of daily living.[1] According to the National Center for Assisted Living (NCAL), almost one million Americans now make their home in assisted living facilities.[2]

A. Overview of Documentation in Assisted Living

In the past, documentation requirements in assisted living (AL) settings were not as stringent as in other areas of long-term care. However, as the popularity of AL has expanded, the awareness of the need for increased documentation has also increased due to the varying levels of acuity. AL facilities may or may not have licensed nurses providing or managing the care aspects of the residents/clients. Residents in AL can be relatively independent, needing only minimal assistance with bathing and dressing. Conversely, an assisted living resident might need much more oversight due to safety and behavioral issues. Therefore, documentation will depend on several factors such as the state regulations, levels of acuity, and the type of mandated staffing requirements.

B. Importance and Purpose of Documentation in Assisted Living

The importance and purpose of documentation has become increasingly identified in AL. Staff in these settings are not immune to liability. Common areas of concern include medication management, accidents and injuries, nutrition and behaviors that result in harm to the resident or result in resident-to-resident abuse. The more complex resident or levels of care offered increase the need to establish continuity of care through care planning and communication between caregivers, designated family members, physicians and pharmacies.

> In a Florida case, an assisted living resident was left unsupervised on the front porch of the facility. She fell near the sidewalk of a street. The staff of the facility was allegedly unaware that the resident had left the premises until an unknown man came in to report that one of the residents had fallen on the street. She suffered lacerations, fractures, and closed head injury due to the fall and died two and one half weeks later. The jury returned a $377,500 verdict, finding the facility ninety percent at fault and the resident ten percent at fault.[3]

The facility is obligated to identify how a resident is managing self-care and safety. This enables identification of resident needs as they increase to a level higher than the AL facility can provide. Family members are often not ready to see their loved one make the transition to skilled care, and may argue that the care can still be provided in the AL environment. Without the documented progression of decline and discussions with appropriate parties, it is more challenging to justify a higher rate level (for the care) or provide the

rationale for moving the resident out of the facility to an intensified level of care.

Medication management is an area of risk in AL facilities. It is important to keep in mind that medication management may not always be managed by licensed nurses. This may be accomplished through paraprofessionals (medication technicians), family members who fill the medication boxes and the residents who self-administer.

Healthcare provider appointments are not always coordinated with the AL staff which can lead to medication errors and/or medication interactions. Therefore, a prudent facility staff will need to have clear systems to ensure pertinent communication occurs between the residents, their responsible parties and healthcare providers to facilitate staff awareness of new orders or changes as a part of the care planning process. Therefore a reviewer will need to explore a multifaceted approach to identify how a medication error occurred.

C. Regulations Pertaining to Assisted Living Medical Records

Each state has different regulations regarding the documentation required in assisted living. However, assisted living still has gray areas including what is classified as a medical record. States may have admission and discharge requirements which include clinical diagnoses, conditions and/or behaviors of which documentation will need to support but such records may not be kept as a part of the medical record file. It may stay in the admissions office, executive director's files or the nurse consultant's files.

The National Center for Assisted Living (NCAL) compiled an updated state regulatory review in 2009. Unlike nursing homes, there is no Federal standard governing the practices in assisted living facilities. The directory details resident assessment and medication management requirements.[4] In general these are the two primary areas identified as medical records. Unless there is a state mandated assessment form, facilities may use their own documents or utilize forms from a recognized supplier like the Med-Pass or Briggs companies. The state regulations will also mandate who can administer medications. Some require licensed nurses while others do not. Facilities may also require that residents administer their own medications. These practices are based on the facility's operating license or care level. Some facilities that have dementia units have additional documentation requirements regarding assessments and plans of care, while others do not.

There are other regulations that contain implications for content in the medical records. For example, some facilities may allow a resident to be treated for stage I and II pressure ulcers and catheter care. Therefore the reviewer would need to know:

- the scope of care and services that is allowed at the facility by regulations,
- who is to provide that type of care, and
- where that documentation should be found.

If a home health nurse is providing this care, none of this nurse's documentation may be found in facility records.

D. The Components of Assisted Living Medical Records

The following sections describe records which may be present in an assisted living chart.

1. Resident information sheet

This sheet contains the demographic data regarding the resident including possible insurance information, who to contact in the emergency, physicians, admission and discharge dates, hospital choice, etc.

2. Physician assessment

If required, a medical examination must be completed upon entry to the assisted living facility by a physician, nurse practitioner or physician assistant. Generally the examination covers a review of the health systems, functional status, activity tolerance, psycho-social assessment and dietary needs. Depending on which state, there may be a timeframe in which the assessment should occur. For example, in West Virginia, this assessment cannot be completed more than 60 days prior to admission, or more than five working days after admission, followed by an annual medical assessment thereafter.

3. Resident assessment

In those states that do not require a medical assessment, a resident assessment is still obtained before or soon after admission. Various states have mandated forms; for example, Rhode Island requires a registered nurse to complete the resident assessment.[5] Other states may not have a mandated form but the state must approve the facility's form to ensure the required baseline functional status has been assessment. This is the case in New Mexico.

4. Service plan

The assisted living service plan is found in most facilities. It serves as a central tool to identify:

- the functional status of the resident,
- the services required or that the resident desires,
- who is to perform the services,
- where the services will be provided, and
- the goals/expectations.

The service plan may be as simple as a one page document[6] or multiple pages depending on the depth and complexity if an assessment is included. See Figure 12.1. The assisted living facility may also utilize this plan to determine fee increases or decreases, as many AL facilities bill the resident according to the amount of care needed.

5. Other possible forms

A medication self-administration assessment form may be present in an AL chart. This type of document provides a format for the appropriate staff to evaluate if the resident can explain what the medication is, the name of the medication, and if she can safely self-administer medications. Depending on the regulations of the state and policies and procedures of the facility, this may initially be conducted by the physician and reviewed quarterly by the staff or just conducted by the staff.

An Activities of Daily Living form may be used by the staff if residents are assisted with bathing or dressing. It may reflect if the resident ate in the dining room, required housekeeping services, had changes in condition, went out for appointments, and so on.

12.3 Long-Term Acute Care Hospitals (LTACHs)

Long-term acute care hospitals, in general, are defined per Medicare law as facilities that have an average inpatient length of stay greater than twenty-five days. These hospitals typically provide extended medical and rehabilitative care for patients who are clinically complex and may suffer from multiple acute or chronic conditions. Services may include comprehensive rehabilitation, respiratory therapy, cancer treatment, head trauma treatment, and pain management.[7]

With changes in acute care hospital reimbursement, more pressure has been placed on acute care hospitals to discharge patients "quicker and sicker." Not all of these patients can be adequately treated in less intensive environments. The majority of revenue for long-term acute care hospitals comes from Medicare and Medicaid due to the patient population they serve. The oldest long-term acute hospitals cared for patients recovering from chronic diseases and tuberculosis. Today some of those hospitals still exist. Long-term acute care can be provided in several different settings such as within acute care hospitals called hospitals within hospitals or as a satellite facility or as a separate hospital altogether. Long-term acute care hospitals make up a small provider group within the Medicare program.

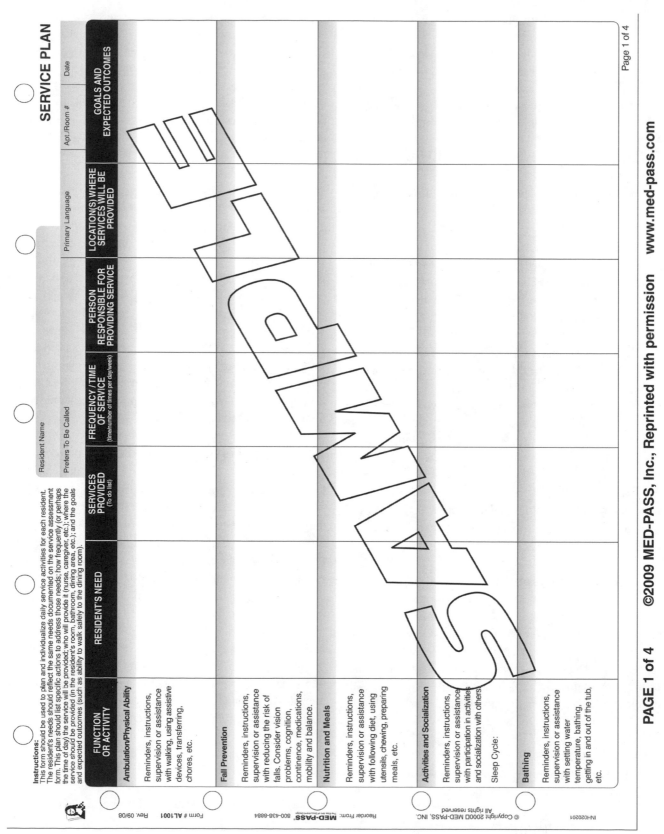

PAGE 1 of 4   ©2009 MED-PASS, Inc., Reprinted with permission   www.med-pass.com

Figure 12.1

Resident Name

Apt./Room #

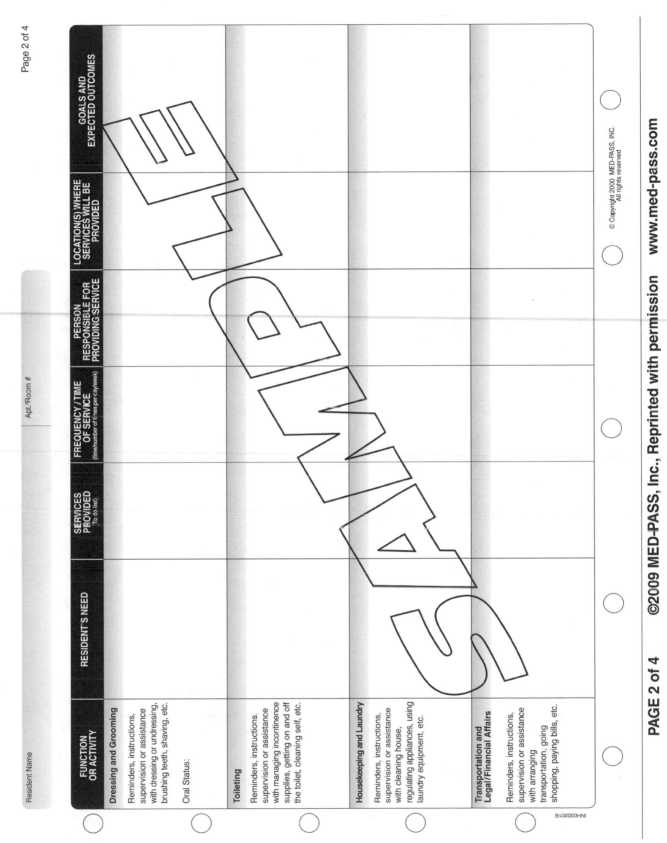

FUNCTION OR ACTIVITY	RESIDENT'S NEED	SERVICES PROVIDED (To do list)	FREQUENCY/TIME OF SERVICE (time/number of times per day/week)	PERSON RESPONSIBLE FOR PROVIDING SERVICE	LOCATION(S) WHERE SERVICES WILL BE PROVIDED	GOALS AND EXPECTED OUTCOMES
Dressing and Grooming Reminders, instructions, supervision or assistance with dressing or undressing, brushing teeth, shaving, etc. Oral Status:						
Toileting Reminders, instructions, supervision or assistance with managing incontinence supplies, getting on and off the toilet, cleaning self, etc.						
Housekeeping and Laundry Reminders, instructions, supervision or assistance with cleaning house, regulating appliances, using laundry equipment, etc.						
Transportation and Legal/Financial Affairs Reminders, instructions, supervision or assistance with arranging transportation, going shopping, paying bills, etc.						

INH02020018

PAGE 2 of 4   ©2009 MED-PASS, Inc., Reprinted with permission   www.med-pass.com

Figure 12.1 *(continued)*

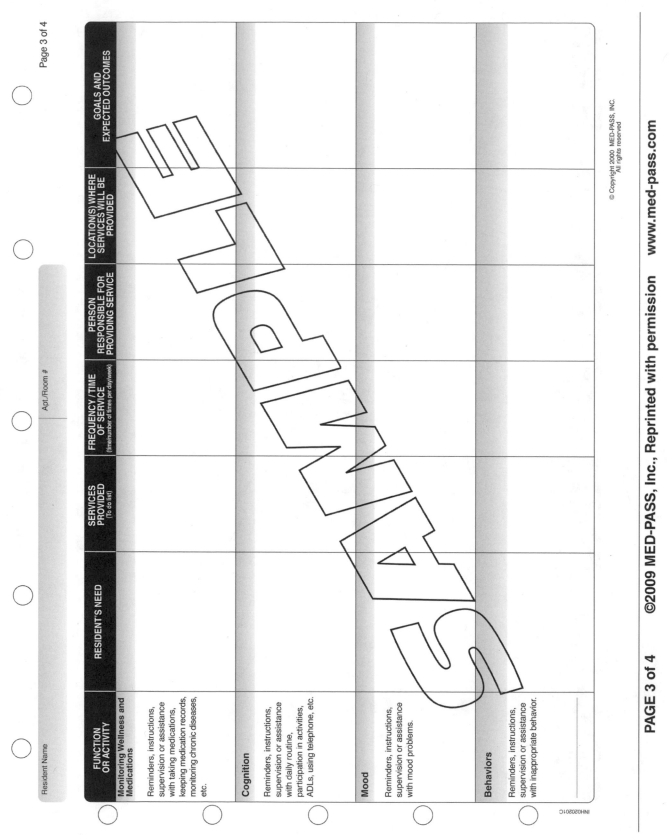

Figure 12.1 (continued)

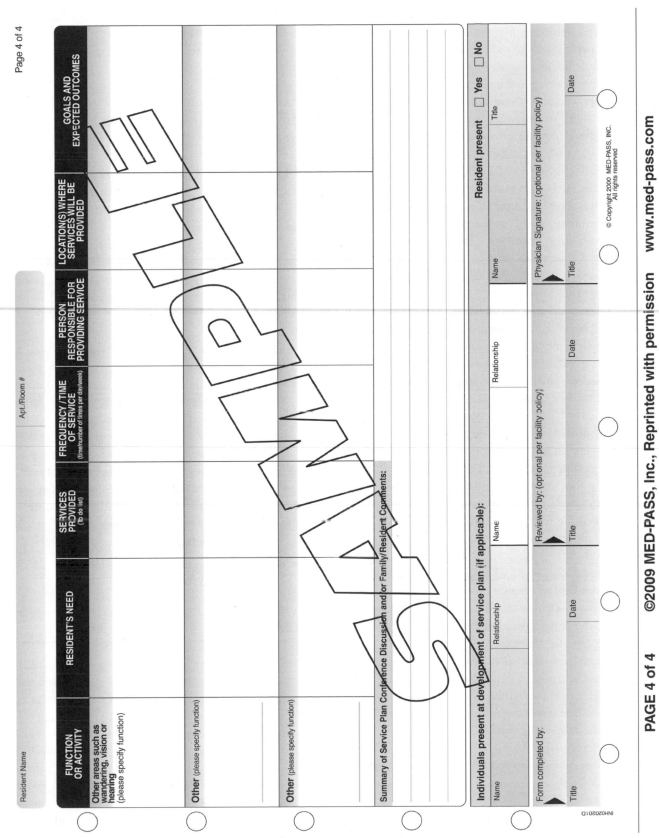

Figure 12.1 (continued)

Patients admitted to LTACHs in most of the cases, have already spent a significant amount of time in the short-term acute care hospital setting and required intensive care services. Hospital intensive care units are utilized for short stays for individuals who are medically unstable. The ICU is not an optimal option for those patients in need of treatment requiring extended or prolonged medical attention. With the changes in the healthcare environment and the escalating costs associated with ICU hospitalization, the LTACH provides a cost-effective alternative to short term acute hospital care. This is effective for patients who have a need for a longer hospital stay due to the existence of multiple medical problems, injury, trauma or unexpected medical complications or who have a need for extensive wound care and management. Often, these patients are too ill to move into rehabilitation, a skilled nursing facility, or sub-acute residential settings.

Patients stay an average of 25 days at an LTACH to receive the specialized medical and nursing care they need to maximize their medical status and level of independence before being transferred to the next appropriate care facility or discharged home. Often patients are transferred to an LTACH unit straight from the intensive care unit of the acute care hospital. The LTACH can continue the established plan of care and provide the necessary complex clinical and medical services on an extended basis and at a lower cost. The goal is to treat patients for a more extended period of time allowing them to recover and then return home or to a skilled nursing facility or nursing home.

Conditions for which admission to LTACH should be considered include:

- Ventilated patients who may possibly be weaned; the underlying disease process may vary,
- Trauma—Critical stabilization has been completed but the patient requires continued acute care (orthopedic, tongs, halo),
- Extensive wound care due to infected/complicated wounds, use of wound Vacuum Assisted Closure (VAC), or less extensive wounds but with additional medical needs requiring active treatment,
- Diabetic/vascular stasis ulcers,
- Post surgical fistulas,
- Dehiscence (failed wound closure) requiring open healing,
- Post flap surgery (3 or more days after surgery)
- Transplant patients—Patients awaiting transplants but too sick to be managed at lower level of care,
- Osteomyelitis (bone infection) patients on IV antibiotics,

- Bacteremia (bacterial blood infection), and
- Neutropenia (low white blood cell count) requiring special nutritional monitoring and build up in preparation for chemotherapy.

Long-term acute care hospitals are considered acute care hospitals and are required to abide by all standards, rules and regulations governing acute care hospitals.

12.4 Long-Term Care Diversity

According to a July 2, 2009 U.S. News & World Report article by Avery Comarow there are over 15,500 nursing long-term-care facilities currently in the United States.[8] In a typical year approximately 3.2 million Americans spend time in a nursing facility. However, the differences in long-term care are still confusing to some consumers, healthcare professionals, and attorneys especially when all levels of care are found within a Continuing Care Retirement Community (CCRC).

Long-term care facilities (nursing homes, nursing facilities, skilled nursing facilities, nursing centers) provide a higher level of 24-hour licensed nursing care oversight than AL. A long-term care facility may provide skilled nursing care or intermediate and custodial care. Specialized care units or dedicated facilities, for example, for dementia residents, also fall under the auspices of long-term care. However, dementia specialized care can be increasingly found in assisted living facilities. While not as common, long-term acute care hospitals also exist. The LTACHs are different than the traditional nursing homes as they provide a higher level of sub-acute and rehabilitation care.

TIP: Because of these subtle but distinct differences, it is important to clarify the type of long-term care facility involved in order to apply the correct regulations and standards of care.

Long-term care provides a variety of services that include medical and non-medical care to people who have chronic illnesses or disabilities. Most long-term care assists people with support services such as activities of daily living like dressing, bathing, and using the bathroom. Long-term care can be provided at home, in the community, in assisted living or in nursing homes and to any age group. Family caregivers are the main providers of long-term care services in all states. Medicare will pay for limited nursing home and home health services, but only for a limited time after a major acute care episode.[9]

A. Intermediate or Custodial Care

Custodial care (non-skilled care) is care that assists clients with activities of daily living, for example, bathing, dressing, eating, receiving medications, and so on.[10]

B. Skilled Care

Skilled care is provided or supervised by registered nurses to residents who need skilled nursing or skilled rehabilitation staff members to manage, observe, and evaluate care. All needs are taken care of with this type of service. Examples of skilled nursing care are giving intravenous injections, managing new tube feeding care, new oxygen therapy, care of pressure ulcers and surgical wounds. Any service that could be safely performed by an average non-medical person (or one's self) without the supervision of a registered nurse is not considered skilled care.[11]

12.5 Subacute Care

Subacute care is simultaneously a new and an old concept. It is new in the hospital setting but has long been provided in the long-term-care facility or chronic care hospitals as "skilled nursing." The concept of subacute care in the hospital sprang up as a result of the push that began in the early 1980s to discharge residents more quickly. The "quicker and sicker" phenomenon created a demand for a setting that could provide care when the resident's needs are too complex to be managed at home or in a traditional long-term-care setting which provides supportive care only.

A. Definition

Subacute care is defined as the bridge between the hospital and the home or long-term-care setting. The types of resident conditions that can be appropriate for a subacute unit include those listed in Figure 12.2. Examples of the type of population in these facilities include

- the resident with chronic obstructive lung disease who has both diabetes and liver disease,
- the resident who becomes debilitated after significant gastrointestinal bleeding, and
- the resident who has had a stroke and needs significant help with most activities of daily living but also has heart disease.[12]

Subacute care is a level of care, not a freestanding setting.

Types of Patient Conditions or Treatment Needs that are Appropriate for Subacute Care

- Postoperative
- Chemotherapy
- Total parenteral nutrition
- Complex wound care
- Intravenous therapy
- Dialysis
- Tube feedings through the nose or stomach
- Psychiatric care
- Rehabilitation after an amputation, spinal cord injury, head injury, burns, trauma, stroke, or a myocardial infarction
- Work conditioning
- Pain management
- Long-term ventilator therapy
- Hospice care for terminally ill patients
- AIDS
- Need for suctioning through the nose, mouth, or tracheostomy

Figure 12.2

TIP: The subacute care may be provided either in hospital beds that have been converted to a subacute status or in a nursing home that is staffed with a sufficient number of registered nurses who have been prepared to care for patients with higher requirements for nursing care.

The pressure to admit residents to subacute care units rather than hospitals is fueled by several factors, including

- the desire to control costs by providing care in a less costly environment than an acute care hospital;
- the trend to discharge patients from the hospital more quickly;
- the need to provide rehabilitative services to permit a resident to return home;
- improvements in technology that permit complex monitoring and care to be administered outside of hospitals;
- advances in medical care that have reduced the mortality rates of catastrophic illness (stroke, heart failure), although survivors of these illnesses may develop disability and complications which require care; and

- residents, nurses, and physicians becoming more comfortable with receiving and providing care in non-acute settings.[13]

Long-term-care facilities have been in the subacute care market for many years. In these units, registered nurses and licensed practical nurses provide the majority of care. This is in contrast to the intermediate care units where supportive care is provided by nursing assistants or licensed practical nurses and overseen by registered nurses. The average subacute care resident requires four to eight hours of nursing care a day, in comparison with the two or three hours per day usually provided to intermediate care nursing home residents.[14] In order to successfully and safely provide nursing care, the subacute care nursing staff must be able to manage the technology and multiple medical problems of residents in these types of units. Subacute care facilities must be prepared to anticipate, identify, and prevent or manage common risk factors and complications of acute medical episodes or chronic illness.

B. Standards of Care for Subacute Care Units

Subacute units are treated as if they are skilled nursing units and are thus governed by state and federal regulations.[15] Aspects of the delivery of subacute care are guided by general standards of nursing care. For example, the care of the subacute resident receiving tube feedings would be the same regardless of whether the resident is located in a hospital or in a long-term-care facility.

There is little in the risk management literature about the risks associated with subacute care. The risks associated with providing subacute care affect both long-term-care facilities and hospitals. These risks center primarily on the ability of the facility to provide the appropriate level of care with staff who have been educated to manage the complex needs of the residents.

TIP: Some residents in subacute care units are younger than those in intermediate long-term-care units. An award could, therefore, be potentially higher because of the economic losses sustained by an employed individual or one responsible for dependent children.

The staff of long-term-care facilities who have converted some of their beds to subacute ones are recognizing the added risks associated with providing the higher level of care required by these residents.

Staff nurses providing subacute care need a blend of acute care and long-term-care skills. Since a physician is not always on the premises of a subacute care unit, the nurses need excellent physical assessment skills, the ability to prevent and recognize complications, and good clinical judgment concerning when to contact the physician. Many long-term-care facilities are hiring nurses from the acute care arena and teaching them how to function in a long-term-care setting. The nurses learn how to involve the resident and family in care planning, record the extensive documentation required in long-term care, and act more independently without an on-site physician. The line that divides subacute care and acute care will continue to blur as subacute care becomes more and more acute.

TIP: The attorney who is researching subacute care cases may not find it easy to locate cases labeled as "subacute care." As subacute care units become more widespread, the case law will begin to identify cases as having occurred on a subacute care unit.

12.6 Overview of Documentation in Long-Term Care

It is important to become familiar with the contents of a long-term care record in order to perform a review. All of the pertinent documents should be at hand prior to conducting a risk management, quality assurance or medical-legal review. This can be challenging in long-term care as information is decentralized from the medical record or not filed with the record for an extended period of time. For example, some facilities do not keep ADL (activities of daily living) flow sheets after a period of time because they are not mandated by the Federal Regulations. Therefore, the reviewer needs to ask for the medical record policies and a list of all items considered a part of the medical record.

In addition, during a review, it is important to ask for the policy regarding documentation for the area of investigation. For example, if there has been a fall or accident, request the fall or accident protocol and related facility documentation requirements.

The 24-hour report is often overlooked as a source of information for attorneys and legal nurse consultants. This document is not placed in the medical record, and will include information regarding other residents that may need to be redacted. It is often kept for years and may include important information regarding communications, changes in conditions and information that was passed onto the nursing team. Since nursing facility interactions with residents, family members, the interdisciplinary teams, consultants, ombudsman, and assigned staff are fluid, information often is documented and recorded in ways that work for the culture and dynamics of organization based on care delivery systems.

12.7 The Importance and Purpose of Documentation in Long-Term Care

Communication is an imbedded function of compliance with the federal and state regulations. The medical record should reflect ongoing communication with the resident, family members, physicians, and interdisciplinary team. The care plan, MDS, and progress notes are essentially communication boards for all interested persons to rely upon. An absent piece of significant information can result in inadequate, inappropriate, or delayed care, or services. Frequently the only way to trace communication lines is through the medical record.

If diligent and substantial communication compliance is not recorded, it can be difficult to defend that an interaction, conversation, or planned process actually occurred. It is common for some facilities to use communication books or journals to facilitate communication. However, these are often not a part of the actual medical record and may be discarded according to facility policy, which may destroy "proof" later needed if a situation comes into question.

The importance of the medical record cannot be overstated. It is the central tool by which liability, damages, regulatory issues, and clinical reimbursement are measured. The medical record should represent a comprehensive catalog of information regarding the resident. In addition, it serves as a communication vehicle to promote continuity of care. See the example below.

> Margaret Jones lost greater than five percent of body weight during the last month and greater than eight percent over the past two months. The medical record reflected that the licensed dietitian saw the resident within two days after the weight loss was known the first month and again after the second month. The dietitian ordered calorie counts and supplements which were documented. The staff made the physician aware of the concerns and the nurse practitioner assessed the resident accordingly. The family was informed and encouraged to bring in from home items that the resident might enjoy. The resident was questioned several times by the nursing staff regarding her decrease in appetite and but the resident did not voice any physical complaints that could be contributing to her weight loss. She was also assessed for possible depression, which did not seem to be an issue. The care plan was updated to reflect the added supplements and to offer additional snacks and the resident was discussed during the weekly weight loss committee meeting. On month three there was no additional

> weight loss. All of these facts were well documented in the medical record.

The quantity of nursing note entries can be significantly less than acute care records and is dependent on the level of care provided. If a custodial care resident does not have any unusual occurrences, a nursing entry may be made only monthly. The discrepancy between the medical record and the actual resident's condition and treatment can open the door for litigation and possible fraud charges. See the examples below.

> Gloria Juarez was admitted to a skilled Medicare reimbursed bed for rehabilitation and care monitoring after an abdominal surgery. The medical record did not reflect consistent assessment of her abdominal incision, bowel sounds, or meal consumption. Within eight days, Gloria was readmitted to the hospital with a wound infection, fecal impaction, and nausea. The resident stated her symptoms were present for approximately three days. The nursing notes did not reflect adequate care monitoring in relation to the resident's diagnoses and needs. The negative outcome with lack of documentation could expose the facility to allegations of Medicare fraud because the resident did not receive the care that Medicare paid for.

> Sarah Kendrick was described in the nursing notes as needing assistance of two people for all transfers in some entries and maximum assistance in other notes. The physical therapy evaluation and notes indicated the need for two-person assistance and the use of a mechanical lift. The care plan stated she needed maximum assistance but did not indicate any assistance devices or how many people were needed to assist the resident. A certified nurse's assistant attempted to transfer Sarah alone. A fall resulted that injured both the resident and the assistant. The nurse assistant was new and not aware how much assistance was required for transferring the resident. The chart reflects discrepancies regarding transfer assistance. The documentation discrepancies could provide supportive evidence of lack of continuity of care, which contributed to the injuries of Sarah and the staff member.

12.8 Regulations Pertaining to Long-Term Care Medical Records

There are specific federal regulations that address medical records in the nursing home. The reviewer must have a clear understanding of the regulations when evaluating the clarity, continuity, and accuracy of the medical record. They are as follows:

- The facility must maintain clinical records on each resident in accordance with accepted professional standards and practices that are complete, accurately documented, readily accessible, and systematically organized.[16]
- The facility must retain clinical records for the period of time required by state law, or five years from the date of discharge when there is no requirement. For a minor, the time is three years after the resident reaches the legal age under state law.[17]
- The facility must keep confidential all information contained in the resident's records, regardless of the form or storage method of the records, except when release is required by transfer to another healthcare institution, law, third-party payment contract, or the resident. This regulation also guides that the clinical record must contain the following: significant information to identify the resident; a record of the resident's assessments; the plan of care and services provided; the results of any preadmission screening conducted by the state; and progress notes.[18]

In addition to the federal regulations, individual state requirements must also be identified and taken into consideration during medical record reviews. In general, most of the state regulations mimic the federal regulations. However, a state regulation may require specific documentation that would take precedence; for example, the state may impose a time for a physician to sign and return telephone orders. Some facilities are also certified by The Joint Commission, which has specific guidelines for long-term-care facilities. Therefore the reviewer will need to check those specifics when applicable.

TIP: The Joint Commission website[19] is an important source of information about standards and patient safety goals.

12.9 Admission and Care Planning Documents

Many facilities use their own format for the initial assessment and then complete the MDS. However, as MDS computer programs have evolved, some facilities use a modified version of the MDS for the initial assessment. The initial assessment may include a flow sheet to document the condi-

tion of the skin if the resident is admitted with pre-existing skin breakdown. Photographs may be taken to document the status of the skin on admission or when breakdown occurs. They may or may not be included in the main record. Check the policy regarding obtaining photographs, or review the admission consents regarding photographing for medical reasons and ask specifically for all related photographs. While wound photography used to be the practice of choice, it is becoming a less common practice for various reasons. Some of those reasons are the use of the photos in litigation against the facilities, poor photo quality, and inconsistent following of the facility policy regarding the interval times the photos are to be taken.

TIP: Look for dates on photographs and request to see the originals.

This section discusses the use of the admission assessment, MDS, RAPs, and care plans.

A. Admission Assessment
1. Purpose
Information gathered in the admission assists in providing the data needed to begin the interim care plan and complete the MDS. The admission assessment includes data about when the resident arrived at the facility, from where (home, acute care, another facility), and what kind of condition the resident was in based on a complete nursing assessment. In order to identify the new resident's needs, most long-term-care facilities complete an abbreviated assessment of the resident on admission. The facility's staff is expected to provide for the resident's safety based on this initial assessment. A number of lawsuits have arisen out of injuries sustained by residents before the comprehensive MDS is completed. The adjustment to a new environment can create or increase the resident's confusion and risk for falls.

2. Mechanism
The resident, family, and certified nursing assistants all play an integral role in the comprehensive assessment and care planning process. Communication between licensed nursing personnel and certified nursing assistants is critical since the CNAs provide the majority of direct personal care to residents.

Additional assessments regarding fall risk and pressure ulcer risk should be conducted during the admission process. More information is provided later in this chapter about additional assessments. Unless contraindicated by physician orders, upon admission the nurse should actually remove dressings to assess incisions, pressure ulcers, and so on in order to accurately assess and document the appearance. A complete assessment, depending on facility policies and procedures, is completed within four to twenty hours from admission time. Physician orders are verified by phone if not signed by the primary physician as part of the admission process. In the case of a Medicare admission, the nurse must ensure that the Medicare certification by the physician has been completed regarding the purpose for the skilled care. The admission assessment is a permanent part of the medical record. It may be done in a narrative format or standardized form. The nurse who completed the assessment should sign and date it.

3. Content

Areas that are covered in the admission assessment include:

- admission weight,
- vital signs,
- allergies,
- skin condition,
- treatments and procedures required,
- mobility status,
- supportive devices or assistance needed for activities of daily living,
- medications,
- hearing and vision assessments and observations,
- nutrition,
- patterns of sleep,
- continence or incontinence,
- discharge evaluation (future plans), and
- orientation to facility.

B. Minimum Data Set

The MDS is a federally developed form that is designed to obtain comprehensive information about the resident, so that key problems can be identified through the Resident Assessment Protocol and a care plan developed.

1. Definition

There are a few forms of documentation that are unique to long-term care. A standardized national assessment tool called the Minimum Data Set (MDS) is one of them. The items in the MDS standardize communication about resident problems and conditions within facilities, between facilities, and between facilities and outside agencies. The Resident Assessment Instrument (RAI) incorporates the Minimum Data Set and RAPs (Resident Assessment Protocol).

TIP: RAI is a federally mandated process that must be adhered to by all nursing facilities receiving Medicare or Medicaid payment for services.

The Resident Assessment Instrument is not required for facilities that accept private payment only. There are certain core items of this process that are minimum requirements; some states adopt only the minimum, while other states have added additional data to the process. The Resident Assessment Instrument is intended to produce a comprehensive, accurate, standardized, and reproducible assessment of each long-term-care facility resident's functional capacity. The MDS is a multi-page collection (including the face sheet) of resident information. There are approximately 500 items regarding demographic, physical, mental, and psychosocial function information. "Every item on the assessment must be answered. If it is not answered, it is considered not assessed. A comprehensive care plan cannot be developed without a comprehensive assessment."[20]

2. Purpose

Providing care to residents of a long-term-care facility is complicated and challenging work requiring clinical competence, observational skills, and assessment expertise from all disciplines to develop individualized care plans. The Resident Assessment Instrument helps facility staff gather definitive information about a resident's strengths and needs, which must be addressed in an individualized care plan. It is intended to produce a comprehensive, accurate, standardized, reproducible assessment of each resident's functional capacity. It also assists staff to evaluate goal achievement and revise care plans accordingly by enabling the facility to track changes in the resident's status. As the process of problem identification is integrated with sound clinical interventions, the care plan becomes each resident's unique path toward achieving or maintaining his highest practicable level of well-being.[21]

The RAI helps facility staff to look at the resident holistically as an individual for whom quality of life and quality of care are mutually significant and necessary. Interdisciplinary use of the RAI promotes this emphasis on quality of care and quality of life. Facilities have found that involving disciplines such as dietary, social service, physical therapy, occupational therapy, speech language pathology, pharmacy, and activities in the RAI process has fostered a more complete approach to resident care and strengthened team communication.[22]

3. History

CMS (Center for Medicare and Medicaid Services) formally known as HCFA (Health Care Finance Administration) used an interdisciplinary process to develop the MDS. The tool was created by experts (who represented many professional disciplines), the nursing home residents, the nursing home industry, and consumer groups. The project team worked together with expert clinicians, consultants, a national advisory board, and hundreds of reviewers from nursing homes across the country. More than fifty draft versions of the MDS were refined and reviewed. Several major tasks were involved in the development of the Resident Assessment Instrument (RAI), such as determining which areas of a person's health status and functioning should be assessed in the MDS and how to organize the elements within a workable, conceptual framework.[23]

4. Timing

Regulations require that a MDS assessment be performed at admission, quarterly, annually, and whenever the resident experiences a significant change in status. For residents in a Medicare Part A stay, the MDS is also used to determine the Medicare reimbursement rate. These assessments are performed on the 5th, 14th, 30th, 60th and 90th day of admission.[24] Nurses, CNAs, social workers, recreational therapists, and the dietitian participate in the completion of the MDS. Data are gathered from the medical record as well as from the caregivers from all shifts.

Staff members must systematically monitor resident status between annual assessments. The quarterly review focuses assessment on a particular subset of MDS items to enable staff to detect gradual changes in resident status. This subset has been defined by CMS as a minimum quarterly assessment. This core of critical indicators helps staff track resident decline or improvement. The quarterly review also provides a basis of information to determine whether or not the care plan needs to be revised.

If a significant change in the resident's status is identified, either through the quarterly review process or at any other time, a complete MDS should be documented and the care plan revised. According to the HCFA "Final Rule" dated June 1998,[25] a "significant change" has been further defined and clarified as "a decline or improvement in a resident's status that will not normally resolve itself without intervention by staff or by implementing standard disease-related clinical interventions, that has an impact on more than one area of the resident's health status, and requires interdisciplinary review or revision of the care plan." Prior to the completion of the MDS, the onset of a suspected significant change should be documented in the progress notes.

All interventions and resident responses must be carefully documented. If the care providers believe that the change in clinical status may not be major or permanent, then substantial rationale for the decision not to complete a new MDS assessment must be documented as well. If by the fourteenth day after onset of change there is not sufficient evidence to prove response to treatment, then a full MDS for significant change must be completed. Significant change can be anything positive or negative, such as the return of the ability to walk or the use of one's hands to grasp small items; the loss of ability to perform two or more activities of daily living; a serious complication; or improved behavior, mood, or functional status, to the extent that the existing care plan no longer matches the current needs of the resident.[26]

The timing of the non-Medicare assessments is summarized below.

- *Admission (Initial) Assessment*—Must be completed by fourteenth day of a resident's stay.
- *Annual Assessment*—Must be completed within twelve months of most recent full assessment.
- *Significant Change in Status Assessment*—Must be completed by the end of the fourteenth calendar day following determination that a significant change has occurred. A "significant change" is defined as a major change in the resident's status that is not self-limiting, affects more than one area of the resident's health status, and requires interdisciplinary review or revision of the care plan.
- *Quarterly Assessment*—Set of MDS items, mandated by the state (contains at least CMS established subset of MDS items) which must be completed no less frequently than once every three months.

5. Accountability and mechanism

Data are gathered from the medical record as well as from the caregivers from all shifts. The process of performing an accurate and comprehensive assessment requires that information about residents be gathered from multiple sources. It is the role of the interdisciplinary team members participating in the assessment process to validate information obtained from the resident, resident's family, or other healthcare team members through observing, interviewing, and reviewing to ensure accuracy. Similarly, information in the resident's record is validated by interaction with the resident and direct care staff. Review the signature section of the document to identify who participated in the completion of the MDS.

The following sources of information must be used in completing the RAI:

- review of the resident medical record,
- communication with and observation of the resident,
- communication with direct-care staff,
- communication with licensed professionals,
- communication with the resident's physician, and
- communication with the resident's family.

State computerization requirements became effective June 1998. Facilities must enter information from the resident assessment into a computer, in accordance with CMS-specified formats. At least monthly, the facility must transmit electronically the information contained in each resident assessment to the state.[31]

6. Future directions

A newer version of the MDS was released in October 2009 after years of input and revisions. The goals of the MDS 3.0 revision were to introduce advances in assessment measures, increase the clinical relevance of items, improve the accuracy and validity of the tool, and increase the resident's voice by introducing more resident interview items. Providers, consumers, and other technical experts in nursing home (NH) care requested that MDS 3.0 revisions focus on improving the tool's clinical utility, clarity, and accuracy. CMS also wanted to shorten the tool while maintaining the ability to use MDS data for quality indicators, quality measures, and payment (resource utilization groups-III [RUGs-III] classification).[27] In addition to improving the content and structure of the MDS, the RAND/Harvard team effort also aimed to improve user satisfaction. User attitudes are key determinants of quality improvement implementation. Negative user attitudes toward the MDS are often cited as a reason that nursing homes have not fully implemented it in targeted care planning.[28]

C. Resident Assessment Protocol

Once the MDS is completed, a second unique form called the Resident Assessment Protocol (RAP) is completed. The RAP is basically a decision tree based on the data collected in the MDS. For example, if certain items are checked on the MDS, the RAP will lead the nurse to the conclusion that a specific problem is likely to exist and that a plan of care may need to be developed to address this issue. The RAPs are structured, problem-oriented frameworks for organizing MDS information and examining additional clinically relevant information about an individual. RAPs help identify social, medical, and psychological problems and form the basis for individualized care planning. The process of identifying problems must be completed within fourteen days after admission to the facility.

D. Care Planning

The care plan addresses key resident problems, the desired outcome, and the interventions needed to address the problem.

1. Federal requirements

Nursing homes that receive federal funds are required to comply with federal laws that specify that residents receive a high quality of care. OBRA 1987, also known as the Nursing Home Reform Act, specifies that a nursing home:

(1) Must develop a comprehensive care plan for each resident that includes measurable objectives and timetables to meet a resident's medical, nursing, and mental and psychosocial needs that are identified in the comprehensive assessment. The care plan must describe the services that are to be furnished to attain or maintain the resident's highest practicable physical, mental, and psychosocial well-being as required.

(2) A comprehensive care plan must be—(i) developed within 7 days after completion of the comprehensive assessment; (ii) prepared by an interdisciplinary team, that includes the attending physician, a registered nurse with responsibility for the resident, and other appropriate staff in disciplines as determined by the resident's needs, and, to the extent practicable, the participation of the resident, the resident's family or the resident's legal representative; and (iii) periodically reviewed and revised by a team of qualified persons after each assessment.

(3) The services provided or arranged by the facility must—(i) meet professional standards of quality; and (ii) be provided by qualified persons in accordance with each resident's written plan of care.

2. Purpose of a care plan and accountability

An individualized plan is developed to outline the need requirements and approaches for the care of an individual in a healthcare setting. The plan will state the approaches and the person responsible to complete or oversee these tasks (for example, "a nursing assistant will help Mrs. Jones walk to each meal to build her strength"). The care plan is prepared by the interdisciplinary team, which consists of nursing staff, physician, therapy staff, social services, activities staff, and dietitian or designee. Each discipline representative should complete an assessment. A care conference is conducted to discuss the findings and the resident's problems, strengths, and needs. The resident or family should be included in the care conference before the final determinations for care are established. The resident, family or responsible party should have input to the care plan, but this frequently does not occur. Responsible persons or departments are designated to implement and carry out each approach and intervention. Sometimes there is more than one discipline designated as responsible.

3. Basic components of the care planning process

After a comprehensive assessment is performed, the resident's strengths and weaknesses are identified. The resident's needs and problems are delineated. This includes anything of concern to the resident or a lack of something useful to, required by, or desired by the resident. Nursing diagnoses may be included on the care plan. Typically the plan defines the resident's needs, such as "self care deficit, dressing/grooming." The care plan may include a statement of potential problems, such as "potential for injury: cuts, related to attempts to shave self and poor coordination." The plan may include a statement of resident desires or strengths, such as "resident desires to be independent with all ADLs."

Next, the care plan team determines an appropriate goal. There are seven steps to the goal setting process.

- *Clarify the problem*—The problem is clearly defined and carefully limited so the goal can be easily directed at the problem.
- *Make an assessment*—The care plan team considers all factors that may be relevant to the resident's ability to achieve the goal.
- *Estimate final goal*—The goal may be a stepping-stone to the outcome.
- *Analyze goal stages*—The care plan team determines the successive stages through which the resident would normally progress to achieve the goal.
- *Identify proximate goals*—The care plan team identifies the first significant measurable stage the resident can be expected to achieve beyond the present condition.
- *Set a time frame*—A realistic estimate of the time it will take to achieve each approximate goal is made, and a goal evaluation date is defined.

- *Write an effective goal statement*—The plan states goals in concise, understandable, and measurable terms. They must be realistic for that resident.

The next step in the care planning process is determining approaches and interventions useful in meeting the stated goal. The plan may refer to carrying out standardized protocols, such as the falls prevention program (Figure 12.3), pressure ulcer prevention protocol (Figure 12.4), or the protocol for a resident at nutritional risk (Figure 12.5). The plan is documented to communicate it to the entire interdisciplinary team, include nursing assistants and all front line staff. The plan is carried out as defined. It should be followed precisely by the discipline listed for each approach and intervention.

Evaluation is the last step in the care planning process. If the interventions do not result in the desired goals, the plan of care must be modified. This should be done in conjunction with the goal date and at a maximum every ninety days. Revision needs to occur at any point there is a new problem or need identified, there is a significant change in resident status, the interventions are not appropriate to move toward the stated goal, or the goal is inappropriate for any reason.

In a Tennessee case, the 89-year-old nursing home resident fell eight times in 16 months, with seven falls documented. The plaintiffs claimed that most of the falls occurred during the demented resident's trips to the bathroom. An x-ray taken seven days after the last fall showed he had sustained a hip fracture. The resident was taken to the hospital for surgery and died thereafter. The plaintiff claimed that the facility failed to implement interventions between falls, such as placing skid mats in the bathroom, lowering his mattress, and instituting a toileting program. The plaintiffs also claimed the decedent received insufficient pain medication, and developed a stage IV heel pressure ulcer, leg contractures, and urosepsis. The defendants argued the decedent was properly assessed as to his risk for falls and numerous and appropriate interventions were added to his care plan. The defendant claimed the decedent continued to fall because he would get up without calling for assistance despite his demonstrated ability to use the call button. The jury awarded $33.9 million including over $29 million in punitive damages.[29]

Falling Star Program (Fall Prevention Program)

Policy: It is the policy of this facility to provide the highest quality care in the safest environment for the residents at the facility.

Procedure:

A. All residents will be assessed for their fall risk at the time of admission, quarterly, and upon a significant change using the Fall Risk Assessment.

B. When a resident is placed on the fall prevention program, an identification reminder will be implemented to help alert the staff to increase their awareness of the resident's safety needs.

C. Residents who are assessed by the use of the fall risk tool or by the IDT (interdisciplinary team) to be at risk for falls will be identified by a star on the nameplate outside their door, and a star on their wheel chair and/or on their walker (as indicated). A star will also be placed on the resident's care guide. The stars will be updated weekly, according to needs by the unit manager, per IDT team discussion. Blue stars will indicate a risk for falls and yellow stars will indicate risk for falls and high risk for injury.

D. A fall/fall risk care plan will be written and implemented, or updated accordingly.

E. When a resident falls, a complete assessment will be performed by the charge nurse/supervisor. The fall will be documented in the nurses' notes, and on the 24 hour report. A post fall assessment will be completed. (This is an internal performance improvement document).

F. The charge nurse will implement appropriate interventions at the time of the fall.

G. The resident will be assessed by the nurse for 72 hours post fall. These findings will be documented in the nurses' notes.

H. The IDT will assess the resident in 24 to 72 hours.

I. Any resident who has fallen will be assessed by the IDT and will be followed by the fall committee until discharged by the committee, or a minimum of 4 weeks.

J. The fall intervention list will be as least restrictive as possible. Some of the devices may require pre-restraining assessment, MD order, and consent form signed by the resident or responsible party. These interventions may be used.

    1. Stable and strong non-skid footwear
    2. Specialized mattress (perimeter etc.)
    3. Specialized chair cushions (pommel etc.)
    4. Low beds
    5. Mats on the floor-only when in bed
    6. Therapy screen or evaluation
    7. Call light within reach; reminders to residents to use when they are capable of understanding
    8. Wedge cushions
    9. Rearrangement of room furniture-to avoid hazards and clutter
    10. Use of a room closer to the nurses station
    11. Placement at the nurses' station or other area of high visibility
    12. Verbal cues and reminders
    13. Adequate lighting
    14. Individualized bowel and bladder program
    15. Individualized toileting program
    16. Activities of interest
    17. Referral to restorative program
    18. Distraction
    19. Environment free of clutter

Figure 12.3

20. Placement of devices within reach at all times (walker, cane, wheelchair, etc.)
21. Night light
22. Review of medication and notification of MD if medication needs to be adjusted
23. Provision of assistance with transfers and ambulation
24. Placement of glasses and hearing aides are within reach at all times, in good/clean condition, assist with applying if needed
25. Placement of adaptive equipment (canes, walkers etc.) are within reach at all times, encourage, and remind use
26. Audiology consult
27. Optometry consult
28. Bed alarm
29. Chair alarm
30. Lap buddy
31. Self release seat belt
32. Half side rail for mobility or positioning
33. Monitoring of blood sugar, if applicable
34. Offering food and fluids, if not contraindicated
35. Comfort checks
36. If restless at night (or any time) and gets OOB, provide a distraction and/or activity

K.   Fall Checklist (to be completed after a resident has fallen)
    _____ Assessment head to toe, document assessment in IDT notes.
    _____ Notify physician, document notification and any orders.
    _____ Notify family, document notification and any concerns voiced.
    _____ Complete incident report.
    _____ Complete post fall assessment.
    _____ Add to 24 hour report sheet.
    _____ Update fall care plan or add episodic care plan.
    _____ Document every shift for 72 hours after a fall.

Figure 12.3 (continued)

Pressure Ulcer Prevention

Prevention, in addition to being the best cure, is less costly than treatment both in terms of human suffering and financial costs.

I. Education

A.   The incidence of pressure ulcers and other complications will be reduced through educational programs.

B.   Appropriate education will be provided for all caregivers, so they will have the knowledge to provide quality care.

C.   Program components: The educational program for the prevention of pressure ulcers will be directed at all levels of healthcare providers, patients, families and caregivers. The educational program for prevention of pressure ulcers includes information about the following items:
1.   Etiology and risk factors for pressure ulcers
2.   Risk assessment tools and their application
3.   Skin assessment
4.   Selection and/or use of support surfaces
5.   Development and implementation of an individualized program of skin care
6.   Demonstration of positioning to decrease risk of tissue breakdown
7.   Instruction on accurate documentation of pertinent data

II. Pressure Ulcer Prevention

A.   Risk Assessment:
1.   Residents will be assessed upon admission, re-admission, quarterly, upon significant change in condition, and as needed for risk of pressure ulcer development, utilizing the Norton Plus Skin Assessment tool.
2.   Applicable interventions will be implemented per the Risk Assessment Protocol, care planned, and individualized as indicated.

B.   Preventative Skin Care: All identified residents will have preventative skin care measures utilized for care.

C.   Support Surfaces: Residents will be placed on appropriate support surfaces.

D.   Positioning:
1.   Residents will be positioned in the basic anatomical position while in bed and repositioned per individual tissue tolerance.
2.   When positioning patients' in a sitting position, postural alignment, distribution of weight, balance, stability, and pressure reduction/relief will be considered.

III. Wound Prevention: Appropriate measures will be taken for the prevention of vascular leg ulcers and skin tears.

IV. Infection Control:

A.   Body Substance Isolation (BSI)/Universal Precautions (UP) will be employed for all patient care.

B.   Clean technique will be utilized for all wound care, unless otherwise indicated.

Figure 12.4

Nutrition at Risk Program Protocol

1) All residents will be assessed for nutritional risk by the dietitian with the Nutritional Risk Review upon admission, quarterly, and at other times as indicated (i.e., significant change).

2) All residents will be weighed weekly for 4 weeks upon admission. All residents will be weighed at least monthly thereafter unless the physician orders otherwise or they are considered at nutritional risk by meeting additional criteria and/or have been determined to be at risk by the IDT.

3) The following additional criteria shall be used to identify residents at nutritional risk.

   A. Residents with pressure ulcers.

   B. Residents on TPN (Total Parenteral Nutrition) or tube fed, until weight and nutritional status are stable.

   C. Residents on dialysis.

   D. Residents with unplanned weight loss:

      1. Loss of 5% of weight in one month.

      2. Loss of 10% of weight in six months.

      3. Any resident showing progressive unplanned weight loss.

   E. Other indications of nutritional risk may include:

      1. Residents with an admitting diagnosis or history of malnutrition/dehydration.

      2. Residents with unresolved feeding problems.

      3. Residents on a fluid restriction.

      4. Residents with unusual diet orders (clear or full liquids).

      5. Residents with severe or chronic vomiting and diarrhea.

      6. Residents with bizarre eating habits.

      7. Residents with complaints of hunger (not associated with obesity).

      8. Residents with taste complications.

      9. Residents with unstable medical condition (i.e., poorly controlled diabetes) whose nutritional status is compromised or is expected to be compromised.

      10. Physical functioning and structural problems (ability to feed self and ability of resident to obtain or finish food before it becomes unpalatable).

      11. Increased level of activity demanding increased calories.

      12. Alterations in taste, smell, chewing, or swallowing.

      13. Availability/unavailability of adaptive equipment.

      14. Dining environment.

      15. Residents with any other situation that the nursing/dietary staff identify that could indicate nutritional risk.

4) Residents who have been identified at nutritional risk by the interdisciplinary team shall be placed on the NARP and added to the Nutrition at Risk Tracking Log by the dietitian or dietary manager. This will be communicated to the nursing department at the weekly meeting, if not before. The unit manager or designee will be responsible to notify the physician and responsible party, as indicated.

5) All residents who are identified at nutritional risk will be discussed by the interdisciplinary team at the weekly quality assurance meetings and the interventions will be care planned and implemented accordingly.

6) The consultant dietitian will review and assess residents at nutritional risk, at minimum, once a month, and enter an appropriate progress note.

7) If, despite appropriate intervention(s) by dietary and nursing staff, the resident is not receiving sufficient nutritional support to meet his/her metabolic needs, the physician should be contacted for medical intervention (i.e., appetite stimulants, NG tube, gastrostomy tube, TPN, hospitalization, and so on.) and the responsible party notified to discuss the IDT and physician recommendations.

8) Residents will remain on the NARP until discharged by the IDT. If the resident is stable without any identified issues, the IDT may choose to discharge him from the program.

Figure 12.5

4. Effectiveness

According to the National Coalition for Nursing Home Reform, a good care plan should:

- be specific to that resident,
- be followed as an important guideline for providing good care for the resident,
- be written so that everyone can understand it and know what to do,
- reflect the resident's concerns and support her well-being,
- use a team approach involving a wide variety of staff and outside referrals as needed,
- assign tasks to specific staff members, and
- be re-evaluated and revised routinely.

5. Types of care plans and timelines for completion

There are several types of care plans. An *initial care plan* should be initiated upon admission to a facility. This is not expected to be a comprehensive plan. However, it must include minimal care requirements (e.g., assistance as needed with ADLs), type of diet, fall care plan if the resident is at risk for falls, pressure ulcer prevention care plan if the resident is at risk for pressure ulcer development, or any resident specific known concerns.

A *standard care plan* is a comprehensive plan initiated no later than seven days after completion of the initial MDS or the twenty-first day in the facility. An *acute or episodic plan* is a care plan that addresses an acute or temporary problem. This should be implemented at the onset of any new issue. A *discharge or post-discharge plan* is developed. Regulations require that a post-discharge plan of care be developed with the participation of the resident and his family, which will assist the resident to adjust to his new living environment.

E. Additional Nursing Assessments

TIP: Since the MDS is a Minimum Data Set, there are additional assessments which are generally obtained when a resident is admitted to a nursing home.

- *Admission Assessment*—An assessment performed by an admitting nurse. This may include a brief history, a head-to-toe physical assessment, and a head-to-toe skin assessment.
- *Fall Risk*—An assessment to obtain an objective score for the resident's risk of falling. Quarterly as-

sessments are also conducted with the MDS and after falls.

- *Pressure Ulcer Risk*—An assessment to obtain an objective score for the resident's risk of developing pressure ulcers. Quarterly assessments are also conducted with the MDS and as needed.
- *Bowel and Bladder Assessment*—An assessment of a resident's continence status and ability to be retrained, if incontinent.
- *Physical Restraint Assessment*—An assessment required if a physician orders a physical restraint of any kind, or there is a perceived need to restrain the individual. If utilized, quarterly assessments must be conducted with documented efforts to use the least restrictive measures necessary.
- *Self-Administration of Medication*—If a resident desires to administer her own medication of any kind, an assessment to determine competence of the individual to do so is made.
- *Nutrition Assessment*—A comprehensive assessment completed by a licensed dietitian of the resident's nutritional status and any potential risk for nutritional or hydration issues. Quarterly assessments are also conducted with the MDS and as needed.
- *Activities Assessment*—An assessment performed by an activity interdisciplinary team member to determine a resident's interests for leisure activities and ability to perform them and what cognitive level activities need to be planned. Quarterly assessments are also conducted with the MDS and as needed.
- *Social Service Assessment*—An assessment of the resident's social history and psychosocial needs. This is done at admission and quarterly with the MDS, as well as when substantive information is obtained.
- *Mini-Mental Assessment*—An assessment, generally performed by the social worker, psychologist or designee, to determine the resident's cognitive ability.
- *Depression Assessment*—An assessment, generally performed by the social worker or designee, to determine if the resident has any indications of depression. Quarterly assessments are also conducted with the MDS and as needed.
- *Pain Assessment*—Conducted upon admission utilizing a numerical scale, Wong-Baker faces or thorough history taking from families or behavioral expressions especially in residents with advanced dementia.

- *Restorative/Rehabilitation Nursing Assessment (Functional)*—If the physician orders any therapy, there should be an assessment by the designated professional (e.g., physical therapist, occupational therapist or a speech pathologist). Generally, if there is no therapy ordered, each therapy discipline will complete a screen to determine if the resident has skilled therapy needs. If no skilled therapy needs are found, there should be a functional assessment completed by the nursing staff to determine the resident's functional ability, to determine if any restorative nursing programming is suitable, and to determine the type of assistance needed. Periodic re-evaluation is conducted to see if resident continues with the need or can be discontinued.

12.10 Nurses' Notes

Nurses document progress notes on a frequent basis in the beginning of the admission and infrequently thereafter. Review the facility policy regarding admission documentation and post-incident documentation. Most require at least 48-72 hours of documentation on each shift. Notes may be recorded in different colors such as red, green, and blue to differentiate shifts, although this is not the standard. Nursing notes are to be maintained on each resident in accordance with accepted professional standards and practices. They must be complete and accurate.[30] State regulations will require at minimum the same as the federal regulations but may also have additional requirements.

A. Format and Frequency

Use of narrative nursing notes continues to be a common practice in long-term care, although computerized charting protocols are increasing the mixture of the two. Many long-term-care staff complete a narrative summary at a designated time each month. The summary is comprehensive, including vital signs, and supports the current plan of care. The responsibility for writing these summaries is often rotated monthly among shifts. Some facilities use a standard monthly summary form that includes areas that are checked off or circled. These forms often include an area for narrative notation on the lower half of the page or on the back to allow the nurse the opportunity to record any additional information not covered by the form or that needs further explanation. The frequencies of routine summaries vary from facility to facility. A weekly summary routine is also used by some facilities. In addition to the summaries, nursing progress notes should be generated between these scheduled times as follows:

- when there is a change in condition or in the care plan,
- when there has been an incident or accident,
- when the resident refuses care or treatment,
- when a physician/nurse practitioner/consult is contacted,
- when new orders are received,
- in accordance with facility policies and procedures,
- in accordance with recognized standards (wound care, pain management, diabetes care),
- when communications, permissions, and so on occur with family, and
- when there is a resident or family complaint.

B. Content

Nurses serve as the primary coordinators of services in nursing homes. If a resident has any appointments, leaves the facility, or has services provided by others (dialysis, wound care clinic), this information is documented in the nursing notes. Nurses in long-term care often deliver services generally provided by other departments in acute care facilities. For example, nurses perform inhalation therapy and venipuncture. References to these services may be found within the nursing notes or on treatment sheets. Family teaching, conflicts, and discussions are often initially addressed in the nursing notes. Refer to Appendix A of this book or see Iyer[31] for a detailed handbook of abbreviations.

If a resident is in a Medicare skilled bed, the documentation should include a daily assessment along with specific documentation regarding the covered skilled care. For example, diabetic monitoring and progression towards rehabilitation goals or pain management are recorded in the record. There are Medicare requirements for documentation for additional situations in addition to clinical assessments, for example, justification for ambulance transfers, special beds for pressure ulcer care, and the use of oxygen.[32]

Nursing documentation should also be congruent with the physician's orders regarding assessments. For example, an order may direct the nurses to monitor for signs and symptoms of shortness of breath or dyspnea every shift and record. Facilities in general have policies that govern certain aspects of care and how often and how long assessments and observations are to be done. For example:

- if a resident falls, follow-up assessments are to be performed every shift for seventy-two hours, and
- if a resident starts new medication, assessment of effectiveness and monitoring for any adverse reactions are performed.

As is true of all medical records, nursing notes are expected to provide an accurate picture of the status of the resident.

In a New Mexico case, the plaintiff alleged the records were false. The plaintiff's decedent was 78-years-old. She complained of dizziness and nausea at the nursing home. No vital signs or blood counts were taken. The next day, the decedent was found unconscious with blood on her sheets, pillows, and adult diaper. The plaintiff claimed the blood-soaked articles were removed and the decedent was cleaned up before her family was contacted. The decedent's daughter claimed that she was told her mother had died of a heart attack. The chart entry on the death date noted only that the decedent was found without respiration and no mention was made of her bloody condition. An autopsy found that the death was due to a gastrointestinal hemorrhage and that she had probably been bleeding internally for several days. The plaintiff claimed that several entries in the decedent's chart were false, including a notation that the decedent had received an insulin shot an hour after her death, and late entries regarding bleeding were made by nurses who were not even on duty. The jury returned a $54 million verdict which included $4 million in compensatory damages and $50 million in punitive damages. Eighty percent of fault was assessed against ManorCare and twenty percent was assessed against two certified nurse practitioners who contracted with the company. An appeal was expected.[33]

C. Progress Toward Care Plan Goals

Once a care plan has been generated, the nursing notes should reflect

- whether or not the care plan interventions are being followed,
- what the resident's response is to the interventions,
- whether the care plan goals remain appropriate,
- whether the care plan will continue as written, or
- whether the care plan will be revised.

See below for an example of a comprehensive nursing note.

Resident continues to tolerate 1800 calorie diabetic diet at all meals. Consumes 80–90 percent of each meal independently. Does not like sugar free pudding snacks at HS. Dietary made aware and will start an alternative tonight and monitor. Nursing will continue to discuss signs and symptoms of hyper/hypoglycemia with resident to assist her in being able to tell staff when she is not feeling well. Will continue teaching during medication administration to resident. Continues on accucheck testing AC and HS. Resident cooperative. No changes to care plan at this time.
—Jane Darcy, LPN

12.11 Additional Nursing Documentation

A variety of other documents are generated by nurses and CNAs. Commonly used ones are described below.

A. Activities of Daily Living Flow Sheets

Activities of daily living (ADL) flow sheets are used in many facilities by the nursing assistants to sign off by the end of their shift the activities of daily living that were completed for each resident. Some facilities are now discontinuing the use of these flow sheets, since there are no federal requirements mandating their use. Even though there is no federal requirement for these sheets, some states may require ADL documentation.

Due to time constraints, issues with illiteracy and language barriers of nursing assistants, the completion of these daily records are often found lacking. Therefore, some facilities are investing in computerized programs with kiosks that nurse assistants can utilize to document ADL care that utilize pictures of activities that can be clicked. However, if a facility utilizes these forms, it is expected that the documentation will be complete and accurate.

B. Medication Administration Records (MARs)

All facilities should have MARs to record all medication administered to a resident. This includes routine as well as PRN (as needed) medication. Every time a medication is administered, the nurse should initial the corresponding box on the MAR. If a routine medication is not given for any reason this box should be initialed and then circled with the explanation of the reason it was not given and recorded on the reverse side of the MAR. When a PRN medication is given, the reason is to be documented, generally on the back of the MAR, followed by a response to the medication, e.g., "complaining of a headache, Tylenol given per physician's order, resident stated relief in one-half hour."

C. Treatment and Administration Records (TARs)

All facilities should have TARs to record treatments provided to that resident. This includes routine as well as PRN (as needed) treatments. Every time a treatment is completed, the nurse should initial the corresponding box on the TAR. If a routine treatment is not performed for any reason the box should be initialed and circled with an explanation of why it was not provided and recorded on the reverse side of the TAR. When a PRN treatment is given, the reason should be documented, generally on the back of the TAR along with a response to the treatment, e.g., "Complaining of an itching on bilateral arms and legs, Sarna lotion applied per order, resident received instant relief."

D. Wound Flow Records

Most facilities use flow sheets for significant wounds including pressure ulcers. If the facility does not use flow sheets, this information should be documented in the nursing progress notes. These sheets or the documentation should be updated weekly and follow the National Pressure Ulcer Advisory Panel (NPUAP) guidelines.[34] The information should include:

- type of wound,
- location of wound,
- measurements of wound—length × width × depth,
- description and type of tissue of the wound bed,
- description of the tissue surrounding the wound,
- presence or absence of any drainage, to include a description of the drainage (viscosity, color, odor, amount),
- presence or absence of pain,
- presence or absence of signs and symptoms of infection, and
- overall status, whether the wound is improving, deteriorating, or status quo.

For additional information on pressure ulcers, refer to Chapter 26, *Skin Trauma*, and Chapter 27, *Controversies in Skin Trauma*.

E. Meal Intake

Nursing homes are required to monitor the nutritional status of residents, but there is, at least at the federal level, no requirement to monitor meal consumption percentages.

TIP: Most facilities monitor meal intake on residents who are at nutritional risk, who are new admissions, or who have weight issues. Other facilities record the meal percentage intake for all residents.

In a Virginia case, the plaintiff's decedent was admitted to the defendant's nursing home with heart problems, diabetes, peripheral vascular disease and issues with nutrition and dehydration. The plaintiff claimed the death was unavoidable due to the decedent's pre-existing condition. The defendant disputed the cause of death listed on the death certificate—dehydration. The defendant claimed that the death was due to heart failure. The plaintiff claimed that the facility staff did not properly record intake and output and those records that were available indicated that output far exceeded intake for the ten days prior to death. The plaintiff also claimed that when the decedent was hospitalized on previous occasions, he had been dehydrated on admission. The nursing home's records failed to record implementation of various treatments and medication orders. These records also included notes regarding care when the decedent was not at the facility and even after his death. An $850,000 verdict was returned.[35]

F. Behavior Monitoring

Facilities are required to monitor the patterns of residents with behavior issues. Many of these residents are prescribed mood-altering medications to control this behavior. The type of behavior exhibited, the triggers (if known), frequency, and the types of interventions used to alter that behavior need to be documented. The majority of facilities use flow sheets, while others may document in the progress notes.

G. Bowel Movements

Virtually all nursing homes monitor and document residents' bowel movements. This allows staff to intervene appropriately to prevent, to the extent possible, any untoward effects from constipation. If not monitored and if appropriate interventions are not taken, a resident can acquire a fecal impaction. This is considered a sentinel event. A "sentinel health event" is a quality indicator that represents a significant occurrence that should be selected as a concern, even if it applies to only one or a few residents. This translates to a further review of a sentinel event when the facility has a certification survey.

12.12 Ancillary Services Documentation
A. Interdisciplinary Care Planning Meetings

When the team gets together to discuss the status of the resident, specific care planning meeting notes may be generated, as well as records of communications with family members. The family member or designated responsible party should be invited to these meetings. If they were there, their signatures should be on the sign-in sheet and if the family cannot attend, the facility should contact them by phone, e-mail or letter to give the updated information. This should also be documented in the record by the MDS coordinator, Director of Nursing or social worker.

B. Laboratory Results and Diagnostic Studies

Blood and urine tests are performed periodically. X-rays may be performed in the event the resident falls or develops respiratory symptoms, or for other reasons. In comparison to hospital charts, this section of the medical record may be thinner. Also, it sometimes takes a longer period of time to obtain routine labs or radiological services if not ordered stat. This is because nursing facilities may only have lab pick dates two to three times per week and receive mobile radiology services versus sending the resident to the hospital. Even when nursing facilities are located next to a hospital or connected with a hospital group, this does not always result in fast service. It is very common for nursing facilities to date, time and initial when lab results or radiological services are phoned or faxed to the physician. This information should be recorded in the nursing progress notes, but sometimes is recorded only on the result. Some services are set up with the results being sent directly to the physician's office with a copy sent to the nursing facility. It is important to ask for the facility policy or protocol regarding how results are handled when reviewing the record if there is a question or concern about timeliness of getting the order completed or about notification of the physician.

C. Physical, Recreational, Speech, and Occupational Therapy

The initial assessment and notations regarding therapy provided (if any) are documented by the therapists. The format for charting usually includes the initial assessment and a record of ongoing treatments based on assessed needs, resident participation, and physician approval orders. It is important for the therapists to record their visits to residents receiving skilled care. Therapists document in minutes to be included in the MDS and for billing purposes. If residents no longer meet the skilled criteria for therapies but could benefit from an additional maintenance program, they will be turned over to the restorative nursing program. This program is overseen by a licensed nurse. Certified nurse assistants with special training deliver the restorative plan of care and document the resident's participation.

D. Respiratory Therapy

Documentation of treatment by respiratory therapists may be included in the medical record if the facility employs or contacts with the therapists. Generally this is seen in facilities that provide ventilator care and may also include administration of nebulizer treatments and multiple dose inhalers. However, most licensed nurses administer respiratory treatments and will document this on the treatment sheet.

E. Graphic Records

Vital signs (temperature, pulse, respirations, blood pressure, weight) are recorded on admission to the facility and then may be infrequently documented thereafter. The weight is usually recorded monthly; it may be on the nurse assistant care form or found under the dietary section of a record. Most vital signs are not recorded in the typical graph seen in hospital charts. Instead, they are usually recorded in columns. If weights or blood pressures are ordered daily or weekly, they may be found on medication or treatment sheets, especially if coordinated with medications.

TIP: Thoroughly search the records for weight and vital sign documentation before assuming it is not present.

F. Consents

The facility may use forms to document immunizations, side rail use, permission or refusal to use restraints, photo imaging and other types of consents. It is important to review who signed the consents if it is not the resident, and if the individual actually has the legal authority to sign. The facility staff is responsible for determining and adhering to wishes of the resident regarding end of life care, termination of life support, and cardiopulmonary resuscitation.

In a Florida case, the plaintiff's decedent, age ninety-two, suffered from dementia and lived in a nursing home. At the time of the woman's admission to the home, she provided a copy of her living will and advanced directive, which included directions not to resuscitate her when she was in the end stage of her illness. The decedent later became non-communicative and suffered from multiple seizures. When she became unresponsive, the paramedics were called. Because there was no do not resuscitate order in the chart, the paramedics resuscitated her and transferred her to the hospital, where she was placed on a ventilator for several days before her death. The plaintiff claimed the nursing home was negligent for failure to comply with the decedent's end-of-life instructions by failing to put a do not resuscitate order in the chart. A $150,000 verdict was reached.[36]

G. Transfer Forms

A form should be filled out when the resident is transferred from a hospital to the facility or vice versa. On admission, this document generally includes ADL information, medications, treatments and any follow-up appointments. Upon discharge, it includes why the resident is being sent to the hospital or home (with or without services), medications, treatments, follow-up appointments, and contact numbers of the primary physician and nursing facility should there be any problems.

12.13 Physician Documentation

Chapter 21, *Physician Documentation in Hospitals and Nursing Homes*, addresses some of the components of medical documentation about residents. This section covers history and physicals, progress notes and orders.

A. History and Physical

The initial history and physical is typically handwritten by the physician and may be quite brief in comparison to the history and physical written when a resident is admitted to the hospital.

B. Progress Notes

Federal regulations govern the provision of physician services. A regulation states that a physician must personally approve in writing a recommendation that an individual be admitted to a facility. Each resident must remain under the care of a physician. It further states that the facility must ensure that: (1) the medical care of each resident is supervised by a physician; and (2) another physician supervises the medical care of residents when the attending physician is unavailable. The physician must make visits. The physician must (1) review the resident's total program of care, including medications and treatments, at each visit; (2) write, sign and date progress notes at each visit; and (3) sign and date all orders.[34]

There may be additional physician service requirements per state licensing requirements regarding who qualifies under physician services and the frequency of visits.

It is quite common for the physician to see the resident only once a month, or every two months unless the nurse notifies the physician of a problem that requires a visit. A physician may designate an advanced practice nurse or physician assistant to see the resident after the initial history and physical. A resident should be seen every thirty days for the first ninety days following admission and every sixty days thereafter. Depending on state regulations, the physician can designate physician extenders for every other visit thereafter. However, this does not prohibit a physician from seeing the resident if a condition necessitates it or if a resident, family, facility staff, or covering practitioner requests the physician to come to the facility. The physician may not routinely see the resident on a weekly basis. Therefore, it is not uncommon to find sparse physician progress notes.

C. Orders

There are federal guidelines that govern the way physicians prepare orders in a nursing home. C.F.R. § 483.20 (a)[37] states that at the time each resident is admitted, the facility must have physician orders for immediate care. C.F.R. § 483.40 (b)[38] states that the physician must (3) sign and date all orders. There may be additional physician service requirements, per state licensing requirements. For example, some states require that telephone orders be signed within a certain time frame or that transfer orders be verified by the facility if the discharge physician is not the same as the admitting physician or her partner(s).

Different types of orders exist. *Standing orders* are used by some facilities for routine matters, e.g., milk of magnesia for constipation, wound care protocols, or routine laboratory studies. Even though these orders may be "standing" and signed by the medical director or attending physician, before execution of an order a nurse must notify the physician and write a telephone order for her to sign. Currently most facilities are doing away with standing orders and placing any PRN (as needed) orders on the monthly physician order sheet. *Monthly physician orders* are provided for ongoing needs for a resident, e.g, routine medications, wound or respiratory treatments, or routine laboratory work. These orders should be reviewed, signed, and dated monthly by the attending physician.

Verbal or telephone orders are given by a physician to a licensed professional, e.g., registered nurses, licensed practical nurses, or licensed therapists. These orders are written by the person who receives them, and the physician signs and dates the order at a later time. The initial orders provided by the physician may be handwritten or typed. Many facilities have moved to computer documentation of physician orders, resulting in orders that are printed each month and signed by the doctor. The physician must sign these orders. Telephone orders are handwritten by nurses and then signed by the physician. Orders may also be faxed to the facility from the doctor's office.

All physicians' orders should include the resident's name, the date the order was written, the date the physician signed the order and, if it is a verbal order, the name of the person who received the order. Medication orders should include the name of the medication, the dosage of the medication, the frequency and route of administration, the medical reason for the order, and a correlating diagnosis for that particular medication. Certain orders also will need an assigned time period, e.g., antibiotics, and narcotics.

Treatment orders should include the type of the treatment, generic or brand name of needed treatment, the location for the treatment, the duration, when indicated, the medical indication for the treatment and the frequency of the treatment. Orders for tests such as laboratory studies, x-rays, and special services must specify medical necessity and frequency.

TIP: Federal regulations require that the physician be notified promptly of diagnostic test results. The facility should have specific policies and procedures regarding what information can be faxed versus what should be called to the physician. It is common for physicians to initial the laboratory printout to indicate that it has been seen.

D. Consultations

Consultants commonly document on a specific consultation note when the resident is visited. However, their documentation is sometimes found within the regular physician progress notes as a consultant note. If the resident goes out of the facility for a consult, a form is sent with the resident for the physician to complete. Often physicians do not complete the form but send the dictated notes to the facility. The nurse should document if the resident does not return with a summary of the visit. Podiatrists, consultant pharmacists, wound care specialists, psychiatrists, and dentists are common consultants.

12.14 Medicare Documentation

When a resident is admitted to a facility for the purpose of receiving skilled nursing services, a physician order and a completed certification form are required. In order to receive certified skilled care services, the resident must be receiving services by licensed therapists and registered nurses participating in the care. In some states, specially trained licensed practical or vocational nurses who pass certification can perform some intravenous care and treatment. However, if this occurs in the absence of training or is not allowed, a Medicare violation could be alleged. The medical record should reflect that observation, services, and assessments were delivered in accordance with the physician orders and higher level of care. For additional specifics, review the State Operations Manual (SOM).[39]

12.15 Discharge Documentation

Discharge documentation may be a dictated, or more commonly a handwritten, document which includes entries from several types of professionals: the physician, nurse, speech and recreational therapists, social services, nutritionist, and so on. The inclusion of several professionals' documentation in the discharge summary sets this document apart from an acute care medical record where typically only the physician documents the discharge summary when a resident leaves a hospital.

A resident may be discharged for several reasons from the nursing home facility.[40] They are as follows:

- the safety of individuals in the facility is endangered,
- the facility cannot meet the resident's needs,
- the health of individuals in the facility would otherwise be endangered,
- the resident's condition has improved to the point of no longer needing care provided by the facility,
- the resident failed after reasonable and appropriate notice to pay for a stay at the facility, or
- the facility ceases to operate.

In any of these situations, a discharge summary recapitulating the resident's stay should be found within the medical record.[39]

The discharge summary must also include a final summary of the resident's status to include items in the comprehensive assessment at the time of discharge. The summary is available for release to authorized persons and agencies with the consent of the resident or legal representative. This should be done to ensure that appropriate discharge planning and communication of necessary information are relayed to the continuing provider. In addition, a post-discharge plan of care must be developed with participation of the resident and family member(s) that will assist the resident to adjust to his new living environment.[41]

The care plan part of the discharge summary should reflect some forethought about the resident's anticipated needs early enough to address adequately the discharge needs. If family members need instruction or training there should be facility documentation to support that it was done and the effectiveness. If additional resources are needed after discharge, these should be addressed and the family assisted in the location and coordination of services if necessary.

12.16 Careless Documentation

Misleading or inaccurate documentation may occur when the staff is careless in documentation. Careless documentation may occur when the individuals involved in documenting on a long-term-care medical record are inattentive to the task at hand. Examples of this type of documentation may include the following.

- The MDS is incomplete because the nurse fails to perform the assessment. This is detected by reviewing the MDS and comparing the information with the observations of the nursing and ancillary staff (therapists) and the physician.
- Quarterly reviews are overlooked. This is detected by calculating how many quarterly reviews should have been completed based on the admission date.
- The nurse documents that the resident is swallowing medications, yet the progress notes show that the resident is unresponsive.
- The record reflects that the resident continues on antibiotic therapy as ordered with signs and symptoms of adverse reaction but fails to include the actual assessment of whether the system is responding to the treatment.
- The resident is transferred to a hospital, yet the staff continues to document as if the resident were still in the nursing home. This type of careless documentation is easy to detect by comparing the date the resident was discharged and the dates on which entries are made in the medical record. Careless documentation betrays a lack of attention to detail or borders on tampering with the medical record, as discussed in Chapter 15, *Tampering with Medical Records*, in Volume I, and illustrated by cases within this chapter.

12.17 Summary

Residents may receive care in a variety of long-term care facilities, which ranges from custodial to subacute. The medical record forms the basis for the communication of important information about the resident to the staff, primary care team, regulatory bodies and reimbursement parties. The staff is expected to complete a variety of forms, some of which are specific only to long-term care. The reviewer must take into account that information may be located in common parts of the record. Therefore it is imperative to read every page before asserting that documentation is not there.

In addition, it is important to become familiar with the Code of Federal Regulations (CFR) which contains all of the federally mandated regulations that all facilities must comply with if the facility is to receive Medicare and Medicaid funding. It is also just as important to remember that if a facility is totally private pay, CFR and state regulations will apply only in relation to owning and operating requirements. However, private pay facilities should be delivering care based on current gerontological nursing standards.

Endnotes

1. http://www.alfa.org.

2. http://www.medicare.gov/LongTermCare/Static/Home. asp.

3. Laska, L. (Editor) "Failure to properly supervise woman of porch of facility," *Medical Malpractice Verdicts, Settlements, and Experts*, July 2009, pg. 30.

4. http://www.ahcancal.org/ncal/resources/Documents/2009_reg_review.pdf (accessed 10/19/09)

5. http://www.rules.state.ri.us/rules/released/pdf/DOH/DOH_2869.pdf Appendix C (accessed 07/23/09).

6. http://health.utah.gov/hflcra/forms/ALServicePlan.PDF (accessed 10/19/09)

7. http://www.medicare.gov/LongTermCare/Static/Home. asp.

8. http://health.usnews.com/articles/health/best-nursing-homes/2009/10/05/best-nursing-homes-rankings-honor-roll.html, (accessed 10/19/09)

9. AARP Across the States: Profiles of Long–Term Care and Independent Living, 2009

10. http://www.medicare.gov/LongTermCare/Static/Home. asp (accessed 10/19/09)

11. *Id.*

12. Levenson, S. "Subacute Settings: Making the Most of a New Model of Care." *Geriatrics*. 53 (7), July 1998, p. 69–74.

13. *Id.*

14. Andreola, N. and S. Pauly-O'Neill. "Subacute Care: Rising Star or Supernova?" *The Nursing Spectrum*. February 6, 1995, p. 4–7.

15. Micheletti, J. and T. Shlala. "Understanding and Operationalizing Subacute Services." *Nursing Management*. June 1995, p. 49–56.

16. Code of Federal Regulations 483.75 (1) (1).

17. Code of Federal Regulations 483.75 (1) (2).

18. Code of Federal Regulations 483.75 (1) (3) (4) (5).

19. 24. http://www.jointcommission.org.

20. Cavallaro, R., J. Newman, and P. Iyer. "Long-Term-Care Documentation" in Iyer, P. and N. Camp. *Nursing Documentation: A Nursing Process Approach.* Fourth Edition. Flemington, NJ: Med League Support Services, Inc. 2005.

21. http://www.cms.hhs.gov/quality/mds20.

22. *Id.*

23. *HCFA Resident Assessment Instrument Training Manual and Resource Guide.* American Health Care Association. Washington, D.C. 1990.

24. http://www.cms.hhs.gov/QualityInitiativesGenInfo/05_HowDataAreCollected.asp, accessed 10/19/09

25. HCFA Final Rule 1998 online.

26. http://www.cms.hhs.gov/Nursinghomequalityinits/25_NHQIMDS30.asp, accessed 10/19/09

27. *Id.*

28. *Id.*

29. Laska, L. "Failure to provide proper care for resident with history of falling blamed for hip fracture which led to pressure ulcers, leg contractures, infection, and urosepsis," *Medical Malpractice Verdicts, Settlements, and Experts*, January 2008, pg 27

30. Code of Federal Regulations 483.40.

31. Iyer, P. *The ABCs of Medical Abbreviations.* Flemington, NJ: Med League Support Services, Inc., 2009, www.medleague.com

32. Code of Federal Regulations 483.20.

33. Laska, L. "Failure to respond to resident's complaints of dizziness and nausea," Medical Malpractice Verdicts, Settlements, and Experts, March 2008, p. 35

34. http://www.npuap.org/, accessed 10/19/09

35. Laska, L. "Failure to properly care for resident blamed for death," *Medical Malpractice Verdicts, Settlements, and Experts*, March 2008, pg. 33

36. Laska, L. "Failure to place do not resuscitate directive in nursing home chart, *Medical Malpractice Verdicts, Settlements, and Experts*, February 2008, pg 30

37. See note 32.

38. Code of Federal Regulations 483.40 (b).

39. http://www.cms.hhs.gov/SurveyCertificationEnforcement

40. Code of Federal Regulations 483.10.

41. Code of Federal Regulations 483.20 (d) (3) (ii).

Additional Reading

Iyer, P. "Roots of Patient Injury" in Iyer, P., Levin, B., Ashton, K., and Powell, V. (Editors). *Nursing Malpractice.* Fourth Edition. Tucson, AZ: Lawyers & Judges Publishing Company, pre-publication (to be released 2010).

Braun, J., M. Lubin, and E. Allen. "Inside the Nursing Home" in Iyer, P. (Editor). *Nursing Home Litigation: Investigation and Case Preparation.* Second Edition. Tucson, AZ: Lawyers and Judges Publishing Company. 2006.

Chapter 13

Medical Surgical Records

Sally Russell, MSN, RN

13.1 Introduction

The practice of medical surgical nursing involves providing nursing care to patients from adolescence to old age, and in a variety of settings. These settings include (but are not limited to) acute and subacute facilities, ambulatory and outpatient areas, residential facilities, and skilled care facilities. Nurses working with this group of patients care for people with illnesses of multiple body systems, as many (if not most) of these patients will have more than one disease process occurring at the same time. For example, it is common for the medical surgical nurse to care for a patient who simultaneously has a respiratory and gastrointestinal disease. Medical surgical patients may range in age from twenty-one to over 100. The nursing unit may provide care to patients with a wide variety of medical or surgical problems. A patient who has had a hernia repaired may be in a two-bed room next to a patient with acute pancreatitis.

The staffing mix of a medical surgical hospital unit usually consists of a nurse manager (a registered nurse) and a complement of registered and practical nurses. Nurse technicians, called multi-skilled technicians or nurse's aides, are also found in some institutions as part of the staffing. A unit clerk (ward clerk or unit secretary) assists with answering phones and medical records assembly and management.

TIP: As the nursing shortage deepens, hospitals continue to struggle to provide adequate numbers of professional staff. The attorney should be alert to the background of nursing personnel (RN, LPN, aide) involved in providing care. Staffing records kept by nursing administration may be useful in some cases.

The nursing process is a primary structure for the framework for care. Refer to Chapter 15, *The Nursing Process and Nursing Records*, for an understanding of the nursing process. Assessments are essential and should be reflected in the ensuing plan of care. Given the fact that many hospitalized medical surgical patients have dysfunctions in more than one system simultaneously, the assessments of these people cannot always be focused on only one body system. Total head-to-toe assessments will be necessary (perhaps frequently during the admission).

Standards of care define the nursing profession's accountability to the public and the patient outcomes for which nurses are responsible.[1] The Academy of Medical Surgical Nurses' *Standards of Medical-Surgical Nursing Practice*[2] consists of "Standards of Care" and "Standards of Professional Performance." These are minimal standards for the medical surgical nurse, not maximum. Standards of care are not specific about such things as how often the vital signs should be taken for a specific diagnosis in the postoperative period as there are too many variables in the medical surgical patient for that to be possible. Documentation of patient care is driven by the "Standards of Care" which include assessment, diagnosis, outcome identification, planning, implementation, and evaluation. As minimal expectations of patient care, each of these components should be evident in documentation.

Assessments and documentation related to each body system are reviewed in the material that follows. There are also sections outlining information that should be evident when patients have common concerns and complications. Obviously not all the included symptoms or concerns will be evident in every patient. The text covers the major areas that nurses should consider when assessing the patient. Documentation of the care provided to some patients will include focused assessments on more than one, if not all, body systems.

When perusing charts for information about care given to the medical surgical patient, the reviewer should find that assessments and interventions were carried out as the patient needed—rather than on a scheduled routine only. Depending on the charting methods used, information may be scattered throughout the chart as opposed to being in a particular place.

TIP: Unfortunately, it is not as common for flow sheets and specific charting forms to be used on medical surgical units as it is in critical care areas. Before determining that an omission in charting has occurred, the entire medical record will need to be looked at for places that the medical surgical nurse has placed documentation.

13.2 Respiratory System

Respiratory diseases are common reasons for people to be admitted to medical surgical units. Respiratory complications are also common. Patients who should be observed closely for the development of respiratory complications include patients who are

- postoperative,
- affected by a compromised immune system,
- elderly, and
- on immune system suppressants such as steroids, anti-inflammatory, and chemotherapeutic drugs.

Documentation should reflect a concern for these potential complications, with increased assessments being made for respiratory abnormalities. Refer to Figure 13.1 for respiratory assessments.

The following interventions used in the care of these patients should be recorded:

- coughing and deep breathing exercises,
- use of incentive spirometers,
- respiratory treatments,
- ambulation,
- fluids,
- nutrition, and
- protection from exposure to infections (isolation if necessary).

Many of the patients found on medical surgical units are those with known respiratory diseases; the expected documentation should include assessments and nursing interventions. The following section discusses common respiratory pathologies. Medical surgical patients admitted to a hospital for something unrelated to the respiratory system may be at risk for respiratory complications, creating a need for specific assessments and interventions.

A. Chronic Obstructive Pulmonary Disease

Chronic obstructive pulmonary disease, or COPD, refers to a group of diseases that cause airflow blockage and breathing related problems. It includes emphysema, chronic bronchitis, and in some cases asthma.[3] Chronic emphysema may result in a "barrel chest," or an overinflation of the lungs which results in a round chest. Home oxygen use may become necessary. Chronic bronchitis results in the constant production of mucous, which needs to be raised and spit out, referred to in medical records as a "productive" cough. Asthma may lead to acute attacks, characterized by gasping for breath and high anxiety levels.

Respiratory Assessments

Assessments and potential findings include:

- **Lung sounds**—Look for documentation of those not heard before (crackles, rhonchi, wheezes, pleural friction rub, stridor).
- **Respiratory rate**—Normal adult values are 16-20.
- **Dyspnea (difficulty breathing) or tachypnea (rapid heart rate)**—The reviewer should be able to determine that these are new and not normal for this patient.
- **Cough**—If productive of sputum, the record should note when the cough is most prominent, the color of sputum, and whether coughing clears the sound. If fluid is noted with each cough, the type of fluid, color, amount, and consistency should be included in documentation.
- **Dyspnea**—How much activity it takes to cause dyspnea and what makes it ease should be noted. Also the nurse should note whether it has been increasingly a problem and over what period of time.
- **Pillows**—The chart should record how many pillows the patient needs to breathe comfortably while lying in bed, or the angle of the bed if the head of bed is elevated.
- **Cardiovascular**—Blood pressure, dysrhythmias (irregular heart rate), and perfusion of extremities should be documented.
- **Neurological**—As the brain is sensitive to decreasing levels of oxygen, changes in mentation will be an early clue to hypoxia. Assessments for decreasing level of consciousness, increasing irritability, and symptoms of cerebral hypoxia should be recorded. Increasing the available oxygen and assuring that the airway is clear are paramount.

Figure 13.1

The medical treatment plan may document the use of bronchodilators with steroids in addition to treatment measures already discussed. Respiratory therapy notes will record the use of inhalers or other treatments, along with an evaluation of effectiveness. Documentation should note any side effects of medications. Documentation of patient education is also essential. Nurses typically teach patients with respiratory illnesses about breathing techniques, how to use the inhalers, and lifestyle modifications necessary to manage the disease, especially if this is a new diagnosis.

Assessments of the respiratory, cardiovascular, and neurological systems should be documented. The respiratory and cardiovascular systems are interrelated, and a severe or chronic problem in one of the two will have inevitable effects on the other. The neurological system may consequently show dysfunction, especially in mentation, since the brain is very sensitive to oxygen deficit.

The medical records of a patient being treated for an acute worsening of COPD should note if heart failure was present. Hypertension and heart failure are not uncommon, especially in long-standing COPD. Heart sounds may be difficult to hear as the lung sounds will be so loud, but the effort should still be made and documented. Interventions for heart failure would include

- notifying the physician,
- elevating the head of the bed,
- decreasing fluid and sodium intake, and
- administering medications such as diuretics, cardiac glycosides, and antihypertensives.
  - *Diuretics* are used to decrease fluid volume in the body or blood stream and are commonly used to decrease the workload on the heart. Examples of these drugs are Lasix and Bumex.
  - *Cardiac glycosides*, such as digoxin or Lanoxin, decrease the workload of the heart by decreasing the rate and the contractility of the heart muscle and are commonly used for people with heart disease.
  - *Antihypertensives* are used to lower blood pressure and work in a variety of ways. (There are a number of classifications of this medication each working in different ways to lower blood pressure.)

Table 13.1
Commonly Used Medical Surgical Medications

Drug Classification	Example	Used for
Diuretic	Furosemide (Lasix®)	Decreasing fluid volume in the blood vessels
Cardiac glycoside	Digoxin (Lanoxin®)	Decrease the work load of the heart, decreasing heart rate
Antihypertensives Calcium channel blockers	Verapamil (Calan®)	Decreases blood pressure, decreases heart rate,increases vasodilation of arterial blood vessels
Beta blockers ACE (Angiotensin Converting Enzyme) Inhibitors	Propranolol (Inderal®) Captopril (Capoten®) Enalapril (Vasotec®)	Decreases blood pressure, decreases fluid volume
Narcotic analgesic	Morphine Sulfate	Decreases pain, increases venous dilation, decreasing blood return to heart

Anti-inflammatory
    Steroids
    Non-steroidal
	Corticosteroid (Cortone®)
	Ibuprofen
	Aspirin
		Decreases inflammation
		Decreases pain
		Decreases fever

Calcium Vitamin D analog	Calcium carbonate (Caltrate®) Doxercalciferol	Supplement for important body element Increases ability of body to absorb calcium
Anticoagulants	Warfarin sodium (Coumadin®) Heparin (Heparin®) Enoxaparin (Lovenox®)	Treat and prevent blood clots
Erythropoietin	Epoetin alpha (EPO®)	Stimulates red blood cell production—a natural protein produced in the kidneys

Refer to Table 13.1 for definitions of several commonly used medical surgical medications.

Medical records may note the presence of gastrointestinal complaints, such as constipation, especially if it is causing shortness of breath or dyspnea by placing pressure on the diaphragm. Interventions could include laxatives and increased oral or intravenous fluids. Neurological assessments and interventions should focus on the patient's thought processes and ability to comprehend information. Assessment of the patient for changes in mentation or irritability, which may indicate long-standing hypoxia (low oxygen level), should be noted in the documentation.

B. Tuberculosis

Tuberculosis is a continuing problem in health care even though at one point it looked like it would disappear. Not only did it not disappear, it has become resistant to multiple drugs, making it difficult to treat. Symptoms of tuberculosis include

- persistent productive cough,
- low grade fever,
- weight loss, and
- chills/night sweats.

TIP: Since multi-drug resistant strains are becoming more common, treatment will include giving drugs in varying combinations for longer periods of time. It is imperative that healthcare providers follow the CDC requirement of two negative sputum specimens prior to considering the patient noninfectious to others.

C. Complications
1. Pneumonia

Pneumonia is a complication of particular concern to the elderly, those with immune deficiencies and those who have had surgery. Continuing surveillance of patients at high risk is essential. Specific information about a cough should be documented, and if the cough is productive, information about the consistency, color, and amount of sputum should be evident. Fever and chills are common. These symptoms may not be present in patients with immune systems that are weakened by age or physiology. Complaints of fatigue and weakness should be noted—including how much activity precipitated the complaints or symptoms. Entries that document the changes in the bronchial breath sounds would be signs that the caregivers recognized the potential of this complication occurring. Noting absence of breath sounds could indicate that the lower airways of the lungs were full of fluid or exudates.

Treatment for pneumonia includes antibiotics and fluids. An assessment for the effectiveness of, and sensitivity to, the antibiotics should be made and documented when the medication is started as well as during the course of treatment.

2. Pneumothorax

Pneumothorax is a condition in which the lung has collapsed either because of air entering through a hole in the chest or a hole in the lung allowing air to collect in the pleural space. Tachypnea (fast respiratory rate) and tachycardia (fast heart rate) are the hallmark symptoms of pneumothorax. Assessments of heart and lung sounds should be done frequently if pneumothorax is a potential or suspected complication.

Diminished movement of chest wall should be observed for and reported if noticed. Breath sounds on the affected side should be evaluated. Decreased or absent breath sounds would be expected. Pallor is indicative of hypoxia and should be documented if present. Cyanosis would be a sign of very severe and long-standing hypoxia. The medical record may refer to the patient as having blue lips or fingertips, two areas where cyanosis is commonly noted. Collections of free air in the tissue, known as subcutaneous emphysema, may be found around the clavicle or jaw line as the free air in the pleural cavity rises. In addition to palpating the clavicular and jaw line areas, the nurse or physician may record that palpation around chest tubes and tracheostomy tubes identified the presence of free air.

Indications of a tension pneumothorax that should be found in the documentation include

- hypotension,
- distended neck veins, and
- point of maximal impulse (the place on the chest wall where the heart beat can be felt) having migrated from the normal palpation area (5th/6th intercostals or between the ribs space in the left midclavicular line).

Changes in the location of the point of maximal impulse should not only be documented but also immediately reported.

Chest tubes (abbreviated as CT) may be inserted to expand the lungs to treat a pneumothorax. The tubes are connected to a drainage device that exerts suction and collects fluid and air. The nurse should assess for and document the presence of lung sounds. As the lung re-expands, air will be heard throughout lung fields. Positioning the patient in an upright position to facilitate reinflation of the lung is important. The medical record may note that the patient was positioned in "High Fowlers," or the "HOB" (head of bed) was elevated.

3. Respiratory failure

Symptoms of impending respiratory failure may include

- increasing disorientation to an end point of a coma,
- increasing dyspnea (difficulty breathing) and shortness of breath,
- tachypnea (rapid breathing),
- increased blood pressure, and
- tachycardia (rapid heart rate).

Treatment is aimed at supporting the respiratory and ventilatory effort. Recognition of impending respiratory failure is important, and documentation should include those methods used to facilitate respirations, including oxygen, positioning, and alerting others to the need for life support.

A forty-year-old man was involved in a motorcycle/car collision in which he was thrown from the motorcycle. He sustained a brain injury. After almost three weeks he was sent to rehabilitation. His arms, legs, and chest were restrained because medical personnel feared his movement could remove a tracheostomy tube and a feeding tube. His jaw was wired shut. A sitter was with him constantly to make sure he did not pull out his tubes. On one day the plaintiff's breathing became labored and his color changed. The sitter put on the call light to get help. It took several minutes for a nurse to arrive. The nurse tried to suction his trach tube; it was quickly determined that his tube was plugged. Before a physician could arrive the patient turned blue. He was resuscitated but suffered brain damage. A $2.1 million verdict was returned.[4]

The medical record would have shown the sequence of events leading up to the arrest. Appropriate and timely intervention is needed in the face of a deteriorating situation.

4. Atelectasis

Atelectasis is a collapse of the small alveoli (the airways from which oxygen moves into the blood stream).

TIP: Any postoperative patient who cannot ventilate adequately enough is at risk for atelectasis.

As atelectasis can be a risk factor for respiratory failure, prevention strategies for atelectasis are imperative. Symptoms are

- low grade fever,
- inspiratory crackles,
- tachycardia and tachypnea, and
- diminished or absent breath sounds over those alveoli that are atelectic.

Treatment includes having the patient take deep breaths, requiring the use of incentive spirometry, or administering ventilatory treatments.

5. Pulmonary embolism

Pulmonary embolism is a blockage of the vessels carrying blood to the lungs. The most common causes are blood clots originating from the large veins in the legs, arms, right side of the heart, or pelvis. A second common cause is emboli created from fatty marrow from long bones that have been fractured or opened for hip replacements. Those at risk should be closely observed for the following symptoms:

- hypotension,
- dyspnea with tachypnea,
- substernal chest pain,
- complaints of anxiety or feelings of impending doom, and
- hypoxemia (decreased oxygen levels in the blood stream).

Symptoms can be subtle and confused with other conditions. Death may rapidly occur when large blood vessels in the lungs are obstructed, causing lung infarction (loss of blood supply). A less lethal potential complication of pulmonary embolism is right sided heart failure (cor pulmonale) because of the increased pressure the right ventricle has to work against.

Treatment includes support of respiratory effort—oxygen, positioning, and potentially even mechanical ventilation. Pharmaceutical treatment will depend on the type of embolism. Heparin and Coumadin are used for blood clot emboli, for instance, while anti-inflammatory drugs may be used if the blockage is caused by a fat emboli.

The major way to improve mortality caused by pulmonary embolism is to prevent the clots from occurring. Medical surgical records should include documentation that preventative measures were used.

- Leg exercises (pointing the toes towards the ceiling and the floor).
- Sequential compression leg boots which inflate and deflate to stimulate circulation.
- Support stockings, called antiembolism or TEDs.
- Anticoagulants—Heparin, Lovenox, Fragmin, Coumadin, Aspirin.
- Placement of a filter in the vena cava.
- Early ambulation after surgery.

The importance of the medical record to document the carrying out of orders was a crucial factor in the following case.

A Maryland case involved a fifty-nine-year-old woman who underwent bladder suspension surgery at St. Joseph Medical Center. After surgery, sequential compression devices were placed, and an order was given that the woman be walked around the hospital and that the compression devices be used when she was not walking. On the day after surgery the compression devices were taken off for the patient to use the bathroom and were never replaced. The plaintiff claimed that the patient was not ambulated or placed in the devices for the remainder of her three-day stay in the hospital. Within days of returning home the woman died of pulmonary thrombo-embolism due to deep vein thrombosis. The defendant maintained that the decedent was ambulated and that the compression devices were used, although the nurses could not recollect their actions. The medical records did not support the defense's contentions. The defense also claimed that the deep vein thrombosis developed after discharge. The jury returned a $1,750,000 verdict.[5]

Refer to Chapter 25, *Respiratory Care Records*, for more information.

Cardiovascular Assessments

Assessments and potential findings include:

- **Heart sounds**—Note documentation of those not heard before (new rhythm, extra heart sound).
- **Blood pressure**—Changes in blood pressure should be evident by reviewing the recorded results.
- **Medications**—The chart should record appropriate/safe dose, desired effects, signs of adverse reactions, or reactions that indicate interactions between drugs.
- **IV drips**—Look for appropriate/safe dose, desired effects, and signs of adverse reactions.
- **Electrolyte and enzyme levels**—Were they reported to the physician by the nurse if abnormal, and was assessment done to determine effects of abnormal levels?
- **Oxygenation level**—The chart should document arterial blood gas and pulse oximetry levels, changes in color of mucous membranes in the mouth, and assessment of the fingernails for evidence of inadequate oxygenation. Be aware that cyanosis (a bluish color indicating inadequate oxygenation) is a very late sign of this condition when in fact a pale color to the skin and mucous membranes should have been noted much earlier because that is a much earlier sign of inadequate oxygenation.
- **Complaints of chest pain, fatigue, shortness of breath**—Were they followed up?
- **Dependent edema** (swelling in areas of the body that are in a dependent position such as the sacrum, arms, and legs)—The chart should note the location, severity, and resolution of edema.
- **Urinary output**—A decrease will be first clue to decreasing cardiac output. Was the decrease recognized, documented, and reported?

Figure 13.2

13.3 Cardiovascular System

Heart and blood pressure related problems are frequent reasons for patients to be admitted to medical surgical units but may also be complications that arise from other causes. Postoperative myocardial infarctions and hypertension because of severe pain may occur. The medical records of the patient with a disorder of the cardiovascular system should contain information from the cardiovascular assessments. Figure 13.2 displays elements of cardiovascular assessments. Cardiovascular dysfunction is commonly seen on medical surgical units.

A. Congestive Heart Failure (CHF)

Congestive heart failure caused by left-sided heart failure is often a complication of hypertension or myocardial infarction, both of which, as mentioned before, are common reasons for patients to be admitted to medical surgical units. Symptoms of this type of CHF would include

- anxiety,
- shortness of breath,
- dyspnea,
- tachycardia and tachypnea,
- jugular distension (enlarged neck veins),
- oliguria (drop in urine output), and
- abnormal heart sounds.

The nurse caring for this patient must always be aware of the potential for pulmonary edema and perform astute respiratory and cardiovascular assessments.

Treatment is aimed at decreasing the workload of the left ventricle. Pharmacologic treatment would consist of drugs that decrease the amount of fluid with which the heart must work. Such medications include diuretics and venous dilators.

TIP: Evaluation of the patient should focus on the effectiveness or side effects of the medications, and determine if the left heart failure is worsening.

Right-sided heart failure is usually a complication of pulmonary hypertension (pulmonary emboli or COPD). Symptoms to observe are

- anxiety,
- anorexia (loss of appetite),
- nausea/vomiting,
- dependent edema (collecting in the sacrum, arms, or legs),
- liver engorgement or tenderness, and
- ascites (collection of fluid in the abdominal cavity).

Treatment of right sided failure should be aimed at decreasing the symptoms of the right sided heart failure as well as clearing the obstruction to forward flow of blood. Diuretics to decrease dependent edema will also treat the cause of the pulmonary hypertension.

B. Peripheral Vascular Disease

Peripheral vascular disease can be either arterial or venous in nature. Those with diabetes are particularly prone to peripheral vascular disease, and careful assessments and interventions are imperative. Documentation of assessments along with evaluations of the outcomes should be evident in the patient's chart. Peripheral vascular disease can occur in the arms and the legs but is more common in the legs.

Arterial vascular disease will present in a variety of ways but usually includes

- pale, waxy, whiteness of the extremity,
- numbness and pain,
- decreased hair growth of that extremity, and
- pain when the legs are elevated.

People with arterial occlusion or perfusion problems will prefer their legs in a dependent position, such as hanging off of the mattress or on the floor when the patient is sitting in a chair. Refer to Chapter 27, *Controversies in Skin Trauma*, for more information on ulcers caused by either arterial or venous vascular disease.

Treatment may be aimed at removing the obstruction to arterial blood flow. If the problem is a blood clot, and a drug to dissolve the clot is given, assessment must then include observing for bleeding from other sites. If the obstruction is caused by plaque formation, treatment may be surgical. Unrelieved obstruction can result in tissue death. For example, the medical record may include notations that the patient's toes turned black due to gangrene. When blood flow to a larger area of the foot is stopped, the physician may describe the foot as "demarcating" or developing into two sections—dead tissue below a level of healthy tissue.

Surgical treatment may include performance of a bypass. Commonly a blood vessel is used to bypass the obstructed area. Postoperative assessments would include

- taking vital signs,
- assuring that no drop in blood pressure occurs which could cause collapse of graft material,
- determining if blood flow is adequate as measured by palpating the pulse or using a Doppler machine to hear the pulse, and

Table 13.2
Peripheral Pulses Locations

Artery	Location
Carotid	Side of the neck
Brachial	Inner elbow
Radial	Wrist
Femoral	Groin between leg and trunk
Popliteal	Behind the knee
Posterior tibialis	Behind the ankle
Dorsalis pedis or pedal	Top of the foot

- assuring that compression of the bypass graft does not occur from tight clothes.

Refer to Table 13.2 for the locations of pulses.

TIP: Pulse quality is recorded on a scale of 1+ to 4+. Normal is 2+. A pulse of 4+ is bounding or full. A pulse of 1+ is a bit diminished.

If bypass grafting is unsuccessful, an amputation may be needed. The patient will likely undergo a series of fittings for prosthetic devices until the stump reaches its final dimensions. A great deal of patient education is necessary prior to the patient being released, and documentation must include what was taught and the patient's response to that education.

Venous difficulties in the legs are common in people who stand for long periods of time, such as those who work on factory lines. Symptoms that would be noted would be

- rubor (a reddish purple color, especially when the legs are in a dependent position), brownish pigmentation around the ankles, and
- an aching sensation if the legs are dependent. (These people prefer to have their legs elevated.)

Treatment will include those actions that will encourage draining of legs. The medical record should show evidence that the patient was taught about using compression stockings, elevating legs, and that avoiding standing for long periods of time is important.

C. Hypertension

Hypertension is defined by the blood pressure. Two numbers make up the blood pressure. As blood is pumped through the body, it exerts pressure on the walls of the arteries. The systolic blood pressure is the pressure against these walls when the heart contracts, and the diastolic blood pressure is the pressure when the heart relaxes. Normal blood pressure is below 120/80. High blood pressure, also called hypertension, occurs when the systolic pressure is consistently over 140 mm Hg, or the diastolic blood pressure is consistently over 90 mm Hg.[6] Hypertension is characterized as primary or secondary. Primary hypertension, also known as essential hypertension, is a chronic disease. Secondary hypertension is caused by inadequate pain medication, anxiety, or another disease. Hypertension is a common phenomenon on medical surgical units. Healthcare providers should recognize that even those people with primary hypertension can experience an elevation in blood pressure from pain or increased fluids.

Blood pressures are recorded in several places within the medical record. They may be found on the

- frequent vital sign sheets,
- graphic records,
- physician progress notes,
- fetal monitoring strips,
- anesthesia preoperative assessment,
- anesthesia intra-operative records,
- post-anesthesia recovery room records,
- same day surgery records,
- nursing admission assessment,
- nursing flowcharts,
- nursing narrative notes,
- home care nursing assessment,
- clinic visit records,
- physician office records,
- history and physical,
- emergency medical technician's notes, or
- triage record or emergency department records.

TIP: In some cases, the recorded value is taken by the person who entered it into the chart. In other cases, the blood pressure may have been taken by one person, such as an aide or nurse, and repeated within the chart by someone else, such as a physician. While the nurse may delegate to an aide the act of taking blood pressure, the nurse is still responsible for taking action on changes in blood pressure that need to be addressed.

In the hospital setting, the nurse should take the blood pressure frequently in the postoperative time period, document what was found, and note the abnormalities. Many hospitals define the frequency of vital sign assessment following surgery. Changes that would signify bleeding (dropping blood pressure, rising pulse) should stimulate further evaluation.

Pain should be assessed, especially if no other cause of hypertension is evident. An assessment for other symptoms should also be completed especially if a significant, quick rise in pressure occurs, or the patient complains of a headache, an increase in urinary output, or blurred vision. Treatment is always aimed at reducing blood pressure. Positioning to increase the patient's comfort may assist. Drugs to reduce blood pressure include diuretics, calcium channel blockers, beta blockers, and ACE inhibitors. Assessment of the effectiveness of the drugs, the existence of side effects, and drug interactions is paramount.

D. Complications

The following are some of the cardiovascular complications that may occur on a medical surgical unit. Liability issues arise when these crises are not promptly recognized and treated.

1. Myocardial infarction

Myocardial infarction, particularly in the postoperative time period, occurs when a portion of the heart muscle dies due to interruption of blood supply, often by a clot. Symptoms that should be noted in the documentation include

- complaints of chest pain (often described as feeling like an elephant is standing on the chest),
- fatigue,
- shortness of breath,
- changes in blood pressure, and
- an increase in pulse rate.

In many cases the pain may be subtle or even completely absent (called a "silent heart attack"), especially in the elderly and diabetics. Often, the pain radiates from the chest to the arms or shoulder; neck, teeth, or jaw; abdomen or back. Sometimes, the pain is only felt in one of these other locations.[7] Although the medical surgical nurse does not make a medical diagnosis, the nurse is expected to recognize these symptoms as being of concern. Prompt notification of a physician is required. The nurse is expected to continue to check the skin color and the patient's mentation level.

Diagnostic tests may be performed to rule out a myocardial infarction. These may include the following:

- arterial blood gases and/or pulse oxygenation levels to evaluate oxygenation,
- electrocardiogram to look for characteristic changes,
- enzyme levels, for instance, troponin,

- serum myoglobin (a protein released into the blood when the heart muscle is damaged),
- sodium (an increase would cause fluid retention),
- potassium (an increase will cause muscular irritability, including cardiac; a decrease will cause loss of muscle tone with cardiac standstill when potassium less than 2.5 mEq),
- calcium (a decrease will cause hyperactive deep tendon reflexes and increased bleeding), and
- magnesium (a decrease will cause muscular irritability, while an increase will cause loss of muscle tone from sedation).

With 25 percent of the cardiac output being delivered to the kidneys, a decrease in the urinary output occurs when the cardiac output decreases, so urinary output is monitored. Oxygen is typically administered, the head of the bed is elevated, and analgesics are given. Documentation about desired effect or signs of adverse reactions to medications should be noted. Medications may be administered by intravenous infusions. (Medical records refer to this as an "IV drip.") The rate of the IV infusion should be documented.

Treatment is aimed at managing pain, reducing the workload on the heart, and preventing fatal arrhythmias. Patient anxiety can add to the stress on the heart. Nurse's notes may describe interventions used to reduce the stress of the patient and family.

> In a Texas case, *Robinson v. Lawrence Quan MD and Karunakar Reddy MD*, a fifty-six-year-old woman was admitted to the hospital with difficulty breathing and chest pains. She underwent serial EKGs and enzyme studies. She went into respiratory arrest eight days after admission and died after transfer to another hospital. The plaintiffs claimed that EKGs indicated a myocardial infarction which the defendants failed to diagnose or treat. The plaintiffs also alleged inadequate monitoring. The hospital settled before trial for a confidential amount. The jury returned a defense verdict as to the physicians.[8]

TIP: Recognition of the symptoms of myocardial infarction and notifying the medical care team are important to a positive outcome.

---

2. Hemorrhage or hypovolemia

A failure to detect or report signs of hemorrhage may result in death. This is of particular concern when the patient has undergone trauma or surgery. The medical team is expected to investigate symptoms consistent with bleeding. Symptoms commonly noted are

- increased pulse rate,
- increased respiratory rate,
- decreased systolic blood pressure,
- pale skin,
- decreased level of consciousness, and
- decreased urinary output.

When a loss of blood, especially an acute loss, occurs, many assessments and interventions are necessary. An assessment of the level of consciousness should be documented. Monitoring of the vital signs with recognition of changes that may be indicative of fluid loss is essential. The nurse is expected to assess the fluid volume level by looking at the hematocrit, specific gravity, and serum osmolarity when available and notifying the medical care team of abnormal results.

> A woman who underwent a laparoscopic assisted vaginal hysterectomy was given Morphine about twenty-five minutes after she was extubated. Her respiration was assisted by an oxygen mask. About forty-five minutes later her blood pressure began to decline. It dropped to 86/51 over the next two and one half hours. A nurse eventually contacted a gynecologist to report the low blood pressure but no action was taken until the gynecologist received a second report about the low blood pressure two hours later. When the gynecologist examined the patient she was drowsy and unresponsive. Epinephrine was administered and a blood test revealed a dangerously low hemoglobin that was almost incompatible with life. Exploratory surgery showed there were two bleeding blood vessels. The damage was repaired but the plaintiff suffered brain damage. The hospital was the only defendant at trial and it conceded liability. A $9 million settlement was reached.[9]

Treatment is primarily aimed at decreasing the blood/fluid loss. IV fluids and blood transfusions, oxygen, and vital sign monitoring are necessary along with treating the hemorrhage site.

3. Arterial blockage

A blockage of an artery can occur in any body organ. Specific assessments for specific blockages are listed below.

Neurological Assessments

Assessments and potential findings include:

- **Level of consciousness**—The brain is very sensitive to declining levels of oxygenation. The change in status and cause (if determined) should be noted. The term may be referred to as LOC and is often charted as "A&Ox3" or "patient alert and oriented x3." This refers to the patient being oriented to person (knows who he is), place (where he is), and time (the current date or year). "A&Ox4" refers to the patient being able to recall the events leading up to the present. There should be clear documentation of confusion and level of function.
- **Glasgow Coma Scale**—The Glasgow Coma Scale is used in a variety of clinical circumstances to record a baseline assessment of the patient's neurological status. A score of 15 is the best value and 3 is the worst. See Chapter 7, *Emergency Medical Services Records*, for the scale. Nurses should document changes in assessment.
- **Pupil changes**—The term PERLA refers to "Pupils Equal and Reactive to Light and Accommodation." When a light is shined in the eyes the pupils should constrict in reaction to that stimulus. Accommodation refers to the change in the pupil when the patient focuses on an object that is near. Often the term PERL will be used, leaving off the accommodation. It is not possible to assess accommodation if the patient is not conscious or is unable to follow commands. Therefore, not seeing the A on this terminology does not necessarily mean a lack of assessment by the healthcare practitioner.
- **Symmetry and strength of facial muscles**—Drooping facial muscles and weakness will be seen if the patient has a diagnosis of CVA or Bell's Palsy.
- **Respiratory status**—This is completed for those with muscular weakness such as muscular sclerosis, amyotrophic lateral sclerosis, or myasthenia gravis.

Figure 13.3

- An arterial blockage of the leg requires observation for changes in color (pallor), temperature (coolness), and a decrease in the strength of the pulses. Complaints of pain should be documented and reported.
- A kidney arterial block may be detected by a drop in the urinary output as well as complaints of flank pain.
- An arterial block of the lungs will cause an increased respiratory and cardiac rate along with chest pain and increased blood pressure.
- Other body organs suffering from circulation blockage manifest the complication through severe pain and evidence of decreased blood flow.

Treatment will be aimed at increasing arterial blood flow, removing the blood clot if possible, and the use of tPa or streptokinase to break down the clot.

4. Cardiac tamponade

Cardiac tamponade is the compression of the heart caused by blood or fluid accumulation in the space between the myocardium (the muscle of the heart) and the pericardium (the outer covering sac of the heart).[10] It is a complication of trauma or coronary angiography. This condition is characterized by

- decreased cardiac output,
- a muffling of heart sounds,
- a narrowed pulse pressure (decreased systolic blood pressure with increased diastolic blood pressure—narrowing the differences between the pressure caused by the heart contracting and the pressure that exists when the heart is relaxed), and
- increased respiratory difficulty if the lung space is impinged.

Treatment will be directed to removal of blood accumulating in the pericardial space. Assessment must include documenting if the heart sounds are more distinct and if the pulse pressure returns to normal following the procedure.

13.4 Neurological System

Neurological dysfunction is frequently noted in patients seen on medical surgical units. For example, cerebral vascular accidents are a common cause of admission to medical surgical units. Neurological assessments should be documented in the medical record. Common elements of these assessments are found in Figure 13.3.

A. Cerebral Vascular Accidents

Cerebral vascular accidents (CVAs) may manifest with one-sided weakness and a degree of aphasia. Aphasia is an impairment of language, affecting the production or comprehension of speech and the ability to read or write.[11] Expressive aphasia denotes an inability to speak. Receptive aphasia refers to an inability to comprehend.

The severity of the weakness and the type of aphasia should be clearly noted in the documentation throughout the patient's time on the medical surgical unit. Dysarthria refers to a group of speech disorders resulting from weakness, slowness, or incoordination of the speech mechanism due to damage to any of a variety of points in the nervous system.

There are several terms that may be used when referring to patients having experienced a CVA. A brief description of the most frequently used terms follows.

- *Hemiplegia*—paralysis of one side of the body.
- *Hemiparesis*—weakness of one side of the body.
- *Unilateral neglect*—a phenomenon in which the patient ignores the side of the body that has been affected.

The medical record may note that the patient had dysphagia or difficulty swallowing. An assessment of the patient's ability to swallow is absolutely essential. The foods given when oral feedings are begun should have some substance to decrease potential for aspiration (inhalation of food into the lungs) as the patient learns to eat again. In a case of severe dysphagia, the patient may require the insertion of a feeding tube through the wall of the abdomen into the stomach. The tube is referred to as a PEG (percutaneous endoscopic gastrostomy) tube or a simply a gastrostomy tube.

The safety of the patient who has suffered a CVA is paramount. Look for evidence of evaluation of the risk for falls or skin breakdown. Physical therapists and nurses use splints to maintain good body alignment in order to preserve muscle function and prevent contractures (bending of the extremity towards the body, resulting in loss of joint function).

Treatment is multifaceted for the patient experiencing a CVA. Documentation should reflect that rehabilitation has begun immediately and that attention is paid to positioning, nutrition, caring for self, and communication. (Refer to Chapter 24, *Rehabilitation Records*, for additional details.)

Decreasing intracranial pressure will be a prime treatment. This involves

- positioning the patient with the head elevated,
- increasing the oxygen being given,
- providing medications to decrease fluid retention, and
- infusing IV fluid and nutrition.

Documentation of the patient's emotional state and the grieving (and how that is manifested) of both patient and the significant others should be noted. The records should contain documentation of patient education and emotional and physical support that is given.

B. Degenerative Disorders

There are a number of degenerative disorders that are neurological in origin. The nursing assessments and interventions are similar in these situations, although there are certainly some that may be focused on the specific disorder experienced by that patient. The medical record should note safety issues related to the muscular atrophy and weakness and the degree to which the patient experienced these problems. Staff should be aware that a patient having difficulty swallowing is in danger of aspiration, and a patient with an inability to clear her own respiratory tract because of muscle weakness or mucous plug development is at risk for acute respiratory difficulty. Symptoms of acute respiratory difficulty can be detected by completing respiratory assessments on an ongoing basis and by observing the patient's ability to clear the respiratory tract. The procedures used to clear the respiratory tract, how often they are used, and the result of those efforts should also be evident in the documentation of the care of the patient.

TIP: The potential for respiratory tract occlusion is always present; education of the caregiver who will be with the patient is essential.

Treatment is aimed at supporting the respiratory system and maintaining a clear airway. The most common cause of death in those with musculoskeletal degenerative disorders is pneumonia, so protecting these patients is important.

C. Complications

High risk neurological occurrences on medical surgical units are described below.

1. Increased intracranial pressure

Increased intracranial pressure can occur when patients have experienced head trauma, cerebral vascular accidents, or fluid overload. The Glasgow Coma Scale is used to determine the extent of increased intracranial pressure. It measures the verbal, motor, and eye opening ability of the patient. It is important to note trends, especially decreasing scores of this assessment as it means that increasing pressure is occurring. The patient's level of consciousness is affected by increased intracranial pressure. The first capability that is lost is knowledge of the time (day, week, or year). The second capability that is lost is the place where the patient is located. Lastly, the patient loses the ability to identify himself. Healthcare providers continue to assess and document neurological status when a patient is totally disoriented. Incremental deterioration of the patient's condition may occur if the intracranial pressure rises. The medical record will include documentation of the length of time it takes to get from one stage to the next. Treatment will be recorded. The responses of the patient will be used to determine needed interventions. Blood pressure will be assessed. An increase in the blood pressure may cause an increase in intracranial pressure. Treatment is aimed at decreasing the intracranial pressure using IV fluids, diuretics, and positioning.

2. Seizure activity

Seizure activity can occur as a result of epilepsy, reactions to drugs, or increased intracranial pressure, among other things. The medical record may note that the patient has experienced an aura (warning symptoms present before a seizure). When clonic (thrashing movement of the arms and legs) movements are noted, safety measures should be taken. It is helpful if the duration of both the tonic (a stiffening and rigidity of the body's muscles) and clonic stages of the seizure was noted, although that is not often possible. The presence of incontinence of urine or stool during or following the seizure will be recorded and is significant for determining the depth of the unconsciousness. Any paresis or paralysis present following the seizure is also important to note along with the cognitive status and behavior exhibited. Maintaining the safety for the epileptic patient is paramount.

> In a Pennsylvania case, *Andrew Gentile v. University of Pennsylvania*, the forty-nine-year-old plaintiff with a seizure disorder was admitted to the defendant's epilepsy unit for studies to determine if he was a candidate for brain surgery. He was weaned off his medication and sleep deprived in order to induce seizure activity. Hours after his first in-hospital seizure, the plaintiff struck his head and injured his back in the bathroom. The plaintiff claimed that he should not have been allowed to use the bathroom unaccompanied. The defense asserted that letting epilepsy patients use the bathroom is common and appropriate. The defense also noted that the plaintiff made no claim of back pain until thirty-six hours later. The jury returned a $3 million verdict.[12]

Renal Assessments

Renal assessments may include:

- *Urinary output*—amount, color, clarity
- *Blood pressure*
- *Edema*, especially dependent
- *Medications*—many cause renal toxicity
- *Cardiac output*—as 25 percent of cardiac output goes to the kidneys, a decrease could cause a significant impact on renal function
- *Pain*—severity, location, related symptoms
- *Blood urea nitrogen, serum creatinine, and uric acid*—as diagnostic tools used to determine the ability of the kidneys to remove known waste products
- *Glomerular filtration rate*—as the definitive measure of renal function

Figure 13.4

Immediate treatment of the seizure may involve intravenous administration of Versed, Valium, or Phenobarbital. Long-term treatment of seizure disorders is accomplished with anticonvulsants such as Dilantin, Tegretol, or Depakote. Documentation of the time it takes the patient to regain cognitive, motor, and mental abilities should be noted. Although not all seizures are caused by a disorder known as epilepsy, it should be noted that a dreaded complication of an epileptic seizure is one in which the seizure activity does not slow down or stop, known as status epilepticus. Patients in this state are at risk for experiencing brain damage because of a lack of oxygen to the brain. Healthcare providers must always be alert to this complication and thoroughly document all treatment and pharmacologic interventions.

13.5 Renal System

Both acute and chronic renal problems can affect the care of a patient on a medical surgical unit. Acute renal dysfunction can be a reason for admittance to the hospital, but acute dysfunction is also a complication that can occur with many serious illnesses (for instance MI and sepsis). Refer to Figure 13.4 for details about renal assessments. Common renal dysfunction and pathology along with the documentation that should be expected is described below.

A. Kidney Stones

Kidney stones can cause severe pain and can be formed by any number of chemicals.

TIP: Pain (renal colic) is the hallmark symptom of a renal stone when a stone has left the kidney and is traveling down towards the bladder.

The medical records should document the location and radiation (where it travels to) of the pain and whether the pain comes in waves coinciding with the peristaltic waves in the ureters. Many people describe renal colic as being the worst possible pain. The pain may be severe enough to cause shock with hypotension, tachycardia, and diaphoresis (sweating) as well as nausea and vomiting. The presence of blood in the urine, called hematuria, should also be noted.

Treatment is first aimed at pain control. The type and amount of opioid (narcotic) given, how frequently it is needed, and the effectiveness of pain relief should be documented. Antiemetics may be given also to control nausea and vomiting. An increase in fluid intake is usual in order to attempt to flush the obstruction, with the amount and type of fluid recorded. Patients should be taught how to strain their urine in order to collect the stone. Once found, the stone is sent for testing to determine its chemical composition. Patient education, including the foods and drugs the patient was instructed to use or avoid once the type of stone was known, should be recorded as well.

Lithotripsy may be used to break up the stone. This treatment involves some risks associated with fluid administration, as the following case illustrates.

In a Texas case, *Gillespie et al. v. McKenna Memorial Hospital et al.*, a forty-seven-year-old woman underwent lithotripsy for removal of a kidney stone. The procedure took over six hours. The patient died twelve hours later from fluid overload caused by absorption of the irrigating fluid, by the resulting hyponatremia, hyperkalemia, pulmonary edema, general tissue edema, acidosis, renal failure, and other conditions. The plaintiffs claimed that the defendants committed numerous acts of malpractice related to the irrigating fluid used, including the use of distilled water rather than saline as the sole irrigant. They failed to protect the patient from the known dangers of extravasation and absorption and failed to keep track of the volume of irrigating solution used. They failed to verify that adequate drainage of the bladder was taking place during the procedure. The defendants settled for a confidential amount following mediation, with all the defendants contributing to the settlement.[13]

B. Incontinence

Incontinence is commonly abbreviated in medical records as "inc." If the patient is incontinent of stool and urine, the medical record may refer to this as "B & B" for bowel and bladder. Incontinence is an increasingly common concern. Causes of stress incontinence such as sneezing, coughing, or laughing should be noted. If the incontinence is an ongoing problem, the condition of skin in the perineal area should be assessed along with the wound and skin assessments, and the interventions used should be documented. The home remedies the patient and family have been using should also be noted and documented.

C. Bladder Cancer

Visible, painless hematuria is a first symptom of bladder cancer 85 percent of the time. The amount of urinary output and the color or the urine (along with the brightness of color whether yellow or red) should be evident in the documentation. Patients will complain of pelvic pain and frequent urination when the cancer is advanced. Treatment may include chemotherapeutic medications directly instilled into the bladder or removal of the bladder.

D. Infections

Infections can occur anywhere within the renal/urologic system. Thorough assessments help to determine the locus of the infection as well as the severity. Pain complaints when the infection is in the kidney are typically found in the costovertebral (at the bottom of the rib cage in the back) area and present as flank pain. The pain will be particularly severe during urination when cystitis (bladder infection) is present. Cystitis is marked by complaints of heaviness in the back and lower pelvic region. Kidney and bladder infections cause fever and chills. If the pain is severe enough, hypertension results, particularly if chronic glomerulonephritis (kidney infection) is the original diagnosis. In the elderly population, a change in mental status is often a sign of urinary tract infection.

The nurse documents the color of the urine (whether clear, cloudy, or evidence of blood), the amount voided with each micturition (urination), as well as a daily total, and complaints of bladder spasms during the voiding process. Treatment will include antibiotics and increased fluids. A decrease in pain and discomfort should be noted. Education aimed at prevention of further episodes should be done.

E. Complications
1. Chronic kidney disease

Chronic kidney disease (CKD) usually insidiously occurs over a great number of years. There are several stages to this renal dysfunction.

- renal insufficiency,
- renal failure, and
- end stage renal disease.

Renal insufficiency occurs when there is a loss of renal function and an inability to concentrate urine. Often there are no symptoms, but a rising blood urea nitrogen and serum creatinine may give evidence if these are noted. If the workload on kidneys is increased (e.g., due to hypertension) there may be increased serum electrolytes, nocturia (urinating in the middle of sleeping hours), and anemia. Renal failure is known to be present when there is evidence of renal disease with symptoms such as hypertension, anorexia, nausea, and even skin changes (both color and texture). In this stage there is clear evidence that the kidneys are unable to keep up with maintaining internal balance, and increased assessments should have been completed.

TIP: End stage renal disease (ESRD) occurs when less than 15 percent of the nephrons are still functional.

At ESRD there will be a need for dialysis to maintain life. Recording urinary output is vital. Metabolic manifestations that should be assessed are

- hypoproteinemia (not enough protein in the serum),
- abnormal glucose levels,
- acidosis,
- cardiovascular manifestations such as hypertension,
- pericarditis (inflammation of the heart sac),
- hypermagnesemia (elevated serum magnesium levels) causing weakness and cardiac arrest, and
- arrhythmias from hyperkalemia (elevated serum potassium levels) and acidosis.

Dermatologic manifestations that may be noted are

- pruritis (itching),
- burning sensations,
- poorly healing wounds,
- a yellowish-gray color skin,
- evidence of bruising, and
- dry skin and brittle nails.

Skin care with non-drying agents is provided. Infected wounds are treated. Hematological manifestations often seen in these patients are anemia and evidence of bruising. Anemia is corrected, and patient education is provided about preventing trauma which might cause bleeding.

Gastrointestinal manifestations include

- a metallic taste in mouth,
- a urine odor to breath,
- complaints of nausea and anorexia,
- esophagitis and gastritis, and
- bowel irregularities.

As the nausea and vomiting have direct implications for nutrition, good mouth care and anti-nausea agents are necessary along with small, frequent meals.

Common neurological manifestations of chronic kidney disease are

- decreased level of consciousness,
- personality changes with increased irritability and labile emotions,
- peripheral neuropathy, and
- muscle changes with twitching and jerking or nocturnal cramps.

Women may experience a cessation of menses; men experience impotence. Both men and women report a decreased libido.

Respiratory symptoms include infections, thick sputum, a depressed cough reflex, and tachypnea. Increased fluids and expectorants may be used, depending on the severity of the symptoms and the efficacy of other treatment. Renal osteodystrophy, a thinning of the bones because of calcium loss, leaves bones weak and susceptible to fractures, creating major skeletal concerns in patients with chronic renal failure. Attention to patient safety issues is important to prevent injury. Pathological fractures (caused by the disease process in the presence of minimal or no trauma) can occur. Activated vitamin D and calcium supplements are commonly used in these patients to decrease the effects of the osteodystrophy.

The treatment of chronic renal failure is complicated and involves many professionals. Chronic renal failure is treated through either hemodialysis or peritoneal dialysis. Peritoneal dialysis uses the membrane in the abdominal cavity to pull waste products and excess fluid off the body by infusing a highly concentrated fluid into the cavity. The medical record should note that the nurse checked the patency of the shunt or access for hemodialysis, or of the peritoneal dialysis catheter, and for signs of infection at any of the insertion sites. Patient education includes information about coming to a dialysis center for treatment or how to do peritoneal dialysis. Management of fluid and electrolyte levels, and anemia and assurance of adequate nutrition are important.

2. Acute renal failure

TIP: Acute renal failure occurs as a result of some other major trauma or illness. Hypoperfusion (decreased blood flow) is the most common cause, but every patient with poor cardiac function, hypotension, and hypovolemia (decreased blood volume) no matter the cause should be considered at risk for acute renal failure.

Assessment of renal function is necessary in the care of most medical surgical patients. A second common cause of acute renal failure in medical surgical patients is nephrotoxicity (damage to the kidneys). The recognition that many medications are likely causes of nephrotoxicity should be a priority. The progression of acute renal failure is in three stages.

- Oliguria, in which fluid restriction to prevent fluid overload is often necessary.
- Diuresis, during which the major concern is hypovolemia.
- Recovery stage, which will take up to an entire year to reach.

A cardiovascular assessment should include

- listening to heart sounds for presence of extra heart sounds (S1 and S2 are normal. S3 and S4 are extra sounds),
- listening for friction rub (a sound caused by the pericardial membranes being dry and rubbing against each other),
- recording heart rate and regularity,
- determining blood pressure,
- observing for presence of peripheral edema, and
- evaluating fluid and electrolyte levels.

Pulmonary assessments should include listening to the lung sounds for crackles indicating an accumulation of fluid. An assessment for increased intracranial pressure should include a check of the level of consciousness.

Gastrointestinal assessments should include

- taking a nutritional history,
- noting nausea, vomiting, or diarrhea, and
- listening for bowel sounds.

Skin or integumentary assessments should focus on evidence of infections.

Musculoskeletal Assessments

Musculoskeletal assessments include:

- Gait
- Symmetry of extremities
- Posture
- Variations in skin color, nodules, masses, swelling
- Deformities following injury or disuse
- Palpation
- Range of motion

Figure 13.5

The treatment of acute renal failure is multifaceted and includes dialysis, medications, and fluid management. Hemodialysis is the most typical type of dialysis used for acute renal failure. Assessment for patency of the access device used for dialysis and for signs of infection around the catheter insertion site is imperative.

TIP: The medical record should note the amount of weight lost during dialysis and symptoms of fluid instability following treatment.

It is common to use medications to treat the anemia, the fluid and electrolyte imbalances, and the acidosis. Because of the renal dysfunction, dosage adjustments are often necessary, requiring careful assessment of efficacy and side effects. Fluid management is complex; differences in the amounts of fluid given during the oliguric and diuretic stages are not static, nor can they be determined for every person the same way but instead depend on the cause of the acute renal failure and the response to the immediate treatment. Patient teaching to prevent nephrotoxicity should be done, even if that is not the immediate cause of the acute renal failure. The patient's recovery may be delayed if toxic drugs are taken.

13.6 Musculoskeletal System

Medical surgical patients may have disorders of the musculoskeletal system. The potential of having to assess the musculoskeletal system is everpresent. Refer to Figure 13.5 for key assessments. Common patient problems and the documentation that should be expected are explained below.

A. Fractures

Many people with fractures will complain of acute pain with muscle spasms if the fracture affects a long bone. Paresthesias (numbness and tingling) of the area sometimes occur, especially if swelling and ecchymosis are evident at the fracture site. The healthcare team should assess for crepitus, the grinding of pieces of bone, by either palpation or auscultation. Movement of fracture fragments should be observed for when first doing the total assessment following the fracture. This is often present immediately after a fracture and before the bone has been stabilized.

The fracture will be set, if possible. Some fractures cannot be immobilized with a cast, such as fractures in the ribs, scapula, and vertebral body. If a closed reduction is done, the nurse must assess for compartment syndrome. If an open reduction is performed, an assessment for symptoms of osteomyelitis (bone infection), such as pain and heat at the fracture site, should be done. Osteomyelitis is treated with six weeks of IV antibiotics. Patient teaching should include how to care for the cast or how to walk safely with crutches.

Compartment syndrome is a high risk complication. Any patient with a cast or an extremity wrapped with a pressure dressing or who has had surgery on an extremity should be observed for the development of this syndrome. Assessment should focus on the extremity distal (below) to the fracture, cast, or pressure dressing. If the patient exhibits pain or paresthesias, paralysis, a weak or absent pulse, or if the extremity is pale in color and cool to touch, documentation should record the complaints and symptoms, and a report should be made to the medical team.

Elevation of the extremity is the first intervention. If compression of nerves and blood vessels continues, complaints of pain on the distal end of the extremity will worsen as will the coolness and paleness of the extremity. If treatment is not started quickly, the patient may lose the extremity.

Skin Assessments

Skin assessments include:
- Skin color changes
- Lesions—color, location, size
- Moisture
- Edema (swelling)—where located, distribution
- Vascular markings
- Elasticity
- Hair growth, or lack thereof
- Nails—presence, color, shape, thickness, clubbing (bent)

Figure 13.6

B. Osteoporosis

Osteoporosis can be either pathological with other disease states or physiological as occurs with the aged. Symptoms of osteoporosis include fractures, progressive spinal deformities causing a loss of height, and sometimes muscle atrophy.

Treatment is aimed at increasing calcium intake and educating about foods high in calcium. Teaching should include information about the efficacy of weight-bearing exercises. Refer to Chapter 17, *Orthopaedic Records*, for additional information.

13.7 Integumentary System

The integumentary (skin) system is particularly vulnerable in elderly patients because the skin thins as we age. Patients who are confined to bedrest or who are incontinent or have draining wounds are also at risk for injury to the skin and should have focused attention paid to prevent that injury. Refer to Figure 13.6 for details about skin assessments.

Disruption of the integumentary system is a common patient problem, and a description of documentation that should be expected when this occurs follows.

A. Infections

Infections of the skin can be caused by any number of microorganisms. Bacterial infections are more common in the lower extremities and manifest with erythema (redness) and edema. The skin is hot and tender to touch. Treatment of bacterial infections is carried out with antibiotics and surgical debridement (cutting off dead tissue) if needed. Medical records should describe the debrided site and the efficacy of the treatment.

Viral infections of the skin present symptoms three to seven days after contact. The patient will exhibit tenderness and pain with a mild paresthesia. Commonly patients will describe a burning feeling prior to the appearance of lesions. Lymphadenopathy (enlarged lymph nodes) with flu-like symptoms may also be seen in patients with viral infections of the skin. Moisture barrier creams are used to treat the skin.

There is increased attention being paid to the development of hospital-acquired infections. Some of the antibiotic-resistant organisms can be difficult and expensive to treat. Prevention of intravenous catheter and Foley catheter related infections are targeted as quality and patient safety measures.

The following case shows the devastation associated with a delay in treating an infection.

A sixty-one year-old man was sentenced to thirteen months in prison. While incarcerated, he repeatedly sought attention for dizziness, fever, genital pain, swelling, and itching. The plaintiff claimed he was told that he had an allergic reaction and was given antihistamines and steroids. He was later diagnosed with necrotizing fasciitis, which was identified as Fournier's Gangrene. The plaintiff claimed he was not given a physical exam until after the gangrene developed. By the time the plaintiff was airlifted to a hospital the bacteria had spread to his pelvic region and surgery was performed which removed several pounds of flesh, including his penis and one testicle. The plaintiff will require reconstruction surgery, which will include the use of skin from a thigh to make a replacement penis. A $300,000 settlement was reached.[14]

B. Cancer

There is a relatively high incidence of skin cancer in the United States. Various kinds of skin cancer are known, and it is important that documentation of abnormalities be thoroughly carried out.

Basal cell carcinoma is usually seen as a single lesion on exposed skin. The lesion will be raised with a well-defined border, while ulceration occurs with crusting as time goes by. These cancers usually have a slow but continuous growth, so an assessment over time should be made. Even though medical surgical nurses do not usually see patients over a long period of time, it is important that the assessment of lesions on the skin be made and teaching be done to encourage patients to examine their own skin. Treatment of basal cell carcinomas is normally done by excising the growth.

Squamous cell carcinoma is usually manifested as a single superficial lesion which develops a crust. These cells have a rapid growth rate, and metastasis occurs almost exclusively via the lymphatic system. Treatment of squamous cell carcinomas is done by excising the lesion, followed by radiation and chemotherapy.

Malignant melanoma is increasing because of exposure to the sun. Lesions should be assessed for

- asymmetry,
- border irregularity,
- color variation within the lesion, and
- a diameter greater than 0.6 cm.

Metastasis occurs via lymphatic and venous systems. Treatment is completed using radiation and chemotherapy along with biopsy and excision of the lesion. Patient and family education should focus on sun protection, risk factors from sun exposure, and minimizing the effects of the treatment by radiation or chemotherapy.

C. Complications
1. Skin breakdown and ulcers

Erythema of intact skin may be a first clue to skin breakdown. It should be noted whether blanching with pressure occurs. A more thorough assessment should include whether the skin loss involves the epidermal, dermal, or the subcutaneous layer of the skin. Pressure sores may progress until bone, muscle or tendons are exposed. Open sores may become infected, resulting in blood infection and death.

TIP: Prevention of skin breakdown and ulcer formation in medical surgical patients is primary.

Evidence that a patient was turned frequently, kept dry, and had skin care frequently done is essential and should be recorded in the record. Shearing occurs when a body is dragged over the sheets, which may occur when not enough people are used to reposition a patient higher in the bed. Documentation of the number of people used to reposition a patient should be noted.

A twenty-five year-old quadriplegic developed a Stage IV pressure sore on his sacrum, a Stage III pressure sore on his right hip and a Stage II pressure sore on his right heel during a hospital admission. The sores progressed to osteomyelitis. He died a year later of urosepsis. The plaintiff claimed the decedent was not properly turned, which led to the pressure sores. The defendant claimed the decedent could not be turned because he was noncompliant. The jury found negligence and awarded $57,585.09 for the Medi-Cal lien. They awarded nothing for pain and suffering or attorney fees.[15]

2. Burns

Major burns are treated in burn units, but there are a number of patients with burns who are found on general medical surgical units when the percentage of skin involved is not extensive enough to require intensive care. The depth of burns should be documented along with an estimation of the size of the burn. Assessment for evidence of respiratory dysfunction would be especially important if the patient is burned on the face or was trapped in an enclosed space during a fire. Cardiovascular and hematological abnormalities such as anemia and congestive failure should be observed for following a severe burn. With severe burns, gastric dysfunction such as ileus (paralyzed bowel) may also occur. Refer to Chapter 26, *Skin Trauma*, and Chapter 27, *Controversies in Skin Trauma*, for additional information on the topic of skin trauma.

13.8 Endocrine System

The endocrine system is scattered throughout the body, which makes assessment and diagnosis of endocrine abnormalities difficult. Each of the endocrine glands has the potential to create disturbances in the other glands of this system. Many have symptoms that are similar. It is sometimes difficult to determine which endocrine gland is causing the symptoms noted, and whether that gland is the primary disturbance or is just reacting to a disturbance in another of the endocrine glands. The most common disturbances are discussed in this section although this is not a complete accounting of endocrine abnormalities. Refer to Figure 13.7 for a listing of endocrine assessments. Common endocrine dysfunction and the documentation that should be expected are discussed below.

Endocrine Assessments

Endocrine assessments include:

- General appearance
- Height
- Weight
- Fat distribution
- Muscle mass
- Skin
- Edema
- Hair distribution

Figure 13.7

A. Hyperthyroidism

Hyperthyroidism results in increased metabolic rate, causing tachycardia, tachypnea, and arrhythmias. Congestive heart failure is a potential complication of this increase in thyroid function. Other symptoms are

- warm moist skin,
- thinning and fine hair,
- excessive sweating and heat intolerance, and
- a loss of weight, requiring increased caloric intake.

Exophthalmos (bulging eyes) with Grave's disease (an autoimmune form of hyperthyroidism) may necessitate the use of artificial tears and care of the eyes because of the inability of the eyelids to close over the eyeball. Documentation of the treatment and patient education to prevent injury to those with this eye problem should be found in medical records.

Hyperthyroidism is treated with antithyroids. Radiation therapy is one type of treatment. Assessment of the effectiveness of treatment and education about returning to the physician's office should be included in the documentation.

B. Hypothyroidism

Hypothyroidism causes a slow-down in metabolic rate. Symptoms may be

- lethargy,
- constipation,
- decreased bowel sounds which will cause a need for increased fluid and stool softeners,
- weight gain because metabolic rate is slow,
- a cold intolerance, requiring a warmer room,
- arthralgias (painful joints),
- dry hair with a tendency to fall out, and
- cardiomegaly (enlarged heart).

Severe cases of hypothyroidism can cause myxedema (severe loss of thyroid hormones) with symptoms as above, only to a greater degree. Periorbital swelling, pleural effusion, ascites, severe hypothermia, and respiratory failure are potential complications of hypothyroidism. Treatment typically includes giving the patient Synthroid, a thyroid hormone. It is necessary to teach the patient that it may be a month before the effects of medication can be seen and felt which requires that the patient continue to take the drug even though no effects are being noted.

C. Diabetes Mellitus

Diabetes mellitus is increasingly being noted in both children and adults. Dietary habits in the United States, coupled with the incidence of obesity, are felt to be implicated in this increased incidence. Type I diabetics are insulin-dependent. Type II diabetics are adult-onset diabetics whose blood sugars are controlled through diet or oral medication. Symptoms generally noted are

- increased serum glucose,
- increased urine output, and
- increased thirst.

The medical record will reflect monitoring of blood sugars, either through blood withdrawals or the use of glucometers to obtain a blood drop to test. Monitoring may occur as often as four times a day, with insulin doses adjusted based on results. Insulin pumps are increasingly common and permit the enhanced regulation of blood sugar through continuous administration of insulin into the tissues.

Chronic complications found in those with diabetes must always be considered if the patient has been diabetic for any period of time. Assessments of those with diabetes should include an attempt to detect complications and to provide safety. Hypertension, edema, proteinuria, and renal insufficiency would be evidence of renal disease, known to be caused by diabetes. Disturbances of the sensation in the hands and feet causing diminished ability to feel pain or touch, unsteadiness, and an unsteady gait may be evidence of neuropathy.

Retinopathy (disease of the retina), cataracts, and glaucoma in the eyes require documentation of safety measures taken to prevent injury when they are present. The medical record should include documentation of activities to prevent injury such as support while walking, testing bath water before stepping into a bathtub, use of night-lights during the night, etc. Orthostatic hypotension (low blood pressure when rising from a lying position) and arrhythmias from cardiac neuropathies are possible and should be noted if found. Delayed gastric emptying requires care in providing some medications as drugs that are absorbed through the gastric mucosa may have more time to get into the blood stream and cause increased blood levels.

Hypoglycemic unawareness (a low blood sugar which has no symptoms which the patient is aware of) is a complication that can occur when the body's warning system is unable to function and hypoglycemia occurs following insulin injection. Hypoglycemia can cause seizures and death.

Accelerated cardiovascular disease is evident in those with diabetes, and assessment should always include a cardiovascular assessment to determine whether hypertension, arrhythmias, cerebrovascular dysfunction, or peripheral vascular disease are evident. Diabetics may have a myocardial infarction without any noticeable symptoms.

Treatment is aimed at

- maintaining glucose levels, fluid, and electrolyte levels, and
- preventing ketosis (increased acids in the serum because of breakdown of fats), hypoglycemia, or hyperglycemia.

The chart will contain documentation of the treatment: medications, fluid regulation, the time that treatment started or that the dosage was increased, and the effectiveness of the treatment.

D. Complications

Patients at high risk for endocrine occurrences on medical surgical units, and specific documentation are discussed below.

1. Diabetic ketoacidosis

Diabetic ketoacidosis is a complication seen usually in those with Type I diabetes. Signs to observe for would be hyperglycemia (usually above 250) and metabolic acidosis. Symptoms will be the same as for diabetes mellitus.

- polyuria (increased urinary output),
- polydipsia (increased thirst),
- polyphagia (increased hunger) evident,
- nausea and vomiting, and
- abdominal pain with muscle irritability related to the acidosis.

Sometimes there is a fruity smell to the breath which may be confused with the smell of alcohol. The medical records should define the severity of any of the symptoms noted and the level of awareness of the patient during the assessment.

Treatment is aimed at correcting the hypovolemia, stopping the production of ketones, and decreasing the level of the blood sugar. Insulin is the primary treatment. It is administered in units. The chart should contain documentation of the type and amount given along with the effectiveness.

2. Hyperosmolar, hyperglycemic nonketotic syndrome (HHNK)

Hyperosmolar, hyperglycemic nonketotic syndrome is usually found in those with Type II Diabetes (non-insulin dependent) and may be diagnosed in people who are not even aware that they are diabetic. It is usual to find hyperglycemia with blood sugars over 600 (normal blood sugar is 80 to 120), and with some serum hyperosmolality over 300 mOsm/dl. Acidosis and severe dehydration are potential complications, with symptoms of difficulty with mentation related to the severe hypovolemia.

Treatment is aimed at correcting hypovolemia and decreasing the blood sugar, and documentation should be expected to reflect that.

TIP: Insulin is the primary treatment of hyperosmolar, hyperglycemic nonketotic syndrome, with fluid volume replacement a second primary requirement.

3. Hypoglycemia

Hypoglycemia is common even in people who are not taking insulin. The first set of symptoms is considered cardiogenic in nature.

- tachycardia,
- shakiness,
- diaphoresis, and
- palpitations.

If the stimulation of these body systems does not increase the blood sugar, the neuroglycopenic symptoms will occur with symptoms such as impaired thought processes, stupor, and seizures. The primary treatment is to increase blood sugar. Expected documentation includes assessments of vital signs and mentation and whether they return to normal.

A Virginia diabetic received an erroneous dose of Insulin the night before she was to be discharged. Her blood sugar fell to 12. When the error was discovered she was in a diabetic coma. She died a month later. The case was settled without filing suit. The hospital agreed to write off all of the hospital bills and not submit them for payment by any health insurer or other sources. The hospital also agreed to reimburse the estate for expenses related to investigation and pursuit of the legal claims. A $1,650,000 settlement was reached.[16]

13.9 Gastrointestinal System

Nausea and vomiting are such common occurrences on medical surgical units that they can be missed as a signal of gastrointestinal complications. Gastrointestinal assessments are included in Figure 13.8. Common patient problems and the documentation are described below.

A. Duodenal and Gastric Ulcers

A gastric ulcer can be located anywhere in the stomach and upper portions of the small intestines (duodenum). In the presence of a duodenal ulcer, pain is most common when the stomach is empty. If bleeding occurs, coffee ground appearing emesis may be noted. Gastric ulcers, on the other hand, are more likely to exhibit with pain being more common directly after eating. Bright red blood may be vomited. Treatment most often includes pharmaceutical agents aimed at decreasing gastric acidity. Documentation should focus on the symptoms noted and the patient education needed.

Gastrointestinal Assessments

Gastrointestinal assessments include:

- Skin—scars from old abdominal surgeries, spider angiomas (enlarged vessels) of the abdomen
- Skin color, particularly jaundice
- Visible peristalsis or aortic pulsations (not normally seen in adults)
- Bowel sounds—hyper or hypo-active
- Ascites
- Palpation of abdominal masses
- Abdominal distention and tenderness
- Nausea, vomiting, constipation, esophageal reflux complaints
- Weight loss or gain
- Presence of blood in the stool, called "occult blood" if not visible and melena if it can be seen

Figure 13.8

TIP: The medical record may contain an order to collect stool for testing for "occult" (hidden) blood. Melena is blood that is visible in the stool. Old gastric blood is described as "coffee grounds," whereas fresh bleeding is red. Old lower intestinal blood is described as "tarry."

B. Gastrointestinal Obstruction

Gastrointestinal obstruction can occur with mechanical obstruction or with paralytic ileus. Projectile vomiting is common, causing a need for placement of a nasogastric tube (NG) for suction to decompress the stomach and to safeguard the lungs from the risk of vomit entering the lungs. No food or fluid should be given by mouth until it is determined that the obstruction has been relieved.

During obstruction, sequestration (accumulation) of fluid into the GI tract can occur, with reported cases of patients having two to three liters of fluid in the small intestine. It is commonplace to insert a nasogastric tube (NG) to decompress the stomach and to safeguard the lungs from vomiting and inhalation of vomit. The amount of fluid obtained from the nasogastric tube suction is essential to know because replacement volume may be needed. Symptoms of hypovolemia due to fluid movement from vessels into GI tract include

- abdominal distention,
- increased peristalsis with high pitched bowel sounds,

- abdominal cramping with increased discomfort related to peristalsis, and
- hypovolemia related to the sequestration of fluid into the GI tract.

Treating hypovolemia and reducing the effects of obstruction will be the focus of assessments and interventions. NG tube placement and symptoms of fluid and electrolyte abnormalities, if those occur, should be noted in the chart.

C. Hepatitis

There are several viruses that cause hepatitis. Prevention of the transmission of hepatitis to others is important. Symptoms of all forms of hepatitis are similar and include

- malaise,
- low grade fever,
- headache,
- jaundice,
- liver enlargement and tenderness, and
- anorexia and nausea.

Treatment is focused on the prevention of transmission as well as alleviating the symptoms being experienced by the patient. Antibiotics and IV fluids may be used to treat the symptoms, and an assessment of the effectiveness should be documented.

D. Chronic Pancreatitis

Chronic pancreatitis can occur in those who have had

- pancreatic trauma,
- chronic infections, and
- alcoholism.

A common symptom of pancreatitis is unrelenting mid-epigastric pain which patients may complain is bad but not the worst they have experienced. Hypocalcemia may be present. An increased bleeding tendency will occur with a decrease in serum calcium. Nutritional deficiencies that can be seen in these patients include steatorrhea (fat in the stool) which indicates

- fat malabsorption,
- weight loss from both fat and protein malabsorption, and
- symptoms of diabetes mellitus.

The medical record should include documentation concerning these symptoms as they provide clues to the damage to the pancreas. Treatment will focus on the discomfort being experienced by the patient, the nutritional disturbances, and the inflammatory process.

E. Acute Pancreatitis

Acute pancreatitis is a common diagnosis on medical surgical units. Many theories exist as to the causes of this, but none have been proven as yet. The patient will complain of severe mid-epigastric pain which is so significant that abdominal guarding is noted. It is common for symptoms of shock to be present, caused both by pain and by hypovolemia. Symptoms of hypovolemia occur as fluid sequesters (collects) in the retroperitoneal space, sometimes in the amount of three liters, much of which comes from the vascular space. Respiratory difficulty may occur from the fluid, causing compression upward into the diaphragm, so assessment should include a thorough respiratory assessment as well.

Reducing pain is the first priority of treatment. Shock could occur, so a complete assessment of volume, bleeding, and pain is always necessary. Volume replacement consisting of administration of blood components and intravenous fluids, as well as calcium to increase the clotting ability, will be included in any treatment plan. NG tube placement will be done, and the patient will need to be kept from eating or drinking in order to rest the pancreas during the healing process. It is common for those with acute pancreatitis to have gastritis as well, so medications may include those that will protect the gastric mucosa. Total parenteral nutrition (nutrition given through the intravenous route) for nutritional support is common. Assessments focus on tolerance to the increase in volume. Care is taken to maintain sterile technique while handling the access to the venous system. Refer to Chapter 11, *Intravenous Therapy Records*, for more details.

In a Michigan case, the patient went to the hospital suffering from acute pancreatitis. She was treated by the surgeon, who ordered fluids. There was no documentation that the plaintiff was given fluids by the nursing staff as ordered, and it was unclear whether the orders had been followed. The defendant visited the patient the next day. Although there was no improvement, no additional fluids were ordered. The patient died that day. The plaintiff claimed that the defendant should have recognized that the patient had not received the prescribed fluids and ordered an increase in fluids. The defendant contended that appropriate fluids were ordered and that the patient's outcome might not have been altered with additional fluids. The hospital settled for $150,000 before trial. A defense verdict was returned for the physician.[17]

13.10 Summary

When medical surgical patients are being cared for, careful documentation is essential. Not only is a focused assessment necessary—focused on the reason for the admission—but the assessment should also include those other body systems that could be affected by the disease process being experienced or that are affected by a chronic disease that was present prior to the current illness. It is not possible, in today's medical surgical units, to care for patients with only one pathophysiologic change, which increases the difficulty of providing complete documentation.

Endnotes

1. American Nurses Association. *Standards of Clinical Nursing Practice*. Second Edition. Kansas City, MO: Author. 1998.

2. Academy of Medical Surgical Nurses. *Scope and Standards of Medical-Surgical Nursing Practice*. Third Edition. Pitman: Author. February 2005.

3. http://www.nlm.nih.gov/medlineplus/copdchronicobstructivepulmonarydisease.html. Retrieved May 14, 2005.

4. Laska, L. "Failure to Timely Clear Tracheostomy Tube for Man Recovering from Brain Injury in Motorcycle Collision." *Medical Malpractice Verdicts, Settlements, and Experts*. October 2009, p. 18.

5. Laska, L. "Failure to Use Compression Devices as Ordered Following Bladder Suspension Surgery." *Medical Malpractice Verdicts, Settlements, and Experts*. February, 2005, p. 17.

6. http://www.nlm.nih.gov/medlineplus/ency/article/000153.htm. Retrieved May 14, 2005.

7. http://www.nlm.nih.gov/medlineplus/ency/article/000195.htm. Retrieved May 14, 2005.

8. Laska, L. "Failure to Timely Treat Bleeding following Hysterectomy" *Medical Malpractice Verdicts, Settlements, and Experts*. July 2009, 20.

9. Laska, L. "Doctors Fail to Order Proper Tests and Nurses Fail to Inform Doctor of Change In Status In Woman Following Fall While on Coumadin." *Medical Malpractice Verdicts, Settlements, and Experts*. April 2005, p. 21.

10. www.nlm.nih.gov/medlineplus/ency/article/000194.htm. Retrieved May 14, 2005.

11. www.aphasia.org/NAAfactsheet.html. Retrieved May 14, 2005.

12. Laska, L. "Epilepsy Patient Allowed to Use Bathroom Unattended Hours After Seizure." *Medical Malpractice Verdicts, Settlements, and Experts*. March 2005, p 21–22.

13. Laska, L. "Woman Dies After Endoscopic Lithotripsy Procedure for Removal of Kidney Stone." *Medical Malpractice Verdicts, Settlements, and Experts*. April 2003, p. 58.

14. Laska, L. "Failure to Diagnose necrotizing Fasciitis in Prisoner." *Medical Malpractice Verdicts, Settlements, and Experts*. April 2009, p. 10.

15. Laska, L. "Failure to Turn Man Blamed for Development of Pressure Sores." *Medical Malpractice Verdicts, Settlements, and Experts*. August 2009, p. 20.

16. Laska, L. "Error in Administration of Insulin to Diabetic Leads to Diabetic Coma and Death." *Medical Malpractice Verdicts, Settlements, and Experts*. August 2009, p. 21.

17. Laska, L. "Failure to Ensure that Sufficient Fluids Were Given to Woman with Acute Pancreatitis." *Medical Malpractice Verdicts, Settlements, and Experts*. February 2005, p. 21.

Chapter 14

Medication Records

Michael T. Lennon, PharmD, MBA, RPh, JD

14.1 Introduction

The purpose of this chapter is three-fold:

- to acquaint the attorney with the role of the pharmacist in a patient's care and treatment;
- to help the attorney understand the medication-related portions of the medical record in evaluating the propriety of the patient's medical course and outcome; and
- to help the attorney recognize any medication related errors or omission that might give rise to liability.

Because the proper evaluation and screening of a potential legal claim requires a thoughtful and rigorous review of the entire medical record, emphasis is placed on the interplay between the different types of medication related documentation contained in the medical record.

This chapter should not be construed as containing any opinions regarding the standard of care of the average qualified pharmacist. Neither should it be considered as an exhaustive review of all aspects of medication related practices. Rather, it should be identified only as a brief orientation to the subjects discussed, for use and reference by attorneys and other legal professionals in reviewing a patient's medical records. Such a review of medical records, of course, should be only one of several factors that the attorney weighs in judging the merits of a potential or pending case.

14.2 Overview of Pharmacy Practice

Traditionally, pharmacists have suffered the distinction of being the underutilized "stepchild" in the American healthcare system. Because recent trends have begun to rectify this misperception, a brief overview of the current professional landscape for pharmacists follows.

A. Education and Training

If one were to ask the average American citizen how long a pharmacist must study before gaining licensure, the answer would likely not come as quickly as if the question were asked about lawyers, physicians, or nurses. This question, asked of twenty legal professionals in Boston in November 2004, yielded the average answer of "three years," with the high answer being "four years."

TIP: The requisite course of study for pharmacists in an accredited pharmacy school is six years, including several on-site clinical rotations. Beyond this, before a pharmacy school graduate may sit for a state board licensure examination, many states require the candidate to complete and document more than 1,500 hours of extracurricular, supervised clinical work in various settings, including hospitals, community pharmacies, investigational facilities, and long-term-care institutions.

Over the past twenty years, there has been a fundamental shift in the focus of pharmacy education. This shift has resulted in the expansion of the formerly standard five-year curriculum to the current six-year program. While pharmacists are still required to study chemistry, biology, anatomy, physiology, pharmacology, microbiology, therapeutics and the like, greater emphasis is now placed on training pharmacists to play a more active role in "disease state management." For this reason, pharmacists are now required to study such advanced subjects as hematology, oncology, infectious disease, geriatrics, gastroenterology, gynecology, obstetrics, cardiology, and pulmonology. Beyond this, there is a discrete subset of pharmacists who choose to pursue certification in such specialized disciplines as diabetes management and anticoagulant therapy.

TIP: For several reasons, the scope and extent of a particular pharmacist's education and training can be an important piece of information for the attorney to discover, especially when the propriety of a pharmacist's acts or omissions is at issue.

B. "Pharmaceutical Care"

Until the beginning of the current century, the entry level degree for pharmacists to practice in the United States was a Bachelor of Science in Pharmacy (B.S.Pharm.). If a pharmacist wished to pursue a graduate degree in the same field, a Doctorate in Pharmacy (Pharm.D.) is the doctoral level degree. This advanced field of study involves two to three years of clinically oriented coursework combined with several clinical rotations in designated teaching hospitals.

TIP: Today, the entry level degree for a pharmacist is the six-year Pharm.D. Consequently, recent graduates have the strange distinction of holding a doctorate as the only degree required to practice. Commensurate with the advent of this unique and perplexing new construct, pharmacy academics have invented and attempted to promote the novel concept of pharmaceutical care.

The underlying precept of pharmaceutical care is as follows: Because pharmacists have been trained in the precepts of disease states and the clinical management of disease states, they are qualified to participate fully in the healthcare team. Such participation includes consulting with physicians, nurses, and other medical professionals regarding proper medication choice, dosing, and monitoring. By virtue of performing in this elevated capacity, pharmacists (especially community pharmacists) are taught to consider their customers as "patients."

With rare exception, however (e.g., administering vaccines in select states), a pharmacist's license simply does not confer on the pharmacist the privileges of administering medication, much less diagnosing, treating, or otherwise evaluating any pathologic condition. In essence, then, the true scope of pharmaceutical care is limited to providing pharmaceutical advice. Of course, providing advice to other medical professionals regarding the myriad aspects of medications has been the traditional role of pharmacists since the turn of the previous century. So, what has changed, other than the degree designation and the still little known catchphrase of pharmaceutical care? From a healthcare standpoint, arguably little has changed.

TIP: From a legal standpoint, however, one can surely envision a heightened duty of care, new theories of liability, and an expanded pool of potential tortfeasors in certain cases of medical (or pharmaceutical) negligence.

14.3 Pharmacists' Roles and Responsibilities

Pharmacists have many options regarding their chosen career path. These options include community practice, hospital practice, long-term-care practice, academia, investigational research, and pharmaceutical sales, to name but a few. The most popular career choices, and the roles and responsibilities attendant thereto, are discussed briefly below.

A. Hospital Practice

Hospital pharmacy practice is markedly different from other types of pharmacy practice. With regard to the dispensing function, hospital pharmacists regularly deal with certain dosage forms that are virtually foreign to community pharmacists. When reviewing the pharmacy-related portion of medical records, the attorney should be able to recognize and understand the different ways of administering these medications, and be able to evaluate the legal implications of professional improprieties.

1. Unit dosing

The term "unit dosing" refers to individually packaged, single doses of medication, in contrast to the "bulk packaging" of medications seen in the neighborhood drugstore. In the hospital setting, patients are billed for each dose of medication that is dispensed for the patient's use. If any of the unit doses are not ultimately administered to the patient, that patient's account is credited accordingly. Reasons that a dose might go unused can include death or discharge of the patient, a medication error, unavailability of the patient at the designated time, or a change in medication orders.

Because medications are almost always administered by the nursing staff, they have been traditionally stored in a locked medication cart. The mobile medication cart is wheeled around to patients' rooms by the nurse charged with administering the medications. The pharmacy is responsible for restocking the medications. Unit dosing allows for ease of inventory, ease of administration, and, when stock is sufficiently low, ease of ordering or replacement. Examples of different unit dose dosage forms include tablets, mini-intravenous (IV) bags, capsules, caplets, injections, suppositories, and troches (large tablets that are lodged and slowly absorbed through the inside of the cheek).

With the advent of technology, many facilities now use computerized drug dispensing carts. Each medication is stored in a drawer. Removal of the drug creates an electronic record used for keeping a running inventory of each patient's medications.

2. Intravenous administration

Intravenous (IV) administration of medication is an option when, for example:

- a particular medication is unstable, and thus unavailable, in oral (by mouth) form;
- an immediate therapeutic effect is desired or necessary;
- a patient is unable to swallow due to unconsciousness or pathology;
- a patient's digestive tract cannot adequately tolerate a particular medication;
- a patient's hydration (fluid) status needs to be stabilized, maintained, and monitored; or
- a patient is allergic to the chemicals (e.g., preservatives, fillers, dyes) in an oral dosage form.

TIP: The injection or infusion of a medication directly into a patient's vein is associated with risks.

If a volume of air makes its way into the bloodstream, or the wrong medication or dose is given, the consequences can be catastrophic. For single-dose injections, the size of the needle, the size of the syringe, and the rate of administration must be correct, and the injection site must be sterilized. In all cases, a sterile technique is critical to avoid the introduction of dangerous pathogens into the bloodstream. Just as importantly, care must be taken to find a patent vein for use as an injection site. There are certain medications that, if mistakenly injected into the surrounding tissues (extravasation), can cause tissue necrosis (death) fairly quickly. If this happens, emergency intervention is required. Refer to Chapter 11, *Intravenous Therapy Records*, for additional content on this topic.

Several components of continuous infusions of fluid (IV drips) must be correct:

- the diluent (e.g., normal saline, half-normal saline, 5 percent dextrose in water);
- the quantities of medications; and
- the rate of infusion.

Any error in calculation (drip rate, patient's lean body mass, patient's kidney function) can lead to a disastrous result.

An Ohio case had severe repercussions for both the patient and the pharmacist. A pharmacy technician made a base solution with too much sodium chloride. The pharmacist failed to note the error. The child received the chemotherapy solution, developed severely elevated sodium and died. The pharmacist had faced a backlog of orders, was dealing with short staffing, did not have normal meal breaks, and felt rushed. The pharmacist was sentenced to 6 months in prison, 6 months of home confinement with electronic monitoring, 3 years of probation, 400 hours of community service, a $5,000 fine, payment of court costs, and loss of his license.[1]

3. Parenteral nutrition

Some patients are unable to take food by mouth. Various reasons for this can include invasive gastric (stomach) surgery, prolonged unconsciousness, or significant esophageal disease. In these situations, it is within the pharmacist's purview to prepare liquid nutritive compounds for infusion into the patient's veins. Meticulous sterile technique is critical. Because some of the orders for these compounds can contain more than two dozen ingredients, attention to detail is extremely important. Such ingredients can include amino acids, minerals, lipids, enzymes, and vitamins. The amounts and proportions of the ingredients are carefully considered by the prescriber, and so should be just as carefully measured by the pharmacist preparer. A miscalculation in the measurement and incorporation of certain ingredients, such as iron, can lead to potentially toxic blood levels and other complications.

TIP: These solutions can be described in the medical records alternatively as hyperalimentation ("hyperal"), total parenteral nutrition (TPN), or peripheral parenteral nutrition (PPN). A facility might use preprinted order forms to facilitate the ordering of these solutions.

B. Community/Retail Practice

Most people are familiar with retail pharmacy practice—the community pharmacist in the local drugstore is the most visible and accessible of all healthcare professionals. Appointments are not necessary, and in most states there is no charge to talk with the pharmacist. Because of their accessibility and willingness to speak with customers for no fee, drugstore pharmacists are considered to be very trustworthy. Indeed, opinion polls routinely place pharmacists as among the top echelon of the most trusted professionals. Along with that level of trust, however, comes the responsibility of accurately dispensing prescribed medications and providing reliable advice to the general public, day in and day out.

1. Dispensing

As one might suspect, there is no magic involved in filling a prescription. In the most simplistic terms, the pharmacist:

- reads the prescription (this alone takes a special time-honed skill);
- locates the big bottle of medication;
- moves the medication from the big bottle to a smaller bottle;
- types and affixes a label to the smaller bottle; and
- collects the money.

This is the equivalent of production-line factory work that countless customers in thousands of drugstores witness first hand, every day. What is not seen, and is thus vastly underappreciated, is the decisionmaking process that the pharmacist must use before dispensing a single dose of any prescription medication. The following questions illustrate what a pharmacist must ask before "collecting the money."

- Is the pharmacist confident she has correctly understood the name of the medication?
- Is the dose prescribed appropriate for the customer's age/weight/ability to tolerate side effects?
- Will the medication interact negatively with any other of the customer's medications?
- Will the medication increase the therapeutic effects of any other of the customer's medications?
- Will the medication interact with any types of foods or liquids such that the customer should be so warned?
- Is the customer allergic to the medication or any similar class of medications?
- Are there any warnings that the law requires the pharmacist to give to the customer?

When one considers the potential consequences of failing to consider these factors and address any potential problems with a prescription, the pharmacist's true role as the final gatekeeper becomes clearer. Indeed, the process is much less mechanistic than is commonly perceived. When one further considers that the average community pharmacy routinely dispenses several hundred prescriptions every day, the importance of constant vigilance and unflinching attention to detail becomes apparent.

The universal starting point for a pharmacist is developing the skill to decipher and interpret accurately the prescriber's handwriting. While many hospitals and some of the more sophisticated physician's offices have adopted policies and procedures requiring computer generated, printed prescriptions, many prescriptions are still written by hand.

TIP: Only after having assisted in filling several thousand prescriptions does a pharmacist-in-training develop the requisite skill to perform this most fundamental of tasks. It is only through experience that pharmacists learn to recognize that certain dosing schedules (e.g., four times daily) are inappropriate (and sometimes dangerous) for certain medications. In such cases, the pharmacist owes a duty to the customer to consult with the prescriber and either clarify the prescriber's true intent, confirm the accuracy of the prescription as written, or recommend a more appropriate dosing regimen.

Although the legal requirements vary from state to state, as a basic proposition, a complete prescription must contain the following minimum information:

- name of medication (the pharmacist has to be vigilant for "sound-alike" drugs);
- dose of medication (the pharmacist has to question any dose that falls outside the usual range);
- quantity of medication (this is usually preceded by "Disp." or the # symbol);
- dosing regimen (this pharmacist has to be careful interpreting Latin abbreviations, still in wide use);
- prescriber's identity (frequency leads to familiarity with handwriting); and
- refill designation (increased legal restrictions with potentially addictive drugs).

When dealing with prescriptions for certain tightly controlled substances, the pharmacist must make sure that the prescriber's federal Drug Enforcement Administration (DEA) number appears on the face of the prescription. This is a seven-digit number, preceded by two letters, which is assigned exclusively to the prescriber by the DEA and used to track physicians' prescribing habits and to monitor these drugs' dissemination.

Once any prescription is filled, whether for a controlled substance or a non-controlled substance, the prescription form must be securely stored for a legally mandated period before it may be destroyed. In contrast, physicians are only required to keep copies of prescriptions written for certain categories of controlled substances. For this reason, prudence cautions that the dispensing pharmacy should maintain at least a copy of each filled prescription well beyond the minimum time required by law.

Attorneys wishing to review a list of all medications dispensed to a patient may request a computerized printout, which is commonly available at most pharmacies. This useful printout identifies the name and dose of the medication, the number of doses dispensed, and the name of the prescriber. Each pharmacy used by the patient must be individually queried for a list of prescriptions.

TIP: As of this writing, there is no efficient way to contact one source which will provide a list of all medications provided to the patient collated from every drugstore the patient has visited.

---

2. Customer consultation

In the early 1990s, the federal government mandated that all pharmacy customers whose prescriptions were paid for with federal funds be offered individual counseling with regard to each prescription dispensed.

The law does not require the pharmacist necessarily to "counsel" the customer, but rather only to extend the offer. Soon after the enactment of this law, several states followed suit, requiring offers to counsel for all prescription medications paid for with state funds (welfare). The rationale behind these laws is straightforward: If customers were to understand more about the proper use of their medications, they would be more likely to take the medications as prescribed, thus lowering government expenditures for unnecessary hospitalizations and treatment. Expanding this rationale to the overarching goal of controlling healthcare costs in general, several states have gone even further and enacted laws requiring pharmacists to offer to counsel all of their prescription customers, without regard to method of payment.

Topics for counseling regarding medications can include

- identification and description of the intended therapeutic effects;

- identification and description of possible side effects;
- warnings regarding possible side effects (e.g., do not drive; take with food);
- identification of potential interactions with other medications;
- explanation of the prescribed dosing schedule;
- description of proper medication storage procedures; proper administration techniques for creams, ointments, patches, inhalers, or nebulizers; and
- identification of any expiration dates beyond which the medication should be discarded.

A blind man brought a prescription for two boxes of 25 microgram Fentanyl patches to the defendant pharmacy. The pharmacy dispensed two boxes of 50 microgam Fentanyl patches. The plaintiff was unable to detect the dosage error before using the medication. The plaintiff applied the narcotic patches over the course of a week as prescribed and suffered a debilitating overdose. In addition to extreme discomfort, confusion, nausea, and lethargy, the overdose caused permanent worsening of the plaintiff's sleep apnea, necessitating numerous sleep studies and supplemental oxygen therapy during sleep. The pharmacy admitted the error but disputed the damages. A $200,000 settlement was reached.[2]

In practice, many dispensing errors can be avoided by simply confirming the medication name, dose, and dosing schedule with the customer. By way of illustration, the author recently handled a professional negligence case against a pharmacist and her chain pharmacy employer involving the wrongful dispensing of a blood pressure lowering medication. The customer had been taking the specific medication for a significant period, but yet she was given and ingested tablets containing four times the prescribed dose. As a result, the patient suffered an episode of severe hypotension (low blood pressure) followed closely by acute renal failure. This dire event required emergency, life-saving intervention and a hospital stay until the patient was ultimately stabilized.

While customers are not required to accept the offer to counsel, those who do are arguably entitled, under common law negligence principles, to rely on the pharmacist's competent advice. The law is still developing with regard to this construct. Some states hold pharmacists to the common law duty of due care in these situations. Other states adhere to the outmoded "learned intermediary doctrine," which effectively shields pharmacists from liability. Specifically, this doctrine holds that a patient's physician functions as a learned intermediary between the drug manufacturer and the ultimate user of the manufacturer's product. Accordingly, the duty to warn patients about any foreseeable adverse side effects lies exclusively with the physician.

Under this arguably Draconian doctrine, the pharmacist acts as a mere conduit and thus cannot be held liable for failing to warn customers of potential adverse effects of the medications dispensed. Some courts have limited the scope of the doctrine to cases where the pharmacy does not provide any written information to customers regarding the customers' medications. Because most computerized pharmacies now offer this service, an effective advocate can reasonably argue that the pharmacy has thereby affirmatively imposed upon itself a duty to warn.

TIP: In such cases, especially where a pharmacist or pharmacy is a potential tortfeasor, make sure to request copies of all written materials that were provided to the injured customer at or around the time of dispensing.

For an in-depth discussion of the learned intermediary doctrine and its shrinking parameters with regard to pharmacists, see *Cottam v. CVS Pharmacy*, 436 Mass. 316 (2002). Given the recent transformation in pharmacy education and practice as described above, a persuasive argument can be made for holding pharmacists to a higher standard of care commensurate with the profession's evolving status.

C. Long-Term Care Practice

In recent decades, the average age of the United States population has risen, largely due to the maturation of the so-termed "baby boom" generation. As a result, the nursing home population has likewise risen over the same period. All indications are that this trend will continue for the foreseeable future.

In light of this trend, it is not surprising that nursing homes far outnumber hospitals in this country. Because the vast majority of nursing homes are largely dependent on reimbursements from the federal Medicare program and state Medicaid programs, the long-term-care industry is extensively regulated by several government agencies. The procurement, administration, and monitoring of prescription medications is watched particularly closely by the government.

1. Monitoring and consultation

Under federal law, Medicare eligible nursing homes must have a pharmacist on-site at least once a month to review each patient's medication regimen. Failure to comply with this requirement can result in a deficiency, or sanction,

from government inspectors, along with the potential of a monetary penalty. As part of the duties in reviewing each patient's medical record, or chart, the consulting pharmacist must assess the clinical necessity of each medication by confirming that the physician has documented a corresponding diagnosis. Additionally, for each medication, the pharmacist must assess the propriety of the

- choice of medication itself;
- choice of dose;
- route of administration;
- frequency of administration; and
- risk/benefit ratio of the side effect profile.

Beyond this, federal law requires the monitoring of periodic blood levels of certain medications (e.g., anticonvulsants, iron supplements, warfarin sodium, digoxin, lithium carbonate) at specific intervals (e.g., weekly, monthly, twice yearly). It is the pharmacist's responsibility to recommend that this monitoring take place as required by law.

If the pharmacist has any concerns regarding any aspect of the nursing home patient's medication regimen or monitoring schedule, he should document those concerns in the patient's chart. Such documentation can include

- written recommendations to the supervising physicians for a dose adjustment;
- an adjustment in monitoring parameters; and
- discontinuation or substitution of a particular medication.

The ultimate decision rests with the prescriber, but the pharmacist's specialized knowledge will certainly help to inform this decision.

TIP: Failure to recognize and act upon certain medication related irregularities can arguably give rise to corresponding liability on the part of the pharmacist.

---

2. Inservice training

Beyond the consulting role described above, long-term-care pharmacists often serve in an educational capacity. Because a large proportion of long-term-care nurses are licensed practical nurses (LPNs) rather than registered nurses (RNs), these nurses' knowledge surrounding medication issues can be limited. With a view toward improving patient care in the long-term-care setting, many consultant pharmacists offer inservice training, or educational lectures, to these nurses. These lectures can pertain to, among other subjects:

- proper medication administration and storage procedures;
- clinical indications for certain classes of medications; and
- proper documentation for administration and side effect monitoring.

In addition to this educational role, pharmacists are often called on to participate on a nursing home's quality assurance committee. This committee is required by law to meet at specific intervals, several times per year. In this capacity, the pharmacist can help to formulate and modify policies and procedures regarding all medication related issues in the nursing home setting.

3. Dispensing

The medication dispensing function in the long-term-care field is most often separate from the consulting function described above. Moreover, because a single pharmacy often provides dispensing services to scores of nursing homes, it is not uncommon for these pharmacies to dispense exclusively to nursing homes and be closed to the general public. Procedurally, each nursing home serviced by a particular pharmacy typically transmits to the pharmacy a weekly order on behalf of all of the nursing home's patients. Each transmitted prescription, once filled, is delivered to the nursing home on a designated day of the week. Medications that are needed on a more expedited basis are delivered within twenty-four hours. Certain emergency (stat) orders can be delivered within hours of transmission. Because this unique type of dispensing can involve the processing of thousands of prescriptions per day, extreme care must be taken to ensure that each prescription is filled and accurately dispensed. Toward this end, the dispensing pharmacists try to put in place effective safeguards to minimize the chance of error. Of course, in the event of a pharmacy error, discovery of such internal policies and procedures will be useful to the attorney.

14.4 Medication Related Records

It is no secret that most physicians' handwriting is notoriously difficult to decipher. Medication related records, in particular, tend to be among the most difficult records to read because abbreviations and acronyms are the norm. To appreciate the full picture of a patient's clinical course and treatment, the attorney must not overlook these important, and sometimes critical, portions of the medical record. It is likewise important that the attorney review the various medication related portions of the record in conjunction with one another.

A. Physician's Orders

In the hospital and long-term-care settings, once a physician has evaluated a patient and recorded her clinical impressions, the doctor might conclude that a prescription medication is indicated as part of the overall treatment plan. Nurse practitioners and physician's assistants also have authority in some states to order medications. Prescribers are required to document such orders in a section of the medical record reserved for this purpose. At times when the prescriber is off-site and is contacted by the treating nurse regarding a change in condition or an emergent situation, the prescriber can issue a telephone order. The transcribing nurse then writes down the order, reads it back to the prescriber, and initials the confirmed order. (Refer to Chapter 10, *Patient Safety Initiatives and Medical Records*, in Volume I, for details on telephone orders.) Without the authority of a medication order, a pharmacist cannot dispense any medication unless he is doing so on a "refill" basis. Once the medication order is received by the pharmacy, it is processed, dispensed, and delivered to the appropriate person (usually a nurse).

It is the pharmacist's duty and responsibility to make sure that the medication as delivered completely complies with the medication order as written or dictated by the prescriber. If there is any question regarding the propriety or accuracy of any aspect of the medication order (e.g., choice of medication, dose, route, frequency, duration), the pharmacist must make every reasonable effort to determine that the medication as dispensed will not harm the patient.

TIP: In this situation, due diligence can include contacting and questioning the prescriber, recommending a change in the order, or, if warranted, refusing to fill the order.

When reviewing the medication orders, the attorney should look for the initial order for each medication, all orders increasing or decreasing the dose of medication, and any order discontinuing ("d/c'ing") the medication. If there is a liability question regarding the ordering, administering, or monitoring of any medication, it is helpful to construct a timeline to view the relevant periods and any events that occurred during those periods. One should remember that such liability questions might not be readily apparent at the time of the initial client interview. Instead, such questions can arise in the course of reviewing the medication related records. For this reason, it is possible for a careful review of these records to uncover a separate theory of liability not previously contemplated or to be the touchstone when deciding whether to accept or to decline a case (if the attorney is a plaintiff's attorney).

B. Nursing Notes

This section of the medical record can be substantial, both in quantity and in content. Nurses are the healthcare professionals most involved with the hospitalized or long-term-care patient on a daily basis. Accordingly, their documentation concerning a patient's signs, symptoms, general affect, and other matters should be carefully and meticulously scrutinized.

Nurses' observations and impressions are routinely charted by the treating nurses and supervising nurses on each of the two or three daily nursing shifts. By reviewing these notes in depth, the attorney can identify trends, both in treatment and in a patient's response to treatment. In the medication context, reading the nursing notes in conjunction with the medication orders can reveal a story that might go undiscovered if those sections were read in isolation.

By way of illustration, consider the case of a physician's order for, and a nurse's administration of, an unusual dose of an antihypertensive (blood pressure lowering) drug. If this administration is followed closely in time by a precipitous drop in blood pressure, resulting in hypotensive shock (as documented by the nurse), the cause and effect scenario might constitute the difference between a plaintiff's verdict for professional negligence and a defense verdict predicated on an "unfortunate medical result." Similarly, one could easily imagine how failing to read and evaluate the physician's orders and the nursing notes in combination could lead to the plaintiff's attorney's rejection of a potentially meritorious case.

C. Medication Administration Record (MAR)

This section of the medical record is typically the least difficult portion of the record to read, especially in long-term-care charts, as its template is usually computer-generated on a weekly or monthly basis. The patient's previously ordered medications are printed in a list format, on a grid. When a new medication is ordered, the nurse simply writes in the new order by hand at the bottom of the grid.

Organizationally, the scheduled medications and their doses and frequencies are listed first (e.g., metoprolol 50mg twice daily). "As needed," or "PRN" medications (e.g., diazepam 5mg three times daily as needed for anxiety), are listed next or on a separate page. Unlike orders for scheduled medications, PRN orders require the administering nurse to assess the clinical need for the medication on a situational basis. One-time-only medications are listed in a separate section of the record. The fourth category of orders listed on the MAR is termed "treatments." These orders include such things as topical preparations (e.g., creams, ointment, sprays) and oral inhalers. In some hospitals and nursing homes, the treatments are not set apart but rather are interspersed among the scheduled and the PRN medications as appropriate. The same is true for injectable medications. In some nursing home settings, the treatments are recorded on treatment administration records.

Convention dictates that when a nurse administers a dose of medication to a patient, in manually documented records, the nurse writes her initials on the MAR in a small box, denoting the medication given and the shift during which it was given. Computer generated records may print the name or initials of the nurse who administered the dose. If a medication is held for some reason (e.g., per physician's orders, because the patient is too lethargic or refuses the medication), the nurse draws a circle in the appropriate box so as to indicate the omission of that dose. The nursing notes should contain an explanation of why the drug was withheld. If a partial dose is given, that too should be so indicated. If a medication is to be given at specific intervals, such as every three days, the boxes for the days that the medication is not needed are crossed out. If a medication is discontinued, a series of Xs should be placed in the remaining boxes for that scheduled period so as to prevent the inadvertent administration of a non-prescribed medication. In an exercise of added caution, some facilities also require the nurse to write "d/c" after the final dose administered and to highlight conspicuously the discontinued medication and all of the dosing boxes for that period on the MAR. Yellow highlighter copies well, but unfortunately some facilities permit the use of other colors which show up as black streaks when copied.

TIP: The specific sites of intramuscular or subcutaneous injections are also recorded. Some facilities establish standard abbreviations for these sites and list them on the medication administration record. Identification of the site can be crucial in a case in which a patient suffers an injury from an improperly administered injection.

With the advent of outcome-based medicine, beginning in the early 1990s, there has been an increased focus on documenting the effects of medications, once given. This documentation includes not just the intended therapeutic effects but also any side effects complained of or observed, whether expected or unexpected. If, in the prescriber's opinion, a medication's untoward effects outweigh its clinical benefit, appropriate steps should be taken. In the same vein, if there is no evidence that a medication is producing the desired therapeutic effect, it should be adjusted, substituted, or discontinued.

The corollary to this rationale is obvious. The effects of medications must be closely monitored and documented so as to determine the efficacy of continued use. Indeed, this is the only way to ensure that ineffective or wasteful medications are not continually used without inquiry. In the long-term-care arena, nurses are mandated by law to document in detail the side effects of certain classes of psychoactive drugs, including antidepressants, antipsychotics, sedatives, and hypnotics ("sleeping pills").

Like the physician's orders and the nursing notes, the MAR is an integral part of the attorney's review of medication related records. A review of the MAR can confirm whether a particular dose of medication was given at the appropriate time; whether a discontinued medication was administered after the time it was supposed to be stopped; and whether there was a clinically significant gap between the time a medication was ordered and the time it was administered. Thinking more expansively, information contained in the MAR can reveal overuse of a PRN medication, without any follow-up as to the reason for the underlying increase in symptomatology. It can also reveal the absence of PRN administration of a medication in the face of obvious symptoms requiring the need for the medication. It is not difficult to imagine a liability theory emerging from any of these types of scenarios.

D. Other Sources of Medication Documentation

Medications can be recorded in a number of places within the medical record. These include

- emergency medical services records;
- emergency department orders and nursing notes;
- anesthesia records;
- procedure records (e.g., endoscopic, radiological, or cardiac procedures);
- post-anesthesia care unit (PACU) records;
- same day surgery unit records;
- critical care nursing flow sheets;
- patient-controlled analgesia (PCA) flow sheets;
- nursing notes;
- medication-specific flow sheets, such as flu and pneumovaccines;
- diabetic flow sheets listing insulin doses;
- anticoagulation sheets for heparin and warfarin sodium; and
- intravenous medication/fluid flow sheets.

In some facilities, these medications might not also be recorded on a medication administration record. Consequently, it is essential to request and review all possible sources of medication documentation.

E. Internal Documents

The formal medical record does not reflect the entirety of medication related documents that might be important to the reviewing attorney. Although each potential case must be considered within its own contours, one should not rest on the presumption that the standard request for medical records, accompanied by the requisite authorization, is the end of the inquiry. If liability is potentially grounded on a medication related issue, one should consider exploring all available facility specific documentation, including, without limitation:

- medication requisition sheets;
- pharmacy policies, procedures, and protocols;
- nursing policies, procedures, and protocols;
- intravenous medication calculation notes;
- drug product professional inserts;
- quality assessment (QA) committee meeting minutes, notes, and reports (if discoverable);
- incident related correspondence and reports;
- pharmacy consultants' written recommendations and notes;
- continuing education and inservice materials; and
- personnel files.

While most of these types of records are not routinely available in the absence of a pending lawsuit, many states allow the filing of a Bill of Discovery, or some similarly termed mechanism, by which a putative plaintiff can discover documents to determine whether a good faith basis exists for a cognizable claim before instituting a civil action. If a case is already in suit, however, a request to produce the above-listed documents is but one of many discovery tools at the plaintiff's attorney's disposal.

TIP: Though certain of these documents (particularly those maintained by hospitals) might be protected from discovery pursuant to a statutory peer review privilege, this is not always the case for similar documents maintained by long-term-care facilities. A careful reading of all controlling federal statutes and regulations, in conjunction with the applicable state statutes and regulations, might yield unexpectedly helpful arguments for use in a motion to compel the production of such documents.

F. Commonly Used Abbreviations

Any chapter dealing even tangentially with medication related records would be incomplete without a chart of the more commonly seen abbreviations and acronyms familiar to pharmacists and other medical professionals. Refer to Figure 14.1 for a list of commonly used abbreviations. They are representative, but certainly not exhaustive. Refer to Chapter 10, *Patient Safety Initiatives and Medical Records*, in Volume I, regarding "Do not use" medication abbreviations.

14.5 Legal Considerations

While reviewing an individual's medical record, the attorney must orient the review depending on the nature of the case. In the screening of a potential professional malpractice case, the medication related records can point to possible liability as against the hospital pharmacist, the community pharmacist, the long-term-care pharmacist, the administering nurse, the charge nurse, the prescriber, or the facility administration. As detailed above, however, the attorney can only extract maximum value from the records if they are read in their totality and with an appreciation of the relationship as between the different sections of the record.

If the purpose of the review is to analyze the causation dynamic or to evaluate the nature and extent of injuries and damages in a general negligence case, the focus should be on the clinical indications, quantities, and long-term effects of the medications identified in the record. For example, in some cases it is helpful for advocacy purposes (or in the case of defense counsel, to refute damages) to determine the number of doses of pain-relieving medication taken by a patient since the time of the initial injury and expected to be taken in the future. Similarly, the number of injections to which a patient has been subjected can help to chronicle effectively the true experience of a tedious and undeserved hospitalization.

If a permanent orthopaedic injury is likely to require continuing treatment with an anti-inflammatory medication, one should consider obtaining an expert opinion regarding the expected cost and side effect profile of that drug over the long term. If a client's injury related medication regimen is complicated, consider consulting with a pharmacist expert who can advise the attorney as to any interactions or dangers associated with the medication. Unlike other types of experts, pharmacist experts tend to be relatively inexpensive and are usually eager to help. Remember, too, that because most people can identify with their neighborhood pharmacist, a practicing pharmacist can often make a more credible and effective witness than can an overly credentialed academic one.

14.6 Summary

Medical records contain a wealth of information regarding a client's presenting status, treatment course, and outcome. Only when the attorney reviewing the records appreciates the full gamut of the patient's clinical experience can she be in the best position to convey the necessary details of that experience to an adjuster, mediator, arbitrator, judge, or jury. In all cases, the attorney who can understand and effectively convey the medication related aspects of a client's care and treatment has gained an appreciable advantage over an attorney who cannot.

Endnotes

1. "Ohio Government Plays Whack a Mole With Pharmacist." *ISMP Medication Safety Alert!* August 27, 2009

2. Laska. L. "Blind man Dispensed 50 Microgram Fentanyl Patches, Instead of the Prescribed 25 Microgam Patches." *Medical Malpractice Verdicts, Settlements, and Experts*. October 2009, p. 37.

Commonly Used Abbreviations

QD	once daily	AC	before meals	PR	rectally
QOD	every other day	PC	after meals	PV	vaginally
BID	twice daily	HS	at bedtime	D/C	discontinue/discharge
TID	three times daily	PO	by mouth	Δ	change
QID	four times daily	IV	intravenous	SOS	may repeat
PRN	as needed	IM	intramuscularly	WF	with food
Q4H	every four hours	SC/SQ	subcutaneous	NOC	at night
Q6H	every six hours	SL	under the tongue	SS	sliding scale

Figure 14.1

Chapter 15

The Nursing Process and Nursing Records

Patricia Iyer, MSN, RN, LNCC

15.1 Overview of Documentation

Nurses have long viewed documentation as a vital part of professional practice. In her early writings Florence Nightingale described the need for nurses to record "the proper use of fresh air, light, warmth, cleanliness, and the proper selection and administration of diet," with the goal of collecting, storing, and retrieving data to manage patient care intelligently.[1] In Nightingale's time, documentation was used primarily to communicate implementation of medical orders, not to observe, assess, or evaluate the patient's status (as it is today).

During the 1930s, Virginia Henderson promoted the idea of using written care plans to communicate patient care information. Nursing documentation is influenced by The Joint Commission on Accreditation of Healthcare Organizations (JCAHO), which was established in 1951; it was first known as Joint Commission on Accreditation of Hospitals (JCAH) and is now known as The Joint Commission. This was part of the trend toward formalization of nursing standards, and so documentation became a way to evaluate nursing care. Although we now view nursing documentation as essential to nursing, medical records personnel did not always view it as such. Consequently, nursing documentation was discarded after a patient's discharge.

Since the early 1970s, nursing documentation has become crucial, reflecting changes in nursing practice, regulatory agency requirements, and legal guidelines. Nursing documentation has moved forward as a mechanism for determining monetary reimbursement for care. With the development of the nursing process as a framework for practice, documentation evolved to become an essential link between the provision and evaluation of care.

15.2 Why Do Nurses Document?

A. Professional Responsibility

Professional responsibility and accountability are among the most important reasons for accurate documentation. Documentation is part of the nurse's overall responsibility for patient care. The clinical record facilitates care, enhances continuity of care, and helps coordinate the treatment and evaluation of the patient. One of the most significant professional functions of the registered nurse is the evaluation of the patient's responses to nursing care. Professional nurses are responsible for managing increasingly complex patient issues and coordinating patient care among many levels of healthcare workers. Documentation must clearly communicate a nurse's judgment and evaluation of the patient's status. The nurse's ability to make a difference in patient outcomes must be demonstrated in practice and in charting.

B. Legal Protection

Another crucial reason for charting is that nursing documentation may be used in medical or nursing malpractice cases. If a suit proceeds, nursing documentation may provide valuable evidence about a patient's condition and treatments. Documentation may be critical in determining whether a standard of care was met. (Standards of care are defined by nursing organizations and regulatory agencies among other entities.) Nursing organizations have developed frameworks for providing and documenting nursing care.

TIP: Jurors and attorneys usually view the patient's chart as the best evidence of what really happened to a patient.

Timely, accurate, and complete charting helps the patient secure better care and protects the nurses, physicians, and healthcare organizations from litigation. Documentation should be done deliberately and carefully, with the understanding that the chart is a legal document.

C. Regulatory Standards

The Joint Commission is probably the most notable healthcare regulatory agency. It accredits eight out of ten hospitals and more than 10,000 other healthcare organizations. Accreditation by The Joint Commission permits the facil-

ity to accept Medicare funds. Additional accrediting bodies exist. The American Osteopathic Association is also a private company with Medicare deeming authority; it accredits more than 200 hospitals in 31 states. DNV is a new organization given authority to accredit hospitals as of 2008.[2]

Discussing documentation without addressing The Joint Commission requirements is impossible. Part of The Joint Commission standards address nursing documentation; therefore nurses must know the current requirements to maintain compliance with the standards. In recent years The Joint Commission has embraced the concept of performance improvement, emphasizing the importance of outcomes and a multidisciplinary approach to care. This approach has changed the way many organizations structure patient care and, as a result, has altered documentation methods.

A healthcare facility must comply with the documentation regulations issued by the department of health of that state. These standards vary from state to state and can be obtained by contacting the state department involved with surveying healthcare facilities.

Federal regulations may also affect documentation standards; for example, the Center for Medicare and Medicaid (CMS) issues requirements that affect the delivery of care to Medicare and nursing home patients. Depending on the type of facility, accreditation standards of other regulatory agencies may apply.

D. Reimbursement

The evolution of managed care has changed the environment in which nurses work. In the past nurses did not have a strong focus on cost containment. At one time, only a few items on a supply cart were chargeable. Today, some facilities require an accounting of every wound dressing and every incontinence pad. This emphasis on cost is increasing the awareness of not only *what* care is necessary but also *how* that care can be most efficiently provided.

Third-party payers such as Medicare, Blue Cross/Blue Shield, and other private insurance companies are increasingly interested in documentation. They scrutinize the clinical record to determine whether the billed services were necessary and to verify that they were delivered appropriately. With the advent of prospective payment systems (PPS) and DRGs, documentation has become critical. Accurate, thorough documentation facilitates appropriate DRG assignment and reimbursement.

Peer review organizations (PROs) and case management committees monitor length of stay, services rendered, and appropriateness of care. Unless there is thorough documentation by the healthcare provider to justify treatment and services, the healthcare agency could lose substantial revenue through denied reimbursement. For example, documentation helps to justify the need for services when the patient charges exceed the allotted cost or the length of stay is increased for a particular DRG. Progress notes play an important role in this review process.

Complete and thorough documentation is critical to accurate DRG assignment and reimbursement. The complexity of patient problems and the intensity of patient needs must be documented to ensure complete reimbursement. Regardless of the clinical setting, the nurse must be aware of documentation issues as they relate to reimbursement.

Quality of care and patient safety issues increasingly affect reimbursement. The United States government made a decision that it will not pay Medicare or Medicaid dollars for certain never events that occur in a hospital. Their definition of a never event is a "serious and costly error in provision of health services that should never happen." This nonpayment stance is echoed by many private insurance companies. There are facilities not affected by the rule: rehabilitation hospitals and units, psychiatric hospitals and units, long-term care hospitals, children's hospitals, cancer hospitals, Maryland waiver hospitals and religious nonmedical healthcare institutions.

As of October 1, 2008, CMS stopped payment for hospital-acquired conditions/never events unless the hospital can provide documentation the condition was present on admission. This includes conditions that were clearly present but not diagnosed until after the admission took place. There needs to be clear and consistent documentation in the chart, including in the history and physical. Only a physician can authorize a coder to give a "present on admission indicator." Inconsistent, missing, conflicting or unclear documentation must be resolved by the healthcare provider. Poor documentation has a profound impact on the ability of the organization to code, bill, and collect on diagnoses that were present on admission.

TIP: Some risk management organizations recommend healthcare facilities develop standardized assessment tools and admission checklists to facilitate identification of present-on-admission indicators.

15.3 Trends in Charting

Although documentation practices and healthcare procedures are rapidly changing, some conclusions can be drawn about trends in charting.

A. Reduction in Duplicate Charting

It is increasingly difficult to justify recording the same information in many places in the medical record. Forms are being designed to reduce and eliminate duplicate charting.

B. Bedside Charting

The immediate recording of pertinent data reduces duplicate charting and improves the accessibility and accuracy of information. Resistance to keeping records at the bedside is fading as healthcare professionals change their practices and perceptions about bedside records. In order to be compliant with HIPAA regulations, facilities that keep records at the bedside must protect them from the casual examination by those not involved in the patient's care.

C. Multidisciplinary Charting

As the distinctions between departments begin to blur, a renewed team approach can affect documentation systems. Patient-focused care, which involves placing multiskilled workers at the patient's bedside, has stimulated a rethinking of documentation systems. Multidisciplinary forms and shared progress notes are emerging. Another growing trend is to use the same admission database, which has a multidisciplinary focus. This format consolidates the assessments of several disciplines.

D. More Uniformity in Documentation

Joint Commission standards require that the same standard of care be used for patients with similar or identical needs, regardless of their location in a hospital. For example, a woman recovering from anesthesia after a cesarean birth should receive the same monitoring in the postanesthesia recovery room as she would in the labor and delivery suite. Nursing department staff members should be scrutinizing forms to ensure that a uniform standard of care is reflected in the design of the forms.

E. Computerized Documentation

The computer has gained acceptance as a vital tool in the healthcare environment. Nurses in administration have recognized the advantages of using computers for documentation and are now purchasing software and hardware. Refer to Chapter 6, *Computerized Medical Records*, in Volume I, for additional information.

F. Compliance with Patient Safety Goals

The latest trend affecting documentation is the need to establish the ability of the facility to demonstrate that it meets The Joint Commission National Patient Safety Goals. The Joint Commission has phased in national patient safety goals that address important sources of error, such as surgery on the wrong site, medication errors, falls, and so on. See Chapter 10, *Patient Safety Initiatives and Medical Records*, in Volume I, for additional information.

15.4 Initial Database: Admission Assessment

The first step in the nursing process is assessment. The standards of care for assessment are defined by a number of regulatory agencies and professional nursing associations, including the American Nurses Association (ANA) and The Joint Commission. The ANA's standard for assessment[3] includes measurement criteria that focus on the following: The registered nurse

- collects data in a systematic and ongoing process,
- involves the patient, family, other healthcare providers, and environment, as appropriate, in holistic data collection,
- prioritizes data collection activities based on the patient's immediate condition, or anticipated needs of the patient or situation,
- uses appropriate evidence-based assessment techniques and instruments in collecting pertinent data,
- uses analytical models and problem-solving tools,
- synthesizes available data, information, and knowledge relevant to the situation to identify patterns and variances, and
- documents relevant data in a retrievable format.

Careful assessment and documentation of the patient's needs may enhance the effectiveness of nursing care by

- describing the patient's needs to make accurate nursing diagnoses and set priorities, thereby using nursing time effectively,
- facilitating the planning of interventions,
- identifying the patient's factors that will enhance recovery and promote discharge planning, and
- fulfilling professional obligations by documenting important assessment information.

TIP: A facility's staff may use a variety of databases to identify each patient's physical, psychological, and social needs. One established practice in an acute-care facility serving a number of different patient populations is the use of several types of admission assessments.

Some databases may include forms used for the patient seen in the following units or departments: same day or outpatient surgery, renal dialysis, pediatrics, short-stay admission, medical-surgical, critical care, emergency department, labor and delivery areas, and ambulatory care.

The initial database should be designed for the most common population cared for in the clinical area. For example, if most patients admitted to a hospital medical-surgical unit are elderly, the database should focus on common problems seen in this population, such as high risk for impaired skin integrity, falls, and sensory impairments. The use of these assessment tools has become commonplace in acute-care facilities.

The following are standards of care that nurses should follow to complete the initial assessment. Attorney review of medical records should reveal that these strategies were used by the nurses.

1. The nurse should describe the physical assessment findings in sufficient detail. The nurse should avoid the use of words such as "a little" and "a lot," which are open to interpretation and must be clarified to be meaningful.
2. Nursing documentation should contain descriptions of what is seen, heard, felt, and smelled during assessment. The nurse should not interpret the patient's behavior unless these conclusions can be validated; for example, writing "patient crying during interview" is better than "patient crying because she is depressed" unless this conclusion can be verified.
3. The nurse should use the patient's own words when describing the patient's chief complaint. This will provide others with insight into the patient's level of understanding and reaction to the illness. The nurse should describe the onset, treatment, and present nature of the problem.
4. The chart should contain documentation of symptoms that the patient denies and the negative findings from the physical examination. This may assist with the formulation of nursing diagnoses.
5. If the patient cannot provide information during the initial assessment, the nurse should note the reason; for example, note that the patient was confused and unable to provide a history. Leaving a section blank may imply that the form was not completed because the nurse was in a hurry or lacked the knowledge and skills to complete the assessment. The nurse should try to obtain the information from available family members or close friends. Both The Joint Commission and the ANA standards of practice mention the need to obtain (and document) data from significant others when indicated.
6. Pediatric assessment forms may be divided into specific age or developmental groups. Forms are commonly developed for the following age groups: infant to three years, four to twelve years, and thirteen to eighteen years.

7. It is important for the initial assessment to contain a section for recording allergies. Administration of medications to which the patient has a known allergy may cause an allergic or fatal anaphylactic reaction. The nurse should document the patient's description of the allergic response and help the patient distinguish between an allergic reaction and side effects. Although duplication in charting is discouraged, the recording of allergies is an exception. Allergy information should be placed on the assessment form, the medication administration record, the treatment kardex, and the front of the chart.

8. Registered nurses (RNs) may delegate aspects of the initial data collection to licensed practical nurses (LPNs). Typically, LPNs take vital signs, height, and weight, and provide instructions to orient the patient to the new environment. However, RNs are still responsible for completing the admission assessment.

15.5 Priority Assessment Issues

The increasingly complex healthcare needs of patients and shortened lengths of stay have highlighted the need for efficient collection of data. The initial encounter with the patient should focus on the following five priority "Ps" of assessment:

- Problems
- Patient's risk for injury
- Potential for self-care following discharge
- Patient and family education needs
- Pain

A. Problems

An important purpose of collecting data at the time of initial assessment is to identify the patient's priority nursing diagnoses or problems. The initial database should be carefully analyzed to determine if the admitting nurse gathered the applicable information. The initial assessment collects data on the patient's chief complaint. Questions are typically included to identify the aggravating and alleviating factors. It is common to ask the newly hospitalized patient if others in the household depend on the patient for care, so as to identify needs best addressed by the social services personnel. The patient may be asked about how the illness has affected her life, specific religious or cultural needs, and the language of choice. Other questions are incorporated into the database depending on the needs of the patient and the specific clinical area. For example, a psychiatric unit may have an admission assessment geared to the needs of that population.

B. Patient's Risk for Injury

The second priority "P" is the identification of the patient's risk for injury. A second purpose of the initial assessment is to detect and document factors that may contribute to patient injury. This commonly includes identifying the patient's risk for falls, pressure ulcers, suicidal or violent behavior, physical or emotional abuse, or substance abuse.

1. Falls

Patient falls account for a large percentage of all incidents reported by acute and long-term-care facilities. Consequences of falls include prolonged hospitalization, increased healthcare costs, and liability problems. The elderly are at particular risk for injuries resulting from falls. More than one third of adults over the age of 75 fall each year. The fall rates are two to three times higher in institutionalized patients.[4] Accidents are the fifth leading cause of death in those older than sixty-five years. Fifty percent of all fractures that occur in institutionalized older persons are hip fractures. Twenty five percent of those who have a hip fracture in an institution die within a year following the fracture.[5] Falls are a complex geriatric syndrome. They have multiple precipitating causes and predisposing risk factors. A fall may be the first indicator of an acute problem, such as an infection, postural hypotension, or a cardiac arrhythmia. A fall may stem from chronic disease, such as Parkinson's, dementia, or diabetic neuropathy. A fall may be a harbinger of the progression of age related changes in vision, gait and strength. Elders are at higher risk if they have weakness, have a history of prior falls, have a physical restraint, including side rails, are newly admitted to the facility, or are at risk for falls due to the aging process, disease processes, psychological factors or medications. There are significant interactive effects of the risk factors. Figure 15.1 lists characteristics that should be considered when the nurse identifies the patient at risk for falls.

TIP: The patient's risk for a fall must be assessed and documented on admission to an acute or long-term-care facility and during the initial visit of a home care nurse.

Falls have been found to be more common during the first few days of admission. Factors that can contribute to the increased incidence of falls after the patient's arrival may include an unfamiliarity with the environment, acute illness with accompanying weakness and disorientation, sensory deprivation caused by the absence of hearing aids and glasses, feelings of helplessness in a fast-paced environment, and the disruption of normal patterns of elimination.[6]

> ## Risk Factors for Falls
>
> - Medications such as sedatives, anticonvulsants, diuretics, antihypertensives, narcotics
> - Chronic disease processes such as arthritis, neurological impairments, orthopaedic disorders
> - Decreased ability to walk
> - Altered sensory perception such as blindness, deafness, decreased vision
> - Altered elimination (incontinence, frequency, nocturia/frequent urinating at night)
> - Depression (loss of interest, weight loss or gain, sleep disturbance, hopelessness, decreased concentration, fatigue)
> - Diarrhea
> - Mental confusion
> - Dizziness/vertigo
> - Male gender
> - History of substance abuse
> - Cumulative result of several risk factors
> - A history of a previous fall is the most valid predictor of future falls

Figure 15.1

A number of documentation tools have been developed to identify the patient at high risk for falls. The Hendrich II fall assessment form is a commonly but not universally used model. It has been validated in a large case control study. It is brief tool that includes high risk medications and focuses on interventions for specific areas of risk rather than on a single, summed general risk score.[7] Commonly, points are assigned to certain risk factors. This type of form should be used on admission or whenever a significant change in the patient's health status increases the risk for falls. Admission assessment forms that include a method to assess the patient's risk for falls remind nurses not to overlook this important risk factor. Refer to Figure 15.2 for some of the factors that are analyzed after a fall has occurred.

Many hospitals have a falls assessment that is usually reviewed on a daily basis and sometimes every shift. The recommended frequency is a daily risk assessment. It is performed to determine a history of falls, the patient's cognitive status, the patient's mobility capabilities, secondary diagnoses and so on. There are points that are given to these factors in some of the facilities to identify whether the individual is at low risk, moderate risk, or high risk for a fall. Some institutions do not give a point value: they want nurses to be aware that when they are reviewing these areas, they should implement measures to help prevent the fall.

Falls are considered never events by CMS. The alert nurse notes a history of a fall prior to admission, and looks for signs of injury. Although the nurse is not expected to make a medical diagnosis, the nurse is required to detect abnormalities and report them to the physician for ordering the appropriate diagnostic tests. Care associated for a fall-related fracture that is present on admission to a hospital and documented by the physician will be reimbursed.

2. Pressure ulcers

One of the recurring concerns in nursing practice is the prevention of pressure ulcers. Like falls, pressure ulcers are costly, both clinically and financially. Pressure ulcers lengthen hospitalization time and increase healthcare costs and the risk of death from sepsis. Several studies found mortality rates as high as 60 percent for older persons with pressure ulcers within one year of hospital discharge.[8] A few studies have been done to evaluate the impact on the quality of life of the patient with a pressure ulcer. Pressure ulcers produce endless pain, restrict life activities and require significant amount of coping on the part of the patient. The endless pain is caused by: the increase in pain that occurs as a result of moving, leading patients to lay still; the pain associated with dressing changes and debridements; and the pain caused by alternating air mattresses. Pressure ulcers can cause depression, and feeling burdensome, powerless, inadequate, and worried. Wound odor affects the patient and others. Pressure ulcers can cause emotional distress in patients. A survey of patients with pressure ulcers showed that some patients believed healthcare professionals did not fully appreciate the pain of the ulcers and their complaints of pain were ignored. Patients may be too frightened to discuss pain with the doctor but may open up to a nurse, some other allied healthcare personnel, or a family member.[9,10] Family members may equate the development of pressure ulcers with poor nursing care and initiate a lawsuit, alleging that neglect led to the skin breakdown. This eventuality is increasingly more likely as the public realizes that "never events" represent quality of care issues. CMS identifies the development of Stage III and IV pressure ulcers as never events—something that should not occur. The ulcer should be staged using the commonly accepted system presented in Figure 15.3.

TIP: A number of risk factors are associated with the development of a pressure ulcer, including immobility, hypoalbuminemia, obesity, decreased hemoglobin, nutritional factors (such as inadequate dietary intake and impaired nutritional status), infection, incontinence, altered level of consciousness, and fracture.

Documentation is key. The nurse should assess and document after a fall:

Integumentary System: The nurse should observe the patient for bruises, lacerations, or abrasions.
Musculoskeletal System: The nurse should note any pain or deformity in the patient's extremities, particularly the hip, arm, leg, or spine. A cardinal sign of a hip fracture is seen when one of the patient's legs is externally rotated, abducted, and shortened compared with the other leg.
Cardiovascular System: The nurse should assess the patient's blood pressure while the patient is lying down and sitting (or standing, if permitted). The nurse should look for a drop of 20-30 mm Hg in the patient's systolic blood pressure, which might indicate orthostatic hypotension. The nurse should check the patient's pulse for irregularities.
Neurological System: The nurse should assess the patient for any obvious neurological changes, such as slurred speech, decreased strength in the extremities, or changes in mental status.

The expert will review a number of factors, including the patient's mental status at the time of the fall. Was the patient alert and oriented at the time of the fall? What did she state at the time of the fall? The expert will look for statements by the patient such as, "I know I should have used my call light to call for assistance."

The expert will look to see if the patient was identified as a risk for fall. Was the bed in its lowest position? Were there lights on in the room or lights under the bed to help light the areas as well? Did the patient have anti-skid slippers on? Were environmental precautions in place? What medications did the patient received prior to the fall? Did any of these medications have dizziness as a side effect?

How soon was the individual found after he had sustained a fall? What was done at the time of the fall? What did the assessment reveal? Was there an injury? Did the healthcare professional communicate the findings to the physician? Were X-rays ordered and performed?

How soon was that injury treated? If the patient fell and hit his head, was the chart reviewed? Was the individual on anti-coagulation blood thinner such as Heparin or Coumadin? Was this communicated to the physician so that diagnostic scans could be performed, if warranted, to see if there was some type of bleed in the head?

Was there a change in mental status after the patient was returned back to the bed? What were the vital signs?

Were there specific conditions which contributed to the fall? Was the person assessed and monitored?

Modified from Levin, B. "After the Fall'" teleseminar, http://www.medleague.com/teleseminars/after_the_fall.htm

Figure 15.2 *Expert witness analysis of a fall.*

Stages of Pressure Ulcers

Stage 1

Pressure ulcer is an observable pressure-related alteration of intact skin whose indicators as compared to an adjacent or opposite area on the body may include changes in one or more of the following: skin temperature (warmth or coolness), tissue consistency (firm or boggy feel), and/or sensation (pain, itching).

The ulcer appears as a defined area of persistent redness in lightly pigmented skin, whereas in darker skin tones, the ulcer may appear with persistent red, blue, or purple hues.

Stage 2

Partial thickness skin loss involving epidermis, dermis, or both. The ulcer is superficial and presents clinically as an abrasion, blister, or shallow crater.

Stage 3

Full thickness skin loss involving damage to, or necrosis of, subcutaneous tissue that may extend down to, but not through, underlying fascia. The ulcer presents clinically as a deep crater with or without undermining of adjacent tissue.

Stage 4

Full thickness skin loss with extensive destruction, tissue necrosis, or damage to muscle, bone, or supporting structures (e.g., tendon, joint, capsule). Undermining and sinus tracts also may be associated with Stage IV pressure ulcers.

Source: http://www.npuap.org.

Figure 15.3

To meet CMS requirements, the physician must assess the patient within a narrow window of time after admission—two days with no provision for weekends or holidays. Pressure ulcer prevention protocols, once formulated for the patient, must be documented. Without proper documentation, the legal and financial burden shifts to the provider. The physician is responsible for this initial documentation.

Two commonly used pressure ulcer risk scales—the Norton scale and the Braden scale—have been extensively tested. Their use provides a consistent format for system-atically assessing risk factors for pressure ulcers. Each uses different parameters and methods of scoring. The Braden scale is the most widely used tool in the U.S. It is easy to use, has been clinically validated, and requires minimal training. It addresses many of the issues that can affect the risk of pressure ulcers.

TIP: No pressure ulcer risk assessment tool captures all of the risk factors that can contribute to the development of pressure ulcers.

Obtaining a thorough patient history is important to ascertain such contributing factors as age, medications, and medical conditions, including a history of pressure ulcers. More than 100 risk factors of pressure ulcers have been identified in the literature. However, a hierarchy of risk factors has not been determined. Medical conditions include diabetes, multiple sclerosis, peripheral vascular disease, cerebral vascular accident, sepsis and hypotension. Additional risk factors are age 70 or older, current smoking history, dry skin, low or high body mass index, impaired nutrition or malnutrition, impaired mobility, altered mental status, urinary and fecal incontinence, physical restraints, and malignancy.

Either the Braden scale or the Norton scale or some variation thereof may be incorporated into the admission assessment or used on skin integrity assessment forms. Some facilities have developed a separate form for ongoing documentation of the pressure ulcer stages that can be used on admission or whenever the patient's condition deteriorates.

Nurses are expected to document the condition of the patient's skin on admission and periodically thereafter. The Institute for Healthcare Improvement, which made pressure sore reduction one of the 12 interventions in the 5 Million Lives Campaign, recommends daily reassessment of risk for pressure ulcer development. The frequency with which such reassessment should be done varies with the health status of the individual, but the trend is towards daily assessment in acute care, and assessment of skin of a home healthcare patient at each visit. Long-term care patients should be assessed on admission, and then every 48 hours for the first week. The majority of pressure ulcers developed within the first two weeks of admission.

There should be clear expectations of staff conducting the risk assessment, which include which nurse is responsible for performing and documenting the first assessment and subsequent assessments. This should be defined as who and which shift is responsible for doing the assessment. Refer to Figure 15.4 for elements of documentation about pressure ulcers.

Elements that Nurses Should Document When Assessing Pressure Sores

— Location, size, color of the wound
— Amount and type of exudate
— Odor
— Nature and frequency of pain
— Color and type of tissue and character of the wound bed, including evidence of healing or necrosis
— Description of wound edges
— Stages

Figure 15.4

If the patient becomes less mobile or other risk factors appear, the risk of developing a pressure ulcer should be reviewed. "Accurate and complete documentation of all risk assessments ensures continuity of care and may be used as a foundation for the skin care plan."[11] The size (in inches or centimeters), depth, location, and appearance of any existing pressure ulcers should be described. In November 2004, The Centers for Medicare and Medicaid Services issued guidance to surveyors involved in visiting nursing homes. The new information replaced Tag F314 and added language to F309. (This revision can be found on the CMS website.) Some of the key findings of these changes are summarized below. The author of this chapter has added some comments in parentheses. Attorneys are urged to review the complete document for all the pertinent points. The document concludes with a protocol for surveyors to use to evaluate a pressure ulcer development in a facility.

- Directions for documentation are provided in the intent of §483.25. At the time of the assessment and diagnosis, the clinician is expected to document the clinical basis of the ulcer (e.g., underlying condition contributing to the ulceration, ulcer edges and wound bed, location, shape, condition of surrounding tissues) which permit differentiating the ulcer type, especially if the ulcer has characteristics consistent with a pressure ulcer but is determined not to be one.

- Unavoidable pressure ulcers are defined for the first time. "An unavoidable pressure ulcer occurs when the facility staff evaluated the resident's clinical condition and pressure ulcer risk factors, defined and implemented interventions that are consistent with resident needs, goals, and recognized standards of practice, monitored and evaluated the impact of interventions, and revised the approaches as appropriate." (Note: documentation in the medical record should support that all of these components were carried out.)

- The staff should perform a complete assessment in order to prevent pressure ulcers and to identify the resident with pressure ulcers. An admission assessment helps to identify the resident at risk of developing a pressure ulcer or one who entered with pre-existing signs. These are defined as a very dark area that is surrounded by profound redness, swelling, or hardness. This suggests that deep tissue damage has already occurred.

- It may be harder to identify redness in a resident with darkly pigmented skin. Other signs should be sought, such as bogginess, hardness, coolness, increased warmth, or skin discoloration.

- A resident with a pressure ulcer who continues to lose weight either needs more calories or correction, where possible, of conditions that are creating a hypermetabolic state. Continuing weight loss and failure of a pressure ulcer to heal despite reasonable efforts to improve caloric intake may indicate that the resident is in a multisystem failure or an end-stage or end-of-life condition warranting additional assessment of the resident's overall condition. (Note: some residents have terminal illnesses, such as undiagnosed cancer, which causes uncontrollable weight loss.)

- It is critical that each resident at risk for hydration deficits or imbalance, including the resident with a pressure ulcer or at risk of developing an ulcer, be identified and that hydration needs are addressed. (Note: documentation about fluid intake should be reviewed.)

- Some studies have found that fecal incontinence may pose a greater threat to skin integrity than urine, most likely due to bile acids and enzymes in feces. (Note: review the medical record to determine if the resident was incontinent of bowel and bladder.)

- The care plan for a resident who is reclining and dependent on staff for repositioning should address position changes to maintain the resident's skin integrity. This may include repositioning at least every two hours or more frequently depending on the resident's condition and tolerance of the tissue load (pressure).

- Wheelchairs are often used for transporting residents, but they may severely limit repositioning options and increase the risk of pressure ulcer development. Wheelchairs with sling seats may not be optimal for prolonged sitting during activities or meals. Available modifications to the seating can provide a more stable surface and better pressure reduction. (Note: review the medical record to determine how long the resident was sitting in a wheelchair each day.)

- The resident's heels and elbows are particularly vulnerable to pressure due to their small surface area. It is important to pay particular attention to reducing the pressure on these areas. (Note: the medical record should include documentation of the use of heel protectors and elevation of the heels while in bed.)

- Staff should remain alert on a daily basis to potential changes in the skin condition. A resident who complains of pain or burning at a site where there has been pressure should be evaluated.

- Components of assessment of an ulcer include
  - differentiate the type of ulcer,
  - determine the ulcer's stage,
  - describe and monitor the ulcer's characteristics,
  - monitor the progress towards healing,
  - monitor for potential complications,
  - determine if the ulcer is infected,
  - assess, treat, and monitor pain, if present, and
  - monitor dressings and treatments.

- With each dressing change or at least weekly (and more often when indicated by wound complications or changes in wound characteristics), an evaluation of the pressure ulcer wound should be documented. At a minimum, documentation should include the date observed and
  - location and staging,
  - size, depth, presence, location, and extent of any undermining or tunneling/sinus tract,
  - exudate (drainage): color, odor, and approximate amount,
  - pain, if present: nature, frequency (episodic or continuous),
  - wound bed: color, type of tissue, evidence of healing (granulation tissue) or necrosis (slough or eschar), and
  - description of wound edges and surrounding tissue (rolled edges, redness, hardness/induration, maceration).

- If the ulcer fails to show some evidence of healing within two to four weeks, the ulcer and the resident's overall condition should be reassessed.

- If photographs are used, they should be taken in compliance with a protocol that addresses frequency, consistent distance from the wound, type of equipment used, means to assure digital images are accurate and not modified, inclusion of the resident identification/ulcer location/dates, and so on within the photographic images, and parameters for comparison.

Some facilities are using the additional precaution of photographing all pressure ulcers found at the time of admission. Such photographs should be dated. These data may be needed if there is a question about whether a pressure ulcer developed before or during the current hospitalization. The photographs and documentation also establish a baseline to evaluate changes in skin integrity. Some defense attorneys are discouraging the use of photographs. Nursing facilities have grappled with the use of photographs in the facility for a number of years. Most defense attorneys do not like pictures because they provide graphic demonstration of the injury, certainly enough to surprise and even shock most jurors who are unfamiliar with this type of wound. However, photographs may be taken by the plaintiff and will most certainly be presented as evidence in the case.[12] Chapter 26, *Skin Trauma,* and Chapter 27, *Controversies in Skin Trauma*, cover this topic in more detail.

3. Suicidal tendencies and violence

A third aspect of identifying the patient at risk for injury involves patients with a potential for harming themselves or others. The Joint Commission focused on this problem in 1998 with the release of a Sentinel Event Alert, which cited incomplete or infrequent patient assessment as one of the root causes.[13] Nurses often detect symptoms of emotional or psychiatric problems. In 2007, The Joint Commission added a National Patient Safety Goal related to suicide: *The Organization Identifies the Safety Risks Inherent in its Patient Population (Implemented January 1, 2007) A. NPSG.15.01.01 Identification of Patients at Risk for Suicide (Hospitals, Behavioral Health).*

When concern arises about the patient's emotional stability, the nurse should document the following: any information provided by the patient concerning previous psychiatric problems, treatments, or hospitalizations; the patient's perception of the situation; and the nurse's assessment of the patient's interpersonal strengths and limitations. Consider the following example:

Patient admitted with chief complaint of rectal bleeding. States he was hospitalized at State Hospital in 1999 because he wanted to kill himself. Says he still has these thoughts and keeps a loaded gun at home. Patient has been receiving outpatient counseling at local mental health clinic. Lacks insight into his problems.

Given this assessment, the nurse would identify the patient's risk for injury and initiate appropriate interventions, including notifying the physician of the patient's comments. The nursing assessment should include data about risk factors for violence. A psychotic patient or patient with a history of violence, substance abuse, or suicide attempts may be more prone to violent outbursts. Questions about these risk factors should be included in the database. Although these factors are commonly incorporated into the database for a patient with a psychiatric diagnosis, any patient may have these risk factors. The nursing assessment must show that the presence of signs indicating a potential for violence has been noted. If warranted by the patient's condition, further documentation should indicate that action was taken to protect the patient and others from harm.

Documentation should include

- direct quotations from the patient, family, or visitors related to suicidal thoughts, actions, and motives,
- data gathered about the patient's risk factors for suicide,
- actions taken to remove items that could harm the patient, and
- names of individuals who were notified about the concerns, such as the attending physician or supervisor.[14]

See Chapter 22, *Psychiatric Records*, for more information.

4. Abuse

People of all ages may be the victims of abuse, from young children to the elderly. Abuse may fit into one of four categories: physical, psychological, financial, or neglect.[15] Nurses encounter victims of abuse in a variety of settings, including the office, the home, the workplace, the emergency department, and acute and long-term-care settings. Over the course of the last several years, Joint Commission standards have highlighted the need to identify possible victims of abuse.

In general, those who are most likely to be abused are dependent on the abuser. Risk factors for elder abuse include the following: both the victim and the abuser having a history of mental illness; shared living arrangements; family history of violence; dependency; and lack of financial resources. Poor health and cognitive impairment on the part of the victim can also contribute to the risks.[16] The abuser may be under unusual stress or have psychiatric or substance-abuse problems. Adult victims of abuse are typically isolated from contact with others who would intervene if they knew about the abuse. The nurse should suspect abuse whenever the patient refers to violence in the home or has injuries inconsistent with the explanation of the patient or family. Bruises in areas covered by clothing, cigarette burns, and unusual fractures may raise the suspicion of abuse.

Abused young children may be more likely to be underweight and anemic from neglect. The patient's interactions with family members should be observed, because the victim may exhibit fear in the presence of the abuser. In these situations, the nurse is advised to interview the patient privately. The nurse should look for evasion when the patient or family is questioned about how the injury occurred. The attorney reviewer, paralegal, or legal nurse consultant, should find evidence in the medical record of documentation of the patient's explanations about the cause of the physical problems.

The description of the nature of the injuries and the patient's behavior should be precise. For example:

(Adult female) patient has a variety of yellow-green and black-blue bruises over her breasts and abdomen. Patient avoided eye contact and said she was injured when she walked into a door.

TIP: The integumentary section of the assessment form should contain documentation of the size, shape, and appearance of bruises, lacerations, or injuries in unusual areas such as the neck or genitals.

The nurse may document pattern injuries that are left when an object used to strike a person leaves an imprint, or parallel injuries, such as bruises on both arms in the same area. Burns should be described; for example, cigarette, iron, rope, and immersion burns may be noted.[17] Many facilities include a specific section on the admission assessment form that provides an area to document any concerns about abuse or neglect.

Photographs are sometimes taken with the patient's permission to preserve evidence of the appearance of the bruises. The attorney may request copies of these photos. Nurses may be obligated to fulfill legal obligations to report suspected cases of abuse. The medical record should include the following: consents from the patient, parent, or legal guardian for collection of information and evidence, as needed; data regarding notification of authorities; and referrals made to community agencies. Reports completed in investigatory agencies may be contained in the medical records or might need to be separately requested.

5. Substance abuse

The abuse of substances is an increasingly common problem in our society. Patients with substance-abuse problems may be encountered in all areas of nursing care. Substances that are commonly abused include narcotics, sedatives, alcohol, and street drugs. The desire to use narcotics may be based on positive reinforcement (the desire for a high) or negative reinforcement (the desire to alleviate pain or discomfort, including that of withdrawal). Prescription drug abuse is on the rise in the United States. The dimensions of this issue are enormous. The 10 percent of the population that drinks the most heavily accounts for 50 percent of the alcohol consumed in the United States. Many of the medications that elderly patients take, including antidepressants and tranquilizers, interact with alcohol, often synergistically. Such interactions can result in aspiration pneumonia, falls, hip fractures, and motor vehicle accidents. Substance abuse is often misdiagnosed in the elderly because symptoms such as changes in cognition, behavior, or physical functioning tend to be attributed inaccurately to an underlying medical condition or simply old age. The leading cause of death among people between fifteen and twenty-four years old is violence, including accidents, homicides, and suicides. Many of these deaths can be attributed to the use of drugs and alcohol.

Part of nursing assessment includes inquiring about and documenting drug and alcohol use. The nurse should specifically ask about the amounts and frequency of alcohol use and other drug use in the past month, week, and day. Details should be documented, including how old the patient was when the substances were first used, the duration and intensity of use, and patterns and consequences of use. If the patient denies recent use, the nurse is expected to ask about previous history to determine whether the patient has ever abused alcohol or used other drugs. Even currently substance-abusing clients in denial may be willing to reveal excessive substance use in the distant past. Use of multiple prescriptions from several doctors and the use of illicit drugs should be specifically investigated. Key signs of substance abuse include consumption of five or more drinks at a time, or use of marijuana more than five times in the client's life. (Statistically, using marijuana more than five times seems to correlate with an increased likelihood of substance abuse.)

Four key questions—also known as CAGE—that healthcare professionals ask include the following:

1. Have you felt that you ought to **cut** down on your drinking or drug use?
2. Have people **annoyed** you by criticizing your drinking or drug use?
3. Have you felt bad or **guilty** about your drinking or drug use?
4. Have you **ever** had a drink or used drugs first thing in the morning (eye opener) to steady your nerves, get rid of a hangover, or get the day started?

Medical consequences of alcohol and drug use should be documented. The medical record may document the patient's level of insight about the correlation between the medical complications of substance abuse and the use of substances. The patient may be asked about the effects of drug or alcohol use on the patient's life. Problems may exist with his health, family, job, or financial status or with the legal system. The patient may admit to a history of blackouts or motor vehicle accidents. The medical records should contain documentation of information regarding the treatment the patient has received for the abuse problem and the effectiveness of the treatment.

The medical records should be carefully evaluated when there is a suspicion of drug-seeking behavior. Characteristics that correlate with abuse or suspected abuse are

- rapid increases in the amount of a medication such as an opioid, central nervous system depressant, or stimulant,
- frequent requests for refills before the quantity prescribed should have been used up,
- doctor shopping in an effort to obtain multiple prescriptions for a drug that is being abused,[18]
- emergency department visits for a variety of subjective painful conditions that are always accompanied by a request for a specific analgesic regimen (along with outpatient prescriptions),
- long lists of undocumented drug allergies,
- repeated claims that a prescription was lost,
- a pattern of making verbal contracts with treating physicians that are not kept,
- discovery of a patient who is rifling through drawers in an emergency department to steal needles or syringes,[19]
- visiting a physician without an appointment to get a prescription renewal,
- frequent calls to the physician's office requesting prescription renewals, and
- frequent requests for drug or dose escalation.

Drug-seeking behavior may be suspected when a pattern of entries like these—based on actual medical records—is found in office or clinic records:

- Patient states he lost his bottle of Percodan (oxycodone) and needs a new prescription.
- Patient states she accidentally spilled her Percocet/Tylox on the floor and needs a new prescription.
- Patient wants a new prescription for MSContin (morphine) because her husband has been taking her supply.
- Pharmacy called: When patient brought script to drug store, it looked like the number "1" was changed to "4". They refused to fill prescription. Dr. Kipp was informed.
- Patient arrived without an appointment. He stated his back pain was severe and he wanted an injection for pain.
- Mr. Piller has called the office three times in the last three days seeking a new prescription for pain medication. He states the Tylenol #3 (acetaminophen with codeine, 15 mg) does not work and he would like to have a script for Percodan (oxycodone).
- Mr. King is allergic to Demerol (meperidine), morphine, Talwin (pentazocine) and Nubain (nalbuphine).
- Mrs. Witter says she would like to have a prescription for Percocet.

When appropriate, the nurse should perform a psychosocial assessment. This process would include information about the

- motivation to change or accept treatment,
- obstacles or resources that would impact recovery, including substance abuse by other family members,
- religious and spiritual beliefs,
- history of physical or sexual abuse,
- sexual history and orientation,
- leisure and recreational activities and childhood history,
- military service and financial status,
- social, peer-group, and environmental setting from which the patient comes,
- family circumstances, including the composition of the family group,
- current living situation, and
- other social, ethnic, cultural, health, and emotional factors.

C. Potential for Self-Care Following Discharge

Assessment and documentation of discharge planning needs to begin at the initial encounter with the patient and continue throughout the provision of care. It is important for the nurse, case manager, and physician to identify the patients who are most likely to need assistance with discharge planning. A high-risk group in one facility may not be so in another facility. The types of patients and the services they require vary with location, socioeconomic status, and support systems of the populations served by the facility. These factors should be taken into account when discharge planning questions are designed and incorporated into assessment tools. Sources of information, such as family members or significant others, are usually needed to complete the database and document discharge needs.

TIP: When gathering information from sources other than the patient, the nurse should clearly document the name of the person, the data provided by the person, and the person's relationship with the patient.

Assessment of discharge needs is particularly important when a patient has been readmitted within a short time for the same condition. A medical negligence suit may revolve around the issue of whether adequate discharge instructions were provided at the end of the first admission. Reimbursement problems may result if a regulatory group, such as a peer review organization, determines that faulty discharge planning or premature discharge was a factor in the readmission. The results of the previous discharge plan, the stability of the patient's health, the patient's understanding of self-care, and the patient's knowledge of community resources should be evaluated. In addition, the patient who has no family or friends to depend on for support may need referral for discharge planning.

The documentation of self-care abilities provides information about the patient's needs to those involved in discharge planning. The initial assessment form provides a central source of information needed for discharge planning. A variety of healthcare professionals use these data, including nurses, physicians, dietitians, social workers, discharge planners, case managers and therapists. With all information centrally located, health workers can easily retrieve data through the clinical record.

Patients are sometimes labeled as uncooperative by the medical and legal systems for not following prescription directions, appointment slips and other written instructions. "Health literacy" is defined as the degree to which individuals have the capacity to obtain, process, and understand basic health information and services needed to make appropriate health care decisions. People with low health literacy are less likely to understand written and oral health information and to be able to navigate the healthcare system. Superimposed on depression, lost income, pain and other symptoms, low functional health literacy can sabotage the efforts of the patient to obtain medically necessary treatment. Although health literacy affects people from all backgrounds, the problem is more acute in those who are older, non-white, immigrants, and those with low incomes. Approximately 44 million adults in the United States are functionally illiterate and an additional 54 million have marginally better reading and computation skills. This information suggests that many injured people may have difficulty understanding prescriptions, informed consent documents, insurance forms, and patient education materials, most of which are written at a high school level. The recommended reading level for all health education materials is 5th to 6th grades. Many individuals with low reading skills are loathe to admit to their deficits and go to great lengths to avoid admitting they have trouble reading. Often they cover this by saying they forgot their glasses.[20]

D. Patient and Family Education Needs

The fourth priority "P" is assessment of patient and family education needs. The assessment of learning needs provides the foundation for the individualized teaching plan. The data collected during the first interaction with the patient are supplemented and validated by subsequent encounters with the patient. The following three factors are important in the documentation of assessed learning needs:

1. *Health beliefs*, *attitudes*, and *social factors* may help or hinder the patient's ability to follow the medical regimen. Examples of factors that may help the patient follow treatment recommendations include a willingness to follow the healthcare regimen, understanding from a supportive family, and the individual's belief that she is in control of her own destiny. Examples of factors that may *hinder* the ability to follow treatment recommendations include superstitions, poverty, language barriers, cultural practices, illiteracy, old wives' tales, and the belief that fate and luck control one's destiny instead of the individual. These could be documented in the following manner:
    *   **Health beliefs**. Patient believes that copper bracelets reduce arthritis symptoms and refuses to take anti-inflammatory agents.
    *   **Attitudes**. Patient states that there is no point in learning how to do care for his colostomy because he is going to die anyway.

*   **Social factors**. (Adult) patient has completed third grade and is unable to read.

2. The *ability to learn*, *follow directions*, and *recall information* may be hindered by several factors, including the effects of aging, sensory deficits, cognitive limitations, the effects of sedation and analgesics, sleep deprivation, pain, stress, memory loss, limited attention span, impaired judgment, and sensory overload. These could be documented in the following manner:
    *   **Ability to learn and follow directions**. Patient is a college graduate who owns a dry cleaning business. Patient is hard of hearing and does not have a hearing aid with her.
    *   **Ability to recall information**. Patient is unable to recall names or types of medications she is taking. Patient states that physician told her what she is taking but that she can never remember these details.

3. *Readiness to learn about condition, self-care measures*, and *priority learning needs* may be hindered by several factors, including lack of motivation, denial of the need to learn, substance abuse, self-destructive patterns, depression, anxiety, stress, fear of change, and social isolation. These could be documented in the following manner:
    *   **Readiness to learn**. Patient says she wants to learn how to manage her asthma.
    *   **Self-care measures**. Patient states that he does not want to learn how to change colostomy bag, saying, "My daughter takes care of that."
    *   **Priority of learning needs**. Patient says she is very interested in finding out how to do CPR for the sake of her infant.

The assessment of learning needs is usually documented on the initial assessment form. Documentation continues on the progress notes or patient education flow sheet as new information is gained. The key points that should be documented are listed in Figure 15.5.

The description of patient-education needs may be documented in appropriate sections of the initial assessment form (decentralized documentation) or in one section labeled "Teaching Needs" (centralized documentation). With *decentralized* charting of teaching needs, pertinent comments may be placed in specific categories of data. However, in this approach the information that identifies learning needs is scattered throughout the form, and the information must be retrieved from several places to develop a teaching plan. *Centralized* charting of teaching needs is typically presented as a summary statement at the end of an assessment form. The section labeled "Teaching Needs" acts as a cue to remind the nurse to address patient education needs. Using this format the nurse can synthesize all the information provided by the patient and identify the high-priority teaching needs. If this format is used, sufficient space for documentation must be included on the form. Patient education needs that are identified after admission to the hospital or after care is initiated may be documented in progress notes or on a centralized form.

E. Pain

A variety of specialized assessment instruments and techniques have been developed to assist healthcare providers in complying with the national standards. These techniques include the use of screening scores, screening tools and algorithms to drive pain assessment and reassessment. Screening pain scores (a pain intensity rating at the time of patient visit or admission) can be used to get a baseline indication of pain level upon hospital admission or with each ambulatory care visit.

Patients contribute to the undertreatment of pain for a number of reasons. They may be fearful that the pain is an indication of a worsening health problem, and therefore believe if it is not reported, and ignored, it will go away. They may be concerned about distracting healthcare providers from other issues ("You're so busy, I hate to bother you…"). Pain may not be reported because it will signal the discomfort or expense of testing and treating the problem causing the pain. The patient may not report pain because of a fear of being labeled as a complainer. Some patients are fatalistic and believe they are meant to endure pain. Others may infer that the healthcare provider should know that the condition is painful and would provide relief if it were available. The stoic individual may be reluctant to seek treatment, believing that it is better to tough it out rather than admit to what is perceived as a weakness: needing help. This individual is taught not to complain. As the author's stoic grandfather used to say, "It does not make any difference whether you complain or not—it won't change a thing. So why complain?" Medical records typically state the patient denied pain, although the nurse may observe objective signs of pain.

Each patient should be assessed for the presence of pain, pain intensity, and barriers to pain assessment. To make the process easier, simple screening questions may be added to admission forms that ask if pain is present and if so at what intensity, if the patient has had any prior problems with pain management, or if the patient has had severe pain for longer than twenty-four hours. If the patient indicates pain, or responds positively to these questions, a more detailed and comprehensive pain assessment should be carried out. Refer to Figure 15.6.

Elements that Nurses Should Document When Assessing Patient Education Needs

Chief complaint: knowledge of disease process, reason for seeking health care; awareness of signs and symptoms as they relate to primary diagnosis

Diet: knowledge of dietary restrictions, adherence to diet

Medications: ability to describe medications, including purpose, schedule, and side effects; adherence to medication regimen; use of over-the-counter medications or illegal drugs

Physical activity: awareness of the impact of activity on disease as well as how disease affects lifestyle

Treatments: ability of the patient or significant other to manage continuing care needs after discharge

Figure 15.5

Pain Assessment Documentation

- Level of pain
- What causes it
- Where is it
- Radiation (where does it travel)
- Nature of the pain- sharp, dull, aching, throbbing, pressure, heavy
- Onset and duration
- What aggravates the pain
- What alleviates the pain
- What are the effects of the pain: mood changes, sleep disturbance, depression, loss of concentration, anxiety, anger, decreased activity, interference with relationships or employment
- What is the patient's goal of pain management, including the level of pain

Figure 15.6

Some individuals are not able to provide a description of pain. The healthcare professional must then use other signs to assess pain level. Interpretation of the patient's facial expressions, behavior and body movements is less accurate than the individual's report of the level of pain.

The elderly may not be able to verbally communicate pain due to dementia. A resident of a nursing home suffered a fractured leg when she was dropped by two nursing aides. The leg was so badly shattered that it had to be amputated. This confused patient could not ask for pain medication in the days following surgery. Review of the medical record showed that the nurses did not provide pain medication to this patient, although an order for medication had been written by the physician. The failure to administer pain medication was below the standard of care.

Interpreters must be available to assist in communication about pain with patients who speak another language.

Patients in ICU can experience discomfort as a result of untreated or intractable pain, invasive procedures, mechanical ventilation, prone positioning, sleep deprivation, adverse drug events, and alcohol and drug withdrawal. The resulting agitation and anxiety can lead to difficulty breathing, patient-ventilator dys-synchrony, elevated blood pressure and heart rate, combative behavior and posttraumatic stress disorder. Observe for moaning, grimacing, rigidity, wincing, eye closing, and fist clenching.

Some critical care patients are able to self report their pain levels. However, those that are intubated or comatose are much more difficult to assess. The use of behavioral scales has been tried with modest success. Researchers have found that critical care patients experienced a high level of pain and that these patients had recall of their critical care pain experiences. A rule of thumb with patients who are unable to report pain is to assume that pain is present if the patient is experiencing a condition which is normally painful.

The medical record may contain assessment data such as these two statements:

1. His knee felt like it had been hit with a sledge hammer hard enough to drive it up into his thigh.
2. The pain was squeezing, clamping pressure—as if steel clamps were squeezing his legs all the time.

There is a growing recognition by attorneys that failure to assess, treat and manage pain is professional negligence. Specific theories of liability include failure to refer to a pain specialist, infliction of emotional distress, and failure to provide informed consent by not discussing alternatives to treatments for pain. In all cases, analysis of medical records, prescriber orders, medication administration records,

and nurses' and other professionals' documentation will be used to analyze liability and to determine the damages. See Chapter 18, *Pain Assessment and Management*, for more information on pain documentation.

F. Reassessments

TIP: Once the admission assessment is completed, the process of ongoing reassessments begins. Facility policy defines how frequently patients are reassessed.

The intervals vary depending on the acuity of the patient regular standards, and the type of care that is needed. Significant changes in the patient's condition, responses, and diagnostic testing trigger the reassessment process. Reassessments are documented in the progress notes and on a variety of flow sheets.

15.6 Components of the Planning Process

Although the formats and methods may change, planning care remains a key step in the nursing process. With accurate and thorough planning, the nurse is able to provide individualized care. Expressing the plan of care in writing promotes continuity and consistency of care. A plan of care based on the admission assessment and subsequent nursing diagnoses provides the nurse with information essential for the provision of high-quality care and helps the attorney and expert witnesses determine if the standard of care was followed.

The planning phase of the nursing process is preceded by formulating nursing diagnoses. Next, the nurse is involved in establishing desired patient outcomes, selecting appropriate interventions, and documenting the plan of care. Each of these components is discussed in the following text.

A. Standardized Nursing Language

TIP: Standardized terms are used by nurses to promote consistency in describing the patient's problems, nursing treatments, and desired outcomes.

The benefits of using standardized nursing language include

*   providing a mechanism for clearly defining and evaluating nursing care,
*   promoting continuity of care,
*   having the ability to incorporate standardized terms in computerized documentation systems,
*   identifying the most effective nursing interventions.[21]

- providing connections that link nursing assessment databases with expected patient outcomes and nursing interventions,
- creating an awareness of nursing's distinct role in the healthcare team, and
- reducing confusion created by use of different terms to describe the same behavior.[22]

The three standardized nursing languages discussed in this section include nursing diagnoses, outcomes, and interventions. These are known as NANDA (North American Nursing Diagnosis Association) nursing diagnoses, NOC (Nursing Outcomes Classification), and NIC (Nursing Interventions Classification). A brief discussion of each system is provided below. NANDA's nursing diagnoses are most widely used, although there are a few other systems of identifying nursing diagnoses.

B. Nursing Diagnoses

A nursing diagnosis is a clinical judgment about individual, family, or community responses to actual or potential health problems/life processes. A nursing diagnosis provides the basis for selection of nursing interventions to achieve desired outcomes for which the nurse is accountable.[23]

Health-promotion and wellness nursing diagnoses also exist. A *health-promotion nursing diagnosis* is a clinical judgment of a person's, family's or community's motivation and desire to increase well-being and actualize human health potential, as expressed in their readiness to enhance specific health behaviors such as nutrition and exercise. Health-promotion diagnoses can be used in any health state and do not require current levels of wellness. This readiness is supported by defining characteristics. Interventions are selected in concert with the individual/family/community to ensure the ability to reach the stated outcomes.[24] A *wellness nursing diagnosis* describes human responses to levels of wellness in an individual, family, or community that have a readiness for enhancement. This readiness is supported by defining characteristics. "As with all diagnoses, nurse-sensitive (sensitive to nursing interventions) outcomes are identified and nursing interventions are selected that will provide a high likelihood of reaching the outcomes."[25]

1. Basis for diagnosis

The nursing diagnosis as written usually consists of two components: human responses (or problems) and related factors. The human response is a term used to define a problem that the nurse has identified through assessment. The vast majority of human responses identified by NANDA define problems that nurses are licensed to treat because they are qualified by virtue of their education. An example of a nursing diagnosis is "risk for injury related to dizziness." (See www.nanda.org for current information on how to obtain the list of approved nursing diagnoses.) Each diagnosis has a label or name, a definition, and defining characteristics.

2. Nursing diagnosis classification

After gathering and analyzing assessment data, the nurse formulates the nursing diagnosis by selecting the appropriate human response from the list of accepted nursing diagnoses. If the nurse is unable to locate a human response on the NANDA list (or other system in use at the facility), he should develop a statement that defines the patient's problem.

Related factors are the factors that appear to show some type of patterned relationship with the nursing diagnosis. Such factors may be described as antecedent to, associated with, related to, contributing to or abetting. Only actual nursing diagnoses have related factors.[26] Related factors can be reflected in physiologic responses and influenced by psychosocial and spiritual elements. The identification of related factors is just as important as the correct identification of the human response. In the diagnostic process, whereas the human response guides the selection of the appropriate outcome, the related factors guide the choice of interventions. If the nurse cannot identify the related factors because of insufficient data, the term *unknown etiology* can be used to indicate that more data are needed; for example, "anxiety related to unknown etiology."

The term *related to* links the human response and the related factors. This relationship implies that if one part of the diagnosis changes, the other part may also change.[27] "Related to" does not express a direct cause-and-effect relationship.

The human response may be associated with a wide variety of related factors, such as "activity intolerance related to deconditioning" or "activity intolerance related to anemia." In this example the human response is the same but the interventions reflect the difference between related factors.

NANDA's diagnoses are assigned a code for use in computerized medical record systems. The Doenges/Moorhouse Diagnostic Divisions include

- Activity/Rest,
- Circulation
- Ego integrity
- Elimination
- Food/Fluid
- Hygiene

- Neurosensory
- Pain/Discomfort
- Respiration
- Safety
- Sexuality
- Social interaction
- Teaching/learning[28]

Nurses may add to the body of knowledge of nursing diagnoses by submitting a diagnosis for acceptance to the Diagnosis Development Committee of NANDA.

3. Evaluating the diagnosis

The American Nurses Association Standards of Practice[29] state that the registered nurse is expected to analyze the assessment data to determine the diagnoses or issues. The measurement criteria for this statement include that the nurse derives the diagnoses or issues based on the assessment data, validates the diagnoses or issues with the patient, family, and other healthcare providers when possible and appropriate, and documents diagnoses or issues in a manner that facilitates the determination of the expected outcomes and plan.

TIP: In a nursing negligence claim, the attorney and expert witness may need to review the nursing diagnoses to determine if they are applicable to the patient. The evaluation may encompass the diagnoses documented on the care plan as well as the actions the nurse took in a certain situation.

---

a. The diagnosis should be based on the assessment data. There should be support in the medical record for the basis for the diagnosis. For example, a nursing diagnosis of "confusion, risk for acute" may appear in the record of a critically ill patient who has been subjected to constant noise, lights, and activities that interfere with sleep.

b. The diagnoses should address the needs of the patient. Validating the diagnoses with the family or patient would involve a discussion between the nurse and these parties. The nurse might say, "These are the issues I see as a problem. Do you agree?" This discussion may be documented by nurses as "Verified with patient that his anxiety is preventing sleep. Discussed stress reduction interventions."

c. Diagnoses are documented in a variety of care planning formats. The patient's diagnoses should be updated as new problems emerge. An outdated diagnosis that is no longer valid should be marked as not being current.

C. Outcomes

In the planning phase, the nurse establishes patient outcomes, which provide a mechanism for evaluating the patient's progress and changes in the patient's status.

1. Basis for outcomes

Outcomes are based on the nursing diagnoses and direct the nursing care. With an increased emphasis on evaluating outcomes of care, the nurse must obtain the knowledge and develop the skills to formulate effective outcomes. The reviewer of the medical record should see evidence that the nurse identified outcomes for care.

2. Nursing Outcomes Classification

The Nursing Outcomes Classification[30] is a comprehensive, standardized classification of patient outcomes developed to evaluate the effects of nursing interventions. Standardized outcomes are used to

- provide a standardized language for nursing
- facilitate appropriate selection of nursing interventions
- define and predict outcomes nurses can achieve with their patients
- facilitate communication of nursing treatments to other nurses and providers
- standardize and define the knowledge base for nursing curricula and practice
- assist administrators ineffectively planning for staff and equipment resources
- enable researchers to examine the effectiveness and cost of nursing care
- assist educators in developing curricula that better conform with clinical practice
- promote the development of a reimbursement system for nursing services
- facilitate the development of computerized information systems
- communicate the nature of nursing to the public.[31]

The Nursing Outcomes Classification is periodically updated. Each outcome has a

- definition,
- list of indicators that can be used to evaluate patient status in relation to the outcome,
- a target outcome rating,
- place to identify the source of data,
- a five-point Likert scale to measure patient status, and

- short list of references used in the development of the outcome.

Each outcome has a unique number that can be used in computerized clinical information systems. The 385 outcomes are grouped into thirty-one classes and divided into seven domains for ease of use. The domains are

- Functional Health,
- Physiologic Health,
- Psychosocial Health,
- Health Knowledge and Behavior,
- Perceived Health,
- Family Health, and
- Community Health.

A few examples of outcomes include

- 1211 Anxiety Level: Severity of manifested apprehension, tension, or uneasiness arising from an unidentified source.
- 0210 Transfer Performance: Ability to change body location independently with or without assistive device.[32]

TIP: Outcomes in the Nursing Outcomes Classification have been linked to several other systems used to define patient problems including systems used in home care, nursing homes, and have been linked to nursing diagnoses and nursing interventions.

---

3. Evaluating the outcomes

The American Nurses Association Standards of Practice[33] address the formation of outcomes. The registered nurse is expected to identify the expected outcomes for a plan that is individualized for the patient or the situation. In order to do so, the registered nurse is expected to involve the patient, family, and other healthcare providers in formulating these outcomes. The outcomes should be culturally appropriate and include a consideration of the risks, benefits, costs, current scientific evidence, and the nurse's clinical expertise. Other factors that influence the formulation of outcomes include the patient's values, ethical considerations, the environment, or the situation. There should be a time estimate for attainment of the outcomes. Outcomes should provide direction for continuity of care for other healthcare providers and settings that will be involved in the care of the patient. The outcomes should be modified based on changes in the status of the patient, the success of the outcomes, or changes in the situation of care. Measurable goals should be documented as the outcomes.

Guidelines for the Formulations of Outcomes

Outcomes should be:
- patient oriented
- realistic
- measurable and observable
- clear and concise
- mutually established
- time bound

Figure 15.7

The outcomes are evaluated to determine if they are applicable to the patient and achievable. (Figure 15.7) These guidelines, coupled with the ANA standards, provide a framework for evaluation of the outcomes.

a. Outcomes should be *patient-oriented*. Outcomes describe the expected behavior that should occur when the patient and family have resolved the nursing diagnosis. An example of an outcome is: "No evidence of skin breakdown over bony prominences exists." Outcomes are now clearly phrased to define patient behaviors, not nursing behaviors.

b. Outcomes should be *realistic*. The nurse must be realistic in writing patient outcomes because a partial change in behavior may be the only goal attainable. In addition, a short patient stay may limit what can be accomplished in the healthcare facility. Some outcomes may have to be completed after discharge, extending the continuum of care into the patient's home environment.

c. Outcomes should be *measurable* and *observable*. Without measurable patient outcomes the nursing process cannot be completed. The nurse should avoid using the terms *understands* and *appreciates* because these terms are difficult to measure. The following outcomes are *inappropriately* worded:

- The patient understands diabetes.
- The patient appreciates the importance of taking insulin.

These outcomes are *correctly* worded:

- The patient can describe the signs and symptoms of hypoglycemia.
- The patient demonstrates correct insulin injection technique.

Only when outcomes are measurable can the nurse determine whether they have been achieved.[34]

d. Outcomes should be *clear* and *concise*, written in a way that is easily understood by both staff and patients. The nurse should avoid lengthy, ambiguous wording, and use simple language to communicate what is expected of the patient.

e. Outcomes should be established *mutually* between the nurse and patient because mutual goals facilitate active participation and communication of expectations between the nurse and the patient. The probability of a patient achieving the goals is enhanced if she is included in the planning process.

f. Outcomes should be *time bound*. The inclusion of a time frame directs the evaluation of outcome achievement at a predetermined interval. Time frames can be stated in a number of ways (for example, "within two hours," "within three days," "throughout hospitalization," "within one month," or "by the time of discharge"). The nature of the outcome and a realistic evaluation of the probability of achieving it should be considered when establishing the time frame.

D. Interventions

After the nursing diagnoses and outcomes are established, interventions that help the patient achieve the outcomes should be selected and documented.

1. Basis for interventions

An intervention is defined as "any treatment, based on the clinical judgment and knowledge that a nurse performs to enhance patient/client outcomes."[35] Figure 15.8 outlines the characteristics of appropriate interventions.

Guidelines for Formulation of Interventions

Interventions should be:

- generated from the related factors
- specific
- individualized
- realistic
- dated and initialed

Figure 15.8

TIP: With an increasing number of part-time, per diem, and float pool nurses caring for patients, accuracy and completeness of the nursing interventions are essential.

---

2. Nursing Interventions Classification

Creating a standardized method for classifying nursing interventions has become increasingly important with the development of computerized nursing information systems. Before nursing documentation could become fully computerized, a common language had to be established to clarify and communicate the role of the nurse in healthcare settings. Chapter 5, *Charting Systems*, in Volume I, provides additional information on computerized documentation.

The NIC project, developed in 1992 by researchers at the University of Iowa, is a comprehensive, research-based, standardized classification of interventions. It is useful for clinical documentation, communication of care across settings, effectiveness research, productivity measurements, competency evaluations, reimbursement, and curricular design. The Classification includes interventions that nurses perform on behalf of patients, both independent (not requiring physician order) and collaborative interventions. They include both physiological and psychosocial activities.

Examples of NIC Intervention Labels and Definitions are

3140   Airway management: facilitation of patency of air passages.

5390   Self awareness enhancement: assisting a patient to explore and understand his/her thoughts, feelings, motivations, and behaviors.

There are 514 interventions in the fourth edition of the classification system. Each intervention has a unique code and is accompanied by specific activities. These are grouped into thirty classes and seven domains. The domains are

- Physiological: Basic,
- Physiological: Complex,
- Behavioral,
- Safety,
- Family,
- Health system, and
- Community.[36]

3. Evaluating the interventions

The identification of interventions is addressed by the American Nurses Association Standards of Practice.[37] A standard requires the nurse to develop a plan that prescribes strategies and alternatives to attain the expected outcomes. The nurse can demonstrate fulfillment of this standard by developing an individualized plan that considers the patient characteristics or the situation (such as the age and culture of the patient). The plan is to be developed in conjunction with the family, patient, and others as appropriate. The nurse includes strategies that address each of the identified diagnoses or issues, which may include interventions for promotion and restoration of health and prevention of illness, injury, and disease. The plan should provide for continuity of care and incorporation of an implementation pathway or timeline. The patient, family, and others are consulted to establish the priorities. Current statutes, rules, regulations, and standards are reflected in the plan. For example, use of restraints should conform to policies regarding obtaining orders, releasing the restraints at intervals, and offering food and elimination opportunities. The plan should also integrate current trends and research affecting care, consider the economic impact of the plan, and use standardized terminology to document the plan.

Appropriate care of a patient may hinge on correct identification of nursing actions. The attorney reviewing a medical record of a plaintiff will find the medical record replete with documentation of interventions. Evaluation of the plan should reflect the ANA standards and points below.

a. As stated previously, the interventions are generated from the related factors in the nursing diagnosis. For example, the nursing diagnosis "risk for impaired skin integrity related to immobility" should prompt the nurse to develop interventions to treat the immobility, such as turning the patient or moving the patient out of bed. By treating immobility the nurse may be able to prevent skin integrity problems.

b. Nursing interventions should be specific. The interventions are meant to direct the care provided by the nursing staff. Therefore action verbs should be used to communicate the expectations for care and the frequency of interventions. Nurses often write vague interventions such as "encourage fluids" and leave the specifics to the discretion of the caregiver. Specific interventions such as "give 200 ml of juice every two hours while awake" are more meaningful.

c. Interventions should be individualized. The purpose of planning care is to assist nurses in addressing differences in the care of patients with similar problems. Interventions should be based on the patient's individual needs. For example, a child and an elderly person may both have the same nursing diagnosis; however, the interventions would differ, perhaps significantly, because of differences in the patients' ages and development.

d. Interventions should be realistic for the patient and nurse and should consider the patient's length of stay, the patient care resources available, and the expected outcomes. Implementing the interventions in the time allotted with the available staff should be possible. The interventions should be realistically phrased to reflect available resources and current nursing literature.

e. All interventions should be dated and initialed, which enables the nurse to establish accountability for professional practice and provides other caregivers with an opportunity to obtain clarification from the person who initiated the interventions.

In summary, the planning phase of the nursing process has three components: the formulation of nursing diagnoses, the establishment of patient outcomes, and the selection of appropriate interventions.

15.7 Care Planning
A. Purpose

TIP: The purpose of the plan of care is to provide a core of information on the patient's nursing diagnoses, outcomes, and planned interventions.

The plan of care is a communication tool for everyone involved in patient care. The interaction of nurses with one another is limited, so they rely heavily on the plan of care to ensure continuity of care for the patient. Because of increases in cross-training efforts designed to contain costs, nurses assigned to work in areas where they have little practical experience can benefit from written plans developed by expert clinicians.[38] The plan of care should guide care and document the planning phase of the nursing process.

The plan of care should be based on the admission assessment and should be initiated during the admission process (or shortly thereafter). The introduction of the diagnostic related grouping (DRG) designations decreased length of stay, necessitating rapid assessment and interventions for patient problems. Once the plan of care has been established, it must be updated regularly to remain current and useful. A number of individuals review care plans, and the information obtained helps to validate admissions, services provided, length of stay, and DRG assignment, and to ensure the delivery of high-quality care. Care plans are also used as part of the evaluation of liability of healthcare professionals. Insurance companies, peer review organizations (PROs), regulatory agencies, malpractice attorneys, and utilization management personnel routinely read the plan of care and associated documentation.[39] The identified nursing diagnoses, outcomes, and interventions may be compared with the documentation in the progress notes. Such an evaluation may be used to determine whether the patient's significant problems were identified and whether nursing measures were effective in relieving them. Additional documentation, including flow sheets and progress notes, may be reviewed to verify that the nurse carried out the plan of care.

B. Individual Care Plans

Care plans have undergone a metamorphosis over the years. (See Figure 15.9.) Individual care plans are created for each patient based on individual needs. This approach was the only option when the concept of care planning first emerged. The nurse collected data at the time of admission, identified problems, and formulated the individualized, handwritten plan of care. The format is usually a three-column design with column headings: *Patient Problems/Nursing Diagnosis*, *Patient Outcomes*, and *Nursing Interventions*. Although time consuming to create, the individualized plan of care should reflect the pertinent needs of the patient or nursing home resident.

C. Standardized Care Plans

As nursing continued to change, the pendulum swung from using individual care plans to using standardized care plans in an effort to meet the needs of both nurses and patients. The term *standardized care plan* refers to a preprinted plan of care for a group of patients with the same medical or nursing diagnosis. Certain commonalities exist among patients with the same diagnosis, which allows nurses to establish standards of care for particular groups of patients. Standardized care plans are kept in files in a facility or printed from a computer.

D. Modified Standardized Care Plans

The standardized care plan evolved into a more meaningful tool when it was modified to include spaces for individualization. The plan of care can be modified by

- adding the related factor and the signs and symptoms to the nursing diagnosis,
- adding frequency to clarify the time frames stated on the outcomes,
- adding frequency, amount, time, and patient preferences to the nursing interventions, and
- documenting nursing diagnoses, outcomes, and interventions specific to the individual patient.

Evolution of Care Planning

Individualized care plan: handwritten; contains basic nursing interventions and medical orders; often discarded when the patient is discharged.

Standardized care plan: preprinted plan based on nursing diagnosis or disease process; no space for individualization; not consistently reviewed or revised.

Modified standard care plan: preprinted plan consists of nursing diagnosis, outcomes, and interventions; space available for individualization; provides more flexibility.

Multidisciplinary care plan: used initially in long-term care and psychiatric settings; provides a place for each discipline to document its plan; used during team conferences to discuss patient progress.

Clinical paths: a predetermined, multidisciplinary plan of care written to address the medical diagnosis; predicts outcomes and interventions for specified time intervals; includes teaching and discharge planning; may be used as a documentation tool as well.

Figure 15.9

Modified standardized care plans reduce the amount of time needed for care planning (compared with individualized care plans). Their quality is usually higher because they are written by clinical experts, and they can be used as a clinical teaching tool for nurses unfamiliar with the setting or patient population. While modified standardized care plans are an improvement, they can be quite lengthy, and they must be designed to include only the essential information. Using the word-processing capabilities of computers, the nurse can edit standardized care plans to produce an individualized document, one which incorporates the standard of care and is based on the needs of the patient.

E. Multidisciplinary Care Planning

Another phase in the evolution of care plans has been the emergence of multidisciplinary care plans, which have been used most commonly in long-term care and psychiatric settings. However, multidisciplinary care planning and documentation has become more widespread with the trend toward collaborative practice. In addition, the emphasis on quality improvement and the use of cross-departmental teams to address patient care issues (as recognized by The Joint Commission) lends itself well to a multidisciplinary approach.

Any of the following disciplines may be involved in contributing to a multidisciplinary plan of care: physicians, nurses, case managers, dietitians, respiratory therapists, speech pathologists, dietitians, physical therapists, adjunctive therapists, occupational therapists, cardiac diagnostic technologists, wound ostomy continence nurses, radiological technologists, pharmacists, and pastoral care.

F. Practice Guidelines

TIP: Practice guidelines (also referred to as protocols) describe the management of patient-care issues, such as skin integrity, safety, postoperative care, or administration of specific medications.

The practice guidelines may address independent nursing care or collaborative practice issues; for example, the practice guidelines for patient safety may outline independent nursing assessment and interventions intended to protect the patient from harm. Practice guidelines for the management of patients receiving chemotherapy, however, describe medical orders and associated care along with the independent nursing management of the patient. The interdependence of this type of practice guideline reflects the collaboration of the healthcare team in the management of a specific patient problem.

The medical record may reflect the use of practice guidelines or protocols through the use of a flow sheet. The flow sheet may list the protocols applicable to the patient and provide the nurse with a place to initial or sign that the protocol was in effect on a specific date. This system prevents the need to write out or select a plan of care from the computer. In a nursing negligence case, the attorney should request a copy of the practice guidelines or protocols in effect at the time of the issue that led to a suit.

G. Clinical Paths

The clinical path is a proactive, multidisciplinary set of daily prescriptions for the care of a specified patient population from the time of preadmission to post discharge. The clinical path identifies key nursing interventions, treatments, consultations, diagnostic tests, teaching, and discharge planning activities and indicates when these must occur to achieve the desired outcomes within the expected LOS (length of stay). This form of care plan works best when the LOS and clinical outcomes can be predicted and defined.

As stated, the clinical path is the communication tool used to guide the care of the patient from the time of admission to discharge. Clinical paths help to determine a predictable sequence of interventions to avoid oversights that might compromise effective discharge planning.[40] The clinical path is used on every shift on each consecutive unit to plan and monitor the flow of care.

The most common clinical path format is set up in a grid. Across the top of the page is the time frame (for example, preadmission, day 1, day 2, day 3). Down the left side of the paper are events, treatments, and outcomes. If an event spans more than one day, a solid or dotted line with an arrow on the right end is used in the grid to indicate this. The expected LOS for the DRG often is defined at the top of the page.

15.8 Documentation of Discharge Planning

This section addresses discharge planning in terms of why, when, and how it should be documented. The prospective payment system has increased the importance of early discharge planning. If discharge needs are not identified in a timely fashion and discharge arrangements are delayed, the patient will remain in the facility and receive services longer than necessary or will be prematurely discharged without receiving adequate preparation. Documentation of discharge planning may be scrutinized by the peer review organization (PRO) if the patient is readmitted with the same diagnosis shortly after discharge. Readmission due to a complication or inadequate preparation for going home may result in liability concerns.

Healthcare professionals are expected to perform discharge planning as early in the process as possible. Discharge needs should ideally be considered before a patient is admitted.

Some facilities use a form with cues that remind healthcare providers to implement and document discharge planning. Discharge planning is often included on a separate form in the medical record. This form usually describes the following:

- initial assessment of the need for discharge planning,
- attempts to place the patient in the appropriate facility for continuing care or to arrange for home care as needed, and
- data provided by family members during interviews.

Communication between care providers and discharge planning/case managers is essential for successful discharge planning.

15.9 Documentation of Implementation

Documenting implementation involves charting the interventions selected to meet the patient's needs. The interventions may be derived from the written plan of care, standards of care, protocols, or clinical paths. Charting interventions using a flow sheet or progress notes records information used to monitor the care that the patient received. Documenting implementation offers evidence of the care rendered, facilitates appropriate reimbursement, and promotes continuity of care.

The documentation of implementation is a broad subject. The chapters covering specialty area documentation, which comprise the middle third of this book, address the charting of interventions in a variety of settings, from obstetrics to nursing homes. This chapter focuses on standards for implementation and evaluation.

15.10 Implementation of the Plan

The American Nurses Association Standards of Practice[41] state that the nurse should document implementation and any modifications, including changes or omissions, of the identified plan (of care).

A. Flow Sheets

Providing and documenting interventions is an integral part of nursing practice. A considerable amount of time is required to chart pertinent findings, patient safety interventions, and psychosocial care, not to mention the routine, repetitive aspects of daily care. To ease the burden and reduce the length of narrative charting, flow sheets were created. Flow sheets are used to collect assessment data, document nursing interventions, or both. Figure 15.10 outlines several uses for flow sheets.

TIP: If used correctly, flow sheets can save the nurse considerable time when charting. Documentation of routine and repetitive aspects of patient care and assessment occupies much of the nurse's time.

This routine data lends itself well to flow sheets. The nurse should avoid repeating flow sheet data in the progress notes, because this practice defeats the purpose of using flow sheets and creates unnecessary work.

It can take a reviewer who is unfamiliar with a flow sheet some effort to study the format and extract information. There is no uniformity between institutions in terms of design of flow sheets. While some flow sheets have keys to explain the use of the form and approved abbreviations, other flow sheets offer no explanations. Sometimes the facility has a policy and procedure that directs the staff on how to complete the form. This information can be requested during the discovery phase of a lawsuit.

Purpose of Flow Sheets

- To provide quick, efficient documentation of data or interventions
- To consolidate data that would otherwise be scattered throughout the medical record
- To facilitate continuity of care
- To reduce duplication in charting
- To protect the legal interests of the patient and the nurse
- To provide an immediate assessment of the patient's status
- To provide for easy comparison of baseline assessment data with subsequent assessment findings
- To document information that will lead to an evaluation of the patient's progress in achieving outcomes

Figure 15.10

Nursing care records should provide a complete database of patient status and nursing care interventions for a specified time period (usually twenty-four hours). If the form is designed to permit easy comparison of patient status from one shift to the next, the reviewer will be able to identify quickly significant changes in patient status. Some flow sheets include key terms to provide cues for care. For example, nursing care records in medical-surgical units often include a section for documenting whether the side rails were up or down and whether the call bell was within reach of the patient. Restraint flow sheets are often used as well. These serve as reminders to the nurse to address important safety issues.

Failure to complete a flow sheet can lead to the inference that the required care was not administered.

B. Provision of Comfort

Nurses spend a significant portion of their time addressing pain and suffering. Nursing interventions designed to reduce these problems are documented in the medical record. Table 15.1 provides names of commonly used medications for pain and suffering. Injuries and illnesses can profoundly disrupt the life of an individual and his family. There are many causes of suffering which may be referenced in medical records. These are just a few:

- Being in unfamiliar surroundings: Exposure to new sights, sounds, smells, people contribute to stress.

- Loss of independence: The inability to care for one's own needs, on either a temporary or permanent basis.
- Role disruptions: The alteration in one's usual roles and responsibilities.
- Separation from loved ones or peers: The disruption in normal relationships imposed by isolation in the hospital, nursing home or at home
- Sensory overload: Constant exposure to lights, noise and being touched.
- Disruption in routines: Alteration in lifestyle due to the need for medical treatment or by injuries.
- Inadequate understanding of one's health situation: Not receiving or being able to comprehend what is happening or going to happen or the prognosis.

- Loss of one's ability to protect one's body from the view of others.
- Loss of control: Surrendering control of one's body and life to others.
- Boredom: Lack of variety in one's daily routine.
- Fearful anticipation of surgery or procedures: Stress caused by worrying about upcoming unpleasant events.
- Disfigurement/change in body image: Alteration in appearance caused by trauma, surgery, burns and other causes.
- Loss of recreation: Inability to participate in hobbies or other relaxing activities. For children, disruption in play activities can be profound.
- Lost opportunities: The inability to participate in chances to improve one's life.

Table 15.1
Provision of Comfort: Pain Relievers

Type of Drug	Examples
Nonsteroidal Anti-Inflammatories (NSAIDS)	Aspirin, Voltaren, Dolobid, Ansaid, Lodine, Motrin, Advil, Nalfon, Indocin, Orudis, Toradol, Relafen, Mobic, Daypro, Anaprox, Naprosyn, Feldene, Clinoril, Tolectin
COX2 Selective NSAIDS	Celebrex
Opioid Analgesics	Stadol, Morphine (MS Contin, Roxanol), Demerol, Codeine, Methadone, Sublimaze, Dilaudid, Nubain, Roxicodone, Percocet, Percodan, Codeine, Levo-dromoran, Darvon
Neuropathic Pain Relievers	Pamelor, Klonopin, Tegretol, Neurontin, Depakote

Other Categories of Drugs Used to Treat Suffering

Patients may require a variety of medications to relieve symptoms. The most common types are listed below.

Type of Drug	Purpose	Examples
Anti-Anxiety	To reduce anxiety	Ativan, Xanax, Librium, Klonopin, Tranxene, Valium, Serax
Antidepressants	To reduce depression	Zoloft, Elavil, Anafranil, Norpramin, Sinequan, Tofranil, Pamelor, Vivactil, Nardil, Parnate, Celexa, Prozac, Luvox, Wellbutrin, Serzone, Remeron, Desyrel, Effexor, Paxil
Antidiarrheals	To reduce diarrhea	Lomotil, Immodium, PeptoBismol, Kaopectate
Antiemetic	To prevent emesis or vomiting	Compazine, Tigan, Reglan
Antipyretic	To reduce itching	Benadryl
Hypnotic	To promote sleep	Ambien, Benadryl, ProSom, Dalmane, Doral, Restoril, Halcion, Sonata
Laxatives	To treat constipation	Milk of Magnesia, Metamucil, Citrucel, Fibercon, Surfak, Colace, Dialose, Mineral Oil, Citronesia, Magnesium Hydroxide, Fleets Phoshosoda, Glycerine, Lactulose, Golytely, Dulcolax, Cascara, Castor Oil, Senokot
Neuromuscular Blockers	Paralyze the diaphragm	Tracrium, Nimbex, Nuromax, Mivacron, Pavulon, Zemuron, Anectine, Norcuron

- Loss of control over bodily functions: Incontinence of bladder and bowel, inability to eat, breathe on one's own, get out of bed, or wash oneself contribute to a feeling of helplessness.
- Disruption in communication: The presence of a ventilator, tracheostomy, stroke or head injury impairs communication.
- Restraints: Restricted movement prevents adjusting position or touching one's body, for example to scratch the face.

Suffering may be manifested through emotional and psychological reactions. The patient may be anxious, fearful, or agitated. Some patients are particularly enraged by the helplessness, lack of control and enforced passivity that disease (or injury) confers. The patient may feel helpless, hopeless, powerless, lonely and isolated. Depression and withdrawal from others may occur. Posttraumatic stress disorder may result after a traumatic event, such as the development of quadriplegia or being burned as a result of nursing negligence. Physical symptoms of suffering may appear in the form of a rapid breathing rate, ulcers in the stomach, insomnia, irritable bowel syndrome (cramping and diarrhea), headaches, asthma attacks, depression, withdrawal and so on. In the context of litigation, it is important to neither overemphasize nor underestimate the suffering that accompanies injury. Medical records are used to substantiate the presence of suffering. Documentation of medications administered to alleviate symptoms that cause suffering, analysis of the charting of healthcare professionals, and understanding of medical equipment and procedures are useful in defining the face of suffering. See Iyer, P. (Ed.) *Medical Legal Aspects of Pain and Suffering*[42] for extensive information on this subject.

Outcomes that fit into the relief of pain and suffering include the following:[43]

- relief of symptoms, such as anxiety or agitation, through the use of medications and therapy,
- improved ability to cope with stressful situations,
- improved ability to function and prevent further disability,
- a sense of physical, mental, and emotional well-being,
- appropriate expression of feelings, and
- improved interactions and communication with family, staff, and friends.

15.11 Documentation of Referrals

The American Nurses Association Standards of Practice[44] state that the nurse utilizes community resources and systems and collaborates with nursing colleagues and others to implement the plan. There is increasing emphasis on the need to provide for continuity of care. The resources that are used are dependent on the needs of the patient and the available services. For example, the medical record may document that a patient who underwent a mastectomy or formation of a colostomy was referred to support groups. Patients are increasingly being directed to obtain education through the Internet.

Advanced practice nurses, defined as nurse practitioners or clinical nurse specialists, may be available to offer an expert level of consultation. These nurses, as well as wound ostomy continence nurses, may complete their documentation on consultation forms or write progress notes in the medical record. Case managers and social workers may fill out their own forms to guide decisions regarding discharge or placement in nursing homes.

15.12 Documentation of Evaluation

Patients are assessed to gather pertinent data needed to identify and document the patient's high-priority nursing diagnoses. Development and documentation of the plan of care follows. The plan of care provides a written framework for the delivery of care. Progress notes and flow sheets are used to document the delivery of care. Evaluation is the final step of the nursing process, and it flows from the outcomes defined in the plan of care. During evaluation, the nurse makes a clinical judgment regarding the resolution of a problem and the achievement of an outcome.[45]

TIP: The terms "evaluation" and "assessment" are sometimes inappropriately interchanged. Assessment involves collecting data. Evaluation involves making a judgment based on the data.

The American Nurses Association Standards of Practice[46] address evaluation by stating that the nurse evaluates progress towards attainment of outcomes. The registered nurse is expected to conduct a systematic, ongoing, and criterion-based evaluation of the outcomes. This means that specific criteria guide the evaluation process. The patient and others are involved in the evaluative process. The nurse evaluates the effectiveness of the planned strategies in relation to the patient responses and the attainment of the expected outcomes. The medical record should contain documentation of the results of the evaluation. The nurse uses ongoing assessment data to revise the diagnoses, outcomes, plan, and implementation as needed. The final step is to disseminate the results of the evaluation to the patient and others involved in the care or situation, as appropriate, in accordance with state and federal laws and regulations.

This chapter discusses five aspects of evaluation documentation: why, what, when, where, and how outcomes are documented.

A. Why Outcomes Are Documented

Clinical records contain documentation of the evaluation of a patient's status for several reasons. Societal factors have placed new emphasis on the achievement of outcomes, which has increased the scrutiny of evaluating documentation. The definition and evaluation of outcomes or results is a fundamental activity in any type of organization, including healthcare agencies. Traditionally, outcomes have not received as strong an emphasis in health care because of the difficulty associated with defining and measuring both the process of care and the results. Healthcare organizations find it easy to hide behind the rationalizations that the existing care processes are too complex to measure and that the human variables that influence outcomes, such as preexisting disease, cannot be controlled.

The current healthcare environment forces us to examine more closely the effectiveness of treatment at both the societal and individual levels. As the cost of health care continues to rise, the attention being directed to the evaluation of patient care outcomes as a way to define the quality of health care is increasing. The nursing shortage has increased the emphasis on justifying the staffing mix (ratio of licensed to unlicensed personnel) and educating of the staff.

The most common reason for evaluating and documenting the achievement of outcomes is to determine the results of specific care and treatment of individual patients and families. Another purpose is to test or improve the effectiveness of services provided by a healthcare organization to a specific patient population. This area is addressed by case management and quality assurance/improvement programs, allowing a facility to determine if the length of stay (LOS) can be reduced while maintaining the quality of the outcomes. Comparison of an organization's outcomes with those of other organizations allows an organization to better understand and improve its own systems. The more closely outcomes are studied, the more apparent it becomes that they are affected by many complex variables.

B. What Outcomes Are Documented

Outcomes fall into one or more of the domains defined in Table 15.2. Outcomes can be measured on different levels and for different purposes. Several difficulties currently complicate the measurement of outcomes, including the lack of the following:

- agreement concerning a common set of elements to use to create a database for measuring outcomes,
- agreement on precise definitions of outcomes,
- systematic documentation regarding the achievement of outcomes, and
- communication between agencies (for example, between home care and acute-care facilities), which prevents measurement of long-term outcomes.

C. When to Evaluate Outcomes

Evaluation is categorized as either formative or summative. Formative evaluation occurs on a periodic basis during the provision of care, whereas summative evaluation occurs at the end of an activity, such as an admission, discharge, or transfer to another area, or at the end of a specific time frame, such as the end of a teaching session.

1. Formative evaluation

The frequency with which a nurse evaluates progress depends on the following factors: policies, regulatory standards, healthcare setting, charting system, standards of care/practice guidelines, nursing diagnosis or problem, time frame specified by the outcome, condition of the patient, and nursing interventions. Policies of a healthcare agency may dictate the frequency with which the nurse should document an evaluation of the patient's progress. This policy may be defined in a number of ways. The agency may have general documentation policies that dictate the frequency of evaluation (for example, a requirement that the plan of care be evaluated hourly, daily, and weekly). It is common for nursing notes to be written on a weekly basis in a nursing home. This frequency would not be acceptable in an acute care facility, where notes are written in some cases on a minute-by-minute basis (in a critical care unit) or at least daily on a medical-surgical unit. Policies may be based on regulatory standards set by the state or federal government or by accrediting bodies.

The charting system used by the facility may define how often the nurse should document an evaluation. For example, as discussed in Chapter 5, *Charting Systems*, in Volume I, problems, interventions, and evaluation (PIE) charting recommends that outcomes be evaluated every eight hours and summarized once every twenty-four hours. The format of the medical record forms may also dictate the frequency of charting outcomes. Standards of care and practice guidelines may specify how frequently outcomes are to be evaluated. For example, a practice guideline for treatment of impaired skin integrity may suggest that the nurse evaluate and document the condition of the patient's skin every eight hours.

Table 15.2
Domains of Outcomes

Domain	Definition
Physiological Status	Documentation of assessment parameters, including blood pressure, breath sounds, blood glucose levels, skin integrity, healing of pressure ulcers, and response to treatment
Psychosocial Status	Behavior of the patient and family, including observations about anxiety level, interactions with others, attitudes, and coping mechanisms
Functional Abilities	The ability to perform activities of daily living, including toileting, grooming, cooking, bathing, and walking
Patient Satisfaction	Reactions and perceptions of the patient and family to the quality of nursing care
Knowledge of Self Care	Understanding of the patient and family regarding treatments, symptoms to be reported to the healthcare provider, self-care measures to maintain good health, and diet
Symptom Control	The ability of the patient, family, or nurse to control symptoms such as pain, fatigue, nausea, constipation, diarrhea, and itching
Satisfaction	Perceptions of the patient and family concerning the quality of care being provided
Home Maintenance	Daily functioning of the patient and family in the home, including cooking, cleaning, shopping, and paying bills
Goal Attainment	Comparison of the expected outcomes of care with the actual outcomes, measured at designated intervals or at discharge
Safety Maintenance	Prevention of falls, skin breakdown, medication errors, accidents or injuries, infections, unplanned readmissions, sentinel events (described in Chapter 15, *The Nursing Process and Nursing Records*), and other complications
Length of Stay (LOS)	Patient's actual LOS compared with the expected LOS

The type of nursing diagnosis or problem may influence the frequency of evaluation. When defining the patient's nursing diagnosis, as discussed earlier, the nurse identifies the most important (high-priority) problems. The human responses with the greatest effect on the patient's well-being are given the highest priority. The patient's basic physiological needs, including the need for food, air, elimination, and circulation, are usually the most urgent. These needs generally should be addressed before concentrating on psychosocial needs. The frequency of evaluation will vary as the patient's condition changes and as new diagnoses are made.

The time frame tells the nurse when to evaluate the outcome. The inclusion of time frames, such as "within twenty-four hours," "by the time of discharge," or "by the third teaching session," provides a great deal of guidance for the nurse who will be evaluating the outcomes. Time frames are also defined in critical paths.

The condition of the patient may dictate how frequently the nurse evaluates the patient. The failure to perform timely and appropriate evaluations often forms the basis of a negligence suit. The increased acuity of patients who are ad-mitted to facilities, coupled with fewer nurses to perform evaluations, creates a recipe for trouble. Complications can rapidly occur, and if not detected in time result in permanent injuries. Skilled evaluation of a patient's condition is necessary to detect signs of bleeding or respiratory distress, for example.

Nursing interventions may specify how frequently the patient's status should be monitored or other nursing actions should be taken. For example, the nursing intervention of auscultating breath sounds every shift indicates that the clinical records should contain a description of breath sounds. Specific, clear interventions facilitate documentation by outlining the expected nursing actions.

2. Summative evaluation

Summative evaluation is typically performed at the time of transfer or discharge of the patient. It is common, for example, for rehabilitation settings to determine multidisciplinary goals to be achieved at specific intervals during care (formative evaluation) and at the time of (discharge summative evaluation). The medical record then defines how the patient achieved the goals.

3. Discharge forms

The needs of the patient should be evaluated at the time of discharge from a healthcare facility. These needs will direct the provision of continuing care. Different types of discharge forms are discharge summaries and discharge instruction sheets. Discharge summaries are used in some facilities and are intended to document the completion of the discharge process to ensure that all appropriate steps have been completed. They are *not* meant to summarize the course of the illness. They can be designed as a quick checklist with space provided for commenting on significant items.

Discharge instruction sheets list discharge instructions for diet, treatments, medications, activities, and follow-up appointments. The follow-up appointment information should specify who the healthcare provider will be and when the patient is to be seen, for example, "Patient is to see Dr. Feller in two weeks." Usually these forms have two copies: one for the patient and one for the medical record. The record should include a notation that these instructions were provided to the patient or a place for the patient to sign to confirm that the instructions were received and understood. Discharge instruction sheets are used in a variety of healthcare settings. These sheets are important in that they document the fulfillment of the nurse's professional responsibility to provide instructions, and they shift the responsibility for following these instructions to the patient. Malpractice suits initiated because of poor outcomes provide evidence that in some situations, it is better to arrange follow-up after the patient is discharged than to leave aftercare to the patient or family's discretion. Specific instructions given in a language that the patient can understand are better than general advice. A written record of the conversation with the patient at the time of the patient's discharge can be vital in defending the actions of healthcare professionals.

TIP: The use of discharge instruction sheets has raised issues in some settings about the degree of communication and collaboration between nurses and physicians.

Sometimes confusion exists as to which discipline is responsible for discharge teaching and instructions. These issues must be resolved in order to promote cooperation and to facilitate documentation of discharge teaching.

4. Post-discharge evaluation

In some healthcare settings, documenting calls to patients following discharge to evaluate their status is common. This may be done in the ED (emergency department), the outpatient surgery department, the medical procedures unit, or any other unit. These forms usually consist of a series of questions about the patient's status and a space to fill in any instructions that were given to the patient. Often there is an area for the nurse to document information about the patient's satisfaction with her experience in the unit. Policy should dictate how many attempts should be made to reach the patient before abandoning the effort. Each attempt to reach the patient should be documented to indicate that the effort was made. The absence of a report of follow-up phone calls in the medical record could be interpreted as a failure to make such calls.

D. Where Outcomes Are Documented

The evaluation of outcomes is documented in flow sheets and in progress notes. Chapter 5, *Charting Systems*, in Volume I, discusses the various charting systems and how evaluation is documented in each type of system.

E. How Outcomes Are Documented

Progress notes document the patient's status in relation to the desired outcomes. The patient's responses are compared with the outcomes defined by the plan of care. The following are some concepts typically addressed in the progress notes, including some examples of evaluative comments:

- progress toward achieving outcomes (for example, "incision shows no sign of infection"),
- response to prn (as needed) medications (for example, "verbalized relief of pain 45 minutes after injection of morphine" or "vomiting subsided 1 hour after received compazine [prochlorperazine]"),
- responses to change in activity (for example, "able to walk from bed to bathroom without becoming dyspneic"/short of breath),
- tolerance of treatments or position change (for example, "unable to tolerate having head of bed raised to 90 degrees to 45 degrees, blood pressure dropped and began to sweat," or "complained of pain when Foley catheter was inserted"),
- ability to perform activities of daily living, particularly those that may influence discharge planning (for example, "unable to wash self independently because of left-sided weakness" or "requires a walker to ambulate to bathroom"),
- response to diet or advancement of diet (for example, "consumed all of full-liquid lunch, stated she was hungry, and wanted more solid food"), and
- reduction in pain (for example, "pain level was reduced from 7/10 to 2/10 after Morphine was given").

F. When Outcomes Are Not Achieved

Patients do not always achieve the outcomes established by the healthcare team. Changes in condition, unrealistic outcomes, and other factors affect the achievement of outcomes. Lack of cooperation with the medical treatment team and plan of care may occur in any healthcare or home setting. The medical term of "noncompliance" defines a person who refuses to listen to the healthcare providers, and displays behavior that is harmful to his physical health. This behavior may also be harmful to a legal claim. There are extrinsic and intrinsic reasons why people do not cooperate with care recommendations after an injury. *Extrinsic* factors are out of the patient's control. It has been the author's experience after reviewing hundreds of medical charts of injured patients that these individuals often get caught in a downward spiral. The inability to work may result in the loss of a job, loss of healthcare insurance, sometimes the loss of a car, and greater difficulty affording medical care, insurance premiums, or co-payments. Medical records may state the family members became the transporters, a role that may interfere with their own work and family responsibilities. The needs of dependents may impinge on the patient's ability to participate in the medical plan of care. Childcare or elder care responsibilities, for example, may conflict with office and therapy appointments. Additionally, long waits for care at doctors' offices or therapy centers or confusion about scheduling appointments discourage compliance with treatment. Missed appointments can set up a climate in the doctor's office of annoyance and even hostility. Patients may be punished by judgmental and negative healthcare providers who are irritated by missed appointments.[47]

Healthcare providers may be less than sympathetic to the injured patient who displays stress or acts out when in pain. Encountering negativity and punishment further discourages the patient from keeping appointments. In extreme cases, physicians discharge patients from their practices. This usually results when the behavior of the patient is so out of bounds as to be unacceptable. Patient behavior that may result in being "fired" by the medical practice includes repeated instances of missed appointments, displays of anger, failure to follow instructions, or abusive behavior towards physician or staff.

Intrinsic issues interfering with treatment are varied. Lack of knowledge of the consequences of not following treatment recommendations may factor into noncompliant behavior. Some patients' lack of understanding of the nuances of the care that has been prescribed is due to low education level or intelligence. The necessity to follow a complicated course of treatment often dissuades injured individuals. The author has worked on cases involving people who have had a near-death experience that renders them compliant, at least for a time. This is the acceptance/denial phase commonly experienced when confronted with certain injuries, especially those that require changes in lifestyles, adherence to protracted periods (perhaps a lifetime) of care, and specific treatment. Individuals who have had a near-death experience may be so appreciative of their survival that they vow to mend their ways, and they do, for a time. Most patients, however, soon return to the business of living and all it entails. Job and family stresses become their primary concerns once again, and health matters fade into the background. It is human nature, especially in our current culture, to do what we want and to be in control of our own lives. Anything that interferes with this, especially a condition that requires ongoing attention, is deemed problematic. That which necessitates our daily involvement frequently is met with even more resistance. In our "instant everything" society, we expect immediate results, and we want them yesterday.[48]

Energy resources are limited by chronic pain. It is most difficult to be an optimistic participant in care for a healthier life when day-to-day stresses are overwhelming. Dysfunctional families, difficult living situations, poverty, long working hours in a tense environment, or problematic parenting issues are examples of factors that can leave injured individuals physically and emotionally exhausted, and are often mentioned in medical records. When patients face these external challenges, they simply are unable to expend either time or energy to manage complex or chronic conditions. All of this becomes a vicious cycle of despair and withdrawal from anyone who would try to intervene because even that requires their time. When they feel hopeless, they fail to return phone calls, skip medical appointments, and ignore symptoms.[49] Many medications have unpleasant side effects, discouraging adherence to a treatment regimen. Individuals who have lost their independence, role identity, and control may become depressed, resulting in lowered adherence to the treatment plan. Flares of pre-existing mental illness, such as bipolar disease, schizophrenia, or depression, may paralyze the will to participate in therapy. Pre-existing alcohol or substance abuse patterns may also worsen in the face of injury.

Religious convictions may hold people back from taking advantage of ordered therapy. Some individuals take a fatalistic view of medical treatment. Cultural beliefs may conflict with the treatment regimen. Language barriers impede understanding of instructions for self-care. Faced with the experience of having pain worsened by therapy, some patients opt to not willingly place themselves in a setting where they will feel worse—at least short term. Vigorous physical therapy may cause pain to flare.

Close inspection of medical records by a legal nurse consultant provides the attorney with essential information about compliance with the treatment plan. Medical records include details and reasons for noncompliance. The uncommon event of a physician discharging a patient from the medical practice is invariably documented in the form of a letter to a patient.

Effective use of the nursing process should result in a revision of the plan of care after the nurse and patient reach an agreement about the achievable goals and the realistic interventions.

15.13 Summary

The medical record serves as a vehicle for communication within the clinical realm of health care. It becomes an essential element in establishing the condition of the patient and the nature of the treatment plan. The success of litigation is often heavily dependent on the nature and amount of documentation. The details of assessment focus on the problems, patient's risk for injury, potential for self-care following discharge, and patient and family education needs. Admission and ongoing assessment forms are designed to fit a number of formats and models. Interpretation of assessment information guides the rest of the nursing process.

This chapter provides information on the diagnosis and planning phase of the nursing process. Planning must be deliberate and thoughtful to be effective. To facilitate the documentation of planning, various methods are discussed, including traditional approaches, such as care planning, and current trends, including using case management and clinical paths to manage patient care. Documentation of planning should include both discharge and education needs to manage patients effectively in the hospital and at home. Planning patient care provides an opportunity for nurses to define nursing practice and set the standards for excellence.

Documenting implementation of the nursing process is essential to providing a clear, chronological description of events during the patient's hospitalization. Evaluation of the patient's status is an important ongoing part of the nursing process. Clearly defined outcomes direct how and when to evaluate the achievement of expected outcomes, provide a framework for documentation, and are increasingly being used as a tool to evaluate the performance of the nursing staff and as a basis for comparison with other healthcare agencies. The scope of patient education documentation has broadened to include documenting that the patient, family, or both comprehended the teaching that was provided to them. (Patient education forms now include this concept.) Documentation of implementation and evaluation provides the basis of establishing that the standard of care was followed.

Endnotes

1. Seymour, L. *Selected Writings of Florence Nightingale*. New York, NY: Macmillan. 1954.

2. Commins, J. "Accreditation's New Player," *HealthLeaders,* March 2009, p. 12-13.

3. American Nurses Association. *Standards of Nursing Practice*. Washington, D.C.: The Author. 2004.

4. Matsumura, B. and Ambrose, A., "Balance in the Elderly," *Clinics in Geriatric Medicine*, 2006, pages 395-412.

5. Komara, F. "The slippery slope: reducing fall risk in older adults," *Primary Care: Clinics in Office Practice*, Vol. 32, No. 3, September 2005.

6. Iyer, P. "Preventing Falls in the Elderly." *S Calif Nurs News*. October 1988, p. 155.

7. Gray-Miceli, D. "Fall risk assessment for older adults: the Hendrich II Model," Issue 8, 2007, www.hartfordign.org

8. Lyder, C. and Ayello, E., "Pressure ulcers: a patient safety issue," in *Patient Safety and Quality: An Evidence-Based Handbook for Nurses*, AHRQ, 2008.

9. Hopkins, A., Dealey, C., Bale, S. et al., "Patient stories of living with a pressure ulcer," *Journal of Advanced Nursing*, Vol. 56 No. 4, November 2006, p. 345-353.

10. Spilsbury, K., Nelson, A., Cullum, N. et al., "Pressure ulcers and their treatment and effects on quality of life: hospital inpatient perspectives," *Journal of Advanced Nursing,* Vol. 57, No. 5, 2007, p. 494-504.

11. U.S. Department of Health and Human Services. *Pressure Ulcers in Adults: Prediction and Prevention*. Rockville, MD: The Author. 1992.

12. Myers, S. "A Practical Guide to the Defense" in Iyer, P. (Editor). *Nursing Home Litigation, Investigation and Case Preparation*. Second Edition. Tucson, AZ: Lawyers and Judges Publishing Company. 2006.

13. http://www.jointcommission.org/SentinelEvents/SentinelEventAlert/sea_7.htm

14. Calfee, B. "Documenting Suicide Risk." *Nursing 96*. July 1996, p. 12.

15. Lynch, S. "Elder Abuse: What to Look For, How to Intervene." *Am J Nurs*. 97(1), 1997, p. 27.

16. *Id*.

17. *Id*.

18. "Prescription-Drug Abuse." January 21, 2003. www.mdconsult.com. Retrieved August 13, 2004.

19. Geiderman, J. "Keeping Lists and Naming Names: Habitual Patient Files for Suspected Nontherapeutic Drug-seeking Patients." *Annals of Emergency Medicine*. 41: 6, June 2003.

20. President's Editorial, *New Jersey Nurse*, May/June 2009.

21. Keenan. "Use of Standardized Nursing Language Will Make Nursing Visible." Michigan Nurses Association. www.minurses.org/prac/snl/snlvisible.shtml. Retrieved February 15, 2004.

22. Clingerman. "Overview of the Standardized Nursing Languages: NANDA, NIC, and NOC." Michigan Nurses Association. www.minurses.org/prac/CENandaNicNoc.shtml. Retrieved February 15, 2004.

23. North American Nursing Diagnosis Association (NANDA). *Nursing Diagnoses: Definitions and Classifications 2001–2002*. Philadelphia, PA: The Author. 2001.

24. NANDA International, *Nursing Diagnosis Submission Handbook*, 2008.

25. *Id*.

26. *Id*.

27. Taptich, B., P. Iyer, and D. Bernocchi-Losey. *Nursing Diagnosis and Care Planning*. Second Edition. Philadelphia, PA: WB Saunders. 1994.

28. 2009-2011 Nursing Diagnoses, www.scribd.com/doc/13679817/Nanda_nursing diagnosis list

29. See Note 3.

30. The University of Iowa College of Nursing. Nursing "Outcomes Classification." www.nursing.uiowa.edu/centers/cncce/noc/nocoverview.htm. Retrieved February 15, 2004.

31. The Center for Nursing Classification, http://www.ncvhs.hhs.gov/970416w6.htm

32. Moorhead, S., Johnson, M, Maas, M. and Swanson, E. (Eds.) (2008) *Nursing Outcomes Classification* (NOC) Fourth Edition, St. Louis: Mosby/Elsevier

33. See Note 3.

34. See Note 27.

35. McCloskey, J. and Bulechek, G. "Nursing Interventions Classification (NIC)—Current Status and New Directions." www.cac.psu.edu/~dxm12/mccart.html. Retrieved February 15, 2004.

36. "Nursing Interventions Classification." www.nursing.uiowa.edu/centers/cncce/nic/nicoverview.htm. Retrieved February 15, 2004.

37. See Note 3.

38. Greenwood, D. "Nursing Care Plans: Issues and Solutions." *Nurs Manage*. 27(3), p. 33. 1996.

39. *Id*.

40. Giuliano, K. and C. Poirier. "Nursing Case Management: Critical Pathways to Desirable Patient Outcomes." *Nurs Manage*. 22(3), p. 52. 1991.

41. See Note 3.

42. Iyer, P. (Ed.) *Medical Legal Aspects of Pain and Suffering*, Tucson, AZ: Lawyers and Judges Publishing Company, 2003

43. Eggland, E. "Documenting Psychiatric and Behavioral Outcomes." *Nursing 97*. April 1997, p. 25.

44. See Note 3.

45. See Note 22.

46. See Note 3.

47. Husain-Gambles, M. Missed appointments in primary care: questionnaire and focus group study of health professions, *British Journal of General Practice*, Feb 01, 2004: 54(499), p. 108-113.

48. Mullahy, C. The challenge of noncompliance for case managers, *The Case Manager*, Volume 16, Number 2, March/April 2005.

49. *Id*.

Chapter 16

Obstetrical Records

Joanne McDermott, MA, RN

16.1 Introduction

An obstetrical record is a unique and dynamic document. This record chronicles the status of both the mother and fetus during the prenatal and the intrapartum periods. Following the birth, there are two pertinent medical records, consisting of the postpartum and newborn records. In order to develop a comprehensive picture of a birth experience, an examiner would need to review thoroughly all of these documents in detail. This chapter assists in the understanding of the obstetrical portion of these records.

16.2 Health History/Initial Pregnancy Profile

The initial prenatal visit is important for the documentation of a baseline of data, composed of a comprehensive health history and obstetrical exam. A plan of care is developed that should take into consideration physical, emotional, and psychosocial needs of the pregnant client. The timing of the first visit is important, as early and regular prenatal care increases the likelihood of having a healthier infant.[1] As ongoing assessments continue during the pregnancy, the plan of care should be revised based on the individual needs of the client. Any pre-existing medical condition needs to be evaluated in light of the physiological changes that accompany pregnancy. The client's history of respiratory ailments, cardiac disease, hypertension, and endocrine disorders will need to be evaluated and documented so that follow-up examinations can assess for any potential complications to the mother and fetus. See Table 16.1 for the recommendation on the frequency of visits during the prenatal period.

Table 16.1
Frequency of Prenatal Visits

Up to 28 weeks	Every 4 weeks
28 to 36 weeks	Every 2-3 weeks
36 weeks to birth	Every week

Figure 16.1 *Example of pregnancy history.*

Table 16.2
Gravida and Para

Term	Definition
Gravida	A woman who is pregnant. Also refers to total number of pregnancies.
Para (parity)	The number of pregnancies in which the fetus or fetuses have reached viability.
Viability	Capacity to live outside the uterus; about 22-24 weeks or fetal weight greater than 500 grams.

Table 16.3
Example of Language for Describing
Obstetrical History

$G_4T_2P_0A_1L_2$

G_4 Pregnant for the fourth time

T_2 Two term deliveries

P_0 No preterm deliveries

A_1 One miscarriage

L_2 Two living children

A. Pregnancy History

A history of all previous pregnancies needs to be well documented in the prenatal record. This would include any previous complications, routes of delivery, fetal size, and positions. See the example in Figure 16.1. These factors can have implications for the management of the present pregnancy. There is specific terminology used in identifying each previous pregnancy's outcome, called gravida and para. See Table 16.2. Gravidity and parity information may be recorded in the client's records in several ways. The acronym GTPAL is used for the description of a commonly used five digit system.[2] The first digit represents the total number of pregnancies, the second digit represents the total number of term births, the third digit indicates the number of preterm births, the fourth identifies the number of miscarriages or abortions, and the fifth is the number of children currently living. See Table 16.3.

B. Medications

A complete list of prescription medications and over-the-counter medications should be noted in the prenatal record. The healthcare provider reviews and provides guidance regarding what medications the client can take. The vast majority of medications necessary for the management of various medical and surgical complications commonly encountered in pregnancy can be used with relative safety.[3] A physician or nurse practitioner would review the risks versus benefits and individually prescribe for each client.

C. At-Risk Behaviors

Any behavior that can jeopardize the health of the mother and fetus is considered to be an at-risk behavior. These behaviors include tobacco use and substance use and abuse, which include alcohol and prescription, non-prescription, and illegal drugs. Other behaviors that increase risk would be engaging in unsafe sexual activity, remaining in domestic abusive situations, missing prenatal appointments, and not complying with the antenatal plan of care.

During the first prenatal visit, at-risk behaviors should be recorded and relevant counseling and teaching provided. By having the at-risk behaviors well documented in the prenatal record, ongoing follow up with the client can be continued at subsequent visits. Clients should be counseled about the perinatal implications of their actions and the potential adverse outcomes. These clients should be referred to appropriate assistance programs, and continued follow up concerning their risk factors should be well documented in the medical record.

D. Risk Status

A high risk pregnancy is one in which the life or health of the mother and/or fetus is jeopardized by a disorder or complication. The problem occurs either coincidental with or is unique to the pregnancy.[4] Identifying a pregnancy as high risk is a function of prenatal care. Besides the at-risk behaviors described previously, there are many other conditions that put a mother and fetus at risk. These include pre-existing medical conditions such as diabetes or cardiac disease and complications directly related to the pregnancy. Examples would include gestational diabetes, placenta previa, placenta abruption, gestational hypertension, preeclampsia, fetal illness, and fetal anomalies.

A client identified as at risk is scheduled at more frequent intervals for prenatal care. The frequency of the visits would be dependent on the client's individual condition. There also could be antenatal testing ordered for fetal surveillance. Medical record documentation related to antenatal tests is illustrated in Section 16.5.

E. Sociocultural/Psychosocial

TIP: Prenatal care records should reflect the client's support systems, education, occupation, and any cultural practices that have relevance to the perinatal period. These entities will have an effect on how the client is able to learn, identify any occupational hazards to the pregnancy, and respect cultural heritage and preferences in the childbearing process.

Examining psychosocial issues is an integral part of the prenatal care plan. Family conflicts, financial concerns, and barriers to health care should all be addressed. The prenatal period is also a good time to begin educating the client about postpartum blues, as more than 70 percent of women manifest this phenomenon. Any history of depression should be well documented in the prenatal record, as these women will be at increased risk for postpartum depression, a more serious condition. Any referrals made to community agencies or other resources should be documented in the medical record.

F. Physical Examination

A thorough physical examination should be documented during the initial prenatal visit. There are many physiological changes that the woman will undergo during the course of the pregnancy, and the initial physical examination provides the baseline for assessing subsequent changes.[5] A review of the mother's health is documented with any abnormalities identified.

Documentation of baseline vital signs includes blood pressure, pulse, height, and weight. A baseline blood pressure is significant in that a rise in blood pressure can be indicative of gestational hypertension (pregnancy-induced hypertension) and preeclampsia. Refer to Section 16.14 for a discussion of these conditions.

G. Pelvic Examination

The pelvic examination is multifaceted. It begins with an external inspection and palpation. Any abnormal findings are documented, such as discharge, lesions, trauma, and inflammation. Internal examination consists of a speculum exam, which is used to view the vaginal vault and cervix. The cervix is inspected for position and appearance. This examination is usually performed at the first visit and not repeated unless there is a medical indication to do so. Specimens are obtained for screening of infections, and a pap smear is obtained. Refer to Section 16.5 for a description of the specific tests performed in the initial prenatal visit.

16.3 Estimating the Date of Birth

When a pregnancy has been confirmed, one of the first determinations made is when the woman will give birth. This date has been identified by a few different acronyms. Traditionally, it was coined the EDC, which stands for Estimated Date of Confinement. The term confinement historically represents the six-week period between the day of birth and the end of the postpartum period, when women were expected to absent themselves from society and remain at home to recover.[6] Times have changed, and so has the terminology.

TIP: Estimated date of delivery, or EDD, is a term that is often used. Presently, the term estimated date of birth (EDB) is being used. By including "birth" in the term, it promotes a more positive perception of both pregnancy and birth.[7]

There are several methods used in estimating the date of birth. One of these is Nägeles Rule. To calculate the EDB using this method, the healthcare provider first determines the first day of the woman's last menstrual period. From this date, subtract three calendar months, add seven days and one year. See Table 16.4 for an example of Nägeles Rule.

If there is a question regarding the dating of the pregnancy, an ultrasound examination is performed. An ultrasound examination is considered to be consistent with menstrual dates if there is gestational age consistency to within one week when performed at six to eleven weeks, or within ten days when obtained at twelve to twenty weeks.[8] There is an increase in the margin of error the later in the pregnancy that the ultrasound is performed.

Table 16.4
Nägeles Rule Example
(Calculation of Due Date)

LMP = July 5, 2005

Formula: -3 months + 7 days + 1 year

7	5	2004
-3	+7	
4	12	2005

EDB is April 12, 2005

16.4 Prenatal Flow Sheet

TIP: Look for trends in the data recorded on flow sheets.

It is important to have a flow sheet for documentation of perinatal data for each subsequent visit. This allows for analysis of comparison data in the ongoing assessment of both the mother and fetus. There are commercially prepared antenatal records available, and the American College of Obstetricians and Gynecologists (ACOG) has a form that they suggest. Healthcare providers can create their own system of prenatal documentation. The information needed to facilitate optimum prenatal care needs to be clearly apparent in the medical record in whatever form is used. The components of a prenatal flow sheet are described in this section, and there is an example of prenatal flow sheet documentation in Figure 16.2.

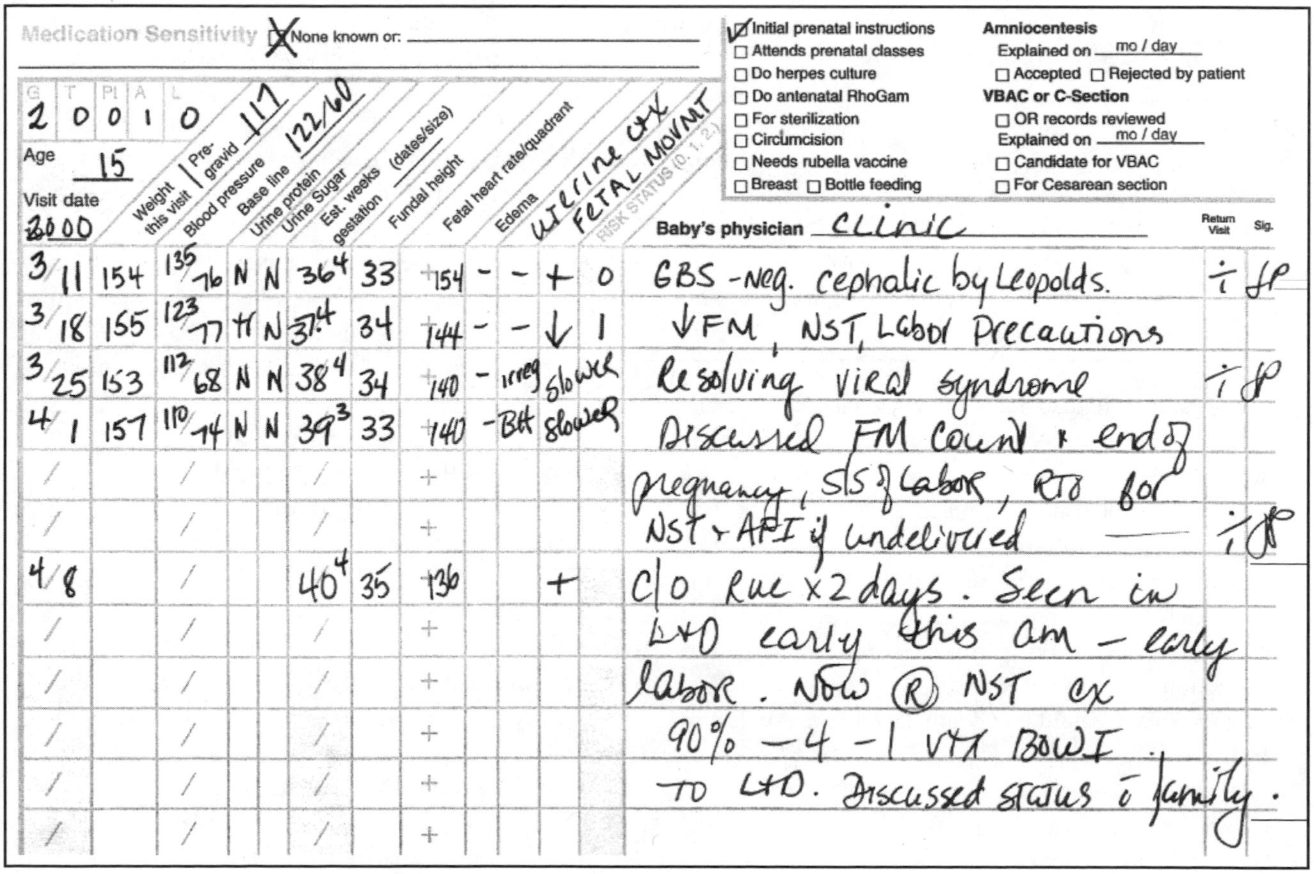
Medication Sensitivity ☒ None known or:

G 2 T 0 Pl 0 A 1 L 0

Age 15

Visit date 2000

Weight / Pre-gravid 117

Blood pressure / Base line 122/60

☑ Initial prenatal instructions
☐ Attends prenatal classes
☐ Do herpes culture
☐ Do antenatal RhoGam
☐ For sterilization
☐ Circumcision
☐ Needs rubella vaccine
☐ Breast ☐ Bottle feeding

Amniocentesis
Explained on mo / day
☐ Accepted ☐ Rejected by patient
VBAC or C-Section
☐ OR records reviewed
Explained on mo / day
☐ Candidate for VBAC
☐ For Cesarean section

Baby's physician CLINIC

Visit date	Weight this visit	Blood pressure	Urine protein	Urine Sugar	Est. weeks gestation	Fundal height	Fetal heart rate/quadrant	Edema	Uterine ctx	Fetal movmt	Risk status (0, 1, 2)		Return Visit	Sig.
3/11	154	135/76	N	N	36 4	33	154	-	-	+	0	GBS -Neg. cephalic by Leopolds.	÷ i	[illegible]
3/18	155	123/77	tr	N	37 4	34	144	-	-	↓	1	↓FM, NST, Labor Precautions		
3/25	153	112/68	N	N	38 4	34	140	-	irreg	slower		Resolving viral syndrome	÷ i	[illegible]
4/1	157	110/74	N	N	39 3	33	140	-	BH	slower		Discussed FM count + end of		
/		/			/		+					pregnancy, S/S of Labor, RTO for		
/		/			/		+					NST + AFI if undelivered —	÷ i	[illegible]
4/8		/			40 4	35	136			+		C/O RUC x2 days. Seen in		
/		/			/		+					L+D early this am – early		
/		/			/		+					labor. Now Ⓡ NST cx		
/		/			/		+					90% –4 –1 vtx BOWI.		
/		/			/		+					TO L+D. Discussed status c̄ family.		
/		/			/		+							

Figure 16.2 *Example of documentation on prenatal flow sheet.*

Table 16.5
Recommendations for Weight Gain in Pregnancy*

Underweight	28–40 pounds
Normal weight	25–35 pounds
Overweight	15–25 pounds

*Data adapted from Cunningham, et al. (1997). *Williams Obstetrics* and Lowdermilk and Perry, *Maternity and Women's Health Care*, Eighth Edition.

A. Weight

On each visit the client is weighed. Recall that on the first prenatal visit a baseline weight had been recorded. Each subsequent weight should be compared to the previous weights, and the trend should be evaluated.

The range of weight change in pregnancy is wide, with there being no simple figure for weight change that can be regarded as normal.[9] However, the Institute of Medicine has published studies on weight gain during pregnancy and made recommendations that are illustrated in Table 16.5.

When there are trends in weight loss, lack of weight gain in second and third trimesters, or excessive weight gain, especially in short timeframes, further assessment should be undertaken. Conditions such as hyperemesis gravidarum (excessive vomiting prenatally), a fetus that is small for gestational age, a fetus that is large for gestational age, gestational diabetes, and preeclampsia (high blood pressure induced by pregnancy) could be a concern. A more in-depth evaluation, such as lab studies and ultrasound, would provide further data. Nutritional counseling should be documented in the prenatal record as well.

B. Blood Pressure

Documentation of the initial baseline blood pressure is an important marker, as the physiological changes that occur in pregnancy will have an effect on maternal blood pressure. In the first trimester, blood pressure usually remains the same as the pre-pregnancy level but then gradually decreases up to about the twentieth week of gestation. During the second trimester, blood pressure decreases about 5-10 mmHg in both the systolic and diastolic pressures. Beyond the twentieth week, a gradual return to first trimester blood pressure occurs by the end of the pregnancy.[10]

There are specific conditions in pregnancy that can be hallmarked by changes in blood pressure. Hypertensive disorders of pregnancy are the most common medical complications reported.[11] An elevated blood pressure can be one of the first signs of preeclampsia. Hypertension is defined as systolic blood pressure (top number in a blood pressure) greater than 140 mm/Hg, or a diastolic blood pressure greater than 90 mm/Hg (bottom number in a blood pressure). It also is concerning if there is an elevation of 30 mm/Hg systolic or greater, or 15 mm/Hg diastolic or greater.

C. Urine Testing

TIP: A urinalysis is obtained during the initial visit, and the laboratory performs a microscopic examination to identify the presence of significant bacteria in the urine.[12] Urinary tract infections (UTI) are a risk factor for preterm birth, and early detection is important.

At each subsequent prenatal visit, it is customary to have the woman provide a urine specimen, which is evaluated for protein and glucose. Many healthcare providers will also check for ketones.

Proteinuria (protein in the urine) can be a symptom of preeclampsia. Glucose in the urine can signify gestational diabetes or uncontrolled diabetes mellitus. Ketone bodies can be present in situations of dehydration and also found in the presence of hyperglycemia that has progressed to diabetic ketoacidosis, which is an acute emergency situation. The presence of moderate to large amounts of leukocytes in the urine can be significant for infection, and a clean specimen is usually sent for culture and sensitivity for diagnostic purposes. If an infection of the urinary tract is present, treatment is initiated with antibiotics. Due to the increased risk of preterm labor with infections, a follow-up culture and sensitivity would be needed to ensure that the infection has been eradicated.

D. Estimated Gestational Age

See Section 16.3 on estimated date of birth. At each prenatal visit, the estimated gestational age (EGA) is recorded, and assessment is made of the correlation between the gestational age and the physical exam. It is important that the EGA be recorded accurately, because there are laboratory tests and clinical findings that are based on gestational age. If the EGA is in error, certain test results will be inaccurate. There also could be a concern over intrauterine growth restriction.

There are many clinical findings in the determination of the estimated gestational age.[13] Included in these findings are

- menstrual history, LMP (last menstrual period),
- first uterine evaluation: date, size,
- date fetal heart rate first heard and method,
- fundal height (defined below),
- estimated fetal weight, and
- ultrasound results.

E. Fundal Height

The fundal height (FH) is the measurement of the height of the uterus above the symphysis pubis. It can be measured after the 12th week of pregnancy, when the uterus grows out of the pelvis and becomes an abdominal organ. It is used as one measurement of fetal growth and provides a gross estimate of gestational age. From about the 12th to the 36th week, the height of the fundus in centimeters (cms) is approximately the same as the number of weeks of gestation.[14] The height of the uterine fundus reaches the maternal umbilicus at about twenty weeks of gestation and the xiphoid process (tip) of the sternum by thirty-six weeks.[15] After approximately thirty-six to thirty-eight weeks of gestation, the fundal height becomes slightly lower. This phenomenon is called lightening. Lightening is a distinctive event representing that the fetal head has descended to or even through the maternal inlet of the pelvis.[16]

F. Fetal Heart Rate

TIP: In essentially all pregnancies, the healthcare provider can first auscultate the fetal heart rate (FHR) with a fetal stethoscope between sixteen to nineteen weeks.[17]

However, with the use of amplified Doppler to detect FHR, it can often be detected at approximately twelve to fourteen weeks gestation. There are many variables that can interfere with the ability to detect the FHR by either method, including patient size, placental location, fetal activity, fetal position, and acuity of the examiner's hearing. Once the FHR can be detected, it is documented at each subsequent visit. If there is difficulty assessing the FHR, an ultrasound would be performed to evaluate fetal well-being.

The average baseline FHR in the normal fetus at twenty weeks of gestation is 155 beats per minute; at thirty weeks, 144 beats per minute; and at term, 140 beats per minute. Variations of twenty beats per minute above or below these levels are considered normal. The baseline FHR normally ranges from 110 to 160 beats per minute.[18]

TIP: Maternal fever increases maternal pulse, and will cause an increase in fetal heart rate.

G. Fetal Position/Presenting Part

During the prenatal visits in the third trimester, fetal position is evaluated. This is usually accomplished by abdominal palpation, but it can also be determined by other means. These include vaginal examination, FHR auscultation, and ultrasound. Presenting part refers to the part of the fetal body that is felt first by the examiner during a vaginal examination.[19] The most common presentations are: cephalic or vertex (vtx), which is the fetal head presenting; breech (br) signifies buttocks or feet presenting; and shoulder or transverse lie.

H. Fetal Movement/Quickening

Quickening occurs on the day the pregnant woman becomes conscious of slight, fluttering movements in her abdomen. It represents the perception of life by the mother. In other words, it is the day the mother first felt fetal movement.[20] This occurs between sixteen and twenty weeks gestation and is also used as a marker for fetal age.

After the experience of quickening, fetal movement should be documented at each subsequent visit. Any absences of fetal movement, or marked change in fetal activity, needs to be further evaluated by the healthcare provider because decreased fetal movement can be of concern for fetal well-being.

TIP: Documentation of decreased fetal movement needs immediate referral for antenatal testing.

16.5 Prenatal Testing

In the best interest of both maternal and fetal health, certain lab tests should be routinely performed in pregnant women. The results are important in the plan of care for the pregnant woman, as well as for the newborn.[21] The newborn record should have the maternal prenatal lab work included to ensure an optimal care plan to promote the well-being of the infant. The initial lab work is done as early as possible in the pregnancy. A review of routine prenatal testing follows.

A. Hemoglobin and Hematocrit

The hemoglobin count is a measure of the total amount of hemoglobin in the peripheral blood. The hemoglobin concentration reflects the oxygen-carrying capacity of blood. Decreased hemoglobin levels can indicate anemia.[22] Normal values for a non-pregnant woman range from 12-16 g/dl. Physiological changes in pregnancy create a hemodilutional effect on hemoglobin levels, so that concern for anemia does not occur until the hemoglobin decreases to 10 g/dl or less.[23] Hematocrit values are also affected by the physiological changes of pregnancy in the same manner. Normal range for non-pregnant females is 37 to 47 percent, while pregnant women's value will be greater than 33 percent as a normal. The hematocrit measures the packed red blood cell volume.[24]

B. Blood Type and Rh

All pregnant women should have blood typing and Rh factor determination. Hemolytic disease of the newborn can be prevented by Rh typing during pregnancy. If the mother is Rh negative, she should be advised that she is a candidate for Rhogam. Rhogam reduces the chance of fetal hemolytic problems during subsequent pregnancies. During the pregnancy, the Rh negative mother is given a prophylactic injection of Rhogam at twenty-eight weeks. As the blood type of the fetus is unknown, it could be Rh positive. If there had been any mixing of maternal and fetal blood, maternal antibodies develop that create problems in subsequent pregnancies with Rh positive fetuses. Rhogam is also administered to Rh negative pregnant women who experience invasive procedures, such as amniocentesis, chorionic villi sampling, or trauma.[25]

C. Sexually Transmitted Disease (STD)

Routine screening for chlamydia, gonorrhea, hepatitis, and syphilis is performed as part of the initial screening process.[26] STDs can complicate pregnancies through miscarriage, fetal congenital infections, or preterm labor and can have devastating effects on the fetus. Early detection and treatment for the pregnant woman are critical.

TIP: Opinions vary related to having routine prenatal HIV screening.

The Institute of Medicine (IOM) has recommended universal but voluntary screening. The American Academy of Pediatrics (AAP) and the American College of Obstetrics and Gynecology (ACOG) have recommended that all pregnant women be tested. The Centers for Disease Control (CDC) recommends that all pregnant women be counseled and encouraged to be tested for HIV infections.[27] This would allow women to know their infection status for their own well-being and also to reduce the risk of perinatal HIV transmission.

D. Group B Betastrep (GBBS)

There are specific risk factors for GBBS infections, and these include women with preterm labor, premature rupture of membranes, ruptured membranes for greater than eighteen hours, previous birth of a child with GBBS disease, or maternal fever during labor. A woman with any of these factors would receive intrapartum antibiotics as prophylaxis. The CDC, ACOG, and AAP recommend obtaining vaginal cultures at thirty-five to thirty-six weeks of gestation. Any woman who has a positive culture would be treated with an-

tibiotics in labor.[28] Treating women in labor for positive cultures, and those that have risk factors for GBBS, is done for the well-being of the infant. If a newborn becomes infected, the result could be sepsis, pneumonia, meningitis, and death. All prenatal records should have clear documentation of the woman's GBBS status. There needs to be follow-up assessment of this status when the woman is admitted in labor, so that antibiotic treatment can be initiated.

TIP: GBBS status should be recorded on prenatal and on labor and delivery admission records.

In a New York case, an obstetrician noted the pregnant patient had a positive group-B streptococcus infection, and that appropriate measures would be needed during delivery, including administration of intravenous antibiotics. Three days later, the mother went into labor. The covering obstetrician did not remember the positive group-B streptococcus result and antibiotics were not given until the following day. Ancef was used because the mother's chart incorrectly identified her as being allergic to Penicillin. The plaintiff child developed a fever, was lethargic, not feeding and ultimately diagnosed with a stroke that affected the left side of his body. Multiple deviations were alleged. The case resulted in a $17 million settlement during trial.[29]

E. Gestational Diabetes Screening

Gestational diabetes is defined as carbohydrate intolerance of variable severity with onset during pregnancy.[30,31] There are several factors that are known to increase maternal risk in the development of gestational diabetes. See Table 16.6 for a list of these risk factors. Through prenatal assessment, if any of these factors is identified, screening for gestational diabetes becomes an important antenatal assessment. Many healthcare providers will routinely screen all pregnant women for gestational diabetes between twenty-four and twenty-eight weeks of pregnancy.[32] The test is performed at this point in gestation because pregnancy hormones decrease the mother's ability to utilize insulin, and this effect increases as the pregnancy progresses. If the diagnosis of gestational diabetes is made, nutrition counseling and glucose monitoring are begun. If diet alone does not control maternal blood sugars, then insulin is started. There would be an increase in frequency of the prenatal visits, as well as further antenatal testing to monitor fetal well-being and growth. If the gestational diabetes is not well controlled, there is a risk of fetal macrosomia (large baby).

Table 16.6
Risk Factors for Gestational Diabetes*

- Maternal age older than 30 years
- Obesity
- Family history of Type 2 diabetes
- Obstetric history of an infant weighing more than nine pounds
- Hydramnios
- Unexplained stillbirth, miscarriage, or an infant with congenital anomalies
- Other factors include hypertensive disorders, recurrent monilial vaginitis, and glucosuria on two consecutive visits to the clinic

*Adapted from Lowdermilk and Perry, *Maternity and Women's Health Care*, Eighth Edition.

Table 16.7
Indications for Antenatal Ultrasounds*

- Confirm pregnancy
- Determine gestational age
- Detect multiple gestations
- Measure amniotic fluid volume
- Detect congenital abnormalities
- Monitor fetal growth
- Confirm placenta placement
- Detect placental maturity
- Determine fetal statue
- Biophysical profile
- Determine fetal size

*Data compiled from Pagana, K. and Pagana, T. (1998). Manual of Diagnostic and Laboratory Tests and Lowdermilk, D. and Perry, S. (2004). *Maternity and Women's Health Care.*

TIP: Macrosomia refers to a fetus who at birth weighs 4500 grams or more.

F. Maternal Serum Alpha Fetal Protein

Maternal serum alpha fetal protein (MSAFP) testing is performed as a screening tool for open neural tube defects, such as spina bifida.[33] The test has the greatest sensitivity when performed at sixteen to eighteen weeks gestation, although it can be performed from fifteen to twenty-two weeks.[34] If the screening test is abnormal, further diagnostic testing would need to be performed.

All women need to be provided the information about the test early in the pregnancy, so that they can make an informed decision as to whether to have the test performed. This would not apply to a woman who seeks prenatal care late in the pregnancy, after the 22nd week, as the test would not be accurate at that time.

G. Ultrasonography

TIP: Diagnostic ultrasonography is considered to be an important, safe technique in antepartum fetal surveillance.

Table 16.7 lists some of the indications for obstetrical ultrasounds. The data provided from the sonogram will assist the healthcare providers in their ongoing care of the woman and her fetus.

H. Amniocentesis

An amniocentesis is the aspiration of amniotic fluid from the amniotic sac.[35] This procedure can be performed in the second and third trimester. An indication for amniocentesis in the second trimester is for genetic analysis of the amniotic fluid. This identifies chromosome abnormalities and metabolic defects. It also can be used to evaluate fetal condition when the woman is sensitized to Rh positive blood, diagnose intrauterine infections, and look for amniotic fluid alpha fetal protein when the MSAFP is elevated. During the third trimester, common indications for amniocentesis are to determine fetal lung maturity and to evaluate the fetal condition in the presence of maternal Rh isoimmunization.[36]

Amniocentesis is also a procedure that is sometimes used in the treatment of hydramnios, also called polyhydramnios. Polyhydramnios is a condition in which the volume of amniotic fluid exceeds 2000 milliliters during the last half of the pregnancy. Amniocentesis is performed to reduce the amniotic fluid volume in women who are experiencing severe discomfort from the pressure of the extra fluid. However, in most cases, conservative management is sufficient. This includes bedrest in the left lateral position to encourage placental perfusion (blood flow) and diuresis (urine production).[37]

I. Nonstress Test (NST)

The nonstress test (NST) is used to evaluate fetal well-being by measuring fetal heart rate accelerations. It is a non-invasive test performed with the use of an external fetal monitor to record the fetal heart rate. The ability of the fetal heart rate to accelerate is felt to be an indication of a fetus who is not acidotic as a result of hypoxia or neurological depression. The result of a NST is documented as either reactive or non-reactive. Reactive criteria include two or more FHR accelerations of fifteen beats per minute or more, each lasting fifteen seconds or more, and all occurring within a twenty-minute time frame. See Figure 16.3 for an example of a re-active NST. A non-reactive NST would be one that does not meet the above criteria. If a non-reactive NST is determined, then further evaluation of fetal well-being would need to be performed.[38]

J. Contraction Stress Test (CST)

The goal of the CST is to identify how a fetus responds to stress. Uterine contractions (stressor) decrease uterine blood flow and placenta perfusion. If the decrease is sufficient to produce hypoxia in the fetus, a late deceleration in the fetal heart rate will result. See Section 16.8 for a discussion on FHR decelerations.

The results of a CST are documented as positive when there are decelerations with contractions and negative if there are no decelerations. A healthy fetus would have a negative CST test. The contractions can be obtained through either breast stimulation or an infusion of oxytocin. The goal is to obtain three uterine contractions of good quality ob-served within a ten-minute period. If the CST is positive, continued monitoring and further evaluation of fetal well-being is indicated.[39]

K. Biophysical Profile

The biophysical profile (BPP) evaluates fetal status on the basis of five components.[40]

- fetal heart rate,
- fetal breathing movement,
- fetal movement,
- fetal muscle tone, and
- amniotic fluid volume.

The fetal heart rate reactivity is measured with the NST rather than with the visualization of the heart rate during the procedure. The status of the fetal well-being at the time of the procedure is documented through a scoring system. Each of the five components is assigned 2 points, and is scored as either 2 or 0. A score of 8 or 10 with an acceptable amount of amniotic fluid is normal. Refer to Table 16.8 for an explanation of the grading criteria for a BPP.

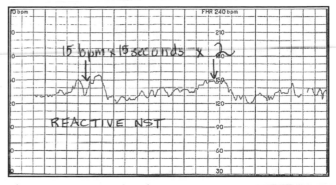

Figure 16.3 *Example of reactive NST—two FHR ac-celerations that increase ≥ 15 bpm over baseline and last for ≥ seconds in a twenty-minute period.*

Table 16.8
Biophysical Profile Grading Criteria*

Component	Criteria for score of 2
FHR reactivity tested with NST	Two FHR accelerations of at least 15 bpm above baseline, at least 15 seconds in duration in a 20 minute time frame.
Fetal breathing movements	At least one episode of fetal breathing lasting a minimum of 30 seconds within a 30 minute time frame.
Fetal body movements	The presence of at least 3 episodes of fetal movement within a 30 minute period.
Fetal muscle tone	At least one episode of active extension with return to flexion (i.e., opening and closing of hand)
Amniotic fluid volume or index	A pocket of amniotic fluid that measures at least 2 cm in two planes perpen-dicular to each other

*Data adapted from American Academy of Pediatrics and American College of Obstetricians and Gynecologists. (2002). *Guidelines for Perinatal Care* and Pagana, K. and Pagana, T. (1998). *Manual of Diagnostic and Laboratory Tests.*

TIP: Decreased amniotic fluid requires follow up even if BPP score is 8 to 10.

L. Amniotic Fluid Volume/Amniotic Fluid Index

The terms *amniotic fluid volume* and *amniotic fluid index* are often used interchangeably, but they do refer to different measurements. Volume refers to the amount of amniotic fluid estimated in millimeters. Amniotic fluid index refers to the measurement in centimeters of the pockets of amniotic fluid observed during an ultrasound examination. Assessment of amniotic fluid index is used as an indication of long-term placental function. Through ultrasound, a semi-quantitative assessment is made of amniotic fluid depth. A value of less than or equal to five is considered indicative of significant oligohydramnios.[41] The term oligohydramnios refers to an abnormally low amount of amniotic fluid.[42]

Insufficient fluid surrounding the fetus increases the potential for cord compression, fetal hypoxia, fetal malformation, and fetal demise. Oligohydramnios is associated with amniotic fluid leakage, placental insufficiency, postmaturity, intrauterine growth restriction, and major congenital abnormalities of the fetal kidney and lungs.

16.6 Intrapartum Care

Much obstetrical litigation revolves around the question of whether negligent intrapartum care caused a negative outcome. The goal of intrapartum care is a safe birth experience for the newborn and mother. Ongoing risk assessment and surveillance of the mother and fetus are essential.

TIP: The medical record should reflect the documentation of assessments, plans of care, interventions, and evaluation from the time of admission to recovery from the birth experience.

A. Admission

A pregnant woman presenting to a labor and delivery unit should be evaluated in a timely fashion.[43] An obstetrical nurse may perform the initial evaluation, which would include documentation of maternal vital signs, FHR, uterine activity, and cervical exam if appropriate. Prompt notification of the healthcare provider is needed if any of the following signs are identified[44]

- acute abdominal pain,
- vaginal bleeding,
- temperature of 99.4 or higher,
- preterm labor,

- preterm premature rupture of membranes,
- hypertension, or
- non-reassuring FHR.

Other areas that need to be documented in the medical record on admission are included in Table 16.9.

Table 16.9
Labor and Delivery Admission Documentation*

- Estimated date of birth
- Cervical dilation and effacement
- Fetal presentation and station
- Status of membranes
- Vital signs
- Fetal heart rate
- Contractions, onset and frequency
- Previous pregnancy history
- Date and time of patient's arrival
- Date and time of notification of the provider
- Previously identified risk factors
- Pertinent information from the prenatal record
- GBBS status
- Recent infections
- Use of any medications
- Time and amount of recent food or fluid
- History of allergies
- Urinary protein and glucose
- Estimated fetal weight

*Data adapted Iyer, P. and Camp, N. (2005). *Nursing Documentation*, and American Academy of Pediatrics and American College of Obstetricians and Gynecologists. (2002). *Guidelines for Perinatal Care.*

B. Labor Progress Record

Labor progress records are often flow sheets that provide an overall view of maternal and fetal condition during the process of labor and birth. However, in hospitals that use electronic charting, one of the only areas recorded on the flow sheet is the interpretation of the electronic fetal monitoring strip. See Section 16.7. The American College of Obstetricians and Gynecologists (ACOG) and the American Academy of Pediatrics (AAP) have established guidelines for the frequency of documentation of the fetal heart rate in labor. These are dependent on whether there are any risk factors present. Table 16.10 describes these guidelines.

Table 16.10
Frequency of Fetal Heart Rate Monitoring*

No risk factors	Determine and record the auscultated FHR just after a contraction at least every 30 minutes in the active stage of the first stage of labor and at least every 15 minutes in the second stage of labor.
Risk factors present	During the active phase of the first stage of labor, the FHR should be determined and recorded at least every 15 minutes just after a uterine contraction. If electronic fetal monitoring (EFM) is in use, tracing should be evaluated at least every 15 minutes. During the second stage of labor, the FHR should be determined and recorded at least every 5 minutes if auscultation is used, or EFM tracing evaluated at least every 5 minutes.

*Data adapted from AAP and ACOG's Guidelines for Perinatal Care (2002).

Table 16.11
Stages of Labor*

First stage	Onset of regular contractions to full dilation of the cervix.
Second stage	From the time cervix is completely dilated to the birth of the baby.
Third stage	Lasts from the birth of the baby until the placenta is delivered.
Fourth stage	Lasts about two hours after delivery of the placenta.

*Adapted from Lowdermilk, D. and Perry, S. (2004). *Maternity and Women's Health Care.*

Vital signs should be recorded at regular intervals, at least every four hours. Blood pressure monitoring is performed more frequently in high risk patients and patients receiving analgesia or anesthesia. Maternal temperature assessment is increased to at least every two hours in the presence of ruptured membranes. Most hospitals have policies and procedures that instruct on frequency of vital signs related to specific conditions, such as patients with epidurals and patients on oxytocin infusions.

Documentation of the course of a woman's labor should include

- the presence of the healthcare providers,
- fetal status,
- maternal position changes,
- cervical status (degree of dilation) and fetal position and station (location within the birth canal),
- oxygen and drug administration,
- frequency, duration, and quality of contractions,
- amniotomy (artificial rupture of membranes) or spontaneous rupture of membranes, and
- bearing down progress in the second stage of labor.

Refer to Table 16.11 for a review of the stages of labor. All entries made into the medical record should include the date and time of occurrence. Labor and delivery is a dynamic process, and action will take precedence over the act of documentation. As soon as possible, the physician and nurses should accurately record all events.[45]

The case described below illustrates the importance of close monitoring of the mother and fetus during labor.

The plaintiff mother was in her thirty-sixth week of pregnancy when she presented to the hospital in labor in February 2006. An external fetal monitor was placed about two hours after her arrival and the fetal heart tracings were deemed non-reactive due to decreased variability with a heart rate of 160-170 beats per minute. The infant had decreased tone with poor suck and grasp. The plaintiff alleged failure to timely delivery and failure to timely being monitoring at the time of the patient's presentation to the hospital. The child was diagnosed with cerebral palsy, cortical impairment, and developmental delays. A settlement was reached with the obstetrician for $2.1 million prior to trial. A jury returned a $77 million verdict.[46]

16.7 Electronic Fetal Monitoring

When using electronic fetal monitoring (EFM), it is important that the healthcare providers accurately interpret the tracing and document appropriately. The mode of monitoring can be either external or internal. This is reflected on the flow sheet and is automatically printed on the tracing. The FHR baseline, variability, presence and types of any decelerations, and presence or absence of FHR accelerations are documented on the flow sheet. Refer to Figure 16.4 for an example of charting on a labor and delivery flow sheet. Many flow sheets will also include a column for interpretation of the tracing as either reassuring or non-reassuring. Whenever there is a change in the rate or pattern of the FHR, it is important to document this event and also to document a subsequent return to reassuring findings.

All monitor strips should have patient identifying information, including the date initiated. The time should appear automatically on the tracing, and the printout runs at a speed of three centimeters per minute. Refer to Figure 16.5 for an example of EFM timeframes. It is important that the internal clock in the EFM be calculated to the Labor and Delivery unit clocks, as even small discrepancies in time can become critical.

TIP: Timing of events in labor and delivery can be critical. Review times from the external fetal monitor and compare to medical record notes.

There are many instances where documentation is done on the EFM tracing itself. Examples of documentation on the EFM tracing are illustrated in Table 16.12. Many monitors have electronic charting systems where the nurse documents on a keyboard or with a stylus, and the data are printed out directly on the tracing. After the delivery, the nurse can print out the annotated notes for the medical record. Anything that is handwritten directly on the tracing would still need to be recorded in the medical record.

16.8 Non-Reassuring Fetal Heart Rate Patterns

Fetal heart rate patterns are usually identified as either *reassuring* or *non-reassuring*.[47] Some authors also include the categories of *compensatory* and *ominous*. The fetus obtaining sufficient blood flow has a reassuring pattern. Documentation of a *reassuring* pattern includes

- normal FHR baseline between 110 to 160 beats per minute,
- presence of short-term variability,
- spontaneous accelerations, and
- absence of decelerations, with the exception of possible early decelerations.[48]

Refer to Figure 16.6 for examples of decelerations. A *non-reassuring* pattern indicates that the fetal status is deteriorating due to hypoxia and the continuing depletion of oxygen reserves, which increases the fetal risk of metabolic acidosis.[49] Decreased FHR variability can be diagnostic of chronic hypoxia. Figure 16.7 illustrates minimal FHR variability. Immediate measures are needed to optimize fetal oxygenation, notify the physician, and determine the probable etiology. Interventions to increase fetal oxygenation include changing maternal position, delivering ten liters of oxygen via face mask, and hydrating as indicated. If a non-reassuring pattern persists, preparation for delivery is initiated.

	Time →	1115	1130	1200	1215	1230	1245	1300	1315	1330	1345	1400	1415
Uterine Activity	Monitor Mode	E	E	E	I	I	I	I	I	I	I	I	I
	Frequency	3-4	2-4	2-4	3-4	3-4	2-3	2-3	2-3	2-3	2-3	2-3	2-3
	Duration	60	60	60	60	40-60	60	60	60	60	60	60	60
	Peak IUP												
	Resting Tone												
	Intensity												
	MVUs												
Fetal Assessment	Monitor Mode (Strip #___)	E	E	E	I	I	I	I	I	I	I	I	I
	Baseline (FHR)	140's	140/150	140's	140's	140's	160	120-140	120-140	120-130	80-120's	120's 90	90-120
	STV	+	+	+	+	+	+	+	+	+	+	+	
	LTV	+	+	+	+	+	+	+	+	+	+	+	+
	Accelerations						+						
	Decelerations		V	V				V	V L	V L	V	V	
	Membranes/Fluid	I	I	I	AROM	MEC	MEC	MEC	→	→			

Figure 16.4 *Example of monitoring uterine activity and fetal assessment on a labor and delivery flow sheet.*

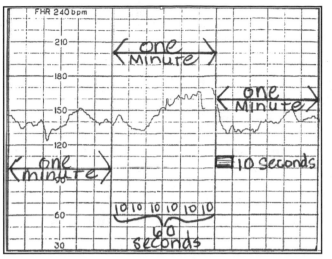

Figure 16.5 *Example of EFM tracing time frames when set at speed of 3 centimeters per minute, a standard setting.*

Table 16.12
Documentation on EFM Tracing*

- Scalp or acoustic stimulation
- Vital signs
- Medications
- Anesthesia and analgesia
- Fetal movement
- Pushing efforts
- IV fluid bolus
- Rupture of membranes
- Maternal movements and position changes
- Vaginal examinations and examiner
- Delivery mode and time
- Apgar score
- Other interventions that might affect the FHR or UA tracing (i.e., Foley catheter insertion, emesis, coughing, effleurage)

*Data adapted from Iyer, P. and Camp, N. (2005). *Nursing Documentation.*

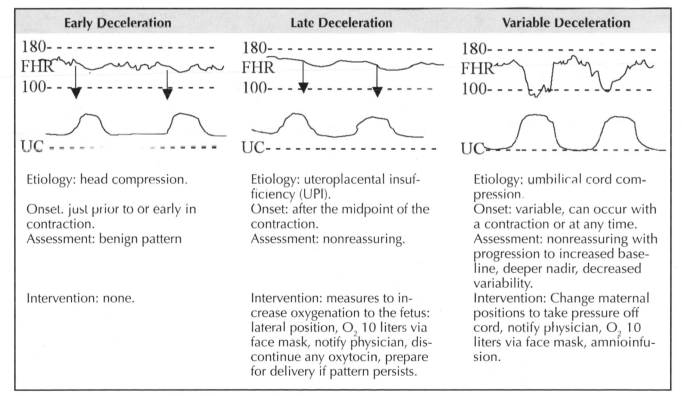

Early Deceleration	Late Deceleration	Variable Deceleration
Etiology: head compression.	Etiology: uteroplacental insufficiency (UPI).	Etiology: umbilical cord compression.
Onset: just prior to or early in contraction.	Onset: after the midpoint of the contraction.	Onset: variable, can occur with a contraction or at any time.
Assessment: benign pattern	Assessment: nonreassuring.	Assessment: nonreassuring with progression to increased baseline, deeper nadir, decreased variability.
Intervention: none.	Intervention: measures to increase oxygenation to the fetus: lateral position, O₂ 10 liters via face mask, notify physician, discontinue any oxytocin, prepare for delivery if pattern persists.	Intervention: Change maternal positions to take pressure off cord, notify physician, O₂ 10 liters via face mask, amnioinfusion.

Figure 16.6 *Explanation of fetal heart rate deceleration patterns.*

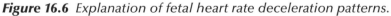

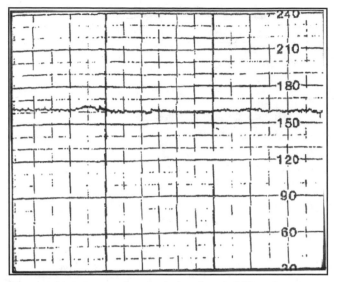

Figure 16.7 *Example of minimal variability. Decreased variability can be related to fetal hypoxia.*

Figure 16.8 *Example of an ominous tracing. FHR shows absent STV and wandering baseline which is significant for CNS injury. The infant died at two days old with multiple systems failure.*

Absent short-term and *long-term variability* is an extremely ominous finding. The FHR tracing would appear as a smooth line. The baseline can be unstable, called a wandering baseline. A fetus that displays this pattern is most likely metabolically acidotic. Figure 16.8 shows the strip of a fetus with severe metabolic acidosis.

The documentation of the communication between the physician and nurse about changes in variability should include the time, the person informed, what information was discussed, and the response given. Any lack of response or action should be documented, as well as the nurse's follow-up action, and any initiation of the chain of command if necessary.[50] The following case shows the importance of communication in the labor and delivery setting.

The plaintiff mother was admitted to the hospital for induction of labor on the day before her due date.

An emergency cesarean section was performed during the evening of the next day. The child was diagnosed with mental retardation and cerebral palsy. The plaintiffs alleged a failure to properly interpret fetal monitoring and signs of intrauterine fetal distress and failure to timely perform a cesarean section. The plaintiffs also alleged the physicians were not timely informed of intrauterine fetal distress. The physicians were dismissed from the case and the matter proceeded against the hospital only. A $2.5 million settlement was reached.[51]

16.9 Pitocin Induction and Augmentation

TIP: An *induction* of labor is when the woman is not in labor, and she comes to the hospital to have her labor induced. An *augmentation* of labor is done when a woman is in labor, but she is not progressing in an acceptable pattern.

A patient undergoing either a Pitocin (oxytocin) augmentation or induction needs to have a nurse clinically evaluate and document the effect of the drug at least every fifteen minutes.[52] This assessment includes evaluation of uterine activity and fetal status. Each hospital's labor and delivery department should have written protocols for preparing and administering Pitocin. The indications for the induction or augmentation of labor should be documented in the medical record. The methods for assessment of the woman and the fetus before and during administration of oxytocin should be specified.[53]

Fetal heart rate monitoring should be documented as described in Table 16.10 for the at-risk patient in active labor. It is also important to monitor and document the response of the uterus to the Pitocin. Pitocin protocols should provide a standing order to discontinue the Pitocin if there is hyperstimulation of the uterus or for any nonreassuring FHR patterns. *Hyperstimulation* of the uterus is defined by Murray as the interval between the contractions being less than one minute and contractions occurring closer together than two minutes apart.[54] Even if the fetal heart rate is reassuring with hyperstimulation of the uterus present, hyperstimulation should *not* be allowed to continue. The fetal oxygen reserve can diminish, with a subsequent nonreassuring FHR pattern appearing. It is not safe practice to allow hyperstimulation to continue to the point where the fetus shows signs of stress. Sadly, saying "pit to distress" has been heard by labor and delivery nurses, but this practice is not defensible. Fetal advocacy should be a primary concern of everyone involved in the patient's care.

TIP: Documentation of contractions should reflect at least one minute of uterine relaxation between contractions.

The risk of uterine rupture increases when oxytocin is used. Signs and symptoms of uterine rupture include

- abdominal pain,
- no fetal descent, or a higher fetal station (associated with extrusion of fetus into the abdomen),
- maternal tachycardia (rapid heart rate),
- maternal hypotension,
- referred shoulder pain,
- vaginal bleeding,
- erratic FHR pattern,
- FHR decelerations or bradycardia (slow heart rate),
- sudden maternal anxiety and restlessness, and
- rectal pain or pressure.[55]

Nursing assessment of any of these conditions needs further timely intervention and notification of the physician, as uterine rupture is a life-threatening event for both the mother and fetus. In the case described below, a uterine rupture occurred with devastating neurological damage to the infant.

A woman who had a previous cesarean section was pregnant and in the defendant hospital for labor and delivery. Pitocin was administered, and during the resultant labor, her uterus ruptured. The baby detached itself from both the uterus and placenta. After an emergency cesarean section, the baby was found to have been without oxygen for an indeterminate amount of time and to have suffered cerebral palsy. The plaintiffs claimed that the hospital, doctors, and nurses were negligent in administering Pitocin and that the defendant doctor was not kept properly informed of changes in the fetal monitor strip. The doctor claimed that he did not remember ordering the Pitocin and that he did not believe he would have ordered it under the circumstances. The jury found that the defendant doctor was not negligent but that the hospital was negligent and awarded the plaintiff $1,587,000 in damages.[56]

16.10 Analgesia and Anesthesia

Pharmacologic analgesics can be used to decrease the pain of contractions for the laboring woman. The physical condition of the patient and the status of the fetus must be evaluated, as narcotics are potentially depressing to both the mother and the fetus. This can result in diminished short or long-term variability.[57] Documentation of decreased variability after pain medication would be an accepted finding, providing a reassuring FHR pattern was noted prior to the administration of the medication.

Epidural anesthesia is a common labor relief choice in today's obstetrical environment. When epidural anesthesia is administered, the FHR pattern is assessed and documented according to established guidelines before and after the procedure and during the procedure if possible.[58] The hospital's procedure concerning care of the patient in labor with epidural anesthesia would state the assessment parameters required in that institution. Maternal hypotension is a common occurrence after an epidural is administered, and frequent maternal blood pressure monitoring and documentation are important. Fetal heart rate bradycardia occurs with precipitous drops in maternal blood pressure. Correction of the decreased blood pressure is needed immediately, and documentation should illustrate what interventions are taken, e.g., maternal position change, IV fluid bolus, anesthesia notification, and possible medication (ephedrine) administration to increase blood pressure. The decreased FHR should respond to maternal blood pressure recovery. Documentation should include the effect of all actions taken and the return of the FHR and maternal blood pressure to normal range. The pain relief and decreased sensation effect of the epidural should also be documented.

16.11 Cesarean Sections

TIP: In relation to the performance of cesarean sections, there is the "thirty minute rule," which infers that hospitals should have the capability of beginning a cesarean section delivery within thirty minutes of the decision to operate.[59]

The time the decision is made should be reflected in the medical record, usually found in the physician's progress notes and the nurse's notes. In an emergency situation the documentation will probably be retrospective, but it still should indicate the timing of events as accurately as possible. The following case demonstrates how the delay in the timing of the cesarean section resulted in severe brain damage in the infant.

An eighteen-year-old expectant mother carrying her fetus at thirty-one weeks gestation presented to the defendant hospital because of symptoms of early delivery. Her fetus had been diagnosed earlier in the breech position. Between midnight and 1:00 A.M., a hospital nurse telephoned the mother of the expectant woman and stated "We have got to get your daughter ready for an emergency C-section." The defendant obstetrician spoke with a nurse shortly after 1:00 A.M. and allegedly ordered a stat cesarean, although such an order did not appear in the medical record. The doctor reached the hospital about 1:45 A.M. but did not commence the cesarean until around 2:50 A.M. The two nurse employees of the defendant hospital did not attempt to reach the on-call obstetrician, notwithstanding that both supposedly admitted knowing that the fetal monitor strip was nonreassuring. Apgars at birth were 1 and 4. The infant suffered brain damage with lack of ability to ambulate, speak, self-feed, or to care for himself. The case was settled in mediation for $3,250,000.[60]

The lack of documentation in the medical record of the stat order for the cesarean section, and the subsequent delay in performing the operation, were critical components in this case.

The literature today discusses the subject of elective primary cesarean sections, but that is beyond the scope of this chapter. Primary cesarean sections usually have medical indications, such as non-reassuring fetal status, cephalopelvic (fetal head/maternal pelvis) disproportion, failure to progress, breech or transverse lie, placenta previa, placenta abruption, and active herpes genital infection.

ACOG developed criteria for medical record documentation in the case of a cesarean section for nonreassuring fetal status. This criteria set states that the medical record should document the presence of certain indications of non-reassuring fetal status. These include persistent and severe variable decelerations with poor recovery or loss of beat-to-beat variability, persistent late decelerations, recurrent prolonged decelerations, scalp pH indicative of progressive fetal acidemia, and prolonged bradycardia.[61]

In May 2000, the FDA approved the use of intrapartum fetal oxygen saturation monitoring as an additional method of assessing fetal oxygen status during labor. The data obtained can help the healthcare provider decide whether it is safe for labor to continue or if interventions are needed.[62] Documentation of the fetal pulse oximetry reading is printed directly on the FHR tracing.

TIP: There has been a trend away from fetal blood sampling during labor to determine fetal oxygenation status. It is a technically difficult procedure and has a high false positive incidence.

Many perinatal centers have turned to scalp stimulation as an indicator of fetal well-being.[63] The premise of this test is that the well-oxygenated term fetus will respond to scalp stimulation with a FHR acceleration that is at least 15 beats per minute above the baseline value that lasts longer than 15 seconds. Fetal scalp stimulation is not done during a deceleration. It should be done in between contractions from the FHR baseline.

There are certain actions that should be documented in the medical record prior to the performance of a cesarean section for non-reassuring fetal status. These are:

- repositioning the patient,
- discontinuing uterine stimulants,
- correcting uterine hyperstimulation if present,
- performing vaginal examination,
- correcting maternal hypotension associated with regional anesthesia if present,
- notifying anesthesia and nursing staff of the need for emergency delivery,
- monitoring FHR in the operating room prior to preparation of the abdomen, and
- ensuring that qualified personnel are in attendance for resuscitation and care of the newborn.[64]

Lack of progress (failure to progress) is a major single indication for cesarean sections. There are many reasons for lack of progress, including disproportion, uterine inertia, and prolonged labor. When lack of progress is diagnosed, the medical record should reflect the indication for the lack of progress. This could be no dilation of the cervix or lack of descent of the presenting part for at least two hours with the patient in active labor. Active labor indicates that the cervix is at least four centimeters dilated, with contractions at least every two to three minutes apart lasting thirty seconds or more. The strength of the contractions is also factored into the active labor phase. To effect cervical change, contraction strength should be documented as at least 50 mmHg internal pressure as measured by an intrauterine pressure catheter or inability to indent the fundus of the uterus on palpation.

If the diagnosis of failure to progress is made, the medical record should reflect that interventions had been taken in an attempt to stimulate the labor. These include rupturing membranes and augmenting labor with oxytocin. Prior to the surgery, a vaginal examination should be performed to reconfirm lack of progress.[65]

16.12 Vaginal Birth after Cesarean (VBAC)

A woman who has undergone a cesarean section is not necessarily precluded from undergoing a subsequent vaginal birth. A VBAC is associated with a small but significant risk of uterine rupture with poor maternal and fetal outcomes.[66] The occurrence of uterine rupture depends on the number, type, and location of the previous incisions. A discussion between the healthcare provider and the woman and her family identifying the risks and benefits of VBAC is recommended by ACOG, and this should be well documented in the medical record.[67] The following case is a good example of informed consent and the importance of close monitoring of a patient undergoing a trial of labor after a cesarean birth.

> The injured plaintiff's mother had a history of two previous cesarean births. For her third pregnancy, she received care from a certified nurse midwife, and she consented to attempt a vaginal birth after prior cesarean (VBAC). She presented to the hospital two days prior to delivery in early labor and was sent home. She returned the next night again in early labor and was sent home. In this visit, she informed the nursing staff that she did not want to go forward with the vaginal birth, as she was in too much pain. They instructed her to consult her midwife the first thing in the morning. Before this could happen, her water broke, and she presented to the hospital around 7 A.M. The physician supervising the midwife was informed of the plaintiff's presence at the hospital in labor. He claimed that he did an evaluation of the patient around 8:00 A.M., confirmed what he understood to be her desire for a VBAC, ordered Pitocin to augment the labor, and then told the nursing staff to contact the midwife for further management. Around 5:30 P.M. there was sustained bradycardia of the FHR. The physician arrived at the hospital to see a different patient and at that time was notified of the bradycardia. He diagnosed a uterine rupture and delivered the patient by cesarean at 5:50 P.M. At delivery, the uterus was found to be ruptured vertically from mid fundus to cervix. The baby was "floating" in the abdomen, and the placenta was 95 percent detached. The infant was resuscitated and transferred to a tertiary hospital with a diagnosis of acute hypoxic ischemic brain injury. The child is now two and a half years old and cannot walk or speak. The plaintiff contended that she had never properly consented for a VBAC in that she did not know of any fetal risks associated with the procedure and would not

> have consented had she been properly informed. The hospital settled prior to trial for $3,000,000. The jury awarded a plaintiff verdict in the amount of $6,800,000, plus prejudgment interest of approximately $900,000.[68]

This case illustrates the importance of documenting informed consent delineating the risks of a VBAC. It is especially important to document the uterine and fetal response to the oxytocin, as uterine rupture is a known complication of a trial of labor after a cesarean section and oxytocin infusion. The communication between the nurses, physician, and midwife is another area that should have been carefully recorded, as well as ongoing maternal and fetal assessment.

A woman who is a candidate for VBAC should receive appropriate counseling regarding the risks of the procedure, and she may decline a trial of labor. She would then be scheduled for a repeat cesarean section.

TIP: Prior to the procedure, the medical record should have documentation of the type of previous uterine incision, the patient counseling, and evidence of fetal maturity.[69]

16.13 Labor and Delivery Summary

The labor and delivery summary form provides the pertinent information specific to the individual birth experience. Refer to Figure 16.9 for an example of documentation on a labor and delivery summary form. Important areas to review on this form are

- the time of birth,
- rupture of membranes,
- stages of labor,
- medication administration,
- intrapartum events,
- type of monitoring (internal, external),
- induction (starting labor) or augmentation (assisting with) of labor,
- sex of infant,
- Apgar scores,
- any resuscitative measures taken,
- presence of meconium, cord blood pH sampling results,
- any specimens to lab,
- placenta disposition, and
- names of all personnel in the delivery room.

Labor Summary

G 2 T 0 Pt 0 A 1 L 0 Type and Rh A+

Presentation — Position: L O T

☑ Vertex
☐ Face or brow
☐ Breech
☐ Transverse lie ☐ Compound
☐ Unknown

Intrapartum Events ☐ None

☐ No prenatal care
☐ Preterm labor (≤ 37 wks.)
☐ Postterm (≥ 42 wks.)
☐ Febrile (≥ 100.4°)
☐ PROM (≥ 1 hr. before onset of labor)
☑ Meconium +2
☐ Foul smelling fluid
☐ Hydramnios
☐ Abruption
☐ Placenta previa
☐ Bleeding-site undetermined
☐ Toxemia (mild) (severe)
☐ Seizure activity
☐ Precipitous labor (< 3 hrs.)
☐ Prolonged labor (≥ 20 hrs.)
☐ Prolonged latent phase
☐ Prolonged active phase
☐ Prolonged 2nd stage (> 2.5 hrs.)
☐ Secondary arrest of dilatation
☐ Cephalopelvic disproportion
☐ Cord prolapse
☐ Decreased FHT variability
☐ Extended fetal bradycardia
☐ Extended fetal tachycardia
☑ Multiple late decelerations
☑ Multiple variable decelerations
☑ Acidosis (pH < 7.2)
☐ Anesthetic complications
☐ ______
☐ ______

Induction ☐ None
☐ ARM ☐ Oxytoc. ☐ ______

Augmentation ☐ None
☑ ARM ☑ Oxytoc. ☐ ______

Monitor ☐ None

	FHT	UC
External	☑	☑
Internal	☑	☑

Medications — Total dosage

Delivery Data

Method of Delivery

Cephalic
☑ Spontaneous — Type
☐ Low forceps
☐ Mid forceps
☐ Rotation ______ to ______
☐ Vacuum extraction

Breech
☐ Spontaneous
☐ Partial extraction (assisted)
☐ Total extraction
☐ Forceps to A.C. head

Cesarean (details in operating notes)
☐ Low cervical: transverse
☐ Low cervical: vertical
☐ Classical
☐ Cesarean hysterectomy

Placenta
☑ Spontaneous
☐ Expressed
☐ Manual
☐ Adherent
☐ Ut. exploration

Blood loss
☑ < 500 ml.
☐ ≥ 500 ml.
Specify amount, detail in Remarks (______ ml.)

Configuration
☐ Normal
☑ Abn. Small
If weighed: ______ gms.

Cord
☐ Nuchal cord x ______
☐ True knot
☒ Umbilical vessels
Cord blood: (to lab) (refrig.) (discard)
For: ☑ Type & Rh ☐ Coombs ☑ VDRL ☐

Episiotomy ☑ None
☐ Median — Suture
☐ Mediolateral ______
☐ Other ______

Laceration ☐ None
① ② ③ ④ Degree Perineal
☒ Vaginal 1° Ⓤ.
☐ Cervical
☐ Uterine rupture
☐ Other Lt. periurethral

Surgical Procedures ☐ None
☐ Tubal ligation ☐ Curettage
☐ Other ______

Delivery Data (cont.)

Delivery Anesthesia ☐ None

1 = Local 2 = Pudendal 3 = Paracervical
4 = Epidural 5 = Spinal 6 = General

No.	Agent/Drug	Dose
4	See anes.	
	Record	

Administered by: ______

Delivery Room Meds. ☐ None

Agent/Drug	Dose	Route
pitocin	10 u	IM
Time 0330 A	Sig.	
Agent/Drug	Dose	Route
Time : A P	Sig.	
Agent/Drug	Dose	Route
Time : A P	Sig.	

Chronology

	Date	Time
EDC	4/4/00	
ADMIT TO HOSPITAL	4/8/00	14:58
MEMBRANES RUPTURED	4/8	22:48
ONSET OF LABOR	4/8	10:30
COMPLETE CERVICAL DIL.	4/9	01:15
DELIVERY OF INFANT	4/9	0330 A
DELIVERY OF PLACENTA	4/9	03 47 A

Infant Data

Apgar Scores

	Heart rate	Respiration	Muscle tone	Reflex irritation	Skin color	Totals
1 min	2	0	0	1	1	4
5 min	2	1	1	1	1	6

Resuscitation ☐ None [spontaneous respiration]
☑ Oxygen
☑ Bag and mask 0331
☑ Intubation 0338
☐ Ext. cardiac massage
☐ Other SUCTION
9 mins. to sustained respiration

Infant Data (cont.)

Medications ☐ None
☐ Volume expander
☐ Sodium bicarbonate
☑ Drug antagonists
☐ Umbilical catheter
☐ Other NARCAN .4 IM 0335

Medications checked below were administered in the delivery room. Otherwise reference the Newborn Flow Record.
☐ Erythromycin 1/2%
☐ $AgNO_3$ 1% or ______
☐ Aqueous Vitamin K IM
Admin. by: ______

Initial Newborn Exam
☐ No observed abnormalities
☐ Gross congenital anomalies
☑ Mec. staining ☐ Trauma
☐ Petechiae ☐ Other

Describe Ø meconium below cords

Basic Data
ID bracelet no. ______
Hospital record no. ______
☑ Male ☐ Female
Birth order: 1 of ① ② ③ ④
Weight 5# 6 7/8 oz
Length 17 1/2"

Output
☐ Urine
☑ Meconium
☑ Gastric ______ (ml.)

Transferred:
☐ To newborn nursery
☐ With mother
☒ To NICU
☐ ______

Deceased:
☐ Antepartum
☐ Intrapartum
☐ Neonatal (in delivery room)

Date 4/9/00 Time 04 10 A

Remarks: placenta to pathology

Figure 16.9 Example of labor and delivery summary.

Table 16.13
Criteria for Apgar Scoring

Sign	0	1	2
Heart rate	Absent	Below 100	Over 100
Respiratory effort	Absent	Slow, irregular	Good, crying
Muscle Tone	Flaccid	Some flexion of extremities	Active motion
Reflex irritability	No response	Grimace	Vigorous cry
Color	Blue, pale	Body pink, extremities blue	Completely pink

Table 16.14
Hypertensive Disorders of Pregnancy*

Type	Description
Gestational hypertension (Pregnancy induced hypertension)	Blood pressure elevation detected after the 20th week of pregnancy without proteinuria.
Pre-eclampsia	Pregnancy specific syndrome that usually occurs after 20 weeks gestation and is determined by gestational hypertension plus proteinuria.
Eclampsia	The occurrence of seizures in a woman with pre-eclampsia that cannot be attributed to other causes.
Chronic hypertension	Chronic underlying hypertension that antecedes pregnancy.
Pre-eclampsia superimposed on chronic hypertension	Chronic hypertension with new proteinura or an exacerbation of hypertension.

*Data adapted from Cunningham, et al., 1997, *Williams Obstetrics* and Lowdermilk and Perry, (2004), *Maternity and Women's Health Care*.

A. Apgar Scoring System

The Apgar scoring system is based on five criteria, and each criteria is assigned 0 to 2 points. See Table 16.13 for an example of an Apgar scoring system. A total score of 0 to 3 indicates severe distress and the need for immediate vigorous resuscitative measures. Infants with Apgars of 4 to 7 are in moderate distress and may require resuscitation, and infants with Apgars of 8 to 10 usually only require observation.[70]

B. Cord Blood Analysis

Cord blood analysis is frequently used to examine the metabolic status of the infant right at the time of birth. ACOG considers an umbilical arterial pH less than 7.00 to reflect pathologic fetal acidemia. Because the fetus has a remarkable adaptive ability to maintain cerebral perfusion, it has been suggested that the pH value, the degree of resuscitation needed, and a five minute Apgar score of greater than five could be a better predictor of the degree of fetal insult.[71]

16.14 Complications in Pregnancy

There are a multitude of conditions that can complicate a pregnancy. These can be pre-existing conditions. Others may be related to the pregnancy. Many complications in pregnancy can frequently occur with little or no warning, and some are life threatening. This section will describe three complications of pregnancy that are commonly seen in the perinatal setting:

- hypertension in pregnancy,
- premature labor, and
- post term pregnancy.

A. Hypertension in Pregnancy

TIP: Hypertensive disorders of pregnancy are the most common medical complications of pregnancy.[72]

There are different definitions for the presentation of increased blood pressure in pregnancy. Refer to Table 16.14 for these definitions. In the United States, pregnancy-associated hypertension is a leading cause of maternal death.[73] Preeclampsia predisposes the woman to potentially lethal complications. These include eclampsia, abruption placentae, disseminated intravascular coagulation (DIC) (uncontrolled widespread bleeding), acute renal failure, hepatic failure, adult respiratory distress syndrome, and cerebral hemorrhage.

Preeclampsia can be a great danger to the fetus as well. Increased blood pressure decreases placental perfusion, which can result in intrauterine growth restriction, fetal hypoxia, and possibly intrauterine fetal death. An elevated blood pressure is often the first sign of preeclampsia to appear. The prenatal record would reflect an increase in blood pressure greater that 140 systolic over 90 diastolic, or greater than 140/90. Another clinical manifestation of preeclampsia is proteinuria.

TIP: The presence or absence of protein in the urine should be documented at each prenatal visit. An amount greater than or equal to plus one ($\geq$ +1) on urine dipstick measurement in at least two random urine specimens, collected at least six hours apart, is clinically significant.[74]

The following case illustrates a failure to treat timely preeclampsia and the resultant damages:

The plaintiffs claimed that the defendants failed to diagnose and treat timely the plaintiff for preeclampsia, allowing the condition to progress to a seizure stage and impair oxygenation to the fetus. The defendants maintained that they met the standard of care and that the infant's impairment was associated with his premature birth at thirty-two weeks. The mother testified that she began to experience headache, chest pain, nausea, blurred vision, and abdominal pain. She called the defendant hospital group at 9:30 P.M. and was told to lie down and call back if her symptoms persisted. At 11:30 P.M., she called the obstetric group again and this time was advised to go to the hospital. The plaintiff arrived at the defendant medical center at 12:15 A.M. The mother alleged that the nurse did not appear to appreciate the severity of her symptoms and that a non-stress test showed the fetus was non-reactive at that time. At 4:00 A.M., the nurse first called the defendant obstetrician. The nurse called the defendant obstetrician again at 6:00 A.M. that morning. The defendant testified that if he had a clear understanding at that time of everything that was wrong with the mother and baby he would have come to the hospital immediately. The nurse testified that she would have reported all of the plaintiff's symptoms and test results to the doctor when she called.

The defendant obstetrician's partner arrived at the hospital at 6:30 A.M., diagnosed preeclampsia, and ordered that the plaintiff be transferred to a larger hospital that would be better equipped to perform a cesarean at thirty-two weeks gestation. Before the transfer, the mother's condition worsened and she suffered a three-minute seizure and an emergency cesarean section was performed. The experts testified that the lack of timely treatment deprived the fetus of needed oxygen. The child was six years old at the time of the trial and had suffered from hypoxic damage with seizures, has mild brain damage, and physiological impairments. A $4,100,000 verdict was awarded.[75]

In this situation, when the nurse testifies that she "would have" reported all of the patient's symptoms when she called the doctor, documentation of the symptoms reported and the physician's response needed to be in the medical record.

TIP: A variant that women with preeclampsia can develop is called *HELLP syndrome*. The acronym HELLP derives from the characteristic symptoms exhibited. These are: H=Hemolysis, EL=Elevated Liver enzymes, LP=Low Platelet count.[76]

The following case demonstrates that these conditions need timely treatment. Rapid delivery of the infant is often indicated for severe preeclampsia and in women with HELLP syndrome.

In this Massachusetts case, the plaintiff claimed that the plaintiff mother was showing ominous signs of preeclampsia during the last four to six weeks of her pregnancy. The defendant did not order an ultrasound or twenty-four hour protein testing, but prescribed Labetalol and performed weekly follow-ups. The plaintiff claimed the plaintiff child was not timely delivered, resulting in intrauterine growth retardation, spastic quadriparetic cerebral palsy, and profound mental retardation. The plaintiff also claimed that proper monitoring and ultrasound evaluation would have resulted in the diagnosis of intrauterine growth retardation and an earlier delivery would have avoided the injuries to the child. The defendant claimed the child's injuries were not consistent with, or the result of, preeclampsia. A $4 million settlement was reached.[77]

**Table 16.15
Risk Factors for Preterm Labor***

- Previous preterm labor or birth
- Cervical incompetence
- Diabetes
- Hypertension
- Anemia
- Multifetal pregnancy
- Hydramnios
- Vaginal bleeding
- Placenta previa
- Abruption placentae
- Infections
- Premature rupture of membranes
- Poor nutrition
- Smoking
- Substance abuse
- Inadequate prenatal care

*Data adapted from Cunningham, et al., 1997, Williams Obstetrics and Lowdermilk, and Perry, (2004), *Maternity and Women's Health Care.*

B. Preterm Labor

Evaluation of risk factors for premature labor should be well documented in the prenatal record. See Table 16.15 for risk factors associated with preterm labor and birth. Patients at risk for preterm labor require close surveillance, as early detection and timely intervention can improve outcomes. There are clinical assessments that can assist the healthcare provider in identifying a woman who may be at risk for preterm labor. Testing for fetal fibronectins can be used in an effort to predict who might experience preterm labor. This test has a high negative predictive value, meaning it may be possible to predict who will not go into preterm labor but not predict who will. This means that if a woman tests negative, she has a decreased risk of having preterm labor. If the test is positive, her risk of preterm labor is high, but she may or may not go into preterm labor. Measurement of cervical length by ultrasound is another tool used in the prediction of preterm labor. There are studies that suggest a shortened cervix precedes preterm labor.[78]

The diagnosis of preterm labor needs to be confirmed prior to the initiation of *tocolysis*. Tocolysis is the term for "inhibition of uterine contractions."[79] ACOG has determined three indicators for the confirmation of preterm labor. These are

- gestational age of at least twenty weeks but less than thirty-seven weeks,

- regular uterine contractions at frequent intervals, and
- documented cervical change or appreciable cervical dilation or effacement.

Documentation in the medical record should include cervical status, initiation of complete bedrest, and adequate hydration. A urinalysis should be on record to rule out urinary tract infection as a potential etiology for preterm labor. The woman's GBBS status should be recorded, and if unknown, a culture should be sent. The gestational age and fetal status should be well documented in the medical record.[80] The most common medications used in the treatment of preterm labor are magnesium sulfate or beta-adrenergic agonists, Terbutaline, and Yutopar. Magnesium sulfate blocks neuromuscular transmissions, resulting in uterine relaxation. Terbutaline and Yutopar inhibit contractility of smooth muscle.

During medication administration, it is important for the healthcare providers to document uterine contractions and fetal heart rate, fluid intake and output, and close observation of the patient for complications of tocolytic therapy.[81] Maternal heart rate and lung sounds are important parameters to include in documentation, as abnormalities in these areas can indicate complications of the drug therapy used to inhibit uterine contractions. Lab studies are done at intervals specific to what medication is being used to inhibit contractions and should be noted in the medical record. The medications used can become toxic and create electrolyte imbalances that would require prompt intervention.

C. Postterm Pregnancy

TIP: Postterm pregnancy is defined by ACOG as a pregnancy lasting more than two weeks beyond the confirmed estimated date of delivery.

The diagnosis can be confirmed by estimating the length of gestation from an initial clinical examination early in pregnancy, with uterine size compatible with the estimated dates. Another way to confirm pregnancy dates is having an ultrasound performed before twenty-four weeks of gestation.[82]

There are many risks to a pregnancy that goes postterm. *Intrapartum asphyxia* and *meconium aspiration* are attributable to postterm pregnancy.[83] The fetus can pass meconium, or fetal stool, into the amniotic fluid. If the fetus aspirates (inhales) this fluid, pneumonia can occur in the newborn. Postterm pregnancies significantly increase labor inductions, cesarean deliveries, macrosomia (large baby), and shoulder dystocia.

A diabetic woman who received prenatal care provided by a community health center was followed by nurse midwives and family practice physicians. The plaintiff claimed that the pregnancy was high risk due to her history of delivering two large babies, her advanced age, and symptoms of gestational diabetes. The plaintiff maintained she should have been referred to an obstetrician or a perinatologist. On the day of delivery the plaintiff claimed that the nurse midwives covering the deliveries failed to come to the hospital to evaluate the mother. A nurse midwife arrived about forty minutes prior to delivery and had difficulty delivering the baby due to shoulder dystocia. A second nurse midwife arrived and performed maneuvers which delivered the baby. The infant sustained brain damage. A trial was conducted on the issue of damages only. The judge awarded about $20 million. A post-trial settlement of about $18.2 million was reached.[84]

Oligohydramnios (decreased amniotic fluid) that is associated with postterm pregnancies poses increased risk to the fetus as a consequence of cord compression. Uteroplacental insufficiency in postmaturity is associated with late decelerations. It is important that the medical record reflect careful surveillance of fetal well-being in postterm pregnancies.

ACOG has recommended management for postterm pregnancy. This plan of care includes having the patient monitor fetal movement and report any reduction, antepartum fetal testing, delivery for nonreassuring indications, and consider cesarean delivery for sonographically estimated macrosomia.[85]

Documentation should always describe fetal status and measures taken when there is a non-reassuring fetal heart rate tracing. If the obstetrician is unable to intervene, further action by calling another physician and using the chain of command is needed. The medical record should reflect all actions taken.

16.15 Anesthesia Record

If a patient undergoes a cesarean birth or receives an anesthetic agent while in labor an anesthesia record would be completed. Important information recorded on this form includes

- amount, type, and times of anesthetic agents,
- all medications given and times,
- record of intake and output during procedure,
- types of fluids infused,

- blood transfusions,
- estimated blood loss, and
- time anesthesia began and ended.

The patient's vital signs and oxygen saturation levels are recorded throughout. The times of incision and birth are often written on this record also. In situations where the timing of events is critical, comparing the OR record, labor and delivery summary, and anesthesia record with the physician's and nurses' notes can assist in development of a timeline. It may also identify time discrepancies.

16.16 Operative Record

A cesarean section is a surgical procedure, for which an operative record would be completed. The operative record includes important times, such as

- time in room,
- prep time,
- anesthesia times,
- incision time,
- birth time,
- closure time, and
- time out of room to recovery.

Other information recorded in the operative record includes

- surgical counts,
- type of operation,
- record of intake and output,
- transfusions, and
- estimated blood loss.

Any equipment in use, as well as model numbers, such as an electrical cautery, infusion pumps, and blood warmers would appear in the operative record. The names of staff present, such as surgeon, assistant, scrub nurse, circulating nurse, anesthesiologist, and nursery personnel would also be documented. This form is usually a general operative record and is not specific to the obstetrical area. A labor and delivery summary form would still be completed.

16.17 Post-Anesthesia Care Unit (PACU)

Documentation in the recovery room, or post-anesthesia care unit, reflects the physiological status of the postpartum woman in regards to

- vital signs,
- oxygenation,

- pain,
- movement,
- level of consciousness,
- incision condition or dressing site, and
- intake and output.

Any medications the patient receives are included on this form. Another very important area that needs to be documented for a postpartum woman is the amount and type of vaginal bleeding, called *lochia*, and the position and consistency of the uterine *fundus* (top of the uterus). Documentation of the fundus would appear in terms of its position in relation to the woman's umbilicus, using a centimeter or fingerbreadth measurement, and noting if it is above or below the umbilicus. In the first twelve hours after birth, the uterus is usually about one centimeter above the umbilicus.

The consistency of the uterus has to be firm, as this indicates the muscle is well contracted, and bleeding from uterine *atony* will be controlled. Uterine atony refers to a relaxed uterine muscle. Documentation would appear as FF (fundus firm) 1/u (one centimeter above the umbilicus), which looks like *FF 1/u*. On the second day postpartum, the uterus would most likely be below the umbilicus, and charting would appear as *FF u/2*, or two fingerbreadths below the uterus. If the fundus is at the level of the umbilicus, charting would be *FF@u*. The fundal height decreases approximately 1 to 2 centimeters a day, and within ten to fourteen days, the uterus can no longer be palpated abdominally, as it returns into the pelvic cavity.

TIP: Assessment and documentation of bleeding are critical in the recovery period, as the greatest risk for early postpartum hemorrhage is in the first hour after birth.

Immediate measures must be taken in the presence of a postpartum hemorrhage, and determining the etiology is critical. The most common reason for a postpartum hemorrhage is uterine atony. Documentation of an atonic uterus can appear as "boggy," meaning it is not contracting well and feels soft and mushy. Fundal massage and increased intravenous pitocin is the treatment, as well as notification of the physician if these measures do not result in a contracted uterus. There are other uterine stimulants that can also be ordered and given. The medical record should include

- estimated amount of blood loss,
- pre-hemorrhage hemoglobin and hematocrit,
- post hemorrhage hemoglobin and hematocrit, and
- volume expanders and transfusions.

Close monitoring of maternal blood pressure, pulse, and respirations needs to be reflected in the charting. In the presence of a firm, well-contracted uterus and continuous bright red vaginal bleeding, a potential etiology could be cervical and/or vaginal tears and lacerations. Also, if the new mother is complaining of rectal pressure with or without pain, there could be a hematoma forming and this would require prompt medical attention.

Bleeding can be revealed by vital sign changes. In the presence of hypovolemia (decreased blood volume), pulse rate and respirations increase, and blood pressure will decrease. Reviewing the documentation of the trends in these vital signs can alert the staff to a potential bleeding problem. Close observation and early intervention is needed as excessive postpartum bleeding can lead to shock and maternal death. During the immediate postpartum period, maternal blood pressure and pulse should be recorded at least every fifteen minutes for the first hour or more often as indicated.[86]

16.18 Computerized Charting

Many hospitals and clinics use computer documentation systems, and it is anticipated that many more will follow. There are antenatal care systems that allow linkage to the hospital setting, so if the expectant mother is admitted, the healthcare provider can have immediate access to the woman's prenatal records. This provides for safe, continuous, and individualized care through the antenatal, intrapartum, and postpartum period. Electronic charting is a fast growing practice. However, with whatever charting system is used, the documentation needs to reflect the dynamic and continuous process of assessment, diagnosis, planning, interventions, and evaluation.

16.19 Commonly Used Obstetrical Abbreviations

Obstetrics seems to have a language of its own, with a variety of acronyms and abbreviations. Be aware that some of the "shorthand" that is seen in medical records derives from no known abbreviation list. It is simply made up by the author. Sometimes looking at the context of what is written can help to identify the shorthand, and then again, often the documentation remains illegible. The only source would be the authors, and sometimes even they have trouble deciphering their notes. For example, in Figure 16.2, the author writes "c/o ru?". Is the last letter l, e or c? An experienced obstetrical nurse would most likely be able to decipher this as "complains of regular uterine contractions," observing that the patient is four centimeters dilated and being sent to Labor and Delivery. Other abbreviations used in Figure 16.2 include:

FM—fetal movement

¬FM—decreased fetal movement

S/S—signs and symptoms

RTO—return to office

NST—non-stress test

AFI—amniotic fluid index

Cx—cervix

Vtx—vertex

BOWI—bag of water intact

BH—Braxton hicks contractions

Circled R—reactive in this instance, commonly refers to right

16.20 Summary

A careful review of an obstetrical record should tell the story of the birth experience, through the prenatal, labor, delivery, recovery, and postpartum periods. The newborn record would also need close review. If the infant is admitted into the Neonatal Intensive Care Unit, there could potentially be volumes of records. Assistance with the review of these records from legal nurse consultants who are experienced in these specialties is extremely beneficial.

In the future when a medical record is requested, a CD-ROM may be handed over. There is so much occurring with new and improved technological advancements in documentation systems that there will be many changes. A new trend in health care is the use of PDAs (personal digital assistants). Nurses are starting to provide shift reports by beaming information from one nurse to the next. They can also synchronize their data with the hospital's system to add information directly to the medical records.[87] For the reviewer of medical records, adapting to the various documentation practices can provide a challenge. But it is a challenge that must be faced, so that medical record reviewers of today do not go the way of the dinosaurs tomorrow.

Endnotes

1. American Academy of Pediatrics and American College of Obstetricians and Gynecologists. *Guidelines for Perinatal care*. Fifth Edition. p. 77. Washington, D.C.: The Author. 2002.

2. Lowdermilk, D. and S. Perry. *Maternity and Women's Health Care*. Eighth Edition. p. 348–349. St. Louis, MO: Mosby, Inc. 2004.

3. Cunningham et al. *Williams Obstetrics*. p. 1046. Stamford, Connecticut: Appleton and Lange. 1997.

4. *See* note 2.

5. *Id*, 415.

6. Venes, D. (Editor). *Taber's Cyclopedic Medical Dictionary*. Nineteenth Edition. p. 470. Philadelphia, PA: F.A. Davis Company. 2001.

7. *See* note 2 at 398.

8. *See* note 1 at 90.

9. *See* note 3 at 233.

10. *See* note 2 at 356–357.

11. *Id*, 837.

12. *See* note 3 at 230.

13. *See* note 2 at 417–418.

14. *Id*, 416–417.

15. Blackburn, S. *Maternal, Fetal, and Neonatal Physiology*. Second Edition. p. 131. St. Louis, MO: Saunders. 2003.

16. *See* note 3 at 280.

17. *Id*, 232.

18. *See* note 15 at 288.

19. *See* note 3 at 254.

20. *Id*, 23.

21. *See* note 8.

22. Pagana, K. and T. Pagana. *Manual of Diagnostic and Laboratory Tests*. p. 255. St. Louis, MO: Mosby, Inc. 1998.

23. *See* note 2 at 357.

24. *See* note 22 at 251.

25. *Id*, 119.

26. *See* note 3 at 1317.

27. *Id*, 1329.

28. *See* note 1 at 311.

29. Laska, L. "Failure to Properly Treat Mother Positive for Group-B Strep at Time of Delivery." *Medical Malpractice Verdicts, Settlements, and Experts*. June 2009, p. 31-32.

30. *See* note 3 at 1205.

31. Murray et al. *Foundations of Maternal-Newborn Nursing*. Third Edition. p. 705. Philadelphia, PA: W.B. Saunders. 2002.

32. *See* note 2 at 466.

33. McDermott, J. "Obstetrical Nursing Malpractice Issues" in Iyer, P. (Editor). *Nursing Malpractice. Third Edition*. Tucson, AZ: Lawyers and Judges Publishing Company, Inc. 2006.

34. *See* note 3 at 923.

35. *See* note 30 at 226.

36. *See* note 2 at 226.

37. *See* note 6 at 1703–1704.

38. *See* note 3 at 1013, 1017.

39. *See* note 2 at 831.

40. *See* note 22 at 255.

41. *See* note 1 at 105.

42. *See* note 6 at 1499.

43. *See* note 1 at 126.

44. *Id*, 127.

45. *See* note 32 at 150.

46. Laska, L. "Failure to Timely begin Monitoring at Mother's Arrival to Hospital and Failure to Timely Deliver Child." *Medical Malpractice Verdicts, Settlements, and Experts*. July 2009, p. 31.

47. *See* note 3 at 367.

48. *See* note 30 at 288–289.

49. *Id*, 289.

50. Iyer, P. and N. Camp. *Nursing Documentation: A Nursing Process Approach*. Fourth Edition. Flemington, NJ: Med League Support Services, Inc. 2005.

51. Laska, L. "Failure to Timely Deliver Child with Cord Wrapped Around Neck." *Medical Malpractice Verdicts, Settlements, and Experts*. August 2009, p. 31.

52. Simpson, K. and P. Creehan. *AWHONNS Perinatal Nursing*. Second Edition. p. 346. Philadelphia, PA: Lippincott. 2001.

53. *See* note 1 at 135.

54. *See* note 30 at 133.

55. *Id*, 187-188.

56. *McClung v. Memorial Hermann Hospital Systems d/b/a Memorial Hospital—The Woodlands, Affiliates of Gynecology, Obstetrics and Fertility, P.A. and James Meyers, M.D.*, Harris County (TX) District Court, Case No. 1999-29377.

57. *See* note 1 at 138.

58. *See* note 2 at 435.

59. *See* note 30 at 147.

60. Laska, L. (Editor). "Delay of Cesarean Results in Infant's Severe Brain Damage." *Medical Malpractice Verdicts, Settlements, and Experts*. March 2003, p. 35–36.

61. American College of Obstetricians and Gynecologists, Committee on Quality Assurance. *ACOG Criteria Set*. Cesarean delivery for nonreassuring status. Washington, D.C.: The Author. May 1998, Number 33.

62. *See* note 58 at 406.

63. *Id*.

64. *See* note 61.

65. *Id*.

66. *See* note 52 at 355.

67. *Id*, 356.

68. *Alexia Marquez v. George Small, M.D., Dora Kissi, CNM*, San Bernardino County (CA) Superior Court, Case No. SCVSS 079948.

69. American College of Obstetricians and Gynecologists, Committee on Quality Assurance. *ACOG Criteria Set.* Repeat Cesarean Delivery. Washington, D.C.: The Author. December 1995, Number 13.

70. American College of Obstetricians and Gynecologists, *ACOG Practice Bulletin.* Premature Rupture of Membranes. Washington, D.C.: The Author. January 1998.

71. *See* note 32 at 138.

72. *See* note 52 at 110.

73. *See* note 2 at 837.

74. *Id*, 841.

75. *Randy Ross and Catherine Ross, Individually, and as p/n/g of Randy Charles Ross, a Minor v. James A Crozier, M.D., Tri-State OB/GYN, Inc., and the Medical Center of Beaver, a Pennsylvania Hospital Corporation*, Beaver County (PA) Court of Common Pleas, Case No. GD 10387-19999.

76. *See* note 15 at 274.

77. Laska, L. "Failure to Properly Monitor Woman with Signs of Preeclampsia and Timely Deliver Child." *Medical Malpractice Verdicts, Settlements, and Experts.* January 2009, p. 36.

78. *See* note 73.

79. *See* note 6 at 2201.

80. American College of Obstetricians and Gynecologists, Committee on Quality Assurance. *ACOG Criteria Set.* Tocolysis in Premature Labor. Washington, D.C.: The Author. June 1998, Number 34.

81. *Id.*

82. American College of Obstetricians and Gynecologists, Committee on Quality Assurance. *ACOG Criteria Set.* Postterm Pregnancy. Washington, D.C.: The Author. August 1995, Number 10.

83. *See* note 3 at 828.

84. Laska, L. "Failure to Treat Pregnancy as High-Risk Despite Woman's History of Large Babies." *Medical Malpractice Verdicts, Settlements, and Experts.* June 2009, p. 30.

85. *See* note 82.

86. *See* note 52 at 435.

87. Armour, K. "PDAs in Nursing." *Lifelines.* 8(3), June–July 2004, p. 246.

Chapter 17

Orthopaedic Records

Barbara J. Levin, BSN, RN, ONC, LNCC and Howard Yeon, MD, JD

17.1 Introduction

Orthopaedic surgery is a specialized branch of surgery focusing on disorders of the musculoskeletal system, including bones, joints, muscles, tendons, and ligaments. Orthopaedic problems are very common. The principal goal of orthopaedic surgical procedures is to maintain or restore pain-free function (posture, mobility, and dexterity) of the axial skeleton and the extremities.

There is a significant nexus between orthopaedics and litigation. This is true more frequently in orthopaedic surgery than with most other medical specialties. Musculoskeletal injuries frequently result from motor vehicle collisions, workplace accidents and other traumatic events giving rise to tort claims. Even when orthopaedic injuries do not themselves generate litigation, orthopaedic surgeons frequently determine degrees of physical impairment or workplace disability that dictate insurance compensation benefits; these issues also may give rise to legal actions.

TIP: Orthopaedic injuries generally are not life threatening, but they can have a significant effect on a patient's activities and level of independent function.

A growing volume of medical literature documents a high incidence of long-term disabilities associated with orthopaedic injuries. Despite successful surgery and objective bone healing, the majority of patients are unable to return to their pre-injury occupation after severe lower extremity fractures.

Example: Mrs. Smith was in a motor vehicle accident and sustained a severe open tibia fracture in which the bone broke through her skin. After nineteen surgeries, she had an above-the-knee amputation to her left leg. Her lifestyle had been significantly affected by the lengthy hospitalizations and rehabilitations required for her numerous surgeries. After limb salvage surgery failed, she was further functionally affected by her use of a prosthetic limb.

This chapter provides a structured overview of the most important aspects of the orthopaedic patient's medical records. Essential elements of the initial evaluation for both trauma and elective surgery patients, the operative plan, and postoperative care are highlighted. Though there are significant differences in the approach to each group of patients, due to the mechanism and acuity of their injuries, there are many areas where care issues overlap.

17.2 Orthopaedic Definitions and Terminology

A. Bones

A basic understanding of orthopaedic physiology and pathophysiology is fundamental to deciphering orthopaedic patients' surgical records. The outpatient or hospital chart contains a limited but initially daunting vocabulary of specific terms and abbreviations that is best understood relative to basic orthopaedic surgical principles. In this section, we introduce the basic vocabulary of orthopaedics relevant to bone, cartilage, joints, and fractures.

Five basic tissues constitute the musculoskeletal system.

- *Bones* form a strong structural framework.
- *Ligaments* are dense fibrous connective tissue that attach bones to each other.
- *Cartilage* lubricates articulations between bone surfaces.
- *Skeletal muscles* generate locomotive forces.
- *Tendons* are bands of dense fibrous tissue that attach muscle to bone.[1]

Muscles are generally described by their function.

- *Flexors* are muscles that bend a limb.
- *Extensors* are muscles that straighten a limb.
- *Abductors* are muscles that move a limb away from the midline of the body.
- *Adductors* move a limb towards the midline of the body.

The skeleton consists of 206 bones of varying morphologies that protect vital organs including the brain, heart, and lungs and provide rigid internal scaffolding upon which muscles can exert forces resulting in mobility. Bones are composed of Type I collagen protein mineralized with calcium salt. The outer layer—cortex—of bones is composed of dense, parallel collagen fibers called "lamellar" bone. This hard outer cortex provides much of the bone's structural stiffness and strength, while the inner canal of the bone

contains a trabecular network of "cancellous" bone that is responsible for a bone's shock and stress absorbing properties. Though the precise function of each bone depends on its anatomic location, the skeleton's principal function is to provide structure and support for the purposes of protection of vital organs and for locomotion. The skeleton also is important for electrolyte homeostasis, as it is the body's main reservoir for elemental calcium.

TIP: Most orthopaedic issues can be generally classified as either acute injuries (for example, fractures, dislocations, sprains or muscle tears resulting from a traumatic event) or chronic degeneration resulting from prolonged wear and degeneration of joint cartilage.

Bones are morphologically divided into four categories:

- long bones (e.g., femur),
- short bones (e.g., metacarpals),
- flat bones (e.g., sternum), and
- irregular bones (e.g., vertebrae).

The varied shapes of bones reflect their different functional roles.

- Long bones act as lever arms allowing muscles to exert their force at a distance.
- Short bones bridge small distances.
- Flat bones are effective as protective shells.
- Small rounded bones called sesamoid bones, for example the kneecap or patella, are embedded within tendons, and they provide the tendon with additional mechanical advantage.
- Irregular bones include the facial bones, vertebrae, and ilium. These highly specialized bones serve dual functions as protective barriers and as important structural components of the axial skeleton.

B. Joints

Joints are simply defined as areas where two or more bones intersect. Though motion may occur at a bone-to-bone junction, motion is not a prerequisite for an articulation to be called a joint.

C. Cartilage

Cartilage serves to support overall musculoskeletal functioning in addition to muscle and bone.[2] Articular cartilage is largely avascular (without a dedicated blood supply) and covers opposing ends of bones with the synovial joint. Cartilage has a limited capacity for repair and regeneration because it is largely avascular. Cartilage can be vulnerable to wear as seen in degenerative joint diseases.[3]

D. Fractures and Healing

A fracture is generally defined as a break in any part of the bone. In children, fractures sometimes preferentially occur at the growth plate where immature bones are the weakest. When bones are injured, a tightly regulated molecular cascade is activated that ultimately leads to the restoration of intact bone at the fracture site. Four distinct stages of fracture healing have been described.[4]

1. Fracture hematoma.
2. Inflammation with neovascularization (formation of new blood vessels).
3. Reparative phase with callus formation and ossification.
4. Remodeling into mature bone.

In the first stage, fracture hematoma, a collection of clotted blood—the hematoma—forms around the injured bone. This blood is released both from injured vessels in the surrounding soft tissue and also from blood vessels found within the bone itself. The process of hematoma formation typically takes approximately one to three days. Specific growth factors and molecular signals called "cytokines" are released by cells adjacent to and within the zone of injury, and this leads to the second stage—inflammation with neovascularization. Neovascularization specifically refers to the growth of new blood vessels into the bone and surrounding injured tissue in response to specific growth factors including fibroblast growth factor (FGF) and vascular endothelial growth factor (VEGF). Once blood supply has begun to be restored, the reparative phase of bone healing begins, and cells near the fracture form a fibrous and later bony bridge, or callus, across the fracture site. Generally, it takes three to four weeks for fracture fragments to be bridged by cartilage or fibrous tissue, and subsequent ossification (hardening) of the bridging tissue requires an additional two to three weeks. At the end of this reparative stage, the structural integrity of the bone is restored, but the new bone "callus" at the fracture site is histologically more disorganized than the original bone. Finally, in the remodeling phase, the bone callus is slowly replaced by an organized structure that more closely resembles the original bone. Remodeling may take months to years, depending on the extent of bone modification needed, the function of the bone, and the functional stresses on the bone.[5]

The time required to complete the four steps of bone healing may be affected by various patient- and injury-spe-

cific factors. The age of the patient and the anatomic location of the fracture are important considerations. Adults generally require a longer healing time than children. Other factors that may retard the healing process include compromised blood supply to the area, for example in patients with severely comminuted (shattered bone) fractures with abundant surrounding muscular damage. Excessive swelling of tissues surrounding the fracture site can also impede the supply of blood to the area. Inadequate immobilization allows relative motion of the fracture fragments and results in pain and a greatly diminished ability of the bone healing apparatus to bridge the fracture site. Metabolic disorders and significant medical comorbidities (illnesses) may also hinder the healing process. Certain medications, including steroids and nonsteroidal anti-inflammatory drugs, can also impede healing under certain conditions.

During the healing process, the orthopaedic surgeon will typically perform and review serial x-rays to evaluate the progress of bony healing, to ensure that the fracture remains acceptably well aligned, and to verify that any implanted hardware remains stably fixed. The medical records of the orthopaedic surgeon typically indicate that these x-rays are taken onsite or at a nearby diagnostic facility. In addition, the clinical examination is repeated to assess for tenderness with palpation at the fracture site. A fracture is considered healed when there is radiographic evidence of a bony union of the fragments and there is minimal or no tenderness to palpation at the fracture site. Refer to Chapter 10, *Diagnostic Testing*, to review specific information related to radiographic testing.

17.3 Traumatic Injuries
A. Mechanism of Injury

Personal bodily injury attorneys and other legal professionals are commonly called upon to review medical records of patients who sustain musculoskeletal injuries. When injuries result from a motor vehicle collision, assault, or workplace accident that generates a tort claim, attorneys need to cull several key pieces of information from the medical record including the

- cause of the patient's injuries,
- breadth and seriousness of the injuries,
- extent of medical or surgical treatment necessary to address the injuries, and
- the resultant long-term disability associated with the injuries.

In other cases, attorneys representing insurance companies or employers review medical records to ascertain whether patients are receiving the appropriate level of disability benefits. Finally, when there is a question of medical malpractice, plaintiffs' and defendants' attorneys review the written medical record to determine whether the appropriate standard of care was met. In this section, we summarize key aspects of the evaluation, treatment, and follow up of patients with traumatic musculoskeletal injuries; we also frame an orderly, chronological approach to reading the trauma patient's medical record.

TIP: One key piece of information contained in the trauma patient's medical record is the mechanism of the patient's injury.

Attorneys reviewing the record in the context of tort injury or disability claims should focus on the mechanism of injury because it is germane to causation. The mechanism of injury may be documented in multiple places in the written record including the on-scene report of the emergency medical transport (EMT) team and the history written by the admitting physician or nurse. Please refer to Chapter 7, *Emergency Medical Services Records*, and Chapter 8, *Emergency Department Records*, for additional information. According to the National Trauma Data Bank (NTDB), motor vehicle traffic collisions cause 48.5 percent of traumatic injuries and account for the largest number of hospital days and intensive care unit (ICU) days. The severity of injuries arising from motor vehicle collisions is reflected in the high 7.5 percent case fatality rate. Falls are the second most common cause of traumatic injury, accounting for 16.7 percent of cases reported by the NTDB. Though injuries from falls are generally less severe, they still result in the second leading number of hospital and ICU days utilized with corresponding 3.93 percent case fatality.[6]

Mechanisms of injury associated with musculoskeletal trauma vary according to age. In younger patients, a high energy mechanism is usually required to fracture strong, well-mineralized bone. Among the elderly, however, a simple fall from standing height may result in a fracture through weak, osteoporotic bone. Injuries sustained from high-energy impacts frequently involve multiple organ systems, including the neurological, cardiac, and gastrointestinal systems.

The mechanism of injury is illustrated in the following case.

The plaintiff was standing in a parking lot waiting for his daughter to clear security at the entrance to the truck stop. He had his back to the defendant's vehicle. The plaintiff contended that the defendant negligently backed up without making proper, con-

tinual observations. The plaintiff was struck, fell to the side of the truck and was not run over by the wheels. He was taken to a local hospital where the fractured scapula was diagnosed. His wife flew to New Jersey and drove him back to Utah in his tractor trailer. The jostling during the trip was extremely painful. He developed severe radiating cervical pain shortly after the accident. Upon his return to Utah, a herniation at C3-C4 was diagnosed. He underwent surgery to the shoulder and a cervical fusion involving the use of a titanium cage. He contended that despite the fusion, he continues to suffer severe pain from the herniation and requires narcotic medication. The plaintiff's orthopedist asserted the pain would continue permanently. He lost both his vehicle and his home. The case settled for $1.5 million.[7]

B. Initial Clinical Examination

Initial clinical examination of the musculoskeletal trauma patient requires the careful and systematic assessment of the axial skeleton, pelvis, and extremities. Over the past decade, the coordinated evaluation, assessment, and early treatment of severely or multiply injured patients have become largely standardized. The development of validated early assessment and treatment protocols is intended to facilitate early respiratory and hemodynamic stabilization, ensure an adequate work-up, and improve recognition of serious, occult (hidden) injuries. Initial in-hospital evaluation follows a paradigm including immediate assessment of the patient's airway, breathing, and circulation—the "ABCs." Other early observations include a general assessment of the patient's overall mental status, notation of penetrating injuries, and recording of the patient's vital signs (temperature, heart rate, blood pressure, and respiratory rate). Only after the patient has been stabilized from a respiratory and hemodynamic standpoint is the orthopaedic surgeon called upon to perform a secondary survey to identify less acute musculoskeletal injuries.

1. Documentation of initial work-up

Documentation of the initial work-up of trauma patients generally consists of an emergency room physician's note, nurse's note, and various other notes from physician consultants such as a general surgeon, neurosurgeon, plastic surgeon, or orthopaedic surgeon. The emergency room physician and nursing notes should contain specific information regarding the early assessment and treatment of the patient including the initial evaluation of the patient's ABCs, fluid resuscitation, and any medications given. Attorneys reviewing the medical record should follow this early series of events with the understanding that the initial management of trauma patients should adhere to a well-defined decision tree. Please refer to Chapter 8, *Emergency Department Records*, for additional information.

2. Secondary survey

"Secondary" survey refers to the subacute examination and evaluation of trauma patients for musculoskeletal injuries that were not the focus of the initial treatment because they did not pose a threat to the patient's respiratory or cardiovascular stability. A thorough secondary survey begins with a careful examination of the entire body to ensure that there are no breaks in the skin that may represent an open fracture (a fracture in direct communication between bone and the outside environment). After it is determined whether there are any open injuries, the orthopaedic surgeon will palpate all of the bones in the extremities to test for areas of tenderness suggestive of fracture. This is necessary because a patient with a painful injury at one location may be unaware of a less severe but still significant fracture at a different location unless the second area is specifically palpated.

TIP: Review of a hospital chart may show that a series of x-rays was ordered after the initial evaluation of the patient was completed. A fractured wrist, finger, or toe may be diagnosed days later.

The secondary survey also includes putting the joints of the upper and lower extremities through a physiologic range of motion while testing for joint laxity or pain that could signify a fracture, or a tendinous or ligamentous injury. Examination of the extremities also includes assessment of motor strength in major muscle groups.

- deltoid,
- biceps,
- triceps,
- wrist extensors,
- wrist flexors,
- finger flexors,
- finger abductors.
- quadriceps,
- hamstrings,
- anterior tibialis,
- extensor hallucis longus,
- gastrocnemius / soleus complex, and
- peroneal muscles in the lower extremities.

TIP: Strength is graded on a scale from 0 to 5 with 0 being no movement, 5 being full strength, and 3 being only enough strength to counteract gravity.

Sensation testing is performed by applying light touch in all practicable spinal nerve distributions—usually from the fifth cervical nerve root to the first sacral nerve root.

To evaluate the axial skeleton, the secondary survey includes palpation of the bony pelvis and the spinal vertebrae posteriorly. The cervical spine has historically been an area where serious injuries have been missed—with potentially disastrous consequences such as paralysis or even death. Recently, protocols for assessing and clearing the cervical spine from injury have been developed. Though there is some disagreement in the orthopaedic literature regarding appropriate evaluation of an unconscious patient, most agree that in awake, alert patients, palpation of the cervical vertebrae posteriorly, a thorough neurological examination including assessment of rectal tone, and a series of radiographs including CT and sometimes MRI are essential to rule out an occult injury. A hard cervical collar is kept in place until a bony or ligamentous injury to the cervical spine is ruled out.

3. Radiographic studies

Radiographic studies are essential early tools in the assessment of the orthopaedic trauma patient. Current protocols generally call for x-rays of the cervical spine, chest, and pelvis to be obtained for patients who experienced a significant trauma. In addition to these standard films, if a fracture is suspected during the secondary survey, x-rays consisting of views of the bone in question from at least two perpendicular planes are evaluated. X-rays are also taken of the joints flanking the fractured bone to reduce the risk of a missed associated injury. Figure 17.1 demonstrates the importance of radiographs taken in two perpendicular planes. The knee dislocation is clear on the lateral view (right image) but difficult to appreciate on the AP (anterior/posterior) view (left image).

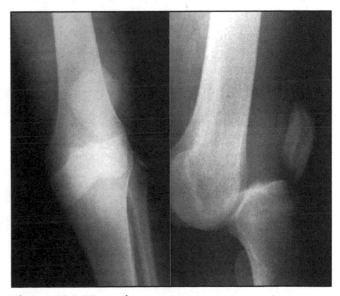

Figure 17.1 *Views for x-rays.*

Radiographic studies are documented in two ways in the medical record. First, the images themselves are saved either as hard copy images on film or as digital images on the hospital's computer storage system. Second, films are read and interpreted by the physicians such as orthopaedic surgeons who initially ordered the studies and by radiologists who are specially trained to interpret a broad spectrum of imaging studies. Documentation of the ordering physician's interpretation of the study should be present in the physician's consultation note, while the radiologist's interpretation is generally contained in a formal report.

The issue of radiographic studies and knowledge of the results was prominent in the following case.

A fifty-six year-old patient was admitted to the hospital with a diagnosis of staphylococcus aureus septicemia infection in the blood which led to a spinal epidural abscess. On the fourth day the defendant neurosurgeon diagnosed the patient with paraparesis and paraplegia of the legs and ordered a thoracic MRI to rule out a compression lesion to the patient's thoracic spine. The defendant radiologist read the MRI as negative. Three days later another MRI was performed and presented some elements of compression. Another neurosurgeon, not a defendant, performed surgery. The plaintiff recovered some use of her legs and now suffers paraparetic weakness in her legs. The plaintiff claimed that the delay in diagnosis resulted in paralysis and that more timely surgery would have resulted in a full recovery. The defendants claimed that the plaintiff's neurological deficits were the result of the staph septicemia and ischemic changes, which adversely affected the blood supply to her spinal cord and caused the neurological deficits which could not be treated surgically. Two other physicians and the hospital had settled previously with the plaintiff for undisclosed amounts. A defense verdict was returned. [8]

4. Laboratory studies

Laboratory studies are another important source of information about the patient with musculoskeletal injuries. A standard panel of laboratory studies ordered for a trauma patient includes a complete blood count (white blood cell count, red blood cell count, hemoglobin, hematocrit, and platelet count), a complete electrolyte panel (sodium, potassium, chloride, bicarbonate, blood urea nitrogen, creatinine, and glucose), and a coagulation panel (partial thromboplastin time, prothrombin time). Generally, the cell count is useful to determine whether the patient has lost a significant amount of blood, which would be reflected in a low hematocrit and hemoglobin. Electrolytes are checked to determine the basic metabolic equilibrium of the patient, and the coagulation panel is important to ensure that surgery, if needed, can be performed without excessive blood loss. Laboratory values are also recorded in physicians' and nurses' notes both to acknowledge the results and to facilitate the recognition of upward or downward trends. Please refer to Chapter 10, *Diagnostic Testing*, for additional information on laboratory values. Refer to Figure 17.2 for a typical trauma consultation report.

C. Define Injury
1. Open versus closed fracture

Once a fracture is confirmed radiographically, the most significant first assessment is whether the fracture is "open" or "closed"—or in other words, whether the fracture is associated with a break in the skin. A useful and ubiquitously used classification system is that of Gustilo and Anderson.

- Grade I open fractures are described as having associated open wounds less than 1 centimeter with minimal soft tissue injury and a clean wound bed; these open fractures are generally thought to result from a sharp spike of bone penetrating the skin from inside to out.
- Grade II injuries have an open wound greater than 1 centimeter in length with a moderate associated soft tissue injury, and the wound bed is moderately contaminated.
- Grade III open fractures generally have wounds greater than 10 centimeters in length, but these injuries are further subclassified as:
  - Type A—with minimal stripping of the soft tissues surrounding the bone
  - Type B—with extensive soft tissue stripping probably requiring a soft tissue flap to close or cover the wound
  - Type C—with an associated major vascular injury. [9]

INITIAL ORTHOPAEDIC TRAUMA CONSULTATION

Date _____ / _____ / _____   Time _____

Seat Belt (Y/N) Air Bag (Y/N)   LOC (Y/N) _____

HPI _____

_____

_____

PMH _____

_____

Allergies _____

Medications _____

Vital Signs: BP _____ HR _____

RR _____ Temp _____

Neuro _____

Glasgow Coma Scale _____

General Evaluation Exam – – **Sensorium** - Awake NL ❑ / Awake impaired ❑ / Unconscious ❑

Airway - Intubated Y/N _____ **Breathing** - Stable ❑ / Unstable ❑ **Circulation** - Stable ❑ / Unstable ❑

Musculoskeletal Exam

	Normal		Abnormal		**Comments**
	R	L	R	L	
Neck	❑		❑		
Spine	❑		❑		
Clavicle	❑	❑	❑	❑	
Shoulder	❑	❑	❑	❑	
Arm	❑	❑	❑	❑	
Elbow	❑	❑	❑	❑	
Wrist	❑	❑	❑	❑	
Hand	❑	❑	❑	❑	

	Normal		Abnormal		**Comments**
	R	L	R	L	
Pelvis	❑	❑	❑	❑	
Hip	❑	❑	❑	❑	
Thigh	❑	❑	❑	❑	
Knee	❑	❑	❑	❑	
Leg	❑	❑	❑	❑	
Ankle	❑	❑	❑	❑	
Foot	❑	❑	❑	❑	

Vascular Exam Palpable; Non-palpable; Doppler;/

	Radial	Ulnar	Fem	Pop	DP	PT
R						
L						

LAB RESULTS:

OTHER LABS:
❑ BBS

Neurological Exam (Upper extremity motor)

	Deltoid (C5/MC)	Wrist flx (C7)	Wrist ext (C6)	Fing flx (C8)	Fing abd (T1)	Thumb ext (PIN)	1st DIP Flx (AIN)	Index abd (U)	Thumb abd (MM)
R									
L									

	Quad (L3/Fem)	Ant Tib (L4/DP)	EHL (L5/DP)	Peroneal (S1/SP)	GS (S1/T)		Quad (L3/Fem)	Ant Tib (L4/DP)	EHL (L5/DP)	Peroneal (S1/SP)	GS (S1/T)
R						L					

Figure 17.2 Trauma consult. (Reprinted with permission of Dr. Vrahas, Dr. Harris, and Dr. Suzanne Morrison, Boston, Massachusetts.)

INITIAL ORTHOPAEDIC TRAUMA CONSULTATION

Rectal Tone - Normal ❑ / Absent ❑
Bulbocavernous - Present ❑ / Absent ❑

Other significant findings (sensory, etc.):
_____
_____
_____

Trauma Series

	POS	NEG	N/A		POS	NEG	N/A	Findings:
Lat C-Spine	❑	❑	❑	CXR	❑	❑	❑	_____
AP Pelvis	❑	❑	❑	Judet/In-Out	❑	❑	❑	_____
C-Spine CT	❑	❑	❑	OOC Lat	❑	❑	❑	_____
Head CT	❑	❑	❑	Chest CT	❑	❑	❑	
Abd/Pelvic CT	❑	❑	❑	Pelvic Recons	❑	❑	❑	_____
TLS Plain Films	❑	❑	❑	TLS CT Recons	❑	❑	❑	_____

Additional Films

Films	Findings	Films Needed
1.		1.
2.		2.
3.		3.
4.		4.
5.		5.
6.		6.
7.		7.

C-Spine Status: Injured ❑   Clearance Pending* (leave collar on) ❑   Cleared (remove collar) ❑

*Plan for Clearing Spine_____
_____

Summary of Injuries and Plan

General
1.
2.
3.
4.
Musculoskeletal
1.
2.
3.
4.

Print Name_____ Signature:_____ ID # ❑❑❑❑❑

Date/time _____ / _____ / _____ , _____ : _____ AM PM   Beeper #:_____

Orthopaedic Attending: _____ , MD.   Beeper #:_____

Figure 17.2 *Trauma consult. (Reprinted with permission of Dr. Vrahas, Dr. Harris, and Dr. Suzanne Morrison, Boston, Massachusetts.) (continued)*

Complications of open tibial fractures include compartment syndrome, non-union, and infections. Additionally, amputations are a well-known complication.[10] A variety of the most common and serious orthopaedic complications are discussed in detail in a subsequent section of this chapter. Figure 17.3 is an x-ray of a open grade one femur fracture. Figure 17.4 is a photo of the open femur fracture. The skin is punctured and there is minimal soft tissue injury. Figure 17.5 offers examples of various types of fractures.

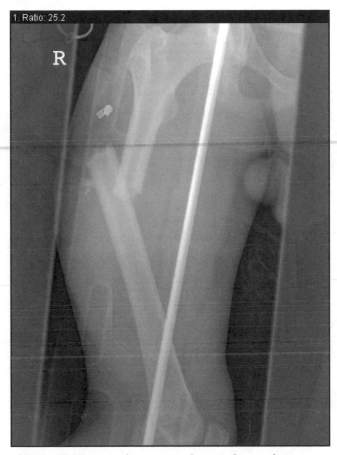

Figure 17.3 *X-ray of open grade one femur fracture.*

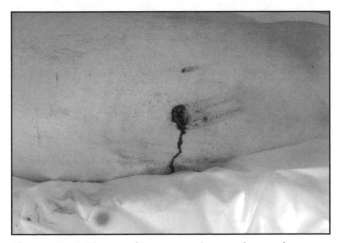

Figure 17.4 *Photo of open grade one femur fracture.*

a. Treatment of fractures. Open fractures require treatment with intravenous antibiotics soon after initial presentation. Recent studies in the orthopaedic literature suggest that the time between the initial injury and the first dose of antibiotics may be the most important factor in determining the overall risk of infection.[11] Tetanus prophylaxis should also be routine when patients have an outdated or unknown inoculation status. The choice of antibiotic or combination of antibiotics depends on the nature of the injury and the degree of contamination of the wound and underlying skin. Open fractures also generally require surgery due to an unacceptably high risk of infection if left untreated. Even when a fracture pattern would not otherwise require operative fixation using hardware such as screws and a plate or pins, the fracture still should be copiously irrigated and all hypovascular soft tissues should be debrided in the operating room. The timing of such irrigation and debridement procedures for open fractures is controversial at this time and it depends to some extent on the severity of the injury and the Gustilo grade.[12] As a rule, open fractures should be irrigated and debrided within twelve to twenty-four hours. For unstable open fractures, rigid fixation of the fracture fragments using appropriate orthopaedic hardware implants has also been shown to be essential both for fracture healing and also for clearing infection. Figure 17.6 is a photo taken in the operating room of an open grade one femur fracture after an irrigation and debridement procedure. Figure 17.7 is an x-ray of the ORIF (open reduction internal fixation) used to treat the same open grade one femur fracture.

b. Infection rates. Despite prompt irrigation and debridement within hours of patient presentation, infection rates are high, especially for open fractures with a significant concomitant soft tissue injury. Infection rates for appropriately treated open tibial fractures are provided as an illustrative example.

- Grade I—infection rate 0 to 2 percent.[13]
- Grade II—infection rate 2 to 7 percent.[14]
- Grade III—infection rate 10 to 25 percent.[15]
- Grade IIIA—infection rate 7 percent.[16]
- Grade IIIB—infection rate 10 to 50 percent.[17]
- Grade IIIC—infection rate 25 to 70 percent.[18]

In cases where the wound and underlying bone become chronically infected, amputation unfortunately is a well described complication.[19]

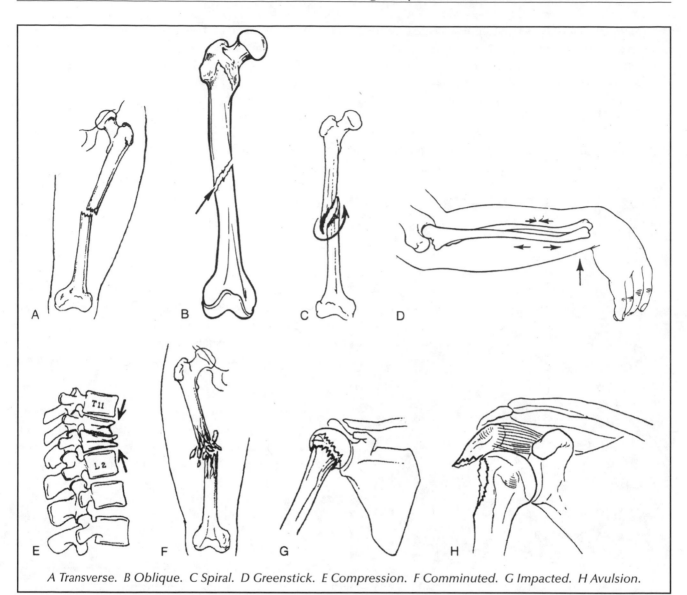

A Transverse. B Oblique. C Spiral. D Greenstick. E Compression. F Comminuted. G Impacted. H Avulsion.

Figure 17.5 *Types of fractures. (Reprinted from DePalma's The Management of Fractures and Dislocations, 3rd Edition, Elsevier, 1981.)*

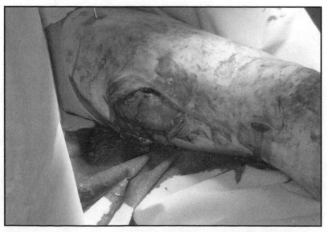

Figure 17.6 *Photo of the irrigation and debridement procedure.*

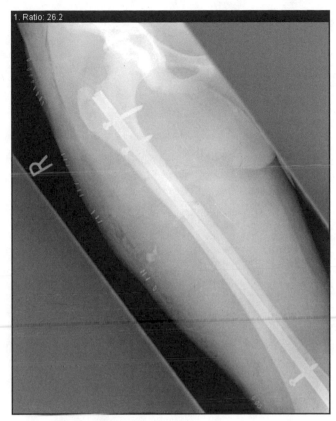

1. Ratio: 26.2

Figure 17.7 X-ray of the ORIF.

2. Classification of fractures

Discussion of specific treatments for the myriad types of fractures and other orthopaedic traumatic injuries is beyond the scope of this chapter. In general, orthopaedic surgeons describe fractures based on the bone involved, the pattern of the fracture, whether there is involvement of the adjacent joint, and whether there is an associated dislocation. Examples of common fracture patterns are

- *complete fractures*, where there is a break across the entire cross-section of the bone, dividing it into distinct fragments,
- *incomplete fractures*, where the break involves only one side of the bone while the other cortex is intact (seen mostly in children),
- *spiral fractures*, where the fracture line winds longitudinally around the bone,
- *oblique fractures*, where the fracture line crosses the bone at an acute angle, and
- *transverse fractures*, where the fracture line crosses the bone perpendicular to its long axis.[20]

Notably, the Academy of Orthopaedic Surgery (AO) and Professor Maurice Muller have developed a comprehensive classification system and nomenclature for fractures by as-

signing a number to every bone in the body and descriptive numbers and letters to describe the pattern and location of the fracture.[21] Figure 17.8 shows the Academy of Orthopaedics fracture types.

Once fractures are appropriately classified, corresponding treatments can be broadly classified as operative or non-operative, requiring reduction or not requiring reduction, and needing or not needing fixation. To define these terms, "reduction" refers to restoring the normal anatomic alignment of the bone or joint. Reduction may be possible in some cases without an operation—"closed reduction," but in other cases, "open reduction" with a skin incision and direct manipulation of the bone ends is necessary. Fixation refers to the use of hardware or specialized devices to hold the reduced bone in its corrected alignment. Fixation can either be "internal," where the hardware is completely under the skin and soft tissues, or "external," where a series of pins and screws is drilled through the skin into the bone and an external apparatus is applied to hold the pins in the appropriate alignment. A popular combination is "open reduction internal fixation" or "ORIF," referring to an operative procedure in which the fracture is reduced through an incision and indwelling hardware is placed on the bone.

3. Past medical history and physical examination

Indications for operative treatment of fractures include

- prevention of infection,
- protection of soft tissues from further instability-related damage,
- restoration of anatomic alignment, and
- restoration of limb function.

Patient factors may influence the orthopaedic surgeon's choice of operative technique. Qualities such as age, baseline activity level, associated injuries, and medical comorbidities such as diabetes determine whether a patient is a suitable operative candidate or whether more conservative management is preferable. This fact highlights the importance for orthopaedic surgeons to obtain and document a full medical history and to keep abreast of the patient's other injuries. The decision between operative and non-operative management may involve patient preferences where either treatment method may be successful. With some fractures, operative management may allow less time in a cast, earlier mobilization, and faster return to work and normal activities. Non-operative management usually avoids the risks inherent with anesthesia and surgery, including bleeding, nerve injury, and infection.

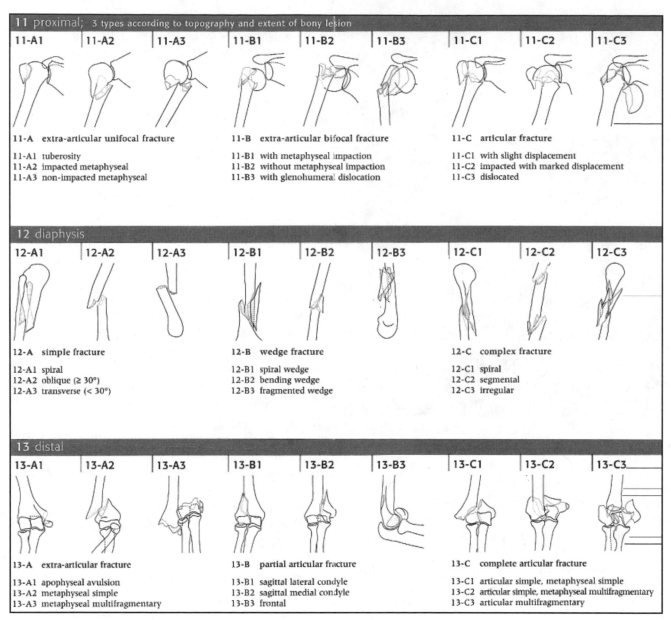

11 proximal; 3 types according to topography and extent of bony lesion

| 11-A1 | 11-A2 | 11-A3 | 11-B1 | 11-B2 | 11-B3 | 11-C1 | 11-C2 | 11-C3 |

11-A　extra-articular unifocal fracture

11-A1　tuberosity
11-A2　impacted metaphyseal
11-A3　non-impacted metaphyseal

11-B　extra-articular bifocal fracture

11-B1　with metaphyseal impaction
11-B2　without metaphyseal impaction
11-B3　with glenohumeral dislocation

11-C　articular fracture

11-C1　with slight displacement
11-C2　impacted with marked displacement
11-C3　dislocated

12 diaphysis

| 12-A1 | 12-A2 | 12-A3 | 12-B1 | 12-B2 | 12-B3 | 12-C1 | 12-C2 | 12-C3 |

12-A　simple fracture

12-A1　spiral
12-A2　oblique (≥ 30°)
12-A3　transverse (< 30°)

12-B　wedge fracture

12-B1　spiral wedge
12-B2　bending wedge
12-B3　fragmented wedge

12-C　complex fracture

12-C1　spiral
12-C2　segmental
12-C3　irregular

13 distal

| 13-A1 | 13-A2 | 13-A3 | 13-B1 | 13-B2 | 13-B3 | 13-C1 | 13-C2 | 13-C3 |

13-A　extra-articular fracture

13-A1　apophyseal avulsion
13-A2　metaphyseal simple
13-A3　metaphyseal multifragmentary

13-B　partial articular fracture

13-B1　sagittal lateral condyle
13-B2　sagittal medial condyle
13-B3　frontal

13-C　complete articular fracture

13-C1　articular simple, metaphyseal simple
13-C2　articular simple, metaphyseal multifragmentary
13-C3　articular multifragmentary

Figure 17.8 *AO depicting fracture types. (Reproduced from Miller AO Classification of Fractures/Long Bones Edition 2004/I, ISBN 3-905363-03-8, with permission of AO Publishing, ©2004 by AO Publishing, Switzerland.)*

TIP: If multiple treatment modalities are possible, the medical record should document that the surgeon fully discussed the alternatives with the patient.

4. Postoperative care

Postoperative care is an important facet of the treatment plan when operative management of orthopaedic trauma is warranted. By far the three most prominent factors determined by the surgeon for the immediate postoperative period are

- the activity level that the patient will be allowed to attain—for example the amount of weight the patient is allowed to place on the injured extremity,

- the duration of antibiotic coverage—depending on wound contamination, and
- the type and duration of prophylactic anticoagulation.

Orthopaedic patients are predisposed to potentially dangerous deep vein thrombosis (blood clots) for multiple reasons, including the fact that broken bone releases pro-clotting factors and that patients with orthopaedic injuries tend to have impaired mobility and thus have more sluggish venous circulation. To protect patients from this potentially dangerous complication, anticoagulant medications ranging from aspirin to Lovenox to Coumadin (warfarin) are prescribed by orthopaedic surgeons for their patients until the patients regain adequate mobility.

a. Impairment versus disability. As patients heal from their injuries, orthopaedists are called upon by patients and their insurance providers to assess functional impairment based on injuries. Impairment refers specifically to the surgeon's assessment of deficits in the patient's strength, sensation, or endurance due to objective weakness or pain. Determination of a patient's functional impairment requires examination of the patient's extremities and spine. Generally, the more proximal the injury, the greater the functional impairment. For example, a distal foot or toe injury is considered less serious than an ankle or knee injury.

Occupational disability, on the other hand, is a related but distinguishable assessment, usually made by an insurance company, relevant to a patient's capacity to perform tasks in a workplace setting. Though disability is based on the surgeon's evaluation of physical impairment, this is an important legal distinction. For example, a great toe amputation might cause relatively little functional impairment, but if the patient were employed as a dancer or sprinter, the associated occupational disability would be very high.[22]

The following case highlights long-term disability.

In this action, the plaintiff contended the defendant driver negligently failed to make adequate observations as she was entering the parkway. The plaintiff wife sustained a bimalleolar fracture of the left ankle which required hardware and surgery. She also sustained a head trauma and a mild traumatic brain injury. She maintained she will permanently suffer very significant pain and that she lost a great deal of independence formerly enjoyed. She had to give up her job. The plaintiffs had lived on the second story of a two family home and had to move into her daughter's home where they reside on the first floor. The plaintiff husband suffered a fractured hip. Since he had pulmonary fibrosis, he could not undergo the indicated hip surgery. The plaintiffs contended the husband suffered extensive pain and difficulties ambulating during the final 400 days of his life, until dying from the pulmonary fibrosis. There was a claim that the accident exacerbated this condition or contributed to the death. The jury awarded $1.5 million to the wife, $500,000 gross verdict to the hospital reduced by 20% comparative negligence.[23]

The following case illustrates extensive orthopaedic injuries one person endured and the various factors weighed to assess damages.

The plaintiff was in his early 40s. He underwent the insertion of a bone implant after a femoral defect was discovered during arthroscopic knee surgery to remove loose fragments. He contended that when he exhibited signs and symptoms of infection twelve days after placement of the implant, the defendant orthopedic surgeon negligently failed to excise the implant. The plaintiff contended that as a result, the implant remained in place for seven months and the patient suffered the formation of an abscess and chronic osteomyelitis. When surgery was ultimately performed seven months later, a portion of the femur had become infected and required excision along with the removal of the implant. He contended he will suffer permanent severe pain and difficulties ambulating, be permanently susceptible to flare ups of the osteomyelitis, and that it is probable that he will ultimately require an above the knee amputation. Prior to trial, the plaintiff settled with the supplier of the graft for $250,000. The jury found the defendant orthopedic surgeon 60% negligent, the settling tissue supplier 30% liable, and attributed 10% to the preexisting condition. They rendered a gross award of $3,500,000 which was reduced to $2,100,000.[24]

17.4 Essential Elements of the Musculoskeletal Trauma Patient's Medical Record

This section summarizes in outline form the concepts discussed in detail above and identifies key information that should be contained in the hospital and outpatient record for a musculoskeletal trauma patient. This list is not intended to be definitive, as different parts of the medical record gain in relative importance depending on the nature and severity of a particular injury; but this outline should provide a solid early reference.

1. Record of EMS, Police, Fire Department—Key observations at the scene of injury
   a. Time of injury
   b. Presumed mechanism of injury (motor vehicle collision, fall, assault)
   c. Patient's initial physical examination
      • Mental status
      • Hemodynamic and respiratory stability

- Obvious injuries or deformities
- Blood loss at the scene of injury (relevant to calculating total blood loss)
- Vital signs (heart rate, blood pressure, respiratory rate, temperature)

  d. Time in transit to hospital
- Medications or other treatments provided in transit
- Trends in vital signs or any changes in the physical examination

2. Initial Hospital Evaluation—Records of emergency department physicians and nurses

  a. Time of presentation of patient

  b. History of injury taken from EMS/Police/Transport
- Patient's past medical history (medical comorbidities)
- Patient's at-home medication regimen
- Known drug or other allergies
- Relevant family history

  c. Patient's updated physical examination
- Mental status
- Hemodynamic and respiratory stability (ABCs)
- Vital signs

  d. Initial radiographs

  e. Initial laboratory results

3. Secondary Hospital Evaluation—Records of consultants including the Orthopaedic Surgeon

  a. Time of consultation

  b. History of injury / past medical history as reported by patient or by other physicians

  c. Complete physical examination
- Orthopaedic evaluation should focus on the neurological, muscular, and distal pulse exams

  d. Documentation of review of radiographic and laboratory data and associated significant abnormal findings

  e. Documentation of known or suspected injuries
- Provisional stabilization of fractures (usually with a plaster splint)

  f. Assessment and plan
- Summary statement including the patient's age, significant past medical history, mechanism of injury, time of injury, list of non-orthopaedic injuries, list of orthopaedic injuries, recommendations regarding treatment of orthopaedic issues
- Recommendations for additional studies where necessary

- Recommendations for urgent or non-urgent operative or non-operative management

4. Operative Record (when relevant)

  a. Documentation of communication between surgeon and patient regarding treatment options (e.g., operative versus non-operative)

  b. Written documentation of informed consent

  c. Documentation of side and site verification

  d. Documentation of preoperative dose of antibiotics

  e. Name of surgeon

  f. Name of anesthesiologist

  g. Name of assistants

  h. Preoperative diagnosis

  i. Procedure performed

  j. Anesthesia record
- Fluids/blood/plasma infused
- Intraoperative monitoring
- Medications given/times

  k. Intraoperative findings

  l. Intraoperative complications

5. Postoperative Record

  a. Documentation of full neurologic and vascular examination
- Notation of any changes between preoperative and postoperative neurovascular status

  b. Daily physician and nursing notes
- Wound status (benign/erythematous (red)/draining)
- Vital signs
- Plan
- Activity level—referral to work with physical therapy
- Specified weight bearing status
- Anticoagulation regimen (medication and duration)
- Antibiotic treatment—(medication and duration)

  c. Daily physical therapy note (refer to Chapter 24, *Rehabilitation Records,* and Chapter 23, *Physical Therapy Records*)

6. Discharge plan

  a. Discharge to home versus rehabilitation center

  b. Discharge medications

  c. Follow-up plan with surgeon and other consulting physicians

17.5 Elective Orthopaedic Procedures

Elective orthopaedic surgical procedures include a vast array of techniques developed to address acute or chronic musculoskeletal disorders. Procedures are classified by their anatomic location—hand, elbow, shoulder, hip, knee, ankle, foot or spine—or based on the technique used, for example, joint replacement, arthroscopy, or joint fusion. The focus is on the most frequently performed elective orthopaedic procedures and the highlighted issues unique to this procedure. Please refer to Chapter 4, *Analyzing Medical Records*, in Volume I, for additional information.

A. Arthroplasty

According to the Centers for Disease Control (CDC), at least seventy million Americans are affected by chronic arthritis.[25] Arthritis is also the leading cause of disability according to the CDC, especially among the elderly, with 17.5 percent of all disability attributable to this single diagnosis. In the early 1970s, orthopaedic surgeons began treating severe, disabling arthritis with arthroplasty—joint replacement. Over the past four decades, joint replacement, usually of the knee or hip, has become one of the most popular and successful orthopaedic surgical procedures with over 700,000 cases performed per year according to Solucient, the company that maintains the nation's largest healthcare database. To assist the reader in understanding why joint replacement is so effective, a brief explanation of the pathophysiology of arthritis is included.

Figure 17.9 displays the various body movements produced by muscle contraction. This is helpful terminology to understand when reviewing orthopaedic medical records.

Physicians, nurses, and physical therapists use the scale shown in Figure 17.10 when examining the strength of the extremities. This is a helpful scale to refer to when reviewing orthopaedic medical records.

Arthritis is a chronic degenerative process and a natural consequence of aging. With advancing age, the chemical and cellular composition of cartilage found in joints changes; the water content of articular cartilage, which determines its mechanical properties, increases, leading to softening and degeneration of the cartilage. Previous fractures or subtle injuries such as repeated bone bruises suffered during athletics may predispose some areas of cartilage to premature wear and speed the degenerative process. As damage to cartilage within joints accumulates, subjective pain results, and patients are diagnosed with arthritis.

Initial symptoms of arthritis commonly respond to weight loss, activity modulation, and occasional nonsteroidal anti-inflammatory medications. As the joint derangement ("arthrosis") worsens, however, pain intensifies, and more aggressive modalities such as directed physical therapy or steroid injections into the affected joint may be necessary. Eventually, even these treatments fail to be effective, and the patient begins to become debilitated due to pain and stiffness. It is often at this stage that patients are referred to an orthopaedic surgeon for a joint replacement procedure. Notably, the most appropriate time for referral is after non-operative measures have been exhausted but before the patient has become sedentary, inactive, or otherwise disabled as a consequence of arthritis.

B. Office Visit—Initial History and Physical

Unlike orthopaedic trauma patients who usually meet their orthopaedic surgeon in the hospital or emergency ward, patients with musculoskeletal disorders caused by chronic degeneration generally are referred to their orthopaedic surgeon in an outpatient office setting. Reflecting this difference, the most informative preoperative medical records for these patients are generally contained in the office rather than the hospital chart. Despite this difference, however, similar aspects of a thorough history and physical examination should be documented in the office record. Range of motion is often documented in orthopaedic surgeons' or physical therapists' notes. Figure 17.11 shows the normal range of motion.

Orthopaedic surgical evaluation of a patient with chronic joint pain from arthritis requires a detailed history. The history should include a chronology of the patient's symptoms and an assessment of the patient's level of independent function including the patient's ability to walk without use of a support aid such as a cane or walker. Other elements of the patient's past medical history including significant medical comorbidities such as peripheral vascular disease, coronary artery disease, or diabetes are also important to elicit during the initial evaluation, as knowledge of these factors enables the surgeon and anesthesiologist to optimize the patient's medical condition for the surgical procedure. Comorbid medical conditions may also alter the orthopaedic surgeon's operative plan; for example, an intraoperative tourniquet may not be used on a patient who has severe peripheral vascular diseases with highly calcified arteries due to the increased risk of vascular injury with use of a compressive device. After a thorough history is obtained, the orthopaedic surgeon also must perform and document a complete physical examination, especially of the extremity where surgery is proposed.

TIP: Essential elements of this examination include a record of any preoperative leg length discrepancy, any preoperative joint stiffness ("contracture"), a distal pulse exam, and a complete neurological examination including distal motor and sensory function.

As the vast majority of joint replacement surgeries are performed on the lower extremities, the lumbar spine should also be assessed to ensure that the hip or knee pain is not actually radicular pain originating from lumbar spine pathology.

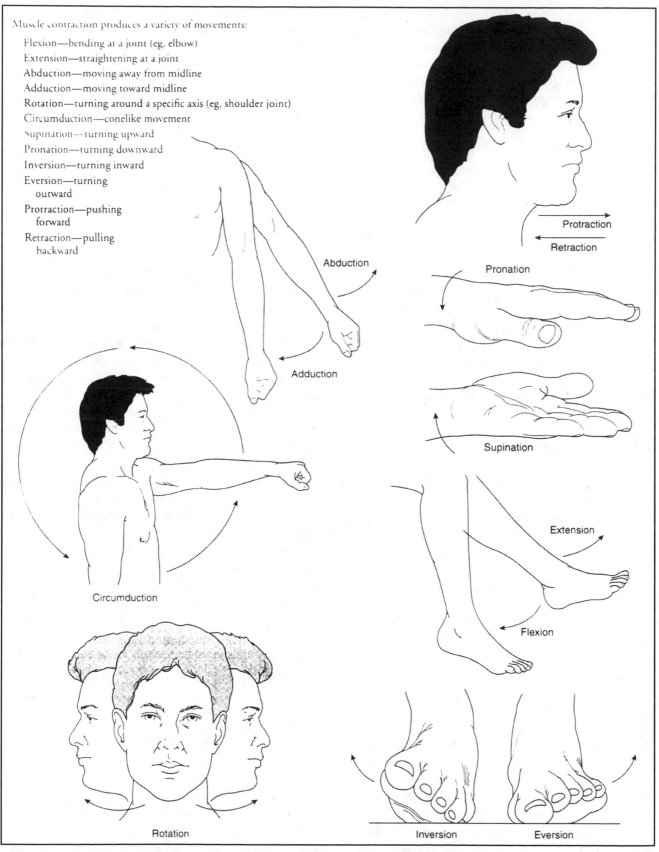

Muscle contraction produces a variety of movements:

Flexion—bending at a joint (eg, elbow)
Extension—straightening at a joint
Abduction—moving away from midline
Adduction—moving toward midline
Rotation—turning around a specific axis (eg, shoulder joint)
Circumduction—conelike movement
Supination—turning upward
Pronation—turning downward
Inversion—turning inward
Eversion—turning outward
Protraction—pushing forward
Retraction—pulling backward

Figure 17.9 *Body movements produced by muscle contraction. (Reprinted with permission of Lippincott Williams and Williams, Textbook of Medical-Surgical Nursing, Smeltzer, 2002, p. 1770.)*

0	Zero	(0)	No palpable contraction of muscle
1	Trace	(T)	Palpable contraction of muscle; no joint motion
2	Poor	(P)	Complete ROM with gravity eliminated
3	Fair	(F)	Complete ROM against gravity; no added resistance
4	Good	(G)	Complete ROM against gravity; some added resistance
5	Normal	(N)	Complete ROM against gravity with full resistance

Figure 17.10 *Grading muscle strength—Lovett scale. (Reprinted with permission from Orthopaedic Nursing, Maher, Salmond, Pellino, 2nd Edition, Elsevier, 1998, p.179.)*

Normal Range of Motion
(Shown in Degrees)

Cervical Spine
Flexion: 80-90
Extension: 70
Side flexion: 20-45
Rotation: 70-90

Thoracic Spine
Forward flexion: 20-45
Extension: 25-45
Side flexion: 20-40
Rotation: 35-50
Costovertebral expansion*
Rib Motion*

Lumbar Spine
Forward flexion: 40-60
Extension: 20-35
Side flexion: 15-20
Rotation: 3-18

Shoulder
Elevation through abduction: 170-180
Elevation through forward flexion: 160-180
Lateral rotation: 80-90
Medial rotation: 60-100
Extension: 50-60
Adduction: 50-75
Horizontal adduction and abduction: 130
Circumduction: 200

Elbow
Flexion: 140-150
Extension: 0-10
Supination (forearm): 90
Pronation (forearm): 80-90

Wrist
Abduction (radial deviation): 15
Adduction (ulnar deviation): 30-40
Flexion: 80-90
Extension: 70-90
Pronation: (forearm): 85-90
Supination (forearm): 85-90

Hip
Flexion: 110-120
Extension: 10-15
Abduction: 30-50
Adduction: 30
Lateral rotation: 40-60
Medial rotation: 30-40

Knee
Flexion: 0-135
Extension: 0-15
Medial Rotation (tibia on femur): 20-30
Lateral Rotation (tibia on femur): 30-40

Ankle
Plantar flexion: 50
Dorsiflexion: 20
Supination: 45-60
Pronation: 15-30

*Maneuvers other than measuring arcs of motion are used for assessment in these instances.

Figure 17.11 *(Reprinted with permission from Management of Lower Extremity Fractures. NAON, Williamson 1998, p.50.)*

Radiographs are another essential element of the outpatient orthopaedic evaluation. In the case of severe arthritis, at least two views of the affected joint should be taken in planes oriented 90 degrees to each other—for example, an anterior-posterior view and a lateral view. Weightbearing views are also helpful in delineating the appearance of the joint under physiologic loading stresses. Key radiographic findings in severe arthritis include: joint space narrowing, especially in weightbearing views, the appearance of bony nodules at the rim of the joint ("osteophytes") and the appearance of small, dark cysts just below the cartilage layer ("subchondral cysts"). Severe osteoarthritis is diagnosed when the joint space is completely absent on the weightbearing radiograph, and scarred ("sclerotic") bone without any normal cartilage is rubbing against another surface of sclerotic bone in the joint. Severe or "end-stage" osteoarthritis is an important finding that should be documented in the chart of any patient for whom a total joint arthroplasty is recommended.

C. Preoperative Workup

In addition to the medical history, specific laboratory tests also partially comprise the preoperative standard of care. A standard panel of preoperative laboratory tests prior to an elective orthopaedic procedure should include a urinalysis to rule out occult urinary tract infection (UTI), a complete blood count to ensure that there are normal red blood cells, white blood cell and platelet counts, an electrolyte panel, and a coagulation panel to confirm that the blood clotting times are within the normal range and that surgery can be performed without excessive bleeding. Depending on the patient's age, other studies including a chest x-ray, an electrocardiogram (ECG), and even a stress test may be appropriate for preoperative evaluation.

When patients have multiple medical problems, especially cardiac problems such as coronary artery disease, valvular disease or heart failure, or pulmonary problems such as chronic obstructive pulmonary disease (COPD) or chronic bronchitis, most orthopaedic surgeons will consult with the patient's primary care physician or other medical specialists to safeguard that the patient will tolerate the procedure safely. Despite the high demand for joint replacement surgery, the surgery itself is an elective procedure, and all medical issues should be thoroughly investigated prior to surgery.

D. Informed Consent

Once the orthopaedic surgeon has completed an evaluation, she is responsible for discussing all available treatment options with the patient. If the surgeon's recommendation is for a joint replacement surgery, the patient should be informed that it is an elective procedure that is intended to eliminate the patient's joint pain and maintain an acceptable range of motion. It should also be emphasized that pain and concomitant stiffness or disability are the only indications for joint replacement surgery.

TIP: In the absence of the symptom of chronic pain, even a joint with the radiologic appearance of severe osteoarthritis does not warrant surgical replacement.

Joint replacement techniques have improved significantly since their introduction due in large part to superior design of the implanted prostheses and the refinement of surgical techniques. The current medical literature suggests that hip or knee replacements are successful with good or excellent results in well over 95 percent of cases. As with any surgery, however, there continue to be significant risks associated with the procedures, including infection, nerve injury, hardware loosening, and dislocation. Documentation of a full discussion of potential risks is an important part of the orthopaedic patient's preoperative record. Only after such a discussion can the patient's consent for the procedure be deemed a valid "informed consent." Once a patient with severe osteoarthritis has decided to proceed with a joint replacement surgery, appropriate informed consent should be documented in the medical record.

E. Review of Orthopaedic Surgery Records

The operative record for joint replacement cases contains a few important specialized pieces of information. These include:

- routine documentation of the appropriate side and site,
- preoperative antibiotics and preoperative diagnosis,
- details of the surgical approach (anterior, lateral, or posterior), and
- the size, composition, and manufacturer of the implants used.

Components used for total joint replacement are manufactured from a variety of metals, including cobalt chromium and titanium. From these metals, components of varying sizes and designs are fashioned to provide orthopaedic surgeons with a wide array of joint replacement options. In addition, the articulating surfaces of the joint replacement are generally made of other materials such as polyethylene plastic, ceramic, or metal alloys. A final important consideration is whether bone cement is used to hold the components in place or whether "porous-coated" implants with specialized surfaces allowing bone to grow directly into the metal are employed. Notably, many of the components currently in use have been the subject of peer-reviewed papers documenting success rates in large series of patients. Please refer to Chapter 20, *Perioperative Records*, for additional information.

F. Postoperative Orthopaedic Records

Postoperative medical records for joint replacement patients include hospital records from the patient's usually brief hospital stay immediately post-op and subsequent office records documenting the patient's progress over the following weeks and months. Once the patient's medical condition has stabilized postoperatively and the pain has been adequately controlled, the patient is started (usually on postoperative day one) on a physical therapy regimen. The goal activity level for each patient is determined by several factors including the type of component used and whether or not bone cement was used. For example, a patient with a cemented component may be cleared to put as much weight as possible on the hip or knee on the first postoperative day while a patient with a "porous-coated" implant may only be cleared to rest a toe on the ground (commonly abbreviated as TTWB for "toe touch weight bearing") on the operative side for the first six weeks.

TIP: In every case, the precise activity level should be specified by the surgeon in the referral to physical therapy.

Other postoperative considerations during the initial hospital stay include the duration of antibiotics given to the patient and the type of anticoagulation prescribed. Many surgeons will give antibiotics for twenty-four hours postoperatively and continue anticoagulation for up to six weeks after the surgery. In any event, these considerations should also be clearly specified in the medical record.

As a result of the high volume of elective procedures performed by orthopaedic surgeons, especially those specializing in joint replacement, patients' postoperative regimens are largely determined by protocol and discussed with patients prior to surgery. This includes:

- the postoperative physical therapy regimen,
- prophylactic anticoagulation,
- occupational therapy review of activities of daily living (ADLs) and provision of equipment (if necessary),
- duration of hospital stay, and

- scheduled follow-up return visits to the outpatient clinic.

Prior to discharge from the hospital, the therapeutic plan, relevant instructions and scheduled clinic visits are reiterated to the patient, recorded on patient education forms, and documented in the written discharge summary. Typically, patients are assessed by the operating surgeon in the outpatient clinic two weeks after the date of surgery to assess wound healing and to remove sutures or surgical staples in the skin. At six weeks, the patient returns to the clinic where early progress with physical therapy and postoperative radiographs are assessed. Patients who are recovering well at this visit may not require further evaluation for one year. Individuals with other illnesses may be transferred to a rehabilitation setting for further treatment or to a subacute unit in a nursing home for a short-term stay. Review of records generated by these facilities will provide a picture of how the patient progressed in rehabilitation.

The following case illustrates how a postoperative total knee replacement patient developed an infection requiring long-term antibiotic treatment.

Mr. Hanson was a 57-year-old mechanic who was admitted for an elective right total knee replacement. The only dose of antibiotic was administered within 30 minutes prior to surgery. Postoperative orders were written and did not include antibiotics. On postoperative day five, Mr. Hanson had a temperature of 102 and was discharged home with Vicodin (pain medication), which has acetaminophen in it. He returned to the hospital three days later with a reddened, infected knee. He was readmitted to the hospital and required a PICC line placed for six weeks of antibiotics. He was unable to drive and work during this time. This case settled during mediation. The physician had the responsibility to order the antibiotic and the nursing staff shared in responsibilities. This physician's routine treatment was to administer 3 doses of antibiotics to his total knee replacement patients, yet the nursing staff did not question the lack of antibiotic orders.

17.6 Essential Elements of the Elective Orthopaedic Patient's Medical Record

This section summarizes in outline form the concepts discussed in detail above and identifies key information that should be contained in the hospital and outpatient record for an orthopaedic patient undergoing elective surgery. This list is not intended to be definitive, but its outline should provide a reasonable factual framework. Please refer to Chapter 4, *Analyzing Medical Records*, in Volume I, for additional information.

A. Initial Evaluation
B. Referral from primary care physician or self-referral Presenting complaint (e.g., joint pain)
C. Patient's complete medical history
    1. Baseline activity level
        •   Use of walking aids
        •   Athletics/exercise tolerance
    2. Significant comorbidities (diabetes, heart disease, peripheral vascular disease, bone metabolic diseases)
        •   Current medication list
        •   Family history
        •   Social history (tobacco or alcohol use)
D. Patient's physical examination
    1. Vital signs (heart rate, blood pressure, respiratory rate, temperature)
        •   Patient's weight
        •   Antalgic gait (limping or preferentially shifting weight away from a painful extremity or joint)
    2. Thorough neurovascular examination of extremities
        •   Distal pulses (usually dorsalis pedis—top of foot, and posterior tibialis—behind the ankle, in the lower extremity)
    3. Assessment of the arthritic joint
        •   Initial range of motion
        •   Any joint instability
        •   Any fixed deformity
E. Initial radiographs
    1. Overall joint alignment
    2. Radiographic signs of arthritis
        •   Narrowed joint space
        •   Osteophytes
        •   Subchondral cysts
    3. Initial laboratory results
        •   CBC, electrolytes, coagulation panel
    4. Assessment and plan
        •   Synthesis statement including the patient's age, significant past medical history, diagnosis (severe osteoarthritis), list of nonorthopaedic injuries, recommendations
    5. Consultations with other physicians regarding preoperative risk factors
        •   Medicine—if evidence of cardiac or renal issues
        •   Cardiology—if chronic or serious cardiac issues

•   Hematology—if evidence of clotting disorder
6. Operative Record
    •   Written documentation of informed consent
    •   Documentation of side and site verification
    •   Documentation of preoperative dose of antibiotics
    •   Name of surgeon
    •   Name of anesthesiologist
    •   Name of assistants
    •   Preoperative diagnosis
    •   Procedure performed
    •   Anesthesia record
    •   Fluids/blood/plasma infused
    •   Intraoperative monitoring
    •   Medications given/times
    •   Intraoperative findings
    •   Intraoperative complications
    •   Estimated blood loss
F. Postoperative record
    1. Documentation of full neurological and vascular examination
        •   Notation of any changes between preoperative and postoperative neurovascular status
    2. Daily physician and nursing notes
        •   Wound status (benign/erythematous (red)/draining)
        •   Vital signs
        •   Plan
            a. Activity level referral to work with physical therapy and specified weightbearing status
            b. Anticoagulation regimen (medication and duration)
            c. Antibiotic treatment (medication and duration)
            d. Critical paths (day-by-day listing of treatment and expected goals)
    3. Daily physical therapy note
    4. Pain levels recorded in nursing notes or on flow sheets and medications given to reduce pain as recorded in recovery room and on postoperative nursing unit
    5. Patient education form or notes
G. Discharge plan
    1. Discharge to home versus rehabilitation center or subacute unit
    2. Discharge medications
    3. Follow-up plan with surgeon and other consulting physicians

17.7 Orthopaedic Complications
A. Compartment Syndrome

A compartment is defined as an area in the body where muscles, nerves, and blood vessels are encompassed within tissues such as bone or fascia. There are forty-six anatomic compartments within the body, thirty-six of which are located in the extremities.[26] The following muscle compartments of the leg are the most frequently involved with this syndrome, and include: anterior, lateral, superficial posterior, and deep posterior.

Compartment syndrome is a condition in which elevated pressures within a confined space—the muscle compartment—compromise the circulation and function of tissues within that space.[27] There are a myriad of causes of compartment syndrome which include

- complications of open and closed fractures,
- arterial injury,
- temporary vascular occlusion,
- excessively tight dressing, splint, or cast,
- snake bite,
- drug overdose,
- burns,
- acute and chronic exertional states,
- gunshot wounds,
- leakage from venous and arterial access,
- pulsatile lavage,
- contusions in hemophiliac patients, and
- intraosseous fluid replacement in an infant.

Whether compartment syndrome is caused by excessive external compression such as from a tight cast or dressing, or internal compression forces as with vascular injury or exuberant swelling, the final common pathway is compression of intracompartmental vessels and nerves leading to muscle ischemia and soon thereafter muscle necrosis.[28] Figure 17.12 lists potential causes of compartment syndrome.

1. Types of compartment syndrome[29]

Compartment syndromes can be classified into three etiologic categories:

- acute compartment syndrome,
- chronic/exertional compartment syndrome, and
- crush syndrome.

a. Acute compartment syndrome. Acute compartment syndrome is the most prevalent and generally occurs within one week after traumatic, high-energy injuries. Fractures of the tibia, supracondylar humerus, and forearm are the most

Potential Causes of Acute Compartment Syndrome

√ Fractures

√ Direct compartment trauma

    Surgery

    Venomous bites

    Crush wounds

    Postischemic swelling

    Electrical injuries

√ Edema formation

    Prolonged tourniquet time

    Vascular obstruction

    Thermal injuries

    Excessive use

√ Coagulopathies resulting in bleeding into a compartment

    Anticoagulant therapy

    Hemophilia

√ Other causes

    Constrictive dressings

    Gas gangrene

    Use of pneumatic antishock garments

    Intravenous infiltration

    Drug overdose

Figure 17.12 *(Reprinted with permission of NAON, Management of Lower Extremity Fractures, Williamson, 1998, p.36.)*

frequent predicate injuries due to the relatively small amount of swelling that the compartments around these bones can accommodate. The following is an example of a clinical case.

Susan White was in a motor vehicle accident and sustained a right tibia and fibula fracture. She was treated with open reduction internal fixation (ORIF). During the first postoperative day, Susan complained of increased pain which was unrelieved by pain medication. In addition she exhibited pain with passive movement of the great toe and decreased sensation in the first web space of the toe. The orthopaedic team was notified by the nursing staff about these symptoms, and the lower extremity muscle compartment pressures were measured.

The pressures of the right leg included anterior compartment 50 mmHG (millimeters of mercury) lateral 45 mmHG; superficial posterior 30 mmHG; deep posterior 38 mmHG. Normal pressures are considered 0 to 10 mmHG. The orthopaedic team promptly brought Susan to the operating room to perform a four-compartment fasciotomy to release the intracompartmental pressures and restore tissue perfusion. It was noted in the operating room that all the muscles were pink and healthy. Susan was returned to the orthopaedic floor after the surgery and had a full recovery.

b. Chronic compartment syndrome. Chronic compartment syndrome results from an increase in compartment pressure due to exertion from exercise. The increased pressure, usually occurring bilaterally, leads to ischemia and resultant pain causing the individual to rest after the activity. Once the activity is stopped, intracompartmental pressures decrease until the individual begins to exercise again. The following is a clinical scenario.

John Smith was admitted to the General Hospital with complaints of "calf pain with numbness of his feet in varied areas." John explained to the staff that he recently began a regimented program for bodybuilding and thus was lifting 160 pounds and increasing at a rapid rate. Upon evaluating him in the emergency room, the physicians determined that he had "chronic compartment syndrome" and was admitted to the hospital for full bed rest with monitoring of his legs. The medical staff and nursing staff continually monitored his neurovascular assessment. Surgical intervention was warranted for both legs, and thus a fasciotomy was performed on each leg. John had a full recovery.

c. Crush syndrome. Crush syndrome is a systemic manifestation of prolonged muscle compression and compartment syndrome. This is also referred to as rhabdomyolysis and is seen more commonly in major traumatic injuries. A multi-system approach is taken when healthcare providers are caring for this population since renal failure and cardiac issues can result from the release of myoglobin, a protein found in muscle cells. Serum potassium levels must also be monitored carefully as widespread cellular damage leads to the release of intracellular potassium into circulating blood.

TIP: While reviewing the medical record of an individual who has been diagnosed with compartment syndrome, it is important to understand that timely diagnosis and treatment are vitally important. Prompt diagnosis and treatment of compartment syndrome prevent irreversible muscle necrosis and neurologic injury. "Muscles can tolerate four hours of ischemia well, but by six hours the result is uncertain; after eight hours the damage is irreversible."[30]

2. Diagnosis

Diagnosis of compartment syndrome, though essential to prompt treatment, can be difficult for multiple reasons. Patients suspected of having compartment syndrome often have a serious known injury at the same site. Complaints of pain and altered sensation may thus be attributable to the bony injury or to a compartment syndrome. Although there are signs and symptoms thought to be classically found in compartment syndrome—specifically the "6 Ps" (see Figure 17.13)—some of these symptoms, especially pallor, paralysis, and pulselessness, manifest quite late in the evolution of a compartment syndrome when significant tissue necrosis has already occurred. Although the compartment pressure measuring device is a useful tool, readings can vary even within a single compartment and depending upon user technique. (See Figure 17.14.)

TIP: Evaluate the medication sheets to establish how often and how much pain medication was delivered to the patient.

In addition, if the patient has a patient controlled analgesia (PCA) pump, review the PCA sheets for subjective complaints of pain; review pump settings to see if there were any changes made to increase the delivery of medication; note amounts of medication delivered to the patient; establish number of attempts of medication delivery—how many times did the patient press the button to obtain more pain medication; and amounts of actual doses delivered to the patient. Evaluate the nursing notes to review the patient's subjective responses to the pain medication. Many facilities will use a pain scale—0 (no pain) to 10 (worst pain). Obtain the facility policies and procedures for pain management. Please refer to Chapter 18, *Pain Assessment and Management*, for additional information.

The Six Ps

Paresthesia—There are complaints of numbness and/or tingling.

Pain—The pain is out of proportion to injury.

Pressure—The skin may be tight and shiny upon observation. Fracture blisters may be present. The compartment may feel tense and warm upon palpation. Review the physician and nursing notes regarding their assessment of the extremity. If the physicians suspect an elevation in compartment pressures, often they will measure the pressures of the compartments. Many trauma centers have a Stryker device to measure for compartment syndrome. The premise of this test is to measure the pressures in the compartments. By utilizing the Stryker pressure device, normal pressures are noted to be 0-10 mmHG.[31] Pressures of 30-45 mmHG are critical.[32] Another option for measurement includes diastolic pressure minus 30 mmHG with 30 mmHG as an absolute value. The Stryker device uses an 18-gauge needle which is inserted directly into the compartment and a measurement is recorded. Figure 17.14 is an example of an intracompartmental pressure monitor.

Pallor—This is a late sign. Normal capillary refill is less than three seconds. Capillary refill is measured when one presses on the nail beds or the fingers or toes and measures how long it takes to transform from a "blanching" to a "pink" tone. Capillary refill greater than three seconds is abnormal and thus is a late sign with compartment syndrome. Due to the lack in capillary perfusion, the skin on the extremity may feel cool.

Paralysis—A decrease in blood supply to the muscles leads to progressive paralysis.

Pulselessness—This is a late sign indicating a lack of arterial perfusion.

Figure 17.13

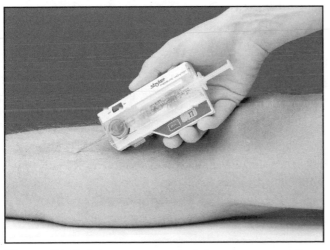

Figure 17.14 Intracompartmental pressure monitor (courtesy of Stryker).

TIP: "While malpractice claims involving compartment syndrome were uncommon, they resulted in a high rate and amount of indemnity payments. Early fasciotomy not only improves patient outcome but is also associated with decreased indemnity risk."[33]

Recognizing the signs and symptoms of compartment syndrome is of paramount importance for the medical and nursing staff. Monitoring the neurovascular assessment closely and noting any changes is key in the successful outcome of treating this process. The nursing staff must communicate the patient's subjective complaints along with the objective findings to the physicians. Continual assessment is pivotal to the successful diagnosis and treatment of compartment syndrome, especially when a one-time assessment may be ambiguous for the reasons discussed above.

The following case demonstrates how the failure to inform a physician of a patient's pain and neurovascular changes resulted in a loss of muscle and tissue of the leg.

Ms. R. was a 19-year-old woman who underwent knee surgery to remove a benign tumor. Upon examination after surgery, Ms. R. had no complications and a normal neurovascular status. During the night, Ms. R. complained of feeling as though her leg felt like it would "explode." She repeatedly complained of pain below her knee and in her foot and had abnormal neurovascular assessments. She was administered increasing amounts of pain medication. Two residents were contacted by the nursing staff but did not come to the hospital to evaluate Ms. R. The attending physician was never contacted. In the early morning, Ms. R was evaluated by the attending surgeon who diagnosed a compartment syndrome. An emergency fasciotomy was performed. Ms. R. required several debridements due to necrotic tissue and muscle below the knee. She lost about ninety percent of the muscle in her leg, and has a foot drop and severe nerve dysfunction. Ms. R. claimed that the delay in diagnosis and treatment of her compartment syndrome caused extensive muscle and tissue death. There was a plaintiff verdict $14.8 million.[34]

3. Treatment

Treatment of compartment syndrome includes a surgical procedure—fasciotomy—that opens the skin and fascia surrounding the swollen compartment to relieve the pressure. The fascia is a thin connective tissue wall that separates adjacent muscle groups from each other. Incisions are made lengthwise along the fascia, and there may be multiple incisions made depending upon the number of compartments involved. Once the fascia is released, surgeons thoroughly evaluate the compartmental contents for signs of devitalized tissue, ischemia, or frank necrosis. Intraoperative observations can vary from healthy appearing muscle and connective tissue to necrotic tissue. There are times when the patients return to surgery to have debridements performed to remove this "dead tissue or muscle."

After a fasciotomy, the released fascia and skin are usually not closed with sutures, and the individual is placed in a bulky dressing. Bed rest is ordered for several days to promote a decrease in swelling so that the skin incisions can ultimately be closed. In many cases, even when the swelling has subsided completely, the skin edges are so severely retracted that direct closure of the skin incisions are not possible. In those cases, surgical options include skin grafting, use of a vacuum dressing, or merely allowing the skin to regrow over the open area, resulting in healing by secondary intention.

4. Prevention

Prevention of compartment syndrome is the primary goal for healthcare providers. When reviewing the medical records, the attorney or legal nurse consultant may note that the staff loosened the dressings or bivalved a cast on the patient. This helps to decrease the external pressures placed on the extremity. Another example of staff intervention includes a patient who is complaining of symptoms and is on a CPM (continuous passive motion) machine which is used after a total knee replacement. The staff may have decreased the flexion on the machine or may have even removed the machine. This helps decrease the external and internal pressures of the knee area.

TIP: The attorney should consider hiring a legal nurse consultant to review the medical records of a client with compartment syndrome. A useful work product is a detailed chronology to best review the timing of the complaints, the symptoms present, and the treatment rendered.

There can be medical-legal aspects relative to the diagnosis of compartment syndrome. Some clinical variables are associated with monetary recovery for the plaintiff.

- "Physician documentation of abnormal finding on neurological examination but no action taken."[35]
- "Poor physician communication."[36]
- "Increased number of cardinal signs (pain, pallor, pulselessness, paralysis, or pain with passive stretching)."[37]
- "Increased time to fasciotomy—this was the most prominent risk factor for an indemnity payment."[38]

While malpractice claims for compartment syndrome are uncommon on a per-surgeon basis, they represent an area of significant potential liability. Orthopaedic surgeons must remain vigilant with regard to compartment syndrome in both the inpatient and outpatient setting. When fasciotomy is performed within eight hours after the presentation of symptoms, a successful defense is likely.[39]

The following case signifies the importance of communicating neurovascular changes on a patient.

The eighty-seven year-old decedent was admitted to the defendant hospital for a laminectomy. Surgery was successful, but she developed severe pain and other symptoms, including numbness and incontinence. The nurses did not call the orthopaedic surgeon. During regular rounds the next morning the orthopedic surgeon found the decedent with numb legs and in extreme pain. He ordered a stat CT scan, which revealed an epidural hematoma which was compressing the nerves. He asked for an operating room emergently, but the hospital did not provide one until mid-afternoon. A massive clot was removed during surgery. The decedent became paraplegic due to the failures of the nurses and the hospital in providing the decedent with timely surgery. The woman died during the pendency of this matter. The defendant claimed that any delay in the surgery made no difference in the outcome and that the decedent's paraplegia could have been caused by her advanced age and profession of spinal disease. A $1.8 million verdict was returned. [40]

B. Delayed Union/Nonunion

TIP: Delayed union is a continuation of or an increase in bone pain and tenderness beyond a reasonable healing period. Healing of fractures is slowed but does not completely stop. Nonunion occurs when fracture healing has not taken place for four to six months after the fracture occurs and spontaneous healing is unlikely.[41]

A patient's health history can contribute to this delay or nonunion of the bones. Smoking and drinking alcohol can delay the healing process. In addition, there are various medications that can also contribute to a delay including steroids and nonsteroidal medications. Evaluation of the medical records will reveal additional health issues as well as a description of the injury. A patient who has a comminuted fracture (a fracture which has greater than three fragments) may have some degree of delayed union. (See Figure 17.15.)

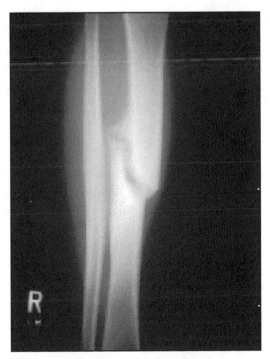

Figure 17.15 *X-ray of delayed union.*

Imagine dropping a brittle candy bar on the floor and seeing the many pieces. How would one put this back together again? Now consider this candy bar as the bone which is in numerous pieces. Surgeons use various pieces of hardware to pull the pieces together and may be unable to attach each piece together.

The following case portrays a woman who developed a nonunion.

Mrs. Smith was a twenty-seven-year-old woman who slipped and fell on top of a metal block while shopping and sustained a comminuted tibia fracture. The legal nurse consultant noted that Mrs. Smith told the emergency room staff that she "always falls while wearing this particular type of high heeled shoes." Mrs. Smith had an ORIF (open reduction internal fixation) procedure and was advised to remain non-weightbearing on the right leg. Additionally, the physicians advised Mrs. Smith to stop smoking. Several follow-up appointments and x-rays occurred. Initially, there was evidence of healing. Mrs. Smith became non-compliant with her follow-up care by continuing to smoke and by placing weight on her right leg. The bone fragments were no longer healing. Mrs. Smith needed subsequent surgeries including placement of a bone graft over the various bony defect sites. In addition, one of the fracture fragments formed a "malunion" as it was healing in the incorrect area. This fracture fragment had moved. The legal nurse consultant advised the attorney of this information, and the attorneys determined that there was "contributory negligence" in this situation due to the client admitting that she falls in her shoes often and also she was noncompliant with her care. The attorneys determined the value of the case had decreased from their original interview with the client and refused the case.

C. Infection

TIP: "Antibiotics are given for the purpose of preventing infection when infection is *not* present but the risk of postoperative infection *is* present."[42]

Recognizing the signs of an infection is important in rendering treatment. It is common to see an elevation in a patient's temperature soon after surgery. Immobility and the use of general anesthesia can contribute to this fever. In order to counteract the effect of general anesthesia on the lungs, the nursing staff will typically request the patient to perform breathing exercises in addition to using an incentive spirometer. This exercise will help to expand the lungs and exhale the general anesthesia used.

All patients who undergo surgery have the potential to develop an infection. Protecting the patient from infection is a primary goal. Maintaining a sterile field in the operating room with aseptic technique and good handwashing techniques will help decrease the risk of spreading infection.

Perioperative antibiotic use is generally recognized as an essential adjunct to minimize postoperative wound infections. In general, an initial dose of intravenous antibiotics (IV) should be administered prior to the start of surgery, and routine prophylaxis includes two additional postoperative doses given eight hours apart over the following twenty-four hours. Where the procedure requires use of a tourniquet, the IV dose should be given at least fifteen minutes prior to inflation of the tourniquet to ensure that the antibiotic has penetrated tissues at the surgical site. Though surgeons have historically been willing to extend the course of prophylactic antibiotics beyond twenty-four hours when the patient has indwelling tubes or surgical drains, current evidence does not support the use of prophylactic antibiotics beyond the initial twenty-four hour period.

D. Deep Vein Thrombosis/Pulmonary Embolism

A brilliant nineteenth century pathologist, Rudolf Virchow, was the first person to recognize that blood clots in the pulmonary artery begin as venous thrombi elsewhere. He stated: "The detachment of larger or smaller fragments from the end of the softening thrombus which are carried along by the current of blood and driven into remote vessels gives rise to the very frequent process on which I have bestowed the name of Embolia." This was the beginning of Virchow's triad which includes

- hypercoagulability,
- stasis, and
- injury to the vessel wall.[43]

A deep vein thrombosis (DVT) is a thrombus that usually forms in the deep veins of the calf or the proximal (popliteal, femoral, or iliac) veins of the leg. It can also form on the upper extremities. The most serious complication of DVT is the pulmonary embolus. Ninety percent of all clinically significant PEs can be traced to the lower extremity DVT.[44,45] Any increased viscosity or hypercoagulability in the blood increases the likelihood of thrombus formation. Venous stasis is the decreased blood flow through the vessels. Immobility or inactivity can impair venous return. Decreased muscle

tone and activity in the legs causes pooling and dilatation. This can result in the development of a thrombus. Vascular wall injury may be present with patients who have had a traumatic injury. The normal smooth vessel will become damaged, and thus clotting factors will be triggered.

There are numerous risk factors involved with this diagnosis. Trauma increases the propensity to develop a hypercoagulable state. See Figure 17.16 for specific examples.

The best way to prevent a DVT is for the healthcare providers to identify the patient's risks and determine which preventative measures can be used. The medical records should show that measures were used. These include

- early ambulation,
- compression stockings or Ace bandages if the patient is too obese for compression stockings,
- intermittent compression boots which squeeze the veins in the legs,
- foot compression devices,
- plantar flexion and dorsiflexion of the feet,
- deep breathing exercises to help the large veins empty, and/or
- anticoagulation medications such as aspirin, Fragmin, Lovenox, or Heparin.

Risk Factors for the Development of Deep Vein Thrombosis

- Obesity
- Age (greater than 60)
- History of cardiac disease (atrial fibrillation, rheumatic heart disease, hypertension, myocardial infarction, or congestive heart failure)
- Cigarette smoking
- Use of oral contraceptives
- Immobility
- Chronic pulmonary disease
- Carcinoma
- Varicose veins
- Prior deep vein thrombosis or pulmonary embolism
- Trauma or surgery involving pelvis, hip, or knee (especially hip fractures)

Figure 17.16 (Reprinted with permission of NAON, Management of Lower Extremity Fractures, Williamson, 1998, p.38.)

TIP: The nurse's role includes assessing and notifying the physician if risk factors are present.[46]

Trauma and total joint replacement patients are at higher risk of developing a DVT versus the general population. DVT rates for hip and knee reconstruction are 40 to 70 percent without anticoagulation. Diagnostic and prevention measures can prevent the thrombus from becoming a pulmonary embolism.

There are approximately 630,000 cases of pulmonary embolism diagnosed per year. It is estimated that pulmonary embolism is the major cause of 100,000 deaths and contributes to 100,000 other deaths in patients with serious coexisting diseases such as heart disease and cancer. Approximately 11 percent of patients with an acute pulmonary embolism die within one hour. Of the 536,000 patients who survive at least one hour, only 29 percent have a diagnosis and treatment plan initiated.[47]

TIP: The vast majority of patients (187,000) die because of failure to diagnose.[48]

The following case exhibits the failure to diagnose a pulmonary embolism.

Mr. Borr was admitted to the General Hospital for a redo right total knee replacement. His health history included obesity, previous right lower extremity DVT, and smoking. Postoperatively, Mr. Borr had difficulty with mobility and thus was not out of bed for three days. The nursing staff documented use of the Ted stockings for only twenty-four hours and then these were removed.

Initially Mr. Borr received Coumadin for anticoagulation, and then this medication was not transcribed to the new medication sheet. Thus, Mr. Borr only received anticoagulation for three days. On post-op day six, Mr. Borr had tachycardia (heart rate 144); tachypnea (respiratory rate 32); and complaints of chest pain. The nursing staff contacted the physician and communicated the complaints of chest pain to the physician. The physician requested an EKG, medication for the chest pain, administration of valium (a sedative), and oxygen to be given. Dr. Peet evaluated the patient and determined that Mr. Borr may be having a "heart attack" and thus requested continuous telemetry monitoring, oxygen use, laboratory work, and monitoring. The following four hours of documentation stated that Mr. Borr's heart rate increased to 150, respira-

tory rate remained at 32, and there were increased complaints of chest pain. There were no additional calls to Dr. Peet. Mr. Borr coded five hours after the initial complaints of chest pain and expired. In deposition, Dr. Peet explained that he was not contacted by the nursing staff about the additional symptoms and that he was unaware that Mr. Borr was no longer receiving Coumadin. (Unpublished settlement.)

Mr. Borr was a high-risk candidate for a deep vein thrombosis because of his history of a DVT, current immobility, as well as having had a right total knee replacement. In addition, anticoagulation therapy was initiated and then abruptly stopped. Objective symptoms were present and these included tachycardia, tachypnea, chest pain, and EKG changes.

TIP: When reviewing medical records with questions specific to a pulmonary embolism, it is important to inspect the medication records and compare these with all the physician orders.

Discharge planning may affect the management of a patient at risk for pulmonary embolism. The medical records should include physician and nursing progress notes and social service or discharge planning/case management documentation regarding the plan for post-admission care. The following case unveils the issues regarding discharge planning and the lack of a follow-up plan.

Mrs. Jones was a thirty-one-year-old woman who was involved in a motor vehicle accident. She sustained traumatic injuries which included a right femur fracture, right radial/ulnar fracture, left tibia/fibula fracture, left olecranon fracture, and a pelvic fracture. She had several surgeries to align the various fractures. Initially she was placed on Heparin injections and Coumadin for a total of five days. These medications were not reordered. After fifteen days in the hospital, Mrs. Jones was discharged to her home with limited visiting nursing services. Mrs. Jones was not out of bed during her entire hospitalization and was transferred home via an ambulance. Mrs. Jones's mother was the caretaker and placed her daughter on bedpans, and assisted with meals, bathing, and repositioning. Three days later, Mrs. Jones had an acute pulmonary embolism and died. The nursing staff and physicians were defendants in this matter. It was determined that the nursing staff should not have discharged Mrs. Jones to her home. Instead Mrs. Jones should have been transferred to a rehabilitation facility. The discharge plan was inadequate in many areas including mobility. There were no home services for physical therapy nor any anticoagulation administered. The physicians failed to evaluate Mrs. Jones for two days prior to discharge and failed to continue with administering anticoagulation to Mrs. Jones. (Unpublished settlement.)

E. Fat Emboli

A major cause of morbidity and mortality following trauma and long bone fracture is fat embolism syndrome, which was first described in the late 19th Century.[49] In 1970, Gurd proposed three major diagnostic criteria for fat emboli syndrome

- petechial rash,
- respiratory distress, and
- cerebral signs.[50]

While respiratory distress associated with fat emboli syndrome is caused by widespread pulmonary intravascular fat deposition and occlusion, petechial rash (red spots) and neurological dysfunction are consistent with systemic microvascular occlusion. Indeed, histologic examination of brain and subcutaneous tissue from patients with systemic fat emboli syndrome reveals widespread microvascular occlusion by fat emboli. Several authors have postulated that fat is miscible (refers to the solubility of fat droplets in water) enough to pass through the pulmonary circulation, especially in areas of physiologic shunting (West's zone III).[51–53] Under this theory, fat emboli syndrome is caused by the release of marrow into the circulation, causing a manifestation of adult respiratory distress syndrome. Prompt diagnosis and supportive therapy are given to prevent a potentially lethal course; these include oxygen therapy and perhaps mechanical ventilation. Approximately 60 percent of cases occur within the first twenty-four hours after trauma, and 90 percent of all cases present within seventy-two hours.

The following case demonstrates prompt diagnosis and treatment.

Mrs. Shaffer was a 52 year old woman who was involved in a motorcycle accident. She sustained bilateral femur fractures and had bilateral open reduction internal fixation (ORIF) surgeries. On postoperative day two, Mrs. Shaffer's oxygen saturations began decreasing to the 85-87% range.

She developed a petechial rash and had confusion. The nursing staff communicated these findings promptly to the orthopaedic surgeon and the Rapid Response Team. (RRT is a team of clinicians who bring critical care expertise to the bedside). Together, they evaluated Mrs. Shaffer and transferred her to the Intensive Care Unit where she was diagnosed with fat emboli syndrome. She was eventually intubated since her respiratory status declined. She remained in the Intensive Care unit for 5 days and was transferred back to the orthopaedic unit. She progressed well with her rehabilitation and was discharged home.

F. Hemorrhage

There is a higher incidence of hemorrhage noted with the following conditions

- revision arthroplasty,
- multi-level anterior/posterior spine procedures,
- multi-trauma, and
- patients with identified risk factors.[54]

When examining a medical record where there has been an incident of hemorrhage, the attorney and legal nurse consultant should review the objective symptoms. The documentation of a physical examination may include the following

- pallor,
- cool, moist skin,
- tachycardia, possibly irregular pulse,
- decreased blood pressure,
- rapid shallow breathing,
- decreased urine output,
- abnormal drainage from wounds,
- frank bleeding from wound or surgical incision, and/or
- restlessness.[55]

Hemorrhage is most likely to occur within forty-eight hours after surgery. Slippage of a suture or dislodging a clot are two causes of hemorrhage. Once the cause is detected, the physician would determine the course of treatment which may include any or all of the following

- lab work (CBC, clotting studies),
- rebandage/pressure dressing application,
- suture,
- medication administration (such as Vitamin K),

- blood transfusions, and
- surgery.

G. Constipation/Ileus

A common complication occurring in the postoperative or immobile patient is constipation, which is an abnormal infrequency of defecation or the passage of abnormally hard stools or both.[56] The causes may be minor or serious and include those patients who have had a change in oral intake, opioid or narcotic intake, as well as other drug therapies, stress, and lack of fluids. The longer the feces remain in the bowel, the drier they become, thus causing constipation and possibly hemorrhoids.

A treatment plan is individualized once the caretaker determines the cause. Common remedies to prevent or treat this include having the patient increase fluid intake, encouraging activity, and increasing fruit and vegetable intake, as well as taking stool softeners such as Colace daily. Additional treatments may include Senna, Fleet enemas, or Dulcolax suppositories. Each medication has a specific mode of treatment whether it be a stool softener, laxative, or other.

It is important for the healthcare providers to document the bowel sounds and the times the patient has a bowel movement. Daily bowel evaluations are made on each shift and include feeling the abdomen—noting if it is soft or distended or hard and listening to bowel sounds. A distended or hard abdomen requires a further assessment to determine if this is due to constipation or other reasons. A treatment plan would then be initiated. It is important for the team of healthcare providers to monitor the patient's bowel pattern and determine if the patient developed an ileus: mechanical, dynamic (a stricture or obstruction causes the blockage), or adynamic (dysmotility of the intestine) obstruction of the bowel. These obstructions may be partial or complete and can be manifested by abdominal pain, emesis, and obstipation (which is pain followed by explosive diarrhea and is often seen in a partial obstruction). There may be high-pitched bowel sounds and tenderness. The rectal exam may reveal fecal impaction. Diagnostic tests, which would be ordered by the physician, may include a KUB (kidney, ureter, bladder x-ray), physical exam, and lab work. Treatment may include nasogastric suction (a tube inserted usually through the nose to the stomach and then attached to low wall suction to decompress the stomach), intravenous fluids, and bowel medications. Patients should not be eating during this time.

TIP: When reviewing medical records of patients who have had bowel problems, the attorney and legal nurse consultant should review the objective symptoms which the patient exhibited. In addition, they will note the scheduling of the narcotics and the reasons the patients were taking them. Were the bowel sounds monitored regularly and were they present? Were the changes in bowel sounds communicated to the physicians? Is there documentation regarding the times the patient had bowel movements? Was the abdomen soft or hard and distended? Was the patient experiencing nausea or vomiting? What was the color of the emesis? Was there blood in the emesis?

The following is a clinical scenario of a patient who had postoperative bowel issues.

A forty-four-year-old man was admitted to General Hospital to have an anterior L4-L5 laminectomy procedure. Postoperatively, the patient did not have bowel sounds. The staff was aware and yet they allowed the patient to have a clear liquid diet. The patient's abdomen was growing larger daily. Four days later his abdomen was hard, tight, shiny, and distended. There were no bowel sounds noted. It was later discovered that the patient was an alcoholic and was treated according to the hospital alcohol pathway which included Ativan administration. The patient began seizing during the night and required a large amount of Ativan—27 mg within a few hours. The nurse evaluated him in the morning and found him quite somnolent. The nurse communicated her concerns to the charge nurse who also evaluated the patient. The charge nurse did a full examination and noted the patient to be using his abdomen muscles to assist with breathing. He was not managing his oral secretions well, and thus the head of the bed was raised and his mouth was suctioned. Due to concerns about his respiratory status, the physician team and nursing supervisor were contacted. A set of blood gases was sent and a nasogastric tube was inserted. Approximately 2.5 liters of bile material flew out of the patient's mouth like a geyser. The RICU (respiratory intensive care unit) team and anesthesiologist were contacted to intubate this patient since it was evident that he aspirated contents into his lungs. It was determined that this situation could have been avoided if the nursing staff had closely monitored the patient's bowel activity and reported the findings earlier.

17.8 Nursing Care Plans

Nursing care plans are an important part of the medical records. The initial step to designing this care plan includes the nurse performing an accurate and comprehensive assessment. Typically the care plan consists of four parts:

- patient's problem or nursing diagnosis,
- goals or expected outcomes which describe results achieved within a period of time,
- nursing interventions, and
- evaluations of the established goals.

In the acute care setting, nurses will continually assess and make revisions to the care plan. Once the assessment is completed, the nurse will then design a problem list. This list will include actual and potential problems followed by interventions. Please refer to Chapter 15, *The Nursing Process and Nursing Records*, for further information.

A nursing care plan should be written within twenty-four hours of admission. The care plan should be applicable for the patient, readily available, specific, and updated as the patient's needs change. The following is an example of an orthopaedic care plan.

A postoperative forty-seven-year-old patient who sustained a right tibia/fibula fracture may have the following diagnosis and plan of care.

Alteration in mobility:

1. Assist the patient with repositioning, maintain body alignment.
2. Keep the right leg elevated.
3. Assist the patient with ambulation and progress with physical therapy.
4. Monitor bowel activity.

Alteration in comfort:

1. Encourage the patient to verbalize his pain on a pain scale 0 to 10 (0–no pain; 10–worst pain).
2. Evaluate the source and character of the pain.
3. Assess for any changes in neurovascular assessment.
4. Medicate the patient and monitor the pain level after the administration of the medication.
5. Provide diversional activities.

Alteration in tissue perfusion:

1. Monitor the incision and dressings.
2. Monitor the drainage from the hemovac drainage device.
3. Monitor the vital signs.
4. Assess the neurovascular status.
5. Apply antiembolic stockings as ordered.
6. Monitor the laboratory results.

A. History and Physical

Upon admission to the hospital or same day surgery unit, the nurse will obtain the patient's history. The following are details an attorney and legal nurse consultant may find within this section.

- Biographic information—age, gender, occupation, living situation. (Determine if there is someone at home who can assist post discharge. If the patient has stairs in the home, the patient may require a physical therapy consult to train on the stairs if she has a lower extremity injury.)
- Admission complaint—description of the musculoskeletal problem (throbbing, dull, piercing, swelling) and any aggravating factors (pain with movement)
- Health history—diseases or illnesses, surgical data, injuries, allergies
- Current status—mobility status, diet, exercise
- Family history—diseases and illnesses included
- Social history—drug and alcohol use

The following case is an example of a situation in which the patient's health history was not shared with the nursing assistant who was assisting the patient.

An eighty-two-year-old man underwent complete blood transfusions at a Virginia hospital six to eight times each year over the course of four years. The transfusions required him to lie in a hospital bed for approximately eight hours after the procedure, after which he would be discharged to the care of his daughter. At the end of one of the transfusion procedures, the nurse assigned to the patient asked a nursing assistant to transfer him from the bed into a wheelchair. The nursing assistant was not informed of the plaintiff's history of chronic obstructive pulmonary disease, congestive heart failure, osteoporosis, prostate cancer, and Type II diabetes. The nurse in charge also failed to tell the assistant that the plaintiff was prone to falling and had a documented history of balance, coordination, and gait difficulty. The only information provided to the nurse assistant by the charge nurse was that the patient was ready for discharge. The assistant assessed the situation and determined that the patient was an elderly, frail man sitting on the edge of a bed. According to the plaintiff's daughter, the assistant brought the wheelchair to the side of the bed and simply stood behind it as the plaintiff attempted to slide off the edge of the bed to stand, pivot, and sit in the wheelchair. At deposition, the assistant testified that she placed her hand on his side during the transfer. The assistant testified at trial that she grasped his upper and lower arm with both her hands to offer assistance. The plaintiff lost his footing and balance and twisted his left knee severely enough to tear the medial meniscus that required surgery several days later. The plaintiff underwent physical therapy and fully recovered in thirty days. The patient was eighty-four at the time of the trial and was not called to testify. The jury awarded him $250,000.[57]

Physicians and nursing staff perform physical assessments that typically include a "head-to-toe" assessment. These include an examination of the respiratory and cardiac systems as well as musculoskeletal system. Once the clinicians evaluate the nature of the patient's complaints and orthopaedic problems or injuries, cause of the incident or the mechanism of injury, this will allow them to narrow the focus of their assessment.

A thirty-year-old woman who was driving her car hit a stone wall. The energy from the velocity of travel was transferred through the point of impact—her legs—and shattered her pelvis.

The practitioner assesses the musculoskeletal system in a systematic fashion; this helps decrease the chances of missing an injury. A basic assessment includes inspecting and palpating the musculoskeletal system. Inspection of the body will include noting

- ecchymosis,
- color,
- swelling,
- capillary refill,
- temperature,
- sensation,
- pain,
- movement, and
- open wounds.

A neurovascular assessment as well as wound assessment will also be included. Positioning of the patient is important to observe and document.

A seventy-eight-year-old woman fell in her home. She was admitted with a diagnosis of a right hip dislocation. Due to this woman's extensive health history, she required a medical consultation prior to having surgical intervention. She was admitted to the orthopaedic floor, and her right leg was noted to be externally rotated and shorter than the other extremity. A Buck's boot was placed with five pounds of weight to assist with decreasing the pressure on her hip.

Most of the time, diagnostic studies are performed in the emergency room but may also continue once the patient is admitted to the floor or unit.

Immobilization devices such as Buck's traction may be used to decrease the pressure on a hip if this is the area in question. Other types of immobilization devices used include splints, casts, Jones dressing, and Ace bandages. Areas may be immobilized to prevent further injury to the site.

TIP: When an attorney reviews medical records of an individual who sustained an orthopaedic injury, it is important to note the admission assessment. This document will reveal the modality of injury, the individual's prior ambulatory status, the individual's current mobility status, as well as the health history.

B. Neurovascular

Disruption of neurovascular integrity can occur after surgical interventions. Prolonged awkward positioning in the operating room, manipulation of the tissues, inadvertent severing of the nerves, or tight bandages can be a few of the contributing factors.[58] Because there are known risks for orthopaedic procedures, it is also vital for the healthcare providers to evaluate on a continuous basis any changes in neurovascular assessment and to communicate these findings to the physician.

When an attorney or legal nurse consultant evaluates the orthopaedic client's medical records, it is expected that neurovascular assessments performed would be documented. These would include evaluation of the color, sensation, and movement of the extremity. In addition, pulses would be evaluated and documented. After an orthopaedic injury or procedure, the patient is at risk for neurovascular dysfunction. It is imperative that there be assessments and documentation of a baseline neurovascular assessment. The attorney or legal nurse consultant should find an assessment of vascular integrity, neurologic integrity, and pain status at regular intervals, and changes by healthcare providers should be reported.[59]

TIP: When reviewing medical records of someone who has had a compromise in neurovascular assessment, it is important to determine if there were changes in pulses. Did the physician and nurses have difficulty obtaining the patient's pulse? Did they need to use a Doppler ultrasound to determine if blood flow or pulses were present? This device is more sensitive than palpation for determining pulse rate and is especially useful when a pulse is faint or weak.

Documentation may include descriptors of pulses such as: strong, thready, weak, bounding, or diminished. Figure 17.17 will assist the reviewer understand components of neurovascular assessments.

It is also important to review neurovascular assessments post epidural or spinal anesthesia. Postoperative orthopaedic patients should be evaluated and monitored in the post anesthesia care unit and then on a regular basis in the postoperative unit such as an orthopaedics or medical surgical unit. The healthcare providers will be evaluating the patient for any decrease in movement and sensation and noting if there is a change in color. This will be documented either on a neurovascular sheet or within the physician or nursing progress notes.

TIP: The healthcare providers should also compare one extremity to the opposite.

Figure 17.18 reflects the assessment of peripheral nerve function.

Neurovascular Scale—Lower Extremity

Vascular Assessment: Dorsalis Pedis/Posterior Tibial

Capillary Refill	Nail Bed Color	Pulses	Skin Temperature
2+ = Brisk	P = Pink	N = Normal/Palpable	W = Warm
1+ = Diminished	Pa = Pale	Ab = Absent	Cl = Cool
0 = No refill	C = Cyanotic	D = Doppler	Cd = Cold

Neurologic Assessment

Nerve	Movement	Sensibility
Tibial	Plantarflexion	Sole of foot
Peroneal	Dorsiflexion	Dorsal space great toe
Femoral	Straight leg raise	Anterior thigh

Movement

N	= Normal
D	= Diminished
Ab	= Absent

Movement

√	= Normal
Nu	= Numbness
T	= Tingling
D	= Diminished (paresthesia)
Ab	= Absent

Assess the extremity for sensation, motion, and vascular status.

Figure 17.17 (Reprinted with permission of NAON, Management of Lower Extremity Fractures, Williamson, 1998, p.50.)

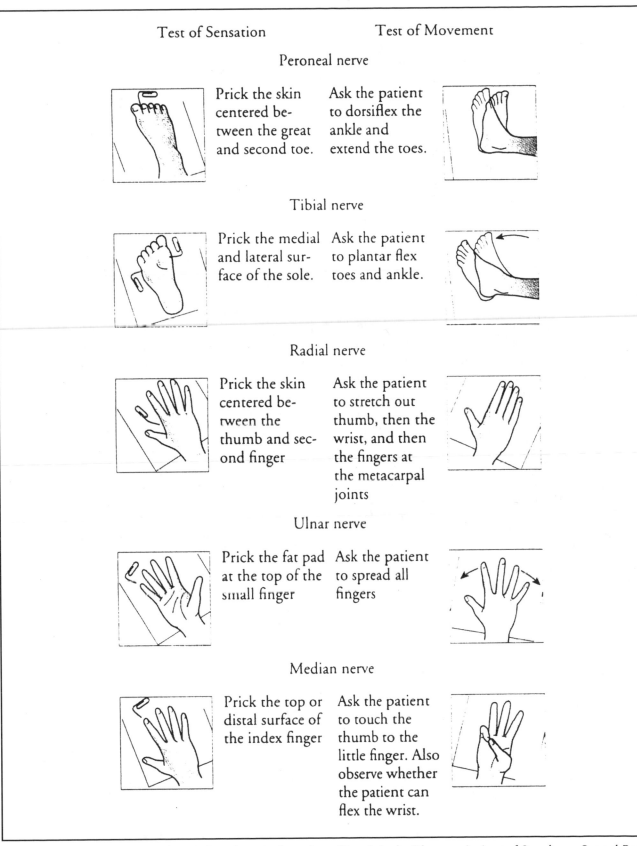

Figure 17.18 *Assessment of peripheral nerve function. (Reprinted with permission of Smeltzer, S. and Barre, B. Textbook of Medical Surgical Nursing, 9th Edition, Lippincott, 2000, p.1774.)*

TIP: Some physicians write orders for performing neurovascular assessments. Some physicians' or facilities' policies may include monitoring every fifteen minutes times four (written as "q 15 min X 4"), every hour times four (written as "q 1' X 4") then every four hours (written as "q 4"). The nursing staff can always increase the frequency of the evaluations without a physician order but cannot decrease them.

An example of documentation of a postoperative total hip replacement patient who had spinal anesthesia follows.

Mr. Hill arrives on the general orthopaedic floor at 11:30 A.M. via his bed. He is alert and oriented times three. Breath sounds are clear. Oxygen saturations wearing O$_2$ 2 liters per nasal canula are 97–98 percent. He has been instructed on incentive spirometry. Vital signs per data sheet. He has been oriented to the call bell system. Mr. Hill is able to move his arms without difficulty and has intact sensation. Mr. Hill has sensation to his thighs and knees. He is able to move his thighs. He is unable to feel or move his feet. Spinal level of L4 (lumbar 4th level) noted. (L4—refers either to the fourth (of usually five) lumbar vertebrae, numbered from proximal to distal. It can in other contexts also refer to the fourth lumbar nerve root that exits at the level of the L4 vertebra.) The feet are warm and capillary refill is less than three seconds. Abductor pillow intact. He has intact bowel sounds. The Foley catheter is draining yellow urine. PCA Morphine is at 1/6/0. (These numbers denote that the patient is able to have 1mg morphine every six minutes per the patient as necessary. There is no basal rate for this patient.) Mr. Hill has been instructed on the use of the PCA. At this time, he denies any pain. Will continue to monitor.

In the following situation, the nurse testified that she was unaware of the hospital policy for postoperative care.

Mrs. Smith was admitted to the orthopaedic floor after a right total knee replacement. Upon arrival to the orthopaedic floor, Mrs. Smith's right leg was in a continuous passive motion machine (CPM) which moves the leg slowly extension/flexion 0 to 30 degrees. The physician orders requested the nurse to increase the flexion 10 degrees every two hours until 50 degrees. Mrs. Smith has an epidural catheter and was complaining of increasing amounts of pain to the right leg. The nurse increased the amount of epidural pain medication being delivered to Mrs. Smith. Mrs. Smith explained that she felt "something metal" digging behind her right leg. The nurse did not evaluate this complaint and administered a sleeping medication to Mrs. Smith. By 8 A.M. the next day, Dr. Roy attended Mrs. Smith and found her to have a right foot drop. The knob of the CPM machine had pressed against Mrs. Smith's peroneal nerve, and she sustained permanent right foot drop. During deposition, the nurse explained that she was unaware of the hospital policy and procedure for performing neurovascular assessments. The only assessment the nurse performed on Mrs. Smith was immediately upon arrival to the floor as a postoperative patient. (Unpublished settlement.)

C. Vital Signs

The recording of vital signs, which includes temperature, heart rate, blood pressure, respiratory rate and pain, is part of every physical exam. These measurements are obtained, recorded, and evaluated. Pain is considered the fifth vital sign since further evaluation is warranted when a patient complains of pain. The patient is questioned about the location of pain. Healthcare providers should not assume that the site of injury or surgery is the area which is causing pain.

Mr. Baglione was a forty-nine-year-old who had a total knee replacement. His health history included significant cardiac disease and thus the anesthesiologist determined that this patient should have a spinal anesthetic. Post surgery, the physician orders stated to "Initiate heparin 800 units intravenously per hour eight hours post surgery." The nursing staff initiated this medication immediately upon arrival to the floor. During the following hours, Mr. Baglione was complaining of increased pain. The nursing staff thought this pain was located in his knee. The nursing staff did not ask the patient specific questions such as location or intensity of the pain. Instead, they contacted the anesthesia pain service and requested an increase in narcotics via PCA pump. The patient's PCA pump was set at 2/6/1—(Mr. Baglione could receive 2 mg morphine every six minutes and then had a basal rate of 1 mg—which meant that in addition, he was receiving 1 mg morphine at a continuous rate).

The pain was decreasing during the night shift. The physicians visited the patient at 7:30 A.M. and found the patient had no sensation or movement from his nipple line down (also known as thoracic 4 level). After an emergency MRI, the diagnosis was a caudal (toward the head) bleed in the spinal column from the original site of the spinal anesthetic. The physicians learned at this time that the initiation of heparin therapy began too soon after surgery. In addition, the nursing staff failed to monitor the patient's neurovascular assessment. The defendant nurse stated she was performing neurovascular assessments initially and was following the physician orders which stated "Perform neurovascular assessments every 1 hour times 4 then every 8 hours." The defendant nurse explained that since the order later stated every eight hours, she did not feel she should increase the frequency. (Unpublished settlement.)

Please refer to Chapter 18, *Pain Assessment and Management*, for additional information.

D. Intake and Output

Accurate intake and output (I&O) records help evaluate a patient's fluid and electrolyte balance. The fluid intake reflects the fluids the patient is taking by mouth, intravenous therapy, and bladder irrigations. The fluid output includes all the fluids which leave the patient's body. These include urine, stool, vomitus, drainage from devices such as hemovac, Jackson-Pratt (JP) drain, chest tubes, and nasogastric tubes.

Indicators of Neurovascular Compromise

Circulation
    Color: Pale or cyanotic
    Temperature: Cool
    Capillary refill: More than 3 seconds
Motion
    Weak
    Paralysis
Sensation
    Paresthesia
    Unrelenting pain
    Pain on passive stretch
    Absence of feeling

Figure 17.19 (Reprinted with permission of Smeltzer, S. and Barre, B. Textbook of Medical Surgical Nursing, 9th Edition, Lippincott, 2000, p.1775.)

Postoperative patients will be closely monitored initially to maintain hydration and observed for blood loss. Additionally, the urine output will be monitored, and usually the nursing staff contacts the physician if the urine output decreases to less than 30 cc per hour. Many postoperative orthopaedic patients have Foley catheters initially, which are later discontinued once they are no longer needed.

TIP: If a patient has a Foley catheter and a PCA pump, generally the PCA will be discontinued prior to or at the same time that the Foley catheter is removed. Narcotic administration of PCA can make voiding independently difficult and thus the PCA is usually discontinued.

17.9 Summary

This chapter has been designed to educate the attorney, paralegal, and legal nurse consultant about the nuances within the orthopaedics field. There are many facets of this field and we suggest the references and additional reading sections for resources to further assist the reader on these types of cases.

Endnotes

1. Phipps, W. and F. Monahan. *Medical Surgical Nursing: Health and Illness Perspectives*. p. 1447–1449. St. Louis, MO: Mosby. 2003.

2. Maher, A., S. Salmond, and T. Pellino. *Orthopaedic Nursing*. Second Edition. p. 162. Philadelphia, PA: W.B. Saunders Company. 1998.

3. *Id.*

4. Smeltzer, S. and B.G. Bare. *Brunner and Suddarth's Textbook of Medical-Surgical Nursing*. p. 1766. Philadelphia, PA: Lippincott Williams and Wilkins. 2000.

5. *Id.*

6. American College of Surgeons, National Trauma Data Bank. 2004. http://www.facs.org/trauma/ntdb/ntdbannual report2004.pdf.

7. $1,500,000 Recovery, *Morris v. Lucchesi*. Docket No. MRS L_834-06; 1-08" *New Jersey Verdict Review and Analysis*. Volume 28, Issue 10, March 2008.

8. Laska, L. (Editor). "Death From Bilateral Pneumonia After Lumbar Surgery and Discharge from Defendant Hospital." *Medical Malpractice Verdicts, Settlements, and Experts*. December 2003.

9. Brumback, R.J. and A.L. Jones. "Interobserver Agreement in the Classification of Open Fractures of the Tibia." *Journal of Bone and Joint Surgery.* August 1994, 76(8), p. 1162–6.

10. Dee, R. et al. *Principles of Orthopaedic Practice.* Second Edition. McGraw-Hill. 1997.

11. Skaggs, D. et al. "The Effect of Surgical Delay on Acute Infection Following 554 Open Fractures in Children." *Journal of Bone and Joint Surgery.* January 2005, 87(1), p. 8–12.

12. *Id.*

13. Dee, R. et al. *Principles of Orthopaedic Practice.* Second Edition. McGraw-Hill. 1997.

14. *Id.*

15. *Id.*

16. *Id.*

17. *Id.*

18. *Id.*

19. *Id.*

20. Schoen, D. *Core Curriculum for Orthopaedic Nursing.* Fourth Edition. p. 378–383. Pitman, NJ: Anthony J. Jannetti, Inc. 2001.

21. www.ao-asif.org.

22. Miller, R.T. *Evaluating Orthopedic Disability, A Commonsense Approach.* Second Edition. p. 979. Oradell, NJ: Medical Economics Company, Inc.

23. $1,500,00 Verdict, *Sharkey v. Hagan*, Docket No. ESX-L 2338-04, *New Jersey Jury Verdict Review and Analysis.* Volume 28, Issue 9, February 2008.

24. $3,150,000 Verdict, Rubino, Docket No. GLO-L-0925-04, *New Jersey Jury Verdict Review and Analysis.* Volume 29, Issue 1, June 2008.

25. http://www.cdc.gov/nccdphp/arthritis/index.htm.

26. *See* note 2 at 212.

27. *See* note 20 at 177.

28. *Id.* 213.

29. *Id.* 212.

30. Whitesides, T. and M. Heckman. "Acute Compartment Syndrome: Update on Diagnosis and Treatment." *Journal of the American Academy of Orthopaedic Surgeons.* Volume 4(209), p. 209–218. 1996.

31. Ross, D. "Acute Compartment Syndrome." *Orthopaedic Nursing.* Volume 10 (2), p. 33–38. 1991.

32. Hoover, T.J. and J.A. Siefert. "Soft Tissue Complications of Orthopaedic Emergencies." *Emergency Medicine Clinics of North America.* Volume 18(1), p. 115–139. 2000.

33. Bhattacharya, T. and M. Vrahas. "The Medical-Legal Aspects of Compartment Syndrome." *The Orthopaedic Forum.* April 2004, Volume 86-A, (4), p. 864–868.

34. Laska, L. (Editor). "Failure to inform Attending Physician of Pain and Neurovascular Changes Following Knee Surgery-Compartment Syndrome Causes Loss of Most of Muscle and Tissue of Leg-$14.8 Million Illinois" *Medical Malpractice Verdicts, Settlements, and Experts.* June 2009.

35. *Id.*

36. *Id.*

37. *Id.*

38. *Id.*

39. *Id.*

40. Laska, L. "Nurses Fail to Inform Surgeon of Pain and Numbness Following Laminectomy." *Medical Malpractice Verdicts, Settlements and Experts*, November 2009, p. 16.

41. *See* note 20 at 182.

42. http://www.aaos.org/wordhtml/bulletin/aug04/fline2.htm.

43. Dalen, J. "Pulmonary Embolism: What Have We Learned Since Virchow?" *Chest.* October 2002, Volume 4.

44. Roman, M. "Deep Vein Thrombosis: An Overview." *Med-Surg Matters.* Winter 2005, Volume 14, Issue 1.

45. Aquila, A. "Deep Vein Thrombosis." *The Journal of Cardiovascular Nursing.* Volume 15, p. 25–44. 2001.

46. *See* note 43.

47. *See* note 42.

48. *Id.*

49. Pell, A. et al. "Fulminating Fat Embolism Syndrome Caused by Paradoxical Embolism Through a Patent Foramen Ovale." *New England Journal of Medicine.* 329(13), p. 926. 1993.

50. Gurd, A. "Fat Embolism: An Aid to Diagnosis." *Journal of Bone and Joint Surgery.* 52-B, p. 732. 1970.

51. *See* note 49.

52. Sulek, C. et al. "Cerebral Microembolism Diagnosed by Transcranial Doppler During Total Knee Arthroplasty." *Anesthesiology.* 91(3), p. 672. 1999.

53. Watson, A. "Genesis of Fat Emboli." *J Clinical Pathology* [Suppl] (R Coll Pathol). Volume 4, p. 132. 1970.

54. *See* note 27.

55. *Id.*

56. *See* note 1 at 1063.

57. Laska, L. "Torn Medial Meniscus of Knee During Bed-to-Wheelchair Transfer of Man—$250,000 Award in Virginia." *Medical Malpractice Verdicts, Settlements, and Experts.* November 2003.

58. *See* note 4 at 357.

59. Williamson, V. *Management of Lower Extremity Fractures.* p. 93. Pitman, NJ: Anthony J. Jannetti, Inc. 1998.

Additional Reading

Browner, Jupiter, Levine, and Trafton. Skeletal Trauma: Basic Science, Management and Reconstruction. Fourth Edition. Elsevier. 2008.

Brozenec, Sally A. and Sally S. Russell. Core Curriculum for Medical Surgical Nursing. Third Edition. Pitman, NJ: Anthony J. Jannetti, Inc. 2004.

Canaley, Terry. Campbells Operative Orthopaedics. Tenth Edition. Mosby. 2003.

DePalma's The Management of Fractures and Dislocations. Third Edition. Elsevier. 1981.

Iyer, Patricia and Levin, Barbara. Nursing Malpractice. Lawyers & Judges Publishing Company, Inc. 2007

Kurkowski, Christina M. Orthopaedic Operating Room Manual. Pitman, NJ: Anthony J. Jannetti, Inc. 2003.

NAON. Core Curriculum for Orthopaedic Nursing. Sixth Edition, Pearson Custom Publishing. 2007

http://www.cdc.gov/nccdphp/arthritis/index.htm Center for Disease Control.

Chapter 18

Pain Assessment and Management

Yvonne D'Arcy, MS, RN, CRNP, CNS

18.1 Introduction
A. Issues Related to Chronic Pain

Persistent or chronic pain is defined as pain that lasts beyond the normal healing period, usually beyond three to six months.[1] It has become such a national issue that the United States Congress has created the national Decade of Pain Control and Research to highlight issues related to pain management. In the United States today, there are 85 million Americans with pain and only 6,000 pain specialists to meet the needs of both patients and other healthcare professionals seeking help with these patients. This gross disproportion of need versus ability to meet patient expectations has created a situation of crisis proportions.

Chronic or persistent pain impairs everyday living in areas such as sleep, concentration, social activities, and full work productivity. There is a dramatic increase in the ability to perform these activities if pain is well controlled and a decrease when it is not controlled.[2] Loss of productive time for patients experiencing chronic pain can cost up to $60 billion, including the reduced work performance that patients with chronic pain have when their pain is not well controlled.[3] An issue that is not often discussed is the lack of self-esteem and the depression that affects chronic pain patients. When chronic pain is not well controlled, approximately 56 percent of patients are irritable, 40 percent feel depressed and 15 to 20 percent feel worthless and unable to cope.[4] Overall, one out of eight individuals in the United States loses productive time from work related to pain.[5]

TIP: The most common reason a patient comes to see a healthcare provider is pain. The cause may be an acute musculoskeletal injury, diabetic neuropathy, migraine headache, abdominal pain, or osteoarthritic pain. No matter what the cause, patients hope that the healthcare provider will have a solution to the condition that is limiting productive time and affecting their quality of life.

B. Acute Pain

Acute pain is short in duration and usually has an identified cause, such as trauma, from which the patient expects to recover.[6] For most hospitalized patients pain is common. In a survey, ninety-nine out of one hundred patients reported pain, and approximately 33 percent rated their pain in the moderate to severe range.[7] Some conditions such as sickle cell or migraine headache pain have a cyclic presentation with periodic exacerbations of acute pain.

Pain causes changes in the nervous system.[8] With continued pain impulses, the body activates specialized pain facilitators and neurons that process pain impulses faster.[9] By treating acute pain adequately the activation of these pain facilitators can be minimized.

When acute pain is inadequately treated, difficult to treat chronic pain conditions can develop. This may include reflex sympathetic dystrophy (RSD), more commonly called complex regional pain syndrome (CRPS). To treat these conditions a multimodal approach using both pharmacological and non-pharmacological methods is needed.[10] The pain and suffering that patients with this syndrome endure is difficult to measure; additionally the emotional and financial consequences are severe. The current goal in healthcare today is to treat acute pain aggressively to avoid the creation of chronic conditions and to limit the effect of pain on the individual.

C. Differences Between Acute and Chronic Pain

Acute pain is brief pain from which a patient knows he will recover no matter how severe the intensity of pain being experienced. Chronic pain, however, becomes a trait, and the experience is incorporated into the patient's being.

TIP: Depression is more common with chronic pain, whereas anxiety is more common with acute pain. These two types are very different and have very different consequences for patients.

One misconception among healthcare providers is that all pain is the same. Nothing could be further from the truth. Patients with chronic or persistent pain may not appear to be in as much pain as they are reporting when they present to a healthcare setting. Patients with acute pain often present with grimacing, moaning, or protecting the injured area, while chronic pain patients may present with no overt signs of pain, yet report high pain intensity scores. Acute pain is also tied to injury, trauma, or post-surgical pain. The cause is readily apparent. Chronic pain, however, may be present with no detectable source of pain on scans or x-rays. This does not mean that the patient does not have pain from a source such as soft tissue damage that is not detectable on scans. Patients who present to healthcare providers with this type of chronic pain run the risk of having their complaints of pain disbelieved and minimized, leading to further decreases in self-esteem.

Patients with acute pain may have a short period of recovery time and then be able to return to work. Chronic pain patients, on the other hand, experience life-changing pain and may never be able to return to work. People with migraine headache or sickle cell anemia may have flares or acute periods of pain when a migraine headache or sickle cell crisis occurs. This cyclic pain can create the same type of pain sensitization as continuous chronic pain. The effect on the ability to work may be similar with both types of chronic pain. Patients who are absent from work repeatedly for chronic pain conditions, either continuous or cyclic, run the risk of losing jobs and using all of the allotted vacation time for treatment of their pain. Because of the effect chronic pain has on work performance it can cause financial ruin and bankruptcy if it is allowed to remain untreated.

18.2 National Guidelines for Pain Management
A. The Joint Commission (TJC)

Because of the severe implications of chronic pain and the need for adequate treatment of pain in general, The Joint Commission (TJC), the body which accredits a variety of healthcare organizations, developed pain management guidelines which state that all patients should have their pain adequately assessed and treated. These national guidelines have created a national standard for pain management that affects all types of healthcare practices. TJC guidelines further state that pain must be documented at regular intervals and that pain should be reassessed after pain medication to measure efficacy. Each institution should have an interdisciplinary group of practitioners such as nursing, pharmacy, rehabilitation services medical staff, risk management, and quality assurance that oversees that development of the pain management process and pain management outcomes. This group is also responsible for ensuring that the institution has a policy that determines pain management practice and complies with TJC pain management guidelines. Figure 18.1 is an example of such a policy. These documents can be obtained through discovery.

South Miami Hospital

BAPTIST HEALTH

IP No.: 2320

Interdepartmental

SUBMITTED BY: _____

SMH Pain Committee
Chairperson's Signature

APPROVED BY:
Name:
Department: VP of Patient Services

EFFECTIVE DATE: 10/96

REVIEW DATE(S): 8/99, 3/01

REVISION DATE(S): 9/99, 7/01, 7/02, 5/04, 2/05

APPROVED BY: _____
CPC Committee

APPROVED BY: _____
IP Committee

SUBJECT: PAIN MANAGEMENT

POLICY STATEMENT:

To provide an environment, which supports satisfactory pain control for all patients, and to provide adequate resources for the staff to assess and manage pain.

PROCEDURES FOR IMPLEMENTATION:

SUPPORTING STRUCTURE

- An interdisciplinary pain committee meets regularly to discuss ways to improve pain management and to monitor progress. This committee develops and/or reviews pain-related policies, guidelines, standards of care, educational materials, and pain-related data.
- The hospital's commitment to pain management is to be included in any patient rights materials published by the hospital.

STAFF EDUCATION

- Education about basic pain assessment and management is to be included in all nursing orientations and new graduate courses.
- Education about common myths associated with pain and specific pain-related information as it relates to the role of the nursing assistant is to be included in orientation programs.
- Inservices about pain are to be conducted as requested by non-nursing departments such as physical therapy and respiratory therapy.
- Basic pain courses are to be held regularly.
- Inservices on pain-related topics are encouraged.

Page 1 of 4

Figure 18.1 *Pain management policy. (Reprinted with permission of South Miami Hospital.)*

- Nurses are encouraged to take additional courses in order to become Pain Resource Nurses for their units.
- Pain-related reference tools and materials are to be available on each nursing unit, emergency departments, pre-and post-operative areas and outpatient departments.

PATIENT EDUCATION

- The *Patient Pain Tips* sheet is to be given to all adult patients.
- Other pain related information should be given as needed.
- New or revised patient education materials should be presented in an understandable manner is appropriate to the patient's abilities, and comprehension evaluated.
- Patients are to be considered partners in their care; therefore education is two-sided. The patient's opinion about how to manage his/her pain should be considered in the assessment and management of pain.

PAIN ASSESSMENT

- Pain assessment is primarily a medical and nursing responsibility; however, licensed health care professionals, such as physical therapists and respiratory therapists, while performing their therapeutic interventions, may assess for the existence of and severity of pain. All members of the health care team have a responsibility to report pertinent pain-related information to the nurse caring for the patient.
- The components of a basic pain assessment of an alert individual include: pain location(s), description/quality, intensity/severity (0-10 numerical pain rating scale or other age-specific scale), patient's pain goal using the severity scale, aggravating/relieving factors, impact pain has on quality of life (sleep, work, etc.), and assessment of the pain site. The following questions may also be helpful: why the patient believes he/she has the pain and what he/she believes would relieve the pain.
- The patient's personal, cultural, spiritual, and ethnic beliefs should be considered when assessing pain.
- The patient's report of pain is the best indicator of its existence; however patients may not be able to report pain. The following hierarchy is suggested when attempting to determine the existence and severity of pain:
    - Patient's self-report
    - Pain behaviors
        - Age-specific scales are to be used when appropriate, e.g., N-PASS (NICU), NIPS (newborns), FACES (ages 3-7)
    - Reports from those close to patient
    - Physiologic measures
        - Are the least sensitive measures.
        - Are usually absent in chronic pain.
- Pain shall be assessed, documented and addressed:
    - On admission
    - After any painful procedure or event
    - At each new report of pain

Figure 18.1 *Pain management policy. (Reprinted with permission of South Miami Hospital.) (continued)*

IP No.: 2320
Interdepartmental

- At each report of inadequate pain control.
- REASSESSMENT of the same pain should include determination of severity, assessment of pain site, and patient's satisfaction with treatment.
- FREQUENCY OF PAIN REASSESSMENT: The type and severity of pain shall determine the frequency of pain reassessment. For example, a patient with acute chest pain should be reevaluated every few minutes; whereas a patient with low level arthritis pain requires less frequent reassessments. Documentation of the reassessment of patients with well-controlled pain should be at least every twelve hours or more often as determined by the nurse or physician.

PAIN MANAGEMENT

- See the *Pain Reference Tools* for guidelines on range orders and for other pain-related information.
- Range orders for analgesics: PRN range orders for opioids (e.g., morphine 2-8 mg IV q 2 h PRN pain) are commonly used to provide flexibility in dosing to meet individual patient needs because wide variability exists in patients' responses to analgesics. Range orders enable necessary and safe adjustments in doses based on individual responses.[1]
  Analgesic selection should be individualized and the following factors considered when an analgesic is prescribed: type of pain, location, severity, description, aggravating/relieving factors; patient's pain goal; presence or absence of comorbidities; anticipated duration of pain (procedural vs chronic); and concomitant use of sedating drugs.
  Choosing a dose from a range order:
  - The maximum dose within the range order should not be greater than four (4) times the minimum dose.
  - Use the <u>lower</u> dose of an opioid range order:
    - ❖ When the patient has already been receiving this dose and it has been effective.
    - ❖ When giving the first several doses of an opioid. Opioid naïve patients are the most vulnerable to the side effects of opioids. Conduct a brief pain history to learn patient's previous experiences with analgesics.
  - If the lower dose of an opioid range order is ineffective (approximately 30 minutes after IV administration and 1 hour after IM or PO administration) and the patient has no side effects, the nurse should consider administering additional opioid as long as the total amount administered does not exceed the upper dose of the range order. Notify the physician for additional orders if pain is not controlled.
  - More rapid upward titration may be indicated in acute, severe pain or in the dying patient, but this action must be specified in the physician orders and the rationale noted in the patient care record.
  - The higher dose of a range order is usually indicated if the patient has been requiring this dose to adequately manage current pain and he/she has been tolerating this dose without having side-effects.
  Determining the frequency of a range order:
  - Frequency range orders such as q 4-6 hours PRN are to be discouraged because the only time interval that matters is the first one (q 4 hours PRN); therefore, the pharmacy will enter only the first number into the patient's profile.
- The patient's personal, cultural, spiritual, and ethnic beliefs are to be considered in the plan of care.
- Non-pharmacological interventions are to be used as indicated and appropriate.

Figure 18.1 *Pain management policy. (Reprinted with permission of South Miami Hospital.) (continued)*

- Placebos are not to be administered unless a patient is enrolled in a clinical trial and has signed informed consent.
- Reports of unrelieved pain are to be reported to the attending physician for change in regimen. If this effort fails, nurses are to use the following hierarchy to advocate for the patient: Call
  - Another physician on the case
  - Pain resource nurse if available
  - Nurse manager or supervisor
  - Chief of staff for that service
  - Ethics consultation.
- Consultation with pain experts is to be encouraged should the patient have complex or unrelieved pain.
- Discharge planning is to include consideration of pain management.

DOCUMENTATION

- Documentation should include the following:
  - Pain assessment (see above),
  - Pharmacological and non-pharmacological interventions used,
  - Patient responses to pain-relieving interventions,
  - Patient education e.g., Pain Tips Sheet was given to patient,
  - Discharge teaching.

DATA COLLECTION AND MONITORING

- All patient care areas are to monitor progress by collecting data, e.g., chart audits and patient satisfaction questionnaires.

REFERENCES:

American Pain Society and the American Society for Pain Management Nursing. (2004) Consensus Statement on *The Use of 'As Needed' Range Orders for Opioid Analgesics in the Management of Acute Pain* .
2005 JCAHO Standards
American Geriatrics Society (2002). The management of persistent pain in older persons. *Journal of the American Geriatrics Society* 50 (S6), 205-224.
American Pain Society (2003). *Principles of Analgesic Use in the Treatment of Acute pain and Cancer Pain.* Skokie, IL: American Pain Society.
McCaffery, M. & Pasero, C. (1999). *Pain: Clinical Manual* (2nd Ed). St. Louis: Mosby.

Figure 18.1 Pain management policy. (Reprinted with permission of South Miami Hospital.) (continued)

Internet Resources

The American Academy of Pain Management
www.aapainmange.org

The American Academy of Pain Medicine
www.painmed.org

American Academy of Pediatrics
www.anp.org

The American Chronic Pain Association
www.theacpa.org

American Geriatric Society
www.ags.org

The American Pain Association
www.ampainsoc.org

The American Society of Pain Management Nurses
www.aspmn.org

International Association for the Study of Pain
www.halcyon.com/iasp

Joint Commission
www.jointcommission.org

National Cancer Institute (NCI) for National Cancer Coalition Network (NCCN) guidelines
www.nccn.org

National Headache Foundation
www.headaches.org

Oncology Nurses Society
www.ons.org

Figure 18.2

Another area of the TJC pain management guidelines indicates that barriers to pain management must be assessed. This includes linguistic barriers, limitations on comprehension such as illiterate patients, and those who are hearing or visually impaired. A method that is commonly used to deal with these impediments to pain assessment is the use of translation telephones. Both the patient and the caregiver can speak and have the phone translators repeat the informa-

tion in a second language. It is also important for the facility to provide sign language interpreters for deaf patients. When reviewing pain management documentation, it is essential to note whether or not this assessment for barriers was done and plans were developed to overcome the barriers.

With the development of these national guidelines for pain management, consumers have also become more aware of what they can expect when they have pain. They can search the Internet to see what the best method of pain relief is for their particular condition. When faced with information from a website, it is important to review the source of the information to make sure it is clinically relevant and taken from medically reliable sources. The websites listed in Figure 18.2 provide medically reliable information.

The original JC pain management guidelines were published in 1999. In 2003, the TJC pain management guidelines were revised and patient safety was incorporated into JC national guidelines. This means that institutions must maintain good medication safety practices to include control of opioid medications and record the medications being used correctly so there is no drug diversion. Medication records must have allergies to medications clearly listed so that patients are not given a medication to which they had a true allergic reaction, such as anaphylaxis, in the past.

Each institution also must ensure that abbreviations used for orders are standardized and that look-alike drugs such as morphine sulfate MS04 and magnesium sulfate MGS04 are correctly identified. This means that morphine sulfate must be written out in its entirety so it cannot be confused with magnesium sulfate. Other examples of questionable abbreviations are "qd" to be written as every day, and mcg and mgs, micrograms and milligrams, and "u" for units as used for insulin orders.

TIP: Each institution has a set of "do not use" (or some other designation) abbreviations. Documentation compliance is measured by chart review with the results kept as an ongoing database.

Another aspect of patient safety related to medications is the use of pumps to deliver medication and intravenous fluids. Each institution should have guidelines for pump usage and maintenance. Pumps that are used to deliver pain medication and intravenous fluids such as saline should have a mechanism that does not allow for free flow of medications. To obtain information about the type of pump and what safety mechanisms each machine has, it is necessary to review the purchase information, maintenance records, and maintenance logs from the clinical or biomedical engineering department.

Defense attorneys should have access to all orders and records that include medications and nursing documentation. The TJC institutional review process focuses on compliance with the policies as they are written for the institutions. Defense attorneys should request the policies and procedures along with information on pumps and maintenance if needed so that it is possible to determine if the staff caring for the patient correctly documented and monitored medication and machines according to the guidelines set out in individual policies. Attorneys can make good use of pain management documentation and biomedical records to prove that the institution is in compliance with its policies and TJC pain management guidelines. Table 18.1 shows some of the dangerous abbreviations.

B. Additional Pain Management Guidelines

A higher level of interest and compliance with national standards was fostered in professional organizations with the publication of TJC pain management guidelines. This ongoing interest highlighted the need for specialized pain management standards for specific populations and difficult-to-treat pain conditions.

The American Pain Society (APS) has taken over the original work done by the AHCPR in 1992 and 1994 when the *Acute Pain and Cancer Pain* guidelines were written by that organization. The more recent pain management guidelines by the APS are a revision of the *Principles of Analgesic Use in the Treatment of Acute Pain and Cancer Pain*, *Sickle Cell Pain Management* guideline, and *Arthritis Pain Management* guideline. Organizations that have guidelines for their specific populations include the American Geriatric Society (AGS), National Cancer Institute (NCCN), American Academy of Pediatrics, and the American Academy of Pain Medicine (AAPM). The American Society of Addiction Medicine (ASAM) deals with issues related to treating patients who have addictive disease yet need treatment for pain. A position paper on treating patients with addictive disease is available on the APS website and is endorsed by the APS, AAPM, and ASAM.

TIP: Plaintiffs' and defense attorneys, paralegals, and medical record professionals should be able to access these specialized guidelines by using each organization's website for the most current version of the guidelines. By reviewing these practice guidelines, legal professionals should have a good basis for understanding what is expected in the treatment of individuals within each of these specialized groups.

18.3 Elements of Pain Assessment

One of the most difficult aspects of pain assessment is the subjectivity of the pain report. There is no doubt that asking a patient to discuss pain and rate the pain intensity is the best method of assessing pain; however, the meaning of the pain is difficult to translate from patient to healthcare provider. Self report is still considered to be the best standard for pain assessment.[11] "Pain is what the patient says it is," and neither behavior nor vital signs can substitute for self report.[12] Patients expect that when they tell healthcare providers about their pain and rate the pain using a standard pain assessment scale, that they are believed. They expect the healthcare provider to try to determine the best method for pain relief given the totality of the patient's presentation. They do not expect that continued high pain ratings will be seen by healthcare professionals as "drug seeking" or "addiction," nor do they expect that such terms will be documented in their charts. Medical record specialists, lawyers, legal nurse consultants, and paralegals reviewing progress and nursing notes in patients' charts should be aware that such terms are rarely if ever justified. It is incumbent on healthcare providers to treat each patient's report of pain with respect and attempt to relieve the pain using techniques appropriate for the condition.

Since assessment is the key to adequate pain control, it is important that healthcare and legal professionals understand the elements of pain assessment. These include but are not limited to

- location,
- intensity,
- duration,
- description,
- aggravating or alleviating factors, and
- functional impairment including sleep and activity.

Baseline assessment data should be recorded upon the patient's admission to the hospital. Figure 18.3 provides an example of the first page of an admission database. The central section of the form provides a section to describe the nature of the pain. A section on page two of this form offers a place to document the patient's pain history. (Figure 18.4)

Table 18.1

Suburban Hospital
12 Dangerous Medical Abbreviations

Do Not Use

Dangerous Abbreviation/ Dose Expression	Intended Meaning	Misinterpretation	Correction
Zero after decimal point (1.0)	1 mg	Misread as 10 mg if the decimal point is not seen	Do not use terminal zeros for doses expressed in whole numbers.
No zero before decimal dose (.5 mg)	0.5 mg	Misread as 5 mg	Always use a zero before a decimal when the dose is less than a whole number.
U or u	Unit	Read as a zero (o) or a four (4) causing a 10-fold overdose or greater. (4 U seen as 40 or 4u seen as 44).	Unit has no acceptable abbreviation. Write "unit"
IU	International Unit	Mistaken as IV (intravenous) or 10 (ten)	Write "international unit"
µg	Microgram	Mistaken for "mg" when handwritten	Use mcg or write "microgram"
MSO4	Morphine sulfate	Mistaken for magnesium sulfate	Write "morphine sulfate"
MgSO4	Magnesium sulfate	Mistaken for morphine sulfate	Write "magnesium sulfate"
MS		Could mean morphine sulfate or magnesium sulfate.	Write out the name of the drug intended.
Q.D.	Once Daily	Mistaken for QOD	Write "daily"
Q.O.D	Every other day	Mistaken for QD; the period after the Q can be mistaken for an "I" and the O can be mistaken for an "I".	Write "every other day"
A.S., A.D., A.U. and O.S.; O.D.; O.U.	Latin for left, right or both ears. Latin for left, right or both eyes	Mistaken for each other (e.g. AS for OS; AD for OD; AU for OU)	Write "left ear," "right ear" or "both ears." And "left eye," "right eye" or "both eyes."

Shaded cells are the new abbreviations (per JCAHO's minimal list), Update effective January 2004

SUBURBAN HOSPITAL
PATIENT DATABASE

☐ Major   ☐ Mend   ☐ Trauma

ED Triage RN*†

PATIENT PLATE

Name   DOB / Age

Date	Time

Admitted from: _____ Via: _____ Accompanied by:

Medication Allergies	☐ NKDA		Reaction	Other Allergies ☐ None	Reaction
				☐ Latex/Adhesive, If yes refer to latex policy	
				☐ Dyes/Contrast/Metals	
				☐ Food (List)	

T Oral/Tympanic/R	P	R	BP	O2 Sat/O2	HT. WT. Lb/Kg ☐ Measured ☐ Stated	Fingerstick Glucose: ☐ NA	Tetanus: ☐ < 5 years ☐ > 5 years ☐ Unsure ☐ NA LMP: ___ ☐ Denies Pregnancy

Chief Complaint or History of Present Illness _____

PMD: Referred by:

ED Triage Level: ☐ Emergent (I)   ☐ Urgent (II)   ☐ Non-urgent (III)   **Triage Protocols:**   ☐ Yes   ☐ No

Past Medical History: Surgical History: Date:

Medications	Dose	Frequency	Last Dose	Meds/Vitamins/OTC/Herbals	Dose	Frequency	Last Dose

Pain Assessment on Admission Score _____ on ☐ Numeric 0-10 Scale   ☐ Faces Scale   ☐ Behavioral Scale

Location _____   Duration _____

Quality   ☐ Dull   ☐ Ache   ☐ Sharp   ☐ Tight   ☐ Intermittent   ☐ Constant   ☐ Radiating   ☐ Other

*Better with _____   Worse with _____

VISION:
☐ No Problem
☐ Glasses/Lenses
☐ Cataracts
☐ Glaucoma
☐ Impaired

HEARING:
☐ No Problem
☐ Hearing Impaired
☐ Hearing Aid
☐ R ☐ L

SPEECH:
☐ No Problem
☐ Limitations
☐ Language
☐ Interpreter

DENTITION:
☐ No Problem
☐ Upper   Full-Partial
☐ Lower   Full-Partial
☐ Bridges/Crowns
☐ Capped/Loose Teeth

DISCHARGE PLANNING:
Do you live in a ☐ NH*   ☐ Assisted Living*   ☐ Group Home*
☐ Shelter*   ☐ Detention Center*   ☐ Homeless*   ☐ NA
Do you anticipate changes to your prior living arrangements? ☐ Yes* ☐ No
Are you currently receiving home care services? ☐ Yes* ☐ No
If Yes or asterisk, Social Services Consulted ☐

PSYCHO-SOCIAL / FUNCTIONAL RISK ASSESSMENT:

Does the patient appear malnourished/underweight?   ☐ Yes ☐ No ☐ If yes, consult PMD or ☐ Dietary Consult

In the past year, has anyone threatened or physically harmed you in any way?   ☐ Yes ☐ No ☐ If yes, refer to Crisis (CIS) or ☐ Info given

Has the patient (if over 65) received the pneumococcal vaccine?   ☐ Yes ☐ No ☐ If no, refer to PMD

Patient describes recent changes in mobility/ADLs/communication/swallowing ability?   ☐ Yes ☐ No ☐ If yes, refer to PMD or ☐ PM & R Referral

A.   Do you smoke?   ☐ Yes ☐ No   ___ Pk per day x ___ years Date Quit ___
B.   Do you drink alcohol?   ☐ Yes ☐ No   Amount ___ Frequency ___ Last Drink ___
C.   Do you use other substances?   ☐ Yes ☐ No   Amount ___ Frequency ___ Last Use ___
ED   Has the patient had an unexplained persistent productive cough lasting longer than 3 weeks?   ☐ Yes ☐ No ☐ If yes, refer to ID

SIGNATURE (initial any changes)	TITLE	DATE	TIME	PRINTED
SIGNATURE (initial any changes)	TITLE	DATE	TIME	PRINTED
SIGNATURE (initial any changes)	TITLE	DATE	TIME	PRINTED

SUBURBAN HOSPITAL
Healthcare System
8600 Old Georgetown Road
Bethesda, Maryland 20814
PATIENT DATABASE
FORM 1-1097 (03/03)

Figure 18.3 Admission database with a section to document the nature of pain. (Courtesy of Suburban Hospital, Bethesda, MD.)

SUBURBAN HOSPITAL
PATIENT DATABASE/ASSESSMENT

Part Two
Page 2 of 2

✓ Denotes YES   PATIENT PLATE

MUSCULOSKELETAL HISTORY ☐ Denies current or prior problem	MUSCULOSKELETAL ASSESSMENT:
☐ Arthritis _____ ☐ Joint Replacement/Prosthesis _____ ☐ Back/Neck Problems _____ ☐ Muscular Dystrophy _____ ☐ Fracture _____ ☐ Amputation _____ COMMENTS: _____	☐ Outpatient NA ☐ Paralysis ☐ Equal ROM/Strength ☐ Deformity PROBLEM/PLAN OF CARE _____

HEMATOLOGY/ONCOLOGY HISTORY   ☐ Denies current or prior problem

☐ Bleeding Disorder _____
☐ Anemia _____
☐ Blood Product Transfusion _____   Reaction _____
☐ Cancer _____
☐ Immune Deficiency _____   ☐ Designated Donor Blood
COMMENTS _____

PROBLEM/PLAN OF CARE _____

VASCULAR DEVICE   ☐ NA   Location: _____
Site(s) without signs or symptoms of infection, inflammation, infiltration or hematoma.   Type: _____
Device is patent (all lumens) & intact   Site Appearance: _____

Signature/Title (initial any changes)	Date/Time
Signature/Title (initial any changes)	Date/Time

FOR INPATIENT USE ONLY

NUTRITIONAL SCREENING: (1 or more yes(s) = initiate dietary consult in computer)

Pressure Ulcer	☐ Yes ☐ No	Patient requests diet education	☐ Yes ☐ No		
Tube Feed/TPN/PPN	☐ Yes ☐ No	> 75 years of age and having surgery	☐ Yes ☐ No		
Appetite loss > 5 days	☐ Yes ☐ No	Pregnant/Breastfeeding and requests			
Unintentional weight loss	☐ Yes ☐ No	additional information	☐ Yes ☐ No		
		Newly diagnosed DM or dialysis patient	☐ Yes ☐ No		

PSYCHO-SOCIAL RISK ASSESSMENT:

• Do you drink alcohol?
• Use Other Substances? (Questions answered on page 1, if yes, then complete 1-4) or ☐ NA
1. Have you ever felt you ought to Cut down on your drinking/drug use?   ☐ Yes ☐ No
2. Have people Annoyed you by criticizing your drinking/drug use?   ☐ Yes ☐ No
3. Have you ever felt bad or Guilty about your drinking or drug use?   ☐ Yes ☐ No
4. Have you Ever taken a drink or used a drug first thing in the
   morning to steady your nerves or get rid of a hangover?   ☐ Yes ☐ No
Scoring two "YES" answers contact Crisis Intervention Services (CIS) by computer consult or
at extension 3027.

1. Have you on more than one occasion during the last few weeks felt anxious, frightened, uncomfortable or uneasy, in situations where most people would not feel that way?   ☐ Yes ☐ No

2. Have you been consistently depressed or down, most of the day, nearly every day for the past two weeks?   ☐ Yes ☐ No

Scoring one "Yes" answer on questions 1 or 2 contact Crisis Intervention Services (CIS) by computer consult or at extension 3027.

FALL-RISK ASSESSMENT: ☐ Patient does not meet criteria

☐ Place on Safety Protocol (only one check needed)
  ☐ Pronounced Decrease in Strength/Mobility
  ☐ Changes in Mental Status (i.e. confusion)
  ☐ History of Falls in the Last Six Months

☐ Place on Safety Protocol (two checks needed)
  ☐ Age Over 70 Years   ☐ Orthostatic Hypotension
  ☐ Urinary Frequency or Urgency   ☐ Visual Deficit
  ☐ First 48 hours on Diuretics, Laxatives, Tranquilizers, Anti-Anxiety Meds
  ☐ Narcotics/Barbiturates, Hypnotics, Anti-Psychotics, Anti-Depressants

PAIN HISTORY: Current Pain Score: _____
Have you ever had difficulties with pain management in the past?   ☐ Yes ☐ No
Have you had > 5 on the pain scale in the last 24 hours?   ☐ Yes ☐ No
If yes, consult the Pain Specialist at x3765 or beeper 576 or consult in computer.

ADVANCE DIRECTIVES:

☐ Yes ☐ No   ☐ Inquiry deferred due to medical condition
If yes, ☐ Living Will ☐ Power of Attorney for Health Care
Copy of Advance Directive on chart?   ☐ Yes ☐ No
If copy not available name of Agent/Relationship: _____

Family requested to provide copy?   ☐ Yes ☐ No
Copy from previous medical record still current? ☐ Yes ☐ No
If no, ☐ Printed information offered to patient
☐ Patient wishes assistance in completing Advance Directive

Signature/Title (initial any changes)	Date/Time

SUBURBAN HOSPITAL
Healthcare System
8600 Old Georgetown Road
Bethesda, Maryland 20814
PATIENT DATABASE/ASSESSMENT
FORM 1-1095 (03/03)

Figure 18.4 *Admission database with a section to document the pain history. (Courtesy of Suburban Hospital, Bethesda, MD.)*

TJC states that patients should be involved in the plan for treating their pain. Patient involvement is demonstrated by indicating a pain goal for the patient and documenting that the patient is in agreement with the goal. For patients with chronic or persistent pain, each sequential pain assessment should indicate progress towards the goal if the plan for treatment is effective. TJC pain management guidelines indicate that pain should not be a limitation to progress in the rehabilitation setting. This type of pain goal approach is very useful for patients who are being seen by physical therapists, when meeting a pain goal indicates ability to function in the rehabilitation process.[13] Legal specialists should look for the pain goal on the intake form for the rehabilitation center or physical therapy department and the subsequent ongoing documentation at each visit, or at least daily for inpatients.

Acute pain assessment should have all the elements of the pain assessment, but subsequent assessment may consist only of intensity scores. An example of this type of process occurs when a patient is being admitted for surgery. The initial intake form will have a complete pain assessment, while in the postoperative unit, pain ratings may focus on pain intensity. The source, location, and radiation of the pain are fairly evident as the surgical site, but the caregiver must verify this. A documentation entry should be made to address the additional pain complaint should the pain be located in another area. Lawyers, paralegals, legal nurse consultants, and medical records specialists should examine the admitting record to assure that the pain documentation is entered. All current pain medications should also be listed on this form. Subsequent pain ratings will be entered on forms such as daily flow sheets from nursing units using the scheduled assessment regimen described in the institution policy. For patients who cannot self report pain, such as nonverbal Alzheimer's patients, information about pain should be obtained from family members, nursing home records, and the use of a behavioral pain scale.

Chronic or persistent pain patients require a more extensive form of pain assessment. There are specific tools for chronic pain patients that are commonly used in pain clinics. These pain assessment tools include sections on coping, family relationships, spirituality, and psychological elements. These tools are commonly used in chronic pain treatment settings. When assessing a patient with chronic pain, it is helpful to have the family or significant other included in the pain assessment because the chronic pain patients may not be aware of how the continued pain is affecting relationships. Husbands and wives of chronic pain patients may not tell the spouse how angry, frustrated, or depressed they are by the continued effect of chronic pain

on home life, finances, or loss of sexual companionship. Children may not share the loss they feel when a parent with chronic pain is unable to participate in school activities in the same way their classmates' parents can. Unless the pain assessment addresses these issues and allows an opportunity to share these feelings, important information will be missed. Since depression is common, antidepressants such as Prozac, Effexor, or nortryptyline are often used to help both patients and family members with coping, but these may also lower libido. Legal professionals should make sure that questioning of the plaintiff (patient in pain) covers not only the location of the pain but documents the effect of the pain on the patient's life.

A. Location

There are several methods for having patients describe the location of pain. The usual method of determining the location is to ask the patient where the pain is and have her point to the painful area using one finger. Gentle palpation by the healthcare practitioner can also be used to determine the area that is painful. Using a body diagram which allows the patient to mark the painful area is a helpful method of locating pain. If the patient marks a painful area in the low back and indicates that it goes down the leg this could be an indication of a radicular pain caused by a ruptured disc. Attorneys should use these diagrams and ask questions about what types of tests were ordered to help diagnose the pain and obtain these results as well.

Some practitioners will have the patients use a diagram to color in the area of pain and include a color code with red, for example, being severe pain. At the same time, radiation of the pain may be determined by asking the patient if the pain extends beyond the painful area or if the pain moves to another area with activity (e.g., pain that radiates down a leg when the patient stands).

B. Intensity

The zero to ten pain intensity scale is the most common method of determining pain intensity or severity. This scale is an eleven-point Likert-type format with a zero through ten scale, with zero being no pain and ten being the worst pain possible. Pain scales may be documented on a flow sheet. For example, Figure 18.5 is an example of a form used in a medical surgical setting. The pain assessment score, quality, frequency, location, and duration are to be documented. The patient may be asked to rate the present pain, the worst it got and the best it got. These three descriptors are commonly used in physical therapy settings. (Figure 18.6) A Visual Analog Scale (VAS) form is used in both research and clinical settings. In research settings, the patient is asked to mark on

MEDICAL/SURGICAL FLOWSHEET
Page 2 of 4

Date:					PATIENT PLATE	
Assess at least every 8 hours:	TIME:					
∅ = Not Assessed WNL						
Document abnormal findings	INIT.					
NEUROLOGICAL ASSESSMENT: Pt. alert and oriented to person, place and time. Behavior appropriate to age and situation. Follows verbal commands. Pupils equal and reactive to light. Active ROM of all extremities with symmetry of strength. Verbalization clear and understandable. Sensation present in all extremities without paresthesia, numbness or tremors. Swallowing without coughing or choking on liquids or solids unless NPO. Document sleep patterns every 24 hours.						
CARDIOVASCULAR ASSESSMENT: Regular apical pulse. Capillary refill < 3 seconds. Peripheral pulses are present in all extremities. No edema. No calf tenderness.						
RESPIRATORY ASSESSMENT: Pt. has spontaneous respirations 12-20 minute at rest, quiet and regular. Breath sounds clear and audible in all lobes bilaterally. Absence of cough or sputum. Document oxygen therapies (i.e., Nebs, CPPD, etc.)						
MUSCULOSKELETAL ASSESSMENT: Active ROM in all joints with symmetry of strength. Absence of joint swelling and tenderness.						
INTEGUMENTARY ASSESSMENT: Skin color normal for patient's ethnic group. Skin warm, dry and intact. Mucous membranes moist. No evidence of erythema. Document if Pressure Ulcer Progress Sheet in use. ☐ Initiated ☐ Maintained						
GENITOURINARY ASSESSMENT: Urine output is quantity sufficient ≥ 30cc/hr if on I & O. Document color and consistency. No odor present. Continent without frequency, urgency or burning on urination. No bladder distention. No vaginal or ureteral discharge. Document Foley, Voided, HNV, Ostomy, etc.						
GASTROINTESTINAL ASSESSMENT: Bowel sounds active. Abdomen soft, non-distended and without pain on palpation. Tolerating PO intake without nausea and/or vomiting. Document Ostomy. Date of last BM: _____						
PAIN ASSESSMENT: Score pain on a scale of 0 (No Pain) to 10 (Worst Pain) / 10. Reassess and document pain intensity, quality, frequency, location and duration on flowsheet.						
VASCULAR DEVICE: ☐ None If yes, Assess Q2° Document on IVT Record.						
A-V GRAFT: Palpable bruit or thrill. No ecchymosis or edema.						

Figure 18.5 *Medical surgical nursing flow sheet with area to document the pain assessment. (Courtesy of Suburban Hospital, Bethesda, MD.)*

SUBURBAN HOSPITAL   Name: _____
OUTPATIENT PHYSICAL THERAPY   MR #: _____
SPINE EVALUATION

Date of Evaluation: _____   Referring MD: _____
Date of Onset: _____   Diagnosis: _____
Treatment Order: _____

SUBJECTIVE:
Chief Complaint/Hx of injury: ☐ gradual   ☐ traumatic   ☐ MVA   if yes, date: _____
_____

Patient Goal: _____
Pertinent Past Medical History: _____

Meds: _____
Prior PT/Treatment/Studies: _____
Pain: present: 0 1 2 3 4 5 6 7 8 9 10   worst: 0 1 2 3 4 5 6 7 8 9 10   best: 0 1 2 3 4 5 6 7 8 9 10
    Description: _____
    ↑d with: _____   ↓d with: _____
Prior Level of Function: _____
Current Level of Function: _____

OBJECTIVE:
Inspection/Observation: _____
Posture:

C/S curve ☐ ↑d ☐ ↓d ☐ normal	ASIS position ☐ ↑d L / R ☐ symmetrical
T/S curve ☐ ↑d ☐ ↓d ☐ normal	PSIS position ☐ ↑d L / R ☐ symmetrical
L/S curve ☐ ↑d ☐ ↓d ☐ normal	Iliac crest height ☐ ↑d L / R ☐ symmetrical

Head position   ☐ neutral   ☐ flexed   ☐ extended   ☐ rotated L / R   ☐ lateral flexed L / R
Scapula   ☐ elevated L / R   ☐ depressed L / R   ☐ protracted L / R   ☐ winging L / R   ☐ normal
Shoulder   ☐ elevated L / R   ☐ depressed L / R   ☐ forward L / R   ☐ normal
UQ/LQ screen: _____

ROM/MMT

MOTION/MUSCLE TESTED	AROM L	AROM R	MMT L	MMT R	COMMENTS

Neuro Signs: _____
DTR : ☐ intact to testing   ☐ deficit noted at: _____
Sensation: ☐ intact to testing   ☐ deficit noted at: _____

Figure 18.6 *Physical therapy form with section to record pain assessment. (Courtesy of Suburban Hospital, Bethesda, MD.)*

a 100-centimeter line where the pain is located. The farther the patient marks the line to the right, the greater the intensity of pain. In clinical settings the most common method for rating pain intensity is to ask the patient to give a number that best describes the pain; one to three being mild pain, four to six being moderate pain, and seven to ten being severe pain. This intensity scale is used for reassessment after pain medication to indicate how effective the pain medication is for relieving the patient's pain.

Research indicates that elderly patients do best with a pain scale that is vertical, similar to a thermometer that has the zero pain rating at the bottom and the ten pain rating at the top. It is felt that the elderly patient conceptualizes the meaning of the rating scale best when it moves from bottom to top.[14,15]

C. Duration

To determine duration of pain the healthcare practitioner can ask the patient questions such as "Do you remember when the pain first started?" and "How long does the pain last?" It is an important part of the pain assessment to determine when the pain started and how long it has lasted. By asking about duration it is possible to see if pain has been allowed to remain untreated for a long period of time. Pain that has been untreated will be more difficult to reduce in intensity.

TIP: For legal professionals it is important to determine by chart review what the pain levels were at the diagnosis of the pain and how long they remained elevated. Pain assessment should take place regularly, and interventions should be aimed at safely reducing the pain in the shortest period possible.

D. Description

A patient describing the pain provides a more individual picture of the pain. This is one of the best ways a patient can convey the experience of pain to the healthcare provider. The patient's chart should contain the actual words the patient uses to describe the pain. It is an extremely powerful element of the pain assessment when the patient describes the pain like "a knitting needle stuck in the leg" or "burning fire across my chest." The descriptors a patient uses can be an indication of what type of pain the patient is experiencing and help to differentiate whether it is musculoskeletal or neuropathic. Musculoskeletal pain is often described as dull or achy while neuropathic pain is best described as pins and needles, numbness, burning, or tingling. A list of common descriptors that patients use to describe pain can be found in multidimensional pain instruments used to assess chronic pain.

The importance of this element in the pain assessment should not be overlooked by healthcare professionals. If a patient gives clear indicators that the pain may be neuropathic, it will require the addition of medications such as Neurontin (gabapentin) or an antidepressant to treat that type of pain. Nerve blocks provided through the services of an anesthesia pain clinic are additional neuropathic treatment modalities. Careful analysis of the verbal descriptors used by a patient may be the key to determining if the best combination of treatment options was offered the patient.

E. Aggravating or Alleviating Factors

When asking a patient what makes the pain better or worse, the healthcare provider should inquire about and document the use of the over-the-counter or homeopathic remedies a patient is taking. Most patients will attempt pain relief using something they have at home. Some of these simple actions are applying heat or cold, topicals such as Ben-Gay, or herbal remedies such as vitamin supplements. A healthcare provider's non-judgmental approach when asking the patient about these items allows the patient to feel comfortable enough to share information. This is especially important when herbal, homeopathic, or nutritional supplements are being taken since in some cases there is the possibility of a drug interaction.

F. Functional Impairment

One of the best measures of pain and pain relief in chronic pain patients is impairment of functional activity. If pain is not well controlled they will lose the ability to maintain any semblance of normal activity in their lives. Pain is dynamic. It usually increases with activity. However, for some chronic pain patients it may increase with sitting. Many chronic patients have not received the pain control they need, and therefore they may suffer from deconditioning which further decreases the level of activity they can tolerate. Some patients use a continuous pain medication such as MS Contin (extended release morphine) or a Duragesic patch with additional medication for breakthrough pain with activity.

Since sleep can be very disturbed in chronic pain patients, they commonly suffer from fatigue, which can decrease the ability to concentrate. Many patients with arthritis cannot get comfortable for any length of time in a laying position, causing them to reposition themselves throughout the night and interrupting sleep. Adjusting doses of pain medication to allow for a dose at bedtime can help provide a better quality of sleep.

TIP: The functional impairment of chronic pain also has an economic impact. If patients cannot fully function they will lose jobs that require regular attendance. Chart entries should be reviewed to evaluate if the amount of pain medication was sufficient to improve functionality and allow the patient to sleep.

G. Case Study

Steve, age forty-two, was the driver of a motorcycle that struck a guardrail on the interstate highway at high speed while he was trying to avoid another vehicle stopped in his lane. As a result of the accident Steve sustained a fractured femur, chest trauma, and fractured ribs that required the placement of a chest tube. Although Steve has recovered from his fractured femur he is seeking help from a pain clinic for a burning pain at the site of his fractured ribs and chest tube that keeps him up all night.

Steve tells his story:

"If I had it to do all over I wouldn't have gotten on that bike. I really should have known better at my age. I just never thought anything bad would happen to me. I never even saw the guardrail coming. When I woke up in the hospital I was in the intensive care unit. I was really afraid I was going to die. My wife and children were so upset. They came to see me every day. Now they are just tired of my complaining about my pain. They all think I should be better but I don't know how to tell them about what it feels like to have this pain in my chest all the time. I feel like a blow torch is burning my chest all the time. Nothing seems to make it better and I have not had a decent night's sleep in months. My wife is getting tired of sleeping in our bed alone. I spend most of the night sitting up in a chair."

"Nobody can tell me what the pain is from. Everyone thinks the pain should be better now and they can't understand why I still have pain eight months after the accident. My boss sure does not understand. He told me I am going to have to find another job if I can't drive a truck because I still need to take pain medications. I guess I will have to file for disability if I cannot get some help at this pain clinic. None of the other doctors know what to do and the pain medication they gave me just does not do the trick. I feel like I am at the end of the line."

This case illustrates some of the issues surrounding a patient living with chronic pain. The pain has a neuropathic component judging by the descriptors the patient used. When the chest tube was inserted there may have been nerve damage or the fractured ribs could have caused some nerve damage. The patient is very depressed about his situation and he is suffering from a heavy impact on his self esteem and functionality. The patient's family seemed to be very supportive at the onset of the accident, but now they are tired of the constant pain complaints, and the family relationships are suffering as a result.

Chart review should include examination of the level of pain the patient has been reporting over the last eight months and the types of medications that were used to treat the pain. Since the pain has a neuropathic component, a neuropathic medication like Neurontin, an antidepressant, or a topical such as a Lidoderm patch should have been included in the medication regimen.

TIP: Lawyers should also explore the full aspect of the case to include loss of job and family relationships when considering what should be included in a potential lawsuit.

H. Pain Goal

Encouraging the patient to determine a pain goal gives both the patient and the healthcare professional a guide to what the patient's expectations are for pain relief. For some patients, it may be impossible to relieve all of the pain. Pain reduction may be a more realistic goal. To set a pain goal the patient is asked what level of pain he thinks is realistic. Once the pain goal is set, subsequent chart entries should reflect progress toward achieving the goal. If subsequent pain ratings are above the pain goal, the chart should reflect any possible reasons such as improved pain relief allowing the patient to participate in increased activity. Any changes in pain medications should also be documented in the patient's record.

The patient and the healthcare practitioner should agree on the pain goal. The pain rating of the patient should fall under the identified pain rating. This would be an indication of stable pain with stable doses of pain medication.

18.4 Pain Instruments

There are a variety of pain tools designed to measure pain. Some pain scales that measure just intensity are appropriate for acute pain, and some scales use a combination of pain intensity ratings, functional measures, and quality of life indicators and are appropriate for assessing chronic pain. Legal professionals should make note that the pain scale being used to assess pain is correct for the patient's pain type. Reliability and validity data are published in the original article describing the scale. Patient populations and usage parameters can also be found in the original research. Each tool being used to measure pain should be reliable and valid. In order for the pain rating to be accurate, only a pain scale designed to measure pain in the particular population that the pain instrument was developed and tested in should be used. Adult pain scales should be used only for adults, and pediatric pain scales should be used in pediatric patient populations.

For patients who do not speak English, pain scales should be provided in the language that the patient speaks, or translators should be used. The Agency for Health Care Policy and Research, AHCPR (now the Agency for Healthcare Research and Quality, AHRQ) *Acute Pain Guidelines* and the *Cancer Pain Guidelines* are available in Spanish. In *Pain: A Clinical Manual* there are selections of pain scales in a variety of languages.

There is a selection of behavioral scales that the healthcare provider can use with patients who cannot report pain in the usual fashion. Although self report is the gold standard for pain assessment, pain assessment tools such as the Checklist of Nonverbal Pain Indicators (CNPI) provide help with assessing pain in nonverbal patients.[16] This tool is a list of behaviors such as grimacing, restlessness, and moaning that indicate pain. Other pain scales such as CRIES, FACES, FLACC, and NIPS are used for children and infants. These pain scales are based on crying, oxygen saturations, and sleeplessness. A pain scale that accommodates for resistance to ventilation can be used for critically ill, intubated patients. This pain scale, the Payen Behavioral Pain Scale (PAYEN-BPS), has good correlations to standard pain ratings even when patients are receiving sedation with medications such as propofol (Diprivan). Although these pain scales can be used to detect the presence of pain, if at all possible a self report should be used.

TIP: It is also wise to remember that if the patient has a condition that is normally painful and the patient cannot self-report pain, a trial of pain medication should have been provided.

A. One-Dimensional Pain Assessment Instruments

1. Numeric Pain Intensity Scale (NPI)

The most common one-dimensional pain scale is the NPI. (Figure 18.7) As described earlier in the chapter there is no right or wrong number for rating pain on this zero to ten scale. Most often a pain rating of three is considered the pain

level where patients can participate in activity. For chronic or persistent pain patients, a higher numeric pain rating may still allow activity. No matter what number the patient reports as the pain level, that is the pain rating that should be accepted and documented in the chart or record. Regular reassessment of pain should be aimed at measuring the efficacy of pain interventions by a decrease in the rating of pain.

2. Visual Analog Scale (VAS)

The visual analog scale (Figure 18.8) is based on a 100 millimeter horizontal line with zero at the left end of the line and ten at the opposite end of the line. The patient is asked to mark on the line where her pain level is located. Although this is a simple form for a pain scale there are some drawbacks to using this scale. Visually or cognitively impaired people have difficulty using this scale. Researchers found that elderly patients had difficulty marking on the line and at times marked above or below that line rather than directly on the line.[17,18]

3. Verbal Descriptor Scale (VDS)

The VDS (Figure 18.9) uses words such as agonizing, excruciating, or uncomfortable to describe the patient's pain or rankings such as mild, moderate, or severe pain. Improvement in pain is evaluated by asking for a descriptor after a pain intervention. If pain which was ranked as severe falls to moderate or mild pain, intensity is considered to be improved and the pain intervention effective. Feldt, Ryden and Miles found a 73 percent completion rate in a group of cognitively impaired patients. Additionally some studies have shown that some adult patients actually prefer this scale.[19]

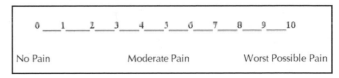

Figure 18.7 *Numeric pain intensity scale.*

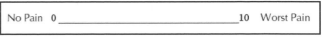

Figure 18.8 *Visual analog scale.*

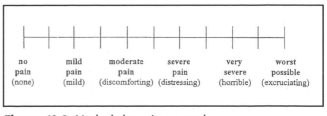

Figure 18.9 *Verbal descriptor scale.*

One of the difficulties with using the scale is that the patients being questioned must have a functional level high enough to use the words and understand their meaning. This eliminates people such as children, cognitively impaired, intubated, unresponsive, or geriatric patients who have an impaired mental functional status.

4. Combined Scale

In order to maximize the potential for using a numeric or verbal descriptor scale, there are several versions of a combined numeric and verbal descriptor scale. This can be done as a vertical or horizontal line with descriptors listed along the line. One such configuration is the thermometer pain scale. This is a vertical presentation combining the NPI with verbal descriptors in a thermometer format. (Figure 18.10)

B. Multidimensional Pain Assessment Scales for Chronic Pain

There are two multidimensional pain scales that are commonly used to assess chronic pain: The McGill Pain Questionnaire (MPQ or short form SF-MPQ) and the Brief Pain Inventory (BPI). These scales are designed not only to measure pain intensity but also to have diagrams for pain location, pain descriptors, and indicators for mood. These tools are used either as a self report tool or as an interview format.

1. McGill Pain Questionnaire (MPQ)

The McGill Pain Questionnaire was originally designed using a long form to assess pain in oncology patients.[20,21] (Figure 18.11) It has been revised to a shortened form which is quicker and easier for the patient to use but still supplies the majority of the information from the original tool. The patient is asked to select from a list of pain descriptors that are weighted for scoring. The tool also includes a VAS and a present pain intensity scale (PPI). Gracely[22] and Graham[23] report that the MPQ is useful for determining some elements of the pain experience but lacks the ability to translate the meaning of the verbal descriptors from the list of words that are more representative of syndromes.[24]

TIP: As one of the earliest multidimensional pain scales, the McGill Pain Questionnaire has been widely used and there are many studies to support the reliability and validity of this instrument.

The pain scale has also been translated into several languages which has widened its applicability. Clinically, it has been used to study post-procedural pain, experimentally in-

duced pain, and in a large number of medical and surgical areas with children over the age of twelve. As one of the first multidimensional pain scales it sets a standard against which other instruments are measured.

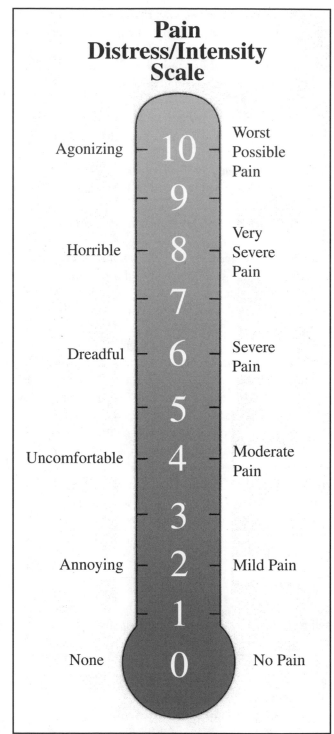

Figure 18.10 *Thermometer-combined verbal descriptor and numeric pain intensity scale.*

McGill Pain Questionnaire (MPQ)-Short Form

Short-Form McGill Pain Questionnaire

PATIENT'S NAME: _____   DATE: _____

	NONE	MILD	MODERATE	SEVERE
THROBBING	0) _____	1) _____	2) _____	3) _____
SHOOTING	0) _____	1) _____	2) _____	3) _____
STABBING	0) _____	1) _____	2) _____	3) _____
SHARP	0) _____	1) _____	2) _____	3) _____
CRAMPING	0) _____	1) _____	2) _____	3) _____
GNAWING	0) _____	1) _____	2) _____	3) _____
HOT/BURNING	0) _____	1) _____	2) _____	3) _____
ACHING	0) _____	1) _____	2) _____	3) _____
HEAVY	0) _____	1) _____	2) _____	3) _____
TENDER	0) _____	1) _____	2) _____	3) _____
SPLITTING	0) _____	1) _____	2) _____	3) _____
TIRING/EXHAUSTING	0) _____	1) _____	2) _____	3) _____
SICKENING	0) _____	1) _____	2) _____	3) _____
FEARFUL	0) _____	1) _____	2) _____	3) _____
PUNISHING/CRUEL	0) _____	1) _____	2) _____	3) _____

VAS

NO PAIN ├─────────────────────────────────────┤ WORST POSSIBLE PAIN

PPI

0	NO PAIN	_____
1	MILD	_____
2	DISCOMFORTING	_____
3	DISTRESSING	_____
4	HORRIBLE	_____
5	EXCRUCIATING	_____

© R. Melzack 1984

The short-form McGill Pain Questionnaire (SF-MPQ). Descriptors 1–11 represent the sensory dimension of pain experience and 12-15 represent the affective dimension. Each descriptor is ranked on an intensity scale of 0 = none, 1 = mild, 2 = moderate, 3 = severe. The Present Pain Intensity (PPI) of the standard long-form McGill Pain Questionnaire (LF-MPQ) and the visual analogue scale (VAS) are also included to provide overall intensity scores.

Figure 18.11 McGill pain questionnaire.

2. Brief Pain Inventory (BPI)

The Brief Pain Inventory (BPI) is a simpler and easier to use pain scale than the MPQ. It has been determined to be reliable and valid.[25] The instrument can be used as a self report or interview format. The instrument has a pain intensity rating: present pain, worst pain, and best pain in the last month. There is a body diagram for the patients to use to locate the pain. The final elements are a functional assessment and questions related to pain medication efficacy. The original author of the scale, Dr. Charles Cleeland, continues to expand the functional section to provide some focus on the effect of fatigue on chronic pain patients.

The BPI (Figure 18.12) has been used extensively for chronic pain assessment outside of the United States and has been translated into a variety of languages. This flexibility has allowed the BPI to be used with many different patient populations. Although this tool is simple and easy to use it is designed to measure chronic pain and has not been validated for acute pain measurement. The major drawback to this pain scale is the need for the patients to have a minimal ability to comprehend the pain scale and respond to the questions with accuracy.

Attorneys and legal nurse consultants should be aware that each pain scale has a particular population for which it has been tested and found reliable. Even though the chronic pain scales contain some elements of acute pain measurement, such as a pain intensity scale, the remainder of the tool is designed to get at the meaning and measurement of chronic pain. Each pain tool should be used only for the population for which it was intended. This becomes an issue as we examine behavioral pain scales where inappropriate attempts have been made to use pediatric pain scales with cognitively impaired older adults.

3. Neuropathic Pain Scale (NPS)

The Neuropathic Pain Scale is designed for use with patients who have a neuropathic pain syndrome such as postherpetic neuralgia (PHN) or Reflex Sympathetic Dystrophy (RSD), also called Chronic Regional Pain Syndrome (CRPS).[26] Patients with these types of pain syndromes often have altered sensation in the affected area such as extreme sensitivity to cold, which may be missed on evaluation by using a standard pain scale. Identifying pain as neuropathic is a very critical element in pain assessment since treating neuropathic pain requires the addition of medication, such as Neurontin, specifically designed to treat neuropathic pain.

The NPS has ten questions that are designed to measure the elements of: pain sharpness, heat/cold, dullness, intensity, overall unpleasantness, and surface versus deep pain. The ten questions are scored using an eleven-point scale where zero is the lowest rating and ten is the highest rating. If a patient has pain that is suspected to have a neuropathic component, using this scale helps the practitioner define the source and type of pain resulting in a more effective treatment plan.

C. Behavioral Pain Rating Scales

One of the newest developments in pain assessment is the proliferation of pain scales based on patient behavior for use with specific populations. It is wise for all practitioners and legal professionals to realize that self report of pain is still the accepted standard for pain assessment.

TIP: With the implementation of TJC pain management guidelines, there is a requirement to measure pain in all patient populations. This includes infants, critically ill intubated patients, and patients who are cognitively impaired such as non-verbal Alzheimer's patients. These patient populations are not able to self report but are entitled to pain assessment.

---

1. The Checklist of Non Verbal Pain Indicators CNPI—nonverbal adults

The Checklist of Non Verbal Pain Indicators[27] is a list of behaviors that have been identified as indicative of pain. This list includes such pain behaviors as: facial grimacing, vocalization such as moaning, and movement. Although behavioral indicators are not ideal for assessing pain, they do give an indication of whether pain is present or not. A drawback to the CNPI is that there is no trigger to treat pain. It serves to identify pain but does not have the ability to quantify pain intensity which would be a stimulus for triggering treatment.

2. Payen Behavioral Pain Scale (BPS)—critically ill intubated patients.

A recent addition to behavioral pain scales is the Payen-BPS used for critically ill intubated patients.[28] The scale includes a four-point measurement of facial expressions, upper limb movement, and compliance with ventilation. This scale also has good correlation with a standard pain intensity scale even when the patient is being sedated with medications such as propofol (Diprivan). By using this scale, patients whose pain was previously thought to be unmeasurable can be assessed for pain. By adding the four-point pain scores in the three areas, an estimation of pain is possible, giving a trigger for treatment.

BRIEF PAIN INVENTORY

Date _____ / _____ / _____   Time: _____

Name: _____ _____ _____
          Last   First   Middle Initial

1) Throughout our lives, most of us have had pain from time to time (such as minor headaches, sprains, and toothaches). Have you had pain other than these everyday kinds of pain today?

   1. Yes   2. No

2) On the diagram, shade in the areas where you feel pain. Put an X on the area that hurts the most.

   Right   Left   Left   Right

3) Please rate your pain by circling the one number that best describes your pain at its WORST in the last 24 hours.

   | 0 | 1 | 2 | 3 | 4 | 5 | 6 | 7 | 8 | 9 | 10 |

   No   Pain as bad
   Pain   as you can
                                         imagine

4) Please rate your pain by circling the one number that best describes your pain at its LEAST in the last 24 hours.

   | 0 | 1 | 2 | 3 | 4 | 5 | 6 | 7 | 8 | 9 | 10 |

   No   Pain as bad
   Pain   as you can
                                         imagine

5) Please rate your pain by circling the one number that best describes your pain on the AVERAGE.

   | 0 | 1 | 2 | 3 | 4 | 5 | 6 | 7 | 8 | 9 | 10 |

   No   Pain as bad
   Pain   as you can
                                         imagine

6) Please rate your pain by circling the one number that tells how much pain you have RIGHT NOW.

   | 0 | 1 | 2 | 3 | 4 | 5 | 6 | 7 | 8 | 9 | 10 |

   No   Pain as bad
   Pain   as you can
                                         imagine

7) What treatments or medications are you receiving for your pain?

   _____

   _____

8) In the last 24 hours, how much relief have pain treatments or medications provided? Please circle the one percentage that shows how much RELIEF you have received.

   | 0% | 10 | 20 | 30 | 40 | 50 | 60 | 70 | 80 | 90 | 100% |

   No   Complete
   relief   relief

9) Circle the one number that describes how, during the past 24 hours, pain has interfered with your:

   A. General activity

   | 0 | 1 | 2 | 3 | 4 | 5 | 6 | 7 | 8 | 9 | 10 |

   Does not   Completely
   interfere   interferes

   B. Mood

   | 0 | 1 | 2 | 3 | 4 | 5 | 6 | 7 | 8 | 9 | 10 |

   Does not   Completely
   interfere   interferes

   C. Walking ability

   | 0 | 1 | 2 | 3 | 4 | 5 | 6 | 7 | 8 | 9 | 10 |

   Does not   Completely
   interfere   interferes

   D. Normal work (includes both work outside the home and housework)

   | 0 | 1 | 2 | 3 | 4 | 5 | 6 | 7 | 8 | 9 | 10 |

   Does not   Completely
   interfere   interferes

   E. Relations with other people

   | 0 | 1 | 2 | 3 | 4 | 5 | 6 | 7 | 8 | 9 | 10 |

   Does not   Completely
   interfere   interferes

   F. Sleep

   | 0 | 1 | 2 | 3 | 4 | 5 | 6 | 7 | 8 | 9 | 10 |

   Does not   Completely
   interfere   interferes

   G. Enjoyment of life

   | 0 | 1 | 2 | 3 | 4 | 5 | 6 | 7 | 8 | 9 | 10 |

   Does not   Completely
   interfere   interferes

Provided as an educational service by *Endo Laboratories*

Figure 18.12 *Brief pain inventory. (Reprinted with permission of Charles S. Cleeland, Ph.D., ©1991 Charles S. Cleeland, Ph.D.—Pain Research Group. All rights reserved.)*

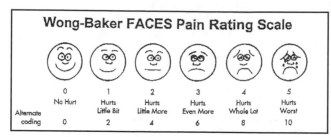

Figure 18.13 Wong-Baker FACES pain rating scale. (Reprinted with permission from Wong D.L., Hockenberry-Eaton M., Wilson D., Winkelstein M.L., Schwartz P.: Wong's Essentials of Pediatric Nursing, Sixth Ed., St. Louis, Mosby, 2001, p. 1301. ©Mosby.)

3. FACES—children and adults

One of the older behavioral pain scales is the FACES scale originally developed for use in pediatric populations who were unable to use the numeric pain rating scales. The six faces are aligned with a happy (or no pain) face at the left and the tearful (or most pain) face at the right. (Figure 18.13) The patient is asked to point to the face that best represents the patient's pain. This rating will not convert to a numeric pain rating but it does indicate the presence of pain and how severe the pain may be. Recent research indicates this scale may be applicable to adult and cognitively impaired patient populations.[29]

4. CRIES—infants

Since infants are unable to rate their pain, observing behaviors and using physiologic indicators are the only way to get some indication of pain. The CRIES scale assesses infants' pain using observations of **C**rying, **R**equires O[2], **I**ncreased vital signs, **E**xpression, and **S**leeplessness. The behaviors are rated and scored, with a higher score indicating greater distress and pain. This scale (Figure 18.14) is specifically designed for use with neonatal postoperative pain. Additional pediatric pain scales are the FLACC and the NIPS for neonates.

TIP: No matter which pain scale is used to assess pain, the rating and the type of scale being used should be indicated in the patient's record. Pain scales that are designed to be used with adults should be used only with adult patients, and scales designed for use with pediatric patients should be used only for pediatric patients. This ensures that the reliability and validity of the pain scales are preserved and that rating of pain is accurate.

18.5 Documentation

Each institution should have a policy that outlines what pain scales should be used to assess pain in patients and how often

the pain should be assessed.[30] In the acute care setting, pain is assessed on admission and at regular intervals usually no less frequently than every shift. For long-term facilities there should be an admission assessment and a regular assessment at least each day. For outpatient settings pain should be assessed at each visit. The key to this regular assessment is to provide a method of measuring pain management efficacy and ensuring that the interventions being used to treat the pain are effective. Initial assessments of pain always include the elements of assessment such as location, radiation, intensity, quality, and aggravating or alleviating factors.[31] The healthcare professional is expected to document the patient's description of pain and the essential factors of the assessment. Without a complete documentation of assessment, the institution cannot prove that pain was assessed in its patients.

The importance of the assessment and documentation process is illustrated in a recent litigation heard in a North Carolina court, *Faison (Administratrix for the Estate of Henry James) v. Hillhaven Corp. et al.*

Mr. James, age seventy-five, was a patient who had a pathological femur fracture related to a diagnosis of prostate cancer. While he was hospitalized his pain medication regimen was Roxanol 150 milligrams seven to eight times per twenty-four hours or every three to four hours around the clock, with breakthrough medication which controlled his pain. He continued this regimen at home until he was admitted to the nursing home.

When the resident was admitted to the Hillhaven facility, the administrator documented that she felt that the patient did not need that much pain medication and she felt that the patient was addicted to morphine. The pain medication was decreased and a mild tranquilizer was substituted, and the admitting nurse decided to wean the patient from Roxanol. Given that the patient had a terminal illness and the admitting physician had determined that the overall goal was pain relief, the actions of the nursing staff were inexcusable. Mr. James lived for twenty-three days at the nursing home during which time the patient's family thought he was receiving his pain medication according to the schedule prior to admission to the nursing home. In the twenty-three days of his stay in the nursing home he received Roxanol only sixty times, and the medication did not relieve his pain adequately according to the patient's report. He was given the medication for an average of three times in a twenty-four-hour period instead of the seven to eight times per twenty-four hours in the preadmission regimen.

CRIES Scale

	0	1	2
Crying	No	High pitched	Inconsolable
Requires O₂ for sat >95	No	<30%	>30%
Increased vital signs	HR and BP = or <preop	HR or BP ↑ <20% of preop	HR or BP ↑ >20% of preop
Expression	None	Grimace	Grimace/grunt
Sleepless	No	Wakes at frequent intervals	Constantly awake

Neonatal pain assessment tool developed at the University of Missouri-Columbia. Copyright S. Krechel, MD, and J. Bildner, RNC, CNS.

CODING TIPS FOR USING CRIES

Crying	The characteristic cry of pain is *high pitched.* If no cry or cry that is not high pitched, score 0. If cry high pitched but baby is easily consoled, score 1. If cry is high pitched and baby is inconsolable, score 2.
Requires O₂ for sat >95%	Look for *changes* in oxygenation. Babies experiencing pain manifest decreases in oxygenation as measured by TcO₂ or oxygen saturation. If no oxygen is required, score 0. If <30% O₂ is required, score 1. If >30% is required, score 2. (Consider other causes of changes in oxygenation, such as atelectasis, pneumothorax, over-sedation)
Increased vital signs	NOTE: Take blood pressure last as this may wake child, causing difficulty with other assessments. Use baseline preoperative parameters from a nonstressed period. Multiply baseline HR × 0.2 and then add this to baseline HR to determine the HR, which is 20% over baseline. Do likewise for BP. Use mean BP. If HR and BP are both unchanged or less than baseline, score 0. If HR or BP is increased but increase is <20% of baseline, score 1. If either one is increased >20% over baseline, score 2.
Expression	The facial expression most often associated with pain is a grimace. This may be characterized by brow lowering, eyes squeezed shut, deepening of the nasolabial furrow, open lips and mouth. If no grimace is present, score 0. If grimace alone is present, score 1. If grimace and noncry vocalization grunt are present, score 2.
Sleepless	This parameter is scored based on the infant's state during the hour preceding this recorded score. If the child has been continuously asleep, score 0. If he or she has awakened at frequent intervals, score 1. If he or she has been awake constantly, score 2.

Figure 18.14 CRIES. (Reprinted with permission of Judy Bildner, RN, CNS, MS, University of Missouri–Columbia.)

The lawsuit was filed by the estate of Mr. James. According to the North Carolina Department of Human Resource (DHR), the Hillhaven Corp. had endangered the health, safety, and welfare of Mr. James, and a fine was levied against the nursing home. The nursing home was also cited for deficits in pain assessment. The defendant was found to have caused increased pain and suffering for the patient prior to his death. The jury awarded $7,500,000 in compensatory damages and $7,500,000 in punitive damages.[32]

With TJC pain management guidelines, the plaintiffs could have also included the lack of reassessment after medication administration in their lawsuit. TJC pain guidelines indicate that pain must be reassessed after interventions such as pain medication to ensure that the treatment is effective for pain relief. Mr. James' repeated statement that his pain was not being relieved would have allowed for an additional element in the complaint.

Lawyers, paralegals, and legal nurse consultants should examine medical records for certain elements which are critical for accurate assessment and documentation.

- Each entry should be timed and dated.
- There should be a pain intensity rating and an indication of which pain scale is being used.
- The additional factors should be recorded: location, duration, radiation, and quality of pain.
- The admission assessment should include a list of any current medications being taken for pain.
- The admission orders should include these pain medications unless contraindicated by the patient's condition.
- Each administration of pain medication should be followed by a reassessment of pain intensity within fifteen to thirty minutes for parenteral pain medication or thirty minutes to one hour for oral pain medications.
- In addition to the pain rating, a sedation scale such as the Ramsey scale should be used in acute care settings to measure the level of sedation in the patients.

The Ramsey scale is a commonly employed five-point scale that indicates the level of alertness in patients. The Ramsey scale can demonstrate that the patient has no sedation related to the use of analgesic medications. If the Ramsey scale shows sedation with pain medication, there should be subsequent dose reductions, oxygen use, more

frequent monitoring, and in more serious cases the use of a reversal agent such as Narcan (nalaxone). Chapter 9, *Critical Care Records*, presents this scale.

A. Issues with Documentation

1. Lack of time

Nurses are being asked to care for more patients who are sicker and have higher acuities. These increased patient demands mean that nurses and staff caring for patients have less time to complete assessments and documentation. Physicians in outpatient settings are being asked to see more and more patients in shorter periods of time. Follow-up appointments in medical offices may be scheduled for every fifteen minutes allowing little time for complete assessment and less time for documentation.

TIP: The inability to document fully the assessment data leaves the nursing and medical staff open to legal action when patients start litigation.

---

2. Bias

All healthcare providers have bias. They are all products of family values and societal conditioning. The key to minimizing bias is to make the healthcare provider aware of his personal bias and create active strategies to address the issue. Providers raised in a family where complaints of pain were dismissed as not important may tend to treat patients the same way. Healthcare providers who have bias must be aware of the patient's right to pain assessment and adequate treatment and comply with the requirements to the best of their ability. If medical providers believe patients are addicted when they use opioids regularly, as in the *James v. Hillhaven* case, they must be made aware that this belief is not in compliance with the current state of pain management practice and TJC pain management guidelines. Healthcare professionals are still held legally accountable for their actions and biases despite their beliefs about the patient's presentation or statements about pain.

3. Lack of education and preparation to manage pain

Physicians spend a large amount of time in medical training associating with physicians who have been trained years earlier. Outdated attitudes about the dangers of using opioid medications may be perpetuated by failure to stay current with pain management information. Nurses receive on average only four hours of pain management education in basic nursing programs, while physicians receive only one hour of training in pain management. This helps to explain the current state of pain management in the United States.[33]

In 2001, a California jury awarded $1,500,000 to the family of an eighty-five-year-old man against a physician who allegedly failed to treat the patient's pain adequately in the days before he died from lung cancer. William Bergman's family alleged that he was denied proper pain medication during a five-day medical stay at Eden Medical Center in Castro Valley, California, where he was admitted in February 1998 because of back pain. His treating physician, Dr. Wing Chin, is an internal medicine specialist.

The Bergman family and expert witnesses who testified on behalf of Mr. Bergman's estate alleged that he should have been given high doses of morphine but, instead, was given lower doses of Demerol which is not recommended for the treatment of cancer pain. Dr. Chin, who had been practicing for thirty years at the time he treated Mr. Bergman, admitted that he was not aware of most developments related to palliative care and had no knowledge of new guidelines for pain management. Dr. Chin testified that he did not remember reading federal guidelines on cancer pain management sponsored by the Agency for Health Care Policy and Research in the 1990s, even though the guidelines were mailed by the California Medical Board to every doctor in the state in 1994.

This case is significant not only because of the amount of the jury verdict, but because it is the first reported case of liability for a physician's undertreatment of pain. It is also notable that it was brought as an "elder abuse case," rather than as a medical malpractice case, presumably to avoid California's $250,000 cap on noneconomic damages, such as pain and suffering, in medical malpractice cases (California Welfare and Institutions Code, 1999). However, after trial the judge reduced the $1,500,000 jury award to $250,000 in order to be consistent with the medical malpractice cap. As permitted by California law, the attorney for the Bergman estate requested attorneys' fees in the amount of $353,871. The trial judge awarded 1 1/2 times the requested fees, explaining that the fee enhancement "makes such cases economically feasible to encourage attorneys to take up the cause of abused elderly persons." With interest, the total jury award and attorneys' fees amounted to $893,888.[34]

Physicians may be reluctant to prescribe opioid medications if other members of their practice do not support the use of opioids. In trying to be compliant with pain management guidelines, these practitioners may feel pressure from their peers to be less generous with opioids even though they are indicated by the pain rating of the patients. Since physicians and nurses receive so little pain management training and may not understand how to use pain medications, they are at risk of undertreating pain.

4. Fears of addiction

One of the biggest issues with the use of opioids in pain management is "opiophobia" or the fear of opioids.[35] Since there is often confusion between patients who are dependent on opioids versus patients who are true addicts, healthcare providers can tend to undertreat pain. This undertreatment of pain can create a phenomenon called "opioid pseudoaddiction."[36] This condition is evidenced when a patient whose pain is being undertreated displays what are perceived to be addictive behaviors such as "clock watching," asking for pain medication each time it is due. When the pain is treated effectively, the addictive behaviors stop and the patient goes on to recovery of normal functioning. More information on addiction and pain management can be found in Section 18.7.B.

B. Undertreated Pain Cited as Elder Abuse

No matter what the cause of undertreatment of pain, patients are seeking legal action in the courts, and plaintiffs' attorneys are adding negligent pain management as an allegation in a complaint.

In a recent case against providers at Mt. Diablo Hospital Medical Center in Concord, California, both the facility and the healthcare providers were cited by the Compassion in Dying Federation as not providing adequate pain management for the plaintiff, a dying patient who needlessly suffered. The plaintiffs settled for a confidential amount with Mt. Diablo Medical Center and the defendant physicians. Bayberry Care Center, the long-term facility where the patient died, paid $80,000 and agreed to give the staff sixteen hours of CME in pain and palliative care to be completed by June 2005.[37]

Additionally, the Medical Board of California filed formal charges against one of the physicians on behalf of the federal Centers for Medicare and Medicaid Services (CMS) and issued a Class A Notice of Deficiency to Bayberry Care Center.[38]

In 1997, a South Carolina federal judge found against a Veteran's Administration hospital and awarded the estate of a patient $125,000 for pain and suffering, in addition to other damages, in part because the hospital failed to "properly monitor, treat and care for" the patient which caused his "continued decline, distress, pain, suffering and eventually death" from laryngeal cancer. The court noted that the patient's final weeks in the VA Hospital were filled with pain and suffering, both physical and emotional. While his pain and suffering really began during the period from July through November, his physical and emotional pain and suffering was many times worse during his final hospitalization. During this final period, for example, pain medicine was ordered for him but never given.[39]

Since the patient was consistently reporting high levels of pain, one might expect he would be receiving regular pain medication. He received no pain medication or insufficient medication to control his pain. This highlights the concept that even if there is a good compliance with documenting pain, healthcare practitioners must act on the pain ratings. It is not enough to document the pain rating without following the documentation with an intervention aimed at treating the level of pain the patient is reporting. See Braun[40] for more information on pain mismanagement litigation.

18.6 Commonly Used Pain Medications

Pain medication should be given according to the patient's report of pain. Table 18.2 lists pain medications, starting doses, and the level of pain for which the medication should be used. Allergies to pain medication should be clearly documented in medical records. When a patient indicates an allergy it should be a true allergy such as anaphylaxis rather than an intolerance or side effect such as nausea.

Two medications which are no longer recommended for use are Demerol (Meperidine) and Darvocet (Propoxyphene). Not only do these medications offer poor pain control they have significant side effects. Demerol is no longer considered a first line pain medication.[41] It needs to be dosed at high levels to produce analgesia which in turn creates side effects such as nausea and sedation. Additionally, it has a metabolite called normerperidine that can accumulate in the central nervous system and can cause seizures. The daily dose of Demerol is limited to a maximum of six hundred milligrams per day, and it should be administered for as short a time as possible.

Each tablet of Darvocet contains fifty milligrams of propoxyphene and 650 mgs of acetaminophen also known as Tylenol. It was once a very popular pain medication because it was considered "safe." The majority of the pain relief is provided by the acetaminophen. Some healthcare providers dose the medication with two tablets every four hours which provides a high level of acetaminophen. Additionally, Darvocet has a metabolite, norpropoxyphene, that can cause cardiac arrhymias. If a patient is using this pain medication for pain relief it should only be used for mild level pain, and the total amount of acetaminophen should be monitored.

18.7 Specialty Pain Assessment and Documentation

There are some populations of patients that require special pain assessment and documentation. Chronic or persistent pain patients may be unable to get adequate pain relief with the use of regular pain medications and interventional methods provided by anesthesia-based pain clinics. These patients are candidates for implanted pain relief systems such as spinal cord stimulators and (under the skin) morphine pumps. The pre-implantation assessment for these patients requires an earnest trial of different pain medications at varying doses with documented inadequate pain relief. Patients should also be screened by a pain psychologist to ensure that they will be able to tolerate having an implanted mechanism.

Spinal cord stimulators consist of a battery (similar to a pacemaker battery) and a catheter that has several electrical poles. The catheter is placed into the epidural space at the site of the nerves innervating the painful area, and the battery provides a mild electrical current. This current can be intensified or moderated according to the patient's need. The patient has a handheld programmer that can turn the stimulator on or off. The goal of the spinal cord stimulator is to make the pain more tolerable and increase function and quality of life.

TIP: Documentation for these patients should include: location of the catheter, pain intensity, names of poles being used, and the intensity the patient is requiring to make the pain tolerable. One very important key to determining the success of the modality is the increase in functionality the patient experiences once the catheter is placed.

The implanted morphine pump is another modality for pain control. This consists of an intrathecal catheter attached to an implanted computer-powered pump that has a program controlling the delivery of morphine.[42] A patient who is a good candidate for this modality is one whose pain medication doses have reached such high levels that the patient is unable to tolerate the oral doses. Prior to the permanent implantation, the patient should have trial doses of intrathecal morphine to determine the settings for the pump once it is implanted. The implantation requires a surgical procedure. The pump computer system is activated directly or soon after implantation. The patient has no control over the medication delivery once the pump is activated. Interrogation of an implanted morphine pump can be generated by a computerized programmer located in the physician's office. The programmer can program the pump, change prescriptions, and generate data. The data included in an interrogation are:

Table 18.2
Commonly Used Pain Medications

Type of Medication	Level of Pain	Name of Medication	Dose	Comment
Oral	Mild: level 1 to 3	Acetaminophen	325 to 650 mgs. every 4 hours.	Daily maximum dosage of acetaminophen not to exceed 4000 mgs. total.
Oral	Mild: level 1 to 3	Tylenol #3	Codeine 30 mgs. and acetaminophen 325 mgs. One or two tablets every 4 or 6 hours.	Maximum daily dosage of acetaminophen not to exceed 4000 mgs. Codeine commonly causes nausea or constipation.
Oral	Moderate: level 4 to 6	Lortab/Vicodin (Hydrocodone)	Hydrocodone 5/10 mgs. with acetaminophen 325/500 mgs. One or two tablets every 4 to 6 hours.	Daily dosage limited by acetaminophen.
Oral	Moderate: level 4 to 6	Percocet/ Percodan (Oxycodone)	Oxycodone 5 mgs. with 325 mgs. acetaminophen or aspirin.	Maximum daily dose limited by acetaminophen.
Oral	Moderate: level 4 to 6	Oxycontin	Extended release oxycodone. Starting dose 10 mgs. dose every 12 hours.	Patients may have difficulty finding oxycontin in chain drugstores. This medication has been a target for robbery in pharmacies and some do not stock it. Unfortunately this medication, which provides excellent pain relief, has been abused. Patient deaths attributed to oxycontin are associated with abuse of multiple substances such as alcohol, benzodiazepines, or other opioids.
Oral & parenteral	Severe: level 7 to 10	Morphine, Roxanol (elixir)	Can be used orally or parenterally. Starting dose is 5 to 10 mgs. orally, 2 to 5 mgs. parenterally. PCA doses usually start at 1 mg	
Oral	Severe: level 7 to 10	MS Contin	Extended release morphine. Starting dose 15 mgs. every 12 hours.	
Oral & parenteral	Severe: level 7 to 10	Dilaudid (Hydromorphone)	Can be used orally or parenterally. Oral starting dose 2 mgs. every 4 to 6 hours. Parenteral dose starts at 0.5 mgs. or 1mg. PCA doses start at 0.2 mgs. every 8 to 10 minutes.	

Table 18.2 (continued)

Type of Medication	Level of Pain	Name of Medication	Dose	Comment
Oral & parenteral	Severe: level 7 to 10	Methadone (Dolophine)		Used for chronic pain and extended use causes increased drug half life. Less expensive option for chronic pain than other extended release medications.
Oral & parenteral, transdermal	Severe: level 7 to 10	Fentanyl	Duragesic patches-starting dose 25 micrograms applied transdermally and changed every 3 days. PCA doses start at 10 to 25 micrograms every 8 to 10 minutes.	Actiq oralet, oral transmucosalfentanyl, for use with opioid dependent oncology patients only.
Oral NSAIDS Non-selective	Mild	Motrin (Ibuprofen) Naprosyn Lodine	Start as low as possible for short periods of time only.	Have the potential for causing GI bleeds.
Oral COX2 selective NSAIDS	Moderate	Celebrex		Spares the lining of the stomach and does not affect platelet aggregation reducing the potential for bleeding. Questions about increased risk of stroke and heart attack are arising.
Oral medications for neuropathic pain	Moderate	Tricyclic antidepressants • Amytriptilin (Elavil) •Nortryptyline		Pain management regimens typically require a multimodal approach, especially for treatment of chronic or persistent pain.
Medications for neuropathic pain		SSRIs (Selective Serotonin Reuptake Inhibitors) • Prozac • Effexor Antiseizure medications • Neurontin • Trileptal		Medication doses often do not provide long lasting pain relief. Combination medications are limited by the total amount of acetaminophen. One alternative is the addition of non-steroidal pain medication can have an opioid-sparing effect and provide added pain relief.

- patient name,
- pump number, medication,
- dose delivery rate,
- activation of alarm, and
- next fill date.

A patient with this type of pump requires frequent visits to the physician's office. There the pump is refilled directly through the abdominal skin since the pump itself is placed very close to the dermal layer in the abdominal wall below the beltline.

A. Case Study

Roy is a forty-five-year-old truck driver with intractable low back pain. His truck was rear-ended during a multi-car crash. He is currently unemployed because his back pain makes it impossible for him to sit for long periods of time. He has been taking large doses of pain medication that have improved his pain relief but do not allow him to sleep well or to sit for any length of time. He has been asked by his pain physician if he would consider having an implanted morphine pump placed. Roy's response is positive: "I'll try anything that will help." A psychological assessment is performed. Roy receives patient education about the implantation of a morphine pump. Roy comes in for a trial of intrathecal morphine, and the correct dose is determined and documented in his record.

Roy arrives at the surgical center for the placement of the intrathecal catheter and pump. The pain physician programs the pump and fills it with morphine. Once the pump is started, the patient should see a decrease in pain, and he will only need some breakthrough pain medication for exacerbations of pain.

When Roy is asked about his activity at his return visit to the pain physician, he says "I think this is going to work. At first it felt funny not to be taking all the pain medication I had before but now I can sit for short periods and I hope I will be able to go to physical therapy so that I can get more active. I even sleep better at night now. I only need a few pain pills now and then. It's not like it was before at all."

By using modern technology, there are options for giving better pain relief and increasing functionality. This case illustrates that even intractable low back pain patients have better options for pain relief.

B. Addicted Patients or Patients with a History of Drug Abuse

Patients who are addicted to illicit drugs, prescription drugs, or alcohol or have a history of drug addiction have the same right to pain assessment and pain treatment as patients who do not have an addictive history.[43,44] Addicted patients can be treated effectively and have their pain relieved. These patients may require higher doses of pain medication to relieve pain, but with careful titration pain can be controlled.

Often healthcare professionals are uncomfortable providing opioids to addicted patients for pain relief. They may fear they are furthering the patient's addiction or readdicting the patient if the patient has a history of past substance abuse. A study of physicians' prescribing practices[45] found that relatively few physicians would prescribe opioids to a patient with a history of drug abuse because they feared regulatory oversight.

TIP: At times, patients who are dependent on pain medication are mistakenly classified as addicts. When assessing pain in an addicted patient, an open and nonjudgmental attitude can elicit an open and honest drug history by the patient. This history can be used to help titrate pain medications for these patients. For the patient with a history of drug addiction, a frank discussion about pain management goals and treatment options can lead to effective pain control that is satisfactory for the patient and healthcare professionals caring for the patient.

Healthcare providers should be aware that true addiction is rare. Addicts take drugs for the psychological effect, not pain relief. They would take opioids even if they had no pain. They like the euphoric effect the opioids provide and have no control over their drug use. Opioid-dependent patients need opioids to control pain and increase functionality. They would not take opioids if they did not need them to control pain. Mistakenly, many patients who are dependent on opioids to maintain a good quality of life are classified as addicts or drug seeking by healthcare providers. Dose increases may be a result of tolerance rather than an indication of addiction. A good knowledge of definitions for tolerance, dependency, and addiction are helpful to make sure patients are not unjustly classified as addicts. Note the definitions that follow.

Tolerance—Tolerance is a state of adaptation in which exposure to a drug induces changes that result in a diminution of one or more of the drug effects over time.[46]

Physical dependence—Physical dependence is a state of adaptation that is manifested by a drug-specific withdrawal syndrome that can be produced by abrupt cessation, rapid dose reduction, decreasing blood level of the drug, or administration of an antagonist.[47]

Addiction—Addiction is a primary, chronic, neurobiological disease, with genetic, psychosocial, and environmental factors influencing its development and manifestations. It is characterized by behaviors that include one or more of the following: impaired control over drug use, compulsive use, continued use despite harm, and craving.[48]

C. Case Study

Diane, age forty-two, is a patient who has end stage breast cancer. She is also a heroin addict. The medical resident has reservations about starting a morphine PCA when she is admitted to the hospital for pain control. When asked why he feels he cannot order morphine for this patient, he says "How do I know I won't make her addiction worse? I don't know what the DEA would say about this either. I don't think they would like me ordering drugs for a drug addict." When the resident is reminded of TJC regulations, he reluctantly orders a morphine PCA pump. Diane's pain becomes manageable as the medication is titrated up. After several days in the hospital she is able to go home with a 33 percent increase in her oral pain medications.

This case demonstrates that healthcare providers can be reluctant to provide opioids to patients who are addicts. There is a risk addicts may be undertreated in an effort to control their use of opioids. Even though these patients require more pain medication than patients who are not addicts, their pain can be controlled. Encouraging healthcare providers to provide adequate pain medication for these patients can be difficult, but keeping the focus on pain relief rather than the addictive disease is helpful.

D. Overtreatment of Pain

A critical element to any pain assessment is the amount of pain medication the patient was taking regularly prior to the admission. Patients who are not taking any opioid pain medications are considered to be *opioid naïve*. When healthcare providers determine what type and dose of pain medication to give opioid naïve patients, it is critical to recognize the need to monitor the effects of the medication. The first dose of opioid medication is always the most important since it is impossible to predetermine what dose of medication may cause over-sedation in any individual patient. The patient may be unknowingly very sensitive to pain medication or conversely have a high medication requirement to maintain

pain control. The patient's response to any pain medication should be the key to future doses.

In such situations, regular and frequent pain assessment and medication adjustments must be made and recorded. Sedation scales such as the Ramsey scale should be used to monitor the sedating effects of opioid medications. Opioid doses should be decreased if sedation increases. Failure to monitor progressing sedation and decrease medication doses may result in significant respiratory depression requiring reversal with Narcan.

Co-administering other sedating medications such as antiemetics such as Compazine or Reglan to alleviate nausea or vomiting or antipuritics such as Benadryl to alleviate itching or allergic reactions can intensify the sedative effect of opioids. The overall cumulative effect of combining sedating medications should always be considered. Less sedating antiemetics such as Zofran are a better choice if there is a risk of increasing sedation.

Oxygen saturations should be maintained at least at 92 or 94 percent in a postoperative patient. Respiratory rates should be greater than eight breaths per minute. Normally patients may require supplemental oxygen by nasal cannula for a short period of time after surgery as they recover from anesthesia. Pulse oximetry is not considered to be a fail safe method to prevent over sedation but rather used for patients who have preexisting conditions that would predispose them for over sedation.[49] Anyone reviewing the medical record should be able to determine what the oxygen levels for a patient were and if oxygen was in place. Respiratory therapy and nursing notes provide important data.

Overall, oxygen monitoring methods such as O_2 saturations are inaccurate indications of sedation. Young patients in particular can maintain a good oxygenation level until very shortly before respiratory arrest due to their unimpaired cardiac and respiratory systems. A better source of information about a patient's respiratory status while on opioids is a CO_2 monitor used to measure carbon dioxide levels on expiration. Rising CO_2 levels indicate increasing respiratory depression.

TIP: If over sedation is suspected, a check of arterial blood gases (ABG) can indicate the status of oxygenation for the patient. Opioid over sedation should be suspected in patients with a CO_2 level greater than forty five.

In an Arizona case, the eighty-one year-old woman was admitted to Tucson Medical Center for treatment of sciatic pain after a fall. Fifteen milligrams of morphine sulfate controlled release tablets (MS

Contin) twice a day, was prescribed. Shortly before the decedent was transferred to a skilled nursing facility for pain management and rehabilitation, an increase in the MS Contin to thirty milligrams was ordered. The hospital's case manager recorded the increase of MS Contin to thirty milligrams, twice a day, without striking out the previous order for fifteen milligrams twice a day. The plaintiff claimed the long-term care facility administered forty-five milligrams of morphine twice a day. The woman died from acute morphine intoxication a couple of weeks after admission. The verdict resulted in a $600,000 recovery.[50]

18.8 Summary

Pain assessment and documentation are important elements in adequate pain management. It does not help the patients if the pain management stops with the assessment and documentation. The healthcare provider must act on the patient's report of pain and then document pain relief after the intervention.

National pain management guidelines and specialty population pain guidelines provide direction for assessment and documentation. In order for pain relief to improve, all caregivers must learn pain assessment skills and use pain assessment techniques that will help determine pain levels for patients. Documentation of pain ratings are mandated by JC pain management guidelines. Attorneys, legal nurse consultants, and paralegals will find information on pain assessment in medical records. Use of the national pain management guidelines to determine compliance for pain assessment and documentation will provide support for chart review and litigation that will determine how pain is managed for all patients.

Endnotes

1. American Pain Society. *Principles of Analgesic Use in the Treatment of Acute Pain and Cancer Pain.* Fifth Edition. Glenview, IL: American Pain Society. 2003.

2. Roper Starch Worldwide, Inc. "Chronic Pain in America: Roadblocks to Relief." 1999. http//ampainsoc.org. Retrieved on May 2004.

3. *Id.*

4. Stewart, W.F. et al. "Lost Productive Time and Cost Due to Common Pain Conditions in the U.S. Workforce." *JAMA.* 290, p. 2443–2454. 2003.

5. *Id.*

6. *See* note 1.

7. D'Arcy, Y.M. A Three Site Comparison World Congress on Pain. Vienna, Austria. August 1999.

8. Agency for Health Care Policy and Research. *Acute Pain Management: Operative or Medical Procedures and Trauma.* Rockville, MD: U.S. Public Health Services. 1992.

9. Chevlan, E. "Opioids: A Review." *Current Pain and Headaches Report.* 7, p. 15–23. 2003.

10. Berry, P.H. et al. (Editors). *Pain: Current Understanding of Assessment, Management and Treatments.* Reston, VA: National Pharmaceutical Council, Inc. 2001.

11. *See* note 1.

12. McCaffery, M. and C. Pasero. *Pain: A Clinical Manual.* St. Louis, MO: Mosby. 1999.

13. Joint Commission on Accreditation of Healthcare Organizations. *Pain Assessment and Management: An Organizational Approach.* Oakbrook Terrace, IL: Joint Commission. 2000.

14. Herr, K. and L. Garrand. "Assessment and Measurement of Pain in Older Adults." *Clinics in Geriatric Medicine.* 17(4), p. 1–22. 2001.

15. Herr, K. and P. Mobily. "Comparison of Selected Pain Assessment Tools for Use with the Elderly." *Applied Nursing Research.* 6(39). 1993.

16. Feldt, K.S. "The Checklist of Non-Verbal Pain Indicators (CNPI)." *Pain Management Nursing.* 1(1), p. 13–21. 2000.

17. *See* note 14.

18. *See* note 15.

19. Feldt, K.S., M.B. Ryden, and S. Miles. "Treatment of Pain in Cognitively Impaired Compared with Cognitively Intact Older Patients with Hip Fractures." *Journal of the American Geriatrics Society.* 46, p. 1079–1085. 1998.

20. Melzack, R. "The McGill Pain Questionnaire: Major Properties and Scoring Methods." *Pain.* 1, p. 277–299. 1975.

21. Melzack, R. "The Short-Form McGill Pain Questionnaire." *Pain.* 30, p. 191–197. 1987.

22. Gracely, R.H. "Evaluation of Multidimensional Pain Scales." *Pain.* 48, p. 297–300. 1992.

23. Graham, C. et al. "Use of the McGill Pain Questionnaire in the Assessment of Cancer Pain: Replicability and Consistency." *Pain.* 8, p. 377–387. 1980.

24. Daut, R.L., C.S. Cleeland, and R. Flannery. "Development of the Wisconsin Brief Questionnaire in the Assessment of Cancer Pain: Replicability and Consistency." *Pain.* 8, p. 377–387. 1983.

25. *Id.*

26. Galer, B.S. and R.H. Dworkin. *A Clinical Guide to Neuropathic Pain.* Minneapolis, MN: Healthcare Information Programs, a Division of McGraw-Hill Healthcare Information. 2000.

27. *See* note 16.

28. Payen, J.F. et al. "Assessing Pain in Critically Ill Sedated Patients by Using a Behavioral Scale." *Critical Care Medicine.* 29(12), p. 1–11. 2001.

29. Wong, D. and K. Nix. "Use of the FACES Pain Rating Tool with Adults." *American Journal of Nursing.* 2004 (in press).

30. *See* note 13.

31. *See* note 10.

32. Vaglienti, C. and M. Grinberg. "Emerging Liability for the Undertreatment of Pain." *Journal of Nursing Law.* Vol. 9, Issue 3, Fall 2004, p. 7–17.

33. Weissman, D.E., D. Joranson, and M.B. Hopwood. "Wisconsin Physician's Knowledge and Attitudes About Opioid Analgesic Regulations." *Wisconsin Medical Journal.* December 1991, p. 671–675.

34. *See* note 32 at 9.

35. Weissman, D. and J.D. Haddox. "Opioid Pseudoaddiction: An Iatrogenic Syndrome." *Pain.* 36, p. 363–366. 1989.

36. *Id.*

37. *See* note 34.

38. *Id.*

39. *Id.*

40. Braun, J. "Pain (Mis)management Litigation" in Iyer, P. *Nursing Home Litigation: Investigation and Case Preparation.* Second Edition. Tucson, AZ: Lawyers and Judges Publishing Company, Inc. 2006.

41. *See* note 1.

42. Kumar, K. "Continuous Intrathecal Morphine Treatment for Chronic Pain of Nonmalignant Etiology: Long Term Benefits and Efficacy." *Surgical Neurology.* 55(2), p. 79–86. 2001.

43. American Academy of Pain Medicine, American Pain Society, American Society of Addiction Medicine. Definitions related to the use of opioids for the treatment of pain. Consensus statement. 2001.

44. American Society of Pain Management. Nurses Position Statement: Pain Management in Patients with Addictive Disease. 2002. Available at www.aspmn.org.

45. *See* note 33.

46. *See* note 43.

47. *Id.*

48. *Id.*

49. McCaffery, M. and C. Pasero. *Pain: A Clinical Manual.* St. Louis, MO: Mosby. 1999.

50. Laska, L. "Failure to Check Prescription for Morphine at Time of Admission." *Medical Malpractice Verdicts, Settlements, and Experts.* January 2009, p. 30.

Chapter 19

Pediatric Records

Susan G. Engleman MSN, RN, APRN, BC, PNP, CLCP

19.1 Introduction

An attorney may request to analyze a child's medical records for a number of reasons. One may be directly related to an injury that is believed to have occurred during treatment by a medical professional; or it may be that the attorney is trying to establish damages that occurred in another setting. Although many of the record types found in the chart of an adult may be similar to those found in the child's medical records, there are some specific to children. In addition, the content of the record may not be the same. As is the case with adults, a poor outcome in a child does not establish liability. Unfortunately, a child may have a poor outcome even while the standard of care is strictly followed. When a poor outcome occurs, the medical records of the child must be carefully reviewed by a knowledgeable professional to determine whether the standard of care was indeed observed. This chapter focuses on the examination of the pediatric medical record for the non-medically trained professional.

Pediatrics is the specialty of caring for children. The age that constitutes "child" varies from institution to institution and provider to provider, but most consider anyone under sixteen years of age a pediatric patient. Other settings will care for children until they are twenty-one years of age. In certain situations, even adults are cared for in pediatric beds or institutions and/or by pediatric providers. As medical technology and expertise has progressed, some adults who previously would have died during their adolescence are now living into adulthood.[1] Because healthcare providers for adults are unfamiliar or uncomfortable with these disease processes, adult patients may continue to seek care from their pediatric providers.[2] Specifically, those patients with congenital heart defects, cystic fibrosis, and muscular dystrophy are often seen in the pediatric setting despite their age.

Medical records are used in legal cases to establish the presence or lack of liability and causation as well as damages.[3] The medical records related to a time period in which an alleged event occurred must be requested and reviewed. If liability and causation are established in those records, it may then be important to review the medical records of the child prior to the injury in question in order to establish the child's status pre-injury. This is, of course, necessary when determining the damages in the case. At that point the attorney will need to decide how many prior records will be important. This decision is often guided by the child's medical history. If the history related is that of a normal childhood prior to the injury, only the most recent pediatrician's records may be needed; however, if the history is complex, the records dating back to the child's birth may be essential. If the child is known to have pre-existing medical issues, records specific to diagnosis of that particular disease process will most likely be necessary.

TIP: If the child had a complicated birth history, records requested should include those related to the birth itself. The prenatal records for that child may also be important.

19.2 Basic Tips for Non-Medical Professionals Reviewing Medical Records

Reviewing a medical record can be a daunting task for a non-medically trained professional. Like many professions, the medical profession has its own language, understandable to those belonging to its ranks but difficult for laypeople. For the non-medical professional planning to review medical records on a regular basis, the purchase of several texts may be helpful. A good medical terminology textbook and a medical dictionary will be invaluable. If the medical records to be reviewed are pediatric in nature, the latest edition of a basic pediatric nursing textbook will be essential. In addition, the latest edition of a pediatric medication guide may also be handy.

Another document that may be useful is a copy of the hospital's official abbreviation list. Most hospitals maintain a policy or booklet listing those abbreviations approved for use by healthcare providers within that particular institution. This is not to say that other abbreviations may not appear in the record, but this official document will give a listing of a great many of those abbreviations within that particular record. This may be requested from the hospital in discovery.[4]

It is helpful to use a systematic method to review medical records. One suggested method is the following:

- first attempt to organize the record,
- place all *like* records together and then in chronological order either beginning with the first date or the last date and working in the opposite direction,
- attempt to get an overview of the course of events that occurred with the patient,
- read the discharge summary, and
- read the physician's progress notes from beginning to end.

If the purpose of reviewing the medical record is to evaluate the care given to the patient by medical professionals, one should attempt to pinpoint a timeframe in which the injury occurred or a deterioration in the child's status was evident. See Chapter 3, *Obtaining and Organizing Medical Records*, and Chapter 4, *Analyzing Medical Records*, both in Volume I, for additional information.

Once a timeframe is determined, the review should become more focused. Each section of the records related to

that particular timeframe and just prior to it should be reviewed in detail. Read the nurses' documentation noting the flow of what occurred. Check the provider's orders against the documentation of each professional to ensure that each order was carried out as written. It may be at this point that a pediatric medical professional may be contacted in order to serve as a consultant to the attorney in determining whether standards of care were breached by the providers.

19.3 Why Are Pediatric Patients Different?

TIP: Children are not just small models of adults. The main concept to keep in mind when dealing with the pediatric population is not the size of the child but the *lack of maturity* of the child. This relates both to the child's physiological development as well as the psychological. This immaturity affects much in the child's care.

The child's lack of communication skills significantly affects the child's care. Unlike an adult patient who is able to deliver a complete history of her symptoms as well as give a detailed description of them, the child is often unable to specifically complain of his symptoms or give any information regarding them. In addition to this, the healthcare provider needs to be aware that the developmental level of the child not only affects the child's ability to communicate in general, but it also colors the reliability of the information delivered as well.[5] For example, an infant can only cry to indicate that there is a problem. Obviously this age group is unable to assist with any specifics whatsoever. A toddler may answer questions for a healthcare professional, but the provider must be aware that at times the child will reply negatively to every question asked. These responses are appropriate to that child's developmental level, but it will not assist the healthcare provider to gather specific data related to the child's symptoms. As for the child who is a preschooler, he may give answers to questions that seem far-fetched and unrealistic. This may relate to the child's propensity for magical thinking which is also developmentally appropriate. Fortunately, once children reach school age, they are often able to respond with more information regarding symptoms. The medical record may provide more detailed histories from older children. It is always important to remember that the responses that the child gives are based upon previous experiences that are often very limited.[6] For example, the child must have had some type of experience with pain in order to compare it to the present complaint. If the child has only experienced the pain of a scraped knee, then he will only be able to describe pain related to a surgical insult in terms of that scraped knee. See Chapter 18, *Pain Assess-*

ment and Management, for more information about assessing pain in children.

Another important aspect to consider in the care of the child is the presence of parents in the healthcare situation. Adults care for themselves and most often do not rely on others to speak for them. Children, who are often unable to advocate for themselves, rely heavily on their parents to meet their needs. One generally assumes that a parent knows the child better than anyone else. When the child is unable to communicate the parent is considered the most reliable spokesperson.[7] Of course, there are instances when this may not be so, such as in the case of a child abused by the parent; however, it is generally true. Given this, healthcare providers often interview parents and use the parent's judgment when the child is unable to speak for himself. Caregivers who typically care for adults may not take the word of a parent as seriously as would a pediatric healthcare professional. If a parent relates that the child "is not acting right," it would behoove the professional to question the parent closely to gain further information and then use that information to carefully assess the child for signs and symptoms that a problem exists.

Another aspect in which children differ psychologically is in their coping with illness or hospitalization. Coping mechanisms are often very individually driven and must be viewed in terms of the child's developmental level; however, there are certain mechanisms that are almost always seen in the pediatric population. Most children who are ill or injured want the close presence of their most trusted caregiver—a parent.[8] Most are frightened by the "medical world" whether it is the doctor's office, an outpatient diagnostic testing center, or a hospital. The child may act out or become withdrawn as a reaction to this fear. Normalizing routines and foods as well as providing comfort items may help to combat the child's fears.[9] The medical record may describe the behavior of the child as "regressed."

TIP: Most children regress or revert to an earlier stage of development when stressed or hospitalized.[10] This occurs because in seeking comfort, the child returns to behaviors most familiar and most comfortable. This is why the child who has recently been weaned from the bottle prior to hospitalization will often refuse to drink from anything other than a bottle once hospitalized. Another example of this is the child who has recently been potty-trained reverting to wetting the bed in the hospital.

The pediatric patient differs in a myriad of physiological manners as well.[11] The child is smaller, has immature organ systems, and experiences a higher metabolic rate.[12]

All systems function closer to their maximum capacity than an adult's in order to meet these normally high metabolic demands. In the face of illness, metabolic demands are increased even more, especially with fever, infection, injuries, or burns. Although children generally have healthy hearts and healthy lungs which allow them to compensate for deficits, their immature systems have fewer reserves when stressed, leading to the possibility of rapid decompensation.

The immaturity of the immune system puts the child at a higher risk for infection, especially when very young. The immature gastrointestinal system has decreased motility, an increased incidence of reflux, as well as an absence of some of the enzymes necessary for the digestion of certain food products. The immature liver is less able to metabolize toxic substances or produce large stores of clotting factors.[13]

An infant's body contains proportionally more water than an adult's. A full-term infant's body weight consists of up to 75 percent water while an adult's may be as little as 60 percent.[14] This explains why fluid loss in the infant or small child may quickly lead to dehydration. Measuring and recording intake and output can be crucial. A child's higher metabolic rate leads to the need for a higher cardiac output. So, in addition to dehydration, fluid losses in the face of other insults may lead to hypoxia, or inadequate oxygen levels to support vital organs. In addition, children's hearts have half the contractile fibers of the adult heart as well as low chemical stores. Stress may lead to rapid cardiac deterioration.

The respiratory system of an infant or child is anatomically and physiologically different from that of an adult. These differences, including the size and maturity of the airways, often lead to an increased number of respiratory illnesses in the child.[15] Because of the structure of the infant's chest, the child is almost completely reliant on the movement of the diaphragm to breathe. The reviewer of a pediatric medical record may note documentation that there were difficulties during intubation. The placement of an artificial airway down the trachea, or intubation, is difficult in the infant and small child because of the size of the tongue being large in relationship to the mouth. In addition, the cricoid ring acts as a cuff because it is the narrowest point of the child's airway until the child is approximately eight years of age. This then negates the need for a cuffed endotracheal tube.[16] Because the lining of the airway is loosely attached, it is more susceptible to the formation of edema than that of the adult. Edema can form on either side of the epithelium, and this can lead to extensive narrowing of the airway during respiratory illnesses. These differences are usually seen in children younger than school age and lessen as the child ages.

The infant's or small child's cardiovascular system is also immature. The heart is smaller than an adult heart, and the musculature is immature. There are a number of factors that accelerate the metabolic rate when a child is ill. When the metabolic rate is increased, the body generally responds by raising the cardiac output or the amount of blood pumped to the body. This is true of the child as well as the adult. The adult's body is able to boost cardiac output to meet a higher metabolic demand by both raising the heart rate and the stroke volume or the amount of blood pumped into the aorta with each beat of the heart. The child, however, has very little ability to increase the stroke volume. When stressed, the child's heart is reliant upon a rapid heart rate to raise cardiac output. This is only successful to a point. If the child's heart rate is too high, the ventricle, which pumps blood to the body, is unable to fill adequately with blood, and the amount of blood pumped to the body is actually decreased.

Because of all their physiologic differences it is important to recognize that children who are ill will generally have abnormal vital signs. The ranges of normal vital signs for children vary as the child ages. As discussed above, cardiac output is raised in the child through the mechanism of increasing heart rate. Illness of an even moderate severity may cause a substantial acceleration of metabolism, leading the child to become tachycardic or experience an increase in heart rate. In addition, a higher need for oxygen will cause the child to have an increased respiratory rate or tachypnea. Changes in blood pressure do not normally become an issue in children as quickly as they do in the adult patient. Because children have normal healthy arteries without any build up of plaque and the like, they are able to constrict their vessels very effectively even in the face of loss of substantial fluids and thus maintain a normal or near-normal blood pressure for a prolonged period of time.

A suit was brought against a hospital when a four-year-old boy admitted to the hospital for liver disease died following a liver biopsy. Upon review of the chart, it was noted that the child was admitted to the pediatric intensive care unit for monitoring immediately following the biopsy. The physician ordered the vital signs to be monitored every fifteen minutes for two hours, then every thirty minutes for two hours, and then hourly for two hours. The first set of vital signs was taken at 1200, the second set was taken at 1220, and the third set was taken, at 1300. At 1400, another set of vital signs was taken and it was then noted that the blood pressure had dropped at 1220 and was continuing to drop. The physician was notified at 1400, and the child was taken to the operating room shortly thereafter. Upon opening the abdomen, it was found that the child had bled from the biopsy site, losing a large portion of his blood volume. He suffered a cardiac arrest and could not be resuscitated. This case settled prior to trial for an undisclosed amount. (Unpublished settlement.)

A child may lose up to 45 percent of total blood volume before the blood pressure drops substantially. Increasing tachycardia, decreasing urine output, and poor peripheral perfusion would result from such an occurrence. However, if these compensatory measures go unrecognized, by the time decompensation occurs, the child will be critically close to death. Therefore, hypotension, or low blood pressure, is designated as a late sign of shock in the pediatric population. Consequently, it should be recognized that shock can be present despite a normal blood pressure.

Because children have specific physiological differences from adults, it is important that medical personnel caring for them be intimate with the details of these differences. Personnel well versed in the care of children recognize these differences and make their assessments and judgments based upon normal ranges appropriate for children. For example, a nurse familiar with the care of children would not make the assumption that a child is *not* in shock based upon the child's blood pressure measurements. Instead, this evaluation would focus more heavily upon the child's capillary refill, level of tachycardia, the strength of peripheral pulses in the arms and legs, and urine output. It is important when reviewing medical records of a child to obtain information regarding the experience of the medical personnel caring for children. Many medical-legal issues may result when personnel caring for children are not familiar with these physiologic differences. For example, a medical surgical nurse who is pulled to work in a pediatric unit may lack the knowledge to provide care according to the standard of care.

19.4 What Should the Child's Chart Contain?

The complexity of the medical record will vary related to the setting in which the child received care. The medical record from a physician's office is generally straightforward and brief, whereas the record for an inpatient admission may be very complex. Children may also have records from diagnostic testing as outpatients, outpatient therapy records, psychiatric outpatient or inpatient settings, school health records, and home health medical records. The medical records will lead one to numerous other sources for healthcare information.

A. Outpatient Records

TIP: The most obvious choice from which to obtain information regarding a child's health would be the child's primary care provider (PCP) or pediatrician.

The office record from this setting should contain some type of intake form in which information is gathered from the caregiver. The form may be a history form that is filled out by the parent, or it may be a form used by a professional who interviews the parent and records the information. If the physician was involved from the time of the child's birth, the record may contain selected records from the newborn hospital admission. From that point forward, most pediatricians' records contain a note related to each visit, an immunization record, laboratory or radiology results, and a medication record if the child takes any medications chronically.

Documentation from each visit should contain specifics related to the child's complaint; however, the child's weight should be recorded at each visit and plotted on a growth chart. Medications prescribed for the child should be based upon the most current weight. The child's vital signs should be recorded at each visit. A physical examination should be documented for the child unless the visit is related to a psychosocial issue. Differential diagnoses or diagnoses that may be a possible cause of the child's symptoms should be followed up with appropriate testing to narrow the list to a final diagnosis. Any diagnostic testing ordered should be followed up with results. If results are abnormal, documentation should reflect the course of action taken by the healthcare provider, especially if results are returned after the patient has left the office. This may include referral to a pediatric subspecialty physician. Instructions given for care of the child at home should be documented, including signs and symptoms that should prompt a return for further professional health care. Similarly, if the child is hospitalized, portions of the hospital medical records, at least the discharge summary, are included.

Referral to a specialist occurs when a specific medical issue extends beyond the scope of practice of the primary care provider (PCP). Notes from the specialist may become a part of the referring physician's record. These may be as brief as one office visit; however, they may contain results of further diagnostic testing or even a surgical procedure.

TIP: One item that may appear in the outpatient record that is rarely seen in other medical records is the telephone message.

Many office charts contain copies of telephone messages taken by secretarial personnel or answering services and handed off either to a physician or nurse for follow-up. In a large office this particular task may be delegated to one nurse each day. The nurse receives the messages, decides whether she or the physician must return the call, prioritizes the return calls, and then gets back to the caller. The chart should contain documentation of what the caller was instructed to do based upon the information gathered during the telephone call. If medical care was sought outside of the office related to one of these calls, some type of follow-up regarding that care should be documented in the chart even if it does not occur until the child's next office visit.

TIP: Whereas an adult may have outpatient testing in a number of different settings, it is not uncommon for the diagnostic testing of a child to occur in a hospital outpatient setting. Caring for children requires some specialization and is often much more time consuming than testing for adults; therefore, there are few freestanding outpatient centers willing to invest in this often expensive endeavor. It is important, therefore, to request outpatient records from hospitals, as well as inpatient records because they may be filed separately.

Children may be referred for a number of therapy types. The most common types of therapies received by children are physical, occupational, and speech therapy. These may be delivered through a hospital outpatient setting, a home care company, a stand-alone therapy center, or through the child's school system. These records contain an initial evaluation of the child related to the particular therapy as well as ongoing documentation of each visit with the child.

B. Emergency Room Records

Emergency room visits typically yield brief records. If the emergency room visit resulted in a hospital admission, the emergency room record becomes a portion of the chart for that particular inpatient admission. It is important to remember that although patient flow from an emergency room to an inpatient hospital bed appears to be seamless, the emergency room is considered an outpatient area, separate from the inpatient units. For a straightforward emergency room visit, the record generally contains information regarding triage of the child, a nursing record, a physician's record, results of diagnostic testing performed during that visit, and discharge instructions given to the child's caregivers.

Specifically, the emergency room record should contain information regarding how the child arrived to the hospital. If the child was brought in by ambulance, the name of the ambulance company should be contained in the chart. A copy of the ambulance record should be placed in the emergency room chart, but if missing and significant should be requested from the EMS provider. There should also be information about how the child was triaged. Triage is a French word meaning "the sorting and allocation of treatment to patients according to a system of priorities designed to maximize the number of survivors."[17] The nurse sees the child upon arrival to the emergency room to prioritize the child's care based upon the acuity of all patients present within the emergency room waiting area. This determines the order in which the physician will see patients. Vital signs including the child's temperature, pulse, respiratory rate, and blood pressure should be recorded and then followed up on as appropriate. A weight should be obtained and recorded. Both the nurse's and the physician's record will contain a brief history obtained regarding the past medical history as well as the current complaint followed by a physical exam. The physician then writes a plan and orders for the nurse to carry out. These orders may be

- instructing parents in care at home after discharge from the emergency room,
- requiring the patient to remain in the emergency room for a period of time while interventions are carried out, or
- leading to admission to the pediatric unit.

Just as in the outpatient chart, there should be a differential diagnosis with testing completed to rule in or rule out a number of those differentials. Results of diagnostic tests should be documented. One should be able to determine from the records that the physician in charge of the care of the child was made aware of any abnormal results, that these results were considered as the differential diagnosis was made, and that follow up for the particular abnormality was considered as well. Appropriate monitoring of the child based upon the child's acuity level should be documented throughout the child's emergency room stay. This could include frequently obtaining vital signs, placing the patient on a cardiac monitor, respiratory monitor, or pulse oximeter, or frequently recording levels of consciousness. Both the potential diagnosis as well as the acuity level of the patient should drive monitoring.

If the child is discharged from the emergency room, documentation regarding the education given to the caregivers of the child should be contained in the chart. This should include information regarding any further treatment to be carried out, any medications to be given, and what signs and symptoms should prompt the caregiver to return to the emergency room with the child.[18] If the child is being admitted as an inpatient, the record should contain documentation of a

report being called to the inpatient nurse from the emergency room nurse as well as the time the child was transported to the floor. In addition, there should be documentation regarding the mode used to transport the patient, including the type of monitoring used. It should also be evident as to whether the appropriate transport personnel were used. See Chapter 8, *Emergency Department Records*, for additional content.

C. Inpatient Hospital Admission Records

A child is admitted to the hospital when the child is deemed too ill to be treated as an outpatient. Consent for treatment should be obtained from the legal guardian unless the child arrives in critical condition and needs emergency intervention. In life-threatening conditions, healthcare providers will generally administer the necessary interventions to sustain life and have general consents signed at a later point in time.[19]

Hospital records are the most complex of medical records, but the level of complexity will depend upon the severity of the illness or injury sustained by the child and the length of the hospital stay. Records obtained from a hospital setting generally have a specific method of organization. It may be advantageous when requesting the medical record to ask for the medical records departmental policy and procedure for organization of the medical record as well.

The hospital record format may be somewhat different from hospital to hospital, but the content is essentially the same. A face sheet with demographic data is generated upon admission to the hospital. Specifically, this should delineate with whom the child lives and who is financially responsible for the child's health care. If the child is seen first in the emergency room, there may be two face sheets: one from the emergency room visit and one generated once the child is admitted. There should be consent for treatment forms that were signed by the child's legal guardians. There may be two sets of these: consent for treatment in the emergency room as well as upon admission to the hospital. From the point of admission forward, throughout the inpatient stay there are two parallel strands of documentation, one written by the nurses and one written by the physicians. In addition there is documentation by ancillary staff and results of diagnostic studies.

There is generally some type of admission data form completed by the admitting nurse with the help of a parent or guardian as well as an admission history and physical completed by the physician. From the history and physical, the physician admitting the patient generates a medical plan and writes orders. Admitting orders may vary based upon the institution. In some institutions, if the child is admitted through the emergency room, the emergency room physician may generate admission orders. In other institutions, the physician accepting the child for inpatient care will write or give the orders over the phone. Nurses will develop a nursing plan of care upon completing their admission database. This care plan should coincide with the medical plan of care.

Following the admitting process, documentation is generated in several fashions. Ongoing physician documentation is usually limited to three formats: progress notes, physician orders, and consultation notes. Generally, any physician seeing the patient writes progress notes. Hospital medical staff bylaws regulate physician practice within the institution and address the frequency that notes must be written. Healthcare prescriber orders are prepared in three ways. The prescriber may physically write the order, or the order may be written by a licensed caregiver (usually a nurse, pharmacist, or respiratory therapist) after having been received either verbally or over the telephone. The third method is through preprinted order sets created by the physician specifically for use with his patients. When a physician requests consultation with another physician, the physician being asked to see the child then generates a consultation note.

TIP: Consultants have differing roles in different institutions. In some institutions, consultants may write orders as they see fit. In other institutions, only the admitting physician writes orders. The consultant will write recommendations for the child in a note but not as orders.

Ongoing nursing documentation following the admission of the child generally includes several specific documents. Nurses often have a flow sheet upon which a twenty-four-hour period of nursing care is documented. A flow sheet will usually contain vital signs, neurological vital signs, intake and output, ongoing nursing interventions, and a nursing assessment of the patient. Narrative notes may be contained on the flow sheet or documented separately. These may be written in chronological order including the nurse's assessments, plans, interventions, and evaluations of the child. A second format would be that of a summary note documented at the end of the nurse's shift, which would include those happenings during the shift that the nurse found significant. A third method of documentation would be Charting by Exception. In this particular method the nurse would document only those findings and happenings that would be defined as outside of normal parameters.[20] In other words, in assessing the child, the nurse would make no notation of normal findings upon physical examination. She would document only those findings outside of normal. See Chapter 5, *Charting Systems*, in Volume I, for more details on Charting By Exception.

Once admitted to the hospital, the nurse completes an assessment of the child and gathers a history from the parents. As previously discussed, the child will generally have abnormal vital signs, including tachycardia and tachypnea. The temperature may be elevated if the child is suspected to have an infection.[21] Unless the child is critically ill, one would expect the blood pressure to be close to normal. The monitoring of the child should be in line with the acuity of the child's illness, not just the physician's orders.

TIP: The standard of care for the monitoring of vital signs for the child admitted to the pediatric intensive care unit is usually at least hourly, whereas monitoring on the general pediatric unit is usually performed every two to four hours.

The nurse's admission assessment of the child is generally a comprehensive one. The illness or complaint with which the child is admitted will generally direct the assessment. If the child is unable to relate his complaints due to developmental status or condition, then the nurse must use her knowledge base related to the mechanism of injury or illness to assist in guiding the direction of the assessment. For example, if a child were injured by a fall from a second-story balcony in which he hit his head, the nurse would focus the assessment on the neurological system, looking for signs and symptoms of changes in level of consciousness. The nurse should suspect that the child could develop increased intracranial pressure. The assessment of this patient should include frequent vital signs, frequent checking for pupillary reaction in the eyes, and regular measurement of the Glasgow Coma Scale.

The mechanism of injury was especially important in the case of a three-year-old child injured in an accident in her backyard. While playing with several older siblings, a concrete bird bath was knocked from its pedestal, hitting the child in the head and then landing on her abdomen. Upon presentation to the emergency room, the child was alert and awake. The CT scan of her head was read as normal. She was admitted to the pediatric unit for monitoring overnight. The nurse continued to assess her neurological status carefully; however, the child vomited several times throughout the night and the nurse documented that the mother had concerns that the child had internal injuries. Early in the morning the child began to cough up blood. When the physician contacted asked for the results of her abdominal CT scan he was told that no one had ordered that. An x-ray of the abdomen revealed "a shadow suspicious for bleeding." The child was taken to the operating room but arrested in the holding area and could not be resuscitated. On autopsy it was found that the child had suffered a laceration to her spleen and had bled internally from this injury. The hospital and the physician settled with the family prior to trial for a confidential amount. (Unpublished settlement.)

It is in this type of situation that it becomes important to determine the level of competence of the professional assessing the child. If the child is admitted to a specialty unit in a children's hospital, one should expect that this professional would be highly competent in using the mechanism of injury to guide the assessment. This may not be the case if the child is admitted to a hospital with no dedicated pediatric services. If the child develops a complication due to this healthcare encounter, the issue may relate back to the decision regarding admission of the child to that particular facility versus transfer to a tertiary care children's hospital.

Regardless of the setting in which a child is treated, the assessment of the child should focus on certain specifics related to the physiologic differences between adults and children. The level of consciousness is one of the most important factors for a healthcare professional to ascertain. It can be difficult to recognize changes in the level of consciousness if the healthcare professional does not have previous experience with the child. A change in the level of irritability would be an important clinical sign. A previously placid infant who becomes fussy may be displaying the first indication that a change in the level of consciousness is occurring. Often this change in the infant will be noted by the parent who may relate something as simple as, "He is just not acting himself." The pediatric healthcare provider needs to stop and listen, question, and assess. Other changes in the child's neurological status should be identified. The records of a child should reflect these actions.

TIP: In a respiratory illness, one of the most important factors to consider is the work of breathing necessary to maintain the child's oxygenation status. "Work of breathing" is an expression used frequently in pediatrics to denote symptoms implying more effort needed of the musculature.

When a child has respiratory distress, work of breathing (often abbreviated "WOB") will increase the metabolic rate. Work of breathing may be characterized by increased respiratory rate, abdominal muscle retractions, nasal flar-

ing, head bobbing, and grunting.[22] When these symptoms are noted, documentation should reflect reporting of these symptoms to a physician followed by orders for rapid intervention. These interventions may include

- administering of oxygen,
- repositioning,
- administering respiratory medications by inhalation,
- suctioning of the airways,
- performing chest physiotherapy,
- using a pulse oximeter,
- using non-invasive mechanical ventilation, or
- intubating the airway followed by mechanical ventilation.

The pulse oximeter reads the amount of oxygen attached to hemoglobin traveling in the peripheral circulation. A sense of false security is often assumed based upon these numbers. If the number on the monitor is an acceptable one, the healthcare provider may not assess the work of breathing necessary to achieve that number on the monitor. In the pediatric population, this can be a very dangerous practice. Compensation for a respiratory illness is achieved by increasing the work of breathing which in turn increases the child's metabolic rate, leading to an increase in the child's oxygen consumption. If this cycle persists without intervention, the child, with less respiratory reserve than the adult, will tire rather quickly. Once tired, the child will decompensate rapidly.[23]

The small child does not generally require a cuffed endotracheal tube for intubation of the airway. The child has a physiologic cuff in the form of the cricoid cartilage. There are some cases in which the cuffed tube may be required, but it is the exception rather than the rule.[24] The size of the endotracheal tube that is placed is important because over time, if the cuff is inflated to too great a degree, left inflated for too long, or if an endotracheal tube of too large a size is placed, the child may have tracheal damage leading to scarring and stenosis (narrowing). This may then require a tracheostomy tube to be placed and surgical intervention in the form of a tracheal reconstruction.

The child is generally able to maintain a normal blood pressure even in the face of fluid loss. In the adult population, the healthcare professional relies more heavily on the patient's blood pressure to assess the cardiovascular status. The child is able to compensate for losses in fluid by vasoconstricting or narrowing the diameter of the blood vessels and by increasing her heart rate. Therefore, blood pressure becomes a late sign of shock in the pediatric population and one that indicates decompensation.[25] The peripheral perfusion is the important assessment parameter to evaluate in the child. This is done by assessing the child's capillary refill by simply depressing the child's nail bed gently until it becomes white, either on the hand or the foot, and counting the seconds until the pink color returns. Three seconds or less is considered within normal limits. This may be documented in the medical record as "cap refill < 3 secs." If the refill is depressed or greater than three seconds, peripheral pulses should also be assessed. Pulses are graded on a scale of 1 to 4, with 4 being a bounding or very strong pulse. Treatment for decreased perfusion should be initiated. Generally the first line of action is to give a child fluid. The appropriate fluid to use to resuscitate a child is either Normal Saline or Lactated Ringers. Using a solution containing glucose is inappropriate. Fluid boluses generally are given in increments of 10 milliliters per kilogram of body weight. If the child is very dry, the first bolus may be 20 milliliters per kilogram. Fluid resuscitation is generally continued until perfusion improves and the child's kidneys begin to make urine.[26] The medical record should contain prescriber orders for fluids. IV administration records or critical care flow sheets should document when the fluids were given and how much was infused.

Children dehydrate more easily with fluid loss because of their proportionally larger surface area exposed to the environment, as well as the larger percentage of body water. Because of this, the child's intake and output is another parameter that is assessed very closely. Signs and symptoms of dehydration include decreased urine output, a sunken fontanel (or soft spot in the skull) in an infant, delayed capillary refill, absence of tears when crying, dry mucous membranes, and poor skin turgor.[27] Fluids given to the child either by mouth or by intravenous infusion are carefully monitored, and diapers are weighed to obtain urine output amounts as well. Urine output for the child should be at least 1 milliliter per kilogram of body weight per hour. As with vital signs, trending of output is more important than the measurement within a one-hour time frame.

Infusion pumps are used to deliver most fluids and medications in the pediatric population. Medications are often given in their most concentrated forms in order to avoid administering large amounts of fluid along with medications. In addition, amounts from any drainage device are also carefully recorded. Children may be weighed daily if their diagnosis warrants it. These measures should be clearly documented. In addition to the flow sheet, nurses generally note the administration of medications on some type of medication administration record or MAR. Education of the patient and family is another important area of documentation for the nurse. This education should center on two areas of care: the care being rendered to the child in the hospital and preparing the family to care for the child once discharged. A discharge instruction form is used by the nurse to give specific written instructions to the caregivers. This is generally a duplicate form, signed by the nurse and the parent with one copy remaining with the chart and the second copy being given to the family.

Beyond physician and nursing care, a number of specialty therapies are delivered by other trained professionals, including respiratory care, physical therapy, occupational therapy, speech therapy, and dietary. Each of these professionals also documents in the child's record. Each professional performs an assessment or evaluation of the child followed by a brief plan for care related to the professional's specialty service. In addition, the therapist documents the interventions and the child's response to those interventions.

Other records found in the chart include results of diagnostic testing, surgical reports, cardiac arrest resuscitation documentation, and autopsy reports. Diagnostic results will generally include laboratory results as well as the results of various radiological studies. Various other diagnostic studies may be included as well. One should be aware that the pre-printed normal parameters often found on the results forms are generally the parameters for adults. There are laboratory studies that have differing normal parameters related to the age of the patient. Please refer to Chapter 10, *Diagnostic Testing*.

Surgical records include documentation related to anesthesia, nursing care in the holding area, operating room, and post-anesthesia recovery room as well as the reports related to the procedure itself. Generally a pathology report would be generated related to any tissues excised during a surgical procedure. If the child experienced either a respiratory or cardiac arrest event, a record of the emergency interventions and the patient's responses to these interventions would be documented on a "code" record. If the child expired, usually the physician records a death note, and if an autopsy is performed it may be part of the record as well. Refer to Chapter 18, *Autopsy Reports*, in Volume I, for more information.

D. Pediatric-Specific Documents

Within the medical record there are several items that are important specifically to the care of children. If the child is young, the history of the pregnancy from which the child resulted may be pertinent. This is also true of the birth history as well. Both of these items may be especially important in the child less than one year of age.

All children's records should include a vaccination history and a history of childhood illnesses as well as information regarding recent exposures to such.[28] This information is often necessary when trying to establish a differential diagnosis. In addition, the child's weight and height should be recorded. If the child is less than two years of age, the child's head circumference should be documented also. This information should not just be verbally taken from family members because medications and other therapies are administered based upon these measurements. The measurements should then be plotted on a growth chart in order to note if the child is growing properly.[29] Lack of growth is often one of the first symptoms that a child is harboring a chronic health problem. It is important to note that it is the trend in the child's growth that should be followed rather than at a specific point in time.[30] For example, it may not be pertinent that a child is at the fifth percentile for weight and height if that particular child has been plotted at that percentile throughout his lifetime. It may be important though if the child was previously at the twentieth percentile and has now fallen into the fifth percentile.

19.5 Red Flags in the Chart

A red flag is something that stands out in the documentation that may warrant further investigation and could be linked to the deterioration of the child. A red flag may be absence of an item listed in Section 19.4 regarding what should be in the chart. There are red flags that are generic to pediatric care in general, and then there are red flags that are specific to certain types of charts. This section will address each of these.

TIP: It is generally the extremes in documentation in charts that are most noteworthy. One should carefully review a chart when there are large gaps in documentation or when there is an abundance of documentation surrounding a specific incident.

A. Generic Red Flags
1. Vital signs

Vital signs are often red flags in pediatric records. A lack of documentation of scheduled vital signs just prior to a child's deterioration is a definite red flag. In addition, trends in vital signs going unrecognized are common red flags in pediatrics. A continuing trend of increasing tachycardia (increasing heart rate) and increasing tachypnea (increasing respiratory rate) with a decrease in oxygen saturation readings often precedes a respiratory arrest if intervention fails to occur in a timely fashion. In a shock state, a child will become increasingly tachycardic with decreasing peripheral perfusion and decreasing urine output. Without receiving interventions, the child may become hypotensive and then bradycardic, possibly suffering a cardiac arrest.[31]

In reviewing the case of an eight-year-old male with a history of cerebral palsy admitted to the hospital for osteotomies with spica cast placement, it was apparent that vital signs were not appropriately taken nor analyzed. For the first ninety minutes postoperatively, the nurse documented that she was unable to obtain a blood pressure. The child was extremely tachycardic with the lowest heart rate recorded at 177 beats per minute. When taking into consideration that the child's temperature was normal and he was medicated with morphine during this period of time, this level of tachycardia should have been extremely worrisome. There was no further documentation by the nurse. The child's follow-up documentation consisted of a resuscitation sheet when he was found without respirations or pulse. The child was not successfully resuscitated. This case was settled for an undisclosed amount prior to trial. (Unpublished settlement.)

2. Medication errors

Other generic red flags in pediatrics relate to the administration of medications.[32] The omission of medications may be a red flag. The attorney or legal nurse consultant should carefully check the orders and verify that they were carried out. For example, if the child was ordered to receive respiratory therapy treatments every two hours, the respiratory therapy notes should reflect that this occurred. If it did not occur and the child's deterioration was respiratory in nature, it is possible that those two happenings were linked. This is not always the case, but those types of things should be noted in the record review. In addition, it is important to check to ensure that medications ordered were the medications given. Even the lay press has printed stories regarding this issue. The similarity of drug names can easily lead to a medication error, especially when verbal orders are given.[33]

Pediatric medication errors often relate to dosages. Because children are small, dosing of medication is most often based upon the child's weight in kilograms.[34] Doses of medications for children should be carefully written. There should be no decimal points in a dose that requires a whole number of milligrams to be given.[35] For instance, 10 milligrams should not be written 10.0 milligrams. This of course can be mistaken for 100 milligrams, a ten-fold error. By the same token, medications that are portions of whole numbers should be reflected with a zero and a decimal point prior to the dosage.[36] For example, .25 milligrams should be written 0.25 milligrams so as not to mistake the dose for 25 milligrams, another very large error. Refer to Chapter 10, *Patient Safety Initiatives and Medical Records*, in Volume I, for more information about "Do not use abbreviations." When deterioration of a child seemed to coincide with the administration of a medication, the dosage should be carefully checked using a pediatric drug manual and working out the dosing based upon the patient's weight as listed in the chart.

TIP: Giving the child the medication by the wrong route can also lead to medication errors. There are many medications that have differing solutions for different routes. Giving the intravenous medication by mouth is usually not harmful; however, giving the oral solution via the intravenous route may be fatal.

Even when the solutions are the same, differing routes may require very different dosing; therefore, giving the oral dosing of a particular medication by the intravenous route may lead to a toxic dose being administered. Chapter 14, *Medication Records,* provides additional information.

3. Code resuscitation records

When a code sheet or arrest record is in the chart, it is important to investigate the circumstances that led to the emergency event and determine whether everything that could have been done to prevent the arrest was in fact done. A respiratory arrest, if not immediately and appropriately treated, will be followed by a cardiac arrest.

TIP: A cardiac arrest should be prevented at all costs since a child who suffers a respiratory arrest without cardiac arrest has a 75 percent chance of being discharged from the hospital, often with a good neurological outcome. The child who sustains a cardiac arrest in the hospital has only a 24 percent chance of survival. In addition, the child who survives a cardiac arrest is likely to have severe neurological deficits.[37]

---

4. Transfers

The investigation of the transfer to a higher level of care should look into what occurred prior to that transfer. If the patient went to surgery before the transfer then it may have been a planned event and, therefore, not a red flag. However, if the patient's condition deteriorated and she was subsequently transferred to another unit or another hospital, careful investigation regarding those circumstances should ensue.

5. Telephone calls

A red flag may be raised by repeated documentation that a physician was called regarding a child's status in a short time frame. This is concerning if there were no physician's orders obtained or the physician did not come to assess the child. This often occurs when a nurse or other healthcare professional such as an intern or resident is attempting to advocate for a child and is unsuccessful in having the physician act as the nurse would like.

TIP: Often the phrase "No orders received" is written by the nurse to indicate that although status changes were reported to the physician, no orders were given to the nurse in order to intervene on the child's behalf.

---

6. Chain of command issues

There are generally two chains of command in hospitals. One is the hierarchy that is the hospital's chain of command, and the other is the chain of command for physicians. In most hospitals, staff nurses caring for the patient at the bedside have a charge nurse who is responsible for the nursing unit and for the patient care being delivered during his shift. Above that person is generally some type of nurse manager who reports to a nursing director. The nursing director often has a "substitute" on off-shifts who may be referred to as the house supervisor. A chief nursing officer is generally responsible for all nurses within the hospital.[38] The physician chain of command may be very abbreviated in a private hospital where private physicians must answer only to the chief of staff; however, in teaching institutions, there is a complex hierarchy. Medical students often see patients but are generally not allowed to write orders independently, at least in the pediatric setting. The students are supervised by interns who are in their first year of practice. After having completed the first year practicum out of medical school, the physician becomes a resident and is generally known by the year of residency currently completing. Above residents are fellows who are physicians who have completed a residency but are now obtaining several more years of training in a subspecialty. Above these physicians is the attending physician who is the leader of the medical team. In addition, most teaching hospitals also have a chief of staff and a pediatric department head.

When a nurse has attempted to advocate for a patient and the physician is being unreceptive, the nurse may choose to move up either of the chains of command in order to achieve what she feels is necessary for the patient. Obviously, as with any hierarchy, this is not implemented for small complaints. This generally occurs when the nurse feels that there is a good possibility of harm to the patient if intervention does not take place.[39] Repeated calls to the same physician without appropriate response may warrant moving up the chain of command, especially if the patient is in jeopardy due to the lack of response from the physician. This may also occur when the nurse feels that an order that has been received is inappropriate. The first intervention should be a discussion with the physician writing the order; however, if that physician is insistent or refuses to be responsive, the nurse may then initiate the chain of command. Documentation of use of the chain of command should appear in the chart.[40]

B. Office Red Flags

In outpatient records, red flags could include

- an incomplete history or physical examination,
- a poorly formulated differential diagnosis,
- failure to follow up the differential diagnosis with appropriate diagnostic studies,
- failure to follow through with abnormal results of diagnostic studies, or
- failure to respond appropriately to a telephone call from a parent reporting abnormal findings.

C. Emergency Room Red Flags

Red flags in the emergency room record may be similar to those of the outpatient record. Problems with triage are red flags specific to the emergency center. Triage demands that a nurse quickly and accurately assess the level of acuity in a child. This is an area that can be rife with problems. Delays in care or deterioration of the child can occur if the patient is inappropriately triaged.[41]

In addition, another problem that may occur in a busy emergency center is the failure to monitor a child at an appropriate frequency. This monitoring may take the form of

- a neurological assessment,
- level of consciousness,
- vital signs,
- peripheral perfusion, or
- respiratory status of the child.

Medical and nursing documentation should provide data about these assessments.

Another issue that is a source of liability for the emergency room is the use of discharge instructions given to the patient and family. When a child is discharged from the emergency room, the documentation should include any instructions given to the parent regarding the ongoing care necessary at home to either prevent worsening of the illness or help the child to return to health. Discharge instructions should also include the specific signs and symptoms that the parent may note if the child is worsening and the actions the parent should take if these signs and symptoms are noted.

The signs and symptoms for which the parent should return to the emergency center should be explicitly spelled out.[42]

Two issues of importance may occur at the time of transition from the emergency center to the inpatient unit: the continuing of appropriate monitoring and the reporting of accurate information from one level of care to the next. The first issue regards the removal of the child from a cardiorespiratory monitor or pulse oximeter for transfer as well as the transport of the child by an inappropriate level of caregiver, such as a technician rather than a licensed professional. These transport decisions should be guided by the acuity of the child. Some children may be transported by an unlicensed caregiver; however, if the child required cardiorespiratory monitoring or pulse oximetry in the emergency room and had orders for continuing monitoring on the floor, the child should be monitored en route and transported by a licensed caregiver. Deterioration of the child while en route to the inpatient room is not uncommon.

The second issue may occur when the emergency room nurse gives an inaccurate or incomplete report to the nurse on the inpatient unit. Under-reporting regarding the acuity of the child is a more critical issue for the patient's safety than over-reporting. This occurs when the nurse diminishes the level of acuity or leaves out important information, therefore leaving the inpatient nurse unprepared for the arrival of a child who is sicker than the child for whom she prepared.

D. Inpatient Red Flags

Many of the above red flags, including those generic pediatric red flags, may be present in the inpatient hospital records as well. Those issues regarding monitoring frequency and the child's acuity level are especially prevalent. In addition to this is the absence of documentation regarding the notification of a physician in light of changes in the child's status. This may be related to vital signs, other changes in physical assessment, or the results of diagnostic testing.

TIP: Generally, a physician should be notified of any change in the child's condition, emergence of new signs and symptoms, abnormal laboratory or other diagnostic test results, inability to carry out physician's orders, or any medication or treatment errors.

19.6 Failure to Recognize Compensatory Mechanisms
A. Compensation for Respiratory Illnesses

Many of the medical-legal issues that occur in the pediatric population are related to the failure to recognize those physiological compensatory mechanisms discussed previously. There are several common pathways in which children deteriorate to a state severe enough to sustain injury or die. Three examples of those are discussed in this section.

Respiratory illnesses make up a large portion of the diagnoses for which children are seen in a medical setting. As discussed previously, children are more prone to respiratory illness related to the physiologic differences from the adult population. In the pediatric record, it is important to look carefully for the signs and symptoms of respiratory compensation that may have been overlooked when the child deteriorated related to respiratory distress. In addition, respiratory symptoms may be exacerbated by medications if the child was receiving analgesics or pain medications or anti-anxiety medications.[43] These medications should be administered with extreme care to the child with respiratory compromise as they decrease the respiratory drive which acts as the compensatory mechanism for respiratory illness. It is important to review the records for this issue.

The early signs and symptoms that may be documented include an increasing respiratory rate, an increased heart rate, and an increase in the work of breathing, often followed by decreasing oxygen saturations if the child was monitored by pulse oximetry. Saturations above 94 percent are generally considered within normal limits. Increased work of breathing may be documented as retractions of any type (deep inward movements of the abdomen when the child breathes), grunting, head bobbing, or nasal flaring.[44] Other indicators of distress may include a need to be positioned in an upright manner or an infant who is unable to suck appropriately. Later signs might include

- lethargy,
- inability to talk,
- failure to respond to a painful procedure such as a blood withdrawal,
- confusion, or
- deterioration of color.

TIP: These signs often indicate that the child's compensatory mechanisms are failing or the child is tiring. If intervention is not immediate, a respiratory arrest is likely imminent.[45]

Physicians and nurses should certainly be aware of the early signs of respiratory distress; however, any late symptoms should cause a physician to react by examining the child. The child should be placed in an upright position with her head elevated. Oxygen should be started or the flow increased, and if indicated, the child may need immediate bronchodilator medications administered. Ultimately, a child who has deteriorated to this point may require an artificial airway in the form of an endotracheal intubation with mechanical ventilation.[46] It is always preferable to intubate a child electively rather than emergently. There is a risk of hypoxia during any intubation process, but it is much smaller in a controlled and planned intubation rather than an emergent situation.[47] In the emergent situation the child may have already suffered a respiratory arrest in which case the child has sustained some level of hypoxia.[48]

B. Compensation for Hypovolemia

Another frequently encountered problem in the pediatric population is that of dehydration which can deteriorate to hypovolemic shock. This may occur by a number of mechanisms. It may be as simple as the child having a diarrheal illness, or it may be as profound as internal bleeding sustained in an accident. Obviously the rate that shock occurs in these two situations varies greatly; however, the signs and symptoms of compensation are the same. As fluid is lost and the child becomes dehydrated, the heart rate increases to maintain the child's cardiac output at the same level. If necessary, because of continuing loss or failure to replace the lost fluid, the peripheral circulation will constrict, decreasing the blood flow to the periphery of the body and maintaining the flow to the vital organs. The extremities then become cooler, the capillary refill becomes slower, and the peripheral pulses weaken somewhat.[49] These are early signs of hypovolemia.

If the process continues, due to failure to stop the fluid loss or the lack of fluid being replaced, the child's condition will deteriorate. The heart and respiratory rates increase, and the amount of urine output decreases as the circulation to the kidneys lessens. The blood pressure generally remains within normal limits although it may decrease somewhat. The point of decompensation in the child with shock is more difficult to predict than that of the child with respiratory failure. Some children can compensate for quite some time in this state, others for only a short period of time. Acidosis occurs related to the progressive tachycardia, tachypnea, and failure of the kidneys to function appropriately.[50] Decompensation is related to the level of acidosis. Hypotension is a late sign and is generally followed closely by bradycardia if intervention does not occur rapidly. Other late signs may include lethargy, confusion, hallucinations, and a decreased level of consciousness with failure to respond to painful stimuli.

The attorney or legal nurse consultant may be involved in reviewing a pediatric record of a child who suffered damages or died following an illness or injury that would lead to dehydration. The record should be carefully examined for the signs and symptoms of compensation listed above. In addition, the chart should be analyzed by an expert witness to determine if the appropriate treatment measures were initiated. Again, although the physician should have been made aware of the initial signs and symptoms of dehydration, the physician should certainly respond emergently if the child is deteriorating with shock.

TIP: Tachycardia and tachypnea are common signs in the ill child; however, decreased urine output in conjunction with these may indicate dehydration.

Fluid replacement should be initiated, and fluid loss should be halted. If the fluid being lost is blood, normal saline may be the initial fluid used as replacement, but this should be followed with blood products.[51] Fluids are generally initiated at 10 milliliters per kilogram of body weight; however, in the child decompensating with shock, fluids may be started at 20 to 30 milliliters per kilogram. Fluid resuscitation is usually continued until the child's capillary refill improves and the child begins to make urine.[52] Other measures that may be initiated include oxygen administration, placement of a second intravenous catheter or central line, and a urinary catheter. Depending upon the severity of the child's acuity, the child may be transferred to a pediatric intensive care unit. In addition, the child may require intubation and mechanical ventilation if there is fear that the child will develop respiratory distress related to fluid resuscitation.

C. Compensation for Increased Intracranial Pressure

Head injuries constitute another big category of injuries that are sustained by children. This is due to the disproportionately large head that the child, especially the child under school age, has as compared to the adult.[53] The child's head is heavy and may act as a projectile if the child is not restrained. This is especially true in some types of motorized accidents such as those involving a car, boat, ATV (all terrain vehicle), or jet ski. Missing the signs and symptoms indicating that there was compensation for increasing intracranial pressure can be catastrophic in a child with a head injury. It is important to recognize that even despite the best of care the child with a head injury may sustain serious neurological damage. Often the injury is multifocal, with massive cerebral edema in addition to bleeding. A hematoma in the brain from a head injury that is caught in a timely fashion may be evacuated surgically. These children may have an opportunity to recover with only minor neurological deficits.[54] This of course depends upon the severity of the initial injury.

The signs and symptoms of increased intracranial pressure often begin very subtly.[55] One of the first signs is an increase in irritability. This is often very difficult for the healthcare professional to detect; however, parents generally do take note of these changes. Their concerns are often expressed to the nurse in terms of, "He's not acting right." Following this, the child will generally demonstrate a decrease in the level of consciousness and will either be difficult to arouse or will fall back to sleep without ongoing stimulation.[56] The pathophysiologic cause of this is the swelling in the brain.

A nine-year-old girl was admitted to the hospital for intravenous antibiotics for mastoiditis. Following her admission she had several episodes of emesis and complained of a headache. The night shift nurse documented that the child was irritable and that even though she was easily arousable she fell back to sleep without stimulation. She further documented that the child would "cry out every now and then" in her sleep. Early in the morning hours the child, who had no prior episode of bed-wetting, was incontinent of urine. The child's status was not recognized until she became unresponsive and required emergent intubation. She suffered irreversible brain damage. The case was settled confidentially prior to trial. (Unpublished settlement.)

There are three substances located within the bony enclosure of the skull: the brain, blood, and cerebrospinal fluid. When swelling of the brain occurs or when a hematoma or collection of blood forms, this causes the pressure within the skull to increase. As this pressure increases, the blood vessels in the brain constrict in order to take up less space, thus decreasing the amount of oxygen getting to the brain tissue. The area of the brain that controls one's level of consciousness is very sensitive to the lack of oxygen. The vasoconstriction causes irritability and then a decreasing level of consciousness. The child's pupils may become unequal or unreactive to light. The child may experience increasing headache, and vomiting may occur. As swelling increases, the child's level of consciousness may continue to decrease until he becomes unarousable even to painful stimuli.[57] Later signs of increased intracranial pressure may include seizures, hypertension, and bradycardia (slow heart rate).

TIP: The physician caring for the child with a head injury should be notified of any change in the child's level of consciousness, especially if the parent is noting a change in the child.

The amount of time that the body can compensate in the child with a head injury may be very short. The more rapid the decompression of the swelling, the more likely the child is to have a better neurological outcome. Prompt recognition is the key to treating this child. Any change in level of consciousness will generally prompt the ordering of a stat immediate CT scan of the brain. If the child is deteriorating quickly, mannitol will be ordered. This is a medication that pulls fluid from the brain tissue and into the vascular spaces in order to decrease the swelling rapidly. For the child with a severe injury, an intracranial catheter may be placed in the ventricle of the brain to measure the intracranial pressure. If this is the case, the child may have suffered a very severe brain injury and may not be expected to live.

Compensatory mechanisms may also be recognized in adults; but in children, they are critical. Deteriorating adults tend to worsen over a period of time. Children decline in a very rapid manner. This is of course a matter of perspective, however. If one looks at the child's course and recognizes the compensatory mechanisms at work, then the course of the deterioration may not be considered so short. However, if one does not recognize the compensatory mechanisms for what they are, then the child appears to decompensate rapidly indeed.

19.7 How Do I Know if I Need a Pediatric Expert?

In any medically based lawsuit the attorney will require assistance from several medical professionals even if the attorney is a medical professional. Having become familiar with just some of the differences found in the pediatric population through reading this chapter, hopefully it has become clear that the necessary professional will be one with a pediatric background. This might be a pediatric nurse or a pediatrician. Nurses should judge the care given by nurses. Pediatricians should analyze the care given by other pediatricians, and pediatric subspecialty physicians should look at the care of like subspecialists.

Although consultants may be personnel no longer participating in the clinical arena, expert witnesses should be persons who are actively involved in clinical care of patients. Attorneys should ensure that they are aware of the amount of clinical involvement of professionals prior to hiring them. It is also important to understand in what type of setting that pediatric professional works. Generally, the standards for pediatric care are set in children's hospitals; personnel utilized to render opinions regarding such care are often found in the same settings. It is important to study carefully the curriculum vitae of the persons being considered to analyze pediatric medical records. Specifics to inspect include educational background, certifications, experience base, professional affiliations, as well as public speaking and publications. It is beneficial for an expert to hold at least a bachelor's degree in the specialty. When the professional has advanced education, it is preferable that it is related to pediatrics. Experience outside the specialty area of pediatrics would not be uncommon; however, the majority of the expert's professional experiences should be in the pediatric arena, especially the most recent experience or the experience during the timeframe of the care being evaluated. Professional affiliations should also reflect an interest in children and related areas. Public speaking and publications in the specific issue at hand may be advantageous; however, it is important to be aware of the specific stance the professional has taken on these matters both in public discussions as well as in written format.

19.8 Conclusions: "Proceed with Caution"

The attorney who is contemplating a pediatric case needs to be aware of the specific nature of dealing with a case that pertains to a child. From the very beginning, when meeting with a family for the first conference, the plaintiffs' attorney needs to be aware of the differences, both in the physical nature of the child and in the emotional nature of the case. Any family seeking legal recourse against the medical system will come to the attorney with some level of emotion because harm has come to someone they love. In the case of a child, there will most likely be grief and anger and often at a greater level as the parent feels some level of responsibility for being unable to protect the child from the injury. It is critically important for the attorney to remain somewhat neutral despite the story told. Many times the records may not bear out the story as perceived by the family. This is not to say that the story is not completely true, but the family must understand that the law is based upon the evidence and what facts can be proved. The only promise that should be made to a family initially is to perform a thorough investigation. This investigation should be waged in a knowledgeable fashion using true pediatric experts, so that the least that is gained by the family is a better understanding of what happened to their child.

Endnotes

1. Morad, M. et al. "Adolescence, Chronic Illness and Disability." *International Journal of Adolescent Medicine and Health.* 16, p. 21–27. 2004.

2. Madge, S. and M.A. Bryon. "Model for Transition from Pediatric to Adult Care in Cystic Fibrosis." *Journal of Pediatric Nursing.* 17, p. 283–288. 2002.

3. Iyer, P. "Nursing Documentation" in Iyer, P. and Levin, B. (Editors). *Nursing Malpractice, Third Edition,* Tucson, AZ: Lawyers and Judges Publishing. 2006.

4. *Id.*

5. Hockenberry, M.J. "Communication and Health Assessment of the Child and Family" in Wilson, D., M.L. Winkelstein, and N.E. Kline. (Eds.) *Wong's Nursing Care of Infants and Children.* p. 139–169. St. Louis, MO: Mosby. 2003.

6. *Id.*

7. Hockenberry, M.J. "Family Influence on Child Health Promotion" in Wilson, D., M.L. Winkelstein, and N.E. Kline. (Eds.) *Wong's Nursing Care of Infants and Children.* p. 64–102. St. Louis, MO: Mosby. 2003.

8. Algren, C. "Family-Centered Care of the Child During Illness and Hospitalization" in D. Wilson, M.L. Winkelstein, and N.E. Kline. (Eds.) *Wong's Nursing Care of Infants and Children.* p. 1031–1100. St. Louis, MO: Mosby. 2003.

9. *Id.*

10. Haiat, H., G. Bar-Mor, and M. Shochat. "The World of the Child: A World of Play Even in the Hospital." *Journal of Pediatric Nursing.* 18, p. 209–214. 2003.

11. Laskowski-Jones, L. and D. Salati. "Responding to Pediatric Trauma." *Dimensions of Critical Care Nursing.* 19, p. 2–8. 2000.

12. Hockenberry, M.J. "Health Promotion of the Infant and Family" in Wilson, D., M.L. Winkelstein, and N.E. Kline. (Eds.) *Wong's Nursing Care of Infants and Children.* p. 493–553. St. Louis, MO: Mosby. 2003.

13. Pineiro-Carrero, V. and E. Pineiro. "Liver." *Pediatrics.* 113, p. 1097–1106. 2004.

14. *See* note 12.

15. *Id.*

16. Perkin, R.M. and D.W. van Stralen. "Intubation" in Perkin, R.M., J.D. Swift, and D.A. Newton. (Eds.) *Pediatric Hospital Medicine: Textbook of Inpatient Management.* p. 874–878. Philadelphia, PA: Lippincott Williams and Wilkins. 2003.

17. Tepas, J. "Triage, Trauma Scores, and Transport" in Buntain, W.L. (Editor). *Management of Pediatric Trauma.* p. 57–68. Philadelphia, PA: W.B. Saunders. 1995.

18. Macaulay, C. Adkins, D., Saville, M. and E. Barker. "Emergency Nursing Malpractice Issues" in Iyer, P. and Levin, B. (Editors). *Nursing Malpractice, Third Edition,* AZ: Lawyers and Judges Publishing. 2006.

19. *Id.*

20. *See* note 3.

21. Newton, D.H. "Fever" in Perkin, R.M., J.D. Swift, and D.A. Newton. (Eds.) *Pediatric Hospital Medicine: Textbook of Inpatient Management.* p. 134–137. Philadelphia, PA: Lippincott Williams and Wilkins. 2003.

22. Perkin, R.M. and J.D. Swift. "Wheezing" in Perkin, R.M., J.D. Swift, and D.A. Newton. (Eds.) *Pediatric Hospital Medicine: Textbook of Inpatient Management.* p. 171–174. Philadelphia, PA: Lippincott Williams and Wilkins. 2003.

23. *Id.*

24. *See* note 16.

25. Novotny, W.E. and R.M. Perkin. "Shock" in Perkin, R.M., J.D. Swift, and D.A. Newton. (Eds.) *Pediatric Hospital Medicine: Textbook of Inpatient Management.* p. 199–208. Philadelphia, PA: Lippincott Williams and Wilkins. 2003.

26. *Id.*

27. Fiordalisi, I. and L. Finsberg. "Diarrhea and Dehydration" in Perkin, R.M., J.D. Swift, and D.A. Newton. (Eds.) *Pediatric Hospital Medicine: Textbook of Inpatient Management.* p. 191–198. Philadelphia, PA: Lippincott Williams and Wilkins. 2003.

28. *See* note 6.

29. de Onis, M., T. Wignhoven, and A. Onyango. "Worldwide Practices in Child Growth Monitoring." *Journal of Pediatrics.* 144, p. 461–465. 2004.

30. Hockenberry, M.J. "Physical and Developmental Assessment of the Child" in Wilson, D., M.L. Winkelstein, and N.E. Kline. (Eds.) *Wong's Nursing Care of Infants and Children.* p. 170–239. St. Louis, MO: Mosby. 2003.

31. *See* note 25.

32. O'Donnell, J., Iyer, P. and Benjamin, D. "Medication Errors" in Iyer, P. and Levin. B. (Editors). *Nursing Malpractice, Third Edition.* Tucson, AZ: Lawyers and Judges Publishing. 2006.

33. Pickert, C.B. "Iatrogensis and the Risks of Hospitalization" in Perkin, R.M., J.D. Swift, and D.A. Newton. (Eds.) *Pediatric Hospital Medicine: Textbook of Inpatient Management.* p. 40–42. Philadelphia, PA: Lippincott Williams and Wilkins. 2003.

34. *Id.*

35. *See* note 32.

36. *Id.*

37. Novotny, W.E. and R.M. Perkin. "Cardiac Arrest and Resuscitation: Infant and Child" in Perkin, R. *Pediatric Hospital Medicine.* p. 183–190. Philadelphia, PA: Lippincott Williams and Wilkins Publishing Company. 2003.

38. Rottkamp. J. "An Inside Look at Today's Health Care Environment" in Iyer, P. and Levin, B. (Editors. *Nursing Malpractice, Third Edition.* Tucson, AZ: Lawyers and Judges Publishing. 2006.

39. Greenwald, L. and M. Mondor. "Malpractice and the Perinatal Nurse." *Journal of Perinatal and Neonatal Nursing.* 17, p. 101–109. 2003.

40. *See* note 3.

41. Macaulay, C., Adkins, D, Saville, M. and E. Barker. "Emergency Nursing Malpractice Issues" in Iyer, P. and Levin. B. (Editors). *Nursing Malpractice, Third Edition.* p. 483–527. Tucson, AZ: Lawyers and Judges Publishing. 2006.

42. *Id.*

43. Katz, A.L. and E.N. Grayck. "Respiratory Failure" in Perkin, R.M., J.D. Swift, and D.A. Newton. (Eds.) *Pediatric Hospital Medicine: Textbook of Inpatient Management.* p. 273–276. Philadelphia, PA: Lippincott Williams and Wilkins. 2003.

44. Winkelstein, M.L. "The Child with Disturbance of Oxygen and Carbon Dioxide Exchange" in Wilson, D., M.L. Winkelstein, and N.E. Kline. (Eds.) *Wong's Nursing Care of Infants and Children.* p. 1303–1342. St. Louis, MO: Mosby. 2003.

45. *See* note 43.

46. *Id.*

47. *See* note 16.

48. *Id.*

49. *See* note 25.

50. *Id.*

51. *Id.*

52. *Id.*

53. James, H. "Pediatric Head Injury: What is Unique and Different." *Acta Neurochirurgica Supplementum.* 73, p. 85–88. 1999.

54. Perkins, R.M. "Minor Closed Head Injury" in Perkin, R.M., J.D. Swift, and D.A. Newton. (Eds.) *Pediatric Hospital Medicine: Textbook of Inpatient Management.* p. 672–677. Philadelphia, PA: Lippincott Williams and Wilkins. 2003.

55. Vanore, M. "Care of the Pediatric Patient with Brain Injury in an Adult Intensive Care Unit." *Critical Care Nurse Quarterly.* 23, p. 38–48. 2000.

56. *Id.*

57. *Id.*

Chapter 20

Perioperative Records

Jo Anne Kuc, BSN, RN, LNCC

20.1 Introduction

Surgical procedures are not confined only to the operating room. Bronchoscopies and colonoscopies that were once done in the operating room are now performed under light intravenous sedation in the endoscopy department. Uterine artery embolization for treatment of uterine fibroids is done under sedation in radiology. Pacemaker insertions can be performed under sedation in the cardiology department. Regardless of the operating room setting, the perioperative period involves patient care provided during the preoperative, intraoperative, and postoperative phases.

Healthcare professionals face tremendous challenges when patients present for surgery in less than optimal condition. Patients who are nutritionally compromised, have suffered a traumatic injury, are in shock, have infections, are immunocompromised, or are very young or old have increased surgical risk factors. Healthcare professionals working in the perioperative setting must possess specialized critical thinking skills and document patient care in accordance with established standards of care. This chapter deals with documentation related to the healthy adult surgical patient in the perioperative setting.

20.2 Preoperative Period

The preoperative period begins the moment the patient is scheduled for surgery and terminates when the patient is transported to the surgical holding area. Documentation centers around the primary goals: ensuring the patient is stable to undergo surgery, identifying risk factors which can lead to perioperative complications, and performing interventions to ensure an optimal surgical outcome. The preoperative period is divided into two phases—preoperative screening and the pre-surgical phase.

TIP: Regardless of the type of anesthesia administered or if the surgery is inpatient or outpatient, all surgeries begin with preoperative screening.

Preoperative screening starts one to two weeks prior to elective surgery and includes two primary components: preoperative diagnostic studies and a patient interview.

A. Preoperative Diagnostic Studies

The surgeon or attending physician is responsible for ordering the necessary lab work prior to surgery. The type of diagnostic studies depends upon the surgical procedure, the patient age, health status, and potential risk factors. For example, when a fifty-three-year-old diabetic is scheduled for an outpatient gastroscopy, the doctor may order a stat glucose level the morning of surgery.

In addition to diagnostic studies that the surgeon may order, the surgical facility will require mandatory preoperative diagnostic lab tests or x-rays. An example of a mandatory preoperative diagnostic study is a pregnancy test done on women of childbearing age prior to any surgical procedure. A list of mandatory preoperative tests is found in the policies and procedures of each surgical facility.

Preoperative diagnostic studies must be done within fourteen days prior to surgery. It is the responsibility of the outpatient nurse to review the results of preoperative lab work and report abnormalities to the ordering physician. In the event of an abnormality, the outpatient nurse documents on the preadmission form the name of the doctor notified of the abnormality including date and time, orders rendered by the doctor, corrective action taken, and patient notification. For example, an abnormal preoperative EKG would be documented: "June 2, 2009, 13:30. Dr. Jones notified of Q waves in lead II and lead III on the 6/2/09 12 Lead EKG. Orders received for cardiology referral with Dr. White for stress testing. Surgery cancelled. Patient called at home at 2:15 P.M. and informed of 6/5/09 cardiology appointment."

B. Patient Interview

Outpatient surgical nurses use a preoperative assessment tool to conduct the pre-surgical interview. An example of a pre-surgical interview form is contained in Figure 20.1. Interview forms vary among institutions but the content generally includes:

- demographic patient information,
- preoperative skin preparation such as showering with antiseptic soap,
- instructions to abstain from oral intake after midnight the evening before surgery,
- list of patient medications including prescription, over-the-counter medication, and herbal supplements,
- medications the patient is allowed to take the morning of surgery,
- review of the patient's medical history,
- allergy list (drug, food, environmental, and latex),
- inquiry of previous adverse anesthetic experiences,
- postoperative instructions (turning, coughing, deep breathing), and
- information on how pain needs will be measured (using a pain scale) and met.

The nurse should also document instructions given to the patient about the removal of makeup, prosthesis, fingernail polish, and jewelry prior to coming to the hospital. The patient is instructed not to bring any money on the day of surgery, and to bring a picture I.D. such as a driver's license. The nurse then provides the patient with instructions as to what time to arrive for surgery and the location of the pre-surgical unit. It is important for the preoperative form to also include the name of the person who will be accompanying the patient to the hospital and the name of the individual who will help care for the patient at home.

Ideally, a copy of patient instructions which has been signed by the patient should be maintained in the medical record. This allows for later reference and for continuation of patient teaching by other members of the nursing team. Furthermore, it provides proof that information was provided in the event of auditing or legal reviews.[1]

20.3 Pre-Surgical Phase

TIP: All documentation during the preoperative preparation phase will come under scrutiny when an adverse intraoperative event occurs.

From the moment the patient arrives for surgery in the outpatient surgical unit, until the time she leaves the surgical holding area for the operating room, documentation must reflect that the patient was sent to surgery in optimal condition.

A. Preoperative checklist

Most facilities use a checklist to ensure that required steps in the preoperative preparation are completed. The nurse who performs a review of the diagnostic studies may be located on a nursing unit if the patient is already hospitalized. An individual may come to the facility from home or another institution, such as a nursing home. In this event, the ambulatory surgery nurse is involved in the pre-surgical assessment. The term "pre-surgical nurse" is used in this chapter to refer to the role of the nurse in either the ambulatory care unit or on the hospital unit.

Prior to sending the patient to surgery, the nurse performs a second check verifying: 1) the patient's name, birth date, proof of ID via driver's license, and physician orders for surgery, and 2) all preoperative diagnostic studies to ensure that laboratory, x-ray, and EKG results are within normal limits. However, liability goes one step further as the nurse can also be held responsible for not questioning the doctor on the need for additional laboratory work. For example, a patient on anticoagulant medication is at risk for intraoperative bleeding and should have a partial thromboplastin (PT) and partial prothrombin time (PPT) done prior to surgery. If the physician forgets to order coagulation tests, it is the nurse's responsibility to alert the surgeon and anesthesia professional that these tests are needed. Similarly, the patient may have a new onset of symptoms or abnormalities such as chest pain or shortness of breath. Symptoms such as these prompt the need for cardiac clearance prior to surgery. The nurse is required to alert the surgeon and anesthesiologist of any new patient abnormalities and inquire if special medical consultations are needed for surgical clearance.

PLEASE CHECK ONE:

☐ ONE DAY ☐ OUTPATIENT SURGICAL PATIENT

PRE - OPERATIVE FLOW SHEET

DATE	UNIT	ARRIVAL TIME	BY ☐ AMBULATORY ☐ WHEELCHAIR ☐ STRETCHER ☐ CARRIED

ACCOMPANIED BY	RELATIONSHIP	CALL FOR RIDE ☐ YES ☐ NO	24 HR SUPERVISION ☐ YES ☐ NO

DRIVER	PHONE NO.	SECONDARY PHONE NO.

PERSONAL ITEMS	DISPOSITION OF PERSONAL ITEMS ☐ FAMILY ☐ CASHIER ☐ CLOSET ☐ OTHER
PROSTHESIS	DISPOSITION OF PROSTHESIS ☐ FAMILY ☐ CASHIER ☐ CLOSET ☐ OTHER

YES	N/A	OR CHECKLIST	YES	N/A	OR CHECKLIST	PRE-OPERATIVE MEDICATION
		HISTORY AND PHYSICAL ON CHART			CBC	ANTIBIOTICS REQUIRED ☐ YES ☐ NO
		IDENTIFICATION BAND			UA	
		CONSENT SIGNED			CHEST X-RAY	
		SIDE RAILS UP			EKG (WHEN REQUIRED)	
		INSTRUCTED TO CALL NURSE			CHEM PROFILE (WHEN REQUIRED)	
		VOIDED			BETA SUB (WHEN REQUIRED)	
		NPO SINCE:			BLEEDING PROFILE / PTT / PT	
		PRE AND POST OP INSTRUCTIONS GIVEN			OTHER	

HEIGHT	WEIGHT	ALLERGIES → MARK ALLERGIES	ANALGESIC SCALE

PHYSICAL DISABILITIES

SURGICAL PROCEDURE

INITIALS

NO PAIN ———————— WORST PAIN

0 1 2 3 4 5 6 7 8 9 10

PAIN SCALE RATING

TYPE OF PAIN
B - BURNING
T - THROBBING
A - ACHE
R - RADIATING
S - SHARP
N - NON-RADIATING

PATIENT ASSESSMENT

T	P / Ap	R	BP RIGHT	BP LEFT	PAIN SCALE	TYPE OF PAIN	LOCATION
INITIALS							

PSYCHOSOCIAL	LOC.	COLOR/SKIN TEMP	LUNG SOUNDS	BOWEL SOUNDS	PULSES				OTHER
					RIGHT FEMORAL	LEFT FEMORAL	RIGHT PEDAL	LEFT PEDAL	

CURRENT MEDICATIONS YOU ARE TAKING - (INCLUDE OVER-THE-COUNTER MEDICATIONS AND ANY HERBAL MEDICATIONS) / OR SUPPLEMENTS

MEDICATION	DOSE	TIME	INITIALS	MEDICATION	DOSE	TIME	INITIALS

TREATMENTS

NURSING PROGRESS NOTES:

TRANSPORTED TO ☐ CARDIOLOGY ☐ OR ☐ ENDOSCOPY ☐ RADIOLOGY ☐ CATH LAB	PER ☐ STRETCHER ☐ WHEELCHAIR	TIME : ☐ AM ☐ PM
FAMILY DIRECTED TO WAITING AREA ☐ YES ☐ NO ☐ N/A	RN SIGNATURE	

1984 (3/02)

Figure 20.1 *Preoperative screening form. (Reprinted with permission from Ingalls Health System, Harvey, IL.)*

POST OPERATIVE FLOW SHEET

| TIME RETURNED | RECEIVED BY | | INTAKE | | OUTPUT | | | ☐ N/A |

| IV FLUIDS (SOLUTION AMOUNT LEFT) | | | DISCONTINUED (TIME) | BY |
| IV SITE ASSESSED | | | | |

VITAL SIGNS / PATIENT ASSESSMENT

TIME	B/P	T	P	R	INITIALS	TIME	L.O.C.	COLOR/SKIN TEMP	LUNGS	ABD	DRSG	PAIN	NAUSEA	DRAINAGE	INITIALS

DISCHARGE GUIDELINES

ACTIVITY   ☐ B/R   ☐ BRP   ☐ AMBULATE   ☐ WRITTEN DISCHARGE INSTRUCTIONS GIVEN FOR:

VOIDED   ☐ YES   ☐ NO   ☐ N/A   _____

VITAL SIGNS STABLE   ☐ YES   ☐ NO   ☐ N/A   ☐ VERBALIZES UNDERSTANDING

TOLERATES FLUIDS   ☐ YES   ☐ NO   ☐ N/A   STATUS: ☐ GOOD ☐ FAIR ☐ SERIOUS ☐ CRITICAL

DRESSING DRY AND INTACT   ☐ YES   ☐ NO   ☐ N/A   DISPOSITION: ☐ WHEELCHAIR ☐ STRETCHER ☐ AMBULATORY ☐ CARRIES

ABSENCE OF EXTENSIVE BLEEDING   ☐ YES   ☐ NO   ☐ N/A   ☐ TRANSFERRED TO _____

INITIALS

PROGRESS NOTES

_____

_____

_____

_____

_____

_____

_____

_____

_____

_____

_____

_____

_____

_____

_____

_____

_____

_____

SIGNATURE	INITIALS	SIGNATURE	INITIALS
SIGNATURE	INITIALS	SIGNATURE	INITIALS
DISCHARGED BY		TIME	
	R.N.		AM PM

Figure 20.1 *Preoperative screening form. (Reprinted with permission from Ingalls Health System, Harvey, IL.) (continued)*

Prior to sending a patient to surgery, the pre-surgical nurse documents complete vital signs, including blood pressure readings in both arms. This is done because blood pressures can vary greatly between arms. The patient's allergies are again verified and clearly documented on the chart, and an allergy band is placed on the patient's wrist. The surgeon may order a type and cross match for blood in preparation for surgeries when a patient may experience a significant blood loss. The patient should have a plastic "blood band" placed on his arm indicating that a type and cross match was done.

The nurse verifies that the patient remained "NPO" (nothing by mouth) after midnight. The nurse then completes the pre-surgical checklist which includes: ensuring a *comprehensive* history and physical is dictated and is on the chart, that all prosthetic devices, hairpins, hairpieces, dentures, glasses, contacts, jewelry (including body jewelry such as nipple rings, tongue studs), and undergarments have been removed. Fingernail polish is removed to permit the anesthesiologist to assess nail bed color.

Frequently, certain operative procedures require preoperative intravenous antibiotics or eye drops to be administered prior to surgery. The preoperative checklist should include an area to record preoperative medication including the name of the medication, dosage, route, and time of administration. Figure 20.2 is an example of the preoperative checklist.

TIP: The Joint Commission has a standard that addresses a thirty-day time frame for completion of a history and physical before hospital admission.

Any significant changes in the patient's condition subsequent to admission must be recorded.[7]

B. Informed Consent

The nurse verifies that the operative consent is correctly worded and signed by the patient.

Consent forms and their wording also differ between institutions. One thing that remains constant, however, is that it is the surgeon's responsibility to explain the operative procedure, surgical risks, alternative methods of treatment, and expected surgical outcomes to the patient. Performing surgery without proper surgical consent is ethically wrong, legally risky, and a violation of the patient's personal rights.[3] It is the duty of the nurse to ensure that the operative consent is accurately worded, the procedure is correctly spelled, and the surgical site is correct, and to witness the signature of the patient or designee.

TIP: More than one consent may be required for surgery. Examples of other surgical consents include anesthesia consent, consent for blood products, sterilization, or for radiation therapy. The surgical facility's policy and procedure manual contains a list of consents required for surgery.

20.4 Intraoperative Nursing Documentation

Patients are transported from the pre-surgical area into the surgery holding area where intraoperative documentation begins. The operative period extends from the time the patient enters the operative holding area until the patient arrives in the post-anesthesia care unit. In the holding area, a third check is done verifying the patient's demographic information and understanding of the surgery to be done. The nurse also ensures that diagnostic studies are within normal limits, the surgical consent has been properly executed, that all prosthetic devices have been removed, and that the patient understands the surgical procedure. The holding area is also where the anesthesiologist or CRNA (certified registered nurse anesthetist) interviews the patient, performs the pre-anesthesia assessment, assesses the patient's airway, explains the anesthesia being administered, and ensures that it is safe to proceed with surgery.

In 2004, The Joint Commission mandated standards focusing on proper patient identification and prevention of wrong site surgery. The Association of Operating Room Nurses (AORN) also formulated a position statement on correct site surgery.[4] Beginning in 2004, surgical records had to include entries that the patient was properly identified and that the surgical site was marked by the physician.[5]

Although correct identification of the surgical site is a basic standard of care, wrong site surgery continues to occur. In a South Carolina case, a man in his fifties had a history of bilateral bunions on each small toe. He elected to have a right foot bunionectomy instead of the proffered simultaneous bilateral bunionectomy offered by the surgeon. About two thirds of the way through the procedure, the operating room staff realized the surgeon was operating on the left foot instead of the right foot. While the plaintiff was still unconscious, his wife got notification and gave permission for the right foot to be done at the same time. The plaintiff alleged negligence in the performance of surgery on the wrong foot. The defendants admitted liability but disputed damages. A $47,500 verdict was returned against the surgeon and hospital.[6]

PREOPERATIVE CHECKLIST

PATIENT PREPARATION

		YES	NA
1.	ANTIMICROBIAL BATH/SHOWER: X1_____Evening Before Surgery	☐	☐
	X1_____Morning of Surgery	☐	☐
2.	ANTIMICROBIAL BATH/SHOWER AM_____X1 Day Before Surgery	☐	☐
	FOR CABG: PM_____X1 Day Before Surgery	☐	☐
	AM_____X1 Day of Surgery	☐	☐
3.	ORAL HYGIENE	☐	☐
4.	ALL CLOTHING REMOVED	☐	
5.	ITEMS WITH METAL ATTACHMENTS REMOVED	☐	☐
6.	OPERATIVE AREA PREPPED / CLIP FOR CABG AM OF SURGERY	☐	☐
7.	JEWELRY REMOVED (PIN RELIGIOUS MEDAL TO GOWN)	☐	☐
8.	BODY PIERCING JEWELRY REMOVED	☐	☐
9.	DENTURES/PARTIALS REMOVED	☐	☐
10.	ARE TEETH CROWNED?	☐	☐
11.	GLASSES, CONTACT LENS REMOVED	☐	☐
12.	WIG REMOVED	☐	☐
13.	MASCARA AND FALSE EYE LASHES REMOVED	☐	☐
14.	VOIDED OR CATHETERIZED AND CHARTED	☐	☐
15.	I.D. BAND IN PLACE	☐	
16.	NPO SINCE _____ AM ☐ PM ☐	☐	☐
17.	ANY PROSTHESIS REMOVED	☐	☐
18.	SURGICAL SITE MARKED	☐	☐

DATE_____   _____
SIGNATURE AND TITLE (RN)

ALLERGIES ASSESSMENT

		NA	YES	NO	NAME/LIST
1.	ALLERGY BAND IN PLACE	☐	☐		
2.	FOOD OR DRUGS	☐	☐	☐	_____
3.	OTHER ALLERGIES	☐	☐	☐	_____

DATE_____   _____
SIGNATURE AND TITLE (RN)

PRE-OPERATIVE ANTIBIOTICS

		NA	YES	NO
1.	REQUIRED FOR PROCEDURE		☐	☐
2.	SCHEDULED ANTIBIOTIC SENT TO O.R. WITH PATIENT		☐	
3.	MUPIROCIN NASAL OINTMENT TO EACH NARES / ORDER CABG PATIENT	☐	☐	☐

MEDICATION	DOSE	TIME DUE

DATE_____   _____
SIGNATURE AND TITLE (RN)

PRE-OPERATIVE MEDICATIONS

☐ NOT APPLICABLE

		YES	NO
1.	BP_____PULSE_____RESP_____ AT TIME OF PRE-OP GIVE		
2.	SIDERAILS UP AFTER PRE-OP GIVEN	☐	☐
3.	ADMINISTERED AND CHARTED	☐	☐

DATE_____   _____
SIGNATURE AND TITLE (RN)

CHART PREPARATION

		NA	YES	NO
1.	VITAL SIGNS CHARTED		☐	
2.	HISTORY AND PHYSICAL ON CHART		☐	☐
3.	SIGNED SURGICAL CONSENT ON CHART		☐	☐
4.	INTERIM SUMMARY ON CHART	☐	☐	☐
5.	NAME PLATE ATTACHED TO CHART		☐	☐
6.	CONSULTATION, IF REQUIRED	☐	☐	☐
7.	STERILIZATION CONSENT, IF REQUIRED	☐	☐	☐

DATE_____   _____
SIGNATURE AND TITLE (RN)

LAB AND TEST RESULTS ON CHART

		NA	YES	NO
1.	H & H		☐	☐
2.	URINALYSIS		☐	☐
3.	CHEST X-RAY	☐	☐	☐
4.	CHEM 7 (40 AND OLDER)	☐	☐	☐
5.	CHEM 12 CABG	☐	☐	☐
6.	PREGNANCY TEST FROM MENARCHE TO MENOPAUSE		☐	☐
7.	PARTIAL THROMBOPLASTIN, IF REQUIRED	☐	☐	☐
8.	BLEEDING TIME, IF REQUIRED	☐	☐	☐
9.	E.C.G., IF REQUIRED	☐	☐	☐
10.	TYPE OR SCREEN	☐	☐	☐
11.	NASAL CULTURES, IF REQUIRED	☐	☐	☐
12.	BGM FOR CABG PATIENT	☐	☐	☐

DATE_____   _____
SIGNATURE AND TITLE (RN)

Form #516 (5/03)

Figure 20.2 *Preoperative checklist form.*

A. Operating Room Nursing Care Plans

Operating room nursing records contain several forms and follow documentation standards set forth by the Association of Operating Room Nurses (AORN). One such form is the "surgical care plan" which is generally a standard computerized form of potential surgical risk factors and patient care goals. An example of a surgical plan of care is found in Figure 20.3.

1. Alteration in skin integrity

Injury to the skin can occur from transportation of the patient from the cart to the OR table, patient positioning, inadequately padded OR tables, skin preparation, operating room equipment, and prolonged operative times. Therefore, description of the patient's skin on arrival to the operating room and at discharge should be done. The OR nurse should document any rashes, bruising, and wounds upon arrival to the operating room as well as any observations of unusual skin lesions that arise during or immediately after the surgical procedure. Documentation of the type of antiseptic skin preparation used should also be recorded.

2. Potential for injury related to positioning and chemical hazards

Safe patient positioning requires knowledge and teamwork. The position must be safe for the patient while permitting the surgeon optimal surgical exposure. Recording the surgical position, repositioning, positioning devices, and padding is crucial. AORN has a position statement regarding proper patient positioning and the operating room nurse's responsibility. This comprehensive position statement includes practice recommendations such as:

- Preoperative assessment for positioning needs should be made before transferring the patient to the procedure bed.
- The perioperative nurse should actively participate in monitoring patient body alignment and tissue integrity based on sound physiologic principles.
- After positioning, the perioperative nurse should evaluate the patient's body alignment and tissue integrity.[7]

The twenty-seven year-old plaintiff was scheduled for a loop electrosurgical excision procedure with cone biopsy. Due to errors by the pharmacy technician, circulating, and scrub technician, one hundred percent acetic acid was applied to the vaginal area instead of the proper five percent solution. The pure acetic acid caused significant vaginal and rectal burns. The plaintiff was transferred to the burn unit of a major hospital and diagnosed with second-degree burns to the vaginal and urethral surfaces. The plaintiff recovered, but was left with scarring on her buttocks. The plaintiff also alleged posttraumatic stress syndrome. An investigation revealed that the three defendants had each failed to identify the undiluted acetic acid and heed clear warnings on the bottle or notice its distinctive odor. A $475,000 settlement was reached.[8]

B. Intraoperative Nursing Notes

TIP: Documentation of intraoperative nurse's notes is performed by the circulating nurse.

The thoroughness of the operative nurse's notes varies among institutions and is generally two pages in length. Figure 20.4 is an example of an operative nursing record. This form is not the benchmark by which to measure other operative nurse's notes, but it is a good example of how one hospital incorporated significant information to show adherence to standards of care. The following information should be included in the operative nurse's notes:

- patient's condition upon transport to and from the OR, and by whom,
- patient position, types of positioning devices, protective measures taken, and names of those involved in patient positioning,
- surgery and anesthesia start and stop times and time of surgical incision,
- skin condition, antimicrobials used for skin preparation, and individual performing the skin prep, and
- location and use of electrosurgical instruments, lasers, cautery, and monitoring devices.

TIP: Many surgical departments maintain a laser log. Information contained in the laser log includes type of laser used, beginning and ending times of use, length of use, wattage, and operator's name.

- IV site, location, size of cannula, IV solutions used, and time of administration,
- medications administered, including dosage, route, and by whom,
- tourniquet on and off times, inflation duration and individual responsible for application and monitoring. (Patients have sustained permanent injuries when tourniquets have been on for long durations or improperly applied.)

NURSING DIAGNOSIS	INTERVENTION	GOALS	Initials
INDIVIDUALIZED PLAN OF CARE			
1. Actual impairment of skin integrity.	1. Protect area of skin impairment 2. Prep impairment area with care if part of surgical site.	1. Patient should not have further impairment of skin integrity.	
2. Alteration in respiratory function	1. Position to enhance ventilation. 2. Assist anesthesia as needed.	1. Patient should maintain adequate respiratory functioning.	
3. Actual impairment of mobility.	1. Assistance/care in patient transfers. 2. Maintain body alignment -use padding and supports.	1. Patient should have no further impairment of mobility.	
4. Alteration in Comfort - Pain.	1. Thorough evaluation of pain. 2. Pain medication as needed.	1. Patient should remain comfortable and as free from pain as possible.	
5. Grieving: Loss of body part/loved one.	1. Supportive care - allow patient to express feelings/concerns.	1. Patient should be able to address grief during surgical period.	
6. Confusion / Disorientation	1. Orient patient as necessary. 2. Explain interventions before they occur.	1. Patient should remain oriented to person, place and time.	
7. Alteration in nutritional status.	1. Record accurate urine output and wound irrigation fluid. 2. Strict asepsis should be maintained.	1. Patient's nutritional status should remain within normal limits.	
8. Alteration in sensory acuity, hearing impairment.	1. Assist individual's hearing loss, if any. 2. Speak clearly and distinctly. 3. Allow patient to wear hearing aid to O.R.	1. Patient should understand surgical procedure and the intervention planned.	
9. Alteration in sensory acuity; visual impairment.	1. Assess individual's vision loss, if any. 2. Speak as approaching patient. 3. Explain environment.	1. Patient should understand surgical procedures and the intervention planned.	
10. Actual communication impairment; language barrier.	1. Utilize translator when doing pre-op teaching; have translator accompany patient to O.R.	1. Patient should understand surgical procedures and the intervention planned.	
11. Alteration is skeletal integrity - impaired metal parts.	1. Care in transferring / positioning. 2. Ground device placed appropriately away from metal implant area.	1. Patient should not have further impairment of skeletal integrity.	
12. Alteration in body image due to implanted device.	1. Assurance / reinforcement pre-op teaching. 2. Supportive care - encourage patient's expression.	1. Patient should be aware of and able to adjust to body image changes.	

13. Alteration in cardiac status: Pacemaker.	1. Placement of grounding device:
	  A. Away from pacer site..
	  B. Ensure path between electrodes does not pass through heart.
	2. Continual monitoring of patient's pulse during procedure.
		1. Patient should have no further alteration in cardiac status.	

1. Standard of Care met as reflected by the written Standards of Care for Peri-operative practice.

2. Individual Care Plan implemented to meet the standard of care.

3. Initial those that are applicable.

4. Enter NA for the remaining items. There can be no blanks on form.

Figure 20.3 *Operative care plan. (Reprinted with permission from Ingalls Health System, Harvey, IL.)*

NURSING DIAGNOSIS	INTERVENTION	OUTCOME	Initials
STANDAF AN OF CARE			
1. Potential for knowledge deficit / anxiety related to surgical intervention	1. Identify patient 2. Verify consent 3. Verify surgical site 4. Provide information and supportive pre-operative teaching when applicable to patient, parents and significant others. 5. Confirm operative procedure with the surgeon. 6. Support patient during induction.	1. Demonstrates knowledge of procedure. 2. Prevent surgical site error.	
2. Potential for injury related to positioning, chemical and electrical hazard.	1. Check and document skin integrity pre and post operatively. 2. Provide positioning devices that are clean, free of sharp edges and padded where applicable. 3. Position safely maintaining good body alignment. 4. Position properly to prevent obstruction to respiratory, circulatory and neurological functions. 5. Ensure proper use of electrical cautery dispersive pad. 6. Determine patient's allergy to medications, latex and dyes.	1. Patient's skin integrity and mobility should be maintained.	
3. Potential for injury related to equipment and physical hazards.	1. Assure adequate instruments, equipment and supplies. 2. Assure all instruments and equipment are functioning properly before use. 3. Monitor room environment, control temperature, humidity and electricity. 4. Organize OR routines to minimize delays. 5. Perform adequate surgical counts.	1. Patient should be free of adverse effects from lack of, or improper use of measures and equipment.	
4. Actual impairment of skin integrity with possible infection.	1. Maintain OR aseptic technique. 2. Follow proper scrubbing procedures. 3. Minimize room traffic flow. 4. Enforce OR dress code. 5. Follow universal precautions. 6. Administer IV antibiotic per protocol when applicable.	1. Patient should be free of surgical wound contamination and/or cross contamination.	
5. Potential for depletion of body fluids and blood loss.	1. Record medications given and report same to anesthesia. 2. Insert foley catheter if necessary; assist anesthesia in measuring / recording intake and output. 3. Display sponges and suction for observation by anesthesia. 4. Record irrigations and inform anesthesia. 5. Assist anesthesia and other OR personnel in blood transfusion, auto transfusion and document on the intra-operative record.	1. Patient's blood, fluids and electrolyte balance should be maintained.	
6. Alteration in self care post-operatively.	1. Transfer patient from O.R. bed to cart with sufficient staff and moving device. 2. Maintain body alignment, use padding and supports, if necessary. 3. Assist with the safe transfer from OR to PACU, Critical Care/patient's room or One Day Surgery. 4. Maintain the integrity of dressings, drain and IV lines. 5. Communicate pertinent information relative to patient's condition and surgery to PACU, unit/floor nurse for post-operative care.	1. Patient should have a coordinated, safe transport to PACU, ODS, Critical Care or patient's room and RN to RN communication of patient's physiological and psychological condition to provide continuity of care.	
7. Alteration in comfort in local procedure; Pain.	1. Provide information/instructions prior to and throughout the procedure. 2. Provide supportive care. 3. Monitor for reaction to drugs/local anesthesia and for physiological and behavioral changes. 4. Keep OR room quiet and conversation appropriate. 5. Maintain privacy, confidentiality and personal dignity. 6. Assess physiological baseline status and monitor throughout procedure including vital signs. 7. Monitor O_2 saturation with pulse oximeter and administer O_2 inhalation when necessary.	1. Patient should have professional, efficient care providing optimal comfort and safety during local procedure.	

INITIALS	NURSING SIGNATURE	

2322 Rev. 2/02

Figure 20.3 Operative care plan. (Reprinted with permission from Ingalls Health System, Harvey, IL.) (continued)

OPERATIVE NURSES RECORD   PAGE 1

DATE_____ARRIVED PRE-OP_____

PRE-OPERATIVE ASSESSMENT

PATIENT IDENTIFICATION: ☐ VERBAL   ☐ CHART   ☐ BRACELET

VERIFICATION OF SURGICAL SITE: ☐ VERBAL   ☐ CONSENT   ☐ DOCTOR'S ORDER   ☐ IF REQUIRED, SITE INITIALED   ☐ HISTORY AND PHYSICAL ON CHART

PATIENT'S UNDERSTANDING OF SURGERY:_____

RECEIVED WITH: ☐ NG   ☐ 02   ☐ EKG MONITOR   ☐ FOLEY CATHETER   ☐ RESTRAINTS   ☐ IV's/ACCESS CATHETERS   SITE / STATUS_____

PROSTHESIS / IMPLANTS_____ DISABILITIES_____ ALLERGIES_____

CURRENT BEHAVIOR: ☐ CALM/RELAXED ☐ APPREHENSIVE ☐ COMMUNICATIVE ☐ RESTLESS ☐ CONCERNED ☐ QUIET/WITHDRAWN ☐ OTHER_____	**PRE-OP ANTIBIOTIC / MEDS.** _____ _____ _____
ORIENTATION: ☐ ALERT ☐ CONFUSED ☐ ORIENTED ☐ LETHARGIC ☐ NON-RESPONSIVE ☐ OTHER_____	_____ _____

SKIN   TEMPERATURE: ☐ WARM   ☐ HOT   ☐ COOL
     MOISTURE: ☐ DRY   ☐ MOIST   ☐ DIAPHORETIC
     COLOR: ☐ NORMAL ☐ PALE   ☐ FLUSHED   ☐ MOTTLED/CYANOTIC   ☐ JAUNDICED ☐ _____
	_____
	_____
	TIME STARTED_____BY_____

COMMENTS:_____ RN SIGNATURE_____

INTRA-OPERATIVE PHASE

OR ROOM #:   TIME PT. ENTERED OR: ANESTHESIA START: OPERATION START TIME: SURGICAL TEAM TIME OUT:

SURGEON_____

ASSISTANT_____

ANESTHESIOLOGIST_____

ANESTHESIA: ☐ GENERAL   ☐ LOCAL   ☐ SPINAL
     ☐ MAC   ☐ BLOCK   ☐ EPIDURAL

CORRECT PATIENT, PROCEDURE, AND, WHERE APPLICABLE, SURGICAL SITE VERIFIED PRIOR TO INCISION.   ☐ YES   ☐ NO

PROCEDURE_____

CIRCULATOR	IN	OUT	SCRUB	IN	OUT

PRE-OP DX_____

POST-OP DX_____

POSITION: ☐ SUPINE ☐ PRONE ☐ JACKKNIFE ☐ LITHOTOMY ☐ LATERAL RI._____ Lt._____	**ARMS:** ☐ SIDE ☐ ARMBOARD/TABLE ☐ ACROSS CHEST ☐ AX. ROLL ☐ SUPPORTS ☐ OTHER	**POSITIONING DEVICES** **LEGS:** ☐ ORTHO HOLDER ☐ SLING STIRRUPS ☐ ALLEN STIRRUPS ☐ FOAM KNEE REST ☐ SAFETY STRAP ☐ BEAN BAG	☐ KIDNEY REST ☐ RT. ☐ LT. ☐ CHEST ROLL(S) ☐ WILSON FRAME ☐ ANDREWS TABLE ☐ LILAC SUPPORTS ☐ FX TABLE ☐ MAYFIELD HEADREST ☐ FOAM HEADREST ☐ LATERAL POSITIONERS ☐ OTHER

ANTIEMBOLIC DEVICE USED ☐ SCD ☐ TED HOSE ☐ OTHER	ESU#_____☐ N/A ☐ MONOPOLAR ☐ BIPOLAR ☐ COAG_____ ☐ CUT_____ ☐ GROUND:_____ ☐ APPLIED BY:_____ SKIN CONDITION PRE-OP ☐ WNL POST-OP ☐ WNL ☐ SEE PROGRESS NOTES	**SURGICAL PREP** ☐ IODINE SCRUB ☐ IODINE PAINT ☐ DURAPREP ☐ PHISOHEX ☐ CHLORAPREP ☐ NONE ☐ OTHER_____

Figure 20.4 *Operative nurses notes. (Reprinted with permission from Ingalls Health System, Harvey, IL.)*

INTRAOPERATIVE NURSES RECORD   PAGE 2

URINARY CATHETER: ☐ N/A

SIZE:

COLOR/CHARACTER:

INSERTED BY:

BLANKET TEMPERATURE CONTROL: ☐ N/A

UNIT #   MANUAL ☐

SETTING: AUTO ☐

TOURNIQUET: ☐ N/A

LOCATION: ☐ RT. ☐ LT. ☐ ARM ☐ LEG

PRESSURE:

TIME UP   TIME DOWN

PRE-TOURNIQUET ASSESSMENT:

PULSE PALPABLE ☐ YES ☐ NO

DOPPLER SIGNAL ☐ YES ☐ NO

SKIN CONDITION ☐ WNL ☐ SEE PROGRESS NOTES

IMPLANTS - PROSTHESIS - INTERNAL STAPLES   ☐ SEE IMPLANT SHEET

TYPE	SIZE	LOT / SERIAL #

SPECIMEN ☐ YES ☐ NO
1.
2.
3.

FROZEN SECTION ☐ YES ☐ NO
1.
2.
3.

CULTURE ☐ YES ☐ NO
1.
2.
3.

SPONGE	NA	CORRECT YES	NO	CIRCULATING R.N.	SCRUB
				1. 2. 3.	
SHARP				1. 2. 3.	
INSTRUMENT				1. 2. 3.	

IRRIGATION_____ ☐ NONE

MEDICATIONS_____ ☐ NONE
_____
_____
_____

OBSERVERS:_____

IF UNRESOLVED, ACTION TAKEN:

_____ SURGEON NOTIFIED   _____ X-RAYS TAKEN IN OR

PROGRESS NOTE:
_____
_____
_____
_____
_____

DRAINS / PACKS   ☐ NONE

☐ PENROSE   ☐ CHEST TUBE

Location_____   Location_____

☐ JACKSON PRATT   ☐ PACK

Location_____   Location_____

☐ HEMOVAC   ☐ OTHER

Location_____   Location_____

LOCAL CASE: MONITORED c̄ ☐ EKG   ☐ AUTO BP   ☐ PULSE O₂

PROCEDURE TOLERATED: ☐ GOOD   ☐ FAIR   ☐ POOR

POST-OPERATIVE PHASE

WOUND CLASSIFICATION: ☐ CLEAN   ☐ CLEAN CONTAMINATED   ☐ CONTAMINATED   ☐ DIRTY / INFECTED

OPERATION END TIME_____

TRANSFERRED VIA: ☐ CART ☐ BED   WITH: ☐ O₂ ☐ AMBU ☐ MONITOR ☐ NONE

DISCHARGED TO: ☐ PACU ☐ SDS ☐ ICU ☐ RM ☐ OTHER

SIGNATURE	INITIALS	SIGNATURE	INITIALS	SIGNATURE	INITIALS

Form #2079 (11/04)

Figure 20.4 Operative nurses notes. (Reprinted with permission from Ingalls Health System, Harvey, IL.) (continued)

- estimated blood loss and other drainage output,
- sponge, sharps, and instrument counts,
- surgical procedure performed as stated by the surgeon, location of incision, and special devices used such as lasers,
- implants or devices inserted, including lot number and manufacturer,
- site and sizes of drains, catheters, and packing if applicable, and
- specimens and cultures obtained and disposition.

TIP: Specimens are double-checked for disposition when sent to Pathology. Additionally, this information is recorded in the operating room log book.

- wound classification including size, color and drainage. Pressure ulcers should be classified according to the following universal system:

  Stage I ulcer—non-blanchable redness with the skin unbroken.

  Stage II ulcer—redness of skin with partial thickness loss of the first few layers of skin, which can look like an abrasion, blister or shallow crater.

  Stage III ulcer—full thickness skin loss with drainage or black subcutaneous tissue. This is generally a deep crater.

  Stage IV ulcer—full thickness skin loss with extensive tissue destruction. Muscle, tendons, or bone may be visible.
- type of surgical dressing applied, and
- individuals in the operating room and their roles including physicians, relief staff, observers, or sales personnel.

C. Surgical Roles

It is essential to understand the roles of the operating room nurses when analyzing operative records. The scrub nurse has multiple responsibilities—assisting with patient positioning, setting up and maintaining a sterile field, and assisting the surgeon during the operation. Documentation of patient positioning was undoubtedly a factor in this case:

A forty-seven year-old man underwent surgery to treat a tissue mass in his colon. The plaintiff was placed in the lithotomy position for surgery, but there was a delay in finding a surgeon to perform the surgery. The surgery was begun that evening and finished about twelve hours after the plaintiff was placed in the lithotomy position. When his legs

were taken down there was no blood flow. The left leg was saved; the right leg was amputated above the knee. The plaintiff alleged negligence in leaving his leg in an elevated position for twelve hours, leading to vascular compromise. The defendants claimed the plaintiff was only in a low lithotomy position and that position was safe for a lengthy period. The defendants also claimed the plaintiff's underlying severe vascular disease which was unknown when the surgery was started was the cause of the injury. A defense verdict was returned.[9]

The circulating operating room nurse is responsible for a multitude of tasks such as obtaining surgical equipment, monitoring asepsis, positioning the patient, counting the sponges and needles, and completing the operative nurse's notes. More detailed information on documentation can be found in: *Recommended Practices for Documentation of Perioperative Nursing Care Standards, Recommended Practices, and Guidelines*, from AORN. However, the following is a partial list of items which requires special documentation:

- identification of persons providing perioperative patient care (i.e., name, title, signature of persons responsible for care);
- placement of electrosurgical unit (ESU) dispersive pad and identification of the ESU and setting used during the surgical procedure;
- placement of tourniquet cuffs, including the type of unit, pressure settings, and inflation and deflation times;
- use of lasers, including name of laser unit, name of surgeon and support staff members, type of laser used, surgical procedure, the lens used, length of laser time, and wattage; and
- placement and location of implants (e.g., medical devices, synthetic and biologic grafts, tissue, bone) including the name of the manufacturer or distributor, lot and serial numbers, type and size of implant, and expiration dates as appropriate, and other information required by the Food and Drug Administration.

The surgical team may include a surgical technologist in lieu of a scrub nurse. This is a person who has completed one to two years of an intensive surgical operating room course. If the surgical technician is certified, "CST" will follow her name on the OR nurse's notes. Many surgeons also use CSTs as first surgical assistants while others work with registered nurses who are certified as surgical first assistants (SFAs).

The Association of Surgical Technologists has developed standards of practice for SFA. The SFA must demonstrate specific skill competencies, possess educational experience, and have completed 350 surgical cases. First Assist Specialists (FAS) are those individuals who have demonstrated competency in a certain surgical specialty. Detailed information regarding competencies, qualifications, and education can be found at www.surgicalassist.org.

The legal issues surrounding SFAs are complicated. The role of the non-physician SFA, whether a registered nurse, physician assistant, or CST, is not specifically addressed in the Centers for Medicare and Medicaid Services (CMS). CMS does not pay for SFA services at teaching hospitals which have training programs related to surgery and where a qualified surgical resident is available. Exceptions to this rule exist if the surgeon certifies that a surgical resident is not available to assist in the surgery.

Legislation at the state level for all non-physician SFAs is vague if it exists at all. Generally speaking, CSTs acting as first assistants are doing so under the broad authority of physicians. The basis for CSTs serving as first assistants is usually found in state medical practice acts or through the states' Attorney General Offices. The underlying principle is that "Physicians/surgeons may delegate to non-physicians those tasks normally carried out by another physician when performed under the direct supervision and in the physical presence of the physician and once the physician and/or employer has made a reasonable determination that the person to whom those tasks are to be delegated has the appropriate skills and knowledge to safely perform those tasks." This principle supports the discretion of the physician in determining who will assist and to what extent throughout the conduct of his case, as long as this does not violate state law or hospital policy.[10]

D. Surgical Counts

Every so often the media airs a story of an individual with a retained surgical instrument or sponge. Therefore, counting of surgical instruments merits special discussion. There are four separate counts of items placed on the sterile table such as sponges, sharps (needles), instruments, and sterile towels or special packing used during rectal or vaginal procedures. The first surgical count is performed by the person who assembles and wraps the items for sterilization. This is generally done in the central processing department. Some facilities enclose a copy of the tray inventory count sheet in the instrument tray before sending it to the surgery department. The second count is done by the scrub person and the circulating nurse who count the items together before the operation begins and as each additional package is opened and added to

the sterile field. Any item placed in a wound, such as packing towels, is recorded. A useful counting method is as follows:

1. As the scrub person touches each item, she and the circulating nurse number each item aloud until all items are counted.
2. The circulator immediately records the count for each type of item on the count record. Preprinted forms are helpful for this purpose.
3. Additional packages should be counted away from counted items already on the table in case it is necessary to repeat the count or to discard an item.
4. Counting should not be interrupted. The count should be repeated if there is uncertainty because of interruption, fumbling, or any other reason.
5. If either the scrub person or the circulator is permanently relieved by another person during the surgical procedure, the incoming person should verify all counts before the person being relieved leaves the room. People who perform the final counts are held accountable for the entire count.[11]

A fourth or final count is performed when the body cavity is closed or during skin closure. The circulating nurse documents on the operating room record what was counted, how many counts were done, and if the count was correct. In the event of an incorrect count, the nurse immediately informs the surgeon and the entire count is repeated. Trash cans and laundry hampers are checked for missing items.

TIP: If the missing item cannot be located, an x-ray should be taken of the patient before leaving the operating room suite. The circulating nurse then generates an incident report, and the patient should be informed.

Retained surgical objects can cause devastating complications such as adhesions (scarring), bowel obstructions, perforation of organs, infection, and death. The following Texas case is one of many lawsuits filed for a retained surgical object:

In *Rita Bateman v. Good Shephard Hospital, et al.*,[12] the plaintiff, a fifty-one-year-old woman, entered Good Shephard Hospital in January 2001 to undergo a hysterectomy. After surgery, Ms. Bateman complained of abdominal pain, and it was discovered that three of the fifteen sponges used during the operation had been left in Ms. Bateman's abdomen. They were removed twenty-days later after the hysterectomy. The plaintiff alleged the sponges produced adhesions, which led to a build up of scar tissue, which in turn led to a bowel obstruction. At trial, the jury found Good Shephard Hospital negligent and awarded the plaintiff $332,000. The jury did not find the surgeon negligent.

E. Adverse Events

Finally, the circulating nurse should record any adverse intraoperative events on the intraoperative nurse's record. In addition, the 1991 Safe Medical Device Act requires that when a device has caused or contributed to a serious illness or patient injury, the facility must file a report within ten days to the manufacturer or to the Food and Drug Administration if the manufacturer is not known. The FDA requires the following information:

- names of the operator or operators,
- nature of the problem,
- error that occurred in using the equipment,
- user's training related to equipment design,
- manufacturer's instructions, and
- hospital's policies and procedures[13]

F. Pitfalls in Documentation

Needless to say, documentation of events in the operating room can make or break a case. The following have been identified as pitfalls in operating room documentation:

- Omission of information (blank spaces) may be construed as a "cover-up" or failure to provide care. A way to decrease liability is to document "N/A" if not applicable.
- Paraphrasing or recording personal opinions should be avoided. It is recommended to document only factual information.
- The use of overly broad terms such as "apparent absence of foreign bodies" or "skin appears intact" should be avoided. Definitive statements such as "skin intact" leave no room for doubt.
- Retrospective charting should be avoided whenever possible. Late entries due to unintentional omissions, if not done properly according to the facility's policies and procedures, might be construed as altering the record.
- Improper use of abbreviations on the operating room record and abbreviating on consent forms create confusion. Hospital-approved abbreviations should be used on the OR nurses notes and at no time should consents contain abbreviations. For example, a total abdominal hysterectomy should

not be abbreviated as "TAH." Also, the name of the surgeon should be listed and not the medical group he belongs to such as "PQR group."

- Illegible handwriting places doubt about the credibility of the author and complicates interpretation of medical records.
- Incorrect spelling can lead to confusion and misinterpretation of the facts.
- Improper error correction through the use of heavy markers or white out makes it look as if the author is trying to hide something. Errors should be crossed out with a single line per hospital policy.
- If a signature is incomplete, or status (MD, RN, etc.) omitted, questions can arise as to who authored the document.[14]

20.5 Documentation of Anesthesia Care

Anesthesia may be administered by an anesthesiologist or a certified registered nurse anesthetist (CRNA). Anesthesiologists are physicians who have completed four years of medical school plus four years of residency in anesthesia. Some complete an additional two years in an anesthesia fellowship specializing in a particular field of medicine such as obstetrical or pediatric anesthesia. CRNAs are highly skilled registered nurses with a master's degree in nursing who possess a background in critical care medicine and who have completed a three year CRNA program and have passed the CRNA certification exam. Approximately 65 percent of anesthesia in the U.S. is administered by CRNAs.

TIP: Analyzing anesthesia records is *extremely* challenging.

Physicians are notorious for poor penmanship, and space limitations on the anesthesia record can further affect handwriting legibility. With a multitude of information to document and limited space on the anesthesia records, omissions can occur. Difficulty in interpretation of the anesthesia record is compounded by specialized anesthesia abbreviations, symbols, and anesthetic agents.

Just like all healthcare professionals, the anesthesia professional is required to document in a timely manner. However, in the clinical setting, anesthesia interventions and assessments occur almost simultaneously, and even the best anesthesiologist finds it difficult to document contemporaneously.

The anesthesia record itself can be broken down into three major areas: pre-anesthesia evaluation, intraoperative record, and post-anesthesia assessment.

A. Pre-Anesthesia Assessment

The anesthesia evaluation is done during the preoperative interview and incorporates the following:

- patient identification and date,
- medical history,
- anesthetic history,
- medication history,
- social/medical history,
- allergies,
- patient examination,
- airway examination and classification,
- review of diagnostic and imaging studies,
- assignment of the American Society of Anesthesia physical status classification (see Figure 20.5),
- vital signs, height, and weight,
- the proposed anesthesia technique, including risks and benefits,
- counseling note that the patient was informed of the type of anesthesia and consented to the proposed anesthesia and questions were answered, and
- name of surgical procedure and surgeons.

TIP: Evaluation of the airway is *the* most important part of the pre-anesthesia assessment.

American Society of Anesthesia Physical Status Classification

ASA 1   Patient is normal and healthy.

ASA 2   Patient has mild systemic disease that does not limit activity (e.g., controlled hypertension or diabetes).

ASA 3   Patient has moderate or severe systemic disease which does not limit activities (e.g., stable angina or diabetes).

ASA 4   Patient has severe systemic disease that is a risk to life (e.g., severe heart failure, recent heart attack).

ASA 5   Patient is morbid and has substantial risk of death within 24 hours with or without intervention.

E   Emergency status: in addition to noting the above ASA classification, any patient undergoing emergency surgery is rated with an "E" to denote emergency.

Figure 20.5

It is vital to recognize a difficult airway before an airway mishap occurs in the operating room. Because of the potential loss of airway during deep sedation and the possibility of inducing a state of apnea (lack of breathing), it is important for the anesthesiologist to identify which patients may have a difficult airway to manage. Difficult airways can occur from the following structural problems:

- congenital or acquired facial and upper airway deformities,
- small mouth,
- trauma to the face or teeth,
- airway tumors, abscesses, or fistulas,
- cervical spine immobility, or
- burns or radiation to the head or neck.

Facial features that can cause mask ventilation difficulties are listed below.

- Lack of teeth can cause upper airway structures to collapse, making it difficult to obtain a good seal with the airway mask,
- Beards can interfere with obtaining a good seal of the airway mask, or
- The airway in obese patients can collapse by excessive oropharyngeal subcutaneous tissue. Obese individuals also have lower chest expansion, requiring higher pressures to maintain ventilation.

Next, the anesthesia professional assesses the patient's tongue and pharyngeal size; also known as the Airway Classification System. The anesthesia professional evaluates the size of the tongue in relation to the size of the oral cavity and grades the airway by how much of the pharynx is obscured by the tongue. The procedure is performed with the patient sitting with the head in neutral to slightly extended position. The patient opens her mouth as wide as possible and protrudes her tongue as far out as possible. The anesthesia professional classifies the airway by what is seen:

Grade I—able to see the soft palate, fauces, entire uvula, and tonsillar pillars

Grade II—able to see the soft palate, fauces and uvula

Grade III—able to see the soft palate and base of the uvula

Grade IV—able to see only the soft palate.[15]

Some pre-anesthesia evaluation records have diagrams illustrating each of these grades.

While it is the standard of care for an anesthesiologist to use the American Society of Anesthesia Airway Classification System to grade the airway, this grading system has limitations. The ASA Airway Classification System does not consider spine mobility and the fact that arching of the tongue obscures the uvula. Therefore, although it is the standard of care to use the ASA Airway Classification System, it alone cannot predict the degree of intubation difficulty.

B. Intraoperative Anesthesia Documentation

The major portion of the anesthesia record is occupied by a vital sign grid and a series of boxes and columns designated for specific purposes. The anesthesia record is a time-based record of events. Documentation is dependent upon the type of surgical procedure performed and intraoperative monitoring devices used.

In addition to monitoring basic patient care elements of blood pressure, pulse, respiration, oxygenation level, and temperature, the anesthesia professional is responsible for observing and documenting a multitude of other monitoring devices. Invasive arterial blood pressure monitoring is done via the radial, ulnar, brachial or femoral arteries. A central venous pressure catheter is used to monitor filling pressures of the right ventricle and provide an assessment of the intravascular volume and right ventricle function. Pulmonary artery devices, commonly called *Swan Ganz* or *PA catheters*, monitor a variety of heart pressures including left ventricular pressure important in critically ill patients or those with significant heart problems. Intracranial pressure monitoring can guide surgical and anesthesia decisions during neurological cases. Data from any monitoring devices should be recorded at regular intervals on the anesthesia record.

A detailed discussion of the anesthesia record is beyond the scope of this chapter. There are various anesthesia texts that describe anesthesia documentation in more detail. The American Society of Anesthesiologists also has *Standards for Basic Anesthetic Monitoring* which apply to all anesthesia care. The guidelines are intended to encourage quality patient care but may be exceeded at any time based upon the judgment of the responsible anesthesiologist.[16]

The anesthesia documentation includes

- check of the anesthesia equipment, drugs, and gas supply,
- starting and ending time of anesthesia,
- type of airway (e.g., endotracheal, nasal), size of endotracheal tube, size of laryngeal blade used,
- method of intubation (direct vision or blind),
- number of intubation attempts,
- utilization of a stylet or Magill forceps,

- use of anesthesia ointment, lubricant, or spray,
- whether it was a traumatic or smooth intubation,
- type and dosage of anesthesia induction agent used (general, spinal, epidural, block),
- paralytic agents used, dosage, and time administered,
- vital signs, including temperature and pulse oximetry recorded every five minutes,
- intravenous fluids, blood transfusion, and intraoperative medications given including dosage and time,
- intake and output including estimated blood loss,
- intraoperative lab work or arterial blood gases,
- clamping time of major vessels,
- tourniquet on and off times and level of inflation,
- intraoperative complications,
- name of reversal medication given including dosage and time, and
- patient's condition at the end of anesthesia including vital signs, pulse oximetry, if the patient was extubated, and that the airway was stable and the patient was oxygenating well.

In cases of an adverse anesthesia event, with or without patient injury, a complete account of the facts should be recorded. The primary anesthesia professional must document all relevant information of the event, and existing entries in the chart must not be altered.

The following case contains allegations related to intraoperative monitoring.

> The sixteen-year-old plaintiff was taken to surgery for a collapsed lung. An attempt was made to establish a double lumen airway during surgery. The plaintiff suffered cardiopulmonary arrest and hypoxic brain injury during the operation and required resuscitation. She was placed on a ventilator while in a coma for several weeks. She claimed the defendant anesthesiologist failed to adequately monitor oxygenation and ventilation. The plaintiff also alleged negligence in the failure to establish and complete a double lumen tube endobronchial intubation. The plaintiff suffered brain damage resulting in dystonia and ataxia of the extremities and is in need for assistance with her daily functions. The defendants denied any negligence. An $869,999 settlement was reached.[17]

C. Postoperative Anesthesia Documentation

It is the responsibility of the anesthesiologist or CRNA to ensure that the patient emerges safely from anesthesia and is safely transported to the post-anesthesia care unit. Upon arrival to the post-anesthesia care unit, anesthesia personnel provides the post-anesthesia care nurse with a patient report including the patient's name, medical history, surgery performed, anesthetics administered, intraoperative medications given, intake and output, estimated blood loss, lab work drawn, and any intraoperative complications that arose.

TIP: The anesthesia professional documents the initial vital signs upon arrival to the post-anesthesia recovery unit, the patient's general condition, and any immediate orders. The anesthesiologist is responsible for the patient while in the care unit and for ensuring the patient is stable for discharge.

Following the immediate post-anesthesia recovery unit period, the anesthesiologist or CRNA will see the patient within twenty-four hours (or prior to discharge from same-day surgery) and document the patient's recovery from anesthesia.

20.6 Post-Anesthesia Care Unit Documentation

The post-anesthesia care unit (PACU), commonly called "Recovery Room" or "PAR" (post-anesthesia recovery) is referred to as Phase I recovery. The PACU is a critical care unit. Nurses must be certified in Advanced Cardiac Life Support and possess specialized knowledge for caring for critical patients and of anesthetic agents. The primary goal of the PACU nurse is to ensure that the patient emerges safely from anesthesia. PACU records are generally flow charts which allow for rapid and complete patient assessment with an area for additional narrative documentation.

A. Assessment

Depending upon the facility, vital signs and pulse oximetry are recorded every ten to fifteen minutes. All PACU documentation is done in accordance with American Society of Perianesthesia Nurses (ASPAN) standards and follows the nursing process of assessment, diagnosis, planning, intervention, and evaluation. Figure 20.6 is a good example of a comprehensive PACU record which includes identifying:

- patient information,
- anesthesia method,
- date and time of arrival into the PACU,
- name of surgeon and anesthesiologist,
- surgical procedure,
- level of consciousness,

- skin, respiratory, circulatory, and neurological assessment,
- drains or tubes,
- vital sign section,
- IVs, monitoring devices,
- intake and output,
- Aldrete (pronounced all-dret-ee) scoring system (or similar scoring system indicating the patient is stable for discharge),
- pain management,
- condition at discharge,
- unit being transferred to and PACU discharge time, and
- names of PACU nurses.

B. Complications

Patients emerging from anesthesia are at high risk for complications. Anesthetic agents, individual health problems, patient age, and emergency surgeries are but a few factors that influence the incidence of postoperative complications. Complications which commonly occur in the immediate postoperative period are discussed below.

- Hypotension (reduced blood pressure) can result from blood and fluid loss, decreased cardiac output, intraoperative medications, or infection. Close recording of vital signs and pulse oximetry allows for rapid intervention in the PACU.

In a Colorado case, a fifty-nine year-old man with cirrhosis underwent a laparoscopic gallbladder surgery. The patient began extensively bleeding after the removal of his gallbladder. The surgeon believed he stopped the bleeding and sent the patient to the recovery room. The patient showed signs of shock and signs that he was bleeding. He returned to the operating room, and the surgeon was unsuccessful in stopping the bleeding. The patient died. The plaintiff claimed there was a lack of informed consent in continuing the surgery after the cirrhosis was found. A $211,037 verdict was returned on the wrongful death claim. The defendant received a defense verdict on the informed consent claim. A confidential post-trial settlement was reached.[18]

Regardless of the hospital policy, facilities and nurses can be held liable if vital signs and pulse oximetry are not frequently recorded during critical situations.

**POST-ANESTHESIA
CARE RECORD**

ANESTHESIA: ☐ GENERAL ☐ MAC ☐ SPINAL ☐ EPIDURAL ☐ OTHER_____

ID BAND ☐

DATE_____ ARRIVAL TIME_____ ☐ A.M. ☐ P.M.

SURGEON	ANESTHESIOLOGIST
OPERATION	
ADMITTING NURSE	PRE-OP BP & PULSE
PRE-OP MEDICAL HX	ALLERGIES

INITIAL ASSESSMENT

SKIN	COLOR	VENTILATION		BREATH SOUNDS	APICAL PULSE	CIRC PULSES
☐ WARM	☐ NORMAL	SPONTANEOUS _____	ASSISTED _____	RIGHT LUNG	☐ REG	RADIAL L___ R___ PEDAL L___ R___
☐ COOL	☐ PALE	LABORED _____	E.T. _____		☐ IRREG	FEM L___ R___ POP L___ R___
☐ TURGOR ___	☐ FLUSHED	REGULAR RATE + RHYTHM ___	T. PIECE _____	LEFT LUNG	☐ MONITOR	4+ - BOUNDING
☐ MOIST	☐ MOTTLED	EQUILATERAL _____	VENTILATOR _____			3+ - NORMAL
☐ DRY	☐ JAUNDICE	O₂ RX N/C _____	FIO₂ _____	CL - CLEAR		2+ - PALPABLE BUT OBLITERATED WITH FINGER PRESSURE
	☐ CYANOTIC	MASK _____	RATE _____	CO - CONGESTED	RHYTHM	1+ - THREADY AND INTERMITTENT
		L/M _____	VOLUME _____			0 - ABSENT

TUBES	I.V.	CONSCIOUS LEVEL	NEURO - SIGNS	SAFETY
N/G _____	L ___ R ___	1) ALERT _____ LETHARGIC _____	EXTREMITY MOVEMENT	☐ ISOLATION
FOLEY _____ GASTROSTOMY _____	CENTRAL R _____	2) ORIENTED TIME _____ PLACE _____ NAME _____	UPPER ☐ R ☐ L	(TYPE)
BULB _____ CHEST _____	LINE L _____	3) OBEYS SIMPLE COMMANDS_____	LOWER ☐ R ☐ L	
SUCTION DRAIN _____	SITE _____	4) RESPONDS TO VERBAL STIMULI_____	SENSATION	_____
OTHER _____	P.A. _____	5) RESPONDS TO PAIN PURPOSEFULLY_____	UPPER ☐ R ☐ L	
_____	ARTERIAL LINE _____	6) RESPONDS TO PAIN NON-PURPOSEFULLY_____	LOWER ☐ R ☐ L	_____
		7) NO RESPONSE_____	PUPILS EQUAL - REACTIVE	

TEMP F / RESP. PULSE 0 20 40 1 hr. 20 40 1hr. 20 40 1 hr. 20 40 1hr.

POST-ANESTHESIA ORDERS

102 — 200
101 — 180
100 — 160
99 — 140
98 — 120
97 — 100
96 — 80
95 — 60
94 — 40
93 — 20
92 — 0

02 SAT

CODE: TEMP = ● BLOOD PRESSURE = ✕ PULSE = X RESP = O

ANESTHESIOLOGIST

INFUSION RECORD	BLOOD BANK NO.	TYPE	TOTAL VOL (CC)	TIME BEGUN	SOLUTION LEFT	INTAKE				
						PARENTAL	BLOOD/BLOOD PRODUCTS	PIGGY BACKS	PO	TOTAL INTAKE
						OUTPUT				
						URINE	SUCTION	EMESIS	MISC.	TOTAL OUTPUT

Form # 894 (665) Rev. 11/02

Figure 20.6

TIME	HGB	HCT	pH	PO2	PCO2	Na	K	FBS	X-RAY	BGM		M.D. NOTIFIED

TIME	MEDICATIONS	REMARKS

POST ANESTHESIA RECOVERY SCORE

		MINUTES							
		IN	20	40	60	80	100	120	OUT
ABLE TO MOVE 4 EXTREMITIES VOLUNTARILY OR ON COMMAND = 2 / ABLE TO MOVE 2 EXTREMITIES VOLUNTARILY OR ON COMMAND = 1 / ABLE TO MOVE 0 EXTREMITIES VOLUNTARILY OR ON COMMAND = 0	ACTIVITY								
ABLE TO BREATHE AND COUGH FREELY = 2 / DYSPNEA OR LIMITED BREATHING = 1 / APNEIC = 0	RESPIRATION								
BP = 20 OF PREANESTHETIC LEVEL = 2 / BP = 20-50 OF PREANESTHETIC LEVEL = 1 / BP = 50 OF PREANESTHETIC LEVEL = 0	CIRCULATION								
FULLY AWAKE = 2 / AROUSABLE ON CALLING = 1 / NOT RESPONDING = 0	CONSCIOUSNESS								
ABLE TO MAINTAIN O2 SATURATION > 92% ON ROOM AIR = 2 / NEEDS O2 INHALATION TO MAINTAIN OXYGEN SATURATION > 90% = 1 / O2 SATURATION < 90% EVEN WITH O2 SUPPLEMENT = 0	OXYGEN SATURATION								
	TOTALS								

ANALGESIC SCALE

NO PAIN — 0 1 2 3 4 5 6 7 8 9 10 — WORST PAIN

PAIN SCALE RATING
PATIENT VERBALIZES UNDERSTANDING OF PAIN SCALE ☐ YES ☐ NO

QUALITY OF PAIN
B - BURNING R - RADIATING
T - THROBBING S - SHARP
A - ACHE P - PRESSURE
D - DULL C - CRAMPING
ADMISSION_____
LOCATION_____
DISCHARGE_____

REPORT GIVEN TO _____ TRANSFERRED TO: _____
TIME OF DISCHARGE _____ AM PM DATE _____ SIGNATURE _____ R.N.

Figure 20.6 (continued)

- Bronchospasm (closing of airways in lungs) and laryngospasm (closing of throat) are considered respiratory emergencies. Documentation should include the auscultation of lung sounds, description of noisy respirations, use of accessory muscles for breathing, skin color, oxygen flow rate, pulse oximetry reading, and notification of the anesthesia professional, treatment intervention, and condition of patient after resolution.

- Cardiac dysrhythmias (irregular heartbeat) or heart failure can occur as a result of underlying cardiac problems or stress on the cardiovascular system during surgery. Documentation includes cardiac rhythm upon arrival and the type of dysrhythmia. A cardiac rhythm strip should also accompany the narrative description of an abnormal cardiac rhythm that develops during the PACU stay, along with notification of the anesthesiologist and other consultants as deemed necessary, and interventions. Finally, another cardiac rhythm strip is obtained prior to PACU discharge.

C. Discharge Criteria

TIP: Patients who have received general or spinal anesthesia should remain in the post-anesthesia care unit for a minimum of one hour.

Patients receiving monitored anesthesia care (MAC) remain in the PACU for a minimum of twenty minutes. However, the length of time a patient stays in the PACU is based upon patient stability. PACU discharge criteria are dependent upon the following:

- the return of protective airway reflexes so that the patient is able to defend her own airway (the patient must be alert enough to swallow, cough, turn her head or reposition herself),
- stable vital signs, heart rhythm, and oxygen level; significantly, the respiratory rate must not only be of a normal rate, but the depth of respirations should be normal,
- alertness, and the patient's ability to summon help from the nursing staff,
- control of pain,
- return of motor/sensory function (is the patient able to move her extremities and is she without numbness, tingling, or weakness),
- normal or near-normal body temperature, and
- surgical dressings are dry and intact, or no overt drainage.

Aldrete Scoring System

Consciousness	fully awake	= 2
	responds to name	= 1
	no response	= 0
Activity	moves all extremities	= 2
	moves two extremities	= 1
	no movement	= 0
Respirations	full respirations	= 2
	limited breathing	= 1
	no respirations	= 0
Circulation	BP within 20 percent preop	= 2
	BP 20-50 percent preop	= 1
	BP 50 percent or less preop	= 0
Oxygenation	> 92 percent on room air	= 2
	> 92 percent with oxygen	= 1
	< 92 percent with oxygen	= 0

Figure 20.7

Prior to discharge from the PACU, the anesthesia professional must provide written documentation that the patient is stable and able to be discharged back to the ambulatory care center or to a medical/surgical unit. Many PACUs use the Aldrete scoring system to evaluate that a patient has recovered from anesthesia and is stable for discharge. Patients are evaluated upon admission to the PACU, at twenty minutes, at thirty minutes and every thirty minutes thereafter. A perfect Aldrete score is 10. However, normal healthy patients must achieve a score of 8 or above in order to be discharged from the PACU. Scoring using the Aldrete system is shown in Figure 20.7.

Both overmedication and respiratory depression played a role in the unfortunate clinical outcome of the next case.

A fifty-one-year-old Hispanic woman underwent rotator cuff repair. The anesthesiologist used a combination of a local block plus general anesthesia. In the post-anesthesia care unit, the patient was moaning in pain but was never conscious enough to rate her pain. The PACU record reflected the nurse administered an excessive amount of IV narcotics over a one-hour period. A more than 30 mmHg drop in blood pressure occurred. The last respiratory rate was recorded at nine breaths per minute, indicating the patient was not stable for discharge. The PACU nurse discharged the patient to a surgical floor where the patient had a respiratory arrest, suffering irreversible brain damage. The PACU record contained numerous deficiencies in documentation, and the case was settled prior to trial (unpublished settlement).

When the patient is ready to leave the PACU, the nurse conducts a final assessment to ensure the patient is stable and alert and all dressings are dry. The nurse calls a report to the receiving unit—either the outpatient surgery center for discharge home, or to the medical/surgical unit if the patient is admitted. The PACU record reflects the time the report was called and the nurse who received the report. The PACU record must contain a complete patient assessment and any special instructions given to the receiving nurse. Some hospitals require the PACU nurse to accompany the patient to the floor, while other institutions have transporters who transfer the patient to the receiving unit. Although it is the responsibility of the PACU nurse to determine that the patient has safely emerged from anesthesia, the PACU nurse does not determine home readiness.

20.7 Outpatient Surgery Discharge

Post-surgical patients transition from the immediate PACU (Phase I) to the Phase II area (ambulatory surgery unit or outpatient surgery unit) prior to discharge or to a medical/surgical unit for hospital admission. The Phase II recovery area allows for continued patient monitoring. Outpatient nursing documentation reflects that the patient is stable for discharge, vital signs are stable, pain is controlled, and the patient is able to retain food and fluids without nausea, walk without dizziness, and urinate.

Patient and family teaching includes documentation of discharge instructions which specify activity level, dressing care, pain management orders, activity restrictions such as refraining from driving or operating machinery for twenty-four hours, abnormal signs to be alert for and immediately report to his doctor, and follow-up appointment information. For patients with whom there is a language barrier, an interpreter may be used or instructions may have to be provided in their language.

Appropriate provision of discharge instructions was raised as an issue in the following case.

A thirty-two-year-old woman suffered a postoperative wound infection following laparoscopic surgery. She alleged the ambulatory care nurses failed to provide appropriate discharge instructions regarding signs and symptoms of infection and proper incision care and follow-up instructions

with her surgeon. A copy of the patient discharge instruction sheet revealed the patient and her husband were given verbal and written instructions on signs and symptoms of infection, medication, activity restrictions, and proper follow up with the surgeon along with the surgeon's phone number. More important, however, was the follow-up phone call that was made to the patient on the third postoperative day when the patient denied any postoperative problems or signs of infection. After receipt of the follow-up phone call form, the plaintiff's attorney dismissed the claim.

Only the patient's surgeon may authorize hospital discharge. The majority of the times, the discharge order and prescriptions are generated while the patient is still in the PACU. The surgeon relies on the outpatient nursing staff to ensure that the patient is stable and ready for discharge home.

The discharge record should include the time of discharge, mode of discharge (per wheelchair, ambulatory, and so on), and name of the family member or significant other who accompanied the patient. It is important to document that the patient was discharged with all belongings and prescriptions. The discharge instruction sheet is signed by the patient or significant other. A copy of the discharge instruction sheet is given to the patient; one is kept in the patient chart, and one is sent to the surgeon. Figure 20.8 is an example of an outpatient surgical discharge form.

A well executed discharge instruction sheet is key when patients allege improper hospital discharge. Although many hospitals conduct follow-up outpatient surgery calls, The Joint Commission does not require this. The *Comprehensive Accreditation Manual for Ambulatory Care* allows a facility to define what data and information are gathered during assessment and reassessment.

TIP: Many hospitals and surgical centers conduct follow-up phone calls and record important recovery information provided by the patient. This form may not be kept as part of the patient record and must be requested separately.

20.8 Summary

Thousands of surgical procedures are performed each day without incident, yet even the simplest of surgeries carries inherent risks. From neonatal surgery to geriatric surgery, lives are saved through the skill of surgeons and the dedication and expertise of perioperative nurses. The perioperative nurse acts as a patient advocate at a time when the patient is unable to perform self-protective measures.[19]

PLEASE CHECK ONE

☐ ONE DAY PROCEDURE   ☐ OUTPATIENT PROCEDURE PATIENT

DISCHARGE INSTRUCTION SHEET

DO NOT WORK WITH ANY ELECTRICAL OR MECHANICAL DEVICES FOR 24 HOURS.	☐ YES	☐ NO
DO NOT OPERATE ANY MOTORIZED VEHICLE FOR 24 HOURS AFTER SURGERY.	☐ YES	☐ NO
DO NOT TAKE TRANQUILIZERS OR SLEEPING PILLS FOR 24 HOURS AFTER SURGERY.	☐ YES	☐ NO
DO NOT DRINK ALCOHOLIC BEVERAGES FOR 24 HOURS AFTER SURGERY.	☐ YES	☐ NO
DO NOT MAKE IMPORTANT DECISIONS OR SIGN IMPORTANT DOCUMENTS FOR 24 HOURS AFTER LEAVING THE HOSPITAL (UNTIL YOUR FULL MENTAL ALERTNESS RETURNS)	☐ YES	☐ NO

FOR 1-2 DAYS FOLLOWING YOUR ANESTHESIA AND SURGICAL PROCEDURE, YOU MAY EXPERIENCE THE FOLLOWING: SORE THROAT, NECK AND JAW DISCOMFORT, MUSCLE ACHES, NAUSEA, LIGHT HEADEDNESS. SHOULDER PAIN MAY OCCUR AFTER LAPAROSCOPIC PROCEDURES. IF THESE SYMPTOMS PERSIST LONGER THAN 2 DAYS, PLEASE CONTACT YOUR PHYSICIAN.

IF YOU HAVE ANY TROUBLE BREATHING, HAVE HEAVY BLEEDING, OR ANY OTHER PROBLEMS AFTER LEAVING THE HOSPITAL, CALL YOUR PHYSICIAN IMMEDIATELY. IF YOU CANNOT REACH YOUR PHYSICIAN, GO IMMEDIATELY TO THE EMERGENCY ROOM.

SPECIAL INSTRUCTIONS RELATING TO YOUR SURGICAL PROCEDURE

BATHING:
☐ NO RESTRICTION   ☐ SHOWER ONLY FOR _____ DAYS   ☐ SPONGE BATH ONLY FOR _____ DAYS

DIET:
☐ NO RESTRICTION   ☐ OTHER: _____

ACTIVITY:
☐ RESUME NORMAL ACTIVITY   ☐ LIGHT ACTIVITY FOR DAYS

☐ DO NOT OPERATE A MOTORIZED VEHICLE FOR ____DAYS   ☐ BEDREST FOR _____HOURS

☐ NO LIFTING, PUSHING OR PULLING FOR _____DAYS

MEDICATIONS:
☐ REVIEW / RESUME HOME MEDS

☐ INSTRUCTED ON PRESCRIPTION RECEIVED

_____

_____

☐ NO ASPIRIN FOR _____DAYS

WOUND CARE: ☐ DO NOT REMOVE DRESSING

☐ CHANGE / REMOVE DRESSING AFTER _____ HOURS   ☐ WATCH INCISION FOR REDNESS, SWELLING OR DRAINAGE

SPECIAL INSTRUCTIONS:

_____

_____

POST-OP PHYSICIAN VISIT: DATE   OFFICE PHONE NUMBER:

SIGNATURE: PHYSICIAN / RN   DATE

I HAVE RECEIVED A COPY OF AND HAVE VERBALIZED UNDERSTANDING OF THE ABOVE INSTRUCTIONS.

PATIENT OR AUTHORIZED PARTY   RELATIONSHIP   DATE

PHYSICIAN / RN   DATE

ORIGINAL-CHART   YELLOW COPY-PATIENT/SIGNIFICANT OTHER   PINK COPY-PHYSICIAN'S OFFICE

1705 4/97

Figure 20.8 *Outpatient surgical discharge form.*

The perioperative environment is a fast-paced arena. Documentation is streamlined, using a combination of pre-printed standardized forms, checklist charting, graphs, and narrative notes. However at all times, documentation of patient care must be done in accordance with the clinical condition of the patient, hospital policy, agency standards, and standards set forth from professional perioperative organizations.

Clear and concise documentation in accordance with the standard of care may not prevent a lawsuit but speaks volumes in a court of law. This chapter has covered several areas of perioperative care and documentation, but by no means is the chapter inclusive. Additional information on perioperative care can be found from governmental agencies, professional perioperative organizations, and articles and books.

Endnotes

1. Burden, N. *Ambulatory Surgical Nursing*. p. 201. W.B. Saunders Co. 1993.

2. Joint Commission on Accreditation of Hospital Organizations. www.jcaho.org.

3. See note. 1

4. AORN. AORN Position Statement on Correct Site Surgery. *2003 Standards, Recommended Practices and Guidelines*.

5. *See* note 3.

6. Laska, L. "Bunionectomy Performed on Wrong Foot." *Medical Malpractice, Verdicts, Settlements, and Experts*. November 2009, p. 34

7. AORN. Recommended Practices for Positioning the Patient in the Perioperative Practice Setting. *2003 Standards, Recommended Practices and Guidelines*.

8. Laska, L. "Full-Strength Acetic Acid used in Loop Electrosurgical Excision with Cone Biopsy." *Medical Malpractice, Verdicts, Settlements, and Experts*. October 2009, p. 16

9. Laska, L. "Man Has No Blood Flow in Legs After Being Left in Lithotomy Position for Twelve Hours." *Medical Malpractice, Verdicts, Settlements, and Experts*. June 2009, p. 48

10. Association of Surgical Technologists. www.ast.org.

11. Fortunato, N.H. *Operating Room Technique*. p. 447. St. Louis, MO: Mosby. 2000.

12. Laska, L. "Sponges Left in Abdomen After Hysterectomy." *Medical Malpractice, Verdicts, Settlements, and Experts*. May 2004, p. 53.

13. Groah, L.K. *Perioperative Nursing*. p. 315. Norwalk, CT: Appleton and Lange. 1996.

14. Fairchild, S.S. *Perioperative Nursing Principles and Practice*. p. 392–393. Philadelphia, PA: Lippincott. 1996.

15. Barash, P.G., B.F. Cullen, and R.K. Stoelting. *Clinical Anesthesia*. Second Edition. p. 557. 1992.

16. American Society of Anesthesiologist. *Standards for Basic Anesthetic Monitoring*. October 2003. (www.asahq.org)

17. Laska, L. "Brain Injury from Lack of Oxygenation During Surgery for Collapsed Lung in Teenager." *Medical Malpractice, Verdicts, Settlements, and Experts*. June 2009, p. 3.

18. Laska, L. "Gallbladder Surgery Continued Even After Cirrhosis Identified." *Medical Malpractice, Verdicts, Settlements, and Experts*. June 2009, p. 45

19. Meiner, S.E. *Nursing Documentation, Legal Focus Across Practice Settings*. p. 172. SAGE Publications. 1999.

Chapter 21

Physician Documentation in Hospitals and Nursing Homes

Jeffrey M. Levine, MD

21.1 Introduction

Understanding what the physician writes in medical records kept in hospitals and nursing homes is essential for retrospectively analyzing medical events, assessing quality, analyzing the patient's condition and treatment, and determining deviations from the standard of care. This chapter introduces the reader to physician documentation. It reviews the forces that shape the standard of care, including medical school training, reimbursement requirements, medical staff bylaws, accreditation bodies, and applicable regulations.

21.2 Physician Roles and Responsibilities for Documentation

The backbone of care is delivered by the primary care provider. Consequently, the documentation of internists and family practitioners is generally broader in scope than single-system focused specialties. This section introduces basic descriptions of documentation found in medical charts by primary care providers, consultants, pathologists, and radiologists. It then describes considerations relevant to academic or teaching environments.

A. The Primary Care Provider: History and Physical, Orders, Progress Notes
1. History and physical

The primary care provider is responsible for the initial history and physical examination (H&P), orders, daily notes, and the timely dictation of a discharge summary. The timing of required documentation is dictated by hospital bylaws and accreditation standards. Many institutions require a formally dictated H&P, while others provide a multi-page form for handwritten completion. Components of a H&P for a newly admitted hospital patient include:

Chief Complaint—A concise statement describing the symptom, condition, or diagnosis that is the reason the patient presented to the hospital.

History of Present Illness—A chronological description of the patient's illness from initial development to the present.

Past Medical History—A review of past illnesses including diagnoses, hospitalizations, and operations or procedures.

Allergies—Includes medications and food items.

Social History—Includes marital status, living arrangements, occupational history, use of drugs, alcohol (sometimes written ETOH), or tobacco, sexual history if appropriate, and other relevant social factors. Drug use may be abbreviated as IVDA (intravenous drug abuse). Smoking history may be calculated in packs per year or referred to as pack/years.

Review of Systems—An inventory of appropriate body systems which is generally directed toward relevance regarding the chief complaint but can include other symptoms.

Medications—A list of medications the patient is currently taking, both prescription and over-the-counter, including the reason for the medication, dosages, and how often. This list should also include "alternative medicine" modalities such as herbs and supplements.

Physical Examination—This begins with vital signs and should present an inventory of physical findings, with special emphasis on those relevant to the chief complaint. Sometimes the physician records what the nurse has documented instead of taking a new set of vital signs. With the advent of denial of reimbursement for the development of ""never events," the physician is obligated to document the presence of certain complications on admission in order to verify that the patient was admitted with these pre-existing problems. For example, the physician must document the presence of a stage III or IV pressure ulcer. See Chapter 14, *Preventing Healthcare-Acquired Conditions Means Never Having to Say You're Sorry,* in Volume I.

Laboratory Values—These can sometimes be depicted by shorthand notation for specific tests, examples of which are given in Figure 21.1.

Impression and Plan—This provides a summary statement of the patient's presumed diagnoses, as well as diagnostic and treatment plan. Problems are sometimes listed numerically, with separate plans designated for each.

2. Physician orders

Physician orders are the primary directives for day-to-day medical care of the patient. As such, they should be dated, timed, clearly written, and unambiguous. Medication orders, for example, should incorporate instructions regarding dosage, timing, and route of administration. Orders that are unclear or incomplete should be questioned by nurses and/or pharmacists. These general rules apply to all healthcare settings.

a. Admitting orders. Admitting orders usually designate the particular service to which the patient is admitted, such as a medical or surgical floor, telemetry unit, ICU, and so on. Other items in the admitting orders include directives for vital signs. It is appropriate to record major allergies in the orders section as well as in the history and physical. An order is required to involve each consulting subspecialty that assists in management of the patient. Admitting orders generally include "The Five D's." These are:

Diagnosis—Identifying the reason the patient is in the hospital. Some physicians will add the resident's condition or expected prognosis.

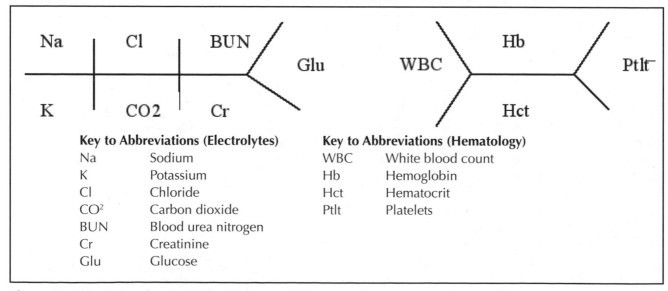

Figure 21.1 *Physician shorthand for laboratory values.*

Disposition—Specifying whether the patient must stay in bed, sit in a chair at the bedside, or ambulate freely.

Diet—Including caloric content and restrictions (e.g., diabetic, low sodium, etc.). Tube feeding orders should incorporate formula type, rate of administration, and water flushes.

Diagnostics—Including blood tests, x-rays, etc.

Drugs—Including name of medication, dose, route of administration, and administration schedule. A preferred practice is to include with each medication the appropriate diagnosis that justifies its use. This section might include daily wound treatments, ventilator settings, intravenous orders, catheter care, etc.

b. Day-to-day orders. Daily orders as well as admitting orders are entered onto order sheets. Many hospitals have computerized physician order entry (CPOE) systems that are replacing order sheets. Certain interventions such as those for intravenous fluids, Heparin drips, total parenteral nutrition (TPN), peripheral parenteral nutrition (PPN), and antibiotics may require separate pre-printed order sheets. The purpose of these is to ensure proper management as well as accuracy and completeness of information such as rationale for treatment, caloric intake, dosages, and stop dates. Others which require separate forms may include orders for do not resuscitate (DNR), post-partum management, patient controlled analgesia pumps, and critical care unit admissions. Other special order sets may exist.

The standard of care requires the physician to be precise in orders. Nurses are expected to carry out the orders or to question ones that are incomplete, imprecise, or inappropriate.

TIP: In order to satisfy federal regulations regarding restraint reduction, some skilled nursing facilities require specific order forms for physical restraints such as wrist restraints, vest restraints, and bedrails.

Order forms may include information such as mandatory informed consent, non-restrictive alternatives previously attempted, and medical symptoms for which the restraint is ordered.

Some nursing homes employ *standing orders*. This is a pre-printed list of medications and interventions that covers a wide variety of symptoms and illnesses (e.g., laxatives for constipation, antacids for gastric upset, antihistamines for allergy, antipyretics for fever, etc.). Standing orders that encompass such a variety of symptoms represent a "cookbook" approach to medical care, with the result of relieving the physician of visiting the nursing home to examine the resident and avoiding phone calls for new treatments. Because of the lack of individualization involved in standing orders, the use of standing orders is strongly discouraged by this author. This must be distinguished, however, from preprinted order sheets commonly found for specific situations such as PCA (Patient Controlled Analgesia) pumps, TPN (Total Parenteral Nutrition), antibiotics, and some specialized care units.

Telephone orders are those which are given when the physician is not present. They require date, time, and countersignature, usually within twenty-four hours depending on medical by-laws. Though sometimes necessary, telephone orders may be overused, particularly in some nursing homes. A consequence of too many telephone orders is the appearance of non-involvement by the physician. A telephone order is documented as "TO (name of prescriber/name of nurse who took the call)." For example, a nurse records "TO Dr. Rahman/B.Tully, RN."

Verbal orders are given in person by a physician, advanced nurse practitioner, or physician's assistant to a nurse. The order is documented as "VO (name of prescriber/ name of nurse who took the order)." For example, a nurse records "VO Dr. Rahman/B.Tully, RN."

In a Virginia case, the plaintiff injured his arm in a fall. He was seen in the emergency department of a hospital. The defendant orthopaedic surgeon was promptly contacted by phone. The defendant admitted the plaintiff and assumed care at about 4:00 A.M. The defendant's only verbal order upon admission was to place the arm in a splint pending his examination and reduction of the dislocation. At the time the plaintiff was in the emergency department, he was able to move his fingers and had a good distal pulse and capillary refill. The defendant did not see the plaintiff until about 1:40 P.M. During the interim, the plaintiff experienced severe pain, swelling, and the gradual loss of feeling and sensation in his hand and fingers. Several calls were made to the defendant, who continued to see patients at his private practice and did not respond to the hospital's attempts to contact him. The plaintiff developed compartment syndrome from the elbow to the hand, which led to permanent damage to the nerve and muscles. The plaintiff claimed the defendant should have urgently reduced the elbow dislocation, which would have prevented the compartment syndrome. The defendant claimed that the nerve injuries occurred acutely from the fall. The plaintiff's surgeon has recommended amputation of the arm, which is dysfunctional and deformed. A $900,000 settlement was reached.[1]

3. Progress notes

TIP: Following the initial H&P, the primary care provider or covering physician should write daily progress notes up to discharge. Frequency of notes is dictated by hospital by-laws, federal regulation (in skilled nursing facilities), and accreditation bodies such as The Joint Commission.

The daily progress note should offer an assessment, including timely responses of the patient to treatment, changes in medications, results of diagnostic tests, discussions with consultants and family members, as well as development of new problems. Physicians may note the results of laboratory studies.

In the following case, the plaintiff alleged that the surgeon failed to provide appropriate postoperative care. No doubt the medical record would have been a key exhibit.

In this Virginia case, a four-year-old child underwent a nephrectomy and reimplantation of her ureter into her bladder. In the early postoperative period she did well, but between postoperative day one and day two she developed a distended abdomen and began having noticeable breathing difficulties. This was first noted at 4 A.M. on day two. The first notation of a distended abdomen was five hours later. By the afternoon, the child was having retractions, nasal flaring, and decreased oxygen saturations. The physicians who saw her during the day did not order any studies until mid-afternoon. There were delays in drawing blood and obtaining the results. Despite not having the lab results, the anesthesiologist gave anesthesia for the procedure to remove fluid from her abdomen. The child's heart stopped and she died. During the resuscitation, the lab results were rushed to the operating room. They revealed a deadly high level of potassium. The plaintiffs alleged multiple deviations. A $1.2 million settlement was reached.[2]

4. Discharge summary

The discharge summary is generally dictated and typed, and a chart is not considered complete until this document is entered. Most hospitals provide dictation and transcription services for completion of discharge summaries. Notes that are transcribed (including discharge summaries, radiology reports, surgical reports, etc.) are usually accompanied by shorthand notation including DD (date dictated), DT (date transcribed), and DR (date revised). These dates are sometimes critical in chart review when reconstructing complex events.

B. Consultants, Procedure-Oriented Specialties, and Non-Primary Care Personnel

Consultant documentation (e.g., surgery, neurology, endocrinology, etc.) usually begins with a handwritten note in the progress notes section, followed by a complete note on a consultation form. Because consults are often "cc'd" to the referring physician, these notes are usually typed. This form appears in the "consultation" section of the chart and provides proof of the initial complete encounter for reimbursement purposes and satisfaction of hospital by-laws. Subsequent consultant notes are usually handwritten into the progress notes section with a header designating the doctor's subspecialty.

Consultants often rely on what they are told by other healthcare providers who have interacted with the patient. A strong defense is created when the information is recorded; this is often not the case when a plaintiff files a claim alleging injury because of lack of communication and appropriate action by providers.

In an Illinois case, a twenty-nine year-old woman who had lupus went to the emergency department with complaints of dizziness, chest tightness, chest pain, difficulty breathing, vomiting, a temperature of 104 degrees and fainting at home. She was examined; a chest x-ray was performed; and blood work showed an elevated white blood cell count. She was given medication and discharged with instructions to follow up with her rheumatologist the next day. The emergency department physician called her rheumatologist and was told that the patient had drug-seeking behavior in the past. The woman refused to leave the hospital, pleading that she needed help and could not see. Security escorted her outside. She died at home of an arrhythmia two hours later. The plaintiff alleged an inadequate history was taken and that the consultant failed to come to the hospital and ask appropriate questions to determine the patient's presenting symptoms. The consultant denied being told the woman had fainted at home and had difficulty breathing and chest pain. A defense verdict was returned for the consultants. The hospital and emergency department doctor settled for $1,950,000 before trial.[3]

Sometimes the consultant writes orders for medications and diagnostics. From a continuity standpoint, this practice may become problematic because it can bypass the attention of the primary care provider. In addition, the primary care provider might disagree with consultant recommendations. Some facilities may have by-laws placing limitations on consultant orders.

Procedures such as echocardiography or endoscopy of the gastrointestinal tract are reported on a pre-printed page where anatomical descriptions and sometimes photographs are included in the chart.

An operative report is generated for procedures taking place in an operating room. This is a typed summary that reports information including surgeon's name and assistants, preoperative diagnosis, postoperative diagnosis, and a detailed recounting of the procedure with operative findings. It includes the type of anesthesia, estimated blood loss (EBL), and complications. Procedures requiring an anesthesiologist are accompanied by the anesthesiologist's preoperative assessment and flow sheets of medications and vital signs. Anesthesia notes and flow sheets are often presented in pre-printed forms with checklists. Procedures performed at the bedside, such as wound debridements and spinal taps, are generally accompanied by a handwritten "procedure note" in the progress notes section. This note is much less formal than the operative note but should contain reasons for the procedure, anesthetic used, fluids or specimens sent to the laboratory, and how the patient responded. Chapter 20, *Perioperative Records*, should be consulted for more information.

Pathology reports describe tissues or biopsies. Any body part or physical item removed during procedures and operations is sent to the pathologist, such as abnormal tissue taken during endoscopy, bone segments removed during operations for fractures, and amputated body parts. The reports are composed of "gross" and "microscopic" findings. The gross section is simply a physical description of the tissue with special notation of clinically relevant portions such as skin margins of tumor resections; the microscopic report sometimes adds separate sections for special stains or chemical treatment of the tissue.

Accurate evaluation of specimens is essential for guiding the treatment of a patient, as the next case illustrates.

In an Illinois case, the plaintiff had significant bleeding three weeks after giving birth. She underwent a D&D for bleeding. The pathology report came back with no evidence of retained tissue. The plaintiff claimed the defendants were negligent in not diagnosing retained placental tissue. The plain-

tiff developed Asherman's syndrome, leaving her unable to become pregnant. The same hospital pathologist who issued the initial report later re-examined the tissue slides and admitted there was retained placental tissue and she made an error in the original report. A $731,124 verdict was returned.[4]

Radiology reports are written descriptions of findings seen on x-ray, ultrasound, CT, or MRI. Some reports include a shorthand form of indicating whether a dye was used: "with or without contrast" or simply "c or s" with a dash above the letters. Reports are composed of a section which describes the findings in visual detail (i.e., description of specific physical structures noting normal and abnormal findings) followed by a brief summary of diagnostic findings (i.e., the significance of the abnormalities, sometimes with further diagnostic recommendations). In some cases, the radiologist will document the time the procedure was done. This is most common on x-ray reports. The nursing notes may also be used to determine timing of tests when an accurate chronology of events is essential. Reports of invasive procedures such as angiograms contain more detail regarding anesthetic and contrast material. Radiology reports should include the time that the procedure was performed. Chapter 10, *Diagnostic Testing*, covers this area in more detail.

C. Miscellaneous Documents

There are several critical documents which require physician involvement and signature but may not receive proper attention from the provider. Often, they are perceived as peripheral to the process of care, and their importance is therefore overlooked. The result of improper attention to these items can be disastrous should litigation arise. These documents include informed consent for surgery and other invasive procedures, advance directives (ADs), and discharge instructions.

1. Informed consent

TIP: Informed consent reflects the concept that a cognitively intact adult has the right to decide whether to allow violation of his body's integrity.[5]

When informed consent is presented to a patient or family, it is the duty of the provider to instruct the patient on all major side effects and poor outcomes that can be expected. This conversation can be difficult and long, and it is often presented in rushed fashion, particularly in emergency situations. The informed consent form generally requires a physician signature.

An operative consent requires identification of the type and location (right versus left) of surgery to be performed.

> In *Anonymous Sixty-One-Year-Old Man v. Anonymous Surgeon*, the plaintiff was at extremely high risk of cancer of the colon because of multiple polyps within the right colon and a family history of colon cancer. The right colon was technically difficult to monitor with colonoscopy. To reduce the plaintiff's risk of developing colon cancer, removal of the right side of the colon was recommended. The plaintiff met with the defendant surgeon prior to the procedure, and the plan for right hemicolectomy was discussed and agreed upon. On October 31, 1997, the plaintiff presented to the hospital for performance of a right hemicolectomy. When he awoke from surgery, he learned that the defendant had performed a left hemicolectomy. Because his remaining right colon contained multiple polyps, his right colon was subsequently also removed. As a result, he had almost no colon and experienced multiple diarrhea-like bowel movements per day. The defendant denied that the removal of the left colon was an error, arguing that he performed merely a "partial" colectomy. The defendant also argued that he needed to evaluate the plaintiff's colon at the time of surgery, and he had waited until that point to determine what portion of the colon to actually remove. The defendant further stated that that was his surgical plan all along—despite what was written in the medical records and what he discussed in detail with the plaintiff prior to surgery. The case was eventually settled for $1,000,000, according to a published account.[6]

In this case, presumably the medical records defined the plan to remove the patient's right colon. The operative consent would have been a crucial document.

2. Advance directives

Advance directives can include instructions on resuscitation preferences, artificial nutrition and hydration, and prolongation of life in futile situations. Although critical documents, these are often not presented for execution when caring for persons with advanced illness. Even when present, the documents may be lost, overlooked, misunderstood, or disregarded by physicians. The advance directive form may not require a physician signature, but an order needs to be signed to place it in effect if the patient is hospitalized or placed in a nursing home. This is specifically required for Do Not Resuscitate (DNR) requests.

3. Discharge instructions

Discharge instructions should be specific and include precautions to be taken by the patient as well as medication dose, schedule, and route. When discharge instructions are insufficient, this document can serve as an important jury exhibit should the patient have a poor outcome.

D. The Issue of Physician Handwriting

The poor quality of physicians' handwriting is common fodder for jokes, but doctors, the public, and regulatory bodies are wakening to the fact that this is no laughing matter. Medical information cannot be abstracted for quality review or billing purposes if documentation is illegible. A recent report by the Committee on the Quality of Health Care in America has drawn attention to the high prevalence of errors in day-to-day medical care delivery, with a major source attributable to illegible, poorly written, or difficult to interpret prescriptions.[7]

In 1998, nearly 2.5 billion prescriptions were dispensed in the United States, at a cost of roughly $92 billion.[8] Several points in the medical care system are prone to error including prescribing, dispensing, and unintentional non-adherence by the patient. As new medications are introduced there is increasing risk of confusion with proliferation of new generic and trade names written into prescriptions. Older persons are at particular risk for medication errors simply due to an increased number of prescriptions per patient. Many medication errors are preventable, particularly those related to illegible prescriptions.

The following case exemplifies what errors can occur with poor handwriting.

> Dr. Ramachandra Kolluru, a Texas cardiologist, was treating Ramon Vasquez for a heart condition. Dr. Kolluru prescribed 20 milligrams of Isordil (isosorbide dinitrate) every six hours for coronary artery vasodilatation. The doctor's handwriting was unclear to the pharmacist, who filled the prescription with 20 milligrams of Plendil (felodipine), a blood pressure drug with a maximum recommended dosage of 10 milligrams.
>
> Mr. Vasquez died one day after taking his new medication, which equaled a 16 percent overdose of felodipine. The Odessa, Texas, jury ordered the cardiologist and the dispensing pharmacy to pay $450,000. The primary issue at trial was not the quality of care the physician delivered, but illegibility of the prescription.[9]

Factors Contributing to Poor Penmanship

- Distractions
- Uneven writing surface
- Incorrect posture when writing
- Lack of enough room
- Rushing
- Wrong chair or desk height
- Forms with inadequate space to write
- Poor penmanship style

Figure 21.2 *(Adapted from Health Care Facility Risk Management Practice Tip, August 2002. http://medicalmutual.com/risk/tips/HCF/23.html.)*

Many factors contribute to poor physician penmanship. (See Figure 21.2.) The current healthcare environment, where managed care encourages maximum numbers of patients to be seen by physicians, presents an additional risk factor for poor physician handwriting. Several solutions have been offered, including handwriting classes for physicians and computerized physician order entry (CPOE) systems.[10] Computerized systems have been shown to decrease prescription errors by as much as 50 percent by sending the order directly to the pharmacy and incorporating alert monitors that screen for drug misuse, allergies, and interactions.[11] Use of a CPOE would directly eliminate handwriting related errors and is already incorporated into many hospitals.

E. The Teaching and Nonteaching Hospital Staff

The academic environment of the teaching hospital presents a new layer of documentation that is not often understood by persons outside this system. The system of medical training contains a hierarchy of doctors-in-training, with each level having different responsibilities for documentation.

The intern is the "entry level" position in the hierarchy. The intern's notes are generally more detailed and are designated as "IPN" or "intern progress notes" or "MIPN" meaning "medical intern progress notes." Interns are also designated as first-year residents, and residents often label their notes as "PGY1," "PGY2," etc. acknowledging the year of post-graduate training. In similar fashion, medical students often precede their notes by "MS3" or "MS4" depending upon the year of training. Medical students generally do not write notes in the medical chart until their third or fourth year of education.

Interns and residents may preface their notes with the initials IOC (Intern on Call) or ROC (Resident on Call).

When a nurse requests an evaluation of a patient, the doctor's progress note may begin CTSP "called to see patient." An intern or resident may end the note with a signature and an identifying number.

The academic system often relieves the attending physician of performing day-to-day tasks of history writing and daily progress notes. However, the attending physician is required to supervise doctors in training and is permitted to bill for these primary care services. Countersignatures of intern and resident notes are sometimes required by medical by-laws. Medicaid and Medicare have specific requirements for documentation by attending physicians for billing purposes. Services are billable only if presented with adequate documentation along with the supervising/teaching physician's countersignature. These rules state that the supervising/teaching physicians must personally document the following:[12]

- that they performed the service or were physically present during key or critical portions of the service when they were performed by the resident, and
- their participation in the management of the patient.

A physician may be employed by the hospital to see patients when attending physicians are not available. For example, this person may insert Foley catheters, and central intravenous lines, order medications, or evaluate critically ill patients. This "house officer" may sign notes as "H.O." This role is more common in non-teaching hospitals.

21.3 Forces That Shape Documentation

It is necessary to examine the forces which shape physician documentation in order to understand it. Elements are found in education, government regulations, reimbursement requirements, and standards set by the institutions in which physicians practice. This section provides an introduction to each of these.

A. Educational Considerations

American medical schools teach the "Problem Oriented Medical Record" developed by Larry Weed, M.D. This sometimes goes under the name of "Weed System" and is coupled with "SOAP" notes that provide an easy-to-follow format. The Problem Oriented Medical Record was developed as a method for organizing, clarifying, and communicating clinical data and medical reasoning. Each problem is to have a designation on the "subjective" nature of the complaint, followed by a list of "objective" findings, then an "assessment" and a "plan" to deal with the problem.

TIP: A problem is defined as anything, including social problems, which requires work-up or other form of management. The system was designed to present a logical, easily followed progression of medical decision-making.

The problem oriented SOAP notes are often found in medical records, but the system is impossible to enforce. Hurried physicians usually adapt a simplified SOAP format, omitting one or more of the designated line items. Some physicians disregard this system entirely, using simply "one-liners" in their medical documentation.

B. Regulatory and Reimbursement Considerations

Insurance companies cannot pay doctors or hospitals for their services without documentation of services. Every physician service must be matched by written documentation that justifies payment for that service. It is therefore critical to understand the federal legislative forces that shape the requirements for physician documentation. This section introduces relevant concepts contained in the Health Insurance Portability and Accountability Act (HIPAA), Current Procedural Terminology (CPT) coding, the Prospective Payment System (PPS), and Diagnosis Related Groups (DRGs).

1. HIPAA

HIPAA is a federal law enacted in 1996 and is considered the most significant healthcare legislation since Medicare in 1965. Its intent was to reform the health insurance market and simplify healthcare transactions and processes. For providers and insurers, intended benefits were reducing processing time for claims and improving accuracy and quality of data and reports.[13] This discussion presents HIPAA's impact on billing and coding which directly influences requirements for physician documentation. According to HIPAA, all physicians must use standardized code sets and identifiers when reporting professional services. Please refer to Chapter 9, *Health Insurance Portability and Accountability Act (HIPAA)*, in Volume I, for more information.

2. CPT coding

Coding standards were intended to improve efficiency of the healthcare system by standardizing electronic transmission of billable transactions. The medical code sets include those referring to diseases and causes of injury (ICD-9 or International Classification of Diseases, 9th Revision), and physician services (CPT or Current Procedural Terminology codes). The CPT coding system provides a uniform language for medical services and standardizes information a physician must include in her documentation justifying the code that allows payment.[14] The codes provide the basis for electronic claims processing and guidelines for review of medical care.

TIP: According to Current Procedural Terminology, all medical services are identified by unique five-digit codes.

There are hundreds of codes which apply to primary care physicians, anesthesiologists, surgeons, radiologists, pathologists, etc. The section pertinent to most physicians is the Evaluation and Management section. This section alone encompasses 298 codes, from numbers 99201 to 99499. For further detail, the reader is referred to the CPT coding manual which contains the entire set of guidelines for reporting procedures and services.

For reporting purposes there are three to five levels of professional service for each physician encounter. Each level reflects a different reimbursement, and documentation must therefore justify the specific code. These levels are intended to reflect the amount of time the physician spends with the patient. Encounters can be classified into broad categories including office visits, hospital visits, and consultations. Levels of service include examinations, evaluations, treatments, conferences, and preventive care.

The coding descriptors recognize three key components when selecting a level of service. These are

- history,
- examination, and
- complexity of medical decision-making.

When determining the complexity of decision-making, the nature of the presenting problem is graded from minimal to high severity. In order to qualify for a particular level of E/M service (evaluation and management) the physician's documentation must provide justification in all of the key components of history, examination, and medical decision-making. Each level of complexity infers an amount of time spent with the patient.

Mrs. Jones is an elderly diabetic who presents to the emergency room with pneumonia and is admitted to the medical floor. She is seen by her physician who performs a history and physical examination. Mrs. Jones' diabetic condition was worsened by her infection, and she is also noted to have anemia and a new leg ulcer.

There are three coding levels for an initial hospital visit, each representing different reimbursement for Mrs. Jones' physician. Mrs. Jones' medical problems are of high complexity, and to justify the appropriate reimbursement her physician must include in his documentation the following elements:

- a comprehensive history,
- a comprehensive examination, and
- an assessment and plan which reflect medical decision making of high complexity.

In this case, the physician's documentation will justify code 99223, designating seventy minutes of time.

3. DRGs

Hospitals as well as physicians need to get paid for their services. The Social Security Amendments of 1983 (Public Law 98-21) established the Prospective Payment System (PPS) for inpatient services provided for Medicare beneficiaries. This system allows a hospital to be paid a fixed amount intended to cover the cost of service delivery to a particular treatment category or Diagnosis Related Group (DRG). The DRG system is a statistical classification of illnesses and injuries that assists insurance companies to determine ahead of time which payments are most appropriate.

Hospital payment under the DRG system is largely dependent upon physician documentation. For example, the physician must provide written documentation that justifies the necessity for hospitalization. If the record does not reflect appropriate justification for services, the hospital risks denial of payment for those days. In similar fashion, if a patient stays longer than expected for a particular DRG, the hospital risks non-payment for those days if documentation does not support the need for services. These regulations apply as well to days spent in intensive care units. The DRG system has engendered a new breed of hospital-based nurses—the case managers—part of whose job is to examine documentation and enforce physician compliance with length-of-stay requirements.

TIP: Some healthcare providers seeking to increase profits will inaccurately code their patient encounters. This is illegal and is known as medical insurance fraud.[15]

The most common medical insurance fraud involves billing for services that were never delivered. The second most common medical insurance fraud is the scheme of upcoding to obtain a higher reimbursement than one is entitled. There are numerous variations on the theme of medical insurance fraud, with the common denominator of misrepresenting facts to receive payment. Please see Chapter 8, *Billing and Coding*, in Volume I, for more information on billing fraud.

In summary, physician documentation must justify the CPT code to obtain reimbursement for a particular medical service. Three key components (history, examination, and medical decision-making) must be documented in the record to support a specific level of service. The level of service is intended to reflect the amount of time the physician is expected to spend with that patient. In addition, the physician's documentation must justify inpatient services under the PPS system so the hospital can obtain reimbursement.

C. Hospital Requirements for Documentation

Requirements set by hospitals for physician documentation are sometimes found in the medical by-laws. The by-laws are essentially a "procedure and policy manual" for medical personnel. To complete their credentialing, physicians receive and sometimes sign receipt of the by-laws. The booklet contains a variety of standards, including procedures for appointment, granting of privileges, dues, disciplinary procedures, medical malpractice insurance requirements, risk management, informed consent, supervision of physicians-in-training, peer review, and obligations to attend certain meetings.

Guidelines for physician documentation as stated in the medical by-laws can range from vague statements regarding overall quality standards to specific instructions on orders, countersignatures, wording of orders, timing for chart completion, and acceptable format for admission notes, progress notes, consultations, and discharge summaries. Enforcement of the by-laws varies greatly from hospital to hospital, but often comes under the scrutiny of accreditation bodies such as TJC (The Joint Commission).

D. Nursing Home Requirements: The Nursing Home Reform Amendments (OBRA'87)

Minimum standards for physician documentation in skilled nursing facilities required by federal law are presented in Figure 21.3. The relevant statute is C.F.R. 42 §483.40 Physician Services. The statutes are accompanied by Guidance for Surveyors, and the guidelines which apply to this statute are also presented in the figure. Keep in mind that these are only *minimum* standards and may be enhanced by state law or requirements of the facility.

For example, some facilities require a pre-printed monthly progress note to be filled out to ensure that adequate attention is paid to issues such as presence of infection, skin condition, presence of pain, or physical restraint.

Regulatory Requirements for Physician Documentation in Skilled Nursing Facilities

§ 483.40 Physician services
A physician must personally approve in writing a recommendation that an individual be admitted to a facility. Each resident must remain under the care of a physician.

(a) *Physician supervision.* The facility must ensure that—
(1) The medical care of each resident is supervised by a physician; and
(2) Another physician supervises the medical care of residents when their attending physician is unavailable.

(b) *Physician visits.* The physician must—
(1) Review the resident's total program of care, including medications and treatments, at each visit required by paragraph (c) of this section;
(2) Write, sign, and date progress notes at each visit; and
(3) Sign and date all orders.

(c) *Frequency of physician visits.*
(1) The resident must be seen by a physician at least once every 30 days for the first 90 days after admission, and at least once every 60 days thereafter.
(2) A physician visit is considered timely if it occurs not later than 10 days after the date the visit was required.

Guidance to Surveyors: Guidelines for § 483.40(b)
Total program of care includes all care the facility provides residents to maintain or improve their highest practicable mental and physical functional status, as defined by the comprehensive assessment and plan of care. Care includes medical services and medical management, physical, occupational, and speech/language therapy, nursing care, nutritional interventions, social work and activities services that maintain or improve psychosocial functioning.

Figure adapted from The Code of Federal Regulations (C.F.R.) Chapter 42, Nursing Home Reform Amendments.

Figure 21.3

21.4 Accreditation Requirements

The Joint Commission is an independent, not-for-profit accrediting body that develops standards and evaluates compliance. It currently accredits 17,000 healthcare organizations including hospitals and long-term-care facilities.[16] Their standards include such topics as quality, safety, patient rights, performance improvement, and requirements for physician documentation.[17]

TIP: Not all facilities are JC accredited, but those that maintain accreditation are subject to an additional layer of documentation requirements.

For each standard there is a stated rationale and elements of performance which are reviewed when the facility is surveyed. Consult the current *Hospital Accreditation Standards* for regulations that pertain specifically to physician documentation. Standards change periodically, so the manuals from the year in question should be consulted.

The Joint Commission is committed to improving patient safety through the accreditation process.[18] Part of this patient safety initiative involves the yearly establishment of patient safety goals. The organization's achievement of these goals is evaluated during an announced or unannounced survey visit. Please review Chapter 10, *Patient Safety Initiatives and Medical Records*, in Volume I, for additional information.

21.5 Summary

It is essential to understand physician documentation to analyze a medical chart. The physician brings years of scientific and technical training and expertise to the care of a sick individual, and medical roles vary. Documentation should ideally translate this technical knowledge into a coherent record reflecting what was done, why it was done, and how the patient responded. Influences such as education, site of practice, regulations, reimbursement, and institutional by-laws all affect the written matter in a medical document. These forces reflect the effect of law and society on the expression of applied medical science. It is helpful to have an understanding of these factors when reconstructing medical events from a written record.

It is also important to know that documentation has its limits. A written document may not reflect a caregiver's empathy, compassion, and bedside manner. The written documentation will probably not detail the eye-to-eye relationship between the doctor and patient. The physician's history and physical may not completely encapsulate all the complex psychosocial factors that make up a human being, and which may have led to the illness at hand. Limitations in medical knowledge and technology must also be taken into consideration. Constraints of time must also be noted, and the prioritization of what is documented often depends on the training, judgment, and expertise of the writer.

Endnotes

1. Laska, L. "Failure to Urgently Treat Dislocated Elbow Blamed for Development of Compartment Syndrome and Nerve Injury." *Medical Malpractice Verdicts, Settlements, and Experts*. October 2009, p. 31-32.

2. Laska, L. "Failure to Respond to Child's Respiratory Difficulty and Abdominal Distention Blamed for Death." *Medical Malpractice Verdicts, Settlements, and Experts*. October 2009, p. 46.

3. Laska, L. "Failure to treat Lupus Flare-Up." *Medical Malpractice Verdicts, Settlements, and Experts*. October 2009, p. 10.

4. Laska, L. "Woman Suffers Bleeding After Birth." *Medical Malpractice Verdicts, Settlements, and Experts*. June 2009, p. 31.

5. *Surefire Documentation: How, What, and When Nurses Need to Document*. St. Louis, MO: Mosby, Inc. 1999.

6. Laska, L. "Left Hemicolectomy Performed Instead of Right Hemicolectomy." *Medical Malpractice Verdicts, Settlements, and Experts*. September 2003, p. 57.

7. Institute of Medicine. *To Err is Human: Building a Safer Health System*. Washington, D.C.: National Academy Press. 1999.

8. *Industry Profile and Healthcare Factbook*. Reston, VA: National Wholesale Druggists' Association. 1998.

9. Charatan, F. "Family Compensated for Death After Illegible Prescription." *British Medical Journal*. 319, p. 1456. 1999.

10. Raschke, R.A. et al. "A Computer Alert System to Prevent Injury from Adverse Drug Events: Development and Evaluation in a Community Teaching Hospital." *JAMA*. 280, p. 1317–1320. 1998.

11. Bates, D.W. et al. "Effect of Computerized Physician Order Entry and a Team Intervention on Prevention of Serious Medication Errors." *JAMA*. 280, p. 1311–1316. 1998.

12. Medicaid Update. November 2003. http://www. health. state.ny.us/nysdos/mancare/omm/1199med.htm.

13. *HIPAA: A Short and Long-term Perspective for Health Care*. Chicago, IL: American Medical Association. 2003.

14. *CPT 2003 Professional Edition*. Chicago, IL: American Medical Association. 2003.

15. *Health Care Fraud and Abuse*. Chicago, IL: American Medical Association. 2003.

16. JCAHO. www.jcaho.org/news+room/faqs/index.htm.

17. Hospital Accreditation Standards. Chicago, IL: JCAHO. 2004.

18. JCAHO. www.jcaho.org/accredited+ organizations/patient+safety/medical+errors+disclosure.

Chapter 22

Psychiatric Records

Wanda K. Mohr, RN, FAAN, PhD

22.1 Introduction

The terminology used in the practice of psychiatry is very specific to psychiatric conditions and illness. Unlike some areas of medicine, psychiatric terminology is rarely used in the context of other medical disciplines. A working knowledge of psychiatric terminology and systematic medical classification of diseases is important in a legal-historical sense, because all that remains after a person's hospitalization is the medical record and peoples' imperfect memories. The medical record, in the way it is written, can serve as a valuable tool for defense and plaintiffs' attorneys, in that individuals doing the writing and recording often reveal a great deal about their competence, biases, and assumptions that affect the care of patients.

This chapter examines the language of psychiatry. It traces the development of the American Psychiatric Association's *Diagnostic and Statistical Manual of Mental Disorders* (DSM)[1] and describes the diagnostic process, the DSM's uses, and its shortcomings. In addition it discusses the use and misuse of psychiatric jargon and describes how psychiatric data are recorded in the medical record.

22.2 The Development of the *Diagnostic and Statistical Manual of Mental Disorders*

TIP: Published by the American Psychiatric Association, the DSM is the standard classification of mental disorders used by mental health professionals in the United States.

There have been six editions of this collection of psychiatric nomenclature, each edition designated by a number. These are

- DSM I,
- DSM II,
- DSM III,
- DSM IIIR (third edition revised),
- DSM IV, and
- the current DSM IV-TR (text revision).

The DSM has its genesis in the U.S. War Department's Technical Bulletin 203 of 1946 (Medical 203),[2] The Standard Classified Nomenclature of Disease of 1942,[3] and the Veterans Administration Nomenclature.[4] The Medical 203 contained forty-seven mental illness diagnoses, and it most heavily influenced what was to become DSM I.

In keeping with the basic Freudian (psychoanalytic) spirit of the times, DSM I, which was published in 1958, expressed a diathesis stress model. Diathesis, which refers to the constitutional predisposition to illness or abnormality, was conceived along psychoanalytic lines. At the time, environmental stress was viewed as likely to contribute to non-physiological disorders, which were divided into neurotic, psychotic, and character disorders. DSM I, containing sixty separate disorders, did not include a separate section for disorders of children and barely mentioned the subject.[5]

The second edition of the DSM was issued in 1968. It contained the same basic structure and conceptual framework as the first edition. However, DSM II included a section on children's disorders. This edition was 134 pages long and listed 182 separate mental disorders, which were classified in nine major groups. Disparate conditions such as depression, obsessive compulsive disorder, and dissociative disorders were all seen as different ways of dealing with internal conflict.[6] It was not until the development of the modern DSMs that the psychoanalytic framework and nomenclature were discarded, and for all intents and purposes subsequent DSMs strove to be theory neutral.[7]

DSM III, published in 1980, included 265 diagnostic categories.[8] It emphasized diagnostic criteria that were meant to be neutral with respect to etiology and designed to be usable across many different theoretical orientations. The listing of explicit criteria immeasurably improved the reliability of diagnostic agreement between clinicians. In 1987, the American Psychiatric Association published a revision to the third DSM entitled DSM III R. DSM III R was meant to correct inconsistencies in DSM III and to include new evidence for diagnostic criteria. DSM III R expanded the diagnostic categories to 296.[9]

The fourth edition of the DSM (DSM IV) was published in 1994 and contained 365 diagnoses, nearly an 800 percent increase over a fifty-one-year period.[10] The addition of new sections and disorders has resulted in numerous critics of the modern DSMs questioning whether or not these new disorders were the result of a process of scientific discovery or the result of economically driven invention processes. They note that the overproduction of mental health professionals has accompanied the expansion of the diagnostic nomenclature. Aside from this question, the DSM IV represented a leap forward in psychiatry in that it has eschewed the distinction between the mental and physical, considering it passé.

TIP: A completely new DSM (DSM V) is tentatively scheduled for publication in 2012.

The American Psychiatric Association revised its text in 2000 because of new research information developed since the 1994 publication of DSM IV. These text revisions (DSM IV-TR) are minor and limited to criteria for *Personality Change Due to a Medical Condition*, several of the *Paraphilias (Sexual Disorders)*, and *Tourette's Disorder*. In the latter two, it was no longer necessary that the person with the disorder suffered distress or impaired functioning.[11–13]

22.3 Use and Structure of the *Diagnostic and Statistical Manual of Mental Disorders*

The DSM is intended to be applicable in a wide array of contexts and used by clinicians and researchers of many different orientations including biological, psychodynamic, cognitive, behavioral, and interpersonal. The manual is de-

signed to be used in settings that include inpatient, outpatient, partial hospital, consultation-liaison, clinic, private practice, primary care, and with community populations. It is used by psychiatrists, psychologists, social workers, nurses, occupational and rehabilitation therapists, counselors, and other health and mental health professionals. It is a necessary tool for collecting and communicating among professionals.

A. Components

The DSM consists of three major components: the diagnostic classification, the diagnostic criteria sets, and the descriptive text. The diagnostic classification is the list of the mental disorders that are officially part of the DSM system. Making a diagnosis consists of selecting those disorders from the classification that best reflect the signs and symptoms that are afflicting the individual being evaluated. Associated with each diagnostic label is a code, which is typically used by institutions and agencies for data collection and billing. These diagnostic codes are derived from the coding system used by all healthcare professionals in the U.S., known as the ICD-9-CM.[14]

Each disorder included in the DSM has specific components.

- A set of diagnostic criteria that indicates what symptoms must be present (and for how long) in order to qualify for a diagnosis.
- Symptoms or conditions that must not be present (inclusion and exclusion criteria).
- Descriptive text that accompanies each disorder. (The text of the DSM systematically describes each disorder under the following headings: diagnostic features, subtypes and/or specifiers, recording procedures, associated features and disorders, specific culture, age and gender features, prevalence, course, familial pattern, and differential diagnosis.)

B. Axes

TIP: The DSM uses a five-axis system to give a more comprehensive picture of the client's functioning.

The five axes are as follows:

- *Axis I*—Clinical disorders consists of all relevant major psychiatric disorders (such as schizophrenia, bipolar disorders, and major depression).
- *Axis II*—Personality disorders and mental retardation. (Personality disorders as defined in the DSM

IV-TR are "deeply ingrained maladaptive, lifelong behavior patterns.")[15]

- *Axis III*—General medical conditions that are identified on the basis of a comprehensive history and physical examination, evaluation of symptoms, mental state examination, and supplementary assessment instruments. These include any medical condition such as diabetes, hypertension, cystic fibrosis, and so on.
- *Axis IV*—Psychosocial and environmental problems (these can include stressors such as a recent death of a loved one, being a victim of a crime, going through a divorce, or losing one's job, among others).
- *Axis V*—Global assessment of functioning (GAF), written as numbers (0-100) meaning "current functioning"/"highest level of functioning in past year" with 100 being the highest optimization of functioning and 0 being the lowest.

Many patients have more than one diagnosis on the first three axes. This is called co-morbidity. Co-morbidity is defined as two or more medical conditions that occur at the same time.[16] From a psychiatric point of view, co-morbidity means the coexistence of a psychiatric disorder, such as depression, anxiety, or a psychotic condition with a chemical dependency disorder. These co-morbid conditions are also called dual diagnosis. The term co-morbidity tends to imply that the illnesses are equal, though they may not be. Disorders are listed in their order of importance for disposition and care. The multiaxial assessment helps to optimize re-assessments of patients' conditions over time. It also affords a refinement of the validity of clinical diagnosis and can serve as an outcome measure of therapeutic intervention.

22.4 Validity, Reliability, and Limitations

TIP: Although the DSM is universally used as a classification system, it has serious limitations.

The categories are descriptions, not explanations. One must guard against the tendency to think that something has been explained when, in fact, it has only been named.[17] In other words, giving a condition a label does not explain or confer any reality to it other than the name itself and the cluster of behaviors subsumed under it.

Also, as convenient as the DSM system is, its categories imply that sharp dividing lines exist between "normal" and "abnormal" behaviors and among different disorders. The reality, however, is that such categories are not so neat and some scholars argue that they are artificial. For example, three patients may suffer from the same disorder; however, manifestations and the personal experience of that disorder will differ for each client. While the DSM has criteria that specify that an individual must have, for example, six out of eight symptoms over the course of a month, it is not flexible enough to account for the individual who might have five of the eight over the course of three weeks and be in distress. Moreover, the DSM diagnostic categories differ somewhat from the taxonomies of other illnesses (e.g., hypertension, diabetes mellitus).[18] Although research is available to support most of the major psychiatric illnesses, many of these categories lack an empirical foundation. They were agreed upon by "expert" consensus and therefore are subject to question. Indeed scholars both within and outside the psychiatric profession have criticized the DSM system.[19,20] An example of such criticism and unanswered questions concerns the number of symptoms necessary for the diagnosis. If a person meets all the criteria but one for the diagnosis, does she actually have the condition?

In particular, the diagnostic labels given to children have been found troublesome in that they were derived from adult categories. The most problematic issue related to this practice is that the diagnoses are not based on a body of research on children; rather, they are derived from disorders that may have very different manifestations in adults. Depression is one such example, because depression in children has very different clinical manifestations than it does in adults. Moreover, making child categories downward extensions of adult categories is problematic because it assumes that children are little adults and that they can have the same adult illnesses. The reality is that some diagnoses are specific to children, while some are specific to adults.

Another caveat is that the DSM criteria may not be uniformly applicable to all cultures. Most studies upon which the DSM criteria are based were conducted in the United States or Canada. The DSM lists a number of specific cultural syndromes, but that list is by no means comprehensive.

The criticisms of the DSM among scholars also include

- It fails to clarify the exact relationship between Axis II and Axis I disorders and the way chronic childhood and developmental problems interact with personality disorders.
- Its differential diagnoses are vague, and the disorders are insufficiently demarcated, resulting in excessive co-morbidity, especially on Axis II and in the area of childhood disorders.

- It contains little discussion of what distinguishes normal character from personality disorders.

- Numerous disorders contain a "not otherwise specified" addition. This is a catchall addendum applied when all of the criteria for a certain disorder are not present.

- It does not speak to life circumstances, biological and psychological processes, and lacks an overarching conceptual or explanatory framework.

- It is heavily influenced by fashion, prevailing social mores, and by the legal and business environment.[21]

Attorneys should keep these questions and criticisms in mind and recognize that there is a dearth of documented clinical experience regarding both the disorders themselves and the utility of various treatment modalities. Judges and attorneys can often be awed by medical and/or psychiatric testimony and grant it some special cachet of truth. But the sin too often committed by mental health professions is reification. A concept is believed to be real, rather than hypothetical, and it is then used to explain behavior which is then used to show how real the concept is. This is simply bad logic and worse science, and attorneys should always raise the issue of the validity of these postulated diagnostic entities.

Other questions that arise about the DSM are in the area of its reliability. Diagnostic reliability concerns the likelihood that different users will assign the same diagnosis. High diagnostic reliability suggests that if the DSM guidelines were followed, different psychiatrists would give the same label to a given person. A central claim about the DSM is that it is a highly reliable system. However, Kutchins and Kirk say the following about the claim of reliability for the DSM: "No study of the DSM as a whole in a regular clinical setting has shown uniformly high reliability. And most studies, including the DSM field trials themselves, provide little evidence that reliability has markedly improved, much less been 'solved' as a problem."[22]

TIP: There is still not a major study available that shows that the DSM is used with high reliability by mental health clinicians in the practice setting.

The issue of the validity of the diagnostic categories is also not discussed often in the professional literature. Yet the validity of any construct cannot exceed what is allowed by its reliability. Serious questions about reliability lead to questions about the categories' validity.

Finally, the DSM system is not fixed. It is always a "work in progress" and should be thought of in that way. A new edition is tentatively scheduled to be published in 2012. As knowledge expands, categories will appear, and old ones may be revised, refined, or eliminated altogether. Because the manual omits a disorder, it does not mean that it does not exist.

22.5 The Diagnostic Process

Diagnosis involves gathering information and forming and revising hypotheses about what might be wrong with a patient. The steps are not carried out in a rigid sequence, and even once a firm diagnosis has been made, it is possible for this to be corrected. Sometimes, no firm diagnosis is made. In "DSM-speak" this is coded as *provisional* or *deferred*. There are specific guidelines taught to all physicians in terms of steps to be followed in diagnosing particular conditions and distinguishing between conditions with similar presentations (differential diagnosis). Differential diagnosis is a list of all diagnoses possible for any given patient.[23] Traditionally they are arranged in order of likelihood, with the most probable diagnosis listed first. The DSM contains criteria for each diagnosis, as well as differential diagnoses for each condition.

The act of diagnosis is one of problem solving.[24] In this process, the clinician uses his knowledge of disease processes and logical inference to deduce what medical condition(s) may underlie a set of symptoms and what conditions may be ruled out. The system of *if-then* rules that guide this process are sometimes called *production rules*. These can be all-or-nothing type rules (assuming that the causal chain between the psychiatric condition and the signs or symptoms is either present or absent), or they can be *probabilistic* (recognizing that the process is often variable and one thing does not always lead to another).

In order to ask meaningful questions, it is helpful for attorneys to understand that competent clinicians keep in mind several principles in formulating a diagnosis. These include the principle that an excellent and careful history, taken from patients and augmented by collateral information, is more useful than cross-sectional observations. Another principle concerns signs and symptoms. *Signs* are what the clinician observes, whereas symptoms are patient complaints. While symptoms are important, discrete observations with the clinician's clarification and description of her observations are more valid in making a diagnosis.[25] Symptoms can often be distorted by patient and clinician interpretation. For example, a patient may deny having auditory hallucinations, but during the interview he may pause, cock his head, and appear to be listening to something.

Another major principle is that objective assessments are superior to subjective judgments. Such objective measures should include structured interviews, psychological testing with objective (as opposed to projective) testing,[26,27] accurate history, and laboratory data. All of these data should be employed in assessing patients. Attorneys should be aware that the least important element in the equation is *clinical judgment* or *clinical prediction*. Research on the issue of clinical versus actuarial (statistical) prediction has been stunningly consistent. Four decades of research consisting of over a hundred research studies has shown that in just about every clinical prediction domain that has ever been examined (psychotherapy outcome, parole behavior, college graduation rates, response to electroshock therapy, criminal recidivism, length of psychiatric hospitalization, and many more), actuarial prediction has been found to be superior to clinical prediction. In a variety of clinical domains actuarial prediction is more accurate than the clinician's prediction, even when the clinician has more information, personal contact, and interviews with the patient.[28]

TIP: The implications of these studies for attorneys are their potential ability to discredit witnesses who rely heavily on *clinical judgment, professional experience,* or *intuition* for their opinions as opposed to relying on data.

22.6 The Medical Record—From Diagnosis to Discharge

According to *The Patient Care Partnership* of the American Hospital Association, each patient has a right to obtain a copy of information from the hospital's records about her care.[29] Accrediting agencies such as The Joint Commission (TJC) also require each patient to have a medical record.[30] Documentation may be in (but is not limited to) the form of

- narrative notes,
- checklists,
- SOAP notes (recording information by subjective data, objective data, assessment, and plan), or
- clinical pathways.

Records may be kept manually or electronically. Records are legal documents that can be used in court; therefore, all notes and progress records should reflect descriptive, nonjudgmental, and objective statements. Examples of significant data include here-and-now observations of the patient through the use of the critical assessment, an accurate report of verbal exchanges with patients, and a description of the outcomes of the care provided. Verbal communication should be straightforward, forthright, descriptive, without opinion, and limited to those involved in the client's care and treatment.

The medical record generally begins with a face sheet with basic identifying information, including the patient's name, address, telephone number, date of birth, gender, ethnicity, religion, education, marital status, employment status, insurance coverage, and next of kin.

The history of psychiatric and general medical illness should be recorded, as far as possible, in chronological sequence, noting significant events, ages, and dates. A family history of mental and general medical disorders and treatment should be collected for all known first and second degree relatives, including children, on both sides of the family. Personal, developmental, and social history should be recorded chronologically. In addition to narrative statements, key milestones, and critical events may be recorded in a structural manner.

The record of the symptom and mental status examination should cover all important areas for mental activity and behavior (e.g., appearance, overt behavior, mood and affect, speech and thought process, thought content, perception, sensorium or alertness, memory, judgment, and insight). One commonly used is the Mini Mental Status Exam.

TIP: The Mini Mental Status Exam is a brief standardized method by which to grade cognitive mental status. It assesses orientation, attention, immediate and short-term recall, language, and the ability to follow simple verbal and written commands. Furthermore, it provides a total score that places the individual on a scale of cognitive function.

Personalized descriptions (as opposed to professional pronouncements) should be presented. The record should contain examples of the patient's own words and narratives that the patient is informed, gives consent, and is actively engaged in his treatment. A comprehensive medical history and physical examination should be conducted. The results of a clinical diagnostic assessment and its linkages to care are generally recorded in narrative form under standard headings, such as the categories seen in Figure 22.1.

Because patients are in a psychiatric setting does not mean that they do not need medical care. Psychiatric patients often have chronic co-morbid medical conditions and do not attend to their healthcare needs. The importance of a comprehensive assessment and the tragic ramifications for the patient and family can be illustrated by the following case report (all names in case reports are fictitious):

Structure of Diagnostic Assessment

- Sources of information: who or what is the basis for the information (e.g., the patient, family, previous records)?
- Chief complaint or reason for evaluation: elicited from the patient and recorded verbatim from what the patient responds (what the patient responds in the assessment may not be the focus of treatment).
- History of present illness: what is the proximal reason for the patient's seeking help at this point in time?
- Past psychiatric and general medical history.
- Family history: particularly important to ascertain heavy genetic loading for certain psychiatric conditions, such as alcohol dependence, bipolar disorder, suicides in the family, or schizophrenia.
- Personal, developmental, and social history: including criminal and substance abuse history.
- Symptom and mental state evaluation.
- Comprehensive medical history and complete physical examination: especially important with a psychiatric population because their physical health tends to be poor.
- Supplementary assessments: these would include psychological testing, educational testing, neuropsychological testing, among others.
- Comprehensive diagnostic formulation: this should include diagnoses on all five axes, as well as differentials.
- Comprehensive treatment plan: this should include input from all disciplines involved in the care of the patient.

Figure 22.1

James Tarver

For the past five years of his life, James Tarver was free of the acute exacerbations of bipolar disorder (manic depression) that had so troubled him in his late teens and early thirties. At age forty-three, he was living in a community residence, attending a day program and mental health clinic, and had not required hospitalization in nearly a decade. With the exception of having high cholesterol, he was in good health, and was maintained on a medication regimen of Risperdal and Lithium. He had also stopped drinking heavily and had maintained sobriety for seven years. He had been a two pack a day smoker for the past twenty-five years. At 5'8" he was obese, weighing 225 lbs.

On the day after Christmas, with no warning, Mr. Tarver left his residence by climbing out of his bedroom window. A note which he had left in his room indicated that he was being commanded by voices. He had apparently stopped taking his medications.

The next day, Mr. Tarver was found and brought back to his residence. An on-call psychiatrist at his clinic was consulted, and a decision was made to admit Mr. Tarver to a local hospital that day.

Upon admission, Mr. Tarver complained of hearing the voice of God talking to him. Admission assessments described him as psychotic, paranoid, overly active, and sexually preoccupied. A short medical history and review of systems (physical examination) was done and documented.

Mr. Tarver was restarted on Lithium and Risperdal. Over the next two weeks his medication levels were adjusted as his clinical status dictated. During this period, Mr. Tarver continued to complain of hearing voices and exhibited high levels of activity. On occasion, he became hostile, verbally assaultive, or extremely anxious, and required additional medications on an "as needed" (PRN) basis. Notes show that he was compliant with his treatment regimen.

His activity levels began to decline, his sleeping improved, and, by early January, Mr. Tarver was reportedly in better control and not bothered by the "voices." Although still occasionally disorganized, he was less anxious, and on January 19th, the plan was to discharge him the next day to the custody of his sister.

The Incident

That evening at 11:30 P.M., Mr. Tarver was having trouble sleeping and approached the nurses' station, asking if he could go to the dining room and make himself some tea. The nurse agreed, and he and another patient went to the dining room. Several minutes went by, and at 11:45 P.M., the nurse went down the hall to the dining room to look for Mr. Tarver. She found him talking with the other patient and eating toast and ice cream. She told Mr. Tarver that she had told him that he could only make himself a cup of tea and that this was not socialization time. She directed him to return to his room. Mr. Tarver responded using profanity and refused to follow the nurse's directive. She repeated her request, and in response Mr. Tarver continued with his profanity and became visibly agitated. After repeating her request a third time, Mr. Tarver left the dining room with his ice cream and went back to the unit, loudly berating the nurse and the other staff members. He paced about the unit in an agitated manner, and the nurse summoned hospital security for "a show of force." Mr. Tarver threw the container of ice cream at the nurse. Four staff members and security personnel restrained him in a prone (face down) position. Mr. Tarver continued to struggle while being held. At one point, the staff members released one of Mr. Tarver's arms, thinking that he had quieted down. He continued to thrash about, and the arm was restrained once again. The nurse called the psychiatrist who gave her an order for an intramuscular injection of Ativan (a tranquilizer). She drew up the medication and returned to Mr. Tarver, who was lying quietly in the restraint and told him that she was giving him an injection. She administered the Ativan and left to discard the empty syringe. When she returned, she addressed Mr. Tarver and found him to be unresponsive and not breathing. His color was dusky, and he had no pulse. Cardiopulmonary resuscitation (CPR) was initiated and 911 called. Paramedics arrived within twelve minutes of his having been found unresponsive. He was defibrillated, and Advanced Cardiac Life Support (ACLS) was initiated, and he was taken to the emergency room of the hospital.

Despite resuscitative efforts, Mr. Tarver could not be revived. At one point he was successfully defibrillated, but eventually he had to be placed on a respirator. Within twenty-four hours of his admission to the emergency department he was taken off the respirator and pronounced dead.

The medical record from his stay in the cardiac care unit documented EKG findings consistent with a myocardial infarction, as did serial enzyme changes. His autopsy documented narrowing blockages in his cardiac arteries and myocardial damage. Mr. Tarver had died of a heart attack.

Although there were many errors made in the treatment of the patient in the above vignette, an especially egregious one was the failure to conduct a comprehensive assessment of a patient who was clearly at risk for having a heart attack: he was a middle aged, obese male who smoked. At no point in the chart was there any documentation that the psychiatric physician considered anything but his psychiatric condition, an inexcusable lapse of the standard of care which is meant to be comprehensive and consider the whole patient.

Thus, all comprehensive diagnostic formulation that incorporates the information obtained through the standardized and diagnostic processes should be recorded. The clinical chart should include a systematic treatment plan, based on the comprehensive diagnostic formulation. Treatment plans should be individually developed and involve engagement of the patient, measurable objectives that are connected to signs and symptoms, and periodic evaluation.[31,32] What this implies is that there should be a clear justification for the use of one form of treatment versus another.

Tying interventions and treatment to signs and symptoms is an indication that thoughtful and precise treatment planning has taken place. Interventions and treatments are bound to fail when they are not developed on the basis of individuals' development and sensitive to their various cognitive, social, and emotional needs. The process of individual assessment and treatment is often an unrealized ideal. The use of checklists, structured interviews, and standardized treatment plans and evaluation instruments, though efficient, runs the risk of practitioners building assessments and asking questions that are devoid of context, thereby omitting many important portions of clinical reality. Checklists tend to be filled out with expediency as opposed to expertise and thoughtful reflection. Many staff members do not know the definitions of psychiatric terminology. A dramatic example of such ignorance was portrayed in a CBS Sixty Minutes II story entitled "Unsafe Haven" and aired on April 21, 1999,[33] in which the registered nurse who was training a mental health aide was filmed choosing from a list of psychiatric terms that she clearly did not understand to describe a patient's behavior. Also, because they lack context, checklists make it that much more difficult to reconstruct the events of a person's hospitalization, especially given the unreliability of memories. For example, a nurse might record on a checklist that a patient responded in the affirmative to the question: "Have you attacked a member of your family?" Such activity is understood very differently in different contexts (e.g., the repeated abuse of the patient's mother, by his father, and his trying to intervene in the domestic violence situation).

TIP: Lack of context is a serious drawback of current assessments in many mental health settings. Attorneys should be aware that failure to provide comprehensive assessment and individual treatment planning may waste much time and resources while interventions are tried and fail.

Various forms (electronic, computer, and paper) and methods (narrative and problem oriented) are used in charting and progress notes. In most institutions all disciplines use the same progress notes, although some still maintain the physician's progress notes separate from those of the rest of the treatment team. The medical record and what it contains has one primary purpose: communication. The medical record is the single most important communication tool in the health care and treatment of patients. Types of information that should be communicated can include

- medical and nursing assessments,
- specialty consultations,
- treatment modalities, the basis for their use and their outcomes,
- patient responses to treatment modalities,
- laboratory and other diagnostic testing results,
- physician orders,
- care plans,
- discharge plans, and
- summaries.

Most charting systems also permit a narrative entry for the practitioner to include information that may be unique to the patient, shift, or event, which may not adequately be explained by the checklist. For example, specific charting is needed in the case of a violent episode leading to a patient being placed in seclusion or restraints.

Regardless of the type or system of documentation, consistency, completeness, and accuracy are key components of a complete medical record. The medical record is a road map of decisions, rationales, treatments, and patient outcomes. In order for it to be maximally informative as a

treatment planning tool, it must contain accurate and complete information. In its optimal form, the medical record relates patient management in sufficient detail for all members of the healthcare team to evaluate those decisions in a critical fashion. This information, or its absence, is what makes the medical record valuable as a litigation device.

The medical record is a legal document designed to provide an overview of the patient's state of health before, during, and after a particular therapy.[34] This overview is normally compiled in different steps.

- Notes are made during daily rounds.
- Particular events or changes in health condition are subsequently entered into the hospital database and coded according to the DSM system.
- The entire body of information is summarized in a cumulative report at the time of patient discharge from the hospital.

Each step depends on the physician's and other professionals' time resources, experience, and routine with paperwork and may be susceptible to neglect and data loss if documentation cannot be carried out immediately.

22.7 The Multidisciplinary Team and Documentation in the Medical Record

The multidisciplinary team is the mainstay of treatment in psychiatric settings. The team constitutes of a group of professionals from diverse disciplines who come together to provide comprehensive assessment and consultation in patient care. While their primary purpose is typically to help team members resolve difficult cases, teams may fulfill a variety of additional functions. They can promote coordination between agencies and identify service gaps and breakdowns in coordination or communication between agencies or individuals. They also enhance the professional skills and knowledge of individual team members by providing a forum for learning more about the strategies, resources, and approaches used by various disciplines. Each discipline has its own perspective, mandates, and resources. Each discipline also addresses different elements of the patient's difficulty, contributes to the treatment plan, and records their activities and observations in the medical record. Table 22.1 illustrates modalities and aspects of patient care and staff members responsible for those modalities. The medical record should clearly indicate the fulfillment of the activities commensurate with the responsibility of each treatment team member.

Table 22.1
Responsibilities of the Psychiatric Team

Professional/Staff Member	Modalities/Responsibilities
Psychiatrist	Admission evaluation/orders • Precautions • Diagnostic examination Relationship interventions • Individual meetings, daily rounds • Formal psychotherapy (individual and/or group) • Special therapies • Special procedures (e.g. orders for seclusion and restraint) Therapeutic milieu • Team meetings • Patient staff meetings • Special in-patient meetings (e.g., eating disorder groups, incest survivors) Somatic therapies • Pharmacotherapy • Other somatic therapies (e.g., ECT/Electroconvulsive Therapy) Discharge planning and referrals
Nursing Care Staff	Nursing assessment and care plan Relationship interventions • Individual meetings • Patient/staff group meetings • Social competency development Therapeutic milieu • Impulse control observation and reinforcement • Patient government and unit meetings Activities of daily living • Personal hygiene, sleeping patterns, nutrition Somatic therapies • Medication administration • Medication education • Effects of all somatic therapies management Health teaching (patient education) Discharge planning
Activity therapist	Activity therapy evaluation • Strengths, weaknesses, and impairments evaluation • Occupational-vocational assessment skills building) Activity therapies (e.g., recreation and leisure skills, music) Discharge planning • Vocational rehabilitation

Table 22.1 (continued)

Professional/Staff Member	Modalities/Responsibilities
Clinical social worker	Social work assessment and plan • Family assessment • Legal history (arrests, and so on) • Contacts and working with family, friends, employers, teachers, and so on Relationship interventions • Family therapy • Individual meeting with patients Discharge planning • Family casework • Collateral resources contacts
Psychologist	Diagnostic testing • Basic psychological assessment • Neuropsychological assessment Relationship interventions • Formal psychotherapy
Others 　Chaplain 　Vocational counselor	Religious counseling and spiritual guidance Vocational assessment, counseling, training

22.8 Psychiatric Terminology and Accuracy in Communication in the Medical Record

Jargon, the specialized language of a trade or profession, functions as a kind of shorthand means of communication between members of the professional group. Jargon can often be efficient and descriptive as a means of communication, but it can be obfuscatory, pretentious, or employed to make the ordinary seem extraordinary or profound.[35] Psychiatric jargon, as opposed to data-based observations, is not theory neutral because it is an interpretation of behavioral events.

TIP: The appendix of the DSM has a glossary of commonly employed psychiatric terms, and attorneys are encouraged to familiarize themselves with this terminology during their evaluation of cases.

An important assumption that underlies the way in which most mental health providers use psychiatric jargon is that the label, qualifier, or descriptive term means the same thing to all practitioners and is consistently applied to the same phenomenon. This flawed assumption creates serious barriers to attaining accurate and reliable assessments, recording of progress, and predicting reliable treatment outcomes. For decades there has been little agreement among mental health practitioners regarding the basic events of psychopathology, psychotherapy, and psychiatric interventions. Assessments,

labels, problems, and interventions are defined differently depending on the disciplinary lens through which they are viewed. This reality can distort the clinical picture which the experts and attorneys are asked to evaluate and act upon.

The popular psychotherapist Carl Rogers, like many professionals, wrote that he had assumed that all therapists were talking about the same constructs and events but attaching different words or labels to them. However, he subsequently concluded that not only were practitioners applying different labels to the same phenomena, they were also applying the same label to different phenomena.[36]

Ideally, jargon terms should be followed by an objective observation (data) that justifies using that term. Thus, if a note in the chart indicates that a particular patient was secluded or restrained because he was engaging in aggressive behavior and that he was a threat to himself or others, the professional who makes such a note should describe the aggressive behavior. For example, was the patient kicking or choking someone or merely cursing loudly and making obscene or threatening gestures? The charting should justify why these behaviors constituted a threat such that it became necessary to subject the patient to a potentially deadly intervention (seclusion or restraint). The term *aggressive behavior* is subject to multiple interpretations, just as is being a threat to oneself or others. The term is often used as a shorthand way to justify restraining a patient. These terms should be described and defined by the professional who is recording the events in the medical record. An operational definition of aggressive behavior would justify the use of the label as to what the person making the entry really means. It would break down the term to a series of discrete and objective descriptive observations. Accuracy in communication is important in a legal-historical sense, because all that remains of a person's hospitalization is the medical record and the inaccurate and unreliable memories of all who are concerned with his care.[37]

22.9 Uses and Misuses of Terminology

In addition to using a data-based language that provides an accurate picture of the patient's treatment, psychiatric professionals and staff are charged with being nonjudgmental. However, too often the medical record can say more about how the staff views the patient than about her condition. In a classic study by Rosenhan that was conducted over thirty years ago, several sane graduate students had themselves admitted to various psychiatric facilities by complaining of hearing voices and no other symptom.[38] Thereafter, they were instructed to act "normally" and not mention voices again. Each found himself or herself admitted with a severe diagnosis, and labeled as "crazy." All of their actions and behaviors were described in the medical record as being derived from their presumed pathology.

Mohr and colleagues conducted a study in which they coded a total of 4,321 entries made by registered nurses in psychiatric medical records.[39] The number of nonpejorative adjectives used to describe patients was outnumbered by pejorative adjectives by three to one. Examples of pejorative descriptors included: manipulative, argumentative, controlling, defensive, defiant, disruptive, attention seeking, whiney, and superficial.

In a second example, Mohr studied over 500 medical records and described nine categories of entries made by registered nurses or other staff members.[40] Only 1 percent of entries reflected any kind of positive assessment of patients. In contrast, more than 20 percent of entries emerged under categories designated as pejorative, inane, punitive, and nonsense. Examples included:

- "is controlling and engages in power plays with staff" (pejorative),
- "time out given for aggressive behavior" (punitive),
- "redirected frequently" (inane because it says nothing of substance), and
- "Pt. lying in bed with eyes closed. Appears to be asleep. Affect is flat." (Nonsense because affect is an emotional reaction to a stimulus, and one must be awake to exhibit affect.)

TIP: Careless or unprofessional (judgmental, critical, or biased) documentation can make the best of care look inadequate.

Substandard charting may be a signal to astute attorneys that there was a failure to meet standards of care or worse.[41] Objective documentation such as describing behavior and using direct quotes must be present to show evidence of the use of proper procedures and to demonstrate that adequate professional care was given. Its absence constitutes a red flag signaling that further investigation should take place.

22.10 Documenting Special Circumstances in the Medical Record

There are special circumstances that merit particular attention in terms of documentation in the medical record. These include issues of therapeutic misadventure and untoward outcome, threats of suicide or homicide, and the use of force for aggressive or violent behavior. The following cases illustrate how poor documentation resulted in legal consequences.

A. Angelo Rivera (A Case of Therapeutic Misadventure)

Therapeutic misadventure is defined as injury or an adverse event caused by medical management rather than by the patient's underlying condition. Therapeutic misadventure was at the root of the case of Angelo Rivera. Angelo Rivera was a sixteen-year old who became psychotic, paranoid, and otherwise began to exhibit idiosyncratic behaviors. His mother drove him to a local emergency room, and en route he tried to jump out of her car. In the emergency room he was diagnosed as having schizophrenia and transferred to a prestigious inpatient psychiatric facility. He received a psychiatric evaluation but no medical evaluation because the medical consultant deemed him "too disoriented" to assess. He was diagnosed with schizophrenia, started on a high potency neuroleptic (Haldol) and, because of his disoriented state, was placed in seclusion.

Mr. Rivera continued to manifest psychotic symptoms which failed to respond to the Haldol within forty-eight hours, whereupon the psychiatrist raised the dose. Again he failed to respond, continued to be disoriented, and developed severe akathesia and dystonias (severely uncomfortable drug-induced side effects of antipsychotic medication), which were treated with Cogentin (an antiparkinson agent). The side effects did not remit. Again his Haldol was increased, and he remained in seclusion. On day 10 of his stay, he was still in seclusion, and nurses' notes observe that he was having trouble swallowing and that he was drooling.

The physician notes were negligible and merely reflected the clinical situation. Ativan (a sedative) was added to his medication regimen on an as needed basis for his "agitation." On day 14 of his stay, he was still secluded, and in addition to the above symptoms, notes by the nurses indicate that he was also ataxic and stumbling about. The psychiatrist speculated that Mr. Rivera might have neuroleptic malignant syndrome and called for a medical consultation. He continued him on his medication, and nurses continued to administer his medications. The medical consultant saw Mr. Rivera, and during the assessment, he found that his blood pressure was 160/120, pulse was 110, and his temperature was 102 degrees. He ordered Inderal (a beta blocker) for his hypertension and Tylenol for his fever. At this point the nurses began to take Mr. Rivera's vital signs every four hours. The record indicates that despite the beta blocker and antipyretics, Mr. Rivera continued to exhibit extreme lability of his vital signs. Two days after this, Mr. Rivera was found to have a fever of 104.6 degrees and was in extremis. His blood work indicated a CPK (a blood enzyme) that was elevated to 1500 (normal being up to 231), and he was transferred to an acute care facility where the diagnosis of neuroleptic malignant syndrome was made. Neuroleptic malignant syndrome (NMS) is a life-threatening side effect of antipsychotic medications. It is characterized by labile blood pressure, pulse and high fevers, severe akathesias and dystonias, difficulty swallowing, drooling, ataxia, disorientation, and intractability of psychosis. The treatment for NMS is immediate discontinuation of the offending agent, in this case the Haldol, and other supportive treatment. Because his NMS was neither recognized nor treated, Mr. Rivera's condition proved intractable to conventional treatment, and he was transferred to a major medical center. His condition today is consistent with organic brain damage, and he is on disability.

Although the issues in this case reflect more than therapeutic misadventure, they do illustrate that Mr. Rivera had a rather rare untoward reaction to a medication that could not have been foreseen but should have been recognized by his caregivers. The consultant opined the following about the nursing care in this case:

> You have asked me to evaluate the standard of nursing care rendered by the nurses involved in the care of Mr. Rivera during his stay at (name of institution). My opinion in this case is that Mr. Rivera was ill served by all of the professionals caring for him at (name of institution), and specifically that the nursing caring fell well below the standards of care as articulated by the American Nurses Association (ANA) Standards of Psychiatric and Mental

> Health Nursing Practice.[42] In addition, the nurses failed in their ethical obligations to Mr. Rivera in a number of areas, specifically violating at least two of the principles as articulated in the American Nurses Association Code of Ethics[43] that was operational at the time of Mr. Rivera's hospitalization. Moreover, the nurses did not live up to the standard of what would be expected of a reasonably prudent professional nurse in the same circumstances. I will expand on all of these areas in turn.

> The ANA Standards of Psychiatric and Mental Health Nursing Practice Standard I states that: *The psychiatric mental health nurse collects health data.* The rationale for this standard is that comprehensive assessment of the client and relevant systems enable the psychiatric mental health nurse to make clinically sound judgments and plan appropriate interventions with clients.[44] The nurses involved in Mr. Rivera's care failed to assess properly his condition and in some instances *did not appear to know what they were observing.* An example of this is contained in a note that reads "Patient having trouble swallowing, no signs of EPS." Indeed, dysphagia (trouble swallowing) is a sign of EPS (extra pyramidal side effects from the medication), as well as an indicator of NMS. Another example of failure to collect health data is the issue of the flow sheets from seclusion. Mr. Rivera was in seclusion during most of his stay. There is no concrete, operational indication as to the necessity for seclusion. What little there is has to do with his "disorientation" and "confusion." Disorientation/confusion is not a cardinal symptom of schizophrenia. While people with schizophrenia have been known to become confused, it is not typical of them to remain confused. Psychiatric nurses should know this, and the nurses caring for him should have questioned it and documented their concerns. The second issue has to do with his being in seclusion despite the documentation of his disorientation. Removing a patient from his environment and placing him in an environment devoid of reality-based environmental stimuli should have served to increase his disorientation rather than decrease it.

> The nurses repeatedly failed in their own institution's protocols for gathering data (e.g., vital signs) during patient seclusion. They failed to obtain vital signs until quite late in his tenure at the facility. They documented that Mr. Rivera was ataxic (stumbling about) and indeed that he had fallen, and yet they administered Ativan to him. The reasonably prudent nurse would know that ataxia is a contraindication to administering a benzodiazepine such as Ativan. Indeed it would increase his ataxia and put him at increased risk for more falls. These are only a few examples of substandard care under Standard I.

The ANA Standards of Psychiatric and Mental Health Nursing Practice Standard II states that: *The psychiatric mental health nurse analyzes the assessment data in determining the diagnosis.*[45] The rationale for this standard is that the basis for providing psychiatric mental health nursing care is the recognition and identification of patterns of response to actual or potential psychiatric illnesses and mental health problems. The nurses involved in the care of Mr. Rivera failed to recognize several key signs that indicated that his diagnosis and treatment were inadequate. They also failed to recognize his developing neuroleptic malignant syndrome. Nurses are taught to make observations in the interest of treatment and treatment modification and to analyze and synthesize data. These nurses did none of those. They duly checked off their flow sheets, but they made the most cursory observations; there were no notes that indicated that they were doing in-depth holistic assessments. They seemed to be operating by rote and stimulus response type thinking, rather than on intelligent and thoughtful assessment. Nurses are also taught to make observations with the goal of avoiding potential problems. The reasonably prudent nurse would have observed that this patient's symptoms were unrelenting despite neuroleptics (a sign of potential NMS), that he was exquisitely sensitive to neuroleptics (again a sign of potential NMS), and that he was disoriented (a sign of improper diagnosis). While there is ample room to lay the responsibility for this tragic misadventure at the foot of his physicians, nurses are also expected to be accountable for their professional practice and judgment and to advocate for their patients, especially in the event that those patients are being subjected to incompetent care. There is nothing in the chart to indicate that any nurse took a strong stand with respect to Mr. Rivera's deteriorating condition.

B. Richard Morose (A Case of a Suicidal Patient)

Richard Morose was a thirty-three-year-old, single male patient who committed suicide while on a four-hour therapeutic pass from the hospital prior to anticipated discharge. He had been hospitalized with a diagnosis of major depression, single episode, and suicidal ideation. He steadfastly denied suicidal thoughts or impulses after admission. He experienced moderate to severe depression, anhedonia (lack of pleasure), global insomnia, loss of appetite, hopelessness, and agitation. Mr. Morose signed a suicide prevention contract, promising to inform the psychiatrist or staff immediately of any suicidal thoughts or impulses. His energy level improved after antidepressant treatment was started.

The psychiatrist and the hospital were sued by the patient's parents for wrongful death. In court, the plaintiff's expert testified that a suicide risk assessment would have determined that the patient was a significant suicide risk and no pass should have been issued. The expert found no evidence in the medical record that a formal suicide risk assessment was conducted before the pass was issued. She opined that not recording a suicide risk assessment was a violation of the standard of care. She further testified that the patient was at greater risk of suicide after administration of an antidepressant drug because the patient now had more energy to carry out the suicidal intent. Finally, she opined that the psychiatrist should not have relied on a no harm contract to prevent suicide in lieu of performing a suicide risk assessment.[46]

The defendant psychiatrist testified that Mr. Morose's willingness to sign a no harm contract indicated the presence of a therapeutic alliance and the motivation to get well. The psychiatrist further testified that he had performed a formal suicide risk assessment that indicated a low to moderate suicide risk. It was an oversight on his part not to record the suicide assessment, and in his judgment the therapeutic benefits of a pass outweighed the risk of suicide.

The defense psychiatric expert testified that the psychiatrist met the standard of care by assessing the risk of suicide and weighing the suicide risk against the therapeutic benefits of a pass. On cross-examination he admitted that the suicide risk assessment should have been recorded. The expert concluded by stating that a patient who is intent upon committing suicide cannot be stopped from doing so by the psychiatrist and the hospital.

The jury found for the plaintiffs and awarded monetary damages. When they were polled by the defense attorney after rendering the verdict, they indicated that the lack of documentation of the psychiatrist's decision-making process prevented them from giving credibility to his testimony.

C. Jason Johnson (A Case of Death Proximal to Restraint)

Jason was fourteen years of age chronologically at the time of his death. He was a complicated youngster who had a history of numerous risk factors during his early development. His Department of Health and Human Services (DHHS) records and various medical records documented an unstable home life with an absent father, physical abuse and neglect, exposure to sexual abuse/misconduct at the hands of others, and multiple out of home placements. Jason's mother was functioning at a level consistent with mild mental retardation and had a long history of involvement with DHHS. Jason and his brothers and sisters have been in the custody of DHHS, which terminated parental rights for several of his siblings. Jason had been in foster care a number of times and also placed with his grandmother because his mother was not capable of caring for him. He had a lengthy history of externalizing and aggressive acting out behaviors and had psychological counseling and residential placements for these issues and for his sexualized behaviors. The first reports of oppositional and destructive behaviors surfaced when he was about six years old. The first reports of inappropriate acting out appeared when he was in a partial hospitalization program at age seven, and he continued to act out sexually and aggressively through a series of hospitalizations and residential placements. He was diagnosed with a long list of mental disorders, including oppositional defiant disorder (ODD), depressive disorder, attention deficit hyperactive disorder (ADHD), dysthymic disorder, adjustment disorder with mixed emotional features, posttraumatic stress disorder (PTSD), and conduct disorder, which were all considered part of his differential diagnoses. His global assessments of functioning (GAFs) ranged from the 30s to the 40s. He was on Ritalin (methylphenidate) for a number of years for his ADHD, and it kept his ADHD symptoms under control. He also took Benadryl for sleep at bedtime.

He had been tested in several ways. His I.Q. was found to be borderline to low average at various times. Neurological and educational testing indicated that he was functioning at low levels across a number of competencies including perceptual problems, reading comprehension problems, and memory difficulties and deficits. He had significant depressive features. His adaptive behaviors were found to be in the low range. Various psychologists also found him to be easily distracted and to have poor planning abilities and low frustration tolerance. His verbal receptive skills were moderately low, as were his coping and interpersonal relationships. He frequently acted out in an aggressive manner toward his peers and the staff.

On the day that Jason died, his primary "therapist" in the residential treatment facility was a staff member with no professional degrees, but who had a bachelor's degree in psychology. This person received a report that Jason had acted out and hit a peer in school. When Jason returned from school to the residence, the staff member was heard to yell at him: "I'm sick of your behavior. We need to talk." Jason proceeded to his room and closed the door. Shortly thereafter, the therapist followed Jason and found him sitting on his bed doing his homework. He observed that Jason had a pencil in his hand, and the therapist demanded that he give up the pencil. They had words over the pencil and the situation escalated to the point that Jason threw the pencil at the therapist, who promptly moved to restrain him physically and called for staff backup. Another male therapist came into the room to assist, and together they held Jason down on his bed in a prone position while a nurse ran to get a sedative order.

Jason was heard to yell "I can't breathe" two or three times and then was noted to become still. Thinking that he had become "compliant," the two therapists released him, turned him over, and found his face to be dusky blue. They initiated CPR to no avail, and Jason was pronounced dead in the emergency room of the acute care hospital to which he was transported.

The psychiatric expert opined in part that: "With respect to the fatal restraint incident itself, it indicates to me that staff members engaged Jason in a power struggle—known in the literature as a "coercion-aggression cycle." There is no indication on the medical record that (name of therapist) tried to thoughtfully defuse or de-escalate the situation in an individually appropriate way nor in any of the narratives or depositions that I read. Indeed he did say that he observed that Jason was becoming increasingly agitated and that he continued to counsel him...the fact remains that (name of institution) was acting in loco parentis and had an obligation to competently treat, protect, and to do no harm. They did none of these. Indeed the medical record indicates that they were out of compliance with their own policies on the use of restraints and restraints were applied to him despite their own recommendations that his behavior be managed without engaging in a power struggle. They were to be fully aware of the dangers of a prone restraint in that there had been reports in the professional literature and in the newspapers of children and adults dying proximal to the use of restraints."

D. Kevin Allen (A Case of Proper Documentation)

Kevin Allen, a thirty-four-year-old man was admitted involuntarily to a psychiatric unit because of an explosive personality. He began to threaten a fellow patient, and the following chart entry was made:

> Mr. Allen came into the day room, stood in front of his roommate who was seated and stated loudly to the roommate: *What do you think you're doing with my radio? I told you I was going to beat the crap out of you if you touched it again!* This writer (referring to the nurse writing the note) identified that there were two other staff members in the day room for assistance if necessary and asked another nurse to request additional assistance. Speaking in a calm voice this writer approached the patient and offered alternatives of moving away from the conflict or going to his room to calm down. Other

patients were asked to leave the immediate area. Mr. Allen was asked to walk to a quiet area of the unit to decrease stimulation, and he was offered a PRN medication. He refused and stood in the hallway with his fists clenched and yelled, *I'm going to fight you to the death!* This writer and four staff members restrained Mr. Allen physically using the Crisis Prevention Institute (CPI) technique. Mark Smothers (mental health aide) observed and monitored the restraint and Mr. Allen's physical condition. Mr. Allen struggled against the hold for approximately 5 minutes and then stopped. He was assessed and J. Janus RN administered IM Haldol after ascertaining that Mr. Allen was responsive and that he was receptive to being sedated.

Key elements of the documentation in the above case include the use of quotations, specific interventions attempted to decrease agitation, specific verbal and nonverbal patient responses, and steps taken to ensure everyone's safety.

The above examples do not exhaust the cases in which precise documentation is particularly important. Others include instances of duty to warn, sexualized behavior of patients, reporting abuse, and patients signing out against medical advice. They do illustrate the importance of documenting fully the facts surrounding unusual occurrences and incidents and when failure to do so leads to legal, and in some instances, criminal liability.

22.11 Summary

Documentation is a record of occurrences, observations, and planning related to patient care. It is important that all significant occurrences, situations, actions, and interventions, including the resolutions and treatment outcomes, be recorded in a factual, nonbiased manner because they inform and guide other healthcare workers. Documentation also provides important information that aids in providing the rationale for treatment given. Characteristics of a good medical record are illustrated in Table 22.2.

The eminent psychologists, Robyn Dawes[47] and Paul Meehl[48] observed that many mental health professionals have slipped into uncritical modes of thinking. These uncritical modes of thinking are often reflected in uncritical documentation.

The medical record should contain no generalized opinion or evaluative statements that cannot be backed up with discrete observations. As noted in this chapter, research indicates that this ideal is not always met.

Table 22.2
Characteristics of Good Medical Records

Accurate	Factual
Clear	Legible
Complete	Objective
Concise	Relevant
Descriptive	Timely

Endnotes

1. American Psychiatric Association. *Diagnostic and Statistical Manual of Mental Disorders*. Fourth Edition. Washington, D.C. 1994.

2. War Department. "Nomenclature of Psychiatric Disorders and Reactions." War Department Technical Bulletin. Medical 203. *Journal of Clinical Psychology*. 2, p. 289–296. 1946.

3. Barton, W.E. *The History and Influence of the American Psychiatric Association*. Washington, D.C.: American Psychiatric Press. 1987.

4. Houts, A.C. "Fifty Years of Psychiatric Nomenclature: Reflections on the 1943 War Department Technical Bulletin." Medical 203. *Journal of Clinical Psychology*. 56 (7), p. 935–967. 2000.

5. *Id.*

6. *Id.*

7. *See* note 3.

8. *Id.*

9. *Id.*

10. *Id.*

11. Paraphilia refers to a condition in which sexual arousal centers around objects and situations that are not part of societally normative arousa or activity patterns (e.g. fetish).

12. Tourettes Disorder is a rare disorder characterized by repetitive muscle movements and vocal outbursts.

13. American Psychiatric Association. *Diagnostic and Statistical Manual of Mental Disorders Text Revision.* Fourth Edition. Washington, D.C. 2000.

14. World Health Organization. *International Classification of Diseases.* Ninth Revision. Clinical Modification (ICD-9-CM). 2003.

15. Personality disorders are pervasive chronic psychological disorders, which often negatively affect a person's life, including work, family, and interpersonal relationships. Personality disorders exists on a continuum so they can be mild to more severe in terms of how pervasive and to what extent a person exhibits the features of a particular personality disorder. Those with a personality disorder possess several distinct psychological features including disturbances in self-image; ability to have successful interpersonal relationships; appropriateness of range of emotion, ways of perceiving themselves, others, and the world; and difficulty possessing proper impulse control. There are ten different types of personality disorders that are listed in the DSM.

16. *See* note 1.

17. Mohr, W.K. and M.J. Regan-Kubinski. "The DSM and Child Psychiatric Nursing: A Cautionary Reflection." *Scholarly Inquiry for Nursing Practice.* 13(4), p. 305–318. 1999.

18. The word "taxonomy" refers to a system of classification or nomenclature that is used by a profession.

19. *See* note 17.

20. Caplan, P.J. *They Say You're Crazy: How the World's Most Powerful Psychiatrists Decide Who's Normal.* Reading: Addison-Wesley. 1995.

21. *Id.*

22. Kutchins, H. and S.A. Kirk. *Making Us Crazy: DSM—the Psychiatric Bible and the Creation of Mental Disorders.* p. 22. New York, NY: The Free Press. 1997.

23. Swartz, M.H. *Textbook of Physical Diagnosis: History and Examination.* Cambridge, UK: Elsevier Science. 2001.

24. *Id.*

25. *Id.*

26. A test which requires an individual to respond to indistinct stimuli. The best known projective psychological test is the Rorschach, or inkblot test. The patient is asked to look at each blot and to say what it looks like or what it could be. Because the stimulus is ambiguous, the patient must impose her own structure. In doing so, thoughts, feelings, and themes, some of which are unconscious, are projected into the material. Projective tests tend to have lower validity and reliability than objective tests. That is, they are less stable and have lower relationships with other criteria.

27. Hunsley, J. and J.M. Bailey. "The Clinical Utility of the Rorschach: Unfulfilled Promises and an Uncertain Future." *Psychological Assessment.* 11(3), p. 266–277. 1999.

28. Dawes, R.M. *House of cards: Psychology and Psychotherapy Built on Myth.* New York, NY: The Free Press. 1994.

29. American Hospital Association. Chicago, IL. 2003. Catalog no. 157759. www.aha.org.

30. Joint Commission on Accreditation of Healthcare Organizations. http://www.jcaho.org/index.htm.

31. Olson, J.N. and W.K. Mohr. "The Lost Art of Accuracy: A Contextual Approach to Assessment." *Journal of Psychosocial Nursing and Mental Health Services.* 40 (10), p. 38–45. 2002.

32. Woody, S.A. et al. *Treatment Planning in Psychotherapy: Taking the Guesswork Out of Clinical Care.* New York, NY: The Guilford Press. 2003.

33. http://www.cbsnews.com/stories/1999/04/15/60II/main43232.shtml.

34. *See* note 23.

35. Lutz, W. *Doublespeak.* New York, NY: Harper Perennial. 1990.

36. Rogers, C.R. "The Necessary and Sufficient Conditions of Therapeutic Personality Change." *Journal of Consulting Psychology.* 21, p. 90–103. 1957.

37. *See* note 31.

38. Rosenhan, D.L. "On Being Sane in Insane Places." *Science.* 179, p. 250–258. 1973

39. Mohr, W.K. and M.J. Noone. "Deconstructing Progress Notes in Psychiatric Settings." *Archives of Psychiatric Nursing*. 11 (6), p. 325–332. 1997.

40. Mohr, W.K. "Deconstructing the Language of Psychiatric Hospitals." *Journal of Advanced Nursing*. 29 (5), p. 1052–1059. 1999.

41. Morgan, N.E. "The Current Litigation Crisis and Tort Reform." *Journal of American Medical Record Association*. 58 (1), p. 19–21. 1987.

42. American Nurses Association. *A statement on psychiatric mental health clinical nursing practice and standards of psychiatric mental health clinical nursing practice*. Washington, D.C. 1994.

43. American Nurses Association Code of Ethics with Interpretive Statements. Washington, D.C. 2001.

44. *See* note 42.

45. *Id.*

46. There is no empirical evidence that a "no-suicide" contract is efficacious or that it affects a person's desire to commit suicide.

47. Dawes, R.M. *House of Cards: Psychology and Psychotherapy Built on Myth*. New York, NY: The Free Press. 1994.

48. Meehl, P.E. "Why I Do Not Attend Case Conferences" in Meehl, P.E. *Psychodiagnosis: Collected Papers*. p. 225–302. Minneapolis, MN: The University of Minnesota Press. 1973.

Chapter 23

Physical Therapy Records

Gwen Simons, PT, JD, OCS, FAAOMPT

23.1 Introduction

The physical therapist's records are an excellent source of evidence in malpractice, personal injury, workers' compensation and disability cases. Physical therapists are experts in diagnosing and quantifying movement impairments and dysfunctions that result in disabilities. Thus the physical therapist is commonly used as an expert to identify and quantify damages. This chapter discusses the physical therapist's qualifications and scope of practice and gives case examples of how the physical therapy records may be used as evidence in a case. Physical therapy documentation is described so that legal professionals know how to spot valuable evidence in the physical therapy record.

23.2 What is Physical Therapy?

Physical therapy is an area of specialty within health care. The physical therapist treats patients and clients across the continuum of care in settings such as: critical and intensive care units, outpatient clinics, long-term care facilities, school systems, and the workplace.[1] The American Physical Therapy Association's (APTA) *Guide to Physical Therapist Practice* (hereinafter "the Guide") describes in great detail the physical therapist's body of knowledge and provides practice parameters for common problems that physical therapists treat.

The Guide defines physical therapy as the "…examination, evaluation, diagnosis, prognosis, and intervention provided by physical therapists/physiotherapists. Physical therapy includes diagnosis and management of movement dysfunction and enhancement of physical and functional abilities; restoration, maintenance, and promotion of optimal physical function, optimal fitness and wellness, and optimal quality of life as it relates to movement and health; and prevention of the onset, symptoms, and progression of impairments, functional limitations, and disabilities that may result from diseases, disorders, conditions, or injuries." The terms "physical therapy" and "physiotherapy" are synonymous.

A. Education and Licensure

Physical therapists are licensed healthcare providers in all fifty states. To obtain a license to practice physical therapy, the physical therapist must graduate from a CAPTE[2] accredited program or have equivalent foreign education. CAPTE accredited programs follow "The Normative Model of Physical Therapists Professional Education."[3] The entry level for physical therapy education has changed over the last twenty years from a bachelor's degree to a doctorate in physical therapy (DPT) degree. Currently physical therapy programs must offer a master's degree to be accredited; however, more than 8 percent of the programs have converted or plan to convert to the entry-level DPT degree. Many practicing physical therapists are returning to "transitional" DPT programs to upgrade their degree to the doctorate degree merely because the DPT is becoming the recognized standard even though physical therapists with bachelor's degrees had an equitable physical therapy education and still meet (or exceed) minimum licensure requirements.

The Federation of State Boards of Physical Therapy administers the only national licensure exam. Therefore, there is a national standard for entry level education and licensure even though each state licensure board sets its own passing criteria for the exam.

The *physical therapist assistant (PTA)* is a graduate of a physical therapist assistant associate's degree program accredited by the Commission on Accreditation in Physical Therapy (CAPTE). The PTA assists the physical therapist in providing physical therapy interventions to carry out the treatment plan. The PTA does not perform examinations or make decisions to change the treatment plan and functions under the direction of the physical therapist. In general, the PTA does not require on-site supervision unless it is required by the payer or the state licensure act. PTAs must be licensed or certified in most but not all states. In some settings, the physical therapist may be assisted by non-licensed personnel called *physical therapy technicians* ("techs") or aides. Occasionally these support personnel have other degrees or certifications, such as an athletic training certification (ATC) or an exercise physiology degree. The Physical Therapy Practice Act in each state governs the use of such non-licensed personnel when they are working in a physical therapy setting regardless of whether they have other degrees or certifications. In most states, non-licensed personnel have a very limited role in caring for the patient and are prohibited from independently performing or billing for physical therapy services. Documentation is not typically done by non-licensed support staff unless they are merely checking off flow sheets or exercise records. Therefore, each physical therapy note should be signed by either the physical therapist or the PTA. A red flag should go up about whether the licensure laws were complied with and the standard of care was met where documentation is done by non-licensed support staff.

B. Practice Settings

According to the Guide, physical therapists provide services in a broad range of inpatient, outpatient, and community-based settings where physical therapists practice, including the following:[4]

- Hospitals (for example, critical care, intensive care, acute care, and subacute care settings)
- Outpatient clinics or offices
- Rehabilitation facilities
- Skilled nursing, extended care, or subacute facilities
- Homes
- Education or research centers
- Schools and playgrounds (preschool, primary, and secondary)
- Hospices
- Corporate or industrial health centers
- Industrial, workplace, or other occupational environments
- Athletic facilities (collegiate, amateur, and professional)
- Fitness centers and sports training facilities

The physical therapist may play a slightly different role and have different responsibilities for the patient in each of these settings. For instance, in acute care and rehabilitation facilities, the physical therapist is one member of the patient care team. Care must be coordinated between multiple providers, and all team members have a responsibility for knowing what care the other team members are providing with regard to how it may impact their individual treatment plans.

In any inpatient setting (hospital, rehab, subacute, extended care or skilled nursing facility), the physical therapists are generally responsible for teaching the patient how to safely transfer from the bed to the wheelchair and bedside commode or in and out of a car. They are also responsible for teaching the patient how to walk with assistive devices. The physical therapist assesses the patient's need for assistance and documents it in the patient's record. Other team members, such as nursing staff, may rely on this information to know how much assistance to give the patient and whether the patient requires the assistance of more than one person. Each facility will have policies and procedures about how this communication between team members should occur.

TIP: Typical documentation on the level of assistance required will read "Max assist of 2," meaning two people were required to give maximum assistance to the patient, or "stand-by assist of 1," meaning the physical therapist only had to stand near the patient for safety purposes. When the physical therapy documentation states that two people are needed to assist with transfers or gait training, it is a safety risk to both the healthcare provider and the patient to attempt the transfer or gait training without having a second person available.

In home care, the physical therapist is responsible for educating the caregiver on how to assist the patient with transfers, gait and other elements of patient care, including carrying out a home exercise program. The documentation should reflect that the caregiver was instructed and that the caregiver's ability to carry out the instructions was assessed.

In the primary education system, physical therapy services may be provided to students with learning and/or physical disabilities. The purpose of physical therapist in this setting is to maximize the child's learning potential. The physical therapist works with the student and consults with the teacher on, for instance, positioning the child in the wheelchair properly for class instruction, transferring the child in and out of the wheelchair or providing pressure relief. The physical therapist may also provide traditional rehab services in a treatment room at the school or the student may receive these services outside the school.

Outpatient physical therapy is one of the most utilized settings. Patients may receive outpatient care in the outpatient department of an inpatient facility or, more likely, in a free-standing outpatient facility. Many physical therapists who own their own private practices specialize in specific patient populations, such as geriatrics, pediatrics, orthopaedics or neurorehabilitation. The large majority of patients seen in an outpatient setting have musculoskeletal (orthopaedic) injuries or conditions that cause pain. The goal for treatment in these settings is generally to return the patients back to the prior level of function or at least maximum safe function.

Physical therapy services in an industrial setting are aimed more specifically at returning injured workers to work or preventing work-related injuries. The physical therapist may also provide injury prevention education, ergonomic and job analyses and employment screenings designed to match the worker to the job. The physical therapist may also consult on reasonable accommodations for workers who have temporary or permanent disabilities.

Much like the industrial setting, physical therapy services for athletes are aimed at returning the athlete to play, minimizing risk of re-injury and maximizing performance. Similar services may be offered in gyms and fitness centers to people who want to stay healthy and fit and may or may not have special needs. Services in these settings focus on individualized exercise prescription specific to the person's medical condition, pre-existing impairments and athletic (function) performance requirements.

C. Scope of Practice

The physical therapist's licensure act in each state defines the legal scope of practice for licensed physical therapists practicing within its borders. Even though the physical therapist's education and licensure exam are nationally standardized, the scope of practice, rules and regulations and licensure board interpretations may differ from state to state. Many states have adopted some components of the *Model Practice Act*[5] (MPT) developed by the Federation of State Boards of Physical Therapy. The MPT describes the physical therapists' scope of practice as follows:

"Practice of physical therapy" means:

1. Examining, evaluating and testing individuals with mechanical, physiological and developmental impairments, functional limitations, and disabilities or other health and movement-related conditions in order to determine a diagnosis, prognosis and plan of treatment intervention, and to assess the ongoing effects of intervention.

2. Alleviating impairments, functional limitations and disabilities by designing, implementing and modifying treatment interventions that may include, but

are not limited to: therapeutic exercise, functional training in self-care and in home, community or work integration or reintegration, manual therapy including soft tissue and joint mobilization/manipulation, therapeutic massage, prescription, application and, as appropriate, fabrication of assistive, adaptive, orthotic, prosthetic, protective and supportive devices and equipment, airway clearance techniques, integumentary protection and repair techniques, debridement and wound care, physical agents or modalities, mechanical and electrotherapeutic modalities, and patient-related instruction.

3. Reducing the risk of injury, impairment, functional limitation and disability, including the promotion and maintenance of fitness, health and wellness in populations of all ages.

4. Engaging in administration, consultation, education and research.[6]

The Guide describes the physical therapists' scope of practice similarly, stating that physical therapists:

- "Diagnose and manage movement dysfunction and enhance physical and functional abilities,

- Restore, maintain, and promote not only optimal physical function but optimal wellness and fitness and optimal quality of life as it relates to movement and health.

- Prevent the onset, symptoms, and progression of impairments, functional limitations, and disabilities that may result from diseases, disorders, conditions, or injuries."[7]

D. Restrictions on Providing a "Medical" Diagnosis

In some states, physical therapists are prohibited from providing a "medical diagnosis," but this should not be confused with the physical therapist's diagnosis of movement dysfunctions and impairments *which may result from* a medical diagnosis.

TIP: The physical therapist may not diagnose the underlying medical problem that is the source of the movement dysfunction or impairment; but the physical therapist does identify, quantify and qualify the movement dysfunctions, impairments and resultant disabilities that result from the medical diagnosis.

For example, a typical physical therapist diagnosis may be "Impaired Joint Mobility, Motor Function, Muscle Performance, Range of Motion, and Reflex Integrity Associated with Spinal Disorders"[8] which could be the result of a medical diagnosis of a herniated disc, spinal stenosis, spondylolisthesis or any other spinal problem that causes these impairments. This physical therapy diagnosis is differentiated from the physical therapy diagnosis of "Impaired Joint Mobility, Motor Function, Muscle Performance, and Range of Motion Associated With Localized Inflammation,"[9] which may be caused by a muscle strain, ligament strain, tendinitis, joint inflammation or any other inflammatory condition.

23.3 The Physical Therapist's Documentation
A. Examination and Documentation

TIP: The physical therapist is required by law to perform a physical therapy examination (sometimes referred to as an evaluation) on each patient on the first visit.

The Guide describes the examination as a "comprehensive screening and specific testing process leading to diagnostic classification or, as appropriate, to a referral to another practitioner." The examination is divided into three steps:

1. Taking the patient's history.
2. Performing a systems review where the physical therapist screens the cardiovascular/pulmonary, integumentary, musculoskeletal, and neuromuscular systems and the communication ability, affect, cognition, language, and learning style of the patient.
3. Performing tests and measures that are "used to rule in or rule out causes of impairment and functional limitations; to establish a diagnosis, prognosis, and plan of care; and to select interventions" within the physical therapist's scope of practice.[10]

Historically the physical therapist's documentation was done in the traditional "SOAP" format. In that documentation style, the patient's subjective reports are under the "S" (for "Subjective") part of the note. The systems review and the tests and measures are under the "O" (for "Objective") part of the note.

After the physical therapist does the examination, she *evaluates* the results to come up with the physical therapy diagnosis, prognosis, and plan of care (which includes the physical therapist's interventions or referral recommendations). The Guide refers to this process as the physical therapist's *Evaluation*. In the SOAP note format, the physical therapy diagnosis and prognosis would be documented

under the "A" (for "Assessment") part of the note. The plan of care for the patient would be documented under the "P" (for "Plan") part of the note. Refer to Chapter 5, *Charting Systems*, in Volume I, for more information.

B. Subsequent Physical Therapy Treatment Notes
Medicare and other payer rules have driven the need for documentation to be done in different formats in different settings. Frequently the physical therapy documentation merely reflects what interventions were delivered in a daily "treatment record" or "encounter note." These notes primarily record what treatment was delivered for payment purposes but do not always record the patient's subjective complaints or progress. However, under most state laws and Medicare rules, the physical therapist is required to document a "progress note" or "re-evaluation" at least every 30 days (or less under some state laws) if the daily treatment notes do not record objective measurements and progress.

TIP: The progress note/re-evaluation contains tests and measures and an evaluation of the patient's progress toward the treatment goals since the initial examination or last re-evaluation.

This is the best place to start the search for medical evidence in the physical therapy record if the daily notes are devoid of objective measurements or evidence. Daily notes should not be overlooked, however. If the patient's condition changes, a new injury occurs, or there is a negative response to treatment, the physical therapist should document it on the day it was discovered rather than saving it for the monthly progress report.

23.4 Evidence in the Physical Therapy Record
Regardless of the format used for documentation, all physical therapy documentation has one thing in common: it quantifies the patient's function. The focus of physical therapy interventions and treatment goals is on maximizing the patient's function and moving the patient toward independence. While the reduction or elimination of pain may also be a goal, safe function *despite* pain is paramount. Therefore, the physical therapy record is frequently a good source of evidence of whether the patient's subjective reports of pain are truly disabling. The medical-legal reviewer should look for statements in the assessment (or evaluation) that say "pain is out of proportion to objective findings" or "signs and symptoms are not consistent with subjective complaints."

Since independence is always a goal, the physical therapist has an expectation of compliance and effort. When the patient is not compliant or shows signs of giving a sub-maximal effort, the physical therapist is likely to document it. The physical therapist may also use words such as "self-limiting," "pain-focused," or "sub-maximal effort" to indicate that the patient's subjective perception of the pain may not be reliable or credible. This does not mean the physical therapist thinks the patient is exaggerating or "faking" the injury but is an indication that the physical therapist has not observed enough objective signs to support the patient's limitations or reports of pain.

The physical therapist may also document comments the patient makes that indicate the patient's motivation for limiting activities, such as "my attorney told me I should not go on my hiking trip" or "my attorney told me I should continue to wear my neck brace, so I put it back on." This is not the evidence the attorney wants to see in the record if she is representing the patient. These entries in the record are particularly damaging when the objective findings indicate that the patient *is* capable of safely doing more, or the attorney's advice contradicts the medical provider's advice. On the other hand, where the patient's subjective complaints are consistent with the medical/physical findings, the physical therapist's documentation can help give credibility to the patient's reported disabilities.

Many physical therapists are now using various standardized pain and function questionnaires to measure the patient's progress. Some of the most frequently used questionnaires include the Oswestry Low Back Pain Disability Questionnaire,[11] the Neck Disability Index,[12] the Fear Avoidance Behavior Questionnaire,[13] and the Lower Extremity Functional Scale.[14] These questionnaires have been published in the research as reliable measures of patients' perceptions of their disabilities. They are used as an objective measure of the patient's subjective pain and perception of function when they are used intermittently throughout the course of a patient's treatment.

The documentation of objective tests and measures tells the reader whether the patient has made or is making improvements. However, sometimes it is difficult to decipher the importance of these measurements by merely reading the notes. A good physical therapist will document the interpretation and evaluation of the tests and measures in the patient's medical record. At a minimum, the physical therapist should document the patient's progress toward the goals at discharge. Where progress was not satisfactory or goals were not met, the physical therapist should document an opinion about why. Did the patient not have potential to meet the goals (perhaps the goals were unrealistic)? Does

the patient require other medical care or consults? If the physical therapy notes indicate a lack of progress and no analysis of the reasons why or need for referral back to the physician, substandard care may be suspected.

23.5 The Physical Therapist as an Expert Witness

Since physical therapists do not usually provide the medical diagnosis, they are not thought of as causation witnesses per se. But after the diagnosis is made by a qualified expert (usually a physician), the physical therapist may be the expert of choice to quantify the disabilities and impairments that result from that diagnosis. However, the physical therapist can definitely provide a professional opinion about whether an impairment or disability is the result of a particular medical diagnosis. This is important where there is a question about whether the disability is from a recent injury or another pre-existing medical condition.

For instance, take the case of a worker who injured his back at work but also has high blood pressure and cardiovascular conditions. After substantial rehab, he is still not able to perform the essential job functions of lifting 30 pounds frequently throughout the work day. However, according to the physical therapist's tests and measures, his residual disability is not due to low back pain, poor lifting techniques or lack of back or leg strength. It is due to an unsafe elevation in heart rate and blood pressure with this type of work activity. The effects of the work-related injury have ended and the employer may no longer be liable for the non-work-related disability.

TIP: Evidence in the physical therapy record may help an attorney determine whether a defendant or employer is responsible for the plaintiff's disabilities/damages.

The physical therapist is also skilled at analyzing risk factors and mechanisms of injury to determine whether they are consistent with the impairment/disability. While this is a causation analysis with regard to biomechanics, it does not require the physical therapist to make a medical diagnosis.

For example, a bus driver is diagnosed as having carpal tunnel syndrome bilaterally, which she claimed was work related. A job analysis by the physical therapist revealed that there were significant risk factors for carpal tunnel syndrome on the right side because the bus driver had to open and close the door with this hand, requiring repetitive forceful gripping, wrist extension and forceful pressure on the carpal tunnel aspect of the hand. There were no significant risks for carpal tunnel in the left hand, however. The vibration on the steering wheel was not significant and no forceful grip or excessive wrist movement was required. Without additional information, the physical therapist could not identify another cause for the carpal tunnel on the left, but the physical therapist could definitely form an opinion that the work *was not* the source of the carpal tunnel syndrome on the left.

TIP: The physical therapist can provide an opinion on whether the work risks or the mechanism of injury are consistent with the resultant disability.

The physical therapist is also frequently asked to give an opinion on whether the plaintiff is exaggerating his symptoms and is really disabled. Over the years many tests have been devised to try to identify whether a patient is "malingering" or is a "symptom magnifier." A full discussion of the validity of such tests is beyond the scope of this chapter, but the attorney should know that many of these tests are unreliable, invalid or have been misused and therefore do not provide a good basis for the professional's opinion. These tests are particularly unreliable when used in a vacuum.[15] The physical therapist's opinion about the patient's pain, effort and maximum safe functional abilities should be based on the record as a whole, including the medical record, the physical therapist's physical (or musculoskeletal) exam and functional testing. Recent research indicates that the physical therapist can reliably identify a sub-maximal versus a maximal safe effort by observing biomechanical and physiological signs,[16] but limitations in performance must still be correlated to the medical record. When the medical record and/or physical exam findings do not support the limited performance, the credibility of the patient's self reports and self-assessment of his abilities may be questioned but his motivations cannot be determined.

TIP: The attorney should investigate the basis of the physical therapist's opinion where the patient's effort, motivation or credibility has been negatively labeled.

23.6 Summary

The physical therapy records provide an excellent source of evidence to establish whether a plaintiff/patient is entitled to compensation and if so, to identify and quantify the damages or compensation due. Where appropriate, the physical therapist may also be a good choice for an expert witness to testify to the impairments, pain, functional loss and disabilities that result from any type of injury, disease or medical problem.

Endnotes

1. *Guide to Physical Therapist Practice*. 2nd ed. Alexandria, VA: American Physical Therapy Association; 2003

2. Commission on Accreditation of Physical Therapy Education (CAPTE) is the only accreditation agency recognized by the United States Department of Education (USDE) and the Council for Higher Education Accreditation (CHEA) to accredit entry-level physical therapist and physical therapist assistant education programs. Information on CAPTE can be obtained at http://www.apta.org/AM/Template.cfm?Section=CAPTE3&Template=/TaggedPage/TaggedPageDisplay.cfm&TPLID=65&ContentID=49490 (accessed on November 16, 2009).

3. *A Normative Model of Physical Therapist Professional Education*: Version 2004 (American Physical Therapy Association).

4. See note 1.

5. The Model Practice Act for Physical Therapy: A Tool for Public Protection and Legislative Change (4th Ed.), Federation of State Boards of Physical Therapy. (available at https://www.fsbpt.org/download/MPA2006.pdf (accessed November 16, 2009).

6. *Id*. at Article 1, Section 1.01 (D).

7. See note 1.

8. *Id*.

9. *Id*.

10. *Id.*

11. Fairbank JCT, Pynsent PB, Disney S. "Oswestry Disability Index version 2.1a." Available at: www.ortho-surg.org.uk/odi/. Accessed 11/16/2009.

12. Hoving JL; O'Leary EF; Niere KR; Green S; Buchbinder R, "Validity of The Neck Disability Index, Northwick Park Neck Pain Questionnaire, and Problem Elicitation Technique For Measuring Disability Associated With Whiplash-Associated Disorders." *Pain.* 2003; 102(3):273-81.

13. Waddell G, Newton M, et al. "A Fear-Avoidance Beliefs Questionnaire (FABQ) and The Role of Fear-Avoidance Beliefs in Chronic Low Back Pain and Disability." *Pain.* 1993; 52: 157-168.

14. Binkley JM, Stratford PW, Lott SA, et al. The Lower Extremity Functional Scale (LEFS): scale development, measurement properties, and clinical application. *Physical Therapy.* 1999;70: 371-383.

15. Fishbain DA; Cutler RB; Rosomoff HL; Rosomoff RS. "Is There a Relationship Between Nonorganic Physical Findings (Waddell Signs) and Secondary Gain/Malingering?" *Clin J Pain.* 2004; 20(6):399-408.

16. Reneman MF, Fokkens AS, Dijkstra PU, Geertzen JH, Groothoff JW. "Testing Lifting Capacity: Validity of Determining Effort Level by Means of Observation." *Spine.* 2005; 30: E40-E46.

Chapter 24

Rehabilitation Records

Jane O'Rourke, MSN, RN, CNAA

24.1 Introduction

Rehabilitation is an area of specialty within health care. The scope of rehabilitation is the diagnosis and treatment of individuals with problems stemming from altered functional ability and lifestyle. The goal of rehabilitation is to assist the individual with a disability or chronic illness in the restoration and maintenance of maximal health and function. The professional members of the rehabilitation team are skilled in treating alterations in functional ability and lifestyle resulting from disability and chronic illness.

Documentation in the rehabilitation setting is focused on *function*. Function is defined as the degree to which an individual is able to perform the required tasks of the day. For each individual the set of required tasks is different.

TIP: The purpose of an individual program of rehabilitation, be it inpatient, outpatient, or as part of homecare services, is to improve function. For some this means to be able to return to work after sustaining an injury, and for others it means to be able to climb steps.

24.2 The Rehabilitation Team

In addition to the physicians (physiatrists) and nurses, the major players on the rehabilitation team are physical therapists (PT), occupational therapists (OT), and speech therapists (ST).

A. Physical Therapy

Physical therapy is initiated following a physician referral. A physical therapist evaluates, treats, or prevents disability, injury, disease, or other conditions using physical, chemical, or mechanical means. The primary focus of care is to assist the person to achieve the greatest degree of independence feasible. Physical therapists are graduates of accredited programs and are licensed and registered in their state of practice. Physical therapy assistants (PTA) are graduates of accredited programs and are usually certified or licensed in their state of practice.

B. Occupational Therapy

Occupational therapy is administered on the referral of a physician. An OT assists individuals to cope with the effects that illness, injury, and aging have on their ability to achieve productive and satisfying lives. The focus of OT is to maximize independence in daily activities, prevent further disability, and to maintain health through the use of selected relevant and meaningful activities. An occupational therapist is a graduate of an accredited program and is licensed and registered in the state of practice. Certified Occupational Therapy Assistants (COTA) are graduates of accredited programs and are licensed and registered in the state of practice. COTAs are supervised by OTs.

C. Speech Therapy

Speech and audiology therapists provide a full range of assessment, treatment, and consultative services for individuals with disorders of speech, language, hearing, and swallowing. Service is initiated through the referral of a physician. Speech and audiology therapists are dedicated to the improvement of an individual's communication ability and oral pharyngeal function (i.e., swallowing). The speech therapist identifies, evaluates, diagnoses, prescribes, develops, and implements preventative and treatment services for patients with disorders of speech, language, cognitive communication, and swallowing. Augmentative and alternative communication systems are established as appropriate.

Speech therapy is often required for a rehabilitation patient if she has sustained any insult which interferes with the vasculature or musculature required for speaking and eating. A speech therapist is involved also if the patient has an inability to transmit or process the spoken word.

TIP: The speech therapist is required to treat receptive aphasia (inability to comprehend the spoken word) and expressive aphasia (inability to put a particular thought of a word into a spoken word). Patients who have sustained a head injury or stroke usually require these services.

Another priority for the ST is treating patients with swallowing disorders. Swallowing evaluations are done by the ST. The most basic swallowing evaluation is to offer the patient foods and liquids of varying consistency. For the patient having problems, thicker substances are easier to swallow than thin or watery substances. Video Fluoroscopy is performed in selected cases to view the exact swallowing process as it is happening under continuous video. The video will allow the ST and physician to see the actual level and musculature involved. Specific diets and feeding directions are given based on the ST evaluation. The proper ST evaluation of swallowing will prevent an aspiration and possibly associated pneumonia. ST evaluation and treatment are essential for certain patients in a neurorehabilitation setting.

D. Audiology Therapy

Audiology services include evaluation and diagnosis of auditory and vestibular competencies, identification, evaluation, diagnosis, prevention, and rehabilitation for patients with peripheral and central auditory system dysfunctions as well as selecting, fitting, and prescribing amplification, assistive listening, and alerting services. Speech therapists are licensed and certified in their states of practice.

24.3 Scope of Documentation

Through documentation, a clinician presents a clear picture of how a patient was able to function at the beginning and end of the program, realistic goals and expected outcomes of the program, treatments performed to reach the determined goals, and patient response to the treatment. Some of the areas considered in the ability to function include the following basic activities:

- bathing,
- grooming,
- dressing,
- eating,

- ambulation,
- transfers (bed to chair, chair to toilet etc),
- toileting,
- cognitive skills (comprehension, memory, ability to solve problems),
- expression, and
- social interactions.

The patient's ability to perform in each of the categories is described in detail to determine the components of therapy, degree of independence, and level of safety. (Frequently used rehabilitation abbreviations appear in Figure 24.1.) The details of these assessments should be looked at closely, and concurrence among disciplines (or lack of concurrence) is essential information. Refer to Chapter 3, *Obtaining and Organizing Medical Records*, in Volume I, for more information about rehabilitation records.

A. Degree of Assistance Needed

Mrs. Green was admitted to a neurological rehabilitation unit following a left side cerebrovascular accident (CVA or stroke). The physical therapy documentation reflected that Mrs. Green required *maximum assistance of two people when transferring from the bed to the wheelchair*. At 10 P.M. on the evening shift, the registered nurse directed the nursing attendant to bring Mrs. Green to the bathroom. The nurse informed the aide that Mrs. Green required a wheelchair to take her to the bathroom and that the *maximum assistance of one person* was sufficient.

The nurse was basing her decision for direction on the documentation of the day shift nurse which described Mrs. Green as requiring the *maximum assistance of one person while transferring*. Mrs. Green lost her balance while the aide was transferring Mrs. Green from the bed to the wheelchair. The aide tried to stop Mrs. Green from falling. In the process, the aide hurt her shoulder. Mrs. Green fell and sustained a right hip fracture.

In reviewing the chart one may feel that the plan was not followed because based on the PT note the patient would need two people to perform a transfer safely. The transfer was done in accordance with the day shift nursing note. In the consideration of patient safety, the majority of healthcare providers reviewing these notes would feel that this patient would not have sustained an injury had the more conservative approach to transfer been taken.

Partial List of Common Abbreviations Used in the Rehabilitation Setting

A/P	anterior to posterior		IPTX	intermittent pelvic traction
AAROM	active assistive range of motion		IR	internal rotation
ABD	abduction		KAFO	knee-ankle-foot orthosis
Abds	abdominals		L/S	lumbar spine
AC	acromioclavicular joint		LB	low back
ACL	anterior cruciate ligament		LBI	low back injury
ADD	aduction		LBP	low back pain
ADL	activities of daily living		LE	lower extremity
AEA	above elbow amputee		Max	maximum
AFO	ankle-foot orthosis		MCL	medial collateral ligament
AKA	above knee amputee		MFR	myofascial release
AMB	ambulated		Mim	minimum
ANK	ankle		Mod	moderate
AROM	active range of motion		MTX	manual traction
ASIS	anterior superior iliac spine		MVA	motor vehicle accident
Asst	assistance		NDT	neurodevelopmental technique
B	both / bilateral		NWB	non-weight bearing
BEA	below elbow amputee		OOB	out of bed
BKA	below knee amputee		P/A	posterior to anterior
C/S	cervical spine		PENS	percutaneous electrical nerve stimulation
CHI	closed head injury		PF	plantar flexion
CP	cold pack		PNF	proprioceptive neuromuscular facilitation
CPM	continuous passive motion		PROM	passive range of motion
CR	axillary crutches		Prox	proximal
CR TR	crutch training		PTX	pelvic traction
CTLSO	cervical-thoracic-lumbar-sacral orthosis		PUW	pick up walker
CTX	cervical traction		PWB	partial weight bearing
CVA	cerebral vascular accident		Q-cane	quad cane
DD	developmentally delayed		Quads	quadriceps muscles
DDD	degenerative disc disease		RA	rheumatoid arthritis
DF	dorsiflexion		RCT	rotator cuff tear
DJD	degenerative joint disease		ROM	range of motion
DME	durable medical equipment		SACH	solid ankle, cushion heel
DTR	deep tendon reflexes		SBA	stand by assistance
DVT	deep venous thrombosis		SCI	spinal cord injury
EMG	electromyography		SEWHO	shoulder-elbow-wrist-hand orthosis
EO	elbow orthosis		SLR	straight leg raise
ER	external rotation		SO	shoulder orthosis
E-Stim	electrical stimulation		SPC	single point cane
Ext	extension		TA	transfer activities / training
FBWP	full body whirlpool		THR	total hip replacement
FIM	functional independence measure		TIA	transient ischemic attack
Flex	flexion		TKR	total knee replacement
FWB	full weight bearing		TTWB	toe touch weight bearing
Fx	fracture		TX	traction
GT	gait training		UE	upper extremity
HP	hot pack		US	ultrasound
I	independent		WC	wheelchair
ICTX	intermittent cervical traction		WNL	within normal limits
IE	initial evaluation		WP	whirlpool

Figure 24.1

Accidents and injuries may occur to both patients and caregivers during patient transfers. Providing the correct level of assistance required is key to accident prevention. The discrepancy in the amount of assistance offered among professional caregivers is a common occurrence for many reasons. Patients' varying levels of fatigue at different times of the day and response to encouragement are two of the major reasons for different assessments. The administration of medication, particularly for pain, is another significant reason for different assessments. Communication and the ultimate agreement among clinicians are paramount in deciding on the one safe and effective care plan for the patient.

B. Functional Assessment

Clinicians use numerous methods and varying detail when documenting function. The following note illustrates the detail of function assessment.

> Ms. Harper was a forty-nine-year-old woman who was admitted to the neurological rehabilitation unit from the head injury unit eleven days after she sustained a subdural cerebral hematoma and multiple lower limb fractures. She understood approximately 80 percent of what was said to her in simple and slow sentences. She required occasional cues with complex information and could not process abstract concepts. Her affect was flat most of the time and improved only when her family visited. She required assistance with verbal communication approximately 25 percent of the time when she appeared to be searching for words. She demonstrated reasonable judgment.
>
> Ms. Harper was able to make her own food choices and could feed herself once her tray was set up for her. (She could open her utensils and condiments and cut her food items). Ms. Harper was able to complete her own grooming activities with minor cuing in the form of reminders. Although she could shower herself, she required supervision for safety. She was able to dress her upper and lower body but required help to have her shoes tied. She was able to ambulate twenty-five feet with supervision due to an unsteady gait when fatigued. She was independent with toileting. Ms. Harper would only initiate interaction with family and required prompting for all other social interaction.

The above note is only part of what could be described about a patient in a rehabilitation setting. Rehabilitation focuses on function and how it can be improved.

> **TIP:** What should be noted on review of documentation is agreement among the clinicians of each discipline and a detailed explanation of why the assessments were not in agreement.

For example, during the PT session, the patient walked to the toilet with minimal assistance of one person, but during the night hours the patient stated she could not get up and wanted to use a bedpan. Many patients are more motivated in a 10 A.M. PT session than at 2 A.M. when they need to go to the bathroom. The discrepancy should be noted and explained. A similar situation occurs when a patient is motivated to dress herself during an OT session but insists that a nurse aide dress her in the morning before breakfast.

C. Complex Rehabilitation Needs Management

The concept of team coordination is central to rehabilitation therapy. The clinicians treating the patient communicate and set collaborative goals. The patient is very much a part of the team and makes substantial contributions to the goal setting process whenever possible. The collaboration should be evident in the chart review. The rounds report document is valuable in that it should be inclusive, timely, and reflective of treatment and response. A typical team rounds report would include information specific to a particular disability. Typically the rounds report is a permanent part of the medical record and serves as the actual functional documentation toward goal achievement.

> Mr. Walker was a twenty-one-year-old college senior who sustained a high cervical spine injury as a result of an accident while riding on an All Terrain Vehicle. Mr. Walker was the passenger. The driver did not sustain any injury. Mr. Walker was awake and alert. He required a ventilator to breathe and had no motor function and sensation from his neck down. Mr. Walker was seen by psychiatry daily and expressed a desire to end his life if he were able to do it. He had supportive parents and a twenty-year-old fiancée who visited regularly. Mr. Walker had an admission to the acute hospital for pneumonia since rehabilitation started. When he returned from the acute hospital, a stage IV sacral decubitus ulcer was noted.

The team rounds report in this case would be reflective of specific issues present with a spinal cord injured patient. Clearly emotional indicators would be documented such as affect, statements of self harm ("refused to speak with fiancée when she visited or patient continues to say that he no longer has a reason to live"). Respiratory status on the ventilator would be described in detail ("remains on continuous mechanical ventilation with acceptable blood gases and clear lungs"). Methods of transfer are significant in terms of safety and the prevention of complications. The transfer for Mr. Walker is passive. (He would not be actively participating in the transfer.) The rounds note would probably reflect that the transfers from the bed to any other surface would be achieved through the use of a mechanical lift. Documentation should be reviewed to identify if the transfer required one or two persons to complete. As previously discussed, accidents may occur on transfer, and safety cannot be overemphasized.

A treatment plan for the decubitus ulcer is imperative. Patients who are not able effectively to shift their body weight will readily sustain skin and tissue breakdown at the pressure points. Spinal cord injured patients are at high risk for skin breakdown. Appropriate measures to prevent prolonged pressure on any one area of the body are required. Mr. Walker has already developed an ulcer. The expectation in this case is that the rounds report and clinician notes reflect assessment of the ulcer (such as size, depth, stage, color, drainage, and effectiveness of the present treatment). (Refer to Chapter 27, *Controversies in Skin Trauma*, for more information about pressure sore documentation.) Since Mr. Walker was paralyzed from the neck down, therapy will be passive to prevent atrophy of the muscles. The therapy input to the rounds report may include information regarding spasticity, which is often an issue for the spinal cord injured patient.

Bowel and bladder function should be addressed from admission and included in the rounds report and clinician notes. Urinary elimination will include methods of catheterization and various measures to assess a healthy bladder (documentation of color of urine, and amount of urine obtained at each catheterization). Bowel elimination is a planned program which includes specific times and particular agents to stimulate evacuation (use of suppositories, enemas, and so on).

Rounds reports will include information regarding short- and long-term goals and patient and significant other teaching in anticipation of discharge. An example of a short-term goal for Mr. Walker is "Patient will be receptive to a discussion of realistic discharge planning." Mr. Walker's emotional needs are a priority as he is a young man with severe life changes. A realistic discussion of life after the hospital is an important step in recovery and not easily achieved. An example of a long-term goal is "Patient will demonstrate an understanding of safety measures regard-

ing infection prevention." Teaching is paramount to aid Mr. Walker in accepting what has happened and what adjustments need to be made to maintain the highest quality of life possible. Refer to Fried and Fried[1] for more information about spinal cord injured patients.

As one may imagine, discharge planning for Mr. Walker will be challenging. A safe placement in a different environment is the responsibility of the discharging institution. Several discharges occur that are not safe in retrospect. A discharge that places an individual in a setting where she may harm herself, be harmed or neglected, or not have her basic needs met is unsafe. Inadequate discharge planning was a factor in this patient's death:

A quadriplegic was placed into an assisted living facility that offered twenty-four-hour attendants. The man was relatively stable upon admission into the program but required intermittent catheterization and bowel elimination assistance. He died in his apartment four days after his placement. The widow and her children sued the disability services agency, the apartment corporation entities, and two nurses for negligence. Among other allegations, the plaintiffs alleged that a nurse was not present on the day of his admittance, and that his admission was approved by a registered nurse by telephone, without any screening or approval physical examination. The plaintiffs also claimed that no written assessment was made of his condition on admission, no nurse assessed him during the four days, and that the program did not have attendants who were trained to perform catheterizations or bowel programs. The plaintiff's pathologist concluded that his death was caused by a severe urinary tract infection acquired from non-sterile and improper catheterizations. The matter settled for $7,500,000.[2]

TIP: Thoughtful and safe discharge planning is the standard of care. Review the details in the chart to determine what arrangements had been made.

Consider what occurred when Mr. Walker was sent home:

Mr. Walker was to be discharged home because his parents were taught how to take care of him. The doorways of the house were widened to accommodate a wheelchair, and a ramp to bypass the front steps of the house was installed. When Mr. Walker arrived home all went well until his parents began suctioning him via a tracheostomy tube. The electrical power then failed. The battery backup on the suctioning machine did not work. The vendor supplying the equipment did not know when the battery was checked. Mr. Walker was put back on the ventilator, which had a three-hour battery backup. The load of the required equipment was not anticipated, and the battery on the suction machine failed. Subsequent to this event, Mr. Walker had to be brought to the local emergency room to be suctioned. He was then returned to the rehabilitation facility and admitted until the issues in the home could be corrected.

D. Complication Recognition

Jackie, twenty-six years old, was admitted to the acute rehabilitation unit which specializes in traumatic brain injury. She was stuporous but could be aroused. Each day she seemed more awake and alert. On the eighth day of her admission, she was able to sit in the chair for long periods of time and follow simple directions. Jackie was clearly making excellent gains in a short period of time. As a result of her progress her prognosis was very good for a full recovery from her head injury.

Jackie's primary nurse on the evening shift went on vacation. One evening when a covering nurse was caring for Jackie, the patient became very aggressive, refused to eat, and seemed restless when returned to bed. The nurse consulted with the house physician who came to see Jackie when it was reported that she seemed to have vomited clear fluid onto the pillow and her blood pressure was 138/84 (her usual blood pressure had been running 110-116/68-74). The physician requested that Jackie be kept NPO (nothing to be taken by mouth) until her attending physician saw her in the morning.

When the night nurse took report at midnight, she was concerned about the information she received about Jackie since she was making steady progress since the first day of her admission. The night nurse immediately went into Jackie's room to do an assessment. Jackie could not be aroused, and her blood pressure was 178/70. The night nurse immediately called Jackie's primary attending neurologist, and Jackie was transferred to the acute hospital emergency room with a diagnosis of increased intracranial pressure and extension of a cerebral bleed. Jackie required emergency neurosurgery. Her condition was questionable postoperatively in that she was still comatose three hours after the surgery.

The clinicians caring for head injury patients require expertise to identify the subtle changes that may indicate a life-threatening condition such as increased intracranial pressure. The changes in the patient's condition are noted in the physician and nurse progress notes, flow sheets reflecting blood pressure, temperature, pulse, respiration, and neurological assessments done at defined intervals. In this case, the nurse did not know what Jackie's norm was and did not seek out the information when she noted what might have been a change in the patient's condition. The physician was not a neurologist and should have consulted the primary attending physician about Jackie's illness. "The failure to treat" resulted in a life-threatening situation with a questionable prognosis.

A ninety-three year old man admitted to a rehabilitation unit required Methadone for back pain. Prior to admission, the patient received Methadone for pain relief. The plaintiff claimed the nurses in the rehabilitation unit administered excessive doses of Methadone. The patient died several days later of aspiration pneumonia. The plaintiff claimed that the actual cause of death was Methadone toxicity, or that a medication error caused or contributed to the aspiration. The defendant claimed that the dose administered was still within the therapeutic range, that there were no clinical symptoms of methadone toxicity noted in the records or lab results and that prior to admission the patient had exhibited aspiration and swallowing difficulties. A $400,000 settlement was achieved.[3]

TIP: Complications of therapy and negative outcomes are a reality in rehabilitation as in other areas of healthcare.

E. Scope of Services

Mr. Sanders was a fifty-four-year-old gentleman admitted to an acute rehabilitation unit following a left below-the-knee amputation. He was a diabetic and had a history of high blood pressure for the last eight years. He was making good progress in therapy. On the fourth night of his admission, Mr. Sanders became very lightheaded and almost passed out. The staff put him in bed, took his vital signs, and called the covering house physician. The nurse was taking an EKG as the physician entered the room. Mr. Sanders was having a cardiac arrhythmia which the physician treated with medication. The patient was transferred to the cardiac rehabilitation unit where he could be placed on constant cardiac monitoring.

At 3 A.M., Mr. Sanders called the nurse saying he did not feel well just as the nurse noted Mr. Sanders was again having arrhythmias. The physician was called. Mr. Sanders' blood pressure was dropping. The physician decided to continue attempting to treat him with cardiac medications. After twenty minutes Mr. Sanders became less alert and short of breath. The physician then decided to call 911 and transfer Mr. Sanders to the acute hospital emergency room. Mr. Sanders was wheezing and needed a chest x-ray and stat blood work. This was not available. Just as the paramedics arrived, Mr. Sanders went into cardiac arrest. CPR was started, and several unsuccessful attempts at intubation were made. Other emergency drugs were given, and Mr. Sanders was defibrillated by the paramedics. Mr. Sanders did not survive the cardiac arrest.

The scope of care is the framework by which a facility operates. Mr. Sanders was placed on the rehabilitation facility's cardiac monitoring equipment as a means of administering emergency treatment for a cardiac arrhythmia, not for monitoring during cardiac rehabilitation therapy sessions. The chart would have contained actual strips of heart rhythm and the clinician's interpretation and action based on those strips. The strips were crucial in deciding on the appropriate course of treatment for a patient. The strips should be coordinated with the clinicians' (physician and nurse) progress notes.

Mr. Sanders should have been transferred to an acute facility that has the support of a twenty-four-hour laboratory, radiology, pharmacy, specialists, and equipment appropriate for his acute (not rehabilitation) needs. Valuable time was lost, and care was compromised.

F. Injury Prevention

Falls, with and without fractures, dislocations, and the development of thrombi and emboli are among the most common injuries. The following case studies reflect some of these issues.

Mr. Bard was a sixty-two-year-old gentleman who was admitted to the acute rehabilitation hospital following a left hip replacement. Mr. Bard was in the physical therapy area. He was climbing four stairs with the physical therapist at his side. He had done this same exercise the previous day without complication. Mr. Bard fell during the activity and complained of slight pain in his left hip. He was examined by the physician who felt the patient could return to therapy after an x-ray of the left hip was done. The rehabilitation physician felt the x-ray was unremarkable, asked that the x-ray be forwarded to the radiologist, and requested that the patient return to therapy. Mr. Bard resumed therapy in time for the one and one-half hour afternoon session. He complained of moderate pain that evening and he was given Percocet with relief. The next morning, Mr. Bard was given Percocet prior to therapy and attended his full morning therapy session. At 12 P.M. Mr. Bard complained of severe pain and the physician was called. The physician contacted the radiologist who interpreted the x-ray as a fracture of the femur below the level of the prosthesis. A second x-ray was taken after Mr. Bard complained of severe pain. The fracture was displaced. Mr. Bard returned to the hospital for an open reduction internal fixation.

The available services in the rehabilitation setting need to be clearly coordinated with the care provided to patients. If the radiologist with the appropriate expertise was not available to read the x-ray at a time proximal to the patient's fall, the patient should not have gone to therapy. Mr. Bard would not have dislocated the fracture if he did not go back to the same therapy regimen after the fall. The first fall probably could not have been prevented, but the dislocation could have been. The documentation of the incident is reflected in the PT progress notes but may also be described on a particular form used to document incidents such as falls. Typically this incident form is not part of the medical record, and the record will not contain reference to this form being completed. A healthcare facility usually does not want this information to become readily available for review.

Mrs. Morton, a sixty-two-year-old woman, was admitted to a rehabilitation hospital after a bilateral knee replacement. She was receiving aspirin 81 milligrams by mouth each morning. The aspirin was originally ordered by her orthopedic surgeon with the intention to have it continued in the rehabilitation hospital to prevent the development of venous thromboembolus. On the third day of admission, Mrs. Morton was being assisted out of bed when she suddenly collapsed. She was noted to be in cardiopulmonary arrest; CPR was initiated and a code was called. All appropriate resuscitative measures were taken. Mrs. Morton did not survive the arrest.

The medical examiner took the case and an autopsy was performed. Mrs. Morton had a confirmed pulmonary embolism which was noted to be the cause of death. When the case was reviewed it was identified that the patient was not being anticoagulated according to evidenced-based guidelines. (The hospital had adopted evidence-based guidelines as a clinical protocol.)

In summary, this patient expired as a result of the facility not following what they have already established to be best practice. Communication among caregivers along the continuum of care is imperative to achieve the desired outcome. The lack of an aspirin order should have been challenged by the "now responsible clinicians" with specific expertise.

24.4 Summary

The core of rehabilitation treatment and care is based on the concept of team. The individual being treated is part of that team. For members of the team to work effectively they need to communicate on levels of progress, treatment plan, safety, and expected outcomes. The medical record should reflect a concurrence of information, and inconsistencies should be noted as significant.

Endnotes

1. Fried, G. and K. Fried. "Spinal Cord Injury" in Iyer, P. (Editor). *Medical Legal Aspects of Pain and Suffering*. Tucson, AZ: Lawyers and Judges Publishing Company, Inc. 2003.

2. Laska, L. "Failure to Properly Attend to Quadriplegic." *Medical Malpractice Verdicts, Settlements, and Experts*. April 2004. 42–43.

3. Laska, L. "Methadone Overdose During Rehabilitation Blamed for Death." *Medical Malpractice Verdicts, Settlements, and Experts*. August 2009, 21.

Chapter 25

Respiratory Care Records

Hilary J. Flanders, MPH, RN-BC, RRT

25.1 Introduction

Respiratory diseases are common in the United States today. They may be acute or chronic in nature, and they "rank among the highest in prevalence, incidence, morbidity and mortality, and resource utilization of all diseases in the United States."[1] Respiratory illnesses may be life-threatening, requiring complex professional medical treatment. This chapter outlines factors contributing to the urgency and intricacy of the diagnosis and treatment of patients who require professional respiratory care. This chapter covers some relevant respiratory concepts, symptoms, diseases, equipment, diagnostic tools, treatments, and documentation guidelines.

A. Anatomy of the Respiratory System

People have two lungs which are situated within the chest cavity. The left lung has two lobes and the right lung has three lobes. Air is inhaled into the lungs and carbon dioxide is exhaled out of the lungs via tubes known as the trachea, the right mainstem bronchus, and the left mainstem bronchus.[2] The pleura are smooth, filmy sheets of tissue. A layer of pleura lines the interior of the chest cavity, and the other coats the exterior of the lung. In the pleural space, between the pleura, a small amount of fluid is secreted. This liquid helps the pleura slide smoothly past one another when the lungs inhale and exhale. The two pleural layers "provide low friction surfaces to enable the lungs to expand and contract easily with as little friction as possible."[3]

When we take a breath, air is inhaled through the mouth or nose, passes through the pharynx and larynx, flows down the trachea, and enters the lungs via a bifurcation that divides into the right and left mainstem bronchi. Further sub-division of the airway occurs, which leads to smaller and smaller branches ending in a tiny sac called the alveolus.[4] Gas exchange takes place at these alveoli—oxygen is taken up by the blood in exchange for carbon dioxide, which is subsequently exhaled. (See Section 25.1.B.) The ribs are bones that keep the wall of the chest rigid. Intercostal mus-cles (between the ribs) move the ribs up and back enabling the lungs to inflate and deflate during inspiration and expira-tion. The primary muscle used for breathing, however, is the diaphragm. The diaphragm moves downward and allows the lungs to fill with air. It moves back in an upward direction when one exhales.[5] See Figure 25.1

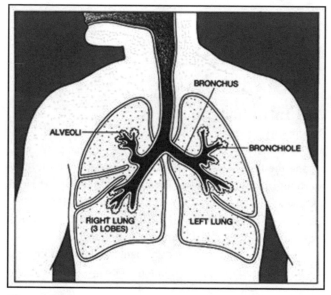

Figure 25.1

The two lungs are physically separated by the medi-astinum. This compartment in the center of the chest holds the heart (and its vasculature), the esophagus, the trachea, the phrenic nerve, the vagus nerve, the thymus gland, and lymph nodes.[6] Intercostal nerves which supply the intercostal muscles "run in a groove underneath the ribs together with the intercostal vein and artery, the vein being uppermost, then the artery, and below that the nerve."[7] The diaphragm is innervated by the phrenic nerve. This nerve runs through the neck along the midline of the chest (the mediastinum) and then spreads out across the diaphragm. Therefore, dam-age to one's mediastinum or neck can be life-threatening, causing diaphragmatic paralysis, which constitutes an acute respiratory emergency.[8]

B. Principles of Gas Exchange and Circulation

Cells (and therefore tissue) within the human body will die if they are not properly oxygenated. The lungs absorb oxygen

from air (which contains 21% oxygen), and excrete carbon dioxide out of the body. This occurs when "carbon dioxide diffuses across the alveolar wall from the respiratory capil-laries into the alveoli and is exhaled."[9] Oxygen is circulated throughout the body via red blood cells. It has an affinity for the hemoglobin within these cells, and readily attaches to it. Oxygenated blood comes from the lungs via the pulmonary veins to the left atrium and ventricle to the aorta. The aorta pumps this oxygen-rich blood to the rest of the body where it is absorbed.

When the body's cells deplete the oxygen from the blood, the blood travels back toward the heart through the peripheral veins. Then, by way of the vena cava and the pul-monary arteries, the deoxygenated blood flows through the right atrium and ventricle, and back out to the lungs. From there, the cycle starts again.[10]

25.2 Types of Patients Who May Require Respiratory Care

Difficulty breathing is considered one of the most frighten-ing experiences a human being can face. People of all ages may encounter respiratory problems at some point in their lives. Examples include tiny neonates who are born prema-turely, children with asthma, adults with lung cancer, and elderly patients with emphysema. At all ages, individuals may experience serious trauma or surgery which interferes with respiratory function. Attorneys may be involved in liti-gating cases involving patients who suffer fractured ribs or crushing chest injuries as a result of a personal injury, for example. A critically ill patient may be placed on a ventila-tor. Additionally, litigation may center on respiratory injury caused by healthcare providers. For example, tube feeding solution may improperly infuse into the lung instead of the stomach; a patient may inhale vomitus; or an anesthesiolo-gist may improperly intubate a patient, resulting in brain damage due to lack of oxygen.

Professionals who provide respiratory care sometimes specialize in the care of patients from one age group. For example, pediatricians only care for children, and geriatri-cians only care for the elderly. However, pulmonologists, emergency physicians and paramedics care for patients of all ages. The next section further discusses the types of pro-fessionals who provide respiratory care in the United States today.

25.3 Professionals Who Provide Respiratory Care in the United States

Physicians, respiratory therapists, nurses, EMTs/paramed-ics and others provide care for respiratory patients. Many of these healthcare professionals have the education and expertise to treat patients with respiratory dysfunction. In most situations, respiratory care is delivered by an interdisciplinary team including several of these provider types.

A. Physicians

Physicians are responsible for diagnosing illnesses as well as prescribing and administering treatment(s) for patients who are sick or injured. Doctors who routinely treat respiratory patients include (but are not limited to) general and family practitioners, general internists, pulmonologists, thoracic surgeons, anesthesiologists, emergency physicians, otolaryngologists, pediatricians, and neonatologists. Some of these physicians have extensive training and experience in meeting the complex needs of respiratory patients, but some do not.

B. Respiratory Therapists

The level of responsibility and the amount of knowledge and expertise necessary to be a respiratory therapist has increased and evolved over the years.[11] Respiratory therapists are part of an interdisciplinary team that cares for respiratory patients. They evaluate and treat patients with respiratory dysfunction under the general supervision of a physician. Evaluation includes taking a patient's history, performing a physical examination, and performing relevant diagnostic testing.

TIP: Treatment(s) may include providing oxygen, aerosolized medications, mechanical ventilation, and even cardiopulmonary resuscitation (CPR).

Regular assessments of their patients are performed, and respiratory equipment is checked and maintained.

The minimal educational requirement for becoming a respiratory therapist is usually an associate's degree, although bachelor's and master's programs also exist. Two levels of certification are available from the National Board of Respiratory Care: Certified Respiratory Therapists (CRTs) are entry level practitioners, and Registered Respiratory Therapists (RRTs) are advanced practitioners.[12] Medical records may contain either of these two designations.

C. Nurses

Registered nurses (RNs) coordinate the care of patients. They establish care plans for individuals with respiratory disease, and evaluate their progress. Tasks that an RN may perform include "administering medication, including careful checking of dosages and avoiding interactions; starting, maintaining, and discontinuing intravenous (IV) lines for fluid, medication, blood, and blood products; administering

therapies and treatments; observing the patient and recording those observations; and consulting with physicians and other health care clinicians."[13] Nurses perform diagnostic testing and participate in the analysis of results. They educate patients about their conditions, and provide support and advice to patients and family members as needed.[14]

RNs are typically educated via diploma, associate's degree, or bachelor's degree programs. Nurses who care for respiratory patients may work in doctor's offices, emergency rooms, medical/surgical floors, operating rooms, intensive care units, home care companies, rehabilitation centers, as well as many other possible locations. While most nurses are prepared to manage most aspects of chronic respiratory care, some have additional specialized training and experience in providing respiratory care in acute or emergency situations.

D. EMTs/Paramedics

EMTs and paramedics are first responders to medical emergencies. They are usually sent to the scene of an emergency via a 911 dispatcher where they frequently assist firefighters and police officers. EMTs and paramedics assess the condition of the patient(s) involved and attempt to determine the cause of the emergency. In addition, any underlying medical problems and/or medications that a patient has taken must be determined if at all possible. Under formal medical protocols and direction, they provide appropriate emergency care while transporting the patient to a medical facility to receive further care. Emergency care, even outside the hospital setting, is provided under the direction of an emergency physician.[15]

EMTs may have any of three levels of certification: "EMT-Basic, EMT-Intermediate, and EMT-Paramedic."[16] Tasks that each level of practitioner is permitted to execute vary by state. It can take 1-2 years of training to achieve the highest level, EMT-Paramedic, and students can receive an associate's degree at this point in many college-based programs. In addition to the academic program, paramedics must have an extensive amount of clinical/field experience and pass a certification examination.[17]

EMTs and paramedics administer oxygen and provide CPR as needed. Paramedics may administer some emergency medications, and may perform endotracheal intubation when a patient cannot breathe.

E. Others

There are other medical professionals who care for respiratory patients. These include (but are not limited to) physical therapists, occupational therapists, recreation therapists, and speech-language pathologists.

TIP: In clinical settings, various technicians and personal care aides also provide hands-on care to respiratory patients under the direction of a physician or nurse.

25.4 Clinical Issues

A. History and Physical

Clinicians caring for respiratory patients are expected to take an accurate patient history, perform a thorough physical exam, and document these processes accurately and completely. In routine situations, the patient's medical chart is reviewed for information regarding the patient's current illness, past medical problems, lifestyle, individual habits, environmental and occupational history.[18] The patient's smoking history is documented in "pack years." A person who smoked 1 pack of cigarettes a day for 20 years would have a 20 pack year history of smoking, as would a patient who smoked two packs a day for 10 years. Obviously, in emergency situations, such information may not be available.

If possible, the patient should be interviewed. The patient's identity should be verified. The reason for seeking medical care and the history of the current illness should be confirmed and documented. Changes in orientation level, cough (including type and amount of sputum), changes in breathing pattern, and any type of chest pain should be described. In some circumstances, a family member may provide this information, and the clinician would record the source of the information.[19]

During the physical exam, the respiratory clinician inspects, palpates (feels with hands), percusses (taps over the skin's surface to assess internal structures), and auscultates (listens to, usually with a stethoscope) the patient. Abnormal findings would be recorded, including adventitious breath sounds (such as crackles or wheezes), asymmetrical chest expansion, accessory muscle use (use of additional muscles to help with inspiratory and expiratory efforts), lower extremity edema, distention of the jugular vein, cyanosis (bluish tissue discoloration), and clubbing (enlargement of the tips of the digits).[20]

Vital signs, including temperature, heart rate, blood pressure, respiratory rate, and oxygen saturation, are taken and recorded. Appropriate laboratory work, imaging studies, and pulmonary function testing should be ordered and when available, documented and reviewed.[21]

B. Common Symptoms/Chief Complaints

The respiratory clinician is responsible for assessing patients thoroughly and documenting findings carefully. The following are key symptoms to be noted as part of the formal history and physical evaluation for each patient.

1. Cough

Coughing is a protective response that guards against aspiration, and/or a way to clear secretions in the lungs (i.e., sputum). Coughing is often the first symptom seen in asthma, postnasal drip, pneumonia, bronchitis, lung cancer and tuberculosis.[22]

A patient's cough "should, at least initially, be described as to severity, length, frequency, inciting factors (if known), relationships to body position, smoking, known allergens or other inciting factors, past attempts (successful or not successful) at therapy, and type and volume of sputum production."[23] Sputum characteristics are often indicative of particular diagnoses.

In addition, the time of day that the cough occurs, and whether the patient experiences pain with the cough, are significant.[24] It would be appropriate for a respiratory clinician to take a detailed history, examine the chest, take a chest x-ray, and measure the function of the lungs. (See Section 25.6.E.)[25]

An Illinois plaintiff alleged the decedent, age sixty-three, went to an internist many times for complaints of coughing. Seasonal allergies were diagnosed and over-the-counter medication was recommended. In 2000, after the decedent coughed up blood, she complained to the internist she felt tired and suffered from body aches and shortness of breath. The internist recommended a stress test, which was normal, and then began treating the patient for asthma. Her symptoms worsened. In 2002, she went to an emergency room and underwent a chest x-ray, which revealed Stage IV lung cancer with metastasis. She died of her disease; the plaintiff alleged a delay in diagnosis of lung cancer. A $1.05 million settlement was reached.[26]

2. Hemoptysis

Hemoptysis is coughing up blood. Common diagnoses associated with this symptom include tuberculosis, lung cancer, pulmonary emboli, bronchiectasis, pneumonia, and acute tracheobronchitis, although sometimes there is no overt explanation for it.[27, 28] Sputum that is streaked with blood should be sent to the laboratory and tested for tuberculosis, other infection, and neoplastic cells.[29]

3. Chest pain

There are several types of chest pain that a patient can experience. The first is angina pectoris, which is chest pain or tightness generated from ischemia (reduced blood flow) to the coronary arteries. Radiation of the pain to the shoulders, neck and left arm often occurs. If the pain cannot be relieved by rest and is accompanied by sweating, nausea and vomiting, this strongly suggests that the patient is having a myocardial infarction (heart attack).[30]

Pleuritic chest pain, or pleurisy, is caused when the pleura become inflamed and rub against one another. The resulting pain "is often sharp, gnawing, nonradiating, localized, and worsened by deep breathing or coughing."[31] Pleurisy is commonly found with pneumonia, as well as other pulmonary disorders.[32]

In cases of chest wall pain, the chest itself hurts, and can be palpated from the exterior of the chest. Possible causes include rib fractures, costochondritis (inflammation of the cartilage of the ribcage), and herpes zoster (shingles).[33]

TIP: It is important to determine the cause of chest pain. If the pain is related to cardiac function, this could be an emergency situation.

When a patient has chest pain, the clinician should take vital signs (temperature, heart rate, blood pressure, respiratory rate, and oxygen saturation, if possible), listen to the lungs and heart, and look for swelling of the ankles (which might indicate heart, liver, or renal failure). If cardiac problems are known or suspected, a resting EKG should be done, and a cardiac stress test should be considered. A chest x-ray may be warranted, particularly if the patient is having pleuritic chest pain and feeling ill. If the x-ray is within normal limits and it is suspected that the patient has a pulmonary embolus (a sudden blockage in an artery of the lung), then further imaging techniques (such as a CT scan) will be necessary to know how to proceed with care.[34]

4. Dyspnea

Dyspnea is defined as "air hunger resulting in labored or difficult breathing, normal when caused by vigorous work or athletic activity."[35] There are many possible pulmonary and cardiac reasons for this shortness of breath.[36]

An Ohio woman with a history of right leg pain and shortness of breath was diagnosed with possible pulmonary embolism, pneumonia or fluid overload. She was sent to the hospital and admitted. The physician ordered STAT blood work and diagnostic testing, but there was a delay in treatment. The patient died. No autopsy was initially done, but the body was later exhumed. The cause of death was a saddle pulmonary embolism. The decedent's sister worked in the defendant's office and obtained a copy of the records without the knowledge of the defendant. After suit was filed, the defendant's records were provided during discovery; they differed from the original which had been given to the sister. The defendant had added that on the second office visit he tested for a Homan's sign and also tested for calf tenderness, both of which alleged tests were negative. These entries were added after the death and at least six weeks after the office visit. The defendant also made alterations to the first office visit records as well as the hospital records. The defendant denied liability. A $5.85 million settlement was reached.[37]

The clinician should take a detailed history of the patient with unexplained dyspnea. In addition, the clinician should evaluate that patient's lungs and heart, assess vital signs, and look for swelling of the ankles. Pulmonary function tests may also be helpful in the diagnostic process. Other useful tests may include a chest x-ray, EKG and echocardiogram (a type of cardiac ultrasound), oximetry, blood tests, and a CT scan.[38]

Dyspnea can be associated with abnormal breath sounds, such as stridor and wheezes. Stridor may occur if a patient's upper airways become obstructed. Stridor is usually characterized by a loud, high-pitched inspiratory noise that is often audible without a stethoscope. Stridor may occur with laryngeal edema (swelling), cancer of the bronchus, or tracheal stenosis (narrowing of the trachea).[39]

Wheezes are high-pitched, musical noises that are typically more evident during the expiratory phase. They occur when airways narrow and the patient's airflow becomes turbulent. Wheezing is common in chronic bronchitis, asthma, and left-sided heart failure.[40]

C. Common Lung Conditions/Complications and Management Techniques

1. Pneumothorax

Pneumothorax is the collapse of a lung, either partially or completely, because of the escape of air into the space between the pleura, which deflates the lung. It is often abbreviated as PTX. It can occur from a variety of causes including trauma, insertion of central (venous) lines, chest compressions, mechanical ventilation, cystic fibrosis, asthma, and lung biopsies. Occasionally, it happens spontaneously.[41]

The affected patient is short of breath and has chest pain on the side of the chest where the pneumothorax has occurred. The respiratory clinician would find the patient's breath sounds to be diminished, and observe decreased chest movement, on the affected side. With percussion (a tapping technique used by clinicians), a hyperresonant note (loud and low-pitched) may also be present. A pneumothorax can be definitively diagnosed by a chest x-ray.[42]

A chest tube was inserted into a New York woman with a pneumothorax 13 hours after her condition was diagnosed. The procedure caused episodes of oxygen desaturation. The plaintiff subsequently underwent two other re-inflation procedures. Several days later she was awakened from a medically induced coma; she was blind. Plaintiffs alleged the blindness was caused by a failure to timely treat the pneumothorax. A $9.1 million settlement was achieved.[43]

Small pneumothoraces may resolve on their own. Current medical literature indicates that patients with small pneumothoraces should still be observed in the hospital. Patients with larger pneumothoraces should have a chest tube inserted to reinflate the lung.[44] Very specific guidelines exist for physicians and nurse practitioners who insert chest tubes. Failure to insert the tube properly can jeopardize the patient. Errors can be made by inexperienced clinicians and/or improper technique(s) that result in the chest tube being inserted into the wrong space.[45]

2. Pleural effusion

A pleural effusion is the accumulation of fluid between the pleura. This fluid may consist of transudate (extravascular fluid), pus from an infection, blood, or chyle (lymphatic fluid). Circulatory and inflammatory disorders are typically the causes. Examples include trauma, infection, or malignancy.[46]

Clinicians may establish the likelihood of this problem by taking a history, doing a physical examination, and analyzing imaging studies. Confirmation of the presence of a pleural effusion can be made by thoracentesis (a needle puncture into the pleural space to drain fluid). Appropriate treatments include performing a thoracentesis, inserting a chest tube, resolving the underlying disorder, or allowing the fluid to absorb back into the lymph vessels.[47]

25.5 Respiratory Equipment and Medications
A. Oxygen Therapy

Oxygen therapy is necessary when there is evidence or suspicion of acute hypoxemia (low level of oxygen in the blood). Increasing the amount of oxygen in the alveoli can help diffuse more oxygen into the circulatory system.[48] Oxygen therapy is intended to alleviate hypoxemia by increasing tension in the alveoli and increasing the oxygen being transferred to the blood. This relieves labored breathing, and decreases the stress on the heart muscle.[49]

Symptoms of hypoxemia include elevated heart and/or respiratory rate, increased depth of breathing, diaphoresis (sweating), accessory muscle use, cyanosis (blue/gray discoloration of tissue), and/or mental confusion. Depending on the underlying cause of hypoxemia, the clinician will need to choose the appropriate amount of oxygen to administer, and titrate as needed.[50] See Figure 25.2.

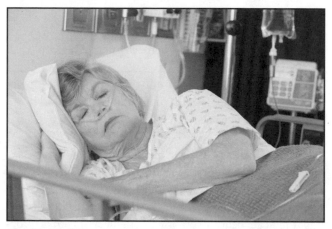

Figure 25.2

Nasal cannulae are plastic tubes that are attached to an oxygen source. They have two prongs that rest in the nostrils, and are capable of delivering supplemental oxygen concentrations of up to approximately 40% (depending on the flow rate of oxygen and ventilatory pattern). The medical record often contains the abbreviation NC for nasal cannula. Most patients tolerate this therapy well and find it reasonably comfortable.[51]

However, there are risks of scarring with the use of cannulae.

A California infant was awarded $385,000 after he underwent several plastic surgeries to correct scarring from a nasal cannula. The plaintiffs alleged the staff at the hospital at which he was born taped the tubing of the nasal cannula on his face too tightly, causing severe pressure necrosis.[52]

Simple masks are made of plastic and are placed over the patient's nose and mouth. A tube at the bottom of the mask is attached to an oxygen source. This mask can provide oxygen concentrations of approximately 55%.[53] Patients often find oxygen masks to be uncomfortable, and they can interfere with dietary intake.[54]

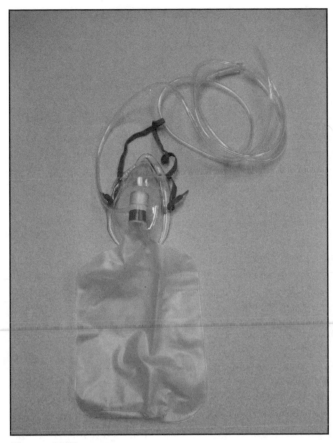

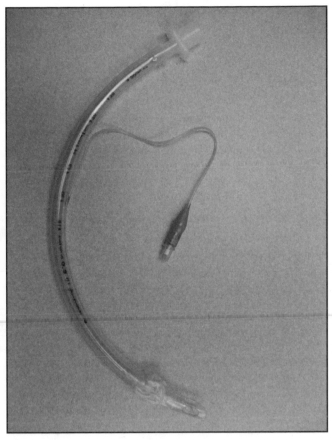

Figure 25.3   *Figure 25.4*

Venturi masks provide the patient with various oxygen concentrations. They can deliver oxygen concentrations from 24-50%, depending on how the clinician adjusts the device. They are also made of plastic and go over the patient's nose and mouth.[55]

Partial rebreather and nonrebreather masks provide higher concentrations of oxygen, and are needed for patients with more severe hypoxemia. Partial rebreathers can provide less than or equal to 60%, and nonrebreathers provide approximately 100% oxygen. There are other oxygen therapy devices that can provide 100% oxygen, such as mechanical ventilators and tracheostomy masks.[56]

The medical record often contains abbreviations for these pieces of equipment. For example, a partial rebreather mask is often charted as PRB, and a nonrebreather mask as NRB. Refer to Figure 25.3.

Risks associated with oxygen therapy include oxygen toxicity, hypoventilation in patients with Chronic Obstructive Pulmonary Disease (see Section 25.7), constriction of the vasculature in the lungs and kidneys, development of retrolental fibroplasia (fibrous tissue behind the lenses of the eyes), and flammability of the gas itself. Fires in the operating room may be associated with the use of oxygen

and a spark from electrocautery. Clinicians should use only as much oxygen as the patient needs, and should monitor oxygen saturations and arterial blood gases to titrate oxygen appropriately. (See Section 25.6.) COPD patients on oxygen should be monitored closely. In addition, patients on oxygen should not smoke, as this may start a fire.[57]

B. Artificial Airways and Airway Management
1. Endotracheal Tube

If a patient is in respiratory failure, medical professionals (i.e., physicians, paramedics, some respiratory therapists, nurse anesthetists, and some advanced practice nurses) are qualified to perform endotracheal intubation to prevent damage from hypoxia (a situation where the body does not have enough oxygen).[58] An endotracheal tube (ETT) is usually made of malleable plastic. It is passed into the trachea via the mouth or nose utilizing specialized tools (such as laryngoscope and Magill forceps). Refer to Figure 25.4.

The patient can be ventilated and oxygenated via this ETT. The size of the tube is determined by the size, weight, gender and anatomy of the patient. The patient will be unable to speak because the ETT goes through the vocal cords. The steps of this invasive procedure include pre-oxygenating the patient with 100% oxygen, administering a sedative and a paralyzing drug, applying pressure to the cricoid area on the neck (to prevent the tube from entering the esophagus, as well as to prevent vomiting and aspiration into the lungs), inserting the ETT, and confirming placement of the tube.[59] Proper tube placement is indicated by observing bilateral chest excursion, listening with a stethoscope for bilateral breath sounds, using a CO_2 detector to make sure that this gas is being exhaled, and checking for oximetry readings between 98% and 100%. (See Section 25.6.D.) In addition, the clinician should listen over the stomach with a stethoscope to make sure that no air flow noises are evident. Definitive confirmation of tube placement is made by a chest x-ray.[60]

There are many possible complications from this procedure. During endotracheal intubation, there can be physical trauma to the tissue, perforation of the airway, injury to the spinal cord, spasms of the bronchi and bronchioles, spasms of the larynx, hemodynamic instability, increased intraocular or intracranial pressure, improper esophageal intubation as well as many other possible problems. After the ETT is confirmed to be in the proper place, the patient may have issues with airway obstruction, mucous plugs, aspiration of fluid into the lungs, pneumothorax, dislodgement, or disconnection of the tube. When the patient is extubated (the ETT is removed), laryngeal swelling, aspiration of fluid from the mouth or stomach, or cuff malfunction may occur. After extubation, the patient may experience additional difficulties. These may include, but are not limited to, hoarseness, laryngeal swelling, throat pain, vocal cord dysfunction, tracheal stenosis (narrowing of the trachea), tracheomalacia (tracheal collapse), and nerve injury.[61]

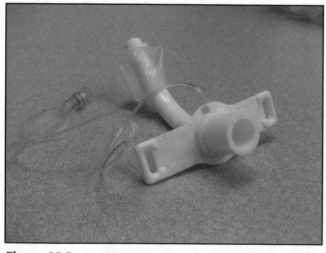

Figure 25.5

2. Tracheostomy tube

A tracheostomy involves an artificial airway surgically placed in the trachea. This artificial airway, called a tracheostomy tube, is made of hard plastic or metal, and comes in various shapes and sizes. Some have cuffs and some do not. Note Figure 25.5.

A tracheostomy is indicated when long-term airway management becomes necessary. For instance, it may be required if a patient is in a coma or needs to be on a ventilator for an extended period of time. Additional indications might be to circumvent a blockage of the upper airway, to improve pulmonary toilet (the removal of phlegm), and to reduce the risk of aspirating oral secretions or stomach contents into the lungs.[62]

Traditionally, tracheostomies have been performed in the operating room, but they may also be inserted percutaneously (through the skin) as a bedside procedure. If possible, the procedure should be discussed with the patient and/or family preoperatively. Therefore, consent can be given, and questions and concerns can be addressed.[63]

TIP: After the tracheostomy tube is placed, the patient should be closely monitored for increased respiratory secretions, oxygen saturation, work of breathing, and cyanosis (a blue hue to the skin that is a result of hypoxia). Vital signs, anxiety level, condition of the surgical site, and signs and symptoms of infection should also be assessed.[64]

Clinicians should be on the lookout for a large amount of bleeding, or persistent oozing of blood after a tracheostomy. A little bleeding postoperatively is considered normal. Bleeding may indicate that a blood vessel is damaged and needs further attention from a surgeon. If an artery is involved, this problem can be deadly.[65]

To prevent obstruction, healthcare providers need to suction a tracheostomy tube when the patient cannot clear secretions. (See Section 25.5.B.4.) In addition, the air that the patient breathes through the tube should be warmed and humidified, and the patient should be properly hydrated.[66]

The tracheostomy tube may become dislodged inadvertently. If this happens within one or two days postoperatively, it is considered an emergency because the surgical tract has not matured. The complete formation of this tract takes approximately five to seven days, and surgical sutures should stay in place at least this long. Accidental dislodgement of the tube may occur via a forceful cough, excessive or careless handling of the tube (by the clinician or the patient), or suctioning.[67]

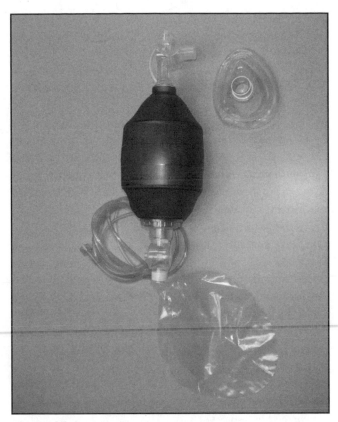

Figure 25.6

Methods of preventing dislodgement include the proper use of cloth ties that secure the tube, and patient/family education about tracheostomy care. If the patient is depressed, anxious, or agitated, then the need for medications for these conditions should be evaluated.[68]

Occasionally, subcutaneous emphysema may occur when a tracheostomy tube is placed. This is caused by air that is inadvertently introduced into the tissue in the neck and/or chest. It bulges the skin, and produces crepitus (an odd, crackling sound and sensation) with palpation. Subcutaneous emphysema is often disturbing to the patient and visitors.[69]

Further complications include tracheal stenosis and tracheomalacia. In addition, a tracheoesophageal fistula could occur from excessive cuff pressure (greater than 25 cm H_2O). This fistula is a communication between the esophagus and the trachea that is a result of tracheal erosion. It causes air to go into the stomach, which predisposes that patient for aspiration of stomach contents, which can cause a pneumonia. The cuff pressure(s) should be assessed per the institution's policy to prevent significant damage to the airway. This is a task that is usually performed by the respiratory therapist.[70]

A speaking valve (made by the Passy-Muir company, and often abbreviated in medical charts as PMV) can be fitted to a tracheostomy tube in order to enable audible speech.

Regaining the ability to speak is often an important part of recovery for patients with tracheostomies, but PMVs can be dangerous for patients who are severely unstable, unconscious, have significant airway obstruction, have copious secretions, are at a high risk for aspiration, or cannot tolerate deflation of the cuff.[71]

3. Purpose of bag valve mask

The bag valve mask (or "Ambu" bag) is used during resuscitation of patients with nonexistent or inadequate respirations. It is attached to a source of 100% oxygen, and applied to the patient's airway. If the patient has an ETT or a tracheostomy tube in place, the bag is attached directly to the artificial airway and squeezed repeatedly to ventilate the patient. If the patient has no artificial airway, then a face mask is attached to the bag and placed over the patient's nose and mouth. Two clinicians may need to perform this task jointly to get an adequate seal when the bag is squeezed. Patients with artificial airways that require extended support will need to transition to mechanical ventilation as soon as possible. See Figure 25.6.

4. Guidelines for endotracheal suctioning

When a patient with an artificial airway has secretions that cannot be expectorated (coughed up), the healthcare professional may need to perform endotracheal suctioning. Guidelines for this invasive procedure include: pre-oxygenating with 100% oxygen for more than thirty seconds, hyperventilating by bag valve mask or ventilator (optional), and utilizing pulse oximetry (in the hospital setting). Actual suctioning occurs when the suction catheter is inserted into the patient's trachea and negative pressure is applied as the catheter is pulled out of the airway. Sterile technique should be used by the clinician.[72]

The amount of negative pressure should be the lowest that effectively removes the secretions. Each suctioning pass should not exceed 15 seconds. After patients are suctioned, they should again receive 100% oxygen, this time for a minute or longer. They may also be hyperventilated. The clinician should monitor the patient for negative reactions to the intervention, and repeat as often as needed to maintain a patent airway.[73]

Possible complications associated with endotracheal suctioning include respiratory arrest, cardiac arrest, hemodynamic instability, increased intracranial pressure, pulmonary bleeding or hemorrhaging, infection, atelectasis (deflation of the alveoli), hypoxia, and constriction of the airways. Blood-tinged secretions documented in medical records are sometimes associated with tissue damage from suction-related trauma. Despite these hazards, there are very few contraindications, as a patent airway is necessary for survival.[74]

C. Mechanical Ventilation
1. General principles

Mechanical ventilators are used in acute care hospitals, rehabilitation hospitals, and long-term and home care settings.[75] Acute goals of providing mechanical ventilation include improving gas exchange in critically ill patients, as well as easing labored respirations. Examples of patients who would require the use of a ventilator might be those in respiratory failure, those with neurological dysfunction, or those who are comatose. Mechanical ventilation can be categorized into invasive and noninvasive.[76]

A District of Columbia case involved a twenty-seven year-old quadriplegic who required the use of a ventilator at night. He was arrested for possession of marijuana and placed in jail. The medical staff at the jail did not provide a ventilator for him. On his first day in jail he suffered a respiratory crisis and was taken to the hospital, where he was seen by Dr. William Vaughn. He initially planned to admit the patient and place him on a ventilator, but after speaking with the medical staff at the jail, he was released back there with a prescription for oxygen by nasal canula. On the fourth day, the patient suffered another respiratory crisis and was returned to the hospital. This time he was seen by Dr. Rotimi Ilyomade. Despite a PCO[2] reading of 56, he was not placed on a ventilator. He gradually declined and died five hours later. None of the defendants seriously alleged the death was from any cause not related to negligence. All defendants paid a total of $4.6 million.[77]

Classic, invasive mechanical ventilators push air into the lungs via an artificial airway to facilitate breathing. Positive pressure techniques are divided into volume-control and pressure-control modes. Volume-control modes provide an exact volume with each breath, but the pressures exerted on the lungs may vary. Pressure-control modes provide an exact pressure, but the volumes are variable.[78]

Complications of conventional mechanical ventilation include injury to the alveoli from barotrauma (damage from high pressures) and volutrauma (damage from large volumes). In addition, it may cause a patient to have a pneumothorax, arrhythmias, decreased perfusion (blood flow) in the kidneys, or reduced urine production.[79]

Noninvasive mechanical ventilation utilizes either positive pressure or negative pressure. In noninvasive positive pressure ventilation (NPPV), air is introduced via a full face mask, nasal mask, or plastic mouthpiece to apply pressure to the airway. This modality is used for the same purpose as conventional mechanical ventilation. However, patients who are reluctant to be intubated may opt for ventilators that provide NPPV.[80]

Complications of NPPV may include necrotic areas on the face from chafing of the mask, aspiration, distention of the stomach, dry mucous membranes, eye infections, and lack of ability to remove secretions effectively. A properly fitting mask is essential when using NPPV to prevent air leakage and protect against skin damage and eye damage.[81]

Noninvasive negative pressure techniques physically manipulate the outside of the chest to improve ventilation. They are useful for patients with chronic respiratory or neuromuscular conditions. Negative pressure can help correct elevated hypercapnia (elevated CO_2 levels in the blood) and hypoxemia, and reduce the incidence of respiratory failure. Examples of devices that provide noninvasive mechanical ventilation include the iron lung, the chest cuirass, and the poncho. These devices can be problematic if the patient has claustrophobia, if the patient cannot stay supine, or if the airway becomes obstructed. In addition, if the patient's abdomen or chest are covered (as with the chest cuirass), clinicians do not have direct access to the patient for assessment and treatment purposes.[82]

Clinicians should be extremely careful with the use of sedation in patients on any noninvasive ventilator. The risks associated with oversedation (aspiration, low blood pressure, and inadequate breathing) need to be weighed against the risks of anxiety and ventilator asynchrony.[83]

2. Ventilator modes and settings

Most patients who require traditional, invasive mechanical ventilation receive assist-control (A/C), intermittent mandatory ventilation (IMV), and/or pressure-support ventilation (PSV).[84] In assist-control, the ventilator delivers a set volume or pressure at an established frequency and flow rate. The patients are able to initiate extra breaths as needed, but they remain at the same volume or pressure no matter how many are triggered.[85]

IMV features a fixed frequency of breaths along with a set volume or pressure, but the patient is allowed to have spontaneous respirations between mandatory ventilator breaths.[86] This mode is usually synchronized (SIMV) to prevent disruption of the patient's own breathing effort.[87]

PSV is indicated when a low level of pressure is needed to enhance each spontaneous respiration. The pressure level selected depends on the patient's respiratory rate.[88] The patient is essentially breathing on his own; however the ventilator provides a boost to the patient's inspiratory phase. This mode is contraindicated if spontaneous respirations are inadequate or absent.[89]

Another common mode of ventilation is continuous positive airway pressure (CPAP). In this mode, positive end expiratory pressure (PEEP) is applied continuously to increase pressure on the airways and alveoli, but additional ventilatory support is not provided. Clearly, this mode is also not appropriate if the patient's spontaneous respiratory effort is poor.[90]

Common ventilator settings include the respiratory rate, tidal volume, minute volume, inspiratory flow rate, sensitivity, PEEP, and oxygen concentration. Audible alarms are set on the ventilator to warn clinicians of issues like apnea (lack of breathing), high pressure, and a disconnected ventilator. Consult Table 25.1.

Frequently, new methods of ventilation become available. Manufacturers of mechanical ventilators come up with different acronyms for these modes, but they employ the same basic principles as earlier positive pressure modes.[91]

Occasionally, the patient will fight or "buck" the ventilator, which is usually caused by "a mismatch between the patient and ventilator inspiratory and expiratory times."[92] It is often distressful for the patient, and may prolong the amount of time that mechanical ventilation is required.[93] Choosing the correct ventilator modes and settings, the right amount of sedation, and an appropriate pain control regimen should reduce the incidence or severity of this problem.

D. Respiratory Medications
1. Bronchodilators

Bronchodilators are medications that help relieve bronchoconstriction (narrowing of the airway). Categories of bronchodilator medications include beta-adrenergic agonists, anticholinergics, and methylxanthine derivatives.[94]

a. Beta-adrenergic agonists

One class of bronchodilators, the beta-adrenergic agonists, functions by relaxing the smooth muscles of the small airways. The short acting Beta2-agonists, such as albuterol or levalbuterol, are considered rescue medications for asthmatics. Patients with COPD (see Section 25.7) are usually prescribed a more routine maintenance schedule for these drugs.[95] Asthmatics that use their rescue medication more often than twice per week should have a steroid added to their regimen.[96]

Long acting Beta2-agonists, such as formoterol or salmeterol, are used as maintenance medications for COPD and asthma patients. They are also prescribed for individuals who have exercise-induced asthma or nocturnal asthma. These medications should not be confused with rescue therapy drugs, and a rescue inhaler should also be prescribed.[97]

Possible side effects of Beta2-agonist bronchodilators include palpitations, tachycardia (rapid heart rate), anxiety, and tremors. Allergic reactions to inhaled aerosols have been reported among people who have sensitivity to peanuts or soybeans.[98]

b. Anticholinergics

Another class of bronchodilators is the anticholinergic class. They function by reducing the secretion of mucus and relaxing the smooth muscles, particularly in the large airways. The short-acting anticholinergic medication, ipratropium bromide, is also considered a rescue inhaler. However, its effect occurs in about fifteen minutes rather than just minutes required for Beta2-agonists. Albuterol and ipratropium bromide are frequently given together to maximize the bronchodilator effect.[99]

Table 25.1
Examples of Common Ventilator Settings with Definitions

Setting	Definition
Respiratory Rate	# of breaths provided by a ventilator in 1 minute
Tidal Volume	Amount (volume) of gas a ventilator provides in a single breath
Minute Volume	Respiratory Rate x Tidal Volume
Inspiratory Flow Rate	Rate or speed that gas is pushed through the ventilator circuit into the lungs
Sensitivity	Amount of inspiratory force necessary for the patient to trigger a breath from the ventilator
PEEP	Positive end expiratory pressure (helps improve gas exchange by maintaining pressure continuously in the airway and keeping alveoli open)
Fractional Inspired Oxygen (FIO$_2$)	Percent oxygen provided by the ventilator (21%-100%)

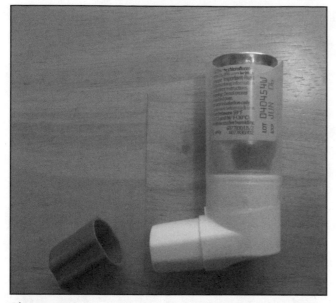

Figure 25.7

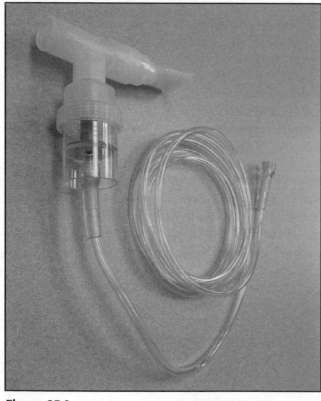

Figure 25.8

Long-acting anticholinergics, such as tiotropium, are used for maintenance of COPD patients with the expectation of reducing exercise intolerance over time. Again, a rescue inhaler should also be prescribed for the patient to provide prompt relief if needed. Possible side effects of anticholiner-

gics include nervousness, dry mouth, cough, and unpleasant taste.[100]

Inhaled medications must be delivered correctly to be effective. Clinicians are responsible for instructing patients how to use their metered dose inhalers or nebulizers properly and for monitoring their compliance over time.[101] Figure 25.7 and Figure 25.8 provide more details.

c. Methylxanthine derivatives

Theophylline is not used very much in current practice. This medication (which comes in the oral or IV form) can have more serious side effects than other bronchodilators, including seizures and death. It has many food and drug interactions, and blood levels need to be monitored closely.[102]

2. Anti-inflammatory medications
a. Steroids

TIP: Corticosteroids are the most powerful anti-inflammatory medications available today.[103] Steroids are frequently administered via the intravenous (iv), oral, inhaled, or nasal routes.

---

3. Intravenous (IV) and oral

IV and oral steroids can be used to battle inflammatory respiratory conditions like asthma. Examples include hydrocortisone and methylprednisolone. These medications are not designed to be used for long periods of time, and need to be tapered down slowly.[104, 105]

Possible side effects of IV and oral steroid use depend on the dose and duration of use. They include high blood sugar, impaired healing, fluid retention, mood swings, electrolyte imbalances, osteoporosis, headache, blurred vision, and eye problems. If oral steroids are rapidly withdrawn, an insufficiency of the adrenal gland may occur. Symptoms of this insufficiency include fever, nausea, dyspnea, joint soreness, fatigue, muscle weakness, anorexia, dizziness, and fainting.[106]

4. Inhaled

Inhaled steroids can be used for ongoing treatment of inflammatory respiratory conditions. Examples include beclamethasone, budesonide, fluticasone, flunisolide, and triamcinolone.[107]

Since they are inhaled and not taken orally, any side effects experienced are localized. Possible side effects include coughing, hoarseness, and oral yeast infections. The patient should be advised to rinse the mouth after using these products to prevent or reduce these effects.[108]

5. Nasal

Like inhaled steroids, some of the same steroids may be used nasally for ongoing treatment, and side effects are not typically systemic. Side effects may include headache, epitaxis (nosebleeds), dryness and nasal irritation.[109]

b. Leukotriene D4 receptor antagonists

Leukotrienes cause bronchoconstriction, and can also trigger inflammation and edema. Zafirlukast and montelukast block leukotrienes. They are used to control symptoms of persistent severe asthma, or to help wean the dose of oral corticosteroids. Montelukast can also be used to treat allergic rhinitis (irritation of the nasal passages) or sinusitis.[110]

Gastrointestinal discomfort and dizziness are possible side effects of Leukotriene D4 Receptor Antagonists. In addition, these medications can elevate the enzymes of the liver, so liver function tests should be performed regularly. This drug is not effective for emergency use.[111]

c. Mast cell stabilizers

These medications (cromolyn sodium and nedocromil sodium) are used to prevent bronchoconstriction when used prior to contact with an identified trigger. The inflammatory responses from allergens and exercise are inhibited by these inhaled medications. Possible side effects include nasal irritation, and a foul taste in the mouth. This medication may be taken on a regular schedule for mild asthma, or twenty to thirty minutes prior to exercise for those with exercise-induced asthma.[112]

6. Antibiotics

Antibiotics are commonly used to treat respiratory infections. They may be administered via the oral, inhaled, or IV route.[113] Amoxicillin and Vancomycin are examples.

Possible side effects of antibiotics are skin rashes, nausea, vomiting, diarrhea, as well as allergic responses. Vaginal or oral candidiasis (yeast infection) may occur when a patient is on antibiotic treatment. Severe, persistent diarrhea from *Clostridium difficile* may be caused by antibiotic therapy.[114]

The misuse and overuse of antibiotics promotes drug-resistant bacteria. Improper use of these medications may include treating infections that are not caused by bacteria, using too many antibiotics simultaneously, failing to change from IV to oral medication when appropriate, failing to take an accurate history of the patient's allergies, and failing to anticipate possible drug-drug interactions.[115]

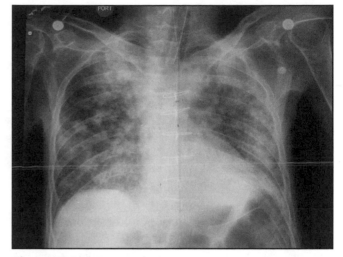

Figure 25.9

25.6 Diagnostic Tests
A. Imaging Studies

Imaging studies that are commonly used in respiratory care include the chest x-ray, the CT scan of the chest, and the MRI of the chest. Please see Chapter 10, *Diagnostic Testing*, for details about these diagnostic tests. Proper interpretation and handling of films is essential. See Figure 25.9.

A Massachusetts case involved a patient who had a thirty-year history of smoking. In 2001, he went to the defendant, a family physician, with respiratory complaints. A nodule in the upper lobe of the lung was seen on CT scan. The defendant misplaced the results of the scan and the patient was not informed of the findings. The next year the patient developed pneumonia. During treatment of his pneumonia, x-rays revealed changes in the lower lymph areas. Another CT scan was not performed until December 2003. This revealed a mass in the right lobe. The patient was then diagnosed with stage IV lung cancer; he died five months later. The plaintiff claimed the defendant was negligent in failing to inform the decedent of the result of the 2001 CT scan and in failing to advise the decedent to follow up within three months of that scan. The plaintiff claimed that an earlier diagnosis would have resulted in a better prognosis. The defendant claimed that an earlier diagnosis would not have changed the outcome. A $650,000 settlement was reached.[116]

B. Bronchoscopy

Physicians use bronchoscopes for diagnostic and therapeutic purposes. They are manufactured in a rigid model, and also in a bendable fiber-optic design. This tool allows the clinician to visualize the airways for irregularities, to biopsy tissue from suspicious lesions, to aspirate sputum to send for microbiological analysis, and to visualize the larynx. In addition, bronchoscopy can be used to clear tenacious secretions, to remove foreign materials from the tracheobronchial tree, and to staunch bleeding in the bronchi.[117]

The first step in the procedure is to topically anesthetize the back of the patient's throat. Then, the bronchoscope is advanced through the mouth or nose (or artificial airway) and into the lower airways via the trachea. If necessary, bronchial washings can be collected and/or lung tissue can be biopsied. Also, excessive secretions can be removed via aspiration.[118]

The patient should have nothing to eat or drink for eight or more hours prior to the procedure to inhibit aspiration of stomach contents into the lungs. After the procedure, the patient should not eat or drink until the anesthetic has subsided and the gag reflex returns, usually at least two hours.[119]

Possible complications of this procedure include throat pain, laryngospasm (muscular contraction of the vocal cords), aspiration of fluid into the lungs, and hemorrhaging. Clinicians should monitor for airway obstruction or bloody sputum after a bronchoscopy is performed.[120] Some facilities provide a form with a preprinted drawing of the lungs to facilitate the documentation of the findings of the test.

C. Laboratory Studies

1. Arterial blood gases (ABG)

The management of the arterial blood gas (ABG) is critical to clinicians who care for patients with respiratory disorders. This test is often ordered when a patient has signs and symptoms of respiratory dysfunction. Clinicians must have specialized training to develop the expertise required to collect, analyze, and interpret the results of this blood test.[121]

From this one lab test, clinicians are able to determine patients' acid-base level (pH), how well they are ventilating ($PaCO_2$), and how well they are oxygenating (PaO_2). They are able to determine whether an abnormal status is caused by an acute or a chronic problem, whether the patient's blood is acidic or alkaline, whether the patient has a metabolic or a respiratory condition, and whether the blood is carrying enough oxygen. Normal value ranges for an ABG are as follows: pH = 7.35-7.45, $PaCO_2$ (partial pressure of carbon dioxide) = 35-45 torr, PaO_2 (partial pressure of oxygen) = 80-100 torr, HCO_3 (bicarbonate) = 22-26 mEq/L, and SaO_2 (arterial oxygenation) = >95%.[122]

TIP: In order to collect an ABG, a trained medical professional (usually a respiratory therapist) must insert a needle into one of the patient's arteries and withdraw a blood sample.

Recommended sites for the puncture are the radial artery (preferred), brachial artery, and femoral artery. The puncture site must be cleaned with an antimicrobial solution. If the radial artery (in the wrist) is the target, then an Allen's test should be performed to make sure there is collateral circulation to the hand from the ulnar artery. An ABG may be done if the Allen's test is found to be within normal limits, the patient is free of severe bleeding disorders, and she does not have an AV fistula (a surgically created hemodialysis access port) above the intended puncture site. Possible complications include bleeding, hematoma and arterial occlusion (blockage).[123] In some circumstances, an indwelling arterial line may be placed to monitor hemodynamic status (heart rate and blood pressure), and make obtaining the blood sample easier and less painful.

2. Microbiology

a. Sputum Culture and Sensitivity, and Gram Stain

If pulmonary infection is suspected, the physician may order a sputum culture and sensitivity (C&S) and possibly a Gram stain. The sputum is collected from the patient via deliberate coughing, suctioning or bronchoscopy and sent to the microbiology lab. The C&S detects the existence of bacteria, and can determine which anti-infective medications are effective to eradicate the infectious organism(s). The Gram stain detects the presence of and identifies the characteristics of Gram negative and Gram positive bacteria.[124]

b. Cytology

Cytology is a sputum diagnostic test that detects the existence of cancerous cells. If malignant cells are found, further diagnostic workup and/or treatment will most likely be necessary.[125]

c. Acid-fast bacillus test (AFB)

This diagnostic test detects the existence of acid-fast bacilli, which indicates the presence of mycobacteria. Usually, when this test is ordered the physician is attempting to determine if the patient has tuberculosis (TB). Often, serial specimens are sent for analysis.[126]

D. Pulse Oximetry

Pulse oximeters are used to monitor oxygen saturation. They are noninvasive monitors that indirectly measure arterial oxygenation (SaO_2). The invention of this technology has reduced the number of invasive ABGs necessary for respiratory patients.[127]

A sensor is placed on a patient's finger, earlobe, toe or forehead. This sensor points light at red and infrared wavelengths through the pulsing capillaries under the skin. It measures the percentage of oxygen absorbed by the hemoglobin in the blood. A normal SpO_2 range for a healthy individual breathing room air is 97-99%. However, levels as low as 95% are considered acceptable by many experts, with even lower acceptable ranges depending on the patient's condition. The monitors and sensor probes come in multiple shapes and sizes.[128] Refer to Figure 25.10.

Indications for continuous pulse oximetry monitoring include patients with unpredictable airways or lung disorders, patients undergoing invasive diagnostic tests (such as bronchoscopy), critical care or respiratory patients who need to be transported, perioperative patients, and those receiving hemodialysis. Spot-checks should be ordered when a patient is on long-term oxygen therapy, or on a chronic mechanical ventilator with a tracheostomy in place.[129]

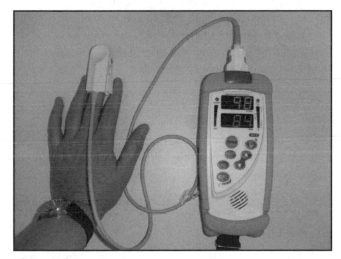

Figure 25.10

E. Pulmonary Function Testing

Pulmonary function testing (PFT) is the use of breathing tests to determine the presence and degree of respiratory dysfunction a patient may have. Progression of overall disease can be tracked over time. In addition, PFTs are often ordered preoperatively to evaluate a patient's risk of respiratory complications after the surgery.[130]

1. Spirometry

Specific lung volumes are measured using an apparatus called a spirometer. Those trained in pulmonary function testing (frequently respiratory therapists) perform the tests and compare them to predicted values for the patient's height, weight, and gender. See the *AARC Clinical Practice Guidelines* for additional details.[131]

2. Peak flow meter

Peak expiratory flow is the measurement of a patient's greatest expiratory flow effort after pulling in as much air as possible. A small plastic meter (peak flow meter) is used. It is recommended that asthmatics measure this flow rate on a daily basis and adjust their medication accordingly. Studies have indicated that using a peak flow meter as indicated reduces visits to the ER and prevents hospitalization.[132]

Although it varies according to height and age, the range of normal values for this test are approximately 380-700 mL. If the patient (or clinician) notes a reduction of 20-50% in peak flow, rescue medications are indicated. If the airflow is compromised by 50% or more, then the patient should be emergently evaluated by a clinician, and emergency treatment should be initiated.[133]

25.7 Respiratory Diseases and Management Techniques
A. Pneumonia

Pneumonia is inflammation in the lungs caused by an infectious agent, such as bacteria, fungi, and viruses. This inflammation causes the airways to become flooded with fluid which thickens, consolidates and interferes with the lung's function, reduces lung volumes, and causes difficulty breathing.[134]

A patient with pneumonia usually presents with a productive cough (sometimes hemoptysis) and a fever. Pleuritic chest pain and breathlessness may be present, and the patient appears extremely ill, often with an elevated heart rate and respiratory rate. The patient may be struggling to breathe. In severe situations, cyanosis may be present, as well as accessory muscle use and decreased chest excursion over affected areas. Percussion will produce a decreased resonance over regions of consolidation. Crackles may be heard by the clinician, which indicate excessive sputum production, and a friction rub may be present if the pleura are inflamed.[135]

The white blood cell count (WBC) will be elevated if the infectious agent is bacterial, but will remain normal if nonbacterial. Chest x-rays vary with the severity of disease. They show zones of increased opacities (white areas) which represent areas of consolidation. ABGs frequently indicate alkalosis of a respiratory nature, and hypoxemia. Sputum cultures are sent to the microbiology lab to determine which pathogen is causing the pneumonia. Sensitivity testing detects which antibiotics can successfully treat the infection.[136]

Treatment of pneumonia may be given in outpatient or acute care settings depending on the severity. If the patient has hypoxemia oxygen therapy may be required. Increased humidity in inspired air can help loosen thick sputum. The appropriate anti-infective medication should be started as soon as possible to treat the infection, and supportive measures (such as intravenous fluid) provided as needed.[137]

B. Asthma

Asthma refers to reversible bronchospasm and swelling of the mucosa complicated by increased pulmonary secretions. The airways become obstructed. Some types of asthma have specific triggers, such as exercise or allergens, and others have no evident cause.[138]

Symptoms vary from mild wheezes to status asthmaticus, a potentially fatal situation where an asthma attack is resistant to standard treatment.[139] Asthmatic patients complain of episodic chest pain/tightness, breathlessness, wheezing, and/or coughing. Between asthma flare-ups, patients may have no difficulty breathing. However, the pattern of symptoms can change throughout a patient's lifetime, and needs to be tracked and monitored in collaboration with medical professionals.[140]

It is sometimes difficult for physicians to diagnose asthma because symptoms vary, and it can easily be confused with other pulmonary disorders. The provider should conduct a detailed interview about current and past symptoms (and triggers), and a physical examination should be performed. Pulmonary function tests such as spirometry and peak flow measurement may be ordered (see Section 25.6.E).[141]

Treatment of asthma may include maintenance medications, rescue medications (see Section 25.5.D), and allergy medications. The correct treatment regimen is dependent on many factors, and may need to be adjusted over time.[142]

C. Chronic Obstructive Pulmonary Disease (COPD)

COPD, which is both incurable and progressive, consists of lung disorders that cause damage from airway obstruction. Most of the time COPD is caused by long-term smoking, but it is occasionally caused by a genetic problem. Two primary examples are chronic bronchitis and emphysema. Some people suffer from both of these types of COPD.[143]

Chronic bronchitis can be described as a condition where a long-term cough causes the airways to become inflamed. The airways narrow, and excess mucous is produced, which causes obstruction of airflow.[144] Emphysema is a condition where the alveoli are progressively destroyed, usually by smoking. Air flow becomes limited when exhaling.[145]

Treatment by a pulmonologist may be recommended if COPD is suspected by a primary care physician. Diagnostic tests may include a chest x-ray, CT scan, spirometry, sputum analysis, and ABG. Non-surgical treatments may include smoking cessation, oxygen therapy, bronchodilators, antibiotics and steroids. Surgical options include wedge resection or lung transplant.[146]

Acute exacerbations (flare-ups) of COPD may cause respiratory failure if not treated promptly. The hospital setting may be warranted to provide additional oxygen, medication and close monitoring.[147]

D. Lung Cancer

Lung cancer causes more fatalities in the United States than prostate, colon, breast and lymph cancers collectively. Approximately 90% of patients with lung cancer are (or were) smokers. Other risks for lung cancer include exposure to radon, asbestos, and second-hand smoke. In addition, gender, familial history, and alcohol consumption may play a role.[148] The cells that make up the lining of the lung become damaged. Initially, the body can repair itself, but with extensive exposure increased damage allows various types of cancer to develop. In the early stages of lung cancer, there are usually no symptoms noted. In late stages, a patient may complain of a persistent cough, hoarseness, wheezing, breathlessness, chest pain, and/or hemoptysis.[149]

TIP: Diagnostic tools used when lung cancer is suspected include chest x-rays, CT scans, sputum analysis, and tissue biopsies. Physicians use staging to define the degree of cancer a patient has. Bone scans, MRI, or positron emission testing (PET) may be used to assist with accurate staging.[150]

Complications from lung cancer may include pleural effusion, metastasis (spreading to other places in the body), and death. The diagnosis is grave, but new treatments targeting specific malignant cells are showing some success in extending life. Early detection improves the chance of survival.[151]

Treatments may include chemotherapy, radiation, surgery, targeted drug therapy (drugs that target cancer cell abnormalities), investigational medications, palliative care or a combination of any of the above. Oncologists, physicians who treat cancer patients, will help the patient decide which therapeutic direction to take.[152]

E. Deep Vein Thrombosis/Pulmonary Embolism

See Section 17.7.D *Deep Vein Thrombosis/Pulmonary Embolism* in Chapter 17, *Orthopaedic Records.*

F. Tuberculosis

Tuberculosis (TB) refers to bacterial infection with an organism called *Mycobacterium tuberculosis*. It is passed from host to host via tiny droplets that are expelled when a contagious person speaks, spits, coughs, sneezes, sings or laughs. TB most often affects the lungs, but it can also attack the kidneys, brain or spine.[153]

Although it was once thought to be eradicated in the Unites States, TB has resurfaced with more drug-resistant, lethal strains. The United States has toughened laws that permit TB patients to be detained, quarantined, and isolated if necessary.[154]

Certain people are at a higher risk for contracting TB than others. Examples include those who are immunocompromised (such as those with HIV infection), substance abusers, healthcare workers, the impoverished, the homeless, and immigrants.[155]

Symptoms of TB include fatigue, fever, chills, poor appetite, weight loss, persistent cough, hemoptysis, and chest pain. Diagnostic testing for TB includes simple Mantoux skin tests and/or more sophisticated blood tests. If evidence of TB is found, further tests such as chest x-rays, CT scans, and/or sputum cultures may be done. Patients may be referred to a pulmonologist (lung doctor) or an infectious disease physician for further care.[156]

Complications of TB may include damage to lung tissue, pain, joint damage, and meningitis. Treatments primarily include medication therapy. However, anti-tuberculosis drugs need to be taken for anywhere from six months to two years.[157]

Physicians need to prescribe an appropriate medication regimen based on the patient's age, medical history, and the area of the body affected by TB. In addition, the type of TB (latent vs. active) and the level of drug resistance need to be considered. Liver toxicity can be a significant problem with these medications, so acetaminophen and alcohol should be avoided during treatment, and liver function should be monitored closely.[158]

G. Pulmonary Fibrosis

Pulmonary fibrosis is a progressive disease where the tissue of the lungs becomes scarred. It is thought that it is brought about by repetitive injury to the alveoli and the spaces between them. This eventually scars the tissue and causes stiffness of the lungs, which results in difficulty breathing.[159]

Possible causes of this type of damage include radiation and chemotherapy, occupational/environmental factors, some medications, gastrointestinal reflux disease (GERD), infections, and autoimmune disorders. Sometimes the etiology is never determined.[160]

Symptoms include a nonproductive cough, dyspnea, fatigue, aching joints and muscles as well as weight loss. The symptoms progressively worsen until the patient becomes breathless while doing basic activities of daily living. Common complications include hypoxemia, elevated blood pressure in the lungs (pulmonary hypertension), heart failure and respiratory failure.[161]

Diagnostic tests include chest x-rays, specialized highly sensitive CT scans, pulmonary function tests, exercise stress tests and oximetry. Many times, definitive diagnosis with pulmonary fibrosis requires a lung biopsy.[162]

Treatment is fairly limited. It includes medicating with combinations of immunosuppressants and providing oxygen therapy. If these do not provide relief, a lung transplant may become the only remaining option.[163]

H. Pulmonary Hypertension

Pulmonary hypertension is a progressive illness where small blood vessels in the lungs narrow or become blocked. Blood flow is impeded in the lungs, which increases the pressure in the pulmonary arteries. As pressure increases in the pulmonary arteries, the heart must pump harder to push blood through the lungs. This causes the muscle of the heart to grow weaker, sometimes leading to complete heart failure.[164]

Symptoms include fatigue, dyspnea, dizziness, syncope (fainting), chest pain, swelling in the lower extremities, cyanosis, and rapid heart rate. Complications include heart failure, irregular heart rhythms, bleeding into the lungs, and blood clots in the lungs.[165]

Diagnostic testing may include an echocardiogram (which allows the physician to visualize the heart using sound waves), pulmonary function testing, a specialized scan that measures the perfusion (blood flow) in the lungs, a CT scan, a MRI, and a lung biopsy. Cardiac catheterization, a procedure where a tube is threaded through the right side of the heart and pulmonary artery, might be recommended to measure pressures and determine which drugs work best on the patient's heart.[166]

Treatment for pulmonary hypertension can be complex. Many medications help reduce the effects of the disease, such as epoprostenol and sildenafil. The right combination for each patient will need to be determined by the physician.[167]

Oxygen therapy often becomes necessary for these patients. Occasionally, lung and heart transplants may be appropriate options for patients with pulmonary hypertension.[168]

25.8 Summary

The skilled care required by respiratory patients is highly complex and often of an emergency nature. The factors presented in this chapter illustrate the significant level of education and experience required to manage a wide variety of urgent and challenging circumstances. Respiratory clinicians are expected to have the advanced practice abilities to respond quickly and correctly in the areas of assessment, diagnosis, mechanical assistance, pharmacological treatment, and stabilization of critical medical situations.

Endnotes

1. Geiger-Bronsky, M. and Wilson, D.J. *Respiratory Nursing, A Core Curriculum.* p. 590. New York: Springer Publishing Company, 2008.

2. Johnson, N.M. *Respiratory Disorders- (Medico-legal practitioner series).* p. 22. London: Cavendish Publishing Limited, 1999.

3. *Id.*

4. Johnson, N.M. *Respiratory Disorders- (Medico-legal practitioner series).* p. 23. London: Cavendish Publishing Limited, 1999.

5. Johnson, N.M. *Respiratory Disorders- (Medico-legal practitioner series).* p. 24. London: Cavendish Publishing Limited, 1999.

6. See note 2.

7. See note 5.

8. *Id.*

9. Johnson, N.M. *Respiratory Disorders- (Medico-legal practitioner series).* p. 25. London: Cavendish Publishing Limited, 1999.

10. *Id.*

11. Kacmarek, R.M. et al. *The Essentials of Respiratory Care, Fourth Edition.* p. xi. St. Louis, Missouri: Elsevier Mosby, 2005.

12. http://www.bls.gov/oco/pdf/ocos084.pdf

13. http://www.bls.gov/oco/pdf/ocos083.pdf

14. *Id.*

15. http://www.bls.gov/oco/pdf/ocos101.pdf

16. *Id.*

17. *Id.*

18. Kacmarek, R.M. et al. *The Essentials of Respiratory Care.* Fourth Edition. p. 325-336. St. Louis, Missouri: Elsevier Mosby, 2005.

19. *Id.*

20. *Id.*

21. *Id.*

22. Barnes, T.A. *Core Textbook of Respiratory Care Practice,* Second Edition. p. 6. St. Louis, Missouri: Mosby-Year Book, Inc., 1994.

23. *Id.*

24. Johnson, N.M. *Respiratory Disorders- (Medico-legal Practitioner Series).* P. 45. London: Cavendish Publishing Limited, 1999.

25. Johnson, N.M. *Respiratory Disorders- (Medico-Legal Practitioner Series).* p. 46. London: Cavendish Publishing Limited, 1999.

26. Laska, L. "Failure to diagnose lung cancer." *Medical Malpractice Verdicts, Settlements, and Experts,* May 2008, p. 27.

27. Barnes, T.A. *Core Textbook of Respiratory Care Practice.* Second Edition. p. 9. St. Louis, Missouri: Mosby-Year Book, Inc., 1994.

28. Johnson, N.M. *Respiratory Disorders- (Medico-legal Practitioner Series).* p. 46-48. London: Cavendish Publishing Limited, 1999.

29. See note 27.

30. Johnson, N.M. *Respiratory Disorders- (Medico-legal Practitioner Series).* p. 57. London: Cavendish Publishing Limited, 1999.

31. See note. 27.

32. Johnson, N.M. *Respiratory Disorders- (Medico-legal Practitioner Series).* p. 58. London: Cavendish Publishing Limited, 1999.

33. See note 27.

34. Johnson, N.M. *Respiratory Disorders- (Medico-legal Practitioner Series).* p. 58-59. London: Cavendish Publishing Limited, 1999.

35. Wilkins, R.L. and Dexter, J.R. *Respiratory Disease, Principles of Patient Care*. p. 395. Philadelphia, PA: F.A. Davis Company, 1993.

36. Johnson, N.M. *Respiratory Disorders- (Medico-legal Practitioner Series)*. p. 52-53. London: Cavendish Publishing Limited, 1999.

37. Laska, L. "Failure to timely treat woman with pain in leg and shortness of breath." *Medical Malpractice Verdicts, Settlements, and Experts*, May 2008, p. 26.

38. Johnson, N.M. *Respiratory Disorders- (Medico-legal Practitioner Series)*. p. 53-56. London: Cavendish Publishing Limited, 1999.

39. Johnson, N.M. *Respiratory Disorders- (Medico-legal Practitioner Series)*. p. 56-57. London: Cavendish Publishing Limited, 1999.

40. *Id.*

41. Johnson, N.M. *Respiratory Disorders- (Medico-legal Practitioner Series)*. p. 177-178. London: Cavendish Publishing Limited, 1999.

42. Johnson, N.M. *Respiratory Disorders- (Medico-legal Practitioner Series)*. p. 178-179. London: Cavendish Publishing Limited, 1999.

43. Laska, L. "Failure to timely diagnose and treat pneumothorax in woman with severe asthma attack." *Medical Malpractice Verdicts, Settlements, and Experts*, December 2008, p. 22.

44. Baumann, M.H. et al. "Management of Spontaneous Pneumothorax- An American College of Chest Physicians Delphi Consensus Statement." *Chest*. February 2001, 119(2). p. 590-602.

45. Johnson, N.M. *Respiratory Disorders- (Medico-legal Practitioner Series)*. p. 181-183. London: Cavendish Publishing Limited, 1999.

46. Kacmarek, R.M. et al. *The Essentials of Respiratory Care*. Fourth Edition. p. 399-400. St. Louis, Missouri: Elsevier Mosby, 2005.

47. *Id.*

48. Kacmarek, R.M. et al. *The Essentials of Respiratory Care*. Fourth Edition. p. 608. St. Louis, Missouri: Elsevier Mosby, 2005.

49. Singh, C.P. et al. "Oxygen Therapy." *Journal, Indian Academy of Clinical Medicine*. July-September 2001, 2(3), p. 178-184.

50. DiPietro, J.S. and Mustard, M.N. *Clinical Guide for Respiratory Care Practitioners*. Norwalk, CT: Appleton & Lange, 1987, p. 64-68.

51. See note 49.

52. Laska, L. (Ed.), "Nasal cannula used for newborn with breathing difficulties secured with tape," Medical Malpractice Verdicts, Settlements, and Experts, July 2008, p. 28.

53. DiPietro, J.S. and Mustard, M.N. *Clinical Guide for Respiratory Care Practitioners*. Norwalk, CT: Appleton & Lange, 1987, p. 64-68.

54. See note 49.

55. DiPietro, J.S. and Mustard, M.N. *Clinical Guide for Respiratory Care Practitioners*. Norwalk, CT: Appleton & Lange, 1987, p. 64-68.

56. *Id.*

57. *Id.*

58. Jagim, M. "Airway Management, Rapid-sequence intubation in trauma patients." *AJN*. October 2003, 103(10), p. 32-35.

59. *Id.*

60. *Id.*

61. Divatia, J.V. and Bhowmick, K. "Complications of Endotracheal Intubation and other Airway Management Procedures." *Indian Journal of Anaesthesia*. August 2005, 49(4), p. 308-318.

62. Geiger-Bronsky, M. and Wilson, D.J. *Respiratory Nursing, A Core Curriculum*. p. 525. New York: Springer Publishing Company, 2008.

63. Geiger-Bronsky, M. and Wilson, D.J. *Respiratory Nursing, A Core Curriculum*. p. 526. New York: Springer Publishing Company, 2008.

64. *Id.*

65. Geiger-Bronsky, M. and Wilson, D.J. *Respiratory Nursing, A Core Curriculum.* p. 526-527. New York: Springer Publishing Company, 2008.

66. *Id.*

67. Geiger-Bronsky, M. and Wilson, D.J. *Respiratory Nursing, A Core Curriculum.* p. 527-528. New York: Springer Publishing Company, 2008.

68. *Id.*

69. *Id.*

70. Geiger-Bronsky, M. and Wilson, D.J. *Respiratory Nursing, A Core Curriculum.* p. 528-530. New York: Springer Publishing Company, 2008.

71. http://www.passy-muir.com/ceu/pdfs/ACourseMaterial.pdf

72. Branson, R.D., et al. "AARC Clinical Practice Guideline, Endotracheal Suctioning of Mechanically Ventilated Adults and Children with Artificial Airways." *Respiratory Care.* May 1993, 38(5), p. 500-504.

73. *Id.*

74. *Id.*

75. Geiger-Bronsky, M. and Wilson, D.J. *Respiratory Nursing, A Core Curriculum.* p. 498. New York: Springer Publishing Company, 2008.

76. Tobin, M.J. "Advances in Mechanical Ventilation." *New England Journal of Medicine.* June 28, 2001, 344(26), p. 1986-1996.

77. Laska, L. "Failure to provide quadriplegic with ventilator during short jail stay," *Medical Malpractice Verdicts, Settlements, and Experts*, June 2009, p. 21.

78. Geiger-Bronsky, M. and Wilson, D.J. *Respiratory Nursing, A Core Curriculum.* p. 497. New York: Springer Publishing Company, 2008.

79. Geiger-Bronsky, M. and Wilson, D.J. *Respiratory Nursing, A Core Curriculum.* p. 518. New York: Springer Publishing Company, 2008.

80. Geiger-Bronsky, M. and Wilson, D.J. *Respiratory Nursing, A Core Curriculum.* p. 499-500. New York: Springer Publishing Company, 2008.

81. Geiger-Bronsky, M. and Wilson, D.J. *Respiratory Nursing, A Core Curriculum.* p. 501. New York: Springer Publishing Company, 2008.

82. Geiger-Bronsky, M. and Wilson, D.J. *Respiratory Nursing, A Core Curriculum.* p. 498-499. New York: Springer Publishing Company, 2008.

83. Gay, P.C. "Complications of Noninvasive Ventilation in Acute Care." *Respiratory Care.* February 2009, 54(2), p. 246-257.

84. See note 76.

85. Geiger-Bronsky, M. and Wilson, D.J. *Respiratory Nursing, A Core Curriculum.* p. 503. New York: Springer Publishing Company, 2008.

86. Tobin, M.J. "Advances in Mechanical Ventilation." *New England Journal of Medicine.* June 28, 2001, 344(26), p. 1986-1996.

87. See note 85.

88. See note 76.

89. Geiger-Bronsky, M. and Wilson, D.J. *Respiratory Nursing, A Core Curriculum.* p. 504. New York: Springer Publishing Company, 2008.

90. *Id.*

91. See note 76.

92. Thille, A.W. et al. "Patient-ventilator asynchrony during assisted mechanical ventilation." *Intensive Care Med.* August 2006, 32, p. 1515.

93. *Id.*

94. Geiger-Bronsky, M. and Wilson, D.J. *Respiratory Nursing, A Core Curriculum.* p. 475-495. New York: Springer Publishing Company, 2008.

95. *Id.*

96. *Id.*

97. *Id.*

98. *Id.*

99. *Id.*

100. *Id.*

101. *Id.*

102. *Id.*

103. *Id.*

104. *Id.*

105. Becker, J.M. et al. "Oral versus intravenous corticosteroids in children hospitalized with asthma." *Journal of Allergy and Clinical Immunology.* Volume 103(4), p. 586-590, 1999.

106. See note 94.

107. *Id.*

108. *Id.*

109. *Id.*

110. *Id.*

111. *Id.*

112. *Id.*

113. *Id.*

114. *Id.*

115. *Id.*

116. Laska, L. "Misplacement of CAT scan report showing nodule in upper lobe of lung results in delay in diagnosis of lung cancer." *Medical Malpractice Verdicts, Settlements, and Experts,* February 2008, p. 22.

117. Geiger-Bronsky, M. and Wilson, D.J. *Respiratory Nursing, A Core Curriculum.* p. 86-87. New York: Springer Publishing Company, 2008.

118. *Id.*

119. *Id.*

120. *Id.*

121. DiPietro, J.S. and Mustard, M.N. *Clinical Guide for Respiratory Care Practitioners.* p. 22-25. Norwalk, CT: Appleton & Lange, 1987.

122. *Id.*

123. Geiger-Bronsky, M. and Wilson, D.J. *Respiratory Nursing, A Core Curriculum.* p. 84-85. New York: Springer Publishing Company, 2008.

124. Geiger-Bronsky, M. and Wilson, D.J. *Respiratory Nursing, A Core Curriculum.* p. 92-93. New York: Springer Publishing Company, 2008.

125. *Id.*

126. *Id.*

127. Valdez-Lowe, C. et al. "Pulse Oximetry in Adults." *AJN.* June 2009, 109(6), p. 52-60.

128. *Id.*

129. *Id.*

130. Geiger-Bronsky, M. and Wilson, D.J. *Respiratory Nursing, A Core Curriculum.* p. 77-78. New York: Springer Publishing Company, 2008.

131. Kacmarek, R.M. et al. *The Essentials of Respiratory Care.* Fourth Edition. p. 344-349. St. Louis, Missouri: Elsevier Mosby, 2005.

132. Geiger-Bronsky, M. and Wilson, D.J. *Respiratory Nursing, A Core Curriculum.* p. 570-571. New York: Springer Publishing Company, 2008.

133. *Id.*

134. Wilkins, R.L. and Dexter, J.R. *Respiratory Disease, Principles of Patient Care.* p. 269-275. Philadelphia, PA: F.A. Davis Company, 1993.

135. *Id.*

136. *Id.*

137. *Id.*

138. Wilkins, R.L. and Dexter, J.R. *Respiratory Disease, Principles of Patient Care.* p. 15-20. Philadelphia, PA: F.A. Davis Company, 1993.

139. *Id.*

140. *Id.*

141. http://www.mayoclinic.com/health/asthma/DS00021/ METHOD=print&DSECTION=all

142. *Id.*

143. http://www.mayoclinic.com/health/copd/DS00916/ METHOD=print

144. *Id.*

145. http://www.mayoclinic.com/health/emphysema/ DS00296

146. http://www.mayoclinic.com/health/copd/DS00916/ METHOD=print

147. *Id.*

148. http://www.mayoclinic.com/health/lung-cancer/ DS00038/METHOD=print

149. *Id.*

150. *Id.*

151. *Id.*

152. *Id.*

153. http://mayoclinic.com/health/tuberculosis/DS00372/ METHOD=print

154. Berlin, L. "Tuberculosis: Resurgent Disease, Renewed Liability." *American Journal of Roentgenology.* June 2008, Volume 190, p. 1438-1444.

155. http://mayoclinic.com/health/tuberculosis/DS00372/ METHOD=print

156. *Id.*

157. *Id.*

158. *Id.*

159. http://www.mayoclinic.com/health/pulmonary-fibrosis/ DS00927/METHOD=print&DSECTION=all

160. *Id.*

161. *Id.*

162. *Id.*

163. *Id.*

164. http://www.mayoclinic.com/health/pulmonary-hypertension/DS00430/METHOD=print&DSECTION=all

165. *Id.*

166. *Id.*

167. *Id.*

168. *Id.*

Additional Resources

American Association for Respiratory Care (AARC) guidelines on their website at www.aarc.org/resources/cpgs_guidelines_statements.

Respiratory Nursing Society's Scope & Standards (Sent to ANA for approval in August 2009).

Chapter 26

Skin Trauma

Kelly A. Jaszarowski, MSN, RN, CNS, ANP, CWOCN

26.1 Introduction

Alterations in skin integrity should be categorized by their etiology using general terms. These general terms include wound, burn, pressure ulcer, incontinence, and ostomics. It is these categories that are explored. This chapter provides a limited overview of each category in terms of etiology, assessment, treatment, documentation, and complications. The information is designed to assist the attorney, paralegal, or legal nurse consultant in interpreting the medical record.

26.2 Wounds

A wound refers to any break in skin integrity. The break in skin integrity may be intentional, such as in the case of surgery, or unintentional, such as a result from trauma. It may be as superficial as an abrasion or as severe as to include multiple layers of skin.

A. Etiology

Drainage from around a tube or drain, improper use of a product, harsh solutions, and incontinence may all cause skin breakdown. A puncture wound may occur as a result of a stabbing. An infection may cause a rash or open area. An important factor in identifying the etiology of the alteration is the location of skin damage. There are five general etiologies of a wound that result in an alteration in skin integrity. General wound etiologies include mechanical, chemical, allergic, infectious, and disease factors.

1. Mechanical factors

Mechanical injuries may occur individually or in combination with each other. These injuries occur as a result of shear, friction, and pressure. A shear injury is created when there is resistance to movement. The classic example occurs when a person slides down in bed after a person sits in bed for an extended period of time with the head of the bed elevated thirty degrees, semi-fowler's position, or higher.

Gravity pulls the torso down while the sacral skin remains in the same position, creating resistance. Hence, shear injuries are commonly identified in the sacral and coccyx areas. This particular type of injury tends to present as a shallow one. However, deep tissue injury may also occur.

Friction injuries occur when the skin rubs against another surface. The injury looks like an abrasion. Tissue injury tends to be shallow and limited to the dermis. Classic locations of a friction injury are the elbow and the heel. Skin stripping or skin tears are also mechanical injuries. With this type of injury, the epidermis is advertently removed. The dermis may or may not be involved. Tape removal may result in skin stripping. Another example of a friction injury is "road rash" as a result of a motorcycle accident.

An injury that results when a force applies pressure to the skin and compromises blood flow to the area is a pressure injury. This particular type of injury typically occurs over bony prominences. For example, lying on one's back in bed compromises blood flow to the occipital, the coccyxgeal (base of spine), and the heel areas. If measures are not taken to relieve the pressure to these bony prominences, a pressure ulcer will result. Pressure ulcers will be discussed in more detail later in this chapter.

2. Chemical factors

Chemical injuries result from the presence of a solution or secretion on the skin that destroys or erodes the epidermis. These injuries may occur in a few hours or after days of repeated exposure. The development of the injury is dependent upon the irritant's strength and the length of exposure to it. Thus the stronger the irritant, the sooner the injury is apparent. Early signs of a chemical injury can be redness or a red rash. Chemical injuries tend to be shallow in nature.

3. Allergic factors

Immunologic responses to an allergen result in an allergic reaction. Allergic reactions may present locally or systemically. These reactions are obvious when the allergen is present. Less obvious reactions occur when the allergen is not present or when the response is obscured by other simultaneously occurring processes. The classic example is an allergic reaction to poison ivy. The plant's substance is not visibly present on the skin. Another example is an allergic reaction to a medication. Local reactions are often referred to as allergic contact dermatitis.

4. Infectious factors

Common classifications of infections are fungal, bacterial, and viral. Infectious reactions may present as a skin rash or as a wound. Fungal infections are marked by pus-

tules, such as in the presence of Candidiasis. Bacterial infections, such as Staphylococcus Aureus, may also present as folliculitis (inflammation of hair follicles). Other types of bacterial infections include toxic shock syndrome, impetigo (a staphylococcal or streptococcal skin infection), and necrotizing fasciitis (death of the fascia). Infection type injuries may also result from viruses. The more common of these include varicella-zoster (chicken pox) and herpes simplex.

5. Disease

Wounds may develop as a manifestation of a disease process or as a complication of treatment. Toxic epidermal necrolysis is a condition that involves the loss of sheets of epidermis over more than 10 percent of the body. This condition is typically the result of a drug reaction. Sickle cell anemia and thalassemia are two blood dyscrasias that can contribute to wound formation. Venous hypertension, arterial insufficiency, and neuropathy may also result in a wound. For example, diabetics experience peripheral neuropathy. Often times an individual may bump the leg or foot and not feel the injury related to the neuropathy. The result is a wound.

B. Assessment

TIP: Wound healing is typically classified as primary, secondary, or tertiary.

Primary wound healing involves closing the wound and restoring the epithelial barrier. Suturing is one technique used to close wounds. Another technique is skin gluing. Wounds left open and allowed to heal by the body filling in the open area with scar tissue are classified as secondary. Tertiary wounds are those wounds managed by delayed closure. Regardless of the wound classification, a thorough assessment needs to be performed by the clinician. This assessment aids the clinician in wound management and treatment.

Classification tools may exist for wounds of specific etiology. Clinicians need to be aware of these tools and use them whenever possible. For example, a classification system is available to assist the clinician in assessing the diabetic foot. Other systems are available for classifying vascular wounds on extremities, diabetic wounds, and pressure ulcers. Use of a tool may assist the clinician in performing a more accurate assessment. Documentation of the assessment findings should include what assessment tools were used.

Nutrition is a component of the initial assessment. The individual should be assessed to determine if the dietary intake meets the body's needs and is conducive to promoting healing. The assessment should be repeated whenever there is a change in the individual's condition. This is especially true if the condition could increase the individual's risk for malnutrition. Some aspects of the nutrition assessment include the individual's current height and weight, history of involuntary weight loss or gain, appetite, dental health, chewing and swallowing difficulties, physical limitations affecting eating, and any psychosocial factors affecting food intake. Each aspect identified as an actual or potential problem should be addressed in the treatment plan.

1. Closed wounds

Primary wounds typically result from surgery where the wound edge approximation appears to have the least obstacles to healing. Hence, the etiology is typically known. Wound assessment includes evaluating the primary dressing, epithelial resurfacing, wound closure, healing ridge, and local changes. The primary dressing provides a barrier to infection, limits local irritation, and provides comfort and support. Its assessment involves determining intactness and presence of drainage. Wound closure involves identifying whether or not the wound is closed with its edges adhered to each other. The healing ridge refers to the hardness (induration) felt beneath the skin, and indicates the accumulation of new tissue. Hence, the lack of a palpable healing ridge is a cause of concern. The site should also be assessed for local changes that might indicate an infection; such as redness, edema, tenderness, and warmth.

2. Open wounds

Secondary and tertiary wounds are open wounds. Wound assessment includes etiology, location, extent of tissue loss, healing phase, wound characteristics, condition of surrounding skin, and presence of pain. The age of the wound should also be assessed. The wound age compared to assessment findings helps to determine whether the wound is on course for healing. Open wounds should be assessed for the presence of foreign bodies as well. A foreign body is any object that would not normally be located there, such as pieces of glass, stones, grass, sticks, metal, and so on.

Location is an important factor in identifying the etiology of a wound. Diabetic ulcers, venous stasis ulcers, and arterial ulcers are all wounds that are primarily located on the lower extremities. Each type of wound has its own identifying characteristics that enable the clinician to classify the wound appropriately. Recognition of wound etiology also assists the clinician in determining whether interventions that promote healing or prevent further complications would be more appropriate. Wound location influences its ability to

heal. Those wounds that are located closer to the upper body or trunk are more likely to heal than those located on a toe.

The extent of tissue loss indicates the mechanism of wound repair and the ability of the involved tissue to regenerate. Wounds involving the epidermis and superficial dermal layers (partial thickness wounds) heal by regeneration. Epithelial, endothelial, and connective tissue all have the ability to reproduce. Wounds that extend through the dermis (full thickness wounds) do not have the ability to regenerate. Full thickness wounds involve subcutaneous tissue and may extend into muscle and bone. These wounds heal by scar tissue formation.

Wound healing is a process that encompasses a series of events. All wounds, regardless of etiology, go through the physiological cascade of events. Wounds that do not heal in a timely manner or go through the healing cascade uneventfully are referred to as chronic wounds. There are three basic phases of wound healing. The first phase is the inflammatory phase. There is an insult to the skin that triggers an acute inflammatory response. Redness and swelling (edema) appear in the injured area. Injured cells release clotting factors in an effort to minimize blood loss. New capillary networks are formed, connective tissue is produced, wound contraction occurs, and epithelialization (new tissue formation) occurs during the second phase of wound healing. This phase is referred to as the proliferative phase. Remodeling, the final phase of wound healing, continues the healing process and can last a year or longer. This phase involves the remodeling of the matrix, network of cells and tissues, to enhance tissue strength.

TIP: Final tensile strength of a scar does not reach the strength of uninjured tissue.

Wound characteristics refer to those dynamics that assist the clinician in describing the wound. Wound measurements include length, width, and depth. Measurements are typically taken in centimeters or millimeters so as to assess the smallest possible change. Multiple measurements may be necessary to derive a better understanding of the actual wound configuration. The type of tissue present in the wound bed needs to be identified. Nonviable (dead) tissue impedes wound healing and must be removed. Areas of tissue destruction, such as undermining and sinus tracts, need to be identified. Wounds with undermining appear to have lips. Tissue extending under intact skin along the wound edges has been destroyed, giving the wound its lip-like appearance. Undermining typically involves a significant portion of the wound edge. Sinus tracts, also referred to as tunneling, are tunnels of tissue destruction. These tunnels can occur in any direction from the wound surface or edge.

Wound drainage is referred to as exudate and should be quantified in terms of amount and type. Odor is a wound characteristic that must be properly assessed. Healthcare providers may refer to the wound as having a foul smell. Wound dressings should be removed from the wound and the area, or at the very least contained. For example, a wound dressing can be placed in a bag and the bag secured shut. The wound should then be irrigated with the appropriate cleanser such as normal saline. Any dressings used to assist in wound cleansing should also be removed from the area or contained. After these measures are instituted, the wound can be properly assessed for an odor.

Surrounding skin, or periwound skin, should be assessed as it provides information regarding the overall health of the individual. Periwound skin assists the clinician in identifying the individual's age, health status, and medication regimen. The presence of periwound moisture indicates the need for exudate containment. It may also signify that attempts at containment have been unsuccessful. The surrounding skin should also be assessed for induration, redness, swelling, warmth, and tenderness. These findings could denote the presence of an infection. Induration, or an abnormal hard spot, could represent deeper tissue destruction.

Pain assessment involves identifying the pain as wound pain or procedural pain. Wound pain could be indicative of an underlying disease process, such as infection. Procedural pain is pain that only occurs as a result of a dressing change or treatment. Measures to eliminate or to minimize the pain should be implemented.

C. Treatment

Identifying the etiology of a wound assists the clinician in determining appropriate measures of treatment. For example, treatment for a wound that has resulted from a chemical irritation would involve removing or containing the irritant. Guidelines exist for pressure ulcers and for wounds when the individual has lower extremity arterial disease or lower extremity venous disease. These guidelines should be incorporated into any treatment plan.

TIP: There are several modalities available for treating alterations in skin integrity. These modalities include hyperbaric oxygenation therapy, negative pressure wound therapy, electrical stimulation, surgical closure, debridement, and topical dressings.

---

1. Hyperbaric oxygenation therapy

Hyperbaric oxygenation therapy is believed to enhance the oxygen carrying and delivery capabilities of the blood.

Systemic and intermittent oxygen is delivered under pressure. Circulation and cellular function to compromised areas may be restored. The result is increased wound site oxygen. Hyperbaric oxygenation therapy is contraindicated in individuals with conditions that may trap oxygen or that pose a risk for oxygen toxicity. Individuals with a history of emphysema and pulmonary disease should not receive hyperbaric oxygenation therapy. There is an increased risk of oxygen toxicity in individuals who have received the medication Bleomycin. Hyperbaric oxygenation therapy use is limited and is not a primary wound treatment modality.

2. Negative pressure wound therapy

Another treatment modality of limited use is negative pressure wound therapy. Controlled negative pressure is used to assist and accelerate wound healing. This type of therapy is also referred to as vacuum assisted closure. KCI (Kinetic Concepts, Inc., San Antonio, Texas) was one of the first companies to market such a device. Their product is called the V.A.C., vacuum assisted closure. As a result, many clinicians refer to negative pressure wound therapy as "vac" therapy regardless of their equipment supplier.

Negative pressure wound therapy is believed to reduce localized edema, decrease bacteria, and help the wound close. The reduction of localized edema increases localized blood flow and promotes the formation of granulation tissue. It is believed that negative wound therapy enhances the body's ability to heal itself. Therefore, candidates for this treatment modality must have the physiological ability to heal. Various clinical conditions that have benefited from this treatment modality include pressure ulcers, diabetic wounds, abdominal wounds, grafts, and flaps. Contraindications for this type of therapy include those individuals whose wounds contain nonviable tissue, who have untreated osteomyelitis, and whose wound margins have malignancy.

3. Electrical stimulation

Electrical impulses are delivered to the wound tissues in the treatment modality of electrical stimulation. It is believed that changes occur at the tissue and cellular levels in a wound exposed to electrical stimulation. These changes, in turn, stimulate the wound healing process. Different types of electrical waveforms and clinical conditions are being studied. Electrical stimulation therapy use is limited and is not a primary therapy modality.

4. Surgical wound closure

Ideal candidates for surgical wound closure are nutritionally healthy, free of wound infections, and possess granulation tissue at the wound bases along with new tissue formation (epithelialization) at the wound margins. Surgical wound closure is a limited treatment modality and is not a primary modality. Wounds caused by pressure are typically the types of wounds that are closed by surgery. Surgical closure techniques include direct closure of the wound and skin grafting. Direct closure may involve flapping of the open area. Skin grafting is addressed in the burn treatment section of this chapter.

5. Debridement

TIP: The removal of nonviable tissue and foreign matter from a wound is referred to as debridement. Debridement can occur naturally as the result of autolysis. Autolysis is the process where the body digests its own tissue.

Debridement can be achieved through mechanical, chemical, and surgical means. Debridement may be classified as selective or nonselective. Selective debridement means that only nonviable tissue is removed. Nonselective means that both viable (healthy) and nonviable tissue are removed. The various types of debridement may be employed in combination or singularly. The frequency of debridement is determined by the wound's presentation.

Mechanical debridement methods for removing nonviable tissue include dressings, irrigation, and whirlpool. Wet to dry are the most commonly used dressings for mechanical debridement. Moist gauze dressings are applied to the wound and allowed to dry. The dry dressings pull both viable and nonviable tissue from the wound. This method, therefore, is considered nonselective and can also be painful. A less painful and tissue damaging alternative is wet to moist dressings. That is, the dressing is applied moist and changed before it becomes completely dry. If the dressing is found to be dry, it is moistened to assist in ease of removal. Irrigation removes tissue by using pressurized fluid. The pressure is high enough to remove nonviable tissue while not harming viable tissue. Whirlpool is used to soften and loosen adherent necrotic tissue and to cleanse and remove exudate. Wounds that can be immersed in water would be potential candidates for this treatment modality.

Chemical debridement removes tissue through the use of enzymes. Enzymes are chemicals that can be applied to the wound to digest the nonviable tissue components or to dissolve the tissue that is holding the nonviable tissue to the underlying wound bed. Santyl ointment is an example of a commercially available product. Clinicians should be aware of the specific indicators for an enzyme before incorporating it into the treatment plan. Some enzymes are not selective

debriders. A solution that has been historically used to debride wounds is Dakin's Solution, which is a diluted sodium hypochlorite solution that is applied to a gauze dressing. The dressing is placed into the wound and removed two times a day. Controversy surrounds this debridement method because the solution is believed to be toxic and to impair wound healing regardless of solution strength.

Maggot therapy debridement is a historical treatment modality that is becoming of interest again related to the multi-resistant strains of bacteria. It is believed that the maggots secrete enzymes that liquefy dead tissue. The maggots ingest the tissue creating a wound bed that has been disinfected and has been stimulated to heal.[1] Maggot therapy involves placing sterile larvae into the wound bed and containing them there. Containment is accomplished by cover dressings. This type of debridement may be repulsive to the individual.

Sharp debridement is a modality that may be classified as conservative sharp wound debridement or surgical debridement. Loosely adherent, nonviable tissue is removed in conservative sharp wound debridement. It is frequently performed at the bedside and in outpatient clinic settings without pre-medication or local anesthesia. However, topical anesthetics are sometimes used. Clinicians specially trained in this modality can perform the procedure. Conservative sharp wound debridement is considered painless and selective. Sharp debridement, on the other hand, is both painful and nonselective. This procedure is an aggressive form of debridement. Large amounts of tissue are typically removed. The procedure can also be performed at the bedside or in an outpatient setting with the individual under a local anesthetic. Surgical debridement, however, is typically performed in the operating room under a general anesthetic.

6. Topical dressings

A wide variety of topical dressings is readily available for treating wounds. Topical dressings are applied on top of or into the alteration in skin integrity and are the treatment of choice. Dressings should be selected based on their performance parameters. A dressing that matches the wound environment and that will provide an environment conducive to wound healing should be selected. Flow charts, algorithms, clinical pathways, and decision trees are available to assist in this selection process. Topical dressings are often used in combination with the previously mentioned treatment modalities.

Generically, dressings are categorized. However, dressings cannot be used interchangeably within the generic category because design and performance variations do exist. One such example is the generic category of hydrocolloid dressings. Variations of hydrocolloid dressings (examples include Duoderm, Restore, and Comfeel) exist in their ability to absorb exudate, their absorbance capacity, the adhesive strength, and the thickness of the dressing. Clinicians need to be aware of the various dressings available and their appropriate uses. Clinicians specializing in wound care management are the ideal resource for dressing selection. Wound care specialists are often consulted to provide treatment plan recommendations or to manage wound care.

D. Documentation

Assessment findings should be documented concisely and objectively. Initial assessment findings should be compared to later findings. Documentation tools have been developed to assist the clinician's documentation of wound characteristics. These tools tend to be institution specific and limiting. Additional narrative documentation may be necessary to describe clinical wound findings better and more specifically. Clinician knowledge and experience could influence documentation accuracy.

OASIS is a documentation tool used in the home care setting. The tool affects financial reimbursement and provides a means for state surveyors and the community to rate the facility. OASIS wound care documentation has been confusing for even the most experienced, specialized wound care nurses. Terminology and defining criteria are not clear. Definitions of wounds and pressure ulcers have been further refined. However, confusion still exists. Clinicians in the home care setting should attend educational offerings to increase their knowledge and enhance the correct use of the document.

Typically, documentation tools incorporate:

- wound size,
- location,
- extent of tissue involvement,
- wound bed tissue,
- presence of exudates,
- presence of infection,
- description of exudate, and
- presence of undermining or tunneling.

Some wound documentation tools ask the clinician to stipulate the type of wound, such as pressure ulcer, and the technique used for the wound care: sterile versus clean. Other tools provide anatomical diagrams for the clinician to mark the location of the wound.

Wound size should be documented in millimeters or centimeters, to assist the clinician in identifying small changes. Centimeters is the most commonly used measurement. If inches are used, the reader needs to be able to convert the measurement into centimeters. One inch is equivalent to 2.54 centimeters. The use of centimeters is also helpful in providing the reader with a visual of the wound when used in conjunction with other wound characteristics.

The presence of undermining and tunneling is often documented in conjunction with wound size. For example, the clinician may document "tunnel noted at one o'clock." The individual's head is the anatomical landmark for twelve on a clock face. The depth of the tunnel should also be noted. Undermining is also documented by location and depth. Documentation in the medical record might read "undermining from twelve to four o'clock with a depth of 1 centimeter at twelve o'clock and 3 centimeters at four o'clock." A similar practice may be used to identify the location of nonviable tissue in the wound. The clinician may document "Necrosis noted at five o'clock measuring 3 cm by 2.5 cm." The extent of tissue involvement should be documented as partial thickness or full thickness or a combination. Any visible anatomical structures should also be noted, such as bone, ligament, or tendon. Other visible structures should also be identified, such as hip replacement hardware.

The frequency of wound documentation is often determined by the institution. Some institutions require documentation of clinical findings with every dressing change and whenever a change occurs in the individual's condition. If the dressing is changed twice a day, then documentation would need to occur twice a day. Other institutions use a frequency of once a week or once a month. Institutional documentation forms, flow sheets, care plans, protocols, or procedures are all sources that may be helpful to the medical record reviewer in determining the institution's prescribed frequency. For example, a home care patient who has skilled nursing visits once a month would have wound documentation once a month. In between visits, the wound is cared for by the individual or caregiver. Thus, there would not be a clinician's assessment.

Wound documentation frequency is related to the types of treatment modalities. Some topical dressings may be left in place for several days or a week. Documentation in these instances would be weekly. Documentation in between the designated intervals could merely say that the dressing had been changed. No indication as to the clinical findings would be noted.

Documentation should also include the treatment modality being used. Treatment modality documentation could be generic or specific. For example, a topical dressing of a hydrocolloid could be a component of the treatment. The clinician could document that a hydrocolloid dressing was applied to the wound or name the specific hydrocolloid dressing used (Duoderm, Restore, Comfeel). Clinicians in these environments are encouraged to document using generic terms. Likewise, different brands of hydrocolloid dressings could be available to choose from at any one time. Clinicians, therefore, need to establish a policy of documenting. One method would be to document based on the dressing's features. For example, the clinician could document that a thin hydrocolloid dressing was applied to the wound. This would be generically documenting while quantifying a feature of the dressing. The clinician could have documented that a thin Duoderm dressing was applied to the wound. Regardless, documentation should occur at regular intervals to capture the information necessary to determine the progress of wound healing.

Education is a key component of any treatment regimen and should be documented. Wound education includes the disease process, the rationale for treatment, the rationale for treatment modality being used, activity guidelines, nutritional management, and community resources. Education methods encompass instruction, demonstration, and the use of media. The method of education employed should be documented along with the individual's response. Response includes the individual's ability to verbalize and to demonstrate the knowledge and understanding of what has been taught. Modifications to the treatment plan should be made based upon education findings. These modifications should also be documented.

26.3 Burns

The structural and functional capabilities of the skin are affected by burn injuries. Burns that are extensive, involving a large body area, affect all bodily systems. Burns may be classified as chemical, thermal, and electrical. Etiology is only one component of the burn assessment. Burn assessment should examine the amount of the body involved and the depth and severity of the injury. Assessment findings influence and guide the treatment plan. A burn treatment plan must address both the physical and psychological needs of the individual.

A. Etiology

Chemical, thermal, and electrical are three classifications of burns with similar pathophysiology and treatment. However, knowledge of the burn's etiology helps the clinician to identify assessment and intervention needs that are specific to that type of burn. An overview of the three types of burn classifications is explored in this section.

1. Chemical burns

Chemical burns occur as a result of exposure to an irritant. Paint removers, drain cleaners, household cleaners, fertilizers, and pool chemicals are all examples of industrial chemicals that can cause a burn. Chemical burns are more likely to be full thickness burns. The deeper tissue damage results from the continued exposure to the chemical. The chemical will continue to injure tissues until it is inactivated. The actual depth of tissue involvement may not be evident for several days after the initial insult. How the injury occurred, the manner and duration of skin contact, the area of the body involved, and the chemical's concentration all contribute to the depth and severity of the injury.

2. Thermal burns

TIP: The most common cause of burns is thermal injuries.

Thermal injuries result from exposure to or contact with a flame, hot fluids, sun, and radiation. The severity of the burn is directly related to the amount of time exposed and the temperature of the irritant. Hot temperatures require less time to inflict injury than those irritants with a cooler temperature. Thermal injuries can range from partial thickness injuries to full thickness injuries. Decreased reaction time, limited mobility and strength, and decreased visibility can all contribute to the extent of the burn injury. Common sources of thermal burns include burning trash or leaves, explosions during motor vehicle, boating, or industrial accidents, mishandling of firecrackers or gasoline, misuse of space heaters, scalding from hot water, and the splattering of liquids. Radiation burns occur as a result of prolonged exposure to the sun or to other sources of ultraviolet radiation, such as tanning beds.

3. Electrical burns

Burns resulting from electrical sources are classified as electrical burn injuries. It is the conversion of electricity to heat that results in tissue injury. The severity of the injury is related to the force, voltage, and to the strength or amperage of the electrical current. Exposure to electrical currents has been shown to produce cardiac rhythm irregularities, cessation of breathing, seizures, and a loss of consciousness. High voltage injuries can result in massive tissue damage or even death. Electrical injuries have an entrance and exit wound. Areas of edema surrounded by areas of shriveled, depressed skin are often noted in low voltage injuries. Higher voltage injuries tend to produce dry, shriveled, and scarred skin.

B. Assessment

As with any type of alteration in skin integrity, burn assessment is a holistic approach. Consideration should be given to both the physical and psychological needs of the individual. Assessment of the extent of the burn injury is performed initially on presentation of the individual. Accurate assessment and documentation are important in determining the course of treatment. Assessment includes examining the need for fluid replacement, the body's systems responses, nutritional needs, and pain and anxiety management. A complete history and physical should be performed and recorded in the medical record.

Vascular changes, fluid shifts, and tissue loss contribute to the need for fluid replacement. Shifts from the vascular compartments to the interstitial spaces result in edema, blisters, and weeping of fluid. There is a decrease in circulating blood volume. Fluid must be replaced to maintain adequate cardiac output, renal perfusion, and tissue perfusion as well as to prevent hypovolemic shock. The amount of fluid replaced is related to the extent of the burn, the depth of the burn, the individual's age, and the individual's medical history.

Extent and depth of the burn, individual's age, and individual's medical history also affect the body's response to the injury. A fast heart rate and a decrease in cardiac output are cardiovascular responses. Blood might be shunted away from the skin, creating an environment conducive to pressure ulcer formation. The individual could develop difficulty in breathing from smoke inhalation or from burn injury to the upper body. The kidneys could quit producing adequate amounts of urine as a result of decreased blood perfusion. Poor circulating blood volume also affects the gastrointestinal tract. An ileus, an area of the bowel that does not function, could occur. The extent and depth of the injury could change over time. Thorough assessments must be performed at regular intervals.

Nutritional needs must be met to minimize weight loss, facilitate burn injury healing, support bodily functions, and prevent death. Again, the individual's nutritional needs are related to the extent and depth of the burn, the individual's age, and the individual's medical history. Drastic increases in metabolic rates have been seen in severe burns. This increased metabolic rate causes an increased need in caloric intake in order to meet the body's demands. A nutritionist would be an ideal resource in these situations and is an integral part of any burn healthcare team.

TIP: Pain management is an essential component of burn care.

Pain should be assessed before, during, and after procedures. Several pain scales exist for determining the extent of pain the individual is experiencing. See Chapter 18, *Pain Assessment and Management*, for details. Different modalities may be required at various intervals. For example, an oral pain medication might control the individual's pain. However during wound debridement, the individual may require something stronger. In these instances, an injection of pain medication may be more appropriate for pain management. Emotional support should be provided to the individual and significant other(s), and coupled with education to decrease fear and anxiety. Decreasing fear and anxiety can help decrease pain.

C. Treatment

The type and severity of the burn injury dictates the plan of treatment. Burn treatment can be as simple as irrigating the exposed skin to remove the chemical irritant. Treatment focuses on controlling microorganism growth, reducing the potential for infection, and preparing the injury for closure. Nonviable tissue provides a medium for bacteria to grow and prevents wound healing. Topical antibiotics, such as Silvadene, are often used to control microorganism growth. Treatment modalities for severe burns include surgical procedures and wound closure techniques. Wound closure techniques include the use of grafts and skin replacements.

1. Surgical procedures

Surgical procedures may be necessary to relieve swelling and pressure. Swelling develops under the nonviable tissue. The swelling causes pressure and can result in poor blood flow to the area (ischemia). Ischemia can result in further tissue death. Neurological and vascular deficits can also occur. Several surgical procedure options exist, including escharotomy, fasciotomy, and burn excision.

Escharotomy refers to the procedure of cutting through the eschar. The incision is only as deep as is necessary to split the eschar. The procedure should not be painful because eschar is nonviable tissue and lacks nerve endings. Pain and anxiety should be managed, so pain medication is often given before the procedure. Another surgical procedure that involves cutting nonviable tissue is a fasciotomy.

TIP: A fasciotomy is often performed when the burn injury extends to the muscle.

Edema develops beneath the fascia and muscle compartments, increasing the risk of tissue and nerve damage. The fascia is cut to prevent this further damage from occurring.

Burn excision aids in reducing infection and in decreasing the body's response to the injury. This procedure is performed to remove nonviable tissue and to expose healthy, or viable, tissue. Thin layers of nonviable tissue are removed until healthy tissue is reached. Burn excision is used in deep, full thickness injuries that may reach into the subcutaneous fat. Fascial excision involves removing burned tissue down to the muscle fascial layer. It is often performed to prepare the wound bed for a graft.

2. Skin grafts

Skin grafts are used for burn wound closure to reduce complications and fluid loss. This expedites the individual's recovery. The procedures used may be permanent or temporary. Autologous skin grafts are considered permanent wound coverings. The graft is taken from another area of the individual's body. Allografts and xenografts are categorized as temporary wound coverings. Another individual (cadaver or allografts) or species (pig or xenografts) serve as the donor for the tissue.

Autologous skin grafts are the most desirable type of grafts as they involve grafting the individual's own skin. Epidermal sheets containing a thin layer of dermis are removed from areas of healthy tissue. The epidermal sheet (graft) is then placed in the burn wound bed. Sheet removal creates a partial thickness wound that should heal within seven to ten days. The thigh, back, and buttock areas are often used as donor sites. Donor sites can be itchy and painful because nerve endings are exposed in partial thickness wounds.

An autograft may be prepared as a sheet or mesh. Sheet grafts are often used on the face, hands, feet, and neck, and provide a more durable covering. Cover dressings are not used with sheet dressings, but are used with mesh grafts to prevent shearing and enhance cellular migration. Mesh grafts involve placing a strip of skin in a device to create a mesh appearance. Epidermal cells migrate between the mesh. Mesh grafts allow for more coverage while minimizing donor sites.

Cadaver-produced graft tissue is used as a temporary covering. Allografts may be purchased fresh or preserved. These grafts foster the formation of new blood vessels in tissues and prepare the wound bed for permanent grafting. Allografts are often used in situations where the extent of burn injury covers a large portion of the body's surface.

TIP: Rejection of allografts frequently occurs.

Other complications associated with allografts include their limited supply, their variable quality, and the transmission of disease.[2]

Xenografts have also been identified to augment the formation of new skin. Xenografts involve the transferring of another species' skin, such as pigs. They are useful on partial thickness burns that will eventually heal on their own. Xenografts are reapplied to the wound bed every three to seven days. If left in the wound too long, the xenograft could become difficult to remove and may become a component of the wound bed.

3. Skin replacements

Skin replacement dressings are another option for treating superficial, partial thickness burns. There are three general types of skin replacements. Biosynthetic skin replacements are readily available and are relatively inexpensive. They are a thin, mesh-like dressing that is applied directly to the wound bed. The wound is then covered with another dressing, such as a compression dressing, until skin replacement adherence occurs. Biosynthetic dressings are left in place until epithelialization occurs and the dressing edges loosen. These loose edges are trimmed.

Biologic skin replacements are composite epidermal skin grafts that include cultured epithelial sheets and cultured epidermis. Cells can be harvested from areas of unburned skin on the individual or from donor skin. The cells are harvested and then expanded. Wound bed epithelialization is induced by the grafts' release of growth hormones. These skin replacement grafts can be fragile and difficult to handle. Burn wounds to be treated with biological skin replacement grafts need to be tended to while waiting for graft development. Typically, a temporary covering will be used to protect the wound and prepare it for the graft.

Synthetic skin replacements have a dermal matrix of epidermal and dermal skin layers. Thus, they are used in full thickness wounds where replacement of the dermal and epidermal skin layers is necessary. Synthetic skin grafts are primarily temporary coverings. They have been used as wound coverings during times of permanent closure planning and until the individual's own cells have an opportunity to grow. Many synthetic skin replacements are in various stages of clinical trials.

D. Documentation

Burn assessment findings and interventions should be documented. The treatment plan should be specific to the individual, with documentation of the interventions and the individual's response to these interventions. Methods of pain management should be recorded, especially variations for pain control during procedures (such as x-ray) and debridement. The reviewer of a medical record may find the clinician's evaluation of how well the patient tolerated burn care. Statements such as "tolerated poorly" may not convey the agony experienced by the patient. Deposition testimony is needed to understand the sensations and level of pain control experienced by the patient. Any modification to the treatment plan should also be documented. The medical record may contain photographs that memorialize the extent of the burn and the severity of the burn over time. Assessment of the zone of tissue damage, burn wound severity, and extent of the burn wound is an integral component of burn wound management. Thorough documentation of these clinical findings guides burn management.

1. Zone of tissue damage

There are three zones of tissue damage.[3] These zones assist with the assessment and documentation of the extent of the tissue damage. The zone of coagulation or zone of clotting refers to the area of greatest damage. It is closest to the heat source and is characterized by coagulation of the cells. Zones of coagulation located above the dermal appendages (nails, hair follicles, nerves, and sweat glands) will heal by reepithelialization. Surrounding the zone of coagulation is the zone of stasis or stopped or diminished flow. The zone of stasis involves the vascular system in the area. This zone is preserved by adequate perfusion and infection prevention. The outermost area, that is usually minimally damaged, is the zone of hyperemia or increased blood. The area appears red because of inflammation and blood vessel dilation (vasodilatation). The zone of hyperemia is similar to superficial, partial thickness burns.

2. Burn wound severity

Burn wound severity refers to the depth of the burn injury. Factors used to determine burn severity include the individual's age, size and depth of the wound, and the location of the burn.

TIP: Traditionally, burns have been classified as first, second, or third degree.

This classification system is being replaced by a more descriptive system that describes the actual depth of the injury.[4]

Superficial burns are those burns that involve the outer cells. They are characterized by inflammation, pain, heat, and redness. These burns typically take a few days to heal.

Superficial, partial thickness burns involve damage to the epidermal layer with the dermal layer still intact. They are characterized by blisters, weeping, and pain. Pain is related to the exposed nerve endings and their sensitivity to air and temperatures.

Partial thickness burns involve damage to the epidermal layer with extension into the dermis. Dermal structures (nails, hair follicles, nerves, and sweat glands) are intact. Pain, weeping, and blanching are present. Partial thickness burns generally take up to two weeks to heal.

Deep, partial thickness burn wounds appear red with cheesy, white patches, large blisters, and pain. These burns are often difficult to differentiate from full thickness burns. Deep, partial thickness burns take longer to heal. Ischemia and infection can cause these burns to convert to a full thickness wound.

Full thickness burns involve the destruction of the entire dermis. The burn injury can extend down into the fat layer. The burned tissue can present as waxy white, gray, brown, or black color with a leathery charred appearance. Pain is not usually present because of the death of the nerve cells. However, pain may be noted at the outer zone areas. Pain then becomes a distinguishing finding between deep, partial thickness wounds and full thickness wounds. Full thickness wounds that result from incinerator type or electrical sources may be classified as fourth degree burns. Damage involves fascia, muscle, and bone.

Burns located on the face, hands, feet, and perineum require close attention regardless of their classification. Some burns to infants and children require more aggressive treatment than burns to an adult. Burns near the eyes, ears, nose, and mouth can result in difficulty breathing due to swelling. Lower extremity burns can interfere with mobility. In some instances, burns to these areas can develop edema, which can delay healing.

3. Extent of burn injury

The extent of the burn injury is determined by using a systematic method such as the Rule of Nines, the Lund and Browder charts, and the Berkow method. Burn injury can also be calculated using the individual's palm. The American Burn Association has a well accepted method of categorizing burns. The method used to determine the extent of burn injury should be documented along with the determined extent of injury.

The more commonly used methods for determining burn injury are the Rule of Nines, the Lund, and Browder charts. The Rule of Nines is a quick, simple method that is based on anatomical regions. The extent of injury is determined by adding the areas of partial and full thickness burns. The burns on the total body surface area are then expressed by a percentage of body surface that was burned. Modifications to this system have been made for children in an effort to incorporate the differences between children and adults.

Many clinicians use the Lund and Browder charts because it is considered more accurate. This method uses charts showing a standard male or female body, child or adult, from the front and back. Burns are then identified as first, second, and third degree. Assessment of the extent of burn injury with this method should be repeated in seventy-two hours to determine any areas that have extended. Burn injury charts may be completed by a rescue squad but are more commonly found in emergency department and burn treatment records.

The American Burn Association categorizes burns as minor, moderate, and major. This method incorporates the percent of total body surface area in relation to the individual's age classification (child, adult, or elderly) and to the type of burn. A cruder method of calculation is the use of the palm of the hand. The palm of the afflicted individual's hand, with fingers closed, represents 1 percent of body surface area. This particular method can be useful in instances involving small, scattered burns.

Computer documentation tools are being developed. Two new computer tools are the SAGE II and the EPRI 3D Burn Vision.[5] The SAGE II method is two dimensional, whereas, the EPRI 3D is three dimensional. Clinicians using the SAGE II program enter information regarding the individual and paint diagrams, using the computer's mouse, indicating the burned body areas. This entered information is then used to calculate body surface areas. It is believed that computer-aided methods will improve percentage of body surface area measurement calculations.

E. Complications

Infection, excessive (hypertrophic) scarring, skin changes, and contractures are all possible complications of a burn injury. The sensations of pain and itching will also return as deep burns heal and nerve endings regenerate. The medical record will note the use of any pain and itching control medications. The presence of a complication should be documented along with the plan of care.

Sources of infection include grafts as well as wound and burn care. Additionally, nonviable tissue is a medium for bacterial growth. Measures to prevent infection include the removal of nonviable tissue, the use of topical antimicrobial agents, and aseptic technique. Some burn care units develop their own antibiotic creams that are known by agency-specific names. The reviewer may need to obtain information regarding the components of these creams. Constant assessment aids in early identification and treatment.

Scarring results when there is an imbalance in skin protein and is related to the individual's age, pigmentation, family history, and injury location. Pressure therapy helps to minimize and prevent excessive scarring but does not prevent all scar tissue formation.

Heat regulation, sensitivity to direct sunlight, sweat, and oil secretion are affected by a burn injury. The epidermis and superficial dermis are involved in split thickness grafts. Grafted skin does not typically include hair follicles and sweat and oil glands. Skin changes include the inability to produce sweat, and the person is unable to shiver.

Excessive scar tissue formation and normal tissue being pulled or stretched results in contractures. Measures used to prevent contractures include pressure garments, splints, and range of motion exercises. Pressure garments and splints may need to be worn for as long as twenty-three hours per day for one to two years. Range of motion exercises can be performed by the individual, the individual's significant other(s), and a physical therapist. Contraction prevention often extends over a period of years.

26.4 Pressure Ulcers

TIP: Bedsores, decubiti, decubitus, decubitus ulcers, and pressure sores are all terms that have been used to describe an alteration in skin integrity from pressure. The more acceptable term, however, is pressure ulcer.

The term pressure ulcer is more accurate and descriptive than decubitus ulcer. Pressure sores are considered preventable events, according to Centers for Medicare and Medicaid Services' position of denying payment for acute care facilities who care for patients with pressure sores that progress to a stage III or IV. The financial implications of denial of payment have sparked a renewed interest in methods of preventing pressure sores. Clinicians caring for individuals with pressure ulcers need to be aware of the guidelines available to assist them. There are six such guidelines available at the time of this writing. One is "Clinical Practice Guideline, Number 15: Treatment of Pressure Ulcers" published by the Agency for Health Care Policy and Research (AHCPR) in December of 1994.[6] Another publication by the AHCPR in 1992[7] is "Pressure Ulcers in Adults: Prediction and Prevention." The European Pressure Ulcer Advisory released guidelines in November 2009 which are available at their site at http://www.epuap.org/. Other sources of standards are useful as well.[8-11]

A. Etiology

Pressure ulcers are areas of localized tissue destruction. The soft tissue is compressed over a bony prominence by an external force over a period of time. The compression interferes with the blood supply to that area, resulting in vascular insufficiency, tissue anoxia, and cell death.[12] Other etiological factors of pressure ulcers are ischemia and reperfusion. Ischemia-reperfusion (I/R) refers to the reperfusion of blood to an area that was previously ischemic tissue, resulting in cellular injury.[13] Common locations of pressure ulcer formation include the buttocks, hips, and heels.

B. Assessment

The assessment of pressure ulcers encompasses individuals with an ulcer as well as those at risk for ulcer development. Assessment involves the entire person and is the basis for the plan of care. This plan of care, depending on assessment findings, will involve prevention or treatment interventions. Aspects of the assessment include overall health status of the individual, nutritional status, pain, and psychosocial health. A complete history and physical should be performed to assist the clinician in obtaining an overall understanding of the individual's health. The history and physical assists with the identification of coexisting disease and medical regimen that could affect the individual's ability to heal or increase the risk for ulcer development. Two examples of such factors are diabetes and systemic steroid use.

Nutritional status is a component of the history and physical. The nutrition assessment includes identifying whether or not the individual is malnourished and has a dietary intake conducive to healing and to meet current bodily needs. Standard measurements used to evaluate nutrition include albumin and pre-albumin. Because of its short half-life of two to three days, pre-albumin is considered a better reflection of protein stores. Serum albumin has a much longer half-life and is, therefore, not considered a sensitive measure of intervention effectiveness.

The goal of pain management is to eliminate its cause or, at the very least, minimize and control the pain. The psychosocial assessment gathers information to assist the clinician in creating an environment conducive to the adherence to the treatment plan.

1. Risk

Risk assessment should be completed by a healthcare professional upon presentation of the individual to the healthcare facility. The assessment should be a component of the initial assessment. Repeated assessment should be performed at designated intervals as well as when a change occurs in the individual's condition. Clinicians should also be aware of high-risk settings and groups.

There are several risk assessment tools available to assist the clinician. The most widely known and used tool is the Braden Scale. The Braden Scale contains six indicators that the clinician rates on a scale of one to four. The overall score, obtained by adding each indicator's rating, determines the individual's overall risk for pressure ulcer development. Total scores can range from four to twenty-three. Risk levels include mild, moderate, high, and very high. A total score of nine or less classifies the individual as very high risk. The Braden Q scale is an adaptation of the original scale and is for use in the pediatric population.

Another commonly used risk scale is the Norton Scale, which has five indicators for the clinician to rate on a scale from one to four. Again, the overall score is determined by adding each indicator's rating. Risk levels include mild, moderate and high, with high being a score of twelve or less. Long-term-care facilities use an assessment tool that is required by all facilities caring for Medicare patients. The assessment tool is called the Minimum Data Set 2.0. However, controversy surrounds this tool. The tool fails to provide an adequate description of the defining characteristics of a pressure ulcer to allow the user to differentiate the pressure ulcer from other types of injuries.[14] The tool also contains an alternative type of ulcer labeled as a stasis ulcer that can create user confusion.

In general, individuals in acute and long-term care are often identified as high risk for skin breakdown. An individual is likely to develop a pressure ulcer within two weeks of admission to an acute care setting.[15] Long-term-care residents are likely to develop a pressure ulcer within the first four weeks of admission.[16] This correlates with individuals over sixty-five years of age being a group at high risk. Other age groups of higher risk are neonates and children younger than five years of age.[17] The head or occiput is the most common site of pressure ulcer development for neonates and children. One other group worth noting is immobile individuals. All individuals with some degree of immobility should be assessed and monitored. Immobility includes individuals who are non-ambulatory, confined to bed or chairs, with limited functioning and range of motion, and require assistance with positioning or mobility. Individuals with spinal cord injuries fall into the limited or immobile group. Spinal cord injured individuals at an increased risk include those who have a previous history of pressure ulcers, surgical repair, young age at onset and duration of injury, and greater difficulty practicing good skin care.[18]

TIP: Individuals with incontinence and poor nutrition are another group of individuals at higher risk for pressure ulcer development.

Assessment should include bowel and bladder habits, toilet programs, treatments, and skin care regimen. Urinary incontinence can result in increased moisture of the skin.

Moist skin tends to break down over time. Fecal incontinence is a factor in skin breakdown because of the bacteria and enzymes contained in stool. Malnourished individuals are at risk due to an inadequate caloric intake causing weight loss and a decrease in subcutaneous tissue. Bony prominences compress and restrict circulation.[19]

2. Presentation

Existing pressure ulcers need to be assessed for their characteristics and for complications. Characteristics include location, stage, size, sinus tracts, undermining, tunneling, exudate, and wound bed tissue. These characteristics are the same as for any alteration in skin integrity, except for staging. Only pressure ulcers should be staged. The widely used staging system is a synthesis of methods and has been enhanced by The National Pressure Ulcer Advisory Panel (NPAUP) and the Wound, Ostomy, and Continence Nurses Society (WOCN). The staging system requires the clinician to be knowledgeable in tissue recognition and differentiation as well as anatomy. Pressure ulcers can not be properly staged in the presence of nonviable tissue, which can prevent the clinician from assessing the full extent of tissue injury. Novice clinicians and clinicians unfamiliar with the staging system may find it more accurate and easier merely to describe their clinical findings.

One other available classification system involves naming the open area as red, yellow, or black. The color of the ulcer bed determines its classification. A classification of red signifies the existence of healthy tissue encompassing the majority of the wound bed. Yellow or black indicates that nonviable tissue occupies the majority of the bed with yellow being slough and black being eschar.

TIP: Slough refers to nonviable or dead tissue that is loose and stringy. Eschar refers to nonviable tissue that is thick and leathery.

Identified pressure ulcers require monitoring and reassessment at each dressing change.

3. Healing

Assessment tools also exist to assist the clinician in monitoring the healing status of the ulcer. These tools encompass several indicators that are monitored and plotted over time to determine improvement or deterioration of the ulcer. These tools include the Pressure Ulcer Scale for Healing (PUSH) Tool, the Pressure Sore Status Tool (PSST), and the Sussman Wound Healing Tool (SWHT).[20]

The PUSH tool was developed by NPAUP as a quick, reliable tool for monitoring pressure ulcers.[21] The tool contains three items for the clinician to classify: ulcer length and width, exudate amount, and tissue type. Each classification correlates with a rating score. The rating scores are then added to determine the overall score. The overall or total score is then plotted on the Pressure Ulcer Healing Chart. Ulcer assessment should be performed at regular intervals. Total scores should show a downward slope on the chart to indicate healing. An upward slope would indicate a deteriorating ulcer. Likewise, no slope would indicate the ulcer has not changed over time. A separate chart should be completed for each ulcer.

Ulcer characteristics as well as overall ulcer status can be monitored using the PSST (Pressure Sore Status Tool).[22] Monitoring individual ulcer characteristics can assist the clinician in determining the effectiveness of various interventions. This tool contains thirteen items to score. The score for each individual item is added together to determine the overall score. Higher overall scores correlate to more severe pressure ulcer status. The overall score is then plotted on the Pressure Sore Status Continuum. The PSST recommends that assessment of the ulcer occur once a week and when there is a change in the ulcer.

Physical therapy technologies for wound healing can be monitored using the SWHT (Sussman Wound Healing Tool).[23] This tool contains nineteen items, ten of which pertain to wound characteristics. The other nine items relate to the wound characteristics such as wound size and extent of tissue damage.

Some clinicians do not use any of these tools to determine pressure ulcer healing and instead compare current clinical findings with previous findings. This method can create interpretation difficulties when the clinicians assessing the ulcer have various education in the field. This is of concern with staging. A pressure ulcer should not be down staged or reverse staged. If the final stage (after all nonviable tissue has been removed) has been determined to be stage III, then the ulcer becomes a healing stage III. It is not restaged as a stage II or I as it heals. Clinical studies support that as ulcers heal they do not replace lost muscle, subcutaneous fat, and dermis before they re-epithelialize.[24] A possible solution to prevent the occurrence of down staging would be for the clinician responsible for pressure ulcer assessment to be highly skilled or educated in the field. Formal wound specialty education is available. Wound, Ostomy, and Continence Nursing Education programs offer this field of study in conjunction with two other specialty areas or separately. Certification as a wound specialist is also available.

C. Treatment

Treatment interventions are based on the actual existence of pressure ulcers and on the individual's risk for development of pressure ulcers. Interventions that are specific to the individual and to the clinical findings should be implemented as early as possible. Prevention measures include interventions that reduce friction, shear, and pressure, manage incontinence, and maintain adequate nutrition. Existing pressure ulcer treatment encompasses the same philosophy as with a wound. Education is a key element of any treatment plan. The individual and significant other(s) should be educated about the cause of pressure ulcers and the rationale of each intervention to be implemented. Individuals need to be aware of the clinician's overall treatment goal.

Risk assessment tools are also useful in identifying potential problem factors, implementing prevention measures to eliminate or minimize their existence. Friction and shear injuries can be reduced by using lift and turning sheets or devices. Injuries resulting from sliding down in bed can be minimized by the head of the bed being maintained at thirty degrees or lower. A basic pressure reduction measure includes turning and repositioning. This measure can be implemented for those individuals who are confined to bed as well as those who sit for long periods of time in a chair. Commercial products are readily available that have been found to reduce or to redistribute pressure. Clinicians need to examine each of these products carefully and incorporate clinical research findings surrounding each product before deciding what products to use as an intervention. Dietary intake should be monitored. Nutritionists should be consulted regarding management of nutrition issues.

A pressure ulcer is a type of wound with treatment measures similar to other wounds. An environment conducive to ulcer healing should be maintained. Interventions should include eliminating or minimizing the cause, providing a physiologic wound environment, and maintaining adequate nutrition. Minimizing or eliminating the cause involves reducing friction and shear, reducing pressure, managing incontinence, and maintaining adequate nutrition. A physiologic wound environment consists of maintaining a moist wound environment and reducing bacterial count and burden. Topical dressings, debridement, hyperbaric oxygenation, negative pressure wound therapy, and surgical closure are all treatment modalities that have been addressed previously in this chapter. Pain management is also a component of pressure ulcer treatment. Pain measures should include those that eliminate or control pain.

D. Documentation

All components of the assessment should be documented. Many standardized forms are available for documenting pressure ulcer characteristics. These forms are typically the same ones used to document a wound. Ulcer size, location, ulcer stage, presence of exudate, infection, nonviable tissue, and undermining and tunneling, and description of exudate are all characteristics to be documented. Color photography is increasing in popularity as a documentation tool. Some defense attorneys, however, discourage the use of photography with worsening ulcers. Photographs are taken at the initiation of treatment and at intervals during the course of treatment. Clinicians need to review their institution's consent authorization forms to determine whether a separate consent is necessary before photographing. Often a copy of the photograph is included with communications sent to the individual's primary healthcare provider.

The frequency of documentation is established by the clinician's institution and by the tool being used. For example, the PSST recommends weekly documentation and whenever a change occurs in the ulcer. Many topical dressings can be left in place for several days or up to one week. Documentation guidelines may recommend documenting ulcer characteristics with each dressing change. Others may recommend a minimum of once a month and when changes are noted in the ulcer. The goal is to provide documentation on a routine basis to enable the clinician to determine ulcer progress and adjust treatment according to the clinical findings.

Ulcer education is similar to education provided to an individual with a wound. Education includes pressure ulcer etiology, the rationale for treatment, the activity guidelines, nutritional management, and community resources. The method of education employed should be documented along with the individual's response. Modifications to the treatment plan, based upon education findings, should also be documented.

E. Complications

Possible complications of pressure ulcers include fistulas, abscesses, osteomyelitis, cellulitis, and bacteremia. A fistula refers to an abnormal passage that can occur internally or externally. An internal fistula is a passage from organ to organ. An external fistula refers to a passage from organ to body surface. An abscess refers to a localized collection of pus usually related to an infection; the area is surrounded by inflamed tissue. Osteomyelitis and cellulitis also are related to an infection. Osteomyelitis refers to the inflammation of bone due to an infection. Cellulitis refers to an inflammation of tissue and is characterized by redness, swelling, and tenderness. Bacteria in the blood is called bacteremia. Interventions should be implemented to treat the complication as soon as it is feasible and as early as possible. Complications should be closely monitored and reassessed for improvement or lack of improvement.

26.5 Incontinence
A. Etiology

The involuntary leakage of stool or urine is referred to as incontinence. Incontinence affects the young as well as the old. Some believe incontinence is a component of the aging process. It is not. Incontinence may result from a variety of conditions. Many of the underlying conditions are treatable. A brief overview of some of the causes are presented and are generally classified as constipation and diarrhea, nerve and muscle damage, and irritants.

Constipation and diarrhea both involve the leakage of liquid stool from the anus. Constipation refers to hard, dry stools. In the presence of hard stools, liquid stool may seep around the hard stool and leak out the anus. Liquid stool, diarrhea, may also leak out the anus in the absence of constipation. This is especially true in the presence of high volume liquid stools. Hard, dry stools can also create an obstruction inhibiting the ability to empty the bladder resulting in urinary incontinence. This inability to empty the bladder can result in urinary retention and overflow.

Nerve and muscle damage impact sensory awareness and sphincter function. Damage to the nerves and muscles render them ineffective. Incontinence is considered a complication of some surgical procedures, especially gynecologic procedures, as a result of nerve disruption. Neurological conditions may compromise sensory awareness. This is true in the presence of multiple sclerosis and spinal cord injuries. There is an absence of sensation and a loss of voluntary sphincter control. Fecal incontinence can result from fecal volume that initiates the rectoanal inhibitory reflex. Pudendal nerve damage from vaginal deliveries or surgical procedures can result in a lack of sensory awareness. Sensory dysfunction can result from cognitive impairment. With cognitive impairment there is an inability to interpret or respond. Chronic constipation can result in a distended rectum with no urge. This chronic distension results in sensory impairment.

Irritants, both dietary and medication, may contribute to urinary incontinence. One such irritant is caffeine. Caffeine also has diuretic affects resulting in an increase in urgency and frequency. Medications that alter neurotransmitters in the lower urinary tract result in the relaxation of the bladder neck and urethra. Examples of medications that may impact continence include ace inhibitors and alpha-adrenergic receptor antagonists. One should keep in mind that alcohol is considered a drug. Alcohol contributes to incontinence by increasing volume, producing sedation, and altering mentation.

B. Assessment

Assessment focuses on identifying the cause. Diaries are often a helpful tool in incontinence. The diary should include what beverages are consumed, what foods are eaten, medications, and voiding/stooling habits of both incontinent and non-incontinent episodes. Additional contributing information includes any activity before an incontinence episode. For example in the case of urinary incontinence, the identification of exercise as an activity prior to an episode would be helpful. This identifies for the practitioner that incontinence may be a result of an increase in intraabdominal pressure with an inability of the urethra to resist and the sphincter being unable to maintain a seal. Interpretation of this kind of data may lead the practitioner to the diagnosis of stress incontinence.

The diary will also help to identify the volume, frequency, and type of incontinence. This knowledge will assist in identifying appropriate treatment measures. Another important factor to identify is whether or not the individual is able to toilet. Toileting ability should be examined in terms of one's mobility, cognitive awareness, and mobility.

Incontinence associated dermatitis (IAD) is a term that is now being applied to skin trauma related to incontinence. Incontinence associated dermatitis describes the response of the skin to chronic exposure to urine or fecal materials, identifies the source of the irritant, and refers to the area of skin larger than just the perineum.[25] Skin that has been exposed may respond by becoming inflamed and erythematous (red), with or without the presence of erosion or denudation. The response is dependent upon the moisture irritant, as well as the duration and frequency of the exposure. Keep in mind that the moisture irritant might be urine, stool (formed or liquid), or a combination of these.

Tools have been developed aimed at providing a more consistent assessment. The Perirectal Skin Assessment Tool is a descriptive tool focusing on skin color, skin integrity, the size of the area involved, and the patient's symptoms while encouraging clinicians to include additional descriptors.[26] A tool focusing on the severity is the IAD Skin Condition Assessment Tool developed by Kennedy and Lutz which examines the amount of area involved, the intensity of the redness, and the extent of erosion.[27] The Perineal Assessment Tool helps to identify an individual's risk for incontinence associated dermatitis by examining the type and intensity of the irritant, the duration of the irritant, the perineal skin condition, as well as contributing factors.[28]

C. Treatment

Incontinence treatment focuses on information gathered during the assessment phase. Treatment should include both the underlying cause as well as the prevention of skin breakdown.

TIP: The key component to treating incontinence is to identify the cause and eliminate, or at the very least, manage it.

Intact skin should be maintained. This is best achieved by minimizing the skin's exposure to the irritant. Skin should be cleansed after each incontinence episode while avoiding scrubbing. No-rinse cleaners are available to assist in this process. Additionally, the skin should be moisturized and protected. Moisturizing and protecting may be achieved using individual products developed specifically for its task or by using products that have both moisturizing and protectant properties. The same approach is true when the skin is red, but intact: protect the skin and minimize exposure.

Protecting the skin and minimizing exposure is also a component of treatment in the presence of erosion and denudation. The damaged skin should be protected from further exposure using products that are available for moist wound healing. Some products that might be selected include hydrocolloids and transparent films. These products support moist wound healing of the irritated skin while protecting it and the surrounding skin from irritation. This goal may also be achieved by the use of a zinc oxide based paste. Zinc oxide based pastes combined with absorption powders are effective treatment options.

Efforts to minimize incontinent episodes should also be a component of the treatment plan. Toileting schedules have been shown to be of benefit. Absorptive products that wick away urine or stool have been used, but should be used with caution. These products should not create an occlusive environment and should be changed promptly. Failure to change these products promptly results in irritant containment along with skin exposure. Containment devices such as pouches and external catheters may be of consideration. Examples of these products include external catheters and pouches. Nutritional support is still another component of incontinence treatment.

26.6 Ostomies
A. Etiology
The term ostomy refers to a surgically created opening. The opening in the body is created to remove body wastes. Often the word itself gives an indication as to where the opening is located. For example, the term colostomy refers to an ostomy created in the large intestine (colon) and is created for

stool removal. Ostomies are not only created in the gastrointestinal tract. They may be created in other areas of the body, such as the genitourinary system. Ostomies are created for a variety of reasons.

Blockage is a common reason for an ostomy creation. The blockage may be related to a disease process such as cancer. Other diseases or conditions that could result in an ostomy include Crohn's Disease, Ulcerative Colitis, Cystitis, Neurogenic Bladder, Megacolon, radiation cystitis, and trauma. An inability to take in enough nutrients by mouth as well as poor nutritional absorption could result in an ostomy in the stomach called a gastrostomy. Jejunostomies may be created in situations where the individual is at risk of aspiration. Congenital anomalies may result in an ostomy in a child. Some of these include Cloacal Exstrophy, Prune Belly Syndrome, Necrotizing Enterocolitis, Malrotation, Meconium Ileus, Hirschsprung's Disease, and Imperforate Anus.

Ostomoies may be permanent or temporary. Temporary ostomies provide relief from the underlying etiology allowing the body to heal before being reconnected. A temporary colostomy may be created in the incidence of diverticulitis. If the diseased portion of the intestine is removed, the proximal end of the colon is then brought up onto the abdomen and cuffed over like a sleeve. This "cuffed" portion of intestine is referred to as a stoma. The distal portion is sewn shut. After a period of time, the two ends may be reconnected (reanastomosed).

B. Assessment
It is important to know what specific type of an ostomy an individual has and what output is expected. A colostomy could result in pasty, in the case of an ascending colostomy, to soft formed stool. The expected output of an esophagostomy would be phlegm or spit as well as whatever liquid the individual may have drunk.

Another important assessment component is that of the ostomy itself. In the event that a stoma is created out of intestine, one would expect to note that the stoma is red and moist. One should note whether or not the stoma protrudes from the skin, is at skin level, or is below skin level.

The periostomal skin or the skin surrounding the ostomy should also be assessed. The periostomal skin should be free from redness and irritation. Redness or irritation may indicate an improperly fitting appliance or an inappropriate dressing type. In this instance, treatment would be to refit the appliance. After identifying the cause and eliminating or reducing it, the next step to treatment is that of the skin itself. Peristomal skin irritation/breakdown is treated using the same principles as skin trauma in general.

C. Treatment

TIP: The key component of ostomy treatment is to prevent periostomal skin irritation.

Ostomy treatment focuses on drainage containment to prevent periostomal skin irritation. Drainage containment may be as simple as applying a dressing over the ostomy. The dressing should be such that it will absorb the drainage. For example, a distal bowel stoma should only secrete mucus. A simple gauze dressing over the stoma may be enough to manage the mucus drainage. Some type of skin barrier such as a moisture barrier ointment may also be needed to help protect the skin.

Another containment treatment option is pouching. Manufacturers have produced pouches specifically designed for ostomies with liquid drainage and those with more solid drainage. The pouches for liquid drainage have spouts for emptying the contents. This pouch design may be connected to larger drainage pouches to enable managing larger volumes of drainage. Pouches for more solid drainage tend to have larger openings with some form of closure clamp.

26.7 Summary

An overview of wounds, burns, pressure ulcers, incontinence, and ostomies has been presented. Consideration needs to be given to the etiology and to assessment findings for each of these phenomena. Etiology and assessment findings are the basis for the plan of care. Many of the treatment modalities are the same. Precise, concise, objective documentation aids in the appropriate identification of the situation and the interventions necessary to meet the established plan of care. Documentation assists clinicians in modifying the treatment plan to reach the ultimate goal of treatment. Documentation is the key communication tool.

Endnotes

1. Sherman, R. "What is Maggot Therapy." Maggot Therapy (Larvae Therapy) Project. www.ucihs.uci.edu/com/pathology/sherman/home_pg.htm. Retrieved July 9, 2002.

2. Patel, R. and A. Trampuz. "Infections Transmitted Through Musculoskeletal-Tissue Allografts." *The New England Journal of Medicine.* 350(25), June 17, 2004.

3. Jordan, B.S. and D.T. Harrington. "Management of the Burn Wound." *Nursing Clinics of North America.* 32 (2), June 1997.

4. Johnson R.M. and R. Richard. "Partial-Thickness Burns: Identification and Management." *Advances in Wound Care.* 16 (4), July–Aug 2003.

5. Neuwalder, J.M. et al. "A Review of Computer-Aided Body Surface Area Determination: SAGE II and EPRI's 3D Burn Vision." *Journal of Burn Care and Rehabilitation.* 23 (1), January–February 2002.

6. *Treatment of Pressure Ulcers.* Rockville, MD: U.S. Department of Health and Human Services. December 1994.

7. *Pressure Ulcers in Adults: Prediction and Prevention.* Rockville, MD: U.S. Department of Health and Human Services. May 1992.

8. *Guideline for the Prevention and Management of Pressure Ulcers.* Glenview, IL: Wound Ostomy and Continence Nurses Society. 2003.

9. *Pressure Ulcers: Clinical Practice Guideline.* Columbia, MD: American Medical Directors Association. 1996.

10. *Pressure Ulcer Therapy Companion: Clinical Practice Guideline.* Columbia, MD: American Medical Directors Association. 1999.

11. Folkedahl, B, R. Frantz, and C. Goode. *Research-based Protocol: Prevention of Pressure Ulcers.* The University of Iowa Gerontological Nursing Interventions Research Center. July 1997.

12. Ratcliff, C.R and G.T. Rodedheaver. "Pressure Ulcer Assessment and Management." *Lippincott's Primary Care Practice.* 3 (2), March–April 1999.

13. Pierce, S.M., T.C. Skalak, and G.T. Rodeheaver. "Ischemia-Reperfusion Injury in Chronic Pressure Ulcer Formation: A Skin Model in the Rat." *Wound Repair and Regeneration.* 8 (1), 2000.

14. National Pressure Ulcer Advisory Panel. *NPAUP Report: The Minimum Data Set-2 (MDS-2) and Skin Ulcer Assessment.* Reston, VA: The Author. April 1996.

15. Langemo, D.K. et al. "Incidence of Pressure Sores in Acute Care, Rehabilitation, Extended Care, Home Health, and Hospice in One Locale." *Decubitus.* 2 (2), p. 42. 1989.

16. Bergstrom, N. and B. Braden. "A Prospective Study of Pressure Sore Risk Among Institutionalized Elderly." *Journal of the American Geriatrics Society.* 40, 1992.

17. Willcock, J. and M. Maylor. "Pressure Ulcers in Infants and Children." *Nursing Standards.* 18 (24), February 25–March 2, 2004.

18. Garber, S.L. et al. "Pressure Ulcer Risk in Spinal Cord Injury: Prediction of Ulcer Status Over 3 Years." *Archives of Physical Medicine and Rehabilitation.* 81 (4), April 2000.

19. Mechanick, J.L. "Practical Aspects of Nutritional Support for Wound-Healing Patients." *The American Journal of Surgery*, 188 (1A Supplement), July 2004.

20. Woodbury, M.G. et al. "Pressure Ulcer Assessment Instruments: A Critical Appraisal." *Ostomy Wound Management.* 45 (5), May 1999.

21. Stotts, N.A. et al. "An Instrument to Measure Healing in Pressure Ulcers: Development and Validation of the Pressure Ulcer Scale for Healing (PUSH)." *The Journals of Gerontology. Series A, Biological Sciences and Medical Sciences.* 10, M795–799. 2001.

22. Bates-Jensen, B.M. "The Pressure Sore Status Tool a Few Thousand Assessments Later." *Advances in Wound Care.* 10 (5), 1997.

23. Sussman, G. and G. Swanson. "Utility of the Sussman Wound Healing Tool in Predicting Wound Healing Outcomes in Physical Therapy." *Advances in Wound Care.* 10 (5), 1997.

24. Wright, K.D. "A Temporary Solution to Reverse Staging: The Skin Care Evaluation Sheet." *Ostomy Wound Management.* 43 (7), August 1997.

25. Gray, M., et al. "Incontinence Associated Dermatitis: Consensus." *Journal Wound Ostomy Continence Nursing.* 34 (1), Jan/Feb 2007.

26. Brown, D. S. "Perineal dermatitis: can we measure it?" *Ostomy Wound Measurement,* 39 (7), September 1993.

27. See note 25.

28. Nix, D. "Validity and Reliability of the Perineal Assessment Tool." *Ostomy Wound Management,* 48(2), February 2002.

Chapter 27

Controversies in Skin Trauma

Steven Charles Castle, MD

27.1 Introduction

Skin trauma may result from a personal injury or medical negligence case. Motor or recreational vehicle or job site accidents may result in abrasions, lacerations, burns, open fractures, puncture wounds, and other types of skin trauma. Pressures ulcers are a leading cause of litigation in long-term care and, to a lesser extent, in hospitals. It is imperative that both legal and medical experts have a depth of knowledge about skin trauma. Damage to the integrity of the skin is a sensitive and personal issue. The effect on physical appearance, self-esteem, and body image (how one feels about appear-

ance) should not be underestimated. Both patients and family members can be affected by changes in the skin integrity of the patient. Wounds add complexity and cost to the medical management of the patient, as well as pain and suffering.

Medical records and photographs are key pieces of evidence in skin trauma cases. The attorney, treating healthcare practitioners, and expert witnesses rely on this evidence to fill in the details about the development of skin trauma, the cause, and the management approach. Medical records reveal medical expectations related to wound management and provide the basis for effective communication with the lay judge and jury. This is a challenge, particularly in settings where documentation is usually extensive, but actual description of the wound and management approach is frequently sketchy at best. Uncovering and disclosing supporting data, such as photographs, becomes essential in skin trauma legal cases. A photograph of a wound is clearly a double-edged medico-legal sword. While a picture is always worth a thousand words, a photograph that has the potential of turning stomachs must always be handled carefully and with skill from both plaintiff and defense perspectives.

A wound refers to a disruption in the integrity of the skin and can be caused from a variety of sources, including trauma, burns (chemical, electrical, and thermal), and infections. This chapter addresses surgical wounds, arterial and vascular insufficiency wounds, diabetic ulcers, skin tears, and pressure sores.

27.2 Surgical Wounds
A. Complications of Surgical Wounds

Surgical wound care is common in the acute care setting. Surprisingly, while there is much more evidence to support care measures related to pressure ulcers, data on management of surgical wounds are limited primarily to anecdotal and small studies. A big reason for this is because of the significant variability of the types of surgical wounds, related to surgical technique, anesthesia, and patient characteristics. The major complications associated with wound care include

- infection,
- dehiscence (disruption of fascia or the fibrous tissue that holds things together, that results in a loss of integrity of the wound closure site),
- nerve damage, and
- fluid collections called seromas (serum-like fluid rich in proteins) or hematomas (collection of clotted blood).

The frequency of wound dehiscence varies but is generally thought to occur in about 1 percent of surgical wounds; it increases to 10 percent of infected wounds and 30 percent of previously dehisced wounds. An infected wound must be opened, drained, inspected, and debrided; and if dehiscence is suspected, debridement may need to be done in the operating room.

TIP: An abdominal wound that dehisces may result in an evisceration (intestines falling out of the incision.) This is always a surgical emergency requiring rapid return to the operating room.

B. Surgical Wound Categories

Surgical wound care management has close parallels with military surgery, which has established basic principles of wound cleansing, debridement, and covering/dressings. Hence, there are two basic types of wound management: healing by primary versus secondary intention, based on whether significant tissue has been lost or not.[1] When tissue loss has occurred, the healthcare team must determine if vital structures such as bone, tendon, nerves, and blood vessels have been exposed and evaluate the degree of soft tissue damage and contamination (exposure to bacteria). If this is minimal, then primary wound closure (healing by primary intention, coverage with skin flaps or delayed primary intention) is the preferred methodology. Secondary healing (healing by secondary intention) refers to the type of healing when there has been significant loss of tissue, exposure of vital structures, or contamination (known as a dirty wound). The wound is left open to heal from the inside out. Tertiary healing occurs when the skin is sutured closed or grafted with skin at a much later date.

In the following case, the plaintiff suffered a devastating infection.

The plaintiff developed a bacterial infection following surgery, which resulted in a below the knee amputation. The patient had a history of insulin-dependent diabetes and peripheral vascular disease. During surgery, the patient developed a hospital-acquired bacterial infection which went untreated by the defendant for almost two months. As a result, the patient endured severe pain, drainage and other symptoms of infection which were ignored by the defendant. The jury awarded $5.8 million in this Rhode Island case.[2]

Issues associated with healing of a traumatic wound may lead to litigation.

A case in California involved the treatment of a traumatic wound to the foot of a twenty-three-year-old man seen in the emergency room for a 6.5 cm laceration on the top of his right foot from a motorcycle accident. The wound was anesthetized, irrigated, and explored. The physician found large flecks of debris and some shredding of superficial tendons. The wound was closed, and the patient discharged. A week later, the man visited his primary care physician because he had a red, swollen, and painful lesion on the top of his right foot, about 4 cm distal to the original laceration. The man was referred to an orthopedic surgeon who performed an incision and drainage a day later and found an infected abscess pocket that contained a 6.5 cm fragment identified as a piece of sock by the pathologist. The plaintiff's experts contended that the wound had not been explored adequately and if it had the subsequent infection would have been avoided. The defendants contended that there had been no communication with the subsequent abscess site and sock fragment, that the continued symptoms were the result of the original crush injury, and that the plaintiff had reported that his sock was intact after the accident. The jury returned a verdict for the defendant.[3]

C. Surgical and Anesthesia Factors that Affect Surgical Wound Healing

Tissues must be handled gently. Healthcare providers should not use any caustic solution that could not be placed in the eye, for example. Serious chemical burns have occurred when a concentrated solution of acetic acid was inadvertently used instead of a much more diluted strength.

Small studies have looked at the operative wound/skin cleansing to provide antisepsis as a factor in surgical wound infections. Six studies showed significant differences between the studies. One study found significantly lower infection rates using chlorhexidine compared to iodine, but no benefit was found in the use of iodophor (a type of iodine) impregnated drapes.[4] In addition, the surgical technique or anesthesia which may cause vasoconstriction due to low blood volume, hypoxemia (low blood oxygen levels), or core body hypothermia can impact wound healing by affecting the amount of tissue damage or necrosis.[5]

The medical record should contain documentation in the anesthesia record and operative report about issues related to anesthesia and surgical technique. The anesthesia record notes important physiological monitoring of blood pressure, pulse, and oxygenation, the intravenous solutions and medications that were given, and general comments about the patient's condition. Similar but less detailed information can be found in the surgical report of operations, and disagreements between the surgeon and anesthesiologist may be referenced. The material used to close the surgical wounds is also a factor related to postoperative complications including risk of infection and dehiscence. The report of operation ("op report") usually describes the type and size of sutures and the method of suture closure used, such as interrupted sutures, figure eight, retention sutures, or running sutures.

A systematic review of medical literature performed by the author found eight randomized controlled trials of various tissue adhesives and sutures for closing surgical wound. There were no significant differences in dehiscence, infection, or satisfaction with appearance (by surgeons or patients), although there was a statistically significant higher rating of appearance by surgeons for use of adhesive versus tape in two trials. This suggests that tissue adhesives, which have been traditionally used more in emergency care settings, should be considered as an alternative to sutures and tape. More study is needed particularly in wound closure areas of high tension as well as a general assessment of the effect on overall health.[6]

TIP: Information about the wound characteristics and how it was managed can be found in the surgical report. Difficulties that might have occurred during the surgery such as a drop in blood pressure or core body temperature, extensive wound contamination, or excessive blood loss might be uncovered by comparing the progress notes of the surgeon and the anesthesiologist and by reviewing the flow charts of the vital signs.

D. Surgical Drains

Another variable in surgical wound healing is related to the use of surgical drains. Drains are important in preventing accumulation of fluid from surgical sites that can result in delays in healing, infection, and dehiscence. Drains usually are placed adjacent to the incision, with a separate drainage puncture (referred to as a stab wound) through the skin and not through the incision itself. A variety of drains are used. A Penrose drain is a flat, beige drain that provides a channel for drainage. (The reader may have encountered a Penrose drain when it was used as a tourniquet for blood withdrawal.) The drainage empties onto the dressing. A Hemovac drain consists of two small pancake-shaped disks attached with a spring. When compressed, the device creates suction to pull drainage out of the wound. A Jackson-Pratt (referred to as "JP") drain is shaped like a football. It also creates suction when compressed. A drain may be attached to a suction canister in the wall next to the bed. A detailed discussion of types and indications of surgical drains is beyond the scope of the chapter.

Nursing staff are responsible for daily drain care, including recording the amount of drainage as well as emptying a drainage collection system. The frequency of emptying typically occurs based on time (every four hours or once a shift) rather than on the accumulation or character of the drainage.[7] However, based on study of the most common types of drains, once Hemovac and Jackson-Pratt drains achieve a 50 percent capacity, the suction generated decreases to 13 to 20 percent.[8]

E. Dressings of Surgical Wounds

Dressing care of surgical wounds can influence healing and risk of infection. The operative report describes the skin preparation, and whether the wound was clean or contaminated (dirty) or irrigated. The surgeon will write a postoperative order about how the surgical wound is to be managed by the nursing staff. Some surgeons prefer to be the first person to remove the surgical dressings, whereas others delegate this task to the nursing staff. When the nurses are involved in dressing changes, the actual method used will be in the nursing progress notes. Occasionally wound care flow sheets that may not be considered a part of the medical record are used, and are kept in a central location on the unit or floor. Commonly used skin care abbreviations include

- DSD—dry sterile dressing,
- NS—normal saline,
- ABD pad—abdominal pad, and
- SSD—Sulfa Silvadene (an antibiotic in cream form).

One study in the medical literature found no difference in a case series of post-surgical wound infections after implementing a standardized clean wound care technique instead of the usual sterile technique. The benefit included a decrease in dressing supply costs. This study involved wounds healing by secondary intention (being left open to heal) in comparison to the primary intention healing.[9] The type of solutions used in cleansing of wounds has been studied, and in addition to the previously mentioned avoidance of caustic agents, normal saline has been a favored solution because it is isotonic (same degree of salinity/density as in blood). However, a recent systematic review of studies that looked at various solutions for wound cleansing found one limited trial that suggested the use of tap water (not sterile but low rates of contamination) reduced the rate of infection, while two others found no difference in the infection rates of patients whose surgical wounds were cleansed with tap water versus sterile solutions.

The type of surgical wound dressing has a profound influence on wound healing, and a critical feature is the maintenance of a moist environment.[10] A recent systematic review was performed by the author on randomized controlled trials that evaluated the effectiveness of dressing and topical agents for surgical wounds healing by secondary intention: fourteen reports of thirteen trials had some important findings.

- Aloe vera supplementation versus gauze suggested delayed healing with the aloe vera, but gauze was associated with significantly more pain than other dressings, and patients were less satisfied with gauze in three trials.[11]
- Gauze is less costly but required more nursing time in comparison to foam.[12]
- There was some evidence of faster wound healing with a plaster cast applied to an amputation stump in comparison to elastic compression in one study, but three others failed to demonstrate a difference in the length of stay.[13]
- Another study looked at the effects of topical vitamin E on the cosmetic appearance of scars. Vitamin E failed to produce any improvement and was associated with a high incidence of contact dermatitis versus the usual skin emollient Aquaphor. Vitamin E is not recommended for use on surgical wounds.[14]

F. Types of Surgical Wound Infections

TIP: Infection is reported to occur in 4 percent of clean wounds and about 35 percent of grossly contaminated wounds.

Meticulous surgical technique to avoid contamination of the wound, removal of excessive tissue damage, and maintenance of good hemostasis (limiting the amount of bleeding) are the first steps in prevention of infection.[15]

Among patients undergoing colorectal surgery, 9 to 27 percent acquired a wound infection, delaying discharge by five to twenty days.[16] Infection of wounds results in delayed and poor healing and even keloid formation (excessive scar formation, more common in darkly pigmented people). Infection may develop when moist dressings are used. Fungal infections are particularly problematic in wounds treated with antibacterial ointments and occlusive dressing.[17] Hence, there is debate over the routine use of topical antibiotic ointments or creams for surgical wounds, which was the subject of a recent systematic medical literature review. Findings indicated that systemic antibiotic use did not promote overall healing, though sample size was small and the effect may have been missed if it exists. The recommendation is to give systemic antibiotics only for clear indications of a systemic or local infection. Topical antibiotics showed more promise, but there was too much significant variability between studies to identify a clear advantage.[18]

Increasingly, attention is being directed to the prevention of facility acquired (nosocomial) infections. The 2005 Joint Commission's National Patient Safety Goals address the prevention and development of nosocomial (institution caused) infections. The emerging recognition that infection control practices should be monitored, altered, or investigated, is reflected in the goal to reduce the risk of healthcare acquired infections. The specific steps for this goal include

- Hand hygiene. Comply with current CDC hand hygiene guidelines.
- Healthcare acquired infection. Manage as sentinel events all identified cases of unanticipated death or major permanent loss of function associated with a healthcare acquired infection.[19]

Refer to Chapter 10, *Patient Safety Initiatives and Medical Records*, in Volume I, and Vance[20] for additional information.

27.3 Psychological Factors Associated with Skin Trauma

Development of a nosocomial infection may be a cause of action, as the following case illustrates. The psychological impact of skin trauma is an important medico-legal aspect that has significant influence on jury verdicts.

A $20 million verdict was awarded to a fifty-year-old woman in New Jersey who blamed a plastic surgeon's contaminated instruments for a disfiguring wound infection following an elective cosmetic face-lift. The procedure was performed in the surgeon's office, and the plaintiff developed painful lesions on her face that did not respond to topical antibiotics. Six years later, despite multiple tests and failed treatments, the diagnosis of *Mycobacterium fortuitum* was made, which is a condition similar to leprosy, with resultant necrosis of facial tissue. Jurors were shown before and after photos and the resultant disfigurement despite two reconstructive surgeries. Additional damage occurred from the inability to entertain her husband's clients, from the hearing loss and arthritis from antibiotics she received for the condition, as well as loss of income for her husband for assisting with her medical treatment. Experts testified that the surgeon did not meet the standard of care of sterilization procedures and had inadequate documentation to refute such assertions. The defense did not dispute the unsanitary conditions but asserted there was a lack of causality.[21]

The psychological impact of skin trauma may include feelings of being ugly, deformed, and disfigured. Medical records may record the patient's anxieties, fears, and alterations in self esteem. Counseling may become necessary to deal with the alterations in body image. Patients who are burned are at particular risk for the negative effects of skin trauma. Often the medical approach to burns is straightforward, but there is limited published data that address this important aspect of skin trauma. Papers have described the theory of the effect of disfigurement associated with burns with recommendations for counseling, especially if the burns are not visible and may actually result in increased depression and anxiety in comparison to visible scars.[22] Another review on the psychological impact of burns discusses both the potential for depression from the disfigurement, reported to be 13 to 23 percent, and posttraumatic stress disorder from the trauma of the burn itself, reported to occur in 13 to 45 percent of cases. Risk factors for depression are pre-burn depression and female gender in combination with facial disfigurement. Risk factors for posttraumatic stress disorder include pre-burn depression, anxiety related to pain, and visibility of burn.

Neuropsychological problems can occur, particularly associated with electrical injuries. Problems in mental areas tend to be more troublesome than physical problems, but the quality of life over a period of years tends to be reported as good. However, there are limited studies on the efficacy of psychological treatments specifically related to burns.[23] A survey subsequent to that review examined the relationship

between scarring, severity and visibility, and body esteem among 2500 members of a national burn survivor support group, of which 361 completed all questions. Visible scarring had a low but significant correlation with perceived stigmatization but not with depression, and other measures of scarring had low correlations with social and emotional outcome variables. Because scar severity and visibility are hypothesized to be relevant to self esteem, a multiple regression analysis was performed, and burn characteristics accounted for less than 20 percent of the variance, while social adjustment measures and depression accounted for the largest portion of variance. In summary, this questionnaire of members of a national support group organization of burn victims suggests that burn scar visibility and severity did not have a strong relationship with social and emotional adjustment variables. Hence, more effort needs to focus on dealing with depression and facilitating social support networks in burn victims.[24]

A New York plaintiff received $1.25 million for pain and suffering associated with a burn. He was a 53-year-old man who went to an acupuncturist. While face down on the table, a heating lamp descended on the pole to close proximity to the plaintiff's back. The plaintiff maintained the defendant acupuncturist negligently left him alone for approximately 15 minutes. The defendant acupuncturist stipulated liability. The plaintiff was awarded a total of $1.4 million.[25]

Although the psychological and physical damages associated with a burn may be severe, a medical malpractice claim cannot succeed without establishing liability, as the following case illustrates.

An Illinois man with a blood alcohol level of .384 was placed in leather restraints in the emergency room of Olympia Fields Osteopathic Hospital. The plaintiff was placed in a cast room that was not directly visible from the main treatment area. About one and one-half hours later the plaintiff was discovered on fire. He was still secured in restraints. A cigarette lighter was found on the floor after the fire. The plaintiff sustained third degree burns to twenty-two percent of his body, including thighs, genitals, abdomen, arms, and hands. He required amputation of about five fingers. The jury returned a verdict of $1,078,600 against the nurse and hospital and reduced it by twenty percent to $862,880.[26]

27.4 Overview of Wounds

Burns from hot water or other substances such as a chemical exposure will have a different distribution and shape than those caused by pressure or by venous or arterial insufficiency. Small circular burns on the arm or leg could be due to cigarette burns. Wounds may be secondarily infected, making recognition of the origin more of a challenge, particularly in a demented person or one who cannot speak (aphasic) to provide a history. Wounds other than those caused by pressure should be staged as either partial thickness (not below the dermis) or full thickness. Refer to Chapter 26, *Skin Trauma*, for definitions of these terms.

Wounds may be caused by arterial or venous insufficiency and may be mistakenly called pressure ulcers by nurses on admission wound care sheets or in documents such as the MDS (Minimum Data Set) in a long-term-care facility. (Refer to Chapter 12, *Long-Term Care Records*, for an explanation of this document.) The risk for wound development and the ability to heal wounds are influenced by the overall health of the tissue and the patient. Wounds not due to pressure typically occur on the lateral aspects of the lower extremities or in the digits of feet or hands. However, the presence of non-pressure types of wounds that document the physiological presence of venous or arterial insufficiency are also risk factors for the development of pressure ulcers.

In medical negligence claims, expert witnesses debate whether pre-existing conditions should have been recognized, whether alternative treatments should have been considered, and the relative risk of these factors on the development of pressure ulcers. Physician experts may be asked to address the question of whether a non-healing or infected wound was a causative factor in the patient's demise. Identifying the correct etiology of a wound will have much to do with the expected wound healing and overall disease trajectory, as will be discussed later. Determining the underlying etiology of a complex wound is difficult in real time and can be nearly impossible in review of photographs after the fact in court cases.

The Centers for Medicare and Medicaid Services, which regulates nursing homes, publishes information to benefit the surveyors who enter nursing homes to examine compliance with regulations. In November 2004, specific definitions were issued by CMS in an F tag appendix for Tag F309.[27] CMS replaced Tag F314 and added new language to Tag F309 to include definitions of non-pressure related ulcers with hyperlinks (www.ahrq.gov, www.npuap.org, www.amda.org, www.medqic.org, www.wocn.org, healthinaging.org, and a CMS site www.cms.hhs.gov/medicaid/survey-cert/siqhome.asp). These guidelines for surveyors af-fect the documentation of long-term-care records and direct the practice of clinicians. The guidelines state that the clinician should document the basis of a skin ulcer at the time of assessment and diagnosis to differentiate wounds that have a similar appearance to a pressure ulcer but are not ulcers. Tag F309 is intended to address quality of care deficiencies not covered by 42 C.F.R. 483.25 (a)-(m), and attempts to clarify what "highest practical" functioning and well-being mean, with respect to the limits of recognized pathology and the aging process as identified in the comprehensive assessment of the resident (for which the MDS is a part but not the sole component of the assessment). Furthermore, this F Tag attempts to clarify and distinguish pressure ulcer wounds from arterial, diabetic neuropathy, and venous insufficiency wounds as discussed below.

TIP: The terminology of this CMS appendix is very detailed, likely beyond the scope of practice of staff, and requires additional training if it is to be used as a guideline for nursing staff. Nursing administrative or educational staff may be required to comment on expected scope of practice for various staff nurses.

A. Arterial Ulcer

A wound may result from inadequate blood flow due to intrinsic blockage of an artery from a variety of disease states or from impaired circulation elsewhere (heart disease or stroke). Distinguishing characteristics include pain that *decreases* with dependency (hanging foot down), location on a distal extremity, and a dry pale wound bed. Other characteristics include diminished pulse in the area, loss of hair, and toenail thickening. Unfortunately, these distinguishing characteristics are rarely documented in the medical record, especially in the long-term-care setting.

B. Venous Insufficiency

Venous insufficiency was previously known as a stasis ulcer, usually occurring on the anterior (front) of the lower tibia or above the medial (inside) ankle. These are the most common vascular ulcers and typically take years to heal. They may recur with minor trauma. These ulcers tend to be painful when the limb is hanging down or the patient is standing, which is referred to as the dependent position. This feature of pain associated with limb position in the dependent position differentiates the venous insufficiency ulcer from an arterial ulcer. There may be minimal to copious amounts of drainage.

The venous insufficiency ulcer is caused by venous hypertension due to one or multiple etiologies including

- obstruction of the vein (from a blood clot, obesity, or tumor) or right-sided failure of the heart (due to lung or heart/heart valve disease),
- impaired ability to move fluid back to the heart due to paralysis or decreased calf muscle strength, or
- generalized edema due to low protein levels in the blood (malnutrition or kidney or liver disease).

Surrounding skin is thickened with a change in skin pigmentation and appearance of flaking/unhealthy. There may be significant edema (swelling), and these wounds are prone to a regional infection of the skin tissue known as cellulitis.

C. Diabetic Neuropathic Ulcer

Diabetic wounds typically refer to specific types of wounds on the soles of the feet, usually under the head of the metatarsals (the bottom of the ball of the foot) and imply impaired sensory nerves in the lower extremities. Underlying diabetes mellitus results in peripheral neuropathy (decreased light touch or proprioception/position sense in the toes). Absence of light touch (abbreviated as LT) may be documented in outpatient records. Proprioception is tested by movement of the toe with the patient's head turned away and recording the number of correct perceptions of moving the toe up or down. Diabetic wounds respond markedly differently from other wounds, in that they tend to be slow or non-healing and can more likely result in osteomyelitis, an infection of the bone. Diabetes also frequently complicates healing of venous and arterial insufficiency wounds.

D. Skin Tears

Medical records may note the development of a skin tear. This is a more common issue in the elderly than in younger patients. Skin tears have been incompletely studied. In an epidemiologic study on adverse and unexpected events in a long-term-care setting, bruises and skin tears were the most commonly reported fall and non-fall related injuries.[28] Aging of the skin itself certainly contributes to this problem, as older adults will recount frequent occurrences of bruising and abrasions with little or no trauma that can be recalled. Studies on human skin using grafting onto special mouse strains have shown that skin from older adults (mean age 70.7 years) has reduced epidermal thickness (the outermost layer of skin), and ability of skin cells (called keratinocytes) to double and repair wounds than younger adults, but that many of these changes are reversed when grafted onto young mice.[29] Hence, the changes in the local environment have a clear effect on the skin; chronic illness will exacerbate the aging changes as well. Any disease that affects circulation, particularly diabetes mellitus or peripheral vascular disease,

and poor nutrition will make the skin more fragile, or as doctors describe it as "friable." One study reviewed 154 skin tears in a long-term-care setting during a six-month period and found that risk factors included stiffness and spasticity of the residents, sensory impairment, limited mobility, poor appetite, polypharmacy (concurrent use of many medications), use of assistive devices, presence of a bruise (ecchymosis), and a history of prior skin tears. This study reported that most skin tears occurred in patient care bedrooms.[30]

Treatment of skin tears is typically provided by non-adherent, non-occlusive dressings, such as Telfa dressings. Other treatment options are similar to those used for skin grafts, including Vaseline gauze, normal saline packs, and non-adherent outer dressings. Dressings should be left intact around five days, unless malodorous or extensive seepage occurs.[31] Methods to prevent skin tears have not been reported other than a screening assessment and approach similar to pressure ulcer prevention. Given this lack of evidence in prevention and management, it is not surprising that there is much inconsistency in terminology or management approach when long-term-care registered nurses were surveyed.[32]

TIP: Skin tears often are quite worrisome to patients and family members, and comments about them may occur in a family log or journal. Review of the nursing notes in particular will often document prior incidents, but plans of care may not specifically address the management of skin care for skin tears.

27.5 Pressure Ulcers
A. Description

Pressure ulcers, also referred to as pressure sores, decubitus ulcers, or decubiti, usually occur over bony prominences. The ulcers are due to compression of blood vessels in the tissue because of persistent pressure, which cuts off the source of oxygen and results in a wound. These are usually graded or staged to reflect the amount of tissue damage. It is often debated when they first developed: from a prior facility, during transfer of a patient, in the emergency department, or during surgery. There is no clinically available test to determine if underlying tissue has been damaged to the point of causing necrosis (death of tissue), although there can be clues for which experts will search the medical records to substantiate a position. However, there are often limited data documenting the start and progression of such wounds.

Correct identification of the stage of a pressure ulcer is important in assessing appropriateness of treatment interventions.[33] As simple as this concept seems, it too has significant inconsistencies and controversies, as discussed below. Refer to Figure 27.1 for the stages of pressure ulcers.

B. Avoidable?

Pressure ulcers have been associated with the concept that care for a patient or resident was poor or inadequate. Pressure ulcers have been accepted as an indicator of quality care by the Centers for Medicare and Medicaid Services (CMS), as is discussed in detail in the next section.

Much work has gone into standardized assessment of the risk of pressure ulcers dating as far back as the Norton Scale developed in 1962. The Braden scale is one of the most commonly used scales in the United States, assessing six main domains:

- sensory perception,
- moisture exposure,
- physical activity,
- mobility,
- nutrition, and
- friction/shear force.[34]

A significant limitation of these scales is the relatively poor positive predictive value (false positive). A poor positive predictive value means that many individuals who screen positive for risk will not develop pressure ulcers. The positive predictive value among seriously ill individuals (prevalence of pressure ulcers of around 37 percent) is only around 20 percent and is as low as 2 percent in the long-term-care setting where the prevalence of pressure ulcers is lower. The significance of a poor positive predictive value means that many individuals are treated with expensive interventions but will never develop the condition.

A second limitation of these scales is the fact that some seriously ill patients identified as at risk and given preventive measures will develop pressure ulcers anyhow, suggesting a floor effect of preventability, meaning a point of diminishing returns despite increased efforts for prevention related to the severity of the underlying illness. This is controversial.[35] The persistent prevalence of pressure ulcers despite significant advances in management and utilization of clinical guidelines suggests that not all pressure ulcers are preventable, though this is also in dispute. In a convenience sample of pressure ulcer management experts, 62 percent of those responding to the survey disagreed with the statement that all pressure ulcers are preventable, and only 5 percent felt that long-term-care facilities had adequate resources to manage pressure ulcers. However, while most felt that pressure ulcers were not necessarily a sign of neglect, 38 percent agreed with the statement that lawsuits were an incentive to facilities to improve the quality of care provided.[36] Finally the recent guidelines for surveyors for Tag F314 attempt to classify avoidable versus unavoidable pressure ulcers, as discussed below.

Stages of Pressure Ulcers

Stage I   Erythematous (reddened) areas of skin that persist even when finger tip pressure is applied (non-blanching), but skin is intact. Stage I pressure ulcers are more difficult to detect in individuals with darkly pigmented skin. *Note:* there is no break in the skin. What is left out of the typical staging description is whether the area of involvement is previously healed skin from a prior scar or healed pressure ulcer or not. Previously damaged tissue is not likely to respond to treatment in the same time frame or manner as previously undamaged skin. Aging has an effect as there is well documented thinning of the skin, flattening of the architecture, and delayed healing, but the presence of various disease states, including diabetes, under nutrition, peripheral vascular disease, and end-stage disease, has much more importance in pressure ulcer risk.[37]

Stage II   Also called "partial thickness," are shallow blisters or erosion of the skin similar to a burn. They do *not* extend below the dermis. Partial thickness is important because of the much higher likelihood and less time for healing. Wounds on the heel may look like a Stage II, with a blister overlying the wound, but typically do involve deeper tissue injury and clinically could be referred to as a deep tissue heel injury. However, most nurses will refer to this as a Stage II wound.

Stage III   A "full thickness" break of the skin below the dermis, but not into deeper tissue. It is difficult to differentiate stages of wounds if there is necrotic tissue, exudates, or drainage. Most guidelines refer to wounds with a scab, otherwise known as an eschar, as "unstageable," but it is highly likely that if an eschar has formed, then the wound extends beyond the dermis. The wound must be cleaned and probed with a cotton tip or gloved finger to know its extent.

Stage IV   Also a full thickness lesion that penetrates into muscle, tendons, or bones. These wounds can lead to systemic infection.

Figure 27.1

The CMS F Tag F314 attempts to clarify avoidable and unavoidable pressure ulcers. It states that a pressure ulcer is primarily caused by "unrelieved pressure that results in damage to the underlying tissue(s)," but friction and shear forces are important contributing factors. "Avoidable" is defined as a pressure ulcer that occurs in a resident when the facility failed to do one or more of the following: "Evaluate the resident's clinical condition and pressure ulcer risk factors, define and implement interventions that are consistent with the resident's needs and goals, and recognized standards of practice; monitor and evaluate the impact of the interventions; or revise the interventions as appropriate."[38] Hence, "unavoidable" is defined as a pressure ulcer occurring even though appropriate/standard of care measures were provided, monitored, and adjusted as needed.

In an Arizona case, a fifty-two year-old man with a history of bladder cancer was admitted to the defendant facility for rehabilitation services. During the thirty-day stay, a preexisting pressure ulcer worsened significantly and became infected. He died ten days later from septicemia. The plaintiff claimed the defendant's staff was negligent in the care of the decedent and that there had been a violation of the Adult Protective Services Act, as well as elder abuse. The defendants claimed the decedent's death was from his bladder cancer. A $1.8 million verdict was returned.[39]

TIP: Wound care nurses may improve the quality of care, but only if the information is disseminated to all staff involved in wound care and prevention. Documentation of training and monitoring of performance of staff are added support to offset the limited documentation of wound care that is common in the long-term-care setting, as well as in acute care.

C. Concept of Standard of Care: A Clinician's Perspective

Standard of care is a legal concept that is not used by and may not be familiar to most clinicians. While it is conceptually simple, a patient being cared for under similar circumstances in a similar setting would have a similar (standard of care achieved) or different (standard of care breached) outcome, it is very abstract in its actual application to specific cases. The other aspect that is unfamiliar to clinicians is that the ultimate decision of this question is by the jury, not the experts, and may have little to do with the actual facts in a given case. The crux of pressure ulcer cases usually comes down to whether care was inadequate or whether this was the unfortunate end stage of irreversible and difficult to manage chronic illness(es).

As mentioned previously, pressure ulcers and wounds are often equated with bad care. However, many nursing home residents are admitted to a long-term-care facility with pressure ulcers, so their progression or the natural progression of a severe underlying and irreversible chronic illness may be equated to poor care. There is significant variability in prospective studies of the development of pressure ulcers in long-term care, with a range of 0.9 percent to over 50 percent.[40] The significant variability in reporting likely has to do with the diversity of residents (severity of illness) as well as the quality of care for pressure ulcer management and prevention: this latter point is discussed in more detail below.

Despite the limitations of current instruments, and the unlikely ability to improve them, risk assessment is the most important element of a pressure ulcer prevention program, and most guidelines recommend assessment on admission, once a week for four weeks, and then quarterly.[41] Studies have shown that facilities that do not use a risk assessment tool had a significantly higher incidence of pressure ulcers, almost double the rate.[42]

Nonetheless, a specific individualized plan of care should be developed for any resident found to be at risk or with an existing wound. This includes

- mobilization of the resident,
- care in transferring patient to avoid shear forces,
- the management of systemic diseases that might affect healing, such as diabetes,
- adequate nutrition and hydration, and
- specific wound care.

If the resident has an existing pressure ulcer, the plan of care should contain the following elements:

- debridement of necrotic tissue or eschar (the "scab" that forms over a wound), except in eschar on heels which are left intact unless infected,
- moist environment but not excessive moisture,
- no topical bactericidal ointments or washes that can disrupt normal healing,
- packing of cavities or holes to promote healing, and
- padding if the wound is over a bony prominence.

Once a plan is developed, the response needs to be monitored and the plan adjusted appropriately.[43] Blisters on the heel are a very different type of injury, and usually the blister is left intact, even once an eschar forms, unless there is evidence of underlying infection.

Applying standard of care criteria is much more of a challenge over time, especially in light of the paradox of extensive charting but actual limited ability to document specific delivery of care. From an expert's perspective, one important aspect to the standard of care question is to identify

- if there is evidence of a change in condition of the resident and whether this is a factor in development or progression of existing pressure ulcers or wounds,
- if this change in condition was recognized by the facility in an appropriate time frame, and
- if it was recognized, did the response to the change in condition match the severity of the change in condition?

D. Clinical Guidelines, the Code of Federal Regulations (C.F.R.) and the Standard of Care

One of the biggest challenges to acute and long-term-care facilities is to incorporate the extensive knowledge and improvements in wound care throughout the facility. Medical experts may state that clinical guidelines and federal regulations are important as guidelines but have limitations in individual application to a complex and varied population. However, there is no question that the many published guidelines in pressure ulcer management have provided a useful framework for nurses to make decisions at the bedside.[44] While the ability to monitor and improve the competency and the quality of the actual wound care delivered at the bedside is a challenge, approaches to assessing the quality of a wound care program have been published.[45]

The CMS Tag F314 further defines and distinguishes various specific aspects of wound care, including description of the wounds, screening assessment and risk factors, and treatment options in detail. Below are terms defined in Tag F314, and other specific aspects of this guideline for surveyors, as it applies to specific assessment and treatment guidelines discussed throughout this chapter.

- Cleansing—remove loose debris, bacteria.
- Irrigation—a type of mechanical debridement, solution delivered under pressure or sprayed on to the wound to remove debris.
- Colonized—bacteria on wound, no evidence of infection.
- Infected—pathogens in large counts that overwhelm usual defenses.

E. Definitions Related to Wound Care
1. Types of debridement

- Autolytic—moisture retentive dressing that allows breakdown of necrotic tissue by natural processes in the body.
- Enzymatic—removal of necrotic material by chemical/enzyme.
- Mechanical—removal of necrotic material by a physical means (pulling bandage/gauze pulling off adherent scab or eschar/necrotic material).
- Sharp—use of a surgical instrument (scalpel or tissue scissors) to remove necrotic/dead debris.

2. Other wound care definitions

- Slough—light, stringy, soft devitalized tissue separating from viable tissue.
- Eschar—thick, leathery, devitalized tissue (dark)—loose or firmly attached.
- Friction—mechanical force on skin from dragging across a surface.
- Shearing—layers of skin rubbing against each other from gravity resulting in damage from tearing, stretching underlying capillaries/blood vessels and tissue.
- Granulation tissue—pink to beefy-red tissue in wound bed, filled with new blood vessels, collagen, fibroblasts (skin cells), and immune cells.
- Tunnel—a channel under skin surface that starts at top of wound edge.
- Sinus tract—cavity or channel under skin that connects the visible wound to an area or pocket under the skin not seen.
- Undermining—destruction and loss of tissue just under the skin margins, making pressure ulcer larger at the base than at the opening.

27.6 Quality of Nursing Care and Documentation in Long-Term-Care Facilities
A. CMS Quality Indicators as they Relate to Prevention of Pressure Ulcers

The Department of Health and Human Services is using the strategy of publicly reporting long-term-care resident outcome measures to administrators of facilities as well as the public in an effort to improve quality via market forces. However, other initiatives have suggested that care in nursing homes will not improve until resources are made available to improve both the number and the training of staff.

Unfortunately, a major limitation of the CMS Quality Indicator initiative is that medical record documentation may be erroneous, in particular about daily care processes, which will be addressed later.

The relevance of lower quality pressure ulcer prevention and care in facilities with higher prevalence of pressure ulcers has been studied.[46] This study compared the care processes of homes with the highest quartile of pressure ulcers reported on the MDS pressure ulcer prevalence quality indicator report to those of homes with the lowest quartile of prevalence of pressure ulcers. This is one criticism of the study, that if the comparison of the development of pressure ulcers in the homes (incidence) might better reflect care processes.[47] In any event, the care processes compared included quality indicators previously published, including

- screening and prevention,
- assessment of pressure ulcers,
- management of the wounds, and
- overall health and coexisting conditions that affect pressure ulcer risk, such as incontinence.

Data about the achievement of quality indicators have been gathered from medical records, direct observation of care, and wireless thigh monitors to assess positioning. Results have been discouraging in the ability to use this quality indicator as a marker for good care, as well as for the need for improving pressure ulcer care in long-term care in general. No difference was found in

- screening (though *none* of the homes fulfilled the quality criteria of screening for pressure ulcers on admission and once a week for the first four weeks),
- documentation of preventive interventions including reposition documentation (documentation of turning every two hours occurred more than 90 percent of the time),
- assisting to the toilet (fewer than two assists per day), or
- feeding assistance or percentage of food consumed.

High pressure ulcer prevalence homes were actually better at quality documentation of the wound characteristics, but no other differences were identified in the management processes for pressure ulcers. There was a wide discrepancy between what was charted and what direct observation and the thigh monitor showed on repositioning. High prevalence homes repositioned only 25 percent of high risk residents.

That was not significantly different from the 19 percent in low risk homes. The average time the high risk resident was in one position was 5.3 hours (in the low prevalence homes) versus 6.0 hours in the high prevalence homes. One very positive outcome is that this study demonstrated that use of a standardized methodology to evaluate pressure ulcer care was feasible.[48]

One of the issues related to repositioning that is rarely discussed in care plans or the medical record relates to patient autonomy regarding positioning. This often relates to patient comfort. The appendix to the C.F.R. guidelines for surveyors discusses the lack of evidence of the benefit of momentary shifts to relieve pressure limited to ten to fifteen seconds. This document also gives guidelines on the resident's right to refuse care and treatment, such as getting out of bed, positioning, and exercising. The guideline provides useful comment on what and how the facility should discuss with the resident and/or legal representative regarding the resident's overall condition, the treatment options, and the consequences of refusing treatment, as well as treatment alternatives if the resident refuses one option.[49] This concept of decisional capacity for medical care options is a complex one, and with little specific guidelines as it refers to care options such as getting out of bed, exercising, or positioning in bed. Hence, management of pain and comfort measures may conflict with positioning and exercise programs. This may be particularly true in end of life care, as wound care provided to these patients is still under the auspices of surveyors and medical liability. Hence it is still important in end of life or comfort care to discuss specific treatment options related to pressure ulcer prevention with the patient and caregiver, and to include consequences of not providing certain elements of care, including the development of pressure ulcers.[50]

B. Staffing Time and Adverse Events Such as Pressure Ulcers

Contrary to expected outcomes, in the acute care setting the prevalence of pressure ulcers has been found to correlate directly with higher nursing hours per patient, suggesting that this is more a marker of a sicker population than it is a marker of residents at higher risk for pressure ulcers.[51] However, a recent survey of ninety-five long-term-care facilities participating in the National Pressure Ulcer Long-Term Care Study throughout the United States demonstrated that residents in facilities with care time by registered nurses of more than fifteen minutes per resident per day and by nurses' aides of more than two hours per resident per day were less likely to develop a pressure ulcer.[52] These staffing ratios are similar to those proposed by the National Citizens' Coalition for Nursing Home Reform of 0.53 registered nursing hours per resident day and a minimum level of total direct nursing staff care of 1.6 hours per resident day.[53]

The discrepancy between staffing times and pressure ulcer prevalence between acute and long-term care could be due to time out of bed. An MDS Quality Indicator on bed-fast patients has been studied[54] to see if differences in care processes could be correlated with this indicator. Facilities in the upper versus lower quartile of reported bedfast residents on the quality indicator were compared to the activity and mobility care provided by nurses for the residents. A combination of medical record review, resident interview, and direct observation was used to assess scores on six activity and mobility care process indicators. The highest quartile of bedfast residents' homes demonstrated a higher proportion of residents described as bedfast (43 percent versus 34 percent) as well as a higher proportion of residents who spend more than twenty-two hours in bed (18 percent versus 8 percent). Of note, all fifteen nursing homes that were studied underestimated the number of bedfast residents. The number of bedfast residents was derived from the Minimum Data Set and defined as the number of residents in bed or in reclining chairs twenty-two hours or more per day, in the immediate four of seven days prior to the MDS assessment. Hence, spending excessive time in bed may be a reflection of differences in the quality of activity and mobility care provided during the times not in bed. Surprisingly, the residents in the highest quartile of bedfast residents showed more activity episodes and reported receiving more walking assistance than the residents in the lowest quartile of bedfast patients.[55] Another study of thirty-four California nursing homes on the effect of staffing time on in-bed times of nursing home residents demonstrated that residents residing in lower staffed homes were nearly six times more likely to have more than 50 percent of observations in bed than in higher staffed homes, even when resident functional level was controlled.[56]

While training is a key component in skills competency, actual measurement of competency is needed. When one staff person is relied on for wound care expertise, there is significant risk as to turnover of that staff member.[57] Despite the high visibility of pressure ulcers as a healthcare problem, studies in The Netherlands have demonstrated that nursing practice in prevention of pressure ulcers is still strongly rooted in old traditions in nursing, and hence a systematic approach is necessary to change nursing thinking and acting with regards to pressure ulcer prevention.[58] These two factors (reliance on a wound care expert and strongly rooted old traditions) are likely contributors to the findings of a medical chart review of thirty-five nursing homes in the De-partment of Veterans Affairs which showed that the six key pressure ulcer prevention recommendations were followed by clinicians only 50 percent of the time.[59]

27.7 Controversies in the Use of Specialized Care for the Prevention and Treatment of Pressure Ulcers

Like a fall related injury or other adverse outcomes, when a pressure ulcer occurs that is associated with a significant adverse health effect, questions of liability may be raised. Issues addressed include whether the patient was identified as being at risk for skin breakdown, whether an appropriate plan of care was developed and implemented, and if the failure of the ulcer to improve resulted in a revision of the plan of care. This inherent liability is further compounded by the limitations of documentation of what actual care was provided, especially in the long-term-care setting where the most hands-on care is provided by staff who do not document and are the least trained (certified nursing assistants/aides).

TIP: Policies, procedures, and routine evaluation of adverse events are extremely important in adding a safety net to liability, but limited resources make implementation a challenge.

One of the interventions often cited on nursing care plans is the use of different pressure-relieving surfaces. Forty-one randomized clinical trials were included in the systematic review performed by the author. One conclusion was that for residents or patients at high risk for pressure ulcer development, consideration should be given to the use of higher specification foam mattresses rather than standard hospital foam mattresses, but that the relative merit of higher technology constant low pressure and alternating pressure mattresses for pressure ulcer prevention was unclear. While consideration should be given to the use of pressure relief surfaces for high-risk individuals in the operating room, the benefit of seat cushions and overlays for use in the emergency room has not been adequately evaluated.[60]

A recent review on the use of topical negative pressure for the treatment of chronic wounds found two small studies with weak evidence suggesting that topical negative pressure may be superior to saline gauze dressing, although the effect of this treatment on cost, quality of life, or pain was not assessed.[61] There are a variety of other specialized treatments with limited or no quality randomized controlled trials in wound healing such as the use of growth factors, hyperbaric oxygen, electrical stimulation, and heat treatments; and hence there is limited support for making recommendations for the benefit of these products.

27.8 Nutritional Support in Wound Healing

Aspects of nutritional care that are well accepted include

- the importance of assessing and monitoring nutritional status,
- the importance of absolute protein intake in wound healing, and
- improvement of protein stores, which is very difficult in someone with extensive wounds, especially if there is active infection.

A recent meta-analysis was completed by the author who reviewed randomized controlled trials (RCT) evaluating the effectiveness of enteral (by mouth) or parenteral (by intravenous) nutritional supplementation on the prevention and treatment of pressure ulcers.[62] Only eight studies were identified that met the criteria of a RCT. There was significant variability in the methods, making it impossible to draw firm conclusions. One trial looked at mixed nutritional supplements, one examined zinc, another protein, and two assessed the effect of vitamin C. The largest study found that nutritional supplements reduced the number of new pressure ulcers. Other case series have reported that stage III and IV ulcers were significantly improved by three weeks of nutritional supplementation that was rich in protein, arginine, vitamin C and zinc.[63] Another comparison study that was not randomized identified that a high protein diet of more than sixty grams of protein per day was associated with improved healing in malnourished nursing home patients with pressure ulcers. Again, it is important to emphasize that these case series reports are not randomized. Randomized clinical trials are extremely challenging to perform due to the significant variability of the population with pressure ulcers, making the risk of a confounding variable likely unless the study is large. The role of feeding tubes in dementia patients is a very controversial issue and beyond the scope of this chapter.

27.9 Summary

Wounds to the skin are an important medico-legal issue because they are visible and hence have a tremendous impact on self-image and pain. Families and juries understand and can relate to skin trauma. Because of the emotional aspects associated with wounds, medical experts and attorneys need to be diligent in addressing the foundation of what led to the wound and the healthcare response to the wound. In post-surgical wounds, factors involved in the surgery and anesthesia, as well as in the approach to management need to be assessed. In non-pressure ulcer traumatic wounds, specific immediate management and follow up are reviewed in the context of underlying disease.

Knowing the underlying disease processes that led to the wound or that affected the ability to heal the wound is essential. A pressure ulcer is a unique and common subset of wounds, and there is much written about the approach to management. Because of the complexity of underlying diseases that contribute to the development of pressure ulcers, the plan of care and expected response must be reviewed on a case-by-case basis. A key factor in pressure ulcer cases is not so much what was done to treat the pressure ulcer but how it was monitored. If treatment was not effective, was evaluation of the context of the wound and subsequent management reassessed? Other wounds also need to be reviewed in the context of disease, particularly arterial and vascular insufficiency. The medical record holds the key for understanding the cause, treatment, and liability associated with skin trauma.

Endnotes

1. Atiya, B.S. et al. "Management of Acute and Chronic Open Wounds: The Importance of Moist Environment in Optimal Wound Healing." *Current Pharmaceutical Biotechnology*. 3, p. 179–95. 2002.

2. "5,800,000 Verdict." *New Jersey Jury Verdict Review and Analysis*. April 2008, Issue 11, p. 28.

3. Laska, L. "Piece of Sock Alleged to be Left in Foot Wound." *Medical Malpractice Verdicts, Settlements, and Experts*. February 2004, p. 16–17.

4. Edwards, P.S., A. Lipp, and A. Holmes. "Preoperative Skin Antiseptics for Preventing Wound Infections After Clean Surgery." *Cochrane Database of Systematic Reviews*. 1, 2005.

5. Tweed, C. "A Review of the Literature Examining the Relationship Between Temperature and Infection in Surgical Wound Healing." *Primary Intention*. 11, p. 119–23. 2003.

6. Coulthard, P. et al. "Tissue Adhesives for Closure of Surgical Wounds." *Cochrane Database of Systematic Reviews*. 1, 2005.

7. Pleat, J. and C. Dunkin. "The Management of Surgical Drains in Plastic Surgical Units." *Nursing Research*. 51, p. 73–75. 2002.

8. Williams, J., D. Toews, and M. Prince. "Survey of the Use of Suction Drains in Head and Neck Surgery and Analysis of Their Biomechanical Properties." *Journal of Otolaryngology.* 32, p. 16–22. 2003.

9. Lawson, C., L. Juliano, and C.R. Ratiliff. "Does Sterile or Nonsterile Technique Make a Difference in Wounds Healing by Secondary Intention?" *Ostomy/Wound Management.* 49, 56–8, 60. 2003.

10. Atiya, B.S. et al. "Management of Acute and Chronic Open Wounds: The Importance of Moist Environment in Optimal Wound Healing." *Current Pharmaceutical Biotechnology.* 3, p. 179–95. 2002.

11. Verneulen, H. et al. "Dressings and Topical Agents for Surgical Wounds Healing by Secondary Intention." *Cochrane Database of Systematic Reviews.* 1, 2005.

12. *Id.*

13. *Id.*

14. Baumann, L.S. and J. Spencer. "The Effects of Vitamin E on the Cosmetic Appearance of Scars." *Dermatology Surgery.* 25, p. 311–315. 1999.

15. Meeks, G.R. and T. Trenhaile. "Surgical Incisions: Prevention and Treatment of Complications." *UpToDate.* 2005.

16. Donnal, B. "Can Anaesthetic Management Influence Surgical-Wound Healing?" *Lancet.* 356, p. 355–357. 2000.

17. Giandoni, M.B. and W.J. Grabski. "Cutaneous Candidiasis as a Cause of Delayed Surgical Wound Healing." *Journal of the American Academy of Dermatology.* 30, p. 981–984. 1994.

18. "Review: Some But Not All Topical Antimicrobial Agents Improve the Rate of Healing of Chronic Wounds." *ACP Journal Club.* 135, p. 55. 2001.

19. www.jcaho.org/accredited+organizations/ patient+safety/05+npsg/05_npsg_hap.htm. Retrieved October 15, 2004.

20. Vance, J. "Infections in the Nursing Home" in Iyer, P. (Editor). *Nursing Home Litigation: Investigation and Case Preparation.* Second Edition. Tucson, AZ: Lawyers and Judges Publishing Company. 2005.

21. Laska, L. "Woman Suffers Tissue Infection Following Cosmetic Facelift Due to Contaminated Instruments." *Medical Malpractice Verdicts, Settlements, and Experts.* May 2004. p. 51–52.

22. Cahner, S.S. "Young Women with Breast Burns: A Self-Help 'Group by Mail.'" *Journal of Burn Care and Rehabilitation.* 13, p. 44–47. 1992.

23. Van Loey, N.E. and M.J. Van Son. "Psychopathology and Psychological Problems in Patients with Burn Scars: Epidemiology and Management." *American Journal of Clinical Dermatology.* 4, p. 245–272. 2003.

24. Lawrence, J.W. et al. "The 2003 Clinical Research Award: Visible vs. Hidden Scars and Their Relationship to Body Esteem." *Journal of Burn Care and Rehabilitation.* 25, p. 25–32. 2004.

25. $1,400,000 Verdict." New Jersey Jury Verdict Review and Analysis," April 2008, Vol. 28, No. 11, p. 30.

26. Laska, L. "Failure to Properly Monitor While in Restraints Placed Due to Disorderly Conduct Caused by Intoxication." *Medical Malpractice Verdicts, Settlements, and Experts.* November 2008, p. 10.

27. CMS Manual System Pub. 100-07 State Operations Provider Certificate, DHHS and CMS. November 12, 2004.

28. Gurwitz, J.H. et al. "The Epidemiology of Adverse and Unexpected Events in the Long-Term-Care Setting." *Journal of the American Geriatrics Society.* 42(1), p. 33–8. 1994.

29. Gilhar, A. et al. "Aging of Human Epidermis: Reversal of Aging Changes Correlates with Reversal of Keratinocyte Fas Expression and Apoptosis." *Journal of Gerontology Series A-Biological and Medical Science.* 59(5), p. 411–5. 2004.

30. McGough-Csarny, J. and C.A. Kopac. "Skin Tears in Institutionalized Elderly: An Epidemiological Study." *Ostomy Wound Management.* 44(3A Suppl), 14S–24S. 1998.

31. Edwards, H., D. Gaskill, and R. Nash. "Treating Skin Tears in Nursing Home Residents: A Pilot Study Comparing Four Types of Dressings." *Int J Nurs Pract.* 4(1), p. 25–32. 1998.

32. O'Regan, A. "Skin Tears: A Review of the Literature." *World Council of Enterostomal Therapists Journal.* 22(2), p. 26–31. 2002.

33. National Pressure Ulcer Advisory Panel. *Pressure Ulcer Staging System.* http://www.npuap.org/

34. *Id.*

35. Bergstrom, N. et al. "The Braden Scale for Predicting Pressure Sore Risk." *Nursing Research.* 36, p. 205–210. 1987.

36. Thomas, D.R. "Issues and Dilemmas in the Prevention and Treatment of Pressure Ulcers: A Review." *Journal of Gerontology: Medical Sciences.* 56A, M328–M340. 2001.

37. Breslow, R.A. et al. "The Importance of Dietary Protein in Healing Pressure Ulcers." *Journal of the American Geriatrics Society.* 41(4), p. 357–62. 1993.

38. Brandes, G.H. and D. Berlowitz. "Are Pressure Ulcers Preventable? A Survey of Experts." *Advances in Skin and Wound Care.* September–October 2001, p. 245–48.

39. Laska, L. "Man's Decubitus Ulcer Worsens and Becomes Infected During Short Stay." *Medical Malpractice Verdicts, Settlement, and Experts.* April 2009, p. 35.

40. Horn, S.D. et al. "Description of the National Pressure Ulcer Long-Term Care Study. *Journal of the American Geriatrics Society.* 50, p. 1816–1825. 2002.

41. Bates-Jensen, B.M. "Quality Indicators for Prevention and Management of Pressure Ulcers in Vulnerable Elders." *Annals of Internal Medicine.* 135(8), part 2, p. 744–751. 2001.

42. Lyder, C.H. et al. "Medicare Quality Indicator System: Pressure Ulcer Prediction and Prevention Module Final Report." Government Report. *Health Care Finance Administration.* Bethesda, MS. November 1998.

43. *See* Note 41.

44. Dowding, C. and C. Thompson. "Using Decision Trees to Aid Decision-Making in Nursing." *Nursing Times.* 100, p. 36–9. 2004.

45. Bates-Jensen, B.M. et al. "Standardized Quality-Assessment System to Evaluate Pressure Ulcer Care in the Nursing Home." *Journal of the American Geriatrics Society.* 51(9), p. 1195–1202. 2003.

46. Bates-Jensen, B.M. et al. "The Minimum Data Set Pressure Ulcer Indicator: Does it Reflect Differences in Care Processes Related to Pressure Ulcer Prevention and Treatment in Nursing Homes?" *Journal of the American Geriatrics Society.* 51(9), p. 1203–12. 2003.

47. Berlowitz, D. "Striving for Six Sigma in Pressure Ulcer Care." *Journal of the American Geriatrics Society.* 51, p. 1320–1321. 2003.

48. Bates-Jensen, B.M. et al. "Standardized Quality-Assessment System to Evaluate Pressure Ulcer Care in the Nursing Home." *Journal of the American Geriatrics Society.* 51(9), p. 1195–1202. 2003.

49. *See* Note 27.

50. Chaplin, J. "Wound Management in Palliative Care." *Nursing Standard.* 19, p. 39–42. 2004.

51. Cho, S. et al. "The Effects of Nurse Staffing on Adverse Events, Morbidity, Mortality, and Medical Costs." *Nursing Research.* 52(2), p. 71–9. 2003.

52. Horn, S.D. et al. "Description of the National Pressure Ulcer Long-Term-Care Study." *Journal of the American Geriatrics Society.* 50, p. 1816–1825. 2002.

53. "National Citizens' Coalition for Nursing Home Reform. Proposed Minimum Staffing Standards Nursing Homes." http://www.nccnhr.org/Updates/rsolution_98.htm. Retrieved March 27, 2001.

54. Bates-Jensen, B.M. et al. "The Minimum Data Set Bedfast Quality Indicator: Differences Among Nursing Homes." *Nursing Research.* 53(4), p. 260–72. 2004.

55. *Id.*

56. Bates-Jensen, B.M. et al. "The Minimum Data Set Pressure Ulcer Indicator: Does it Reflect Differences in Care Processes Related to Pressure Ulcer Prevention and Treatment in Nursing Homes?" *Journal of the American Geriatrics Society.* 51(9), p. 1203–12. 2003.

57. *See* Note 47.

58. Buss Inng, C. et al. "Pressure Ulcer Prevention in Nursing in Nursing Homes: Views and Beliefs of Enrolled Nurses and Other Healthcare Workers." *Journal of Clinical Nursing.* 13, p. 668–676. 2004.

59. Saliba, D. et al. "Adherence to Pressure Ulcer Prevention Guidelines: Implications for Nursing Home Quality." *J Am Geriatr Soc.* 51, p. 56–62. 2003.

60. Cullum, N. et al. "Support Surfaces for Pressure Ulcer Prevention." *Cochrane Database For Systematic Reviews*. 1, 2005.

61. Evans, D. and L. Land. "Topical Negative Pressure for Treating Chronic Wounds." *Cochrane Database of Systematic Reviews*. 2, 2004.

62. Langer, G. et al. "Nutritional Interventions for Preventing and Treating Pressure Ulcers." *Cochrane Wounds Group Cochrane Database of Systematic Reviews*. 1, 2005.

63. Soriano, L.F. et al. "The Effectiveness of Oral Nutritional Supplementation in the Healing of Pressure Ulcers." *Journal of Wound Care*. September 2004, 13(8), p. 319–22.

64. *Id.*

Appendix A

Medical Terminology, Abbreviations, Acronyms, and Symbols

Ann M. Peterson, EdD, MSN, RN, CS, LNCC

Medical Terminology

English words, and most medical terms, are drawn from other languages, most notably Latin and Greek. To determine the meaning of a word it is helpful to understand the basic components—the root, the prefix and the suffix. Generally, but not always, prefixes and suffixes combine with a root of a word derived from the same language, that is, Latin prefixes and suffixes combine Latin roots and Greek prefixes and suffixes with Greek roots.

The root, stem, or base of a word provides the primary meaning. The prefix added to the beginning of the root word changes the meaning. For example, one can add "un" before the root word "pleasant," or add "a" to "symptomatic." The suffix is added to the end of a word to modify its meaning and, often, its part of speech. For instance, adding "ly" to the end of the word "pleasant" changes the word from an adjective to an adverb. Breaking down the various components of a word or phrase will help the reader arrive at a definition. Define the suffix first followed by the prefix and then the root. (See Table A.1.)

Roots

The root provides the basic meaning of a word and can be descriptive (providing color, strength, size, shape, position and quantity) as is shown in the following examples

- Leukocyte describes the *body part* and *color*—white cell.
- Megaloblast suggests *strength* of an abnormally large immature blood cell that develops in large numbers in the bone marrow.
- Bariatrics describe the field of medicine dealing with *size,* i.e., obesity.
- Anklosis indicates the *shape,* i.e., bent or abnormally positioned joint.
- Dextrocardia denotes the *position* of the heart in the right side of the chest.

- Oliguria describes the *quantity* of urine.

Although a root can stand alone, it is usually combined with a suffix. For example gastro, meaning stomach, usually occurs with a suffix. The suffix "itis" means inflammation. Some words, such as gastroenteritis, have more than one root. (See Table A.2.) Prefixes and suffixes connect two consonantal roots with the letter "o", as in "neur + o + logy." However the "o" is dropped when joining to a vowel stem as in the word "neur + itis."

Prefixes

A prefix, generally an adverb or preposition, placed before a word will add to or alter the word's meaning. Consider the words order and **dis**order. (See Table A.3.)

Suffixes

The suffix, added at the end of a word, identifies the part of speech—noun, verb, and adjective. Some, such as phobia, can stand alone. Start with the suffix when attempting to define a word. (See Table A.4.)

Abbreviations and Acronyms
Legibility

An Institute of Medicine report, "To Err is Human: Building a Safer Health System," published in 2000, estimates that, in any given year, as many as 98,000 people die from medical errors that occur in hospitals. Many patient safety experts feel this number is too low. The original Harvard Practice Review studied New York State hospitals. Additional people die of negligence in other settings, such as offices, nursing homes, clinics, and so on. Illegible entries compromise patient safety and lead to disastrous legal ramifications.

In general, written medical documentation should be done in black ink; however, some institutions designate other colors for the evening and night nurses' notes or for telephone orders. Each entry should immediately follow the

565

previous entry without leaving any blank space between the entries. If an error is made, a single line should be drawn through the erroneous words and the words written above followed by the initials of the writer making the correction. Erasures or liquid whiteout are unacceptable. If the note flows over onto a second page, each entry and page in the progress notes and the doctor's order sheet should be preceded by the date and time that documentation was made and should be followed by the writer's legal signature and license initials. For example: John Doe, RN.

Communication and Safety

The goal of medical records is to communicate information about a patient's health and care. Abbreviations, intended to save time and space, can be problematic if illegible or misinterpreted. Many abbreviations have more than one meaning, even within the same discipline, as the following points out.

> "A 49-YO WF was admitted with CP and SOB. She was known to have MS and MI and had an MVR 2 years ago." The first question that arises is whether she is having chest pain or chest pressure. The poor woman also may have multiple sclerosis, but what if she has mitral stenosis? She could have a history of mitral stenosis and mitral incompetence, but maybe she has had a myocardial infarction. One hopes that the physician remembers that she had a mitral valve repair rather than a mitral valve replacement 2 years ago, so she doesn't receive anticoagulants unnecessarily, and so on. Like a physician's handwriting, the interpretation of medical abbreviations often is in the eye of the beholder.[1]

Knowing the field of medical practice will help, but not ensure, correct interpretation of abbreviations and acronyms. To prevent misunderstandings most healthcare facilities offer an official list of authorized abbreviations or use abbreviations recommended by The Joint Commission (formerly the Joint Commission on Accreditation of Healthcare Organizations or JCAHO). Medical personnel should only use standard approved abbreviations, acronyms and symbols.[2]

The concern over the lack of standard medical abbreviations, acronyms and symbols has long been recognized.[3] Given the magnitude of abbreviations, acronyms, and symbols in use (the 2005 *Stedman's Medical Speller* contained 120,000 entries based on more than 72,000 medical words, phrases, and acronyms), it is more practical to address what is NOT accepted. In an effort to reduce the risk to patient safety and professional liability, organizations such as The Joint Commission have published a list of abbreviations, acronyms, and symbols *not* to be used, and encouraged healthcare institutions to prepare a list of approved abbreviations to be used within the medical records. They should not be used on the face sheet, in the final diagnosis, or on the physician's order sheet.

The use of handwritten abbreviations and symbols can jeopardize patient safety due to illegibility and misinterpretation. As the list provided below demonstrates, there can be numerous interpretations, influenced by the practitioner's education, experience, background, writing style (upper case versus lower case, use of periods, and so on) and legibility, specialty area, and patient care setting. In an effort to reduce the risk to patients' safety, institutions and organizations such as The Joint Commission and the Institute for Safe Medication Practices (ISMP) have provided listings of often-misinterpreted abbreviations to be eliminated from all types of clinical documentation, including written laboratory reports.

JCAHO's *2004 National Patient Safety Goals* requires abbreviations, acronyms and symbols used to be standardized throughout the organization (Standard IM.3.10, EP #20). The Joint Commission's approved list of dangerous abbreviations, acronyms, and symbols *not to use* were required to appear on each accredited organization's "Do not use" list beginning January 1, 2004. In 2008, The Joint Commission reaffirmed and renumbered this safety goal as NPSG.02.02.01. The ISMP urges publishers and Information Systems vendors to adhere to a single universal standard and follow the recommended standards in their printed materials and has made available the *List of Error-Prone Abbreviations, Symbols, and Dose Designations* at http://www.ismp.org/tools/errorproneabbreviations.pdf.

Table A.1
Word Components

Word	Prefix	Root	Suffix
Autobiography A story of a person's life written by himself.	*Auto* is from the Greek word meaning "self."	*Bio* is from the Greek word meaning "life."	*Graph* is from the Greek word meaning graph which means "to write."
Angiotensin A chemical in the body that causes blood vessel constriction.	*Tensin* is from the Latin word "tendere" which means "to stretch."	*Angio* is from the Greek word "angeion" meaning "vessel."	
Appendicitis		*Appendix* comes from the Latin word "appendere" which means "to add something."	*Itis* is from the Greek language meaning "inflammation."
Vermiform	*Vermi* is from the Latin word "vermis" meaning "worm."	*Forma* is the Latin word meaning "form."	

Table A.2
Roots

Root	Meaning	Sample Word
acanth-	spine, prickle	**acanth**oma—tumor arising from the prickle-cell layer of the epidermis
aceto-	vinegar cup	**aceta**bulum—cup-shaped cavity that holds the femur head
acro-	extremity, tip, sharp	**acro**megaly—chronic metabolic condition characterized by marked enlargement of the bones of the face, jaw and extremities
adeno-	gland	**adeno**pathy—enlargement of a gland
agon-	contest, struggle	**agon**ist—contacting muscle opposing another muscle
angio-	vessel	**angio**genesis—ability to evoke blood vessel formation
ankyl-	bent, a joint locked in one position	**ankyl**osis—fusion of a joint
arthro-	joint	**arthro**scopy—examination of an interior joint via endoscopy
athero-	meal	**athero**sclerosis—formation of plaques on an arterial wall
azo-	nitrogen	**azo**temia—retention of an excessive amount of nitrogenous compounds in the blood
bac(t)-	rod	**bac**terium—rod shaped organism
balano-	acorn, glans	**balan**itis—inflammation of the glans penis
blast-	bud, sprout	**blast**in—any substance that provides nourishment for cell growth
bleph-	eyelid	**bleph**aritis—inflammation of the eyelids
bol-	throw	**bol**us—a dose of medicine injected all at once intravenously
brachi-	arm	**brachi**alis—muscle of the upper arm
brady-	slow	**brady**cardia—slow heart rate
calco-	heel, spur	**calca**neal—relating to the heel bone
carpo-	wrist	**carp**al—pertaining to the wrist
caus-	burn	**caus**algia—burning pain
cephal-	head	**cepha**lgia—headache
cereb(r)-	brain	**cereb**ral hemorrhage—hemorrhage of a blood vessel in the brain
cervic-	neck	**cervic**odynia—neck pain
chlor(o)-	green	**chlor**oma—greenish malignant neoplasm
chol(e)-	bile	**chol**angitis—inflammation of the bile ducts
chondr-	cartilage	**chrondr**omalacia—softening of the cartilage
chrom-	color	**chrom**otopssia—a form of color blindness
circum-	around	**circum**cision—cutting around
cirrh(o)-	red-yellow	**cirrh**osis—chronic degenerative disease of the liver
cornu-	horn	**corn**—a horny mass, resulting from chronic friction and pressure, over a bony prominence
cost(o)-	rib	**cost**ectomy—surgical removal of a rib
cox-	hip	**cox**a—head of the femur
Cranio-	skull	**crani**um—skull
cubit-	elbow	**cubit**al—pertaining to the elbow
cutane	skin	**cutane**ous—pertaining to the skin

Root	Meaning	Sample Word
cyan-	dark blue	**cyan**osis—bluish discoloration of the skin or mucous membranes due to decreased tissue oxygenation
cysto-	urinary bladder	**cysto**scopy—direct visualization of the bladder
cyto-	cell	**cyto**toxic—poisonous to tissue cells
dacr-	tear (from the eye)	**dacr**yocystitis—infection of the tear duct
dacty-	finger	**dacty**litis—painful inflammation of the fingers or toes
dent	teeth	**dent**ist
derm(o)-, dermat(o)	skin	**dermat**ologist
diplo-	double	**diplo**pia—double vision
dors(i)-, dors(o)-	back	**dors**um—back of
embol-	plug	**embol**us—a quantity of gas, tissue or foreign object that ciculates until it becomes lodged
enceph-	brain	**enceph**alopathy—any abnormality of the brain structure or function
entero-	intestine	**entero**itis—inflammation of the intestine
erythro-	red	**erythro**cyte—red blood cell
equi-	equal	**equi**librium—state of balance
fis-, fid-	split, cleave, divide	**fis**sure—cleft or groove in an organ
fora/foro	hole	**fora**men—opening in a bone
galact	milk	**galact**orrhea—lactation not associated with childbirth or nursing. Symptom associated with pituitary gland tumor.
gangl-	knot	**gangl**ion—knotlike mass of nerve cells
gastr-	stomach, belly	**gastr**ic—pertaining to the stomach
genu	knee	**genu**flect—to bend the knee
gest-	bring forth, produce	**gest**ation—period of time from conception to birth
gingiv-	gums	**gingiv**itis—inflammation of the gums
glauc-	bluish grey	**glauc**oma—disease of the eye with increased pressure within the eyeball
gloss-	tongue	**gloss**odynia—pain in the tongue
gluco-	sweet	**gluco**se—simple sugar found in foods
glute-	buttocks	**glute**al—pertaining to the buttocks
glyco-	sugar	**glyco**genesis—the synthesis of glycogen from glucose
gnath(o)-	jaw	**gnath**ic—pertaining to the jaw
halluc	to wander in the mind	**halluc**ination—a sensory perception not triggered by an external sensation
helm-	worm	**helm**inthiasis—parasitic worm infestation
heme-	blood	**heme**turia—abnormal presence of blood in the urine
hemi-	half	**hemi**paresis—muscular weakness on one half of the body
hepat-	liver	**hepat**itis—inflammation of the liver
hidr-	sweat	**hidr**osos—sweat production
histo-	tissue, web, cloth	**histo**logy—science dealing with the microscopic identification of cells and tissues

Root	Meaning	Sample Word
hydro-	water	**hydro**ps—abnormal accumulation of clear watery fluid in the body
hystero-	uterus	**hyster**ectomy—surgical removal of the uterus
iatro-	physician	**iatro**genic—caused by treatment
ichth-	fish	**ichth**yosis—dry scaly skin condition
idio-	self, personal, private	**idio**pathic—unknown cause
ischi-	hip joint	**ischi**um—one of three parts of the hip bone
iso-	equal	**iso**metric—maintaining the same measurement
jejun-	hungry	**jejun**um—one of three portions of the small intestine
kera-	horny	**kera**tosis—overgrowth and thickening of the cornified epithelium
kerato-	cornea	**kerate**ctomy—surgical removal of the cornea
kyph(o)-	hunch backed	**kyph**osis—abnormal convexity in the curvature of the thoracic spine
lab-	lips	**lab**ia—the lips
lachry-	tear (from the eye)	**lacri**mal—pertaining to tears
lacrim-	tear	**lacrim**al apparatus-structure hat secretes and drains tears from the eyeball
lact-,	milk	**lact**aion—synthesis and secretion of milk from the breasts
lapar-	loin, abdomen	**lapar**otomy—surgical incision into the peritoneal cavity
leiomyo-	smooth muscle	**leimyo**mata—smooth muscle tumor found in the esophagus, stomach, or small intestine
leuco- / leuko-	white	**leuko**cyte—white blood cell
liga(t)-	bind together, bandage	**liga**ments—bands of fibrous tissue that binds joints together and connect bones and cartilage
lingu-	tongue	**lingu**al artery—artery that supplies blood to the tongue
lip(o)	fat	**lip**osuction—technique for removing fatty tissue
lith-	stone	**lith**iasis—formation of calculi or stones in a body cavity or duct
mal(i)	abnormal, bad	**mal**ignant—virulent, destructive
mast(o)-	breast	**mast**ectomy—surgical removal of a breast
melano-	black	**melano**ma—malignant neoplasm-usually black or brown in color
medi- / mid-	middle	**mid**body—middle of the body
meso-	middle	**meso**derm—middle of three layers of developing embryo
multi-	many	**multi**form—more than one shape
my(o)-	muscle	**my**algia—muscle pain
myel(o)-	bone marrow	**myel**ocyte—immature white blood cell found in the bone marrow
myring(o)-	eardrum	**myring**ectomy—excision of the tympanic membrane (eardrum)
narco-	sleep	**narco**lepsy—sudden sleep attacks
necro-	dead	**necro**sis—localized tissue death
nephr-	kidney	**nephr**optosis—downward displacement of the kidney
neur-,	nerve	**neur**ology—science of the nervous system
ocul-	eye	**ocul**ar spot—abnormal opacity In the eye
odon-	tooth	**odon**tectomy—tooth extraction
olfact-	smell	**olfact**ory—pertaining to smell
oligo-	few, scarce	**olig**uria-scant urine

Root	Meaning	Sample Word
onco-	tumor, mass	**onco**logist—physician who specializes in the treatment of cancers
onycho-	nail (finger/toe)	**onycho**lysis—separation of the nail from the nail bed
oophor-	carrying egg	**oophor**ectomy—surgical removal of one or both ovaries
ophth-	eye	**ophth**almoscope—instrument used to examine the interior of the eye
orch-	testis	**orch**itis—inflammation of the testes
ortho-	straight	**ortho**pnea—condition in which a person must sit or stand to breathe comfortably
ossi-	bone	**ossi**cle—small bone within the ear
ot-	ear	**ot**ologist—physician trained in ear disorders
ov-	egg, ovum	**ov**iduct—fallopian tube which serves as a passage for the ovum to the uterus
palpebr-	eyelid	**palpebr**a superior—upper eyelid
peri-	surrounding	**peri**cardium—around the heart
phag-	eat	**phag**ocytosis—process where certain cells engulf and destroy microorganisms and cell debris
phlebo-	vein	**phlebo**tomy—incision of a vein for blood letting
phren-	mind, breath	**phren**ic nerve—one of the nerves that innervates the diaphragm
pleur-	ribs	**pleur**al cavity—the cavity that contains the lings
pneum-	luns	**pneum**onia—inflammation of the lungs
pod-	foot	**pod**iatrist—a physician who treats conditions of the foot
polio-	gray	**polio**encephalitis—inflammation of the gray matter of the brain
poly-	many	**poly**morphous—many shapes
procto-	rectum	**proct**itis—inflammation of the rectum and anus
pyelo-	vat, basin, pelvis	**pyelo**nephritis—inflammation of the pelvis and parenchyma of the kidney
pyo-	pus	**pyo**genic—pus producing
pyr(o)-	fever (cognate to "fire")	**pyr**exia—fever
ren(o)-	kidneys	**ren**al—pertaining to the kidneys
ret(ic)	net	**ret**icular—netlike pattern
rhabdo-	striated muscle	**rhabdo**myoma—tumor of striated muscle
rhino-	nose	**rhino**plasty—plastic surgery to change the nose structure
rub(r)-	red	**rub**ella—fine red viral rash
sacch(ar)-	sugar	**sacch**arine—sugar substitute
sang(ui)	blood	**sang**uineous—pertaining to the blood
sarc(o)-	flesh	**sarc**oma—malignant soft tissue tumor
sclero-	hard	**sclero**derma—autoimmune condition in which the skin becomes firm and fixed to underlying tissues
scoli(o)-	twised	**scoli**osis—lateral curvature of the spine
sebo-	hard fat, skin oil	**sebo**rrhea—skin condition in which there is an overproduction of sebum resulting in oiliness or dry scales
semi	half	**semi**lunar—half-moon shaped

Root	Meaning	Sample Word
soma/somy	body	**soma**totype—body build
spondylo-	spine	**spondyl**itis—an inflammation of any of the spinal vertebrae
sphygmo-	heartbeat	**sphygmo**manometer—device for measuring blood pressure
sten(o)-	narrow	**sten**osis—abnormal narrowing of a bodily passageway
tachy-	fast, swift	**tachy**cardia—rapid heart beat
ten(d)o-	stretch, tendon	**tend**on—band of tissue that attaches muscle to bone
terato-	monster	**terato**logy—study of causes and effects of congenital abnormalities
thel-	breast, covering layer	**thel**arche—the beginning of female pubertal breast development
thromb(o)-	blood clot	**thromb**olytic—pertaining to the dissolution of a blood clot
thyro-	oblong shield	**thyro**id—shield shaped gland
tono-	stretch	**ton**ic—pertaining to nerve fibers that respond to length changes of a muscle spindle
trache-	neck	**trache**a—air passage tube in the neck
tricho-	hair	**tricho**id—resembling a hair
umbilic-	navel	**umbilic**us—navel, depression in the center of the abdomen
ungui	nail, claw	**ungui**s—nail, claw
uro-	urine	**uro**gram—x-ray of the urinary tract
vacc-	cow	**vacc**inia—infectious disease of cattle
vaso-	blood vessel	**vaso**dilatation—distention of a blood vessel
vener-	sexual acts, lusty	**vener**eal—pertaining to sexual intercourse or genital contact
veno-	vein (as opposed to artery)	**veno**us—pertaining to the vein
vert-	turn	**vert**igo—dizziness
vesico-	bladder	**vesic**le—blister
xantho-	yellow	**xantho**ma—yellowish plaque that develops in the subcutaneous layer of skin
xeno-	stranger	**xeno**phobia—irrational fear of strangers
xero-	dry	**xero**derma—chronic dry rough skin
zoo-	animals	**zoo**toxin—poisonous substance from an animal
zygo-	yoke	**zygo**te—developing fertilized ovum

Table A.3
Prefixes

Prefix	Meaning	Sample Word
a	without	**a**symptomatic—without symptoms
a(n)-	without	**an**aerobe—without air
ab-	from	**ab**duct—move from
ab(s)-	away from	**abs**orb—to take up or receive
abdomin(o)-	abdomen, fat around the belly	**abdomen**
acous(o)-	hearing	**acous**tic
acr(o)-	topmost, extremity	**acr**odematitis—skin eruption of the hands and feet caused by a mite
ad-	towards	**ad**duction—move towards
aden(o), anden(i)-	fatty tissue	**aden**olipoma—a fatty tumor
adip(o)-	fatty tissue	**adip**oscyte—a fat cell
adren(o)-	adrenal galnd	**adren**al crisis—life threatening dysfuncion of the adrenal gland
aesthesio-	sensation	**anesthesi**a—absence of normal sensation
alb-	white	**alb**inism—lack of melanim pigment
alg((i)-	pain	an**alg**esic— pain medication
allo-	other, another	**allo**genic—genetically different tissues from same species
ambi-	both	**ambi**dextrous—able to use both hands equally well
amino-	fetal sac	**amnio**tic fliud—fluid that surrounds the fetus
amphi-	on both sides, around	**amphi**theater—room with seats arranged in tiers around a central area
ana-	up to, back, again, movement from	**ana**stomosis—surgical bypass of a vessel or duct to allow flow from one part to the other
andr(o)-	man	**andr**osterone—male sex hormone
angio-	blood vessel	**angio**catheter—a tube inserted into th blood vessel
aniso-	different, unequal	**aniso**cytosis—variable and abnormal size of red blood cells
ante-	before, forwards	**ante**version—abnormal forward tilt of an organ
anti-	against, opposite	**anti**bacterial—substance that destroys or inhibits bacterial growth or replication
ap-, apo-	from, away	**apo**physis—outgrowth, usually from bone
arteri(o)-	the artery	**arteri**ogram—x-ray of an artery using radiopaque medium
arthr(o)-	joint or limb	**arthr**itis—inflammation of a joint
aur(i)-	the ear	**aur**al—pertaining to the ear or hearing
Bene	good	**ben**ign—non-cancerous
bi(s)-	twice, double	**bi**lateral—having two sides
bio-	life	**bio**logic—pertaining to living organisms
blast(o)-	germ	**blast**ogenic—originating in the germ plasm
brachio-	arm	**brachi**al artery—artery in upper arm
brachy-	short	**brachy**dactyly—abnormally short fingers and toes
bronchi-	windpipe	**bronchi**al tree—anatomic branches of the traches

Prefix	Meaning	Sample Word
bucc(o)-	cheek	**bucc**al—inside of cheek
burs(o)-	wine skin	**burs**a—fluid filled saclike cavity between movable body parts
capill-	hair	**capill**ary fracture—hairlike fracture
capit-	head	**capit**at—head shaped
carcin(o)-	cancer	**carcin**ogen-cancer producing substance
cardi(o)-	heart	**cardi**ac—pertaining to the heart
carp(o)-	wrist	**carp**al—pertaining to the wrist
cata-	down	**cata**bolism—breakdown of complex substances to simpler substances
cephal(o)-	head	**cephal**ometry—measurement of the head
cerebell(o)-	little brain	**cerebell**um-posterior part of the brain that controls balance and muscular coordination
cerebro-	brain	**cerebr**um—the largest part of the brain associated with thought, emotions and memory
cervic-	neck	**cervi**x—lower narrow outer part of the uterus that extends into the vagina
chemo-	chemistry	**chemo**therapy—treament of disease with chemicals
chir(o)-	hand	**chir**opractic—manipulation of the spinal column
chlor(o)-	green	**chlor**ophyll—green pigments found in plants
chol(e)-	bile	**chol**angiogram—x-ray of bile ducts
chrom(ato)-	color,	**chrom**atosis—abnormal skin pigmentation
cili-	eyelash	**cili**a—eyelashes
circum-	around	**circum**corneal—area surrounding the cornea
co-,com-, con-	together	**con**fluent—running together
colo-, colono-	pipe	**colo**n—portion of the large intestine
colp(o)-	vaginal canal	**colp**oscopy—examination of the vagina and cervix with a magnifying instrument
contra-	against	**contra**ceptive—serving to prevent pregnancy or conception
cor-	heart	**cor**onary—pertaining to the heart
Cry(o)	cold	**cry**otherapy—treating with cold
cyte-	cell	**cyto**logy—study of cells
de-	from, away from, down from	**de**cease—to depart from life
deca-	ten	**deca**gram—a unit of 10 grams
dextr(o)-	right	**dextr**ocaria—location of the heart
di(s)-	two	**dis**sect—cut apart
dia-	through, complete	**dia**gnose—determine the nature of a problem
di(a)s-	separation	**dia**stasis—forceful separation of two parts normally joined together
diplo-	double	**diplo**pia—double vision
dolicho-	long	**dolicho**cephalicx—long-headed
dur-	hard, firm	**dur**able—lasting, resistant to wear
dys-	bad, abnormal	**dys**phagia—difficulty swallowing

Prefix	Meaning	Sample Word
e-, ec-	out, from out of	**ec**crine—sweat gland secreting outwardly
ecto-	outside, external	**ecto**pic—away from its normal location
em-	in	**em**bed—fix into place
en-	into	**en**case—enclose
endo-	into	**endo**scopy—visualization of the inner cavities of the body
ent-	within	**ent**eric—pertaining to the intestines
epi-	on, up, against, high	**epi**thelium—tissue that covers a surface
eso-	I will carry	**eso**teric—meant for a select few
eu-	well, abundant, prosperous	**eu**phoric—state of well-being
eury-	broad, wide	**eury**thmic—wide variations in rhythm
ex-, exo-	out, from out of	**exo**phytic—tendency to grow outward
extra-	outside, beyond, in addition	**extra**cellular—occurring outside the cell
haplo-	single	**haplo**id—pertaining to a single set of chromosones
hypo-	below, deficient	**hypo**glycemia—low blood sugar
im-, in-	not	**in**ert—not moving
in-	into, to	**in**spiration—drawing air into the lungs
infra-	below, underneath	**infra**clavicular—below the clavicle
inter-	among, between	**inter**mittent—occurring at intervals
intra-	within, inside, during	**intra**muscular—into the muscle
intro-	inward, during	**intro**vert—withdrawn, self-absorbed
iso-	equal, same	**iso**metric—having equal measure
juxta-	adjacent to	**juxta**position—placement side-to-side or end-to-end
kerat(o)	horny	**kerat**osis- hard bump on the skin
macro-	large	**macro**glossia—excessively large tongue
medi-	middle	**medi**an—middle value
mega-	large	**mega**dose—excessively large dose
megalo-	very large	**megalo**cephaly—pathological overgrowth of the brain
meso-	middle	**meso**derm—middle of three layers of an embryo
meta-	beyond, between	**meta**stasis—spread of tumor cells
micro-	small	**micro**cytic—smaller than normal red blood cells
neo-	new	**neo**nate—newborn child
non-	not	**non**compliance—not adhering to therapeutic plan
ob-	before, against	**ob**tund—render insensitive to painful stimuli
oligo-	few	**oligo**uria—diminished amount of produced and passed urine
pachy-	thick	**pachy**cephaly—abnormal thickening of the skull
pan-	all	**pan**acea—cure-all
para-	beside, to the side of, wrong	**para**plegia—paralysis of the lower limbs

Prefix	Meaning	Sample Word
per-	by, through, throughout	**per**cutaneous—through the skin
peri-	around, round-about	**peri**odontal—area around a tooth
pleo-	more than usual	**pleo**morphism—existing in two or more distinct forms during a life cycle
poly-	many	**poly**cystic—presence of many cysts
post-	behind, after	**post**mortem—after death
pre-	before, in front, very	**pre**tibial—area in front of the tibia
pseudo-	false, fake	**pseudo**tumor—false tumor
quar(r)-	four	**quar**tan—occurring on the fourth day
re, red-	back, again	**re**duce—restore to original size
retro-	backwards, behind	**retro**flex—bent backward
semi-	half	**semi**lunar—half moon-shaped objects
sub-	under, beneath	**sub**cutaneous—beneath the skin
super-	above, in addition, over	**super**ficial—pertaining to the surface
supra-	above, on the upper side	**supra**pubic—above the symphysis pubis
syn-	together, with	**syn**ergy—two or muscles, nerves etc. working together
sys-	together, with	**sys**temic—pertaining to the whole
tetra-	four	**tetra**logy of Fallot—congenital heart anomaly consisting of four defects
trans-	across, beyond	**trans**cend—to rise above and beyond
tri-	three	**tri**mester—one of three 3-month periods
uni-	one	**uni**lateral—pertaining to one side
ultra-	beyond, besides, over	**ultra**centrifuge—high-speed centrifuge

Table A.4
Suffixes

Suffix	Meaning	Sample Word
-ac	pertaining to	cardi**ac**—pertaining to the heart
-al	pertaining to	abdomin**al**—pertaining to the abdomen
algia	pain	my**algia**—muscle aches or pains
-ase	fermenter	lact**ase**—enzyme that breaks down milk
-asthenia	weakness	my**asthenia**—abnormal muscle weakness
-centesis	puncture	amnio**centesis**—removal of amniotic fluid
-cide	killer	bacteri**cide**—destruction of bacteria
-c(o)ele	cavity, hollow	cyst**ocele**—protrusion of the bladder into the vaginal wall
-crine	secretion ("separation")	endo**crine** system—network of glands that secrete hormones
-cyte	cell	leuko**cyte**—white cell
-desis	binding	arthro**desis**-surgical fixation of a joint
-ectasis	expansion	bronchi**ectasis**—dilatation of the bronchial tubes
-ectomy	excision	thromb**ectomy**—removal of a blood clot
-emesis	vomiting	hemat**emesis**—vomiting blood
-em(ia)	blood	an**emia**—blood disorder characterized by low hemoglobin levels
-enchyme	filling, infusion	par**enchyma**—essential and distinctive tissue of an organ
-form	shaped like	bacilli**form**—rod shaped like a bacterium
-genesis	origin	sporo**genesis**—formation of spores
-gram	record	electrocardio**gram**—graphic record of the electrocardiograph tracings
-graph	to write	electrocardio**graph**—printout of the electrical activity of the heart
-iasis	full of	ancylostomo**iasis**—hookworm infection
-icle	small	part**icle**—a small piece
-ism	theory, characteristic of	relativ**ism**—"theory that knowledge is relative to the limited nature of the mind and the conditions of knowing"[1]
-itis	inflammation	appendic**itis**—inflammation of the appendix
-ity	makes a noun, of quality	reliabil**ity**—quality of being reliable
-ium, um	thing (makes a noun)	bacter**ium**—unicellular microorganism
-ize	do	social**ize**—act in a social manner
-lepsis	seizure	epi**lepsy**—seizure disorder
-logy	study of, reasoning about	histo**logy**—study of tissue
-lysis / -lytic	breaking down	hemo**lytic**—break down of red blood cells
-malacia	soft	chondro**malacia**—softening of cartilage
-megaly	large	hepato**megaly**—enlarged liver
-meter	measurement	spiro**meter**—instrument for measuring air flow in and out of the lungs
-oid	resembling, image of	aden**oid**—having a glandular appearance
-ol(e)	alcohol	ethan**ol**—intoxicating flammable element in liquor
-oma	tumor/lump	hemat**oma**—blood clot

Suffix	Meaning	Sample Word
-osis	full of	anatom**osis**—joining of two ducts or vessels
-paresis	weakness	hemi**paresis**—weakness on one side of the body
-pathy	disease of, suffering	neuro**pathy**—abnormal condition of the peripheral nerves
-penia	lack	thrombocyto**penia**—reduced number of platelets
-phage	eater	macro**phages**—cells that ingest pathogens
-philia	attraction for	hemo**philia**—bleeding disorder
-phobia	fear	homo**phobia**—irrational fear or aversion to homosexuals
-plasia	formation	hyper**plasia**—abnormal increase in cells
-plasty	re-shaping	mammo**plasty**—plastic reshaping of the breasts
-plexy	stroke	apo**plexy**—hemorrhage within an organ
-plegia	stroke, paralysis	para**plegia**—motor or sensory loss in the lower limbs
-philia / -philo	affection for	cryo**philia**—preference for cold environments
-poiesis	production	erythro**poiesis**—formation of red blood cells
-ptosis	fall	colo**ptosis**—prolapse of the colon
-ptysis	spitting	hemo**ptysis**—spitting blood
-rhage	burst out	hemor**rhage**—bleeding
-rhea	discharge, flowing out	rhinor**rhea**—runny nose
-sis	idea (makes a noun, typically abstract)	synthe**sis**—combination of elements
-static	standing	bacterio**static**—restraining the reproduction of bacteria
-staxis	dripping	epi**staxis**—nosebleed
-stomy	"mouth-cut"	colo**stomy**—surgically created artificial anus
-tresia	Not whole	a**tresia**—absence of a normal body opening
-tripsy	crushing, pounding	litho**tripsy**—procedure for crushing stones in the urinary bladder or the urethra
-tomy	cut	thoraco**tomy**—surgical opening in the chest cavity
-ule	little version	ven**ule**—small vein

1. The Free Dictionary http://www.thefreedictionary.com (accessed 5/12/09)

Abbreviations and Acronyms: Know thy Source

An abbreviation is a shortened form of a word or phrase, used for convenience, which should be readily understood by the reader. Abbreviations may appear as upper or lower case letters and with or without periods. An acronym is an abbreviation of a name or formed from the initial letters of other words. Organization, corporations, famous people and countries often use acronyms—AMA, IBM, JFK, USA, with or without periods, which arc readily recognizable by most readers. Some acronyms form pronounceable words and are readily recognized, such as WHO (World Health Organization) and OPEC (Organization of the Petroleum Exporting Countries).

Medical records are apt to contain multiple abbreviations and acronyms, the definition of some being more obvious than others. ER, referring to emergency room, is a popular abbreviation unlikely to cause confusion. AROM in a note written by a physical therapist means "active range of motion." An obstetrician will use the same acronym to mean artificial rupture of membranes. "BC" in a medical chart can have numerous meanings and the interpretation depends upon the context of the note. Is the writer referring to back care, blood count, birth control, and so on?

As indicated, there are multiple and divergent definitions ascribed to any one abbreviation or acronym. When initially written in a record, the writer should provide a definition to help alleviate confusion and misinterpretation by the reader. To assign the most appropriate meaning of abbreviations in medical records, the reader should first define medical diagnoses and the author's practice specialty.

The following list provides a sampling of abbreviations and acronyms found in medical records. In an effort to assist the reader, when appropriate, the applicable specialty area or type of medical record where the abbreviation or acronym is likely to be used and/or the area the reader can begin researching further information is provided in parentheses. (The author has italicized some notes of explanation in parentheses to assist the reader.)

A

@	at
A	active, assistance
A	arteriole
a	ante/before
A1	aortic first heart sound
A2	aortic second heart sound
A&B	apnea and bradycardia
A&BC	air and bone conduction
A&D	alcohol and drug
A&O	alert and oriented
A&P	anterior and posterior
A&P	auscultation and palpation
A&P	auscultation and percussion
A&W	alive and well
A/	acid-base ratio
A/G	albumin globulin ratio
A/O	alert and oriented
A/T	activity therapy
A/V	arteriovenous
A>B	air greater than bone (*Refers to sound conduction in the ear*)
A1	aortic first sound
A2	aortic second sound
AA	Alcoholics Anonymous
Aa	of each
AAA	abdominal aortic aneurysm
AAAHC	Accreditation Association for Ambulatory Care
AAAASF	American Association for Accreditation of Ambulatory Surgery Facilities
AABB	American Association of Blood Banks
AACME	Accreditation Council for Continuing Medical Education
ACGME	Accreditation Council for Graduate Medical Education
AACPDM	American Academy for Cerebral Palsy and Developmental Medicine
AACR	American Association for Cancer Research
AAE	American Association of Endodontists
AAFP	American Academy of Family Physicians
AAHKS	American Association of Hip and Knee Surgeons
AAHP	American Association of Health Plans
AAHS	American Association for Hand Surgery
AAHSA	American Association of Homes and Services for the Aging
AAL	anterior axillary line
AAMA	American Academy of Medical Administrators
AAMC	Association of American Medical Colleges
AAN	American Academy of Neurology
AAN	Attending admission note
AANOS	The American Academy of Neurological and Orthopaedic Surgeons
AANS	American Association of Neurological Surgeons

AAO	American Academy of Ophthalmology	Ab, ab	antibody
AAOFAS	American Association of Orthopaedic Foot and Ankle Surgeons	AB, Ab	abortion
		AB, Ab	antibiotic
AAOHN	American Association of Occupational Health Nurses	AB, abn	abnormal
		ABA	American Board of Anesthesiologists
AAOM	American Academy of Oral Medicine	Abb	abbreviation, abbreviated
AAOO	American Academy of Ophthalmology and Otolaryngology	ABC	airway, breathing, and circulation
		Abd	abdomen
AAOP	American Academy of Orthotists and Prosthetists	Abd	abduction
		ABE	acute bacterial endocarditis
AAOS	American Academy of Orthopaedic Surgery	ABE	American Board of Endodontics
		ABG	arterial blood gas (Laboratory)
AAO×3	awake, alert, and oriented × 3; i.e., to person, place, and time	ABI	ankle to brachial index (peripheral vascular)
AAP	American Academy of Pediatrics	ABJS	Association of Bone and Joint Surgeons
AAP	American Academy of Pedodontics		
AAP	American Academy of Periodontology	ABL	anticonvulsive blood level
AAP	American Association of Pathologists	ABMS	American Board of Medical Specialties
AAPA	American Academy of Physician Assistants		
		ABO	blood grouping system
AAPA	American Association of Pathologist Assistants	ABOS	American Board of Orthopaedic Surgery
AAPB	American Association of Pathologists and Bacteriologists	ABP	American Board of Pathology
		ABR	auditory brainstem response audiometry
AAPC	antibiotic-associated pseudomembranous colitis		
		ABS	arterial blood pressure
AAPCC	adjusted average per capita cost	Abs feb	while the fever is absent
AAPMC	antibiotic-associated pseudo-membranous colitis	ABTA	American Brain Tumor Association
		AC	acromioclavicular joint
AAPMR	American Academy of Physical Medicine and Rehabilitation	AC	air conduction
		ac	before meals
AAPPO	American Association of Preferred Providers Organization	AC	anterior chamber (may be graded, i.e., 4/4; 3/4; 2/4; 1/4; 0/4) (Ophthalmology)
AAPS	American Association of Plastic Surgeons		
		AC/A	accommodation convergence/accommodation ratio (Ophthalmology)
AAPS	Association of American Physicians and Surgeons	ACA	American Chiropractic Association
AAPSM	American Academy of Podiatric Sports Medicine	ACC	American College of Cardiology
		Acc	accommodation (Ophthalmology)
AARC	American Association for Respiratory Care	ACCP	American College of Chest Physicians
		ACD	anterior cervical discectomy (Orthopedics, Neurosurgery)
AAROM	active assistive range of motion		
AAT	alanine aminotransferase (Laboratory)	ACDF	anterior cervical discectomy and fusion (Orthopedics, Neurosurgery)
AATS	American Association for Thoracic Surgery		
		ACE	angiotensin converting enzyme (Pharmacology)
AAU	acute anterior uveitis		
AAWM	American Academy of Wound Management	ACF	anterior cervical fusion (Orthopedics, Neurosurgery)
AB	American Board of Pediatrics	ACFAS	American College of Foot and Ankle Surgeons
AB	blood group AB		

ACF	antecubital fossa (Intravenous site location)	ACPOC	Association of Children's Prosthetic-Orthotic Clinics
ACG	angle closure glaucoma (Ophthalmology)	ACPP	prostate-specific acid phosphatase (Laboratory)
ACHP	Alliance of Community Health Plans	ACR	adenomatosis of colon and rectum (Gastroenterology; Endocrinology)
ACI	acute coronary insufficiency		
acid phos	acid phosphatase (Laboratory)	ACR	adjusted community rating (Insurance)
ACJ	acromioclavicular joint (Orthopedic)	ACR	ambulance call report
ACL	anterior clavicular line *(Physical assessment term referring to location)*	ACR	American College of Radiology
		ACR	American College of Rheumatology
ACL	anterior cruciate ligament (Orthopedics, Physical Therapy)	ACRM	American Congress on Rehabilitation Medicine
ACLA	American Clinical Laboratory Association	ACRPI	Association of Clinical Research for the Pharmaceutical Industry
ACLR	anterior capsulolabral reconstruction (Orthopedics)	ACS	acute cervical strain; acute cervical sprain
ACLS	Advanced Cardiac Life Support	ACS	acute chest syndrome
ACM	acetaminophen (Pharmacology)	ACS	acute confusional state
ACM	anticonvulsant (Pharmacology)	ACS	American Cancer Society
ACMA	American Occupational Medical Association	ACS	American College of Surgeons
		ACSM	American College of Sports Medicine
ACMV	assist-controlled mechanical ventilation (Respiratory Therapy)	ACSV	aortocoronary saphenous vein
		ACSVBG	aortocoronary saphenous vein bypass graft
ACNM	American College of Nurse-Midwives		
ACNP	acute care nurse practitioner	ACSW	Academy of Certified Social Workers
ACNP	American College of Nuclear Physicians	ACT	activated clotting time (Laboratory)
		ACT	active motion
ACO	acute coronary occlusion	Act	activity, active
ACO	alert, cooperative, oriented	ACT	anticoagulant therapy (Pharmacology)
ACOA	adult children of alcoholics	ACT	anxiety control training
ACOEM	American College of Occupational and Environmental Medicine	ACT	asthma care training
		ACT	atropine coma therapy (Pharmacology)
ACOEP	American College of Osteopathic Emergency Physicians	ACTA	American Cardiology Technologists Association
ACOG	American College of Obstetricians and Gynecologist	ACTA	automatic computerized transverse axial *(scanning)* (Radiology)
ACOM	American College of Occupational Medicine	ACTH	adrenocorticotrophic hormone (Endocrinology)
ACOM	anterior communicating *(Artery)*	ACTS	acute cervical trauma syndrome
ACOMS	American College of Oral and Maxillofacial Surgeons	ACTZ	acetazolamide (Pharmacology)
		ACVB	aortocoronary venous bypass
ACOOG	American College of Osteopathic Obstetricians and Gynecologists	ACVD	acute cardiovascular disease
		ACVD	arteriosclerotic cardiovascular disease
ACOS	American College of Osteopathic Surgeons	ad lib	at pleasure, at discretion, freely as desired
ACP	American College of Pathologists	AD	adjuvant chemotherapy
ACP	American College of Pharmacists	AD	admission and discharge
ACP	American College of Prosthodontists	AD	admitting diagnosis
ACPM	American College of Preventive Medicine	AD	alternating days
		AD	Alzheimer's disease

AD	attending doctor	ADS	alternative delivery system (Insurance)
AD	atopic dermatitis (Dermatology)	ADV	advised
AD	auris dextra (right ear)	adv	against *(Found on prescriptions)*
ADA	American Dental Association	AE	above the elbow
ADA	Americans with Disabilities Act	AE	active and equal
ADA	anterior descending artery (Cardiology)	AE	adverse event
		AEB	as evidenced by
ADASP	Association of Directors of Anatomic and Surgical Pathology	AED	antiepileptic drug (Pharmacology)
ADC	AIDS dementia complex (Psychiatry)	AED	automated external defibrillator (Cardiology, Emergency Medical Services)
ADD	addiction	Aeg	the patient *(Found on prescriptions)*
Add	adduct; adduction	AEG	air encephalogram (Neurology)
Add	addition (Ophthalmology)	AER	auditory evoked response (Neurology)
ADD	attention deficit disorder (Psychology)	AER	average evoked response (Neurology)
ADD	average daily dose (Pharmacology)	AF	adult female
ADEA	American Dental Education Association	AF	African-American
		AF	amniotic fluid (Obstetrics)
adeno-Ca	adenocarcinoma (Oncology)	AF	aortic flow (Cardiology)
ADH	antidiuretic hormone (Pharmacology)	AF	atrial fibrillation; atrial flutter (Cardiology)
ADH·	atypical ductal hyperplasia (Gynecology; Oncology)		
		AFB	acid-fast bacilli (Laboratory)
ADHD	attention deficit hyperactivity disorder (Psychology)	AFC	amniotic fluid cortisol (Obstetrics)
		AFDC	Aid to Families with Dependent Children
ADJ	adjacent		
ADJ	adjoining	A-Fib; Afib	atrial fibrillation (Cardiology)
ADJ	adjust, adjustment or manipulation (Chiropractic)	AFL	artificial limb
		A-Flutter	atrial flutter (Cardiology, Emergency Medical Services)
ADL	activities of daily living (i.e., bathing, dressing, toileting, feeding, and grooming)	AFO	ankle-foot orthoses (Physical Therapy)
		AFP	acute flaccid paralysis (Neurology)
Ad lib	as desired	AFP	alpha-fetoprotein (Obstetrics, Laboratory)
ADM scale	Acceptance of Disability Scale Modified		
		AGA	appropriate-for-gestational age (Obstetrics)
ADM	admission/admitted		
ADM	adrenal medulla (Endocrinology)	AGF	angle of greatest flexion (Physical Therapy)
ADM	advancement of the mandible (Dental)		
ADM	alcohol, drug, and mental disorders	AGG	aggravation
ADM	anterior deep masseter (Orthopedics, Physical Therapy)	AGN	acute glomerulonephritis (Renal)
		AGTT	abnormal glucose tolerance test (Laboratory)
ADM	atypical diabetes mellitus; adult onset diabetes mellitus (Endocrinology)		
		AH	abdominal hysterectomy (Gynecology)
ADM	auditory dominance model (Speech)	AH	arterial hypertension (Cardiology)
admin	administration	AH	auditory hallucinations (Psychiatry)
ADN	attending *(doctor)* discharge note	AHA	American Hospital Association
ADON	assistant director of nursing	AHC	acute hemorrhagic conjunctivitis *(Refers to the eye)*
ADP	abductor pollicis (Orthopedics, Physical Therapy)		
		AHC	acute hemorrhagic cystitis *(Refers to the bladder)* (Urology)
ADP	adenosine diphosphate (Pharmacology)		
		AHC	alternative health care (Insurance)
ADR	adverse drug reaction	AHCA	Agency for Health Care Administration

AHCA	American Health Care Association
AHCPR	Agency for Health Care Policy and Research
AHD	acute heart disease
AHD	antihypertensive drug
AHD	atherosclerotic heart disease
AHD	autoimmune hemolytic disease (Hematology)
AHEC	Area Health Education Center
AHF	acute heart failure
AHIMA	American Health Information Management Association
AHIS	automated hospital information system
AHJ	artificial hip joint
AHM	ambulatory Holter monitor (Cardiology, Diagnostic)
AHMA	American Holistic Medicine Association
AHR	atrial heart rate (Cardiology)
AHRF	acute hypoxemic respiratory failure (Pulmonary)
AHRQ	Agency for Healthcare Research and Quality (formerly AHCPR)
AHS	Academy of Health Sciences
AHS	American Hearing Society
AHS	American Hospital Society
AHT	arterial hypertension
AI	active ingredient
AI	aortic incompetence; aortic insufficiency (Cardiology)
AI	apical impulse (Cardiology)
AI	articulation index (Speech Pathology)
AI	artificial insemination (Infertility)
AI	atrial insufficiency (Cardiology)
AI	autoimmune, autoimmunity (Endocrinology)
AICA	anterior inferior cerebellar artery (Anatomy)
AICA	anterior inferior communicating artery (Anatomy)
AICD	automated internal cardioverter (Cardiology, Emergency Medical Services)
AID	autoimmune deficiency; autoimmune disease (Infectious Disease)
AIDS	acquired immune deficiency syndrome
AIDSDRUGS	clinical trials of acquired immunodeficiency drugs
AIDS-KS	acquired immune deficiency syndrome with Kaposi's sarcoma
AIDSLINE	online information on acquired immunodeficiency syndrome
AIDS-OI	AIDS with opportunistic infections
AIIS	anterior inferior iliac spine
AIMS	Abnormal Involuntary Movement Scale (Neurology)
AION	anterior ischemic optic neuropathy (Ophthalmology)
AIOSM	American Institute of Orthopaedic and Sports Medicine
AIS	adenocarcinoma in situ (Oncology)
AIT	after image transfer (Ophthalmology)
AltSOT	alternate esotrophis (Ophthalmology)
AltXOT	alternative exotropia (Ophthalmology)
AJ	ankle jerk
AJKS	American Journal of Knee Surgery
AJNR	American Journal of NeuroRadiology
AJO	American Journal of Orthopaedics
AK	above knee
AKA	above knee amputation
AKA	also known as
AL	left ear (Not recommended)
alb	albumin (Laboratory)
alk phos	alkaline phosphatase (Laboratory)
ALL	acute lymphocytic leukemia (Oncology)
ALL	allergic; allergy
ALMI	anterior lateral myocardial infarction (Cardiology)
ALOS	average length of stay
ALP	alkaline phosphatase (Laboratory)
ALPC	argon laser photocoagulation (Laboratory)
ALRI	anterolateral rotatory instability (Physical Therapy)
ALS	acute lumbar strain
ALS	amyotrophic lateral sclerosis (Neurology)
ALT	alanine aminotransferase (Formerly SGPT) (Laboratory)
alt	alternate; alternating
alt die	alternate days (Found on prescriptions)
ALTHA	Acute Long Term Hospital Association
alt hore	alternate hours (Found on prescriptions)
alt noc	alternate nights (Found on prescriptions)
alv	alveolar
AM A.M.	before noon
AM	adult male

AM	anteromedial	A-P & Lat	anterioposterior and lateral *(Physical assessment term referring to location)*
AM	before noon		
ama	against medical advice	AP	acute pancreatitis (Gastroenterology, Digestive Diseases)
AMA	American Medical Association		
AMB	ambulate; ambulatory	AP	acute pneumonia (Pulmonary)
AMCRA	American Managed Care and Review Association	AP	after parturition (Obstetrics)
		AP	alkaline phosphatase (Laboratory)
AMD	age-related macular degeneration *(also ARMD)* (Ophthalmology)	AP	angina pectoris (Cardiology)
		A-P	anterioposterior *(Physical assessment term referring to location)*
AMI	acute myocardial infarction (Cardiology)		
AMIA	American Medical Informatics Association	AP	anterior pituitary (Anatomy, Endocrinology)
AML	acute myelogenous leukemia (Oncology)	AP	anterioposterior *(Physical assessment term referring to location)*
AMP	adenosine monophosphate (biochemistry)	AP	aortic pressure (Cardiology)
		AP	apical pulse
amp	ampere *(Unit of electric current)*	AP	appendectomy; appendicitis; appendix
AMP	amphetamine (Pharmacology)		
AMP	amputation	AP	arterial pressure
AMSSM	American Medical Society for Sports Medicine	AP	aspiration pneumonia
		AP	atrial pacing (Cardiology)
Amt; amt	amount	AP	atrioventricular pathway (Anatomy)
ANA	American Nurses Association	APA	American Psychiatric Association
ANA	antinuclear antibody test (Laboratory)	APA	acetaminophen (Pharmacology)
ANAL	analgesic (Pharmacology)	APB	atrial premature beat (Cardiology)
ANES	anesthesia	APC	atrial premature contractions (Cardiology)
ANP	advanced nurse practitioner		
ANRI	acute nerve root irritation	APC	anterior polar cataract (Ophthalmology)
ANS	autonomic nervous system (Anatomy)		
ANT, ant.	anterior	APC	aspirin, phenacetin, caffeine (Pharmacology)
ante	before		
ANX	anxiety	APC	Ambulatory Payment Classification
AO	angle of	APD	afferent pupillary defect (Ophthalmology)
AO	aorta		
AOA	American Osteopathic Association	APH	anterior pituitary hormone (Endocrinology)
AOB	alcohol on breath		
AOD	arteriosclerotic occlusive disease	APH	aphasia (Neurology)
AODM	adult onset diabetes mellitus	APHA	American Public Health Association
AOFAS	American Orthopaedic Foot and Ankle Society	APL	abductor pollicis longus (Orthopedics, Physical Therapy)
AOI	Academia Ophthalmologica Internationalis	APMA	American Podiatric Medical Association
AOM	acute otitis media	APP	Alzheimer amyloid precursor protein (Neurology, Laboratory)
AOPA	American Orthotic and Prosthetic Association		
		APP	appendix
AORN	Association of Perioperative Registered Nurses	Appt	appointment
		APTA	American Physical Therapy Association
AOS	Academic Orthopaedic Society		
AOSSM	American Orthopaedic Society for Sports Medicine	APTT	automated partial thromboplastin time (Laboratory)

aq	water	ASHD	atherosclerotic heart disease
AR	active resistance (Physical Therapy)	ASHNR	American Society of Head and Neck Radiology
AR	admitting room	ASIA	American Spinal Injury Association
AR	aortic regurgitation (Cardiology)	ASIS	anterior superior iliac spine (Anatomy)
ARC	AIDS related complex	ASLME	American Society of Law, Medicine & Ethics
ARC	anomalous retinal correspondence (Ophthalmology)	ASMI	American Sports Medicine Institute
ARD	acute respiratory disease	ASMI	atrial septal myocardial infarction (Cardiology)
ARDS	adult respiratory distress syndrome	ASNR	American Society of NeuroRadiology
ARE	active-resistance exercise (Physical Therapy)	ASO	administrative services only
ARF	acute renal failure (Renal)	ASO	arteriosclerosis obliterans (Vascular)
ARF	acute respiratory failure (Pulmonary)	ASOPA	American Society of Orthopaedic Physician's Assistants
ARF	acute rheumatic fever (Immunology)	ASPNR	American Society of Pediatric Neuro-Radiology
ARM	anxiety reaction, mild (Psychiatry)		
ARNP	advanced registered nurse practitioner		
AROM	active range of motion (Physical Therapy)	ASPRS	American Society of Plastic and Reconstructive Surgeons
AROM	artificial rupture of membranes (Obstetrics)	ASR	age/sex rate (Insurance)
ARP	American Registry of Pathology	ASRT	American Society of Radiologic Technologists
ARRT	American Registry of Radiologic Technologists	ASS	anterior superior spine (Physical assessment term referring to location)
ART	artery		
ART	articulation	ASSH	American Society for Surgery of the Hand
ART	artificial	ASSR	American Society of Spine Radiology
as to	as tolerated	Asst	assistant
AS	anal sphincter	AST	alanine aminotransferase (Laboratory)
AS	ankylosing spondylitis (Immunology)	AST	aspartate aminotransferase (Formerly SGOT) (Laboratory)
AS	aortic stenosis (Cardiology)		
AS; ASC	arteriosclerosis	AST	Association of Surgical Technologists
AS	left ear	AST; Astigm.	Astigmatism (Ophthalmology)
ASA	acetylsalicylic acid (aspirin)	As tol	as tolerated
ASA	American Society of Anesthesiologists	ASTRO	American Society for Therapeutic Radiology and Oncology
ASAP	as soon as possible		
ASC	ascending (Physical assessment term referring to location)	ASU	ambulatory surgery unit
ASCAD	arteriosclerotic coronary artery disease	ASVD	Arteriosclerotic Vascular Disease
ASCO	American Society of Clinical Oncology	AT	achilles tendon (Anatomy)
		AT	activity therapist
ASCVD	arteriosclerotic cardiovascular disease	AT	anterior tibial (Anatomy)
ASD	atrial septal defect (Cardiology)	AT	athletic trainer
ASDP	American Society of DermatoPathology	ATA	American Telemedicine Association
		ATP	adenosine triphosphate (Biochemistry)
ASES	American Shoulder and Elbow Surgeons	ATP	attending physician
		Atr fib	atrial fibrillation (Cardiology)
ASF	anterior spinal fusion (Neurology)	ATR	Achilles tendon reflex (Anatomy)
ASH	American Society of Hematology	ATR	alpha-thalassemia-mental retardation (syndrome) (Hematology, Genetics)
ASH	asymmetrical septal hypertrophy (Cardiology)	Atr	atrophy

ATS	American Thoracic Society
ATS	arteriosclerosis
Atyp	atypical
ATZ	atypical transformation zone (Pathology)
AU	both ears, each ear
Au	gold (Pharmacology, Biochemistry)
AUA	American Urological Association
AUB	normal uterine bleeding (Gynecology)
Aud	auditory
AUDIT	alcohol use disorders identification test
AUG	acute ulcerative gingivitis (Dental)
AUR	ambulatory utilization review
AUS	acute urethral syndrome (Genitourinary)
Aus	alcohol users
aus, ausc	auscultation (Physical Assessment)
AUV	anterior urethral valve (Genitourinary)
AV	anteversion *(Physical assessment term referring to position)*
AV	aortic valve (Cardiology)
AV	artificial ventilation, assisted ventilation (Respiratory Therapy)
AV/AF	anteverted, anteflexed *(Physical assessment term referring to position)*
AV; av	avulsion
AV; A-V	arteriovenous; atrioventricular (Cardiovascular)
AV; Av	avoirdupois (Pharmacology)
AV; Av; av	average
AVA	antiviral antibody (Laboratory)
AVA	aortic valve area
AVA	aortic valve atresia (Cardiology)
AVA	arteriovenous anastomosis (Cardiology)
AVB	atrioventricular block (Cardiology)
AV block	atrioventricular block (Cardiology)
AVC	aberrant ventricular conduction (Cardiology)
AVC	aortic valve closure (Cardiology)
AVD	aortic valvular disease (Cardiology)
AVD	atrioventricular dissociation (Cardiology)
Avdp	avoirdupois (Pharmacology)
AVF	antiviral factor (Laboratory)
AVF	arteriovenous fistula (Cardiology)
AVF	unipolar limb lead on the left leg in electrocardiography
AVG, avg	average

AVH	acute viral hepatitis (Infectious Disease, Gastroenterology)
AVL	automated volt left (Electrocardiography)
aVL	unipolar limb lead on the left arm in electrocardiography
AVM	atrio-ventricular malformations (Cardiology)
AVM	arteriovenous malformations (Cardiology)
AVN	atrioventricular node (Cardiology)
AVO	aortic valve opening (Cardiology)
AVO	aortic valve orifice (Cardiology)
AVO	atrioventricular opening (Cardiology)
AVR	automated volt right (Electrocardiography)
AVR	unipolar limb lead on the right arm in electrocardiography
AVRI	acute viral respiratory infection
AVS	aortic valve stenosis (Cardiology)
AVS	arteriovenous shunt (Cardiology)
AVSD	atrioventricular septal defect (Cardiology)
AVT	Allen vision test (Ophthalmology)
AVZ	avascular zone
AW	above waist
Aw	airway
AW	alive and well
AW	alveolar wall (Pulmonary)
AW	anterior wall *(Physical assessment term referring to location)*
AWOL	absent without leave
AX	axial: axillary *(Physical assessment term referring to location)*
AZT	azidothymidine *(Zidovudine)* (Pharmacology)

B

B; bal	bath
B	bilateral *(May be encircled) (Physical assessment term referring to location)*
B	Black
b	bone
B	born
B	buccal
B&B	bowel and bladder
B&C	biopsy and curettage (Surgery, Pathology)
b/c	because
B/M	black male
B-Mod	behavior modification

BA	blood alcohol
BA	bone age
BA	brachial artery
BA	bronchial asthma
Ba, BA	barium (Pharmacology)
BAB	Babinski's sign (Neurological examination)
BAC	blood alcohol concentration (Laboratory)
Bact	bacteriologist; bacteriology, bacterium (Laboratory)
BaE	barium enema (Diagnostic)
BAER	brain stem auditory evoked response (Neurology)
BAL	blood alcohol level (Laboratory)
BAPS	biomechanical ankle platform (Physical Therapy)
Barb, BARB	barbiturate, barbituric (Pharmacology)
BaS	barium swallow (Diagnostic)
Baso; basos	basophils (leukocytes) (Laboratory)
BAT	blunt abdominal trauma
BB	bad breath
BB	bed bath
BB	bed board
BB	breakthrough bleeding (Gynecology)
BB	breast biopsy (Oncology, Pathology)
BB	bundle branch (Cardiology)
BBB	blood-brain barrier (Anatomy)
BBB	bundle branch block (Cardiology)
BBBB	bilateral bundle-branch block (Cardiology)
BBD	benign breast disease
BBS	benign breast syndrome
BBS	bilateral breath sounds (Pulmonary examination)
BC	back care
BC	birth control
BC	blood count
BC	blood culture
BC	bone conduction (ear examination)
BC	brachiocephalic (Anatomy)
BC	breast cancer
BC/BS	Blue Cross/Blue Shield
BCA	balloon catheter angioplasty (Diagnostic)
BCC	basal cell carcinoma (Oncology)
BCC	benign cellular changes (pap smear) (Pathology)
BCP	birth control pills
BCS	breast conservation surgery

BD	behavioral disorder
BD	Bechct disease (Immunology, Gastroenterology)
BD	belladonna (Pharmacology)
BD	bile duct (Anatomy)
BD	birth date
BD	blood donor
BD	brain dead, brain death
BD	bronchodilation, bronchodilator (Pulmonary, Pharmacology)
BDI-PC	Beck Depression Inventory for Primary Care
BDR	background retinal correspondence (Ophthalmology)
BE	barium enema
BE	below the elbow
BE	benzoylecgonine (cocaine) (Pharmacology)
BE	binocular visual efficiency (Ophthalmology)
BE	blood vessel endothelium (Vascular)
BE	blood volume expander (Hematology, Pharmacology)
BE	both eyes (Ophthalmology)
BE	brisk and equal (neurological examination)
BEAP	brainstem evoked auditory potential (Neurology)
Beh Sp	behavior specialist
Beh Tech	behavior technician
BF	blood flow
BF	bone fragment
bf	boyfriend
BG	blood glucose
BG	bone graft
BHP	benign hypertrophic prostate (Urology)
BHS	beta hemolytic streptococcus (Laboratory)
BHT	blunt head trauma
BI	bodily injury
BI	bone injury
BI	brain injury
BI	burn index (Surgery, Plastic Surgery)
Bic	Biceps
Bicarb	sodium bicarbonate
BID	brought in dead
BID, b.i.d.	twice a day. (Not recommended)
BI; Bilat	bilateral
BILI	bilirubin (Anatomy, Hematology, Gastroenterology)

BIN	twice a night	BOW	bag of waters (Obstetrics)
BIO	binocular indirect ophthalmoscopy (Ophthalmology)	BP	bipolar
		BP; B/P	blood pressure
Biol	biological	BPD	biparietal diameter (Anatomy)
BIP	bronchiolitis obliterans with interstitial pneumonia (Pulmonary)	BPD	borderline personality disorder (Psychiatry)
BIPE	brief psychiatric examination	BPD	bronchopulmonary dysplasia
BiVAS	biventricular assist system (Cardiology)	BPH	benign prostatic hypertrophy (Urology)
BIW	twice a week (Not recommended)	BPI	Brief Pain Inventory
BJ	Bence Jones (proteinuria) (Laboratory)	BPM	beats per minute
BJ	biceps jerk (neurological examination)	BPRS	Brief Psychiatric Rating Scale
BJ	bone and joint	BR	bathroom
BJE	bones, joints, extremities	BR	bed rest
BJM	bones, joints, muscles	BRAP	branch retinal artery occlusion (Ophthalmology)
BK	back		
BK	below the knee	BRB	bright red blood
BKA	below knee amputation; below-the-knee amputee	BRBPR	bright red blood per rectum
		BRP	bathroom privileges
Bkwds	backwards	BRVO	branch retinal vein occlusion (Ophthalmology)
bl cult	blood culture		
BL	bilateral lower lung fields (Physical assessment term referring to location)	BS	blood sugar
		BS	bowel sounds
BL	blood loss	BS	breath sounds
Blad.	bladder	BS	bronchial secretion (Pulmonary)
bld	blood	BSA	body surface area
BLE	both lower extremities	BSA	bowel signs active
BLEED	(Mnemonic for gastro-intestinal hemorrhage)	BSAEP	brain stem auditory evoked potentials (Neurology)
BLS	basic life support	BSC	bedside commode
BM	body mass index (Nutrition)	BSE	breast self examination
BM	blood monitoring	BSI	blood stream infections
BM	body mass	BSL	baseline
BM	bone marrow	BSO	bilateral salpingo-oophorectomy (Surgery, Gynecology)
BM	bowel movement		
BM	basal metabolism	BSR	bowel sounds regular
BM/E	bowel movement with enema	BSU	Bartholin, Skene, urethral (glands) (Anatomy)
BMD	bone mineral density (Diagnostic)		
BMG	benign monoclonal gammopathy (Hematology, Immunology)	BT	bedtime
		BT	bladder tumor
BMJ	British Medical Journal	BT	bleeding time
BMR	basal metabolic rate (Nutrition)	BT	body temperature
BNO	bladder neck obstruction (Urology)	BT	brain tumor
BOE	bilateral otitis externa (External canal ear infection)	BT	breast tumor
		BTB	breakthrough bleeding (Gynecology)
		BTC	basal temperature chart
BOM	bilateral otitis media (Middle ear infection)	BTC	biliary tract complication (Gastroenterology)
BOO	bladder outlet obstruction (Urology)	BTC	body temperature chart
BOP	blood, ova, parasites (Laboratory)	BTD	biliary tract disease
BOS	base of support	BTE	behind the ear (Hearing aid)

BTL	bilateral tubal ligation (Obstetrics/Gynecology)	C/W	continue with
BTR	biceps tendon reflex (Anatomy)	C1- C7	cervical vertebrae (Anatomy)
BTW	back to work	Ca	calcium (Chemistry, Laboratory)
BTW	by the way	CA, Ca	cancer, carcinoma
BTZ	benzothiazepine (Pharmacology)	CA	cardiac arrest
BUE	both upper extremities	CA	caucasian adult
BUN	blood urea nitrogen (Laboratory)	CA	chronological age
BUN/CR	blood urea nitrogen/creatine ratio (Laboratory)	CAB	coronary artery bypass
		CABG	coronary artery bypass graft
BUO	bleeding of undetermined origin, bruising of undetermined origin	CAC	certified alcoholism counselor
		CAD	coronary artery disease
BUQ	both upper quadrants	CAE	carotid artery endarterectomy (Cardiovascular)
BUR	bilateral ureteral occlusion (Urology)		
BUS	Bartholin, urethral, and Skene glands (Anatomy)	CAF	caucasian adult female
		cal	calorie
BV	bacterial vaginosis (Gynecology)	CAM	caucasian adult male
BV	blood vessel	Cap	capitation (Insurance, Administration)
BV	blood volume	caps	capsules
BV	bronchovesicular (Pulmonary)	Car	carbapenem (Pharmacology)
BVD	back vertex distance (Ophthalmology)	CARF	Commission on Accreditation of Rehabilitation Facilities
BVP	back vertex power (Ophthalmology)		
BW	bed wetting	Cat	cataract (Ophthalmology)
BW	below waist	CAT	computed axial tomography (Diagnostic)
BW	biological warfare		
BW	biological weapon	cath	catheter
BW	birth weight	CBC	complete blood count
BW	black woman	CBD	common bile duct (Anatomy)
BW	body weight	CBG	capillary blood gas (Laboratory)
BWS	battered woman syndrome	CBI	continuous bladder irrigation (Urology)
BWX	bite wing x-ray (Dental)		
BX, Bx, biop	biopsy	CBP	comprehensive behavior plan
BZ. BZD	benzodiazepine (Pharmacology)	CBR	complete bed rest
		CBS	chronic brain syndrome
		CBT	carotid body tumor (Oncology)
		CBT	computed body tomography (Diagnostic)

C

c	with		
C	celsius, centigrade, complement	CBV	cerebral blood volume
C	chlorine (Chemistry, Laboratory)	CBV	circulating blood volume
C	clinical	CBZ	carbamazepine (Tegretol) (Pharmacology)
C&C	cold and clammy		
c&d	clean and dry (Assessment)	CC	chief complaint
C/D	cup/disc ratio (Ophthalmology)	Cc	clean catch
C&S	conjunctiva and sclera (Anatomy)	CC	colony count
C&S	culture and sensitivity (Laboratory)	CC	Complicating condition
C/M	counts per minute	Cc	concave
C/O, c/o	care of; complains of	CC	contrast cystogram (Diagnostic, Urology)
C/O	complaint of		
C/S	C sect, Cesarean section (Obstetrics)	CC	corpus callosum (Birth Defects)
C/S	cycles per second	Cc	corrected
c/w	compatible with	CC	creatinine clearance (Laboratory)

CC	critical care	CD	cystic duct (Anatomy)
CC	critical condition	CDC	Centers for Disease Control
CC	Crohn colitis (Digestive Diseases)	CDI (c, d, i)	clean, dry, intact (Assessment)
CC; cc	cc, cubic centimeter (Not recommended)	Cdiff	clostridium difficile (Laboratory)
		CDR	clinical dementia rating
CCA	circumflex coronary artery (Anatomy)	CDT	chronic disorganized type (Schizophrenia)
CCA	common carotid artery (Anatomy)		
CCB	calcium channel blocker (Pharmacology)	CDT	clock drawing test (Psychiatry)
		CE	angle (radiograph), center-edge angle
CCC	Council on Clinical Classification	CEA	carcinoembryonic antigen (Laboratory)
CCCR	closed chest cardiac resuscitation	ceph	cephalic vein (Intravenous site location)
CCCS	condom catheter collecting system		
CCE	cyanosis, clubbing, edema	Cervical dil	cervical dilation (Obstetrics)
CCF	compound comminuted fracture (Orthopedics)	CF	clofibrate (Pharmacology)
		cf	compare, refer to
CCF	congestive cardiac failure (Cardiology)	CF	complement fixation (Laboratory)
CCG	cholecystogram, cholecystography (Diagnostic)	CF	cystic fibrosis
		CFDI	color-flow duplex imaging (Diagnostic)
CCHIT	Certification Commission for Health Information Technology		
		CFM	continuous electronic fetal monitoring (Obstetrics)
CCI	chronic coronary insufficiency		
CCLI	composite clinical and Laboratory index	CFNS	chills, fever, night sweats
		CFR	Code of Federal Regulations
C-collar	cervical collar (Emergency Medical Services)	CG	contact guard
		CGA	contact guard assist (Physical Therapy)
CCM	critical care medicine	CGN	chronic glomerulonephritis (Renal)
CCMS	clean (urine) catch midstream	CGy	centi gray (Unit of radiation)
CCMSU	clean catch midstream urine	CH	chest
CCN	coronary care nursing	CH	chief
CCN	critical care nursing	CH	chronic
CCT	chronic catatonic type (Schizophrenia)	CH	crown-heel (Obstetrics, Diagnostic)
CCU	coronary/cardiac care unit	CHAMPUS	Civilian Health and Medical Program for Uniformed Services (Insurance)
CCW	counterclockwise		
CD	carbon dioxide	CHB	complete heart block
CD	cardiac disease	CHD	congenital dislocation of the hip
CD	cardiac dysrhythmia	CHD	congenital heart disease
CD	cardiovascular disease	CHD	coronary heart disease
CD	caudad, caudal (Physical assessment term referring to location)	Chemo	chemotherapy
		CHF	congestive heart failure
CD	cause of death	CHG	change
CD	celiac disease (Digestive Diseases)	CHI	closed head injury
CD	centration distance (Ophthalmology)	CHO	carbohydrate
CD	color Doppler (Diagnostic)	CHOL	serum cholesterol (Laboratory)
CD	common (bile) duct (Anatomy)	CHR	chronic
CD	communicable disease	CHR	chronological
CD	conduction disorder (Cardiology, Neurology)	CI	cardiac index
		CI	cardiac insufficiency
CD	contact dermatitis (Dermatitis)	CI	cerebral infarction
CD	Crohn disease (Digestive Diseases)	CI	confidence interval (Research)
CD	cut down (Intravenous Therapy)	CIC	crisis intervention clinic

CICU	cardiac intensive care unit	CLINPROT	clinical cancer protocols
CID	carpal instability, dissociative (Orthopedics)	CLL	cholesterol-lowering lipid (Laboratory, Pharmacology)
CID	cervical immobilization device (Emergency Medical Services)	CLMA	Clinical Laboratory Management Association
cig	cigarette	CLP	cleft lip with cleft palate
CIN	cervical intraepithelial neoplasia (grades I, II, III) (Pathology)	ClP	clinical pathology
		CLS	clinical laboratory scientist
CIND	carpal instability non-dissociative (Orthopedics)	CLT	certified laboratory technician; clinical laboratory technician
CIP	clinical investigation plan (Research)	CLT	clotting time (Laboratory)
circ	circulation	CM	cardiac murmur
circ	circumference	CM	cardiac muscle
CIS	carcinoma in situ (Oncology)	CM	cardiomyopathy
CJD	Creutzfeldt-Jakob disease (Neurology)	CM	carpometacarpal (Anatomy)
ck	check	CM	caucasian male
CK	creatine kinase (Laboratory)	cm	centimeter
CKD	chronic kidney disease	CM	cervical mucosa or mucus (Gynecology)
Cl	chest and left arm (Lead in electrocardiography)		
		CM	circumferential measurement
Cl	chloride (Laboratory)	CM	clinical medicine
CL	cholelithiasis (Gastroenterology)	CM	congenital malformation
CL	clavicle (Anatomy)	CM	contrast medium (Diagnostic, Pharmacology)
CL	clear liquid		
CL	clearance	CM	costal margin (Physical assessment term referring to location)
Cl	cleft		
CL	cleft lip	CM	continuous murmur (Cardiology)
Cl	clinic, clinical	CM	tomorrow morning (Rehabilitation)
CL	clinical laboratory	CMA	certified medical assistant
Cl	clonus	CME	continuing medical education
Cl	closed, closure	CME	cystoid macula edema (Ophthalmology)
Cl, Clostr	clostridium (Laboratory)		
Cl	clotting	CMHC	community mental health center
Cl	cloudy	CMO	comfort measures only
CL	contact lens	CMP	cardiomyopathy
CL	corpus luteum (Anatomy, Gynecology)	CMP	competitive medical plan (Insurance)
CL	critical list	CMS	Centers for Medicare and Medicaid Services (Formerly HCFA)
CL; cl	clean		
CLA	cerebellar ataxia (Neurology)	CMS	circulation, motion, sensation
CLA	certified laboratory assistant	CMS 1500	a standard claim form for submission of
Clav	clavicle (Anatomy)		charges (Formerly HCFA 1500)
CLBBB	complete left bundle branch block (Cardiology)	CMT	chiropractic manipulative therapy (Chiropractic)
CLBP	chronic low back pain	CMV	cytomegalovirus (Infectious Diseases)
CLD	complete lower denture	CN	cranial nerve (Often followed by a Roman numeral from I to XII, e.g. CNII) (Anatomy)
CLD	chronic lung disease		
Cldy	cloudy		
CLH	corpus luteum hormone (Gynecology, Endocrinology)	CNA	certified nursing assistant
		CNS	central nervous system
CLIA	Clinical Laboratory Improvement Act	CNV	cranial nerve number 5

CNX	cranial nerve number 10	CPS	Children's Protective Services
CO	cardiac output	CPT	chronic paranoid type (Schizophrenia)
CO	check out	CPT	Current Procedural Terminology (Billing)
CO	childhood-onset		
Co	cobalt (Nuclear Medicine)	CQI	Continuous Quality Improvement (Risk Management)
CO2	carbon monoxide (Laboratory)		
COA	certificate of authority	CR	carrier replacement (Insurance)
COAG	coagulation (Laboratory, Hematology)	CR	clinical records
COB	coordination of benefits (Insurance)	CR	closed reduction (Orthopedics)
COBRA	Consolidated Omnibus Budget Reconciliation Act	CR	complete remission; complete response
COC	certificate of coverage	CR	conditional release
COC	continuity of care	CR	conditioned reflex
COG	center of gravity	Cr	creatinine (Laboratory)
Cog	cognitive	CRAO	central retinal artery occlusion (Ophthalmology)
col ct	colony count (Laboratory)		
COLD	chronic obstructive lung disease (Pulmonary)	Cr Cl	creatinine clearance (Laboratory)
		CR&C	closed reduction and cast (Orthopedics)
comp	complete		
Comp	compound	CRA	clinical research associate
CON	Certificate of Need	CRBBB	complete right bundle branch block (Cardiology)
conc	concentrate		
cont	continue	CRC	colorectal carcinoma
co-ord	coordination	CRC	community rating by class (Insurance)
COPD	chronic obstructive pulmonary disease	CRF	chronic renal failure
COPE	chronic obstructive pulmonary emphysema	CRI	chronic renal insufficiency
		CRNA	certified registered nurse anesthetist
COTA	certified occupational therapy assistant	CROM	cervical range of motion
CP	cerebral palsy	CRP	C-reactive protein (Laboratory)
CP	chest pain	CRRN	certified rehabilitation registered nurse
CP	cold pack	CRT	capillary refill time (Laboratory)
CP&PD	chest percussion and postural drainage (Respiratory Therapy)	CRT	certified
		CRT	chronic residual type (Schizophrenia)
CPAP	continuous positive airway pressure (Respiratory Therapy)	CRT	computerized renal tomography (Diagnostic)
CPB	cardiopulmonary bypass	CRTT	certified respiratory therapy technician
CPD	cephalopelvic disproportion (Obstetrics)	CRVO	central vein occlusion (Ophthalmology)
CPHA	Commission on Professional and Hospital Activities	CS	Cesarean section (Obstetrics)
		CS	cardiogenic shock (Cardiology)
CPK	creatine phosphokinase (Laboratory)	CS	carotid sinus (Cardiology)
CPM	clinical project manager	CS	central supply
CPM	continuous passive motion (Physical Therapy)	CS	cerebrospinal
		CS	cigarette smoker
CPM	counts per minute	CS	conscious sedation (Anesthesia)
CPM	cyclophosphamide (Anti cancer drug) (Pharmacology)	CS	conscious, consciousness
		Cs	consciousness
CPR	cardiopulmonary resuscitation	CS	convalescence, convalescent
CPR	checks with previous results	CS	coronary sclerosis (Cardiovascular)
CPR	C-reactive protein (Laboratory)	CS	coronary sinus (Cardiology)

CS	C-section, Cesarean section (Obstetrics)
CS	current smoker
CS	Cushing syndrome (Endocrinology)
C-section	Cesarean section
CSF	cerebrospinal fluid (Anatomy, Neurology)
CSF	coronary sinus flow (Diagnostic)
CSF-WR	cerebrospinal fluid-Wassermann reaction (Laboratory)
CSG	cholecystography, cholecystogram (Diagnostic)
CSH	carotid sinus hypersensitivity (Cardiology)
CSH	chronic subdural hematoma (Neurology)
CSP	cervical spine
CSP	cyclosporine (Pharmacology)
C-spine	cervical spine
CT	carpal tunnel (Anatomy)
CT	cerebral thrombosis (Neurology, Hematology)
CT	cervical traction (Orthopedics)
CT	cervical-thoracic (Physical assessment term referring to location)
CT	chemotherapy
CT	clinical trial
CT	Computerized Tomography (Diagnostic)
ct	count
CT	cover test (Ophthalmology)
CTA	clear to auscultation (Refers to lung examination)
CTAB	clear to auscultation bilaterally
CTB	confined to bed
CTNB	guided needle biopsy (Diagnostic, Pathology)
CTR	carpal tunnel release (Orthopedics)
CTRS	certified therapeutic recreational specialist
CTS	carpal tunnel syndrome (Orthopedics, Neurology)
Ctx	cervical traction (Orthopedics)
CU	cause unknown
CU	clinical unit
Cu	cubic
CUD	complete upper denture
CULD	complete upper and lower dentures
CUT	chronic undifferentiated type
CV	cardiovascular

CV	cervical vertebra (Anatomy)
CV	color vision
CVA	cerebrovascular accident (Stroke)
CVA	costovertebral angle (Physical assessment term referring to location)
CVAT	costovertebral angle tenderness
CVC	central venous catheters (Intravenous Therapy)
CVD	cardiovascular disease
CVF	confrontation visual field (Ophthalmology)
CVI	Cerebrovascular Insufficiency
CVP	central venous pressure
CVS	cardiovascular system
CVS	chorionic villous sampling (Obstetrics, Diagnostic)
CVAT	costovertebral angle tenderness
CW	caseworker
CW	chest wall
CW	clockwise
CW	close work (Ophthalmology)
CW	crutch walking
CWI	crutch walking instructions
CWP	childbirth without pain
CX	cervix (Anatomy)
CX	consciousness
Cx	culture (Laboratory)
Cx	cervical spine (Chiropractic)
CXR	chest x-ray
cyl	cylinder (refraction) (Ophthalmology)
Cysto	cystoscopic exam (Urology, Diagnostic)
CZP	clonazepam (Klonopin) (Pharmacology)

D

D	day
D	diopter (lens strength) (Ophthalmology)
D&C	dilatation and curettage (Gynecology)
D&E	dilatation and evacuation (Gynecology)
D&I	dry and intact (Wound dressings)
D&V	diarrhea and vomiting
d, /d	day, per day
D/A	date of accident
D/A	date of admission
d/c	diarrhea/constipation
D/C	discharge
D/C	discontinue (Not recommended)

D/DW	dextrose in distilled water (Pharmacology, Intravenous Therapy)	DCI	duplicate coverage inquiry (Insurance)
D/H	drug history	DCIS	ductal carcinoma in situ *(Type of breast cancer)* (Oncology)
D/NS	dextrose in normal saline (Pharmacology, Intravenous Therapy)	DCR	dacrocystorhinostomy (Ophthalmology)
D/O	disorder	DD	developmental disabilities
D/W	dextrose in water (Pharmacology, Intravenous Therapy)	DD	discharge diagnosis
		DD	dry dressing
D/W	discuss with	DDD	degenerative disk disease (Orthopedics)
D1–D12	dorsal vertebrae *(Thoracic vertebrae 1 through 12)* (Anatomy)	DDS	Doctor of Dental Surgery
D1OW, 10%	aqueous dextrose solution (Pharmacology, Intravenous Therapy)	DDx	differential diagnosis
		DEA	diethylamine (Pharmacology)
D5%DW	dextrose 5% in distilled water (Pharmacology, Intravenous Therapy)	DEA	Drug Enforcement Agency
		DEC; dec	deceased
D5%NS	dextrose 5% in normal saline (Pharmacology, Intravenous Therapy)	Dec	decrease
		decel	deceleration
D5LR	dextrose 5% with lactated ringers (Pharmacology, Intravenous Therapy)	Deg	degeneration
		Den	dental
D5W	dextrose 5% in water (Pharmacology, Intravenous Therapy)	Derm	dermatology
		des	describe
DA	degenerative arthritis (Orthopedics, Immunology)	DES	diethylstilbestrol (Pharmacology)
		Dev	deviation
DAB	dorsal abductors (Orthopedics)	DF	dorsiflexion *(Physical assessment term referring to position)*
DAFO	dynamic ankle/foot orthosis (Physical Therapy)	DFA	direct fluorescent antibody test (Laboratory)
DAP	Draw a Person Test (Psychiatry)	DFCS	Department of Family and Children Services
DAPRE	daily adjustable progressive resistive exercise (Physical Therapy)	DFM	deep friction massage
DAPT	direct agglutination pregnancy test	DI	date of injury
DAT	dementia of the Alzheimer's type	DI	diabetes insipitus
DAT	diet as tolerated	Diag	diagnosis, diagnostic
DAT	direct antibody testing (Laboratory)	DIC	disseminated intravascular coagulation (Hematology)
DAW	dispense as written (Pharmacology)		
db	decibel	DICOM	Digital Imaging and Communications in Medicine
DB	disability		
DB; DOB	date of birth	Dict	dictation
DBP	diastolic blood pressure	DIFF; diff	differential *(Blood count)* (Laboratory)
DBW	desirable body weight	Dig	digoxin (Pharmacology)
DBW	diabetic black women	DIL, dil	dilated, dilatation
DC	dioptres cylinder (Ophthalmology)	DIL	dilute
DC	direct current	DIM	diminished
DC	Doctor of Chiropractic	DIP	distal interphalangeal *(Physical assessment term referring to location)*
DC&B	dilation, curettage, and biopsy		
DC; D/C	discharged, discontinue *(Not recommended)*	DIPJ	distal interphalangeal joint (Anatomy)
		DIS	disabled
DCA	deferred compensation administrator (Insurance)	DIS	disease
		Disl	dislocate; dislocation
DCABG	double coronary artery bypass graft (Cardiac Surgery)	disp	disposition, dispense

DIST	distal, distribution	DOE	dyspnea on exertion
DIST	distended	DOH	department of health
DIW	dextrose in water (Pharmacology, Intravenous Therapy)	DOI	date of injury
		DOMS	delayed onset muscle soreness
DJD	degenerative joint disease (Orthopedics)	DON	director of nursing
		DOS	date of surgery
DKA	diabetic ketoacidosis (Gastroenterology)	DOT	date of transfer
		DP	deep pulse
DKB	deep knee bends	DP	diastolic pressure
dl, deciliter	0.01 liters (100 ml)	DP	distal pulses (Physical assessment tern referring to location)
DLA	dorsolateral area (Physical assessment term referring to location)	DP; DPed	dorsalis pedis (Anatomy)
DLE	discoid lupus erythematosus (Dermatology, Immunology)	DPL	diagnostic peritoneal lavage
		DPM	doctor of podiatric medicine
DLS	date last seen	DPR	drug price review (Insurance)
DM	diabetes mellitus	DPT	days per thousand (Insurance)
DM	diastolic murmur (Cardiology)	DPT	diphtheria, pertussis, tetanus immunization
DMD	daily maintenance dose		
DMD	delayed mental development	DR	delivery room
DMD	depression and manic depression (Psychiatry)	DR	diabetic retinopathy (Ophthalmology)
		Dr	dram
DMD	disease modifying drug	DR	dressing
DMD	Doctor of Dental Medicine	DRA	Deficit Reduction Act of 2005
DMD	Duchenne muscular dystrophy (Neurology)	DRE	digital rectal examination
		DRG	diagnosis-related groups (Billing)
DME	durable medical equipment	DRG	dorsal root ganglion (Anatomy, Neurology)
DMSO	dimethyl sulfamethoxazole (Pharmacology)		
		Drng	drainage
DMT	dynamic muscle test (Physical Therapy)	Drsg	dressing
DMV	dorsal metatarsal veins (Anatomy)	DS	dioptres spherical (Ophthalmology)
DNA	deoxyribonucleic acid (Biochemistry)	DSD	dry sterile dressing
DNA	did not attend (clinic)	Dsg	dressing
DNC	dominant-negative complementation (Genetics)	DSG	dry sterile gauze
		DSM	Diagnostic and Statistical Manual
DND	died a natural death	DSM-IV	Diagnostic and Statistical Manual Fourth Edition
DNI	do not intubate		
DNI/DNR	do not intubate, do not resuscitate	DT	date and time
DNKA	did not keep appointment	DT	date of treatment
DNR	do not resuscitate	DT	due to
DNR	dorsal nerve root (Anatomy)	DT	delirium tremens (Neurology, Psychiatry)
DNS	did not show for appointment		
DNS	director of nursing service	DTP	diphtheria and tetanus toxoids with pertussis
DNS	doctor of nursing science		
DO	doctor of osteopathy	DTP	distal tingling on percussion (Physical assessment term referring to sensation)
DO	dorsal outflow (Cardiology)		
DOA	day of admission	DTR	deep tendon reflex/es (Anatomy)
DOA	dead on arrival	DTZ	diltiazem (Pharmacology)
DOB	date of birth	DU	duodenal ulcer (Gastroenterology)
DOD	date of death	DUB	dysfunctional uterine bleeding (Gynecology)
DOE	date of examination		

DUE	drug use evaluation
DUR	drug utilization review (Risk Management)
DUS	divergent unilateral strabismus (Ophthalmology)
DUS	Doppler ultrasound (Diagnostic)
DUS	Dusseldorf (Catheter)
DUs	drug users
Dus	duodenal ulcers
Dv	double vibrations
DV; DVA	distance vision; distance visual acuity (Ophthalmology)
DVD	dissociated vertical deviation (Ophthalmology)
DVERT	domestic violence emergency response team
DVI	deep venous insufficiency
DVI	Doppler velocity index (Diagnostic)
DVP	domestic violence programs
DVP	Doppler velocity profile (Diagnostic)
DVR	double valve replacement (Cardiology)
DVT	deep venous thrombosis
DW	daily weight
DW	dextrose in water (Pharmacology, Intravenous Therapy)
DW	distilled water
DW	doing well
DWI	driving while impaired; driving while intoxicated
DWR	delayed word recall
DWR	desirable weight range
DWSCL	daily wear contact lenses (Ophthalmology)
DX	dextran (Pharmacology)
DX	dicloxacillin (Pharmacology)
DX	discharged
DX	disease
Dx, dx	diagnosis
DYFS	Division of Youth and Family Services
Dysp	dyspnea
DZ	diazepam (Pharmacology)
DZ	dizziness
Dz	dozen

E

EAC	external auditory canal
E	esotropia (Ophthalmology)
EAP	employee assistance program
EBL	estimated blood loss
EBV	Epstein-Barr Virus (Infectious Diseases)

ECCE	extracapsular cataract extraction (Ophthalmology)
ECF	extended care facility
ECG	electrocardiogram
ECHO	ultrasound cardiogram
ECRB	extensor carpi radialus brevis (Orthopedics; Physical Therapy)
ECRL	extensor carpi radialus longus (Orthopedics; Physical Therapy)
ECT	electroconvulsive therapy (Psychiatry)
ED	emergency department
EDC	estimated date of confinement (Obstetrics)
EDI	electronic data interchange
EDTA	ethylendiminetetracetic acid (used in measuring kidney function) (Pharmacology)
EEG	electroencephalogram
EENT	eyes, ears, nose, and throat
EF	eccentric fixation (Ophthalmology)
EF	ejection fraction (Cardiology)
e.g.	for example
EGD	esophagogastroduodenoscopy (Diagnostic)
EHL	extensor hallicus longus (Anatomy)
EIA	essay immunosobent assay (Laboratory)
EIA	exercise induced asthma
EIL	extension in lying (Physical Therapy)
EJ	external jugular (Anatomy)
EKG	electrocardiogram
ELISA	enzyme-linked immunosorbent assay (Laboratory)
Elix	elixir
EM	emergency medical technician
E/M	evaluation and management
EMD	electrical mechanical dissociation
EMG	electromyelogram
EMUO	early morning urine osmolarity (Laboratory test)
EMS	electrical muscle stimulation (Chiropractic)
EMS	emergency medical service
EMV	eyes, motor, verbal response (Glasgow coma scale) (Neurology)
ENDO	endocrine
Endo	endodontics
ENT	ears, nose, and throat
eo	eosinophil (Laboratory)
EOB	explanation of benefits (Insurance)

EOB	edge of bed
EOE	extraoral exam
EOG	electrooculogram (Ophthalmology)
EOI	evidence of insurability
EOM	end of month (Insurance)
EOM	extraocular movement *(Eye muscle)*
EOMB	explanation of medicare benefits (Insurance)
EOMI	extraocular movement intact
EOR	end of report (Emergency Medical Services)
Eos	eosinophil (Laboratory, Hematology)
EOY	end of year
EP	electrophysiology
Epi	epinephrine (Pharmacology)
EPO	Epogen (Pharmacology)
EPO	Exclusive Provider Organization (Insurance)
EPS	extrapyramidal symptoms (Neurology)
ER	emergency room
ER	external rotation (Physical Therapy)
ERCP	endoscopic retrograde cholangiopancrea-tography (Diagnostic)
ERG	electroretinogram (Ophthalmology)
ERISA	Employee Retirement Income Security Act of 1974
ERM	epi-retinal membrane (Ophthalmology)
ERP	end range pain (Physical Therapy)
ES; E-stim	electrical stimulation (Physical Therapy)
Esp	especially
ESR	erythrocyte sedimentation rate (Laboratory)
ESRD	end-stage renal disease
EST	exercise stress test
ETOH	alcohol
et	and
ET	endotracheal
ETA	estimated time of arrival
ETCO2	end tidal carbon dioxide (Respiratory, Emergency Medical Services)
ETOH	ethanol
ETS	endotracheal suctioning
ETT	endotracheal tube
EUA	examination under anesthesia
EV	eversion
eval	evaluation
Ex	exercise
expt	expectorant
Ext	extraction; external

F

F	Fahrenheit
F	female; father
fa	forearm (Intravenous site location)
FADER	flexion, abduction, external rotation
FADIR	flexion, adduction, internal rotation
FASA	Federated Ambulatory Surgery Association
f/b	followed by
F/U	follow up
FB	foreign body
FBR	full body restraint
FBS	fasting blood sugar
FBS&2hPP	fasting blood sugar and 2-hour post prandial (Laboratory)
FEV	forced expectorant volume *(Lung test)*
FDL	flexor digitorum longus (Orthopedics, Physical Therapy)
FD	fixation disparity (Ophthalmology)
FDA	Food and Drug Administration
Fe	iron
FeSO4	ferrous sulfate (Pharmacology)
FFB	flexible fibroscopic bronchoscope (Diagnostic)
FFP	fresh frozen plasma (Hematology)
FFS	fee for service
FFW	front wheel walker Physical Therapy)
FH; F/H	family history
FHL	flexor hallicus longus (Anatomy)
fib	fibula (Anatomy)
FIL	flexion in lying (Physical Therapy)
FIM	functional independence measure (Physical Therapy)
fl	femtoliter (Pharmacology)
Fl	fluid
Flex	flexion
fl tr	fluoride treatment
fluoro	fluoroscopy (Diagnostic)
FM	full mouth
FMX	full mouth x-ray
FNP	family nurse practitioner
FOH	family ocular vision (Ophthalmology)
FOI	flight of ideas (Psychiatry)
FM	family meeting
FOB	foot of bed
FPD	fixed partial denture (Dental bridge)
Fr	French
FRC	functional residual capacity (Rehabilitation)
FRCP	Federal Rules of Civil Procedure

FROM	full range of motion (Physical Therapy)	glu	glucose
FS	fever scan *(Forehead thermometer)*	gm	gram
FS	finger stick	GM	grandmother
FSBG	fasting sugar blood glucose (Laboratory)	GN	graduate nurse
		GP	general practitioner
FSH	follicle stimulating hormone (Laboratory)	gr	grain
		GR	gravida (Obstetrics)
FSIQ	Full Scale Intelligence Quotient	Grad	gradually (Rehabilitation)
Ft	foot	GSI	genuine stress incontinence (Urology)
FTN	full term nursery	GSW	gunshot wound
FTT	failure to thrive	GTC	generalized tonic-clonic *(Seizures)*
funct	function	GTE	great toe extension
FUO	fever of unknown origin	Gtt; gtt, gutt	drop
FVC	forced vital capacity	GTT	glucose tolerance test (Laboratory)
FWB	full weight bearing	Gtube	gastrointestinal tube
Fx	fracture	GU	genitourinary
Fxn	function	GVHR	graft vs. host reaction (Immunology)
FY	Fiscal year	GXT	graded exercise tolerance *(Stress test)*
		Gy	grays *(Units of radiation)*
		GYN	Gynecology

G

g	gram	
G6PD	glucose-6 phosphate dehydrogenase (Genetics)	
g/h	grooming and hygiene	
GA	general anesthesia	
GAD	generalized anxiety disorder (Psychiatry)	
GAF	Global Assessment of Functioning (Psychiatry)	
gastroc	gastrocnemius (Anatomy)	
GB	gallbladder	
GBP	gabapentin *(Neurontin)* (Pharmacology)	
GC	gonorrhea, gonococcus, gonococcal (Infectious Diseases)	
GCS	Glascow Coma Scale (Neurology)	
GE	gastroesophageal (Anatomy)	
GERD	gastroesophageal reflux disease (Gastroenterology)	
GF	glomerular filtration (Renal)	
gf	girlfriend	
GF	grandfather	
GFR	glomerular filtration rate (Renal)	
GGT	gamma glutamyl transpeptidase (Genetics)	
GH	general health	
GH	glenorhumeral (Anatomy)	
GH	growth hormone	
GHAA	Group Health Association of America	
GI	gastrointestinal	

H

H	Hispanic
h	hour
H&P	history and physical
H/A; HA	headache
HAC	Hospital acquired condition
h/o	history of
H2O2	hydrogen peroxide
H2O	water
HAA	Hospice Association of America
HARC	harmonious abnormal retinal correspondence (Ophthalmology)
HbcAb	type B hepatitis core antibody (Laboratory)
HBP	high blood pressure
HbsAb	type B hepatitis surface antibody (Laboratory)
HbsAG	type B hepatitis surface antigen (Laboratory)
HC	hydrocortisone (Pharmacology)
HC	head circumference
HCCA	Health Care Compliance Association
HCFA	Health Care Finance Administration
HCFA 1500	HCFA developed billing form
HCG	Human Chorionic Gonadatropin (Laboratory)
HCL	hairy cell leukemia (Oncology)
HCO3	bicarbonate (Laboratory)
HCP	healthcare plan (Insurance)

HCPCS	Healthcare Common Procedure Coding System (Insurance)	HOP-HAC	hospital outpatient-hospital acquired condition
HCPP	Health Care Prepayment Plan (Insurance)	Hosp	hospital
Hct	hematocrit (Laboratory)	HP	hot pack (Physical Therapy)
HCTZ	hydrochlorothiazide (Pharmacology)	Hpf	high-powered field (Laboratory)
HCVD	Hypertensive Cardiovascular Disease	HPI	history of present illness
HD	Hodgkin's disease (Oncology)	HPLC	high-pressure liquid chromatography (Laboratory)
HDC	high dose chemotherapy (Oncology)	HPV	human papilloma virus (Laboratory, Infectious Disease)
HDL	high-density lipoprotein (Laboratory)		
HEDIS	Health Plan Employer Data and Information Set (Insurance)	HR	heart rate
		HR	high risk
HEENT	head, eyes, ears, nose, and throat	HRT	hormone replacement therapy (Pharmacology)
Heme	hematology		
HEP	home exercise program (Physical Therapy)	hs	at bedtime
		HSA	health service agreement (Insurance)
Hgb	hemoglobin (Laboratory)	HSM	hepatosplenomegaly (Anatomy)
HH	hiatal hernia	HSP	health service plan (Insurance)
HHA	home health agency; home health aide	HST	health service technician
		HSV	herpes simplex virus (Laboratory, Infectious Disease)
HHC	home health care		
HHNK	Hyperosmolor, hyperglycemic nonketotic syndrome	Ht	height
		HTN	hypertension
HHS	Health and Human Services	HTLV	human T-cell leukemia lymphoma virus (Oncology)
HI	head injury		
HI	homicidal ideation	HVD	Hypertensive Vascular Disease
HIAA	Health Insurance Association of America	HVGS	high voltage galvanic stimulation (Physical Therapy)
HICP	Health Insurance Purchasing Cooperative	hw	heparin well (Intravenous)
		Hx	history
Histo	histoplasmosis (Infectious Diseases)	Hyg	hygiene
HITECH	Health Information Technology for Economic and Clinical Health Act	Hz	hertz, cycles per second
HIV	human immunodeficiency virus (Infectious Diseases)	**I**	
		I	incisal
HKAFO	hip, knee, ankle, foot orthosis (Physical Therapy)	I	independent
		I	iris (Ophthalmology)
HJR	hepatojugular reflux (Anatomy)	I&D	incision and drainage
HKB	hinged knee brace	I/J	insight/judgment (Psychiatry)
hl	heparin lock (Intravenous)	I&O	intake and output
HL-A	human leukocyte associated antigens (Laboratory)	I-131	radioactive iodine
		IABP	intraaortic balloon pump (Cardiology)
HM	hand motion vision (Ophthalmology)	IAC	internal auditory canal
HMO	Health Maintenance Organization	IADL	instrumental acts of daily living
HNP	herniated nucleus pulposus (Neurology)	IAPB	International Agency for the Prevention of Blindness
HO	hold order	IBNR	incurred but not reported
HO	house officer	IBW	ideal body weight
HOB	head of bed	ICCE	intracapsular cataract extraction (Ophthalmology)
HOP	hospital outpatient		

ICD	implantable cardiac defibrillator	INNS	International Neuroblastoma Staging System
ICD	International Classification of Diseases	inoc	inoculation
ICD-9-CM	International Classification of Diseases, 9th Edition-Clinical Modification	In Pt	in-patient
ICD-10-CM	International Classification of Diseases, 10th Revision for Clinical Modification	Inpt	inpatient
		int	internal
ICDO	International Classification of Diseases for Oncology	int	intermittent device
		INV	inversion
ICF	intercellular fluid	Invol	involuntary
ICF	intermediate care facility	IOE	intraoral exam
ICF/MR	intermediate care facility/mental retardation	IOL	intra-ocular lens implant (Ophthalmology)
		IOM	Institute of Medicine
ICN	intensive care nursery	IOP	intraocular pressure (Ophthalmology)
ICO	International Congress of Ophthalmology	IOR	ideas of reference (Psychiatry)
ICS	intercostal space (Physical assessment term referring to location)	ip	intraperitoneal
		IP	interphalangeal
ict	icterus (Gastroenterology)	IPA	Individual Practice Association (Insurance)
ICU	Intensive Care Unit		
ICU	intermediate care unit	IPE	initial psychiatric examination
ID	identification	IPF	idiopathic pulmonary fibrosis
ID	intradermal	IPPB	intermittent positive pressure breathing (Respiratory Therapy)
id	same day (Rehabilitation)		
IDDM	Insulin Dependent Diabetes Mellitus	IPPS	Inpatient Prospective Payment System
IDT	interdisciplinary team	IQ	intelligence quotient
ie	that is	IR	internal rotation
IF	inferential	IRBBB	incomplete right bundle branch block (Cardiology)
IF	intrinsic factor		
IFN	Interferon (Pharmacology)	IRM	intermediate restorative material (Dental)
IFOS	International Federation of Ophthalmologic Societies		
		IRMA	intraretinal microvascular abnormality (Ophthalmology)
IgG	immunoglobulin G (Laboratory)		
IK	interstitial keratitis (Ophthalmology)	IRU	inpatient rehabilitation unit
IJ	internal jugular (Anatomy)	IS/IS	intensity of service/severity of illness— (Describes how sick a patient is and the level of healthcare services the patient requires.) (Administration)
IL2	interleukin2 (Pharmacology)		
IM; im	intramuscular		
IME	Independent Medical Evaluation		
IMI	inferior myocardial infarction (Cardiology)	ISP	individual service plan (Insurance)
		IST	intersegmental traction (Chiropractic)
IMM	immunologic	ITB	iliotibial band (Anatomy)
IMO	Integrated Multiple Option (Insurance)	ITP	idiopathic thrombocytopenia purpura (Hematology)
Imp	impression		
IMV	intermittent mandatory ventilation (Respiratory Therapy)	IU	international units (Not Recommended) (Pharmacology)
inc	increase	IUD	intrauterine device (Gynecology)
inf	infiltration	IUP	intrauterine pregnancy (Obstetrics)
INF	intravenous nutritional fluid	IV	intravenous
Inf	infusion	IVC	inferior vena cava (Anatomy)
inj	injection	IVDA	IV drug abuse
inj	injury	IVF	intravenous fluids
INH	isoniazid (Pharmacology)		

IVP	intravenous pyelogram (Diagnostic, Renal)
IWR	ideal weight range

J

JC	The Joint Commission
JCAHO	The Joint Commission on Accreditation of Healthcare Organizations (now The Joint Commission, or TJC)
JCO	Journal of Clinical Oncology
jt	joint
JODM	juvenile onset diabetes mellitus
JRA	juvenile rheumatoid arthritis
JVD	jugular-venous distension
JVP	jugular-venous pulsation (Anatomy)

K

K	keratometry, keratometer reading (Ophthalmology)
K	potassium (Laboratory)
KAFO	knee ankle foot orthosis (Physical Therapy)
KB	ketone bodies (Laboratory)
KCL	Potassium Chloride (Intravenous Therapy Solution)
KCS	keratoconjunctivitis sicca (Ophthalmology)
Kg	kilogram
kj	knee jerk
Klebs	klebsiella (Laboratory)
KOH	potassium hydroxide (Laboratory)
KOR	keep open rate
KP	keratic precipitate (Ophthalmology)
KUB	kidney, ureter, bladder x-ray
KVO	keep vein open

L

L	left (May be encircled)
l	liter
L&D	Labor & Delivery (Obstetrics)
L/R	left hyperphoria (Ophthalmology)
L/RFD	L/R fixation disparity (Ophthalmology)
L1	1st lumbar vertebra, etc. (Total of 5) (Anatomy)
LA	long acting
lab	Laboratory
lac	laceration (Obstetrics)
LAD	left axis deviation (Cardiology)
LAE	left atrial enlargement (Cardiology)

LAH	left atrial hypertrophy (Cardiology)
lat	lateral
lAQ	long arc quad set (Physical Therapy)
Lax	laxative
Lb	pound
LB	low back, lumbar spine
LBBB	left bundle branch block (Cardiology)
LBP	lower back pain
LCL	lateral collateral ligament (Orthopedics, Physical Therapy)
LCM	left costal margin (Physical assessment term referring to location)
LCP	licensed clinical psychologist
LCSW	licensed clinical social worker
LDH	lactate dehydrogenase (Laboratory)
L-DOPA	levadopamine (Pharmacology)
LE prep	lupus erythematosus cell preparation (Laboratory)
LE	left eye (Ophthalmology)
LE	lower extremity
LFT	liver function tests (Laboratory)
Lg	large
LGA	large for gestational age (Obstetrics)
LH	lutenizing hormone (Obstetrics)
LHyperT	left hypertropia (Ophthalmology)
LHypoT	left hypotropia (Ophthalmology)
LiCo3	lithium carbonate (Pharmacology)
Lido	lidocaine (Pharmacology)
LIH	left inguinal hernia
LIMA	left internal mammary artery (Anatomy)
Liq	liquid
LJX	lateral jaw x-ray
LLb	long leg brace
LLC	long leg cast
LLE	left lower extremity
LLL	left lower lobe (Lung) (Physical assessment term referring to location)
LLQ	left lower quadrant (Abdomen) (Physical assessment term referring to location)
LLSB	left lower sternal border (Physical assessment term referring to location)
LM	landmark
LMP	last menstrual period
LMSW	licensed master social worker
LN	lymph node
LO	lens opacities (Ophthalmology)
LOA	left occipito-anterior (Physical assessment term referring to location)

LOA	loosening of associations (Psychiatry)	M	murmur (cardiac)
LOB	loss of balance	M/H	medical history
LOC	loss of consciousness; level of consciousness	M&N	Mydriacyl and neosynephrine solution (Ophthalmology, Pharmacology)
LOM	loss of memory	m/o	month old
LOS	length of stay	mab	median antebrachial vein (Intravenous site location)
LOS	line of sight		
LP	lumbar puncture	MAC	maximum allowable cost list (Prescription drug) (Insurance)
LPC	licensed professional counselor		
LPI	laser peripheral iredectomy (Ophthalmology)	MAFO	molded ankle foot orthosis (Physical Therapy)
LPN	licensed practical nurse	MAL	mid axillary line (Physical assessment term referring to location)
LR	light reflex		
LR	Lactated Ringer's solution (Pharmacology, Intravenous Therapy)	malign	malignant
		MAP	mean arterial pressure
L-S	lumbosacral (Anatomy)	MAO	monoamine oxidase (Pharmacology)
LSB	left sternal border (Physical assessment term referring to location)	MAOI	monoamine oxidase inhibitor (Pharmacology)
LSOT	left esotropia (Ophthalmology)	Mand	mandibular (Anatomy)
L-spine	lumbar spine (Anatomy)	MAST	medical anti-shock trousers
LTACH	long-term acute care hospital	max	maximum
LTG	long-term goal	MBC	minimum bacterial concentration (Laboratory)
LTG	low tension glaucoma (Ophthalmology)		
		MC	metacarpal (Anatomy)
LTM	long-term memory	MCC	major complicating condition
LTR	lower truck rotation (Physical Therapy)	Mcg	micrograms
L-trax	lumbar traction (Physical therapy)	MCH	mean corpuscular hemoglobin (Laboratory)
LUE	left upper extremity		
LUL	left upper lobe (Lung)	MCHC	mean corpuscular hemoglobin concentration (Laboratory)
LUQ	left upper quadrant (Abdomen)		
LV	left ventricle (Cardiology)	MCL	medial collateral ligament (Anatomy)
LVA	low vision aid (Ophthalmology)	MCL	mid-clavicular line (Physical assessment term referring to location)
LVE	left ventricle enlargement (Cardiology)		
LVH	left ventricle hypertrophy (Cardiology)	MCO	Managed Care Organization (Insurance)
LVN	licensed vocational nurse		
LVEF	left ventricular ejection fraction (Cardiology)	MCP; MP	metacarpophalangeal (joint)
		MCR	modified community rating (Insurance)
LVSF	left ventricular shortening fraction (Cardiology)	MCV	mean corpuscular volume (Laboratory)
		MD	medical doctor
LWBS	left without being seen	MDE	major depressive episode (Psychiatry)
Lx	lumpectomy (Surgery)	MDI	metered dose inhaler (Pharmacology)
Lymphs	lymphocytes (Laboratory, Hematology)	MDR	multi drug resistant
lytes	electrolytes (Laboratory)	MDS	Minimum Data Set (Tool to assess nursing home residents' needs and determine Medicare reimbursement)

M

m	meter	MDU	Mallett distance unit (Ophthalmology)
M/A	mood/affect	med	medial (Physical assessment term referring to location)
M; m	male		
M	mother	Med	medicine
M	manifest refraction (Ophthalmology)	Medigap	Medicare Supplement Insurance

Meds	medications	MR	Maddock rod (Ophthalmology)
Medsupp	Medicare Supplement Insurance	MR	mental retardation
MEq	milliequivalent	MR	myofascial release (Chiropractic)
mEq/l	milliequivalents per liter	MRE	most recent episode
met	metacarpal vein (Intravenous site location)	MRI	Magnetic Resonance Imaging
		MRN	medical record number
MET	muscle energy technique (Physical Therapy)	mRNA	messenger ribonucleic acid (Laboratory)
		MRSA	methicillin resistant staphylococcus aureus (Infectious Disease, Laboratory)
mets	metastases (Oncology)		
MFR	myofascial release (Physical Therapy)	MS	multiple sclerosis
Mg	magnesium (Laboratory)	MS	musculoskeleton
mg	milligram (0.0001 gram)	MSE	mental status exam
mg%	milligrams per hundred milliliter of serum or blood	Msg	massage (Physical Therapy)
		MSIII	medical student, 3rd year
MGF	maternal grandfather	MSIV	medical student, 4th year
MGM	maternal grandmother	MSL	midsternal line (Physical assessment term referring to location)
MH	mental health		
MH	moist heat (Physical Therapy)	MSN	master of science in nursing
MHC	mental health center; mental health counselor	MSO	Management Service Organization (Insurance)
MH/CD	mental health/chemical dependency	MSS	medical social services
MH/SA	mental health/substance abuse	MSSU	midstream specimen urine
MI	myocardial infarction (Cardiology)	MSW	master of social work
MIC	minimum inhibitory concentration (Laboratory)	MT	music therapy
		MTP	master treatment plan
min	minimum	MTP joint	metatarsophalangeal joint (Anatomy)
Misc	miscellaneous	MTP	minor treatment protocol
MJ	marijuana	MTP	master treatment plan
ml	milliliter or milliliters	MTX	methotrexate (Cancer drug)
MLE	midline episiotomy (Obstetrics)	MVA	motor vehicle accident
mm	millimeter	MVI	multivitamin injection
mM	millimole	MVM	mobilization with movement (Physical Therapy)
MM	muscle		
MMG	mammogram (Diagnostic)	MVP	mitral valve prolapse (Cardiology)
MMPI	Minnesota Multiphasic Personality Inventory (Psychology)	MVV	maximum voluntary ventilation (Respiratory Therapy)
MMR	measles/mumps/rubella	Mwing	Maddock wing (Ophthalmology)
MMSE	mini-mental status exam	MX	maxillary (Anatomy)
MMT	manual muscle test (Physical Therapy)	Mx	mastectomy (Surgery)
Mn	midnight		
MNU	Mallett near unit (Ophthalmology)	**N**	
mo	month	N	normal
mob	mobilization	N/A	not applicable
mod	moderate	n/v	nausea and vomiting
MOM	milk of magnesia (Pharmacology)	N/V/D	nausea, vomiting and diarrhea
Mono	infectious mononucleosis	N20/02	nitrous oxide and oxygen (Anesthesia)
mono	monocyte (Laboratory)	NA	nurse assistant
mos	months	Na	sodium (Laboratory)
MP	mouth prop (Dental)	NAATP	National Association of Addiction Treatment Providers
MP	metacarpophalangeal joint (Anatomy)		

NACC	National Association of Childbearing Centers	NH	nursing home
NaCl	sodium chloride (Laboratory, Intravenous Therapy)	NHL	non Hodgkin's lymphoma (Oncology)
		NIC	Nursing Interventions Classification
NAD	no acute distress	NIDDM	non-insulin dependent diabetes mellitus
NAG	narrow angle glaucoma (Ophthalmology)	Nitro	nitroglycerin (Pharmacology)
NAGS	neuro apophyseal glides (Physical Therapy)	NK	not known
		NKA	no known allergies
NAHC	National Association of Health Consultants	NKDA	no known drug allergies
		nl	normal
NAHDO	National Association of Health Data Organizations	NLP	no light perception (Ophthalmology)
		NMR	neuromuscular re-education (Chiropractic)
NAIC	National Association of Insurance Commissioners	NMRI	nuclear Magnetic Resonance Imaging
NAD	no acute distress	no.	number
NAD	no abnormality detected; no active disease	noc	night
		NOC	Nursing Outcomes Classification
NANDA	North American Nursing Diagnosis Association	non-par	non-participating provider (Insurance)
		NOS	not otherwise specified (Insurance)
NAS	no added salt	NP	nurse practitioner
NB	newborn	NPA	National Prescription Audit
NBM	nothing by mouth	NPA	non-participating provider approved (Insurance)
NBW	normal birth weight	NPC	no previous correction; near point of convergence (Ophthalmology)
NC	nasal canula		
NCA	nurse controlled analgesia	NPH	neutral protamine hagedorn (Insulin) (Pharmacology)
NCAT	normocephalic atraumatic		
NCPDP	Nation Council of Prescription Drug Programs	NPL	no perception of light (Ophthalmology)
NCQA	The National Committee for Quality Assurance	NPN	nonprotein nitrogen (Nutrition)
		NPO	nothing by mouth
NCT	near cover test (Ophthalmology)	NPN	non-participating provider not approved (Insurance)
NCT	non-contact tonometry		
NCV	nerve conduction velocity (Neurology)	NRC	normal retinal correspondence (Ophthalmology)
ND	neural density filter (Ophthalmology)		
NDC	National Drug Code	NREM	non rapid eye movement (Neurology)
NDT	neurodevelopmental treatment (Neurology)	NS	normal saline
		NS	nuclear sclerosis (Ophthalmology)
NEC	necrotizing enterocolitis (Gastroenterology)	NSAID	nonsteroidal anti-inflammatory drug
		NSCLC	non-small cell lung cancer (Oncology)
NEC	not classified elsewhere	NSFTD	normal spontaneous full term delivery (Obstetrics)
NED	no evidence recurrent disease (Insurance)		
		NSG	nursing
Neg	negative	NSR	normal sinus rhythm
Neuro	neurology	NSS	Normal Saline Solution (Intravenous Therapy)
NeuroSurg	neurosurgery		
NFTD	normal full term delivery (Obstetrics)	NSU	neurosurgey unit
ng	nanogram (0.000000001 gram)	NSVD	normal spontaneous vaginal delivery (Obstetrics)
NG; NGT	nasogastric		
NGRI	not guilty by reason of insanity	NT	nasotracheal

NT	not tested	OP	overpressure (Physical Therapy)
NTE	not to exceed	OPC	order of protective custody
NTG	nitroglycerin (Pharmacology)	OPC	outpatient clinic
NTG	normotensive glaucoma (Ophthalmology)	Ophth	ophthalmology
NVI	neovascularization of iris (Ophthalmology)	OPPS	Outpatient Prospective Payment System
NWB	non-weight bearing (Physical Therapy)	OPV	oral polio vaccine
NWT	normal wearing time (Ophthalmology)	OR	operating room
		ORIF	open reduction internal fixation (Orthopedic)
		Orth; ortho	orthopedic

O

O	occlusal (Surface of tooth) (Dental)	OS	left eye (Not recommended)
O X 3	oriented times three	OSHA	Occupational Safety and Health Administration
O/T; OT	occupational therapy	OT	occupational therapist
O2 cap	oxygen capacity	OTC	over the counter
O2	oxygen	OTR	occupational therapist, registered
O2Sat	oxygen saturation (Laboratory, Pulmonary)	OU	both eyes (Not recommended)
OA	open access (Insurance)	Out Pt	outpatient
OA	osteoarthritis	OTC	over the counter
OB	obstetrics	Oz	ounce
obl	oblique		

P

OBRA	Omnibus Budget Reconciliation Act of 1987 (Defines nursing home standards)	p̄	after (Written with a line drawn over letter)
obs	observation	P	pulse
OBS	Organic Brain Syndrome	P/T	physical therapy
OC	optical center (Ophthalmology)	P2	pulmonic second sound (Anatomy, Cardiology)
OCBZ	oxycarbazepine (Trileptal) (Pharmacology)	PA	physician's assistant
Occ	occupation	P-A	posteroanterior (Physical assessment term referring to location)
OCD	obsessive-compulsive disorder (Psychiatry)	PAAO	Pan American Association of Ophthalmology
od	once a day (Ophthalmology)	PA-C	physician's assistant—certified
OD	right eye (Not recommended)	PAC	pre-admission certificate (Insurance)
OD	overall diameter (Ophthalmology)	PAC	premature atrial contraction (Cardiology)
ODD	oppositional defiant disorder (Psychiatry)	PAGE	polyacrylamide gel electrophoresis (Diagnostic)
OE	otitis externa (Outer ear)	PAL	posterior axillary line (Physical assessment term referring to location)
OH	oral hygiene		
OHT	ocular hypertension (Ophthalmology)	Palp	palpitation
OKC	open kinetic chain (Physical Therapy)	PAO2	alveolar oxygen (Laboratory; Pulmonary)
OM	otitis media (Middle ear)		
OMB	ocular motor balance (Ophthalmology)	PaO2	peripheral arterial oxygen content (Laboratory)
ONH	optic nerve head (Ophthalmology)		
OOA	out of area (Insurance)	PANSS	Positive and Negative Syndrome Scale (Psychiatry)
OOB	out of bed		
OOPS	out-of-pocket-expenses (Insurance)	PAP; Pap	Papanicolaou's smear (Gynecology)
Op	operation		

Par	participating provider (Insurance)	PEG	percutaneous gastrostomy (Gastroenterology)
PARA 1	having borne one child (Number indicated number of children born) (Obstetrics)	PEG	punctuate epithelial granularity (Ophthalmology)
PAT	paroxysmal atrial tachycardia (Cardiology)	PEK	punctuate epithelial keratitis (Ophthalmology)
Path; pathol	pathology	PEJ	percutaneous jejunostomy (Gastroenterology)
PAX	periapical x-ray	Per	through or by
PB	phenobarbital (Pharmacology)	Perio	periodontal (Dental)
PBI	protein bound iodine (Laboratory)	PERL	pupils equal and reactive to light
PBS	phosphate-buffered saline (Pharmacology)	PERRLA	pupils equal, round, reactive to light and
pc	after meals, post prandial		accommodation
PC	posterior chamber; posterior capsule (Ophthalmology)	PET	positron emission computed tomography (Diagnostic)
PCA	patient controlled analgesia	PFM	porcelain fused to metal (Crown) (Dental)
PCH	personal care home		
PCL	posterior cruciate ligament (Anatomy)	PFS	patellofemoral syndrome (Orthopedics)
PCN	penicillin (Pharmacology)		
PCN	Primary Care Network (Insurance)	PFSH	past family social history
PCP	primary care physician	PFT	pulmonary function tests
PCP	phencyclidine (Pharmacology)	Pg	pictogram (0.000000000001 gram)
PCPM	per contract per month (Insurance)	PGF	paternal grandfather
PCR	Physician Contingency Reserve (Insurance)	PGM	paternal grandmother
PCR	polymerase chain reaction (Laboratory)	pH	hydrogen ion concentration (Chemistry)
PCV	packed cell volume (Hematology)	PH	past history
PCWP	pulmonary capillary wedge pressure (Diagnostic)	PH	pinhole (Ophthalmology)
		Phos	phosphorus (Laboratory)
PD	papillary distance (Ophthalmology)	PHR	periodic health review
PDA	patient ductus arteriosis (Cardiovascular)	PI	pulmonary insufficiency
		PID	pelvic inflammatory disease
PDD	pervasive development disorder (Psychiatry)	PIP	proximal interphalangeal (joint)
PDL	periodontal ligament (Dental)	PIP	Personal Injury Protection (Medical expense coverage by the client's own auto insurance carrier) (Insurance)
PDR	Physicians Desk Reference		
PDR	proliferative diabetic retinopathy (Ophthalmology)	PIVM	passive intervertebral motion (Physical Therapy)
PDQ	Physicians Data Query	PJC	porcelain jacket crown (Dental)
PE, PHACO	phacoemulsification (Ophthalmology)	PKU	phenylketonuria (Laboratory)
PE	physical examination	PL	light perception (Ophthalmology)
PE	pulmonary edema	pl ct	platelet count (Laboratory)
PE	pulmonary embolism	plt	platelet
PEC	pre-existing condition (Insurance)	PM; pm	afternoon
Pedi	pediatric	PMG	Primary Medical Group (Insurance)
PEE	punctuate epithelial erosions (Ophthalmology)	PMH	past medical history
		PMI	point of maximal impulse (Cardiology)
PEEP	positive end expiratory pressure (Respiratory Therapy)	PMP	previous menstrual period
		PMS	premenstrual syndrome

PND	paroxysmal nocturnal dyspnea (Cardiology)	PROM	passive range of motion (Physical Therapy)
PNF	proprioceptive neuromuscular facilitation (Neurology)	Prophy	dental prophylaxis
PNS	peripheral nervous system	PRP	pan-retinal photocoagulation (Ophthalmology)
PO; po	by mouth	PQRE	progressive quad resistance exercises (Physical Therapy)
POA	Present on admission		
POAG	primary open angle glaucoma (Ophthalmology)	PS	pulmonary stenosis
		PSA	prostate specific antigen (Laboratory)
POD	postoperative day (Followed by a number)	PSC	posterior subcapsular cataract (Ophthalmology)
POH	previous ocular history (Ophthalmology)	PSI	Patient Safety Institute
polys	polymorphonuclear leucocytes (Also called neutrophils) (Laboratory)	PSIS	posterior superior iliac spine (Anatomy)
		Psy; Psych	psychiatric
POS	point of service (Insurance)	PsychD	Doctor of Psychology
post	after; posterior	Pt; pt	patient
Post-op	postoperative	PT	physical therapy
PPD	purified protein derivative (Pharmacology)	PT	prothrombin time (Laboratory)
		PTA	prior to admission
PPDR	preproliferatuve diabetic retinopathy (Ophthalmology)	PTA	physical therapy assistant
		PTCA	percutaneous transluminal coronary angioplasty (Diagnostic)
PPO	preferred provider organization (Insurance)	PTE	pretrial evaluation
PPRC	Physician Payment Review Commission (Insurance)	Pt Ed	patient education
		PTN	phenytoin (Dilantin) (Pharmacology)
PPS	Prospective Payment System (Insurance)	PTSD	posttraumatic stress disorder (Psychiatry)
PPTL	postpartum tubal ligation (Obstetrics; Gynecology)	PTT	partial thromboplastin time (Laboratory)
PPVT-R	Peabody Picture Vocabulary Test-Revised (Psychology)	Ptx	pelvic traction
		PUD	peptic ulcer disease
PR	per rectum	PVC	premature ventricular contraction (Cardiology)
PRBC	packed red blood cells (Hematology, Intravenous Therapy)	PVD	peripheral vascular disease (Vascular)
PRE	progressive resistive exercise (Physical Therapy)	PVD	posterior vitreous detachment (Ophthalmology)
pre-op	preoperative	PWB	partial weight bearing (Physical Therapy)
prep	prepare for, preparation for	Px	patient
PRICE	protect, rest, ice, compression, elevation (Physical Therapy)		
PRN; prn	as necessary, as needed	**Q**	
PRO	Peer Review Organization, Physician Review Organization (Risk Management)	q	every; each
		Q(x)H	every (x) hours
		QA	quality assurance (Risk Management)
Pro	pronation	qAM	every morning
Prog	prognosis	qd	every day (Not recommended)
PRK	photorefractive keratectomy (Ophthalmology)	qh	every hour (Not recommended)
		qhs	every hour of sleep (Not recommended)

QI	quality improvement
qid	four times per day *(Not recommended)*
QM	quality management
QMB	qualified Medicare beneficiary (Insurance)
qod	every other day *(Not recommended)*
qPM	every afternoon
QS	quad sets (Physical Therapy)
QS	quantity sufficient (Urology)
qSHIFT	every shift

R

R	registration
R	respiration
R	right *(May be encircled)*
R&C	reasonable and customary (Insurance)
R/O	rule out
R/T	related to
RA	rheumatoid arthritis
rad	radius
RAD	right axis deviation (Cardiology)
RAE	right atrial enlargement (Cardiology)
RAH	right atrial hypertrophy (Cardiology)
RAI	Resident Assessment Instrument *(Includes the MDS, RAPS, and the care plan)* (Nursing Home Record)
RAIU	radioactive iodine uptake (Diagnostic)
RAN	resident admission note
RAP	Resident Assessment Protocol *(System that used the MDS to identify and define residents' problems)* (Nursing Home Record)
RAP	retinal artery pressure (Urology)
RAP	right atrial pressure (Cardiology)
RAPD	relative afferent papillary defect (Ophthalmology)
RBBB	right bundle branch block (Cardiology)
RBC	red blood cell (Laboratory, Hematology)
RPB	retinol-binding protein (Laboratory)
RC	rotator cuff (Anatomy)
RCT	rotator cuff tear (Orthopedics)
RCM	right costal margin *(Physical assessment term referring to location)*
RCT	randomized controlled trial (Research)
RCT	root canal therapy (Dental)
RD	registered dietitian
RD	retinal detachment (Ophthalmology)
RDH	registered dental hygienist
Re	regarding

RE	right eye (Ophthalmology)
readm	readmission
recd	received
REIL	repeated extension in lying (Physical Therapy)
REIS	repeated extension in standing (Physical Therapy)
Ret	retinoscopy (Ophthalmology)
retics	reticulocyte (Laboratory)
RFIL	repeated flexion in lying (Physical Therapy)
RFIS	repeated flexion in standing (Physical Therapy)
rehab	rehabilitation
reps	repetitions (Physical Therapy)
resp	respiration
ret	retraction (Physical Therapy)
retic(s)	reticulocyte(s) (Laboratory)
RF	rheumatoid factor (Laboratory)
RFP	request for proposal (Insurance)
Rh	rhesus blood factor (Laboratory)
RHD	rheumatic heart disease
RHyperT	right hypertropia (Ophthalmology)
RHypoT	right hypotropia (Ophthalmology)
RIA	radioimmunoassay (Diagnostic)
RICE	rest, ice, compression, and elevation
RIG	right inguinal hernia
RK	radial keratotomy (Ophthalmology)
RLE	right lower extremity
RLL	right lower lobe *(Lung)*
RLQ	right lower quadrant *(Abdomen)*
RMC	rating method code (Insurance)
RML	right middle lobe *(Lung)*
RN	registered nurse
RNFL	retinal nerve fiber layer (Ophthalmology)
ROM	range of movement
ROP	retinopathy of prematurity (Ophthalmology)
ROS	review of systems
rot	rotation
RP	retinal pigmentosa (Ophthalmology)
RPE	retinal pigmentosa epithelium (Ophthalmology)
RPD	removable partial denture
RPG	retrograde pyelogram (Radiology)
RPh	registered pharmacist
RROM	resistive range of motion (Physical Therapy)
RPR	rapid plasma reagent (Laboratory)

RR	recovery room	SANE	sexual assault nurse examiner
RR	respiratory rate	SAQ	short arc quad set (Physical Therapy)
RRR	regular rate and rhythm (Heart examination)	SB	side bending (Physical Therapy)
		SBA	stand by assist (Physical Therapy)
RRT	Rapid Response Team	SBAR	Situation Background Assessment Response
RS	rhythmic stabilization (Physical Therapy)		
		SBE	subacute bacterial endocarditis (Cardiology)
RSOT	right esotropia (Ophthalmology)		
RT	recreational therapist	SBIS	side bending in standing (Physical Therapy)
RTC	return to clinic		
RUE	right upper extremity	SBO	small bowel obstruction
RUG	Resource Utilization Group (Method that used MDS data to calculate reimbursements) (Insurance)	SBP	systolic blood pressure
		SBS	short bowel syndrome (Gastroenterology)
RUG	retrograde urethrogram (Diagnostic)	SC	sternoclavicular (Physical assessment term referring to location)
RUL	right upper lobe (Lung)		
RUQ	right upper quadrant (Abdomen)	SC; SQ	subcutaneous
RV	residual volume (Respiratory Therapy)	sc	without refractive correction (Ophthalmology)
RV	right ventricle (Cardiology)		
RVE	right ventricular enlargement (Cardiology)	SC anemia	sickle cell anemia (Hematology)
		SCC	squamous cell carcinoma (Oncology)
RVH	right ventricular hypertrophy (Cardiology)	SCI	spinal cord injury
		SC joint	sternoclavicular joint (Anatomy)
RVS	Relative Value System (Method of assigning the cost of a procedure or service) (Insurance)	SCLC	small cell lung cancer (Oncology)
		SCM	sternocleidomastoid muscle (Anatomy)
RVT	rate, volume, tone	SC Trait	sickle cell trait (Genetics)
Rx	prescription, treatment	SCR	standard class rate (Insurance)
		SDA	same day admission
		SDAT	Senile Dementia Alzheimer's type
S		SDH	Subdural Hematoma
S	sign	SE	side effects
S	sister	SEAL	superior epithelial arcuate lesion (Ophthalmology)
S	supervision (May be encircled)		
s	second		
s	without (Written with a line drawn over letter)	sed	sedation
		sed rate	sedimentation rate (Laboratory)
S/P	status-post	SF	stepfather (May be encircled)
S/P	suicide precautions	SGA	small for gestational age (Obstetrics)
S/Sx; s/s	signs/symptoms	segs	segmented neutrophils (Laboratory, Hematology)
S1 & S2	first and second heart sounds (Heart examination)		
		SEM	systolic ejection murmur (Cardiology)
S3 & S4	third and fourth heart sounds (Heart examination)	SG	specific gravity (Laboratory)
		SG	Swan-Ganz (Catheter)
SA	sinoatrial (Cardiology)	SGA	small for gestational age (Obstetrics)
SA	substance abuse	SGIS	side glide in standing (Physical Therapy)
SAC	short arm cast		
SAH	subarachnoid hemorrhage (Neurology)	SGOT	serum glutamic oxaloacetic transaminase (Laboratory)
SAID	specific adaptation to imposed demands		
		SGPT	serum glutamic pyruvic transaminase (Laboratory)
SART	sexual response team		

SH	social history	SP	suicide precaution(s)
SHAPA	social history and psychosocial assessment	SPC	single point cane (Physical Therapy)
		SPF	sun protection factor
SHO	senior house officer	sp gr	specific gravity (Laboratory)
SI	sacroiliac (Anatomy, Chiropractic)	SPIN	standard prescriber identification number (Insurance)
SI	steroid injection		
SI	suicidal ideation (Psychiatry)	SPK	superficial punctuate keratitis (Ophthalmology)
SI/HI	suicidal/homicidal ideation		
SIADH	Syndrome of Inappropriate Antidiuretic Hormone	SQ; SC	subcutaneous (Dermatology)
		SR	superior rectus (Ophthalmology)
SIB	self-injurious behavior	SRN	subretinal neovascularization membrane (Ophthalmology)
sib(s)	sibling(s)		
SIC	standard industry code (Insurance)	STAT	immediately
SICU	surgical intensive care unit	STG	short-term goals
sig:	directions for use, label	STM	short-term memory
sl	saline lock (Intravenous Therapy)	STS	serological tests for syphilis (Laboratory)
sl	slight; slightly		
SL	sublingual (Under the tongue)	SQ	subcutaneous
SLB	short leg brace	ss enema	soapsuds enema
SLC	short leg cast	SS	Social Security
SLE; SLX	slit lamp exam (Ophthalmology)	SSC	stainless steel crown (Dental)
SLE	systemic lupus erythematous (Immunology)	SSD	Sulfa Silvadene (an antibiotic in cream form)
SLH	supportive living home	SSD	social security disability
SLK	superior limbic keratoconjunctivitis (Ophthalmology)	SSI	supplemental security income
		SSN	social security number
SLM	slit-lamp microscope (Ophthalmology)	ST	speech therapy
SLP	speech/language pathologist	Staph	staphylococcus (Biology, Laboratory)
SLR	straight leg raise (Neurology, Physical Therapy)	STAT	immediately; at once
		STD	sexually transmitted disease
S-M	sensorimotor (Neurology)	STJ	subtabular joint (Physical Therapy)
Sm	small	Strep	streptococcus (Biology, Laboratory)
SM	stepmother (May be encircled)	STSG	split thickness skin graft (Surgery)
SMA; SMAC	sequential multiple analyzer (computer)	STW	soft tissue wound
		Subg	subgingival (Dental)
SMI	supplementary medical insurance	sup	supination (Physical Therapy)
SMO	slips made out	Supp	suppository
SMT	static muscle test (Physical Therapy)	Surg	surgery; surgical
SNF	skilled nursing facility	Susp	suspension (Pharmacology)
SO2	oxygen saturation (Laboratory)	SVC	service
SOAP	subjective, objective, assessment, plan (Progress note format)	SVD	spontaneous vaginal delivery (Obstetrics)
SOB	shortness of breath	SVT	supra-ventricular tachycardia (Cardiology)
SOC	social		
SOD	statement of deficiency	SW	social worker
sol'n	solution	Sx	symptoms
SOM	serous otitis media (Fluid behind the middle ear)	Sz	seizure
		Sz D/O	seizure disorder
SPA	summary plan description (Insurance)	SZAF	schizoaffective (Psychiatry)

T

T; temp	temperature
T&A	tonsillectomy and adenoidectomy (Surgery)
T/A	toothache
T&C	type and cross (Hematology, Laboratory)
T&H	type and hold (Hematology, Laboratory)
T&S	type and screen (Laboratory)
T1	1st thoracic vertebra, etc. *(12 total)*
TA	applanation tonometry (Ophthalmology)
Tab, tabs	tablet, tablets
TAC	triamcinolone cream (Pharmacology)
TAH	total abdominal hysterectomy (Gynecology, Surgery)
TAH & BSO	total abdominal hysterectomy and bilateral salpingo oophorectomy (Gynecology)
TANF	Temporary Aid to Needy Families
TAS	therapeutic activity specialist
TAT	Thematic Apperception Test (Psychology)
TAT	turnaround time
TB; Tbc	tuberculosis
TBG	total binding globulin (Laboratory)
TBI	total body irradiation (Radiology)
TBI	traumatic brain injury
TBSA	total body surface area
tbsp	tablespoon
TC	thought content
TCA	tricyclic antidepressant (Pharmacology)
TCDB	turn, cough, deep breathe
TCH	marijuana
TCP	thrombocytopenia (Hematology)
TD	tardive dyskinesia (Psychiatry)
Td	tetanus/diphtheria toxoid
Temp Flg	temporary filling (Dental)
Ted hose	antiembolitic stockings
TENS	transcutaneous electrical neurostimulation (Anesthesia, Pain Control)
TFM	transverse friction massage (Physical Therapy)
TFT	thyroid function test (Laboratory)
TGB	tiagabine *(Gabatril)* (Pharmacology)
THA	total hip arthroplasty (Orthopedics)
Ther ex	therapeutic exercise
THR	total hip replacement

TIA	transient ischemic attack (Vascular)
TIBC	total iron binding capacity (Laboratory)
TID	three times daily *(Not recommended)*
TIW	three times per week *(Not recommended)*
TKA	total knee arthroplasty (Orthopedics)
TKR	total knee replacement (Orthopedics)
TL	temporary leave
T-L	thoracolumbar *(Physical assessment term referring to location)*
TLC	tender loving care
TLC	total lung capacity
tlc	triple lumen catheter (Intravenous Therapy)
TLSO	thoracic lumbar sacral orthosis (Physical Therapy)
TM	tympanic membrane *(ear drum)*
TMJ	temporomandibular joint (Anatomy)
TNF	tumor necrosis factor (Laboratory)
TNM	staging system-primary tumor (Oncology)
TNTC	too numerous to count (Laboratory)
TO	telephone order
TOF	tetralogy of fallot (Cardiology)
Tol	tolerate
TOPV	trivalent oral polio vaccine
TOS	thoracic outlet syndrome (Neurovascular)
Toxo	toxoplasmosis (Infectious Diseases)
TP	thought process
TPA	third party administrator (Insurance)
TPM	topiramate *(Topamax)* (Pharmacology)
TPN	total parenteral nutrition
TPR	temperature, pulse, respiration
TR	therapeutic recreation
Trach	tracheostomy
trans	transfer (Physical Therapy)
trax	traction (Physical Therapy)
Trich	trichomonas (Laboratory)
TSH	thyroid stimulating hormone (Laboratory)
tsp	teaspoon
TT	tetanus toxoid *(Vaccine)*
TT	thrombin time (Laboratory)
TTP	thrombotic thrombocytopenic purpura (Hematology)
TTWM	toe touch weight bearing (Physical Therapy)
TU	tuberculin units

TUR	transurethral resection (Urology)
TURBT	transurethral bladder tumors (Urology)
TURP	transurethral resection of prostate (Urology)
TV	tidal volume (Respiratory Therapy)
TV	trial visit
TVH	total vaginal hysterectomy (Gynecology, Surgery)
TW	thought withdrawal (Psychiatry)
Tx	treatment
tx plan	treatment plan

U

U	uncle (May be encircled)
U&C	usual and customary (Insurance)
UA; U/A	urinalysis (Laboratory)
UAC	uric acid (Laboratory)
UB-92	Uniform Billing Code 1992
UBE	upper body ergometer (Physical Therapy)
UBR	upper body restraints
UCG	urine chorionic gonadotropin (Pregnancy test) (Laboratory)
UCR	usual, customary, and reasonable (Insurance)
ud	as directed
UDS	urine drug screen
UE	upper extremity
ug	microgram (0.000001 gram)
UGI w/SBFT	upper gastrointestinal series with small bowel follow through (Diagnostic)
UGI	upper gastrointestinal
ULTT	upper limb tension test (Physical Therapy)
UM	utilization management
UNK	unknown
UP	ureteropelvic (Anatomy)
UPIN	universal physician identification number
UR	Utilization Review (Risk Management)
URC	usual, customary, and reasonable (Insurance)
UR/QA	utilization review/quality assurance (Risk Management)
URI	upper respiratory infection
Urol	urology
URR	urea reduction ratio (Laboratory test done to determine effectiveness of dialysis treatment in removing blood urea nitrogen)

URTI	upper respiratory tract infection
US	ultra-sound (Diagnostic)
USP	United States Pharmacopoeia
UT	upper trapezius muscle (Anatomy)
UTI	urinary tract infection
UV	ultraviolet
UVR	ultraviolet radiation

V

-ve	negative
+ve	positive
V	vision (Ophthalmology)
V/A	visual acuity
V/Q	ventilation/perfusion (Respiratory Therapy)
VA	Veterans Administration
Va	visual acuity (Ophthalmology)
VAMC	Veterans Administration Medical Center
VCU	voiding cystourethrogram (Diagnostic)
VD	venereal disease
VDRL	Venereal Disease Research Laboratory
VE	voluntary effort
VEF	ventricular ejection fraction (Cardiology, Diagnostic)
VEP	visual evoked potential (Neurology)
VF	visual field (Ophthalmology)
VH	visual hallucinations (Psychiatry)
Vit	vitamin
Vit	vitreous (Ophthalmology)
VMA	vanillylmandelic acid (Laboratory)
VO; vo	verbal order
vol	volume
V-P	ventriculo-peritoneal (shunt) (Neurology)
VPA	valproic acid (Pharmacology)
VPC	ventricular premature complexes (Cardiology)
VR	vocational rehabilitation
VRE	vancomycin resistant enterococcus (Laboratory)
VS; V/S	vital signs
vs	versus
VSD	ventricular septal defect (Cardiology)
vss	vital signs stable
V Tach	ventricular tachycardia (Cardiology)
VTX	vitrectomy (Ophthalmology)

W

W	white

w/	with *(Not recommended)*
w/c	wheelchair
W/F	white female
W/M	white male
w/o	without
w/u	workup
WAIS	Wechsler Adult Intelligence Scale (Psychology)
WAIS-R	Wechsler Adult Intelligence Scale-Revised (Psychology)
WB	weight bearing (Physical Therapy)
WBAT	weight bearing as tolerated
WBC	white blood count
WBT	weight bearing transfers (Physical Therapy)
WD	well developed
WD	working distance (Ophthalmology)
WD/WN	well-developed and well-nourished
WFL	within functional limits (Physical Therapy)
whpl	whirlpool (Physical Therapy)
WISC	Wechsler Intelligence Scale for Children (Psychology)
WISC-R	Wechsler Intelligence Scale for Children-Revised (Psychology)
WISC-III	Wechsler Intelligence Scale for Children-Revised (3rd edition) (Psychology)
wk	week
WN	well nourished
WNL, wnl	within normal limits
WP	whirlpool (Physical Therapy)
WPPSI-R	Wechsler Preschool and Primary Scale of Intelligence-Revised (Psychology)
WPW Syndrome	Wolff-Parkinson-White Syndrome (Cardiology)
WRAT-R	Wide Range Achievement Test-Revised (Psychology)
Wt	weight
WTR	within therapeutic range

X

X	times
X	exoptrophia (Ophthalmology)
X-match	cross match (Laboratory)
XRT	x-ray therapy

Y

YAG	neodymium-yttrium aluminum garnet laser (Ophthalmology)

YO; y/o	year old
yr(s)	year(s)
ytd	year-to-date

Z

ZnO	zinc oxide
ZOE	zinc oxide and eugenol (Pharmacology)
ZSM	zonisamide *(Zonegran)*(Pharmacology)

Symbols

Symbols use characters or letters and characters to abbreviate. The following symbols may be found on a medical record, but like letter abbreviations are open to interpretation and should be used with caution.

&	and
@	t
$\bar{p}$	after *(Written with a line drawn over the "p")*
$\bar{s}$	without
x	except for; with the exception of *(Written with a line drawn above the "x")*
°	degree
0	absent, null
Ø	nothing, none
↑	increase
↓	decrease
+, ive+	positive
(-), -, ive-	negative
(+)	significant
(-)	insignificant
++, 2+	plus two *(Often used to describe reflex response time)*
+++, 3+	plus three
++++, 4+	plus four
<	less than
<	less than or equal to
>	greater than *(Not recommended)*
|	standing
—	lying
l¬	sitting
/	per
X	times
1X	one time, once
i	one
ii	two
iii	three
=	equal to; equals
≠	not equal

±	more or less, indefinite, plus or minus, minimal pain
_+	time interval
≠	no change
%	percent
1°	primary
2°	secondary
~	approximate
?	questionable
O	normal female, living female
n	affected female, deceased female
qs	quantity sufficient
ψ	psychiatric

Endnotes

1. French, P.A., E. Ohman, and Magnus. "The Abbreviated Life of Acronyms." *American Heart Journal*. Vol 137 (4), April 1999.

2. The Use of Standardized Abbreviations, Acronyms, and Symbols is Addressed by JCAHO Standard IM.3 http://www.jcaho.org/accredited+organizations/ health+care+network/standards/field+reviews/net_ids_ mco_im_ xwalk.pdf. Retrieved December 1, 2003.

3. http://www.pubmedcentral.nih.gov/picrender.fcgi?artid =227556&action=stream&blobtype=pdf.   Retrieved December 3, 2003.

Appendix B

Internet Resources

(Accessed May 25, 2005)

Anesthesia

http://www.anesthesiazone.com/anesthesia-glossary.aspx

http://www.asahq.org

http://www.med.umich.edu/anes/tcpub/glossary/
anesthesia_glossary-07.htm#TopOfPage

http://www.usc.edu/schools/medicine/departments/
anesthesiology/assets/GlossaryAnes.pdf

Art/Graphics

http://www.americancorporateservices.com/index.php/
fuseaction/products.details/catid/63/id/365.php

http://www.consultsos.com/pandora/sample2.htm

http://www.doereport.com

http://www.geocities.com/med_smurf/medical/med_clipart.
html

http://webclipart.about.com/gi/dynamic/offsite.htm?zi=1/
XJ/Ya&sdn=webclipart&zu=http%3A%2F%2Fwww.
aperfectworld.org%2Fhealthcare_medicine.htm

Cancer (Oncology)

http://www.cancerindex.org/medterm/medtm3.htm

http://www.mtdesk.com/word-lists/oncology-terms.php

http://uccrc.uchicago.edu/patients/Cancer%20specific%20l
inks.html

http://uccrc.uchicago.edu/patients/glossary.html

Cardiology

http://www.acc.org

http://www.asnc.org/section_73.cfmhttp://en.wikipedia.org/
wiki/Cardiology_diagnostic_tests_and_procedures

http://www.mtdesk.com/word-lists/cardiovascular-terms.
php

http://www.somersetmedicalcenter.com/body.cfm?id=429

Chemistry

http://www.glossarist.com/glossaries/health-medicine-
fitness/medical.asphttp://home.nas.net/~dbc/cic_
hamilton/dictionary/a.html

http://chemistry.about.com/od/dictionariesglossaries/
Chemistry_Glossaries_Dictionaries.htm

Chiropractic Medicine

http://www.acatoday.org

http://www.amerchiro.org

http://chiropracticsitereviews.com/reviews-ch/chiromed-
org.html

http://www.chirobase.org/01General/chiroglossary.html

http://www.chiroweb.com/mpacms/dc/article.
php?id=50405

http://en.wikipedia.org/wiki/Chiropractic

Consent Forms

http://cflegacy.research.umn.edu/irb/consent

http://humansubjects.stanford.edu/general/glossary.html

http://humansubjects.stanford.edu/research/medical/med_consent.html

http://www.omic.com/resources/risk_man/forms.cfm

Dental

http://www.toothinfo.com/dtsplit.htm

http://www.bracesinfo.com/glossary.html

http://www.dentalleaders.com/terms.htm

Dermatology

http://courses.washington.edu/hubio567/lang/index.html

http://faculty.washington.edu/jingfeng/index.shtml

http://www.mtdesk.com/word-lists/dermatology-terms.php

http://www.umm.edu/dermatology-info/glossary.htm

Dictionaries

(See medical terminology.)

Disability

http://www.acils.com/acil/talking.html

http://www.ncbi.nlm.nih.gov/books/bv.fcgi?rid=hstat1.table.18980

http://www.fcc.gov/cgb/dro/504/disability_primer_2-3.html

Ear

http://www.audiologyonline.com/articles/arc_disp.asp?id=285

Education for Healthcare Professionals

http://www.theabr.org/moc/moc_policy.html#standing

http://www.uth.tmc.edu/pathology/medic/professional.html

Emergency

http://firstaid.about.com/od/glossary/Glossary_of_Emergency_Medical_Terminology.htm

http://www.aaem.org

http://www.abem.org

http://www.acep.org

http://www.emory.edu/EEMS/MedicalTerms.html

Endocrinology

http://www.aace.com

http://www.americanhospitals.com/resources/endocrinology.htm

http://www.diabetes.org

http://www.endocrineweb.com/define.html

Ear, Nose, and Throat

http://www.atheadandneck.com/hn

http://www.sph.uth.tmc.edu/Retnet/sym-dis.htm

http://www.hopkinsmedicine.org/wilmer/services/mdc/terms.html

http://www.maculacenter.com/Glossary

Gastroenterology/Liver

http://www.acg.gi.org

http://ahecpinebluff-dl.slis.ua.edu/clinical/gastroenterology/general.htm

http://www.asge.org

http://www.atgastroenterology.com/gi

http://www.gastro.org

http://www.liverfoundation.org

General Medicine

http://www.aafp.org

http://www.abms.org

http://www.ama-assn.org

http://www.aamc.org

Genetics

http://www.geneticsresources.org

http://www.ornl.gov/sci/techresources/Human_Genome/glossary

Guidelines

http://www.aapmr.org/hpl/pracguide/resource.htm

http://www.guideline.gov

Hazardous Waste

http://www.epa.gov/OCEPAterms/hterms.html

http://www.free-training.com/osha/hazcom/Hhaz/84.htm

http://www.wastemanagementcanada.com/Press/
terminology.asp

Healthcare Technology

http://www.acc.org/practicemgt/HealthCareTechnology/
index.cfm

http://www.hctproject.com/welcome.asp

Hematology

http://www.allny.com/health/hematology.html

http://www.bloodbook.com/glossary.html

http://www.free-ed.net/sweethaven/MedTech/Hematology/
hemaGloss.htm

http://www.hematology.org

Iatrogenic Injuries

http://www.chiro.org/LINKS/Iatrogenic_Page.shtml

http://www.iatrogenic.org

Immunology

http://www.ashi-hla.org

http://www.aaaai.org

Infectious Diseases

http://www.cdc.gov/ncidod/id_links.htm

http://en.wikipedia.org/wiki/Infectious_disease

http://www.nfid.org/library

Infusion/Intravenous

http://www.nursefriendly.com/nursing/directpatientcare/
intravenous.iv.therapy/intravenous.infusions.htm

http://www.amm.co.uk

http://www.thebody.com/content/art1786.html

http://www.amm.co.uk

Internal Medicine

http://www.abim.org/default.aspx

http://www.acponline.org

http://www.sgim.org

Laboratory

http://www.ascls.org/labtesting/labcbc.asp

http://www.labtestsonline.org

http://www.martindalecenter.com/Reference_3_LabP.html

http://www.nlm.nih.gov/medlineplus/laboratorytests.html

Library Search

http://ehealthcarebot.blogspot.com

http://www.mdconsult.com

http://www.medscape.com

http://www.urmc.rochester.edu/hslt/miner/digital_library/
evidence_based_resources.cfm

http://www.nlm.nih.gov/mesh/abbrev2003.html

http://www.pubmedcentral.nih.gov

http://www.samlib.com/Associations.aspx

Measurements

http://allchin.net/converter

http://www.convert-me.com/en/convert/weight

http://www.unc.edu/~rowlett/units

Medical Abbreviations and Acronyms

http://www.acronymfinder.com/.http://www.globalrph.
com/abbrev.htm#C&S

http://www.medilexicon.com

http://www.mondofacto.com/dictionary/acronym.html

Medical Codes

https://catalog.ama-assn.org/Catalog/cpt/cpt_search.jsp?_
    requestid=466740

http://www.cdc.gov/nchs/icd9.htm

http://icd9cm.chrisendres.com/icd9cm

http://www.icd9data.com

http://en.wikipedia.org/wiki/List_of_ICD-9_codes

Medical Devices

http://www.fda.gov/cdrh

http://www.fda.gov/oc/ohrt/irbs/devices.html

http://www.tga.gov.au/devices/devices.htm

Medical Terminology

http://nyp.org/glossary/index.html

http://www.cancerindex.org/medterm/medtm15.htm

http://www.iime.org/glossary.htm

http://www.intelihealth.com/IH/ihtIH/
    WSIHW000/9276/9276/209455.html?d=dmtDictionary

http://www.jdmd.com/glossary/abrevae.html

http://www.medic8.com/healthguide/dictionary.htm

http://www.medicalglossary.org

http://www.medinf.mu-luebeck.de/~ingenerf/terminology

http://medmatrix.org

http://www.medterms.com/Script/Main/hp.asp

http://www.mtdesk.com/glossary

http://www.mtdesk.com/word-lists

http://www.nlm.nih.gov/medlineplus/mplusdictionary.html

http://www.osha.gov/SLTC/etools/hospital/glossary.html

http://www.staff.ncl.ac.uk/s.j.cotterill/medtm15a.htm

http://www.webcrawler.com/webcrawler300/ws/results/
    Web/glossary+of+medical+terms/1/417/TopNavigation/
    Relevance/iq=true/zoom=off/_iceUrlFlag=7?_IceUrl=tru
    e&gclid=CPCsw8LGqZoCFQVfFQod6l6R1Q

Medical Links

http://www.asecho.org/i4a/pages/index.cfm?pageid=3577

Medical Symbols

http://dir.coolclips.com/Healthcare/Medical_Symbols

http://www.fotosearch.com/valueclips-clip-art/medical-
    symbols/UNC150

Midwifery

http://www.acnm.org

http://www.studentmidwife.net/educational-resources-35/
    midwifery-glossary-and-definition-terms-41

Military

http://home.att.net/~steinert/united_states_army_general_
    medic2.htm

http://www.gulflink.osd.mil/mrk/mrk_taba.
    htm#TAB%20A%20-%20Abbreviations,%20Acronyms,
    %20and%20Office%20Symbols

http://www.vnh.org

Neurology/Neurosurgery

http://www.aan.com

http://www.lifespan.org/services/neuro/articles/glossary.
    htm

http://www.medic8.com/healthguide/neurologyindex.htm

http://www.neuroguide.com/.http://www.neurosurgeon.org/
    education/glossary.asp

http://www.stroke.org

http://www.strokecenter.org/education/glossary.html

Nutrition

http://open-site.org/Health/Nutrition/Terminology

http://rex.nci.nih.gov/NCI_Pub_Interface/Eating_Hints/eatglossary.html

http://www.nutritiondata.com

http://www.nutritiondata.com/help/glossary

Obstetrics/Gynecology

http://www.abog.org

http://www.acog.org

http://www.healthatoz.com/healthatoz/Atoz/ency/obstetrical_emergencies.jsp

http://www.obgyn.net

http://www.stjohnsmercy.org/healthinfo/test/gyn/default.asp

http://womenshealth.about.com/cs/annualgynexam

http://www.woosterobgyn.com/glossary.cfm

Oncology

http://www.asco.org

http://www.cancer.gov/dictionary

http://www.cancer.org

http://www.cancerindex.org/medterm

http://www.cancernet.nci.nih.gov

http://www.oncolink.upenn.edu

Ophthalmology/Optometry

http://www.aao.org

http://www.aaopt.org

http://www.aoa.org

http://www.ascrs.org

http://www.asoprs.org

http://www.eyeglossary.net

Orthodontics

http://www.astoriadentalorthodontist.com/orthodontics-procedure-terms.htm

http://orthodontics.case.edu/resource.html

Orthopedics

http://www.aaos.org

http://www.cfoo.com/terms.php

http://www.niams.nih.gov

http://orthoinfo.aaos.org/menus/arthroplasty.cfm

http://www.orthopaedicweblinks.com

http://orthopedics.about.com

http://www.sportsmed.org

Pediatrics

http://dwp.bigplanet.com/nurseinform/pediatriclinks

http://www.aap.org

http://www.crashcards.com/pedlinks.htm

http://www.globalrph.com/pediatric.htm

http://www.neuropsychologycentral.com/interface/content/links/page_material/pediatric/pediatric_links.html

Pharmacy Abbreviations, Terminology, and Symbols

http://www2.kumc.edu/pharmacy/medabbreviations.htm

http://www.bumc.bu.edu/Dept/Content.aspx?DepartmentID=65&PageID=7797

http://www.lib.umich.edu/tcp/docs/dox/medical.html

http://www.medword.com/abbrevs-pharm.html

http://perth.uwlax.edu/faculty/gushiken/rth355-002/pharmacology.html

http://www.pharmaceutical-drug-manufacturers.com/pharmaceutical-glossary/http://www.pharmacist.com

Physical Therapy

http://www.aaptnet.org

http://www.apta.org//AM/Template.cfm?Section=Home

http://www.hshsl.umaryland.edu/resources/disciplines/physicaltherapy.html

http://www.nationalrehab.org

http://physicaltherapy.about.com/od/abbreviationsandterms/a/PTabbreviations.htm

http://www.physicaltherapist.com

Plastic Surgery

http://www.beautysurg.com/resources/glossary.html

http://www.plasticsurgery.org

http://www.plasticsurgery.com/plastic-surgery/plastic-surgery-glossary-a1535.aspx

http://www.plasticsurgery.com/procedures.aspx

Podiatry

http://www.apma.org

http://www.epodiatry.com/education_sub3.asp?topic=Foot%20surgery&sub1=Learning%20resources&sub2=Surgical%20techniques

http://www.epodiatry.com/foot_problems.htm

http://www.footandankle.com/podmed

Preventative Medicine

http://www.acpm.org

Pulmonary/Respiratory

http://www.aarc.org

http://www.chestnet.org

http://www.lungusa.org

http://www.medicalglossary.org/therapeutics_respiratory_therapy_definitions.html

http://www.nursefriendly.com/nursing/directpatientcare/respiratory/links/respiratoryjournals.html

http://ruralnurseorganization-dl.slis.ua.edu/clinical/pulmonology/embolism.html

http://www.thoracic.org

Psychiatry/Psychology

http://www.abess.com/glossary.html

http://www.abpn.com

http://www.alleydog.com/glossary/psychology-glossary.cfm

http://www.priory.com/gloss.htm

http://www.psych.org

http://www.psychologymatters.org/glossary.html

Quality Assurance/ Quality Improvement

http://www.ahrq.gov/qual/nhqr03/nhqrsum03.htm

http://www.ihi.org/IHI/Topics/Improvement/ImprovementMethods/Tools

http://www.nahq.org/journal/ce/article.html?article_id=205

http://www.pohly.com/terms_q.html

Radiology

http://www.acr.org

http://www.asrt.org

http://www.mtdesk.com/word-lists/radiology-terms.php

http://www.pamf.org/radiology/tests.html

http://www.radiologyeducation.com/#Guidelines

http://www.rsna.org

Rheumatology

http://www.arthritis.org

http://www.rheumatology.org

Risk Management

http://gsa.search.ucla.edu/search?site=UCLA&client=UCLA&proxystylesheet=UCLA&output=xml_no_dtd&proxyreload=1&q=risk+management (Risk Management Guide)

http://prism.library.cornell.edu/VRC/riskresources.html

Scientific and Medical Terminology and Symbols

http://www.btinternet.com/~ablumsohn/fonts.htm

http://www.medbioworld.com/MedBioWorld/TopicQuery.aspx

http://www.medinf.mu-luebeck.de/~ingenerf/terminology/Term-oth.html#Terminology

http://www.symbols.net/medical

Surgery

http://www.acfas.org

http://www.facs.org

http://www.fascrs.org

http://www.umm.edu/surgery-info/glossary.htm

http://www.surgassoc.com/glossary.html

Toxicology

http://cchs-dl.slis.ua.edu/pubhealth/environment/toxicology.html

http://toxnet.nlm.nih.gov

Trauma

http://www.istss.org/resources/index.cfm

http://www.regionshospital.com/Regions/Menu/0,1592,3795,00.html

http://suicideandmentalhealthassociationinternational.org/griefgloss.html

Urology

http://www.auanet.org

http://www.cornellurology.com/resources.shtml

http://crisp.cit.nih.gov/Thesaurus/00017434.htm

http://www.cornellurology.com/uro/cornell/glossary.shtml

http://www.kidney.org

http://www.urologyhealth.org/glossary/index.cfm?letter=W

Vascular Surgery

http://cvi.med.nyu.edu/patients/treatment-technologies-and-surgery

http://www.nlm.nih.gov/medlineplus/surgeryvideos.html

http://www.svmb.org

http://www.vascularweb.org/patients/NorthPoint/Index.html

Appendix C

Textbook References

Davis, Neil M. (2003). *Medical Abbreviations: 24,000 Conveniences at the Expense of Communications and Safety.*

Dorland, W.A. (2003). *Newman Dorlands Illustrated Medical Dictionary.* 30th Edition. May 2003.

Drake, R. and Drake, E. (2002). *Pharmaceutical Word Book 2003.* Stedmans Word Books.

Kovacs, S. and Galvez Rubino, C.R. (2002). *Stedman's Pathology and Lab Medicine Words.* Stedmans Word Books, 15, June 2002.

Littrell, H.E. (2000). *Stedman's Ob-Gyn Words.* Stedmans Word Books, December 2000.

Stedman, T.L. (2002). *Stedmans Medical Dictionary.* Stedmans Word Books, January 2002.

Stedman, T.L. (1999). *Stedmans Plastic Surgery/ENT/Dentistry Words.* Stedmans Word Books, January 1999.

Stedman, T.L. (2000). *Stedmans Ophthalmology Words.* Stedmans Word Books, 15, January 2000.

Stedman, T.L. (2003). *Stedman's Abbreviations, Acronyms, and Symbols.* Lippincott Williams and Wilkins.

Stedman, T.L. (2001). *Stedman's Cardiovascular and Pulmonary Words: Includes Respiratory.* Lippincott Williams and Wilkins.

Stedman, T.L. (1991). *Stedman's Orthopedic and Rehab Words.* Lippincott Williams and Wilkins.

Stedmans, J. and Haberer, D. (2001). *Stedman's GI and GU Words: With Nephrology Words.* Lippincott Williams and Wilkins.

Stedman's Psychiatry/Neurology/Neurosurgery Words. Stedmans Word Books

Stedman, T.L. (2001). *Stedmans Endocrinology Words.* Stedmans Word Books.

Haberer, D. (1997). *Stedmans Dermatology and Immunology Words.* Stedmans Word Books.

Stedman, T.L. and Groth, D.B. (2002). *Stedman's Surgery Words: Includes Anatomy, Anesthesia, and Pain Management.* Stedmans Word Books.

Beverly, J. and Wolpert, B.J. (2000). *Stedmans Oncology Words.* Stedmans Word Books, 15, June 2000.

Venes, Donald, et al. (Editor). *Taber's Cyclopedic Medical Dictionary.*

Appendix D

Glossary

A

abrasion—when the skin contacts a rough object or surface with sufficient force to rub away part of the surface layers. (Forensics.)

accreditation—recognition that a provider meets standards set by a national accrediting organization such as The Joint Commission.

ACE (Angiotensin Converting Enzyme) inhibitors—medications used to decrease blood pressure and fluid volume.

Activities of Daily Living (ADL)—routine activities needed by a resident to function in everyday life (e.g., dressing, eating etc.).

acute—rapidly developing; severe; short duration.

adnexa—parts accessory to the main organ or structure. (Ophthalmology.)

administrator—person licensed under state regulations and responsible for internal management of the healthcare facility.

Admission-Discharge—report published and distributed daily to key departments in a facility as an information record of all movements of residents within a facility, new admissions, re-admissions, discharges, and transfers.

Admission Register—a chronological listing of nursing home residents according to admission date.

Admitting Diagnosis—statement made by physician at time of admission, which describes the reason for a patient's/resident's admission to the facility.

adjustment—any chiropractic therapeutic procedure, that utilizes controlled force, leverage, direction, amplitude, and velocity, which is directed at a specific joint or anatomical region. Chiropractors commonly use such procedures to influence joint and neurophysiological function. (Chiropractic.)

Advance Directive—written instructions from residents (patients) about the management and provision of care if they become incapacitated.

adverse event—any untoward change in health or medical states.

amblyopia—decreased vision that is not due to organic defects or refractive errors. (Ophthalmology.)

anal verge—opening of the anus on the surface of the body.

annular—equal amount of tissue circumferentially.

anorexia—a loss of appetite.

anoxic encephalopathy—brain damage caused by low oxygen level.

anticholinergic side effects—dry eyes, dry mouth, blurred vision, constipation, urinary retention, behavior changes, and loss of cognitive function.

antiemetic—medication given to control nausea and vomiting.

antihypertensive—medication used to lower blood pressure.

aphakic—absence of the lens of an eye either congenitally, after trauma, or after surgery. (Ophthalmology.)

aphasia—an impairment of language, which affects the production or comprehension of speech and the ability to read or write.

arterial injury—injury to the artery due to catheter insertion. (IV Therapy.)

arterial ulcer—a wound resulting from inadequate blood flow due to intrinsic blockage of an artery from a variety of disease states or from impaired circulation elsewhere (heart disease or stroke).

arthralgias—painful joints.

ascites—an abnormal collection of fluids in the abdominal cavity.

aspiration of food—inhalation of food into the lungs.

assessment—part of progress notes that consist of a health professional's judgment of observations made.

assisted living facility—professionally managed group-living setting that provides housing and assistance with activities of daily living.

atelectasis—a collapse of the small alveoli (the airways from which oxygen moves into the blood stream).

atopy—clinically hypersensitive state, i.e., hay fever, asthma, eczema. (Ophthalmology.)

aura—warning symptoms present before a seizure.

authority—right to act or get others to act within a defined scope.

authorization—investment of legal authority; to sanction the action of someone else acting on behalf of another.

autolytic—a moisture retentive dressing, that allows the breakdown of necrotic tissue (debridement) by natural processes in the body. (Dermatology.)

B

bacterial phlebitis—inflammation of a vein caused by an infection.

balance billing—the amount above the Medicare-approved charge that healthcare providers charge patients for care. (Balanced billing is banned in Connecticut, Massachusetts, Minnesota, New York, Ohio, Pennsylvania, Rhode Island and Vermont.)

bed hold—preservation of a nursing home bed when a nursing home resident is temporarily hospitalized or out of the facility on therapeutic leave.

behavioral intervention—non-drug interventions used to change the resident's (patient's) behavior or environment to lessen or accommodate the resident's (patient's) behavioral symptoms.

Benign Senescent Forgetfulness—age-related memory loss that results from the slowing of neural processes with age.

beta blocker—medication that decreases blood pressure, decreases heart rate, increases vasodilatation of arterial blood vessels.

blepharospasm—spasm of the eyelid muscles. (Ophthalmology.)

bruise—a contusion or blunt soft tissue injury resulting in disruption and leakage of blood vessels without breaking the skin. (Forensics.)

C

calcium channel blocker—medication that widens and relaxes blood vessels.

Call System—a system to allow residents (patients) to communicate with a nurses' station from their rooms and from toilet and bathing facilities.

cardiac arrhythmia—irregular heartbeat.

cardiac glycosides—medication, such as digoxin or Lanoxin, given to decrease the workload of the heart by decreasing the rate and the contractility of the heart muscle.

cardiac tamponade—compression of the heart.

Care Plan—a plan designed to meet all of a resident's (patient's) identified physical, mental, emotional, cognitive, and functional needs. The care plan is generally the result of assessment and collaboration by an interdisciplinary team of provider staff. (Also known as the Plan of Care.)

Case Mix—a system that uses resident (patient) attributes (e.g., functional status in activities of daily living or cognitive ability) to classify residents (patients) for purposes such as reimbursement.

catastrophic injury—injury or illness that permanently alters an individual's functional status.

compression injury—large amount of fluid in the tissue compressing nerve.

catheter embolism—catheter fragment floating in the venous system. (IV Therapy.)

catheter fracture—broken catheter floating in the venous system. (IV Therapy.)

catheter malposition—central catheter located outside vena cava. (IV Therapy.)

catheter related sepsis—blood stream infection related to the catheter. (IV Therapy.)

catheter migration—central catheter moved outside the vena cava. (IV Therapy.)

catheter occlusion—blocked catheter due to blood or drugs. (IV Therapy.)

cellulitis—bacterial skin infection.

census—the number of patients present in a facility at any one time.

certification—approval of a provider to participate and receive payment from the Medicare and/or Medicaid programs. In some states, a system for determining if various individual healthcare professionals are qualified.

Certification/Re-certification—a signed statement indicating the resident's admission/continued stay in the facility is justified. This statement is required on all residents receiving Medicare. (Nursing Home.)

chalcosis—abnormal deposition of copper salts in the tissues.

chemical phlebitis—inflammation of the vein caused by irritating drugs. (IV Therapy.)

chemical restraint—a psychoactive drug used to control behavior and used in a manner not required to treat the patient's medical symptoms by a facility for discipline or convenience.

chronic obstructive pulmonary disease (COPD)—refers to a group of diseases that cause airflow blockage and breathing-related problems.

chylothorax—leakage of lymph fluid into chest cavity. (IV Therapy.)

ciliary injection—redness at the junction of the cornea and sclera. (Ophthalmology.)

clinical pathways—a disease specific patient focused multidisciplinary and interdisciplinary team guide of routine services based on average medical recovery outcomes.

clinical record—pertinent documentation of an individual's health care; must contain sufficient information to clearly identify the patient, to support the diagnosis, to justify the treatment, and to document the results accurately.

clinical résumé—discharge summary. A necessary part of a patient's clinical record; a recapitulation of the resident's course in the facility; to be written or dictated immediately following discharge of the patient.

clinical trial—research study that tests a drug or medical device to determine its safety and effectiveness.

clonic—thrashing movement of the arms and legs during a seizure.

coding—the process of assigning numerical values to diagnoses/problems and diagnostic/treatment procedures recorded in a clinical record, also slang for cardiac or respiratory arrest.

colonized—as in wound, occurs when bacteria are on the wound, but there is no evidence of infection. (Dermatology.)

computer (digital) forensics—the set of methods and techniques used to preserve the authenticity and content of digital information necessary for admissibility of evidence.

concretions—a hardened mass. (Ophthalmology.)

Conditions of Participation—standards set by the federal government for facilities wishing to take part in Medicare/Medicaid programs.

consent—to approve or assent to a particular act, such as treatment.

Consulting or Reviewing Expert—an expert who offers an opinion on a particular subject and is not expected to testify at trial.

Continuing Care Retirement Community (CCRC)—a housing alternative, also known as Life Care Community, that offers progressive levels of care, i.e., fully independent living, assisted living (personal care services) and skilled nursing care.

Continuity of Care Record—a core set of data of the most relevant and timely facts about a patient's health care. It is to be prepared by a practitioner at the conclusion of a health-care encounter in order to enable the next practitioner to access such information. (Computerized Records.)

contracture—chronic loss of joint motion due to structural changes in non-bony tissue, such as, muscles, ligaments, and tendons.

contraindicated drugs—drugs that are in opposition, or against each other; drugs inappropriate in the presence of other symptoms or circumstances.

controlled substance—a drug, substance, or immediate precursor included in Schedules I to V of the Controlled Substances Act (e.g., morphine, acetaminophen with codeine, oxycontin).

cor pulmonale—right sided heart failure.

costovertebral angle—found at the bottom of the rib cage in the back.

crepitus—sound made by grinding of pieces of fractured bone.

crescentic—tissue begins at 1 o'clock and continues to 11 o'clock.

cribriform—multiple small openings, may be covered with a thin layer of epithelium.

cross-matching—testing compatibility of blood and/or tissues.

cut—the result of sharp object coming against the skin with sufficient pressure to result in the division of tissues.

cystitis—bladder infection.

D

decubitus ulcer—outdated term for pressure sore/ulcer.

delirium—a brief acute or sudden state of confusion.

demarcating—death of tissue below a line of healthy tissue.

dementia—clinical state characterized by loss of function in multiple cognitive domains. It must be differentiated from age-related memory loss (i.e., benign senescent forgetfulness).

dependent edema—swelling that collects in the sacrum, arms, or legs.

diabetic neuropathic ulcer—diabetic wounds typically refer to specific types of wounds on the soles of the feet, usually under the head of the metatarsals (the bottom of the ball of the foot) and imply impaired sensory nerves in the lower extremities. (Dermatology.)

dialyzer—artificial kidney.

diastolic blood pressure value—the pressure within the arteries when the heart relaxes.

diastolic—pressure exerted against the blood vessel walls when the heart is at rest. The bottom number of the blood pressure reading.

diffusion—slow steady movement of particles from a solution of high concentration to one of low concentration resulting in an even distribution of particles.

diopters—a unit adopted for calibration of lenses. (Ophthalmology.)

discharge planning—assessment, usually by a social worker on staff, of a patient's function and needs following discharge, and planning, including a smooth transition in moving from one level of care to another, for example from a hospital to a nursing home or from a hospital to home care. The discharge planner also contacts home health agencies to assist the patient in connection with his/her home care.

diuretic—medication used to decrease fluid volume in the body or blood stream, and to decrease the workload on the heart.

documentation—the preparing or assembling of written records.

Do Not Resuscitate Order (DNR)—an order by a physician, following discussion with and informed consent by a legally competent patient or the patient's legal representative, which orders healthcare providers NOT to perform resuscitation on this patient when these procedures are necessary for sustaining the patient's life. A DNR order is frequently initiated by the patient's living will or the legal representative's medical power of attorney.

drug formulary—a preferred listing of medications by the health plan.

Drug Regimen Review (DRR)—the review of drugs, administered to a resident (patient) to determine the effects and the potential for harmful effects.

Drug Utilization Review (DUR)—the review and determination of drug use patterns within a facility.

dysarthria—a group of speech disorders resulting from weakness, slowness, or uncoordination of the speech mechanism due to damage to any of a variety of points in the nervous system.

dysphagia—difficulty swallowing.

dysphasia—inability to verbalize.

dyspnea—shortness of breath.

E

edema—swelling.

electronic medical record—a provider based record of healthcare received within a provider organization. (Computerized Records.)

electronic health record—a community-based record of all healthcare information related to the individual. (Computerized Records.)

electronically stored information (ESI)—a term of art for a class of information that is created or stored in electronic form.

emmetropia—a person with normal vision. (Ophthalmology.)

endophthalmitis—inflammation of the internal structure of the eye. (Ophthalmology.)

enophthalmos—abnormal recession of the eyeball in the orbit.

enzymatic—as in debridement, removal of necrotic material by chemicals or enzymes. (Dermatology.)

epiphora—overflow of tears from obstruction of the lacrimal duct. (Ophthalmology.)

erythema—redness.

essential hypertension—a chronic disease of unknown cause, also known as primary.

eschar—(pronounced es-car) thick, leathery, devitalized tissue—loose or firmly attached. (Dermatology.)

exabyte—a measurement unit for determining the size of an information file. One exabyte = 10^{18} bytes = 1000^6 bytes = 1,000,000,000,000,000,000 bytes.

exophthalmos—bulging eyes.

Extrapyramidal Symptoms (EPS)—abnormal movements of the mouth or tongue, mask-like facial expression, tremors, rigid movements, constant movement of legs or body, tics, blinking, pacing, pill rolling motion of fingers, eyes rolled up, and drooling.

extravasation—leakage of a vesicant solution into the tissue. (IV Therapy.)

F

Federal Register—official government publication; proposed or enacted changes in requirements for participation in Medicare and Medicaid programs are published therein.

fibrin sheath—cellular material on the outer catheter surface. (IV Therapy.)

field case management—case management services provided to a client face to face at home, in an inpatient setting, or at treatment provider's offices.

fimbriated—multiple projections and indentations.

fistula—the surgical joining of an artery and a vein so that the vein enlarges due to the flow of arterial blood. A fistula is a type of access, also known as an *arteriovenous fistula*.

fluid overload—excess fluid in the body causing edema, difficulty in breathing or extra strain on the heart.

foreskin—retractable covering of the glans penis.

fossa navicularis (vestibule)—area between the posterior fourchette and the hymen.

frenulum—where the foreskin attaches to the scrotum.

friction rub—a sound caused by the pericardial membranes being dry and rubbing against each other.

G

glans penis—distal head of the penis.

glomerulonephritis—kidney infection.

Grave's disease—an autoimmune form of hyperthyroidism.

granulation tissue—pink to beefy red tissue in wound bed, filled with new blood vessels, collagen, fibroblasts (skin cells) and immune cells. (Dermatology.)

H

hand-off—communication between care providers when a patient is transferred from the care of one person to another

hematoma—collection of blood under the skin (bruise).

hematuria—blood in the urine.

hemiparesis—weakness of one side of the body.

hemiplegia—paralysis of one side of the body.

hemothorax—leakage of blood into the chest cavity.

heparin—an anticoagulant that slows clotting time.

HIPAA—the Health Insurance Portability and Accountability Act of 1996 that protects the privacy and security of a patient's healthcare information.

hospice care—care of terminally ill persons aimed at relieving pain and managing symptoms rather than curing the disease entity.

hydrothorax—leakage of IV fluid into the chest cavity. (IV Therapy.)

hymen—collar of tissue at the opening of the vagina.

hyperkalemia—elevated serum potassium levels.

hyperopia—farsightedness, focused light rays are behind the retina. (Ophthalmology.)

hypoperfusion—decreased blood flow.

hypovolemia—decreased blood volume.

I

ichthyosis—dryness, roughness, and scaliness of the skin. (Dermatology.)

incident—a deviation from usual and routine activities.

induration—hardness, usually below the skin.

infiltration—accidental leakage of non-vesicant solution into the tissues. (IV Therapy.)

informed consent—disclosure of the risks, benefits, and alternatives of proposed treatment, made by a physician to a patient competent to understand and make an intelligent decision based on the information provided.

intermediate care—basic care including physical, emotional, social and other restorative services under periodic medical supervision. (Nursing Home.)

interoperability—refers to the ability to securely exchange clinical, demographic, and financial data by using a method of capturing, storing, and securely transmitting and receiving data. (Computerized Records.)

iridoplegia—paralysis of the sphincter of the iris, with lack of contraction or dilation of the pupil. (Ophthalmology.)

irrigation—a type of mechanical debridement, solution delivered under pressure or sprayed on to the wound to remove debris. (Dermatology.)

J

jugular venous distension—enlarged neck veins.

K

ketosis—increased acids in the serum because of breakdown of fats.

L

labia majora—outer lips to the vagina.

labia minora—inner lips to the vagina.

lacrimation—secretion and discharge of tears. (Ophthalmology.)

lens subluxation—incomplete or partial dislocation. (Ophthalmology.)

limbus—edge of the cornea where it joins the sclera. (Ophthalmology.)

licensure—process of obtaining a license to meet state and local requirements to operate a healthcare facility.

life-sustaining medical treatment—medical treatment which sustains a person's life functions, including respiratory and cardiopulmonary functions, preventing the person's body from reaching that state where it is declared legally dead.

Life Care Community—see Continuing Care Retirement Community.

Litigation Hold—(also known as "preservation orders" or "hold orders") is a discovery obligation to preserve all data that may relate reasonably anticipated litigation.

Living Will—a document executed by a competent person which governs the withholding or withdrawal of life-sustaining treatment from an individual in the event of an incurable or irreversible condition that will cause death within a relatively short time, and when such person is no longer able to make decisions regarding his medical treatment.

localized insertion site infection—symptoms include redness and tenderness. (IV Therapy.)

Long-Term Care Survey—a resident oriented on-site survey, which focuses on resident outcomes and care. (Nursing Home.)

lymphadenopathy—enlarged lymph nodes.

M

manipulation—a manual procedure that involves a directed thrust to move a joint past the physiological range of motion, without exceeding the anatomical limit. (Chiropractic.)

manipulable subluxation—a subluxation in which altered alignment, movement, and/or function can be improved by manual thrust procedures. (Chiropractic.)

manual therapy—procedures by which the hand directly contacts the body to treat the articulations and/or soft tissues. (Chiropractic.)

maximization—manipulation of data to optimize reimbursement.

meatus—opening of the urethra.

mechanical—as in debridement, removal of necrotic material by a physical means (pulling bandage/gauze pulling off adherent scab or eschar/necrotic material. (Dermatology.)

mechanical phlebitis—vein inflammation caused by catheter movement. (IV Therapy.)

Medical Director—a physician given responsibility to coordinate and supervise the medical activity within that facility.

medication record—individualized record of all drugs and medications given/not given to the resident.

melena—visible blood in the stool.

metadata—information that provides authenticity, history, context, statistics, or other information to assist with data management.

micturition—urination.

mobilization—movement applied singularly or repetitively within or at the physiological range of joint motion, without imparting a thrust or impulse, with the goal of restoring joint mobility. (Chiropractic.)

mons pubis—round fleshy prominence created by the underlying fat pad over the symphysis pubis.

motion segment—a functional unit made up of the two adjacent articulating surfaces and the connecting tissues binding them to each other. (Chiropractic.)

myocardium—the muscle of the heart.

myoglobin—a protein that is released from the heart muscle when damaged.

myopia—nearsightedness, focused light rays are in front of the retina. (Ophthalmology.)

myxedema—severe loss of thyroid hormones.

N

Native file format—the format of information as it is originally stored electronically by an application or computer system.

nerve damage—injury to the nerve.

nocturia—urinating in the middle of sleeping hours.

nursing assessment—valuation of patient needs and lifestyle by nursing service, a process that helps determine nursing care.

Nursing Home Reform—a Federal law contained in the Omnibus Budget Reconciliation Act of 1987 and often simply referred to a OBRA '87, sets the standards of care in nursing home, establishes certain rights for patients, and requires states and the Federal government to inspect nursing homes and to enforce standards.

nursing process—a problem solving and goal reaching strategy, consisting of five steps: assessment, diagnosis, planning, implementation, and evaluation.

O

oliguria—drop in urine output.

ora—zigzag margin of the retina of the eye. (Ophthalmology.)

outcomes—end results of care or a measurable change in an actual state; consequences or results.

P

pannus—membrane-like structure overlying the cornea. (Ophthalmology.)

panophthalmitis—inflammation of all eye structures. (Ophthalmology.)

paresthesias—numbness and tingling.

pericardium—the outer covering sac of the heart.

perineum—area between the vagina and the anus.

persistent vegetative state—an enduring state of grossly impaired consciousness leaving an individual is incapable of voluntary acts.

photophobia—abnormal intolerance to light. (Ophthalmology.)

phthisis bulbi—shrinkage of the eyeball. (Ophthalmology.)

physical restraint—a device that prevents or restricts resident (patient) movement.

Pinch-Off Syndrome—catheter is pinched between collarbone and rib. (IV Therapy.)

Plan of Care—the plan for each patient/resident, in which members of the interdisciplinary team recorded the identified problems, goals, and interventions, to be used for the care of that resident.

pneumothorax—a condition in which the lung has collapsed either because of air entering through a hole in the chest or a hole in the lung allowing air to collect in the pleural space.

policy—basic guides to action; establishes the boundaries of authority.

point of maximal impulse—the place on the chest wall where the pulse can be felt.

polydipsia—increased thirst.

polyphagia—increased hunger.

polyuria—increased urinary output.

posterior fourchette—place where the labia minora meet posteriorly.

pressure ulcers—also referred to as pressure sores, decubitus ulcers, or decubiti, usually occur over bony prominences. The ulcers are due to compression of blood vessels in the tissue because of persistent pressure, which cuts off the source of oxygen and results in a wound. (Dermatology.)

primary wound closure—healing by primary intention, coverage with skin flaps or delayed primary intention. (Dermatology.)

problem list—an index and table of contents to the medical record that lists all a person's problems and diagnoses.

process—the nature and sequence of events in the delivery of care.

prognosis—prediction of course and end of disease, and the estimate of chance for recovery.

Program for All-Inclusive Care for the Elderly (PACE)—a program that uses a multidisciplinary team of healthcare providers to provide health and long-term-care services in an adult day care. PACE participants meet eligibility requirements (fifty-five years of age or older, require adult day care and nursing services regularly).

progress notes—statement about a patient's response to treatment, written by the healthcare professional providing or evaluating treatment.

Prospective Payment System—a payment method in which Medicare rates are set prospectively, before services are rendered, and based upon resource utilization groups. (Nursing Home.)

provider—individual, group, or facility responsible for delivery of health care.

pruritis—itching.

psychosocial assessment—evaluation of a patient's psychological and social needs.

psychotropic medication—medication (i.e., anti-anxiety, antidepressant, antipsychotic, or hypnotic) used to alter an individual's behavior or mood.

pulmonary embolism—a blockage of the vessels carrying blood to the lungs.

pulse pressure, narrowed—decreased systolic blood pressure with increased diastolic blood pressure narrowing the differences between the pressure caused by the heart contracting and the pressure that exists when the heart is relaxed.

Q

Quality—the degree of performance to a standard, it implies achieving the optimal goal.

Quality Improvement—activities performed to determine the extent to which a practice meets certain standards and, if necessary, to initiate a change in practice.

R

read-back—TJC-required process demanding the receiver of any telephone or verbal order, including "critical test results," to *write* down the complete order or enter it into a computer, then *read* it back, and receive confirmation from the person who gave the order. (Exceptions to the "read back" rule may apply in emergency and operative circumstances. Voice mail orders are not acceptable. The healthcare provider must speak directly with the person giving the order and than follow the read back procedure.)

redundant—presents with abundant circumferential tissue that folds back and protrudes.

refraction—deviation of light traversing obliquely a medium of differing density. (Ophthalmology.)

restorative nursing—a program designed to increase a resident's ability to self-care. (Nursing Home.)

Resident Activities—a service in the healthcare facility concerned with recreation and socialization for the residents. (Nursing Home.)

Resident's Rights—a signed document reflecting that a resident is informed of rights in a facility, and that the resident or designee understands those rights; required by law. (Nursing Home.)

Restorative Potential—a physician's estimate of the possibility of a resident's return to optimal functioning levels. (Nursing Home.)

Resource Utilization—a case mix classification for long-term care, to be used as a reimbursement methodology, which will match resources with resident needs. (Nursing Home.)

retinopathy (diabetic)—non-inflammatory disease of the retina manifested by microaneurysms and punctate exudutes. (Ophthalmology.)

rubeosis—new formation of vessels and connective tissue. (Ophthalmology.)

rubor—a reddish purple color, especially when the legs are in a dependent position.

S

secondary hypertension—blood pressure elevation caused by stress, pain, and so on.

septate—a hymen with a band of tissue that bisects the opening.

secondary healing—the wound is left open to heal from the inside out when there has been significant loss of tissue, exposure of vital structures, or contamination. (Dermatology.)

sharp—as in debridement, use of a surgical instrument (scalpel or tissue scissors) to remove necrotic/dead debris. (Dermatology.)

shearing—layers of skin rubbing against each other from gravity resulting in damage from tearing, stretching underlying capillaries/blood vessels and tissue. (Dermatology.)

siderosis—deposition of an iron pigment within the eyeball. (Ophthalmology.)

sinus tract—cavity or channel under skin that connects the visible wound to an area or pocket under the skin not seen. (Dermatology.)

skilled care—a level of care which includes physical, emotional, social and other restorative services with frequent medical supervision and continuous skilled nursing observation or specialized rehabilitation services. (Nursing Home.)

skilled nursing care—care provided under the general direction of a physician and the direct supervision of licensed nursing personnel. The care required cannot safely and effectively be self-administered or performed by the average unsupervised non-medical personnel and may include services such as intravenous injections and tube feeding.

skilled nursing facility—a long-term-care facility, which is staffed, maintained, and equipped to provide continuous skilled nursing observation, assessment and care, restorative and activity programs, and other services under professional direction and medical supervision as needed. (Nursing Home.)

slough—(pronounced sluff) light, stringy, soft devitalized tissue separating from viable tissue. (Dermatology.)

social service—a service that assists the patients and family in adjusting to the facility and environment, arranging for home care, and dealing with psychosocial needs of patients.

specialized rehabilitative services—professional care aimed at restoration of function, usually by physical therapists, occupational therapists and speech/language pathologists. (Nursing Home.)

spinal motion segment—two adjacent vertebrae, and the connecting tissues binding them to each other. (Chiropractic.)

spoliation—the destruction of information that is subject to a discovery request.

stage I ulcer—erythematous (reddened) areas of skin that persist even when fingertip pressure is applied (non-blanching), but skin is intact. (Dermatology.)

stage II ulcer—also called "partial thickness," are shallow blisters or erosion of the skin similar to a burn. They do not extend below the dermis. (Dermatology.)

stage III ulcer—a "full thickness" break of the skin below the dermis, but not into deeper tissue. (Dermatology.)

stage IV ulcer—a "full thickness" lesion that penetrates into muscle, tendons or bones. (Dermatology.)

Standards of Care—criteria that serve as a basis of comparison when evaluating the quality of nursing practice. In a malpractice lawsuit, a measure by which the defendant's alleged wrongful conduct is compared. Acts performed or omitted that an ordinary, reasonably prudent nurse, in the defendant's position would have done or not done.

status epilepticus—continuous seizure activity.

steatorrhea—fat in the stool.

subjective observations—observations that refer to a patient's symptoms, often what the patient says and documented in the medical record.

subluxation—a motion segment, in which alignment, movement integrity, and/or physiological function are altered, although contact between joint surfaces remains intact. (Chiropractic.)

subluxation complex—a theoretical model of motion segment dysfunction (subluxation), which incorporates the complex interaction of pathological changes in nerve, muscle, ligamentous, vascular, and connective tissues. (Chiropractic.)

subluxation syndrome—an aggregate of signs and symptoms that relate to pathophysiology or dysfunction of spinal and pelvic motion segments or to peripheral joints. (Chiropractic.)

systolic—pressure exerted against the blood vessel walls when the heart is contracting; the upper number of the blood pressure reading.

T

tachycardia—rapid heart rate.

tachypnea—rapid respiratory rate.

tears, lacerations—injury produced by blunt force causing tearing, ripping, crushing or overstretching of soft tissues.

terminally ill—an incurable or irreversible health problem from which a recovery can no longer be reasonably expected and the life expectancy, more probably than not, is twenty-four months or less.

tertiary healing—closure of the skin with sutures or grafts at a much later date. (Dermatology.)

tonic—stiffening and rigidity of the body's muscles during a seizure.

tunnel—a channel under skin surface that starts at top of wound edge. (Dermatology.)

twiddlers syndrome—inversion of the port in the pocket. (IV Therapy.)

U

undermining—the destruction and loss of tissue just under the skin margin making a pressure ulcer larger at the base than at the opening. (Dermatology.)

unilateral neglect—a phenomenon in which the patient ignores the side of the body that has been affected.

urethra—opening to the bladder.

V

venous insufficiency—also known as a stasis ulcer, usually occurs on the anterior (front) of the lower tibia or above the medial (inside) ankle. (Dermatology.)

venous thrombosis—blood clot inside the vein.

visual field—the area within which objects are distinctly seen by the eye in a fixed position. (Ophthalmology.)

X

xiphoid process—lowest part of the sternum.

About the Editors

Editors for the First and Second Editions

Patricia Iyer, MSN, RN, LNCC earned her Bachelor of Science in Nursing and Masters of Science in Nursing from University of Pennsylvania. She has earned the certification of Legal Nurse Consultant Certified. Patricia served for five years on the Board of Directors of the American Association of Legal Nurse Consultants, including one year as the President from 2002–2003. Additionally she was the first chair of the Educational Steering Committee (for a term of two years) and received the distinguished Lifetime Achievement Service Award from AALNC in 2005 and Volunteer of the Year Award in 2006. She served as the chief editor of Legal Nurse Consulting, Principles and Practices, Second Edition, the core curriculum of legal nurse consulting. She also served as the chief editor of AALNC's first online legal nurse consulting course. Patricia has edited or coauthored over 125 books, chapters, case studies, articles and online courses. Patricia is president of Med League Support Services, Inc. (www.medleague.com), a legal nurse consulting company in Flemington, New Jersey, which was established in 1989. A devoted entrepreneur, Pat also started Patricia Iyer Associates, a company that provides legal nurse consulting education (www.patiyer.com) and Patient Safety Now (www.PatientSafetyNow.com), which provides education for healthcare providers. She has taught hundreds of attorneys, physicians, nurses and paralegals about medical records and medical-legal topics, and thousands of nurses both nationally and internationally about nursing documentation and risk management. A member of the National Speakers Association, she has taught nurses in Denmark, India, Japan, Canada and Japan. Several chapters in this text were authored or coauthored by Pat.

Barbara J. Levin, BSN, RN, ONC, LNCC obtained her Bachelor of Science in Nursing from Boston University School of Nursing. She is also a certified orthopaedic nurse and has received the recognition of *Clinical Scholar* at Massachusetts General Hospital, Boston, Massachusetts, where she works in the orthopaedic/trauma unit. Barbara draws on a wealth of twenty-five years of nursing experience in a myriad of clinical settings, Barbara is an accomplished speaker and writer, nationally and internationally, and also works with other providers at facilities and organizations to redesign policies and procedures. In addition to her clinical activities, Barbara is an experienced legal nurse consultant providing an educational foundation for her clients in a variety of roles. She has earned the distinction of Legal Nurse Consultant Certified and served as the President of the American Association of Legal Nurse Consultants 2004–2005. In 2007, Barbara received the AALNC Member of the Year award. Barbara served as the Chair of the AALNC Scope and Standards of Practice committee and worked together with the American Nurses Association to design, publish and obtain recognition for the *Legal Nurse Consulting Scope and Standards of Practice*. She also serves as a valued member of the Massachusetts Tribunal, working together with a judge and an attorney, to determine the direction of medical malpractice claims. Barbara, Patricia and first edition editor Mary Ann Shea have worked together on several projects which include teaching two programs to the International Council of Nurses, 2007 conference, in Yokohama, Japan.

Editor for First Edition

Mary Ann Shea, JD, BS, RN earned her Juris Doctor from St. Louis University School of Law, and her Bachelor of Science in Psychology and Associate of Arts in Nursing from Maryville University. She molded her dual law and nursing expertise into the medical/legal arena by practicing in both plaintiff and defense personal injury law firms, serving as a Director of Quality Assurance and Risk Management, being an independent medical/legal consultant on hundreds of cases involving medical analysis, teaching legal nurse consulting courses, as well as presenting hundreds of risk management seminars to medical, legal and nursing professionals nationwide. Mary Ann has been a contributing author in several textbooks, has written informational articles in nursing publications, and has been quoted in medical and legal publications. She is a member of the Missouri Bar, is active on the Solo and Small Firm Practice Committee, and serves as an active member of the Bar Association of Metropolitan St. Louis. Mary Ann also served as President of the American Association of Legal Nurse Consultants from 2003–2004 and continues to provide leadership and professional direction to many of AALNC's chapters and members.

About the Contributors

John A. Amaro, DC, Dipl.Ac. (IAMA), Dipl.Ac. (NC-CAOM) coauthored *Complimentary and Alternative Medicine* and is an internationally known author, lecturer and practitioner beginning his practice of acupuncture and chiropractic in 1971. He has led 13 diplomatic study tours of The People's Republic of China escorting more than 500 doctors and practitioners. He has personally studied acupuncture in nine separate Asian nations. He received Certification in Acupuncture through the Columbia Institute of Chiropractic in 1973 and was certified by the Waseda Acupuncture College in Tokyo, Japan 1974 and the Chinese Medical Institute Kowloon China in 1976. Dr. Amaro studied at the Tai Chung Medical School Taipei, China 1973 where he received Diplomate status from the Shanghai Research Institute of Acupuncture in 1980 as well as Diplomate (Dipl.Ac.) of the National Commission for the Certification of Acupuncture (NCCA) 1985, which has added the designation "Oriental Medicine" making it the NCCAOM.

Dr. Amaro was awarded the prestigious Fellow of the American College of Chiropractic (FACC) in 1997. He has served on the editorial board of The American Chiropractor magazine since 1980. Additionally, Dr. Amaro has been a columnist for the international publication, "Dynamic Chiropractic" since 1988 as well as a columnist for "Acupuncture Today." He has had over 200 articles published internationally.

Dr. Amaro is the Founder of the International Academy of Clinical Acupuncture and The International Academy of Medical Acupuncture which more than 20,000 physicians and assistants have graduated from or taken specific postgraduate work in Euro/Asian acupuncture.

Kathleen C. Ashton, APRN, BC, PhD author of *Critical Care Records*, is a Professor of Nursing in the Jefferson School of Nursing at Thomas Jefferson University in Philadelphia and a Professor Emerita in the Department of Nursing at Rutgers University in Camden, New Jersey. Her research interest is in the area of women and heart disease. She has conducted numerous funded research studies over the past twenty years and has published the results of her work in leading nursing journals. Her clinical expertise is in adult health/critical care nursing and she holds an Advanced Practice license. As a legal nurse consultant, she serves as an expert witness reviewing legal cases for plaintiff and defense firms for over nine years. Currently, she serves as a reviewer for three nursing journals and as a board member for several community and professional groups.

Barbara Mladenetz Weber Berry, MSN, RN wrote the *Home Care Records* chapter. She is the VP of Patient Services at the Visiting Nurse Association of Mercer County, Trenton, New Jersey. Community health nursing was her passion as a student nurse and it became her professional career path for over thirty years. Barbara holds a bachelor's in nursing from the College of New Jersey and a master's in nursing from the University of Pennsylvania with a major in community health nursing and a minor in education. She attained certifications in Nursing Administration, School Nursing and Legal Nurse Consulting from various institutions. Working in many capacities from field nurse to administrator, in both preventive health and morbidity home care programs, has given Barbara a unique perspective about this nursing specialty. In conjunction with this, Barbara is committed to education and exposing students to the field of community health nursing. She was a clinical faculty member in the College of New Jersey's baccalaureate nursing program for over ten years and taught leadership in nursing practice. She has also mentored graduate students pursuing degrees in nursing administration. Barbara currently writes reviews for *Advance*, the bimonthly nursing journal, on topics related to home health care and nursing management.

Gloria Blackmon, AAS, RN, BSN, RN-BC, LNHA coauthored *Long Term Care Records*, formerly *Nursing Home Records*. Based in Maryland, Gloria received an associate's degree in Nursing from Maryville College of St. Louis and a Bachelor of Science in Nursing from the University of Missouri-St. Louis. Her clinical career has included acute medicine, physical rehabilitation, home health and gerontological nursing, in which she holds ANCC certification. Administratively, she has functioned as a coordinator in education and Alzheimer's unit development, a director of nursing in freestanding and hospital based skilled nursing facilities, and is a licensed nursing home administrator. Ms. Blackmon established an independent medical-legal practice in 1996 while she continued a clinical practice. She has worked with Legal Aid, defense and plaintiff counsels. Experienced as an appointed independent monitor by a State Attorney General's office and expert witness, she also provides services to the insurance industry as a loss control analyst and onsite investigator. Ms. Blackmon has given numerous presentations at nursing facilities and to national audiences regarding long term care issues. Frequently published, she has contributed articles to Claims Magazine, LNC Resource, The Medical-Legal Institute Journals and *E-Zine* and textbook chapters in *A Facility Based Risk Management Program—A Practical Guide For LTC Providers*, *Defensive Documentation For Long Term Care: Strategies for Creating a More Lawsuit-Proof Resident Record*, and *Problem Behaviors in Long Term Care*.

Bruce Bonnell, MD, MPH wrote the *Diagnostic Testing* chapter. He is an Instructor in Medicine at the Harvard Medical School in Boston and Chief of Geriatric Medicine at Youville Hospital and Rehabilitation Center in Cambridge, Massachusetts. He has served as medical director of several Boston area nursing homes and is board certified in Internal Medicine and Geriatrics. Dr. Bonnell has practiced at Massachusetts General Hospital, Beth Israel Deaconess Medical Center, Youville Hospital and Rehabilitation Center and Mount Auburn Hospital. His research interests include nosocomial and iatrogenic complications in hospitalized elders. He lives with his wife and four children in Hingham, Massachusetts.

Douglas R. Briggs, DC, Dipl.Ac. (IAMA), DAAPM coauthored *Complimentary and Alternative Medicine*. He received his Bachelors degree in Biology/Natural Science from Messiah College, and his Chiropractic degree from Palmer College in Davenport, Iowa. While earning his graduate degree, he taught in the diagnosis department and studied myofascial therapies. After completing a post-doctoral fellowship, he was awarded Diplomate status through the International Academy of Medical Acupuncture. He then earned a Diplomate from the American Academy of Pain Management, and further credentialing as a Diplomate in behavioral medicine. He currently is the senior associate of First State Health and Wellness. In addition to his full-time practice, he teaches Korean martial arts and lectures on Eastern healing practices. His patients have voted him one of the "Best of Delaware" for both Chiropractic and Acupuncture. He is a founding member of the American College of Chiropractic Acupuncture of the American Chiropractic Association. He has been previously published in the *Journal of Legal Nurse Consulting*, and has contributed articles to the international publications *Dynamic Chiropractic* and *Acupuncture Today*.

Steven Charles Castle, MD wrote *Controversies in Skin Trauma*. He is internationally recognized for his expertise in geriatric care, program development, healthcare professional training and research in managing the complexity of aging. He received a B.A., Summa Cum Laude in Zoology from Miami University, and his M.D. from the Ohio State University. He did a residency in Internal Medicine at Riverside Methodist Hospital in Columbus, Ohio, and a Geriatric Medicine Fellowship at UCLA in Los Angeles, California. Currently, Dr. Castle is Clinical Professor of Medicine at UCLA, and the past recipient of two National Institute on Aging grants studying the effects of disease and chronic illness on immunity. He is also the Clinical Director of the Geriatric Research Education and Clinical Center at the VA Greater Los Angeles Healthcare System where he has been involved in many clinical demonstration projects; including falls prevention programs in the full continuum of care, the use of air-fluidized beds in pressure ulcer care, infection control and detection of infections in long-term care, group chronic care clinics and decisional capacity to return home in cognitively impaired older adults.

Dr. Castle has published more than twenty-five peer-reviewed manuscripts and written several chapters in medical textbooks, and has been awarded over $500,000 in research funds. He has been an invited lecturer all over the country, and in Japan, the Philippines, Germany and Canada. He has been fortunate to be the recipient of several significant awards: "LA's Best Doctors," by *Los Angeles Magazine*, the "Clarence A. Dykstra Award," from The American Society of Public Administration for broad professional and community impact, and many teaching awards at UCLA. Of note, the American Geriatric Society selected him as the Clinician of the Year in 2000.

Stacy S. Cohen, DC coauthored *Complimentary and Alternative Medicine*. He is the founder and president of First State Health & Wellness. He received his first professional degree in psychology from the State University of New York at Albany in 1980 and his chiropractic degree from New York Chiropractic College in 1984. Dr. Cohen is active in the Delaware Chiropractic Society, where he served as president for 1988 to 1993. In 1988, he was voted "Chiropractor of the Year" by his peers. First State Health & Wellness was honored this year as one of the state's most ethical businesses when it earned the 2009 Torch Award for Ethics from the Better Business Bureau of Delaware. Dr. Cohen, along with his wife and business partner, Dr. Lydia Cohen, has developed one of the first and foremost facilities for integrative medicine serving Delaware.

Kimberly Combs, LMT coauthored *Complimentary and Alternative Medicine*. She received her Bachelor of Arts degree from Temple University in 1990 in English with a minor in Education. In 2001 she graduated from Pennsylvania School of Muscle Therapy and is now Nationally Certified in Therapeutic Massage. She is also a licensed massage therapist in Delaware. While in private practice as a massage therapist, Kimberly expanded her training to work as a both a birth and postpartum Doula. While working as a Doula, Kimberly writes and teaches courses she designed in Prenatal, Infant, and Couples massage. These classes are taught for continuing education credits for Delaware. She also teaches continuing education classes for foster parents. Kimberly currently specializes in treating myofascial trauma.

Barry C. Cooper, DDS wrote the *Dental Records* chapter. He graduated from Columbia University School of Dental and Oral Surgery. Currently he serves as an Associate Clinical Professor at the School of Dental Medicine, Department of Oral Biology & Pathology, SUNY Stony Brook, New York. Dr. Cooper is the Past International President of the International College of CranioMandibular Orthopedics (ICCMO). He is a clinician, educator, researcher and author on temporomandibular disorders and electronic measurement devices. Dr. Cooper maintains offices in Manhattan and Hewlett, New York, where he treats patients with temporomandibular disorders.

Yvonne D'Arcy, MS, RN, CRNP, CNS authored the chapter on *Pain Assessment and Management*. Ms. D'Arcy is the Nurse Practitioner for Pain Management and the Pain and Palliative Care Outcomes Manager at Suburban Hospital, Bethesda, MD. Prior to moving to Suburban Hospital Ms. D'Arcy was the coordinator of the Johns Hopkins Oncology Pain Service at the Sidney Kimmel Comprehensive Cancer Center, Baltimore, Maryland. She has also worked for Mayo Clinic Jacksonville, Florida where she was the coordinator of the acute pain service and the supervisor of the Chronic Pain Clinic.

In 1995 Ms. D'Arcy graduated from Winona State University, Winona Minnesota with a Master of Science degree on a clinical nurse specialist track. In 1999, she received a certification as a nurse practitioner from the University of Florida, Jacksonville campus. Currently Ms. D'Arcy holds professional memberships in the American Pain Society, the American Society of Pain Management Nurses and the Oncology Nursing Society. She has served on the Board of Directors for the American Society of Pain Management Nurses and is currently the Chairperson of their Clinical Practice Committee. Ms. D'Arcy writes and presents frequently on various pain management topics and issues both nationally and internationally. Additionally, she has consulted with attorneys as an expert witness.

Susan G. Engleman, MSN, RN, APRN, BC, PNP, CLCP, author of *Pediatric Records*, is an advanced practice nurse who works both as a clinical nurse specialist for Pediatric Services and as a nurse practitioner for the Pediatric Pain Service at Memorial Hermann Children's Hospital, a level one trauma center, in Houston, Texas. In addition, Ms. Engleman is also a certified life care planner specializing in life care plans for children with catastrophic injuries or illnesses and has participated in the field of legal nurse consulting since 1989. Ms. Engleman is adjunct faculty with the University of Texas Health Science Center School of Nursing in Houston, Texas. She earned her Bachelor of Science Degree in Nursing from the University of Evansville in Evansville, Indiana in 1984. She received her MSN in Critical Care Nursing with a focus in Pediatrics in 1989 and a post-Master's Pediatric Nurse Practitioner certificate in 1994 from the University of Texas in Houston. Ms. Engleman has numerous years of pediatric nursing experience in numerous roles practicing in a variety of settings including pediatric intensive care, intermediate care, acute care and home care. Prior to her employment with Memorial Hermann Children's Hospital, she served as Chief Operating Officer with Pediatric Special Care, a home care agency specializing in the care of children with special health care needs. Ms. Engleman is a member of several professional organizations and was the founding chapter president for the Houston Gulf Coast Chapter of the Society of Pediatric Nurses in 1993.

Marjorie Eskay-Auerbach, MD, JD authored the *Independent Medical Examination* chapter. She is a board-certified orthopedic surgeon, fellowship trained spine surgeon and medical-legal consultant. She received her BS in Biomedical Sciences and her M.D. from University of Michigan in Ann Arbor. Dr. Eskay-Auerbach completed her orthopedic surgery residency at the University of Pittsburgh, and her fellowship training in adult lumbar spine surgery in Long Beach, California. She practiced orthopedic spine surgery in Phoenix for nearly ten years, concentrating on the care of patients with work-related injuries and personal injuries primarily related to the adult spine. She attended law school at University of Arizona in Tucson, and became a member of the Arizona Bar in 2001. Dr. Eskay-Auerbach is a frequent CLE lecturer and an instructor for the American Medical Association on the AMA Guides to the Evaluation of Permanent Impairment, Fifth Edition. She is on the Board of Directors of the North American Spine Society, a fellow of the American Academy of Orthopedic Surgery and is certified by the American Board of Independent Medical Examiners. Her practice focuses on medical-legal consultations, independent medical evaluations and case review in the workers' compensation and personal injury arenas.

Mary Fakes, RN, MSN coauthored *Emergency Medical Services Records*. She is the Coordinator, Emergency Nursing Programs at St. Louis Community College in St. Louis, Missouri. In addition, she is the EMS Educational Coordinator at the Eureka Fire Protection District, Support Team, Eureka, Missouri and Director of Education for Lifeline Training Inc. located in Maryland Heights, Missouri. Ms. Fakes' professional responsibilities include the design, coordination and instruction of a variety of specialty programs offered through the various organizations she is associated with and includes diverse areas such as emergency and critical care nursing, legal nurse consulting programs, and a variety of prehospital professional training programs. Ms. Fakes has been licensed as a registered nurse (RN) and Funeral Director for more than twenty years. She received her nursing diploma and BSN at Deaconess School of Nursing in St. Louis, Missouri, and her Master's in Nursing Administration from University of Phoenix. She is an American Heart Association Regional Faculty in the disciplines of Advanced Cardiac Life Support (ACLS), Basic Life Support (BLS) and Pediatric Advanced Life Support (PALS) and has served as a National Faculty member for ACLS. She is a member of Sigma Theta Tau International Honor Society of Nursing. She serves on numerous planning committees for a variety of specialty nursing programs.

Hilary J. Flanders, MPH, RN-BC, RRT is currently a staff nurse in the Respiratory Acute Care Unit (RACU), and a coach for the Electronic Medication Administration Process for Patient Safety (EMAPPS) at Massachusetts General Hospital. She holds a bachelor's degree in Respiratory Therapy from Northeastern University, a bachelor's degree in Nursing from the University of Massachusetts Boston, and a master's degree in Public Health from the University of Massachusetts Amherst. Prior to working at Massachusetts General Hospital, she held several staff and travel

nurse positions in intensive and intermediate care units. She is board certified in Medical-Surgical Nursing and Gerontological Nursing.

Kelly A. Jaszarowski, MSN, RN, CNS, ANP, CWOCN authored *Skin Trauma*. She received her Masters of Science in Nursing from Indiana University. She completed her undergraduate studies at the University of Illinois at Springfield. Ms. Jaszarowski is also a graduate of the Abbott Northwestern Enterostomal Therapy Nursing Education Program. Ms. Jaszarowski has been a Wound, Ostomy, and Continence Nurse Specialist since 1990. She has been a recipient of the Excellence in Clinical Practice award presented by the Delta Omicron Chapter of Sigma Theta Tau recognizing her expertise in the specialty. Additionally, she has been a two-time recipient of the Most Educational Enterostomal Therapy Nursing award presented by her peers. She has also served as an expert witness for several medical malpractice cases.

Ms. Jaszarowski has been very active within the Wound, Ostomy, and Continence Nursing Society (WOCN). She has served nationally as treasurer and secretary as well as a director. Ms. Jaszarowski has been active on the regional level where she has served on a variety of committees as both a member and a committee chairperson. Her clinical practice expertise encompasses a variety of healthcare settings.

Elliott M. Korn, MD is author of *Ophthalmology Records*. He is a board certified ophthalmologist who is a fellowship-trained oculoplastic surgeon. He has been a Medicare consultant and has been involved in workers' compensation cases for the last twenty years. Dr. Korn has written ten original articles pertaining to the usage of the CO_2 laser in ophthalmic plastic surgery. He is currently chairman of the department of ophthalmology of Missouri Baptist Medical Center in St. Louis. He provides expert witness services in the field of ophthalmology and oculoplastic surgery.

Jo Anne Kuc, BSN, RN, LNCC author of *Documentation of Perioperative Care*, has worked in several critical care nursing areas and currently works dual positions in both Acute Pain Management and Post Anesthesia Care. She has lectured on various topics including nursing practice, documentation, and medical-legal issues. Additionally, Ms. Kuc has published a number of journal articles and book chapters. In addition to her clinical practice, Ms. Kuc is President of Midwest Medical Legal Resources, Inc., in Schererville, Indiana. Her company provides various aspects of litigation support to law firms.

Michael T. Lennon, PharmD, MBA, RPh, JD wrote the *Medication Records* chapter. He is a trial lawyer and principal of Lennon Law Offices, located in downtown Boston. His practice concentrates in all areas of personal injury representation, including medical malpractice, nursing home malpractice, and pharmacy malpractice cases. Dr. Lennon is a member of the Association of Trial Lawyers of America, the Massachusetts Academy of Trial Attorneys, the Massachusetts Bar Association, and the Boston Bar Association. He is a graduate of the Massachusetts College of Pharmacy, where he earned his Bachelor's Degree in Pharmacy in 1989 and his Doctorate in Pharmacy in 2001. He is also a graduate of Suffolk University Law School, where he earned his Juris Doctor in 2000, and of Suffolk University Sawyer School of Management, where he earned his Masters in Business Administration in 2001.

Dr. Lennon currently serves as a coach for the Suffolk Law School interscholastic trial teams. He has also accepted several invitations to speak at seminars on the subject of pharmacists' and pharmacies' professional liability.

Jeffrey M. Levine, MD is the author of *Physician Documentation in Hospitals and Nursing Home*. He is president and founder of SeniorHealth Consulting, Inc., a risk-management and medical-legal consulting firm located in New York City. Dr. Levine's professional focus is improving the quality of care delivered to elderly persons. He received his fellowship training in geriatrics at the Mount Sinai Medical Center in Manhattan, where he spent much of his career on the clinical faculty. He is board certified in Internal Medicine, is a Certified Medical Director, Certified Wound Care Specialist, and holds a Certificate of Added Qualifications in Geriatrics. He is a Fellow of the American Geriatrics Society, Fellow of the Gerontological Society of America, and President of the New York Metropolitan Area Geriatrics Society. He is consulting expert to the United States Department of Justice's Special Litigation Group and the New York State Department of Health's Office of Professional Medical Conduct. Dr. Levine is editor of *Medical-Legal Aspects of Long-Term Care*, also published by Lawyers & Judges Publishing Company.

Susan Masoorli, RN wrote the *Intravenous Therapy Records* chapter. She is a registered nurse who is recognized nationally and internationally as an expert in Infusion Therapy and Vascular Access Devices. She is the founder, President/CEO of Perivascular Nurse Consultants, Inc., which is a Philadelphia infusion nursing education company. She has over 30 years of infusion experience in both hospitals and home care. She has conducted over 300 national presentations for various organizations including ONS, INS and AVA and has published over 200 articles related to the practice of Infusion Therapy. She has been chosen as the recipient of the "2000 Nursing Educator Award" by the Pennsylvania State Nurses Association. In addition, she has served as an expert witness for infusion therapy nursing malpractice cases and has functioned as a legal nurse consultant for vascular access device litigation since 1990.

Joanne McDermott, MA, RN authored the *Obstetrical Records* chapter. She has worked in the maternal-newborn area of nursing for over twenty-five years. She received her BSN in nursing in 1975 from the State University of New York and her Masters in Nursing Education from New York University in 1985. She has worked as a staff nurse, assistant head nurse, clinical coordinator, and assistant director of nursing. She is currently an Assistant Professor of Nursing in Kansas City, Missouri. Ms. McDermott has experience in medical risk management as a claims analyst, and has reviewed medical-legal cases as an obstetrical nurse expert witness. She is a member of the Association of Women's Health, Obstetrical and Neonatal Nursing (AWHONN).

Wanda K. Mohr, RN, FAAN, PhD authored the *Psychiatric Medical Records*. She received her doctorate in nursing from the University of Texas at Austin in 1995. Presently she is an Associate Professor of Psychiatric Mental Health Nursing at University of Medicine and Dentistry School of Nursing. She is a certified advanced practice nurse in Child and Adolescent Psychiatric Mental Health Nursing. Dr. Mohr has dedicated her career to studying the effects of exposure to violence on children's development. She is conducting a study employing police officers as first line sentinels in identifying children exposed to violence. She is recognized for her work on institutional violence on troubled children, and has testified before the United States Congress representing national agencies that advocate for children's mental health. She is a recognized leader in the movement to reform conditions in mental health settings, with special emphasis on seclusion and restraint. She has over thirty years of clinical experience with troubled children and their families ranging across a variety of health care settings. Since completing her doctorate in 1995, she has authored over seventy professional journal articles, chapters, and books on the subject of mental health and has been consulted by a variety of state and federal agencies on the issue of children's responses to violence. Dr. Mohr is a fellow in the American Academy of Nursing and has been recognized by her peers by numerous national and international awards. She has conducted seven funded research studies from 1983 to present employing qualitative and quantitative research methods. Dr. Mohr is presently funded by the David and Lucille Packard Foundation to study child exposure to domestic violence.

Scott A. Mullins, AAS, EMT-P coauthored the *Emergency Medical Services Records* chapter. Scott is a Deputy Chief for the Eureka Fire Protection District in St. Louis County, Missouri. He has an MS in Executive Fire Service Leadership from Grand Canyon University, a BS in Fire and Safety Engineering Technology from the University of Cincinnati and is a graduate of the Executive Fire Officer Program at the National Fire Academy in Emmitsburg, Maryland. He was a Regional Faculty for the American Heart Association for the disciplines of Basic Life Support, Advanced Cardiac Life Support, as well as National Faculty for Pediatric Advanced Life Support for the State of Missouri. Deputy Chief Mullins has published articles in Emergency Medical Services Magazine and has been a reviewer for various sections of paramedic textbooks. He recently served as President of the Greater St. Louis Region Fire EMS Officer's Association and was named the Administrator of the Year in 2002 for the Missouri Emergency Medical Services Association. He also is vice president of SAR Training and Consulting Inc. an EMS and medical training and consulting company that offers a variety of programs for corporate and medical provider clients in the St. Louis area.

Jane O'Rourke, MSN, RN, CNAA wrote the chapter on *Rehabilitation Records*. She is the Director of Patient Care Services at one of the largest free standing rehabilitation specialty hospitals in the country. She holds a BSN and MSN from Hunter College and a Nursing Administration Certificate from Villanova. She is certified in Nursing Administration, Advanced by the American Nurses Association. She has twenty eight years experience as a clinician, educator and administrator and serves as adjunct faculty in various schools of nursing. She is a nurse consultant for plaintiff and defense attorneys and reviews medical records for regulatory purposes.

Ann M. Peterson, EdD, MSN, RN, CS, LNCC compiled the Appendix. Dr. Peterson has practiced as an independent legal nurse consultant since 1995. Located in Massachusetts, Dr. Peterson, a certified family nurse practitioner, consults with both defense and plaintiff firms nationwide drawing on her vast experiences as a clinician, educator and healthcare administrator to review and opine on medical malpractice, nursing negligence, and criminal cases. The majority of her work has been in the arena of nursing home litigation. In addition to being a contributor to this text, Dr. Peterson has au-

thored numerous professional articles, edited a professional text, participated in Massachusetts' Medical Malpractice Tribunals, and been an active member of numerous public and professional organizations.

Sally Russell, MSN, RN is the author of the *Medical Surgical Records* chapter. At that time, she had been a medical-surgical nurse for over twenty years, and a member the Academy of Medical Surgical Nurses since its inception, serving as the President in 1994–1995 and then as the Education Director for the past nine years. She has a Master's degree in Medical-Surgical nursing, has worked clinically as a staff nurse, and taught in a diploma school of nursing for fifteen years. Currently she works for Anthony J. Jannetti, Inc, a nursing association management firm as their Director of Education Services, in which capacity she works with several nursing associations as their Education Director. She has presented nationally on a variety of topics for the last twenty years.

Gwen Simons, PT, JD, OCS, FAAOMPT, author of *Physical Therapy Records*, is a lawyer and physical therapist in Scarborough, Maine. She practices law at Simons & Associates Law where she works almost exclusively with rehab providers on practice management, Medicare and health law compliance, and business law issues. As a physical therapist, Gwen is an expert in functional capacity evaluations and performs FCEs in medicolegal cases as an expert witness. She served on the American Physical Therapy Association's FCE task force to revise the Guidelines for FCEs and authored *Legal Issues in Functional Capacity Evaluations (FCEs)* in the *Guide to the Evaluation of Functional Ability* (American Medical Association 2009). She is Board Certified in Orthopaedic Physical Therapy (OCS) and a Fellow in the American Academy of Orthopaedic Manual Physical Therapists (FAAOMPT). Gwen teaches the legal issues course in the Evidence in Motion Executive Management Program for physical therapists. She is also an adjunct faculty member at the University of New England where she teaches health policy in the physical therapy transitional doctorate program. Gwen is the Past President of the Kentucky and Maine Chapters of the American Physical Therapy Association and serves as the Ethics Chair for the American Academy of Orthopaedic Manual Physical Therapists.

Ginny Tucci Starke, MSN, RN coauthored the *Office-Based Medical Records* chapter with her husband, Keith. Ginny owns and operates her own legal nurse consulting business in St. Louis, Missouri, providing information and resources for both plaintiff and defense counsel. She has twenty-four years of experience as a registered nurse and holds a masters degree in cardiac and pulmonary nursing from St. Louis University. Ms. Starke is affiliated with several professional nursing organizations including the Sigma Theta Tau nursing honor society, the American Association of Legal Nurse Consultants, and the National Alliance of Legal Nurse Consultants. She is active in the St. Louis Chapter of the American Association of Legal Nurse Consultants.

Keith M. Starke, MD, FACP coauthored the *Office-Based Medical Records* chapter. He has been a practicing physician for over twenty years in St. Louis, Missouri. He is Board Certified in Internal Medicine and a Fellow in the American College of Physicians. Dr. Starke also serves as Vice President of Medical Affairs for Mercy Medical Group, a large primary care group in St. Louis. He is a member of the American College of Physicians and the American Medical Association.

Dana Stearns, MD wrote *Emergency Department Records*. He is an Assistant Professor of Surgery at Harvard Medical School. He graduated from the Tufts School of Medicine and completed his residency training at the Johns Hopkins Hospital. Dr. Stearns is board certified in Emergency Medicine and an attending faculty in the Department of Emergency Medicine at the Massachusetts General Hospital. His research interests have included prehospital care and medical education. Dr. Stearns is a member of the Program in Medical Education at HMS and is an Associate Master of the William Bosworth Castle Academic Society. He is an undergraduate lecturer and tutor at Harvard and Tufts. Dr. Stearns is a faculty instructor for the Harvard Affiliated Emergency Medicine Residency Program (HAEMR) and presents research and educational topics at several national and international post-graduate continuing medical education conferences annually.

Jill Thomas, RNC, CWOCN, LNHA coauthored the *Long Term Care Records* chapter. Jill graduated from Kings County Hospital Center School of Nursing and has been a registered nurse for over thirty years. The last eighteen years have been dedicated to the long-term care arena. She has been involved in home health care, long-term care hospital and skilled nursing settings. She is board certified in geriatrics and a licensed nursing home administrator. Jill has been a director of nursing services for multiple skilled nursing facilities ranging from 50 to 250 beds. In addition, she has been a consultant to the long-term care industry on a national level for the past twelve years. Jill is Vice President of Product Development for Advance Care Planning, Inc., a national company that has a new unique product. The "Advance Care" is an extensive questionnaire which includes: biographical, end of life wishes, medical history, values preferences and lifestyle information. The web-based HIPAA compliant system produces and stores, for later retrieval, a needs based care plan, and bio for future caregivers.

Angela Tobias, RN, BSN, MSHSA, LNCC, CHCC co-authored the *Long Term Care Records* chapter. Angela received her associate's degree in Nursing from Dalton Junior College in Dalton, Georgia, Bachelor of Science in Nursing from Southern University in Chattanooga, Tennessee, and her Masters Degree in Health Care Administration from Saint Francis University. Her clinical career has included work in general medical surgical, pediatrics and coronary care nursing. She has been in hospital administration serving as a hospital CEO and Corporate Compliance Officer. Angela established her legal nurse consulting practice in 1996 (Nightingale Consulting, LLC) and has provided legal nurse consulting services as well as health care and compliance consulting services across the United States. She has also served as a member of an Independent Review Organization for the Office of Inspector General and has performed multiple health care compliance reviews and internal auditing. She has provided regulatory compliance consulting in the area of Behavioral Health, Physician Practice, Acute Care, DME, Radiology Practice, Long-Term Care and Long-term acute Care. She has written several articles relating to healthcare compliance for a legal nurse consulting newspaper and for healthcare institutions. She has given numerous presentations for health care institutions and has presented to national audiences regarding healthcare compliance and legal nurse consulting.

Howard Yeon, MD, JD coauthored *Orthopaedic Records*. He is a graduate of Harvard Medical School and Harvard Law School. He has published peer-reviewed articles on human molecular genetics and in the field of orthopaedic surgery including total joint arthroplasty and sports medicine. He has also written articles on subjects concerning medical litigation. Previous textbook chapter topics include pharmaceutical litigation and knee structure and function. Dr. Yeon is currently an orthopaedic surgeon in New York.

Index

#5104 Nursing Malpractice, Fourth Edition
(To be released 2010)

Edited by Patricia Iyer and Barbara J. Levin

The new Fourth Edition of Nursing Malpractice is scheduled to be released in 2010. Be sure to order your copy today. This outstanding reference—for the attorney, legal nurse consultant, insurance claim adjuster, healthcare risk manager, or healthcare facility leader involved in a nursing malpractice claim—brings you a wealth of information and resources for your case. This revised and updated edition covers the spectrum of the nursing process—from patient admittance to lawsuit. This title is an excellent and important addition to your nursing malpractice library.

Topics Include

- The foundations of nursing practice
- Medical errors
- Healthcare safety and risk management
- Today's healthcare environment
- Nursing practice
- Nursing and employment law
- Nursing documentation
- Obstetrical malpractice issues
- Neonatal and pediatric malpractice issues
- Emergency care malpractice issues
- Critical care malpractice issues
- Perioperative malpractice issues
- Nurse anesthesia malpractice issues
- Nurse midwife malpractice issues

- Psychiatric malpractice issues
- Medical surgical malpractice issues
- Subacute and long term care malpractice issues
- Assisted living malpractice issues
- Managed care malpractice issues
- Home care malpractice issues
- Medication errors
- Infections in healthcare settings
- Intravenous therapy malpractice issues
- Wound treatment malpractice issues
- Pain and suffering malpractice issues
- Healthcare fraud and nursing
- Nurses serial killers
- Lifecare planning
- Working with vocational experts
- Working with economic experts
- Working with expert witnesses
- Working with Insurance adjusters
- Working with legal nurse consultants
- Screening cases
- The plaintiff attorney's perspective
- The defense attorney's perspective
- Working with the jury
- Demonstrative evidence
- Themes for nursing malpractice cases
- Trial techniques
- Understanding medical terminology

Product Code: 5104 • 8.5"x11" • Casebound

#5643 Nursing Home Litigation: Investigation and Case Preparation, Second Edition

Edited by Patricia Iyer

This comprehensive text is a must-have legal and medical reference for everyone who works with nursing home, assisted living, long-term care, or elder law cases. Each chapter in Nursing Home Litigation Investigation and Case Preparation, Second Edition has been revised and updated while new chapters have been added to provide detailed information on even more issues and cases in nursing home litigation. It is an excellent reference for your nursing home or eldercare litigation team including attorneys representing either plaintiffs or defendants, financial consultants, life care planners, and other specialists with perspectives from experienced attorneys, physicians, nursing consultants, pharmacists, and nursing home experts.

This book is composed of four specialized sections so you can quickly and easily find the information you need. Part One discusses legal strategies you and your team can utilize during the investigation and pretrial phases of nursing home cases including screening cases, special issues unique to assisted living and nursing home cases, and use of Legal Nurse Consultants. Part Two explains the liability issues that arise due to the nature of the nursing home setting including staffing concerns, services provided to residents, administrative liability, direct and indirect medical practitioner responsibility issues. Part Three describes common allegations of injury, illness and other liability issues that occur in nursing home cases including falls, skin trauma, infections, pharmacology issues, pain management, billing fraud, and records tampering. Part Four provides tips for defending nursing home, long-term care and assisted living facilities with information on defense perspectives and strategies on many types of nursing home cases as well as insurance adjusters' perspectives on nursing home cases pertaining to insurance claims.

Product Code: 5643 • 8.5"x11"
Casebound • ISBN: 978-1-933264-00-4

#5813 Nursing Home Litigation: Pretrial Practice and Trials, Second Edition

Edited by Ruben J. Krisztal

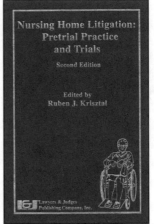

A must-have reference for any professional involved in nursing home cases. The litigation of neglect and abuse of the elderly in assisted living and nursing home facilities is unlike any other personal injury litigation. The second edition of Nursing Home Litigation: Pretrial Practice and Trials has been significantly expanded and will provide you with a detailed step-by-step look at how nursing home cases should be handled.

The book's chapters are organized in a way that will help you with your case from pretrial to trial. The first chapter will give you tips and techniques for writing the demand letter. The following chapters provide insight for both the plaintiff's attorney and defense attorney on topics such as interviewing older witnesses, preparing staff for deposition, demonstrative evidence, voir dire, opening and closing arguments.

Also included is a FREE CD-ROM of actual depositions of nurses, administrators, directors of nursing and upper management in nursing homes.

Topics include

- Handling older witnesses: the defense perspecive
- Preparing nursing home staff for deposition
- The preparation and use of demonstrative evidence
- Fighting fraud in long-term care
- Voir dire, opening arguments and closing arguments
- Punitive damages
- The role of nutrition
- The Medicare "super lein"
- CD-ROM of actual depositions of nurses, administrators, directors of nursing and upper management in nursing homes

Product Code: 5813 • 6"x9"
Casebound • ISBN: 978-1-930056-48-0

#6397 Medical-Legal Aspects of Pain and Suffering

Edited by Patricia Iyer

Written for the healthcare professional, claims adjuster and trial attorney, this book provides detailed information on how to analyze pain and suffering cases. You will read chapters written by legal nurse consultants, physicians and attorneys and see how pain and suffering patients and cases are viewed and treated on all sides. Each section of this valuable text is designed to fully explain each aspect of this hot topic in health care.

This book also explains to you how to understand medical records and commonly used pain assessment tools. It focuses on high-risk populations, pain and suffering in children and cancer pain. The last section is dedicated to your presentation of pain and suffering cases in the courtroom. By combining the clinical information in the first two sections with the legal strategies in the last section, this book becomes a must read for any attorney litigating medical, nursing, or nursing home negligence cases.

Topics include

- Organization and analysis of medical records
- Pain assessment and management
- Chronic pain cancer
- Spinal cord injury
- Wounds and burns
- Life-care planning
- Chronic pain
- Pain and suffering in children
- Trial exhibits
- Ante-mortem damages
- Defense and plaintiffs' perspectives

Product Code: 6397 • 8.5"x11"
Casebound • ISBN: 978-1-930056-39-8

#6230 Medical-Legal Aspects of Long-Term Care

Compiled and edited by Jeffrey M. Levine

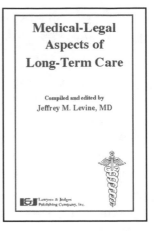

There are currently over 1.7 million elderly persons in nursing homes in America. Because of their medical complexity, this group is prone to poor outcomes such as falls, accidents, pressure ulcers, infections and death. In recent years, damage awards by juries in negligence cases involving elderly persons have soared.

This book is designed as a reference source for attorney and lay persons interested in the topic of neglect and abuse in nursing homes. Its goal is to provide a framework for understanding when a poor outcome is a result of negligence on the part of the caregiving facility and its personnel. It provides a source of information on basic medical aspects of nursing home care, with an emphasis on topics of medical-legal importance.

Topics include

- Introduction to the nursing home industry
- The survey process and the minimum data set
- Understaffing in nursing homes: Causes, consequences and cures
- Dementia and dysphagia
- Pain management; adverse drug events
- Nutrition and hydration
- Wound care
- Psychopharmacolgic medication
- Falls and fall-related injuries
- Bed safety and physical restraints
- Physical abuse and neglect
- Effective risk management
- The role of private accreditation

Product Code: 6230 • 6"x9"
Casebound • ISBN: 978-1-930056-23-7